Contemporary
Literary Criticism

Guide to Gale Literary Criticism Series

When you need to review criticism of literary works, these are the Gale series to use:

If the author's death date is: **You should turn to:**

After Dec. 31, 1959
(or author is still living)

CONTEMPORARY LITERARY CRITICISM

for example: Jorge Luis Borges, Anthony Burgess,
William Faulkner, Mary Gordon,
Ernest Hemingway, Iris Murdoch

1900 through 1959

TWENTIETH-CENTURY LITERARY CRITICISM

for example: Willa Cather, F. Scott Fitzgerald,
Henry James, Mark Twain, Virginia Woolf

1800 through 1899

NINETEENTH-CENTURY LITERATURE CRITICISM

for example: Fedor Dostoevski, George Sand,
Gerard Manley Hopkins, Emily Dickinson

1400 through 1799

LITERATURE CRITICISM FROM 1400 TO 1800
(excluding Shakespeare)

for example: Anne Bradstreet, Pierre Corneille,
Daniel Defoe, Alexander Pope,
Jonathan Swift, Phillis Wheatley

SHAKESPEAREAN CRITICISM

Shakespeare's plays and poetry

Gale also publishes related criticism series:

CONTEMPORARY ISSUES CRITICISM

Presents criticism on contemporary authors writing
on current issues. Topics covered include the social
sciences, philosophy, economics, natural science, law,
and related areas.

CHILDREN'S LITERATURE REVIEW

Covers authors of all eras. Presents criticism on
authors and author/illustrators who write for the
preschool to junior-high audience.

ISSN 0091-3421

Volume 31

Contemporary Literary Criticism

Excerpts from Criticism of the
Works of Today's Novelists, Poets,
Playwrights, Short Story Writers, Scriptwriters,
and Other Creative Writers

Jean C. Stine
Daniel G. Marowski
EDITORS

Gale Research Company
Book Tower
Detroit, Michigan 48226

STAFF

Jean C. Stine, Daniel G. Marowski, *Editors*

Roger Matuz, Jane E. Neidhardt, Marjorie Wachtel,
Robyn V. Young, *Senior Assistant Editors*

Lee Fournier, John G. Kuhnlein, Molly L. Norris, Sean R. Pollock,
Jeffrey T. Rogg, Lisa M. Rost, Jane C. Thacker, Debra A. Wells, *Assistant Editors*

Bridget Broderick, Sharon R. Gunton, Thomas Ligotti,
Phyllis Carmel Mendelson, *Contributing Editors*

Lizbeth A. Purdy, *Production Supervisor*
Denise M. Broderick, *Production Coordinator*
Eric Berger, *Assistant Production Coordinator*
Robin L. Du Blanc, Kelly King Howes, Amy Marcaccio, *Editorial Assistants*

Linda M. Pugliese, *Manuscript Coordinator*
Donna Craft, *Assistant Manuscript Coordinator*
Colleen M. Crane, Maureen A. Puhl, Rosetta Irene Simms, *Manuscript Assistants*

Karen Rae Forsyth, *Research Coordinator*
Jeannine Schiffman Davidson, *Assistant Research Coordinator*
Kevin John Campbell, Victoria Cariappa, Rebecca Nicholaides,
Kyle Schell, Valerie Webster, *Research Assistants*

L. Elizabeth Hardin, *Permissions Supervisor*
Janice M. Mach, *Permissions Coordinator*
Patricia A. Seefelt, *Assistant Permissions Coordinator, Illustrations*
Margaret A. Chamberlain, Mary M. Matuz, Susan D. Nobles, *Senior Permissions Assistants*
Sandra C. Davis, Kathy Grell, Josephine M. Keene, *Permissions Assistants*
H. Diane Cooper, Dorothy J. Fowler, Yolanda Parker,
Mabel E. Schoening, *Permissions Clerks*

Frederick G. Ruffner, *Publisher*
James M. Ethridge, *Executive Vice-President/Editorial*
Dedria Bryfonski, *Editorial Director*
Christine Nasso, *Director, Literature Division*
Laurie Lanzen Harris, *Senior Editor, Literary Criticism Series*

Since this page cannot legibly accommodate all the copyright notices,
the Appendix constitutes an extension of the copyright notice.

Contents

Preface

Literary criticism is, by definition, "the art of evaluating or analyzing with knowledge and propriety works of literature." The complexity and variety of the themes and forms of contemporary literature make the function of the critic especially important to today's reader. It is the critic who assists the reader in identifying significant new writers, recognizing trends in critical methods, mastering new terminology, and monitoring scholarly and popular sources of critical opinion.

Until the publication of the first volume of *Contemporary Literary Criticism (CLC)* in 1973, there existed no ongoing digest of current literary opinion. *CLC,* therefore, has fulfilled an essential need.

Scope of the Work

CLC presents significant passages from published criticism of works by today's creative writers. Each volume of *CLC* includes excerpted criticism on about 60 authors who are now living or who died after December 31, 1959. Since the series began publication, more than 1,700 authors have been included. The majority of authors covered by *CLC* are living writers who continue to publish; therefore, an author frequently appears in more than one volume. There is, of course, no duplication of reprinted criticism.

Authors are selected for inclusion for a variety of reasons, among them: the publication of a critically acclaimed new work, the reception of a major literary award, or the dramatization of a literary work as a movie or television screenplay. For example, the present volume includes Nobel laureate Czesław Miłosz, whose *The Separate Notebooks* and *The Land of Ulro* were recently translated; Philip Roth, who completed his Zuckerman trilogy with the publication of *The Anatomy Lesson;* and Simone de Beauvoir, whose new volume of memoirs, *Ceremonie des adieux,* received much attention from the literary world. Perhaps most importantly, authors who appear frequently on the syllabuses of high school and college literature classes are heavily represented in *CLC.* Nathalie Sarraute and H.D. are examples of writers of this stature in the present volume. Attention is also given to several other groups of writers—authors of considerable public interest—about whose work criticism is often difficult to locate. These are the contributors to the well-loved but nonscholarly genres of mystery and science fiction, as well as writers who appeal specifically to young adults and writers for the nonprint media, including scriptwriters, lyricists, and cartoonists. Foreign writers and authors who represent particular ethnic groups in the United States are also featured in each volume.

Format of the Book

Altogether there are about 750 individual excerpts in each volume—with an average of about 11 excerpts per author—taken from hundreds of literary reviews, general magazines, scholarly journals, and monographs. Contemporary criticism is loosely defined as that which is relevant to the evaluation of the author under discussion; this includes criticism written at the beginning of an author's career as well as current commentary. Emphasis has been placed on expanding the sources for criticism by including an increasing number of scholarly and specialized periodicals. Students, teachers, librarians, and researchers frequently find that the generous excerpts and supplementary material provided by the editors supply them with all the information that they need to write a term paper, analyze a poem, or lead a book discussion group. However, complete bibliographical citations facilitate the location of the original source as well as provide all of the information necessary for a term paper footnote or bibliography.

A *CLC* author entry consists of the following elements:

> • The **author heading** cites the author's full name, followed by birth date, and death date when applicable. The portion of the name outside the parentheses denotes the form under which the author has most commonly published. If an author has written consistently under a pseudonym, the pseudonym will be listed in the author heading and the real name given on the first line of the biographical and critical introduction. Also located at the beginning of the introduction to the author entry are any important name

variations under which an author has written. Uncertainty as to a birth or death date is indicated by a question mark.

- A **portrait** of the author is included when available.

- A brief **biographical and critical introduction** to the author and his or her work precedes the excerpted criticism. However, *CLC* is not intended to be a definitive biographical source. Therefore, *cross-references* have been included to direct the reader to other useful sources published by the Gale Research Company: *Contemporary Authors* now includes detailed biographical and bibliographical sketches on nearly 79,000 authors; *Children's Literature Review* presents excerpted criticism on the works of authors of children's books; *Something about the Author* contains heavily illustrated biographical sketches on writers and illustrators who create books for children and young adults; *Contemporary Issues Criticism* presents excerpted commentary on the nonfiction works of authors who influence contemporary thought; *Dictionary of Literary Biography* provides original evaluations of authors important to literary history; and the new *Contemporary Authors Autobiography Series* offers autobiographical essays by prominent authors. Previous volumes of *CLC* in which the author has been featured are also listed in the introduction.

- The **excerpted criticism** represents various kinds of critical writing—a particular essay may be normative, descriptive, interpretive, textual, appreciative, comparative, or generic. It may range in form from the brief review to the scholarly monograph. Essays are selected by the editors to reflect the spectrum of opinion about a specific work or about an author's writing in general. The excerpts are presented chronologically, adding a useful perspective to the entry. All titles by the author featured in the entry are printed in boldface type, which enables the reader to easily identify the works being discussed.

- A complete **bibliographical citation** designed to help the user find the original essay or book follows each excerpt. An asterisk (*) at the end of a citation indicates the essay is on more than one author.

Other Features

- A list of **Authors Forthcoming in *CLC*** previews the authors to be researched for future volumes.

- An **Appendix** lists the sources from which material in the volume has been reprinted. Many other sources have also been consulted during the preparation of the volume.

- A **Cumulative Index to Authors** lists all the authors who have appeared in *Contemporary Literary Criticism, Twentieth-Century Literary Criticism, Nineteenth-Century Literature Criticism*, and *Literature Criticism from 1400 to 1800*, along with cross-references to other Gale series: *Children's Literature Review, Authors in the News, Contemporary Authors, Contemporary Authors Autobiography Series, Dictionary of Literary Biography, Something about the Author*, and *Yesterday's Authors of Books for Children*. Users will welcome this cumulated author index as a useful tool for locating an author within the various series. The index, which lists birth and death dates when available, will be particularly valuable for those authors who are identified with a certain period but whose death date causes them to be placed in another, or for those authors whose careers span two periods. For example, F. Scott Fitzgerald is found in *Twentieth-Century Literary Criticism*, yet a writer often associated with him, Ernest Hemingway, is found in *Contemporary Literary Criticism*.

- A **Cumulative Index to Critics** lists the critics and the author entries in which the critics' essays appear.

Acknowledgments

The editors wish to thank the copyright holders of the excerpted articles included in this volume for permission to use the material and the photographers and individuals who provided photographs for us. We are grateful to the staffs of the following libraries for making their resources available to us: Detroit Public Library and the libraries of Wayne State University, the University of Michigan, and the University of Detroit. We also wish to thank Jeri Yaryan for her assistance with copyright research.

Suggestions Are Welcome

The editors welcome the comments and suggestions of readers to expand the coverage and enhance the usefulness of the series.

Authors Forthcoming in *CLC*

To Be Included in Volume 32

Pat Barker (English novelist)—*Union Street,* a novel of working-class England told from the perspective of seven women, marks Barker's auspicious literary debut.

Malcolm Bradbury (English novelist, critic, and biographer)—A university professor, Bradbury offers a satirical view of academic life in his fiction, most recently in *Rates of Exchange.*

Philip Caputo (American novelist, journalist, and memoirist)—Hailed for his moving Vietnam War memoir, *A Rumor of War,* Caputo has subsequently published two well-received novels, *Horn of Africa* and *DelCorso's Gallery.*

Amy Clampitt (American poet)—Considered an important new poetic voice, Clampitt received high praise for *The Kingfisher,* her first volume of poetry.

Max Frisch (Swiss-born German novelist and dramatist)—With the recent publication of his novels *Bluebeard* and *Gantenbein,* Frisch has again been lauded for his insight into human nature.

Günter Grass (German novelist, poet, and dramatist)—Grass, whose work centers on contemporary Germany, won international acclaim for his novel *The Tin Drum.* Criticism in the forthcoming volume will focus on his poetry and his recent novel, *Headbirths.*

Thom Gunn (English poet, critic, and editor)—Gunn is noted for combining traditional verse forms with pop culture motifs. He has recently published a volume of new

poems, *The Passages of Joy,* and a collection of autobiographical and critical essays, *The Occasions of Poetry.*

A. R. Gurney, Jr. (American dramatist and novelist)—Praised in both America and England, Gurney's plays often utilize song, music, and offstage characters to examine white middle-class attitudes.

Ronald Harwood (South African novelist, dramatist, and scriptwriter)—After writing plays and novels for twenty years, Harwood achieved international fame with his play *The Dresser,* which has also been adapted for the screen.

Richard Hugo (American poet and essayist)—A critically acclaimed poet who frequently writes of the Pacific Northwest, Hugo is most often praised for his compressed style and highly rhythmic lines.

Julian Symons (English novelist, critic, and poet)—A prominent crime writer, Symons has reaffirmed his stature with several recent mystery publications, including *The Name of Annabel Lee* and *The Tigers of Subtopia.*

Wendy Wasserstein (American dramatist)—Her play *Isn't It Romantic?,* a comedy about two single women during the 1980s, was a recent off-Broadway success.

Yvor Winters (American critic, poet, short story writer, and editor)—One of the most prominent literary critics of the twentieth century, Winters is recognized for his innovative technique for analyzing poetry.

To Be Included in Volume 33

Ayi Kwei Armah (Ghanaian novelist, short story writer, and poet)—Armah's early novels, including *The Beautyful Ones Are Not Yet Born,* indirectly indict colonialism in their description of the cultural and political corruption of postindependence Africa; his later historical novels, *Two Thousand Seasons* and *The Healers,* turn to the past as a model for Africa's future.

Alan Ayckbourn (English dramatist)—A popular and prolific playwright, Ayckbourn is best known for farces that examine middle-class marriage and society, including *Absurd Person Singular, The Norman Conquests,* and *Bedroom Farce.*

Saul Bellow (American novelist and short story writer)—Nobel laureate Bellow's recent volume of short stories, *Him with His Foot in His Mouth,* received an enthusiastic critical response, confirming Bellow's reputation as a thoughtful purveyor of the worth of life.

Art Buchwald (American humorist and journalist)—*While Reagan Slept,* a volume of political humor, is the latest of over thirty collections of Buchwald's syndicated newspaper columns.

Harvey Fierstein (American dramatist)—In his Tony Award-winning plays, *Torch Song Trilogy* and *La cage aux folles,* Fierstein blurs the distinction between homosexual and heterosexual concepts of love, attacking stereotypes through humor and satire.

John Fowles (English novelist)—*Mantissa,* the most recent work by the author of *The French Lieutenant's Woman,* is a dialogue between the writer and his muse about creativity, literary theory, and sex.

Jim Harrison (American poet, novelist, scriptwriter, and critic)—A native of rural northern Michigan, Harrison imbues his prose and poetry with a strong sense of the outdoors. His latest works include *New & Selected Poems 1961-1981* and the novels *Warlock* and *Sundog.*

Stratis Haviaras (Greek-born American novelist and poet)—Haviaras's two highly regarded novels, *When the Tree Sings* and *The Heroic Age,* examine the turbulent events of recent Greek history through the eyes of children.

C.L.R. James (West Indian nonfiction writer, novelist, dramatist, and short story writer)—James is widely recognized in England for his writings on Third World politics. His study of sports and society, *Beyond a Boundary,* has received substantial critical attention in the United States.

Arthur Kopit (American dramatist and scriptwriter)—A prominent figure in contemporary American theater, Kopit has added *Nine* and *End of the World* to his already impressive body of work.

Joyce Carol Oates (American novelist, short story writer, poet, dramatist, and critic)—Recent additions to the canon of this versatile and prolific author include *A Bloodsmoor Romance, The Profane Art, Mysteries of Winterthurn,* and *Angel of Light.*

Pier Paolo Pasolini (Italian poet, dramatist, novelist, and filmmaker)—Regarded by some critics as the most notable poet of post-World War II Italy, Pasolini was a social reformer whose criticism of the Italian government and the Roman Catholic Church incensed most factions of Italian society.

Thomas Pynchon (American novelist and short story writer)—Pynchon's early writing style and initial thematic concerns are evident in *Slow Learner,* a recently published collection of short stories written prior to his three celebrated novels.

Renata Adler

1938-

American novelist, journalist, critic, and short story writer.

A journalist and critic whose articles have been collected in *Toward a Radical Middle* (1969) and *A Year in the Dark* (1970), Adler is also the author of two successful novels. Both *Speedboat* (1976) and *Pitch Dark* (1983) are composed of seemingly unconnected passages that challenge readers to find meaning. Like her nonfiction, Adler's novels examine the issues and mores of contemporary life.

Toward a Radical Middle includes essays on national and international social and political issues. Critics applauded the collection, noting that Adler had skillfully chosen details to provide insight into many of the troubling issues of the 1960s and that she had managed to offer meaningful social commentary without intruding on her subject. *A Year in the Dark* is a compendium of film reviews Adler wrote for *The New York Times*. Although some critics felt that Adler's lack of formal training in film studies diminished her criticism, it was generally recognized that she had expanded the role of a movie reviewer by writing a wide range of articles, from a report on the arts in Cuba to reviews of pornographic and foreign-language films.

Speedboat, Adler's first novel, met with generally favorable response, even though many critics found it difficult to classify the book. They hesitated to call it a novel because the work comprises short scenes that overlap and recall one another without forming a single narrative line. Other critics maintained that *Speedboat* was a unified work and praised its mixture of journalistic reportage and autobiography. The success of *Speedboat* led to great anticipation of Adler's next novel. *Pitch Dark* is the story of Kate Ennis and her attempt to end a nine-year romance with her married lover. Like *Speedboat*, *Pitch Dark* emphasizes particular and apparently disparate moments rather than a sequential narrative. Some critics found *Pitch Dark* solipsistic and charged that Adler did not finally draw the fragments of the novel into one continuously interesting work. Most, however, concluded that Adler was successful in making the pattern of moments both satisfying and effective.

(See also *CLC*, Vol. 8; *Contemporary Authors*, Vols. 49-52; and *Contemporary Authors New Revision Series*, Vol. 5.)

© 1984 Thomas Victor

JACOB BRACKMAN

In excruciating conversations over drinks around the city, during the fourteen months that Renata Adler served as film critic for The New York *Times,* I often found myself serving, by a whoosh of role suction, as her apologist. When anyone else present seemed prepared to champion her critical honor, I'd find myself laying back. Even after a heavy artillery barrage, my reinforcements were timid and lackluster. . . .

Now Random House has published all her *Times* stuff (January, 1968-February, 1969) virtually unreedited, in the precise order of its appearance—nearly two hundred complete pieces of writing: daily reviews, Sunday essays, movie-oriented reports from

New York, Paris, Rome, Venice, Rochester and Havana—under the title *A Year in the Dark.*

Reading through her year in a couple of sittings, I became progressively more ashamed of (and bewildered by) my old soft shoe, since it could scarcely be more clear that Miss Adler was not just far and away the best daily movie reviewer we've ever had, but one of the best film critics as well.

She ideally combined the qualities of reviewer and critic. Once you'd got the hang of her, you could tell just how you'd take to a given movie, whatever liberties of association she'd taken. . . .

Even at her shakiest—when she forced tone (over which she exerts exquisite control) to bear the major burden of her response—she had the most uncanny sense for which details were telling, and what story they told. She unraveled gestures and throwaways most critics never thought to mention. (p. 26)

The assembled pieces show us how movies are now connected up with everything that plays upon our imagination, with politics especially; how close they are, in form and reverberation, to imagination itself. An altogether special shot, montage, or *mise-en-scène* is never lost on her—but she won't celebrate it with any more brouhaha than one would a neatly turned phrase in fiction. She is mainly interested in the ideas behind films, and the atmosphere they create. (p. 28)

In many ways, her scant film experience turned out to be a blessing. With no reservoir of allusion to draw upon, she wasted no space belaboring us with credentials that might testify to the credibility of her judgments. She released us from both the floundering, adjective-strewn misapprehensions of the daily reviewers, from their silly gushing, and from the useless, pedantic effusions of the buffs, who taught us more about penguins than we cared to learn. Miss Adler, in her ignorance, managed to say more interesting things about movies in a year—which will stand forever, one guesses, as her whole career in the movie-critic business—than most critics would manage if they lasted twenty-seven years.

Toward the end of one of her reflective Sunday essays about writing about movies (she disclaimed this kind of "metawriting," but of course ended up doing it often), she said: "Failing everything else, one would like to have one thought, one sentence, one line, that shows a certain tension and effort, something worth reading after you have seen the film, or even if you haven't seen it and will never go." None of her columns is without such a line. Given the mind-mucking ferocity of her consumption and working schedule during that year, it strikes one as an unexpected, breathtaking, touching achievement. That the writing, the *sensibility,* held together through this grueling period, can only be credited to character: something rare and disciplined and proud that takes over the wheel after intellect, stamina, even motivation, have failed.

The thoughtful candor of her introduction succeeds in making this book the journal of a year rather like the years we have all been passing lately—freaky and overloaded, steeped in mediocrity and dangerous doubletalk; lit up by moments that make our hearts jump, recall to us that we are still a bit human. Here Miss Adler writes, "Reviewing movies seemed not at all like reviewing books, more like writing about events, about anything." And later, after enumerating a number of unsatisfying approaches, she adds, "The best criticism I read was still by writers who simply felt moved by film to say something about it—without reverent or consistent strategies, putting films idiosyncratically alongside things they cared about in other ways."

Insofar as the Jesuit rigors of her position allowed, Miss Adler operated that way, not as a film critic, really, but as a writer who allowed movies to comprise the whole of her new experience for a time; set them resonating against the whole of her old experience, and listened even to the faintest echoes. She wrote to different audiences at different moments—many of her pieces, in retrospect, obviously demanded more attention than the thin columns of newsprint, with their border distractions, would permit—but primarily to a literate, decent, vaguely nervous group of people like herself who, she may have imagined, would gather on some appointed corner if things got too bad and discuss what ought to be done. . . .

I was incessantly amazed at how she managed to think through and articulate coherent attitudes toward films within several hours after having seen them. . . .

I intend to stay out of any retrospective discussions of Miss Adler's critical prowess that may be occasioned by this collection, though I am most curious to hear how her nonfans will explain it. I'm not really interested in talking with them, I only want to eavesdrop. Because movies seem to be saying the most fundamental things for us now, even telling us how we should feel about where it's at, one often seems called upon to defend *oneself* in talking about a movie one likes. Attacking a movie someone else likes, one feels somehow engaged in an uncomfortably personal sort of attack. The additional remove in talking about movie *critics* tends to make the whole business impossibly elusive, and unpleasant. So out of tune are certain people with their own subjectivity that, in putting down someone else's response, they seem bent on extirpating a despised aspect of themselves. One can become embarrassed, in casual movie talk, to learn more about people than they wish to reveal. To hear good work deprecated at a time when so little of it is being done anywhere is also, for me, a source of perplexity and embitterment. (p. 34)

Jacob Brackman, in a review of "A Year in the Dark," in Esquire, *Vol. LXXIII, No. 3, March, 1970, pp. 26, 28, 34.*

WILFRID SHEED

[In **"Toward a Radical Middle: Fourteen Pieces of Reporting and Criticism,"** a] collection of essays written originally for The New Yorker, [Adler] appears in several roles: reporter, critic, social philosopher. As a reporter, she occasionally suffers from too much courtesy: she hates to criticize her hosts, the people who let her run the tape recorder, and her point comes through rather too lightly. As a critic, she bites as hard as anyone, but always in the service of an idea, which saves her from bitchiness or any kind of nastiness high. As a social philosopher, she binds up her several selves and explains what they are all up to.

In her Introduction, which doubles as the best essay in the book, she explains herself in terms of her generation. If Norman Podhoretz did this, she would call it a dubious universalization of self; and sometimes it is. Since she thinks rather highly of her generation (and makes one feel mightily proud to belong to it), she is reluctant to admit that it is herself alone that she is talking about at least part of the time. (pp. 12, 14)

The model of what Miss Adler thinks we should be doing is conveyed in her long, harrowing account of the 1965 march on Selma: sober, specific action, absolutely free of bombast. What we shouldn't be doing comes up at the end, when she reports on the 1968 New Politics conference in Chicago, where all manner of Spocks and Coffins endorsed a Black Manifesto, every item of which must have made them wince, for the sake of a crazyquilt united front. The heartbreaking gains and losses of these years convince her that historical progress is made only by inches. But I think this overlooks the way those inches often come in violent spurts: some things must be done fast or not at all. (Not to argue with this book is to waste it.)

Much of her reporting and criticism elaborates on a single theme: her highly personal discovery and acceptance of America. She describes without smirking some of our most vulnerable aberrations: second-drawer hippies and preachers on the Sunset Strip, self-saturated group therapists in New York (a little smirking would have been O.K. here, I think). The rich unexpectedness of this country never ceases to dazzle her, and her observation is keen as a child's.

In criticism, she wheels on the literary anti-Americans, 1930's radicals who have transferred their permanent sneer from politics to culture, and their wise-guy juniors, braying unearned clichés about a society they haven't bothered to look into. At moments, one fears she is about to lapse into the soft-sell celebrations of the C.I.A. intellectuals. (Sure we have problems, but we're working on them every minute.) Yet her position is finally too independent for that. She is, to sum it up crudely, a dead serious radical, who believes that you can't do much for a populace you despise and can't do anything with a bag of cant tied round your neck.

Miss Adler's literary criticism is always at the service of her general ideas, which means that esthetic judgments tend to come in at a slightly irregular angle. So it is good to have the whole Adler in one book. . . . , where we can keep an eye on her. And good of course to have such a gracefully phrased, ardently intelligent book from anyone. (p. 14)

> *Wilfrid Sheed, "Radical Middle," in* The New York Times Book Review, *March 29, 1970, pp. 12, 14.*

RICHARD CORLISS

It was a big mistake for the *New York Times* to ask Renata Adler to replace Bosley Crowther as the paper's movie critic in 1967, and a small disaster for Miss Adler (or Renata, as she became known to the thousands who started following her daily mistakes, laxities of prose, insights and oversights, in a cliffhanging "Perils of Renata" that was usually resolved by Miss Adler's falling off her critical or rhetorical cliff) to have accepted. Somebody at the *Times* must have heard that movies were fashionable, and thought to bestow a little cultural respectability on a medium it had previously recognized mainly as an advertiser. . . .

What nobody seemed to notice was that Renata didn't know much about movies, didn't care much about them, and didn't care to write much about them. At a time when there were far more interested, interesting film critics around (and the *Times* could have had any of them for the asking), the paper chose to use the movies as a guinea pig on which to experiment with someone who was less a New Journalist than a novice. Film 1968 went largely unappraised in the *Times* (except by second-stringer Vincent Canby) as Renata attempted on the job to develop a prose style and a film attitude. Gradually, an Adlerian style *was* discerned. First paragraph: summation. Second paragraph: list of good things in movie. Third paragraph: list of bad things in movie. Final paragraph: critical appraisal of theater décor or ethnological consideration of movie audience. Once in a while she seemed to get her lists mixed up—would you guess that "lyrics like 'Oh, what a lovely, lonely man' and 'There's magic in the wake of a fiasco' and lines like 'Zis is X speaking. X, as in X and pains'" is from a good list or a bad one?

For the answer to that, you'll have to buy Miss Adler's book *A Year in the Dark: Journal of a Film Critic, 1968-1969.* I can't think of another reason for anyone besides Miss Adler owning this book. While you could sympathize with Renata's dis-ease in a job she was bored with and ill-suited for, like an Imperial General forced to work as a café doorman, the only person you need to feel sorry for, once her ephemera was published between hard covers, is the typesetter . . . and maybe the reviewer. If Renata had as bad a time at the movies as she gives us in her book, perhaps she does deserve our sympathy. (p. 370)

> *Richard Corliss, "Perils of Renata, Pearls of Pauline," in* National Review, *Vol. XXII, No. 13, April 7, 1970, pp. 369-70.*

JAMES GILBERT

The last ten or fifteen years have been marked by two prominent notions among intellectuals. Many writers have felt that the essence of the period has been the eruption of hot issues through the fissures and seams of American political compromises. Current political language often sounds like a new geometry developed to measure gaps and distances between groups of people. Without a climate of compromise, politically conscious writers are more often than not compelled to take a position and hold ground as if under attack. Thus, Renata Adler entitled her book of reportage *Toward a Radical Middle,* which says very little about her work in the sixties but quite a bit about the need to locate on the generational battlefield. (p. 580)

The problem of assessing one's own past writings is often as difficult as the actual writing about one's experience. Renata Adler's fourteen pieces of reporting and criticism from 1963 to 1968, despite what she says in her introductory essay, do not amount to a defense of language and nuance, nor offer much proof that the "System" has accommodated anyone out of the ordinary in the past decade, nor that it is getting "better." In fact, Adler is a far better writer than she is a polemicist for the radical middle. Her essays simply do not add up to the position for which she claims to be a spokesman.

If anything, Adler's political position is slightly off center. At her best, as in "The March for Non-Violence from Selma," she has a marvelous eye and ear for detail and tone, and a sympathetic omnipresence recording bits of conversation, faces, movements. In the piece on Sunset Strip in Los Angeles, and the very funny report on the Washington conference of the Independent Committee to End the War in Vietnam in 1965 she adopts a half-serious acceptance of what is happening and then slowly and deftly undercuts the pretense of a Los Angeles cultural happening and a dead serious political convention. Her half-mocking, ironic tone carries the reader to the inevitable absurd conclusion. (p. 581)

After a while, the method and point of view break down. The report on the Black Power march in Mississippi (after Selma) is a stereotyped, outsider's report dismissing white marchers as Drones, reporters as disrupters and "Black Power," as one of those at best, bad, at worst, worse, slogans. There are sympathetic sketches of Stokely Carmichael and, especially, Martin Luther King. But one has the feeling that Adler has tired of it all, sees the marches as boring and repetitive, and will not write about them anymore. This sense is even stronger in her report on the Palmer House meeting of Radical Blacks and whites in 1967, and the debacle of the New Politics Convention. Clearly, by then, she had had it (the no-longer-New-Left was a "vulgar joke," and able to contribute as much to discussion of problems as a "mean drunk to the workings of a fire brigade"). So much did she see this as the signal for the end of the Left, which she scores for polarizing American society, that in the end she doubts the future of New Politics at all. Of course, it was impossible then to predict the Convention of the summer of 1968, or the academic year of 1969 and 1970, and perhaps, also, to foresee that this incredibly absurd gathering would not be the last reunion of those who want to change American society radically. Adler makes much of the breakdown of language and sloganeering. This is a useful gauge for evaluating one level of political activity; but it is also the mark of most politics.

In the end, it is her sense of herself as a writer that Adler puts at the service of the "radical middle." With her stylistic weapons she draws up the defenses of her own generation. She writes herself stylistically and ideologically out of the corner of the Average American. She is closest to making sense out of the early sixties when she writes of Kennedy's politics of glamour, and farthest when she writes of World War II as the last just war of romantic possibility. Surely, from the other side, that is what the Chinese, Algerian, Cuban, Vietnamese wars have been all about. Still it is language that Adler feels she is defending. But when she has finished casting her proxy for clear thought and good style, she speaks of the historical necessity of American internal reconciliation, and to prove the immense possibilities for the future, she writes of the "three of us" who have just come back from the moon. Three men did come back from the moon, but courageous as that was, it has nothing to do with preserving the bonds of social unity in America, and less with language and clarity of thought. If anything, the whole moon extravaganza proved how far we will allow language to be debased in the service of technology, with programmed surprise, historic first words and gimmicky political exploitation.

In the end, one is inevitably convinced that Renata Adler is far different from the middle class she mistakes for a radical middle. She calls her values corny; but her strain of sophistication has no more place in an Iowa cornfield than the *New Yorker,* for which her essays were written, resembles the *Prairie Farmer.* At one point she remarks, "Lacking an idiom entirely our own, we cannot adopt any single voice without a note of irony." Perhaps we must read her the same way. (pp. 581-82)

> James Gilbert, "American Dreams," in Partisan Review, Vol. XXXVII, No. 4, Fall, 1970, pp. 580-85.*

ANNE TYLER

[*Speedboat,* Renata Adler's first novel,] was a wonderfully fresh and thoughtful book, written as if the author neither knew nor cared how other people wrote; she would proceed in her own remarkable way.

Her second novel [*Pitch Dark*] necessarily lacks that element of surprise; we know her by now. But it conveys the same sense of freshness, or originality practiced not for its own sake but because the author is absolutely desperate to tell us how things are just as forthrightly and truthfully as possible. Or maybe it's not so much how things are as what is felt—what her heroine feels upon arriving at the frayed, sad, uncertain end of a love affair.

Even with her opening remarks, Kate—who is the narrator as well as the heroine—shows herself obsessed with getting this story across to us exactly right. Where to start? we hear her wondering, and she begins first one way and then another, discarding whole paragraphs as they prove unsatisfactory. . . .

But she doesn't get them straight; that's not her style. Instead, she presents us with a scattering of fragments, stray bits and pieces that she trusts will come to have meaning for us. Some of the fragments float past over and over, at first unexplained— brief sentences like "Quanta, Amy said, on the train," and "Not here, Diana said, to her lasting regret," and "What do you tell the Sanger people? Lily asked." Eventually these sentences are given a context; it's as if they had to ripen first. Other fragments work more as the refrain in a love song might: "Did I throw the most important thing perhaps, by accident, away?" and "How could I know that every time you had a choice you would choose the other thing?"

Like *Speedboat, Pitch Dark* gives the effect of an intelligent, wry, rather quirky woman lying awake in the small hours, staring at the ceiling and sorting over her life. There's the same reflectiveness, the same insomniac earnestness in her voice, the same eerie immediacy in the recollected voices of others. (p. 27)

At one point, Kate mentions a journal that she kept in her twenties. Her entries covered a Sunday to the Wednesday of the following week; after that she wrote no more. What stopped her, she says, was that when she read back over the journal, it struck her as incomprehensible. "There were no events, few names, no facts, no indication whatever of what *happened,* apart from this gloom, that cheering up, this gloom again." In a sense, Kate could be speaking of *Pitch Dark.* The book is not a narrative of events—although a few events do occur here—but a description of a certain weighted moment in a woman's life.

Can such a moment make for a satisfying novel? That's up to the individual reader, I suppose. If you read these fragments in hope of some forward motion—some conclusive final goal— you'll be disappointed. But if you simply allow them to settle in their own patterns, flashing light where they will, you'll find *Pitch Dark* a bright kaleidoscope of a book. (p. 28)

> Anne Tyler, "End of a Love Affair," in The New Republic, Vol. 189, No. 23, December 5, 1983, pp. 27-8.

PETER S. PRESCOTT

"Pitch Dark" has its clever moments and, in its central section, something that resembles a story, but it's not the witty virtuoso performance that "Speedboat" was. The earlier book was put together like a collage of file cards on which Adler had scribbled whatever jokes, anecdotes and scraps of conversation she could use to define a contemporary sensibility. The architecture of this one is visibly more ambitious, more ambiguous. It is, I think, an anorectic novel: its class, its intelligence and the high seriousness of its intentions don't quite justify its lack of flesh.

Plot and character are for other people's novels; "Pitch Dark" presents a situation that Adler develops by theme and variations. The narrator, Kate Ennis, may be a newspaperwoman in her 40s, but the important thing about her is her tone of voice, her diffidence about telling her story ("I don't know where it begins. It is where I am"), her habit of interrupting herself to repeat obscure sentences as if they were refrains from some as yet unwritten dirge. . . .

Adler's idea of how to build a novel is to make it as fragmented as the lives it reflects. I suspect the easiest way to like "Pitch Dark" is to examine its parts and not worry long about the overall design. Kate's protestations that she doesn't know how to begin her story don't excuse Adler's own early stumblings. Her numbing repetition of perhaps a dozen significant sentences quickly becomes irritating, as do her portentous promises of stories soon to be revealed (a few, in fact, never are). I'm convinced that one or two of these fragments can't be understood from the information provided. And yet most, taken in isolation, or even in an association less strict than their author intended, work very well indeed. Kate is so effective a foil for her author that in one muddled moment her last name appears to be not Ennis but Adler. Beyond the pleasure that these little essays afford—an argument that Penelope was unfaithful to

Ulysses, for instance, or a speculation on how the center of a football team came to wear the towel with which the quarterback dries his hands—there's the pleasure of Adler's prose, as distinctive and controlled as any in American fiction today.

Peter S. Prescott, "Age of Angst and Anxiety," in Newsweek, Vol. 102, No. 25, December 19, 1983, p. 82.

OLIVER CONANT

Plot and characterization are barely bothered with in *Pitch Dark*. The breakup is a foregone conclusion—no suspense there. Adler refuses to begin her novel in any conventional manner. "It's not what I know how to do," she has Kate tell us. She appears anxious to distinguish her writing from the kind of tale where, as Kate remarks with fine scorn, "somebody loves and somebody doesn't, or loves less, or loves someone else, or someone is a good soul and someone is a villain. . . ." This dismissive attitude is problematic. No really great novel has been without these essential ingredients. Nor is *Pitch Dark,* which is not a great novel, free of them: Jake is a kind of villain, the book is filled with love and its diminishment, and Kate, despite her self-deprecation, is meant to seem, and regard herself (especially in comparison to others) as a good enough soul.

There is in Adler a recognizably American wish to write as if the desires of others, the very fact of others, were not constraining on the self and its experience. True, the disquisitions on modern life have a determined, almost dutiful, outward bearing and significance. But parts of the book give one the feeling that the wish to float free had compulsive force. Kate's flight across Ireland is an illustration: The reader can only believe in the symbolic resonances of the events, what they reveal about Kate's state of mind, not in the people she flees from or in her predicament. Indeed, the Irish section of the book has a Kafkaesque nightmare logic, except Kafka nightmares depart from a real world. At its heart, to borrow Kate's observation in a discourse on "the matter of solipsism and prayer," *Pitch Dark* is a "lonely song," and not simply because it is the plaint of a disappointed lover.

As for characterization, even Jake hardly emerges. It is his type that is revealed. . . . Most of the other characters, with their improbable names—Viola Teagarden (based, apparently, on Lillian Hellman), or Leander Dworkin—and their foolish or vicious ideas, are no more than foils for Adler/Ennis' deflating and ironic commentary.

The absence of plot and characterization notwithstanding, Adler clearly does not want her work mistaken for an avant-garde effort. Anyone who refers derisively to a "trendy French philosopher," or who ruminates on "sentimentality in the works of Gertrude Stein," is not marching in that particular formation. There is a story here—consisting of Kate's perceptions—and an old-fashioned ambition to be its teller. Moreover, the discontinuous, journal-like form of *Pitch Dark*—reading at times like a private diary, at times like the attempt of a private diarist to reach for the public concerns of, say Gide's *Journals*—is largely suited to Adler's purposes. Deficiencies in execution, however, heighten the sense of excessive self-consciousness: The voice often seems to be speaking, or muttering, only to itself. More serious, Adler is sometimes lazy; the phrase "the incredible unseen beauty of the Irish countryside," for example, strikes me as a guidebook-style evasion. The opposite problem, a piling on of unnecessary details, is particularly

noticeable in the anecdotes of city life. They have the bemused, deliberately incurious (albeit highly detailed) style of an "impression" in the *New Yorker*'s "Talk of the Town" column. (pp. 17-18)

Pitch Dark shows a mind far happier spinning forth fine threads of argument, exposition and analysis than dealing with the intensity of emotion. Adler is at her sharpest uncovering the irrational aspects of the way we now live: a friend's unthinking romanticization of the PLO, or the weird civility of a publisher's lunch with a convicted murderer. She is very good on what Denis Donoghue recently described, with his customary shrewdness, as the inordinate reliance on the vocabulary of guilt and innocence in the moral imagination of most Americans, especially Americans who think of themselves as intellectuals. "We have the sins of silence here," Adler writes with dismay. "Also the sins of loquacity and glibness . . . of ignorance, and being well-informed. Of carelessness, and of exactitude. Of leading, following, opposing, taking no part in. Very few of us, it seems fair to say, are morally at ease."

Kate Ennis is not herself notably at ease. She has all the recognizable anxieties of the modern intellectual, and then some. *Pitch Dark,* if not ridden with angst, has its share of that omnipresent modern feeling. Still, Adler does seem to me to be unusually secure—even smug—precisely in her moral sense. In political terms, this complacency translates into predictably ungenerous portrayals of any of her characters who are even faintly Left-wing. They are represented as unthinkingly stylish, sentimental, or in love with violence. On the other hand, the two conservatives who figure briefly in the novel, Frank and Marilyn (note the good plain American names), are described as "kind, educated, tolerant, church-going people." These paragons oppose a local effort to reroute trucks that whiz dangerously by their neighborhood because "they so dislike the Sierra Club, Clamshell Alliance overtone."

Radicals have certainly been known to be sentimental, and to worship power and violence. There are decent and humane Right-wingers. It is both refreshing and salutary to find an American writer of stature willing to challenge facile Left pieties. Yet allowing for all this, I could not help feeling that Adler's antipathy to even her "vaguely Leftish" characters is unfair. (The expression "vaguely Leftish" is itself excessive rhetorical overkill.)

Pitch Dark will please those for whom Adler's sensibility is not only attractive but a sufficient guarantee of satisfying fiction, who won't care that this novel is, like the solipsist's prayer Kate speaks of, essentially a "lonely song." To such readers, the substitution of well-turned phrases and finely spun thoughts for emotional intensity or the presence of living, breathing human characters will in fact seem a considerable achievement. Others will admire Adler's evident talent, wit and intelligence, and hope for something more from her in the future. (p. 18)

Oliver Conant, "A Novelist's Lonely Song," in The New Leader, Vol. LXVII, No. 2, January 23, 1984, pp. 17-18.

ROGER SHATTUCK

Nature abhors a vacuum—at least in the little nook of the universe we inhabit. According to continuities and correspondences we cannot easily explain, the descriptive power of that statement appears to extend to some areas of art. . . .

[This is true of] some advanced areas of literature. For a number of years I have kept a list of devices and terms proposed from many sides to replace unity as the central organizing principle, particularly in the novel: digression, parody, marginal discourse, reflexivity, fragment, miscellany, theme and variations, *écriture*, palimpsest, and many more. The peculiar quality of Renata Adler's latest book, like the earlier *Speedboat*, is that, while adopting several of these devices, it insists on describing the vacuum itself. *Pitch Dark* injects into the seemingly vacant life of the author's surrogate narrator-protagonist enough dye to give the emptiness shape and visibility. The dye is compounded of short anecdotes, comic asides, deadpan refrains, and dissertations on far-fetched topics. It shows up the vacant space without filling it, and the resultant style veers rapidly between liveliness and diagnosis. . . .

Pitch Dark is a Book of Questions, often without the usual punctuation, suggesting they seek no answer. Speculation is called for here more than interrogation or detection. . . .

These questions and these brooding, intermittent memories create the effect of a constant hovering. Everything Adler writes in her "novels" hovers among genres, among generations, among farflung places, and among available moral attitudes. . . . Within this strain of hovering and inconclusiveness Adler has succeeded in establishing a magpie niche of her own.

Symmetrical as a triptych, *Pitch Dark* offers three fifty-page, loosely interlocking stories. Using half-page chunks—false starts, vignettes, insistent echoes—"Orcas Island" describes the never-quite-realized breakup of an affair between Kate Ennis, the narrator, and Jake, an older married man. He is vaguely understanding, preoccupied, and always offstage. . . . [Kate's] ruminations in this first section end characteristically with a question: "Did I throw the most important thing perhaps, by accident, away?" By now the reader understands that "the most important thing" can be stated in this frequently repeated form: "But you are, you know, you were, the nearest thing to a real story to happen in my life." . . .

The second section, which gives its title to the book, relates with relatively few interruptions what I read as a diversionary and cautionary tale told from the middle outward. On the way to a friend's loaned estate in Ireland in search of quiet and rest, Kate has a minor car accident whose consequences infect her with a sense of disgust and guilt. She refers to herself as a "tortfeasor." These pages, whose mood of self-isolation may be taken to connect with the first section, held me more by the occasional clarity of detail than by any power in the events. . . .

In "Home," the last section, the prolonged breakup with Jake is brought back into the foreground and compressed into an insistent telephone obbligato. Every third or fourth page one encounters a shred of despairing conversation overheard in London where Kate is working as a journalist. The rest of the time she is either shaping a fragile life in a small house with pond in a New England town within commuting distance of New York, or seeking refuge and solitude on Orcas Island off Seattle. Constant interruptions block any continuity that might be called a story line. The interruptions themselves, on the other hand, rough in a motif that concerns the betrayal of reality by inaccurate reporting. . . .

Meanwhile Jake has a cautious reaction to reading "Orcas Island," the first part of this book you hold in your hand. Gradually it all circles back on itself in an accelerating swirl

so that the last ten pages push nineteen distinct items of flotsam in front of the patient or distraught reader. . . .

By dint of repetition, variations in phrasing and speech patterns, and frequent interventions, Adler has created in *Pitch Dark* a sense of form that could be called cubist. The three sections do not develop a careful self-portrait of the central character. Yet the impulse behind the book is autobiographical, even confessional, rather than novelistic—i.e., genuinely concerned with other people's lives. The reader has to assemble Kate as the sum of her scattered parts—shy-bold, cosmopolitan, idealist, nostalgic, *farouche*. It does not spin a tale in spite of one underlined reference to the Penelope story. Rather it depicts a "mode of vision, a process of gathering odds and ends into a "piece" in both the fictional and the journalistic sense. Two hundred years ago Laurence Sterne had already mastered the art of self-interruption and elaborate detour. In reading Adler I began jotting in the margins "aecp" to designate the occasional voice of an alter ego critic-professor bringing things to a halt, shaking her finger, and breaking any illusion of narrative momentum. . . . The frequent gaps in the prose imply both a fainthearted hope of connection and the kind of total breakdown and fresh start that Sartre detected between every successive sentence of Camus's *The Stranger*. In this inwardly impassioned work by a writer who lived as student and journalist through the Fifties, Sixties, and Seventies, there seems to be no moral center beyond the end of an affair. Sputnik, the sit-ins, the assassinations, the moonshot, Vietnam, Watergate do not even ruffle the surface. How are we to take hold of this antinovel and its predecessor, *Speedboat*, to which it seems to be a close sequel?

I believe these astutely shuffled works take shape and have an effect in two related ways. Despite the lack of reference to major social and political events, the books convey the sense of an era that cohabits uncomfortably with its past. The antepenultimate sentence of *Speedboat* holds out a small key. "I think there's something to be said for assuring the next that the water's fine—quite warm, actually—once you get into it." Next *generation* she means. Even though both novels describe, primarily through fractured form and terse diction, a version of trauma, an ego detached like a retina, still the neurosis is bearable and has its small rewards.

> Roger Shattuck, "Quanta," *in* The New York Review of Books, *Vol. XXXI, No. 4, March 15, 1984, p. 3.*

JOSEPH EPSTEIN

I do not have the attention span to sustain a lengthy depression, but I have of late been reading two novelists who do: Renata Adler and Joan Didion. I think of them as the Sunshine Girls, largely because in their work the sun is never shining. . . . They seem, these two writers, not really happy unless they are sad. They keep, to alter the line from an old song, a frown on their page for the whole modern age. (p. 62)

Of the two, Renata Adler is the less practiced novelist. She has written, in fact, two novels but no narratives. *Speedboat*, her first novel, and *Pitch Dark*, her second, are both composed for the most part of short, journal-like entries, which, in the modernist spirit, a reader has rather to assemble on his own. *Speedboat*, published in 1976, was much praised; it won the Ernest Hemingway Award for best first novel of the year in which it was published. Reading it today, one notices certain affinities with the work of Ann Beattie: a flatness of expression meant to convey a deep spiritual fatigue. On the formal level, the novel seems Barthelmystically influenced, though without Barthelme's intellectual playfulness. (p. 63)

Miss Adler is not telling a story in *Speedboat;* instead she is trying to create a feeling through the thoughts, incidents, and odd happenings that occur to the presence at the center of her book, Jen Fain, who is a working journalist also teaching a film course at a school that resembles the City University of New York. The feeling she is trying to create is one of dislocation, disorientation, depression. "There doesn't seem to be a spirit of the times," Jen Fain remarks on the second page of the book. Miss Adler, though, will soon enough supply one. On that same page she has her character remark, "I think sanity, however, is the most profound moral option of our time." And at the bottom of the page, awaking at the apartment of one of her men friends, she is told, "Just stay here. *Angst* is common." We are, you might say, off and limping. . . .

In *Speedboat* disconnection is a way of life. Rats roam the halls; a Doberman pinscher attacks an old woman. Jen Fain reports: "I knew a deliverer of flowers who, at Sixty-ninth and Lexington, was hit by a flying suicide. Situations simply do not yield to the most likely structures of the mind." And: "There are some days when everyone I see is a lunatic." These passages pile up, and all are written, in the spiritual if not the grammatical sense, in the passive voice.

Having said all this, I must go on to say that I do not find *Speedboat* boring. It ought to be, but it isn't. Perhaps it isn't because, though the book offers none of the traditional pleasures of the novel, it does offer pleasures of a different kind. When it begins to hum, Miss Adler's is a lively mind, which throws off interesting insights. "Lonely people," she writes, "see double entendres everywhere." In a brilliant passage she talks about what she calls "the Angry Bravo," which is what goes on when, in her example, an audience cheers *No, No, Nanette* when in fact behind their cheers is rage at *Hair* or whatever the going triumph of the day is. She is also clever on the unseriousness of certain artists and intellectuals. (p. 63)

The world depicted in *Speedboat* is that of unattached youngish people for whom money is not a serious problem but finding a purpose in life is. They I won't say bound but at least crawl into one another's beds, less it seems out of passion than out of the need for comfort and solace against a cold world. They are distanced from life. Boredom is among their deadliest enemies. They have endless time to spend thinking about themselves. ("'Self-pity' is just sadness, I think, in the pejorative," says Miss Adler's Miss Fain.) Therapy is no help. "In every city, at the same time, therapists earned their living by saying, 'You're too hard on yourself.'" There is a slightly frenetic stylishness about their lives. "Elaine's was jammed"; a man invents a drink called "Last Mango in Paris." Nothing quite holds. Jen Fain avers: "The radical intelligence in the moderate position is the only place where the center holds." But of those who write or argue or say that the center will not hold, I always wonder how they know they are standing in the center—or anywhere near it.

It doesn't take long for *Speedboat* to run out of gas. The book provides no forward motion, nothing in the way of momentum. In a snippet of conversation reported in one of Miss Adler's paragraphs, a man says: "Janine, you know I'm very tired of your *aperçus*." So in time does one grow tired of Miss Adler's, which, in a book without any narrative force, could, any one of them, as easily appear on page 14 as on page 203. Cause

and effect, narrative order, nothing seems to matter. "It all ends in disaster anyway." But then Miss Adler is forthright about not having a story to tell. Toward the close of *Speedboat,* she writes: "There are only so many plots. There are insights, prose flights, rhythms, felicities. But only so many plots."

Friend, here's the bad news: you want to call yourself a novelist, you're going to have to find a plot.

Pitch Dark, Renata Adler's recent novel, does appear to be setting out to tell a story: that of the break-up of an eight-year love affair between another journalist, Kate Ennis, and a married man referred to as Jake. But the story turns out not to be much of a story. As the dust-jacket copy has it, ". . . *Pitch Dark* moves into new realms of feeling." This book, too, peels off into aperçuistical paragraphs; it is interested in making disconnections. It is about, as the narrator of this non-narration says, "my state of mind." This second book of Miss Adler's is more modernist, more avant-garde, in intention than *Speedboat.* The practical consequence is that, within its pages, more puzzles are offered, more elaborate games are played.

Like all contemporary works of modernist intention, *Pitch Dark* is highly self-reflexive—that is, it often talks about itself. Thus, two-thirds through the book Miss Adler writes:

> But will they understand it if I tell it this way?
> Yes, they will. They will surely understand it.
> But will they care about it?
> That I cannot guarantee.

The way that *Pitch Dark* is told is aslant, through indirection. "Do I need to stylize it, then, or can I tell it as it was?" Miss Adler stylizes it, in my view. At the forefront of her book is the affirmation that stories can no longer be told. "For a woman, it is always, don't you see, Scheherazade. For a man, it may be the Virginian. There he goes, then, striding through the dust of midday toward his confrontation. Here I am, of an evening, wondering whether I can hold his interest yet a while."

Throughout *Pitch Dark* lines repeat, meant to convey a refrain-like resonance. "But you are, you know, you were, the nearest thing to a real story to happen in my life," is one such line; "Did I throw the most important thing perhaps, by accident, away?" is another. We cannot know for certain who is saying these lines, Kate or Jake. But the lines recur, as do, among others, these two: "The world is everything that is the case," which is from Wittgenstein, and "And in the second place because," which is the first line of a Nabokov story. Both these lines are there to establish the modernity of Miss Adler's narrator's mind as well as to establish the modernity of her own intention in this book. Of the Wittgenstein line, an epigrammatic couplet by the poet Donald Hall seems particularly pertinent here:

> The world is everything that is the case.
> Now stop your blubbering and wash your face.

For there is a certain high-tone blubbering going on in *Pitch Dark.* In its pages Miss Adler has the portentousness knob turned all the way up. (p. 64)

Miss Adler never does get around to telling the story of Kate Ennis's long love affair with Jake. Instead she shows the sad after-effects of its break-up. Accounts of events, she believes, are lies. What is important are moods, feelings, symbols. So we are given an account of a raccoon who slowly dies of distemper on the stove of Kate Ennis's country house. Is this meant to stand in for the symbolic death of her love affair? So we are given a lengthy, deliberately paranoid account of a trip through Ireland. Is this meant to stand in for Kate Ennis's feeling of utter disorientation after the prop of her love affair is pulled out from under her? So the same lines repeat and resound throughout the book. Miss Adler succeeds in giving her novel a highly claustral feeling. Reading it one feels rather as if one is being asked to play handball in an empty but very small closet.

Bleak, psychologically inconclusive, bereft of the normal pleasures of storytelling, *Pitch Dark* has nonetheless enjoyed a pretty good run in both the popular press and from critics. In part, I suspect, this derives from the autobiographical atmosphere of the novel. In the course of an adulatory piece about her in *New York* magazine Miss Adler implied—and perhaps more than implied—that the love affair that she has not really written about in *Pitch Dark* is one that she herself has gone through. . . . There is also the attraction of gossip. "One morning, in the early nineteen-eighties, Viola Teagarden filed a suit in a New York state court against Claudia Denneny for libel. Also named as defendants were a public television station and a talkshow host." We all know who Viola and Claudia are, do we not? Withholding such obvious names is a fine advance on name-dropping.

As for the critical appreciation of *Pitch Dark*, here Miss Adler has what I think of as the moral minority on her side—that select group of critics who worry about not lending approval to avant-garde endeavor. Roger Shattuck, for example, writing in the *New York Review of Books* [see excerpt above], has remarked that "Adler has created in *Pitch Dark* a sense of form that could be called cubist." Professor Shattuck plays that old shell game of modern criticism, switching genres, in which the critic has to guess under which genre the work lies. "Adler, like many of her contemporaries, abjures fusion, practices simple removal," he writes. "The resulting minimalist genre should properly not be called a novel, for it answers radically different expectations, brings other rewards." Better yet, the book has allowed Professor Shattuck to erect what he calls "the innarratability principle," which has to do with the inability—or, more precisely, unwillingness—of certain modern writers to tell their story straight out.

But to return to the old, perhaps boring, narratability principle, would it be too rude to suggest that Miss Adler has let slip away an extremely interesting story? The story of being a married man's mistress, told from the point of view of the mistress, is after all neither a common nor an unpromising one. What is it about women who enter into lengthy affairs with married men? What do they have to gain? What is it they are afraid of? Why are they so ready to put themselves almost automatically in second place or below? But then this is a story

Renata Adler, given her view that accounts of incidents are lies and that narrative contains the seeds of its own falsity, could never tell. She is among that band of contemporary writers who evidently do not agree with Oscar Wilde's statement: "It must be our faith that there is nothing that cannot be said with words." (pp. 64-5)

With its deconstructionists in literary criticism, its ordinary-language and other philosophers, and its novelists, our age may one day come to be known in intellectual history for its role in the advancement of techniques to prove that reality doesn't exist. Along with their natural gifts of dark temperament, our Sunshine Girls, Renata Adler and Joan Didion, are joined in this enterprise. It is more than a mite depressing.

In search of comic relief while reading the novels of Miss Adler and Miss Didion, I happened upon Nietzsche's little book *Schopenhauer as Educator*—one must take one's laughs where one can find them—where I came upon the following remarkable explanation of why such novels, and the general train of thought they represent, are so depressing:

> Basically, you see, cheerfulness is only to be found where there is victory, and this applies to the works of all true thinkers as it does to every work of art. Even if the content is terrible and serious as the problem of existence itself, the work will have an oppressive and painful effect only in those cases where the half-thinker or half-artist has spread the haze of his inadequacy over it; whereas nothing better or more cheering can happen to a man than to be near those victorious persons who, because they have thought the deepest thoughts, must love what is most alive, and finally, like the wise men they are, turn to the Beautiful. They really *talk,* they don't stammer or gossip; they really live and move, unlike other human beings who lead such a strange mask-like existence. For this reason when we are near them we feel, for a change, human and natural and have an urge to shout out as Goethe: "How marvelous and precious is a living thing! how real and truly adapted to its condition!"

Recall that Nietzsche is here talking about Schopenhauer, the darkest of all modern philosophers. There is plain pessimism and there is heroic pessimism—and of plain pessimism, of the kind Renata Adler and Joan Didion dispense, we have had quite enough. Let, please, the sun shine in. (p. 65)

Joseph Epstein, "The Sunshine Girls," in Commentary, *Vol. 77, No. 6, June, 1984, pp. 62-7.**

Manlio Argueta

1936-

Salvadoran novelist.

Argueta gained attention in the English-speaking world with *Un día en la vida* (1980; *One Day of Life*). This novel depicts the civil strife in present-day El Salvador, particularly the conflict between peasants and the special government force that polices them. Critical reaction to *One Day of Life* was mixed. Some considered it excessively moralistic and one-sided in its presentation of the brutalities inflicted upon peasants. However, others found the novel timely and claimed that it accurately and realistically depicts the social chaos and horrors of civil war. The government of El Salvador banned *One Day of Life* and forced Argueta to leave his native land. Argueta currently lives in exile in Costa Rica.

KESSEL SCHWARTZ

El valle de las hamacas, winner of the Certamen Cultural Centroamericano in 1968, reflects the political and social experience of the author, especially in the years 1959-60. Argueta depicts the all too familiar conflicts in his country and the inevitable identification of idealistic Salvadorean youth with problems in neighboring Honduras and Nicaragua. In his social fiction Argueta avoids direct ideological manifestoes and romantic symbolism without diminishing his concern or conviction. Using chains of associations, interior monologue, and a kind of mythological fusion of past and present history, he lightly touches on the theme of alienation which besets us all. Avoiding punctuation, Argueta uses various forms of address, especially the second person, in his recall and reverie, sometimes indicating them by italics. Done as a series of superimposed layers with flashbacks and interior temporal jumps, many of the events become fully evident only toward the end of the novel.

Essentially the story concerns a group of university students at San Salvador between the ages of eighteen and twenty-five who enjoy drinking, sex, music, and strong language, which the author transcribes in perhaps overabundant detail. Among these students are Raúl Morales, in love with Rosaura; Mauricio Robles, known as el Chatío, her brother; and Jorge. Imbued with a dislike of tyranny, they slip into Nicaragua to take part in guerrilla activities. Mauricio and many of the group are killed and Raúl is captured and mistreated to try to force him to reveal his companion's whereabouts. He is finally released but on his return to San Salvador cannot tell Rosaura about her brother.

At various moments in the story (with a group of revolutionaries or in the jail) Raúl slips in and out of different states of recall, remembering part of his childhood, his friendships, and university days. At times he seems to reexperience, at others to recall and resynthesize remote half-conscious associations as he switches in time and space.

Argueta mercilessly exposes the pretentious political hacks who preach phony law and order and the incredible police brutality against dissenting university students. In his hypocritical and corrupt country, where only the poor pay taxes, there are "clubes para ricos y excusados para pobres." Although Central America is a land of eternal contradiction filled with beautiful geography and invisible men, Raúl and others manage to maintain some of their convictions.

> *Kessel Schwartz, in a review of "El valle de las hamacas," in Hispania, Vol. 54, No. 4, December, 1971, p. 974.*

JIM MILLER

Americans have long seemed content to read novels about themselves: about the absurdities of affluence, the anxiety of adultery, the pitfalls of "midlife crisis." But tastes are changing. Gabriel García Márquez's "One Hundred Years of Solitude" introduced readers to a strange new world of magical happenings and political extremity. . . .

["**One Day of Life**"] recounts 12 hours in the life of a woman named Lupe. She is a 44-year-old matriarch who manages a small plot of farmland on the outskirts of Chalatenango, a bus ride away from the capital city of San Salvador. Much of the book consists of her meandering thoughts as she mulls over the color of the dawn, the freedom of birds in flight, the surprising militance of the local priests since they began saying mass in Spanish instead of Latin. Pious, self-reliant and stubborn, Lupe harbors growing doubts about the necessity of the poverty she endures.

Lupe's reveries are shattered by the appearance of National Guardsmen who are searching for her granddaughter, Adolfina. Through a series of interior monologues set in the minds of Adolfina, her mother, a friend and the "authorities," we learn that the youngster is an activist in a new peasant alliance. Though she is only 15, Adolfina has already participated in a demonstration at a bank, watched the Army retaliate with a blood bath and suffered through the unexplained "disappearance" of her father.

The book's conclusion is gruesome, its message about as subtle as a clenched fist. "They"—as the guardsmen are called—are mindless macho brutes. The poor villagers, in stark contrast, are pious, industrious, upright. In case anyone has missed the point, Lupe declares that "we're all innocent. The only ones at fault for the bad things that are happening are the authorities."

Despite such crude moralizing, "**One Day of Life**" does document a side of the conflict in El Salvador that is rarely reported in America—the squalor, government terror and understandable thirst for vengeance that turn peasants into revolutionaries. (p. 87)

> *Jim Miller, "Listening to Foreign Voices," in Newsweek, Vol. CII, No. 13, September 26, 1983, pp. 87-8.**

ALLEN JOSEPHS

Manlio Argueta's "**One Day of Life**" is . . . all too believable. . . . [Its style] is something I can only call primitive oral realism. Doña Lupe, a peasant grandmother already old at 45, narrates most of it. . . . Interspersed at random in a somewhat confusing narrative scheme are monologues by others, including Lupe's daughter, María Pía and Lupe's granddaughter, Adolfina. There are also two sections related by "The Authorities" and "They." All these monologues are addressed to "you," who is sometimes the reader and sometimes, in the case of Lupe's sections, her dead son, Justino, and her absent husband, José.

The events this testimonial novel depicts—the oppression, torture and murder of *campesinos* by the "Special Forces"—have a grim predictability. In the course of this one day, "you" learn that Justino was murdered and decapitated for helping to organize a demonstration; that María Pía has been crippled by a beating; and that her husband has been captured and tortured and has disappeared. . . . Priests are also tortured, and children die of dysentery, their heads caved in from dehydration. The agent of much of this brutality is Private Martínez, the son of Lupe's poor neighbors, who has become one of "them."

"One Day of Life," which was originally published in El Salvador in 1980 and was subsequently banned there, is both poignant and simplistic. Many of the 40,000 Salvadorans who have been killed recently were *campesinos* like Mr. Argueta's characters. Yet the novel, while eliciting sympathy for these victims, seldom transcends the literal recording of misery. Readers seeking the particulars of that suffering will find this record rewarding, but those searching for a larger discussion of the dilemma facing El Salvador will have to look elsewhere. As brave and engaging as Lupe and her family are, they are incapable of describing the nature of the evil surrounding them. (pp. 15, 26)

> Allen Josephs, "Sorcerers and Despots," *in* The New York Times Book Review, *October 2, 1983, pp. 15, 26.**

CHRISTOPHER DICKEY

In a one-room building behind the archbishop's offices in San Salvador there are high-piled stacks of depositions recording what is known about the last hours in the lives of thousands of people lost to El Salvador over the last four years. . . .

At its best, *One Day of Life,* a novel by exiled Salvadoran author Manlio Argueta, reads as if it were written from those files and drawn from those grisly images. As he tells the story of Guadalupe Fuentes and her family's quotidian ordeals in mountainous Chalatenango province the peasant voices are real with the woefulness and the sheer determination to survive that pervades the Salvadoran countryside. The matter-of-factness of horror is there. . . .

When it works, this book does what virtually no other volume or newspaper story or television report in the United States has even begun to do. It renders the Salvadoran peasant visible. . . . In *One Day of Life* they are presented, at last, as something more than political ciphers.

The ambience of rural poverty—the pervasiveness of the violence, the intimate presence of a repressive system that feeds on the violence—is drawn in telling detail. . . .

And yet there is a great deal about this book, alas, that is so obvious, so banal, so plainly bad as literature and so potentially misleading as politics and sociology, that one hesitates to praise it at all. It is a painfully awkward work that teeters somewhere between art and polemic, truth and lies. It calls itself a novel, but its roots are in propaganda. In much of its intellectual dishonesty, unfortunately, Argueta's book is reminiscent once again of what is to be found at the unofficial Human Rights Commission: the tendency to turn your opponents into demons and your allies into angels, which is endemic to Salvadoran society and nowhere more evident than on the left.

You might expect that with so much real horror at hand the opposition would see no need to report more than the objective truth about what is going on. But reality, as damning as it might be, is somehow never quite adequate to the propagandist's purpose. No one killed is ever so much as a leftist sympathizer, much less a guerrilla. (p. 46)

Argueta is at his worst when he attempts to adopt the voice of a common soldier in El Salvador's *Guardia Nacional,* the agent of repression. He does catch accurately the way soldiers are taught to think of themselves as a separate class. . . . But Argueta cannot resist the kind of arch twist that seems designed to win cheap nods of approval from the left's true believers. . . . (pp. 46-7)

Moreover, while its American publishers . . . are selling *One Day of Life* with the line that it is "as timely a novel as there could ever be about the present turmoil in El Salvador," it is already very much a work of the past. It depicts a time four or five years ago when it was much easier to define the good, the bad, and the ugly in El Salvador without so much as mentioning where the guerrillas might fit into the spectrum. Chalatenango, the setting for the novel, was and is the stronghold of the most radical communist faction in the guerrilla front. . . . But there are no rebels to be seen in Argueta's book. There is only talk about the Christian Federation, known in El Salvador as FECCAS, and there are some revolutionary priests. (p. 47)

Argueta's interest presumably is in showing why a revolution is needed in El Salvador, not in suggesting the sometimes sordid and cynical mechanics employed to bring it about, even if they are a vital part of the lives and deaths his characters would encounter in the scene he has set. I do not mean for a moment to lose sight of the evils committed in the past and still being committed by members of the government Washington backs in El Salvador. "Unfortunately the truth about atrocities is far worse than that they are lied about and made into propaganda," George Orwell wrote more than forty years ago. "The truth is that they happen." But to understand the true horror of those atrocities and, most importantly, to search for some way to bring them to an end, it is important to know propaganda when you see it—whether at the Human Rights Commission, or in a White House press release, or in this novel.

Caught between the repression of the U.S.-backed military and the cynical dogmas of the rebel armies, about all the Salvadoran people can depend on these days to set them free is, in fact, the truth. *One Day of Life,* for all its promise, and all the promises made for it, carries us only a very little way closer to finding out what that may be. (pp. 47-8)

> Christopher Dickey, "A Salvadoran Writer," *in* The New Republic, *Vol. 189, No. 21, November 21, 1983, pp. 46-8.*

EDWARD J. CURTIN, JR.

All suffering is incarnate, doubly so that of the poor and persecuted. Empty bellies, painful early deaths, back-breaking labor, a rifle butt in the face: These are some of the milder tortures administered by the "authorities" to the citizens of El Salvador.

Such oppressive suffering is hard for Americans to visualize, much less believe in or care about, even though their own Government is deeply implicated in the daily carnage. It all seems abstract, unreal, Salvadorans somehow seeming not quite human.

This moving novel, banned by the Government of El Salvador, shatters that illusion. Written by the exiled Salvadoran, Manlio Argueta, *One Day of Life* palpably presents peasants as they struggle through one terrifying day. Murdered at the present rate of about 100 a week, these persecuted people here find a voice.

And a quietly powerful voice it is, one that reverberates in the reader. (pp. 14-15)

The voices of the poor tell a story of the growth of conscience. . . , the discovery of rights and the awareness of exploitation. . . .

Despite the terrifying evil that pervades this book, there is a luminous spirit of hope and resistance that miraculously prevails. It is passed on from person to person despite death and torture and great suffering. "Maybe the spirit is the memory that gets into your head," Lupe muses. It is precisely this spirit, generous, loving, but infinitely determined to resist oppression, that Argueta has artfully managed to portray. (p. 15)

> *Edward J. Curtin, Jr., in a review of "One Day of Life," in* America, *Vol. 150, No. 1, January 14, 1984, pp. 14-15.*

GRACE INGOLDBY

Argueta's 'authorities', like Kundera's, cannot joke or smile lest they be revealed as too absurd. *One Day of Life* is the story of Lupe, grandmother at 40, a peasant woman from Chalate in El Salvador. . . .

The story is a sad one, delicately told, revealing not only Lupe's fate as she is caught in the cross-fire of civil war but also (and as remote from our understanding) the peasant life of birds and flowers and dust, the colours of a country woven in a blanket, infant mortality, hunger, water, a precious commodity offered as a symbolic, superstitious gift to friends and enemies alike.

The mirthless authorities have their say: boys equipped with fast philosophy and automatics who do well to overlook the fact that they rose from the ranks of the people they now subdue. . . . Well-fed and backed by 'the most civilized country in the world' (guess who?), they are brainwashed into believing that the people have been brainwashed too: 'Who is our special enemy? The people.' Lupe's story tells of the silent erosion of normal behaviour, the effects of intimidation and terror that mark, as in Northern Ireland now, a prolonged period of civil war, and of lessons learnt the hard way: Christian goodness must no longer be confused with resignation; stoicism in the face of horror (her son's severed head on a pole) is not only dignified but advisable—never show your fear. Rights are something that Lupe must learn to understand and to fight for, a new way of enduring, a significant if small-scale step forward.

> *Grace Ingoldby, "Lessons in Life," in* New Statesman, *Vol. 107, No. 2766, March 23, 1984, p. 27.**

KEVIN CULLY

In *One Day of Life* we are at last offered a glimpse of what that awful, savage [Salvadoran civil] war must be like from the point of view of the peasants who bear the brunt of it. . . .

We also get an insight into the minds of these brutalised Civil Guard through the letters that one of them writes home. Reading the letters is depressing because they throw into sharp focus the fear and suspicion that the authorities harbour toward their own people. The man is himself a peasant but after months with his "foreign" instructors he regards his own people with icy contempt.

This is a marvellous novel on a tragic situation but the author is not well served by his translator who opts for a very Americanised dialogue.

> *Kevin Cully, "Hard Day's Night," in* Tribune, *Vol. 48, No. 19, May 11, 1984, p. 9.*

Jean M(arie) Auel

1936-

American novelist and poet.

Auel's first novel, *The Clan of the Cave Bear* (1980), and its sequel, *The Valley of Horses* (1982), are considered interesting and original attempts to depict early human history. These stories take place in the Middle Paleolithic age when the Neanderthal and Cro-Magnon species coexisted. The basic conflict in the first of these novels is between a Neanderthal tribe and the Cro-Magnon girl whom the tribe adopts. The girl, Ayla, performs feats which earn her the respect of all but one member of the tribe, who forces her into exile. The second novel continues her story. While *The Clan of the Cave Bear* and *The Valley of Horses* have been faulted for their stereotypical characterizations of the blond, blue-eyed Ayla and her tall, handsome mate, Jondalar, they are also noted for Auel's well-researched and detailed descriptions of survival techniques. The books have been described as "cave operas," since they have some of the characteristics of popular romances and soap operas and have been well received by the public. Auel is planning several more novels with prehistoric settings which will form a series called *Earth's Children.*

(See also *Contemporary Authors,* Vol. 103.)

© *Jerry Bauer*

JOHN PFEIFFER

["**The Clan of the Cave Bear**"] tells the tale of a band of prehistoric hunter-gatherers living on the Crimean peninsula near the shores of the Black Sea. . . . These people, at large some 35,000 years ago, are representatives of a dying breed, among the last of the Neanderthal line.

The band faces new tensions, new troubles, which will ultimately prove its undoing. It has just taken in one of the "Others," a 5-year-old girl foundling named Ayla whose parents have been killed in a recent earthquake. . . . She is a member of the Cro-Magnon species destined to replace all Neanderthals everywhere. (p. 7)

The Neanderthal people are doomed by the structure of their brains. Intelligent and sensitive, they have prodigious memories, care for their weak and handicapped and bury their dead with grave talismans for use in an afterlife. At the height of secret totemic ceremonies, they can probe deep into the racial past, communicating with one another telepathically. But having only rudimentary frontal lobes, the brain centers responsible for foresight and analysis, they are incapable of adapting to major changes. They have reached an evolutionary dead end, living very much as their ancestors lived 100,000 years ago. Everything they do has been done already. They cannot innovate, and that is where the growing girl of the Others shines.

The people are amazed, one spring day near the inland sea, to see Ayla plunging into a swift sturgeon-rich stream to rescue a drowning child. "No one had ever been saved before, once they had been swept away." And no one had ever wielded a sling in rapid-fire fashion, inserting and hurling a second pebble as soon as the first had been released. But Ayla teaches herself that trick, thereby breaking a taboo forbidding women even to

touch hunting weapons, and she uses it to kill a hyena in the act of dragging off a baby boy.

Every success brings Ayla a step closer to tragedy. If she had only been less courageous, less outstanding and admired, the story of her life with the people might have ended happily. She earns the respect of all members of the band—all but one, Brun's son Broud, insecure, jealous and vicious, next in line to be the band's leader and half-aware that he is not the man for the job. He hates her to the point of beatings and rape. Things come to a head suddenly. There is a grim struggle between Ayla and Broud, another earthquake and a bitter final showdown.

When it comes to certain details about the appearance and cerebral apparatus of the Neanderthals, anthropologists may grumble about "**The Clan of the Cave Bear.**" . . . Even literary license cannot justify endowing the Neanderthals with brains having "almost no frontal lobes." Also, they were not bow-legged, and it is rather unlikely that their vocal cords were less developed than ours, or that such a difference would have seriously affected their ability to communicate vocally.

In the last analysis, however, such points do not really matter. There was a great and subtle gap between the Neanderthals and their successors, people like ourselves, and Mrs. Auel has caught its essence beautifully. She has written an exciting, imaginative and intuitively solid book. She is planning five more prehistoric novels (the series is called **"Earth's Children"**). I look forward to reading them as I look forward to her own evolution as a writer and her versions of human evolution. (pp. 7, 20)

> John Pfeiffer, *"Prehistoric Characters,"* in The New York Times Book Review, *August 31, 1980, pp. 7, 20.*

BARBARA MERTZ

So few solid facts are known about [the Middle Paleolithic] period that one can hardly criticize an author for filling in the canyon-sized gaps with speculation, particularly when the authorities themselves disagree. Can one, then, reasonably call [Jean M. Auel's *The Clan of the Cave Bear* and Bjorn Kurtén's *Dance of the Tiger*] historical (or prehistorical) novels, and demand that they conform to the rules governing that genre? I believe one can and must, if only because both authors have followed the rules to the best of their respective abilities. Known fact is not violated; conjecture is based on reasonable inferences.

The biggest problem facing a historical novelist is how to create the sense of an alien culture without losing the basic humanity of the characters. Most writers go too far in one direction or the other, producing modern men and women in funny clothes, or wax figures who gesticulate and move but never live.

One key element is the handling of language. I myself have a sneaking affection for what Josephine Tey contemptuously referred to as "writing forsoothly." An occasional "forsooth" or "by our Lady" reminds me that I am not listening to contemporaries talking. Auel and Kurtén have taken the only sensible approach, since we have no Neanderthal equivalent of forsooth, or of any other word. Their characters speak colloquial English. However, we are made to realize that this is only a convenient fictional device. Auel's Neanderthals have a limited spoken vocabulary, amplified by a complex system of gestures. (Her heroine, a Cro-Magnon orphan adopted by a tribe of kindly Neanderthals, has the dickens of a time unlearning her *Homo sapiens* loquacity in favor of sign language.) . . .

[This approach is] based on what may well be the most questionable scientific theory in either book—a recent study by Philip Liebermann which attempts to prove that the vocal apparatus of Neanderthal man was incapable of producing the full range of modern sound. . . . As Stephen Jay Gould points out in his excellent introduction to the Kurtén book, Leibermann's theory is highly suspect but has not been proven wrong, and therefore it may legitimately serve as a model for a writer of fiction. The significant point is how the two authors use the model. . . . Auel's Neanderthals grunt. They are a good deal more apelike, physically and mentally, than Kurtén's; and Auel's Cro-Magnon heroine is a typical Aryan—blond, blue-eyed, tall and beautiful. (p. 6)

Bear is a prehistoric soap opera—"cave opera" would be an appropriate term. Put the heroine in a bustle instead of a bearskin, and she could walk right into one of the "historical romances" crowding the bookshelves in drugstore and supermarket. Except for a few other stock characters—the motherly wise woman, the surly villain—the rest of the cast is outstandingly undistinguished. The fact that they all have names like Oga and Aga and Uba makes it even harder to tell them apart.

As cave operas go it is a good one—slickly written, carefully researched, very sincere. But that is all it is. (pp. 6, 10)

> Barbara Mertz, *"The Novel Neanderthal,"* in Book World—The Washington Post, *September 28, 1980, pp. 6, 10.**

THOMAS HOPKINS

[Despite] an arid narrative style that would have crushed a less audacious story, Auel has fashioned [*The Clan of the Cave Bear*] . . . with nuggets of archeology and anthropology. (p. 64)

Auel has created a remarkable, speculative portrait of a preconscious world, different from science fiction because of the constant echoes of human experience found there. The documentary effect is achieved by sprinkled passages of Dick-and-Jane anthropology on topics such as herbs, fire transporting or toolmaking. As a narrative technique it's not new: Arthur Hailey has made fortunes serving up thinly novelized instruction manuals to airports or car factories. Auel's pedagogy is more successful because it illuminates a plausible if melodramatic ancestral world oddly comforting in its richness and diversity. Moreover, it will likely reward its sponsors financially, partially because it adheres to the perennially seductive saga format of *The Thorn Birds* and *Shōgun*, or of Dickens for that matter.

But its success will ultimately be due to the affecting character of Ayla, whose life story will bind the *Earth's Children* series together. A sort of Cro-Magnon Katharine Hepburn, she stoically endures innumerable beatings, a rape and ritual banishment at the hands of oafish and inferior males before finally earning the honorific: The Woman Who Hunts. In Ayla, Auel has an engine both familiar and intriguingly alien enough to drive her next five books. (pp. 64-5)

> Thomas Hopkins, *"Perils of a Prehistoric Pauline,"* in Maclean's Magazine, *Vol. 93, No. 40, October 6, 1980, pp. 64-5.*

GROVER SALES

"The Valley of Horses," Jean M. Auel's sequel to her blockbuster novel **"The Clan of the Cave Bear"** set in ice age Ukraine, 30,000 BC, is a well-researched children's story fleshed out with steamy primordial sex, women's lib, soap opera plots and "Me, Tarzan—you, Jane" dialogue.

One must admire the painstaking anthropological research Auel has poured into her proposed trilogy. Even readers turned off by the gimmicky form this novel assumes may find fascination in the technique of human survival in the late Pleistocene Epoch. . . .

[Ayla's] story is entwined with the wanderings of Jondalar, 6-foot-6 superstud making the long trek down the Danube to the Black Sea. Early on, the author telegraphs their cataclysmic coupling, and readers who have stuck it out this far are rewarded with epic copulations.

There may be the sound idea of a novel in all this, but Auel's odd notions of primitive speech are a continual nuisance. . . .

[And] Auel's narrative style seems weirdly at variance with the era she's describing. When Ayla finds she can start fire with flint, "That was the serendipity." Again, when Ayla's cave becomes fetid with the stink of rotting corpses, "She wanted a breath of air untainted by malodorous emanations."

This goes on for 500 pages; the pages are large and the type small.

Grover Sales, "Primordial Passions of Pleistocene Times: The Flesh Is Willing, But the Diction Is Weak," in Los Angeles Times Book Review, September 12, 1982, p. 3.

SUSAN ISAACS

Mrs. Auel is craftsman enough to weave her facts into the fabric of her book ["**The Valley of Horses**"], providing texture as well as information. When Ayla sutures a wound, her patient is no anonymous charity case whose injured leg is just a limb on which the author hangs her research. The wounded man is significant. His appearance marks the end of Ayla's horrible loneliness; he is the first human being she has seen in years.

His name is Jondalar, and he is one of the Others, the first Cro-Magnon Ayla can remember seeing. When he lies unconscious on the floor of her cave, her concern, curiosity and enchantment are both understandable and appropriate. . . .

[Jondalar is] 6 feet 6, with charismatic blue eyes and enough sexual finesse to make Masters and Johnson shout hosannas. And that is the main problem with the novel. While the background seems authentic, the characters seem too good—and too modern—to be true. . . .

Of course, this golden couple (their blondness is stressed almost ad nauseam) is no ordinary twosome; they are archetypes. Although Ayla and Jondalar have particular personalities and concerns, they also serve as models of what humanity was capable of 25,000 to 30,000 years ago. But because the author places too much weight on these characters' shoulders, their credibility is strained. They are superhuman and thus not believable. Jondalar is the ultimate civilized Cro-Magnon, a well-muscled, artistic, spear-throwing Cary Grant. And it is Ayla, and Ayla alone, who invents oral sex, horseback riding, a new technique for making fire and a better way of dragging the kill back to the cave.

But despite those qualifications, "**The Valley of Horses**" is great fun to read. Jean M. Auel has created ancestors who do us all credit. She has gone beyond the cliché of leopard-skin-covered, club-wielding grunters and presented a panorama of human culture in its infancy. Her characters enjoy celebrations, companionship, sex, travel and good cooking. They care for children and animals. They discuss art and religion. They are very much like us, although generally better behaved. And that's the best part of the book, to look back with Mrs. Auel and savor what we might have been.

Susan Isaacs, "Ayla Loves Jondalar," in The New York Times Book Review, September 26, 1982, p. 14.

Russell (Wayne) Baker

1925-

American nonfiction writer.

Baker is a highly regarded, widely read newspaper columnist and humorist. While serving on the Washington bureau of the *New York Times* during the mid-1950s and early 1960s, Baker earned recognition for his wry commentaries on the federal bureaucracy, many of which formed the basis of *An American in Washington* (1961). Since 1962, Baker has written the "Observer" column in the *Times*. The essays in this column satirize such issues as politics, the economy, and popular culture. Baker is especially praised for his insight into the human condition, particularly the daily problems of ordinary people.

Many of Baker's columns have been published in collections: *No Cause For Panic* (1969), *Poor Russell's Almanac* (1972; revised, 1982), and *So This Is Depravity* (1980). In 1979 Baker was awarded the Pulitzer Prize for distinguished commentary for his columns. He is the first humorist to win the award in that category since its inception in 1970. Baker's critically acclaimed autobiography *Growing Up* (1982) earned him another Pulitzer Prize in 1982. The book chronicles Baker's childhood and family life during the Great Depression. The quiet humor and the lack of melodrama in his portrayal of that era prompted critics to compare *Growing Up* to the works of Mark Twain. In a style which is understated yet powerful, Baker describes personal hardships with subtle emotion. *Growing Up* is considered a notable work of Americana. *The Rescue of Miss Yaskell and Other Pipe Dreams* (1983) is a recent collection of Baker's essays.

(See also *Contemporary Authors*, Vols. 57-60 and *Contemporary Authors New Revision Series*, Vol. 11.)

© 1984 Thomas Victor

VIRGINIA KIRKUS' SERVICE

Russell Baker, a *New York Times* Washington correspondent, gets a lot off his chest [in *An American in Washington*] writing about Washington as a tribal entity, filled with bizarre customs. Considerable information is packed into chapters satirizing Society, Bureaucrats, Diplomats, Congress, the Presidency, etc. But the style is difficult, overcrowded with metaphors, and only fairly successful in its humor. . . . A sketch book, in which the individual scenes are sharper than the end view, and more satisfying in its occasional vignettes and insights. (pp. 765-66)

> A review of "An American in Washington," in Virginia Kirkus' Service, Vol. XXIX, No. 16, August 15, 1961, pp. 765-66.

WILLIAM H. STRINGER

The only thing worrisome about [*An American in Washington,* a] wild Lord Bryce's guide on how Washington's denizens behave, is that someone may regard it as true to life.

That said, one can proceed to report that this Coney-Island-mirror view of the waltzings and posings and peccadilloes of Washington's politicians, hostesses, cocktail-party givers, am-

bassadors, congressmen, State Department officials, newsmen and the President himself is witty, sardonic, blasé, irreverent, and often funny.

A lot of American humor these days is not soft and chuckling, poking fun at one's self as well as others, in the Will Rogers tradition. Russell Baker of The New York Times has the wit but not the gentleness. His guidebook portrait of a Washington of rogues, name-droppers, obfuscators and belabored bureaucrats reaches from one end of Pennsylvania Avenue to the other, and provides not a dull moment.

Unfortunately, he wrote before the full flavor of the Kennedy administration set in. Much of the Kennedy Washington is thus unmined. And there's this one warning: Washington is more bearable, humane, kindly, even idealistic, than we're told here. This book is, of course, for laughs.

> William H. Stringer, "Laughter on Pennsylvania Avenue," in The Christian Science Monitor, October 16, 1961, p. 9.

SIDNEY HYMAN

[Russell Baker] has written a book whose laughter better serves the cause of what is truly serious and solemn than any thundering from a pulpit. The author's finely tuned moral and esthetic instincts have been jarred in equal measure by the disfigurements Washington produces in some men, and by the nation's unwarranted fear of its own capital. However, the reformist counter-attack Mr. Baker mounts in **"An American in Washington"** resembles a prose-cartoon, and not the Book of Deuteronomy. It is fluently drawn, epigrammatically succinct, and by turning every instance of the ludicrous into a "rule of prudence" makes the ludicrous all the more apparent.

To put the matter directly, **"An American in Washington"** is offered as a "practical guide to survival" in the nation's capital, and as a contribution to "easing the tensions between the United States of America and the District of Columbia." Why this? Well, says Mr. Baker, most Americans look upon Washington as "an unworthy place where men of mean talents but cunning proclivities conspire to inconvenience people beyond its frontiers." In fact, the widely held notion that the place is "more dangerous than Moscow" helps explain why Presidential hopefuls often promise the country that if elected, "they will work American's vengeance on Washington."

Mr. Baker admits that Washington does indeed have its dangers, and not only for the newly arrived American who thinks he has come to a patch of friendly motherland. Even some of Washington's "most famous men have had knives placed so professionally in their backs that they have learned about it only by reading the next morning's newspapers." Still, says he, when Washington and Washingtonians are looked at in a detached way, it is not the sinister but the silly that is more likely to come into focus. . . .

Chapter and subchapter headings suggest the aspects of Washington life covered by the guide. They include The Importance of Despair, How to Put on the Dog Without Pedigree, The Urgency of Lunch, How to Be a Great President, How to Be a Successful Senator, How to Be Investigated, Hindsighting and Crystal-balling, Esoterica, and a good deal more in this tipsy-turvy vein.

The "practical advice" offered under these headings becomes a galvanic needle in the hide of the censorable. And the needle hits its mark without touching any bones en route, precisely because Mr. Baker appears to be such a stanch defender of the manners and morals he jabs. Here are a few small examples of his technique:

When he offers advice to the socially ambitious, he says: "Be careful about seduction. This is not Hollywood, and anyone caught exhibiting more interest in the libido than the ego is apt to be dismissed as a trifle ordinary." When he stresses how important it is for a man to qualify at least as a "worthy worrier"—the President alone is expected to be a "fully rounded, Renaissance worrier"—Mr. Baker says: "The point to remember is that no one can last long in Washington who is not convinced that something some place is in hellish shape. Those who find it difficult being spooky for sustained periods will prefer Paris or Miami Beach." . . .

When he emphasizes that skill at obfuscating is essential to all activists in Washington, he says: "The mark of a great Obfuscator is an audience debating what he *meant*. The plain talker says what he means; the Obfuscator leaves them guessing."

Much of Mr. Baker's book, in fact, turns on making plain what the obfuscators in Washington circles mean when they use such key words as "implement," "coordinate," "formulate," "function," "finalize," "definitize," "maximize" and "minimize." Nor is this proportion of the book misplaced in emphasis. After all, democratic government is "government by speaking"—which implies an obligation to use words in ways in which they will stand as one with the things they are meant to describe. Mr. Baker therefore performs a heroic service in helping the rest of us—and the Government—understand what we mean when we talk as we do in Washington.

> *Sidney Hyman, "A Guide to Survival," in* The New York Times Book Review, *October 22, 1961, p. 18.*

JOHN MARTIN

Russell Baker is perhaps the funniest newspaper columnist there is, and, after Murray Kempton, the finest stylist in contemporary journalism. Regrettably, his lyrical and wildly inventive social satire has until now been limited to appearances in the drab and leaden columns of the New York *Times*. [*No Cause for Panic*] not only takes him out of the *Times* but should put him on the shelves of connoisseurs of first-rate humor.

Ninety-four of Baker's best are reprinted here. They are topical and they are choice.

There is the foreign ambassador puzzled by American football: "Huge men repeatedly flung themselves beast-like upon a much smaller man who was holding the prolate spheroid." An American official replies: "That, Mr. Ambassador, is called playing the game." (pp. 84-5)

And there is the inimitable Baker fantasy: "Spring came to Washington this week. Naturally there was a cocktail reception for her."

What's puzzling about reading Baker is that it's hard to be sure whether he stays with you or you stay with him. I left him rolling through a bowl game: "Gumcrack up over the ball. Flanker guards roll left, splitback in motion to the right . . . field judge and head linesman ready for the short flare, Simian on the handoff. . . ." (p. 85)

> *John Martin, in a review of "No Cause for Panic," in* America, *Vol. 112, No. 3, January 16, 1965, pp. 84-5.*

GERALD GOTTLIEB

Baker's method [in *No Cause for Panic*] is irony rather than whimsy, sarcasm rather than ranting. His material is the entire United States of America and his talent is of matching size. He is capable of parody, poetry, galloping fantasy, wistful poignancy, and the simple sneer. He holds himself in constant contempt of Congress, and with grisly joy predicts a time when that body, clogged and rusted at last into utter immobility, will be made a branch of the Smithsonian Institution. On the subject of government gobbledygook he writes like a scathing James Joyce working the Washington beat. Testy, inventive, sardonic, he polishes off his book with a glorious gabble of disdain for television. All is suffused with a realistic intelligence, a cold humor, and an even colder irony—not the least of which resides in the title.

Gerald Gottlieb, "They Could Laugh Dying," in
Book Week—The Sunday Herald Tribune, *May 16,
1965, p. 16.**

VIRGINIA KIRKUS' SERVICE

Baker's squibs and brief forays have an uncommon ability to
touch the center of our private perceptions. His subject [in *All
Things Considered*] is the modern U.S. culture as viewed through
the eyes of the *New York Times*—our 100-eyed cultural Ar-
gus. . . . He revamps the plots of *Anna Karenina* by Henry
Miller, *Heidi* by Terry Southern, *Huckleberry Finn* by James
Baldwin, *A Tale of Two Cities* by Joseph Heller, *Wuthering
Heights* by Tennessee Williams, and *The Iliad* by Norman
Mailer, and does it amusingly. Most often, while enjoying
Baker, one has the sense of being *in* even when he is talking
about the relative intelligence of dolphins, cats and men. He
is quite keen on the average American's non-life and disposable
children. His is an assault on middle-class values, and he tilts
with more accuracy than Quixote had. He also has many readers, deservedly.

A review of "All Things Considered," in Virginia
Kirkus' Service, *Vol. XXXIII, No. 15, August 1, 1965,
p. 803.*

ELIOT FREMONT-SMITH

Russell Baker, The New York Times "Observer" columnist,
is one of the two funniest and more enlightening commentators
on the Washington scene. (The other is Art Buchwald.) Mr.
Baker's latest book ["**Our Next President**"] . . . tells "The
Incredible Story of What Happened in the 1968 Elections." It
is not the first spoof on the upcoming Presidential campaigns,
nor will it be the last. . . .

Mr. Baker's new scenario provokes one or two chuckles, but
what is interesting about it is that it is so unfunny. The publishers seem to have recognized this, calling it a "nightmare"
and a "political horror story" and wrapping the book in funereal black. . . .

As a spoof, however (which would provide an edge for the
criticism—otherwise why spoof it up at all?), the tale is oddly
bare-boned, and too often strikes one as a record of surprisingly
missed golden opportunities. Comic mimicry of the various
politicians' rhetorical styles is kept to a minimum, and what
there is seems quite bland. Opportunities for broader laughs
are also missed. There is a funny spot, where General Eisen-
hower repeats his to-endorse-or-not-to-endorse confusion of
1964 (remember William W. Scranton?), and another when
Hubert Humphrey must pretend it's an honor to resign the Vice
Presidency to become Secretary of State.

But more typical is a flat showdown scene at the end of the
book between the Vice President-elect and his furious former
superior, in which Mr. Baker has an inexplicably witless Mr.
Kennedy say to Mr. Johnson, "I am the only President the
country has." Left ready and waiting, and sadly unexploited,
is President Johnson's own comically notorious, real-life assertion, "I'm the only President you've got."

Fate, too, has been less than kind to the comic aspects of this
book; the pre-publication withdrawal of George Romney from
the race has, inevitably, a flattening effect on the early sections
of **"Our Next President"** where Mr. Baker's Mr. Romney is
still plugging determinedly on.

All of which conspires to tempt one to treat this book as serious
after all. Mr. Baker's scenario is set against a background of
racial unrest and urban riots. And certainly, the Constitutional
crisis is a grim prospect. Yet if the scenario is intended to be
convincing, one wonders why the issue of Vietnam is scarcely
mentioned. Not only is it missing from Mr. Baker's imaginary
campaign history, but so also is an explanation of its absence.

It's grasping at straws, I know, but a possible explanation is
that the book is, in fact, neither spoof nor critique, but a
cleverly discreet campaign opener. Could Mr. Baker be running
himself? The thought is a cheering one; perhaps we need a
humorist for President. His opponent? Art Buchwald, of course,
whose own campaign book, succinctly titled, "Have I Ever
Lied to You?" is scheduled for publication on April Fool's
Day. Watch out, George Wallace! Suddenly things are looking
up.

*Eliot Fremont-Smith, "The Making of a Deadlock,
1968," in* The New York Times, *March 4, 1968, p.
35.*

ERWIN D. CANHAM

For a journalist there's nothing, so to speak, like getting ahead
of the news. So [in *Our Next President*] Russell Baker has
written the story of the 1968 presidential election in advance.
He does it delightfully. And in many respects, he could be
right.

In one or two details, the facts have already caught up with
Mr. Baker. He did not anticipate George Romney's pullout.
He did not anticipate Senator Eugene McCarthy's strong showing. But let us not be picayune. The crystal ball is bound to
be clouded here and there.

Mr. Baker is the humor-affairs columnist of the New York
Times' editorial page. Being funny three times a week is a
devastating assignment. Mr. Baker keeps up with it very well
indeed. Often it is real wit, rather than slapstick of the Art
Buchwald variety. . . .

This preview of the 1968 campaign, however, is no exercise
in whimsy. In most respects it isn't funny at all. Especially,
it is no joke when the U.S. constitutional system—which requires an absolute majority in the Electoral College—throws
the election into the House of Representatives and the Senate.
The House, with one vote per state, fails to produce a majority
because George Wallace has taken six states, and they cannot
agree on the highest bidder. So the Senate, with each Senator
voting, chooses the Vice-President who becomes Acting President.

The Acting President turns out to be Robert Kennedy. And he
turns out to be more than Acting, as the mordant last line of
the book attests. Before this stern denouement, however, there
are many adventures. Perhaps the most acid is when President
Johnson dismisses Dean Rusk and forces Vice-President Humphrey to become Secretary of State. That opens the way for
the Democratic Convention to nominate Bobby Kennedy for a
second place. Some of his friends criticize him for taking a
spot on the Johnson ticket, but as Mr. Baker has his mother,
Mrs. Rose Kennedy . . . say (more succinctly than Walter
Lippmann): "Why shouldn't he take it? He's got nothing to
lose."

So it turned out.

Mr. Baker may have performed what some will regard as a great public service. It is well-known that President Johnson bitterly resents it when the newspapers anticipate any of his great decisions. Mr. Baker may have prevented the chain of events he so vivaciously describes.

Pre-history has its virtues.

> Erwin D. Canham, *"Election Pre-Historian,"* in The Christian Science Monitor, *March 28, 1968, p. 11.*

R. Z. SHEPPARD

In the old fairy tale, the grumpy king runs a contest to find a jester who can make him laugh. Unsuccessful contestants go to the block. The winner gets a new suit of motley and the next-to-impossible job of making the king laugh again. In journalism, the dyspeptic despot is usually played by an editor who starts off saying something like "This page is too damn dull. It needs some humor." Serious words are then circulated among the clever headline writers and droll city-room pinochle players that there is an opening for a funny columnist.

If the editors and readers are lucky, they may get a durable broad-ax wit like Art Buchwald. If they are very lucky, they find someone like Russell Baker. . . . At his best, Baker fills his allotted space opposite the editorial page with bizarre, often bleak fantasies about human foolishness. At his second best, he holds a funhouse mirror up to the nature of the consumer state. Baker's "growing family," for example, does not increase numerically but expands through overweight and the excess tonnage of possessions.

Poor Russell's Almanac, [a] . . . collection of columns and comment, is composed largely of such ticklish visions. The more painful versions often have to do with a variety of middle-aged, middle-management saps who have congealed in mid-marriage and mid-mortgage. "Misery no longer loves company," says Baker. "Nowadays it insists upon it." . . .

To use the kind of phrases he lampoons in a piece on reviewers' jargon, Baker is a man of range, sensitive intellect and fertile imagination. He is also a fine stylist whose columns frequently unfurl to defend the language against corruption. But to read 212 pages of him at a sitting is a mistake. He is most effective in his newspaper, where the reader can wade expectantly toward him through bloated accounts of disaster, inhumanity, avarice and hypocrisy. Russell Baker can then best be appreciated doing what a good humorist has always done: writing to preserve his sanity for at least one more day.

> R. Z. Sheppard, *"Daily Sanity,"* in Time, *Vol. 99, No. 3, January 17, 1972, p. 63.*

PHIL ELDERKIN

Reading **"Poor Russell's Almanac"** is a lot like visiting the Internal Revenue Service—with somebody else's tax return!

If you have ever changed a flat tire in the rain, tripped over the flowers on the rug or spilled gravy on your Aunt Agatha's canary, then this book is for you.

Actually, it is not really a book at all but a collection of essays. Russell Baker, the author, is extremely talented at stroking a platitude until it purrs like an epigram.

While Baker tries to pass himself off a genuine character in most interviews, he is really a self-styled one. No man who describes himself as a decaying boy, and still has to duck his head to clear any doorway under six feet, two inches, is not to be trusted.

But if an author can sell his book by first selling himself, I suppose this comes under the heading of good business. Baker has traveled extensively and there isn't much in the way of newspaper writing which he hasn't done. Fortunately it shows.

I highly recommend some of Poor Russell's more literary passages, such as "How to use the FBI to settle a dispute with your plumber." It also has such goody oneliners as: "Security is a suntan in February."

I must admit, after reading this, that I immediately began thumbing through the rest of the book for pictures of Snoopy and was disappointed.

Nevertheless, this is the kind of all-purpose book which can be picked up, a few articles read while waiting for the bus, and then put down. It has the kind of clever humor which makes one think rather than chuckle.

It pokes fun at a lot of people and a lot of things—both real and imagined. But most of the time its poker is dipped in satire rather than poison. . . .

I warn you. **"Poor Russell's Almanac"** is a series of literary boobytraps. The best way to handle them is to read all 212 pages.

> Phil Elderkin, *"Tripping Over the Gravy,"* in The Christian Science Monitor, *February 3, 1972, p. 11.*

KIRKUS REVIEWS

"Observer" columns from Russell Baker are the perfect light-beer chasers for the hard-stuff of daily news—but few of the short pieces in this pleasant, bland collection [*So This Is Depravity*] stand up well to the sterner tests of time and hard-cover compilation. The most obvious sufferers from the format, of course, are dated columns on the political scene—*lots* on Watergate—that are usually common-sensical enough . . . , yet often over-simplified and a bit preachy. But other pieces that *should* be less frayed by time—on inflation, language (the "Have a nice day" craze), the sexual revolution, city living (parking, cabs, noise), marriage, parenthood, taxes—also tend to seem rather limp in retrospect. . . . [When] consciously emulating Mencken or Perelman or Woody Allen, [Baker] consistently lacks the *edge* needed for that darker brand of humor. Still, none of these never-too-long pieces is without a smile or two, especially for those partial to wistful looks back to cleaner, simpler times. And in certain areas, Baker is superb: TV commercials bring out his cleanest swipes; historical whimsies inspire him to glorious flights of anachronism, and one column here is bona fide classic—**"Cooped Up,"** in which the ghost of Gary C. accompanies Baker to movies that have junked all the old Coop-movie values. Less impressive the second time around, then—but Baker fans and others will find it literate, gently amusing bedside reading that's smoothly mainstream all the way.

A review of "So This Is Depravity," in Kirkus Reviews, *Vol. XLVIII, No. 15, August 1, 1980, p. 1033.*

JOSEPH McLELLAN

You can begin quoting Russell Baker in this collection [*So This Is Depravity*], as you can begin reading him, almost anywhere. Open at random to **"The Humble Dollar"** (you will have to track it down; his latest book has no table of contents), and you come up with a small gem:

"The papers keep saying that the dollar is very weak. This is nonsense. The truth is that the dollar is absolutely powerless. I sent one for a pound of cheese the other day and it was thrown out of the store for giving itself airs."

It's all there in that quote: the timeliness, the air of crisis, the sweeping generalization and the quick, absurd illustration that puts everything in context and makes you want to laugh. The Baker technique is easy to reduce to a formula when you have read enough samples. Fortunately for Baker, the formula is difficult to translate into living prose and almost impossible to implement on deadline, several times a week, with consistent quality, as Baker has been doing in his "Observer" column for *The New York Times* since 1962.

The hardest part is the requirement that it should be funny. Some writers have an endless supply of profundity, constantly available at five minutes notice, but very few have professional-quality wit so readily on tap. Many of the most profound have no wit at all. Occasionally, Baker lets up on the comedy and settles for mere seriousness, but he is almost never solemn—for reasons explained in one of the little essays in *So This Is Depravity:*

"Though Americans talk a great deal about the virtue of being serious, they generally prefer people who are solemn over people who are serious. . . . Jogging is solemn. Poker is serious. Once you can grasp that distinction, you are on your way to enlightenment."

Baker's form of enlightenment usually arrives in segments about 2½ pages long—just about right for the rushed, half-awake reader of a morning paper, though they make the continuity seem a bit choppy when spread out in a book. The brevity of its segments probably accounts for the smaller-than-usual design of *So This Is Depravity,* which is chopped down to the page-size of a trade paperback or a volume in the Viking Portable Library. The world probably isn't ready yet for a Portable Baker. He is consistently good and sometimes brilliant in the selections included in this book, but he'll have to wait a while to become a classic.

He does have one of the other qualities of a classic, however: the ability to take the random material of current events and find durable meaning in it. He does this partly through concrete images, which transcend such narrow categories as comedy and solemnity. Any abstract definition reduces the richness of his central image in **"Spaced In,"** for example, which compares life in New York City to the behavior of a driver trying to park a 20-foot car in a 19-foot space. "Trying to fit life into spaces too small for it takes a toll on civilization," he says, and that observation totters on the brink of solemnity. But it doesn't fall over, because we have had several very concrete paragraphs showing a New York driver trying to make

room for himself. . . . This kills all danger of solemnity. It is something like poetry, which is always serious, even when it is comic, but stops being poetry when it starts being solemn.

The latest installment in the continuing intellectual adventures of the "Observer" begins in 1973—just over a decade after the column began—and it escorts the reader through the years of darkest Nixon and Ford up to the present, bouncing around the '70s like a supercharged pinball. The book's tone is set and its title adumbrated by a Latin quotation from Juvenal which has a page all to itself at the beginning: *Nemo repente fuit turpissimus* (roughly, "It takes a while to become utterly depraved"). If you want to sum up the '70s in four words, those may be as good as any.

Baker takes another 300-odd pages to elaborate and annotate Juvenal's pithy observation—not that Baker lacks pith, but English is a wordier language than Latin, and there are so many points to be covered—some quite urgently. A theme for 1980, though it was written four years ago, is his observation on those who abstain from voting because they are "too high-minded to concede that politics is almost always the choice of the lesser evil." . . .

Baker is good all through the book on the potentially disastrous effects of high-mindedness—fortunately, since it was a leit-motif of the decade which he loosely chronicles. He has a keen eye on the way people live in television commercials—on the men named Buck and Mike who are forever dropping their tools and running off for their after-work beer, and on the competition between headache, upset stomach and nagging backache for the status of No. 1 medical problem. The evils of jogging—particularly of jogging others out of their pet vices—move him to put down his martini and his cigarette long enough for a serious (though not solemn) warning. A weakness, I think, but one into which he does not fall too often, is his occasional use of the historical flashback—a piece showing how George Washington would have acted in situations typical of Richard Nixon, or a portrayal of Henry James using his fists like Norman Mailer. These fail to be funny, perhaps through sheer implausibility, but being funny is not his only strength. In this collection, he is particularly eloquent on American money—perhaps because of the horrible things that happened to it in the '70s. There is acute psycho-economic observation in an essay about the turning point that came when he started unconsciously stuffing dollar bills in his pocket like coins, rather than put them in his wallet. And there is a special kind of poetry in an essay about old people shopping—trying to pay '70s prices with money earned in the '60s, deliberating on whether to buy one orange and finally putting it back.

The bedrock of his subject-matter is politics, and he tries to be even-handed about it. "The Democrats have no program" he observed during the 1976 campaign. "Actually, the Democrats may not be a party anymore. I tend to the theory that they are just a memory." On the other hand, "To a Republican, a Republican President is not good enough. He must be The Right Kind of Republican President. The Right Kind of Republican President is the kind for whom independents and Democrats will vote only if the alternative is Attila the Hun."

Both passages, like most of the other material in this book written for nearly a decade of deadlines, seem designed to stand at least a medium-length test of time.

Joseph McLellan, "Russell Baker: Punch Lines on Deadline," in Book World—The Washington Post, *October 5, 1980, p. 5.*

MARY LEE SETTLE

What do you say about a memoir that has made you cry, made
you laugh, brought back streets, sounds and hours of your own
growing up and helped you look at them with more tenderness?
In Russell Baker's **"Growing Up,"** that is what can happen to
anyone who has known, in childhood, the rural South, when,
as the family sat in their rockers in the evening, "nothing new
had been said on that porch in a hundred years." This is not
the dirt-poor South of easy fiction. With sensuous grace, incisive recall and an evocation of daily language that is the
poetry of the inarticulate, he recreates a place where there is
dignity and ambition and an inflexible social and economic
hierarchy run by women. (p. 1)

There are scenes as funny and as touching as Mark Twain's—
the burial of the local bootlegger in a glass coffin, "the fanciest
Mason Jar in Loudoun County," the magic of an indoor toilet,
the shunting of steam trains, the first telephone in the house,
the fantastic luxury of a bathtub with a shower. The acute
simplicity of the scene of the father's death is a masterpiece.

It is a world of blood connections who survive together through
the still, daily terror of the Great Depression. There is Uncle
Charlie, who does nothing but read the paper and hate Roosevelt, so that the young Baker "thought of Republicans as
people who rose from 12-hour stretches in bed to denounce
idlers and then lie down with a good book."

The quest for survival takes the family to New Jersey and then
to Baltimore. One of the most moving characters is Oluf, whose
awkward love letters to Baker's widowed mother reflect the
gradual crushing of an ambitious and kindly man in the Depression. His last letter is his own epitaph and that of thousands
of victims of the time: "I am lost and going and not interested
in anything any more."

The memoir takes Baker through a college scholarship and
wonderful scenes of flight training as a Navy pilot. After the
war he began to write, with an ambition once fed by his mother
and an attractive hope that "writers didn't have to have any
gumption."

In the end, a painfully priggish young man has indeed "made
something of himself," the Pulitzer Prize-winning essayist for
the New York Times whose work is syndicated all over the
country, a part of his life he does not mention.

His is a wondrous book, funny, sad and strong. Above all, it
can make us see that the family cruelties we have suffered are
often cultural and not personal—and that to recognize this is
to begin to forgive. (p. 1, 10)

Mary Lee Settle, "*The Dignity and Ties of Apron-
String America,*" *in* Los Angeles Times Book Review, *October 10, 1982, pp. 1, 10.*

RICHARD LINGEMAN

As we all know from reading the higher fan journalism, funny
people are really deeply unhappy. They had childhoods that
make Charles Dickens's blacking factory seem like Charles
Ryder's golden summer with Sebastian at Oxford.

And so I approached Russell Baker's autobiography, **"Growing Up,"** with high anticipation, expecting a heartening read
about someone more miserable than I am. Alas, I was deeply
disappointed. To come straight out with it, Russell Baker, who
writes funny stuff three times a week for his Observer column
in The New York Times, ruined my day. This is not the kind
of book one can put down with a contented sigh: "That poor
son of a bitch." Instead of being a grim tale of drunken step-
mothers and battered stepfathers, **"Growing Up"** is touching
and funny, a hopeless muddle of sadness and laughter that
bears a suspicious resemblance to real life.

It cannot be said that Mr. Baker lacked the opportunity to open
floodgate after floodgate of pain, sorrow and trauma. His father, a stonemason who liked fixing up Model Ts and drinking
whisky, died of the lethal synergism of diabetes and moonshine
when the boy was still young. Mr. Baker's mother, Lucy Elizabeth, shows considerable promise as a domineering ogre of
the breed that condemns its sons to a lifetime of gnashing and
wailing on analysts' couches. There is a highly promising stretch
of poverty too as young Russell spends much of the Depression
with his sister Doris and their mother living off the kindness
of relatives. Then comes World War II, with Mr. Baker primed
to be one of those smooth-cheeked striplings whom Betty Gra-
ble was always sending off to obscure deaths on Pacific atolls.
Finally, for the Freudians, there is an ambivalent romance with
a beautiful young woman of whom mom strongly disapproves.

But all this promising material yields only the normal miseries
of boyhood and adolescence. There are Depression meals of
macaroni and cheese and creamed chipped beef on toast, to be
sure, but Mr. Baker confesses they seemed adequate at the
time. . . .

Well, all right, Mr. Baker's childhood was tough, but he came
through, and his mother's hectoring may have had something
to do with it. At least, one can't find too terrible her constant
harping at him to "have a little gumption" and "make something of yourself." (p. 13)

[Despite] his mother's nagging, he managed to excel in high
school and win a scholarship to Johns Hopkins, which he left
after a year to enter the United States Navy Air Force. He
never saw combat and managed to avoid cracking up his Piper
Cub trainer, although he made his combat-veteran instructors
wish they were back in Zero Alley. After the war, he graduated
from Johns Hopkins and eased into a successful newspaper
career with The Baltimore Sun. The book ends on a note of
triumph that will send the Freudians fleeing in disarray. Mr.
Baker breaks the Oedipal knot and marries the beautiful Mimi
in defiance of his mother's implacable opposition. Oh yes,
asked his ambition in life on a high school questionnaire, he
wrote "newspaper columnist." As the Germans say, "A fine
Bildungsroman with no *Weltschmerz!*" Well, think how much
poorer American humor would be if he had written "president
of General Motors."

Like all the best humor, Mr. Baker's is grounded in truth and
mellowed by a sense of the sadness in things. His laughs are
distilled from the juices of life. It is a natural comic sense that
comes from playing on a pool table that is slightly out of plumb,
on which the most carefully lined-up shot veers off, leaving
you behind the eight ball. His view of life is also rooted in the
Southern folk tradition, a garrulous culture of extended families
that provided the author some gently eccentric kinfolk. . . .
He draws from a time and a world very much in the American
grain: memories of listening to grown-ups rocking on the porch

and sonorously reciting clichés or of Depression evenings in Baltimore spent around the kitchen table with endless talk and cups of coffee.

These Depression babies were inveterate materialists, the author frankly admits. They dismissed the fermentative brew of ideas in the air—from the Brain Trust's to Mussolini's—as "crackpot." Instead they talked about the furnace and morality and who was the better singer—Rudy Vallee or Bing Crosby. But they had a mystique—a belief in the future that would somehow be better. Lucy Elizabeth's future was her son, for whom "something will turn up." Or as her former boyfriend, Oluf the Danish oleomargarine salesman, wrote in a letter to her, "Well, it will all come out O.K."—just before he lost all his money and disappeared from her life.

Still, Lucy Elizabeth found another man and something did turn up for Russell Baker. I suppose that is more or less the moral of **"Growing Up"** if you're looking for one; this is not exactly "The Education of Henry Adams." But it is not often you read a book that makes you want to congratulate the author for marrying the right woman. It is that involving a book. (pp. 13, 28)

> *Richard Lingeman, "Suspiciously Like Real Life,"
> in* The New York Times Book Review, *October 17, 1982, pp. 13, 28.*

JOE MYSAK

[In *Growing Up*] Russell Baker, the *New York Times* "Observer" columnist, turns his talent to autobiography. The results are as happy as his fellow Baltimorean H. L. Mencken's were when he ventured into the form in his *Days* books. Baker has shown his readers some of this material before—notably in 1979, the year he won the Pulitzer Prize—but the story is especially well told here. . . . This is as much the story of Lucy Baker's struggling against the Depression as it is of her son's growing up, and it is often quite moving. The Bakers' circumstances were somewhat unusual, but the story and the characters are familiar ones. Here are the usual assortment of jobs and ne'er-do-well relatives. There is no character or tale here so fabulous as to be unbelievable, which puts the author in the same realist-humorist category as George Ade, Mencken, and Jean Shepherd, who have all shown American life as it is really lived: routine contentment continually interrupted by high drama and crucial turning points, shot through with desperate comedy. *Growing Up* is a satisfying read, and it will also tell future biographers something about the origins of Baker's humor, his skepticism, and even his ear for quirky dialogue.

> *Joe Mysak, in a review of "Growing Up," in* National Review, *Vol. XXXIV, No. 22, November 12, 1982, p. 1430.*

JOHN LUKACS

[Russell Baker] writes serious funny things usually with the purpose of pointing out absurdities, including economists' prevarications, the pretensions of technology, and government prose that has not noticeably improved during the Reagan monarchy. Whatever the targets of his attacks, Russell Baker is a defender of the greatest heritage of this nation—of which conservatives ought to be more respectful than they often are—the American English language. Within the *New York Times*

Russell Baker compares as a grammarian to the house conservative William Safire somewhat as Red Smith compares to Howard Cosell. But Baker is more than a grammarian. He is a master of the American language.

[*Growing Up*] is a revelation of that fact. In it he recounts the first 24 years of his life as the son of an independent and deep-rooted Virginian family, people as frugal and brave as their American ancestors two hundred years before had been. One paragraph of his description of family life in the Depression is worth everything Studs Terkel ever wrote. The Depression brought families close together. . . . [Baker's] was an unusual family. His childhood was not an unhappy one. I have always thought that Tolstoy's famous first sentence of *Anna Karenina*—"Happy families are all alike; every unhappy family is unhappy in its own way"—was a lot of guff, and that its very opposite is true. (p. 331)

When a writer equipped with a minimum of talent thinks or writes about undramatic phases of his life, he can always fall back on color, and attempt to describe things and scenes in souped-up prose. But writing is not quite like painting, and even in painting, color cannot be altogether a substitute for draftsmanship. Baker's prose is like clear water. His descriptions do not depend on colors; they reflect them. Here is a sentence in which sensitive readers may glimpse that combination of irony and tenderness and natural virtuosity which is the mark of a great writer. Russell Baker's grandfather had 11 sons. His devotion to Christian worship "was remarkable. He required a minimum of two church services each Sunday to keep his soul in sound repair, and after partaking of the Gospel at morning and afternoon servings he often set out across the fields for a third helping at dusk if he heard of a church with lamps lit for nocturnal psalming."

Baker was born in 1925, when H. L. Mencken, another Baltimorean, was proclaiming that an American language had come into being, a language that was more democratic and more straightforward and telling than what the English language, with all of its Latinisms and emasculated suggestiveness, had become. Mencken was wrong. During the twentieth century the American language—including the literary language—became intellectualized and bureaucratized, cumbrous and soggy. Even Hemingway was no exception to this, since his indubitable talent was not matched by sufficient wisdom or integrity. The result was a style that was ephemeral, closer to O. Henry or to Maupassant than to us. But now comes this wondrous apparition—no, a solid reality—in our midst. Here is a modest book, a modest autobiographical story, with a title that is as modest as it is truthful and precise. It is an American classic, containing an *American* style that leaves Hemingway and Mencken and Henry Adams—the prose of the first, the thesis of the second, and the pessimism of the third—behind. It ought to be put before every young American to see what can be done with the great language of a nation. (pp. 331-32)

> *John Lukacs, "An American Classic," in* National Review, *Vol. XXXV, No. 5, March 18, 1983, pp. 331-32.*

PUBLISHERS WEEKLY

As expected, nothing is immune to Baker's unique comedic observations—the MX missile (**"Merrily We Pentagon"**), New Yorkers' dogs (**"Beastly Manhattan"**), Marcel Proust (**"Things Passed"**)—in [*The Rescue of Miss Yaskell*], the title piece being a charming evocation of boyish fantasy. This gathering will entertain first-time readers, refresh the risibilities of fans and do much to elevate the status of the personal essay.

> *A review of "The Rescue of Miss Yaskell: And Other Pipe Dreams," in* Publishers Weekly, *Vol. 224, No. 8, August 19, 1983, p. 60.*

A. J. ANDERSON

Few things soften and grow moldy quicker than collections of stuff written for newspapers. But Baker . . . [survives] very well when pressed between the covers of a book. . . . The 100 or so of his columns tied together [in *The Rescue of Miss Yaskell and Other Pipe Dreams*] have nothing in common except that all are written in an easy, slippered prose. Always observant, Baker is in turn reminiscent, fanciful, serious, thought-provoking, and downright funny. Among his topics are *Brideshead Revisited*, Leo Buscaglia, and "The Male Weepie." Probably there are things that do not interest him, but they must be few and far between. . . .

Many fans will be glad to recover some of their favorite pieces in [this collection]. Good for what ails you.

> *A. J. Anderson, in a review of "The Rescue of Miss Yaskell and Other Pipe Dreams," in* Library Journal, *Vol. 108, No. 17, October 1, 1983, p. 1878.*

Simone de Beauvoir

1908-

French novelist, nonfiction writer, autobiographer, dramatist, short story writer, and editor.

One of the most prominent writers of her generation, Beauvoir was a member of the French left-wing intellectual circle associated with existentialist Jean-Paul Sartre. She is known as both a chronicler of that milieu and a literary explicator of the existentialist philosophy. She also became identified as a leading feminist theorist with the publication of *Le deuxième sexe* (1949; *The Second Sex*), her comprehensive study of the secondary status of women throughout history. Interest in her long-time relationship with Sartre and the controversies elicited by *The Second Sex* have often eclipsed recognition of Beauvoir's fiction. Yet she gained favorable attention for her first novel, *L'invitée* (1943; *She Came to Stay*), and her novel *Les mandarins* (1954; *The Mandarins*) received the Prix Goncourt.

Beauvoir was born in Paris to middle-class parents. Early in her life she rebelled against the restrictions of her family, her class, and her Catholic education, as well as the social disadvantages of her gender. A brilliant student, she earned her degree in 1929 at the Sorbonne, where she also met Sartre, her companion until his death in 1980. Beauvoir taught philosophy until *She Came to Stay* was published, at which time she stopped teaching in order to concentrate on writing.

Beauvoir's life and development are revealed in her several volumes of autobiographical writings. Beginning with *Mémoires d'une jeune fille rangée* (1958; *Memoirs of a Dutiful Daughter*) and continuing through *La cérémonie des adieux* (1980; *Adieux*), these memoirs also provide insight into the social, political, and intellectual climate of the Second World War era. *La force de l'âge* (1960; *The Prime of Life*) is particularly valuable for explaining the development of the existentialist movement and demonstrates the continuing dialogue Beauvoir maintained with Sartre.

The first of her novels of ideas, *She Came to Stay*, poses existentialist questions of choice and consciousness. Another novel, *Le sang des autres* (1944; *The Blood of Others*), is set in France during World War II and focuses on the issue of responsibility in a godless world. *The Mandarins* is celebrated as a *roman à clef* of French existentialists and their associates. Other writings include the nonfiction *L'Amérique au jour le jour* (1948; *America Day by Day*) and *La longue marche* (1957; *The Long March*), based respectively on Beauvoir's travels in America in 1947 and her tour of Communist China after the war.

In addition to documenting the persons and events of her generation, Beauvoir also sought to explain existentialism in several philosophical essays. The most important of these essays is *Pour une morale de l'ambiguïté* (1947; *The Ethics of Ambiguity*). Here she offers an affirmative view of life based on commitment and free choice which complements Sartre's *Being and Nothingness*.

Critics have often concerned themselves with what they perceive as two central ironies in Beauvoir's feminism: her apparent reliance on a man—Sartre—for ideas and insights, and a noticeable bias against women in her writings. In regard to

the former, it has been pointed out that mutual influence is unavoidable in any lifelong relationship; in this instance, Sartre's originality as a philosopher and Beauvoir's ability to synthesize, to document, and to apply complex ideas clearly and accessibly represent different roles. As for the latter irony, several critics have argued that in both her fiction and her nonfiction Beauvoir's depiction of women reveals her anger at their circumstances, not their inherent inferiority.

The publication and recent translation of five early stories collected in *Quand prime le spirituel* (1979; *When Things of the Spirit Come First*) has provided fresh perspectives on Beauvoir, resulting in new appreciation for her lifelong dedication to her art as a means of expressing and recording her development in relation to her era.

(See also *CLC*, Vols. 1, 2, 4, 8, 14 and *Contemporary Authors*, Vols. 9-12, rev. ed.)

JEAN LEIGHTON

The somber thesis of *The Second Sex* that it is a malediction to be a woman finds substantial support in [Simone de Beauvoir's] novels inasmuch as the feminine characters are preponderantly unhappy, divided and neurotic creatures. Though they do not consciously reflect on their fate and submission *qua* woman, most are nonetheless conspicuously marked by a flaw; one suspects that their suffering derives in part from their initial misfortune of being female. The pessimism of *The Second Sex* is thus reinforced in the novels. However, *The Second Sex* also contains the optimistic and even Utopian idea that woman's subjection and role as the passive, "inessential" being has arbitrarily been imposed by the dominant male culture. If woman could become economically independent and as committed to her work as man she might escape the curse of immanence, passivity, and relative "being." "One is not born a woman, one becomes one" expresses Simone de Beauvoir's radical conception that the unhappiness of woman is rooted in culture and not biology. Woman is thus in principle capable of transcending her inferiority, which is man-made. *The Second Sex* appears in that perspective as an exhortation to women to rise from their passivity and indifference and break the chains which enslave them.

The "ideal" of *The Second Sex* is this future emancipated woman, but the vast documentation of the book produces a very negative and uninspiring picture of woman as she has been and actually is. Woman has been sadly impaired by her role as wife, mother, amoureuse, etc. As a result, and ideal theory notwithstanding, by and large the pessimistic element of woman's malediction and inferiority to man dominates the work. This "objective" description does not have to obtain for fictional works. It is there that the ideal woman could be found. Indeed, . . . two of Simone de Beauvoir's fictional heroines, Françoise in *L'Invitée* and Anne in *Les Mandarins,* both modeled on Simone de Beauvoir herself, represent in some measure the emancipated woman. They both have careers that make them economically independent of men and they are also "sympathetic" heroines. They have generosity of spirit, intelligence, some strength, and a grandeur of character that quite sets them apart from the mournful array of *The Second Sex* females whose pettiness, self-pity, passivity, resentment and subtle domination through feminine martyrdom produce such an unsavory impression of women in general. They are also infinitely more prepossessing as human beings than the other "sad" feminine characters of the novels. And yet neither Anne nor Françoise is really an "emancipated" woman, for both suffer from some inexplicable weakness which makes them unable to assert themselves with the full vigor of an authentic, liberated personality. Françoise has an almost pathological dependence on Pierre, while Anne not only is an "amoureuse" whose life is almost ruined by the unhappy end of a love affair, but she succumbs to despair in middle age and contemplates suicide. Both Anne and Françoise for some mysterious reason regard their work as subsidiary and relegate it to a minor role even though it must consume large quantities of time and energy conveniently ignored by the conventions of novel writing.

Possibly the key to Simone de Beauvoir's ambiguous feelings can be discerned in Françoise and Anne, who express her own emotional difficulties. Like Françoise with Pierre, Simone de Beauvoir was exceedingly dependent on the opinions of Sartre; the autobiography continually documents this. . . . Similarly, Anne's love affair (though treated with sympathy and approval she is "une amoureuse" who lets her love life dominate her life) is autobiographical, and her despair in face of the onslaught of desolate middle age is exactly recapitulated in *La Force des Choses* with its chilling finale of "la femme flouée"— an avowal that significantly undermines the entire hopeful thesis of *The Second Sex.* (pp. 208-10)

[One] must conclude that her identification of emancipation with serene independence and strength is perhaps not altogether valid. Simone de Beauvoir suffered from the same weaknesses as her heroines; in the novels these weaknesses are not seen as necessarily reprehensible where they emerge as part of the imponderable complexity of the anguished human condition. Yet according to the implacable standards of *The Second Sex* they must be seen as failings which prevent either heroine from achieving that tranquil state of strength and wisdom so wistfully extolled in *The Second Sex*—that is, the same authenticity and freedom as the male enjoys. Thus Anne and Françoise are in a sense self-criticism on the part of the author. . . . One gets the impression that Simone de Beauvoir's horror of dependence and passivity in women arises both from the undeniable subjugation of women as a class, but also from some weakness or dependency in herself which she deplores. Therefore, she identifies "dependence" and "weakness" with all the classic feminine virtues, excoriates "le dévouement" as a perversion of familial affection, and even casts grave doubts on familial affection itself. Psychological "dependency" is a very complex phenomenon, often not recognized by the victim. The equation of economic independence and inner psychic freedom seems somewhat simplistic, but is perhaps understandable in the light of Simone de Beauvoir's own tendencies. Anne and Françoise both show that economic independence is not enough; Simone de Beauvoir's "ideal" woman remains an ideal.

As for woman as she is, or was yesterday, Simone de Beauvoir frankly confesses that she describes women as she sees them— as "divided beings." Thus Paule, Hélène, Denise, Elisabeth, Régine, Nadine and Xavière and the legion of discontented females of *The Second Sex,* represent the *choice* of Simone de Beauvoir; they are finely etched portraits of various types of femininity and they personify in a compelling way the pessimistic and anti-feminine bias of *The Second Sex:* woman has not only been cruelly oppressed by man, but the limitations on her freedom and the imposition of a specifically feminine role have hindered her from exemplifying humanity at its best. Woman remains inferior, unable to surmount the tragic handicaps of her cultural situation. The heroines of the novels, products of Simone de Beauvoir's imagination, illustrate in a more complex and interesting way the tragic theme of *The Second Sex.* They represent the depth and consistency of her deepest convictions on the subject.

Simone de Beauvoir's theory itself which is, in my opinion, unjust to women, is presented in an extreme and somewhat simplistic manner. . . . Such a rigorously one-sided polemic has difficulty in maintaining itself and there are moments when the weaknesses show through. At such moments Simone de Beauvoir comes precariously close to admitting the insufficiency of her one-sided doctrine. *The Second Sex* staunchly insists that transcendence, action, creativity, and power are the masculine virtues par excellence, and these are what determine human value. Being, passivity, and immanence are feminine prerogatives and they diminish the human value of those trapped in this mode of existence. Action and transcendence are male and good; being and immanence are feminine and bad. Unless women renounce "femininity" and equal men on their own terms, they will continue to be inferior. Essentially, therefore, Simone de Beauvoir seems to equate a person's human value and moral worth with his role: the kind of work one does determines human excellence. . . . [However], to literally equate human worth with power and success does not seem to be very profound. At any rate the undisguised adulation of "masculine" activity becomes not only fatiguing but arouses a certain skepticism; the tone is always extravagant and romantic as though all masculine "action" were the equivalent of adventure and creative genius and not simply going down to the office and earning a living. Does this lyrical rhapsody of masculine activity really ring true?. . . [But at last] Simone de Beauvoir envisages the common run of masculine endeavor . . . in the factory and at the office; throwing her previous arguments to the winds, she becomes eloquent about the moral inferiority of the male. The horrors of conformism, dullness, unimaginative pomposity, and ignoble money-grubbing are seen to be his lot and his situation in turn damages his character almost beyond repair. Everything is reversed and freedom, authenticity, imagination and moral superiority are actually deemed to be encouraged by the freer and more enviable life of "the housewife!" It is a breath-taking switch and Simone de Beauvoir's euphoric description of the positive aspects of woman's traditional role is delightful hyperbole, but decidedly un-Beauvoirian! It is the mere thought of the mediocre run-of-the-mill average specimen of mankind, especially in his middle-class manifestation, that elicits this rare panegyric to woman and the untold benefits of her traditional role. (pp. 210-14)

The most brilliant section of *The Second Sex* is Simone de Beauvoir's analysis of several myths about woman propagated by various male writers. Her sympathetic and astute discussion of Stendhal, who was a feminist, champion, and idolater of women, provides a very penetrating counterargument to her own general denigration of them. Stendhal held that it is paradoxically the oppression of women that enables them (the best of them) to escape the worst faults of their oppressors. Excluded from power, they are able to look with skepticism and irony on all the values the world holds so dear. Like artists, intellectuals or slaves or any group effectively denied power they can judge the true values from the false and be moral critics because they are barred from participation in the always compromised moral paltriness of actual power. . . . Stendhal's heroines embody the qualities he admires most—their role or place in the world of affairs does not coincide with or determine their human worth. . . . These marvelous heroines finally triumph over their subservient condition because they know what the true values are. . . . [Simone de Beauvoir] praises Stendhal because in spite of his romanticism and exaltation of woman she maintains that he actually refuses the myths and embraces the much more satisfying human reality. Here the romantic and realist Simone de Beauvoir joins the romantic but realist Stendhal, and this attitude toward the second sex is perhaps the most appealing of all. (pp. 216-18)

[Still], Simone de Beauvoir's work has become a classic in feminist literature and she deserves to be honored for her very great contribution to women's liberation. If I have been critical of a part of her theory, I must still render her homage for her original, penetrating and sympathetic advancement of the cause. Her analysis of the subtle and insinuating way women are molded by society to accept their inferior role is masterful and devastating. Her perception of how the male-dominated culture tries to transform woman into an "object" who exists primarily to please men has had profound reverberations. . . . (p. 219)

Jean Leighton, in her Simone de Beauvoir on Woman, *Fairleigh Dickinson University Press, 1975, 230 p.*

LAWRENCE L. LANGER

Simone de Beauvoir's *A Very Easy Death* does not qualify as the "ultimate revelation" [that is, a completely honest presentation of another's dying and one's own response to that experience, but it comes close] . . . to a confrontation with

the inappropriate death of a loved one, in this instance her mother. But even in this narrative, disclosure is balanced by unconscious suppression, as we witness how a sensitive literary intelligence (when writing from her own point of view) has difficulty exploring all the implications of mortality. One is tempted to conclude that art alone liberates the imagination to probe the darkest corners of the arena where man contends with the experience of dying—his own and others'. It seems that de Beauvoir's literary intuition taught her this, because she organizes the chronicle of her mother's death around an alternating pattern of present scene and past recall so that the two time sequences flow into each other and memory becomes an important means of confronting death. The patient has a social existence as a mother, a daughter, a wife, a good Catholic, a friend—and these roles sometimes contradict, sometimes reinforce each other. Simultaneously, the author has a multiple existence as daughter, sister, companion of Jean-Paul Sartre . . . , and—vitally important—as the narrator of the events.

Simone de Beauvoir recognizes . . . that when an "other" voice intervenes between the dying and their death, we can never obtain a fully objective portrait, but only an interpretation tempered by the insight and psychological courage of the observer. *A Very Easy Death* . . . is a *dual* account—of how the mother died, and how the daughter adjusted to the fact. For every death necessitates at least two responses, from the victim and from the survivor(s); moreover, these responses often interact, modifying each other. The reaction is further complicated by the survivor's memory [of other deaths]. . . . Indeed, one is led to believe that no confrontation is ever "pure" in the sense of a totally selfless concern for the dying. (pp. 27-8)

During the initial stages of her mother's illness, de Beauvoir verifies through personal experience what as a novelist she must have known all along: the insufficiency *and* necessity of language as consolation to the dying and the survivors. Racked by pain, her mother still utters ready-made phrases about the motives of nurses or how badly "the lower classes" bear adversity: "The contrast between the truth of her suffering body and the nonsense that her head was stuffed with saddened me," the daughter reflects. But Simone de Beauvoir is guilty of seeking similar refuge in words, as she instinctively turns to the platitude that at seventy-eight her mother "is of an age to die," then recognizes that "the words were devoid of meaning, as so many words are. For the first time I saw her as a dead body under suspended sentence." And her heart is wrenched with compassion at the vision of a woman bereft of means to rationalize her situation—only words to extend the deception. . . . (pp. 28-9)

[We] exist in an age when "outliving others" has left an unavoidable patina of guilt on the collective memory of men, and de Beauvoir's sense of regret may be more resonant for the reader than she intends. In an age of atrocity, the terms of the struggle have shifted: it is no longer a contest between dying or living, but, as Simone de Beauvoir shrewdly indicates, between death and torture. If regret is a wasted emotion for those who have died in our century after intolerable suffering beyond our power to alleviate, it intensifies for those like Simone de Beauvoir who witnessed her mother's torment but lacked the will or the means of ending it. . . . Simone de Beauvoir assumes that she has been beaten by the ethics of society, but Sartre, with keener insight, declares that she was beaten by technique, and she finally realizes how accurate he is: "One is caught up in the wheels and dragged along, powerless in the face of specialists' diagnoses, their forecasts, their decisions. The patient becomes their property: get him away from them if you can!'' (p. 29)

As long as death is narrated by an outsider, however close to the victim, the dying voice must be excluded from our range of imaginative perception. . . . [All] we have available to us is experience once removed—unless we find a way of over-hearing the dying voice itself.

Even Simone de Beauvoir's mind has been so saturated by reflected images of death that she finds it impossible to with-stand the steady glare of the reality, and retreats into her own cave at crucial moments, depending on safe and familiar prem-ises to sustain her wavering vision. As the nature and prognosis of the disease seep into her mother's consciousness, Simone de Beauvoir cannot admit that she herself finds it too much to bear or discuss, and unconvincingly shifts the motive to her mother: "The truth was crushing her and when she needed to escape from it by talking, . . . we forced her to say nothing about her anxieties and to suppress her doubts. . . .'' (pp. 30-1)

So even an observer as acute as Simone de Beauvoir has limited access to the experience of dying. . . . Simone de Beauvoir's ultimate insight, the justification for her narrative, appears in her discovery that one is *never* of an age to die, that even the old do not die from age but from *something,* and that whenever death arrives, it is violent and unforeseen: there is no way to *prepare* for a very easy death, because no death is easy. The challenge she flings at the imagination is born of twentieth-century man's experience:

> There is no such thing as a natural death: noth-ing that happens to a man is ever natural, since his presence calls the world into question. All men must die: but for every man his death is an accident and, even if he knows it and con-sents to it, an unjustifiable violation.

Simone de Beauvoir repudiates all formulas for immortality: her mother's death is an end in time, not a beginning in eternity, a lesson on the nature of *our* existence, now that hers is over. . . . My own investigation convinces me that the twentieth-century mind, goaded by the insights of Freud and his successors and harassed by the experience of atrocity, has been less dependent on common assumptions about death than its ancestors, and has struck out in fresh directions to open up vistas that we have yet to absorb. . . . The implications of atrocity, of death as a generally inappropriate end despite its eventual necessity, are making slow inroads on our intelligence and emotions. . . . (pp. 31-2)

Lawrence L. Langer, "The Examined Death," in his The Age of Atrocity: Death in Modern Literature, *Beacon Press, 1978, pp. 1-33.**

NAOMI GREENE

While all the ambivalences in [Simone de Beauvoir's] work may not be attributable to Sartre, so much of her argument is based on Sartrean concepts, so many of the very words and metaphors—particularly those describing female sexuality and existence—she chooses recall his, that it is impossible not to sense his influence throughout *The Second Sex.* After all, no one, least of all de Beauvoir herself, would deny that what could be considered the central concept of *The Second Sex*—

the idea that woman is seen as the "other" both by individual men and by society as a whole—comes from the Sartrean dialectic enounced in *Being and Nothingness.* According to Sartre, the individual ego, in perpetual conflict with other egos or consciousnesses, seeks to assert itself precisely by subduing these other egos. In *The Second Sex* this essential process is described thus: "We find in consciousness itself a fundamental hostility toward every other consciousness; the subject can be posed only in being opposed—he sets himself up as the es-sential, as opposed to the other, the inessential, the object." . . . But, as in the Hegelian master/slave dialectic (where the master *needs* the slave to remain a master), the individual consciousness cannot totally subjugate other egos and turn them into pure objects, for it needs opposition to retain a sense of its own power and being. Taking this process as a starting point, it was de Beauvoir's genius to observe, and take as a central thesis of *The Second Sex* that, in this dialectic, woman is ideally suited to play the role of the "other" since she has always been a "free slave." Woman is:

> a conscious being, but naturally submissive. And therein lies the wondrous hope that man has often put in woman: he hopes to fulfill himself as a being by carnally possessing a being, but at the same time confirming his sense of freedom through the docility of a free per-son. . . . She is a conscious being and yet it seems possible to possess her in the flesh. Thanks to her, there is a way for escaping that im-placable dialectic of master and slave which has its source in the reciprocity that exists be-tween free beings.

(pp. 202-03)

Even if one takes issue with this basic Sartrean dialectic, it is impossible to question the important role it plays in *The Second Sex,* the richness and coherence (if sometimes the rigidity) it lends to de Beauvoir's analysis of the position of women. At the same time, however, this metaphysical or "existential" notion is at the base of many disturbing remarks and judgments concerning woman's sexuality, her "nature," and her behavior patterns. Moreover, although de Beauvoir is constantly at pains to show how existential (i.e., almost invariably, Sartrean) ele-ments are reinforced by the social conditions shaping and con-fronting women, the importance she ascribes to existential fac-tors means that they frequently overwhelm all else, leading her into a certain fatalism. Take, for example, the central notion of the primordial conflict of the two egos in which woman is turned into the "other," into an unchanging *en-soi,* reduced to immanence, to her body, to the image others have of her. From this "otherness" of women, de Beauvoir draws certain conclusions concerning female sexuality: essentially, she ar-gues that woman's status as the "other" means that she is not a free being but, rather, a sexually passive "prey" limited to immanent or corporeal being. Not only does such a conclusion support the traditional view of sexuality which sees man as active and woman as passive but, further, it precludes the possibility of social change. Although throughout *The Second Sex* de Beauvoir repeatedly observes that woman's immanence is both an existential given and a situation reinforced by existing social norms (in this case, woman's "otherness" is reinforced by her social inability to go out into the world where, by doing and creating, she could "transcend" herself and become an evolving *pour-soi*), when it comes to her discussion of female sexuality she virtually dismisses all social factors. Limiting female sexuality to its existential given (that of "otherness," of "prey"), she tells us that if woman tries to escape from her immanent, passive sexuality she will receive little or no pleasure. Further, woman can never be sexually dominant, but can only mimic dominance. Speaking of the "independent" woman, de Beauvoir remarks that:

> If she is proud and demanding, woman meets the male as an adversary, and she is much less well armed than he is. In the first place, he has physical strength, and it is easy for him to impose his will; . . . tension and activity suit his erotic nature, whereas when woman departs from passivity, she breaks the spell that brings on her enjoyment; if she mimics dominance in her postures and movements, she fails to reach the climax of pleasure: most women who cling to their pride become frigid. . . .

But if woman cannot (and, implicitly, should not) transcend this basic existential given of passive sexuality—a given which must influence other behavior patterns—how is she to transcend all the factors condemning her to immanence in the social sphere? And, how can she—as de Beauvoir persistently urges her to do throughout *The Second Sex*—throw off the shackles blocking her way to transcendence?

It is not only Sartre's existential givens (which condemn woman to her existential status of the "other"), but also the world-view behind them, which seems to have influenced this disturbing view of female sexuality. The very language de Beauvoir uses to describe such sexuality—in particular, her frequent metaphors suggesting passivity, heaviness, stickiness, her description of female sexuality as a "bog" or a "trap"—echo Sartre. Instead of words expressing pity or compassion for the plight of women reduced to "prey," her terms suggest recoil and disgust. Throughout *The Second Sex,* female sexuality and corporeality seem to play the same role as unjustified Being in *Nausea* in that they are forever threatening to engulf and absorb man. Sexuality thus becomes the best metaphor for the disturbing world of living matter, if not its most threatening manifestation. One striking passage, full of Sartrean metaphors, describes the viscous nature of female sexuality thus:

> Feminine sex is the soft throbbing of a mollusk. Whereas man is impetuous, woman is only impatient; her expectation can become ardent without ceasing to be passive; man dives upon his prey like the eagle and the hawk; woman lies in wait like the carniverous plant, the bog, in which insects and children are swallowed up. She is absorption, suction, humus, pitch and glue, a passive influx, insinuating and viscous: thus, at least, she vaguely feels herself to be. . . .

No less than Sartre, de Beauvoir establishes a dichotomy between what she views as the repulsive world of living, changing matter (a world incarnated in female sexuality) and an unchanging realm of hardness. This dichotomy emerges quite clearly when de Beauvoir contrasts a young girl's developing sexuality (referred to as "unclean alchemies") with a world of "gold" or "diamond." (pp. 203-05)

[Their] fear of matter and female sexuality probably constitutes the most striking aspect of a world view, common to Sartre and de Beauvoir, which rigidly divides the world into transcendence (the *pour-soi*) and immanence (the *en-soi*), mind and matter, action and passivity, and, ultimately, masculinity

and femininity. And this puritanical, ascetic (and, some would argue, capitalist and Western) world view valorizes "masculine" values, placing, as it does, thought above feeling, doing above quietly existing, transcendence above "nature." Over and over, de Beauvoir echoes Sartre's dictum that man is nothing but his acts and, like him, she defines those acts almost exclusively in terms of the external world: "the reality of man is in the houses he builds, the forests he clears, the maladies he cures." . . . In contrast with man, who creates himself through what he builds and does, woman *is* nothing because she *does* nothing. She becomes narcissistic because "not being able to fulfill herself through projects and objectives, [woman] is forced to find her reality in the immanence of her person. . . . She gives herself a supreme importance because no object of importance is accessible to her." . . . In contrast to the narcissistic, traditional woman who "wallows in immanence" and "attaches extreme importance to her animal nature," the liberated or "modern" woman accepts "masculine values: she prides herself on thinking, taking action, working, creating, on the same terms as men." . . . (p. 205)

De Beauvoir's emphasis upon what she sees as the inherent value of action brings to mind many of the same moral issues raised in the past concerning Sartre. Doesn't the quality of the action count? the reasons one has for committing it? its consequences? Aside from a few passages dealing with the alienation produced by working in a capitalist system (an alienation affecting both men and women), de Beauvoir does not address herself to these issues. Instead, much of *The Second Sex* examines how the world of masculine values has been closed to women and discusses the resulting "female" behavior patterns. Here, too, her argument raises many questionable points, revealing, once again, an uneasy tension between social factors and metaphysical givens. At the core of the tension this time lies that terribly thorny question: was woman locked out of man's world because of her "nature" or because of her "situation," to use the Sartrean terminology? As an existentialist who views man in "situation," who believes that man defines himself by what he does, de Beauvoir tries hard not to attribute everything to an inherent "nature" or "essence," yet its shadow clouds much of what she writes. Not only does she condemn woman to sexual passivity, but, elsewhere, she suggests that woman was denied access to the masculine Eden because of the child-bearing function Nature had assigned her. . . . This firm belief that woman is different from man because of both her sexuality and her maternal function (both of which are often qualified as "animal") does not, however, cause de Beauvoir to take the fatal step and ask if woman's very way of being in the world, her "nature," is different from man's. Instead, divorcing both sexuality and maternity from other modes of behavior, she insists that characteristic female patterns are due to social factors which have closed the masculine world of acting and doing to women.

But the problems do not end with these theoretical difficulties: de Beauvoir's many descriptions of female behavior traits echo existing stereotypes and clichés, even reinforcing them through the dialectical tendency she shares with Sartre to polarize the world so sharply at every turn. . . . More importantly, as feminists have observed, de Beauvoir's pervasive pragmatic, rational, and anti-sexual world-view causes her to ignore or undervalue the positive side of many characteristics associated with women. For example, she repeatedly deplores the fact that woman is more "physical" or, as she says, more "animal" than man. Yet one could argue that in a technological world where man has lost touch with deep feelings and immediate reality, an attachment to the "physical" and the "sensual" is of great value. And a similar case could be made for many of the other "female" characteristics criticized by de Beauvoir. Woman's "lack of a sense of grandeur" and her reluctance to believe in "fixed truths" could be deemed positive qualities in a world where "truth," reason, and grandeur (does one hear echoes of de Gaulle here?) have so often served cruel ideological ends.

It is no coincidence, I think, that many of the qualities de Beauvoir ascribes to women are precisely those often associated with poets. In this respect, de Beauvoir seems once again in accord with Sartre. . . . Much of his wrath is directed against the Surrealists, whose outlook appears diametrically opposed to his own: exalting the immediate, the irrational, the marvelous, they care more about the individual than the group, more about metaphysics than history. Not surprisingly, de Beauvoir derides woman for a similar approach to the world. She laments the fact that woman's inability to grasp the world through "technical skill, sound logic, and articulated knowledge" makes her feel, like "the child and the savage, that she is surrounded by dangerous mysteries" and causes her to seek refuge in a "harmony" which, in de Beauvoir's eyes, is passive and "stationary." And her fundamental disdain for female sensitivity is summed up when she observes that woman has double allegiance—to the "carnal world and the world of poetry."

The ideological prejudices underlying de Beauvoir's dismissal of the "world of poetry" permeate her entire approach to literature and especially to women writers. Judging literature in terms of social commitment (the same terms set forth by Sartre in *What is Literature?*), she insists that the writer's fundamental task is to "contest" the universe, to "found the world anew on a human liberty." And this, like other attempts at transcendence, falls to the lot of men. Women writers may "speak directly to the senses," they may "present experience still warm" or "be attentive to the hidden substance of things," but they are marked by a fundamental weakness:

> Women writers do not contest the human situation, because they have hardly begun to be able to assume it fully. . . .

Although de Beauvoir, like Sartre, demands both political and metaphysical revolt of a writer, . . . [it appears] that she is drawn to writers, like the Russians, in whom metaphysical issues predominate. This preference, in addition to her own philosophical bias (and perhaps a certain French insularity), leads de Beauvoir into some fairly surprising [negative] judgments concerning major English women authors. (pp. 205-08)

The perceptive, sensitive and often independently-minded women described by [such English novelists as Jane Austen, George Eliot, and the Brontës] tower way above most of their counterparts in contemporary fiction, not excluding de Beauvoir's own novels. Even a glance at some of her female characters confirms many of the disturbing ambivalences discernible in *The Second Sex.* Moreover, her female characters, and their various relationships, bring Sartre's fiction to mind. This is particularly true of *The Mandarins* . . . , her long, quasi-autobiographical novel which continues, in a sense, the historical canvas of Sartre's *The Roads to Freedom,* portraying, as it does, the conflicts of personalities, ideas and political loyalties among a group of intellectuals in post-war Paris.

While virtually all the men in this novel are passionately concerned with politics and literature, the three major female char-

acters are curiously untouched by the political fervor seething about them. Instead, as in a romantic novel, each is consumed by sentimental affairs, aware of the outer world only insofar as it touches their men. Each of the three, in fact, appears to illustrate, somewhat schematically, one of the several possible female behavior patterns described in *The Second Sex:* Paule is the "woman in love" (in the novel she is literally driven mad by unreciprocated passion), Nadine is the masochistic, insecure adolescent ready to accept the political beliefs of her current love, and Anne is, at least theoretically, the "independent woman."

Of the three, Anne is by far the most disturbing, since she is supposedly "independent" and, in addition, clearly modelled on de Beauvoir herself. . . . No counterpart of Anne exists in *The Roads to Freedom* but as *The Mandarins* progresses one wonders what, if anything, has been gained. Intelligent and introspective, Anne has nonetheless married a man much older than herself whom she casts in the role of mentor and father. And, although a psychiatrist, she takes little interest in a career which she abandons for months on end to meet her lover in America. In contrast to the detailed descriptions of the professional and political matters facing the men, Anne's work is dismissed by vague references to her clients, most of whom appear to be women with emotional problems.

Worst of all, much of her own narration (and of *The Mandarins* itself) describes her love affair, blow by blow, in terms worthy of romantic stories destined for a female public. (pp. 209-10)

Distressing as the female characters in *The Mandarins* may be, one could argue that de Beauvoir is merely creating some of the "female" behavior patterns described in *The Second Sex,* or that she is simply recording modes of behavior encountered in real life. But if she is attempting to faithfully create various "patterns," why is it that she, like Sartre, seems virtually obsessed by one particular image—that of the "aging" woman clinging to a lover who has become indifferent to her? As for the second hypothesis, it is difficult to believe that in the literary and philosophical milieu of de Beauvoir and Sartre, there were no independent women, no women really interested in politics and literature. It seems far more likely that de Beauvoir's disturbing female characters, like the ambivalencies in *The Second Sex,* stem from deeper sources, not least of which is a philosophical/psychological outlook profoundly influenced by Sartre. (p. 210)

Naomi Greene, "Sartre, Sexuality, and 'The Second Sex'," in Philosophy and Literature, *Vol. 4, No. 2, Fall, 1980, pp. 199-211.**

SIÂN REYNOLDS

[One] realizes how little one knows about Beauvoir from any source other than herself. Few authors can in their lifetime have so firmly controlled the material on which the secondary industry is based.

A further example of this is the publication [in 1979] . . . of *Quand prime le spirituel,* which Gallimard and Grasset turned down in the 1930s, and which Beauvoir decided was worth rescuing from a dusty drawer. . . . [This] loosely-linked collection of five novellas shows almost all the five heroines living through some conflict between their Catholic upbringing and their adolescent or repressed sexuality in the unsettling Paris of the twenties and thirties. The verdict of Grasset's reader—'ce roman manque d'originalité profonde'—may be considered not entirely fair by some readers; in some ways these rather relentlessly written *nouvelles* were groping after a more raw or self-revealing account of woman's experience than, say, a novel by Colette. But while there is some intensity, there is in the end little power.

Why did Simone de Beauvoir so much want to be a novelist? Or rather, why did her acknowledged determination to be a great writer, the driving force of her career, drive her towards fiction? With the exception of *Les Mandarins,* her novels are [less read than her essays and memoirs], . . . yet she kept on writing them. This has posed problems for writers of monographs on Beauvoir. . . . [Some of the studies betray] the uneasiness that has beset (particularly male) writers on Beauvoir's overall achievements: an almost exaggerated respect for the author, with an undercurrent of irritation that bursts through from time to time, perhaps in a sharp reference to her long-windedness (and brevity is indeed not her forte), or in nit-picking of some acerbity (over her incorrect quotation of some American titles). It is as if [several male critics] feel they will be out of line with current pro-feminist attitudes if they criticize Beauvoir's writings too outspokenly. (pp. 206-07)

Is Simone de Beauvoir, who was once unbelievably reviled by the (mostly male) French critics for *Le Deuxième Sexe,* really such a *monstre sacré* that every word of her huge output has to be treated with heavy reverence now that times have changed? Or is the time ripe for some clear-eyed discrimination between the good, the bad, and the indifferent in her writing? (p. 207)

> *Siân Reynolds, in a review of "Quand prime le spirituel," in* The Modern Language Review, *Vol. 76, Part 1, January, 1981, pp. 206-07.*

CATHERINE SAVAGE BROSMAN

The information on the cover [of *Quand prime le spirituel*], which indicates that this is the author's first book and that it is a novel, is somewhat misleading on two counts. . . . The volume is . . . neither her *first* novel nor a novel but rather long stories concerning different characters, among whom there are ties of family or friendship and who thus move in the same milieu. . . . The texts are not arranged in order of composition but rather according to the chronology of the characters' relationships. . . .

One must recognize, as the author does now, that the work is immature for several reasons, some of which she notes in her Preface: absence of fleshed-out male characters, awkward social satire, failure to convey sufficiently either her own drama or that of "Anne," the Zaza of *Mémoires d'une jeune fille rangée.* She could have observed also the excessive and somewhat unconvincing naïveté of the characters, the near-absence of scenic presentation (as opposed simply to summary) in several long passages, weaknesses of structure, and other technical flaws. Clearly, then, this publication is intended, not to bring to light a work of considerable literary merit, but to afford scholars and the author's admirers a chance to assess her early fiction and thus appreciate more both the difficulites of the young writer and her eventual achievement. It is a companion to a forthcoming volume of Beauvoir's other early writings.

The volume offers yet another view of the hated bourgeoisie, which, from her earliest writings, Simone de Beauvoir criticized, even if she was not yet ready to propose substitute values. The depiction would seem caricatural, were it not for the verification afforded by her autobiography. The text is characterized also by romanticism and idealism, which, although the author tried to rid herself of them, persist not only in the critical portraits but also in the dominant ethic of rebellion and self-affirmation, as well as in the style. In both ways this work is a complement to and in some ways a rough draft of both her memoirs and part of her fiction. As one would expect, since she wanted to write about what she knew, it is partly autobiographical. . . .

This volume will interest specialists (on Beauvoir, women writers in France, and the French bourgeoisie); it is much less polished, however, than Beauvoir's later writings, thus demonstrating that one *can learn* to write: she did.

> *Catharine Savage Brosman, in a review of "Quand prime le spirituel," in* The French Review, *Vol. LIV, No. 6, May, 1981, p. 890.*

CAROL ASCHER

[Here is] what strikes me in Simone de Beauvoir, what makes her worth reading and thinking about time after time. Her conflicts are central—for women, for men, for our age—personally as well as politically. Throughout her books there is a tension between being alone, solitary, an individual, and being a part of a friendship, a love, a political group, the world. The issue here is one's ultimate aloneness, but also one's inability as a human being to do anything that is not a social act. . . . There is an essential ambiguity, which we all share, between our real freedom to remake our world, with the responsibility that this implies, and the constraints which at all moments impinge against us. De Beauvoir felt both sides of this ambiguity sharply. She talked about transcendence, acting on one's continually increasing liberties, or its obverse, oppression; or, in psychological terms, about authenticity and bad faith. And there is the strange, contradictory quality of our human condition: our being part of nature, but no longer natural. Here de Beauvoir was most uncomfortable: her mind keen, her will strong, I think she would have wrenched herself from nature if that were possible. (p. 5)

The question of the relationship between de Beauvoir's ideas and those of Jean-Paul Sartre has haunted me throughout [my studies]. . . . [A] recent book on de Beauvoir . . . concludes with the solitary praise that she ought to be considered on her own, rather than as a mere appendage to Sartre. Imagine a book on Sartre whose sole point was that he shouldn't be thought of as merely de Beauvoir's boyfriend. (p. 6)

Still, the reader will want to know: How do her ideas differ from Sartre's? In the moments of petty slander, she was called La Grande Sartreuse. Was she simply a lesser voice, without the enormous philosophical edifice? Or did she have different strengths, take different positions? Several things stand out for me. First, de Beauvoir's study of women transformed dramatically Sartre's ideas of freedom; once *The Second Sex* was published and read by women, her continually increasing sensitivity to women's situation was never deeply shared with him. Second, nowhere in de Beauvoir's writing can one find the celebration of violence, such as appears, for example, in Sartre's introduction to *The Wretched of the Earth* by Fanon, and which he himself modified in his last published interview. Although . . . de Beauvoir raised the possibility, even the necessity for violence, she always did so in the same breath as understanding the irreconcilable sacrifice of real human lives. Third, many have noted that the characters in Sartre's stories and plays are abstract forms sent moving along the page to express philosophical principles. This is never so with de Beauvoir, whose characters are rounded and alive even when they themselves feel captured by metaphysical or political ideas. While de Beauvoir saw life through the grillwork of philosophical concepts, she could also block out the grill at times to see the profusion and contradictory moments that spill out beyond any conceptualization. If she wished life to be held in and pinned down by ideas, she also knew it couldn't.

The question of influence is further complicated . . . because while [Sartre] has said relatively little about his private life as an adult, de Beauvoir has written three volumes covering their fifty years together, much of which details Sartre's intellectual and political development. . . . [For] many years she saw herself as a less imposing figure. Although much of the time she tells the reader that she followed Sartre in his changes in political views, there are also moments when de Beauvoir records an opinion of Sartre's without giving her own. At those moments, one can choose one's interpretation; but my assumption is that she has been intellectually convinced by the arguments, without feeling quite at ease. Her lack of comment on his extreme position on violence is a case in point. (pp. 7-8)

De Beauvoir's books are not finely chiseled. She does not treat language like a precious jewel. Instead, the words rush forth, qualifying others, adding nuance and contradiction, as if a mind is trying to reproduce itself on the written page. When she writes that her goal has always been to reach truth, one senses that she means the very experience of thought itself. Nor is she a lover of form, or of the perfectly wrought plot. Hers are the functional plots, laid down like solid floorwork before the furniture is brought in. Narrative voices differ in order to insert another point of view, not to mystify the reader or to create a refined literary experiment. Yet the very rough surface, which seems both serviceable and meant only for the moment, is part of an honesty, and a digging for what is essential, that defies any quick or easy judgemnt. (p. 8)

[De Beauvoir's] early fiction reinforces our awareness that she tried to work through . . . [a] personal conflict—partly through creating characters who shared her traits. And because she lived in a philosophical world, she conceptualized her fiction, as her life, in existentialist terms.

Between 1943 and 1946, de Beauvoir published her first three novels, *She Came to Stay* (1943), *The Blood of Others* (1945), and *All Men Are Mortal* (1946), her only play, *Les Bouches Inutiles* (1945, still untranslated), as well as her first philosophical essay, *Pyrrhus et Cinéas* (1944, also untranslated). De Beauvoir has called this early period her "moral phase," meaning that she was trying to work out such ethical issues as: what it means to be free or to deny freedom to oneself or anybody else; our responsibility for ourselves and for others, since there is no way we cannot impinge on others; the sources of our guilt; and the effects of our mortality, or our denial of it. Of course, these "moral" issues have their political implications, and so . . . de Beauvoir's transition into an intellectual activist is largely a matter of her pushing certain assumptions a step farther.

Her four works of fiction are disquieting, disturbing books, often physically uncomfortable to read. Each in its own way illustrates some of the basic existentialist principles through describing the opposite of freedom—the various sticky personal and political traps into which we are likely to let ourselves be caught. The (universal?) urge to resist the responsibility, as well as the awesome aloneness, inherent in freedom is elab-

orately investigated. The few moments where characters comprehend their own or others' freedom are incomplete, tenuous, or accompanied by doubt more than jubilation. Thus, by focusing on the ideal, even if largely in its negative, de Beauvoir creates excruciating versions of the limited failure of everyday life.

She Came to Stay, de Beauvoir's first published book, is based on the painful trio that she, Sartre, and her young friend Olga tried to create while de Beauvoir was teaching in Rouen before the war. . . . *She Came to Stay* can be read as a fictional expression of *Being and Nothingness,* also published in 1943. The novel traces Sartre's two "primitive attitudes": the denial of one's own freedom, in which one allows oneself to be an object and to be absorbed by the other's freedom, in the hope that this will be sustaining; and the attempt to possess the other as object, denying her or his freedom, to prevent a threat to one's own sovereignty. Both of these attitudes stem from the "useless passion," the desire to be everything, to be God; both clearly result in conflict, competitiveness, and strife. The only way out for de Beauvoir, as for Sartre, in this early period of their thinking, is through a radical conversion in which one decides to take responsibility for one's own freedom and assumes the freedom of all others. (pp. 49-51)

In contrast to the epigraph of *She Came to Stay* ("Each consciousness pursues the death of the other"), *The Blood of Others* begins with an epigraph taken from Dostoyevsky: "Each of us is responsible for everything and to every human being." These two propositions, which appear to imply opposite attitudes, can also be seen as the attitude of the superego imposed on that of the id. In Sartrian terms, both are the result of the uneasy connection between the self and the other—a connection which, without a "radical conversion" of true freedom, results in relations either of opposition and conflict or fusion. Being responsible for everything, with its sickly guilt, is the other side of the "useless passion," the desire to be God. It is the attempt to leap beyond isolation into a total merging with all others—without retaining the true separateness, and an understanding of each individual's freedom, that true connectedness would imply. (p. 58)

In *All Men Are Mortal,* Simone de Beauvoir continued untangling the threads of our responsibility and freedom. Here, the issue of the self in relation to others is put into excruciating relief by a character who, through a magical potion drunk in the thirteenth century, has already lived seven hundred years. Once again, *All Men Are Mortal* investigates what it means to try to hand over responsibility for one's life to another, or to ask another to give meaning to one's life. But, like *The Blood of Others* and *Les Bouches Inutiles,* this last novel of de Beauvoir's "moral phase" also raises an extension of the opposite question: From what perspective, or with what justification, can one make decisions to save or build for the future at the expense of people who are currently living? (p. 68)

Reading this mythic novel, one has the relentlessly oppressive, page after page experience of being led by the collar into a confrontation with one's mortality. In contrast to most of de Beauvoir's work, which carries an underlying theme of the terror of death, this book examines the horror of endless existence. Here, immortality becomes the symbol of ultimate alienation. Although our mortality constrains us to a limited vision, it is the only vision of meaning, according to de Beauvoir. Beyond the perspective of the present there is no perspective that makes sense of experience. It is hard to imagine anyone reading to the last page of *All Men Are Mortal* and still wanting eternal life. (pp. 68-9)

From *She Came to Stay* To *All Men Are Mortal,* de Beauvoir draws a moral and philosophical picture of the individual's relationships in both the private and the public spheres. Taken together, these works from the "moral phase" offer an ethical as well as the beginnings of a political perspective. Nowhere, including in Sartre's work, do we have a fictional sequence that so carefully investigates the structures of thought and behavior that are used in relationship to oneself, to a friend or lover, and to the larger movements of history. Over the past several decades, a number of writers have made these connections from a psychoanalytic, Marxist, or feminist (which often combines the other two) perspective. But because de Beauvoir makes them from an existentialist perspective—a view we are much less accustomed to in the United States—they cut into our lives in a fresh way. In fact, given our enormous preoccupation with freedom, it is a strange quirk of history, largely attributable to the Cold War, that we have neglected making the connections within an existentialist framework.

With the vision of personal and political freedom as an ideal, de Beauvoir traces how grandiosity leads to attempts to control or conquer, and self-denial results in submission and giving over one's freedom. (p. 73)

Although she had not yet thought systematically about the issues surrounding women's roles, de Beauvoir is clear throughout these early works that the attitudes of controlling or being controlled, or of objectifying or being objectified, are not necessarily gender-related and certainly not based on biology. (pp. 73-4)

Another theme which would be developed more fully in future works is that of the "saint." . . . Jean's obsession with responsibility and guilt in *The Blood of Others* is deeply connected to both a rejection of the world and a wish for conquest and control. From the point of view of grandiosity, Jean Blomart is no different from the early Fosca who took a magic potion to achieve immortality. Both want to live outside the rules that apply to ordinary people. Until his involvement in the Resistance, Jean's politics stem from his urge to cleanse himself personally of the evil which is all around him and in which, as he increasingly comes to understand, he is actually embedded. In a world filled with evil, as de Beauvoir and Sartre would argue, the saint is one who is largely out to clean his own skin. It is only when Jean joins the Resistance that he also gives up this hubris of saintliness. Blood will be spilled, he knows; he will be responsible for things he can't even predict, and which won't be in his control. But as de Beauvoir argues in *Pyrrhus et Cinéas,* there are no acts that do not impinge on others. Knowing this doesn't give us free license, but it changes the notion of responsibility from an individualistic striving for purity to one of being accountable to ourselves and others within the context of a specific situation and our very temporal goals.

The notion that we are all absolutely free is implicit and explicit in these early works. This freedom is abstract and potential for those who do not use it, but it exists just the same. And just as we are each absolutely free, we must respect the absolute freedom of every other person. (pp. 74-5)

Finally, *Les Bouches Inutiles, The Blood of Others,* and *All Men Are Mortal* raise the question of how one is to judge any action, whether violent or nonviolent. When de Beauvoir and Sartre first espoused their ethics of existentialism, a common

and frightened retort was that, without a God or some absolute standard of judgment, the world would simply end in wanton license. These early works, deeply tortured as they are by questions of morality, are an answer to the critics. *Les Bouches Inutiles* shows the silliness—and danger—of reifying the ideal of Useful. *The Blood of Others* criticizes the objectification of communism, pacifism, or even freedom since such goes beyond the specifics of real individuals and real lives. *All Men Are Mortal* illustrates the meaninglessness of any achievement, whether it be a canal, monument, building, or giant country, gained at the expense of rootedness in the present. All attempts to give "absolute meaning" to values are doomed to failure, since "nothing is useful [including freedom] if it is not useful to man; nothing is useful to man if the latter is not in a position to define his own ends and values, if he is not free." (p. 77)

[*The Mandarins*] was written after de Beauvoir had already completed *The Second Sex.* Thus it was also her first novel to reflect the systematic insights she had gained in her study of women. . . . Opening onto the liberation of Paris in late 1944, the novel traces the new hopes for personal freedom and political activity, and the ensuing complications, for a group of Parisian Left intellectuals, as the news of the Stalin regime, the altered realities of political organizing in France, and the threat of a Cold War begin to press down on their lives. While the ethical and political issues posed by the book might seem one-dimensional when expressed philosophically, the novel gives them flesh. . . . (p. 83)

The Mandarins is de Beauvoir's richest, most complex, and most beautifully wrought novel—one that should not be skipped over by anyone interested in de Beauvoir, the postwar period in France, the problem of communism in a European context, or the issues of ethics and political action. More than any novel, it conveys the excitement and urgency of conversations about ethical and political issues. (p. 84)

The Second Sex is a miracle of courage and creativity. . . . The book's clarity of vision makes it comparable to Frantz Fanon's *Black Skin, White Masks,* which also turned reality inside out—in his case to expose the hidden mechanisms of racial opposition.

To fully appreciate *The Second Sex,* one must understand that it was written in isolation from other women thinking about women, as well as almost total isolation from other women intellectuals. Not only was there no lively, or even dormant, woman's movement, but the issues of women's oppression could hardly have seemed the important ones in the late 1940s. Between Hitler, Stalin, and the atom bomb, most French people weren't worrying about the woman question. Also, . . . the existentialist theory she relied upon was riddled with unconscious sexism in its arguments as well as in its casual metaphors. Yet faced with all these wide-ranging and immediate obstacles, de Beauvoir spent two years and a thousand pages detailing the lives of women through the ages. If her language seems overblown at times, or her arguments overshot with endless supporting detail, the historical moment in which she wrote should be remembered. (pp. 144-45)

The Second Sex is the first, and still the only book to offer a dialectic theory which can account for both women's oppression and the possibility of their liberation. Other works which focus on the oppression of women tend to leave the reader with the sense of women as victims, while those describing women's historical achievements lose an analytical grip on the opposing forces and constraints against which those achievements occurred. There is no other book I know of that attempts to make moral judgments about the variety of ways women live in and beyond their constraint. De Beauvoir's model enables her to show how women, through their own acts, are complicitous; yet to say this is not to "blame the victim," a phrase which has become popular on the Left and in the women's movement. Rather, it is to remove the category of victim *per se,* and to give to women the respect due any choosing and responsible individual. (pp. 145-46)

Like *Das Kapital,* or *Being and Nothingness* on which *The Second Sex* was largely based, de Beauvoir's analysis is the product of isolation and the absence of any political movement; and like the other books, its strength derives from criticizing the mechanisms of oppression. (p. 146)

> Carol Ascher, *in her* Simone de Beauvoir: A Life of Freedom, *Beacon Press, 1981, 254 p.*

CAROL ASCHER

[When de Beauvoir wrote the stories now published as *When Things of The Spirit Come First: Five Early Tales,* she] had already removed herself morally and politically from the world she was describing—which may account for her harshness toward the heroines in some of these stories. Already, while teaching in the provinces, she and Sartre had been involved in a long and difficult triangle with one of de Beauvoir's students (the basis of *L'invitée,* her first published novel, translated into English as *She Came to Stay*). They had also been pulled into politics by the Spanish Civil War.

The common theme of these five stories . . . is the existentialist tragedy of placing essence before existence—that is, attempting to dispel the ambiguity and freedom of one's life by setting up an Absolute (God) or absolutes (social customs) on which one relies, making "things of the spirit come first." Some of the stories are roughly structured, while others are told without a complete command of that skill for transforming life and philosophy into art which de Beauvoir would beautifully master in her best fiction, *The Mandarins.* However, all five have an energy and rigor, an honesty of detail and a sense of hitting the bone of a story that are characteristic of de Beauvoir. (p. 314)

Those who wish can read de Beauvoir's characteristically unsparing evaluation of these early stories in the second volume of her memoirs, *The Prime of Life,* where she uses such adjectives as "bloodless" and "labored."

Yet the tales are always interesting and, even in their harshness, pleasing. . . . They describe a claustrophobic world of repression that is difficult for most liberally raised Americans to comprehend. More than her other fiction, more even than *Memoirs of a Dutiful Daughter,* the stories show the refined brutality of Catholic schoolgirl society. They give a window on the closed universe out of which de Beauvoir thrust herself to live her unconventional and politically committed life. (p. 315)

> Carol Ascher, *"Lisa & Marcelle & Anne & Chantal," in* The Nation, *Vol. 235, No. 10, October 2, 1982, pp. 314-15.*

DEIRDRE BAIR

The five stories in ["**When Things of The Spirit Come First: Five Early Tales**"] were written after Miss de Beauvoir had abandoned several complete and partly complete early writings

that were never offered for publication because of what she called "shoddy romanticism." . . .

She had already decided that fiction should be her means of expression and to this end began experimenting with short texts that fictionalized her own experiences as well as those of other women. In the five stories . . . , she wrote about five different approaches along as many different paths toward the discovery of the same personal truths. . . .

Although the five stories are independent entities, the leading characters of some appear as background figures in the others. All the stories deal with the harm done to young women by the excessive religiosity that dominates their backgrounds and constricts the marital and educational opportunities and possibilities of behavior open to them. (p. 12)

These are stories of young women in the process of defining what they want to be; of their youthful attempts to break free of familial, social and religious restraints, to learn to respect themselves as well as to love others, to come to terms with commitments either freely chosen or else imposed, and to dare to flaunt social convention. Miss de Beauvoir writes about the undefinable feelings that presage the first youthful discovery of femininity and concurrent passion. She writes of role models who no longer serve, of friends who disappoint, of men who behave, quite simply, as themselves.

When placed within historical context—the bourgeois French society of the early part of this century—these stories can be read as accurate reflections of that culture, portraying a suffocating insularity requiring great courage for undereducated women to rail against. It is this emotional toll that Miss de Beauvoir conveys so successfully. Despite certain failures of style, there is a realistic cast to these stories that makes the situation of the women tangible. (pp. 12, 44)

With "**Chantal**" and "**Anne**" she takes deliberate stylistic risks that for the most part succeed. . . . "This book is a beginner's piece of work," Miss de Beauvoir writes in the preface, with "obvious faults," and "**Lisa**" comes closest to fitting this judgment.

"**Chantal**" begins splendidly . . . , but it disintegrates when Miss de Beauvoir seems unable to decide whose point of view the narrator should embrace. . . . ["**Anne**"] drifts into jargon once Anne reaches the point at which she must make important decisions about her life. The final outcome, though true to Miss de Beauvoir's life, seems contrived when fictionalized. . . .

"**Marguerite,**" which Miss de Beauvoir calls "a satire on my youth," is the most openly autobiographical of the stories and the one whose details will be most recognizable to readers of the memoirs. This "little bourgeoise trying to act the bohemian" triumphs over religious and familial crises and ends with her explanation of how she came to "try to look things straight in the face, without accepting oracles or ready made values. I had to rediscover everything myself, and sometimes it was disconcerting—furthermore, not everything is clear even now."

The importance of this book today lies in its demonstration of how early in her career Simone de Beauvoir recognized and expressed the ideas that would figure throughout her writing, particularly the question of the forces that determine women's lives. Recently she remarked that she would write no more fiction, nor would she publish any early works other than this one. She feels that her canon is complete and "one book more or less will not change anyone's opinion about the body of my work.''

Her last fiction published before this was **"The Woman Destroyed,"** a collection of three stories about older women who are made vulnerable to suffering by old age, loneliness and the loss of love. Now, with this book about five young women, we have the perfect set of bookends to enclose a remarkable lifetime of writing. (p. 45)

> Deirdre Bair, *"A Conversion to the Real World,"* in The New York Times Book Review, *November 7, 1982, pp. 12, 44-5.*

CAROL STERNHELL

A beacon, a symbol, the author of feminism's most important theoretical text, a great lover, a militant at 76—Simone de Beauvoir seems beyond criticism, creator of one of the most examined lives ever lived. She has had what she wanted, Sartre and writing, writing and Sartre; "I have never met anyone," she says in her memoirs, "in the whole course of my life, who was so well equipped for happiness as I was, or who labored so stubbornly to achieve it." Why then have I always felt so ambivalent, so uneasy, reading her autobiography? Why is this latest installment, *Adieux: A Farewell to Sartre,* so disturbing? . . .

If I've learned anything in feminism's last decade, it's that nobody's emotional life is—or should be—"politically correct." If somebody tells me that she or he is satisfied, it seems worse than churlish to disagree. In the case of Simone de Beauvoir—who more than anyone else made me feel the sheer, transforming power of feminist thought—it seems breathtakingly rude, like spitting at your grandmother. While parts of *The Second Sex* are dated today, 35 years after it was published amid a barrage of hostile reviews, and while feminists have taken issue with everything from the book's existentialist framework to its use of anthropology, nothing even approaches it in scope; de Beauvoir ranges from biology to psychology to literature to history, describing a vast pattern of sexual asymmetry. . . .

And because de Beauvoir's life and work are so thoroughly entwined—she once wrote, "My most important work is my life"—the six autobiographical volumes (including *Adieux* and her moving account of her mother's battle against cancer, *A Very Easy Death*), the fiction, and her more theoretical work (an encyclopedic study of aging, philosophical treatises, travel reports) illuminate each other in unusual ways. . . .

The picture that emerges from de Beauvoir's autobiography—particularly in *Adieux*—is of Sartre at the center of a circle of adoring women. . . . It's hard not to feel that the ideal love was asymmetrical; where he praises her as his "one special reader," she says that meeting him "was the most important event in my life." He recalls his youthful sense of purpose: "I looked upon myself as a genius. It was an idea that came to me very young." She embarks on a life of devotion: "My trust in him was so complete that he supplied me with the sort of absolute unfailing security that I had once had from my parents, or from God." He is his own measure: "And then there were the thoughts of the man alone, a man such as I wished to be, a man who thought only by his own powers and who gave light to the city thanks to what he thought and felt." She puts him at the very center of her life: "For me his mere existence justified the world—though there was nothing that

could perform the same service for him." She writes about him constantly; he's never written about her. . . .

More than any of her other works, *Adieux* is a valentine to Sartre, a poignant account of his last 10 years. As always, de Beauvoir reports the minutiae of their lives . . . , but this time we also learn of Sartre's slow decline, of strokes and failing eyesight, weak legs and bouts of senility. Each detail, tragic or banal, is recorded. . . . The second, and longer, half of *Adieux* consists of "conversations" de Beauvoir conducted with Sartre during the summer and fall of 1974, when her worries about his health (he'd already had minor strokes and could no longer see well enough to read or write) made her eager to preserve his last word on every possible subject. Less conversations, or even interviews, than testimony, these dialogues are intended for posterity. De Beauvoir, who already knows the answers, only wants to capture "his living voice." (p. 6)

The first section of *Adieux,* de Beauvoir's farewell ceremony (the French text is called *La Ceremonie des Adieux*), is as busy and detailed as the earlier volumes of memoirs. It often reads like a diary, and like a diary is written for insiders. If you can't identify Bost, or Lanzmann, or Sylvie, too bad (de Beauvoir's women frequently have only first names, her men only surnames). She has been criticized in the past for this casual arrogance, but I find it endearing; you just have to read the whole autobiography in order, like a 2000-page novel. In *Adieux,* I generally skipped the political episodes I'd never heard of—the coal mines trial, the Burgos trial, the Overney murder. The powerful story here, and de Beauvoir's real concern, is Sartre's painful deterioration. . . .

The contrast between the exalted—their conversations about genius, work, immortality—and the mundane—medications, bedsores, false teeth—is shockingly touching. So is the picture of de Beauvoir, ladylike, meticulously groomed, beautiful, trying to climb under the sheets to lie beside Sartre's gangrenous corpse. It's a perverse gesture, of course, but a lovely one, obsessive and moving at once, like *Adieux.* (p. 7)

> Carol Sternhell, *"Love among the Ruins: Simone de Beauvoir Thinks It Over,"* in VLS, *No. 26, May, 1984, pp. 1, 6-7.*

LORNA SAGE

[*Adieux: A Farewell to Sartre*] is a deliberate affront to conventional notions of privacy and dignity. It's an exact, stoical account of Sartre's disintegration during his last 10 years, and in writing it Simone de Beauvoir is testifying, with a kind of obstinate scrupulosity, to their shared freedom from all such conventional decencies as would—for example—keep a great man's image 'intact.'

'Honesty suited us,' she said in a 1973 interview—as though too much truth might be damaging in less extraordinary lives. And there's something of the same pride in the writing here. Sartre's dying, you are meant to feel, is watchable because he had himself unfolded the possibilities of his experience (in the books, in his political life) so honestly. The book is as much a matter of keeping the record straight as a labour of love, from this point of view, and indeed the refusal of sentimental language is itself part of the pain of the thing. . . . [What] de Beauvoir gives here (and, surely, what she wanted) is the specifically, even absurdly, human. She ends with a dialogue about God—that 'infinite intermediary' Sartre and she had learnt to do without, though His Almighty absence explained why one must face one's freedom, why one must write everything out again, including, or especially, age and death:

> You and I, for example, have lived without paying attention to the problem [of God]. And yet we've lived; we feel that we've taken an interest in our world. . . .

To keep God out, you need to deconstruct the myth of 'the great man,' too. This, or something like it, is de Beauvoir's logic, and she's probably right. 'Adieu'—except that *le bon Dieu* has nothing to do with it, 'this life owes nothing to God.'

> *Lorna Sage, "Last Testament," in* The Observer, *June 17, 1984, p. 22.*

ADRIANNE BLUE

The ruthlessness with which Simone de Beauvoir documents Sartre's deterioration is, at first, appalling. The puddle of piss he leaves on a chair is recorded. So is the dribble on his shirt. Nothing is shameful to de Beauvoir if it is true: the ugliest, the least dignified truth is beauty.

The staccato rat-a-tat of the years of Sartre's faltering final decade, 1970-1980, shatters our and the 19th-century's obsession with immutable Grecian urns, with adolescent 'perfection', with euphemism. This book is an extraordinary achievement, precisely the right encomium for a man whose passion was mind. . . .

Neither [de Beauvoir nor Sartre] ever shies from truth, even when the terse, almost too scrupulous diary which makes up the first third of this 450-page book, and which mentions even the deathbed gangrene and her own drunkenness, gives way to the conversations.

Taped in 1974 after blindness made it impossible for him to write, they show her to be as relentless an interrogator as she is a diarist. Sartre talks about politics, literature, sex. (p. 25)

He speaks of himself and she speaks of him as a man of genius and one looks for irony, but there is none. Yet why should there be? If gangrene is mentionable, surely so is genius. (p. 26)

> *Adrianne Blue, "Minding," in* New Statesman, *Vol. 107, No. 2780, June 29, 1984, pp. 25-6.*

HAZEL E. BARNES

[*The Ceremony of Farewells*] is an account of the decade preceding Sartre's death. The title is itself a recollection of a poignant moment, as Beauvoir explains: "'Then this is the ceremony of farewells!' Sartre said to me as we were leaving each other for a month at the beginning of one summer. I had a presentiment of the meaning these words would one day assume. The ceremony lasted ten years. It is these ten years that I recount in this book." The record is annalistic, the same kind of detailed year-by-year account of events and her reactions to them that Beauvoir employed in the first three volumes of her autobiography. But there her stated intention was to keep herself as the center of focus and to speak of Sartre only insofar as his existence was intertwined with her own. In the preface to *The Ceremony of Farewells* she states that she has recorded these ten years as she had lived them, but that the book is devoted wholly to Sartre. If she has spoken also of herself, it is because "the witness is a part of what he witnesses." The book is dedicated "To those who loved Sartre, love him, will

love him." Indeed, it has been written for them by one who is of them. . . .

[Beauvoir's chronicle] is not a dramatic tale. Prone as Sartre was to look upon his life as a series of conversions, his was not the death of an Ivan Ilych. Perhaps what is most remarkable is the fact that Sartre tried, almost beyond the bonds of realism, not to change his way of life. . . .

I will not attempt to follow the chronology of this tale of inevitable physical and mental decline. Beauvoir does not spare her readers the unpleasant details. She gives specific instances of physical awkwardness and incontinence and spells of mental confusion. I understand that in some feminist circles gossip paints Beauvoir as finally getting her own back, in return for having to put up with Sartre's infidelities. This is slander. The narrative is both factual reporting and a tribute. If she includes trivial details, her purpose is neither to point to the idol's feet of clay nor, as a hagiographer might, to record every word and act as intrinsically precious and of equal value with every other. She wants to show how it was. And if we want to know how it really was when this philosopher grappled with physical ills and death, we should be grateful to her for providing information rather than writing a subjective, impressionistic sketch. Not that she refrains from comment; she does not. But we can test the adequacy of her judgments by the evidence she provides—in the text itself or in the interviews. At some points I think we can discern what she did not record and perhaps did not perceive.

In his book on Baudelaire, Sartre claimed that the poet had the life he deserved. Did Sartre have the death he deserved? At one point Beauvoir seems to answer affirmatively. "What is certain is that the drama of his last years is the consequence of his entire life. . . . Sartre had the decline and the death that his life called for. And that is why, perhaps, he accepted them so calmly." . . . She refers particularly to the fact, acknowledged by Sartre himself, that his high blood pressure, stroke, and eye hemorrhage were in large part caused by his excessive use of stimulants at the time he was writing *Critique of Dialectical Reason* in the late 1950s. Sartre said that it was more important to him to bring that work to a speedy finish than to live longer. He did not, however, anticipate the blindness, and one wonders if he would have been as content with his bargain if he had. Beauvoir remarks on, and Sartre publicly proclaimed, his calm acceptance of a situation that he considered to be due partly to inevitable aging and partly to physiological accidents. To me, however, the narrative itself undermines this notion of calm acquiescence. It hints at periods of despair and at least raises the question as to whether Sartre deliberately worsened his condition or even hastened his death. . . .

I . . . think that his refusal to act more effectively to prevent [his death] was halfway an invitation, a willingness to let bodily events take their course. I believe that the reason behind it was, as Beauvoir indicated, his not wanting life at all unless it continued to include the written objectification of his active, creative thought. . . .

Beauvoir's book, fascinating in its picture of Sartre's involvement in the political activities of France's leftist intellectuals, will probably be most valued as a portrait of the quotidian details of life in the Sartrean circle. One is impressed with the rich ambiance of personal concern and devotion, the love bestowed on Sartre by the remarkably large number of persons with whom he maintained close and constant contact. . . .

Everywhere in *The Ceremony of Farewells,* as in the *Interviews,* one is struck with the profound respect which Sartre and Beauvoir had for each other, something deeper than the obvious affection, companionship, and commonality of values, more bedrock than love. . . .

In a novella, *The Age of Discretion,* written in the 1960s, Beauvoir imaginatively anticipated what she and Sartre would live through in the decade to follow. Although its hero and heroine are by no means a mirror image of Sartre and Beauvoir, we find surprising parallels as well as contrasts between the story and the factual report. . . .

Reality was both better and worse than literary anticipation. Although Sartre and Beauvoir were no longer close to being cult objects, honors continued to pour in. Alien and disillusioned as they felt with regard to contemporary political realities, they continued to find meaning in social action on specific issues. . . .

Blindness was not included in Beauvoir's list of ailments [in the novella], nor a mind not steadily composed. Mental sterility was there. André [the hero] foreshadows Sartre's "I have no ideas," even his sense of frustration in feeling that he ought to apply the new structuralist techniques with which he did not feel at home. . . .

There is one striking parallel. The wife in the story was disturbed and resentful at the easy resignation with which her husband gave in to the tics and thought patterns of old age. Beauvoir's reaction to Sartre is similar. At the first sign of his urinary incontinence, she expected him to be greatly embarrassed. . . . Sartre, however, simply remarked that one must not expect too much when one is old. Beauvoir writes, "I was touched by his simplicity, by this humility so new in him, and at the same time I was pained by his lack of aggression, by his resignation." . . .

I do not mean for a moment to suggest that Beauvoir invented any of this to fit a fictional pattern. It is possible, however, that both her perception and her way of writing reflected it. Or we could go full circle. In her autobiography Beauvoir had

already described how Sartre, by sheer exertion of will, cured himself of a prolonged bout of depression and hallucinatory experiences. Possibly observation of Sartre's willed and effective self-readjustment had inspired the development of André. . . .

At no point either in Beauvoir's narrative or in the interviews is there expressed the hope, so often present in personal farewells, of a reunion after death or a sense that the departed is in any way present to the bereaved. Beauvoir is quite explicit. In her preface she writes, "Here is the first of my books—the only one, no doubt—that you will not have read before it was published. It is entirely consecrated to you, and it is of no concern to you." She goes on to say that her use of the "you" is but a lure, a rhetorical device. She is addressing not Sartre, but his friends. The last paragraph of *The Ceremony of Farewells* has the words, "His death separates us. My death will not reunite us. That's the way it is." . . .

In the last interview [in *Interviews*] Sartre describes how he gradually worked out the full implications of a wholly materialistic atheism. He then acknowledges that there are some advantages for the believer but concludes that belief simply does not fit our knowledge of the world. Moreover, our concept and image of the divine is a projection of our own ideas. God has been made by man. Why should we then try to live and judge ourselves by our own creation? "The true relation to our self is to what we are and not to that self which we have constructed in vague resemblance to us." . . . At the very end Sartre and Beauvoir agree that really they have not been much preoccupied by the subject, have not had many conversations that concerned God. Sartre says, "And yet all the same we have lived, we have the impression of having interested ourselves in our world and of having tried to see it." This modest aim, to look at the world and to understand it as it is, seems to me to have been the driving force in these two persons who have so greatly influenced so many people in the world.

Hazel E. Barnes, "Beauvoir and Sartre: The Forms of Farewell," in Philosophy and Literature, *Vol. 9, No. 1, April, 1985.**

Marvin (Hartley) Bell

1937-

American poet, essayist, critic, and editor.

Bell is among America's most prestigious contemporary poets. His career has been marked by steady development and his work as an editor, critic, and professor has significantly influenced contemporary American poetry. Bell's early poems reveal his interest in language. They are noted for experimentation with style and structure, extensive use of complicated syntax, and clever wordplay; the predominant tone, as G. E. Murray notes, is "breezy charm and wit." As Bell's writing matured, his language became more simple and direct. According to critics, this development heightened the emotional impact of his poems and fostered greater integration of their content and form.

A Probable Volume of Dreams (1969), Bell's first important collection, contains poems reprinted from *Things We Dreamt We Died For* (1966) and other publications. This volume presents his thematic concern with loss and displacement. Bell's relationship with his family, especially his deceased father, and the problems unique to his Russian-Jewish heritage form the basis of much of his poetry. The tone of his later verse suggests a sense of reconciliation and acceptance not found in his early work.

Bell's next two major works, *The Escape into You* (1971) and *Residue of Song* (1974), reveal his increasing preference for emotional depth over technical virtuosity. With *Stars Which See, Stars Which Do Not See* (1977), Bell found what he had sought: "A language that embodies deep feeling and meaningful experience." Bell also discovered a style which enabled him to "write poetry in a way that is accessible to anyone who wants to read it." Of this volume, Bell further stated: "In a very real sense, [this is] my first book." The quiet, graceful tone, the sense of modesty and calm assurance, and the sophisticated maturity of this "first book" have elicited almost unanimous critical approval.

The poem "Trinket" in *Stars Which See, Stars Which Do Not See* exemplifies the simplicity and immediacy of emotion which constitute the strengths of this and subsequent volumes. In this poem, the sight of water oozing through a crack in a fern pot acts as a reminder for the speaker that, as David St. John notes, "It is not in grandeur that the self is to be found," but in the domestic particulars of everyday life. In the same volume, "The Self and the Mulberry" begins with the line: "I wanted to see the self, so I looked at the mulberry." Since *Stars Which See, Stars Which Do Not See* Bell has produced two volumes of poetry—*These Green-Going-to-Yellow* (1981) and *Segues* (1983), a "correspondence in poetry" with William Stafford—and a collection of essays, *Old Snow Just Melting* (1982).

(See also *CLC*, Vol. 8; *Contemporary Authors*, Vols. 21-24, rev. ed.; and *Dictionary of Literary Biography*, Vol. 5.)

ROBLEY WILSON, JR.

Marvin Bell does it [well]—this business of articulating a Jewish heritage—and the opening third of *Things We Dreamt We*

Died For succeeds through sheer feeling in converting the stereotype of the immigrant arrived from Russia into an affective image. The Jewish father becomes the symbol of a past remembered, respected, owed to. "There will always be a Jew in Russia, / to whose grave our very talk / goes back and forth . . . ," says "The Manipulator." "The Coat of Arms" begins: "I am seen in a landscape sometime before / the revolution. . . . / My name is Botsian, and the Jews are in for it." The lines suggest the differences between generations, and the remainder of the poem cries out for continuity. Such poems make for a strong first book.

Other subject matters undercut the strength. What Bell does that I don't enjoy seeing done is: be clever. And he *is* clever, and brittle and glib and elliptical and a player-with-language. He has the gift of lyric, but he often obliges that gift to be only rhetoric. Still the good pieces—"What Song the Soldiers Sang," "The Hole in the Sea," "Believable Linden, Pumpkin, Cherry, Etc."—are worth re-reading, and I hope these mark the poet's best direction. (p. 120)

> Robley Wilson, Jr., "Five Poets at Hand," in The Carleton Miscellany, *Vol. IX, No. 4, Fall, 1968, pp. 117-20.**

ARTHUR OBERG

[From *A Probable Volume of Dreams* through *The Escape into*

You and *Residue of Song*]—the three most important books of Marvin Bell which have been published so far—we discover the poet crafting his poems in structures which keep reminding us just how much artifice is involved, and how much wit is needed to keep the poem afloat and the reader at once near and at bay. What proves telling is seeing which poems from Bell's limited edition of *Things We Dreamt We Died For* . . . get left out of *A Probable Volume of Dreams:* the poems tend not merely to be the weaker ones, but the less distanced ones in which there is insufficient strategy to manage where the poet-father must walk, "foot by foot," both on earth and in heaven.

If the most recent poems of Bell, those still uncollected in book form, have begun to indicate changes in both the life and the art, there are lines of continuity as well as lines of departure. Some of Bell's preferences are ingrained and resonant enough for his best poems, whatever the vintage, for us to know that if they shout back and forth at one another there will be response and commerce. (pp. 4-5)

Stanza by stanza, sequence by sequence, and book by book, Bell reminds us that he is intent on exploring the relationships among love, art, and some public, moral realm which demands faces and postures of another kind. . . .

["An Afterword to My Father," the opening poem in *A Probable Volume of Dreams*,] announces a motif of fathers and sons which will run through all of Bell's work. . . .

Although Bell is never narrowly confessional, it is important to note just how much the death of the father—his profound absence and presence—helps shape Bell's poetry and create possible worlds. *The* father: Bell's own dead father, and his growing sense of himself as a father who has sons and who, like him, will someday die.

The titles of *The Escape into You* and *Residue of Song* present ambiguities of time and person, loss and rescue, treasure and waste which look back toward *A Probable Volume of Dreams*. Bell suggests that as he moves amid father and son, woman and woman, poem as speech and poem as song, he often will be unsure whether there is anything left, whether home has been reached, whether homecoming is desirable or possible. Each of these three books is divided into sections which tell how unlinear life and art are, how "progress" is a deception of the nineteenth century, how increasingly distant the finishing line for the poet-runner proves to be. The choice is in knowing there is no choice, and in acting as if there were choices all along. . . .

If the death of the father sets into motion *A Probable Volume of Dreams* as a book of homage and love, it soon becomes obvious that Bell has more than his father under his heart, or on his mind. . . . The father never disappears in Bell's work, but he is part of a landscape of sons and wife and friends. The dream house which the poems and the poet build toward seeks love as its foundation and song, a place where "all things are possible." The wish proves easier in the making than in the keeping. Repeatedly, poems in this volume break or give the impression of breaking into fragments. Lines are drawn across the page, and across the face. The promised dream proves not to include us, or to offer a home which it is useless to be in. Joy cannot be contained less because it runs over than because it is the nature of joy to go wounded. . . .

It would be easy to extract from *A Probable Volume of Dreams* those poems that push toward the status and shine of anthology pieces: "An Afterword to My Father," "Treetops," "Let's Go, Daddy," "The Perfection of Dentistry," "The Address to the Parents," "Toward Certain Divorce." We could argue about the grouping, but that would be only to be transfixed by the integrity of whole, contained poems and thereby to forget how radically experimental and brilliant the book itself is. The feel or experience of the book is closer to that of going under or around some of the poems . . . in order to determine the network of feelings which at every turn or junction come into view. . . .

In doing a review of *A Probable Volume of Dreams*, I noted about the song which Bell learns to sing that it "is never an easy one, but paradoxical, and when necessary, unengaging." That *unengaging* sense remains for me central to this book and to all of Bell's later work. It is part of a core of meaning which is variously relentless, tough, and irresistible. . . .

By the conclusion of *A Probable Volume of Dreams* the poet suggests that his chances of taking his father down from the pedestal or wall are greater, and that his own chances of "entering the wall" are better than they had been at the ambiguous conclusion of "An Afterword to My Father." Barrier, after all, need not be barrier; and cloud need not be hindrance but protection, halo, and sign.

What Bell discovers in this book is how much looking and looking up he must do, and how "giving in" is not so much weak surrender as it is some strong, gracious embracing of his own life and of the lives of those close to him. (p. 5)

In *The Escape into You* and in *Residue of Song* the poet's two sons Nathan and Jason and his wife Dorothy figure as increasingly telling presences whose possible absence or loss the poet seeks to prevent. . . .

From the poems in *A Probable Volume of Dreams* through those in *Residue of Song* we see not only how related volumes of dreams, love poems, and songs are, but how easily each book could turn into some book of the dead unless the poet is careful to see where and exactly what his kinships are. In *The Escape into You* we soon discover how ambiguous the title is, and how difficult again Bell's poems have a habit of being. . . .

[The] poems in *The Escape into You* function as a sequence which will record a crisis, or many smaller crises, within a marriage and within a poetic self that is still learning to bury the dead and to walk among the living, loving persons who can and must sustain his life beyond the reaches of even the tallest, fullest art.

The Escape into You is not so much the detail-by-detail story of a faltering marriage and a divided poet that come together and hold together when more lasting relationships are worked out as it is the story of the slow, painful coming to awareness of a man who sees what was already there: a wife and sons who keep and have their own separateness even as they love, and a man whose better self needed only a keener looking glass to help make him up and out. What are rescue and escape, grace and craft, warning and dare: these prove leitmotifs in a drama which understands there is no single answer, but answers true for the moment or context which demanded them. For even the people are changing and changeable, not out of weakness but out of the needs and the wants which drive them on. Sons, wife, and husband join in a dance which keeps stopping so that we can see who are the partners, who is calling, and what is the dance. Only to have it all start again.

Just as William Stafford understands the "millions of intricate moves" needed to create "justice," Bell enacts in his poems the endless strategies for locating and establishing love. Love is not easy or cheap in Bell's world. As a result, we find Bell perpetually acknowledging that what the doctor ordered is not what the poet may choose to do, that all that he can do is to say he is having trouble saying how much he loves. . . .

No matter how I address the fact, *The Escape into You* is a painful, exhausting book to read. As metaphysical amorist, Bell leads us to the repeated situation where dressing up is dressing down. The passages are "murky," and the feelings frequently unpleasant and ugly and small. But what saves the book and makes the book an important one is Bell's ability to reveal a radical innocence behind the witty sophistication, and a radical intelligence behind the mock stances of ignorance and foolishness. The wise fool kills off the foolish fool, and long enough before the floating drama-epic-lyric-elegy decides to close down. Only again to tell us we do not have to, and have to, go on. This is the magnanimous act and fact of the book. And it is quintessential Bell. . . .

Poem by poem, *The Escape into You* moves to the turning of "So help me" as colloquialism into a moving, acceptable prayer for help and love. If poetry is "scratching," it also becomes for Bell a means toward finding an instrument and vehicle for his sad, long song. In *The Escape into You* the dead father comes to seem more at rest, and childhood and children and wives sink in more profoundly than they had done before. (p. 6)

With the publication of Bell's next book *Residue of Song* the poet suggests that he has come to some vantage point of both rest and distance. As I read the book, it is a coda to the earlier work. Of all of Bell's volumes published so far, I find it the strongest; and it contains the two poems I return to most in all the books—the title poem "**Residue of Song**" and the last poem in the volume "**The Hurt Trees.**"

If compressed, intricate lyrics are always instructions for performance, *Residue of Song* involves a score which must be played soft, softly. . . .

What the poet comes to with new and renewed eyes is the fact of the dead, wounded father and of his own marriage which has not only survived but deepened since he left off with versing it in *The Escape into You*. For this task Bell knows he needs "a pure mid-country poetry" which is English but which may not sound like English at all: a redeeming language wrung out of Iowa and a lightly hidden Long Island, and unlike the speech that any other American poet has used before.

In the title poem "**Residue of Song**," in "**The Hurt Trees**," and in such poems as the thirteen poems for the father (the *You Would Know* sequence), Bell is able to move beyond what had sometimes been for him a dangerous, debilitating wit to a poised, tough wisdom. These poems possess fuller closure and greater ease without forcing the poet to mark down items for less than they cost. . . . [They] achieve that same suspended time sense which enables the poet and the reader to admit loss and grief *and* to lessen them. . . .

Residue of Song takes more than one look back, and more than one look at what the poet tried to accomplish in *The Escape into You*. . . . *The Escape into You* had attempted to walk the poet home; *Residue of Song* continues that long walk. . . . *The Escape into You* very well might have been subtitled "On Loneliness." And *Residue of Song* aspires in its movement through five sections—*Study of the Letter A, You Would Know,*

Being in Love, Holding Together, and *Song of the Immediacy of Death*—to the feel and the experience of one more long poem in which loneliness and loss again prove central, undeniable facts. . . .

If the unexamined life and the eternally examined life are equally unbearable, Bell moves in *Residue of Song* toward a perspectivism which avoids the sentimental and the nostalgic yet does not deny or profane or imitate happiness as it existed, or now exists, between father and son, father and sons, husband and wife. Bell's poems become his own sacred wood in which he refuses to romanticize hard times or hard knocks. Just as the poet goes to history and pre-history for origins and beginnings, so he now looks up to find his own planets and stars. False heroism, false idealism, and false Romanticism are rejected as the poet learns to trust what is close and familiar, the self is able to hold together because it learns to be with father and sons and wife, to be *together* with them.

Residue of Song shows the poet seeing what love with death should have to do. The dead and the living teach the poet that in time nothing is alien or foreign to him. He finds less of a need to hoard in(to) his poems as much as he once did. A sparer lyric emerges as he is able to say his love for his wife again, and on familiar, local ground. The scene and the air are distinctively American. . . . As lives open and close around him, as the parachute collapses in slow motion, Bell knows that only the close and the familiar and the American can restore the hurt, bleeding trees. . . .

What I see as the defining achievement of *Residue of Song* is a slow distancing of the poet from associations and attractions which prove at odds with an evolving sense of what he wants his own poetry ultimately to be. On the one hand, the sad loneliness which always threatens to undo him—and which I connect with his Jewishness (and with the writing of Bellow, Salinger, and Roth) as much as with a larger American poetry of sadness produced by contemporary poets as different as Lowell, Berryman, Hugo, Ashbery, and James Wright—I find less in evidence here. On the other hand, a preference shared by such poets as Justice and Strand for absence and cancellation seems to be shifting in Bell toward an insistence upon what is close at hand as closest to the heart. . . .

Recent poems of Bell uncollected in book form continue to move toward a simplicity which is no easy simplicity at all. . . . [There] is a new ease and tone . . . which seem part of some hard won awareness of just how close artlessness and ultimate artifice in fact are. (p. 7)

The latest work of Bell shows a predilection, still, for using a poetry of wit in order to address concerns of morality and aesthetics. But what is changed is Bell's ability to join that kind of poem to a poem that is more lyrical, sometimes more lyrically elegiac than he had wished or managed to be before. . . . (pp. 7-8)

The poetic strategies are still elaborate, even when the poet seems to walk most lightly or softly. But "license" now seems in the service of greater good: the "exclusive calculations," "sensational airwaves" and "interchangeable frequencies" of some of the past work have settled into Bell's celebration of the fact that the self has held together, that the wife and sons have not been lost in order to allow the poet to satisfy some false, wilful Romanticism in his own time.

Nor is sadness, or Bell's corner on sadness, gone. But he has begun to see sadness more in terms of joy. If happiness is an unfashionable contemporary American poetics, Bell is unafraid to start writing a new lyric which tells us we had better ascertain ''who is doing the crying,'' and just how happy we are. (p. 8)

Arthur Oberg, ''Marvin Bell: 'Time's Determinant./ Once, I Knew You.''' in The American Poetry Review, Vol. 5, No. 3, May-June, 1976, pp. 4-8.

G. E. MURRAY

The new work of Marvin Bell . . . reflects the effects of major alteration in voice and thematic course. From the breezy charm and wit of Bell's earliest poems, which frequently assumed a vaudevillian aura, and the open-hearted emotional drive of . . . *The Escape Into You* (1971), Bell now achieves a crystallization of sense and style in *Stars Which See, Stars Which Do Not See*. In short, the good news is that Bell has come to create with authority instead of temperament.

This, however, is not immediately apparent. In fact, the first few poems in this volume smack of mediocrity—almost as if Bell tests us by saying, ''if you can survive the bread and water of these early poems, what flaming desserts I have in store for you later.'' And this is exactly the case. After slumping through several merely competent pages, Bell turns on in **''The Mystery of Emily Dickinson,''** writing: ''Sometimes the weather goes on for days / but you were different. You were divine.'' There is conviction to this strange juxtaposition, a rightness that survives and supports the remainder of the book.

Bell's thin collection combines facets of dream, metamorphosis, and work-a-day observation to create something that at first appears to be a separate reality from the one in which we live, but on closer inspection evolves with disquieting affinities to conventional life. . . . [The book's distinctive title piece maneuvers in such a way, drifting] perilously close to prose, but Bell manipulates risk to his advantage, in the end exciting with a rare delicacy of phrasing and shrewd control over the poem's fate. (pp. 969-70)

[Mainly] I am impressed by this poet's increasing ability to perceive and praise small wonders. There is life and health in this book, and if sometimes Bell's expression is quiet and reserved, his talent is not. Altogether, *Stars Which See, Stars Which Do Not See* demonstrates an important transitional phase for the poet—a subdued, graceful vein that enables him to ''speak of eyes and seasons'' with an intimacy and surehandedness that informs and gratifies. . . . I believe Marvin Bell is on a track of the future—a mature, accessible and personalized venture into the mainstream of contemporary American verse, one beyond adolescent caterwauling and psychological minutiae, one at once devoted to craft and substance, vitality and permanence of tone. (pp. 970-71)

G. E. Murray, in a review of ''Stars Which See, Stars Which Do Not See,'' in The Georgia Review, Vol. XXXI, No. 4, Winter, 1977, pp. 969-71.

DAVID ST. JOHN

Stars Which See, Stars Which Do Not See, Marvin Bell's fourth volume, is a disarming book, deceptive in its simplicity and altogether seductive in its beauty. If others have made much of the verbal intelligence and knotty wit in Bell's work, and rightly so, what has most often been ignored is the extreme delicacy of the voice in his most lyric poems. Though Bell's playful, metaphysical intelligence is always pleasing, it is when this intelligence grows most fluid and intimate that the poems most completely succeed. It is this same delicacy, for example, which informs the much anthologized poem **''Treetops''** from Bell's first book, *A Probable Volume of Dreams*. It is the immediacy of this voice and the implicit pleas which draw us to a poem such as **''We Have Known''** from *The Escape Into You,* his second book. . . . (p. 314)

That same sense of being, as readers, invited into the landscape of a *privacy overheard* continues throughout Bell's third book, *Residue of Song*. The fluid self-dialogue of the title poem . . . as well as the intimate address of the sequence ''You Would Know'' (for his dead father) both serve to join us with the experiences Bell seizes. (p. 315)

For some time now, it has seemed as if Bell has wanted to abandon the complications of syntax which have sometimes marked other of his poems, even though they were nearly always genial complications. He has sought a plainer speech, as American and colloquial as Williams'. Since Gary Snyder's haybucker in ''Hay For The Horses'' many poets have tried to appropriate into their poems a gritty, tough-talking American character, and to thereby earn for themselves some similar authority or ''authenticity.'' But in *Stars Which See, Stars Which Do Not See,* Bell has found within his *own* voice that American voice, and with it the ability to write convincingly about the smallest details of a personal history. He has found the maturity to meet with an enviable generosity those otherwise ordinary domestic events and routines of a daily life. . . . And what in some poets has always seemed a Puritan underpinning to our ideas of American speech (''straight talk, no nonsense'') instead reads in Bell simply as a belief that words might possibly mean what they say. Yet this never leads him to contend, as it apparently has others, that beauty in language is the snake-oil of poetry. Nor does Bell ever feel called upon to abandon his intelligence to retain his identity as an American.

Throughout *Stars Which See, Stars Which Do Not See*, the overwhelming concern is for *wholeness*. The poems seek to establish the self in relation to the natural, as in poems such as **''The Self and the Mulberry''** . . . and **''Bits and Pieces of Our Land.''** . . . The poems consider the self's relation to the fragments of the past and the vague promises we name the future, yet they rely on nothing so grand as these summations imply. The poems are invariably located in the moment, the idea arising from the fact. Each seems as earthbound as a prayer, for what but a life on earth prompts us to prayer? (pp. 315-16)

Slowly, through a reading of the book, we assume a trust in the voice of these poems, a trust enhanced by the instances of sheer lyric beauty. (p. 317)

[It] is the daily incident transformed, the minute detail serving as fulcrum to the poem, which informs nearly all of *Stars Which See, Stars Which Do Not See*. Bell has sought out the most physical mirrors for his considerations of the self. He refuses to dazzle us with mysterious possibilities; instead, he is happy now to talk with us plainly, until we feel we understand.

It is in the poem **''Trinket,''** which I take to be the real and secret *Ars Poetica* of the book, that Bell most clearly outlines his methods and concerns. The pacing is deliberate and exact, like the movement of the poem's water through a crack in a fern pot. The poem's humor is measured and human. It is not in grandeur that the self is to be found, but in this minute trickle of water through the cracked, baked earthen pot. It is this trinket, this gift, which is to be found and shared. The poem enacts the same balance of self Bell has sought in all of the book, and the pervasive *presence* in the poem steadies as we, like the water, move slowly out of what contains us. It is this delicate balancing act, between ambition and peace, . . . between our self-consciousness and the natural, which **"Trinket"** allows us to perform. . . . (pp. 318-19)

David St. John, "Oxygen and Small Frictions," in Parnassus: Poetry in Review, *Vol. 5, No. 2, Spring-Summer, 1977, pp. 314-20.*

CALVIN BEDIENT

For [*Stars Which See, Stars Which Do Not See*], Marvin Bell has developed a style that steps among silence in plain shoes, making as little noise as possible. Without becoming flat, the language is held down to simplicity and quietness as if truth itself were a mild thing—Dame Patience, perhaps, or Dame Peace. *Stars Which See, Stars Which Do Not See,* though comprised of not-quite-satisfactory poems, pleases all through by its sociable small music as of wind chimes on Mid-Western porches. The style has a subdued, sweet, and confiding volubility. . . . You cannot help liking poetry that so obviously welcomes you, that is so gentle in itself besides. A remarkable air of sincerity, a gift of humble appreciation, a certain validating awkwardness in the diction and line-breaks, as of one who is more moved than calculating—these are enough to transform the basic style of contemporary poetry into something (as the jacket says) "unique in tone."

Bell has finally trusted himself to be direct. His earlier work twists about uncomfortably, wanting plainness yet resisting it. The poems seem both concentrated and distracted. The perfection of for instance the close of **"Letting in Cold"** from *Residue of Song,* his preceding volume, "No one approaches the father's thoughts / where he stands, at the back door, letting in cold" (to feel the chill of this, one scarcely needs to know that the father is dead), was too rare to make Bell more than "promising."

Is he better than "promising" in the new volume? Perhaps he has overshot the mark, perhaps he has sacrificed too much "charge" for the real but limited virtues of simplicity. Maybe simple verse can be great verse but Bell's seems to look down modestly at the very thought. He has put ambition to an easy death. A child's first grief, "the crack in the fern pot," "the trouble with love," elm trees, catfish, all have in his book the same emotional weight, which is no more, if no less, than that of a flat skimming stone that the hand cups momentarily, before deciding not to throw it. He is in danger of falling into a very wayside of modesty, where even his utmost seriousness has a smiling, palms-up shrugging lightness. Civilized, and genial as all get out, but meanwhile the poetry looks a little helpless. (pp. 119-20)

Frequently Bell's simplicity is . . . impure. Now and again his wit strains or drifts sentimentally. . . . Too, he could occasionally be still a degree more honest. . . . If we see his plainness as a poetic strategy that affects precisely an abdication of strategy, then Bell has yet to perfect its transparency, its complete and wonderful openness as of air.

But in pleasure and justice let us note how very good he can be. For one thing, he has a very subtle and unexpected ear. . . . For another, his language can bear very sensitive implications, . . . [as in] the title poem. (pp. 120-21)

Bell can now deliver for many lines at a time a fine simplicity. (See . . . **"To Dorothy."**) Still there remains for him the problem of sustaining excellence from beginning to end—in poems, in volumes—and, further, that of scale: the size of the sphere and the vigor of the clapper. (pp. 121-22)

Calvin Bedient, in a review of "Stars Which See, Stars Which Do Not See," in Chicago Review, *Vol. 29, No. 2, Autumn, 1977, pp. 119-22.*

DAVID ST. JOHN

What strikes one immediately about Marvin Bell's wonderful new book, *These Green-Going-to-Yellow* . . . is the sense of *quiet* that pervades them and the deceptive understatement of nearly every poem. Even more than Bell's previous book, *Stars Which See, Stars Which Do Not See,* his new collection offers poems that express their fluent and steady peace with the world.

Although many of the poems in *These Green-Going-to-Yellow* are set in distant locales—Hawaii, Tangier, Alaska, Cuba, Italy, Spain, France—they seek not to appropriate the exotica of their surroundings but to recognize the dailiness and immediacy, yet intrinsic *otherness,* of their settings. (p. 227)

Throughout this volume, Bell has chosen a more straightforward and unadorned diction, a diction capable of becoming alternately reflective and immediate. Yet there is still the verbal play and sly wit, the marvelous turns and reversals familiar to readers of Bell's earlier books. Because the poems in *These Green-Going-to-Yellow* are more consistently, more unashamedly narrative than in the past, Marvin Bell's aphoristic gifts have never seemed more successful; interwoven in the narrative fabric of the poems, these moments seem so inevitable and yet so surprising. Bell is constantly able to bring the reader up short with a sudden shift in tone; he has become masterful at quite invisibly shifting the grounds of argument upon the reader, and he often makes his exit in these poems with a disarming and winning directness. . . . [Each] of the poems in *These Green-Going-to-Yellow* holds within it that resolute core of self that Bell recognizes as the one "home" he will carry within himself always and to any distance. This careful, subtle book needs to be read more than once, as with each reading it accrues with power and vision. (pp. 227-28)

David St. John, "Raised Voices in the Choir: A Review of 1981 Poetry Selections," in The Antioch Review, *Vol. XL, No. 2, Spring, 1982, pp. 225-34.**

PETER STITT

As its title—*These Green-Going-to-Yellow*—indicates, Marvin Bell's new book is concerned with aging, decay, mutability, mortality. Its central metaphor, tenuously and enticingly attached to the speaker of the poems, is illness. . . . The sense of illness is not limited to the speaker, nor to humanity in general, but permeates the natural world as well. . . .

[The] poems tend to be relatively long, meditative, accumulative, even discursive. When the method works well, as it does on four or five notable occasions, the results are outstanding. Perhaps the best poem in the book is **"Birds Who Nest in the Garage."** . . . (p. 677)

The construction of this poem is obviously loose; some would call it rambling. The line between success and failure in such structures is a fine one. In **"Birds Who Nest in the Garage,"** success is achieved by the use of not just one but two technical elements that appear consistently from the beginning of the poem to its end: one is the speaking voice, and the other is the image that carries the theme, the bird droppings. In similarly structured poems which fail (and every poem in the book is written in this form), there is only one element used consistently from beginning to end—the speaking voice. What results is a kind of self-indulgence—the reader is asked to attend to a series of unrefined images that matter to the speaker but do not seem to matter much to the poem. . . . *These Green-Going-to-Yellow* is thus an uneven book, not quite what one had hoped for from the author of *Stars Which See, Stars Which Do Not See.* Its poems that succeed are wonderful . . . ([for example] **"Late Naps"** and **"Someone Is Probably Dead"**), but its poems that do not succeed are a disappointment—too casual, not enough lyrical craftiness. (pp. 678-79)

> *Peter Stitt, "Poems in Open Forms," in* The Georgia Review, *Vol. XXXVI, No. 3, Fall, 1982, pp. 675-85.**

PUBLISHERS WEEKLY

The Marvin Bell method of writing a poem consists of producing a terrific first line and then refining all possible sequiturs into a whole, if somewhat mysterious, poem. This technique produces some fine poetry, but does not seem to apply to the composition of essays, which require not only topic sentences but also logical development and conclusive endings. Besides some undistinguished essays and interviews, the pith of [*Old Snow Just Melting*] is a series of 11 columns commissioned by the *American Poetry Review* in which Bell gets wildly excited and tells us everything he knows, practically in one single breath per column, about everything there is to know about poetry. . . . [Bell is] so full of genuine intelligence that it's a pity these random associations couldn't have been ordered into a form accessible to all readers.

> *A review of "Old Snow Just Melting," in* Publishers Weekly, *Vol. 222, No. 22, November 26, 1982, p. 56.*

DAVID BAKER

Marvin Bell does love poetry. He loves the very idea of it. And in *Old Snow Just Melting,* his new collection of essays and interviews, he loves writing and talking about poetry and does so with a joy and an obvious commitment that are contagious. . . .

Old Snow Just Melting . . . brings together twenty-one essays with such titles as "I Was a Boston (Marathon) Bandit (On Assignment)" and "Learning from Translations" and four interviews including "The University Is Something Else You Do" and "Self Is a Very Iffy Word for Me." All were, he points out, done on assignment, including eleven essays written from 1974 to 1978 for *The American Poetry Review,* published here under the title "Homage to the Runner." Even the titles indicate the range of subjects in these pieces, from teaching to Hugo to pain, and the range of attitudes, playfulness-going-to-seriousness (as he might say). (p. 332)

I do think you will be disappointed if you expect, in *Old Snow Just Melting,* a book of criticism. And you will be disappointed if you expect a fully drawn, straightforward statement of poetics; this is more a poetics-in-the-making. If you can give Bell a little room, though, as you do that old friend who takes so long to tell a "simple" story, the one who winds around and

forgets and gestures wildly and maybe even invents a little, you will be doubly rewarded. After all, when your friend finally finishes his story, haven't you learned more than the story itself? Haven't you learned something about your friend?

Now a couple of years old, *These Green-Going-to-Yellow* is to my mind one of Marvin Bell's best books of poetry. . . . In a day of hermit-poets, watered-down confessional poets, self-absorbed poets, diary-poets and poets-of-the-private-language, Bell's richly populated poems are a welcome return back to the world of people. By my count, in fact, all but two of the thirty-one poems in *These Green-Going-to-Yellow* include characters other than the speaker. (p. 334)

What the people in Bell's poems have to contend with is indicated in the title. *These Green-Going-to-Yellow* identifies the natural and inevitable decay of the world: trees die here, and birds, and pigs; the seasons change; people pass away and are missed; wars claim lives faster than ever. Maybe it is only a coincidence, but many of Bell's best poems here are those in which the speaker both admits to loss (or meanness or decay) and then tries to give back something to fill the void. In the beautiful **"The Hedgeapple,"** the speaker and his friends have nearly taken a hedgeapple from a woman's tree. . . . The poem ends in a gesture of unabashed guilt-going-to-generosity, since he cannot bear to have almost stolen "someone else's treasure." . . . (pp. 334-35)

Bell's form is relaxed, even rambling at times. His voice is casual, but is capable of the beauty that clear language can bring. Only infrequently in these poems do I sense Bell allowing his form too much leisure or his voice too much ease. [**"To an Adolescent Weeping Willow"**], though, typifies such temptation. . . . The poem ends with the speaker's realization of the fallacy of his own metaphor—that the easy-moving tree and his hard-working father *aren't* alike. But Bell's language is a touch too easy too. I think Bell is less effective . . . when he depends too much on the momentum and character (even charm) of his style to make up for looseness. In fact, hasn't this been identified as a problem of many poets from the generation just prior to Bell's: that, having struggled to develop recognizable and convincing styles, they sometimes seem satisfied, simply and almost always ineffectively, to imitate themselves? I certainly don't think it's a problem for Bell generally. But I don't want it to become one either. He has come far already, and his poems, at their best, are among our current best. (pp. 335-36)

> *David Baker, "Marvin Bell: Essays, Interviews, Poems," in* New England Review and Bread Loaf Quarterly, *Vol. 6, No. 2, Winter, 1983, pp. 332-36.*

STEVEN RATINER

"Segues" is written by William Stafford and Marvin Bell, two of America's most respected poets. Theirs is an ambitious experiment, and while the quality of the poetry is uneven, their book is a refreshingly novel event on the literary scene. . . .

[The poetry of **"Segues"** began when Stafford and Bell] decided to collaborate on a writing project to strengthen their friendship and explore the ways a poem comes into being. Stafford began the chain of "verse letters," and each successive poem grew out of the subject, tone, or language of the previous one. A long-distance version of the ancient Japanese *renga* (linked verse), their correspondence was a form of mutual inspiration, making a poetic duet from what is usually a private solo performance. The title **"Segues"** is a term for the transitions inside a piece of music that allow one theme to grow into another.

Certainly more is required of a book than the novelty of the poems' call-and-answer progression to make any lasting impression on the reader. Of the 44 poems in the collection, only a handful are strong enough to stand on their own merits. Stylistically, this work is a marked contrast to many of the popular trends in poetry; they have none of the oblique, hard-edged lines, vaguely surreal visions, or self-conscious absorption in the surface qualities of verse. The writing possesses some of the intimacy of letters and the give-and-take of good conversation—two practices nearly extinct in American social life. Stafford and Bell are conversational, even voluble, in their writing, paying most attention to the subject at hand and the emotional tone. At times the relaxed atmosphere of this correspondence brings out their worst tendencies, allowing slack, unfocused lines or thin philosophical pronouncements that dilute the poem's effect. . . .

Bell's poetry usually relies on sudden twists of diction and focus. He adopts some of Stafford's simplicity here in auto-biographical pieces about his family and childhood. By and large, these poems aren't as well crafted as his previous work, displaying less control but providing more emotional involvement.

But in a curious way, **"Segues"** is a better book than the sum of its table of contents. Some of the most interesting moments seem to occur behind and between the actual poems. There is the feeling of true correspondence in these poems—not just the "letter" variety but also the sympathetic reverberation between two visions. . . .

At the conclusion, the sense of culmination is more involved with the poets' bond than the poems' subject matter. But the reader is left with several strong impressions: first, that the book describes a greater human landscape than was initially apparent, implied more than defined by the individual poems in the way flares in a night sky provide glimpses of the broad countryside; second, a reaffirmation that the greatest strength of modern poems lies not in the surface dazzle and linguistic effects, but in the way a work impels a reader's imagination to be involved with the creation of its subject; and third, as these writers discovered, that there is more common emotional ground in the literary arts than the caustic visions that are becoming the sanctioning elements of much contemporary writing.

Steven Ratiner, "Poetry by Post Seals Friendship, Explores Nature of Verse," in The Christian Science Monitor, *November 4, 1983, p. B5.*

William Brammer

1930?-1978

(Also wrote under the name Billy Lee Brammer) American novelist.

Brammer's literary output consists of three short novels published collectively under the title *The Gay Place* (1961). Set in a fictional southwestern state which critics identify as Texas, the three stories—*The Flea Circus, Room Enough to Caper,* and *Country Pleasures*—are loosely based on Brammer's experiences as a senatorial aide to Lyndon B. Johnson during the 1950s. Although each short novel centers on the career of a different young politician, connecting all three works is the character Governor Arthur Fenstemaker. Fenstemaker, who is said to be modeled after Johnson, is a heroic figure who stands in contrast to the self-doubting young politicians.

Although *The Gay Place* was favorably received when first published, it did not receive the widespread recognition that most critics expected. Reissued posthumously in 1978, the work elicited renewed critical appraisal. Critics generally agree that the primary strengths of *The Gay Place* are Brammer's witty and elegant prose style, his ability to recreate the dynamics and complexities of political campaigns, and his realistic depiction of the manners and mores of an elite stratum of society during a distinctive era of American history. Although some critics view Brammer's portrayal of Fenstemaker as overly sympathetic, others contend that his well-developed characters and skillful narration make *The Gay Place* a work of exceptional merit among political novels.

(See also *Contemporary Authors,* Vols. 77-80 [obituary].)

Courtesy of Nadine Eckhardt

VIRGINIA KIRKUS' SERVICE

[*The Gay Place*] introduces a newcomer of considerable stature. But frankly we do not see [Brammer] as a major literary figure or a great discovery. *The Gay Place* depends too much on stock sex situations, indiscriminate changing of partners, free for alls on a superficial charge of excess liquor and license. And yet it will undoubtedly be reviewed as another inside picture of American politics—and an unsavory one on all counts. Brammer has a gift for dialogue, a sharp wit, a keen sense of posing irreconcilables. But as a story-teller he has much to learn. *The Gay Place* is actually three books: *The Flea Circus, Room Enough to Caper* and *Country Pleasures.* The setting throughout is presumably Texas—big, brash, and rich. The personable governor, Arthur Fenstemaker, is a constant in all three stories, and with overlapping minor characters links the three parts into a major portrait of the American political arena. And an arena it is, with victims thrown to the beasts, with shenanigans and extravaganzas arranged for the entertainment of the mob, with questionable manipulations behind the scenes, deals, wire pulling, cheap stunts. . . . Somehow the parts never jell, either on their own or as panels in an overall scene. And somehow one doesn't much care.

A review of "The Gay Place," in Virginia Kirkus' Service, *Vol. XXIX, No. 1, January 1, 1961, p. 30.*

CAROLINE TUNSTALL

"The Gay Place" is made up of three short novels unified by setting and theme. They present the political scene in a Southwestern state that is a reasonable facsimile of Texas; one is not surprised to learn that William Brammer was for some time on the staff of Lyndon Johnson. The three protagonists of these tales are very similar, all members of the not-so-young generation, veterans of World War II, liberal politicians sardonically aware that their liberalism has been compromised by their politics. They use the current intellectual catchwords only half mockingly, distrust themselves more than their foes, and conduct their affairs—of all sorts—to the unceasing sound of record player, jukebox or radio. They owe their drinking to Hemingway, their glitter to Fitzgerald and their sweetness to Salinger. This is not for a moment to deny that they represent very actual types. And for all their likeness, they are sharply differentiated.

"The Flea Circus," first and fullest of the three stories, covers a few days in the life of Roy Sherwood. . . .

"Room Enough to Caper" presents the . . . case of Neil Christiansen. . . . [And] the final story, "Country Pleasures," [features] Jay McGown. . . .

The three stories are in fact three anecdotes in the life of the same man, the governor, Arthur Fenstemaker. . . . He is a devoted husband and brother, a ruthless schemer, a charming rake. He is also the liberal leader who has inspired a generation of younger men. Altogether a successful creation, Fenstemaker is, one suspects, very dear to his author. But after creating his hero, his man of action, Brammer refuses to call him to account. The question of responsibility hangs over the book, today's familiar mushroom cloud in an empty sky.

> *Caroline Tunstall, "Award-Winning First Novel,"*
> *in* Lively Arts and Book Review, *March 12, 1961,*
> *p. 34.*

WIRT WILLIAMS

William Brammer has an authentic, even lyrical, writing talent. He has as intimate a knowledge of operational politics as any serious American novelist. . . . And he is only 30 years old. Situated as he is at the confluence of natural gifts, experience and youth, it would seem inescapable that his political novel would be truly impressive. Instead, it turns out to be no more than interesting and promising—though it will surely rank strongly among the year's first novels. . . . The disappointment comes from a weak grasp of fictional form. In the three installments which make up the book (each, actually, is a short novel in itself), the author shows a sense of the architecture of the novel in only one, the last. . . .

The pin that holds them together is a wise, witty, vulgar, almost saintly superman named Arthur Fenstemaker, the Governor. All through the first novel, **"The Flea Circus,"** float legislators and editors, beautiful women and bemused liberals, as though in some unfocused, dimly remembered dream. The effect is striking, though the structure is slender. . . .

In **"Room Enough to Caper,"** the good, wily Governor tricks his young appointee to the Senate into seeking a full term by election. The last installment, **"Country Pleasures"** is the least ambitious and yet perhaps the most successful of the three. The beautiful, blonde ex-wife of the Governor's assistant, Jay McGown, has cheese-caked her way to film stardom. She is thrown with her former husband when she tries to get him to return to her. As Jay is driven to a crisis in his personal life, the Governor is driven to one in his political career by Federal integration rulings.

Mr. Brammer's great gift is his ability to communicate the poignancy of the passing moment, the sweet sadness of the flight of love and time. When he learns to project vision as well as surfaces, he will be a writer of real consequence.

> *Wirt Williams, "A Political Triptych," in* The New
> York Times Book Review, *March 12, 1961, p. 33.*

JAMES FALLOWS

Eighteen years ago, when he was 31, Billy Lee Brammer published the novel he had written during long late-night stands on Lyndon B. Johnson's Senate staff. The book was called **"The Gay Place"**—not a loaded title then—and, except for riches, it brought Brammer all the sweet glories of early literary success. . . . [Respectful] reviewers proclaimed him the heir to F. Scott Fitzgerald; all the prospects were bright.

One year ago, at the age of 48, Billy Lee Brammer lay dead in Texas, technically the victim of drug abuse, but really undone by the years of frustration that had followed his great success. . . .

[The new edition of **"The Gay Place"**] appears as a kind of memorial edition—a memorial one is almost afraid to read, for fear that the novel will not be as good as memory has made it, or as kind wishes want it to be.

In fact, **"The Gay Place"** is even stronger than it seemed at first. With its era (the late 1950's) passed, its author dead, its central figure (Lyndon Johnson) gone from the stage, it still stands as an independent, lasting work of art that may now receive the fame and following it has deserved all along.

To give the book its most obvious due—that it is one of the best political novels—is almost to undersell its merits, because a "political" novel has come to mean one that makes up for the thinness of its characters with the grandness of their job titles and the implausible nobility or crassness of their thoughts. **"The Gay Place"** is fundamentally a political book, but it is first a superbly controlled work of fiction, its characters vivid, its style elegant and knowing, its political and human insights growing naturally from its characters rather than being strapped crudely upon them. (p. 7)

The figure that holds the book together is Fenstemaker—always prodding the others to act, guiding their lives in unseen ways, running on mysterious supplies of enthusiasm and concern that seem denied to all the rest. The name . . . means "window-maker" in the German still spoken in the Texas Hill Country—conjurer, illusionist, worker of wonders. Fenstemaker is all these things in the book, and Brammer's description of his style is the richest evocation of Lyndon Johnson anywhere in print. (p. 30)

Fenstemaker looms especially large because of the era in which he operates. **"The Gay Place"** etches the mood of the late 1950's as clearly as "Gatsby" does the Jazz Age; nearly all the characters in the book wonder where they should commit themselves, what is happening to them, why it matters at all. Fenstemaker is the one source of energy in this attenuated crowd, the one firm anchor of purpose amid self-doubt.

This may account for what, in retrospect, seems the novel's only flaw. Brammer no more judges Fenstemaker—or Johnson—than a child could judge his father, marveling instead at his energy and purpose, considering them as their own justifications, regardless of their ends. In a later, more passionate era, Johnson's certainty would not win such automatic admiration. Brammer was going to write about that, too, and would have done it well, but his biography of Johnson, commissioned 15 years ago, was left by the wayside, like so much else.

Brammer's death—really, his inability to write anything that came up to his standards after **"The Gay Place"**—was a loss to readers, a sorrow to his friends, a tragedy for himself. But no man can be considered tragic who has left a work like this. (pp. 30-1)

> *James Fallows, "Success Story," in* The New York
> Times Book Review, *January 14, 1979, pp. 7, 30-1.*

GARRETT EPPS

[Billy Lee Brammer's *The Gay Place*] has a special quality that almost transcends questions of literary merit—a richness, a completeness in rendering an entire small world, a satisfying structure of myth and symbol. It is, quite simply, a magical book. (p. 1)

In the novel, Brammer transforms his former boss and mentor [Lyndon B. Johnson] into a moderate governor of decent instincts who is also a symbol of courage and a crazed kind of integrity in a landscape of entropic weariness.

The book's other characters are bewildered, ineffectual provincial liberals, bright young people pursuing an impossible ideal of ease and grace set forth in an epigraph from Ford Madox Ford: "Is there then any terrestrial paradise where, amidst the whispering of the olive leaves, people can be with whom they like and have what they like and take their ease in shadows and coolness?"

The vision of an earthly paradise, Brammer seems to be saying, is an illusion; it has led his cast of "hipster pols" into lives of sexual and alcoholic abandon, the paralysis of thinking without acting. . . . (pp. 1, 4)

Fenstemaker does not rely on the dubious guide of the intellect, but on instinct and larger-than-life sense of purpose, as he sets about his work of "power an' change an' improvement." Like Willie Stark in *All the King's Men*, Fenstemaker possesses supernatural powers and insight; he is by turns the Prophet Isaiah, a "corn-pone Buddha," and Jehovah himself, a heavenly father figure who even arranges the crucifixion and resurrection—over an Easter weekend in Austin—of his own political son, the symbolically named Senator Neil Christiansen.

Indeed, Fenstemaker manages to save two of the young wastrels around him—Christiansen and a legislator named Roy Sherwood. He fills them with his own sense of motivation and sends them forth "to make a change and build a city and save the goddam world from collapse." But in the end, he is overcome by an American mythic figure even more powerful than he, the Hollywood sex goddess. Maddened by lust, he signs the state over to a Mexican tavern owner and dies in a heartstopping sexual excess. . . .

[Though] *The Gay Place* brilliantly lampoons [Lyndon Johnson's] mannerisms and speech and caricatures his sexual appetites, it remains unswervingly faithful to a vision of the best in Lyndon Johnson, to the Johnson of the Voting Rights Act and the Great Society. . . .

Arthur Fenstemaker falls into sexual corruption, but when the real Johnson fell it was into darkness more desperate than that—paranoia, war, the betrayal of many bright dreams for himself and his country. A work of art may stand as partial redemption of its maker's tortured life; *The Gay Place* certainly does. But it may also constitute one small act of restitution by its model. LBJ left us so much that is evil, it seems fitting that he should have helped inspire something as fine as *The Gay Place*. (p. 4)

Garrett Epps, "Deep in the Heart of Texas," in Book World—The Washington Post, *February 4, 1979, pp. 1, 4.*

JOE KLEIN

Political novels usually aren't very good. Most are overstuffed with dashing Kennedyesque characters who go around pouring bourbon over ice, smoking cigarette after cigarette after slim, elegant cigar and screwing their unvaryingly voluptuous secretaries. . . . Worse, most political novels make the tragic mistake of treating politicians as if they were human beings with feelings, emotions and sometimes even principles. This—as any reasonable American realizes in 1979—is giving them far more credit than they deserve. . . .

Billy Lee Brammer's *The Gay Place* is, if you can believe it, a rather hopeful portrait of Lyndon Johnson. . . . While it isn't exactly the classic its fans suppose (Brammer is compared with everyone from Dickens to James Joyce in a series of introductions, forwards and mad gushings prior to the text itself), it still reads pretty well after 20 years, quite an achievement for a political novel. . . .

[Governor Arthur "Goddamn"] Fenstemaker dominates the book without ever becoming the central figure. The effect is something like a clothing store mirror—Fenstemaker is ever-present and all-knowing, wheeling and dealing and cajoling, but always peripheral. He appears briefly, obliquely, takes our breath away and is gone. We never find out what he's really thinking.

Fenstemaker is more a force of nature than a human being, which, I gather, is pretty much what Lyndon Johnson was like. . . .

By comparison, the heroes of *The Gay Place* are distressingly human. They are the first post-war, post-McCarthy generation of Texas liberals. . . .

Their aimlessness is the perfect foil for the mad drive of Arthur Fenstemaker. The young liberals are fascinated by the governor, drawn to him, nonplussed and tickled by him. Somehow he's managed to play the game both more *and* less seriously than they. They sense he is larger, more complete than they'll ever be. His young aide, Jay McGown, wonders why he can't be a *man* like Fenstemaker. But Fenstemaker isn't a man; he's an illusion. Brammer's unwitting triumph was to discover the perfect structure for communicating the exasperating unreality of the master politician. (p. 65)

Joe Klein, "Politicians: Are They Not Men?" in Mother Jones, *Vol. IV, No. V, June, 1979, pp. 65-6.*

Howard Brenton

1942-

English dramatist, scriptwriter, and poet.

Brenton is one of the most controversial playwrights in contemporary English theater. Employing graphic violence and sexuality, coarse language, and black humor, he symbolically and explicitly attacks the political and social structures of Britain. Brenton views theater as a means for presenting his critiques of society: he has stated that his plays are written "unreservedly in the cause of socialism."

Brenton developed his radical style in the experimental theater movement known as "the Fringe" which emerged in England during the 1960s and which included among its contributors Brenton's occasional collaborator, David Hare. The Fringe provided a forum for noncommercial drama, staging plays in pubs, storefronts, and other unusual sites. These plays generally expressed extreme political and social views in unconventional dramatic forms. Brenton drew attention and praise from critics for *Christie in Love* (1969), which centers on John Reginald Christie, a convicted murderer and rapist notorious in England during the 1950s. The policemen in the play represent narrow and repressive values that make them more threatening, for Brenton, than Christie himself, who is presented as reserved and inconspicuous. *Revenge* (1969), the story of a policeman pursued by a criminal, contributed to Brenton's reputation as a forceful and promising playwright. Brenton had one actor play both the policeman and the criminal to underscore his belief that law breakers and law keepers can be similarly oppressive.

The growing recognition of Brenton's work and the eventual production of his plays in established London theaters in no way tamed his social protests. Many Brenton plays of the 1970s portrayed frustrated attempts of political rebels to effect social change. In *Magnificence* (1973), for example, a group of people who peacefully demonstrate for housing reform in Great Britain are treated harshly by the police. Brenton highlights police brutality with an attack on a pregnant woman who later miscarries. Her husband, bent on revenge, kills both himself and the wrong government official, thus accomplishing nothing. The play emphasizes the waste on all sides. Such projections of oppressive authority figures and the hopeless or bungled efforts of those who attempt action also appear in *The Churchill Play* (1974) and *Weapons of Happiness* (1976). According to some critics, these plays contain meaningful statements about the state of contemporary Britain. Others faulted Brenton for presenting simplistic political views without recommending any means toward serious social change. Critical reception was also mixed concerning Brenton's use of startling violent images. Despite these reservations, critics generally continued to regard Brenton as a bold and intriguing playwright.

Brenton became more widely known with *The Romans in Britain* (1981), which provoked a public furor in England because of its scenes of graphic sexual violence. Set in part in Roman-occupied Britain circa 54 A.D. and paralleling the English presence in Northern Ireland, *The Romans in Britain* features the homosexual rape of a Druid priest by a Roman soldier, among other shocking images, to portray Brenton's dislike of

© Jerry Bauer

imperialism. The aesthetic merit of such imagery was debated by government officials, critics, and citizens.

Critics are divided in assessing Brenton's importance in contemporary English theater. While some view him as politically naive and theatrically extravagant, others find his style and his views intellectually challenging and regard him as an innovative and stimulating dramatist.

(See also *Contemporary Authors*, Vols. 69-72 and *Dictionary of Literary Biography*, Vol. 13.)

MICHAEL BILLINGTON

Through such plays as *Revenge* and *Christie in Love*, Howard Brenton has quickly won himself a reputation as one of our most strikingly original young dramatists. However, this new piece [*Fruit*] . . . is so shrill, hysterical and uncoordinated, that it makes one wonder where precisely Mr. Brenton's acknowledged love of excess is leading him.

Admittedly it bears all his familiar trademarks: the relish for grotesque physical detail, the fascination with the corrupting effect of power, the love of theatrical shock tactics. But whereas before his obsession with the narrow dividing line between the policeman and his prey has helped to focus all his dramatic energies, he here seems to be flailing wildly about in all directions. . . . [There] is no dramatic law that says playwrights who preach anarchy themselves have to practise it; and Mr. Brenton gravely weakens a perfectly tenable viewpoint by failing to give the separate scenes an organic relationship and by repeatedly turning to violence as a device for raising the theatrical temperature.

If one is severe with Mr. Brenton, it is because he has so much exuberant natural talent; but here, in spite of the nervy vitality of David Hare's production, one feels that talent is wildly misdirected.

> *Michael Billington, in a review of "Fruit," in* The Times, *London, September 30, 1970, p. 13.*

JOHN RUSSELL TAYLOR

Brenton is, if not resentful, at least rather puzzled at the recurrent comparison of his dramatic method to that of a strip cartoon, since he disclaims any particular interest in strip cartoons or any conscious influence. All the same, the comparison is irresistible. Psychology and explanation are ruthlessly suppressed, dialogue is reduced to the skeleton indications of a cartoon's bubbles, the action of his plays proceeds from image to image with virtually no transitions, no gradations. (p. 217)

[*Christie in Love* (1969) is] a perfect case in point. The action is a sort of Chinese box: on the outside is almost a literal box, a compound of chicken wire scattered with rubbish in which Christie's victims wait to be dug up by the police and in which Christie himself is finally buried. Inside this burial-ground box is another box, that of Christie's interrogation by the police. And in that is another, the flashbacks of his confession. Thus image follows image, image is sometimes superimposed on image, and when the horror becomes too direct the police (representing presumably, among other things, society at large) turn aside into blue jokes, as though to cancel out horror with protective humour. Again, as in strip cartoons, obvious visual equations can be made without inquiring too deeply into the reasonable basis of the equation: it is enough simply to present Christie as a suffering weakling, the police officer as a fascistic thug, and leave it at that.

Much the same approach to drama informs the best-known of Brenton's other plays, *Revenge* (1969). . . . In fact the revenge, or desire for revenge, is twofold: Adam Hepple, a lifelong criminal, conceives a passionate desire to revenge himself on MacLeish of the Yard, the policeman who has always, as he sees it, victimized him. But when he shoots a policeman MacLeish becomes equally impassioned in his vengeful pursuit of Hepple. The tone of the play veers wildly from melodrama to farce, up to a curious conclusion in which both Hepple and MacLeish die quietly in their beds, all passion spent. In performance the roles of Hepple and MacLeish are played by the same actor, doing a succession of quick changes—which all adds to the fun of the thing, if not I think to its significance.

The method is obviously limited, but in a theatre which sometimes seems in danger of sinking altogether under its load of subtlety, refinement and civilization, Brenton's avowed desire to use drama just as a way of 'stirring it up' is enlivening. In practice his method is erratically successful. Two of his short plays, *Heads* and *The Education of Skinny Spew* (1969), show it at its compressionist best. *Heads* is a bleak little comment on the relations of the sexes, in which a monstrous young woman with two possible lovers, a muscleman and an intellectual, briskly decapitates them both and switches heads—only to find that eventually the two resultant men still gang up on her. *Skinny Spew* is the life-story of a Blakean baby who nurtures the urge to revolt in his cradle and develops instantly into a figure of monstrous savagery and determination. Both plays are frightfully funny, and manage perfectly to say what they want to say within their length, without outstaying their welcome. The same cannot be said for *Fruit* (1970) in which Brenton lays about him with too single-minded relish at the expense of all politicians, public figures and people in authority, denouncing them as corrupt from the angle of wholehearted anarchism. The central character is an embittered osteopath who has come across all their secrets in the line of professional duty; this might make a good starting-point for satire, but instead the piece is reduced to an hysterical succession of violent set-pieces, so unorganized that monotony and boredom rapidly supervene.

Brenton is clearly a hit-or-miss dramatist who hits often enough to be worth watching. (pp. 217-19)

> *John Russell Taylor, "Brenton, Heathcote Williams," in his* The Second Wave: British Drama for the Seventies, *Hill and Wang, 1971, pp. 205-22.**

HAROLD CLURMAN

[*Magnificence* is] a social drama in a rougher mode than [those] of the English 1950s.

The play begins with a scene showing a number of young people—several of the working class, an uneducated hippie and a girl emigrated from the BBC—who break into an unoccupied flat as a protest against a housing situation that allows landlords to hold out for high rents while the poor are left virtually homeless. But the police come to evict the "squatters," and though they meet with very little resistance, one of the young women who is pregnant is knocked down and, we later learn, miscarries.

Except for the moment of violence at its end, the tone of the first scene is light enough. (p. 124)

[In later scenes, we learn] that the young man whose wife was struck down by the policeman . . . has just come out of jail, where he was sentenced for a year for having assaulted the policeman in retaliation, and is now consumed by desperate anger. He plans to kill [a] rather inoffensive cabinet minister. . . . This particular person has been picked as the victim of the young man's wrath because he is mistakenly believed to be the minister in charge of housing. The minister is captured while he is peacefully mowing the beautiful rhododendron lawn of his estate. A bundle of explosives is set on his head. But at the last minute the would-be assassin desists from his vengeful and supposedly revolutionary act. He flings the bomb away; it explodes and kills both men.

There are two "points" to this play. The almost incidental one has to do with the wretched state which still exists in housing facilities for the poor. The second is the sad and basic futility, the human waste, of attempting to change such conditions by violence alone. In a sense, however, neither of these themes is conceived to set forth a "thesis." The play dramatizes a sense of anguish among the young who, now that the old aristocracy is gone and the welfare state is governed by a seemingly benevolent conservatism . . . , are made not only savagely resentful of the impasse into which England has fallen but also dreadfully unhappy by their inability to find the effective way to break through and overcome it. (pp. 124-25)

Harold Clurman, in a review of "Magnificence," in The Nation, *Vol. 217, No. 4, August 13, 1973, pp. 124-25.*

HAROLD HOBSON

Howard Brenton has a terrifying imagination that makes his **"The Churchill Play"** . . . a very disturbing experience. It is an experience one would not like to have missed, but it unsettles the foundations of the world on which England unsteadily rests. One of the few matters on which it is still generally assumed that there is a consensus of opinion is that in May, 1940, England found a man who could, and did, save her. The haunting and alarming suggestion made in Mr Brenton's powerful play . . . is that the man England found was the wrong man; that the war of 1939-45 was less Hitler's war than Churchill's; that the British, and especially the Scottish, people were so demoralised by bombing that they bitterly resented Churchill's keeping them at war; and that this was the cause of our loss of empire, and the moment when our freedom went.

Now there is nothing in my experience of the war that can be squared with Mr Brenton's account of the demoralising effect of the German bombing. I was in the east, and most heavily hit, part of London during every raid but two during the entire war: I saw London burn and explode round me: but, with the exception of a couple of foreign journalists, I never heard anyone express even the smallest fear or tension. Mr Brenton was very young at the time, and there is much evidence in his play that he has listened to, and been impressed by, some very lurid stories: stories no doubt factually true, but not because of that necessarily universally truthful. I do not therefore accept as valid his attack on Churchill for allegedly hounding into battle a nation whose spirit was broken. What I do accept is that **"The Churchill Play"** is a work of great aesthetic and intellectual power, a work as impregnably self-defended and ambiguous as was Sartre's when Sartre was at the height of his creative power.

For it is defended, and it is ambiguous. The portrait of Churchill in **"The Churchill Play"** is drawn in such a manner that Mr Brenton could himself repudiate it. **"The Churchill Play"** is set in 1984, when England has become a country of concentration camps. A gentle, bewildered, liberal officer in this camp, Dr Thompson . . . , thinks it therapeutic for the internees to write and present a play of their own. . . . They act their play before a Parliamentary delegation, and it is in this play that the attack on Churchill is made.

It is perfectly possible to maintain that the attack is only what one would expect from political prisoners. But there is no suggestion of a counter-case. The furthest the play will go in defence of the class from which Churchill came is a passage in which Mr Brenton shows, in speaking of the shining youth of Lord Randolph Churchill before he was stricken with syphilis, that he is not indifferent to the grace of an English aristocrat who has been to a great public school.

There is a very moving scene . . . [which] suggests that Churchill was haunted by the fear that he might inherit his father's appalling disease: a suggestion paralleled in my mind by the thought that Mr Brenton himself is haunted by tales of bombing that he heard in his childhood. He is as compassionate towards his internees as William Douglas Home was to the prisoners

in "Now Barabbas." Is this compassion an implicit approval of what they say? Everyone must make up his own mind.

Our two most arresting political dramatists are Brenton and David Storey, because beneath the politics of their work there is a mysterious spirit of poetry. In Storey there are Wordsworthian quietness and regret: in Brenton the wild strangeness of the best scenes in Wilkie Collins's "The Woman in White." This strangeness, in the frantic walk of Captain Thompson, or the inexplicable tale of an incident on an unidentifiable plain told by a Welsh internee . . . , is what makes a Brenton play memorable. The wind is malign, and ever so slightly the bones are ill at ease in their sockets.

Harold Hobson, "Inventing the Past," in The Sunday Times, *London, May 19, 1974, p. 37.**

BARRY RUSSELL

[**The Churchill Play**] is not, in the strictest sense, a 'documentary': Brenton's vision is too personal, and perhaps too romantic, for that. Certainly, there are reconstructions. . . . But these glances into the past, like the more substantial projection forward into the future which gives the play its circumstantial basis, are merely elements in a metaphor which Brenton develops in order to comment on our present. The historic image is poeticised.

The metaphor rests squarely on the idea that just as certain forms of VD can develop unnoticed in the human body until the body rots to death, so the 'body politic' can contract virulent but unseen social diseases which will ultimately destroy it. Inflammation equals inflation: 'Schubert died of the pox . . . it makes artists see things in weird and wonderful ways. Countries are the same . . . inflation, inflammation. Everything's wonderful —till the backbone goes.' . . .

Brenton's play finds its justification on a political, rather than a theatrical level. The theatrical idea is too derivative ('Marat/ Sade'), as is the reinterpretation of Churchill ('The Soldiers') for it to stand solid scrutiny at that level. . . .

Brenton is in the position of many conscientious young liberals today: seeing the danger, but not quite knowing which way to turn.

Sometimes his writing shades off into the same post-Romantic ethic that has given rise to the Great Man syndrome, sometimes he totters on the verge of sensationalism, lacking Brecht's control. But at the heart of his play there is a genuine attempt to pose a problem. . . . [Brenton] may find that his message falls on deaf or already saturated ears, tired of the prophets of doom.

Barry Russell, "Nottingham," in Plays and Players, *Vol. 21, No. 9, June, 1974, p. 55.*

JOHN SPURLING

The Churchill Play is a powerful transference of what is happening in Northern Ireland now to what might be happening in England in ten years' time. Its swift dialogue in a masterful variety of dialects masks a cunning battery of cross-fire, a play about the immediate past is performed within the play, as an implicit criticism of our disregard for present events is contained within a warning of future events we could not so easily disregard. This is a controlled and sophisticated play, a marked advance on Brenton's previously patchy work.

John Spurling, in a review of "Magnificence," in
Encounter, *Vol. XLIV, No. 1, January, 1975, p. 66.*

PETER ANSORGE

'The Theatre', claims Howard Brenton, 'is a dirty place.' And Brenton, as much as any dramatist of recent years, has been associated with an obsessive interest in public and private violence—seeming assaults on all versions of law and order. . . . Brenton has a particular view of the power which lies behind the drama, both past and present, which he most admires. It is obvious, for instance, that dramatists have often been more concerned with portraying individuals who break rather than obey the law. The history of theatre can be read in these terms as a history of some pretty spectacular criminals; from Clytemnestra murdering Agamemnon in his bath; to Oedipus slaying his father; to Hamlet's sudden slaughter of Polonius; to the crimes of a Macbeth unleashing a seemingly endless tide of blood upon his Scottish kingdom. It is only with the rise of the naturalist theatre, in the eighteenth and nineteenth centuries, that the criminal loses his central place on our stages. Now Brenton and many writers of his generation are consciously attacking the norms of the naturalist stage. . . . But, as is often pointed out, the criminal acts presented in the most famous tragedies, like *Oedipus* or *Hamlet,* are nearly always compensated by a moral law which is restored at the end of the drama. Tragedy, one definition runs, is the story of an individual who decides to break the laws of his or her community and is destroyed by following through a particular, extreme course of action. Howard Brenton's plays are peopled with individuals who choose to pursue a perverse, but direct path of action through a world in which there are *no* clear patterns of law and order to judge a man. This can be seen in Brenton's fascination with the figure of the murderer Christie in *Christie In Love* (1969), who pursues a path of erotic fulfilment from his wretched Rillington Place home. It is also present in *Revenge* [1969] where the criminal Hepple and the Assistant Commissioner of Police, Macleish, engage in a game of 'cops and robbers' in a society which judges their criminal concepts as an anachronism. (pp. 2-3)

One feature of Brenton's development as a writer has been his direct involvement in the groups for which he has written. He has been able, through the underground circuit, to find a style of presentation which most closely mirrors his own theatrical preoccupations. . . . For the 1969 and 1970 Bradford Festivals, Brenton produced various environments for his plays *Wesley* and *Scott of the Antarctic. Wesley* was played in a Methodist church showing the father of that religion ending up in a mess of contradictions and moral confusions. In *Scott* an ice rink was utilized to spell out a message about the British Empire. Scott, out to win the ice pole for England's Empire, kept tumbling over on the ice. His party collapsed on the ice—revealing again Brenton's fascination with failed heroes, men who try and 'skate' a straight course through a slippery, confused and clumsy world.

This attempt to produce complete environments for plays, using churches, ice rinks, even swimming pools, is common enough to the underground. But in Brenton's case such experiments served to shape the specific style which he has chosen for writing his most successful work to date. In no work of Brenton's is this clearer than in *Christie In Love.* . . . In the preface to the published version Brenton has written that he wanted 'a kind of dislocation, tearing one style up for another'. Certainly the play depends for its effect on a stylistic contrast, a sort of pressure-cooking of clashing, disparate methods of presentation. The play is set in a pen of old newspapers—ten feet by six feet—which represents the garden in which England's most notorious murderer of the 1950s buried his victims. Two policemen, an Inspector and a Constable, are digging up bodies. Eventually they resurrect Christie himself, who leads the policemen, with the help of a female dummy, through the history of one of his crimes. The policemen are completely artificial characters; dummies themselves, they mirror public distaste for Christie's crimes. The Constable cheers himself up whilst digging for the remains of the corpses by reciting various obscene limericks. The Inspector contents himself by mouthing police platitudes, telling the Constable not to think too deeply about Christie's motivations. As Christie rises from the dead different kinds of horror effects take place. The stage is plunged into darkness, and we are prepared for the rising of a Dracula figure which might occur in a Hammer Horror picture. But the eventual appearance of Christie is a deliberate anti-climax. The murderer seems to be a sad, apparently respectable middle-aged man. The policemen are, in a real sense, disappointed:

> 'I dunno, it's disappointing. Why can't a mass
> murderer be just a bit diabolical. Why can't a
> pervert . . . have fangs or something?' . . .

Indeed Christie in Brenton's play comes across as an entirely naturalistic figure in sharp contrast to the role-playing, artificial policemen. It is here that one can spot a central paradox in *Christie In Love.* For Brenton is concerned with showing the surface of social life in England as something of a sham. His policemen, investigating the Christie murders, can find no real clue to the motivation behind the crimes. They are ventriloquists' dummies, fooling around like music-hall comics, registering their reactions to Christie's corpses as characters out of a horror comic. They do little to reassure audiences about the competence or judgment of their policemen. . . . For a writer like Brenton, authentic characters can only be located beneath the surface of public life—with the monsters buried in our gardens. Christie is a truer character for Brenton than either the Inspector or Constable. For the murderer has been pursuing a true end, the attainment, in however perverse a style, of erotic fulfilment. . . . Obviously Brenton regards the theatre as a place in which the surface 'bounds' of social conduct are broken, and where the monsters resting beneath the surface can make a startling reappearance. But in *Christie In Love,* and this in my view is the weakness of the piece, Brenton never offers us his own verdict on the murderer who so fascinates him. Christie is simply part of a sinister natural process—like the sexual disgust expressed in the Constable's nauseous limericks.

With *Revenge,* also penned in the prolific year of 1969, Brenton continued his highly personal exploration into the nature of England's police force. . . . *Revenge* charts the career of a criminal, Hepple, pursuing a fanatical desire for revenge against the Assistant Police Commissioner, Macleish, who first brought him to justice and Brixton Prison. On his release from jail, Hepple invades the garden of the Assistant Commissioner, planning to murder his old enemy. But two other policemen, PCs George and Albert, are already on Hepple's trail and have discovered the intruder in Macleish's garden—a garden also, of course, was the scene of the crime in *Christie In Love.* Hepple shoots and kills the younger constable, Albert, and is again pursued and imprisoned by Macleish. But in presenting the narrative Brenton introduced one remarkable innovation. Hepple and Macleish are played by the same actor. This immediately deprives an audience of any black and white identification with either policeman or criminal. (pp. 3-6)

In a strong final scene the ghost of the dead policeman visits Hepple in jail. It is now the 1980s and Hepple learns that all the people he knew on the outside have met with bloody deaths. In a scenario which recalls the revenge scenes that conclude so many Jacobean tragedies, Hepple's relatives and criminal colleagues appear in the jail with blood pouring from their mouths. (p. 6)

Obviously Brenton can be accused of all kinds of exaggeration in his view of crimes which lie beyond the bounds of either good or evil. . . . [*Fruit* (1970) suggested] his bitter view of English society is shared by several writers of his generation. *Fruit* was written as an on the spot reaction to the 1970 British General Election which brought the Conservative Party back to power. Brenton has admitted that at the time he was under the influence of a group of French intellectuals known as the 'situationists'. The situationists were, interestingly, very important to the Paris students of May '68. In a series of pamphlets, the situationists have described our present day Western society as 'the Society of the Spectacle'. To many of Brenton's generation, for whatever differing reasons, public life has come to appear more and more as a kind of 'spectacle', a vast game or confidence trick, played by politicians on the public through the mass media. In *Fruit* a Harley Street surgeon is seized by a feeling of total cynicism against the workings of England's parliamentary democracy. To him, as to Hepple at the end of *Revenge,* public life has become a charade, merely 'the turn of a card the fall of a dice'. The surgeon decides to take his revenge when he learns that the new Prime Minister is a homosexual. He attempts to use blackmail to bring down the Government. But he learns that 'the spectacle', the workings of the society he so hates, caters for this kind of attack. No one, least of all the corrupt Prime Minister, is interested in the blackmailer. . . . On the whole the play was dismissed by the critics. . . . It reads a little like one of *Private Eye's* more scandalous gossip columns. It is also written in a very fragmentary way, containing a lot of undigested bitterness. But like David Hare's more subtle *The Great Exhibition* (and Hare directed *Fruit* for Portable [Theatre]) it does reflect the overwhelming political disillusion felt by the generation now working in the underground theatres. (pp. 6-7)

Magnificence (1973) suggested a further development in Brenton's progress as a playwright. . . .

The play was, in fact, a more subtle account of the motivations which can underlie apparently meaningless acts of violence. It charts the Angry Brigade style career of a young man named Jed whose response to the failure of a squatting expedition with a group of friends is, like several Brenton heroes before him, to demand 'revenge'—in this case, vengeance on the political system which has denied the squatters their rights. For his victim Jed chooses a cabinet minister—clearly of the post-1970 Conservative Government—named Alice. The final scene is a confrontation between Jed and Alice in the latter's garden—the scene of so many of Brenton's moments of violence. (p. 8)

Jed has a very personal motive for his actions. While being evicted with his fellow squatters during the first act, Jed's wife is deliberately kicked in the stomach by the bailiff and thus loses her baby. Jed is sent to jail for assaulting the bailiff. Yet the whole sequence, written in a deliberate naturalistic vein, lacks the authenticity of the later scenes. . . . Jed's anger seems less related to the squatting episode during which he hardly

speaks a sentence, than to a more generalized hatred for the political establishment—an emotion clearly shared by the author. Jed wants to leave a violent mark upon the political scene, to touch an area of society with which he has no obvious contact. . . . Running through *Magnificence,* as a kind of high-life sub-plot, is a portrait of Alice's political and social background. A long, enthralling scene is devoted to a homosexual encounter between Alice and a dying ex-minister of the Macmillan era, named Babs, on the backs of a Cambridge college. This refers to another thread of Brenton's more recent writing—a contrast between two kinds of Conservative politician. . . . So in *Magnificence,* the Macmillan-like Babs accuses Alice of being a 'fascist'—representing a party which is now only interested in holding on to power in a rigid, puritanical manner, no longer safeguarding the more populist traditions of Toryism. Like Jed in fact, Babs has come to see political life as a great futile game, a hoax or empty spectacle from which his most cherished traditions and values have been ruthlessly expunged. So, ironically, Babs and Jed represent similar threats to the well-being of Alice.

Critics accused Brenton of either siding too obviously with a group of disgruntled drop-outs or of not providing a clearer ideological context for Jed's actions. He had failed, it was claimed, to provide a clear radical alternative to 'the system'. Yet I think that this is where the honesty of the play resides. Jed's act is not 'magnificent'—but a wasteful outlet for his personal frustrations. The play embodies an individual's demand for instant satisfaction, clear-cut solutions—for 'revenge'. . . . Jed's words reflect important and powerful attitudes of mind which underline many of the plays presented on the fringe between 1968 and 1973. Brenton's ability to bring Jed's frustration ('untouchable being on that silver screen') into the context of an increased sense of militancy ('right through their silver screen') marks out *Magnificence* as a key work of the period. (pp. 8-10)

Peter Ansorge, "Running Wild," in his Disrupting the Spectacle: Five Years of Experimental and Fringe Theatre in Britain, *Pitman Publishing, 1975, pp. 1-21.**

CHARLES MAROWITZ

The poverty of political theatre in England is so great that almost any drama with political intimations gets welcomed as if it were the long-lost grandchild of Bertolt Brecht. It creates a real dilemma for those (like myself) who genuinely hanker for a piece of relevant theatre that isn't ideologically prepackaged and offensively 'all thought out'. *Weapons of Happiness* is about political subjects but, if your definition of political art includes moral fair-play and aesthetic equilibrium, it is hard to clasp it to one's bosom as a 'political play'. . . . I expect a political play to be more than the dramatisation of an author's political loyalties. Left-wing propaganda with its heart-in-the-right-place is still propaganda and, as such, nullified as art—unless it transcends its own biases. *Weapons of Happiness,* during the course of its first act, tantalisingly leads one to expect it may do just that, but by the time its second act has concluded, you realise you are once again being asked to buy a rigid interpretation of life whether it tallies with your conception of life or not. And that, ultimately, is the case against partisanship-parading-as-art, it asks for our approval simply because it's wearing the right pins.

The most interesting thing Brenton has done in the play is to set up a comparison between an old-styled, Cold War Communist and the fuzzily-romantic, left-wing political zealots of today whose notions of revolution are Vanessatised against the hard, grim realities of power-politics. Brenton's 'hero', Josef Frank, was, in fact, one of the 14 defendants in the Rudolph Slansky 'show trial' which was performed in Czechoslovakia in 1952. The real Frank was the Assistant Secretary of the Czechoslovakian Communist Party and executed along with 11 other leading Communists (most of them Jewish, allegedly Zionist) on 3 December, 1952. The Slansky trial was the first Stalinist show-trial to be held in a satellite country and one of the first to be primarily generated by anti-semitism. . . .

In Brenton's play, Frank, a wan Communist phantom, is shown to have emigrated to England and acquired a job in a South London crisp factory in order to achieve anonymity. Against his will he is involved with a group of yobbo-wobblies who attempt a factory sit-in after they learn the business is to be sold and they, declared redundant; an act they easily manage to escalate into an impulse of revolutionary fervour.

Brenton derives a real dramatic tension by pitting a tortured, brain-washed, historically-verifiable Communist leader against the WRP-amateurs who feel the pinch of their oppression but don't know how to relieve the ache. Frank's dogged refusal to play revolutionary games emanates from a kind of funereal world-weariness. Here is a man who knows that behind the pursuit of every political ideal stands the torturer's rack and the vicious circle. The presence of such a man, and all he has endured, powerfully questions the relevance, as well as the methodology, of what nascent British revolution is all about, and Brenton gets a lot of dramatic mileage out of simply confronting the remnants of a true combatant with a group of anti-Establishment zealots who truly, but cluelessly, want to change the world.

Weapons of Happiness begins to go wrong when Mr Stanley, the inveterate factory foreman (the boss's bumboy, a now popular left-wing stereotype) is allowed to become a figure of fun. As they taunt him for having 'sold out' to the management, the crunch of leaden, uncritical value-judgement begins to reverberate around the auditorium. Then we learn that Mr and Mrs Makepeace, the factory owners, are in fact displaced persons from Harrods who sit in expensive fur coats in front of their locked-out factory, soothing themselves out of champagne buckets and being comforted by patronising members of Her Majesty's police. . . .

Brenton's attitude to the 'bosses' (uncritically abetted by his director, David Hare) is to mark them out as fools and villains. By so doing, the workers need reveal no moral superiority whatsoever. They are already the 'heroes' of this rigged social combat; a little naïve perhaps, relying somewhat too heavily on media-made mythology; believing a bit too earnestly that it really matters whether Bob Dylan sells out or not; buying, a bit too wholeheartedly, what I would call the *Time Out* ethic, but nevertheless, the *downtrodden,* the *pure-in-heart* and, ipso-facto, the heroes. (p. 18)

All right, all right, I hear myself saying to myself. Enough facetiousness! Brenton is writing out of his convictions. He passionately believes the worker's lot is not a happy one, and that some kind of drastic social upheaval—like a revolution—will redress a lot of the balances. . . . It just isn't enough to edit out disagreeable or unsympathetic ideas because one doesn't agree with them or finds them unsympathetic. A play is a place where an author's central idea is swung, like a cat by the tail, around all the other ideas it would like to banish or deny. But to banish or deny any set of beliefs involves grappling with them—not simply assuming every right-thinking left-winger automatically perceives the lunacy of capitalism and the degradation of workers' exploitation.

But the real paradox, and I wonder whether Brenton himself sees it, is that his protagonist, Josef Frank, from the little we know of him, was himself a working-class fall-guy. The son of a working-class Czech family, a former volunteer in an International Brigade, a staunch Communist, a champion of the workers, elevated to power by the Communist takeover in Czechoslovakia in 1948 when Gottwald, sensing defeat at the polls, staged the left-wing coup that ultimately brought Soviet domination to that country. . . . (pp. 18-19)

What, I ask myself, is Brenton's equation? If Communist revolution produces the Gottwalds, the Slanskies and the Franks, what does revolutionary British youth have to learn from these examples—other than ferocious self-reliance and profound suspicion of any Marxist-dominated political system? But the inference of *Weapons of Happiness* is that there is an historical route by which exploitation and repression can be stamped out, and in some modified and rehabilitated way, it is the route of Josef Frank. It is the route of an idealised kind of Communism sprinkled with liberal-humanism and devoted to a marvellous kind of self-emancipation founded on the right kind (as opposed to the wrong kind) of class malice. Brenton's play warns us against romanticism, but the real enemy is woolly-mindedness and blinkered-thinking, the deadly habit of refusing to think out your case to its logical conclusion, preferring to stop comfortably midway, just before the moral contradictions cut you down in your tracks. . . .

It is the outrageous political naïveté of writers like Brenton and Hare that makes one's flesh crawl, and it is this naïveté, coupled with their unconscious desire to cash in on fashionable left-wing rhetoric, that ultimately debilitates their works-of-art and makes people like me rush off to see the latest Astaire-Rogers revival, uttering a plague on both your houses. (p. 19)

> *Charles Marowitz, in a review of "Weapons of Happiness," in* Plays and Players, *Vol. 23, No. 12, September, 1976, pp. 18-19.*

OLEG KERENSKY

Brenton is as political as Trevor Griffiths, and perhaps even further to the Left. Like Griffiths, he expresses strong dissatisfaction with present-day Britain but, instead of being naturalistic and relying largely on rational argument, Brenton's plays are fantasies, full of bizarre and theatrical visual effects. The dialogue is often artificial and surrealistic, attempting to show people as they really are, beneath the veneer of conventional behaviour and polite talk. Brenton is obsessed with the violence lurking beneath the surface of apparently respectable upholders of law and order, and with the way this suppressed violence brings the oppressed and the oppressor, the worker and the criminal, the politician and the policeman, closer together than is generally realized. The result is often extremely amusing, as well as frightening. (p. 207)

Brenton's first full-length play to be staged in London was *Revenge*. . . . Its characters and language are highly original, but soon became familiar as typical of Brenton's work. As in his later plays, there are criminals, prostitutes and policemen involved with each other in bizarre situations and using artificial language which is often very funny in its outspoken and exaggerated expression of thoughts which normally remain unspoken. Also, like Brenton's later work, *Revenge* is very theatrical. One actor has several very quick changes to 'double' the roles of Adam Hepple, a notorious ageing criminal, and Assistant Commissioner Archibald MacLeish, the detective who has always hounded him. This doubling, apart from giving the actor a chance to impress the audience with his virtuosity, also underlines the parallel between policeman and criminal. (pp. 207-08)

MacLeish is a figure of farce, a religious fanatic who believes he is one of the Elect and that God is helping his hunt for Hepple. His great scheme is to keep Hepple on the run till he collapses from heart failure, and he vows not to shave till Hepple is caught because 'Al Capone never shaved when he was after a man'. When George, a junior policeman, points out that this is England, not Chicago, MacLeish disdainfully replies that they are 'both foreign parts to a Scot'.

In the end, all the characters die, each in turn spectacularly biting a sack of stage blood and spitting out the contents. So *Revenge* ends like the Jacobean or Victorian melodrama which Brenton is parodying. The deaths also symbolize a dying Britain, or at least the passing of an age. (pp. 208-09)

The social criticism implicit in *Revenge* is overshadowed in the theatre by the play's violence, humour and explicit amorality, so that it's doubtful if many members of the audience are stimulated to question the social system. The same is true of *Christie in Love*. . . . Once again Brenton is concerned with criminals and police, this time with the notorious real-life murderer, John Reginald Halliday Christie, who killed and buried numerous women in and around his house in Notting Hill Gate. (p. 209)

[*Christie in Love*] struck many people as a mere exercise in bad taste. But it does try to show that even a perverted mass murderer is also a human being, and it again underlines parallels between the criminal and the police, one of Brenton's favourite themes, using typical verbal and visual shock tactics. (p. 211)

Magnificence was Brenton's first play to be staged in a full-size London theatre as distinct from an attic or basement. Even so, it only had a short run at the comparatively small Royal Court. Described by Brenton as 'a kind of tragedy', it's about a group of illegal squatters who eventually decide to assassinate a Cabinet Minister. (p. 213)

What the audience may find hard to forgive is the play's obscurity. . . . It is a fault in the construction of *Magnificence* that it fails to make its point, holding the audience's attention while it is in progress but leaving it irritated and dissatisfied. (pp. 215-16)

Brassneck was extremely topical, dealing with nepotism and corruption in local government and in the awarding of building contracts. It was produced when big scandals of this sort were just becoming common knowledge and reaching the courts; as in real life, the officials and building contractors in the play are closely associated with the Labour Party. (p. 216)

The Churchill Play was produced at Nottingham [in 1974]. . . . An italicized note under the title of the play adds: *As it will be performed in the winter of 1984 by the internees of Churchill Camp somewhere in England.* We are in a near-Fascist Orwellian Britain. A group of political prisoners takes the opportunity of a visiting delegation of M.P.s to make their protest through a theatrical performance and to use it as a cover for an escape attempt. . . . The soldiers guarding the camp have been brutalized by shooting down terrorists in Northern Ireland and strikers at home. In the play performed by the prisoners, Churchill rises from his coffin and is depicted in an unfavourable light. . . . When he visits a bombed-out family in the blitz, he is told, 'We can take it. But we just might give it back to you one day', translated in his memoirs as, 'We can take it. Give it 'em back'. (p. 218)

[This] makes a theatrical and frightening vision of the future. The horror, as prisoners are occasionally removed and 'dumped' (murdered) by the guards, is convincing. The tensions between officers, N.C.O.s and various prisoners, and their rough attempts at humour to make life bearable, are well depicted, and so are the three members of the inspecting delegation. But the attempt to belittle Churchill, and the simplistic message that people rather than great men win wars, detract from, rather than add to, the effectiveness of the play. Similar political uncertainty and naivety mar *Weapons of Happiness*.

This play, specially written for the National Theatre, presents an interesting situation, not previously treated in the theatre, and touches an important problem. But the situation is not explored, the problem not tackled. Josef Frank, a historical Czechoslovak Communist leader who was hanged in the Stalinist purges of 1952, is shown as alive and well and living in London. He is working in a potato crisp factory and arousing the curiosity of the young British workers. . . . But the workers are depicted as so stupid and so ignorant of history and revolutionary theory that he is forced to dismiss them as 'children'. There is no real debate about the best way of changing Britain. Although he warns them that their attempt to run the factory themselves, without any expertise, is doomed, there is no serious discussion of how and when workers' control can be practical. Nor is there any exploration of the consequences of violent revolution, and whether it must inevitably breed further violence, political despotism and economic inefficiency, as it has done in the Soviet countries. The workers never learn the truth about Soviet Communism, because Brenton's Frank cannot be bothered to try teaching them. (pp. 218-19)

The implication is that, despite all the faults of their system, Communists are the only people who really care about working people. This gives the play a lamentably weak conclusion; if it is a point of view that Brenton seriously wants to propound, he needs to provide much more argument in support of it.

Weapons of Happiness is further diluted and made less convincing by the introduction of some unlikely and almost incredible sex. Janice, a young half-educated revolutionary, seduces the veteran Frank on the floor of the London Planetarium. . . .

The play is of course partly fantasy, and unites several of Brenton's favourite themes. As in *The Churchill Play,* the subservient police middle-ranks upholding the establishment are irritated by genteel upper-class posing. The factory owner wants to be 'nice' and to be liked by 'his' workers, while at the same time selling the factory behind their backs. Brenton's interest in the police finds a natural outlet. Trivial incidents in Britain, like police questioning about hooliganism in the street, trigger off Frank's memories of brutal police interrogations in Czechoslovakia. In a series of flash-backs, British policemen and bosses become Communist torturers, with a suggestion that the two really have got something in common. (p. 220)

Brenton slightly demurs from the 'political' label attached to his plays, not denying that they are political and socialist, but claiming that all plays are political. 'When they are rightwing, like William Douglas-Home's or Noël Coward's, nobody bothers to call them political'. Brenton's socialism could loosely be called 'Trotskyite'; he describes *Weapons of Happiness* as 'anti-Stalinist and pro-Communist'. (p. 222)

Most of Brenton's plays refer, explicitly or implicitly, to well-known personalities in the news or to topical items from the newspapers. 'It's important to make connections with what the audience already knows. I don't think of myself as writing plays to last, but to be performed at the time I write them.' . . . (pp. 223-24)

[Brenton says], 'The theatre could be something really fantastic, incredibly powerful. At present it's full of dead classics and meretricious rubbish. New plays by writers of my generation are much more interesting and enjoyable—much better—than the classics. The more good writing there is, the more it helps to change the theatre. We've got to change how the theatres are run, how the actors act. But the pressures to get a radical new sort of theatre can only come from the writers.' . . . (p. 224)

> *Oleg Kerensky, "Politics, Mild and Bitter," in his*
> The New British Drama: Fourteen Playwrights Since
> Osborne and Pinter, *1977. Reprint by Taplinger Pub-*
> *lishing Co., Inc., 1979, pp. 206-25.*

PAUL MERCHANT

Howard Brenton's poems follow after ten years of plays, in performance and in print, and at first sight they seem like a new departure. The collection is a sequence of 74 sonnets, and has the kind of completeness and individual authority associated with the traditional sonnet sequence. Yet in two important respects Brenton's poems are at least as organic to his dramatic purpose as those of Brecht and Bond. First, as his title, *Sonnets of Love and Opposition,* suggests, the poems are an attempt to chart his everyday landscape, moral and physical, and the poems operate through actual description more than universal images, so that the sequence has something of the effect of a journal, a record of experience and development over a number of months.

That this experience covers a very wide range of subject matter is one reason for the collection's great interest. The other lies in his use of the sonnet sequence as a form. It is clearly (as Lowell and Berryman have found) an ideal vehicle for a journal; the individual poems are just the length of a manageable single process of argument (two ideas, for example, opposed and then drawn to a conclusion), but Brenton has also found in the sequence its potential as a most direct form of drama.

It reads as a sinuous monologue that amplifies and extends the central speaking voice by contact with various characters who almost meet him in dialogue—members of his family at the closest, a series of archetypes of opposition at the furthest remove—and throughout the sequence the placing is firm and effective, clearly a dramatist's work. . . .

The poems are immediate and raw, but surprising in being scrupulously rhymed and patterned, often rhyming from the centre outwards. The combination of an almost reckless openness and careful craftsmanship is impressive. (p. 51)

> *Paul Merchant, "The Theatre Poems of Bertolt Brecht,*
> *Edward Bond, and Howard Brenton," in* Theatre

Quarterly, *Vol. IX, No. 34, Summer, 1979, pp. 49-51.**

COLIN CHAMBERS

In *Sore Throats,* Howard Brenton has gone further than most of his contemporaries in exploring the intimate, bringing to bear on three fractured people in an unwelcoming South London flat, the social vision that sustains the broader, public canvas of his earlier work. . . . In the wake of divorce, Jack . . . , a chief inspector, has returned to see Judy . . . to claim half her money, and in so doing hits, kicks her and stamps on her head. Enter Sally . . . to look at the flat, knowing, because she works as a telephonist at the *Evening Standard,* that it is to be let. In Act 2, 18 months later, the two women are enjoying 'liberated' liberal sex with all-comers, especially 14-year-old-boys, and Jack returns again, this time from Canada, without having fulfilled his ambition to become a Mountie: his humiliation is rounded off with the closing declaration from Judy of her freedom from sexual and economic oppression. . . .

The power balance and the decay are forcefully, brilliantly highlighted through Brenton's typically tough, vivid language, brutal, disturbing, intense and sometimes comic. But in Act 2, the bruising dialogue gives way to more self-conscious writing like Jack's story of his roadside birth after a motor car crash, as Brenton drifts into the fantasy of the women's so-called liberation and the empty, emotional gesture at the end when the lights go down on Judy about to burn her money and be 'fucked, happy and free'. Part one convinces because Brenton has found a theatrical expression for his perception of reality, despite Jack's stiff style . . . , whereas in the second act both the analysis and its dramatic realisation are shaky. The single bottle on the bare stage when the play opens compared to the forest of empties and other debris of the 'good life' at the beginning of Act 2, sums up the metaphor Brenton is struggling with—marriage today is a love desert, freedom means lots of fruit. It is as relevant to the state of Britain as . . . *The Churchill Play* (the speech on the nation is delivered by the force for change, Sally) and it would be unfair to expect Brenton to fully succeed where many others have not yet feared to tread. Hopefully, he and some of those others will take up this 'experiment in writing' which tackles the personal from a wider social dimension than is usual, seeing links between power, politics and love.

> *Colin Chambers, in a review of "Sore Throats," in*
> Plays and Players, *Vol. 27, No. 1, October, 1979,*
> *pp. 22-3.*

BENEDICT NIGHTINGALE

There have been plays that have used the years 1945 and 1968 to deliver little homilies about socialist hopes raised and dashed. Now, it seems, 1974 must be added to that list. *A Short Sharp Shock* begins with the fall of the Heath government, and proceeds to show the nation succumbing, after a long, strength-sapping bout of Wilsonitis and Callaghanosis, to what the authors fear may be a terminal assault by the bacillus M-Thatcher. . . .

Unluckily, both the voltage and wattage of *Shock* are disappointingly low. It is neither good Brenton nor rousing agitprop. My prescription for socialist stage-drama is painfully simple. Either it must display a trenchant, tough-minded awareness of the contradictions of what is, after all, a very complex subject, namely the possibility of social change in stick-in-the-mud Britain. . . . Or it must draw on some powerful non-intellectual source of energy: a *saeva indignatio,* in whose armoury may be found satire, parody, scathing metaphor, visual and verbal bravura, and whatever other weaponry a high-duty imagination can galvanise into action. . . .

Or, most difficult of all, a combination of the two. This is presumably what *Shock* attempts, with its brusque cuts between a caricature Tory government and the reactions and arguments of a Cockney clan, representing 'the governed'. The leading grotesques are all played by women. . . . The laughter they provoke is not, however, very abundant or savage; and the lines thrust into their mouths are neither particularly inventive nor especially informative. For anyone who skims through a daily paper over breakfast, remembers [Keith] Joseph's strictures on the irresponsibly fertile, and has some minimal grasp of the tenets of Milton Friedman, much of this will seem primary-class stuff: Tory politics 101. . . .

Perhaps the evening needs an injection of that tastelessness it has already, bewilderingly been charged with displaying. I don't know whether the accusation is based on the scene in which [a character] is force-fed with Friedman's semen—a harmlessly jokey reference, this, to the Shockley breeding-bank for Nobel laureates—or on the introduction of the ghosts of Mountbatten and queenmaker Neave to the accompaniment of some unexceptionable sentiments about the British presence in Ireland. If the latter, the objectors surely expose how out-of-touch they are with the way their fellow-citizens think and laugh. They should try comparing Brenton's not-unsympathetic necromancy with the ghoulish Mountbatten jokes current in London schools. . . . [*A Short Sharp Shock* might] have gained from more van-Itallian, Hogarthian, Swiftian, or Scarfean treatment of the principal object of its ire, Margaret Thatcher. . . .

Benedict Nightingale, "Low Voltage," in New Statesman, *Vol. 100, No. 2572, July 4, 1980, pp. 27-8.**

BENEDICT NIGHTINGALE

The first time Edward Bond's *Saved* was staged, it was to an outraged pandemonium in which, I'm sorry to say, the voices of some respected colleagues were shrilly to be heard; the second, only four years later, to general agreement that the stoning-to-death of the baby in his pram was a justifiable illustration of the extremes to which deprivation could push our fellow-citizens. Yesterday's shock-horror headline had become today's challenging masterpiece. It's a familiar enough process; and if I take leave to doubt that *The Romans in Britain* will provide the next instance of its operation, it's more because of scepticism about the whole than disgust at any part or parts, including the private ones so generously on display in the Celtic forests of 54 BC. I was duly sickened by the scene in which a druid is incompetently raped by a Roman soldier, as I was meant to be. It's what is known in the trade as a 'strong image', meaning one that makes you want to swallow your eyes and ears and pretend that such things couldn't happen. The real trouble, however, is that the plaint it's designed to italicise is hardly more sophisticated than that imperialism is a crying shame, not to say a pain in the arse.

Of course, Brenton would argue that it's time for straight talking and not sophistication, when we Anglo-Saxons persist in treating the Celts in a style analogous to that of the Romans two millennia ago. He makes the point with another 'strong image': a roar of helicopters in the pre-Christian twilight, the appearance of British soldiers in khaki, who shoot dead a stone-brandishing slave-girl. . . . [On] trundles their general, who turns out to be Caesar updated, to mouth platitudes about violence being reduced to an acceptable level and (a gratuitous dig at Yeats, this) civilisation not sinking, its great battle lost. Thus ends act one.

Thus, perhaps, ought to end the play. After all, this is its theatrical and political climax, the anachronistic culmination of the invasion whose story Brenton has spent the previous hour telling. He has told it pretty vividly too, with less preciosity of diction than in his recent work and no attempt to idealise the victims of colonialism. His ancient Britons are a superstitious, short-sighted, artlessly cruel lot, admirable only for the energy with which they till their fields, improvise football-games and launch into group discussions about topical issues. But how helpful is it bluntly to identify then with now? . . .

To some extent the play's second act answers this objection. Much of it seems redundant, a picture of post-Roman Britain crumbling as pre-Roman Britain crumbled, this time before the Saxon invader. A high-Tory matron, suffering from a somewhat symbolic plague, is hauled onstage, then killed by her steward, for whom war promises freedom; and two of her household cooks hit the road with two farm-girls, by way of illustrating Brenton's belief, apparent in both *Weapons of Happiness* and *The Churchill Play,* that hope for the future lies in the obscure survivor, the unconsidered skulker, biding his time in the cracks of a disintegrating society. But the act also involves an SAS major lurking in an Irish field, improbably disguised as a yokel and bent on inveigling an IRA godfather within range of his revolver; and here, . . . the play does become more interesting.

Another of Brenton's recurrent notions, evident in *Magnificence* and *Weapons of Happiness,* is that the nob class has lost faith in itself. The mailed fist is rusting, and the iron heart has developed a sort of metallic gangrene, whose outer symptoms are self-doubt and self-loathing; and so it proves here. Confronted with his target, [the SAS major] admits his true identity, rambles incoherently on about the ghosts of the war-dead, accuses himself of wielding 'a Roman spear, a Saxon axe, a British army machine gun', and is promptly shot for his phoney 'humanity'. The scene is tense, theatrically effective and, for what it's worth, more resonant and suggestive than anything preceding it. The question is whether it compensates for the play's intellectual and political crudeness, its sentimental appeals to an Arthurian utopia and, sometimes, a lack of plausibility that lurches towards Pythonesque exorbitance. I fear it doesn't, and I suspect the theatregoers of four or 40 years hence won't judge me too harshly for saying so.

Benedict Nightingale, "Mailed Fist & Iron Heart," in New Statesman, *Vol. 100, No. 2588, October 24, 1980, p. 28.**

STEVE GRANT

[The critic W. Stephen Gilbert] once hesitatingly dubbed Brenton and [David] Hare the Lennon and McCartney of the New Wave. Indeed, the comparison has its point. Brenton is most at home when creating startling and often outrageous *coups de théâtre* or when composing choice, vernacular exchanges for his favourite characters, who are usually villains, policemen or angry, disenfranchised youngsters.

Hare once confessed, albeit wryly, that he can only write about the middle classes; and while it is true that he can pen convincing dialogue for Chinese peasants or zonked-out rock musicians, his most memorable creations stem from the highly articulate but often emotionally sterile bourgeoisie. . . .

Brenton has fewer fears about the content of his plays, seeing himself in the epic theatrical tradition of Brecht, a playwright politicized by his own writings. Even in his most accessible play to date—*Epsom Downs*—Brenton creates a vivid dramatic tension out of his various characters, all imprisoned within the gloriously absurd confines of the Big Occasion and yet all faced with the possibility of change. For Emily Davison, the suffragette who threw herself beneath the King's horse at the Epsom Derby in 1913, change means violent self-sacrifice; for a young homeless couple who have blown their savings on Lester Piggott and the Minstrel, change is realizing that winning the money for a home doesn't finally mean anything; for Jocks, the sacked stable lad, change means an articulation of his embryonic class awareness; for Tillotson, the evangelist, change means rejecting the hypodermic of religion for the bigger if equally illusory thrill of the wager. (p. 118)

[The] expression of inner disenchantment mixed with a muted desire to belong is quite typical of the power and ambiguity of the best of Brenton's work. Indeed, what is not always appreciated by critics of both Brenton and Hare is the conflicts which arise within their plays—conflicts that are not necessarily (though at times they certainly can be) the result of confusion on the part of the dramatist but merely reflections of the complexity of their creations. . . . If the plays are full of contradictions and doubts then that is not necessarily a fault. Both Hare and Brenton are deeply concerned with morality, with the need for compassion and courage, and with the fears and desperations of their contemporaries. It is these features as much as any strident cry for revolutionary change that permeate their work.

Magnificence (1973), Brenton's examination of urban terrorism—a theme he has returned to in *The Saliva Milkshake* (1975) and *Weapons of Happiness* (1976)—exhibits a classic ambiguity. Jed the bomber blows himself up in the bungled course of assassinating a Tory Minister. While the audience strongly identifies with Jed, who has been politicized through his experiences in a brutal squat eviction, it is his companion Cliff who pronounces the supposedly telling verdict. For Jed the act of extreme destructiveness is "magnificent", for Cliff it is "a fucking stupid gesture" which has reduced Jed to "a nothing. A zero. A crank with a tin box of bangs." But with which verdict does the audience identify? Theatrically with Jed, politically (Brenton obviously hopes) with Cliff for whom action is "work, corny work, with and for the people".

Weapons of Happiness and *The Churchill Play* represent Brenton's work at its most expansive. *The Churchill Play,* set in an internment camp in 1984 after a coalition government takeover backed by the military, is a nightmare vision of the future in which Churchill, the pinnacle of National Heroism, is portrayed through a play-within-a-play as a hypochondriac and obsessive, out of touch with the British people and haunted by a spectre of gloom called Black Dog. (pp. 119-20)

[In *Weapons of Happiness,* Brenton extended] his field of vision to take in the bitter example of the Stalinist betrayal in Eastern Europe. The play, impressive in its technical virtuosity, juxtaposes the sufferings of a former Czech Communist leader, Joseph Frank, imprisoned, tortured and tried in the 1952 Slan-

sky show trials (and in reality hanged) with the fumblings and sometimes ludicrous gropings towards political awareness of a group of South London factory workers. There is a perennial problem in the play, namely that the representatives of the contemporary capitalist classes are poor creations indeed, as if Brenton's invention had run out before reaching them. Thus the factory owner (typically it's a potato crisp factory, which makes for much humour but detracts from the play's seriousness) writes poetry and reacts to the occupation of his works by drinking champagne, dissecting his marriage with an equally unbelievable rich-bitch wife ("I would like you all to know back there that he never liked me to touch my breasts") and consuming himself in vitriolic worker-bashing. As Charles Marowitz observed [see excerpt above] the picture is not only uncritical but positively inaccurate.

It seems that on occasion Brenton's love of comedy and violent theatrical confrontation robs him of a much-needed analytical element. There is simply very little contest in the play between the capitalist classes and their real or potential opponents, even though the latter comprise a portentous Czech, a deaf mute, an illiterate, an old lag and a few sullen, inarticulate boys and girls. Nevertheless *Weapons of Happiness* contains much that is good about Brenton's work. It has a dimension that so much political theatre lacks . . . , ranging as it does from the New Testament of Christ to the Cosmos of the Planetarium, from the winter streets of post-war Moscow to the rural landscape of contemporary Wales. At its climax the factory employees start afresh (leaving Frank dead of a heart attack), bent on a slow process of self-help. It is certainly a bleak and tentative conclusion, not without hope but almost a thin, bare gesture when set against the ferocity of Frank's torment. (pp. 120-21)

Brenton's earlier work is notable for its theatrical invention, particularly the intriguing use of environmental elements. Early plays include a portrait of *Wesley,* performed in a suitably denominational church, a version of Rabelais' *Gargantua, . . .* played out in the representation of a giant stomach, and *Scott of the Antarctic,* performed in 1971 on a Bradford ice rink with one professional actor, several amateurs, skaters, a rock band and a performance artist. His first major success, *Christie in Love* (1969), takes a new look at the notorious mass murderer as a clue to society's own sexual hypocrisies. It is most notable for its brilliantly evocative design (a play-pen made out of newspaper) and its effective juxtaposition of various dramatic styles—from the baldly naturalistic to the comically grotesque. Brenton's first full-length play, *Revenge* (1969), though small beer in comparison with later works, has a pleasing comic intensity (as much gleaned from the radio humour of the time as from prior theatrical models) and as well as dramatizing the voice of Brixton Gaol—"Oh England, what will become of you . . . ?"—has both main parts played by the same actor: the old criminal Adam Hepple and his arch-rival, a religious detective inspector named Macleish.

In many of Brenton's earlier plays the obsessional qualities of his central protagonists play a major role in the moral content. . . . Though there are great weaknesses of judgement in some of these early dramatic excursions (what is the author's view on Christie, for example, other than as a barometer of officially sanctioned passions?) the emphasis on the need for individual integrity, the search for codes which transcend the pragmatic or the habitual, is well to the fore. (pp. 121-22)

Steve Grant, "Voicing the Protest: The New Writers," in Dreams and Deconstructions: Alternative

Theatre in Britain, *edited by Sandy Craig, Amber Lane Press, 1980, pp. 116-44.**

HAROLD HOBSON

[Anger, scorn, and shock were aroused] amongst the national critics by Howard Brenton's *The Romans in Britain*. . . . They put up such a show of indignation and moralistic horror as has scarcely been rivalled in Britain since the country lost its senses over the wickedness of Lord Byron. . . . *The Romans in Britain* begins with a haunting picture of the ancient Britons living in freedom and terror in the darkness of pre-Roman conquest, freemen frightened out of their wits at the sight of any unfamiliar face. The Romans come, and impose by implacable force and military superiority some sort of order upon them. In the course of the wild action there is a calm, self-controlled speech by Julius Caesar . . . , the stabbing of a man strung upside down, so that his blood gushes forth to the ground, and an attempted homosexual rape of a naked Druid by a Roman soldier.

It is these two incidents that caused all the furore. No one mentioned that they occupied just about four minutes in a play lasting nearly three hours, or that they illustrated the main theme of the play, namely, that violence is natural to man, whether conqueror or conquered; that man is prone to sin and his heart is full of wickedness. Brenton's is a pessimistic view of human nature, but it is one that has from the earliest times led to the creation of great literature. It was expounded with savagery by Swift, with irony by Thackeray, and with an elegiac grief by the writer of Ecclesiastes. Mr Brenton's hand is clumsier than any of these, but it is powerful. In the second part of the play he makes a comparison between the Romans and the British forces in Northern Ireland, which in its complexity may be interpreted in several different ways. . . . As is customary with Brenton, he draws this example of the governing classes which he hates with considerable sympathy and charm.

The Romans in Britain is as thought-provoking a play as the [National Theater] has ever produced, and the close of the first act, in which the evening of Roman occupation falls with the crashing sound of the breaking of nations is as thunder-striking as anything we have seen or heard upon the stage for some years. There is nothing so impressive, it may be, as the sound of a still, small voice, but the cracking of the heavens comes pretty near to it. (pp. 29-30)

> *Harold Hobson, in a review of "The Romans in Britain," in* Drama, *No. 139, first quarter, 1981, pp. 29-30.*

BEN CAMERON

Brenton has survived the demise of the Fringe and has gained a controversial position unequalled among the writers of the late 1960's. But critical acclaim, commercial acceptance, and diversity of interests have in no way threatened the intensity of Brenton's political commitment. He remains one of Britain's most dedicated political writers and unapologetically states, "All my plays are written unreservedly in the cause of socialism." And though "agit/prop" is a label he eschews, he openly avows, "My purpose is to agitate by satire, by intelligent argument, by writing scenes of verifiable truth . . . and to propagate an idea"; he thus attempts to revitalize the revolutionary's vocabulary while avoiding such stock conventions

as sermons, placards, and facile solutions. In depicting the struggles of people trapped in a world without political or social morality and in avoiding traditional psychological analyses, Brenton establishes himself as a descendant of Brecht. He adheres to the Brechtian imperative of man as the sum of social circumstance and of the drama as the study of social contradictions as manifested in the individual.

Brenton, with this political focus of an unabashed dedication to socialism, uses the theater to investigate revolution. Not surprisingly, early Brenton plays embrace the political or moral rebel as a leading character. *Christie in Love* follows the progression of a love that can find its ultimate expression only in murder; John Christie, in following his own erotic and ethical code, violates all social laws and usual concepts of affection. In *The Churchill Play,* prison inmates who have been incarcerated for various innocuous forms of political protest perform a satirical play for government officials. *The Saliva Milkshake* focuses on the confrontation between a radical-turned-assassin and a liberal acquaintance whose political commitment consists of mere ideological flirtation. And in both *Magnificence* and *Weapons of Happiness,* a radical faction seizes control of a building in an aborted attempt to effect social change. (p. 30)

The curious power of *Magnificence* springs from Brenton's double-edged view of the situation. The energy, fervor, and (in some ways) innocence of the revolutionaries are admirable and compelling; indeed the play is prefaced with Brecht's injunction, taken literally by the characters, to "Sink into the mire. Embrace the butcher. But change the world." At the same time, a sense of frustration permeates the play. Politicians are ineffectual and petty, changing the world becomes impossible, and the eulogy offered by Cliff (Jed's best friend) at the end of the play concludes: "The waste. I can't forgive you that. The waste of your anger. Not the murder, murder is common enough. Not the violence, violence is everyday. What I can't forgive you Jed, my dear, dear friend, is the waste." *Magnificence* is a play of frustration, leaping from the devotion to ideals that sees not only "magnificence" in spilling blood but the simultaneous awareness of the impossibility of a viable, radical revolution.

Weapons of Happiness . . . continues to explore these themes, this time using the historical figure of Joseph Frank, a Czech wrongly convicted of treason and executed during the Soviet spy trials of the early 1950's. Brenton allows his Frank to survive this purge and places him in contact with a group of disgruntled British workers who seize a potato crisp factory and threaten to ruin a corporation. These rebels are more sullen, more violent, and less educated than their predecessors in *Magnificence* and thus link the idealistic rebels of the late 1960's with the punk movement of the late 1970's. Frank can see these revolutionaries only as children playing games they cannot understand. History recalls friends driven to suicide, betrayals, recriminations; revolution, having been crushed before, now seems impossible. . . . Frank's experience counterpoints the naivete of the others throughout, and the revolution, in going underground, continues without waste.

This evolving sense of practicality is intricately related to Brenton's understanding of the failure of the Fringe: he ultimately sees the ruling society as remorseless, inescapable, incapable of coexisting with Brenton's more socialistic perspective. Revolution thus must be achieved from within; it cannot be imposed from the outside. This philosophy makes Brenton an urban guerilla of sorts, a position he has achieved gradually. His early plays focus on the relationship between idealism and power. In the mid-1970's, however, Brenton's characters come to equate power with physical freedom. The inmates of Churchill prison, the rebels who flee the potato crisp factory through the sewer—all battle incarceration and test the tension between spiritual freedom and physical liberty, a tension that emphasizes the importance of civil liberties while measuring ideological commitment in the face of survival. A further step is taken in *Epsom Downs:* power and freedom are defined by money, which is seen not as the root of all evil but as the root of all social attitudes and conceptions of good as well. Though characters realize the social order is corrupt and that life is really without meaning, all classes pursue material gains with the same reckless fervor. Such materialism in turn reinforces existing class structures and obscures more significant goals—a theme that anticipates *Sore Throats*.

In *Sore Throats,* Brenton creates an intricate mesh of money, morals, and marriage; he decries a social framework defined by the materialistic impulse. Characters must choose between survival, implying the acceptance of money and therefore of existing moral and social standards, and freedom, which rejects ethics and finances together. Judy's final line, spoken with a flaming match poised to burn the stack of torn banknotes, is a first step to total freedom through anarchy. There can be no question of these two societies—the materialistic and the anarchic—coexisting. In Brenton's typical fashion, the political problems are raised but not solved.

Such attitudes point to Brenton's socialist origins, yet it would be misleading to cite his social convictions as the source of his dramatic power. Brenton above all is a man of the theater, a poet of extraordinary originality and freshness, a craftsman trained by early experiences in the theater to work with minimal technical facilities, a scholar well versed in theater history. Brenton himself may emphasize the political message of his plays as their defining characteristic, but an American audience unfamiliar with the specific political incidents or structures will be immediately drawn by Brenton, the poet.

Brenton writes out of a rich theatrical heritage and exploits literary allusion, both past and present, to anchor his work. *Magnificence* is a prime example: the rebels call their settlement ''Anarchy Farm'' and pay homage to the Brechtian imperative that precedes the play. In the play within *The Churchill Play,* a gong is struck to prevent obscenities from being heard and thereby frightening the ladies—an echo of *A Midsummer-Night's Dream*—and the 1984 setting clearly evokes Orwell. Brenton's use in *Epsom Downs* of naked men to play horses who refuse to race without a ''fixed idea'' is surely a gibe at *Equus,* and Shakespeare's *Measure for Measure* is readapted to exploit specific parallels to Harold Macmillan and Enoch Powell. History for Brenton offers a rich mine to be tapped, a wealth of associations that can easily be exploited for new and shocking effects. (pp. 30-2)

A Brenton play is likely to strike an audience as a patchwork affair—at one moment violent and angry, at another fanciful and humorous, sometimes painfully realistic, often bizarrely creative. *Epsom Downs,* which combines actors playing helicopters by twirling orange day-glow batons, a ghost of a racing accident victim, and such characters as The Race Track and The Race, curiously fuses the blatantly theatrical with naturalistic confessions of self-doubt or sentimental moments of reconciliation—a fascinating combination typical of Brenton's creative eccentricity.

Sore Throats may be seen by many as an exception to this larger rule of creative audacity. The play lends itself to a nat-

uralistic style of interpretation; the setting (within a single room) places the characters in a world one more often expects of Pinter than of Brenton. Jack, Judy, and Sally continually defy naturalistic conventions of psychological consistency, however, and their violent, savage outbursts are all the more brutal for being set in a mundane bare or garbage-strewn apartment. To read the play naturalistically without seeing the larger juxtaposition of the everyday and the darkly primal is dangerous; the theme of wife-beating, for example, then assumes disproportionate importance, and the lurid violence is reduced to mere psychological expression. Brenton, the man of political conviction, is examining issues of far greater scope and uses violence only in the service of larger social themes.

In *Sore Throats* Brenton achieves a new poetic and thematic power. The language is skeletal, clipped, brutal—a verbal reflection of the physical violence, itself a reflection of a perverted social order. Brenton's characters assault one another with every resource; an apparently civil conversation, a traditional dramatic opening, is allowed a mere three words before the veneer of politeness is stripped aside and seething anger is allowed to surface. Secrets become recriminations, key themes are immediately aired—the role of obscenity as a form of social rebellion, the obsession with sexuality, the primary importance of money, and an inability to separate these. The poetic images are horrifying ones—Judy's desire for adders' heads to replace her breasts—and the verbal texture often hypnotic, as in Jack's tale of the baby. At times the play almost becomes a stark, subtle poem, infused with concentric images, yet the sheer theatricality of the story alone keeps the play continually dramatic.

Even in this darker vision, . . . Brenton's typical dependence on humor, albeit black humor, shines forth. Brenton has often commented on the importance of gag writing as a defining mark of maturity in a playwright, bespeaking a confidence and an ability to manipulate the audience. His early humor is frequently epigrammatic—''You are a politician. You never had a political thought in your life'' (*Magnificence*)—as well as situational. *The Churchill Play* opens with Churchill springing up out of his coffin; the liberal friend in *The Saliva Milkshake* concentrates only on drinking from his friend's lips as she expounds the merits of social revolution; *Brassneck* follows the rise and fall of a powerful family finally reduced to running strip joints and selling Chinese heroin to British school children; the revolutionaries in *Weapons of Happiness* target a potato crisp factory. *Sore Throats* especially recalls those early, comic book-like plays. Jack's desire to mate with a twenty-four hour cash-dispensing machine is humorously macabre but thematically revealing in the obsessive conflation of money and sexuality—a reminder that Brenton is at his most serious when he seems most playful and that he employs the fantastic only in service of seriousness.

This condemnation of society, created through theatrics and humor, makes Brenton's solidly socialistic viewpoint more accessible to his audience. Political conviction, complemented by a growing social awareness and by an increasing poetic power, enables Brenton to transcend the trivial and the glib in political theater. (p. 33)

> Ben Cameron, ''Howard Brenton: The Privilege of Revolt,'' in *Theater, Vol. 12, No. 2, Spring, 1981, pp. 28-33.*

RICHARD BEACHAM

When *The Romans in Britain,* Howard Brenton's latest play, opened last October . . . it led to prodigious controversy, the greatest outpouring of comment and the most intense popular interest that British theater has engendered in years. The production was attacked and defended in Parliament and in the Press. Plainclothesmen attended to determine whether charges should be brought. Its merits were debated in the noble institution of the *Times'* letters page. Local politicians thundered their abuse, and the usual guardians of public virtue displayed their own by picketing outside the theater, and staging disruptive protests during performances inside. In short, we were all treated once more to Macaulay's oft-cited and long-running spectacle of the "British public in one of its periodic fits of morality." (p. 34)

In a number of areas the play, if not breaking much new ground, did at least manage to tread on some highly sensitive subjects. Imperialism has been relatively neglected by British playwrights, considering its enormous impact on the nation's history and psychology. It would seem to be one of those topics which, by unwritten convention, in a society still much-subject to such conventions, playwrights have largely avoided. In Brenton's case, his having taken up the subject is particularly intrusive since he deals with it in the context of subject matter otherwise widely treated and intensely popular: the heritage of Roman Britain and, later, the Anglo-Saxon period. In this play the brutality of events and banality of language are used to debunk history, or, differently perceived, to de-mythologize the popular conception of the past. In fact, Brenton largely displaces the myth of the past with a new saga very much of his own devising. His play is loaded with intentional anachronisms of language and incident, and the rapacious and degraded world which it conjures up is, in its contrivance, every bit as artificial and unhistorical, and as much the projected imagination of the playwright as any rhapsody or idyll ever spun out of the Celtic mists.

The Romans in Britain is, however, a good deal less comely and charming than some previous idylls. Without notable exception, all the characters are brutish or violent, and their actions are predictably unattractive. More than any particularly repugnant theme or unpalatable idea, perhaps it was the relentless ill-humor and nastiness of the piece that offended its critics, prompting one to fume: "This play is a nauseating load of rubbish from beginning to end. It is written in a ludicrous pseudo-poetic yob-talk; such themes as it possesses are banal beyond belief." . . . (pp. 35-6)

The play's abiding theme of imperialism, which casts a lurid light on cherished notions of Roman and Anglo-Saxon Britain, also highlights the latterday troubles in Ireland, without providing much illumination of either's history. The treatment and subject seem calculated more to offend than to provide insight. A rough parallel is predicted to exist between Caesar's forces in early Britain, and Britain's forces in present-day Northern Ireland; but beyond providing a certain thematic continuity to the piece, no argument or dialectic develops from the notion. Out of the reiteration of themes too obvious to deserve repetition (men are acquisive louts, war further dehumanizes them, the powerful oppress the weaker, and the oppressed become the oppressor), nothing of substance emerges to jostle an audience into unsettling new perceptions. Neither our understanding nor our capacity for fresh insight is really enlarged. This is the ill-humor of the play: it nurses its own anger and jealously, with little show of concern for its audience, little attempt to move it and thus to convince it.

Much critical response was devoted to the play's nudity, violence, and sexuality. Reviewers felt that these qualities could

be described in any combination of the one noun and two adjectives to adequately sum up their impression of the play. (p. 36)

Since 1968 a number of quite violent and provocative plays, as well as works with explicit sexual activity of every description, have appeared regularly on the British stage. That none was engulfed in anything like the level of controversy surrounding *The Romans* is surely due in part to the play's content, a confluence of controversial subjects remarkable in a single work. Normally discussion about the merits of a particular play as art, or politics, or even as commerce attracts little public attention and generates little heat. What sparked off and sustained the critics' fire in this case was that, by virtue of being presented at the National Theater, the play was liable to be discussed as "culture." The National Theater has come to occupy a very significant place not only in Britain's theatrical life, but, given difficult times and the prevalent awareness of national decline, also as a sort of icon representing the better aspects of British heritage and achievement. *The Romans* was seen by some as striking deeply at the nation's honour and values not only because of its subject matter, but because the thing was perpetrated within the cultural Holy of Holies. . . .

It may well turn out that the ultimate and unwelcome legacy of *The Romans* will not be a change in moral or artistic or political consciousness, but a less tolerant attitude toward the National Theater itself, which brought forth and nurtured Brenton's invasion. (p. 37)

> *Richard Beacham, "Brenton Invades Britain: The 'Romans in Britain' Controversy," in* Theater, *Vol. 12, No. 2, Spring, 1981, pp. 34-7.*

DIANA DEVLIN

In Howard Brenton's *The Romans in Britain* political parallels are overt: the play is set in 54 AD, 515 AD and 1980 AD. The linking image is of stoning the enemy, and the numerous meanings of that act stop it from being a facile equation—slave woman against male runaway, Celt against Roman, against Saxon, against British army. Each episode is sketched fully enough for us to grasp the mixture of human qualities Brenton is concerned with: brutality, caring, cunning, stupidity, fear, greed. I found the immense scope of the play to be its strength, often having been put off Brenton's work by the dogmatic attitude he takes to a specific event. Here, although there is a problem in accepting the premise that the Romans and Saxons in Britain can dramatically reflect the situation in Ulster today, there is a historical perspective and room for vision and aspiration. We see that perspective make the ideal of civilised peace more attractive but at the same time more difficult to achieve. (p. 55)

> *Diana Devlin, "Plays in Print," in* Drama, *No. 140, second quarter, 1981, pp. 55-6.**

BENEDICT NIGHTINGALE

Back in 1943 J. B. Priestley, who could (I suppose) be regarded as Howard Brenton's political and theatrical grand-dad, wrote a play entitled *We Came to a City*, in which a cross-section of hallucinating citizens were confronted with a socialist utopia. Some winced away in genteel distaste; others eagerly embraced its share-alike lifestyle; and the best and boldest made the trip back to waking reality with the intention of transforming glum old Britain into the new Jerusalem whose glistening avenues they'd briefly trod. Then, anything was possible; now, everything seems impossible; and, if you want a pretty vivid illustration of just how far Icarus has plummeted in the intervening years, compare Priestley's soaring vision with the distinctly nightmarish 'dream-play' [*Thirteenth Night*]. . . . Jack Beaty, an earnest young idealist concussed in a dust-up with rampaging fascists, finds that he is the male lead in what rapidly reveals itself to be an updated version of *Macbeth:* or perhaps one should say *Macbeth* and *Julius Caesar,* since Bill Dunn, as his victim and the nation's Labour PM is quaintly called, hides tyrannical instincts under his folksy manner and at one point appears in a bath-towel adjusted to resemble a shaggy toga.

The parallels are wryly unfurled. Beaty, like his prototype, hesitates, scruples, soliloquises, then feebly and somewhat banally protests 'there must be a massive increase of democracy right through the movement' as he succumbs to the blandishments of his mistress. . . . In only two respects is the Macbeth legend substantially revised. Murgatroyd, alias Macduff, is as corrupt as Labour Party potentates usually are in Brenton plays and, far from bringing principled government back to Blighty, dies drunk in his Californian pool; and it's left to the witches, truculent radicals in leather, to polish off the man-monster whose charisma they originally hoped to exploit. . . .

The ending seems a bit meaningless, . . . and the rest of the play has its lapses, too. Brenton's imaginative grasp of the banter swapped by Cabinet ministers seems unremarkable, as witness the 'you're riding high, Jack, but I'm going to screw you' with which Dunn amiably hails Beaty. Is that really how troubled Foots cope with balky Benns? More importantly, it's quite impossible to believe that even a modern Cicero's spoutings about nuclear disarmament, the Third World, multinationals, Ulster, and so on could incite a British crowd to burn down the American embassy and lynch the ambassador. Recent events suggest that he could inflame skinheads to invade immigrant ghettoes or, conceivably, blacks to raze Scotland Yard; but no demagogue is going to rise to supreme power, as Beaty does, on a pious anti-Americanism. The play is based on a manifestly ridiculous premise.

It is also less politically enlightening than it should be. In a sense, *Macbeth* is a lure and snare for Brenton, because it inveigles him into concentrating on the internal corruption of Beaty as, like his tartan forebear, he steps so far in blood that returning were as tedious as go o'er. His emphasis as a dramatist has hitherto been the present state and future prospects of Britain itself, and I, for one, felt puzzled and mildly swindled by his cursory treatment of a subject so obviously congenial to him and relevant to the rest of us. What's going on outside Beaty's Stalinist eyrie, in the factories, the banks, the workingmen's clubs, the police stations, the streets? How does his Praetorian guard sustain his sway, and how does disaffection become insurrection? Brenton can, of course, argue that this is a 'dream', and therefore bound to be substantially personal and subjective; but that only leaves one wondering if the dream was worth chronicling in the first place. Shakespeare has already said most of what needs to be said about the evolution of Beaty as individual and archetype. (p. 24)

Benedict Nightingale, "Poor Players," in New Statesman, Vol. 102, No. 2625, July 10, 1981, pp. 24-5.*

STEPHEN GRECCO

Howard Brenton has written a dozen plays during the past ten

years, almost all of them controversial. To no one's great surprise, *The Romans in Britain* is not an exception. . . . Brenton's intention seems to be to shock his audience into an awareness of how obscene and absurd the world really is, particularly that part which he inhabits, Great Britain, where he detects violence lurking beneath the surface of apparently respectable people who hold positions of power and leadership. Brenton denies that the play is overtly political, but it is hard to see how it could be viewed otherwise, equating as it does the Roman legions with the British military in Northern Ireland. Described by its author as a "peace play," *The Romans in Britain,* when it isn't straining to be left-wing hip, is largely about survival, of both individuals and groups, and about the dreams and myths we create in order to make survival possible. At the end of the play the story of King Arthur is born, to give voice to the aspirations of the defeated.

Plays for the Poor Theatre, whose title seems to have been inspired by the works of the Polish director Jerzy Grotowski, is a collection of five short plays from Brenton's early involvement in London's "fringe" (off-off-Broadway type) theatre. Several of the pieces smack of 1920s agitprop, but all go beyond the merely tendentious through the playwright's facility for creating highly lyrical language and wildly amusing situations. *Christie in Love,* the best of the group, is concerned with a real-life murderer who killed and buried numerous women in and around his London house. The play, "in the Dracula tradition," is designed to stimulate the audience to question the fairness of the social system, to show the parallels between criminals and the police and to illustrate that even a perverted mass murderer is also a human being. Like so much of Brenton's work, it is frightening, amusing, tedious and thought-provoking.

Stephen Grecco, in a review of "The Romans in Britain" and "Plays for the Poor Theatre," in World Literature Today, Vol. 55, No. 4, Autumn, 1981, p. 673.

STEPHEN BROOK

Howard Brenton's new play *The Genius* will not offend the eye though it does abuse the ear. Trevor Eve, clenched fists by his side, clad in a black suit, and looking altogether like a statue of a Bulgarian hero, rants his way through the ungratifying role of Leo, an American Nobel Prize-winning mathematician who is mysteriously exiled to a Midlands university. 'A prickly little shit', the Vice-Chancellor . . . calls Leo, and takes the words right out of my mouth. Leo creates havoc, warping young minds, borrowing wives, serving urine at garden parties and involving both MI5 and the Kremlin in a tug-of-war for the formulae he's devised that are essential to building a new superbomb. Both play and actors lack conviction. Characterization lapses into caricature, and the issues raised by the play—the moral status of and responsibility for dangerous research, and the limits to which 'genius' is morally entitled to go to achieve its dubious ends—neither cohere nor confound in a stirring way. (p. 30)

Stephen Brook, "Crime Wave," in New Statesman, Vol. 106, No. 2739, September 16, 1983, pp. 29-30.*

Ernesto Cardenal

1925-

Nicaraguan poet, translator, and nonfiction writer.

Cardenal writes most of his poetry in a montage style that unites revolutionary political ideology with Roman Catholic theology. Like other modern revolutionary poets, most notably Pablo Neruda, Cardenal focuses his writing on oppression in society and attempts to motivate his readers to bring about social change. Critics often note that Cardenal has been strongly influenced by the poetry of Ezra Pound. Cardenal's juxtaposition of disparate images, his contrast between lyrical and prosaic passages of poetry, and his emphasis on the relationship between socioeconomics and spirituality are devices employed by Pound in his most important work, the *Cantos*. Cardenal's technical skill and the sociopolitical relevance of his work have led one reviewer to praise him as "probably the most stimulating Latin American poet to have emerged since 1950."

In the 1950s Cardenal became deeply involved in the revolutionary politics of Nicaragua and joined forces with those opposed to the dictatorship of the United States-backed Somoza regime. Converting to Catholicism in 1956, he became a novice at Gethsemeni, a Trappist abbey in Kentucky, where he studied under the well-known religious scholar and poet, Thomas Merton. Cardenal completed his studies in Cuernavaca, Mexico, and was ordained a Catholic priest in 1965. He later cofounded Solentiname, a religious commune on an island in Lake Nicaragua, where he preached Mertonian nonviolence. In 1970, however, Cardenal changed his stance on violence and decreed that militancy would be necessary to achieve the Christian goals of peace and brotherhood desired by the anti-Somozan majority. After the downfall of the Somoza regime in 1979, Cardenal was appointed Minister of Culture for the new government of Nicaragua.

Cardenal's first major work, "La hora 0" (1956; "Zero Hour"), was collected along with seven related poems and published as *Zero Hour and Other Documentary Poems* (1980), a poetic history of events leading to the Nicaraguan revolution in 1979. The use of factual information, crosscutting, and contrast in these poems contribute to a style not unlike that used by documentary filmmakers. Cardenal creates a multilevel narrative in his long poem "El estrecho dudoso" (1966) by using similar techniques. On the surface, "El estrecho dudoso" relates a history of destruction in Central America; through comparisons and juxtaposed images, however, the poem becomes a commentary on contemporary political and cultural exploitation. Cardenal's concern with the decline of spiritual values is also evident in his collection *Homenaje a los indios americanos* (1969; *Homage to the American Indians*), in which the psychic wholeness of extinct Indian civilizations is contrasted with modern imperialism, and in *Oracion por Marilyn Monroe, y otros poemas* (1965; *Marilyn Monroe and Other Poems*), in which commercialization is seen to have replaced emotional spontaneity.

Some critics have denounced Cardenal's poetry as propagandistic and didactic. Many find his Marxist treatises incompatible with his Catholic beliefs. However, most agree that

Cardenal avoids mere agitprop through his strong command of poetic technique and his controlled, fact-oriented approach to potentially melodramatic situations.

(See also *Contemporary Authors*, Vols. 49-52 and *Contemporary Authors New Revision Series*, Vol. 2.)

JACK RIEMER

A Psalter for those who live in the last third of the twentieth century has to be more than a collection of pretty hymns. It has to be a collection of cries that help to express our anguish, our embarrassment at being human, and our sense of awe at both the glory and the grimness of human life.

Ernesto Cardenal is a Nicaraguan poet who understands what the Psalms are and what they mean to this generation. . . . [His] rendition of the Psalms [*Psalms of Struggle*] is not the work of a contemplative but of a man who is deeply involved in the affairs of this world. It is the work of one who knows the meaning of words like police brutality, concentration camps, mafia and terror, and who knows these words not only from books but from his own personal experience.

The reader's first reaction to these renditions of the Psalms is surprise. We are not used to finding words like "dictators" or "gangsters" or "crooked politicians" used as translations instead of "wicked" or "scoffers" or "ungodly men." But if you live with these phrases long enough you begin to realize that they come very close in tone and spirit to the original. You begin to remember that the Psalmists were shepherds and farmers, not ministers, and that they spoke simple Hebrew, not King James or Victorian English as we sometimes tend to think.

There are two kinds of Psalms in this collection that will live long in the consciousness of the reader because of their vividness. One kind is the nature psalm that retells the glory of God's world. . . . Cardenal begins one: "You are clothed in atomic power as in a cloak" instead of with the more familiar "light" and he goes on to recount the saga of creation in terms of what we now know from geology and nature study. (pp. 484-85)

The language here is today's but the content and the mood are those of the original Psalm. The vocabulary is contemporary but the exultation, the sheer wonder at the workings of the world, is biblical.

Equally memorable are those Psalms in which Cardenal expresses his horror at the cruelty and the brutality of human life. His anguished outcries over the rapaciousness of the greedy and the viciousness of the dictators are the work of a man who has lived through some of the atrocities of this century. Hitler, Stalin and Mussolini have been the teachers who have enlightened him to the meaning of many passages in the Psalms and current events are very much in his mind as he writes these paraphrases.

Cardenal mixes metaphors from the old and the new and sometimes the juxtaposition creates a surprising effect. For instance, all of us recognize "Near the rivers of Babylon we sit and weep remembering Zion," but we are caught off guard by the next lines: "Looking at the skyscrapers of Babylon and the lights reflected in the river, the glare of the nightclubs and bars of Babylon and listening to their music." Suddenly Babylon has become simultaneously both the arch-example of evil in antiquity and a metaphor for the big city of today. (p. 485)

Those who are only interested in determining just when it was that a Psalmist lived will dismiss this book as unscholarly but those who care about whether the Psalmists still live and speak today will find this an exciting and suggestive work. (p. 486)

Jack Riemer, in a review of "Psalms of Struggle," in Commonweal, *Vol. XCIV, No. 20, September 17, 1971, pp. 484-86.*

ROBERT D. WELCH

An excellent free verse translation presents . . . [Cardenal's] poems of lost American Indian civilizations [*Homage to the American Indians*]. The poetry is clear, lean, and proselike, making effective use of alliteration, repetition, and allusion. Its sharp imagery focuses upon vanished Indian worlds . . . , contemporary destructive forces . . . , and our need for contact with the wellsprings of Indian vitality. . . . Cardenal's eloquent, evocative poetry is fit homage to the rich heritage left us by the American Indians which, he hopes, may lead to the spiritual rebirth of mankind.

Robert D. Welch, in a review of "Homage to the American Indians," in Library Journal, *Vol. 99, No. 1, January 1, 1974, p. 59.*

ANNE FREEMANTLE

[Cardenal] is both naive and subtle in his notes on Cuba [*In Cuba*]. It is as if St. Francis of Assisi were jotting things down, and St. Francis Borgia were editing the jottings. He praises the Cubans . . . and is impressed because everyone gets the same rations, just as in wartime England, or in China until the food situation eased in the 1960's. He repeats three or four times that over 100,000 people voluntarily gave blood for disaster victims in Peru (in the U.S. press, only Castro's gift of a pint was mentioned—by *Time*). But he also reports, on good authority, that there are 7,000 political prisoners in the Havana jail. (pp. 14, 16)

He puts down what people say exactly. . . .

He is wonderfully clear-sighted: "While we are getting less religious, you are getting more so," he tells Paz Espejo, and she replies, "The greatest danger of the revolution is theocracy." . . .

Cardenal concludes that "now, and in Latin America, to practice religion is to make revolution." He seems convinced that Fidel Castro, with his Greek profile, is completely sincere. The whole book is permeated with the posthumous glow of Che Guevara, who for so many millions is the Christ figure of our time. Poet, priest, perhaps polemicist, Fr. Ernesto Cardenal has certainly written by far the most interesting account yet to appear of contemporary Cuba. (p. 16)

Anne Freemantle, "Poetry, Revolution, and Theology," in America, *Vol. 132, No. 1, January 11, 1975, pp. 14, 16.*

GORDON BROTHERSTON

[Cardenal's] first major work, *Hora 0 (Zero Hour)*, and *Epigrams*, emerge from the 'tropical nights of Central America', an atmosphere thick with dictators, misery and injustice. His anger and his reasons for it are comparable with Neruda's in *Canto general*. But his satire has, precisely, an epigrammatic quality and relies less on exposed feelings than on an exposing intelligence, as in his lines on the dictator of Nicaragua: 'Somoza unveils the statue of Somoza in the Somoza Stadium'. Similarly, instead of launching into invective, he documents his subject with the appearance of painstaking accuracy. The detail of occurrence in his hands acquires an absurd yet undeniable certainty. . . . (p. 174)

Cardenal learned to focus on his subject . . . largely through his deep knowledge of poetry in English, especially Pound's. The detailed and exterior language of the Cantos is unmistakable in *Hora 0*, down to such precise techniques as quoting from magazines like *Time*. (In fact his critics have complained that his verse reads like a translation from English.) (p. 175)

Cardenal's great strength is to have allowed 'facts' of the exterior world to speak for themselves while preserving a firm centre from which to arrange them. In these more recent works the first person is in fact not often formally expressed, is sooner implicit, and powerfully so, in the whole configuration of the poem. . . . [In his *Homage to the American Indians*] he will occasionally interpret their being favourably in terms of his own faith [Catholicism], incorporating them as it were into his universe on slight 'evidence'. . . . But this rarely seems forced in a given poem because of his talent for creating a space in which statements, from diverse sources, are cumulative and not pre-emptive. . . . To make his American credo more immediate, Neruda re-shaped history and geography, placed himself in them as the voice that invokes, censures and extols. . . . By convincing us of the 'objective' truth of his immense erudition, the corollary of his faith, Cardenal fuses experience yet more thoroughly and strives for a specifically prophetic tone. This is especially evident in the poems which draw on the Maya prophecies, or *katuns,* which refer to both past and future from some further point; and in his verses on the death of Merton, perhaps his most fulsome profession of understanding of life and the world. (pp. 175-76)

Among his contemporaries Cardenal is exceptional not just for having a faith of such intensity but for expressing it in terms that are politically so exuberant and accessible. (p. 177)

> *Gordon Brotherston, "Modern Priorities," in his*
> Latin American Poetry: Origins and Presence, *Cambridge University Press, 1975, pp. 169-200.**

F. WHITNEY JONES

[*Homage to the American Indian*] celebrates the spiritual strengths of the American Indian and confesses the spiritual weaknesses of modern America. In a torrent of images and phrases ripped out of context, Cardenal juxtaposes fragments of ancient American life with fragments of modern American life. His technique is that of the documentary film maker who juxtaposes two opposing points of view in such a way that the viewer is encouraged to choose one, in Cardenal's case the ancient American. (pp. 85-6)

Cardenal's view of modern America is limited and, more seriously, dated. It is set in the late sixties, and it is a view created by the media. It is so much a product of the media that most of us can no longer respond to it, and Cardenal's allusions to such recent events tend to fall flat.

His view of ancient America is more generous, perhaps too generous. Whereas he limits his view of recent history to the war in Vietnam, technology, and film fantasies . . . , he tends to cover all aspects of life in ancient America. What is most bothersome is his all-encompassing view of the American Indian, . . . which tends to leave a very blurred impression of a rich and extraordinarily diverse culture.

What Cardenal is really paying homage to is not the several million people who lived on the North American continent before the white European arrived, but to a way of life which celebrates peace above war and spiritual strength above personal wealth. One has a strong sense in reading Cardenal that he is using the American Indian as a vehicle to celebrate those values which are most important to him as a well-educated Trappist monk who has dedicated himself to a life of spiritual retreat.

As didactic poetry, Cardenal's verse is really quite effective. There is an energy in his fragmented syntax which gives force to the poet's sense of moral outrage. . . . *Homage to the American Indian* is strong, energetic, and complex verse by a poet of significant talent. (p. 86)

> *F. Whitney Jones, in a review of "Homage to the American Indian," in* The Southern Humanities Review, *Vol. X, No. 1, Winter, 1976, pp. 85-6.*

GREGORY RABASSA

In Cuba has been called reportage for want of exact definition. It is more than that. It is the compendium of Cardenal's far-

ranging impressions during visits to the island in 1970 and 1971. If we must define things by genre, the closest we can come to is the form practiced in Brazil called the *crônica* (chronicle), which is freer than the essay and broader than journalism, the form used, indeed, by so many of the first Europeans who came to the New World and wrote down their impressions. The Cuban José Lezama Lima has used a variant of this same form as fiction in his novel *Paradiso,* thus remaining true to his title, which is drawn from Columbus' chronicles and only indirectly from Dante. The book is also a kind of auxiliary anthology as Cardenal includes several poems by Cuban writers, most of which are Englished here for the first time.

Just as the old chronicles followed the bent of the events and people described, so does this book take on the shape of Ernesto Cardenal's own interests and inquiries and we find that there is indeed a shape to it and quite natural a one at that, unencumbered by the demands of literary formulas or journalistic columns. One is first reminded of that other remarkable compendium, *The Three Marias: New Portuguese Letters,* but here the single presence makes it all more vivid and the only fiction is the one inherent in fragile words themselves as we go our Odyssean way of lying to Athena. (pp. 127-28)

> *Gregory Rabassa, "The Gospel of Marx According to Omolú and According to Jesus," in* Parnassus: Poetry in Review, *Vol. 4, No. 2, Spring-Summer, 1976, pp. 122-29.**

ISABEL FRAIRE

Upon reading [Ernesto Cardenal's poetry] and being hit on the head by the striking and continuous similarities to Pound's poetry in so much of Cardenal's work, you do not get the impression that he is a young poet feeling his way, learning through imitation; these are not the first, promising efforts of a budding genius. You do not get the impression that he is going on to something else, to "find his own voice," etc. No. This is it. This *is* his own voice, and these poems are no fumbling, no lucky, naïve, "early work." They are memorable poems; rounded, masterful, mature work. This is it, all right. This is Ernesto Cardenal.

There seems to be a problem here.

Ernesto Cardenal copies Pound. Well, he does. Anybody can see that. In that case, why have Cardenal at all? Why not eliminate him and stick to Pound? (pp. 36-7)

Cardenal has something to offer us that Pound does not offer, and it is not just a matter of language. Even a good translation of all of Pound into Spanish could not possibly replace Cardenal's poetry. So something has changed, something has been added, making Cardenal's poetry worthwhile to readers of Spanish and even justifying the translation of his poetry into English. There we have it: there is a similarity, a remarkable similarity, which is the main subject of this article. And there is a difference. The result is poetry worth reading and translating, poetry which moves, which sticks in the mind and even, I would venture to say, is likely to influence some people's view of the world. Ernesto Cardenal *is* a great poet *despite* the fact that he obviously copies Pound. . . .

Cardenal is a great poet, but not an inventor of forms. After all, how many poets are? And . . . he merely took a form, a structure, a pattern which Pound had invented, and used it for his own purposes, filled it with his own content. A Latin American content. (p. 37)

As I see it Cardenal's poetry falls roughly into three batches:

a) The short, epigrammatic poems. No need to overstress Pound's influence here since, guided or not by Pound, Cardenal had recourse to Pound's Latin models, and it is to them that final reference should be made. (pp. 37-8)

Incidentally, these short poems of Cardenal seem to have sparked or, perhaps, reinforced, a whole new trend among some of the younger Latin American poets.

b) The longer, canto-like poems where Pound's influence is unquestionable and unquestioned. Cardenal himself willingly admits it.

c) The rest of Cardenal's poems stemming from various other sources, although nearly always playing very closely on the original models, in a way reminiscent of Pound's personae. In *Cantares Mexicanos I* and *II* and *Netzahualcóyotl* we get a blend of *b* and *c* where, using the basic canto form, he sticks so steadily to the style of the Náhuatl originals, or rather to the Spanish versions of them, that the effect is quite different from either the canto or the Náhuatl poems.

Of these three categories the only one that concerns me here is *b,* since though Pound can hardly be said to have invented the epigram, although he may have reactivated it, we can safely say that Pound invented the Canto. (p. 38)

In the first place, of course, the idea itself: history into poetry, but direct from the *sources* as often as possible and convenient. Since this history can be from any period, including the contemporary, the sources are of all kinds: histories, documents, letters, newspapers, books, anecdotes, personal recollections, etc. Either the exact words, or the style of the original are kept. Where the poet substitutes his own voice for the sources, he usually either imitates them or keeps to a terse, matter-of-fact retelling. This characteristic shows up very clearly on comparing Cardenal's poetry to Neruda's *Canto General.* Setting aside the metrical differences that are immediately obvious, you see an entirely different emotional approach to the matter at hand. Neruda is always exhorting or declaiming or dramatically questioning the reader. He is always present as first-person in the poem. This Whitmanesque attitude is radically different from the "reportage" attitude of Pound and Cardenal, which is strongly reminiscent of Brecht's approach: don't get the spectator emotionally involved, present the material and let him think for himself—but of course they do get the reader emotionally involved, they just go about it differently. This difference is quite enough to explain why, even though the subject matter of Neruda and Cardenal is more than similar—it is, in fact, nearly identical—the poetry is so different.

The dominant tone is usually one of plain statement or quotation: however, at times, it is much more *cantabile.* We get passages of a sustained, descriptive lyricism (or what I would call lyricism) where the intense beauty and harmony of nature or of a certain social order or life style are presented. This is more frequent in Cardenal, perhaps, than in Pound, and in these passages Cardenal indulges in a greater fluidity, linking each line to the next to make the general effect more singing and harmonious and carry the reader forward constantly. In the *reportage* passages the lines coincide more frequently with complete statements, stopping short at the end, achieving in this way a certain finality, and reinforcing the non-subjective

attitude. I suppose one could say that Pound is more frequently choppy and Cardenal more frequently fluid.

The presentation is fundamentally that of the *collage,* the juxtaposition of fragmented material producing frequent and ever richer cross-references and slowly building up several levels of meaning.

The number of lines per canto and the length of the lines follow no set rule.

There are no rhymes at the end of the lines linking them in a set pattern; however, rhymes do occur quite often by repetition of words, or stems of words, or whole phrases, either at the end of lines or at the end of one line and in the middle or even at the beginning of another, or after intervening lines. Where they do occur, these rhymes serve a purpose related to the content.

You sometimes get whole chunks of poetry which seem to follow a rhythmical pattern clearly recognizable to the ear and the emotional response, but difficult or impossible to reduce to metrical rules. . . . [In] reading Cardenal I very often came across lines or sets of lines strongly reminiscent of Pound's from a rhythmical, aural point of view. So close as to be echoes, and often of a very poignant beauty.

Part of the reason for the Poundian ring to many of Cardenal's lines, and probably linked to the rhythm, is the syntactical peculiarity which distinguishes so many of them: inversion of the usual word order, elimination of, say, verbs, or of conjunctions or prepositions, use of nouns or participles instead of verbs, etc. (pp. 38-9)

There is also what I would call Pound's bag of tricks or rhetorical devices:

a) Repetition at long intervals of a single line (or word or phrase) with slight variations, tying the whole poem or series of poems together and giving a sub-theme or meaning. . . .

b) The use of words, phrases or sentences in parentheses as commentaries or reminders.

c) The capitalization of words and sentences either as a kind of visual shouting (Pound either realized or fancied that most people are deaf) or because these words or sentences are brand names or advertisements usually seen capitalized in print or signs.

d) The use of numbers, as a non-poetic intrusion into the poem and as a reference (sometimes ironic) to our number-ridden society, or to stress that what he is telling about actually happened.

e) The use of concrete, factual detail, here again to impress on the reader that what he is telling about actually happened.

f) The insertion of a single emotionally charged line in the middle of matter treated in a different, more prosaic way. . . .

g) The use of names and surnames of individuals, sometimes principal, sometimes very secondary characters.

h) The use of quotations in quotation marks.

i) The way of cutting into quotations, beginning them in midsentence, or breaking them off, thus heightening the dramatic effect and sometimes giving depth by oblique reference to the unquoted part.

j) The use of fragmentation or interruption, applied not only to quotations but to sentences or trains of thought, sometimes for economy, sometimes for drama, sometimes for both.

k) The use of words and sentences in foreign languages.

l) The explanation of same in parentheses next to the original word or sentence.

m) The use of repetition, not as in a) but in immediate or nearly immediate lines, in order to rub something in or explore different variations of meaning. . . .

n) The use of anecdotes as illustrations of meaning or as part of the story.

And, of course, although this has to do with content and not with form, one shouldn't forget the presence in Cardenal of certain recurring themes which form part of the basic conceptual network of his poetry, as of Pound's. These themes are the corrupting effect of moneymaking as the overriding value in a society; the importance of precision and truthfulness in language; the degradation of human values in the world which surrounds us; the search through the past (or, in Cardenal's poetry, in more "primitive" societies, a kind of contemporary past) for better world-models. (p. 40)

It might be pertinent here to indicate the similarity of the uses to which the Canto has been put, first by Pound and then by Cardenal: recreation of historical periods, both ancient and contemporary; biography; catchall for scraps of political, economic, philosophical theorizing; recreation of literary precedents and myths. It might justifiably be argued that Cardenal has used the Canto for all of them, but especially for the first two, in his recreation of the Spanish conquests, the pre-Columbian theocracies, the Somoza dictatorship and contemporary political scene in Central America, and the biographies of tyrants and indigenous leaders. When he uses it to sing the exploits of sixteenth-century conquerors or twentieth-century guerrillas, it becomes, even more than in Pound's hands, a *canción de gesta,* a song of action, and Cardenal rightly steps up the tempo, drops distracting elements, and gets closer to a good cowboy movie than to a Pound Canto in his effects. (p. 41)

And now, perhaps, it is time to point out the differences between Cardenal's cantos and Pound's. These differences can be boiled down to a more *classical* approach, a sparer and more economical and functional use of the resources discovered by Pound. A greater consideration for the reader, and a willingness to seduce him instead of making demands on him.

Where Cardenal uses Pound's break-off, juxtapositions, contrasts, and similar, effective but potentially confusing techniques, he does so more sparingly, leaving the structure much more visible to the naked eye than does Pound, easier to grasp and appreciate esthetically, less cluttered or hazy, and demanding less concentration and effort on the part of the reader.

On occasion, as I mentioned before, Cardenal presents his material in a highly dramatic way, creating a mounting suspense reminiscent of a good adventure movie that completely overwhelms the reader—*any* reader—and makes it impossible for him to put the book down until he finishes the poem. . . .

Cardenal makes few if any demands on the reader's previous education. This does not mean that there are not abundant literary and historical references in his work. (There are, and it is significant that the ordinary Latin American with a middling traditional education spots them easily.) Rather, I mean

that Cardenal has realized Pound's fond hope that the reader would not need anything but the poems themselves in order to understand everything in them. I am afraid Pound was mistaken in this illusion in regard to his own Cantos, but Cardenal seems to me to have succeeded where Pound failed. I think any Spanish or Latin American reader with a secondary or even a good grade-school education—which would ordinarily include a sketchy working knowledge of the Spanish conquest, of the great pre-Columbian civilizations and of the contemporary political scene—needs no reference books for a satisfactory reading of Cardenal's Cantos.

Perhaps another and deeper difference is that Cardenal is rooted in a wider cultural conscience. Where Pound seems to spring up disconnected from his own contemporary cultural scene and to be working against it, putting his roots through books into the past, Cardenal is born into a ready-made cultural context and shared political conscience. Cardenal's past is common to all Latin Americans. His present is likewise common to all Latin Americans. He speaks to those who are ready and willing to hear him and are likely to agree on a great many points. (p. 42)

Isabel Fraire, "Pound and Cardenal," in Review, *No. 18, Fall, 1976, pp. 36-42.*

JAMES J. ALSTRUM

[Ernesto Cardenal's] long narrative poem, *El estrecho dudoso* (1966), has not been adequately studied to date as an artistic whole. Like Pablo Neruda . . . in *Canto General* (1950), Cardenal employs the epic form in his poem to effectively criticize the socio-political realities of Nicaragua prior to the overthrow of the Somoza regime while recreating the traditional history of the colonization of Central America by viewing it as a search for social justice as much as an attempt to find an inland channel through which passage from the Atlantic to the Pacific Ocean could be achieved. Some critics have seen this account in verse of the first century of Spanish colonization as an indirect attack on the military dictatorships and oligarchies (such as the Somoza dynasty) which have dominated most of the region. However, they do not go beyond this observation to appreciate fully the intricate artistry with which Cardenal has intertwined the past and present through myth and history while employing both modern and ancient narrative techniques in his poem. (p. 9)

Cardenal's way of handling his material is not just an interpolation of random texts to create the effect of an ideogram in the manner of Ezra Pound. More importantly, the Nicaraguan poet's abundant use of prefiguration throughout this poem to call the reader's attention to the present situation of his own country and the rest of Central America, represents a clear example of the application of typology—a traditional literary technique first used by the writers of the Bible. Typology contributes to the development of theme and the arrangement and sequencing of historical events in such a way that they acquire a prophetic significance which transcends history. Together with the typological foreshadowing of his poem, Cardenal also relies on other narrative techniques commonly found in prose rhetoric as he attempts to convince the reader of the validity of his prophetic vision. He foresees an inevitable social upheaval which will topple Central America's traditionally tyrannical regimes of terror, and lead to a new order of social and economic justice. The typological juxtaposition of the present and the past as well as the present and the future is not only found in *El estrecho dudoso.* This technique is employed in much of Cardenal's poetry, particularly in books such as *Hora 0, Salmos,* and the poem, **"Apocalipsis."** However, it is in this epic poem where Christian typology and teleology most parallel the Bible as structuring elements which integrate detail and plot with symbolic imagery. As we analyze Cardenal's poem, we must also keep in mind the poet's activist concept of Christianity which is expressed in a poetry of prophetic witness inseparable from his revolutionary political ideology. (pp. 9-10)

Cardenal has combined biblical typology with several narrative techniques to develop his central theme of the heroic quest for social justice which coincided with the Spanish conquerers' futile search for a waterway to link the Atlantic and Pacific Oceans. There are recurring mentions of both the search for the narrow strait and the pursuit of social justice which convert them into the principal motifs of the entire poem. The historic exploration of the isthmus, with the hope of finding a way to connect the oceans, is the predominant motif in the first half of the poem although both quest motifs converge or overlap in several cantos. However, in the final and climactic canto of the poem, the search for social justice has clearly become the dominant motif proclaimed through the repeated outcries for justice of a series of dramatized narrators and an omniscient narrator who constantly intervenes throughout the epic poem. In both an historical context and Cardenal's work itself, the Spanish conqueror fails in his enterprise just as the aspirations of the common people for justice have likewise been frustrated throughout most of Central America's history. (pp. 10-11)

As we view Cardenal's epic as an artistic whole, we will see that two kinds of foreshadowing emerge in which earlier events presage later ones and in so doing attain their fulfillment. I will call this first kind of foreshadowing "internal prefiguration" because it occurs when an initial event within the narrative poem prefigures a similar happening a few years later. For example, Balboa's unjust execution by Pedrarias due to a false accusation is repeated later in the case of Francisco Hernández de Córdoba, who becomes another victim of the tyrant's envy after having founded Nicaragua's two most important colonial cities: Granada and León. The poetic narrator implicitly reminds the reader of the historical parallel between Balboa and Hernández de Córdoba when the latter does not heed the warning of his men nor flees after Pedrarias has falsely accused him of leading an insurrection. . . . The internal prefiguration found in Cardenal's poem is purely literary or textual because it only points toward a recurrence of a parallel event in the narrative poem without having a direct or explicit relationship with a recognizable occurrence in our own time. (pp. 11-12)

Internal prefiguration is often reinforced by the disclosure of important information by the poetic narrator at opportune moments in the poem. For example, after Córdoba's execution, there is a succinct summary of the discoverer's accomplishments which contrast implicitly with the reader's knowledge of Pedrarias' opportunistic exploitation of the achievements of other men for his own personal gain. . . . Here, as in many other parts of the poem, the omniscient poetic narrator has summarized data or privileged information which would not be readily known by the reader in order to influence his appraisal of the men or events depicted from a moral standpoint. Multiple narrators often join with the principal poetic narrator to reveal information gleaned from a variety of sources such as diaries, epistles, government decrees, documents, proclamations, petitions, and private inventories and listings of business transactions. Wayne C. Booth has called the narrative technique of providing different kinds of disclosures, such as those which are found in *El estrecho dudoso,* "reliable commentary." The authoritative manner with which the omniscient narrator speaks as he reveals his information enables the entire poem to acquire an oracular tone reminiscent of the biblical prophets or evangelists. (pp. 12-13)

Cardenal's poem also contains a second kind of prefiguration which is external or extraliterary because it depends on the reader's knowledge of recent Central American history in which there are recognizable ties between the colonial period dealt with in the work and today's political and socio-economic situation in Nicaragua and throughout the region. Often external prefiguration is also coupled with the narrative technique known as "reliable commentary." The poetic narrator intrudes to provide the reader with factual information which will enable him to appreciate better the full significance of the events presented. However, the narrative commentary in *El estrecho dudoso* is seldom impartial or unbiased despite its apparent objectivity because the poet clearly desires to persuade the reader to accept his condemnatory or laudable interpretation of an incident and the moral conduct of the characters involved. Usually Cardenal's poetic narrator intervenes to guide the reader toward a greater awareness of the historical analogies between the past and the present through an explicit mention of the Somoza family or a parenthetical remark which is ironic. The intervention of the omniscient narrator adds an evaluative and often ironic commentary which influences the reader's attitude toward the characters and his emotional response to their actions. The historical figures also reveal their personalities as they are portrayed in the narration of events. Some of the characters may also mask the poet's opinion of the people and events described by becoming his spokesman or being allied sympathetically to another person in the poem. (pp. 14-15)

[In the canto about Predrarias which follows the account of Córdoba's death, both] external and internal prefiguration are joined . . . to foreshadow the concluding canto of the entire poem. At the same time, the poem acquires a prophetic function because the poetic narrator implies that there will be an eventual fulfillment of the promise of social redemption prefigured by the incidents and historic characters of the past. The events depicted in the culminating cantos of the poem suggest that the past history of Pedrarias' Nicaragua will be repeated with the overthrow of the Somoza dynasty. The distinction between the past and present is effectively blurred when the description of León Viejo, as it appears today, submerged under the waters of Lake Managua, is presented in the same context with the revelation that Pedrarias' grave is also found there in the old cathedral next to the tomb of his victim, Hernández de Córdoba. The eerie atmosphere evoked by the description of León Viejo, as a cursed city buried beneath a lake, converts the setting into a ghostly reminder of Nicaragua's heritage of tyrannical evil which will not be allowed to go unpunished. (pp. 17-18)

The employment of a typological narrative strategy to arrange the sequence of incidents and underline a central theme is enhanced by the presence of historic characters who function as dramatized narrators. Most of the heroic figures in the poem act as spokesmen for Cardenal's point of view. Even when they apparently speak for themselves these narrators exemplify the technique which Booth has labelled "telling as showing." Through "telling as showing," the direct intervention of an omniscient narrator is avoided and the characters not only reveal their own personalities but provide information which is credible to the reader due to the character's proximity in time and space to the events described. Although there is no central character in Cardenal's poem akin to the messiah in the Old and New Testaments, there are nevertheless groups of heroic martyrs in constant conflict with an opposing series of villainous exploiters like Pedrarias. In other words, just as in the Old Testament, there is constant struggle between the chosen people of Israel and the imperialist Gentile rulers of antiquity, also in *El estrecho dudoso,* there emerge two clearly opposing forces of victims (mainly the Indians and the common people) and executioners. Such an arrangement of diametrically opposed groups can be simplified further in moral terms as a conflict between the forces of good and evil. (p. 19)

Cardenal wants his reader to see and be moved by the recurring causes of injustice and be able also to identify its perpetrators. Therefore, his epic poem, although well documented, must be stripped of all adornments or hermetic metaphors. A close reading of *El estrecho dudoso* reminds us that today's Spanish American poetry increasingly utilizes the narrative techniques which were heretofore reserved for exclusive use in prose. Although many readers of *El estrecho dudoso* may neither share the faith nor hope on which the poem is based, nobody can deny that, as in the Bible, the Nicaraguan poet seeks to convince men that history contains lessons which have a transcendant significance. The poem also reaffirms the Judeo-Christian belief that there is an inexorable progression of historical events which point toward the ultimate consummation of the Divine Word. Cardenal himself views his poetry as merely the medium for his hopeful message of the transformation of the old order into a new and more just society in which the utopian dreams and Christian values of men like Bartolomé de Las Casas can finally be realized. (p. 24)

> *James J. Alstrum, "Typology and Narrative Techniques in Cardenal's 'El estrecho dudoso'," in Journal of Spanish Studies: Twentieth Century, Vol. 8, Nos. 1 & 2, Spring & Fall, 1980, pp. 9-27.*

ROBERT PRING-MILL

All Cardenal's poetry "debunks," "corroborates," and "mediates" reality. His esthetic principles are clearly ethical, and most of his poems are more than just "vaguely" religious. (p. ix)

[All] eight texts of *Zero Hour and Other Documentary Poems* set out to "document" reality (and so redeem it) in a . . . dialectically visual way: picturing things, peoples, and events in the light of a clear-cut sociopolitical commitment; selecting, shaping, and imposing interpretative patterns on the world, with liberal use of such filmic "editing" techniques as cross-cutting, accelerated montage, or flash frames; and pursuing "the redemption of physical reality" by bringing us "back into communication" with its harshness and its beauty. Poets and cameras can both affect what they record, but whereas a documentary camera's presence conditions the "on-going situation," Cardenal's recording of the present or the past is aimed at helping to shape the future—involving the reader in the poetic process in order to provoke him into full political commitment, thus fostering the translation of the poet's more prophetic visions into sociopolitcal fact. (pp. ix-x)

None of the longer poems is simple, though they all aim at surface clarity, being meant for a wide public. They are strictly "factual," but facts can be double-edged, and their juxtapo-

sitions can also set up further meanings. Cardenal's reader cannot just sit back and "listen" to the words and rhythm: he has to visualize sequences of disparate images (each one a snatched glimpse of reality), noting their pairings and progressions, matching them both with each other and with what is left unsaid—and thereby sharing in the extraction of their fuller "meaning." These poems demand more than just an alert response, because the poet wishes to prod us beyond thought and into action: his texts are never just concerned to document and understand reality, but also to help change it—which is why they have been called "The Poetry of Useful Prophecy." But the data have to be recorded before reality can be reshaped, and the reshaping lies beyond the poems themselves: the changes for which the poet yearns lie in the future. (p. x)

[The environment in **"Trip to New York"** is familiar] and this account of a rushed six-day trip is the closest thing in any of the longer poems to the direct reporting of immediate experience, as in a personal diary. It ought to be read, however, as a deliberately "public" diary, and also *strictly as poetry:* its appearance of uncommitted objectivity is a studied one, achieving its effects (as almost always in his better poems) obliquely, by poetic means—although its "images" *are* real, not metaphorical. They may seem as clear and as immediately revealed as snapshots taken with a Polaroid camera —photos which materialize "before one's very eyes," often still in the presence of the objects photographed (in "real life") against which one is able to control the degree of "likeness" which the camera has captured. But readers cannot match these shots against what they depict, and they have all been carefully selected and assembled. . . . The process is less intellectual than intuitive: when pressed to say *how* he selects which details of "reality" to represent, Cardenal can never rationalize his procedure, saying no more than that he "knows" which details will turn out to be "poetic" in a given context. The shots he uses are, naturally, "angled" (so are a camera's): taken from the poet's individual viewpoint, which always has inherent ethical and moral preoccupations. They have been chosen and grouped (however intuitively) with a sure sense for thematic links and quiet ironies—some of which the poet makes explicit, but not all. Thus it would be rather naïve to take **"Trip to New York"** as no more than a simple diary, or a piece of instant reportage couched in free verse.

Readers would do well to examine Cardenal's methods in the familiar context of that known environment before they move into the half-alien Latin American world of the remaining poems, the first of which—**"Zero Hour"** (**"Hora 0"** or **"La hora cero"**)—is certainly the best-known of all his longer poems. As it is also the one which displays many of his favorite techniques in their most graspable form, it merits examination at somewhat greater length by way of introduction to the much later series of post-Cuban documentary poems. **"Zero Hour"** is in four parts: a brief opening section, in the nature of an introit, establishing the mood of Central American life under dictatorships, followed by three separate episodes. The first one concerns the economic factors underlying the politics of "banana republics"; the second is about Sandino, culminating in his treacherous execution (along with his brother Sócrates and two of his own commanders) on Tacho's orders, within three weeks of peace having been signed; while the third concerns the Conspiración de Abril, an anti-Somozan plot which misfired (in April 1954), in which Cardenal himself took part. (pp. xvi-xvii)

The whole introit depends on swiftly effective contrasts, whose "meaning" is not spoilt by being spelled out: the Guatemalan dictator with "a head cold," while his people are dispersed with phosphorous bombs; a single window of the Honduran dictator's office smashed, provoking an inappropriately violent response from armed police. Such introductory "shots" build up the setting and its atmosphere in the same terms and ways as does the opening sequence of almost any film. Other techniques which will recur appear in the three episodes. Thus the collage of documentary sources in the "economic" sequence, with its oppressive and depersonalizing lists of company names and alienating juxtapositions of contrastive factual details, will become a characteristically Cardenalian technique (one learned from Pound, and which has influenced many younger Spanish American poets through its use by Cardenal). Equally characteristic are the shafts of irony, often dependent on the reversal of an expected phrase—like "Carías is the dictator / who didn't build the greatest number of miles of railroad" (in Honduras).

The Sandino episode brings in many favorite themes: heroic self-abnegation, the purity of motives, and the egalitarian virtues of a guerrilla force "more like a community than like an army / and more united by love than by military discipline"—features he will all use much later as heroic precedents, when depicting the Sandinista *guerrilleros* of the following generation. At one stage, he punctuates the action with repeated snatches of "Adelita" (perhaps the favorite song of the 1910 Mexican Revolution), intensifying the vision of Sandino's forces as a "happy army" since "A love song was its battle hymn." This is a typically filmic use of song. Filmic, too, is the accelerated montage of the death sequence, with its visual and aural crosscutting between parallel actions: the exchanges between Somoza and the American minister (and later between the American minister and Moncada) punctuated by the digging of a grave, a glimpse of prisoners, and the halting of Sandino's car, whose unnamed passengers are hustled off to face the firing squad.

Similar devices are used in the third episode. Cardenal's own entry on the scene intensifies the mood ("I was with them in the April rebellion / and I learned how to handle a Rising machine gun"). Its effect is—characteristically—heightened by the lack of further elaboration, as the "I-was-there" device gives way to the stark understatement of the hunting down and slaughter of Adolfo Báez Bone, whose identification with the land in which his body lies ensures his resurrection in the collective body of his people (a theme which becomes a leitmotif in later poems). The lyrical use of landscape and the seasons to echo or contrast with man's affairs—a striking feature of both the second and the third episodes—is a device which will achieve even greater prominence in "**Nicaraguan Canto**," the "**Oracle**," and both "**Epistles**."

An understanding of how "**Zero Hour**" establishes its points helps greatly with later poems, where the chronological sequence of events is deliberately dislocated by abrupt (but often unspecified) temporal intercutting, while the poetic texture is complicated by far greater use of understated or oblique "symbolic images"—or brief references whose wider connotations only emerge with hindsight, like the thrush which "sings / in freedom, in the North" (in the first few lines of "**Nicaraguan Canto**"): an unstated echo of Sandino, later to be revealed as the first hint of the presence of contemporary Sandinista freedom fighters in the same Northern hills. "**Nicaraguan Canto**" (whose Spanish title—*Canto Nacional*—is as much a Nerudian as a Poundian echo) culminates in one of Cardenal's most

startling *tours de force:* its last nine lines consist entirely of birdsong—not a device which any translator could hope to reproduce with much success.

After the "**Canto**," "**Mosquito Kingdom**" ("***Reino mosco***") provides easier reading, starting with the factual parody of Western pomp at the drunken coronation of a black British-sponsored puppet king as nominal ruler of the scattered nineteenth-century British settlements along the Mosquito Coast (all the way from Belize to Costa Rica), peopled by English-speaking former slaves from the West Indies, the Miskito Indians themselves, and the mixed race born of their intermarriage. The poem jumps forward in time to the pompous ostentation of Cornelius Vanderbilt's huge private yacht *North Star* and Vanderbilt's involvement in the attempted exploitation of that Caribbean coast, and then cuts to a series of sordid and ill-fated dealings among its actual or would-be exploiters. Although the obscurity of this facet of nineteenth-century Nicaraguan local history may puzzle foreign readers, there is no missing the point of Cardenal's satirical devices.

"**Oracle over Managua**" ("***Oráculo sobre Managua***") is a more somber and a far more complex poem. The earthquake which destroyed the city in 1972 is merely the latest stage of a long geological process, and the poem harks back to the long-past eruption which recorded the feet of fleeing prehistoric men and beasts in a layer of volcanic mud which later turned to stone, out at Acahualinca: the site of one of the worst of the shanty-towns which fringe Managua, to which the tourists and the seminarians used to go (their eyes averted from the slums) to view the Footprints. One of these seminarians, the poet Leonel Rugama, became a Sandinista, and in the sections of the poem which are addressed to him Cardenal expresses their shared view of "Revolution" as the natural next stage of "Evolution"—a process started in the stars, millions of years ago, and which will require social metamorphoses as startling as those from caterpillar into chrysalis or chrysalis to butterfly. Rugama was cornered in a house in Managua by the National Guard on January 15, 1970, along with two other young urban guerrillas, and the siege of the house where they holed up was watched by thousands of Managuans—as helicopters, planes, and even tanks were brought in to eliminate them. This small but epic incident in the Sandinista saga is made to interact, at numerous levels and in various complex ways, with the far greater catastrophe of the earthquake, in a highly intricate poetic structure.

After "**Oracle over Managua**," the "**Trip to New York**" ("***Viaje a Nueva York***") seems easy, and neither "**Epistle**" poses such problems of interpretation as the earlier poems because Cardenal's attitudes are stated more explicitly, for patently didactic purposes, while "**Lights**" ("***Luces***") is equally accessible. The visual and associative material used to frame the ideas in these four poems is, however, handled with Cardenal's accustomed skill: shifts of focus or of angle; cuts from close up or detail shots right through to extreme long; jump-cuts for the sake of concision and abruptness; the poetic equivalent of pans and zooms; deft insert shots (to give additional data); the use of flashbacks (and flash-forwards), or of bridging shots (like those of railway wheels or newspapers in films); foreshortening and forelengthening, applied both to space and to time (where films would use the time lapse camera or slow motion); studied relational editing; match-cuts which link two disparate scenes by the repetition of an action or a shape (or a sound)—but most of all the dialectical process of "collisional" montage, which generates fresh meaning out of the meanings of adjacent shots.

Cardenal's highly visual poetry displays the verbal equivalent of each of those effects, and many of his most vivid sequences could almost serve as detailed shooting scripts.

All these devices, together with Poundian textual collage and the full range of more traditional poetic or rhetorical effects, are used in the course of Cardenal's documentary "redemption of reality," which successively "corroborates," "debunks," or "mediates" things, people, and events in a validation process designed to govern what we are to consider "true" and "real" and "meritorious" (or "false"—"illusory"—"contemptible") when viewed from the standpoint of his brave new revolutionary world. (pp. xxviii-xxi)

> *Robert Pring-Mill, "The Redemption of Reality through Documentary Poetry," in* Zero Hour and Other Documentary Poems *by Ernesto Cardenal, edited by Donald D. Walsh, translated by Paul W. Borgeson, Jr. & others, New Directions, 1980, pp. ix-xxii.*

JASCHA KESSLER

The Preface to a volume of poems by Ernesto Cardenal, entitled *Zero Hour and Other Documentary Poems,* says bluntly about the poet that he "is a Catholic Priest and a Marxist poet, and he sees no conflict between these two loyalties." And the poems in this volume, long works that read in English like amalgams of Walt Whitman, Ezra Pound, Pablo Neruda and Allen Ginsberg, amply demonstrate the fusion in his mind of these two institutions, the Church of Rome and the Leninist dogmas of atheistic dialectical materialism, two mirror opposites in philosophy as well as in the real world. Or, if not opposites, then contraries, as William Blake would have put it. Of course, appearances may be misleading: the Catholic Church has an almost two thousand-year history of practical organization of society, of many diverse societies and cultures in fact, of missionary work and conversion of unbelievers to the faith; and likewise, Leninist Marxism, as directed from its infallible, and totalist seat in the Kremlin, has for the 60 years of this century aimed at missionary conversion of whole societies to the dogma of Marxism, which describes itself as "scientific" socialism. The absolutism of both the Church of Rome, if not of most religious beliefs, and the absolutism required of the believers in the faith called "the Revolution," are not formally dissimilar, and the varied techniques of forcible conversion are part of their history. Of course, the Catholic Church has not used armies since Rome was liberated in 1870. . . . But the Marxist revolutionary movements in various parts of the world do not hesitate to use the force of arms to make their materialist cult prevail whenever and wherever possible. . . . And despite the fact that since Cuba became monolithically Marxist, which means that the other Latin power, that of the Catholic Church, must be suppressed, there are many other places below the Border, so to speak, where the social, religious and political struggle for power and ultimate control still go on, and go on in ways almost incomprehensible to the Americans of the Northern Hemisphere. . . .

What I want to convey . . . is my sense of amazement at the really unholy brew that goes into the making of these poems, the fusion and confusion of styles and meanings: the adaptation of Pound's work, especially that of the lifelong failed epic, *The Cantos,* with its hectic crypto-Fascist historiography, and the ideology of the Catholic Worker-Priests, the anti-liberal, anti-bourgeois, anti-capitalist and fundamentally socialist priests of Latin America . . . , as well as the well-trained terrorist-guerrillas sent out by Castro and trained by Russian professionals from the KGB. What it all comes from directly is also partly Pablo Neruda's influence. . . . It is a grotesque and really quite surreal situation, because facts and truths are hardly part of the intellectual makeup or discipline of middle-class revolutionaries. Indeed, Cardenal speaks always bluntly, saying things like:

> There is no communion with God or with
> man if there are classes,
>   if there is exploitation
> there is no communion.

You can hear Pound talking there, disguised as the ghost of the very young Karl Marx, the convert to Christianity. And Cardenal finishes that statement by saying:

> They've told me I talk only about politics now.
> It's not about politics but about Revolution
> which for me is the same thing as the kingdom of god.

All of which does not mean that *Zero Hour* is not an interesting book, or that Cardenal is not an interesting poet, even though one is reading him in translation. Even so, I suspect that he is not writing "poetry" in the usual senses. What we have here are eight "documentary poems," and they are very long pieces in the by-now familiar montage technique. Cardenal does in fact lend himself most easily to being read as an imitator in language of the techniques of the film. He speaks of the "documentary redemption of reality." This is most peculiar terminology indeed; but by now we know that documentary is scarcely synonymous with fact, and that it is part of the illusory power of film itself to seem to be recording the facticity of everyday reality, whereas it is just as highly organized and manipulated an artifact as drama: it is made, like poetry.

One thing is very clear about this whole book, including the long poem about the great earthquake that destroyed Managua, a very vivid poem indeed, and that is that Cardenal has, in his content, if not his form, taken a very long step beyond his two principal poetic models, Ezra Pound and Father Thomas Merton. Pound wanted his poetry to be politically effectual, and he was content to live under Mussolini's Fascist dictatorship and to make violent propaganda broadcasts against the United States during the Second World War. Merton's work is equally forceful, despite his perfect commitment to strict nonviolence. Cardenal is committed himself to violence, to warfare, to a most radical, most militant form of Christianity. He is unequivocal about it: for him Christianity is Marxism, literally. As Minister of Culture now in Nicaragua he is too busy with programs of education and combatting illiteracy to be writing more poems. But since his work in poetry is a form of agitprop, and since he espouses the Leninist principle that "ethics are the esthetics of the future," we may learn a good deal about the mentality and the ideals of Latin revolutionaries, these desperate intellectuals who now represent forces engaged in what may be the last struggle in which we can see an uncynical Marxist revolutionary fervor. It is serious, it is naive, it is unhistorical and unreasoned in the extreme, but it should be understood. It may well be that Cardenal's poems offer us a very clear entrance into the mentality of the men we are facing in the current bloody guerrilla warfare of Central America. Passionate propaganda, and poor poetry though it may often be, it is far better suited for our grasp of the reality these fighters see than what we get from columnists in the newspapers. . . .

It is clearly handy to be a trained priest, and to have available for one's poetry the voices of Amos, Isaiah, Hosea and Jeremiah, and to mix prophetic vision with the perspectives of violent revolutionary Marxist ideology. It makes for an incendiary brew indeed. It is not nice; it is not civilized; it is not humane or sceptical or reasonable. But it is all part of the terrible heritage of Central Latin America. And since these 99 pages of Cardenal's poetry over a period of 20 years and more are now available in English, it is, to my way of reading and reflection at least, far more enlightening than a library of official policy reports and superficial newspaper reporting can ever hope to be.

> *Jascha Kessler, "Ernesto Cardenal: 'Zero Hour and Other Documentary Poems'," in a radio broadcast on KUSC-FM—Los Angeles, CA, April 15, 1981.*

PHOEBE PETTINGELL

The poems of Ernesto Cardenal collected in *Zero Hour* . . . will interest many readers in the United States less as poetry than as political commentary. These verses . . . describe events leading up to the revolution in Nicaragua and the overthrow of the Somoza dictatorship in 1979. . . . [Despite Cardenal's] adherence to the "theology of liberation," he accepts the late Mao Zedong's view that "revolutionary art without artistic value has no revolutionary value." Indeed, how Cardenal attempts to reconcile the demands of poetic creation with revolutionary activity constitutes much of the dramatic tension of *Zero Hour*. . . .

In the title poem, Cardenal fashions a terse commentary on the brutalities practiced by Anastasio Somoza's government. Or, rather, he marshals facts into a cry of outrage against torture, murder and oppression that is all the more hard hitting because such events speak for themselves. . . . In this moving bit of propaganda, our pity and indignation rise as we are forced to watch the cruelty of the powerful against the weak. There are similar pungent images in the poem: Political prisoners strain to hear dance music wafting down from the presidential palace in their effort to block out the screams of those being tortured; in Washington, Franklin D. Roosevelt tells Sumner Welles, "Somoza is a sunofabitch / but he's ours." Nor is Cardenal romantic about the war waged against tyrants: "Glory isn't what the history books teach: / it's a flock of buzzards in a field and a great stink." (p. 11)

Cardenal's most effective voice is the purely dramatic, particularly since he has an ear for conversation somewhat reminiscent of the late Frank O'Hara's. In **"Trip to New York"** the poet flies to Manhattan for a poetry reading and, as the Watergate hearings are being broadcast, visits James Laughlin, his publisher. He discusses politics with members of the American radical Catholic movement, from Dorothy Day to the Berrigan brothers, all the while perceiving [Thomas] Merton's benign ghost hovering over these encounters. Although here, too, Cardenal is unable to resist donning his Marxist spectacles along the way to take a broad look at capitalism, the overall mood of the poem is ruminative, the dialogue perfectly captured, the scene graphically conveyed.

It is unfortunate that Cardenal cannot separate his tracts from his poems. He has the gift of making his characters sound fully human. Only when he ascends the pulpit is that skill lost in a windy rush of rhetoric. Father Cardenal ought to know as a poet, if not as a priest, that no man can serve two masters. Imagination is the freest thing we possess; it cannot be a servant, even to Revolution. (pp. 11-12)

> *Phoebe Pettingell, "Poets of Commitment," in The New Leader, Vol. LXIV, No. 9, May 4, 1981, pp. 11-12.**

HAROLD JAFFE

Except for [Cardenal's] earliest verses which were modeled on Ruben Dario and Neruda, Whitman and Pound are his principal forbears. As with Whitman, there is less compression than extension in Cardenal's most successful poems. The effects usually depend on increment to uncover depth; and the poem is meant to be public, an open window bearing the naked heart. From Pound (whom he translated, and whose influence he has acknowledged), Cardenal derived his method of incorporating disparate matter into a patchwork fabric while avoiding slack. And from Pound he learned to vitalize the rhetorical flourish with lean precise imagery.

Cardenal's moral nature (to revive the useful nineteenth century phrase) more closely resembles Whitman's. He is, after all, a Roman Catholic priest in the tradition of the pre-patristic visionaries. And throughout his writings he refers often and hopefully to the uniting of communism and Christianity, a unity he glimpses in post-Batista Cuba, despite the Castro government's less than sympathetic attitude to practicing Christians. . . .

Revolutionary force is everywhere implicit in Cardenal's most recent volume, *Zero Hour and Other Documentary Poems*. This is an ambitious work of striking originality, which I believe will prove as influential to younger committed poets as Neruda's *Canto General* did thirty years ago. . . .

Because Cardenal wanted these poems to be vehicles for social change, he strove for surface clarity. And given the copious data with which they are suffused, it is remarkable that the poems possess their clear hard surfaces. Clarity, though, was not all Cardenal wanted. Brilliantly implementing what he derived from Pound's method in the *Cantos* with—in [Robert] Pring-Mill's words—"filmic editing techniques like crosscutting, accelerated montage, flash frames" [see excerpt above], Cardenal saturates the reader with history, economics, politics, religion, popular advertisements . . . But these are neither the raw sewage of "facts," nor the customary self-serving compendia of particular data; they are a revolutionary Christian's visionary conversion of fact into reality.

Although the manifest reality of Cardenal's Central America is grim, its future—which to Cardenal is as "real" as its present —appears eminently hopeful. Furious or revolted as Cardenal is over this or that dreadful inequity, he never loses hope. His love, his faith in the disadvantaged, his great good humor, his enduring belief that communism and Christ's communion are at root the same—these extraordinary convictions resound throughout the volume.

> *Harold Jaffe, in a review of "Zero Hour and Other Documentary Poems," in The American Book Review, Vol. 4, No. 2, January-February, 1982, p. 11.*

PAUL BUHLE AND THOMAS FIEHRER

Cardenal patterned his later work after the texts of Ezra Pound, flawed champion of the "documentary" poem. Behind Pound stood Dante, whose cries against encroaching merchant capitalism expressed the spirit of old radical Christianity. Pound hated the modern order but tripped on his fondness for rigid societies (ancient China, fascist Italy) where, he imagined, poets earned special favor. Cardenal has freed himself from this last artistic vanity. . . . Without illusions about some Golden Age . . . , he has recalled the virtues of agrarian communism, brought them forward as proof of Latin America's past and its potential. The poet of liberation theology returns the narrative to its ancient purpose—history, myth, and ritual wrapped up in one. Cardenal the revolutionary activist and modern writer advances the day when poetry will be made by the people in common.

But how does all this square with Christianity, the priesthood in particular, based as it is on psychic and social hierarchy and locked into the crimes of the west? The religious heritage that brings Cardenal close to the *campesinos* and European millenarian movements also throws obstacles in the way of his poetic consistency. A dualism haunts his *Psalms*. . . . The searing critique of imperial economics, of suffering unredeemed by history, stands alongside pitiful laments like those of the Old Testament: "God, our God, why have you forgotten / the wretched of the earth?" Cardenal pleads, apparently without confidence in a reassuring response, or in the people's power to change the world. The Holocaust suggests divine indifference. How could Christianity have aided and abetted sadism and genocide in Europe, in Africa, Asia, and the Americas? Cardenal will not fall into the quietist acceptance of fate. "Blessed be the man who says no to the party / . . . Who will not sit down with gangsters / . . . Blessed the man who coughs at commercials," he spits in the face of businessmen, their supportive generals, politicans, and Church officials. But he can't wholly escape the sense of contradiction. (pp. 10-11)

Paul Buhle and Thomas Fiehrer, "Holy Warriors: Latin America's Moral Majority," in VLS, *No. 10, September, 1982, pp. 8, 10-11.**

Caryl Churchill

1938-

English dramatist and scriptwriter.

Churchill is the most widely performed and published female dramatist in contemporary British theater. Her works challenge social and dramatic conventions and are informed by a strong commitment to socialism and feminism. Churchill is often linked with Britain's "Fringe Theater" movement, which includes such political playwrights as David Hare and Edward Bond. Stylistically complex, Churchill's plays are noted for their innovative techniques, including the manipulation of casting and chronology.

Churchill wrote plays for radio and television during the 1960s. With the rise of the Fringe Theater in the 1970s she found outlets for theatrical performance of her work. Many of her plays were produced at the Royal Court, a subsidized alternative theater, where Churchill became the first female resident playwright.

Churchill first drew significant critical attention with *Objections to Sex and Violence* (1975), which introduced feminist ideology into her work. A female terrorist is the central character in this exploration of the relationship between sexuality, violence, and power. Her next play, *Light Shining in Buckinghamshire* (1976), explores the combination of religious and revolutionary fervor that contributed to rebellion during the Cromwellian era.

Churchill became recognized as an accomplished playwright in both Britain and the United States with *Cloud Nine* (1979), a critical and popular success. Critics praised her wit and inventiveness and several proclaimed her a major talent. The play, set in colonial Africa during the Victorian era and then in present-day London, is a farce in which rampant sexual activity is exposed against a background of genteel Victorian manners. Churchill uses several theatrical devices in *Cloud Nine* to underscore what she believes to be the artificiality of conventional sex roles. Churchill stated that her goal in *Cloud Nine* was to write a play about sexual politics that would not be simply feminist but would reveal how sexual repression, like colonial repression, dehumanizes everyone. She has commented, "I brought together two preoccupations of mine—people's internal states of being and the external political structures which affect them, which make them insane."

Churchill employed similar devices in *Top Girls* (1982), a satire of a society in which the only way for women to succeed professionally is to adopt the worst qualities of men. Her next play, *Fen* (1983), was jokingly referred to as "Bottom Girls" by Frank Rich because it portrays lower-class women whom the women's liberation movement has left behind. In *Fen*, Churchill explores both the political problem of economic exploitation of farm workers and such personal problems as one woman's dilemma of choosing between her lover and her children. Her recent play *Softcops* (1984), an occasionally humorous but predominantly serious work about crime, punishment, and social responsibility, relies heavily on Michel Foucault's *Surveiller et punir* (Discipline and Punish).

© Jerry Bauer

(See also *Contemporary Authors*, Vol. 102 and *Dictionary of Literary Biography*, Vol. 13.)

EDITH OLIVER

In a short-lived curiosity from England—"**Owners,**" by Caryl Churchill—we had on hand a promising dramatist. . . . The play is a farce about hatred, power, despair, baby-selling, arson, and murder (Joe Orton certainly released something in the British psyche) among some working-class people in a North London development. Marion, the despotic wife of a butcher, has very recently made a lot of money in real estate, and the story of her machinations and the anguish she causes those around her is told in a series of short scenes, almost like animated horror comics. The resultant confusion was not necessarily transatlantic, or necessarily a matter of direction; Miss Churchill is not a very firm or clear playwright. She is, however, occasionally clever, although she sounds as if she had learned about the lower orders entirely from old bound volumes of *Punch;* her characters talk like captions. (p. 56)

Edith Oliver, "Suffer, Little Children," in The New Yorker, *Vol. XLIX, No. 14, May 26, 1973, pp. 54, 56.* *

IRVING WARDLE

Like *Owners,* Caryl Churchill's [*Objections to Sex and Violence*] carries a portmanteau title. It is a danger sign. Ownership is a fascinating and timely theme, opening up a perspective of multiple ironies on the possession of property and the possession of people. Likewise sex and violence. . . . But meanwhile, who are the people in the play and what happens to them?

To this question Miss Churchill returns a flimsy and long-winded answer. We are on a beach . . . where Jule, a taciturn urban terrorist, has retired with a boyfriend after being named in a conspiracy charge. What makes a nice girl start blowing people up? I imagine this question was on the author's mind at some stage of the play's composition; but we never find out. Nor do we discover why, having gone into hiding, Jule should have peppered her acquaintances with holiday postcards.

But however improbable their arrival, all the visitors come under the umbrella of the title. To start with, there is sister Annie, who seems to be living the kind of life that caused Jule's rebellion; an executive sex-object, who gets even more inanimate treatment when she junks the typewriter and enrolls as a house cleaner for Mr Big's wife. . . .

Annie, fresh from five years of marital battering, is accompanied by a docile lover who responds to every verbal challenge with dithering equivocation. Others on the scene are a miserable pair of middle-aged Festival of Lighters, the woman scanning the seascape for likely rapists, the man diving into a porno magazine as soon as she turns her back. Then there is a lonely old lady from Watford . . . against whom the husband directs a furtive assault: and, right at the end, Jule's Communist husband, who arrives primed with ideological weapons.

It is all there: liberalism, the National Front, hard-line Socialism, and the terrorist ethic (if that is the word). But theatrically speaking who cares? I suspect that even Miss Churchill does not care very much, as what gets spoken about on stage differs totally from what happens. So far as events and immediate feelings are concerned we are back in the traditional feminine world where personal relationships are all and everything would work out satisfactorily if men would only behave properly. . . .

Jule is confined to holding the rest of the company at arm's length and striding about masterfully in a bathing suit, until faced with the recurring question: "Do you remember how . . . ?" at which, unfortunately, her defences are apt to crumble. This is a difficult time for playwrights; but I doubt whether anything is to be gained from going through the motions of writing about important issues when one has nothing to say.

> *Irving Wardle, "An Unfilled Portmanteau," in* The Times, *London, January 3, 1975, p. 7.*

HAROLD HOBSON

A shabby seaside lodging house; a meek little man bitterly hurt when as a birthday present he is given a child's toy drum; two visitors, one fast-talking, the other viciously sinister; these things, when Harold Pinter's "The Birthday Party" received its famous first production, sent through one a surge of joy and wonder and awe at the revelation of a new dramatist of indisputable genius. . . .

One has something of the same excitement in watching Caryl Churchill's **"Objections to Sex and Violence."** . . . Neither Miss Churchill nor Mr Pinter believes that it is necessary, nor even possible, to explain everything. In "The Birthday Party" we know neither why Stanley is persecuted, nor why everything that Goldberg does to Stanley will eventually be done to Goldberg. In **"Objections to Sex and Violence"** the bikini-clad girl on the beach never gives an adequate explanation of her implacable resolution to say No to society.

This sense of obscurity, this feeling that we live, precariously, in a world beyond rational explanation, is one of the most powerful factors in the work of both authors. Mr Pinter exploits the verbally concrete and ideologically amorphous: "Who watered the wicket at Melbourne?" And Miss Churchill goes so far, in a fascinating disquisition on the possible meanings of the phrase "I believe," as to show that the very words which we use to disperse obscurity are themselves obscure.

> *Harold Hobson, "In Search of Happiness," in* The Times, *London, January 12, 1975, p. 32.**

W STEPHEN GILBERT

Knowing her apprenticeship in radio, I hope it doesn't seem too easy a cavil to say that Caryl Churchill's [*Objections to Sex and Violence*] feels more like a chamber work for voices than a fully realised dramatic event in a medium-sized theatre. Several commentators have noted an uneasiness about the setting up of the duologues which are the play's mode, a lack of conviction in the sheer mechanics of pushing a pair of speakers on and off. Conceived as a radio work, the play would easily shed these minor impediments and the more elusive, perhaps more fundamental problem of its not fully resolved dependence on a setting that is and is not formalised, particular. The lack of conviction that I find is spatial.

The text itself takes the form of a sort of double lobster-quadrille around two Alices, one a young woman extricated from marriage to a down-the-line CP drone and integrating with a small group who may or may not be about to plant bombs, the other an old woman returned to what may or may not be the scene of a sexual adventure that memory and loneliness have rendered idyllic. . . .

Ms Churchill does nothing so crude as to write in parallel lines. The connections are there to be picked up or not. She avoids clearly pinning her characters down with issues. She has a way of sidling up to her themes and giving them a nudge which is both fascinating and maddening. (p. 24)

In the most theatrical image of the evening (and the play's most important lack is the visual realisation of the verbal motifs), Annie has rendered Jule a talking head by burying her up to the neck in the sand, as she used to do in childhood. Mocked for her threat of violence, she stuffs sand in Jule's mouth and flounces off. The image is a small miracle of compression and evocation. Jule is, as it were, raped and murdered. Abandoned in the sand, silenced, violated, she provides a link between the desperate search of Miss Forbes for an unexorcised ghost and the desperate, inarticulate, dead end of anarchic action. . . .

There are many telling moments in the dialogue—Madge's resolute equation of service and force, Eric's merry relation of accident to justice, Jule's husband Terry's careful distinction between passion and action. Ms Churchill is excellent on the instability of words like 'hurt' and 'belief', the absurdity of concepts like 'happiness' and 'non-violence'. But of course these things make for a largely static and wordy piece of theatre. . . . *Objections to Sex and Violence* is less funny, more schematic than Caryl Churchill's previous stage play *Owners,* but it marks a considerable advance. It reminds me at times of the work of Edward Bond, by which I mean the highest praise. The sheer economy and resonance of Bond's stagecraft is unsurpassed amongst contemporary dramatists. Ms Churchill may be going to alter that assessment. At any rate, she's going to be a major dramatist. (p. 25)

> *W Stephen Gilbert, in a review of "Objections to Sex and Violence," in* Plays and Players, *Vol. 22, No. 6, March, 1975, pp. 24-5.*

J. W. LAMBERT

Objections to Sex and Violence was . . . something of a morality play without a moral. Its characters, that is to say, are all firmly representative of some class or attitude of mind, rather too much so for the good of the play, yet deployed with a short-term intelligence which makes them interesting moment-by-moment without leaving behind any clear impression of what Miss Churchill is saying, or indirectly expressing by their interplay. The scene is a rocky beach. . . . It is for some a place of escape, for others a familiar alternative to everyday life or a possible means to recapture lost happiness. (p. 44)

In the background of the play Arthur and Madge, a solid couple in lower-middle-class late-middle-age, brighten their dim routines by expressing disapproval of almost everything, she leading their chorus of disapproval, he echoing, and consoling himself with glum sexual fantasy which suddenly takes an active form when he finds himself sheltering with an old woman if possible even lonelier than he is; she is horrified by his flash of folly—but won't take action against him. . . . Odd that Miss Churchill should write with such essential truth about these two, yet give Madge lines of such crudity. . . . So much, however, for the older generation, a mere chorus of failure. The play is really about a group in their early thirties, some would say leftovers from the Sixties. . . . [Jule, the] figure round whom they revolve—is she a failure too? Well, no—she is an enigma: one of those girls—and they certainly exist in real life—whose sole stock-in-trade seems to be sexuality and contempt, both of which of course exert considerable power on those susceptible to them. We have so often been given impotence as a specious explanation of sadistic authoritarianism that at least it makes a change for Miss Churchill to draw this brutal girl as the only character in her play to have, and make no bones about, a satisfactory sex life. That she is cruel is clear; that she is also an active terrorist is not. Certainly she is also the only character in the play who might become one; and Miss Churchill's conclusion would seem to be that the connection between sex and violence is that both can be satisfactorily exercised at someone else's expense, but that people who don't so exercise them are all failures. . . . (pp. 44-5)

> *J. W. Lambert, in a review of "Objections to Sex and Violence," in* Drama, *No. 116, Spring, 1975, pp. 44-5.*

DONALD CAMPBELL

If I were to be asked to list the plays which have given me most satisfaction this year, [*Light Shining in Buckinghamshire*] would come pretty high on the list. Two features of this production impressed me very much. First of all, there was the complexity of its concern; many important questions were raised and no trite answers offered. On the face of it an account of the English Revolution, this is in fact a genuine study of revolution itself, any revolution. When, towards the end, one of the actors suggests that a great opportunity has been lost, one is not given the feeling that a point is being made, but that a question has been seriously asked. Moreover, an even more important question is asked by the religious beliefs and expectations of the characters—is there a direct correlation between the efficiency of a revolution and the nature of the society that creates it? In other words, what kind of omelette do you get when you break rotten eggs? Parallels with our own time exist in plenty . . . but they operate at several levels and do not exist merely as parallels. The second feature which impresses is the language: spare, uncluttered, colourful when it needs to be, usually low-keyed and neutral, the awareness of the importance of the language is always evident. (pp. 20-1)

> *Donald Campbell, "Traditional Movement," in* Plays and Players, *Vol. 24, No. 2, November, 1976, pp. 20-1.**

DAVID ZANE MAIROWITZ

In the opening moments of *Light Shining In Buckinghamshire* Caryl Churchill gets her sharpened hook into God—the God who first supports Charles I against Parliament, then sides with Parliament against the monarchy and, at all points, backs Property against the common people—and does not relent until she has pulled Him (decidedly *Him* in this case) down to face the social outcasts of the misfired English Revolution. . . .

One of the dramatic virtues of this magnificent play is that it can assume a certain given historical foundation and proceed to de-emphasise specific characters and events. In fact the play's history is rooted wholly in a *collective* consciousness which is its protagonist and hero. This is neither a group of specified individuals moving together or even a defined community experiencing the raising of armies or the aftermath of civil war, but an interweaving of historical and fictional persons appearing and disappearing, together and independently, through the middle of the 17th century, seeking parallel roads to freedom, paths occasionally crossing, reaching similar (if not cohesive) conclusions. Churchill works against their identification: 'there is no need for the audience to know each time which character they are seeing'. Consequently, roles are interchanged so that no one player carries the same character throughout, thereby stressing the collective vision of history even in the staging of the play. Initially this is confusing, but Churchill does not feel constrained by the pre-eminence of personality in our culture (and in our theatre), and twists our comprehension of inter-relationships in her view of events and in her operation of the stage. . . .

Isaiah has the first prophetic word: 'The earth is utterly broken down, the earth is clean dissolved, the earth is moved exceedingly'. Churchill now proceeds to take the world to pieces. With the anticipation of the Millennium (worked out as likely to come in 1650), an army of Christ is raised to fight for Parliament against the monarchy. The poor march and die to justify the overturning of the world's perfect order. Yet this upsets the clerical hierarchy and brings forth a new generation of preachers who even permit questions in church. In one of the play's best scenes, a woman disrupts the service to contradict the preacher, exposing the hollowness of the new 'liberty'. . . .

She is of course ejected and beaten because the preacher cannot go so far as to allow a woman to speak up in church.

So, through the eyes of those who have been misled, we see the revolution backtracking even before it has gone its full progress. Using documentary material, Churchill gives us the Putney Debates of 1647, with a not over-significant Cromwell in the chair, and shows that Property will inevitably rule the day, that Parliament has no intention of stretching its new liberties to embrace common people, and that those who fought with God have been deceived. The only recourse is to upset the pattern of social relations yet again. . . .

The long-range result is an intensification of class awareness, if not yet class warfare. But Churchill's handling of it avoids any trite political traps. Standing old Isaiah on his head, she seems to suggest a possible reconstruction of the broken world, solely from the viewpoint of the downtrodden. . . .

This is no 1967-Instant God-Package, but the existential logic of a dramatic world determined by the social moves of those who have nothing. The result is not a realised political or even social revolution—as it was not in 1647—but the harvest of a revolutionary experience, the collapse of fixed hierarchy, the recognition of betrayal, the beginnings of social doubt. Those who have gathered at the final prayer meeting learn not to expect their freedom to be granted them . . . but that it must be taken, by them, and not in false solidarity with any other class. They are left with an ecstatic solidarity of their own— 'all things in common'—and a sense of power (both men and women) for common future use. . . . (p. 24)

Emerging from successful combat with God, Churchill now takes on the devil, and shows him to be a convenient tool in the historical oppression of women. In *Vinegar Tom,* the witches are those women of all classes who have acted rebelliously or lustily and thereby gained the wrath of the emotionally suppressed community. The women who are unmarried, for one reason or another, are social outcasts and therefore perfect targets for simple jealousy and for religious and political exploitation. (pp. 24-5)

The scenario is more or less familiar. The equation of witchery with social nonconformity has been used before dramatically, reaching a pinnacle perhaps with Miller's *The Crucible.* There are threads in *Vinegar Tom* which provide new feminist dimensions. Miss Betty . . . refuses to marry a man of her father's choice and is in danger of hanging as a witch. But because of her status, her rebellion can be construed as 'sickness' and, in the end, she saves herself by capitulating to the marriage—only a less painful form of woman's torture.

Equally, [a] farmer's wife is as loveless and debased as any of the other women, but she is never a candidate for hanging because she suppresses her anguish and maintains her 'expected' role, instead of protesting. But this side of the play seems only sketched, as are the more dynamic later scenes of actual witchfinding. Instead of dramatic elaboration these themes are expanded by way of song interruptions, to place the problems in a contemporary voice. . . .

The impact is one of estrangement, especially when the lyrics become medically and physically graphic, or when a male Music Hall act . . . [expounds] on the inferior qualities of women. But the playtext is not strong enough to withstand the breaking of its rhythm and antagonism of the musical interludes. Where *Light Shining In Buckinghamshire* gains in power from episodic shots gathering in momentum, . . . [*Vinegar*

Tom] does not override the conflict of its dramatic and musical pitches. Nonetheless, even the pieces of *Vinegar Tom* confirm Caryl Churchill's writing strength, and leave sharp scars if failing to deliver the *coup de grace.*

It is [Churchill's] good fortune—and ours—that she has found two companies (Joint Stock and Monstrous Regiment) who are wholly sympathetic not only with her work, but with her working methods. Both plays were born out of direct textual improvisation with groups of actors who do not fear this kind of laborious give-and-take experience. That this collaboration can produce not just the usual good will, but powerful writing, can bode nothing but good for the dismal, entrenched English theatre. In the case of *Light Shining In Buckinghamshire,* the effort has given us one of the finest pieces of English play writing for years. (p. 25)

David Zane Mairowitz, "God and the Devil," in Plays and Players, *Vol. 24, No. 5, February, 1977, pp. 24-5.*

W STEPHEN GILBERT

[*Traps*] has a title which seems to promise more than the play delivers—or possibly less than the play delivers. Elliptically structured, it features one returning and three regular communards plus a visiting couple. It also features a clock set at real time throughout and a setting . . . which is sited variously in town and country. I take it these things are not gratuitous; Churchill's purpose nonetheless remains obscure. Thus a character accounted dead soon returns without provocation of comment, another entering in a flourish of anal complex repeats the performance later almost word for word before things turn ugly—ludicrously ugly. After the interval, a destroyed plant is restored.

A fascinating script, always several pages ahead of the audience, especially on critics' night, offers plenty of sinewy lines and joyous juxtapositions and Churchill's most confident and creative deployment of stagecraft to date. The result is that one regrets the feeling of exclusion from an enigma where one might have resented being subjected to arbitrary mystification. The clearest thread, on which a repressed bourgeois . . . comes to reclaim his wife and stays to discover with a brittle chirpiness the wonders of communal living ('I only just begin to appreciate how the sun shines on the moon'), works well though it could not be said to astonish. (p. 33)

W Stephen Gilbert, " 'Dusa, Fish, Stas & Vi' . . . and 'Traps'," in Plays and Players, *Vol. 24, No. 6, March, 1977, pp. 32-3.**

ANTHONY CURTIS

[*Cloud Nine*] takes a leaf or two out of what used to be called our island's story and tears them up into shreds. We begin on an outpost of empire in the African jungle *circa* 1900; we end in a London park and a recreation hut *circa* 1979. To highlight the caricature a black is played by a white, a woman by a man, an infant by a grown person. The result is a little bit like an extended Farjeon revue sketch. . . .

Ms. Churchill gives an adroit and amusing exposure of what goes on behind the masks of conventional behaviour. Playwrights who readily avail themselves of the freedom to show things that used to be regarded as disgusting and to mention things that used to be regarded as unmentionable are nearly always utterly humourless about it; or else they have a 'black' sense of humour that leaves me white with boredom. It is refreshing to find in *Cloud Nine* a genuinely funny play arising out of this freedom.

> *Anthony Curtis, in a review of "Cloud Nine," in* Drama, *No. 133, Summer, 1979, p. 57.*

IRVING WARDLE

If any liberationist purpose underlies this diptych of British sexuality under the reign of two dear Queens, Caryl Churchill has wisely left it well concealed. The only didactic point that occurred to me after [viewing *Cloud Nine*] . . . was that its abrupt contrast between seething lust in a Kiplingesque colonial outpost and polymorphous experimentation in modern London illustrated the decline of farce writing in direct proportion to the relaxation of moral taboo.

That begs the question that Miss Churchill wanted to write a farce in the first place. It is a fine piece . . . , but I think Miss Churchill disregards the crude facts of audience psychology by starting the evening with some uproariously coarse jokes at the expense of Victorian pieties, and then modulating into something altogether gentler and non-satirical. Long into last night's the second half, there were uneasy giggles from spectators trying to view a study in sexual evolution as if it were another ludicrous chapter in the history of the White Man's Burden.

However, one can see why Miss Churchill has settled for this arrangement, and why she defies chronology by bringing back her Victorian characters in no more than middle-age in the second act. *Cloud Nine* is an exercize on the theme of ghosts; of the persistence of supposedly discarded moral imperatives. And it makes the point by showing them at the height of their power before examining the variety of modern rebellion against them.

To put that another way, it is about role-playing. Everyone at Clive's African outpost, from his docile wife and commanding mother-in-law to the native houseboy (the most rigidly British of the lot) has a fixed role. In the second act—which moves out of doors into a public park—the characters have to make up their own roles. . . .

[Beyond] the laughs, the real dramatic interest lies in the double approach to character as a fixed or fluid thing. The triumph of the play . . . is that this point is inscribed in the casting.

Roles are doubled, and they change hands from the first to the second acts. . . . The production reaches a brief poetic point of rest in its . . . title [song]. Otherwise it points the way to *Cloud Nine* with a gentle playfulness, satiric without ever becoming censorious, in which sex always retains a human face.

> *Irving Wardle, in a review of "Cloud Nine," in* The Times, *London, September 10, 1980, p. 10.*

CLIVE BARNES

[*Cloud 9* is] a very funny play full of odd dramatic spasms. It probably helps to have an interest in England and its former empire with its setting sun. Yet beyond this, it is fundamentally a play about love relationships to which that fading Empire merely provides the backcloth.

The play is in two distinct parts. The first is Africa in 1880. . . . The second part is London in 1980, although as the playwright

Caryl Churchill is at ambiguous pains to point out, ". . . but for the characters it is only 25 years later."

I'm not sure what that means either. Presumably Miss Churchill is implying that the British pattern of relationships has been colored by Britain's imperial past—a concept that other British playwrights such as David Storey and Peter Nichols have also hinted at. Possible—but probably irrelevant to one's ultimate enjoyment of the play.

Miss Churchill is saying here—despite the imperial background—that all human relationships, if genuine, have their validity. Her fantastic parade of heterosexuals, homosexuals and bisexuals, the relationship of parents with children, the relationships of people with servants, the entire kaleidoscope of relationships, particularly sexual relationships, come under her hilarious yet loving scrutiny.

What I really like about Miss Churchill is not merely her sweetly deft writing skills, although they do help, but her moral inability to put anyone or anything down. She makes judgments on relations and relationships, but she is never judgmental. Perhaps it is actually the quality of discreet acceptance that made the British Empire what it was, and is still maintained in some shadowed shape in British society today. . . .

This is a zany play, but one with terrific wit and humanity to it. It is far from perfect—in fact, it is sometimes positively disorganized. Yet it is a play that has something to say to us today about kindness, affection, perversion and most of all, love.

> *Clive Barnes, "Zany 'Cloud' Has a Bright Silver Lining," in* New York Post, *May 19, 1981. Reprinted in* New York Theatre Critics' Reviews, *Vol. XLIV, No. 14, September 7-13, 1981, p. 192.*

FRANK RICH

["**Cloud 9**"] may not transport the audience all the way to Cloud 9—but it surely keeps us on our toes. The evening's subject is sexual confusion, and Miss Churchill has found a theatrical method that is easily as dizzying as her theme. Not only does she examine a cornucopia of sexual permutations— from heterosexual adultery right up to bisexual incest—but she does so with a wild array of dramatic styles and tricks. . . .

Miss Churchill, as you might gather, is one daft writer. "**Cloud 9**" . . . has real failings, but intelligence and inventiveness aren't among them; we're always interested in what the playwright is up to, no matter what the outcome. . . .

[The first] half of "**Cloud 9**" is about what happens when a very proper colonial British family receives a visit from a pith-helmeted explorer named Harry Bagley. . . . While the natives outside the camp are getting restless, they have nothing on the rakish Harry. He's *really* been too long in the bush. Grabbing every clandestine opportunity he can, this explorer seduces the household's wife (played by a man), schoolboy son (played by a woman) and obsequious black servant (played by a white)— all before getting married to the governess, a lesbian.

What makes this carnal circus funny is the contrast between the characters' manners and deeds. No matter what they do, Miss Churchill's colonials act and talk like true-blue, genteel Victorians. When Harry is caught in a homosexual act, he apologizes by explaining that he is merely the helpless victim of "a disease worse than diphtheria." . . .

The joke does wear thin too quickly. Once we understand that Miss Churchill is stripping bare the hypocrisies of an oversatirized era, Act I becomes stalled. The transsexual casting is also problematic: though the male and female impersonations are amusing, not smirky, they nonetheless serve the unwanted function of announcing the jokes. Nor is the story's farcical structure so strong that it pulls up the slack. Instead of the ingenious clockwork of, say, an Alan Ayckbourn play, Miss Churchill provides a progression of overly similar scenes that steadily reveal each character's particular proclivity.

Act II has its own problems—and pleasures. We re-encounter three members of the 1880 family, as well as four new characters, and find that, in 1980, they are as liberated as their predecessors were repressed. But progress presents its own difficulties. The homosexual schoolboy of 1880, now hitting middle age, is so confused by his love for both his sister and an insolent young male lover that he worries that he might be a lesbian. . . .

Miss Churchill covers this and much more territory by relying on tender monologues. The speeches are very well written, but one hungers for stronger interchanges between the characters. An element of ideological Polyanna-ism also creeps in, for the playwright provides most of her lost souls with happy endings. Is everyone really so much better off in the swinging 1980's? It seems a waste that Act II's wittiest conceit—the ghostly return of characters from Act I—is mainly used to draw mawkish parallels between now and then. . . .

[Betty] delivers a beautiful closing speech in which she graphically describes how she overcame her sheltered 1880 upbringing to take her rightful place in a modern, feminist world of infinite possibilities. "If there isn't a right way to do things," she explains, "you just have to invent one."

By the end, we're terribly moved by this middle-aged woman's brave attempt to reinvent herself—just as we're moved by Caryl Churchill's attempt to reinvent the comedy of manners so that it might do such a heroine justice.

Frank Rich, "Sexual Confusion on 'Cloud 9'," in
The New York Times, *May 20, 1981, p. C30.*

ROBERT ASAHINA

[Act One of Caryl Churchill's *Cloud 9* is] a dizzying and delectable farce. . . .

Her emphasis is on both "white" and "man"—on race and sex, though particularly on the latter. From the first scene, Churchill . . . is clearly intent on upsetting our preconceptions about both. (p. 564)

By mismatching the performers with their stage roles, Churchill underscores the artificiality and conventionality of the characters' sex roles. A clever theatrical idea thus serves a dramatic purpose, and the sexual shenanigans that result give rise to more than just the predictable cheap laughs. . . . [When] the timid Edward finally shows some spunk by dressing down Joshua, his mother cheers . . . , while we are plunged into a jungle of conflicting feelings about what it means for a "boy" (with the quotation marks very much supplied by the casting) to become a man, when masculinity is defined in terms of sexual as well as racial superiority.

We are still reeling from Act One when Churchill throws us for another loop at the beginning of Act Two. It is now one hundred years later, in contemporary London, but the char-

acters have aged only twenty-five years, thus maintaining a continuity with the past that paradoxically underscores the passage of time and the change in mores. (pp. 564-65)

Sound confusing? Well, it is, but Act Two unfortunately lacks the delightful and profoundly disturbing satirical quality of Act One. The second act begins, for example, with Gerry's earnest and explicit monologue about a very brief encounter (homosexual) on a train, and ends with Betty's equally humorless and unembarrassed paean to the joys of masturbation. In between, rather than writing (and casting) against type to jar our expectations and expose the shallowness of sexual stereotypes, Churchill has the characters and the performers fulfill them in the dreariest possible way. (p. 565)

To be sure, it is perfectly legitimate for Churchill to try to impart some seriousness retrospectively by bringing the characters off Cloud 9 to earth after the intermission. We should not expect that the second act will continue in the farcical vein of the first, which is broader than it is deep. But the plodding realism of Act Two seems to be motivated more by political than by aesthetic considerations. Churchill belongs to the loose coalition of vaguely Marxist playwrights in England who emerged in the mid-seventies from the radical theater movement called The Fringe, which arose during the late sixties in reaction against the psychologistic tradition that had dominated the British stage since the appearance of Osborne and Pinter. Along with Edward Bond, Howard Brenton, David Hare and others, Churchill has written plays (several others before *Cloud 9*, which is her first to be produced in America) that are sweepingly critical not only of capitalist society but of the conventions of the bourgeois stage, with its alleged privatization of experience (as in the works of the so-called "angry young men," whose problems, or so it is charged, are more personal than political).

Although the first act of *Cloud 9* is very much in accordance, aesthetically and politically, with this ambitious critique, it nonetheless succeeds as a rather old-fashioned satire, because there is very little at stake. No one today would defend the racist and sexist attitudes of Victorian colonials; the only problem facing a contemporary playwright is coming up with clever new ways of savaging those old beliefs, and Churchill certainly succeeds in doing so.

To oversimplify somewhat, her problem in Act Two, by contrast, is to show how (or whether) sexual behavior is just as entangled with the fate of Empire today as it was a hundred years ago. Yet the blurring of the boundary between public and private over the past century has eliminated the easiest target of the satirist—hypocrisy. Sex is hardly the "dirty little secret" that it was to the Victorians; indeed, there are precious few secrets regarding sexual behavior these days.

So Churchill is seemingly stuck with presenting her characters more or less at face value. Indeed, her avowed liberationist convictions almost force her to take seriously their behavior and attitudes (feminism, radical lesbianism, gay liberation), which seem—regardless of one's personal politics —as richly deserving of satire as any of a century ago (or any others found today). So the caustic witticisms of Act One give way to the didactic exhortations of Act Two, and ideology triumphs over sensibility. (p. 566)

Robert Asahina, in a review of "Cloud 9," in The
Hudson Review, *Vol. XXXIV, No. 4, Winter, 1981-82, pp. 564-66.*

BENEDICT NIGHTINGALE

[*Cloud Nine*] and *Top Girls,* taken together, show that [Caryl Churchill] has evolved into a playwright of genuine audacity and assurance, able to use her considerable wit and intelligence in ways at once unusual, resonant and dramatically riveting.

Top Girls itself opens with the sort of dinner-party you might conjure up in some spectacularly fanciful game of Consequences. In the Prima Donna restaurant, Pope Joan, who supposedly spread her skirts over St Peter's throne in 854, is hobnobbing with a Japanese courtesan, a Victorian lady-traveller, Chaucer's ultra-patient Griselda, and Dulle Griet, whom Brueghel painted invading hell in apron and armour. All suffered, either personally or through the abuse of their children, and all coped with the buffeting of their eras, with extraordinary courage. Each tells her tale, sometimes in excitedly overlapping sentences: a device I first thought was supposed to add realism to [the] . . . production, but later suspected was meant to imply some lack of mutual attention. Women don't listen to each other enough, don't learn sufficiently from their accumulated experience.

Why else should they now be using the limited freedoms they have painfully won as gruesomely as they too often do? That's the question implicitly raised by the dinner-party's hostess, who is celebrating her appointment as managing director of an employment agency staffed by women as tough and callous as herself, if not quite as adept at slotting girls into a male-dominated business universe. Triumph for Marlene, as she's called, has been bought at the cost of great personal mutilation: meaning the loss of love, and specifically of motherhood, through the odd abortion and one big act of rejection. At this point Ms Churchill sensationally but successfully links the world of the employment agency with that of its boss-woman's sister, who toils in a council house to bring up a backward teenager. Unknown to her, this girl is Marlene's daughter. She handed her over, left for London, and now offhandedly dismisses her as 'a bit thick—she's not going to make it'. What use is female emancipation, Churchill asks, if it transforms the clever women into predators and does nothing for the stupid, weak and helpless? Does freedom, and feminism, consist of aggressively adopting the very values that have for centuries oppressed your sex?

The question becomes plonkingly explicit in a climactic row between Marlene and her sister, the one raving about Thatcher and the success-ethic, the other grimly demurring. That exchange sounds too much like mandatory Royal Court indignation, and could safely be toned down. After all, the play as a whole, arguing through and by human observation, leaves us in no doubt that a quivering finger is being pointed at a society whose highest good is 'making it'. It is articulate, eloquent, alive, proof in itself that we can no longer patronise women playwrights as peripheral. I think Caryl Churchill is well on the way to being a major talent.

Benedict Nightingale, "Women's Playtime," in New Statesman, *Vol. 104, No. 2686, September 10, 1982, p. 27.*

JOHN RUSSELL TAYLOR

In *Cloud Nine* you could not always quite produce a logical reason why one thing followed another, but somehow you never doubted that it did. *Top Girls* . . . progresses in a similar zigzag way between present and past, realism and outrageous fantasy.

The connections are just as much (and just as little) there for the reason to apprehend. And yet, to me at least, the pieces in the puzzle remain determinedly separate, never quite adding up to more than, well, so many fascinating pieces in a fascinating puzzle.

One thing about Caryl Churchill, you are never bored. Or hardly ever. Even the scene that sets the attention drifting here, the short glimpse of a present day rustic childhood which concludes a first half primarily taken up with very different things, is not so much boring in itself as too much of a let down after the long first scene, a real virtuoso piece if ever there was one. (p. 22)

[The first] scene is, to begin with, very funny. It also rehearses, directly and indirectly, the themes which will run through the rest of the play: woman's role in relation to men, children lost, stolen or strayed, the question of whether equal is the same as the same in the balance of the sexes. The whole discussion is so bizarre that you actually want to hear all of it—something which the structure of the play's overlapping dialogue effectually prevents. . . . Churchill manages particularly well the sudden transition of tone, as when Joan concludes an hilarious account of how she was caught short in childbirth during a papal procession with the bland observation that of course then she was dragged off into the country and stoned to death: yes indeed, things like that can put a damper on a jolly social evening.

At least, for all its oddity and obscurity, we know what this scene is about. It is difficult to be so sure about the rest. Like most of Churchill's work, it is about nothing simple and easily capsulated. It is not even plugging a simple feminist line. Clearly she must be on the side of women, and all for their escaping from the ridiculous position of total dependency in which Griselda and Nijo in particular are trapped. But her modern career-girls seem to have settled instead for what Osborne calls 'the Brave-New-Nothing-very-much-thank-you'. They have, in a very real sense, taken the place of men, but only so that they can ape men's least appealing traits. . . . Is that what it was all for? . . .

And as for Marlene—well, is she a heroine or isn't she? She seems to start as the model of a woman who can handle herself in a man's world, but gradually, as revelation follows revelation, we begin to wonder. So she has made it, but at what human price? And revelation does follow revelation: the rest of the play after the first scene proves to be fundamentally a good, old-fashioned piece with clues planted and secrets kept and revealed, climaxing in a splendidly sustained session of kitchen-sink drama which puts a situation . . . into Wesker country (literally rustic East Anglia) and lets it rip until we find out all there is to know. The result is achieved, in typical Churchill fashion, by putting the chronologically earliest scene at the end. . . .

Anyway, it is a play which sends you out asking questions and trying to work out, not disagreeably, just what it is you have been watching. Not quite *Cloud Nine,* but it leaves no doubt that Caryl Churchill is a big talent, still developing. (p. 23)

John Russell Taylor, in a review of "Top Girls," in Plays and Players, *No. 350, November, 1982, pp. 22-3.*

FRANK RICH

["**Top Girls**"] is no match for its predecessor ["**Cloud 9**"], but, happily, it is every bit as intent on breaking rules. . . .

The actresses in the company keep popping up in new roles; the setting switches abruptly and at first inexplicably between London and a dreary working-class home in provincial Suffolk; the evening ends with a scene that predates the rest of the action by a year. Miss Churchill also makes abundant use of overlapping, intentionally indecipherable dialogue, Robert Altman-style, as well as of lengthy pauses and stage waits that would make any Pinter play seem as frantic as a Marx Brothers sketch by comparison.

One cannot be too thankful for all these brave gambles, the strangely compelling and somehow moving silences included. Miss Churchill sees the theater as an open frontier where lives can be burst apart and explored, rather than as a cage that flattens out experience and diminishes it. Because of the startling technique and several passages of dazzling writing, **"Top Girls"** is almost always fascinating, even when it is considerably less than involving.

Some of the play's slippage does occur, it's true, when Miss Churchill's experiments run on self-indulgently. It seems unduly perverse that almost every scene must trail off before ending. The fantasy prologue, fun as it may be, is seriously overlong; later on, the author has trouble resisting the urge to lecture. Yet the major difficulty in **"Top Girls"** is a matter of content, not form. To these male American ears, Miss Churchill's new statement about women and men seems far more simplistic and obvious than the fervent pansexuality of **"Cloud 9."**

The message announces itself in that first scene, which proves an almost anthropological search for the ties that bind history's strongest sisters. Like Marlene, the famous icons at her table are "top girls"—courageous women who have "come a long way" by accomplishing "extraordinary achievements." But they've all paid a price for success: They've sacrificed their personal lives and children, been abused by men and lost contact with women who did not become "top girls." And we soon learn that Marlene, the present-day inheritor of their hard struggles for independent womanhood, is worse off yet. In order to fight her way up from her backwater proletarian roots to the executive suite, she has become, figuratively speaking, a male oppressor. . . .

No one can deny that women like Marlene exist. As Miss Churchill ultimately makes too clear, her heroine is partly a caricature of the ultimate British "top girl," Prime Minister Margaret Thatcher. But the playwright seems to beg her complicated issues by showing us only her monstrous heroine at one extreme, and, at the other, the victimized women that the Marlenes of this world exploit and betray. The absence of the middle range—of women who achieve without imitating power-crazed men and denying their own humanity—is an artificial polemical contrivance that cuts the play off at the heart. We're never quite convinced that women's choices are as limited and, in the play's final word, "frightening" as the stacked case of **"Top Girls"** suggests. Even in England, one assumes, not every woman must be either an iron maiden or a downtrodden serf.

Still, we're often carried along by the author's unpredictable stagecraft, her observant flashes of angry wit and pathos.

> *Frank Rich, "Caryl Churchill's 'Top Girls,' at the Public: Lady and the Tiger," in* The New York Times, *December 29, 1982, p. C17.*

BENEDICT NIGHTINGALE

One of the questions Caryl Churchill put to her fellow-feminists in *Top Girls* . . . was this. What have you, or indeed anyone, to offer the woman who hasn't the mental wherewithal ever to overtake the men on the promotion ladder, run her own office, jet off to New York for meetings and California for holidays, and do all the greater and lesser things associated with 'making it' in our sabre-toothed society? By way of illustrating the problem, she introduced a podgy, dim Ipswich schoolgirl, Angie, the unwanted daughter of her high-achieving protagonist, Marlene; and, by way of expanding and expatiating upon it, she now takes us [in *Fen*] to the opposite end of the East Anglian peninsular, to a fen village where Angies are to be found over every other sink, and thwarted and sometimes embittered Marlenes in every second potato patch. . . .

The village girls may, and do, sing little ditties about becoming hairdressers and nurses, but their likely destination is always out there in the wind and rough weather, toiling for the farmers as their grandmothers did and their granddaughters presumably will. Since the five-woman, one-man cast doubles, trebles, even quadruples its roles, we meet a fair spread of such victims, most resigned to being half-buried by the local sod ('what you after, bluebird of happiness?') and one or two putting up some fragile show of resistance ('don't start on me, just because you had nothing yourself').

In the latter category is Angela, who persistently torments her stepdaughter, partly out of personal frustration, partly to goad the girl out of her maddening submissiveness; and in it, too, is Val, who has left husband and children for a farm-labourer, Frank. . . . It would be wrong to give away the precise denouement of a play that powerfully demonstrates Ms Churchill's gift for crispness and tension, for vivid, succinct dialogue that keeps you alert and guessing; but you will hardly be surprised to learn that among these glum tillers and doleful sowers there should eventually appear a Grim Reaper.

You could of course argue that what destroys Val is not so much imprisonment-with-hard-labour in the village, rather an inner conflict that could be found in Kensington, the Cayman Islands, or anywhere else women are trying and failing to reconcile the claims of the sexual and the maternal. In fact, there were several times when I myself wondered whether Ms Churchill wasn't over-simplifying the nature and degree of the blame to be apportioned for the wasted and blasted lives she was showing us. If the City conglomerates gave back the land to the farmers, and the farmers were then forced to distribute it among their serfs, as no doubt should in justice happen, would the quality of life in far-off Fen country really improve as thoroughly as the play implies? Is it so much less paralysing to the mind and spirit to drudge from sun to sun in a potato field which happens to belong to you?

Yet Ms Churchill would no doubt expect us to ask such questions. Her distaste for the economic and social status quo doesn't mean she's relentlessly deterministic when she comes to analyse character and conduct; nor is her play without its complexities, its acknowledged contradictions and uncertainties, its beguiling quirks and intriguing oddities. *Top Girls* is probably the finer work, because it possesses those selfsame qualities in greater abundance and because it has a more unusual and arresting point to make: liberation is only a subtler, uglier form of enslavement if women have to maim, mutilate and be-Thatcher themselves in order to achieve it. But *Fen* offers proof enough of the assurance and skill, intelligence and passion of a dramatist who must surely be rated among the half-dozen best now writing.

Benedict Nightingale, ''Hard Labour,'' in New Statesman, Vol. 105, No. 2710, February 25, 1983, p. 30.*

CLIVE BARNES

[Churchill] is probably more popular in London than in N.Y. and—despite her strong political impulses—at times, accents and places apart, she proves more like an American playwright than most British. For her technique is firmly based on that kind of symbolic realism favored by so many American writers.

Where most playwrights produce a form of dramatic portrait, Miss Churchill, and it can be seen in *Cloud Nine* and *Top Girls* as well as *Fen,* is attempting to suggest a landscape with figures. The background to her plays, their descriptions of the specific worlds outside the players, is extremely important.

Never more than in this richly dense *Fen,* which offers a perfectly straightforward account of a domestic tragedy—the sort of stuff that newspapers as much as dreams are made of—but this story is set against a wonderful psychogeographic picture of the life, times and legends, history, and ecology, of the Fens. (pp. 209-10)

It is a rich, complex tragic picture, often very funny. Because while Churchill is placing her play in its special location, she is telling bizarre anecdotes that all have a strict if peculiar, ring of truth to them.

What is being told means more than what is being said. Churchill seems to beguile us with her technique and then transfix with her passion. We think we know what she is doing—we can understand her minor, placatory gestures to keep us interested with wit, quaintness and comforting cleverness, when like an axe-blow, something hits us. (p. 210)

Clive Barnes, '''Fen' Unearths Passion & Potatoes,'' in New York Post, May 31, 1983. Reprinted in New York Theatre Critics' Reviews, Vol. XLIV, No. 10, June 13-19, 1983, pp. 209-10.

FRANK RICH

[''Fen''] could well be called ''Bottom Girls.'' As the author's ''Top Girls'' told of Marlene, a self-made businesswoman who sells out her provincial working-class roots and humanity for corporate success in London, so the new one examines the less privileged sisters such top girls leave behind. . . .

As befits the shift in focus, the new play contains little of its predecessor's laughter: even as the audience enters . . . , it is swept up in a gloomy mist that pours out from the stage. ''Fen'' is dour, difficult and, unlike either ''Top Girls'' or ''Cloud 9,'' never coy about its rather stridently doctrinaire socialism: it's the most stylistically consistent of Miss Churchill's plays and at times the most off-putting. It is also yet another confirmation that its author possesses one of the boldest theatrical imaginations to emerge in this decade. . . .

As an impressionistic, class-conscious portrait of an agrarian community, the play recalls David Hare's . . . piece about a similar village in nascent revolutionary China, ''Fanshen.'' . . .

The action unfolds on a stunning set . . . : the stage floor is carpeted with the dirt of the potato fields and surrealistically bordered by walls and furnishings suggesting the women's dreary homes. In . . . [the] eerie lighting—all shades of Thomas Hardy dankness, no sunlight—the 90 minutes of scenes loom in the icy dark like fragmented nightmares. One minute the women are picking potatoes in a thunderstorm; then, through startlingly sharp transitions, that dominant image gives way to the sight of two illicit lovers dancing in moonlight or a madonna-like portrait of mother and child or a forlorn Baptist revival meeting.

''We're all rubbish,'' says one of the suffering Baptists, ''but Jesus still loves us, so it's all right.'' As in **''Top Girls,''** Miss Churchill sees one and all as helpless, exploited victims of a dehumanizing capitalistic system. She further feels that women can only escape its clutches, as Marlene did, by adopting that system's most selfish, ruthless traits. . . .

Most of the women in **''Fen,''** however, are laborers, bound to the land by an age-old, oppressive tradition that enslaves them from birth to grave. As Miss Churchill presents these sad serfs, they can only ameliorate their misery in self-destructive ways: by drinking in a pub or gossiping or taking Valium or betraying one another or going mad. Yet if the playwright's definition of these women's choices is rigidly deterministic, her concentrated dramatization of their lives has an open, poetic intensity that transcends the flat tendentiousness of mere agit-prop. . . .

''The earth's awake!,'' says one of [the characters at the conclusion of **''Fen''**]—and it's Miss Churchill who has awakened it. Here's a writer, amazingly enough, who is plowing new ground in the theater with every new play.

Frank Rich, '''Fen,' New Work by Caryl Churchill,'' in The New York Times, May 31, 1983, p. C10.

JOHN SIMON

The unsuccessful work of a gifted and pungent playwright, [*Fen*] is eminently watchable, full of sharp, stinging, tragicomic moments that, however, refuse to coalesce. Shapeliness, to be sure, is seldom what Miss Churchill is after; topsy-turvy jaggedness and intricately lacerating jests are her game. But however you go about it, impact is needed—particularly when political agitation for socialism is the purpose. Yet *Fen,* which examines the lives of a score of women and couple of men in East Anglia's fen, or marsh, country, dilutes its effect doubly: by trying to do too much and do it with far too little.

Five actresses and one actor . . . portray here, as it were, the entire population of a hamlet: the toilers on the earth, the harsh overseers who are themselves exploited, even the ultimate overlord from a Japanese conglomerate. But the subject seems more suited to a semi-documentary film: There are too many characters for us to get truly involved with any (shrewd old Brecht always managed to have a central charismatic figure or two), and played by too few actors, adding to our confusion. Then there is the nonmeshing of the political overplot and the personal stories: a married woman torn between her children and her lover; a stepchild bullied by her stepmother until the two form a sadomasochist couple. Miss Churchill wishes to make the private miseries hinge on social injustice, but the two don't blend compellingly, especially as the play tries to be in so many places simultaneously that it ends up tearing itself to shreds. Provocative shreds, but insubstantial and unsustaining ones. (p. 77)

John Simon, "Soft Centers," in New York *Maga-zine, Vol. 17, No. 24, June 13, 1983, pp. 76-8.**

GILES GORDON

[*Softcops* is] a desperately serious treatise, (and to emphasise that, there's no interval) about crime, punishment and male society. Set in 19th-century France, it features our old, ambiguous friend Vidocq . . . , master-crook turned top cop, and thus Miss Churchill—one of our very best playwrights—can debate as she will whether hierarchical society is responsible for the criminal, or the criminal for forcing society to punish him.

The trouble is that the play is more illustrated lecture than drama, though lots of 'dramatic' things happen. A thief is obliged to hold up for the mob to see, his right hand, painted red; then it's cut off. (p. 27)

Miss Churchill, I suspect unfortunately, read Michel Foucault's *Surveiller et Punir* and so impressed was she by Foucault's ideas that they have taken over and devoured the play she might have written. The book, apparently, analyses the way in which we used to brutalise, torture and physically destroy the criminal classes whereas today we merely observe them. If you believe that, it seems to me, you'll believe anything. Yet Miss Churchill is as sophisticated a writer as we have (there's a nice dig at Brecht: because there are no placards, nobody knows what to think), so dexterous with language and argument, that even the horrors . . . disturb rather than merely disgust. (pp. 27-8)

Giles Gordon, "No Soft Option," in The Spectator, *Vol. 252, No. 8115, January 21, 1984, pp. 27-8.**

ROSALIND CARNE

So intent is [Churchill in *Softcops*] on stating her message that every whiff of humour is imbued with a grim sense of its sinister implications. . . . [The] result is one of the least enjoyable evenings I can remember in three years' regular theatregoing. Enjoyment may not be mandatory, but there are few compensatory factors in *Softcops;* it keeps you guessing, and hoping, but consistently fails to provide what it promises. . . . [When] I left the theatre I felt as if I'd been mentally battered with a blunt instrument. (pp. 30-1)

In a succession of loosely connected episodes, which acts like an ironic moral pageant, the treatment of crime is seen as a form of mass entertainment, part of a government plan to mystify and depoliticise the criminal process. The cast of 12 men take turns at representing the many faces of Vidocq in short sketches, supplemented with cabaret-style exhibitions of torture, execution, incarceration and so forth.

Ms Churchill pays tribute to Michel Foucault's *Surveiller et Punir* for some of the ideas in the play, but she appears to be too enamoured of her source material to see the pitfalls of its dramatic reconstruction. The content is too tortuous and intellectual to work as agit-prop which, in any case, needs much stronger links between auditorium and stage, while a drama of ideologies needs fuller personalities, especially in the theatre of words. (p. 31)

Rosalind Carne, "Punishment," in New Statesman, *Vol. 107, No. 2758, January 27, 1984, pp. 30-1.**

Arthur A(llen) Cohen
1928-

American novelist, critic, theologian, editor, and publisher.

Cohen is considered a leading contemporary Jewish-American literary figure. His novels and scholarly works of nonfiction explore the difficulty of following a traditional Judaic ethos in an increasingly secular America. In his works Cohen exhorts his fellow Jews to practice a more devout life and set aside the materialistic aspects of American Judaism. Built on themes of particular concern to American Jews, Cohen's works have nonetheless been praised as successful depictions of the full range of modern life.

Cohen's early writings were primarily works of Jewish theology. These include *The Natural and Supernatural Jew* (1963), in which Cohen attempted to reconcile Jewish tradition with existentialism. His first novel, *The Carpenter Years* (1967), is the story of a Jew who leaves his family and his religion to adopt the lifestyle of a white Anglo-Saxon Protestant in Langham, Pennsylvania. When his Jewish son comes to Langham, the man must confront both his religious past and the family he left behind. *The Carpenter Years* examines the pressures on the modern Jew to forsake his past and the need to come to terms with his tradition. Although some critics found intriguing Cohen's attempt to develop the novel as a device for moral investigation, most argued that the work was overly didactic and that much of the plot was improbable.

Over the next decade Cohen wrote both fiction and nonfiction, including what has been called his best novel, *In the Days of Simon Stern* (1973). The story of a post-World War II messiah who sets up a haven for victims of the Holocaust in New York City's Lower East Side, this work was praised as an intellectual examination of belief and survival. Another novel, *A Hero in His Time* (1975), tells the tale of a Soviet Jewish poet who comes to the United States and is pressured by his government to deliver a poem that contains a coded KGB message. While some critics viewed the novel as an exercise in farce and praised its engaging humor, others considered it a more serious work in its examination of politics and art.

Acts of Theft (1979), Cohen's next novel, does not deal overtly with Judaism. Instead, it is the story of a European sculptor living in Mexico who steals pieces of pre-Columbian art to sell to collectors. Cohen was praised for providing insight into the creative process and for examining the idea that art is necessarily derived from previously established concepts, thus constituting a form of thievery.

In his recent novel *An Admirable Woman* (1983), Cohen narrates the story of a fictional Jewish scholar who has fled to the United States from Nazi Germany. Although the protagonist is fictional, Cohen has stated that she was inspired by the famed German scholar Hannah Arendt.

(See also *CLC*, Vol. 7; *Contemporary Authors*, Vols. 1-4, rev. ed.; *Contemporary Authors New Revision Series*, Vol. 1; and *Dictionary of Literary Biography*, Vol. 28.)

RICHARD M. ELMAN

[The] Jewish-born protagonist of Arthur Cohen's first novel ["**The Carpenter Years**"], keen to the logic of his own de-

spairing mediocrity, reflects lugubriously about the New York "Jewish mediocrity" he left behind in the middle of the Depression to assume the identity of a Christian functionary in a small Pennsylvania city: "All those people—small merchants and young eager businessmen winding their lives around success, joyless opulence, methodical accumulation, praising their own self-sacrifice, and raising their own children to admire the works which they wrought in despair—were real, but they meant nothing and they had no meaning to offer."

Within the context of the novel, such assertions by Edgar Morrison (Morris Edelman) are intended to simulate the reflections of a morally earnest man at a moment when his whole past is about to be uncovered, revisited upon him by the appearance in Langham, Pa., of the son whom he had abandoned nearly two decades earlier. . . . Clearly, we are meant to sympathize with Edgar's honesty, if not with his choice or with the deceits he must compound to remain a Christian. "What a damned serious man he is," Edgar's minister declares to the second wife, Edwinna, but it's my serious suspicion that the minister is mistaken. As soon as Edgar begins to reflect on why he did what he did it becomes obvious that he is really just a damned prig.

For even though one hates to uphold Jewish mediocrity, the facts are that when this man sought to get out from under the afflictions of his Jewish self-hate by allegedly pursuing his "Jewish destiny" through Christianity, Edgar Morrison left behind a helpless wife and a small child, in the care of his brother Stanley, who had a family of his own, and was, moreover, a firm believer in "joyless opulence" and "methodical accumulation," a man consumed by his own mediocrity and self-loathing, limited and begrudging.

Yet Stanley supported Edgar's wife and child. He diligently sought out his own brother and was able to release him from the bondage which he had imposed upon himself through bigamy. Is it not blind for a moralist to suggest, consequently, that brother Stanley had "no meaning to offer" anybody? If Stanley's ordeal is only to be made incidental to Edgar's crisis of identity, then one can only assume that the thoroughly honest religious man must turn himself into a thoroughgoing fool. . . .

It is a mark of the smugness of this novel that Stanley is an object of contempt; he is "all those people." But, if he is that mediocre, what does that make Edgar? Mr. Cohen lets Edgar off rather easily: he suffers from recurrent fits of Barthian despair, which occasionally drive him out of the house on a bender, and once he visits a prostitute to discuss his great need for "Talk. Need. Love." It's just about that trite. Mr. Cohen's assertion of an elevated discourse for this beery refugee is his chief admission of the absence of any moral exertion within the novel.

As an erudite and skillful essayist on religion in the modern world, he has argued, with some power, that unless Judaism brings forth its messianic vision to offer to a faithless world it is doomed to its own mediocrity. But the reader who accepts such assertions within an essay may still demand experiential proof in fiction. And when one finds that the writer is insensitive to the very possibilities for which he seems to be searching, then not only fiction, but essay itself is called into question.

Which is to say that this religious potboiler is pretentious, asserting archetypes as people and people as archetypes. It is also morally obtuse, written with stilted dialogue and melodramatic excess, and with a contempt for mediocrity that is about as excessive and blind as adoration would be.

I was prepared to accept Edgar Morrison's choice as an option which any man has the right to exercise until I was introduced to that first son, Daniel. Bitter, nihilistic and violent, Daniel is the author's archly ironic comment on the Biblical reverberations in the name, for it turns out that this Daniel has grown up to become an apprentice psychiatrist with a hesitancy about interpreting dreams. And he is, clearly, the future which the novel holds forth as Jewish destiny.

> Richard M. Elman, "Edgar Morrison's Choice," in The New York Times Book Review, *February 5, 1967, p. 45.*

ARTHUR R. GOLD

Can a man who is not a novelist write a good novel? Mr. Cohen is not a novelist. He has mastered the ordinary techniques of modern fiction, the flashback, the controlled point of view, the scene doubling as action and the action doubling as dialogue. But he is content to use these techniques passively, never suggesting that he has something *novel* to contribute to the history of the form.

Yet *The Carpenter Years* is a good novel. It is good because the man who made it, though not imaginatively gifted, has

known how to take advantage of the possibilities of conventional fiction as a medium of discourse and as a tool of investigation. As philosophers use myth, as novelists have sometimes used theology, so Mr. Cohen, a theologian, uses fiction—for purposes foreign to its ends, but proper to his.

What, for example, can we say of Mr. Cohen's main character, Edgar Morrison born Morris Edelman, an imperfect convert to American Christianity, once a failing accountant with Jewish wife and son in New York, now a YMCA director with gentile wife and son in a country town? As a created person, a man with an illegal passport into one's mind and heart, he is not substantial enough to be moving, for he has no life other than that given to him by his all too paradigmatic plot. Knowing him is like never knowing water except at the boiling point. But what has been made to move *in* him moves us deeply—two religions, each troubled, confronting each other in the invented laboratory of a consciousness sensitive enough to respond to them both. . . .

Morrison leaves Judaism because he cannot survive as a failure in a community "where no one was ever let off the hook," and where now the criterion of material achievement has been added to that of moral success. He can survive, but only, of course, as someone else, in the community which at its noblest intimated a confession of failure as the condition of rebirth, and which now, in America, offers the additional lure of anonymity. "As a Christian, as an *echt* American, he could fail and fail quietly, unknown and undiscovered. Soul redeemed in Jesus Christ (that single Man extending his hand to single men) and be buried in the vastness of America." This is a hard, unpleasant view of one religion in its decadence from the point of view of another, equally decadent. But this very unpleasantness commends the novel that contains it. . . .

[In] what I think we must accept as a very fine discrimination among the values possible in such a story, Cohen refuses to make the obvious points. He doesn't argue that an Americanized Jew is bound to be found out and rejected by his Christian neighbors. Morrison's minister and his Christian family continue to adore him for his goodness. Nor does Cohen argue that a man like Morrison will suffer the contumely of a traitor to past and people. The past can't be betrayed, and at the end of the book Morrison and his Jewish son acknowledge each other in wordless compassion. Neither a hypocrite nor an apostate, Morrison has committed only one sin worth thinking about—the sin of shirking his people's legacy of "magnificence," the sin of letting himself off the hook—and the only fate adequate to a sin so subtly defined is precisely not to be let back *on* the hook. His new community accepts him, but does not know him, for he can be known only in his failure. And by those to whom he is known he can neither be addressed nor embraced.

It is a complex formulation of a complex fate, and worthy of study for the sake of fact, not fiction.

> Arthur R. Gold, "What Makes Edgar Run?" in Book Week—World Journal Tribune, *March 12, 1967, p. 4.*

DAVID DAICHES

The details in ["**The Carpenter Years**"] are filled in with skill and care and there is some powerful and occasionally even moving writing. But the author moves uneasily between realism and symbolism. The tone is that of sociological and psychological precision, but the incidents are meant to have symbolic dimensions. As a result, there are two levels of probability at work which, instead of reinforcing each other, tend to destroy or at least weaken each other. The pressures that would make a Polish-Jewish immigrant want to appear as a WASP in an American small town are real pressures, and they result in real conflicts, real timidities, self-deceptions, internal strains. But to have such a person converted to Christianity by a nutty Hebrew Christian before finally landing a job as Presbyterian director of the YMCA in a Pennsylvania town, and to have him in the process commit bigamy and therefore not only expose himself to the criminal law but threaten the whole foundation of his new life—this is not plausible. But who wants that kind of plausibility in a symbolic novel?, it may be asked. Well, I do for one: the tone of the novel demands it. "The dilemma of Edelman-Morrison unforgettably symbolizes the dilemma of religion-hungry Americans in an age when the traditional demands of religion have become a burden few can bear," the blurb tells us. I cannot accept this. The special kind of conformity which Edelman-Morrison practices is insufficiently motivated, inadequately related to a psychological drive which in turn might be made symbolic of the urge to abandon differentiating traditions and seek conformity in modern American society.

I think this is a most interesting novel, in some ways a skillful novel, at some points a powerful novel, but I do not think that it consistently achieves the symbolic dimension the author clearly aimed at. (pp. 95-6)

> *David Daiches, "Symbolic Dimensions," in* Commentary, *Vol. 43, No. 4, April, 1967, pp. 94-6.*

RICHARD HORCHLER

The Carpenter Years is not a successful novel, which makes for particularly keen disappointment because it is—or has—a number of other very good things. Because Mr. Cohen is a thinker, there are important and provocative ideas in the book. Because he is a religious scholar and theologian, there are profound religious perceptions in it. Because he is a twentieth-century American and a believing Jew, there is in it an urgent concern for the spiritual meaning of the modern American experience, to the Jew and the Christian particularly.

But because Mr. Cohen is not a novelist—at least not yet a novelist—his interests, reflections and ideas are only hung on his characters and events, not embodied in them. Mr. Cohen is more interested in certain ideas and problems, it seems clear, than he is in his characters. If he were really interested in Edgar Morrison (Morris Edelman), for example, he would have to have seen a more complete, more believable human being than the one he presents. Morrison-Edelman's story—a monstrous story, twenty years past when we are introduced to him—is simply incredible. This is not to say that a history such as his is impossible, but that it is impossible for the man the author describes. Almost any man is capable of almost any action, of course, but actions to be believable and meaningful to a reader should be part of some kind of development, and in the case of Morrison-Edelman the past and present are linked only by the author's declaration. What we are shown of the character belies what we are told of him, and vice-versa.

At the core of the novel, Morrison-Edelman's flight from his Jewish identity is given some context and whatever measure of plausibility it has is mostly as a kind of theological betrayal, no doubt because this is what chiefly interested the author. The actual human betrayal, however—of wife, child, family, friends,

psychological personhood—is so perfunctorily treated as to be unreal.

It is hard to believe in any of the characters, in fact, and therefore hard to take very seriously the objectively very serious things that happen in the novel. The dialogue, as part of this problem, seldom rings true, although the style is as graceful and sure in the expository passages as we would expect of Mr. Cohen. I am afraid that what he was trying to convey in *The Carpenter Years* would have been clearer—and better realized—in one of his philosophic essays. (pp. 558-59)

> *Richard Horchler, in a review of "The Carpenter Years," in* Commonweal, *Vol. LXXXVI, No. 20, September 8, 1967, pp. 558-59.*

JOHN LEONARD

In ["**Acts of Theft**"], Arthur A. Cohen assigns himself the formidable task of making us believe in an art—sculpture—that we can't see, of evoking space shaped in silence, "essential things," by a piling on of words. That he succeeds should come as no surprise. Mr. Cohen is always ambitious, and almost always succeeds. In his tour de force, "**A Hero in His Time**," he made us believe in a Russian-Jewish minor poet with whose soul Mr. Cohen had no right to be so well acquainted. In his astonishing "**In the Days of Simon Stern**," he made me believe that all of us are Jewish.

Stefan Mauger is Austrian, born with our century, of minor nobility, a young Count whose father goes mad. Educated in and around Vienna, he leaves for Paris to teach himself to paint. He is befriended by the American art critic Clemens Rosenthal—a nice touch, that name—who tells him frankly that, on canvas, Mauger has failed. Mauger knows it. He turns to sculpture and to mythology, to the fixities of ancient Egypt and to the carvings of folk craftsmen. He worships Brancusi, even as he resists Brancusi's influence in favor of his example. He makes masks. . . .

After yet another war, Mauger follows Clemens Rosenthal to New York, marries his mistress and takes off for the Pacific Northwest, where the shamanistic art of the Kwakiutl Indians, "indifferent to measurable time," enrages him: he's not as good as they are. Mauger and his wife, Alicia, escape to Mexico, to Yucatan, where we first meet them. Brancusi has died. Rosenthal, who is about to die, brings the news. Mauger, at work on his "creatures," his bestiary, is confronted by the death of Brancusi, the dying of his friend, and, at the same time, Inspector Mariposa of the Mexico Police.

Mauger, you see, is a thief, specializing in pre-Columbian art. He has organized a major heist from an archeological site. For Inspector Mariposa, who was once a student of archeology, the stolen art . . . is his identity. . . . Mauger, on the other hand, despises the "brutalism" of this art. . . .

In the confrontation of Mauger and Mariposa, the many themes of "**Acts of Theft**" scream together, a distraught chorus—the artist as God, art as theft, the ransom of the past, the ancient made modern, pride and sacrifice. I think it was Rimbaud who said that the poet is a thief of fire. For Mauger, his stealing and his art are "interlocking acts of seizure." We are violated by the gods. We have to make silence out of the noise. It is an idea that might have been found in the notebooks of Dostoyevsky. . . .

We also have some ups and downs. Among the ups: a young Mauger stealing the medical report on his mad father, as if to remind us that knowledge is a kind of theft; the sudden friendship of Mauger and Rosenthal; the first, wonderful, silent meeting between Mauger and Brancusi; the account of the Kwakiutl Indians, their art and their potlatch; a Mexico brilliantly rendered without the heavy breathing of D. H. Lawrence in "The Plumed Serpent." Among the downs: an altogether too casual attitude toward crucial scenes in the novel. Why should Mauger marry Alicia? Rosenthal in Mexico is too convenient and too omniscient. Mariposa and Mauger ought to have had a longer confrontation; they understand each other too quickly; Dostoyevsky would have given them a hundred pages. And Mariposa needs more development to be a worthy adversary.

This, however, is housecleaning and bookkeeping. We believe in Mauger's rage and in his bestiary, that garden of the hieratic crane, the ovum, the eye, the bear, the stone masks and the women and the phalluses. We believe Mauger himself in his solitude, as he tries and fails to burn his way to the truths of wood and stone. He lacks an acceptable metaphysics of the unseen, but if he can smash the Olmec figurine and then allow his own sculptured eye to be destroyed, he may be on his way. Prometheus may steal his genius. We believe because Mr. Cohen has somehow found words that amount to a revelation instead of an excuse.

> *John Leonard, in a review of "Acts of Theft," in* The New York Times, *February 12, 1980, p. C9.*

MARK SHECHNER

Since it's not about Judaism but American Indians, Olmec heads, Mayan pots and Kwakiutl potlatches, **"Acts of Theft,"** Arthur A. Cohen's fourth novel and eleventh book, may appear to be something of a departure from his usual terrain. . . . But **"Acts of Theft"** is about religion, and specifically about the kind of worship that Jews have historically held anathema: idolatry. . . .

Those who buy this book expecting a straightforward drama of crime and detection will find Mauger sadly easy to catch. He drops clues everywhere. This is because, I guess, Mr. Cohen doesn't want the dramatics of pursuit and evasion to distract us from his ruminations on the morality of art. Hence he short-circuits his plot with flashbacks, asides, interior monologues, lectures, the works, for the sake of depth, weight and moral tone.

But rather than challenging the reader, this strategy only exasperates him. Mr. Cohen is basically an essayist starting out with a problem and seeking to concretize it in fiction. Since the problem here is theophany, knowledge of the infinite, Mr. Cohen plies us with vivid and passionate yearnings that overpower his plot and overwhelm his sentences. . . .

The cumulative effect of Mauger's peripatetic religiosity is neither dramatic nor ecstatic but wearily curatorial. . . . As each character's voice dissolves into the general ambience of lecturing and theorizing, his language grows more animated, as if to salvage his individuality by sheer vividness of phrasing. But this vividness itself quickly becomes routine and, at last, simply shrill. Mr. Cohen is not unaware of this difficulty. "I've no vision worth talking about," Mauger allows. "Anyway, talking makes it as stale as yesterday's bread." He adds, apologetically, "Matisse was right: artists should have their tongues cut out."

Is this, then, another one of those long books about the hopelessness of language, or is the author just throwing in the towel? The trouble with **"Acts of Theft"** is that Mr. Cohen wants the sublime but can achieve only the breathless, which works in fiction about as well as it does in religion.

> *Mark Shechner, "Graven Images and Other Temptations," in* The New York Times Book Review, *March 9, 1980, p. 10.*

JOHN NAUGHTON

[*Acts of Theft* is] about a believer in Art, but one who digs his own traps rather than falling into the ready-made ones which plague ordinary mortals. *Acts of Theft* opens in Mexico with a raid on the site of an archaeological dig and the removal of hundreds of priceless figurines. The operation is masterminded by an Austrian aristocrat and artist, Stephen Mauger; when the scene changes to a hunting-lodge in Silesia in the closing years of the 19th century, and the birth of the hero, one gets the sinking feeling that this is yet another Kentucky Fried Novel, constructed according to the formula that permits translation into lavish screenplay with the minimum of effort.

It pays to persevere, though, for Mr Cohen is as serious as his hero, and he has things to get off his chest about the peculiarities of the creative psyche. The balance he has to strike is between dissertation and tale, between an exploration of what it feels like to be an artist of a particular kind and a detective story about an art robbery. The method adopted to keep the book on the rails is to interweave the two themes and to make the detective pursuing Mauger into a kind of mirror-image of the thief. A bit like matter and anti-matter in theoretical physics, if you like; but, in Mr Cohen's case, the collision of the two produces not an enormous bang, but a rather ambiguous whimper.

> *John Naughton, "Smirking," in* The Listener, *Vol. 103, No. 2655, March 27, 1980, p. 419.**

PUBLISHERS WEEKLY

Although Cohen makes very clear in a foreword that all of his characters [in *An Admirable Woman*] "are derived wholly from the imagination," it is impossible to read his fine novel without thinking of the late Hannah Arendt. His "admirable woman" is a brilliant German Jewish scholar who flees Berlin with her gentile husband just in time, going first to Paris, then, none too soon, to America. . . . Cohen's constant probing of what constitutes true brilliance is a fascinating piece of scholarship in its own right, and his portrait of the Nazi era and what it wrought is haunting. To tease just a little, Cohen brings in an offstage Hannah Arendt as a longtime friend of the narrator and then has his "admirable woman" analyze *her*.

> *A review of "An Admirable Woman," in* Publishers Weekly, *Vol. 224, No. 13, September 23, 1983, p. 62.*

ANATOLE BROYARD

In an article distributed by the publisher along with **"An Admirable Woman,"** Arthur Cohen says that Erika Hertz, the heroine of his novel, was "suggested to me by the remarkable personality and intellectual career of an old friend, Hannah Arendt." Reading this, one can see both the promise and the potential difficulties in portraying the philosopher and political scientist who wrote the "Origins of Totalitarianism," and "Eichmann in Jerusalem," as well as several other books. When she died almost eight years ago, Hannah Arendt was regarded as one of the most important political thinkers of her time.

To dress such a woman in fiction, to do her justice in an everyday context, is an ambitious project. Mr. Cohen did not, he says, borrow actual biographical details. Rather, he tried to imagine the kind of life Hannah Arendt had lived. To do this, he would have to capture her conversation, the workings of her mind, the flow of her feelings. But in taking on such a complex character, it is almost as if Mr. Cohen had tried to write a novel about the human condition itself. Miss Arendt had, in fact, written a book called "The Human Condition."
. . .

What one misses in **"An Admirable Woman"** is contact with other people. Erika's career in New York City is more often summarized than dramatized. And after all this sacrifice of the concrete stuff of which novels are made, Mr. Cohen does not succeed much better in conveying the quality of Erika's mind. While his summaries of her books are adequate, he has not given Erika the style, the intellectual texture, of a great woman.

Though one critic accuses Erika's work of suffering from "a surfeit of elegance," Mr. Cohen's notion of elegance makes Erika sound like this: "My life task had been until that moment and remained confirmed thereafter to understand the unspeakable loneliness of human consciousness—the shared faculty of awareness whose every detail defies camaraderie."

It is Erika's defiance of camaraderie that makes **"An Admirable Woman"** a rather schematic or unrealized novel. Mr. Cohen means to portray her as an example of what Kant called a "moral terrorist," but she achieves only a kind of dry, majestic remoteness. On her deathbed Erika says that most of her friends "are growing tired of my steadfastness." For all Mr. Cohen's intelligent exertions, the reader too may grow tired of steadfastness.

> *Anatole Broyard, in a review of "An Admirable Woman," in* The New York Times, *November 17, 1983, p. C25.*

EARL SHORRIS

Not so many years ago, before it became a stew of poverty and boutiques, the Upper West Side of New York was a German university town, and all the inhabitants were Jews. Or so it seemed to someone newly arrived from the Southwest. It was a miraculous town in which a pediatrician spoke of his schoolmate Sigmund Freud and the person on the next bench in Riverside Park browsed in a German edition of Martin Heidegger's "Being and Time." Part of the fascination of this town of the mind is that it was closed to outsiders, surrounded by walls of language and tragic history.

Now, with the university town largely gone, lost, like a person, to time, Arthur A. Cohen has written **"An Admirable Woman,"** a novel in the form of a memoir by the most famous woman of that place in that time. One could not be better prepared than Mr. Cohen to write such a novel, for besides being the author of four other novels, he is a theologian, a historian, an editor and an anthologist. He succeeds in opening the gates of the town, revealing its origins and exploring a kind of life and a kind of marriage in what seemed an elevated, magical town. (p. 9)

Mr. Cohen has written a novel about not-Hannah Arendt. He uses the denial brilliantly to inform the novel and to overlay it with the suspense of a puzzle. The particulars of Erika Hertz, which Mr. Cohen uses so deftly to give a fullness to her, are often the particulars of Hannah Arendt. Erika Hertz is vain about her legs. Hannah Arendt is said to have been vain about her legs. Both women smoke. Both are comfortable using Latin and Greek phrases.

But Mr. Cohen has not written a biography of Hannah Arendt, nor has he intended a biography. Rather, he has used the novelist's imagination to explore fame in the intellectual world, to reveal life overwhelmed by ethics, to take the reader to the miraculous town. All through her memoir, Erika Hertz ponders the quality of admirableness, examines it in relation to each of her attributes. She is a doubter, a critic of herself. A measure of Mr. Cohen's accomplishment is that the reader wants to argue with her, often to insist that she is a "wholly admirable" woman.

Near the end of the novel, Mr. Cohen comes inevitable to the Eichmann trial, for even in the life of not-Hannah Arendt, the drama of the controversy caused by Arendt's book "Eichmann in Jerusalem" and the idea of the banality of evil cannot be ignored. Instead of a parallel that might take the reader into the soul of a person in a storm of conflicting views of history, Mr. Cohen chooses to let Erika Hertz attack her "friend" Hannah Arendt, to accuse her of using "the occasion to be original," of misunderstanding the meaning of the word "banal" in English, of recklessness.

Whether one agrees with Hannah Arendt or Erika Hertz makes no difference, the scene is an act of timidity, and art is not timid. For all its thoughtfulness and its knowing and sure-handed use of the writer's craft, **"An Admirable Woman"** cannot recover from this moment. (p. 49)

> *Earl Shorris, "Not Hannah Arendt," in* The New York Times Book Review, *November 20, 1983, pp. 9, 49.*

J(ames) V(incent) Cunningham

1911-

American poet, critic, and editor.

Cunningham is respected for his finely crafted poetry and for his poetic theories, which stress the value of formal techniques. Early in his career Cunningham wrote in the modernist tradition and was associated with the literary circle surrounding the poet and critic Yvor Winters. By the 1940s, however, Cunningham had rejected modernism as well as romanticism, which he believes is the basis for much modernist verse; he adopted instead a terse and witty epigrammatic style. Cunningham holds that a romantic sensibility can lead only to imprecision and emotionalism, while strict classical formalism encourages clarity, analysis, and objectivity. Often compared to the works of John Donne, Ben Jonson, and Alexander Pope, most of Cunningham's later verse is carefully rhymed and measured with little emphasis on imagery. Rather than the symbolic description employed by the modernists, Cunningham presents direct philosophical and metaphysical commentary.

Cunningham developed his epigrammatic poetry in his collections *The Helmsman* (1942), *The Judge Is Fury* (1947), *Doctor Drink* (1950), *Trivial, Vulgar, and Exalted* (1957), and *The Exclusions of a Rhyme* (1960). Some critics interpret many of the poems in these volumes as considerations of the human fate after death and praise Cunningham's rational approach to the search for meaning in life. In his long poem *To What Strangers, What Welcome* (1964) Cunningham modifies his earlier style by extending his epigrams into a narrative sequence. In this symbolic account of a physical and psychological journey he also experiments with sensory detail. Most critics agree that these devices, combined with his characteristic exactitude and formal restraint, make *To What Strangers, What Welcome* one of Cunningham's strongest works.

In his prose work *In Quest of the Opal* (1950) Cunningham comments in the third person on his own poetry. In that work and in *The Collected Essays* (1976) Cunningham also analyzes the verse of other writers from the Renaissance to the modern period. His long essay *Woe or Wonder* (1951), which was reprinted in *The Collected Essays*, explores the relationship between technical devices and emotional impact in Shakespeare's tragedies. The work is considered an important contribution to the existing body of Shakespearean criticism.

(See also *CLC*, Vol. 3; *Contemporary Authors*, Vols. 1-4, rev. ed.; *Contemporary Authors New Revision Series*, Vol. 1; and *Dictionary of Literary Biography*, Vol. 5.)

EDWARD WEISMILLER

The poems in this brief and beautifully printed collection [*The Helmsman*], difficult as they are to place in the stream of American and English poetry, are of unusual interest. They are the products of a talent which is emphatically and avowedly not modern, but which, though it operates within quite narrow bounds, and intentionally so, is none the less expert and sensitive. Cunningham is a humanist scholar and a philosopher, concerned with choice, the will, wisdom, reason, and nature

viewed both concretely and as an abstraction; yet curiously enough, however abstract the subject-matter may be, the reader is always conscious that it is part of what might be termed the autobiography of the mind producing it. Cunningham's personality, ironic, austere, sharply self-conscious yet objective, is everywhere on the poems. They do not, therefore, seem so much humanistic as literally classical, as though Cunningham were trying to erect in his own sparse works an American Silver Age. (p. 279)

Adopting classical forms and conventions, [Cunningham] enters many of his poems, particularly the title ode, a number of epigrams, and a punning mock elegy. One thinks a little of Housman in his less winsome moods. Rejecting the ways of the "men of wild perceptions," Cunningham says of himself finally:

> Conceptions
> Cold as the serpent and as wise
>   Have held my eyes:
> Their fierce impersonal forms have moved my pen.

It is this poet's particular triumph that, dealing with such conceptions in poems of medium difficulty—he speaks neither to the many nor to an impossible few—he has produced a series of poems cut like jewels. The "fierce impersonal forms" in the minds of many of today's poets might have swollen into turgidity, into mere shapelessness; Cunningham leaves them beautifully precise. . . . Cunningham's unit is typically the stanza, and many of those he contrives are of great beauty; his lines are customarily short, but varied in their shortness, and his rhymes are arranged with so unwearied a diversity and skill that his music, precise as it is, does not repeat itself from poem to poem. Further, he literally almost never relaxes the care with which he enforces or varies his metrical effects, so that he produces some amazing felicities with hovering accents and with trochaic counterpoint to what is basically an iambic rhythm.

It remains to be said that there is something cold about Cunningham's poetry which seldom permits the reader to do more than admire: he regards the poet's experience, but does not enter in. There are occasional passages of natural description— "the tossing forest of one sleepless tree," and the last two stanzas of *The Dog-Days*—which get a quick response from the visual or auditory imagination; . . . and like the last stanza of *The Helmsman* itself, evoke in the reader more than the satisfaction of mere intellectual identification. But the following lines from *Fancy* persist in my mind as more representative of Cunningham's method:

> The hot flesh and passionless mind
> In fancy's house must still abide,
> Each share the work, its share defined
> By caution under custom's guide.

Here as elsewhere one might think of Sir John Davies (less for his Aristotelianism than for his general dealing with philosophic problems in simple lyric terms). But Davies was more moved by his pondering on the soul than Cunningham allows himself to appear; almost certainly the "good sense" which Cunningham claims more than once has taught him to shape his emotion to an intellectual pattern. He remains, of course, an admirable poet, whose technique is superb, but whose chosen austerity often puts a wall of clear ice between himself and the reader. (pp. 280-82)

> *Edward Weismiller, in a review of "The Helmsman," in* Poetry, *Vol. LX, No. 5, August, 1942, pp. 279-82.*

YVOR WINTERS

[The essay from which the following excerpt is taken originally appeared in The Hudson Review *in 1948.]*

J. V. Cunningham is a man who began as a Catholic and who in the process of losing his faith acquired a good deal of philosophical erudition and a restless yet uncompromising mind. Of his original faith he retained, as nearly as I can discover, only a few metaphysical convictions, and those of a type which offer more certitude than consolation. I do not share all of his convictions, and I hold a few convictions which he does not share; yet it seems to me certain that his mind is more lucid, more sure of its own contents, and more profoundly "modern" (if we must have such a mind) than that of anyone else writing poetry today, and it seems to me equally certain that he is more surely a master of his craft, within the forms which he has used, than is any other poet writing today. . . . *[Meditation on Statistical Method]* is not, as I have known occasional readers to think it, a piece of neat light verse. It is a serious comment on a major topic; intellectually, it is absolutely lucid; and it exhibits that combination of passion and irony which is supposed in our time to be essential. In my opinion (and I believe in Cunningham's) passion can get along without irony quite

as well as with it, though not without intelligence. However, passion, irony, and intelligence are all present in this poem, and are beautifully related to each other. (pp. 171-73)

[Such poems as *Meditation on Statistical Method, On the Calculus,* and others in *The Helmsman* and *The Judge Is Fury*] will not appeal to those who consider poetry to be a "revery over remembered sensory impressions." Neither will they appeal to those who share what is popularly regarded as the modern temperament and who have little experience with the modern (or any other) mind. These are not the work of an unhappy adolescent; they are the work of a mature scholar, thinker, and craftsman. And I believe that they will stand the most rigorous comparison with the finest short poems in English. (p. 173)

> *Yvor Winters, "Three Poets (Randall Jarrell, John Berryman and J. V. Cunningham, 1948)," in his* Yvor Winters: Uncollected Essays and Reviews, *edited by Francis Murphy, The Swallow Press Inc., 1973, pp. 167-73.**

LOUIS SIMPSON

There are not so many serious poets in America that we can afford to neglect the collected poems of a talent like [J. V. Cunningham], yet I am afraid that present neglect is what Mr. Cunningham must have—and, to some extent, he has courted it. By reaction, it appears, he has particularly cultivated just those qualities that are likely to repel the publicists of the age. I sympathize with his attitude, for there is no general public worth having, yet I regret that his attitude has constricted his poetry [in *The Exclusions of a Rhyme*]; it is too much in reaction. But before I go into this, I would like to show his advantages.

First, he is a master, in his way. His tight, short, rhymed lines could hardly be improved. . . . The forms and tone of Mr. Cunningham's verse are neo-classic; as far as his style goes, no poet since Swift need have written, and the vernacular does not exist. Exclusions with a vengeance! Now and then an image is admitted, as in **"The Dog-Days."** . . . But there are entire poems which contain no image: they are written as *sententiae*. What are they about? The discipline of the will . . . love, pride, anger . . . the work of art. Dispassion and diffidence are key words. His poems are demonstrations of ideas, and are themselves the ideas they demonstrate. Moreover, there is much grace in his method, and those who have an ear for verse will enjoy his poems for that reason alone. (pp. 284-85)

I admire Mr. Cunningham, as you see, and I am glad that there is one of him in America. But there are other ways of poetry which, I am afraid, Mr. Cunningham would exclude, and this brings me to my main criticism of his verse. It is simply that you cannot show the triumph of discipline over disorder unless you also show the disorder. You cannot produce *Lear* without the storm scene, nor bring Oedipus to Colonus without passing through Thebes. The poet must always fear his own wisdom, the self-examination which says, Why write anything at all? Is not the perfection of understanding perfect silence? Is not the best poem a blank page? When one comes to this resignation, one is abnegating the task that poets, if not philosophers, have, which is to translate the world. The task was not beneath Shakespeare, nor Dante, nor Sophocles; they did not merely give you the epilogue; they also made you see and feel their experience, and so you were able to participate in their wisdom. You had earned the right to be resigned. But Mr.

Cunningham's poems do not often give you the opportunity to earn that right. You may see how he justifies himself in the poem, and yet have no joy in it.

Again—can you turn your back so entirely on the language of your own time and place, neglect the traditions of your own country, without marring your perceptions? In his adherence to English traditions of verse, Mr. Cunningham is excluding— of course, deliberately—all that is specifically American, the traditions of Twain and Whitman and Hart Crane, for example. I wonder if this is not a serious error. For can you really revive antique ways of thought? Can an American writing like a sixteenth or eighteenth century Englishman avoid seeming to be only an American *et cetera?* Poetry is not all a matter of idea and technique; it is also in the air we breathe. I miss in Mr. Cunningham's poetry a local habitation and a name. Sometimes, when Americans try to be like Europeans, their native twang creeps in willy-nilly, producing a slightly ludicrous juxtaposition; or their precision reveals their discomfort. I find it difficult to imagine any Englishman's verse being quite as impeccably formal as Mr. Cunningham's. He has an excruciated sense of poetic manners. But here I find my argument turning against itself, for no one is as pure as the American. No Englishman was ever as proper as Henry James; and Mr. Cunningham, in the excess of his severity, is our old friend the American Puritan.

And like the Puritan he has a sardonic side. The poems, and more strikingly the epigrams, exhibit a standard, old-fashioned way of treating love and lust. It is in these places particularly that I feel the deficiency of the neo-classic, or neo-classic-Puritan, way of dealing with experience. . . . The art of reason also has its inadequacies, and the Romantics, who tried to recreate and heighten experience in their poems, though they might arrive at no explicit conclusion, were not so foolish after all. They made you see again that the world is a delightful place, that the whole is more interesting than the sum of its parts. The pleasures of the reasonable man are always such a little thing—pipe-smoking, or sipping wine, or handling first editions. (pp. 286-87)

> *Louis Simpson, "A Garland for the Muse," in* The Hudson Review, *Vol. XIII, No. 2, Summer, 1960, pp. 284-93.**

THOM GUNN

It is likely that rather few people interested in poetry have read anything by J. V. Cunningham: he was not included in any of the popular anthologies until Allen Tate's, last year; his books have been difficult to obtain, and very few critics have referred to him even in passing. Yet he must be one of the most accomplished poets alive, and one of the few of whom it can be said that he will still be worth reading in fifty years' time.

There are various other reasons for his neglect, of course. One is that though he started writing in the 'thirties, he has used none of the modes popular in the last three decades. Readers accustomed to novelty may be upset by the fact that most of the poems in the present complete collection [*The Exclusions of a Rhyme*] are stylistically as much of the seventeenth century as of the twentieth. However, if this is true, it's also true that they are as much of the twentieth as of the seventeenth—they contain the idiosyncrasies of neither age. His style is close to, say, Rochester's in "Absent from thee, I languish still" or Donne's in "Hymn to God the Father." Anyone who finds such poems can mean anything to him in 1960 should have

little difficulty with Cunningham; anyone who does not might as well return to comic books.

Cunningham writes compactly and plainly, but he is not an especially easy poet. He is about as difficult, in many poems, as the early Lowell, but he is no more difficult, and I find him on the whole a good deal more rewarding. The difficulty comes not so much from obscurity of thought and feeling, as from the concentration of his language, which contains a large proportion of abstract words. And here is another reason why Cunningham is neglected; most critics, conveniently forgetting the language of the *Four Quartets,* regard abstract words with a kind of superstitious contempt. It is true that abstractions can be one of the many ways in which one can avoid saying anything; but very often they constitute the only possible full confrontation of one's subject matter. In using them, a writer is demanding that we take on trust the particulars of a certain class of experience: we may be able to do so, we may not; but there is certainly nothing wrong with the frequent use of abstractions as such, so long as they are kept in control. They are not easy to use with precision, and Cunningham himself runs into difficulties in an early poem **"The Dog Days"**: here the word "love" seems a trifle arbitrary, and the exact relation of love to the light of noon is not altogether clear, except in exclusively symbolic terms. (pp. 125-26)

Turning, however, to a later poem, **"Meditation on Satistical Method,"** we find a masterly control over generalization, a control more typical of Cunningham. (p. 126)

[Cunningham could be said] to have a certain affinity with one of the attitudes of the 'fifties, an attitude to be found, at least, in some of the young English writers: it is an impatience with gratuitous displays of feeling, and ultimately with any kind of phoniness. With Cunningham the impatience most commonly takes the form of exasperation with the Romantic search after experience for its own sake. Rather than be one of the "professionals of experience," he says, "I have preferred indifference." Indifference is itself an evil, of course, being only at the opposite extreme, but at least it is something to be *preferred,* in that it avoids all the further vices that the pursuit of experience will lead to.

Not that Cunningham *is* indifferent: the odd and interesting fact is that in attacking certain forms of passion he is himself being passionate. For it must not be assumed that a modern writer who scans, rhymes, and writes syntactically is less passionate than one who uses sentence fragments and free verse. Cunningham's book is called *The Exclusions of a Rhyme:* and it is true to say that what we have in any poem is not only strengthened but actually defined and realized by the nature of the exclusions that have taken place. Cunningham's awareness of the process gives the inclusions a bare and ferocious energy for which one could search in vain among the violent anthologies of sensation that we often receive from more popular poets. The feeling in his work, moreover, is not restricted to one particular kind: one can find an extremely wide range of it by comparing such different poems as **"On the Calculus,"** **"Elegy for a Cricket,"** **"Haecceity,"** **"Interview with Doctor Drink,"** the dedicatory **"To My Wife,"** and **"The Phoenix."** The last of these exhibits his powers at their most remarkable. . . . The poem, like many of his others, is concerned with the definition of the Absolute, which can be said to both exist and not exist. But it is also about the Phoenix as Phoenix, and he exploits the exoticism of this symbol to the full by controlling it to the full. I cannot find a weakness in the poem and am sure that it ranks among the great poems of the century. (pp. 127-28)

Thom Gunn, "Manner and Mannerism," in The Yale Review, *Vol. L, No. 1, September, 1960, pp. 125-35.**

DONALD JUSTICE

The Exclusions of a Rhyme is in effect the collected poems of J. V. Cunningham. . . . Its publication is therefore an important event, for although his poetry has yet to receive the attention it deserves, Cunningham is, within his limits, the most expert craftsman we have today. (p. 181)

For a career covering nearly thirty years, the body of his work is as small as the level is high. The limits within which he works are the result not so much, perhaps, of the rigorous application of a particular literary theory as of the severe intellectual scrutiny of form and content and their interrelations which the theory demands. At any rate, Cunningham appears deliberately to embrace the limits imposed by the forms he adopts, the series of choices which, as the line that provides the title of this collection implies, may lead through exclusions to definition and understanding. The short poem, which Winters has declared to be supreme among the literary forms, is the province of Cunningham, and one of his most characteristic stanzas is the cramped and difficult dimeter quatrain, which is handled with great authority in such a poem as *Meditation on Statistical Method.* Except for a few interesting experiments with syllables and accentuals, mostly early, Cunningham stays with the iamb, playing subtle and small but very beautiful variations on this base. His attitude is everywhere that of the craftsman. (p. 182)

[It] is as an epigrammatist, of course, that Cunningham is best known. Such specialists are rare in English, and as such he is surely the peer of Landor; in fact, his range in epigram is wider than Landor's, wider perhaps than anyone's since Ben Jonson, the poet in English whose work in this form his seems most to resemble. The title of the most recent group of epigrams, *Trivial, Vulgar, and Exalted,* suggests something of the range, but only extended quotation would demonstrate it adequately.

With the trivial and vulgar Cunningham's manner approaches light verse, but light verse of a fairly serious character, however bawdy and malicious it may be. . . . At the other end of the range the epigram in Cunningham's hands includes less predictable and much more ambitious materials. (p. 183)

Evidently Cunningham draws some distinction between his epigrams and his poems proper, but except where the epigrams are restricted to verbal wit and satirical observation, the grounds of the distinction are by no means clear. There is, indeed, a sense in which all but a handful of his poems could be described as epigrams, or at least as extensions of the epigrammatic method. The "poems" share with the "epigrams" not only the wit, the high surface polish, and the tight form which are among the simpler features of the epigrammatic method but a rational scheme of organization . . . , as well as a constant pressure to condense rather than expand, which, despite the honor officially paid economy as a poetic virtue, has always been uncommon.

Several of his early poems do not quite fit this description. Written during what Cunningham describes as his quest of the opal—the "pursuit of modern feeling, of shadows and blunted light"—such poems as *The Wandering Scholar's Prayer to St.*

Catherine of Egypt and *The Dog-Days* contain the recurring symbols characteristic of much modern poetry, together with a feeling more outwardly attended to than is usual in Cunningham's poems, and some slight inconsecutiveness of detail, so slight indeed that in the work of almost any other twentieth-century poet it might easily escape notice. . . . By the forties the quest was abandoned; as Cunningham himself flatly observes, "He became an epigrammatist."

Somewhere between these two poles of his work lies *The Phoenix,* a poem somewhat outside the main line of his development yet bearing, luckily, the marks of this particular poet. . . . This poem is as rich in sensibility as modern taste could wish. At the same time the rational order remains coherent; the details are related both rationally and emotionally, and in a meter subtle and firmly varied. It is probably Cunningham's masterpiece, and it also seems to me, not at all paradoxically, one of the genuinely original masterpieces of the period. (pp. 183-85)

Donald Justice, "The Poems of J. V. Cunningham," in Poetry, *Vol. XCVII, No. 3, December, 1960, pp. 181-85.*

GROSVENOR E. POWELL

Cunningham writes poetry of controlled statement which suggests the Renaissance masters of the short poem. The development is logical rather than associative, and abstract rather than concrete. The introductory poem to *The Helmsman,* in which the reader is told what he must do if he wishes to read poetry, and in which a scholastic vocabulary carries the meaning, illustrates the style. . . .

When we discover Renaissance influence in a twentieth century poet, we expect it to be metaphysical, but Cunningham is not affected by the usual influences. Although Cunningham's verse displays a certain home-grown pleasure in metaphysical wit, the most easily traceable influence on his poetry is not that of Donne, but of Donne's contemporary, the plain-spoken Ben Jonson. The laconic precision, the rhythm, and the subject matter are frequently the same. . . .

For the casual reader, Cunningham's poetry may provide sufficient pleasure; the verbal wit, the metrical skill, and the precision of statement are apparent in the individual poems considered as impersonal and isolated statements. But Cunningham himself discourages such a reader. In *The Quest of the Opal,* a curious, third person, autobiographical document dealing with the origins of the poems in *The Helmsman,* he speaks of his own attitude toward the reading of poetry. . . . Cunningham suggests clearly that the poems in *The Helmsman* are intended to form a coherent and unified body of work. Specifically, they deal with a definition and resolution of the problem generally thought to be that of the romantic poet.

The problem, to put it simply, is that which arises when the traditional categories of thought are recognized as arbitrary, and when the mind becomes its own place in a sense more terrifying than that intended by Marlowe's Mephistopheles. (pp. 20-1)

The development in Cunningham's first book, *The Helmsman,* is toward a discovery of the following historical fact: a period in which knowledge seems possible appeals to that knowledge; a period in which knowledge seems arbitrary appeals to direct, wordless experience, which as Cunningham discovers, is the appeal to sensibility. Cunningham finally rejects this appeal, but the interest in his poetry lies in the fact that he does not reject it at once. His Irish-Catholic background gave him the habit of solving personal problems through the traditional categories of Thomistic psychology. Although the habit never leaves him, he begins in his earliest published poetry to question the traditional absolutes and to consider the romantic alternatives. That sensibility provides the principal concern of his first book he tells us himself in his prose commentary, *The Quest of the Opal.* Speaking of an early poem, he says:

> The dog-days, then, was the first issue of what he called privately the quest of the opal: the attempt to court and possess, and at the same time disinterestedly to understand, roughly what was then called sensibility: the province of modern art, the deep well of creativity, the secret and sacred recesses of personality, the Gothic chamber of modern psychology, and the fall of light among the teacups. But an opal, particularly the deep fire opal, derives its color and attractions from flaws in the stone. If this were all, the flaws would be virtues. But any accidental sharp knock, as on the side of a basin while one is washing his hands, may cause the stone to crack; and though it remain in its setting for a while, in some unguarded moment the pieces will fall out, and one will have the ring without the jewel, the promise without the fulfilment.

It is necessary, in reading *The Helmsman,* to recognize this abiding preoccupation with sensibility and with lost absolutes. (pp. 21-2)

The progress from Catholic unity through romantic multiplicity is traced for us in *The Helmsman* and *The Judge is Fury.* The mapping of that Las Vegas of the soul beyond romanticism we must postpone until we reach Cunningham's most recent work. Cunningham recognizes that, without the traditional absolutes, there is no reason why one experience should be preferred to another, that to create experience through language is arbitrarily to choose the experience to which he will attend. The alternative would appear to be the appeal to sensibility, but this Cunningham rejects as an appeal to non-verbal experience. As he tells us in *The Quest of the Opal,* "the pursuit of sensibility had been the pursuit of an engrossment in immediacy of experience, but immediacy by definition cannot be talked about, cannot yield a line of verse." This problem is the one developed and resolved in *The Helmsman.* (pp. 22-3)

Cunningham's problem, then, is the modern one of seeing through many illusions without being able to name alternative absolutes. He is reduced to acknowledging that words are necessary intermediaries between experience and perception, without being able to affirm the truth of any one choice or statement. His solution is essentially the same as that of a navigator trying to find his bearings while flying over the North Pole. In these circumstances, the usual absolute becomes meaningless, and the navigator must find his position with reference to an arbitrary pole placed at some other point. It is by inferring hypothetical absolutes that Cunningham is able to conduct his moral navigation through the perceptions of his second book, *The Judge is Fury;* as he puts it at the end of *The Quest of the Opal,* "I am the idea that informs my experience." (p. 23)

This, "the idea that informs my experience," is the hypothetical absolute which Cunningham now substitutes for the absolutes of his Catholic training and the non-verbal absolute of sensibility. It provides the substitute North Pole in terms of which moral bearings will be established in that area beyond Catholic dogma and beyond romantic sensibility. It is with such ideas in mind that Cunningham tells us, at the end of *The Quest of the Opal,* that his second book will develop relationships between the terms sympathy and judgment: since judgment will be in terms of hypothetical absolutes, it cannot occur without sympathy.

Reality and the language which describe it are not the same thing, but for human perception the former can exist only through the medium of the latter. It is never possible to maintain this distinction with any ease. If the self is recognized as the only arbiter of experience and of choice, then one choice is as good as another, or, as Cunningham puts it in **"The Solipsist":** "Your *hence* / Is personal consequence, / Desire is reason." The problem can be solved only by recognizing that, though perception is determined by the scheme of thought in terms of which it is apprehended, the two must somehow be kept distinct. . . .

Cunningham recognizes that irrational experience, experience which evades verbal definition, must be faced and can only be imperfectly mastered in language. He is different from many American poets in that he does not confuse irrational experience with super-rational or mystical experience, as the doctrine of sensibility would suggest that he do, to say nothing of the practice of a poet such as Hart Crane, who could be said to court irrationality as the proper subject of poetry and as a means to God. Cunningham is not a romantic poet, despite the fact that his subject is the problems raised by romanticism. He does not seek the irrationality of experience, and we can assume that he is not comfortable with it. (p. 24)

The style of [Cunningham's] . . . poems may trouble the reader brought up on the view which has gained authority from the critical pronouncements of Pound and Eliot (most impressively stated in Pound's *ABC of Reading*) that only sensory images are capable of producing anything vivid and real. Cunningham would agree with Wallace Stevens' assertion that "The momentum of the mind is all toward abstraction." And, in doing so, he would have ample precedent in the best English poetry of the Renaissance. Cunningham writes "literary" poetry in the good sense in which Stevens did: the language of the poem itself is solidly within a tradition of good writing, and is itself a development of that tradition. Poetry of the past is not present as information or as allusion: Cunningham has assimilated his reading, his mind has been changed by what he has read, and the change is apparent in the maturity of the poetry. This poetry has its native roots in the abstract vocabulary of the greatest poets of the sixteenth and seventeenth century. . . .

The best of Cunningham's poetry, however, uses a style which seems totally mastered from the moment of its first appearance. It is a poetry in which image and statement are so closely joined as to be inseparable from one another. (p. 25)

Cunningham has considered and rejected the dominant literary tendencies of our time. He has seen that they lead to that imprecision of statement which grasps at the ineffable. His own achievement has been that of knowing where he is. The value of this poetry lies in its total honesty to the experience it describes. The mind builds within itself heaven and hell: "I am the idea that informs my experience." In arriving at this position, and in exploring beyond it, Cunningham has written some very great poems. (p. 26)

Grosvenor E. Powell, "The Poetry of J. V. Cunningham," in TriQuarterly - 2, *Vol. 3, No. 2, Winter, 1961, pp. 20-6.*

GEOFFREY H. HARTMAN

[In *Tradition and Poetic Structure,* a] strong and exact mind is at work on rich materials. . . . Mr. Cunningham deals with Statius, Marvell, Dunbar, Nashe, Wallace Stevens, and Shakespeare. The second half of the book is a reprint of *Woe or Wonder* (1951), five essays on Shakespearean Tragedy. The book as a whole is an important step toward a history of the modes of literary artifice. Each chapter shows in a different way how our knowledge of the traditional definition of the species to which a poem belongs aids us to understand that poem, i.e., to value it for the *right* reason. . . . A successful example is the recovery of the distinction between Shakespeare's plot and the modern (plotless) plot. The contemporary reader tends to slight Shakespeare's plot of intrigues and mistakes ("errors") because it is crude and mechanical compared to that of the modern novel. He turns by preference to character or imagery or other evidences of "organic" form. By simply insisting that Shakespeare's plot is what it is, and that it was chosen for what it is, Mr. Cunningham redresses the balance: "To our modern question, What is Hamlet's tragic flaw? or, In what way are we to construe his final death as issuing out of the depths of his personality? we answer: His tragic flaw is Claudius and Laertes. He was coldbloodedly murdered by means of a contrived diabolical plot."

To keep the truly old from misuse is surely as important as to recognize the genuinely new. Historical criticism, according to Mr. Cunningham, is "that act of respect by which we recognize otherness", and aesthetic appreciation "that act of sympathy by which we realize the other and make it our own". I agree with his assertion that both acts are ideally one: our desire for spiritual property is as avid as for material, and one of the things that can both satisfy and chasten it is the study of history. (p. 336)

Geoffrey H. Hartman, "Methods and the Man," in Poetry, *Vol. XCVIII, No. 3, August, 1961, pp. 332-36.**

DENIS DONOGHUE

Goaded by *Tradition and Poetic Structure* I have been doing a little homework on the use of the term "tradition" in literary studies. The results are not comforting. Most critics who use the term seem to have picked up the knack in Madison Avenue; the word is rarely a sign, it's a status symbol, like Saxon Hawk tweeds on men of discernment. Often its presumptive meaning is delivered in a cloud of vague and undeclared politics; the reader feels that something is going on, but he is discouraged from taking a close look. (pp. 476-77)

In this as in most other respects Mr. Cunningham is outstandingly decorous. "Tradition" figures largely in his speech, but he never flashes the term as a fraternity emblem; the word is a word, not a kite. "A tradition is all the ways a particular poem could have been written; it is the potentiality of realized structures, as the rules of chess contain all the games that may be played." . . . Again, it is "form, method, a way of apprehending" . . . and, more narrowly, "the body of texts and interpretations current among a group of writers at a given time and place." . . . For Mr. Cunningham, the notions which constitute a tradition are "principles of order"; they may be related to language as such (in meter, for instance) or to literature as such (as in the conventions of the Petrarchan sonnet, or the idea of tragedy, or the convention of the dream-vision) or they may be taken from sources external to literature (as he shows Marvell, Dunbar, and Nashe using the strict processes of logic for their own poetic occasions, and Shakespeare the strict processes of scholastic philosophy for *The Phoenix and the Turtle*). These matters are cogently presented in *Tradition and Poetic Structure:* the inclusion of *Woe or Wonder* (the best introduction to Shakespeare's tragedies which I have read) discloses the strict coherence of Mr. Cunningham's work and the corresponding fact that these cool, ripe essays make a book, not a miscellany. (p. 477)

Denis Donoghue, "Tradition, Poetry, and W. B. Yeats," in The Sewanee Review, *Vol. LXIX, No. 3, Summer, 1961, pp. 476-84.**

YVOR WINTERS

J. V. Cunningham seems to me the most consistently distinguished poet writing in English today, and one of the finest in the language; to make myself clear, however, I shall have to begin with a few reservations.

Some years ago Cunningham did a very rash thing: he published an essay on his own poems [*The Quest of the Opal*]. I wish he had never written it, but it is interesting and it is in print, and one has to use it. In discussing two of the earliest poems, *The Wandering Scholar's Prayer* and *The Dog-Days,* Cunningham describes them as poems of sensibility, essentially romantic and remote from his natural talent, and he is right. On the first page of his pamphlet, however, he attributes this interest to "the dark pretentions of his early associates who were almost without exception congenital romantics, however classical their creed." I was one of these associates, and, I am sure from conversations with Cunningham, the one whom he had especially in mind. I wish, therefore, to clarify a few points.

Cunningham is a very learned scholar and acute critic in Renaissance literature and in certain fields of medieval literature, and he is an unusually good Latinist. But in the English literature since the Renaissance and in the French language and literature, he is an academic amateur. As nearly as I can understand, he believes that any interest in sensory detail is a romantic trait which involves the irresponsible exploitation of "sensibility." This theory happens to be untrue. We live in a physical universe, and we have senses as well as rational faculties, and the physical universe affects the lives and understanding of most of us profoundly. The large use of sensory perception began in the early romantic movement, but there is nothing romantic about the employment of sensory perception per se, although such perception has often been used irresponsibly. (pp. 3-4)

The Quest of the Opal is troublesome in other ways. Let me quote Cunningham's [later] poem *To the Reader,* which is one of his finest:

> Time will assuage.
> Time's verses bury
> Margin and page
> In commentary.

For gloss demands
A gloss annexed
Till busy hands
Blot out the text,

And all's coherent.
Search in this gloss
No text inherent:
The text was loss.

The gain is gloss.

Cunningham is a textual scholar by profession, and at the level of the vehicle this is an ironic comment on textual scholarship. At the level of the tenor, however, it describes Cunningham's usual way of writing poetry: that is, he draws abstractions from the experience and discards the experience itself. The "text" is the experience; the "gloss" is the poem. If the poem is ironic at the level of the vehicle, it is deeply bitter at the level of the tenor, for the loss is real, and the word *loss* refers not merely to the discarding of the experience but to the personal suffering involved, just as the word *gloss* refers to the wisdom gained from the suffering. The double meanings of these words are not a whimsical imposition of my own; they are clearly evident in the poem, and they are largely responsible for the extraordinary concentration and force of the poem. But in *The Quest of the Opal*, it seems to me, he violates his own principle, for on many occasions he tries to read the text (the experience) back into the gloss (the poem). (p. 5)

There is another aspect of Cunningham's early poetry which bothers me. *The Metaphysical Amorist* is precisely and gracefully written. It has real virtues. But it remains an exercise in wit, interesting for one or two readings but no more. (p. 6)

It is not surprising that the weaker poems of any poet should be early. There are, however, certain surprising facts with regard to [Cunningham's] early work. Even the poems to which I have objected are in many ways distinguished in diction, rhythm, and structure; they are better than most of the poetry which has been published in the last thirty years or in any other comparable period. Furthermore, three of Cunningham's great poems were written within this period: *Poets survive in fame* and *The Phoenix* (both written at the age of about twenty-one); and **Epigram 8** in *The Judge is Fury*. And some of the finest minor poems belong to the same period: *The Symposium, Fancy, The Helmsman, Timor Dei, Choice,* and perhaps others.

It was shortly after these early poems, however, that Cunningham's style hardened into what is perhaps the most remarkable style of our time. *To the Reader* . . . is a good example. Another is *Meditation on Statistical Method*. . . . (p. 7)

[Cunningham's] mature style is what we would call the plain style if we met it in the Renaissance. It is free of ornament, almost without sensory detail, and compact. But it is a highly sophisticated version of the plain style, and is very complex without loss of clarity. . . . It comes closer, perhaps, to Ben Jonson and a few of his contemporaries, than to anyone else. Cunningham has long admired Jonson and has studied him carefully. The resemblance of Cunningham's minor epigrams to the minor epigrams of Jonson may seem very close until one examines the tradition of the epigram throughout Europe in the Renaissance and in the Latin literature preceding: then it becomes evident that we merely have two men working in a common and widespread tradition. (p. 12)

Cunningham's style is in no sense the personal style of some one else, nor is it an archaic style. . . . Cunningham's matter is not that of Jonson or of any other poet of the Renaissance. Some of his epigrams are in the early manner, but few could have been written by an early poet. His work deals with his own matter and with matter which would not have been conceivable in the Renaissance. And he deals with his own matter as effectively as Jonson deals with the matter of Jonson. Jonson's character was a Christian character; a character which I think is no longer possible for an intelligent man. Cunningham's spiritual situation is much more difficult, and by that measure his achievement has been more difficult. Just as the styles of Sidney and Spenser are dated today, the styles of pseudo-mythic hypertension which we find in most of Yeats and Crane, and of aimless associationism which we find in most of Pound and his imitators, will be dated tomorrow. But the style of Cunningham, on the one hand, and the style of the best of Valéry, on the other, will not be dated. The styles and the matter are firm. (pp. 13-14)

> *Yvor Winters, in his* The Poetry of J. V. Cunningham, *Alan Swallow, 1961, 15 p.*

PATRICK COSGRAVE

Though this short volume [*Collected Poems and Epigrams*] contains his entire published output in verse, and though—judged by his own standard—the outstanding poems in it number perhaps no more than half a dozen, Cunningham is, in my judgement, one of the major poets of the century. He is, besides, an outstanding critic and literary scholar, and has written one of the few great (I chose the word very carefully) volumes of Shakespearian criticism [*Woe or Wonder*]. (p. 588)

Cunningham draws his intellectual and emotional sustenance from his studies of the past. In this he is similar to, in some of their periods, his contemporaries, like Eliot, Stevens, Yeats and Lowell, although his poetry looks and sounds very different from theirs and is usually constructed according to different metrical principles. He differs from the others in two obvious respects. First, the specifically contemporary is excluded almost entirely from his successful poems. . . . More commonly, he deals with the contemporary—and especially with modern sexual love—in epigrams which are often both bitter and vulgar, to a degree sometimes unbalanced. Secondly, his scholarly understanding of the past is, naturally, vastly superior to that of the other poets: perhaps only Yeats, in his grasp of his historical Irish source material, rivals him; and Yeats's understanding was much more generalised and impressionistic than Cunningham's, though nonetheless true. Cunningham's involvement with scholarship and with the past is so profound and passionate . . . that he is able to live within their traditions and write out of them: he is a schoolman in much of his work, and his meditations often take on medieval forms and use medieval materials. His major contribution to scholarship, outside his work on Shakespeare, has been in his study of the Renaissance lyric and its medieval origins. In this work he has shown, through a series of remarkable readings . . . the essential part a very simple, and indeed truistic, series of logical statements played in this great Renaissance literature, and how their emotional power came from the profundity of the poets' understanding of these truisms of life and was expressed principally by their command of emerging English metres. Though the intellectual structure of his own poems is often much more complex, Cunningham derived from this study the main principle of his own poetry: that the emotional power of a poem consists especially of a proper response to the rational understanding by the poet of the experience it describes, and that the distinctive characteristic of poetry (as opposed to any prose form) is the capacity to organize appropriate emotion by the use of metre.

Nonetheless, Cunningham is a man of his own time and, as such, as much victim as his contemporaries of the uncertainties, neuroses and chaos of our period of history. He is a pagan, and cannot live out of the teleological context of his forebears. (pp. 588-89)

Cunningham can neither assent to Christian salvation, nor honestly restate pagan stoicism.

His subject . . . is the immortality or not of man. He is, himself, in a sort of scholarly, sentimental historical flux of infinite continuity. . . .

This essence of Cunningham [Yvor] Winters . . . wholly missed. He concentrated rather on the devices Cunningham has set up to avoid the tragedy of his own indecision. Most notable among these is the doctrine of Haecceity, ordaining that nothing perfected is good, but that the essence of value is in possibility, not performance. This enables Cunningham to state his belief in the principle of a vaguely and accidentally continuous search for truth . . . ; it enables him to make statements about experience, and even to judge experience, without committing himself to any final consequences.

Cunningham's personal tragedy in much of his work is his own inability to be more than a civilized purveyor of the attitudes and values he finds in the writers he studies: that is to say, his work states the essence of the quest of other genuine modern poets: that they revere the past, its Godhead and its values of style and utterance, but cannot easily assent to the consequences of this reverence—cannot decide that there is, or is not, an end of life that is more than living. He is superior to most of his contemporaries, first in that his understanding of the material is greater: when he uses a reference, or an ambiguity, it sustains the argument; it is not resonant decoration, as in, say, *The Waste Land* or 'The Quaker Graveyard'; secondly and most importantly, in that his great theme—the immortality or not of man—is never handled with less than skill.

Nonetheless, Cunningham has tried in many ways other than that mentioned, to avoid his dilemma. He has recently attempted syllabic metres . . . which make possible very limited and precise statements about sensory phenomena; he has a doctrine of indifference (which he sometimes calls hatred) to human yearnings, which enables him to dismiss the strivings of men and cultivate his book learning. Once in his career, however, he did manage fully to state what seems to be his most sustaining belief, expressed sentimentally elsewhere: that man's striving after the meaning of life is never ending, and must be attempted rationally; that what is available in the way of evidence for each one of us in this striving is what has been done in the past in this direction, and no more; that, in studying this past, we may have to omit an essence—in his case the belief in God of the writers he studies; but that our striving, the gloss on the text of this essence, is both necessary to us, and a gain in our struggle for understanding. **'To the reader'**, in summarizing all this, is a great poem. . . . (p. 589)

Patrick Cosgrave, "The Poetry of J. V. Cunningham," in The Spectator, *Vol. 227, No. 7478, October 23, 1971, pp. 588-89.*

DENIS DONOGHUE

The **"Collected Essays"** includes everything, presumably, that Cunningham wishes to retain: the famous **"Woe or Wonder"**

(1951), a study of the emotional effect of the major Shakespearean tragedies; **"Tradition and Poetic Structure"** (1960), a collection of essays on problems of literary form; a batch of later essays on questions of style; and, at the end, a remarkable commentary on his own poetry, couched in the third person rather than the first, and published in 1964 as **"The Journal of John Cardan."** . . .

Cunningham is one of the best poets in America, for some things; and . . . he is one of the best critics in America, for the same things. He is a professional poet in Thomas Mann's version of that fate, "a man who finds writing more difficult than most people do"; and also a professional critic, abstemious more often than not because he finds that "there is less to be said about literature than has been said," except for a few things that are still ignored or misunderstood. Most of these few things have to do with poetry, tragedy, style, structure, conventional forms and the poetic meters. Cunningham finds it convenient to state the basic points while commenting upon Shakespeare, Statius, Dunbar, Marvell, Nashe, Chaucer, Donne, Emily Dickinson, E. A. Robinson, Wallace Stevens and himself. What he has to say is usually that there is a certain principle of order governing the poet's work, or failing to govern it sufficiently, and that the reader is a fool if he does not advert to it.

Cunningham loves to show that the facts of the poetic case are sufficiently explained by something palpable rather than by something vague; by an external rather than an internal cause. He thinks that a lot of literary criticism is self-indulgent nonsense, and that the few essential truths are still available to anyone with a decent classical education, reasonable intelligence and a competence in the grammar, logic and rhetoric of Renaissance literature. Like his master, Yvor Winters, Cunningham regards most of the distinctive modern varieties of poetry as decadent.

The merit of Cunningham's criticism is indisputable. He is in touch with crucial themes, perennial rather than novel. He is relentless in the search for lucidity. I surmise that he taught himself to write good English by reading good Latin. He speaks only when he has something to say and when he has taken pains to discover the facts of the case. I hope it will be granted that these are virtues. Cunningham reads poetry, and writes it, in the hope of coming upon "the access of perfection to the page"—the phrase is Wallace Stevens's, a poet whom Cunningham treats somewhat harshly, I think. Cunningham's own style is prescriptive, continuously astringent, and he resents Stevens's facility to the point of refusing to recognize that Stevens put his verses together to keep himself from falling apart. Stevens's bland surface is deceptive, but Cunningham does not want to let himself respond to the struggle between plenitude and void.

At this point, we come upon one of Cunningham's limitations in criticism: His criticism does not respect the need for fresh experience. Cunningham's mind is remarkably powerful, but it is always already made up, and it receives only such new experience as will confirm its judgment. . . .

There is a beautiful sentence in the **"Collected Essays"** in which Cunningham refers to "thought's duty to approximate the wrinkled lineaments of experience and truth"; but I persist in thinking that he would be gratified to remove the wrinkles from his own thought and present it as self-evident in its lucidity. What I miss in his criticism, on the few occasions on which I am conscious of a limitation in it, is not truth or even experience. I miss the wrinkles on the face of intelligence and would welcome any sign that the critic is living in a world of possibility, risk, and error. I wish he would stumble now and again and reveal the price he has had to pay for his lucidity.

Denis Donoghue, "In Love With Severity," in The New York Times Book Review, *August 7, 1977, p. 12.*

ROBERT PINSKY

If there were only one diamond in the whole world, some people might worship it, while others might consider it merely an interesting curiosity. (p. 25)

As this awkward little parable suggests, I admire J. V. Cunningham's poems and epigrams quite a lot. I think that if there were more than one of him—or even if he had successful imitators—his work might be as popular as engagement rings. But he is unique; in many ways his poems have nothing at all to do with modern poetry. And so, honored though he is . . . , I don't believe that nearly as many people read his poems as would get deep pleasure from them.

The lapidary comparison is suggested by the poems themselves: brilliant, portably brief, with a dazzling formal precision and an unmistakable depth of fire. And in the epigrams of social and moral observation, there is the obdurate, cutting point:

> This Humanist whom no beliefs constrained
> Grew so broad-minded he was scatter-brained.
>
>   **(Epigram 43)** . . .

Because they are funny, immediately accessible, and patently masterful in execution, the epigrams that fall into this category—incisive, witty, judicatory—seem effective ways to introduce people who are not yet Cunningham-addicts to his work. . . . [But] one worries that the new reader, whether through wavering attention or prejudice, may think that Cunningham is merely a funny man, the author of a kind of light verse.

So—oversolicitously, perhaps—I feel like pointing out that **"This Humanist"** isolates a serious, irritating moral failure, and that by cracking the whip of two lines and a rhyme the poem manages to isolate that moral failure while making neither too much nor too little of it. I feel tempted to talk about the poem a lot, about its technique, for example: "broad-minded" and "scatter-brained" mean the same thing spatially, so that the second phrase explodes the first one as if from within; "constrained" in its Latin root presents still another version of the same spatial figure; because the rhyme neatly clicks the colloquial, Germanic "scatter-brained" onto the more elevated, Norman / Latinate "constrained," the action of deflation is made more crisp; the focussing "Humanist" defines precisely the right terrain for the observation about facile, bland tolerance; the movement of both pentameter lines is deft and light, not a simple swat on alternate syllables, yet the iambic pulse is utterly firm and lucid . . . and so forth. At the least, such critical analysis dramatizes the poem's brevity, a quality which Cunningham makes into a remarkably effective resource. (pp. 25-6)

These small, lightning-fast operations [the epigrams] are made possible by a special poise, stylistic and personal. The sources of that poise are partly historical: the epigrams of Donne, Jonson, Martial, the European tradition of epigrams, Latin and Vulgate. (Similarly, **"The Helmsman: An Ode"** echoes both

Horace and Vergil, and closely resembles a great Horatian ode in reticence, allusiveness, and power.) In a profound sense, however, the poise is Cunningham's own accomplishment, and not historical. It is an invention which makes his work possible, his creation of the striking, anomalous person who appears, or declines to appear, in the poems. From that imposing person's odd, self-developed moral terrain, the poems can make their quick raids on experience, and on our received ideas about what poetry is. Though the poems are dubious about human character, their force and coherence are based upon a particular, consistent personality.

Aloof, melancholy, passionate about the certitude of definitions, drily resigned to sexual restlessness, urbane, scholarly, worldly, that personality is above all solitary. It is not you or me, and it is not Everyman. This gloomy, fiercely-reasoned and rather devil-ridden rebelliousness toward most of the world seems to have to do with being an Irish ex-Catholic. It is a pessimistic declaration of the individual's separateness from the comfort of received ideas, and from the contemptible toys of the senses. The laconic, ruthless style gives this sour isolation its dignity and a kind of glamour, almost heroic, almost "romantic"—and perhaps even a little melodramatic. . . . (p. 26)

So far I have concentrated on Cunningham's most epigrammatic and reductive manner, in order to suggest the moral presence—the impersonal personality—which underlies those reductions and exclusions. I have tried to fill in the outline of phrases which occur to one, like "passionately cold."

Now I would like to look at some less reductive, more lyrical poems. These are concerned with the largest exclusion, the most fundamental action of angry self-definition, in Cunningham's work. They are concerned with the exclusion of the Absolute, or more precisely, the idea of an Absolute. The poet's definition of himself as distinct from that idea is partly stoical and partly angry and restless. The anger and restlessness have to do with the fact that his chosen patterns of thought and feeling, including his abstract, Scholastic style, are indebted to that primary Abstraction. The old form persists, nourishes, threatens. The early, wonderful, somewhat uncharacteristic poem **"The Phoenix"** deals with this problem. It ends with a superb long sentence, addressed to that "Mythical bird that bears in burying":

> I have not found you in exhausted breath,
> That carves its image on the Northern air,
> I have not found you on the glass of death
> Though I am told that I shall find you there,
> Imperturbable in the final cold,
>
> There where the North wind shapes white cenotaphs,
> There where snowdrifts cover the fathers' mound,
> Unmarked but for these wintry epitaphs,
> Still are you singing there without sound,
> Your mute voice on the crystal embers flinging.

The absence of God is a powerful presence; the muteness a significant voice. More downright and explicit is **"Timor Dei,"** a kind of negative prayer, in the slow, emphatic trimeter of Nashe and Ralegh. The subject is a specific emotion, the Fear of God; the poet does not feel that emotion, but he has known it and can fear its power and its possible return. The reasons for having rejected the absolute have to do with clarity and independence of vision. . . .

Love, the need for another or the need to choose another, from beyond the fence of stoical self-definition, is an important subject for Cunningham. It is the converse preoccupation to [his] passionate independence. . . . Cunningham's poems frequently imply "This poem is by me, not you, and I am different from you: cold and edged where you are warm and tolerant, fiery and possessed where you are indifferent or bemused." It is misleading to call him a love poet, though he returns to the subject often, because his love poems are as obdurate as his others. They too flaunt a tight-lipped, stoical outlook; the poem called **"Choices,"** for example, treats love's constancy as a kind of philosophical concession, even a grudging one. . . . (p. 28)

A warmer, more sustained work on need and love is Cunningham's remarkable sequence **"To What Strangers, What Welcome."** . . .

[The] sense of a flowing, partial, almost arbitrary relationship between the individual and the world [in **"To What Strangers, What Welcome"**] is somewhat different from the harsher, reductive energy of the epigrams. This elusive, affecting kind of material could be dealt with only by a poet whose vocabulary is philosophical, while his obsessions are love and isolation. The terrain is unique, and so is the nature of the talent. That is why they are so striking in combination, and so valuable. (p. 29)

> *Robert Pinsky, "The Poetry of J. V. Cunningham,"*
> in The New Republic, *Vol. 178, No. 4, January 28,*
> *1978, pp. 25-6, 28-9.*

RAYMOND OLIVER

[*The Collected Essays of J. V. Cunningham*] are essentially an account of how literature is written and how it ought to be read; they are, to my knowledge, the most useful account we have, and one of the most profound. I say "literature" because, though all the essays deal with writings in verse, Cunningham's methods and conclusions (except where he discusses meter) apply equally well to prose. His work is useful for its specific conclusions, or findings, and even more so for its methods and their applicability. For Cunningham is not the sort of critic who improvises on the theme of a text, or jolts us with the power of his "readerresponse"; he is a *Wissenschaftler,* a scientist in the best German sense, whose science includes all the literary sensitivity one could wish, but firmly controlled by theory and method and by desire for the truth. (p. 545)

Cunningham's literary doctrines can be stated logically, as a set of axioms, definitions, corollaries, and conclusions. I can best begin, perhaps, by compressing these theories into a dense nexus of propositions, which I will then loosen up and examine part by part. Thus, literary forms are principles of order; they converge to make the structure of a literary work, and this structure is the work itself. The forms, or principles of order, come together in more or less stable configurations known as literary traditions, or styles, of which one main division, prose, is written in sentences, and the other, poetry, in sentences and lines; the poetic line or verse is furthermore determined by the principles of meter. Good poems are definitive statements worth making; and since, in turn, the aim of the formal is to be definitive, which for Cunningham implies brevity, good poems tend to be formal and brief. These are the barest bones of what Cunningham tells us about the nature of poetry; we will now examine the sinews. There is no fat. (p. 548)

Cunningham wants us to understand what any poet, classical or absurdist, is doing when he writes a poem; and in understanding this, we realize that learning to write poetry is analogous to learning to write a foreign language, with the difference that poetry is a language without native speakers. It is more like Latin than like French or German; we begin by deliberately learning the rules of grammar and syntax, and acquiring vocabulary, just as we learn the rules of metrical writing and acquire the special vocabulary, if any, of our poetic tradition. Only later, as we gather skill, does the process of learning begin to seem unconscious, like "second nature": we read a great deal of Frost or Stevens, picking up traits of style and thought and temperament, until what we write looks like Frost or Stevens. Or we read enough Latin so that we can instantly grasp the syntax of subordinate clauses, without having to piece it together like a puzzle; at an even higher level, we can anticipate Horacian or Ciceronian habits of style as we read, and, finally, we can write imitations of Horace or Cicero. For of course this is the old principle of imitation—the point at which the learning of style and of language intersect.

Cunningham does speak of poetic tradition in linguistic terms, but he seems to prefer analogies that have sharp edges, aimed at lacerating the soft sensibilities of the average literary student. Thus a poetic tradition is like chess or logic; we have to learn "the rules of the game." . . . ". . . The rules of poetry, or rather the rules of the various traditions of poetry, are . . . even more complex. Nevertheless, they are describable, and to describe the rules of the game is to define a tradition. A tradition is all the ways a particular poem could have been written; it is the potentiality of realized structures. . . ." (p. 549)

[Cunningham's] prose style, by the way, is . . . concise throughout the essays, which makes it nearly impossible to paraphrase. And his critical method . . . also remains constant, with some allowance for variations in the kind and complexity of the subject matter. This method, whether applied to the dominant poetic styles of the Renaissance or the works of Emily Dickinson, is to abstract and state the implicit principles, or rules, of a given tradition. These rules are procedures governing, theoretically, everything in the poem, from the relative disposition of syllables to the prevailing tone and ethical quality, and including overall as well as local meaning. One difficulty of Cunningham's method, and I think this is a rhetorical rather than substantive difficulty, is that the explicit stating of these "rules . . . by which is stipulated beforehand what kinds of terms, of propositions and successions of propositions are admissible" gives the impression that a poet goes about his business like someone constructing a model airplane from blueprints. We all realize that no matter how high and gracefully the artifact may soar, it was put together with craft and labor; still, we also know that writing a poem, except in a few extreme and dubious cases, is not like mechanically following the directions, step by step, for the assembly of, e.g., a Petrarchan sonnet. Cunningham certainly likes to *épater les critiques*, and cold-bloodedness of a quasi-mathematical sort is one of his favorite devices; but this formal, abstract quality is inherent in his method, and does not invalidate that method. We do not condemn the anatomist because he presents us with a set of bones and muscles and organs rather than a living body.

More to the point, we do not condemn the philologist for abstracting the rules of grammar and syntax from a living language. As I have explained, Cunningham compares literary traditions with chess and logic, but he also relates language and literature intimately; it is characteristic of him that he makes regular use of the old term "philology," implying a fusion of word-study and literary criticism. It is only reasonable to regard language and poetry in this way, since they *are* intimately related—even, from a certain standpoint, identical, if we closely consider the act of reading a poem. . . . Cunningham tells us how poetry behaves, how it is constituted, what it resembles; he does not try to name its essence because he does not believe in objective essences. To write verse is to practice a technique for handling experience: "What a writer finds in real life is to a large extent what his literary tradition enables him to see and to handle." The same could be said, and has been said, about language as such. (pp. 550-51)

The differentia of the poet's language is meter. "Poetry," says Cunningham with the ancient theorists, "is metrical composition"; and "meter is the principle, or set of principles . . . that determines the line." (This is in potential conflict with a sociological definition he also gives: "what that society [of those concerned with poetry] regards as poetry is what I mean by tradition. What it regards as poetry will furnish the rules of the game." But currently the rules of the game, as laid down by "that society," do not normally include meter.) Everything not written in lines is prose. And the flat, minimal definition verges on the prescriptive: in answer to the essay-title "How Shall the Poem Be Written?", Cunningham says directly "in metrical language"—an increasingly rare achievement, he points out, in times like ours, when rhythmical patterns are becoming harder and harder to recognize in poetry. So much, if I may traduce William Carlos Williams, depends upon meter. Yet for Williams and virtually all young poets in America today, much more depends upon such things as red wheelbarrows and white chickens than upon meter, at least traditional meter. For it is a well-guarded secret that verse in the strict sense, hence poetry in Cunningham's sense, is no longer being written, except in a few small enclaves. What we have instead is Poetry, or, more modestly, free verse, and hardly anyone knows what that is. (p. 552)

It appears that poetic style oscillates between careful attention to meter, and careful—or perhaps lavish—attention to imagery. Poetry requires extraordinariness of language; meter can provide it, and so can imagery. Cunningham, with the Renaissance, chooses the former, and most of our contemporaries choose the latter. (p. 553)

Let us say, then, that traditional meter and responsible free verse require an inherent principle or set of principles that generates each line in the poem. For standard accentual-syllabic meter, the principles are roughly these: each line shall consist of (usually) no more than five feet; a foot is a pair of syllables, the first of which has a relatively light stress, the second a relatively heavy one; there may be variations in the patterning of light and heavy stresses within the foot (two lightly stressed syllables followed by one heavily stressed, or vice versa, and others). But Cunningham does not put it this way, for the following reason: "One rejects the textbook distinction between the metrical norm and the rhythm of a line, defined as the actual stress-contour, as a fiction, and a harmful fiction. Meter is perceived in the actual stress-contour, or the line is perceived as unmetrical, or the perceiver doesn't perceive meter at all." I find this account harmfully atomistic and misleading; in fact, I hold with the textbook distinction. It is perfectly true that "meter is perceived in the actual stress-contour" of each line, but it is also perceived within the metrical context of the whole poem—with reference, that is, to the prevailing pattern, "the metrical norm." The issue is more subtle than Cunningham allows. (pp. 553-54)

If you read a poem aloud in such fashion as to compromise between a mechanical, sing-song alternation of stress-unstress, and a perfectly casual, conversational style, you will find yourself expecting—and hearing, even when it's not present—the normal iambic movement, while at the same time you shift the weight of your voice to follow the "actual stress-contour," the variations that occur in each individual line. You hear each line both ways—against the iambic expectation, which it may or may not fulfill, and as it actually is. This counterpointing of artifice and naturalness creates most of the fine effects for which we value our eight hundred years' worth of metrical writing. Those of us who value it, I mean.

Among those who value this tradition, J. V. Cunningham is preeminent. He has stated the case for strict form as well as anyone could do, and stated it with uniquely mordant eloquence. In **"The Quest of the Opal,"** where he meditates in the third person on his own poetry, he writes: "The author, in fact, was only satisfied with a poem when qualification complicated qualification and yet the whole contrivance seemed to achieve stability and absoluteness by a coincidence with some given and simple external form." The effect of "stability and absoluteness" is perhaps the chief desideratum for a poet who wants to combine artifice and naturalness; such poems, when they succeed, appear to be cut out of marble. And notice the word "contrivance," reminding us almost defiantly that the poet, whatever else he may be, is a craftsman. On the specific matter of rhymed versus unrhymed poetry, Cunningham writes with authority as well as precision: "This is not just a difference in effect; it is a difference in what can be said. A word to be rhymed immediately suggests its rhymes, and at the same time rules out all expressions that are not potentially rhymable." Here he echoes the title of his own poem and book *Exclusions of a Rhyme*—a typically provocative title in its logical, stripped-down way.

In all these discussions of form, there are two points of view to be distinguished, both of which Cunningham understands profoundly: the poet's and the reader's. For the poet, rhyme and strict meter are heuristic devices; they are, in the words of Yvor Winters, "forms of discovery." For the reader, and that includes the poet as reader of his own finished work, rhyme and meter lend the "stability and absoluteness" mentioned above—a thinghood, a sense that the words could not have been otherwise. But writing formal poetry is also a traditional act as well as a technique for controlling rhythms precisely. It means and announces "I value the past and belong to it in this way." We hear, and I believe it, that most contemporary poets do not feel rooted in a social or religious tradition; they want to renounce and escape the past. So of course they renounce meter. Cunningham is perfectly contemporary, but in quite a different way.

In a traditional way, for one thing. His present moment is not sui generis, it contains the past. . . . If we put . . . [certain of his statements together], we have Cunningham's formula for excellence in poetry: "The aim of the formal is the definitive . . . the concern for definitiveness is a prejudice for brevity . . . a good poem is the definitive statement in meter of something worth saying." Here we have it: finished, formal, metrical and symmetrical, definitive, brief, and worth saying. Most contemporary poets, who write in free verse and colloquial language, aim for the authority of raw experience; for Cunningham, a good poem has the authority of a bear trap or a Q.E.D. It is a clincher. (pp. 555-57)

Since Cunningham's theory of literary values is a deductive system, closely reasoned and founded on solid axioms, it has great power and coherence; but it also has limitations. The limitations appear especially when the critic encounters modern novelists and story writers. For example, in an interview recorded not long before he won the Nobel Prize, Isaac Bashevis Singer says, "I do the story, and I leave the rest to the reader, or to the critic—let them draw their own conclusions. . . ." A critic of J. V. Cunningham's persuasion might be disturbed by this easy-going attitude toward authorial control and self-consciousness, toward "the author's intentions as realized in the particular text"; but I would not care to deduce that *The Magician of Lubin* (I haven't read it) is a bad book. It seems to be a truth of human nature that we don't always know what we're doing or saying or even writing. This seems especially to be the case in the modern period, where literature—and not just drama or fiction—makes very heavy use of indirection, the obliquely suggestive, and apparent randomness.

Yet these modern works can make sense. To do them justice we need a broad critical theory that does not surrender to a fashionable anarchy of values (cf. the Cunningham epigram "This Humanist whom no beliefs contrained / Grew so broad-minded he was scatter-brained"). I suppose that an adequate approach must aim for a scrupulously historical reading of the text "on its own terms," a reading that the author himself would recognize, and at the same time allow that the text may contain implicit meanings of which the author was unaware; language is far too complicated to be controlled absolutely and always, especially with reference to discoveries that have not yet been made. (pp. 557-58)

Unlike those who insist on "innovative" ideas in literary studies—an attitude that too closely resembles the Detroit attitude toward making and selling cars—Cunningham insists that "one does not make progress in this field"; the point is to understand the poem itself, which involves recovering old meanings and values, not promoting one's own. And just as the critic should adhere strictly to the text, so should the writer be true to experience. For Cunningham, life and literature, ethics and aesthetics, are inextricably wedded, to the great benefit of both. Coherence is a chief hallmark of Cunningham's mind—coherence of a very high order, since the materials he harmonizes are many and complicated. His poems are often glosses on his scholarship, or vice versa. . . . His style in both prose and verse is that of a distinguished epigrammatist; as a scholar, more specifically, he is a master of the summary, the sudden generalization, the ironic aside, the condensed insight, the dazzling précis of intellectual history; he can give odd bits of minute philological analysis bearing clearly on a central point, or judiciously qualify a thesis, or deftly set up an idea or opponent for destruction; he draws easily from his immense learning to adduce parallel texts from the author or period; he handles logic and theory with absolute sureness; and he does all this in the most concise scholarly prose I have ever read. (pp. 558-59)

Raymond Oliver, "'The Scholar Is a Mere Conservative': The Criticism of J. V. Cunningham," in The Southern Review, *Vol. 15, No. 3, Spring, 1979, pp. 545-59.*

Donald (Alfred) Davie

1922-

English poet, critic, editor, and translator.

Davie is well respected for both his creative and his critical contributions to contemporary literature. His belief that the poet "is responsible to the community in which he writes for purifying and correcting the spoken language" is evidenced by the classical formalism of his first volume of poetry, *The Brides of Reason* (1955), and is the focus of his first critical work, *The Purity of Diction in English Verse* (1952). In *The Purity of Diction*, Davie argues for a return to the prose-like syntax, formal structures, and conservative metaphors of the eighteenth-century Augustan poets. In the 1950s Davie was associated with the Movement, a group of poets including Philip Larkin, Kingsley Amis, and Thom Gunn who believed in the importance of these qualities. In contrast to English poets of the 1940s who were influenced by imagism and symbolism, the Movement poets emphasized restrained language, traditional syntax, and the moral and social implications of poetic content.

Davie has described himself as a poet for whom intellectual concerns take precedence over expressions of sensual experience. Some critics, however, note a sensuous attraction to nature in several poems in *A Winter Talent and Other Poems* (1957) which becomes more pronounced and deliberate in *Events and Wisdoms* (1964). Certain critics also assert that many of Davie's most successful poems are suffused with a sense of place and a sense of history associated with place. The most prominent example of this is *The Shires* (1974), a collection composed of forty poems, one for each county in England, in which Davie contemplates the past, present, and future of his native country. Davie's critical interest in other poets often affects his own poetic style. He translated Boris Pasternak's *The Poems of Dr. Zhivago* (1965) and has written critical works on Pasternak, Ezra Pound, and Thomas Hardy. Davie's reviewers attribute his experimental use of metaphor, symbolism, and loosely-structured verse forms to the influence of these poets.

Disillusioned with what he saw as a declining English culture, and feeling himself alienated from English academics who emphasized the separateness of poetry and criticism, Davie moved to the United States in the late 1960s. Many of his poems deal with his ambivalent feelings toward England. Several poems from *In the Stopping Train* (1977) illuminate this tension as Davie attempts to come to terms with the England of his childhood and the England of today. Reviewing this collection, Michael Collins describes Davie's writing as "quiet, restrained, erudite, carefully-wrought—a poetry of statement rather than of image."

Davie's critical works are as highly regarded as his poetry. In *Articulating Energy* (1955), a continuation of the arguments formulated in *The Purity of Diction*, Davie continues to stress the need for reason and clarity in literature. In two full-length works, *Ezra Pound: Poet as Sculptor* (1964) and *Ezra Pound* (1976), and in several essays in the collection *Trying to Explain* (1979), he analyzes the poetry of Ezra Pound. These works are praised for being provocative, insightful, and well-in-

Photograph by Doreen Davie

formed. In two other scholarly books, *A Gathered Church: The Literature of the English Dissenting Interest, 1700-1930* (1978) and *Dissentient Voice* (1982), Davie traces the cultural and literary implications of religious dissent.

Davie has recently published *Collected Poems, 1970-1983* (1983) and a volume of personal recollections entitled *These the Companions* (1982). *These the Companions* deals mainly with the people and places that have had the greatest effect on Davie and his work. *Collected Poems* includes previously published poems as well as a new sequence, *The Battered Wife and Other Poems*. The volume displays the directness and aesthetic control for which Davie has been commended throughout his career.

(See also *CLC*, Vols. 5, 8, 10; *Contemporary Authors*, Vols. 1-4, rev. ed.; *Contemporary Authors New Revision Series*, Vol. 1; and *Dictionary of Literary Biography*, Vol. 27.)

CAROL JOHNSON

[Donald Davie's *New and Selected Poems*] perplexes with flaws of a kind totally unlooked for in the mode he practices. Among several of the better moments of contemporary verse are scattered hypermetric lines for which one cannot imagine an excuse. The most preposterous occurs in "**Reflections on Deaf-**

ness," a mistake from beginning to end, in which however 19 out of 20 lines scan as pentameters. One goes: "Distinguishingly human act of speech contorted." There are others, easily reparable. I make this criticism first off in some amazement that the poet has not done so himself before ever quitting his first draft. Yet alongside the boners, the untractable instants of prose, are some poems the lucid order of which is persistently satisfying. . . . The better poems, like **"Samuel Beckett's Dublin,"** **"On Hearing Russian Spoken,"** parts of **"Remembering the Thirties"** are agreeable . . . because they do not take themselves too seriously. Seriousness in clever poets can be beyond all supposition banal. It is in those poems with pretentions that Mr. Davie tends to go disastrously awry, blundering into hopeless turgidities when he falls, as it seems, out of touch (aural and conceptual) with his intended course. (pp. 520-21)

> *Carol Johnson, "Four Poets," in* The Sewanee Review, *Vol. LXX, No. 3, Summer, 1962, pp. 517-22.* *

THOM GUNN

In some of the reviews of Donald Davie's *New and Selected Poems* there is a certain reluctance to praise, though no good reason is given for the reluctance. He writes in meter, and meter is once again . . . becoming unfashionable: by definition, apparently, its user is an "academic poet." He uses his brain as well as his eyes. He is a sort of symbolist at a time when symbolism is scarcely the up-and-coming thing. Moreover there appears to be an implicit assumption that if you consider, say, Denise Levertov a good poet you cannot also consider Donald Davie good. But there is more than one type of excellence in poetry, and if meter and symbolism have ever been valid devices then they must still be so: to deny such truisms is to be oneself academic in the narrowest sense—confined by historical prejudice and blind to performance.

To one who has eyes to see with, Davie's performance is one of amplitude, variety, and liveliness. The present collection is wisely selected, and should show the American public that he is without a doubt one of the best three English poets of his generation. . . . The early poems are pleasant, and wear better than I would have expected, in spite of an occasional stiffness of movement and a certain over-ingenuity that takes the place of emotion. (pp. 136-37)

There is an astonishing range of perception, feeling, and technique to the poems in the second section, as can be seen from comparing **"Time Passing, Beloved,"** **"The Mushroom Gatherers,"** **"Hearing Russian Spoken,"** and **"Under St. Paul's,"** very different and very good poems. And the most recent poems show an expansion of powers, a secure mastery, whether in the bareness of **"Against Confidences"** . . . or in the rich emblems of **"With the Grain."** In particular I admire **"To a Brother in the Mystery,"** the best dramatic monologue I have read since Edgar Bowers' "The Prince." It . . . not only establishes a dramatic situation fully and plausibly but gives it a meaning that goes beyond the situation. (p. 137)

> *Thom Gunn, "Things, Voices, Minds," in* The Yale Review, *Vol. LII, No. 1, Autumn, 1962, pp. 129-38.* *

CHRISTOPHER RICKS

Most admirers of Pound truckle to his terms; [in **"Ezra Pound: Poet as Sculptor]** Professor Davie succeeds most usefully in describing and elucidating those terms, but he maintains our right to judge the terms themselves, to define the limits of what inherently could be accomplished given Pound's mode. The artistic case against Pound is a real one, both internally in his frequent failure to carry out his own poetic principles, and externally in the limitations of the principles themselves.

Mr Davie's praise of Pound is far more convincing than anyone else's, for two reasons. First, that he actually discusses how Pound uses words and rhythms—instead of paying the usual perfunctory tribute to Pound's 'technical mastery' and then scampering on. Whether Pound is a master of words or not, his is certainly not the kind of mastery which stamps itself at once and self-evidently on our minds and hearts, and the question 'What is Pound at?' is as needed for the style as for the larger concerns. The second source of Mr Davie's authority is his reluctance to exculpate Pound, technically or morally. The callous bigotry of Pound's politics is not evaded, and its appalling poetic consequences are conceded. . . .

There is fervent admiration for Pound's translations, especially from the Chinese, for the *Pisan Cantos* and *Rock-Drill*. The admiration gains from the evidence that the critic is not selling Pound or sold on him. When, for instance, Pound mistranslates, Mr Davie is witty about it, instead of frothing like a pedagogue or claiming that Pound is being superbly 'creative'. He is prepared to offer arguments that are at once precise and tentative. He has the virtue which he praises in Pound, 'the ability to change opinion and confess as much'. . . . As a critical study, the book is notable for its habits of mind—and for its sense of fact, its ability to offer a plausible description of the works in hand. The subtitle, 'Poet as Sculptor', is justified by a very informative account (drawing impressively on the work of Adrian Stokes) of just exactly what Pound meant by invoking the analogy. The twists and turns of the prose works, especially the *Guide to Kulchur* and the translation from Confucius, are traced with a pertinacity that is possible only to the well-informed. A strong case is made that Pound's main poetic intention is to create 'a state of mind in which ideas tremble on the edge of expression.' Recurrent, though not repetitive, use is made of the insight that in metre and rhythm Pound was preoccupied with composition by verse-line rather than by larger units such as the verse-paragraph. One thing saves all these diverse matters from flying apart into just such as *bric à brac* as the *Cantos* themselves: Mr Davie's remarkable gifts (apparent in all his books) as a commentator on style, his ability to say something both new and true about the lines of verse there before our eyes. What we are given is a convincing account of what Pound wished to do, how he wished to do it, and how—intermittently—he did it.

And yet . . . To me it still seems that Mr Davie has been, though not soft, softish on Pound's basic poetic decisions and principles. Why is the translation from Cavalcanti in Canto 36 so impenetrably obscure? Because there are surviving phenomena that are impenetrably obscure, and 'in such cases the most faithful translation is the one making least sense.' This book, it is true, contains what can be said against as well as for Pound, but it does not admit quite how damagingly radical its own objections are. . . . Mr Davie seems to have refrained from drawing the (harsh) conclusions that really follow from his own arguments. . . .

Another leniency is that Pound is often allowed to escape under cover of an antithesis. If Pound were to be praised simply as a talented minor poet, there would be no harm in saying without comment that he gives us *this* rather than *that*. But such antitheses are precisely those which we are not forced to make on behalf of major poets, those poets whom Pound insists that we shall consider his peers. To combine what would seem incompatibles, to unite polar opposites such as novelty and nature—these are the terms of a major poet. So that to defend Pound by quoting his attack on 'those who mistake the eye for the mind' is to admit the smaller standards appropriate to smaller poetry. Why not both the eye and the mind?

The antithetical excuse affects even the admirable account of Pound's insistence on the verse-line. 'Only when the line was isolated as a rhythmical unit did it become possible for the line to be rhythmically disrupted or dismembered from within.' Why 'only when'? It is true that *Pound* was able to achieve an effective internal disruption within the line only by eschewing both enjambment and any larger verse-unit than the line. But the antitheses (verse-member versus verse-line versus verse-paragraph) are exactly those that it is not necessary to invoke for a true master of verse. In Shakespeare, Milton, Wordsworth (and many others), the verse does not find itself having to sacrifice large units in order to achieve small ones, or vice versa. 'For the members of the line to achieve some rhythmical independence of the line, it was essential that the rhythmical impetus through the line as a whole be slackened.' Essential for Pound, yes—but to say so is to deny Pound's claim to high technical mastery. In the work of a real master, impetus would surprisingly coexist with poise, just as local effectiveness would fight not against but alongside over-all effectiveness. Pound's terms, the terms on which Mr Davie correctly asks us to discover what is best in Pound, are by their nature an implicit admission of Pound's drastic limitations.

> *Christopher Ricks, "Davie's Pound," in* New Statesman, *Vol. LXIX, No. 1779, April 16, 1965, p. 610.*

MARTIN DODSWORTH

The fundamental principle of [Ezra Pound's *Cantos* is the] attempt to express ideas only in terms of sensory impression, and by its very nature it was bound to fail. Pound cannot, after all, stop us from inferring wrong ideas from the fact presented; as Yvor Winters has cogently argued, the method leaves us at best with "no way of knowing whether we have had any ideas or not." Pound, the dumb pedlar, sinks under the weight of his pack, a familiar and miscellaneous collection of fragments gathered in a lifetime of travels. He is an ancient mariner who cannot hold us, for he is unable to tell his story coherently.

It is not the least of Mr. Davie's virtues that in his excellent new book [*Ezra Pound: Poet as Sculptor*] he faces squarely such objections to Pound and yet argues convincingly for his status as a major poet of the century. He does not fall into the trap of total commitment to the *Cantos,* and there is no talk of an illusory coherence of design or strength of construction: instead we are made aware of the deeply conflicting elements in the poet's practice. Committed to a language of particulars, Pound is nevertheless fascinated by ideas, as only a dogmatist can be. . . . Although the *Cantos* fail as an epic account of history and in their attempt to establish standards of judgment and a pantheon of heroes, they do often succeed as lyric, the lyric that has to do with time past. "Wherever Pound deals with history successfully, he does so in an elegiac, not an epic, spirit"; and so Mr. Davie rests the burden of his case on the reflective verse of *The Pisan Cantos* and *Section Rock-Drill.*

Mr. Davie is able to seize this essential point about Pound's poetry as it has not been grasped before. . . . (pp. 75-6)

Mr. Davie has written a book that is a necessary companion to Hugh Kenner's pioneer study, *The Poetry of Ezra Pound;* it is well-informed, provocative, and readable. Although it was probably a mistake to begin the book with a discussion of the version of the Confucian Odes—surely not as good as all that— Mr. Davie rarely falters thereafter. Thanks to him, Pound is steadier in the literary stock-exchange, and all the more so for the high value Mr. Davie attaches to creative activity itself— "the great happiness and the great proof of being alive." (p. 76)

> *Martin Dodsworth, "Pound Revalued," in* Encounter, *Vol. XXV, No. 1, July, 1965, pp. 74-6.*

L. S. DEMBO

Mr Davie's book [*Ezra Pound: Poet as Sculptor*] is announced as a "comprehensive critical study" that takes "a straightforward chronological approach" to the career of Ezra Pound and is not burdened with "complex thematic or metaphorical devices." The statement is just, and the book possesses many of the virtues implied, among them a moderate tone and an unlabored pace. On the other hand, it suffers from the defects possible to such an approach; not only is Davie's book not burdened with complex thematic devices, it is burdened with no real unifying principle, except the general one that appears in the metaphor of the title. The work is characterized by a series of arguments, occasionally related, and having a common denominator more in an attitude than a point of view. One might insist that this method has its advantages, especially with a subject so evasive as Pound; nonetheless, it can bring us little more than the isolated illumination, the observation, or the general comparision, while it avoids the problems of explication and interpretation that cannot be avoided in systematic analysis.

Yet, even granting the author has methodology, there is much in this work that is either merely speculative or ill-reasoned. And often Davie's speculations are presented in so confusing a manner that one would be tempted to dismiss them as incomprehensible did they not seem to reduce themselves to oversimplification. (pp. 88-9)

Yet despite its lack of rigor and its frequent confusions, Mr. Davie's book is not wholly devoid of merit. The author does bring to his subject a wide range of reading and he does make his awareness of the canon of Pound criticism evident. But most important is that his comments are at least on the level of critical insight, and even when those insights are spurious they are not without a certain interest. When they are not spurious, as for example in the discussion of Pound's conception of *forma* as an underlying principle in the *Cantos,* they can be illuminating indeed. The work will not, one feels, "take its place as the primary critical study," but it may provide some excellent points of departure for the book that does. (p. 90)

> *L. S. Dembo, in a review of "Ezra Pound: Poet As Sculptor," in* Modern Philology, *Vol. LXIII, No. 1, August, 1965, pp. 88-90.*

THOMAS McKEOWN

[Donald Davie's *Ezra Pound*] stimulates disagreements of a constructive kind. This alone should be enough to recommend it. Davie gets the year of Pound's death wrong (1972, not 1973), the year of first publication of the Urcantos wrong (1917, not 1919), and still manages to produce the most trustworthy and acute introduction to Pound's mind and art that we yet possess. If we cannot always rely on this book for facts concerning dates, we can rely fully upon Davie's ear to pick up sounds and rhythms that we were previously unaware of, and to demonstrate their function in the poem as a whole. Moreover, Davie provides us as well with original interpretations of the reasons behind Pound's methods which square with the poem as it is experienced. (p. 485)

What makes this book so valuable is that Davie's comments are both new and controversial; one feels positively impelled to disagree in some measure with almost everything he says, while his overall sense of Pound's work is both just and convincing. (p. 486)

The heart of **Pound** lies in chapter four ("Ideas in the Cantos"), where Davie offers a splendid enunciation of Pound's use of ideas. "As we start to read the *Cantos*," he says, "we float out upon a sea where we must be on the look-out for waterspouts. These, when they occur, are ideas, the only sort that this poem is going to give us." In magnificent and brilliant analyses of sections from canto 91 ("that the body of light come forth from the body of fire") and canto 74 ("Le Paradis n'est pas artificiel / but spezzato apparently"), Davie records the moments when "strength turns inside out." Using Upward's metaphor of the waterspout, Davie demonstrates how just as in nature "not only does the water swirl upward through the cloud-whirl, but the cloud swirls downward through the sea-whirl," so in these cantos the disembodied imagination swirls downward into the sea-whirl of language, while the sea-whirl of language swirls upward into the cloud-whirl of the imagination. . . . But ideas as Pound uses them are not merely free-floating Utopian aspirations either, for they spring from solid perceptions into the sensualized imagination. Like the waterspout, energy flows in two directions. Davie's inimitable sensitivity to language and his magnificent explication of this notion at work in cantos 91 and 74 make this chapter a joy to read.

Davie's sixth chapter ("Towards a Conclusion") is similarly brilliant. He points out that Pound's poetry is meant to be heard—felt in the ear—rather than read, to be directly and sensually experienced. He shows how Pound follows Dante in focussing on the ability of language to corporealize the abstract idea, to transform "the notional into something apprehensible, or as if apprehensible, through the senses." . . . And of course this is what we need reminding of, that the kind of knowledge Pound's poetry imparts is *sensuous* knowledge. Davie's implication is clear; Ezra Pound is the first poet since Dante. . . . (pp. 487-88)

There are numerous . . . points of controversy in Davie's book . . . which the reader will wish to encounter for himself. And how few books rouse any thought at all? **Pound** succeeds where others have failed, largely because Davie does believe that "the intellectual love of a thing consists in the understanding of its perfections;" his book embodies this love, this sensitivity. And also, it embodies that *hilaritas*, that joy, which some find the most rewarding element in Pound's work. . . . (p. 488)

> *Thomas McKeown, in a review of "Ezra Pound,"*
> *in Paideuma, Vol. 5, No. 3, Winter, 1976, pp. 485-*
> *89.*

IRVIN EHRENPREIS

Donald Davie, in his new book [*Ezra Pound*], takes the *Cantos* very seriously, and tries to dispose of the ideological difficulties by separating the "opinions" from the "ideas" of the poem. He pleads, I think, that the appalling doctrines on politics and race belong to mere opinion or prejudice, and are not central to the meaning, but that Pound's ultimate values (justice, beauty, love, order)—not stated but embodied in processes of rapt vision arising from immediate experience—constitute the ideas or real meaning.

I put the analysis in my own words because Davie's account is troubled and obscure; he may well disagree with the paraphrase. But rather than study his terms and quarrel with his logic, I will make a single, literary comment: that if Pound built his poem as Davie indicates, it is a devastating mark of his failure that the poet's ear should have been so deaf to the impact his "opinions" would make on an audience.

Davie is excellently equipped to write an authoritative introduction to Pound's work. He is an accomplished poet and critic, familiar not only with Pound's writings of every sort but also with the scholarship on them. Though deeply responsive to Pound's verse, Davie is acutely aware of his limitations as a poet. He holds a sane, balanced view of Pound's importance in literary history but does not compromise with his evil banalities.

In an earlier book [*Ezra Pound: Poet as Sculptor*] Davie tried to survey the whole of Pound's output, with very uneven results. The new book is as learned as its predecessor but better defined. Davie fixes on the right topics, concentrating upon the poetry itself and not Pound's criticism. (p. 11)

Yet with all his talents Davie has not served us well. Though short, the book is neither orderly, lucid, nor concise. Davie writes carelessly and fills out his text with lengths of unnecessary quotation, he digresses into peripheral topics, like the relation between birth control and the arts. His inaccuracies undermine his learning—e.g., he will give innocent readers the impression that Pound himself translated the hundreds of lines of Dante in the *Spirit of Romance!* Readers who already know a good deal about Pound will find a number of fresh insights in Davie's book. Others will be disappointed. (p. 12)

> *Irvin Ehrenpreis, "Love, Hate, and Ezra Pound,"*
> *in The New York Review of Books, Vol. XXIII, No.*
> *9, May 27, 1976, pp. 6, 8-12.*

RUSSELL DAVIES

In the stopping train is just as full of jolts as it sounds, largely because Davie so often leaps out of his reverie to hang desperately on the communication-cord. There are some items in his book, to be sure, which appear to proceed according to plan. . . . But other poems here are invaded and overcome by apprehensive clamminess. . . .

'To Thom Gunn in Los Altos, California' sets out with a mock-and-matey-heroic 'Conquistador! Live dangerously, my Byron', but quickly becomes a long shudder at the Californian coastline, the far edge of the world, looking out over the benumbing indifference of the Pacific. 'What am I doing, I who am scared of edges?', Davie ends by asking. The answer is often: looking scared, and in the same sweaty, domestic way as the late Robert Lowell. It's not just the nearness to the surface here of Davie's family, friends and personal habits, or even the occasional red splash of schizophrenia . . . , but the auto-diagnostic impulse, the febrile, pulse-taking fear of self. More sinister, though—because one senses the strain Davie is experiencing in keeping his disgust bottled in images—is **'St Paul's Revisited'**, a 'sermon' on Depravity. . . . [Suddenly] Davie the moralist becomes Davie the unhonoured prophet, and looks not at all at home in this world. It is in the glowering light of [poems] . . . like this that simpler pieces, say **'A Wistful poem called "Readers"'** . . . , take on the glint of paranoia. It all leaves one wondering whether Davie's indignation is now an ingrowing thing, destined to torture him into a last, loud phase as the Angry Old Man. (p. 489)

> Russell Davies, "Ah Well," in New Statesman, Vol. 94, No. 2428, September 30, 1977, pp. 448-49.*

WILLIAM CLARKSON

Donald Davie's excellent *Ezra Pound: Poet as Sculptor* was published in 1964. He has now written a new introduction to Pound [entitled *Ezra Pound*] . . . which duplicates little of his earlier work; it is tightly compressed, thoroughly eccentric, and equally indispensable. Davie surveys Pound's important work, probes much of the major work on Pound, and offers suggestions as to where scholarship had better look next. Despite this scope the book is nothing in the way of a reader's guide, but it includes important contributions to the discovery of Allen Upward's relation to Pound and the *Cantos,* and a brilliant treatment of the Pound sound in a chapter on "Rhythms in the *Cantos.*" . . .

Donald Davie goes a long way toward showing where and why Ezra Pound is better than everyone else. Davie shows too, humanely but clearly, where and why, despite revisions and because of them, Pound is worse. (p. 670)

> William Clarkson, "Ezra Pound Ltd.," in The Sewanee Review, Vol. LXXXV, No. 4, Fall, 1977, pp. 667-70.

DOUGLAS DUNN

Donald Davie's new collection [*In the Stopping Train*] is as nicely fashioned as ever before. His title poem is more subfusc than usual, a sombre but firm performance. It's characteristic of Davie's styles that his poems move neatly to their clinching lines without assuming too much that they should do so. Indeed, his manner is more properly relaxed in *In the Stopping Train* than it was in *The Shires,* where it was relaxed into a state of suave chat. There are five more poems to add to the Shires series, one of them, **"Bedfordshire"**, being perhaps the best of the lot. (pp. 82-3)

[Davie's] points of reference are self-consciously cultural and social. He conducts arguments. A number of his poems in his new book proceed first by asking a question, then answering it, then moving forward until the next question is reached, followed by its answer, followed by moving forward again. The method mimics a state of mind suspicious of bold manoeuvres, of anything unreasonable, intemperate or seemingly immoderate. If he was to imagine something, or speculate, he would tell us first. He wouldn't want to think he was going off his own rails. There is of course an assumption of plain honesty in that manner. But there are times, too, when it looks like a greater degree of circumspection than poetry encourages. His poems strike me as conditioned by criticism of poetry, a

phenomenon of the mid-20th century. If there *is* an academic poetry, this is it.

That is, in style; for I doubt if all that Davie cares to mean is entirely reasonable. In **"In the Stopping Train"**, there are lines close to an admission of his own cosmopolitan deracination. There is doubt; and there is the self-blasphemy of "bad thoughts", bad will and the decency of being wrong. He can own up to the quirks of psychology, self-deception. But in **"Townend, 1976"** his unreasonableness is of a different kind.

In one guise, the poem is a spirited meditation on the idea of a town, taking its cue from Mr Davie's memories of his native Barnsley. The verse is unyielding and quick, argumentative, searching, and highly assured in style; it is brisk, no-nonsense, and perhaps a shade pompous, the ruminations of a discredited civic dignitary. It may be the poem the blurb-writer had in mind when he wrote of Davie's "civic conscience." But **"Townend, 1976"** is a highly contentious political piece. Change appals Mr Davie at the same time as he notes its benefits. . . .

Mr Davie is attacking none other than the welfare state, the institutions of mass democratic society. . . . He admits to a preference for yesteryear when all was in its place and the Barnsleys of the world revelled in their humility and hardship and were approved for doing so. Mr Davie laments an upset to hierarchy, to the existence of mass democracy. The continued fading of one, the continued development of the other, make Mr Davie guilty. He has very little goodwill. He believes the past before he recognises the present, which is neither healthy or wise. (p. 83)

> Douglas Dunn, "For the Love of Lumb," in Encounter, Vol. L, No. 1, January, 1978, pp. 78-83.*

D. E. RICHARDSON

Donald Davie's criticism conveys the sense that the making and criticizing of poems continue to matter. Such critics as Harold Rosenberg have noticed the absence of a genuine avant-garde in the arts today and have even questioned the usefulness of the notion avant-garde. If the notion is dead, and that is perhaps just as well, one misses the sense of historic enterprise which the idea of the avant-garde carried and which is noticeable everywhere in the criticism of such modernists as Pound and Eliot. The modernists, however much they differed on fundamental matters, all hoped to go beyond the failures of nineteenth-century art. Yet scholars of modernism have encouraged us to see twentieth-century poetry as a footnote, an impressive footnote, to nineteenth-century culture.

The Poet in the Imaginary Museum: Essays of Two Decades . . . publishes a selection of Davie's essays dating—despite the title—from 1950 to 1978. It reveals that Davie's mind has from the beginning pushed forward with the same preoccupations although he has modified particular views, as he acknowledges in new postscripts to some of the essays.

Like the early modernists whom he admires, Davie wishes the poet to keep his head in a confusing world by embracing the old role of the artist as artificer or maker, rather than secular prophet, thinker, or creator of alternative worlds. . . . Davie thinks of the poet as working somehow like other artists, and he resorts readily to analogies between poetry and other arts, especially music, sculpture, and architecture. When he talks about liking poems which have been so carefully made that they "can be seen all round" it is obvious that his metaphor is drawn from the art of sculpture.

Davie holds to his staunch aestheticism, unafraid of the shades of Pater or Wilde, because he argues not confusion between religion and art but a genuine art for art's sake. Religion is something else. In a hard-hitting review of the poems of Galway Kinnell, he indicts American poets of the last twenty years for dissipating "the artistic and intellectual riches accumulated by the great decades of American poetry earlier in this century." They have taken "American poetry back out of the twentieth century into the nineteenth, from the astringent and sophisticated world of Allen Tate and Yvor Winters back into the world of Emerson and Whitman." And he goes on to compare the unbelief and anxiety of much contemporary poetry to the "tediously familiar dilemma of those late-Victorians who vociferously 'lost their faith.'"

Davie resists the conception of the poem as primarily the expression or communication of the private anxiety of the poet. While he is sympathetic to the confessional poems of Robert Lowell and to the historical circumstances which made these poems all but necessary, he finally wonders what desperate game Lowell plays with his readers in his last poems and whether Lowell can tell what to chisel away and what to leave in the stone. As an artist, does Lowell know what he is doing?

Davie is not asking for an impersonal poetry characterized chiefly by the New Critical virtues of irony and detachment. Instead he seems to be arguing for the "radiant paradox" embodied for him in Pushkin: "the union of impregnable impersonality and reserve as an artist with eager and vulnerable frankness as a person."

One corollary of Davie's view of the poet as maker is his attempt to see the poet as a member of an international artistic community, a community which clearly exists among sculptors, painters, architects, and musicians but which seems to be less of a reality among poets. This collection of essays reveals that Davie has taken up more than once André Malraux's metaphor of the twentieth-century imaginary museum which makes contemporary the art of all times and places. But in "Poetry and the Other Modern Arts" he finally seems to conclude that the poet can never be so international as the painter although he must somehow escape the danger of becoming provincial in a sense which implies philistinism. The poet is an occasional visitor to the imaginary museum; he doesn't live there because "the art of poetry has not been, is not now, and can never be, an *international* vocabulary. All the other arts nowadays release us from the prisons we were born in; but poetry forces us back inside the iron cage of being of a certain race speaking a certain language." (pp. 577-79)

For Davie, then, the poet is a maker, but a maker using a particular language which places him in relation to a particular culture and possibly a particular place or particular places. Not literary nationalism is at issue here, but principally the exigencies of poetic craft. It cannot be an accident that Davie himself recently published a book of poems entitled *The Shires*, an abbreviated and personal *Poly-Olbion*. (p. 579)

From the beginning of his career Davie's attempt to go beyond the romantic tradition toward a conception of the poet as maker has carried him back to the eighteenth-century poets. *Purity of Diction in English Verse* (1953) is the engaged criticism of a contemporary poet who is trying to write poems which go beyond symbolism and post-symbolism. Davie's *A Gathered Church: The Literature of the English Dissenting Interest, 1700-1930* is a eulogy of the taste and cultivation of eighteenth-century dissenters who were his own forebears, although he writes not as a dissenter but as a son of Dissent. The reader may suspect that Davie is working a thin vein here, and Davie acknowledges his reader's suspicions in what was first delivered as the Clark Lectures at Cambridge in 1976.

The key to what Davie is doing can be found in his earlier book *Ezra Pound: Poet as Sculptor* (1964). There, writing about the relation of genre to subject in Pound's *The Classic Anthology Defined by Confucius*, he states that the central clue to "the entire labyrinth" of Pound's work is that "a question of poetic genre, and of the marrying of genres, is necessarily a question of entertaining certain ranges of perceptions rather than others, and of combining some perceptions with others in unprecedented ways." For all of his aetheticism, or perhaps because of it, Davie's essays move freely to social and cultural questions and increasingly to religion. For example he argues elsewhere that much contemporary American poetry is technically retrogressive because it is filled with religious yearnings which refuse religion's discipline.

The history of dissenting literature since 1700 is for Davie one of decline corresponding to a decline in the intellectual, social, and spiritual awareness of Dissent. Davie locates the characteristic artistic achievements of Dissent not in the century of Milton and Bunyan but in the century of Watts. What the eighteenth-century dissenters achieved in the poetry of their hymns and the architecture of their chapels was *"simplicity, sobriety, and measure,"* which Davie argues are the qualities Calvinist aesthetics demands of the art-object. Calvinist art at its best does not deny sensual pleasure but deploys it "with an unusually frugal, and therefore exquisite, fastidiousness." Using phrases reminiscent of *The Purity of Diction in English Verse*, Davie defends Calvinist aesthetics because "the aesthetic *and* the moral perceptions have, built into them and near to the heart of them, the perception of licence, of abandonment, of superfluity, foreseen, even invited, and yet in the end, fended off." This is almost to see Calvinist art through Confucian spectacles. (pp. 579-80)

Davie has written a persuasive defense of one strand or one moment in dissenting tradition. He has been wise to include in his book photographs of eighteenth-century chapels which reveal the aesthetic discrimination possible among the Old Dissenters. This book, however, is not an exercise in eighteenth-century historical scholarship any more than was *The Purity of Diction in English Verse*. Instead it is a contemporary English poet's investigation into what English art has been and what it might become. It is characteristic of Davie always to ask the artist to fend off provincialism at the same time that he locates himself in particular landscapes; and so it is central to his argument that the dissenting tradition at its best "does not offer an insular alternative to European culture, a way of 'keeping out', but rather a way of 'going in' on special, and specially rewarding, terms."

A Gathered Church may seem to be a work of filial piety by a man once a Baptist. But by locating and defending the aesthetic excellence in dissenting tradition, Davie has written an important chapter in the aesthetic history of England, contributed to the debate about the nature of English culture and its future, and enlarged our understanding of the way religious conviction affects the way an artist makes an art-object. (p. 581)

D. E. Richardson, *"Donald Davie and the Escape from the Nineteenth Century," in* The Sewanee Review, *Vol. LXXXVI, No. 4, Fall, 1978, pp. 577-81.*

E. P. THOMPSON

[*A Gathered Church: The Literature of the English Dissenting Interest, 1700-1930*] is a work of committed criticism. (p. 164)

But the points [of Davie's Clark Lectures collected here] are argued by indirection, allusion, and selection, and we are conducted in no recognizable discipline. Some part of each lecture is given over to rhetorical strategies designed to show that Professor Davie's judgements are endowed with a peculiar privilege denied to other critics. Historians, literary and especially social, are disqualified at the outset, as having no criteria relevant to aesthetic judgement. But much of this book is, quite simply, a rewriting of history, without an appropriate discipline to do so. Aesthetic judgements may be faulted if they conflict with doctrinal considerations, and *vice versa*. By another strategy ('I was there') Professor Davie assumes the privilege of personal association with the tradition. . . . A certain privilege we may allow. I do allow it: Professor Davie has a deep, but narrow, arc of sympathy which may derive from his familial inheritance. But we cannot allow it too far, or we make nonsense of the work of critics and historians, who must, in a sense, always be 'there'. Are we to suppose that only female royalists are privileged to write the history of Queens?

By yet another strategy, political and social interests disqualify the writers Professor Davie dislikes but commend those whom he approves. But none of these strategies is employed consistently; one can watch Professor Davie pause and consider which arrow to select from his quiver. The extension of literary or intellectual traditions to a wide general public is seen as an 'ominous' dilution in one case (the 'veneration' with which Blake is regarded is 'a test case . . . of what happens when a body of difficult but momentous truths is taken "to the people"') and as endorsement of approved values in another (the poetry of Watts is vindicated as forming 'the common anonymous stock of our linguistic inheritance'). There is a kind of engaging snobbery of a high minority tradition about Professor Davie's judgements; a 'linguistic inheritance' remains distinguished, but 'the people' remain always as the vulgar. Yet the aesthetic judgements upon which Professor Davie's ultimate authority rests are seldom demonstrated by attention to the text. They lie, often, somewhere just outside the rim of the lectures, gestured to, as self-evident, through the lecture-theatre window. (pp. 165-66)

This is a very odd book. What is one to make of a study of the 'literature of the dissenting interest' which mentions neither Joseph Johnson, the publisher at the centre of that literature for three vigorous decades, nor (almost) any of the books he published? This is a committed and idiosyncratic tract. Behind all the strategies of doctrinal or aesthetic rigour, there will often be found ulterior political and social judgements as crude as anything to be found on the 'Left'. One is irritated only when Professor Davie rises in the pulpit, in a spotless surplice of critical objectivity, and accuses others of his own sins: 'In the course of my studies I encountered assumptions and contentions of a socio-political kind which I cannot but regard as tendentious to the point of being deliberately misleading.' . . .

Professor Davie is wholly entitled to his commitment. However interested his stance, his work is more interesting to read than many 'disinterested' accounts. But the general reader will gain from it a most abbreviated notion of Dissent, in its literary influence: Watts, Rutherford. Large repairs to the defaced fabric of understanding will have to be made in the seminar and tutorial. The biggest repair of all must be in the very definition of Dissent. For Professor Davie at no point lingers to discuss the critical defining questions. (p. 167)

Of course Professor Davie wishes to provoke argument; he will be disappointed if he does not. And I am glad that we have this book. But it is doing three things, and we must be careful to distinguish between them. First, it is a kind of public polemical meditation, in which the author ponders a particular, and narrow, cultural genealogy which he affirms as his own. I find this procedure valid and often enlightening. Professor Davie is in search of a descent from a genteel and mercantile Dissent of the early eighteenth century, politically accommodating, and endowed with values of *sobriety, simplicity,* and *measure,* values exemplified in Watts's verse and in the chaste neo-classical lines of the eighteenth-century meeting-houses shown in his Plates. In tracing this descent, he becomes fiercely involved in long-forgotten sectarian controversies, and shows a party zeal in the arguments of nineteenth-century non-conformist historiography. I cannot regret this zeal, which illumines much that had become obscure.

Second, and in the course of doing the first, Professor Davie is striking out at a number of lazy notions and received opinions as to Dissent. In particular, he is contesting the notion that the major dissenting tradition can be seen as an easy evolution towards liberal, humanist, or even rationalist conclusions; or, indeed, the notion (for which he holds Christopher Hill and myself responsible) that Dissent can be claimed, wholesale, as part of the pre-history of the Left. Such notions, as he properly shows, can be profoundly condescending, if they pass by or disallow the authenticity of the Dissenters' spiritual and doctrinal concerns. Moreover, the Socinian 'enlightenment' cannot be taken as representative of Dissent as a whole; there were Tory Dissenters as well as Jacobins, and the former may have remained within their gathered churches more loyally than the latter. These points are often well made; and they should be taken.

Third, and intermingled with the first and second, Professor Davie is claiming *his* 'genealogy' as the *true* Dissent, and disallowing all other parts of the tradition. As I have argued, this is preposterous, limiting, and often enforced by dubious rhetorical strategies. In his notes Professor Davie appears as a more candid advocate of party. The Unitarians should be regarded, not 'as merely the Left and liberal wing of English Dissent' but (as 'orthodox' Dissenters saw them) as 'pernicious and alarming heretics'. And he plainly asserts that 'the Arianism of Priestley did far more damage to Dissent than either the hostility of the Establishment or the ambiguous fervour of Methodism'. In somewhat similar terms one has heard a certain kind of Marxist sectarian avow that 'the revisionism of Bernstein did far more damage to Marxism than either the hostility of the State or the ambiguous fervour of Christian Socialists'. I find this kind of prejudgement, which appeals to an original and stationary purity of doctrine, open to the same objection in both cases. For what appears valid from within the doctrine's premises appears as bigotry without.

But doctrines matter. I think they do, and I applaud Professor Davie for thinking likewise. Everything cannot be passed down the academic production-line until it comes out at the end as a highly-wrought and objective 'no answer'. Then how are we to conduct a discourse together, those of us within and those without a given doctrine's premises? I do not see that we must always try; there are times when we should simply make plain our beliefs. But the Clark Lectures are surely a time for an attempt at communication? And it is here that these lectures finally fail to satisfy, for one would suppose that these were offered to auditors on a common ground, and that this ground was aesthetic judgement. But Professor Davie never succeeds in sorting out aesthetic and doctrinal criteria. In the end we are left with an assertion entailed in a doctrinal premise: Robert Hall must be seen as culturally enlightened because he restated the doctrine of the Eucharist.

There is a most interesting passage in the third lecture where Professor Davie discusses paradox. He notes, in Watts and Wesley, the aesthetic force derived from 'the central paradox of a god who is also man'. Such paradoxes (he notes) are at the heart of 'any writing in the centrally Christian tradition'; and he goes on to contrast this with the dialectical way of thought in Blake. I wish he had written more, much more, to such effect, in the area where aesthetic and doctrinal influence intersect. (pp. 168-69)

> *E. P. Thompson, in a review of "A Gathered Church: The Literature of the English Dissenting Interest, 1700-1930," in* The Modern Language Review, *Vol. 75, Part I, January, 1980, pp. 164-70.*

PETER LEVI

The best of Donald Davie's essays [in *Trying to Explain*] are subtle, reasonable and serious discussions of the detail of [Ezra Pound's] work; they range widely, they explain, and they give great pleasure. But they take Pound too seriously as a moral being. He was a poet of great genius, and we read him constantly, but to put it mildly, 'he could not make it all cohere'. Donald Davie is not necessarily right to put the blame for Pound's alienation from England on the amateurism and hopelessness of the British literary culture from 1900 to 1920. The distinction that involves between professional and amateur poets is obscure and doubtful.

Donald Davie is torn between British and American standards. That is part of his interest as an essayist, and what a splendidly trenchant and clear writer, what an impressively rational explainer he is. I failed to find one uninteresting paragraph in this book. Its lucidity makes it easy to disagree with, but even the miscalculation of some of its attacks on the wilder fringe of writers is honourable and endearing. Donald Davie's photograph on the jacket is that of some rare, mid-Atlantic seabird, literary and intellectual and in full spate of explanation. But his phobia against socialism, which he allows to weaken even his case against the fascism of Yeats and Pound, is less sympathetic, and his rage against Dylan Thomas is exaggerated. . . .

But all Davie's prejudices are honest and he stands for rational decency. . . . Donald Davie is within the modern movement a neo-classic writer and critic—a successor to Yvor Winters. That is certainly better than romantic gush or the technical jargon and reworking of earlier writers which is often a mask for chauvinism. But it risks leaving out of account something of the genius and the inwardness, the forceful truth of important writers. Donald Davie is a generous intellectual. Most of what he attacks needs attacking, and he picks his way as carefully and easily as a cat. What fills one with gloom is the juggernaut of the American academic-poetic establishment, the writing schools in which nearly every poet teaches, and the 'on-going act of criticism' which feeds back into poetry. Donald Davie has lived and worked effectively with all that. . . .

Maybe if Ezra Pound had found the teachers and examples that he looked for in vain in England, his greatness really might have been less fragmented. That is a point that Donald Davie makes. . . .

The *Pisan Cantos* are still a greater work of genius and a more moving human document than almost anything else written in English in this century. It may be that Pound's mysterious case says more about the art and origins of poetry than any easier example. Once again, this is something that Donald Davie has understood.

There is a lower level of the quarrel between Pound and the British which is one almost of buffoonery. Davie takes it far too seriously. He minds Max Beerbohm at Rapallo thinking Pound an undesirable acquaintance. . . . Davie minds Maurice Bowra calling Pound 'a bore, and an American bore'. That did not prevent Bowra from knowing and loving the *Pisan Cantos*. It is also, in its way, perfectly true. And if Pound had called someone 'a bore, and a British bore', would we not think it funny? When he beats up the barbarous British in *How to Read*, he still is funny. Donald Davie's reacton is not laughter, but meticulous fairness. On this level of knock-about humour fairness is somehow inappropriate.

> *Peter Levi, "Impresario of the Waves," in* New Statesman, *Vol. 99, No. 2568, June 6, 1980, p. 854.*

P. N. FURBANK

Donald Davie's new book [*Trying to Explain*], a collection of reprinted pieces, is a jumpy one, as is indicated by its fretful title and the expression (faintly exasperated) on his face on the dust-jacket, as well as by a lecture on 'Art and Anger', and 'Second Thoughts' on the same subject, in which he defends anger (with its corollary, contempt) as a salutary emotion and one suitable to great art. Anger, as opposed to hatred, rancour and even indignation, is purgative and goes with clear thought—reasons, he says, why it is unwelcome in democracies where 'contempt is unforgivable, as ultimately hatred isn't'.

You could state all the themes of his book in terms of a question which he has plainly often asked himself: why, being English and predominantly concerned about English, or British, matters, does he live and work in America? Or rather, some answers to that are clear: it is because in England 'the non-academic makers and moulders of literary opinion are judging poetry by standards which are 60 years out of date', and because of the 'arrogant rationalism and authoritarianism of British socialism'.

The question he is really troubled by is, what are the perils for him of his self-exile? This puts him in a good position, involved yet detached, to meditate the case of Ezra Pound, who, though an American, never before and never after felt so much at home as in England . . . , yet eventually quitted the place, in an impatience like Davie's own if more violent, and fared badly ever afterwards.

Davie's thoughts fasten continually upon Pound. He is always wonderfully instructive on the subject, which somehow brings his own ideas on literature, cultural history and politics into focus and into relation; and the six pieces on Pound are the solidest part of the present volume. One of the valuable points he makes in these Pound essays is that the pre-1914 cultured society that Pound met in England, complacent and insular though it was, had a lot to be said for it. . . . Despite this, though, Davie shows convincingly why Pound, in the long run, was probably bound to quarrel with this 'establishment' and feel he must cut loose from it. It was because it was a society 'ineradicably vowed to the idea of the artist as amateur'.

Another and related aspect of Pound's career that Davie discusses, and also identifies himself with, is the role of aesthete. It has been one of the strongest parts of Davie's achievement to vindicate aestheticism, to show it as potentially vigorous, heroic and life-giving—as undoubtedly it is in the great 'modernist' masterpieces—and rescue it from the automatic English belittlement (as 'arid', 'trivial' etc.). Nevertheless, it is in this matter of Pound and aestheticism that worries attack Davie and (I think) confuse him. Is aestheticism, with all the good you can say of it, ultimately anti-human? Is it what led Pound into fascism?

This is a serious enough question in all conscience, and it makes Davie lose his cool and his poise. He is, rightly, desperately anxious to face the ugly facts of Pound's fascism, and he offers us, as a model attitude to this matter, the behaviour of the poet Charles Olson towards Pound at the time of Pound's *débâcle*. And indeed Olson seems to have acted very finely, 'saving Pound's life' as Pound himself said, while refusing altogether to palliate Pound's politics or to allow weak excuses for him, such as would distinguish the man from the poet or would pretend that a poet's views don't matter. But Olson's central judgement upon Pound directly arraigns his aestheticism. (p. 214)

It is honourable in Davie to face this challenge, but his response is defensive-aggressive. Olson insists on separating Pound's fascism from his anti-Semitism, and Davie turns this into an attack upon lefties, who, he says, find it easier and more enjoyable to castigate Pound's anti-Semitism, about which all they have to be is 'indignant', than his fascism, which would require them to define their own political 'positive'. Fair sport perhaps; but meanwhile, rather unnaturally in his case, Davie is recommending Olson's verse for its 'audacity and grandeur of the conception' despite 'solecisms' and 'gaucheries' and 'arbitrary coarseness in diction' on every page, and praising Olson's 'ill-written but splendidly honest verse diatribes against MUSAK'.

From one who makes such claims for literary values, this won't quite do; and what is distorting his judgment becomes clear. It is the problem of 'mass society'. Olson's accusation against Pound is that he and his admirers rejected or ignored 'the single most important human fact between Newton and the Atomic Bomb—the sudden multiple increase of the earth's population, the coming into existence of the MASSES'. Davie's response to this is disturbed and distraught. . . . Davie writes, of Olson's charge against Pound: 'Pound's admirers will protest at this, but they will be wrong. If they ask proof, let them look into their own hearts. Do they not find there (I know I do) just that suffocation Olson speaks of? Just that panicky fear, always on the verge of turning into hatred until we shamefacedly choke it back? The Masses! How can we not fear them, and fearing them, how not hate them? . . . For we cannot feel what we know we *ought* to feel—that "the masses" are "just folks". (It isn't true anyway.) The fear and the incipient hatred are something that we impenitent élitists must learn to live with, not anything we can deny.' (pp. 214-15)

By worrying about fascism in this self-reflecting way, Davie has worried himself into a misreading of Yeats's poem of 1928, 'Blood and the Moon', which he stigmatises as an ugly piece of fascism, lauding the 'innocence' of ruthless, bloodthirsty men-of-action as against the envy and impotence of intellec-

tuals. Davie's error links with the question of 'literary amateurism' referred to earlier. He believes that Yeats would, unlike Pound, have preferred a graceful, aristocratic amateurism for himself, in the manner of Robert Gregory, and blamed a democratic age for making him perforce a professional.

This is surely wrong, and Yeats was always a most committed professional. . . . Davie is ignoring a leading theme of *The Tower* and *The Winding Stair,* which is that the poet may hope, by a life of solitude and dispossession and of back-breaking professional toil and burning of midnight oil, ultimately to achieve, by this totally different route, the same joyous unification of being as is the ancestral birthright of the leisured and endowed. Thus, in 'Blood and the Moon', his mental tower, with its treadmill stair, is a 'powerful' alternative emblem to the brick-and-stone tower of past Anglo-Norman conquerors, and to a great degree a satire on it. . . . Yeats's tone is, in fact, wry but genial and not at all fascist. As so often, he has by some prodigious leap of mind resolved a stark opposition into a being-in-the-same-boat. And Davie has found in the poem what he feared to find, and not what is there. (pp. 215-16)

P. N. Furbank, " "What Are the Perils for Him of His Self-Exile?'' " in The Listener, *Vol. 104, No. 2674, August 14, 1980, pp. 214-16.*

JEROME MAZZARO

Donald Davie's *In the Stopping Train* indicates that [a] tendency toward reduced style [exists in] contemporary English poetry . . . , though for Davie's book . . . one can see the tendency as part of a larger desire to test the language's ability to treat emotions that are often ignored by unitary visions. For Davie, who praises his French teacher for giving him the language of Ronsard, conventional themes provide occasions to see "the whole / Diction kit begin to fall apart," and the interest in his collection lies in the self-consciousness of his efforts to shun the "unlikely . . . enormous, louring resonant spaces / carved out by a Virgil" and gauge his style to "small clearances, small poems." At times, as in **"Father, The Cavalier,"** the efforts add up to nothing more than rhetorical adroitness—the withholding or the correct placing of a word. The work's final "mostly," sentimentalizing the photo, qualifies "unnoticed" but also echoes the assertion / qualification of the poem's second stanza—"A surrogate / Virility, perhaps." **"The Harrow"** creates its tension syntactically by withholding the verb "stir." These techniques work well in the opening half of **"Depravity: Two Sermons"** and in **"Bedfordshire"** to bring irony to the conventions of occasional poems. Although in poems like **"Morning,"** **"To a Teacher of French,"** **"Widowers,"** and **"A Spring Song,"** Davie emerges with a live voice, readers may wonder whether there is not as much artifice in this voice as in one that strives for elegance, and if the reason for Davie's efforts is political rather than artistic. American readers especially may concur with the imagined reader of **"A Spring Song"** that "the sort of acrobatics that this poet / Is good at, we can do without." (p. 465)

[A] self-conscious style, conventional themes, and political intent [are what] one finds in Davie's volume. . . . (p. 466)

Jerome Mazzaro, "At the Start of the Eighties," in The Hudson Review, *Vol. XXXIII, No. 3, Autumn, 1980, pp. 455-68.**

JOHN SEED

This short but vivid and provocative book [*A Gathered Church*] consists of the Clark Lectures given at Cambridge in 1976, with an additional thirty-odd pages of 'Notes' which amplify some of the arguments. Davie is concerned with the Dissenting tradition's contribution to English literature and culture since the late seventeenth century—a contribution which he argues is important if in some ways very limited. His aim is frankly polemical: as he puts it, "clearing the dissenting tradition of various libels that circulate about it."

He ranges widely, looking at writers as diverse as Bunyan, Mathew Green, Isaac Watts, Charles Wesley, William Blake, George Eliot, 'Mark Rutherford,' and D. H. Lawrence. One of his central propositions is that there is an aesthetic specifically linked to religious Dissent. Its characteristic virtues were "simplicity, sobriety, and measure." Important examples are the hymns of Isaac Watts, the prose of 'Mark Rutherford.' This severely restrained poetic echoes more recent poetics such as that of the "Objectivists" in the United States. . . .

But Davie's concern is not narrowly literary. It is the broader cultural role of Dissent and its literature which is the central concern of the lectures: "since what we are concerned with is English culture, our history cannot be a history of ideas, nor a history of events, nor yet a narrowly literary history, but a history of people and the styles in which they have lived." Thus he looks carefully at such Nonconformist intellectuals as Philip Doddridge, Robert Hall, and Charles Spurgeon. (p. 93)

Davie's engagement with his subject is refreshing. His own concern with Dissenting culture, he tells us, stems from a dual allegiance: his Baptist upbringing and his enthusiasm for literature. This book tells us a good deal about Davie's notions of his own work. But if this personal involvement gives the lectures their vigor and movement, it has its price. At times the scope narrows and there is emotional assertion instead of reasoned argument. On the whole problem of the meaning of the word "culture," for instance, he evades the full thrust of Dissenting influence on English historical development by narrowing his flanks: he restricts culture to the literary and spiritual. The relationships between these aspects of culture and the broader social and political dimensions of culture, according to Davie, "are still, as they have always been, too subtle and intricate for our historical scholarship to draw them out with any confidence." This is an evasion. . . .

At the end of his final lecture, Davie threatens that some day he may publish a larger study which will "challenge received notions about the social and political history of English Dissent over the past three centuries." I hope he does. The result will be contentious and important. But a much wider conceptual framework and an attention to the social and political role of nineteenth-century Dissent . . . will be necessary if his revisions are going to be of more than personal significance.

As far as it goes, *A Gathered Church* is a challenge which initiates debate on a whole range of issues in English culture and literature—a challenge also contained in some other recent pieces by Davie. It is a challenge which is already beginning to be taken up. (p. 94)

John Seed, in a review of "A Gathered Church: The Literature of the English Dissenting Interest, 1700-1930," in The South Carolina Review, *Vol. 13, No. 1, Fall, 1980, pp. 93-4.*

NEIL POWELL

[Any account of Davie's] work since 1970 must be at least partly concerned with the tension (at best a creative tension) between Davie and his English audience or, more bluntly, between Davie and England. (p. 39)

The restless, ruminative sense of a mind moving among half-understood echoes and associations informs the poems in *The Shires* [1974]—a far richer book than it at first appears—as well as many of the pieces at the end of the *Collected Poems* [1972] and in Davie's most recent collection, *In the Stopping Train* (1977). The circumstances surrounding Davie's emigration to California in 1968, and the poems written at that time, are outside the chronological scope of this volume; but the perplexed and unresolved tensions with England continue to reverberate. . . .

The responses to England contained in *The Shires* are far from comfortable but they are glancingly, and therefore the more sharply, affectionate: if 'love' has not 'drained away', it has become infinitely complicated. (p. 40)

Behind *The Shires,* inevitably, is **'Essex'**, at whose university Davie was Professor of English and which

> merits
> Better than I can give it
> Who have unfinished business
> There, with my own failures.

The paradox (not, after all, such an unusual one) is that Davie's 'failures' at Essex produced some strikingly successful poems: the pared-down lucidity of his *Essex Poems* (1969), a poetic flavour which has been called American but which might equally be described as East Anglian, continues to influence his work. Alongside this, however, is a more disturbing development which becomes clear from a comparison of the excellent *Essex Poems* with the section of the *Collected Poems* called **'More Essex Poems'**: a slackening of control and, at times, a descent into almost hysterical rancour. *The Shires* is almost (and perhaps surprisingly) free of this, but it disfigures the less successful pieces in *In the Stopping Train* and among Davie's uncollected poems.

The basic problem concerns Davie's relationship with his audience: and this means Davie's relationship with England for, as Michael Schmidt has pointed out, 'Davie's work, all of it, is beamed towards England. He is writing to us and of us. We are his principal concern' . . . [see *CLC,* Vol. 8]. Many of Davie's poems of the late sixties and early seventies chart a loss of confidence in the English audience, exacerbated by the Essex experience and the prevalence of modish, superficial subcultures. One might expect Davie's fury to have abated, given the widening geographical and temporal distance, but if it has (and a poem like **'St. Paul's Revisited'** suggests that it hasn't) there remains as a residue an irritating stylistic mannerism. Davie has always tended to be an exclamatory writer: since *Essex Poems,* though, much of his work has been peppered with obscure and frequently incomplete exclamations: 'They see his face!' (**'The Departed'**); 'Rancour! Rancour! / Oh patriotic and indignant bird!' (**'St. Paul's Revisited'**); 'This West! this ocean!' (**'Seeing her leave'**); 'Now this! / Earthquake!' (**'Gemona-del-Friuli, 1961-1976'**). Such fragments (shored against his ruins, perhaps) seem intended to shut the reader out; and I think that this defensive exclusion, as it seems to be, of the reader is in fact at least as damaging to the poems as the widely-noticed bitterness which goes along with it. Yet, in an obvious sense, this objection of mine is a naive one: I have just, after all, alluded to *The Waste Land* and in the same breath complained, like early critics of Eliot, that Davie's work has become obscure and fragmented. My unease stems from the suspicion that Davie is inclined to give his readers a bumpy ride because he feels that they deserve it and that it will be somehow salutary for them: but the effect of this may be to isolate from the poet just that consensus of intelligent readers which he actually seeks to address. There is, as if acknowledging this difficulty, **'A Wistful Poem called "Readers"'** in *In the Stopping Train* which, far from being wistful, is a laboured joke: Davie admits as much in his laboured title.

A solution to this problem of audience is to talk to oneself. That is partly what seems to be happening in the title sequence of *In the Stopping Train*, where the tension is between the 'I' of the poem and the 'he', 'the man going mad inside me'. (pp. 41-2)

But the relationship between the 'I' and the 'he' is continually shifting, like the equally ambiguous relationship between the 'I' and the 'you' in 'Prufrock'. Perhaps with this model in mind, Davie, like Eliot, astonishes the reader with an abrupt change of perspective at the end of the sequence. . . . The suggestion is perhaps that there is a kind of external social madness which is quite distinct from the internal personal madness. (p. 43)

'In the Stopping Train' may well by now appear to be baffling, so I had better insist that this is not the case. Its sparseness of syntax and imagery, its angularity of thought do in fact produce a frightening lucidity. The sequence frightens in its cannibalistic ability to devour its potential subject-matter as it goes along: it becomes an extraordinarily and designedly *impoverished* piece of writing about lacks, gaps, needs. It is undeniably impressive—and properly the focal point of the book which is built around it—but it is not the kind of thing one would wish Davie to attempt too often.

In the Stopping Train, the collection, is a worried and worrying book, reaching out in its skeletal fashion to various antecedents: to Christopher Smart, for instance, in one of the most vivid and successful poems, **'Morning'**; or, once again, to Pasternak; or to Davie's own earlier work, as when **'A Spring Song'** reshapes the mode of **'Time Passing, Beloved'** only to be reshaped—or 'read'—itself in the adjacent **'A Wistful Poem Called "Readers"'**. In the final poem, **'Townend, 1976'**, Davie is at his best—at once topographically accurate and thoughtful, relating the inner and outer worlds so mercilessly wrenched apart in the title sequence. Here, at last, the tension between Davie and his English subject-matter does become creative. . . . [The opening stanzas of the poem] clearly demonstrate how concrete detail and introspection can work profitably with rather than against each other; they show, too, how successfully Davie's ironic, questioning tone can build upon a clearly visualized starting-point.

Despite this, and despite other distinguished recent poems, Davie's most notable and memorable poetic achievements so far seem to belong to the fifties and the sixties rather than to the seventies. No doubt this is partly a matter of distancing: poetry needs to settle into familiarity before it can be properly judged. But it is also, I think, a matter of Davie's recent preoccupations finding their appropriate expression in his stylish and energetic prose: ideas which can be worked *out* in prose may prove too intractable to work *into* poems. This is not to suggest that poems shouldn't contain ideas—far from it—but to wonder whether the rough edges and fragmented syntax of

some poems in *In the Stopping Train* really do justice to the ideas they try to embody. Where the ideas are linked to a clear external subject—as in much of *The Shires* or in **'Townend, 1976'**—the resulting poetry is coherent and moving. The poet should indeed stand, as Forster said of Cavafy, 'at a slight angle to the universe'; but with Davie the angle sometimes seems to grow uncomfortably wide. (pp. 44-5)

> *Neil Powell, "Donald Davie, Dissentient Voice," in* British Poetry Since 1970: A Critical Survey, *edited by Peter Jones and Michael Schmidt, Persea Books, Inc., 1980, pp. 39-45.*

MICHAEL J. COLLINS

A poem, writes Donald Davie in **"Ars Poetica,"** is "a space / Cleared to walk around in." The definition, better than many, seems to apply particularly to the twenty-eight short poems that make up *In the Stopping Train*. . . . As we read through the poems here, we encounter, as Davie puts it, "small clearances," each of which, with its distinct boundaries, excludes "the turbulence it was cleared from." Each poem, to use Frost's words, seems "a momentary stay against confusion": it takes us, quietly and skillfully, through twenty or forty or fifty lines to a firm conclusion. While we find no "enormous . . . spaces" here (even the six-page poem **"In the Stopping Train"** is really a sequence of short ones), these scanty plots of ground are generally satisfying confines to walk around in.

The poems here have the qualities we expect of Donald Davie: they are quiet, restrained, erudite, carefully wrought—a poetry of statement rather than of image. They are generally public and, in some cases, occasional rather than private or intensely personal. Particular people and places, as they often do with Davie, figure prominently in the collection. . . .

[Davie is] a particularly allusive poet, and as a result, his poems can be, for me at least, difficult to understand without research and rereading. And yet, while some of the poems take time, others are almost immediately accessible and effective. **"To a Teacher of French,"** for example, while certainly not the most ambitious poem in the collection, is a deft, engaging and generous tribute to the "'Fiery' Evans," who gave the speaker the language of Ronsard. *In the Stopping Train,* it seems to me, is a welcome collection, for the poems it includes, while narrowly focused, often grow richer and more resonant as one comes to know them better.

> *Michael J. Collins, in a review of "In the Stopping Train and Other Poems," in* World Literature Today, *Vol. 55, No. 2, Spring, 1981, p. 318.*

MICHAEL KIRKHAM

Davie as a critic has sometimes seemed to the dazed bystander to be in perpetual motion, perpetual transition from one phase of opinion to another. But many of the same issues recur, newly formulated and presented, but the same; the truth may be that he is perpetually oscillating between sets of opposite opinions. It does not matter which. His criticism always vibrates with the immediate and pressing interest that poetry in its technical, moral, social, and spiritual realities has for him; it tingles with an air of urgency that vitalizes literary discussion; not infrequently it gives off a brimstone stench of literary warfare. Sometimes I wish he would retire from the fight long enough to settle the internal conflict of ideas. In the fifties the most intelligent and ardent polemicist for the Movement, Davie was also the quickest to see its shortcomings. The pieces in *Trying to Explain,* mainly about poetry, his own and others', were all published in the seventies; they cover a variety of topics, but in this context what is most striking is the persistence, alongside new interests and some changes of outlook, of Movement attitudes and habits of mind. The moral recoil from the cult of the lyric poet as "one who is absolved from all civic responsibilities and all moral restraints" is as sharp as it ever was. His scorn for "the sublime," in ancient or modern dress, has not relaxed. "Disaffection, resentment, acedia, malaise, 'alienation'—all those fashionable conditions, precisely because in all of them the sufferer 'doesn't know what is wrong with him,' produce in art 'the sublime.'" This comes from an essay in praise of the "clarity" of anger. Is there no room, then, for a *lucid* uncertainty? . . . One of the most interesting essays is about Allen Tate's poetry; as so often with Davie at his best, it discloses a deep division of feeling, a fruitful indecision. He speaks of Tate as a great poet and at the same time deplores his "impatient neglect of the literal meaning of his poems in favour of their symbolical or (his own word) *anagogical* meanings." This is sound radical criticism and is in line with the Movement attack upon the sanctification of metaphor. His way of expressing dissatisfaction with "this besetting fault of Tate's writing" elsewhere in the essay, on the other hand, betrays the weaker side of Movement aesthetics—a concern for getting on good terms with the reader. "One could not fail to remark in [his poems] the lack of that seductive suavity which won us over to Ransom. . . . Ransom, Hart Crane, even in his austere way Winters, were *winning* writers in a way that Tate has seldom deigned to be." One may rate social and civic virtues highly and still judge "suavity" and "winning," words from a vocabulary of social charm to which Davie sometimes resorts, to be too lightweight for the purpose; if they are intended to be faintly self-deprecating or provocative (an English tone that doesn't travel well), then their arch modesty undersells a valuable case. (pp. 475-76)

Michael Kirkham, *"English Poetry Since 1950,"* in The Sewanee Review, *Vol. LXXXIX, No. 3, Summer, 1981, pp. 474-79.**

SIMON RAE

Talk of Donald Davie's 'new' collection would not be strictly accurate. Even parts of the title sequence, *Three for Water Music,* are borrowed from his last volume, *In the Stopping Train,* and the bulk of the book is simply a reprint of his earlier work, *The Shires.* 'Three Poems of Sicily' are shared between the two Mediterranean pieces, **'The Fountain of Cyanë'** and **'The Fountain of Arethusa'** which sandwich the very English ('deuce, Fred Perry serving . . .') **'Wild Boar Clough'**. Myth and personal memories (of childhood, 'Infidel youth' and shrine-seeking maturity) mingle with musings on familiar Davie themes in series of separate poems employing a wide range of imitative styles. Here Davie borrows the metre of Shelley's 'Arethusa' to celebrate not only the original poem, but his own precociousness—and to pay homage to his mother whose love of literature made it possible:

> In a parlour game,
> Required to name
> Mountains beginning with A,
> Proudly, aged ten,
> I pronounced it then:
> The Akrokeraunian Mountain!

The egotistical impulse gains momentum through the rest of the volume, *The Shires* resembling nothing so much as an album of snapshots in which the peripatetic professor features prominently, while the 40-odd counties assume the role of Hall's-Distemper boards. (p. 19)

Simon Rae, *"Light on the Water,"* in New Statesman, *Vol. 102, No. 2633, September 4, 1981, pp. 19-20.**

BARBARA EVERETT

Donald Davie's new sequence of poems, **'Three for Water-Music'** [in the volume of the same title] . . . , refers not only to pleasant 18th-century entertainments by water, but to something like Yeats's 'words for music, perhaps': or like Eliot's *Four Quartets,* to which the sequence declares some relationship. For Davie's three poems lie somewhere between late Symbolist poetry and a more quietly literal tradition of English topography; they are a species of modern half-abstract landscape poem, which locate in the real certain transparencies of thought. They show concept both created and creating, as a fountain might be heard to rise and fall again. And indeed of the poet's three locations which have given rise to epiphanies, the first and last are, in fact, Sicilian 'fountains' or pools, each named after an Ovidian legend of loss of love; the second is a brown pool in a torrential stream between steep English hillsides. The sequence, recording 'Epiphanies all around us / Always perhaps', in a sense finds no answer to its opening question: 'And what's to be made of that?' Any sense of answer or reconciliation is confined to the expressive forms of the poems themselves, which always—like music—imply the silence behind them. . . .

Donald Davie is on occasion a superlative poet, and [*Three for Water-Music*] is one of the occasions. Reticence and a love of the theoretical often combine to make his communications a triumph of style. Even the unegoistic Eliot allows ghosts and Furies to move through his *Quartets,* possessing and obsessing them and directing an imperious control over the reader: there are no such ghosts in **'Three for Water-Music'**, which in fact insists on the absence of any such presences. . . . This absence of the explainable beyond the renewal of the self-containedness of the image . . . gives the sequence its beautiful and tough purity, as of those 'clear-glassed windows / The clear day looking in' which the poet remembers from early Dissenting chapels. But it produces an art always close enough to the tacit to make a reader grateful for the relative 'impurities' (what Davie has called elsewhere, in connection with Wordsworth, 'the smell of the human') in the latter part of this book, which consists of **'The Shires'**.

'The Shires' . . . is a sequence of 40 short or shortish poems lacking the manifest philosophical concerns of the poems that precede it. It offers itself as an easy, even casual topographical record of England, county by county in alphabetical sequence. . . . [This is] an extremely original gazetteer, whose aesthetic nature places it rightly in the same volume as **'Three for Water-Music'**. The very word 'shires' reminds us by its archaism of what we know already—that England like other known places is always slipping into the past, always changing its nature from the remembered. Moreover the 'sense of place' is a feeling often keenest in absence or exile . . . ; like other senses of loss, it occasions self-questioning. . . .

Davie builds up in the end an extraordinarily clear, sharp and pungent sense of England. But he does so by first clearing the ground of illusion (almost every poem begins with a harsh disclaimer, as **'Berkshire'**, 'Don't care for it . . .', **'Derby-shire'**, 'We never made it . . .'). The fragments of memory come to carry truth because the real human topographies, so the poems seem to say, depend on certain stripped and wintry conditions in life itself. Thus Rutland, the 'Joke county, smallest in England', is real because it once held

> my old
> Friend, Bill Partridge. Dead now. Had you
> noticed?
>
> How heavy that weighs, how wide the narrowest
> shire!

Because all space forms itself round the loved, who become more and more, as time passes, the loved dead, all counties really are alike 'the smallest'; just as all these poems begin in their sharp wit of detachment as 'joke' poems—but jokes that nonetheless hold in their bluntness, their fragmentariness, their ridiculously wooden personal allusions, a whole unjokey monumental statement about human limits and human value. Thus **'Leicestershire'** ends impassively:

> At Loughborough, I remember,
> A man too little regarded
> (Dead since), V. C. Clinton-
> Baddeley afforded
> Several views of Yeats.

There is a fine art, given this essentially English context, even in the balanced placing of the hyphen. Everything in **'The Shires'** has a decorous 'English' smallness in this sense, a perfect art of self-containment and throw-away grace and wit, all the effects as tacit as they are taciturn. Indeed, the ironies, silences and negations in Davie's art are clearly conditions of their opposite, as a love of country may dictate a refusal to be mindlessly 'patriotic'. . . .

Davie's work has integrity in the simple sense: it holds together, and preoccupations recur in different forms and throw light on each other alike in verse and in several kinds of critical prose. In both verse and prose his reflections centre on a quality of Christian civilisation that may be seen as 'Pulsing through history and out of it': a tradition of life and belief that seeks a true and classic human standard while setting itself against such aspects of the merely comfortably established as are spurious or vicious. He pursues a definition of existence lived out (in favourite phrases) 'with the grain' but 'against the current'. (p. 5)

> Barbara Everett, *"Poetry and Christianity,"* in London Review of Books, *February 4 to February 18, 1982, pp. 5-7.*

VALENTINE CUNNINGHAM

Donald Davie speaks up for Old Dissent—for its religious life and the literature it generated—with what might be thought of as an aptly persistent dissentience. He naturally believes he must dissent from the bulk of Dissent's usual enemies. Even more, though, he feels led to dissent from some of the most insistent of Dissent's friends. Crustily, he stands between, on the one hand, the scornful majority who borrow the terminologies of Matthew Arnold for their dismissals of all Dissent as barbarously uncultured philistinism, and, on the other, that colonising minority who want to specialise Dissent into the ranks of the progressive and leftist.

It's an awkward, contentious corner to hold out in. Davie knowingly boxed himself into it in his Clark Lectures, *A Gathered Church* (1976), and these more recent lectures and articles [collected in ***Dissentient Voice: Enlightenment and Christian Dissent***] show him still contentedly there, still jabbing foxily away with intent to outrage his chosen opponents. His beloved 18th-century Dissenters, so his argument goes, didn't just happen to hit off a clutch of memorable hymns. Watts and Charles Wesley, Newton and Doddridge wrote their great poems because their religion sited them comfortably within the Age of Reason. Nobody was more intellectually serious and reasonable than Watts and Co., with their abstractions and their theological paradoxes. The Enlightenment was—and enlightenment still is—as much Christian as it is anything. The members of an 18th-century Baptist or Congregationalist church were shaped by a toughly reasoning faith expressed in a strong-minded, plain-speaking poetry. They enjoyed Christ *and* culture. Which is, or so Davie intends, one in the eye for their snobbish, 'cultured' despisers. . . .

Davie's case for Dissent harnesses his powerful hostility towards verbal muddling. Getting us straight about the difference between unorthodox Unitarians and orthodox Dissenters—a distinction Davie shows the tricksy, trimming Unitarians uncandidly and successfully fudging over in the later 18th century—will teach us to care for semantic clarity and precision, to 'take seriously what words say, *each* word, severally and together'—which is just what 'a good poem' does. Furthermore, if we read a Flavel or a Watts attentively, we may be saved from what in a hectic moment Davie sneers at as the soggily warm 'steam' of socialism's assumptions and language.

Davie knows that his egregiously huge conceptual leaps and links are likely to give us pause. They're designed to. Giving, and being given, pause are favourite Davie activities. 'Here we need to pause,' he will say, stopping us from rattling heedlessly on through some difficult stretch of Dissenting history or religious poetry that we'd rather avoid being discomfited by. He loves the unblinkable, the disconcerting, the rebarbatively exact bit of Christian doctrine that one of his favourite hymn-writers hasn't shunned. 'His dying crimson like a robe / Spreads o'er his body on the Tree'; the squeamish Christians who rarely sing these words could do with more of Watts's bleakly uncompromising and orthodox challenges. Flinching softness of doctrine, tolerance, liberalism: they've let the wily Unitarians, and all the other traducers of truth and true Dissent, get away with their language-ruining hypocrisies, prevarications and distortions. Hard sayings, these. But then Davie thinks Anglicans are exhorted in Advent to 'meditate on "the four last things"—Death, Sin, Hell, and Judgment'. No Heaven, you see; only Sin. No wonder Davie has little time for 19th-century Nonconformists—who added to orthodoxy a fifth last thing, the idea of the welcomable rescue of the saints from earth's end-time distresses. They called it the Rapture.

Davie's unwarm, unenraptured kind of Christianity, and the presumptuous critical and social assumptions into whose service it's pressed, are by no means new. T. S. Eliot also made play with the need for orthodoxy in faith and literature, for tradition and monarchism against all liberal practitioners ('knee-jerk liberals', Davie calls them) and democratisers (Davie approves a right-wing Dissenter deploring 'the tyranny of a depraved multitude'). And just as Eliot was cagey about his debt to Arnold and slippery about monarchists like Lancelot Andrewes and the Commonwealth poets Milton and Marvell, so Davie is cagey about his own debt to Eliot—after all, he was an ex-Unitarian turned Anglican—and slippery in lots of his own readings of poems and histories. . . . Davie's sacrifice of 19th-century Nonconformity, and Browning in particular, to the Arnoldians' 'smug grocer' scenario is appallingly sweeping. His put-down of the Rev. Thomas Binney's hymn 'Eternal Light! Eternal Light!' looks wilfully programmatic. His enthusiasm for the 20th-century Calvinist poet Jack Clemo is carefully silent about the grislier aspects of what is essentially second-hand Jack Powys eroticism, about the awful tosh his 'Royal Wedding' poem . . . really is, and about his hot-gospelling admiration for such anti-culture Christians as Oral Roberts and C. T. Studd. On such occasions, one could do with rather more of that candour Davie rightly blames those Unitarians for lacking.

Valentine Cunningham, "Dissenting Davie," in The Listener, *Vol. 108, No. 2775, August 26, 1982, p. 21.*

CHRISTOPHER RICKS

Donald Davie's critical arguments are often happily reminiscential, and his reminiscences are often happily argumentative, so the difference in kind between these two admirable books doesn't make for any great difference of temper. The critical essays which make up *Dissentient Voice: Enlightenment and Christian Dissent* are an act of making good; they fulfil the promise and they repair the deficiencies of Davie's earlier book on Dissent and culture, *A Gathered Church*. The recollections gathered as *These the Companions* are an act of making permanent, with such permanence as time has; they fulfil a promise often made and often kept in Davie's poems but which these days asks, too, for the expatiating element of prose: the exercise of 'the faculty of pious memory'.

There is no reason to question the sincerity of the foreword's concluding insistence: 'For certainly I'm not writing to vindicate myself, if only because in this book I am not the principal character. You must bear with the first person singular only so as to have me introduce you to persons and places and ambiences that have a singularity and a value such as I won't claim for myself.' The trouble is that this is an insistence. The swell and throb of the title, *These the Companions* (as against, say, Charles Tomlinson's recent recollections, *Some Americans*), are evidence, not just that Davie will over-forgive Ezra Pound almost anything ('Lordly men are to earth o'ergiven / these the companions'), but also that he needed to underline the self-abnegation. Sincerity, like patriotism (which Davie has too), is not enough. Moving as these recollections often are, in their evocation of places (the West Riding, the Arctic Circle, Cambridge or California) and of people (Douglas Brown, Yvor Winters, an early love, fellow-sailors), his touch in this prose is less secure than in either the kind of prose which he has most practised or the poems which figure within the book as at once asides and nubs. You may say, and believe, that you 'are not the principal character', but you can't help sounding like it when you use such a locution as 'when I and Sean White took him to Dublin Castle'. . . .

Still, Davie's not being entirely in possession of his means, in a kind of writing relatively new to him, does little to lessen the worth of his living gratitude. Since he is what used to be called a good hater and a bonny fighter ('I am happy in my glittering envelope, and will fight those who would puncture it,' 'I am not prepared to give up my inheritance without a fight'), it is notable that he vindicates such praises in the only way they can be vindicated: by manifesting that he is, too, a man of love. This is not, to put it mildly, a claim usually made for the man. But his love of literature and of literary studies (in descending but not demeaning order); his love of landscape, of rocks and roots (human nature is fine, but scenery is in some respects finer); his love of those who taught him and of those whom he has taught: these are crowned by a feat of the book, its establishing the continuing presence of the people most important to Davie—those so near and dear as not to be companions exactly, his wife and children. They are seldom mentioned, they are indeed, as he says, 'taken for granted'—but not unthinkingly or perfunctorily. Davie's beliefs about privacy, in life and in literature, made it essential that he in no way parade his family, his marriage, his domesticities. He has managed to convey that his family is not at all an element in his book because it is something more important, the element of the book. He has managed to convey, not only that he loves his wife, but that she—who does not get a word in edgeways—loves him, edges and all.

The intimate relation of such covert love to Davie's overt hatreds is akin to his great strength as a critic, his mounting of polemic from which he can then take off, since it is entirely continuous with his more highly imaginative criticism. (p. 5)

It is one of the many paradoxes of Davie's achievement and character that this apostle of temperance, moderation, coolness and privacy should so often *sound* (my emphasis) as if he were in thrall to their opposites. He will say that 'the Cantabrigian ethos . . . leaves no margin for *caprice*', where the weight put upon 'caprice' takes from it all possibility of the free-floating provisional levity which it ostensibly values. He will speak of 'a specifically Cambridge way of putting privileged emphasis on the *verbal* arts', in the act of using italics to do that which he is deploring. Those who believe Davie to be a bundle of contradictions will—as he does—call up the old Essex days, and will recall that he was then publicly described as touched with the wing of madness. Those of us who—through all the trials which he inflicts (most of them putting us justly on trial, others a bit trying)—still hold to the confidence that he is the best, the most fertile, critic of the generations after Eliot, Leavis and Empson will see the most important of these contradictions as paradoxes; will judge that the paradoxes are fecund and revelatory when they are in touch with the Christian paradoxes to which Davie is dedicated; and will believe that, at 60, he is unique in offering so principled a resistance to Yeats's famous slice of neatness: for sometimes we can make out of the quarrel with ourselves nothing but rhetoric; and sometimes we can make out of the quarrel with others poetry.

Davie has so many positive capabilities that it is hard to know just what to make of his so seeming to lack the Keatsian negative one. It is not so much that he reaches irritably after fact and reason, and will not admit an aperçu unless it can be theorised. But he is, by temperament and by conviction, hostile to openmindedness, which he sees as liberalism's dogma. When, in a related thought, Keats said 'that Dilke was a Man who cannot feel he has a personal identity unless he has made up his Mind about every thing,' he prophesied Davie—or rather Davie the critic. Certain things are occluded from such a man. But Davie can reply that ours is not an age in which people are too much or too candidly making up their minds about things, but one in which doubt is the one thing undoubted. Literature is praised as all questions and no answers; interpretation as determinedly indeterminate; and pyrrhonism as the one thing not to be sceptical of.

Granted, tentativeness has access to certain truths, and they are mostly truths by which Davie does not set enough store: but the tentative does not have a monopoly of the truth, and there is such a thing as the falsely tentative, much in evidence. Davie is against slides and glides. *Dissentient Voice* is out to rescue Dissent from its kidnappers. Dissent was not and is not 'a stage on the way to enlightened unbelief', or endemically of the Left; it has often been loyalist and royalist, and the take-over by E. P. Thompson is exposed as the irreligious left-winger's imperialism. Davie is not only stringent, he is cogent. . . . [He] pays Thompson the supreme compliment of taking his statements more seriously than he had taken them himself. Davie is unusual among the most influential critics of our day in both proffering and inviting the compliment of rational opposition.

Where then should he be opposed? Wherever he allows his own polemical powers a license such as he rightly refuses to Thompson's. 'Indeed it is surely obvious that in any age it is the conservatives, wary of departing from precedents embodying the wisdom of the forefathers, who are least complacent about the advances achieved by themselves and their contemporaries.' This has too much rhetorical backing: it is as if he had moved from 'in any age it is the conservatives', to 'it is obvious that in any age . . .', to 'it is surely obvious . . .', to 'Indeed it is surely obvious. . . .' The man who is sceptical about social protest doth protest too much. In any case, there is no reason why those who are 'wary of departing from precedents embodying the wisdom of the forefathers' should not be handsomely complacent as to 'the advances achieved by themselves and their contemporaries', any more than those conservative artists who are—in Eliot's words—original with the minimum of alteration need be any less complacent about their achievement than their maximising rivals. At such moments, Davie is less dissentient than insentient, as he is when he limits his vigilance to 'Leftist politicos', as if there were no such things as Rightist ones. . . . It is not that Davie lacks magnanimity: rather that he wrongly thinks it prudent to ration it.

So when he half-admires Thompson's 'furious impatience', we are alerted to the need on occasion to recall Davie to his own highest standards. Davie deplores 'a tone that is brutal, overemphatic, overconfident': 'It is, above all, impatient and therefore irreverent. And it is certainly to be heard at times in Browning, as in Charles Kingsley, where Gerard Manley Hopkins heard it and characterised it unforgivingly but vividly when he envisaged a man starting up from the breakfast table, his mouth full of bacon and eggs, declaring that he will stand no damn'd nonsense.' Does it matter, except to patient pedantry, that this wasn't exactly what Hopkins said about Browning? (pp. 5-6)

The instance is trivial but the principle is not. For the impatience has become Davie's.

Sometimes, then, like a man who says he will stand no nonsense, he utters some of the kind which goes with saying such a thing. His impatience with England moves him to rhetorical questioning: 'Where else but in England, I ask myself, does a clear-cut disagreement about a professional matter, for instance about the proper diction for poetry, get itself so immediately cross-hatched with shadows thrown from irrelevancies like egalitarian humanism or wounded *amour-propre*?' But this violates Davie's own deepest sense of the issues, for he elsewhere rightly refuses to accept that there is such a thing as 'a professional matter' when it comes to language and its properties and responsibilities. *Purity of Diction in English Verse* took seriously, in themselves, the concepts of purity and chastity; it did not countenance the dehumanised professionalism which would segregate the proper diction for poetry as a purely professional matter. Again, when Davie, as a Christian, dissents from the 'spiritual twilight' which he says he used to share with Leavis and Yvor Winters, he seems to me then to falsify his own clarity when he goes on at once to say: 'I think it has to be the case that such crepuscular uncertainty about First and Last Things disperses itself, like a miasma, through the crevices of thought about apparently quite other things, accustoming us to approximations merely, and twilight zones in our thinking, about such entirely secular matters as the proper language for poetry.' For he cannot with entire honesty—cannot without some self-suppression of the wrong sort—invoke the proper language of poetry as an entirely secular matter. He is defecting from an apophthegm of his own, one that should be as respected by an atheist like me as by a Christian like Davie: 'If he [God] exists, there is no equation that he can be left out of.'

It matters when Davie travesties his opponents, not least because he then wrongs himself too. 'My Voltairean friends . . . surely misjudge when they suppose that dangerous irrationality is peculiar to religious life.' I simply don't believe that anybody as stupid as that has ever been granted the friendship of Donald Davie. Ian Watt and Matthew Hodgart, who are the friends who had just been mentioned in the vicinity of Voltaire, have been able to write as well as they have done about Conrad and about Johnson just because their respect for the Enlightenment has never been so fatuous as to 'suppose that dangerous irrationality is peculiar to religious life.' . . . In so disrespecting those who honourably, even if it were misguidedly, oppose 'dangerous irrationality' in religious life, this ceases to respect itself. Davie has yielded to the one thing which his principles and tone least allow him to indulge: disingenuousness.

'I am, and have always been—let's face it—a prude.' As manipulation, this is a brilliant way into an account of Davie's rejection of erotic vulgarity and sensationalism in art and in life: but as part of a responsible deploring of those vices as a manipulation, it is lamentable. For of course Davie is not saying that he is and has always been a prude: he is saying, without taking the righteous rap for it, that he is and has always been a man of honourable and uncorrupted *pudeur*, of truly sensitive propriety. Naturally this puts him in an awkward position as an autobiographer, for it is a proud claim. But that is what it should be offered as, not with the glissade of a man who, not wishing to sound like a prig, affects to believe that he is a prude.

It is because a great part of Davie's enterprise is the recalling of people to their own professed principles that he himself must not be granted exemption. For otherwise it would be impudence and not audacity in him to have rebuked T. S. Eliot for, of all things, an excessive liberalism. . . . Much of these two books is an engagement with Eliot. Eliot's shade might murmur the words which Kingsley Amis recently used of Philip Larkin: 'Sometimes he seems reactionary even to me.' (p. 6)

Christopher Ricks, "Armadillo," in London Review of Books, *September 16 to October 6, 1982, pp. 5-6.*

LOUIS SIMPSON

The imagination, Donald Davie says, is concerned with "one particular person, in one place, at one time, in one sort of weather." Therefore [in **"These the Companions"**] he is re-creating the individuals, some of them obscure, and the places, some well off the beaten path, that contributed to his growth as a writer. He is speaking of "companions," individuals who have meant something to him personally, rather than those he has met in his career as poet, teacher and critic. Like the Russian novelists he admires, he aims to render things as they were. He is not drawing morals, for, he says, he does not have "the heart for it," but is making a truthful record so that the people, places and times he is describing may invite "different reflections from those of the narrator." In this I think he has succeeded, for as I read about his adventures and considered his reflections, my reflections were frequently very different from his. . . .

[Mr. Davie's frankness] invites a certain sort of reader to feel superior. He says that he has been a "coward before life," a prig and a prude. To write so doubtfully about oneself is to put a weapon in the hands of envy and malice. Most writers only admit to failings—promiscuous sexual activity, for example—that most people do not regard as failings. In reading Mr. Davie's admissions, I had, as it were, to protect him from himself, from his zeal for explaining his limitations. He is not a prig now, if he ever was. He is not a "coward before life." He is a writer, and a writer can't immerse himself in human relationships but must stand a little way off. About prudishness, however, I think he may be right. He tells us that sex is "in the last analysis comical" and that Joyce's "Ulysses," though great, is a "smutty and sniggering book." Apparently he missed the comic passages. (p. 9)

[On] the pros and cons of having an imagination he is an expert. Is it possible, he muses, that the stability of the English—demonstrated by their resistance to the Nazis—came of their inability to imagine defeat? Other peoples with a more vivid imagination (the Poles and Irish, for example) have paid a terrible price for having it. But he asks, is survival the test of the validity of attitudes and ideas? Here, on the verge of chaos or perhaps of a revelation, Mr. Davie ceases to pursue his train of thought.

This is where I find him dissatisfying. Sometimes I get the feeling from Mr. Davie's reflections that I have had in conversations with English men and women, that they retire behind a wall of "good taste." You think you are having a discussion and find you are at a club. "Who outside England," says Mr. Davie, "thinks any longer that the making of a point is what a poem can or should be concerned with?" I could tell him, but he does not stay for an answer. . . .

Speaking of critics who emasculate poetry by treating it as though it were prose, Mr. Davie says, "I could name names, and they would be distinguished ones." Why doesn't he name them?

The trouble with this kind of reticence is that judgments seem to be made on the basis of personal taste rather than thought. Yet Mr. Davie's range of sympathy is impressive. He has written about Ezra Pound at one extreme and Thomas Hardy at the other. . . . Mr. Davie's recollections are very readable, in fact, one is likely to go through them too fast, looking for nuggets. The chapters about Russia during the war, when he was stationed at Polyarno and Archangel on the Arctic Circle, have the realism and a sense of spiritual space corresponding to the immensity of the land that one finds in Russian writing. The people are equally memorable—best of all, a statuesque Russian woman with a can of sugared beer in one hand and a raw fish in the other. Mr. Davie also captures the atmosphere of Trinity College, Dublin, and landscapes in California and Italy. (p. 22)

Louis Simpson, "Friends and Opinions and Influences," in The New York Times Book Review, November 21, 1982, pp. 9, 22.

JOHN LUCAS

If poems were made solely of ideas there would be few more interesting poets than Donald Davie. For his seriousness about ideas is never in doubt: he ponders, questions, argues with himself and others, and it seems inevitable that, reading him, you want to argue back. Davie's [*Collected Poems 1970-1983*] is, in short, remarkable for its prose virtues, although these have more to do with articulate energy than with purity of diction. For he can be very clumsy and his ear is by no means true. This is especially the case whenever he tries to move towards the colloquial or the demotic. It is not merely that his lines lack grace, or that they quite fail to suggest an attentiveness to those rhythms that imply human depths tapped through speech utterance. It is also that although he requires us to be good listeners he is not a good listener himself. This is perhaps a consequence of his donnishness, of a literariness that seems ill at ease with the familiar. At all events there are some remarkably phoney moments in his poetry. 'The beery ram that mounted / His niece and, hissing "Belt up", had her.' How do you *hiss* 'Belt up'? And can you really believe in the desire of a poet to make it new who writes of 'a hulking great villain' or who carelessly repeats 'there's' 'theirs' and 'there's' in the space of three lines?

Well, yes, you can. Because set against these faults, and in spite of a lack of canorousness so great that trying to speak his lines you often feel as though you have a mouth full of pebbles, there are those undeniable merits that keep you reading. In fact, Davie is very readable, perhaps because his literary, donnish qualities compel him to take the reader seriously, so that although you often feel talked at you never feel talked down to. I do not intend this to be faint praise. There are not many poets who can communicate such passionate interest in the written word or who can match Davie's searching out of a variety of frequently surprising verse forms and prosodic techniques, all of which he puts to exhilarating use. At his best Davie is an ambassador for poetry and, whether abrasive or courteous, always candid, open, vulnerable even. Of the poems new to me in this collection I particularly admire **'Artifax in Extremis', 'Well-Found Poem'** and **'Catullus on Friendship'**, with its inimitable, rasping, half-affectionate, half-maddened tone, its very real testimony to the exactions required by a marriage of minds.

John Lucas, "A Mouthful of Pebbles," in New Statesman, Vol. 106, No. 2733, August 5, 1983, p. 23.*

EMILY GROSHOLZ

Donald Davie's latest book, *Three for Water Music*, is a composite of three reflections on water and the long poem **"The Shires,"** Davie's idiosyncratic commentary on each of the English shires. The whole book is dense and finely balanced, another welcome product by one of the master-workers of our language.

In **"The Fountain of Cyanë,"** Davie writes about poetry with the fluency of Dryden, but a wholly modern irreverence for mythical subjects and a reflexive irony towards poetry's ability to gloze over even the most terrible events. The occasion is his visit to the pool of Cyanë in Sicily where, on Ovid's account, Persephone was carried off by the Lord of the Underworld and her grief-stricken companion Cyanë wept herself into a pool. (p. 583)

Considering the springs of inspiration and the poet's way of drawing upon them, Davie argues that poetry requires formality, but not so that it suppresses the anarchic violence which is part of the truth of reality. Language should crack a little for grief into fault-traceries on the perfection of form. Epiphanies "like the closed-off / Precincts all right, but never / When those exult in their closures." Moreover, poetry requires a subject which, though it may not have the necessity of existence, should at least be a postulate useful for making sense of life, one of those permanent myths that explain, for instance, why we endure long winter nights and trust in the return of summer's daughter.

"Wild Boar Clough" attests to Davie's strongly ambivalent feelings about English Protestantism in all its religious, political and cultural ramifications. For a Puritan poet can only be a "Burning, redundant candle, / Invisible at noon." . . . **"The Fountain of Arethousa"** mirrors the poet again, this time with the past behind him. In **"Gratitude, Need and Gladness"** he acknowledges his debt towards the inhabitants of the everyday for the small glories he finds there. Thus it is not Shelley's grandiosity he praises, but rather his own mother's way of reciting Shelley, which first turned him to poetry and to which he turns again now, in memoriam. (pp. 583-84)

> *Emily Grosholz, "Master-Workers and Others," in* The Hudson Review, *Vol. XXXVI, No. 3, Autumn, 1983, pp. 582-92.**

ALAN SHAPIRO

At a time when we are accustomed to thinking about the lives of poets more in terms of marital chaos, alcoholism, and breakdown than in terms of poetry, it is refreshing to read Donald Davie's memoir [*These the Companions*], which not only is an episodic account of events and personalities but also is a serious meditation on his lifelong involvement with literature. The two acquaintances whom he remembers most acutely and generously are F. R. Leavis and Yvor Winters, writers he portrays as puritans in their thinking about art. By *puritan* he means a person of principle, someone for whom not all moral and intellectual judgments are relative, someone who insists "that in the arts, as between the genuine and the fake, or between the achieved and the unachieved, there cannot be any halfway house."

These the Companions is not a book of unqualified praise for puritanism so much as it is a deeply felt reaction against the tendency in himself and in important friends and mentors to divide too brutally the sheep from the goats, the genuine from the fake. What animates his assessment of men like Winters and Leavis and what stands uneasily back of his assessment of his own intellectual and literary habits is a troubled awareness of how an appetite for rigorous and absolute criteria, however necessary, can constrict one's sympathies; yet at the same time he also can acknowledge how sympathy uninformed by principle can degenerate into what he calls "a lax eclecti-cism," a warm diffusive live-and-let-live attitude which in its impact on the practising artist can be just as harmful. Though at times his antithetical thinking seems like mere ambivalence, for the most part it is a form of generosity or evenhandedness. One might even call it a kind of Keatsian disinterestedness, for it enables Davie to enter imaginatively into positions he opposes or distrusts not to evade judgment but to ground judgment in sympathetic understanding, to judge from the inside, not to label and dismiss. (p. lxviii)

Nowhere is Davie's inclusiveness—his refusal to settle for comforting simplifications—more apparent than in his comments on poetry. The writers of his generation, he tells us, fought their way into print "in the teeth of an irrationalist theory of poetry." Though he appears to align himself here with a strictly rationalist view of poetry, in another chapter he insists that art works arise, "not exclusively but necessarily," out of "*caprice* . . . that free-running, freely associating, arbitrary and gratuitous play of mind." In his thinking, poetry integrates both classical and romantic tendencies, the spontaneous and deliberately shaped, the emotional and intellectual. Davie's unwavering commitment to this ideal justifies his bitter response to someone who says he cannot decide whether, as a poet, he wants to be like Doctor Johnson or like Rimbaud: "It is such a clever thing to say, and so shallow! I want to be a poet of *feeling,* as Doctor Johnson is, and Rimbaud also." His own poems . . . illustrate these generous ambitions. On the one hand he can write movingly in the discursive formal style of **"Among Artisans' Houses"**; yet on the other hand he can write with just as much success, with just as much feeling, in the experimental style of **"Petit-Thouars."** . . . (p. lxx)

What *These the Companions* shows us is how unnecessarily pinched and inflexible our judgments and assumptions about poetry are, turning what should be mutually implicatory possibilities into mutually exclusive ones. That Davie refuses to choose exclusively between Johnson and Rimbaud, that he desires to bring the widest range of faculties to bear upon the widest range of experience, is finally what makes his work so troubling and unpredictable to those who seek in it the refuge of simplistic categories. That inclusiveness makes Donald Davie one of the most valuable and engaging poet-critics that we have. (pp. lxx, lxxii)

> *Alan Shapiro, "Generous Puritan," in* The Sewanee Review, *Vol. XCI, No. 4, Fall, 1983, pp. lxviii, lxx, lxxii.*

WILLIAM H. PRITCHARD

There are of course many reasons to be grateful for Donald Davie's continuing presence, but after reading the most recent poems in his volume of collected poems from the years since 1970 [*Collected Poems 1970-1983*] . . . I decided that one of the reasons was that he rhymed. Rhyme, so conspicuously absent in the volumes considered here, is present in Davie's late poem **"Artifex in Extremis,"** which begins with "Let him rehearse the gifts reserved for age / Much as the poet Eliot did" and goes on to explore the consciousness of a dying artist. This exploration is given strength and shape by its rhymes. . . . The new poems from *The Battered Wife* (1982) include, notably, the title poem, **"Screech Owl," "Having No Ear," "Siloam," "Three Beyond,"** and **"Two From Ireland,"** in the last of which the older poet looks back on his younger self, once a don at Trinity College, Dublin. Now, returning in 1977 to the country of the "troubles," he finds himself oddly charmed. . . . As always, to read this poet is to experience intelligence, control, and a quotient of obscurity; but . . . also a lyric of song. The title of one of these poems, **"Having No Ear,"** is about listening to music. But Davie's ear is in his poetry. (pp. 340-42)

> *William H. Pritchard, "Aboard the Poetry Omni-*
> *bus," in* The Hudson Review, *Vol. XXXVII, No. 2,*
> *Summer, 1984, pp. 327-42.**

August (William) Derleth

1909-1971

(Also wrote under pseudonyms of Stephen Grendon and Tally Mason) American novelist, short story writer, poet, nonfiction writer, biographer, critic, editor, and publisher.

Derleth wrote or edited more than 150 books, including poetry, fiction, biographies, histories, juvenile fiction, mysteries, and supernatural tales, during a career that spanned nearly fifty years. While he began his career as a mystery writer, Derleth gained his most serious critical attention for his semiautobiographical "Sac Prairie Saga." These works, which revolve around the people and events in the fictive town of Sac Prairie, Wisconsin, were praised for their attention to detail and their vivid descriptions of nature. Totalling thirty-eight volumes, including poetry, prose, and character sketches, the Sac Prairie Saga evinces Derleth's ability to depict both the peacefulness and the tension in small-town life.

The Sac Prairie series covers the time period from the early 1800s through the mid-1900s. While the works in this series are highly praised for Derleth's descriptions of natural beauty, some critics maintain that his preoccupation with the land indicates a lack of feeling for his characters and makes it difficult to sustain interest in them. Derleth's characters generally are loners who exhibit what he called "the night that is in each of us." Most of Derleth's stories are concerned with the themes of love, courage, and honor and are infused with a wistful, nostalgic tone that often includes gentle humor. Among the more highly praised Sac Prairie works are the novels *Still Is the Summer Night* (1937), *Wind Over Wisconsin* (1938), and *Evening in Spring* (1941), the short story collection *Country Growth* (1940), and two volumes of poetry, *Hawk on the Wind* (1938) and *Man Track Here* (1939).

While he was involved in writing the Sac Prairie works, Derleth began another series, the "Wisconsin Saga." The five novels in this series, *Bright Journey* (1940), *The House on the Mound* (1958), *The Hills Stand Watch* (1960), *The Shadow in the Glass* (1963), and *The Wind Leans West* (1969), often have as their subjects actual people and events in the history of Wisconsin. These volumes maintain the same subdued tone as the Sac Prairie Saga, for Derleth concentrated on similar themes and carefully detailed his settings. However, this series, like the later volumes of the Sac Prairie works, was not well received by critics; they considered his later works monotonous, repetitive, and crowded with superfluous characters and incidents.

Two other series for which Derleth is known are the Judge Peck stories and the Solar Pons mysteries. Also set in Sac Prairie, the Judge Peck works, which include *Murder Stalks the Wakely Family* (1934), *The Seven Who Waited* (1943), and *Death by Design* (1953), are cleverly plotted detective stories that have been well received by devotees of the genre. The Solar Pons mysteries, including *In Re: Sherlock Holmes, The Adventures of Solar Pons* (1945) and *Mr. Fairlie's Final Journey* (1968), have been praised as among the best Sherlock Holmes imitations as well as being entertaining and intriguing in their own right.

Photo-Land © 1983

Although Derleth was recognized as an important regional writer during the 1940s and 1950s, he became better known in subsequent years as the founder of Arkham House, which published a number of well-known writers in the supernatural and fantasy fields, including Robert E. Howard, Lord Dunsany, Robert Bloch, and Algernon Blackwood. Derleth also oversaw the publication of the first novels of science fiction writers Fritz Leiber, Ray Bradbury, and A. E. Van Vogt. His most famous literary association, however, was with H. P. Lovecraft, whose works he promoted for critical and public attention. Derleth also wrote numerous stories based on notes and fragments Lovecraft had left and published them under joint authorship. These works are collected in the volume *The Watchers Out of Time and Others* (1974). Derleth also tried his hand at writing science fiction, but his accomplishments in this field are considered slight in comparison to those in his Sac Prairie series.

(See also *Contemporary Authors*, Vols. 1-4, rev. ed., Vols. 29-32, rev. ed. [obituary]; *Contemporary Authors New Revision Series*, Vol. 4; *Something about the Author*, Vol. 5; and *Dictionary of Literary Biography*, Vol. 9.)

H P [H. P. LOVECRAFT]

Dear A. W.:—

Your novelette *The Early Years* [the initial draft of the novel which was to become *Evening in Spring*] duly came, and I have read it with the closest attention. Truly, it is a splendid piece of work. . . . I knew from your isolated fragments that you had the real stuff of literature at your command; but now that I see some of these arranged in a proper organic relationship, my opinion takes an additional upward soaring! There is profound and subtle beauty, splendidly modulated, in this sequence of dream-glamourous pictures. You have a keen and sensitively selective eye for details and sensations and images, as indeed I realised before. Now I see that you are equally felicitous in arranging these things in a significant, revelatory, and aesthetically satisfying form. It seems to me that you are coming to handle words and sentences more and more skilfully and adequately—you will recall my mentioning, in years past, that carelessness in this field . . . was one result of your overvoluminous writing which ought to be corrected a bit. Time, I imagine, is supplying this correction—for this novelette has passages of beautiful and musical language as well as of poignant imagery and convincing emotion. There is no mistaking the right of this piece to be considered as serious literary expression. (pp. 141-42)

[The] sketches all have the feel of genuine life and sincerity about them. They create a scene and atmosphere with solid reality in every part—even though it be that ethereal reality which depends on mood and subjective vision for its palpable outlines. You are obviously not trying to give a cross-section of the entire lives of the characters in all their complex humanity. What you are doing is to trace a certain line of emotional activity in them—and in this you succeed with admirable completeness. Most certainly I find all the characters clearly outlined—visible and psychologically realisable. Though each one represents a temperament and emotional life antipodally different from my own at their age, I can detect the earmarks of truthful portrayal throughout the story. There is an impression of authentic life—a feeling that some sort of key is furnished to the fumbling and ambivalent thoughts and motivations of a vast proportion of actual adolescents whom one has observed. . . . Certainly, this is a marvellously fine piece of delving into the obscure associative imagery and emotional overtones of a certain part of the stream of consciousness of a certain type of introverted and somewhat hyperaesthetic youth. I can see the differences in intention from the Proust and Joyce schools of fiction, and think on the whole that your attitude is somewhat more conservative than the latter's. You preserve a certain coherence and integration, and exercise a measurable degree of selectiveness despite your departure from the superficial and the conventional. . . . You have the real stuff, and with the progress of time it seems to me over-whelmingly probable that you will produce literature of a major calibre. . . . Yr. most obt. and Hble. servt. HP (p. 142)

> *H P [H. P. Lovecraft], in a letter to August Derleth on April 9, 1930, in his* Selected Letters: 1929-1931, *Vol. III, edited by August Derleth and Donald Wandrei, Arkham House: Publishers, 1971, pp. 141-42.*

H P [H. P. LOVECRAFT]

Dear A. W.:—

. . . *Five Alone* is such a magnificently balanced bit of atmosphere and inevitability that I don't see how any fully awake and sober editor could possibly reject it. The steady growth of your work is surely heartening to see, and I can easily imagine what your place in the literary field will be a decade hence.

About the objection to the odd constructions typified by "she walking out" . . . or "she perfectly natural" . . . , I must say that I am inclined to agree with the pedagogical commentator. These constructions, whatever their abstract syntactical merits, are so conspicuously *unidiomatic* that they tend to attract attention to themselves and thus halt the imaginative progress of the reader. An author's object should be the art which conceals art, hence obtrusive singularity is always to be shunned. . . . This story is certainly a most remarkable piece of work—full of the horror (also to be noted in early New England) of exaggerated instincts in remote and lonely places. I can't think of anything that could be done to better it as a whole. . . .

Best wishes—HP

> *H P [H. P. Lovecraft], in a letter to August Derleth in February, 1932, in his* Selected Letters: 1932-1934, *Vol. IV, edited by August Derleth and James Turner, Arkham House: Publishers, Inc., 1976, p. 11.*

ISAAC ANDERSON

[In **"Murder Stalks the Wakely Family,"** seven] persons living in the little town of Sac Prairie, Wis., receive invitations—they might almost be called commands—to call at midnight on Satterlee Wakely, a man who is hated by virtually everybody who knows him. . . . [The four who accept the invitations] arrive at Wakely's house so nearly at the same moment that they all go in together. They find Wakely dead with a knife stuck through his neck. . . . But this is only the beginning. Three more murders are to follow before Judge Peck . . . discovers the secret that is at the bottom of all the killings and finds the killer. Judge Peck is not a particularly brilliant detective, but he is patient and persistent, and those are the qualities that the case seems to call for.

For the most part the story is told from the viewpoint of Judge Peck and his fellow investigators, but in two places the author departs from this plan and puts himself in the place of the person about to be killed, thus marring the unity of the story for no other purpose, apparently, than to add a slight touch of horror. However, it is not likely that the average mystery fan is fussy about such things so long as he is provided with plenty of bloodshed, and there is no lack of that in this book. (pp. 12, 21)

> *Isaac Anderson, in a review of "Murder Stalks the Wakely Family," in* The New York Times Book Review, *March 18, 1934, pp. 12, 21.*

WILL CUPPY

[In **"The Man on All Fours"**] we have some not unpleasant sleuthing by Judge Ephraim Peck, who appeared in **"Murder Stalks the Wakely Family,"** ferreting out a coil of fatal violence at Senessen House, the seat of the strange clan of mentally deranged and otherwise suspicious folks near Sac Prairie, Wis. Who stabbed Ray Horrell, son-in-law of old Mrs. Gravisa Senessen, matriarch of the house, unless it was maybe the beldame herself? And what caused the rest of the lively doings in the murder mansion? There are sixteen people to watch. . . . Ye author succeeds in keeping his secret to the final chapter, which is as it should be.

> *Will Cuppy, in a review of "The Man on All Fours," in* New York Herald Tribune Books, *November 18, 1934, p. 18.*

ISAAC ANDERSON

The little Wisconsin village of Sac Prairie is the scene of ["**Three Who Died**"], as of the other stories about Judge Peck, who is Mr. Derleth's pet sleuth. The judge and his friend, Dr. Considine, have just returned from a fishing trip. They learn that during their absence two persons have died and a third is at the point of death.

There is, at first, no suspicion of foul play, but larger developments make both Judge Peck and Dr. Considine suspicious, and investigation shows that all three of these persons have been murdered. A puzzling feature of the case is that there is no apparent motive, nor is one discovered until the pasts of the persons concerned have been thoroughly raked over.

The solution at which Judge Peck finally arrives appears to be the only logical one, even though it is one which it would be difficult to prove to the satisfaction of a jury. Fortunately, that is not necessary. Mr. Derleth has pictured a series of rather improbable crimes in a community of people whom it is a pleasure to meet, but who are not particularly exciting.

> *Isaac Anderson, in a review of "Three Who Died,"*
> *in* The New York Times Book Review, *March 31,*
> *1935, p. 14.*

ELIZABETH HART

Whoever conceived the idea for **"Place of Hawks"** has, with the best intentions, done August Derleth a disservice. . . . [The] first sample of his [short stories] to appear in book form is a literary hybrid that misses both ways. Composed of four long stories which together attempt to constitute a unified pattern, it cannot by the most elastic definition of the term he called a novel; as a representative collection of short stories it is a singularly poor job of selection. I am afraid that readers encountering Mr. Derleth for the first time in these pages will notice his faults and overlook his talents, as they would not in a less tricky and arbitrary arrangement.

It is easy to understand the temptation to those responsible for assembling the volume's contents: Mr. Derleth has written an unusual story, a haunting and oddly poetic boyhood memoir of an old Wisconsin family, the last of the line, whose strain has become darkened with an obsession verging on madness and at times slipping over the border. He has written another with the same setting and a somewhat similar subject. . . . It sounds good. It sounds very good. But it just doesn't come off.

The author handicaps himself at the start by choosing to cast all four episodes in the first-person narrative form, and by making the narrator a very young child. This is a mechanism difficult enough to employ naturally in isolated stories; when used as it is here its artificial creakings cannot be disguised. One does not notice any technical strain in **"Five Alone,"** the story with which the book opens; one accepts the little boy who drives around the countryside of Sac Prairie with his doctor-grandfather in the latter's gig, and one accepts his account of how he gradually pieced together the melancholy history of Linda Grell, who tried to escape from the prison of a semi-mad family relationship and found she could not live in her freedom. The overheard conversations, the confidences made to little Steve by people wandering in a world of their own devising, the accidental happening to be with grandfather at all the times when grandfather is summoned to assist the Grells or Linda through a crisis—these devices are woven so skillfully

into the dark, dreamy mood of the story that they are hardly visible to the reader. It is when Mr. Derleth is forced to repeat them and to supplement them with clumsier means of revelation—grandfather talking in his sleep, at great length and most coherently, is one example—that he loses us as participants and believers in the strange lives he is depicting and we become observers of a craftsman whose performance seems a little tiresome, a little bungling.

Monotony and a labored attempt to cure it lie, in fact, rather heavily over the book as a whole. Mr. Derleth's variations on the same theme are not varied enough. His imbecile boys, his octogenarians confusing past with present, his fear-ridden descendants of an insane ancestor turning to suicide as they feel themselves drifting toward the madhouse, his normal folk crushed and bewildered by the burden of caring for an abnormal loved one, are all too much of a piece. It is hard to separate them in one's mind after finishing the book, and it also is hard to disentangle the plot-structure of one story from another because the development of each follows such a fixed pattern, inevitably ending in at least one unnatural death and generally in two or three.

My advice is to read **"Five Alone"** and the title story—which is confused and somewhat padded but contains some remarkably done atmosphere—and put the book aside.

> *Elizabeth Hart, "New and Old World in Recent Fic-*
> *tion: 'Place of Hawks',"* in New York Herald Tri-
> bune Books, *June 9, 1935, p. 8.*

EDITH H. WALTON

In **"Place of Hawks,"** a series of four novelettes so closely interrelated that they practically form a unit, Mr. Derleth deals with the kind of material which William Faulkner has copyrighted, though his point of view is essentially different. Horror and madness are his principal themes, but they are presented sanely, with pity and compassion. . . .

Mr. Derleth has a highly developed sense of form. The pattern which he has chosen to bind his four tales together is so logical and apt that **"Place of Hawks"** resembles a novel rather than the usual collection of stories. His mouthpiece is a young boy, Steve Grendon, who is in the habit of driving round the countryside with his grandfather, a doctor. . . .

Each of the four families whose stories Mr. Derleth tells is burdened with obsessions and clutching vainly at sanity. Linda Grell, knowing that her possessive family is close to madness, struggles without success to escape their hold. Rella Farway, driven over the borderline by her fanatic hatred of the land, involves the whole Farway clan in her mania for destruction. Mrs. Ortell, intelligent and self-sacrificing in her moments of lucidity, solves the problem of approaching madness with a fine dignity. The decline of the Pierneau family, upon whom lies the hidden curse of miscegenation, has a tragic beauty consonant with their past.

To deal credibly with such melodramatic material is not an easy feat. Mr. Derleth brings it off because he is so restrained and so coolly matter-of-fact. By choosing a child as observer he has, moreover, lessened his problem. Steve Grendon, to be sure, tells his stories in retrospect, but he tells only those things which were apprehended by his youthful eyes. Mr. Derleth is consequently under no necessity to trace back the roots of all these pitiful obsessions.

One grasps their essential outlines from Steve's observations supplemented by the comments of his parents and his grandfather, but there is no complex Freudian excavation into the seeds of tragedy. It exists—that is all—and one is convinced of its reality because Mr. Derleth obviously knows these Wisconsin derelicts so well. . . .

Mr. Derleth does not impress one as a writer unduly attracted to the abnormal. He is merely giving a picture of a small prairie community where isolation and inbreeding have done their deadly work, and if the picture seems somewhat highly colored it is because he has chosen to stress the extraordinary rather than the commonplace. **"Place of Hawks"** is a grim but not a morbid book. It may not be realism in the strictest sense, but on its own terms it compels belief.

> Edith H. Walton, *"Family Skeletons," in* The New York Times Book Review, *June 16, 1935, p. 7.*

EDITH H. WALTON

"Still Is the Summer Night," Mr. Derleth's second novel, again has Sac Prairie for a background. This time, however, the emphasis is different [from that in **"Place of Hawks"**]. Though his story ends in violence, though his three young Halders act out a stormy triangular drama, his characters this time are normal and subject to normal passions. They take an active, vigorous part in the life of Sac Prairie—a town which, in the early Eighties, still retained lingering features of a typical frontier settlement. (pp. 7, 18)

On the outskirts of the village, crouching at the edge of the prairie, lay the prosperous Halder farm. Here, in apparent amity, dwelt old Captain Halder, a Civil War veteran; his sons, Ratio and Alton, and Ratio's beautiful young wife, Julie. As the book opens, however, the seeds of disunion and disaster have already been sowed. Handsome, arrogant, fretted by domesticity, Ratio has turned from Julie and is carrying on a sordid intrigue with a village girl. Julie guesses what is happening, and though her first pain has been somewhat stilled, she is angry, wounded, and eager for certitude. Alton, who loves her deeply but silently, is a helpless spectator in this early stage of the drama. . . .

From here on the course of the story is not hard to predict. Having learned to depend on Alton for comfort and sustenance, Julie soon responds to the gentle urgency of his passion. Secretly, they become lovers, and in a year or so, after the cruel death of her own and Ratio's baby, Julie realizes exultantly that she is bearing Alton's child. They must, however, be more discreet than ever, watchful particularly lest they hurt the old man. But Captain Halder, as it happens, has already guessed the situation. Town gossip has brought him word of Ratio's infidelity. His own slow, groping intuition has taught him the truth about Alton, Julie and the paternity of the child. There is nothing, however, for him to do but hold his tongue in sorrowful impotence—fearful that disaster may come, as it does, when Ratio is at last undeceived.

Such is the rather simple plot of Mr. Derleth's novel, uncomplicated by side issues, proceeding forward in an undeviating line. The texture of his tale is enriched, however, by the superb, sensitive descriptions which he gives of Wisconsin landscape and Wisconsin atmosphere. One watches the seasons roll in splendor over Sac Prairie, meaning much to the Halders because they are so close to the soil. He is adroit, also, at giving one the actual feel of a little prairie town in the Eighties. There

are corn huskings, roof raisings, sleigh rides, country dances. State politics are discussed avidly by the graybeards. One is introduced, even, to the older La Follette, then the rising young District Attorney of Dane County. Single-threaded as is the drama of the Halders, they do not play it out in a vacuum.

In many respects, **"Still Is the Summer Night"** is superior to its predecessor. It is unified instead of scattered. It has greater breadth of appeal. It avoids excessive, specialized emphasis on decadence and insanity. One would rather see Mr. Derleth develop in this direction than have him write another **"Place of Hawks."** Unfortunately, there is something a little static and monotonous about this new book of his. It is not as interesting as it should be. Its course is often clogged by superfluous scenes and conversations; the three protagonists are not arresting enough people to carry the frail, familiar burden of his story. In a sense, one is more interested in the genre picture which he gives of a Wisconsin village in the Eighties than in the psychological tension within the Halder household. **"Still Is the Summer Night"** is an honest and well-written book, but it moves slowly and lacks lift. (p. 18)

> Edith H. Walton, *"A Prairie Triangle," in* The New York Times Book Review, *March 7, 1937, pp. 7, 18.*

ZONA GALE

"Still is the Summer Night," by August Derleth, is far more than a regional story with a vivid background. In the story of the lives of its prairie people, it traces, page by page, the invisible pattern, even though it never refers to pattern at all. Even though Julie does not see that she could have acted differently, even though Alton "was not concerned with moral aspects," still the old Greek emergence of cause and effect sets the book far beyond tale-telling.

And Mr. Derleth tells a tale, absorbing enough in itself, and knit with the land. He has Hardy's sense of the soil, the "roll and wheel" of stars, of the seasons, of live things and growing things. These are as vivid to him as are human emotions, and noble.

His special background, once considered so empty, is given its own shapes and colors—the little town on the long river, the raftsmen, the taverns, the show-boat, the talk in the homes, the flow of life in the fields. Political figures of the day move there, but only as bits of color, like the hawks and the hills; so that whatever it was that they did seems to matter not at all. But the four high characters, in their relations to one another, matter much—as if relationship and attitude were all there is to be accounted for, in the end.

In a tale sordid enough in other hands, these three—Julie, her husband, Ratio, his brother whom Julie loves—are like blind, masked figures, moved by primal impulse, unaware of any other urge. There they are, in the Eighties, acting as they might have acted before mind arose, and there is immense reserve of comment upon them—no comments at all, in fact. It is the method of drama—you see them move, no one says anything about what they do, not even they themselves.

Save the father, old Captain Halder. . . .

The old captain is no bondage to standards, but rather he is the universal consciousness, aware that fire burns, that ice melts, that water flows down-hill. He has observed these natural causes, he knows with certainty what to expect of human action; but he himself is intensely human, and far more alive, than the others in his agony at shiftiness, concealment, hypocrisy, violence done to values. His humor, his gusto, his enormous participation make him a really great figure. The confusion and self-irritation and fear of his visit to the cemetery moved by his own blind desire to the right is a chapter memorable, in 1884 or in any other time.

If one has a quarrel with the book, it is that a tangible modern psychology is imposed upon the Eighties. In the Eighties, among people as sensitive as Julie and Alton, there would have been struggle and misery in these decisions, not merely bright complacence. The only imitation of this is when, years after, in a preface and epilogue of power, the old Alton sits at dusk in the still summer night, in that same house at the prairie's edge, watching, and afterwards releasing, a beetle on the face of the old clock, "chased by time." Then he knows that some spectator opened her grave for Julie.

Mr. Derleth one will assess as a writer of power—and in this book he goes far and away beyond his earlier **"Place of Hawks."** He has form and direction and can tell his story admirably—and he has strong sensitivity to his materials.

> *Zona Gale, "Lives of the Prairie People," in* New York Herald Tribune Books, *March 14, 1937, p. 5.*

ROSE C. FELD

To August Derleth the saga of Wisconsin is not a tale of heady conquest, but one of understanding of the suffering and betrayal experienced by two races which could not live together in peace and equality. And, giving meaning to the tragedy of a people doomed to extermination, is ["**Wind Over Wisconsin"**], the story of friendship between two men, Black Hawk and Chalfonte Pierneau, holding each other in high esteem and affection but powerless to stem the tide of affairs which separate them. Each suffered pain and disillusion, but at the end it was the conquering white who found it hardest to swallow the defeat and humiliation of the conquered. . . .

Besides telling the story of Wisconsin of this era, Mr. Derleth tells the story of Chalfonte's courtship of his second wife, but so powerful is the drama and romance of the country that the personal drama is dwarfed by it. Mr. Derleth has recreated the scene with power and with tenderness and the men who walk through it carry their strength and their weakness with unerring direction. A vast amount of historical research has gone into this book, but beneath the scholarship one finds something deeper, a love for the land which is Wisconsin. . . . And because Mr. Derleth is a poet, this book takes on the stature of a singing epic concerned alike with white man and red.

> *Rose C. Feld, "Untamed Country of the 1830's," in* New York Herald Tribune Books, *April 24, 1938, p. 7.*

JAMES GRAY

[In **"Wind Over Wisconsin"**] August Derleth invites inspection of a significant moment in the history of his own state. . . . [He] wishes to throw a bridge across an obscure interval of history, linking the familiar country of the present to the terra incognita of the past. His impulse is honest and admirable; but his execution of the plan is ineffectively engineered.

The chief difficulty lies in Mr. Derleth's inability to bring his characters to life. Each of them wears a label around his neck and shows the strain of carrying it. Chalfonte, American-born son of a French settler of aristocratic birth, is the stout-hearted idealist. Hercules Dousman, fur trader, is the realist with a clear-eyed view of destiny. Black Hawk is the "noble savage." Each of them bears an embarrassing resemblance to the Fourth of July orator, complete with soap-box. There is a flash of purple in every casual utterance.

More disastrous, still, is the fact that the narrative breaks in two. The only link between the part dealing with the Indian campaigns against the settlers and the part dealing with opening of the land is that the central character, Chalfonte, presides with amiable ineffectuality over both. The effect of climax persistently eludes Mr. Derleth's eager efforts. The book collapses into a series of scenes out of a pageant, played by characters all of whom are under-developed, some of whom have been created for the sole purpose of dying melodramatic deaths. Historical figures like Zachary Taylor and Jefferson Davis make irrelevant appearances, seeming to remark in pompous asides to the reader: "Surely, you know how important I am to become." Two perfunctory romances emphasize the anemic character of the whole narrative.

Mr. Derleth seems determined to impress the reader with the cultivation of the early Wisconsin settlers. They quote Pascal to one another. They sigh over the unfortunate demise of "M. Goethe." Their letters from abroad describe neatly the state of European culture. The wind over Wisconsin settles down into a caressing breeze. (pp. 20-1)

> *James Gray, in a review of "Wind Over Wisconsin," in* The Saturday Review of Literature, *Vol. XVIII, No. 8, June 18, 1938, pp. 20-1.*

PERCY HUTCHISON

Although August Derleth, the author of several published novels, has been writing poetry for a decade or more, . . . ["**Hawk on the Wind"** marks] his first appearance in book form as a poet. A marked individuality is the striking characteristic of these pieces, individuality of form as well as of thought. August Derleth has an ear acutely tuned both for meter and rhyme. In respect to the latter he is most subtle. Not merely at first glance at the page but after reading for several lines one believes him to be writing vers libre. Then gradually there intrudes a teasingly pleasing doubt which presently gives way before the perception of the negligently carried rhyme scheme. And the reason the rhyme was not noticed earlier is because, on analysis, the usual sharpness of the effect is found to have been muted by the uneven length of Mr. Derleth's lines. That is to say, unconscious expectancy being thwarted, the mind of the reader has been pleased with the blend of sound without having been halted by it. The result is one of overtones one often misses in more formally rhymed poetry. . . .

August Derleth is from Wisconsin, and the human strength and individuality of those whose lives went to the building of that State are the very soil of much of his verse and the source of his power. Yet here again is subtlety. Mr. Derleth is not writing history, he is writing poetry; and in poetry, as he perceives, it is the thought evoked, rather than the thought exploited, which is more effective. Marquette and Frontenac, Black Hawk and Yellow Thunder; he can use a name and pass on, but an image has been projected into the reader's imagination. Mr. Derleth can even make a railroad the basis of poetic concept.

Another characteristic of these poems is a very general preference for active rather than for what may be termed static subjects. A notable exception is a group of several fairly caustic short-length portraits, a minor Spoon River, called **"Sac Prairie People."** The hawk on the wing, deer in the snow, the latter, incidentally, an exceptionally fine poem; floating clouds, the loping fox—these and kindred themes offer undeniable attraction for this young Wisconsin poet. Yet, lest dwelling on this feature should lead to a conclusion that Mr. Derleth is less than human in his interests, we hasten to say that this is not so. On the contrary, August Derleth's interest in his fellows is very deep and warm. He is caustic only on occasion. **"Perhaps Never"** is an exceptional poem on love, to mention but one title on this theme.

We are convinced by **"Hawk on the Wind"** that here is a young poet with a brilliant future.

> Percy Hutchison, *"The Poems of August Derleth,"* in The New York Times Book Review, *August 14, 1938, p. 2.*

RUTH BYRNS

[**"Hawk on the Wind"** is Derleth's] first volume of poetry. Chosen from hundreds of poems which he has written in the past decade, the selections in this book are an integral part of the story of Wisconsin which Derleth aims to tell in the "Saga."

He is a competent poet. His verse is smooth and pleasant to read, not too experimental in form, and never obscure. He expresses his love of nature and his knowledge of the Wisconsin countryside with delicacy and beauty. He is somewhat preoccupied with an awareness of the passing of time and the inevitable changes that time brings. He says, in effect, this sort of thing again and again. . . . (p. 52)

In his poetry Derleth does not reveal emotional, spiritual or intellectual depth of experience. He is always the observer who describes what he has observed in precise and lovely verse but he does not disclose what he thinks is the meaning of the beauty of nature, of life, of death or of time. (p. 53)

> Ruth Byrns, *in a review of "Hawk on the Wind,"* in Commonweal, *Vol. XXIX, No. 2, November 4, 1938, pp. 52-3.*

EDITH H. WALTON

Clinging still to Sac Prairie—the small Wisconsin town which has been the scene of all his stories—August Derleth has written a brief novelette whose mood is that of poetry and legend. Its patterned prose, its air of melancholy, its rueful echoes from a more idyllic past, all remind one of Willa Cather—and especially of the Willa Cather who wrote "Lucy Gayheart." Renna, however, the hauntingly lovely heroine of **"Any Day Now"** is made of more fiery stuff than Miss Cather's pitiful Lucy. . . .

Of all the men who clustered around Renna, met her at the station when she came home on holiday, made her name a byword for glamour, it was Doctor Joe who was clearly her favorite. Every one, Joe included, expected him to be her choice. When the hour struck, however, one magic midsummer night, Renna could not bring herself to say yes to him. . . . [She] was thwarted by the memory of her big, wonderful mother, who had been so fiercely ambitious for her child. "No young doctor," that dead voice had said. So it was that Renna wan-

tonly denied love—and found too late, when Joe was lost, was married, that she would give anything to retract that denial. So she came, after Joe's death, to live achingly and wholly in the past.

This, in essence, is the very simple plot of **"Any Day Now."** Being an old plot, though a good one, the book would amount to little if Mr. Derleth had not invested it with special graces of atmosphere and style. The glamour which he conjures up, his pictures of quiet pleasures and still, moon-drenched nights in the village of Renna's youth—all this has a kind of enchantment. His story, in a sense, is an elegy for lost beauty, a lament for the havoc wrought by time. As for his prose, though it is too measured, too metrical, and hence a little monotonous, it does have a distinction which is half the charm of the book. **"Any Day Now"** is a very minor threnody, but as an interlude between sturdier novels it shows that Mr. Derleth is continuing to perfect his art. He has gone a long way since **"Place of Hawks."**

> Edith H. Walton, *in a review of "Any Day Now,"* in The New York Times Book Review, *January 1, 1939, p. 6.*

MASON WADE

The promise that was revealed and widely recognized in August Derleth's first book of poems, **"Hawk on the Wind,"** is . . . richly realized [in **"Man Track Here"**]. Mr. Derleth has matured amazingly in a year's time, and now stands well out from the ruck of young poets. He is no imitator, no follower of schools and trends, but displays an originality and independence which made Edgar Lee Masters and Sinclair Lewis single him out as an important figure. His debt, if he has one, is to Walt Whitman and the early Masters; he is the poet of Sac Prairie, a lyrical Lewis.

Mr. Derleth has evolved his own verse schemes, although they take their departure from those of Whitman and Masters. But there is none of the sprawling formlessness of Whitman, or the flatness of much of Masters. He is at all times musical, though as with Gerard Manley Hopkins, it is necessary to attune the ear to his music. Once it becomes familiar, the reader finds no lack of it. He writes largely of things and people, but more of the things of nature that he knows better now than of the people about whom he has much to learn. He is refreshingly free from added ideologies, and very much in the great tradition of English poetry.

> Mason Wade, *"August Derleth's Poems,"* in The New York Times Book Review, *August 20, 1939, p. 9.*

STANLEY YOUNG

Pioneer life in Wisconsin, as August Derleth writes of it, takes on the serenity of rural New England. The perils and heroism and general surcharge of drama that readers . . . have long associated with the winning of the West are oddly veiled by the bland scenes and situations of [**"Restless Is the River"**]. The whole surge and sound of immigrant life appear muffled, and in many pages there is no sound whatever. It may very well be argued that Mr. Derleth's naturalism is nearer to the truth than either the heady romance or the bleak realistic novel on the same subject, but his careful skirting of emotional conflicts and crises leaves a work of good intention with only a sheep-grazing excitement.

The central situation tells of the Hungarian Count Augustin Brogmar, whose liberal sentiments made it necessary for him to flee to America to escape Metternich, and Brogmar's wife, Eleanor, who fled with him and was never able to adjust herself to a new wilderness life. This is a situation familiar to fiction and interesting only in so far as some freshness and new insight are brought to bear upon it. The Countess Brogmar is created in a monotone pattern wherein we are told that the crude life of Wisconsin in the 1840's makes her yearn for the elegance of her past, but her homesickness is so evident from the beginning and continues with so much repetition of incident—it would be distressing to enumerate how many times she sits brooding before the portraits of her patrician relatives—that her death stands out as a somewhat welcome moment. . . .

Most of the book is concerned with Brogmar's business failures. . . . He meets a host of other pioneers who appear and reappear from time to time without much intent or purpose—hazy characters who are not rooted in the story. Only young Ralsa, Brogmar's servant, has full dimension as a minor character.

August Derleth's descriptive powers save this writing from complete barrenness. He has a botanist's knowledge of the flowering land of Wisconsin and takes a lyrical delight in conveying the natural glories and panorama of a virgin country. If his characters and his situations had in them any of the brilliance and illumination of the sunsets he describes so well, this over-long and understated novel would demand anything but harsh criticism. (pp. 6-7)

> *Stanley Young, "Wisconsin Pioneers," in* The New York Times Book Review, *October 8, 1939, pp. 6-7.*

RUTH LECHLITNER

What is important and good in ["**Restless Is the River**"] lies in the interwoven background details, incidents not so much personal as communal. These facets of land development, with attendant intrigues and none too savory politics . . . are necessary to a full picture of the era. Pervasively beautiful, slower to change, are the turning seasons on the prairie itself. But because of the non-selective, diffuse, sometimes lush writing (half as long, the book might be more effective) the significant is often lost among the insignificant, the good color of reality robbed by the synthetically romantic. For the authenticity of its background material, however, and its truly epic score, "**Restless Is the River**" may well be commended.

> *Ruth Lechlitner, in a review of "Restless Is the River," in* New York Herald Tribune Books, *October 15, 1939, p. 12.*

JAMES GRAY

August Derleth has staked out an unchallengeable literary claim upon a part of the state of Wisconsin. He calls his town Sac Prairie. The story of its settling and its development has supplied him with material for a series of historical novels of which there are more to come. And the contemporary life of the same community is reflected in the group of tales that make up ["**Country Growth,**"] his latest volume.

Around the theory of regionalism, Mr. Derleth has put a neat, tight fence, giving to its vague formality an effect of intimacy and coziness. The effect of a comfortable familiarity with the scene is heightened by the fact that many of his stories are told

in the first person from the point of view of a boy, growing up in Sac Prairie and watching with humorous shrewdness the behavior of his Great Aunt Lou, his Great Uncle Joe, and a group of other villagers in all of whom he has the closest kind of neighborly interest.

Mr. Derleth strikes his happiest vein in these unpretentious but often deeply moving folk tales. What seems pretentious in his historical novels, what seems over-wrought in all his longer works of fiction seldom appears in this volume to plague the reader out of his wish to remain sympathetic with his talent. Here he is direct, simple, humorous, and hearty—all without the disquieting trace of self-consciousness that mars his more ambitious work.

Best of all these stories is "**Buck in the Bottoms,**" an enormously appealing account of how the force of goodwill dramatically declared itself against the predatory impulse of village life by saving a handsome buck from destruction. The snowy serenity of the December night offers a picturesque background to a tale in which poetry and folk humor are skillfully blended. The anthologists will reprint this story many times. . . .

Only one story, and that the most carefully and conscientiously wrought of all, betrays Mr. Derleth into some of his unfortunate ways. "**Any Day Now**" is the story of a girl who turns away from love and lives to regret it. The author chants mournfully, lovingly, repetitiously over his theme for seventy-five pages, succeeding only in underscoring its commonplaceness. But when he gives casually of his rich knowledge of village life, August Derleth reveals himself as one of the best equipped and most appealing of our American short story writers.

> *James Gray, "Wisconsin Local Color," in* The Saturday Review of Literature, *Vol. XXII, No. 13, July 20, 1940, p. 10.*

HARRY THORNTON MOORE

There are twenty stories in ["**Country Growth**"], and in each of them the most consistent character in all Derleth's serious writing appears—the Wisconsin landscape, which is conveniently varied . . . by prairie, hill country and cliff-edged river. The people in the stories are the people Derleth knows so thoroughly, the small towners and farmers of the region.

A few of the stories in this book are predominantly lyric in tone, but most of them are traditionally conceived sketches and fables of Sac Prairie inhabitants. "**Goodbye Margery**" and "**Girl in Time Lost,**" which begin and end the book, are examples of the first method; they are subjective idylls about the same love affair, and they skillfully invoke the atmosphere of a small town of yesterday, the hushed heavy summer evenings with the boy and girl walking through the streets, hardly articulate even in quarrel. Many of the remaining stories are lightly comic, with town gossips and shrewd farmers figuring largely in their personnel. Several of these concern a single family, viewed from a boy's angle of vision. "**A Holiday for Three**" is the chronicle of a bicycle tour made by the boy and his great-uncle and another farmer, Gus Elker, who cover an amazing amount of Midwest territory on their odd trip. Although the story is partly spoiled by the forced humor of its ending, the middle parts of it contain some energetic contributions to American humorous literature. Occasionally, in some of the other short stories of these same characters, Derleth tends to create an elaborate story-structure for the sake of an anecdote: the result is barely worth the effort in the title story, but in some of the tales there is a rich center of humor which unites character and anecdote. This is particularly true in **"The Alphabet Begins with AAA,"** the hilarious account of Gus Elker's experience with an AAA representative.

The two most interesting pieces in the book are the longer stories, **"Any Day Now,"** and **"The Intercessors." "Any Day Now"** . . . is the story of a small-town girl growing into unhappy spinsterhood after failing to marry the young doctor she loved. Like almost all women in Derleth's stories, she is sentimentally presented. . . .

The other longer story is also about a lonely woman broken by love; Celia Calden lives out her life in a single house, never going out after the wrenching experience of her first love affair, which turned bitter after she was betrayed. But in later life she emerges twice, on two dramatic occasions which give this story a suspense that is somewhat higher in story interest than **"Any Day Now"**: there is even an old-fashioned sleigh-chase, though it is not melodrama. Both these stories present full pictures of life in an American small town, the hot, dusty summers, the harsh winters, the featureless houses, the surrounding farmlands, the social network in which the lives of the people are interlaced—lives that make good stories, as most of the sections of this book demonstrate.

> *Harry Thornton Moore, in a review of "Country Growth," in* New York Herald Tribune Books, *July 21, 1940, p. 7.*

ROBERT VAN GELDER

[Because] of a curious quality of realism, of common experience, **"Country Growth"** touches the edge of that universality that is the province of the great books. Though Mr. Derleth's stories are not really memorable or major in their effects, they can be honestly recommended not only to good readers but even to . . . book-throwers. . . .

Mr. Derleth takes Sac Prairie, Wis., as his setting, writes of a Main Street as viciously gossipy, false-fronted and backward as Gopher Prairie ever was, but he sees it from the inside, not judging, understanding the necessities behind the seemingly senseless taboos, and not impatient with these necessities. . . .

He writes good stories, and one good thing about them is that they show no trace of manner; they are not, apparently, even self-conscious. It is evident that he is a writer who is in little danger of writing himself out.

Mr. Derleth handles a variety of situations well, but is at his best with humor. He writes humor as it should be written, with natural characters, believable situations, and no straining for effect. The humor is robust, but not with the false heartiness that too many of the regional writers assume. . . .

It should be added that Mr. Derleth does not edit himself any too well. He writes, it is evident, by ear rather than by plan, and has a tendency to waste effects in unnecessary verbiage. But as the fault of so many of his contemporaries is that of straining and cutting until finally the precious quality of their own work scares them, probably Derleth is right in going the other way.

> *Robert Van Gelder, in a review of "Country Growth," in* The New York Times Book Review, *July 21, 1940, p. 6.*

THE CHRISTIAN SCIENCE MONITOR

Though [Derleth's] novels have won for him wider recognition, it is probably true that his short-story techniques is the better. The novels, for all their sincerity and the high quality of their style lack something of drama and sharp emotion. The short stories possess either keener emotional urgency or as a substitute have humor or sympathetic insight. As narratives or as character studies they are interesting, and always they are written with beauty, precision, and a canny selection of details.

Some readers may accuse Mr. Derleth of being sentimental. In his stories of romance and emotion he shows a pronounced taste for the nostalgic and wistful and in the novelette called **"The Intercessors"** a disposition to stress lacrimae rerum—as he says, "time lost, time past, time gone."

This is well enough when it is done with a spontaneity that convinces. But, once in a while, there creeps in a faint suggestion of bookishness and too studied effect. Not often. It certainly does not happen in the lovely little tale of adolescent love which opens [**"Country Growth"**]—**"Good-Bye, Margery."**

Mr. Derleth is not only a novelist and a storyteller, but a poet. This would be evident if **"Hawk on the Wind," "Man Track Here,"** and **"Here on a Darkling Plain"** had never been published. In his prose as well as in his verse he shows the poet's eye. This is especially true when he writes, in words bathed in cool color, about the Wisconsin scene; most of all in innumerable descriptions of the heavens—of sunsets, evening clouds, the afterglow, and the stars. This kind of thing gives perspective to his little tales of little folk.

> *W.K.R., "Sac Prairie Stories," in* The Christian Science Monitor, *July 27, 1940, p. 11.*

HARRY THORNTON MOORE

Like the other books in the Sac Prairie Saga, [**"Bright Journey"**] stands by itself as a separate story. But it does not differ essentially from Derleth's previous novels of man vs. wilderness, and, despite some temperamental variations, [the principal character] Dousman strongly resembles Baron Pierneau, American-born scion of French aristocrats (**"Wind Over Wisconsin"**) and Pierneau's cousin, Count Brogmar, Hungarian patriot exile (**"Restless Is the River"**). There is, indeed, a disturbing sameness, at more than one level, in Derleth's historical novels, and though he can present the background material of his stories vividly—the wilderness, the fresh lakes, the Indians with their dignified poetry of speech, the brave little frontier towns, the "voyageurs" or trappers—the background material comes to give the effect of presenting again and again the same moonrise or forest-clearing or the same conversation between repeated characters. The reader of the entire series begins to wish that August Derleth would concentrate his talent on fewer volumes and strive a little more for depth, a little less for breadth. These restrictions do not apply to the novels when read singly: like the others, **"Bright Journey"** is an excellent and sometimes beautiful presentation of frontier Wisconsin.

> *Harry Thornton Moore, in a review of "Bright Journey," in* New York Herald Tribune Books, *October 27, 1940, p. 20.*

HORACE REYNOLDS

The hero [of **"Bright Journey"**] Hercules Dousman, is a historical character. He was a 12-year-old boy in Mackinac when the British took Fort Michilimackinac in one of the early campaigns of the War of 1812. Later, when he grows up, he paddles up the Fox and down the Wisconsin River to assume charge of the Prairie du Chien post of Astor's American Fur Company. . . . Mr. Derleth's Dousman is almost Sir Galahad on the frontier. He marries the half-breed girl who dies in giving birth to his daughter; always he is the Indian's friend; when the woman he loves leaves [her husband] because of his drinking, he urges her to return to her husband. Realizing that the fur trade is bound to decline, he buys land the value of which went up with every new settler. He foresees that Prairie du Chien will some day become an important grain shipping center. . . .

Mr. Derleth tells his story simply and directly in the calm pace and timeless manner of the old historical novel. He describes with convincing detail the growth of the small trading village into a river town, the retirement of the animals and Indians and the great brigades of French-Canadian trappers before the steady advance of hordes of tree-felling, land-hungry settlers. When he remembers what the greed of men has destroyed, the carrier pigeons and the buffalo, for instance, he regrets that the Dousmans are so few and the slaughterers so many. The sense of place and the sweep of historical events are here better realized than the collision of character with character. As is so often the case with contemporary historical novels, the love story seems a little mechanical and contrived: the private fortunes of Dousman and the woman he eventually marries seem much less real than the public history of the old Michigan Territory. That is well set forth.

> *Horace Reynolds, "The Fur Trade," in* The New York Times Book Review, *October 27, 1940, p. 7.*

KATHERINE WOODS

What Mr. Derleth has done [in **"Village Year"**] is simply to set down the observations that personally interested him day to day or month to month [in and about Sac Prairie]; and his book thus has the distinction and personal appeal of an entirely unforced chronicle from a little American town and a loved American countryside. **"Village Year"** is not a memory of pioneers nor a picture either of revenants seeking rural simplicity or survivors still enisled in it, but an actual evocation of a fairly typical community in its ordinary life today. And because Mr. Derleth has a poetic love for Nature and awareness of Nature's richly varied minutiae, there is often a haunting beauty in these journal entries as the seasons move across the Wisconsin scene. . . .

Most of these country details . . . are of concrete observation rather than mood or symbol.

There are plenty of people to be met, and met again, in this flow of a few village years. And introduction to village neighbors will no doubt give many readers their liveliest interest in August Derleth's book—especially when the characters are odd, like the gentle old man who has taken on the tremendous task of snaring infinities in evangelistic words, or the delightful garden-lover who keeps bees and weaves rugs for sale. These people are sketched with a few lines for the most part and with a proper casualness. But the very slightness of the portraits is

a token of the naturalness which gives the journal its charm and value. . . .

In all this, again, the charm and vitality alike seem to grow from the author's absence of intention. He has had no purpose to be idyllic or grim or dramatic or even complete, but merely to set things down as they come. He is always at his best when he is most at one with his subject—when he seems to stand aside and find his neighbors amusing his readers are least likely to be amused. But happily his journal as a whole is rooted in real oneness with the life it reflects. It is thus that **"Village Year"** is marred by very little of the self-consciousness which can so completely spoil a country record, and at its best it glows with the real mellowness that can only come from the genuineness of effortless sympathy. A number of August Derleth's poems are set down here under the circumstances of their composition. . . . The rhythm of such a journal as this becomes almost inevitably monotonous; inevitably, too, its notes are of very uneven excellence; to be most thoroughly enjoyed it should be read a few pages at a time. A book of instant sensitive responsiveness, **"Village Year"** recreates its scene with acuteness and beauty, and makes an unusual contribution to the Americana of the present day. Its life and its landscape have yielded to change as they must, but their character has kept its persistence.

> *Katherine Woods, "Mr. Derleth's Village Chronicle," in* The New York Times Book Review, *March 30, 1941, p. 4.*

HARRY THORNTON MOORE

In many ways **"Village Year"** is the most satisfactory part of the [Sac Prairie] series yet to appear, for it has the virtues of the others without their weaknesses, and adds a definite quality of its own. It is not intended to be a record of the bridge parties and local visits which are duly reported in the local press but, rather, it is meant to preserve the little things, the daily between-the-lines life of a village. . . .

[Derleth] deepens the value of his village setting by presenting in full the enduring natural background; with the people projected against this the writing comes to have the quality of an old Flemish picture, humanity lively and amusing and lovable in the foreground and nature magnificent beyond. This book is filled with accounts of the author's travels through the Sac Prairie region and his nightly walks to the marshes by the river, where he notes the different bird calls and compares them with the findings of other naturalists. The progress of flowers in the spring is carefully watched, and when the geese go honking south in October, their departure is reported.

All the human figures in these journals are not seen in the humorous light that bathes most of them—there are relatives and friends, young and old, who died as the years pass, and the significance of their lives and deaths is thoughtfully (though not sentimentally) noted. Within such a small concentrated circle of humanity, birth and mortality are emphasized, human values are seen in a different perspective than in a larger group, a personality is more apt to be respected for its own sake than it might be in a huge city. These are among the implications of the book: Zona Gale (whose biography Derleth recently wrote) seems to have given August Derleth a motto for his work when, on a visit to Sauk City, recorded in this portion of his journals, she said: "It seems to me that to be really creative one must live in a small place."

Harry Thornton Moore, "Sauk City, Wisconsin," in New York Herald Tribune Books, *April 6, 1941, p. 20.*

EDITH H. WALTON

"**Evening in Spring**" is a light lyric story, half comic, half tender, which has to do with the ardors and the sorrows of first love. It is the story of how Steve lost his heart to Margery Estabrook while they were both still in high school and of how their young touching idyl—so innocent and so poignant—was thwarted by the meddling and the opposition of their elders. Because Steve was a Catholic while Margery was not, both their families did everything in their power to keep the two apart, hounding them with commands, reproaches, accusations and tears. . . .

As one can gather, this simple, artless story is almost unimaginably old, and it would be difficult to freshen it into vivid life. Mr. Derleth, frankly, has not done so, and where his young lovers and their transports are concerned his book, though gently lyric, is insipid and monotonous. What distinguishes "**Evening in Spring**," what saves it from plain dullness, is first the author's evocative picture of a Wisconsin country town and second his humorous appreciation of character. Such color as there is in this novel is largely provided by Steve's eccentric relatives—from astringent Grandfather Adams, an old love of a man, to that appalling religious zealot, Aunt May. Here Mr. Derleth is in his element, and very funny indeed—but for the rest I cannot hand him so much. Perhaps it is time that he turned his eyes from Sac Prairie and from wistful memories of his boyhood and found something more galvanizing to write about.

Edith H. Walton, "First Love," in The New York Times Book Review, *September 14, 1941, p. 7.*

THE CHRISTIAN SCIENCE MONITOR

[In "**Evening in Spring**" the] idyl of Steve and Margery is full of wistful beauty, enhanced by the author's unfailing consciousness of the poetic qualities of the background. The poet in August Derleth is always near the surface, whether he is writing poetry, fiction, or biography. Skies, hills, trees, marsh, rivers, and wild life make clear images on his sensitive intelligence and affections. The fragrance of corn and clover, of mint and oak leaf are in his nostrils. Hawks riding the wind, owls softly sobbing in the dark, hills surging upward to the sky, trees pressing close upon small houses are constantly in his memory. Through this book winds are ever stirring, a west wind touching Steve's eyes and lips, small breezes scuttering the dry leaves and growing into a wind that tears at the autumn foliage, "a wind that blows over all the earth, a wanderer, too, alone." Loneliness is the motif of this book, the essential loneliness of Steve, despite his love, his boy companions, his myriad kinsfolk and his responsiveness to village life.

Contrasted with a delicate lament for the shattered crystal of first love and with the poetic background is a full gallery of comedy characters, even of burlesques. The people of Sac Prairie are a collection of oddities, not all of them malign but many of them eccentric even in their good nature. In Steve's own family his grandparents and possibly his father are exceptions. Altogether the village characters give proof that August Derleth is humorist as well as poet. His book is both ethereal and, frankly, without abashment, earthy.

The total effect of the book, it must be confessed, is that of patchwork. Here and there it contains bits already published in various magazines, and the final chapter, "Goodbye, Margery," has previously appeared thrice. Though these repeated portions are all, in their various ways, of high quality, and "Goodbye, Margery" is exquisite enough for three times three readings, nevertheless it is impossible not to feel that the book is a complication more than a growth. It is by way of being a sampler to show what the author can do in different moods and materials, admirable for readers who have not heretofore become acquainted with his work, but a source of faint uneasiness to others who would prefer to see him going on to fresh heights.

W.K.R., "Capulets and Montagues in Sac Prairie," in The Christian Science Monitor, *October 11, 1941, p. 11.*

MARGARET DONALDSON

The Oliver Mackenzie, carrying a show boat troupe, plied its way up the Mississippi River each Spring from St. Louis to New Orleans and back again in the Fall. In November, 1916, the season was mild and the old boat traveled up the Wisconsin as far as Sac Prairie, where the captain docked to give a performance of "Uncle Tom's Cabin." They had been nursing the leading lady through an attack of appendicitis and when they reached Sac Prairie she was too ill to play. But a young amateur actress in town who knew the part of Little Eva was recruited for the performance, and when the Oliver Mackenzie steamed away that night Jennie Breen was aboard eager to take the first step toward a great theatrical career. She had no regret about leaving home because she had been badly treated by her parents and she hated little towns, but she was sorry to desert Davey, her childhood sweetheart, who could not leave his mother to follow her.

There are several vivid descriptions of river life and of the Sac Prairie atmosphere, but ["**Sweet Genevieve**"] is a series of predictable incidents taken from the yellow pages of stock. . . . You know that ultimately young love will conquer all obstacles; but if the author makes you believe it, it is because he has drawn a skillful picture of Davey, the boy who waits back home, the only credible character of them all.

The author is at his best when he gives us the flavor of the seasons, the life in the river towns and the refreshing spirit of young love. Many of his observations about the actions of his characters, however, suffer from overamplification. If he's in doubt about your missing the point at any time, he all but draws a picture for you. His style also suffers from top-heavy modifying clauses, the kind that imprison a thought instead of releasing it.

In spite of all that, it is a pleasant story. The easy motion of the river runs through it. You get the small town feeling, and understand not only why Jennie wanted to leave it but also why she wanted to come back. If you like them slow and sweet and sentimental and if you don't mind being able to guess what's going to happen twenty pages ahead of time, then "**Sweet Genevieve**" is for you.

Margaret Donaldson, "Show Boat," in The New York Times Book Review, *May 31, 1942, p. 16.*

WILLIAM ROSE BENÉT

The poetry of August Derleth, a versatile and voluminous poet from Sac Prairie, often reminds of improvisation upon the piano. . . . [**"Rind of Earth"**] is thoroughly American in grain. The poem about the young men in **"Yesterday, Tomorrow, Always,"** the train in **"Transcontinental," "River Going By,"** the American myths in **"Raftsman, Lumberjack,"** the poem about the radio, such things as these not only have flowing theme-molded rhythm, but close observation and the pulse of life. Sometimes I think Mr. Derleth may be too musical for his own good, but, in a day when so few poets seem to give the actual movement of a poem any attention, he restores an element that was badly needed.

> *William Rose Benét, in a review of "Rind of Earth," in* The Saturday Review of Literature, *Vol. XXVI, No. 34, August 21, 1943, p. 11.*

VIVIENNE C. KOCH

There are valuable elements in August Derleth's diligent loyalty to the Sac Prairie region with which his voluminous writings have become identified: He is intimate with the cultural and social history which made that area one of the strongholds of a free-thinking, slavery-abhorring liberalism in the middle decades of the last century. He has a kind of nostalgic ancestor-worship for the resourceful, colorful French and German pioneer stock, who, as refugees from their native lands, combined to give Sac Prairie a moral climate as exhilarating and liberating as the air of the lovely Wisconsin country in which it lay. And, lastly, he has a feeling for the Sac Prairie terrain which is both affectionate and knowledgeable.

Yet, with all this, Mr. Derleth does not make credible his novel of Hasso, a hunchback German émigré, and his search for vengeance. Hasso seeks the murderer of his dearly beloved younger brother, Josef, who had been brutally shot down by a mercenary who fled Germany and who is thought to be living in the Sac Prairie region.

"Shadow of Night" is the slow-moving, discursive account of the psychological conflict that is set up in Hasso, a cultured and naturally gentle man, when he comes face to face with his intended victim, Odo Gebhardt, and finds him to be a hard-working, respected and liberal farmer. But Hasso's internal conflict is unconvincing. The initial premise on which it must rest is never adequately established: namely, Hasso's need to dedicate his life to the pursuit of his brother's slayer. Eventually, one suspects that Hasso's constant vacillation about when and how to achieve retribution is merely a convenient device to enable Mr. Derleth to keep his record of Sac Prairie history going.

And his cunning takes this pattern: there are alternate and recurrent pictures of (a) aspects of the Sac Prairie countryside; (b) Hasso up in his room in the Mellman's house, where he is employed as tutor, pulling out his picture of Josef and swearing eternal, implacable vengeance, and (c) Hasso's various encounters with Odo Gebhardt, each of which alternately weaken and reinforce his determination to kill him. So predictable is the novel's structure that one exclaims, "Now Hasso's going up to his room again to look at Josef's picture!" And that is exactly what he does unless, perchance, he saunters through the fields where insects are eternally "stridulating" and the wind makes an interminable "susurrus" (two of Mr. Derleth's

favorite words and imported in wholesale quantities from his verse-writing vocabulary).

Because **"Shadow of Night"** is liveliest in the journalistic passages describing historical events . . . , one feels that Mr. Derleth's material would have responded more tellingly to straight reportorial treatment. As it now stands, the slender, uninventive, narrative structure fails to carry adequately the double responsibility of history and fiction.

> *Vivienne C. Koch, "Prairie Symbols," in* The New York Times Book Review, *October 31, 1943, p. 20.*

NEW YORK HERALD TRIBUNE WEEKLY BOOK REVIEW

So long identified in poetry with the Wisconsin scene, with his sagas of Sac Prairie told in quiet, conventional, repetitious patterns, August Derleth surprisingly ventures beyond the regional viewpoint and into new forms with [**" And You, Thoreau!"**]. The love scenes in the second grouping, both erotic and symbolic, . . . might be taken, unsigned, as the work of almost any poet published by New Directions except Derleth. The first grouping, "Homage to Thoreau," with its Mid-Western nature images, is more characteristic. But the poems show much more skill and technical variety than Derleth's earlier work. The tribute to Thoreau, too, seems strongly, sincerely felt. . . .

> *"In New Forms," in* New York Herald Tribune Weekly Book Review, *August 5, 1945, p. 8.*

RICHARD A. CORDELL

This latest in the long series of Sac Prairie stories [**"The Shield of the Valiant"**] will add little to the reputation of Wisconsin's most noted regional novelist. The book needs tightening and pruning; the many narrative threads, each interesting in itself, are not skilfully woven into a fabric and pattern of meaning and general interest. The episodic form of the novel lures the author into verbose byways of almost irrelevant anecdote and frequent paragraphs of tedious moralizing. Many tried-and-safe ingredients of popular fiction are here: the banker's son falls in love with a brash but pure girl on the other side of the tracks; the liberal son is at odds with his stuffy, reactionary father; malicious village gossip is the motive power that turns the wheels of the plot; the tolerant, tobacco-loving, Going-My-Way sort of priest is contrasted with the bigoted cleric more Catholic than Christian; there are fights, adultery, and suicides, and brave deeds of the few men of good will in the community. The Gordian knot of indecisions and confusions is cut sharply by Pearl Harbor, a useful deus ex machina to end more than one recent novel.

Derleth's faithful readers will find his good things here, too: his keen knowledge of village and country life, his affectionate descriptions of the Wisconsin River and Valley, the pleasant reappearance of such old friends as Steve Grendon. Many will find, however, the over-all impression of the novel depressing; there is a triviality about Sac Prairie in our time that contrasts with the vigorous and heady life of the community in earlier days.

> *Richard A. Cordell, "Sac Prairie Again," in* The Saturday Review of Literature, *Vol. XXVIII, No. 45, November 10, 1945, p. 43.*

WILLIAM KEHOE

["**The Shield of the Valiant**"] proves once again that one must live in a small town most of his life really to know its over-all pattern, and that Derleth himself is no outsider as far as Sac Prairie is concerned. There is a tie-up between the different lives he describes and the petty intrigues, the malicious gossip and the often desperate attempts to escape loneliness even in a place where there are no real strangers, which is almost always authentic.

Unfortunately the novel also proves again that authenticity isn't the only component of good writing and reading. There are things of authentic importance and others of authentic unimportance; in his frenetic attempt to record every last dance tune that Rena Janney ever sings, and conversation with a dictaphone accuracy, Derleth hasn't taken the time to distinguish between the two. When he does, he will be a far more competent writer, and his books . . . much more widely read.

> *William Kehoe, in a review of "The Shield of the Valiant," in* The New York Times Book Review, *November 18, 1945, p. 13.*

HOWARD HAYCRAFT

[The twelve stories in "**In Re: Sherlock Holmes**"] are all in the pastiche vein and all written by Derleth himself. . . . The resulting book inevitably lacks variety, although some of the individual selections are not without a certain charm and an engaging fidelity in form and spirit to the originals they imitate. A few, like "**The Adventure of the Norcross Riddle**" . . . and "**The Adventure of the Late Mr. Faversham**" . . . are good enough detective stories in their own right; most of the other episodes are over-long and, it must be confessed, a little tedious, even to the confirmed Sherlockian, when read in close sequence.

> *Howard Haycraft, "Holmesian Pastiches," in* The New York Times Book Review, *December 2, 1945, p. 32.*

EMERSON HYNES

"**Village Daybook**" consists of selections over a period from Derleth's diary. If mediocrity and brilliance are marks of authenticity in a diary, this is thoroughly authentic. On May 16, Sac Prairie produced the phenomenon of dogs barking at a car: "Quite evidently the dogs, for lack perhaps of anything better to do, enjoy the chase after cars that pass during the night." I believe it. . . . On the other hand Mr. Derleth records with rare skill the beauty and movement of nature. He never fails to please as he describes the weather, the birds, flowers, fish and animals. One who loves the outdoors will be fully rewarded with his nature passages.

Mr. Derleth has affection for his townsmen and they, evidently, for him. The items of daily gossip and reminiscences add up to a comfortable completeness of village life. Unfortunately, it is largely a surface description. He has not learned to analyze and handle people as effectively as he does Mother Nature. Commenting on an exchange of conversation about the weather on Christmas Day, he reflects, "that the essential pulse of village life beats in just such trivial exchanges, which occur constantly and forever: the talk of weather, of sun and rain, of fog and cloud, of storm and wind throughout every season . . . ." That may be the pulse, but it is a long way from the heart of village life. Weather and other trivia are universal symbols of communication, but each village has its unique secret in the intimate knowledge of the life and background of every citizen, of this we get too little in "**Village Daybook**."

> *Emerson Hynes, in a review of "Village Daybook," in* Commonweal, *Vol. XLVI, No. 6, May 23, 1947, p. 146.*

ANTHONY BOUCHER

Solar Pons is not precisely either an imitation or a parody of Sherlock Holmes. One might almost call him an understudy, and a triumphant one—a necessary replacement filling the abhorrent vacuum created by The Master's retirement. . . .

The first book collection of Pons adventures, oddly entitled "**In Re: Sherlock Holmes**," appeared in 1945, to the deep gratification of all who have read and reread the sixty tales of the Holmesian canon and hungered for something new and yet the same. Now at last we have the long-awaited sequel . . . , "**The Memoirs of Solar Pons**" . . . ; and once again the habitués of Holmes' 221B Baker Street can move to Pons' Praed Street with happy confidence.

The title is misleading; no equivalent of the seemingly tragic Reichenbach disaster befalls Pons. But the eleven stories . . . are all in the grand tradition of magnificently sinister plotting and spectacularly logical deduction. Each devotee will have his favorite; this department elects "**The Adventure of Ricoletti of the Clubfoot**." A passing Watsonian reference to this gentleman and his abominable wife has long titillated readers. The story as Mr. Derleth reveals it could not have been conceived along more nobly classical lines.

> *Anthony Boucher, in a review of "The Memoirs of Solar Pons," in* The New York Times Book Review, *August 26, 1951, p. 20.*

JOHN HOLMES

[August Derleth] has made a new collection of his poems ["**Rendezvous in a Landscape**"] in four groups, "Homage to Thoreau," "Homage to Robert Frost," "Homage to Psyche," and "Homage to Edgar Lee Masters." The first is the longest and the best poem in the book. The poet uses brief prose passages from Thoreau's "Walden," and plays poetic variations on each one, expanding that severe economy into the wealth of its implications. This is done with genuine love and admiration, and with genuine creation. Twenty-eight poems are offered to Frost, also with sincerity, as homage.

They are Derleth poems on the sort of themes Frost might have written, and thus to gather them is to run the risk of sounding like a lesser Frost, and Mr. Derleth unfortunately does. They are beyond question his own experience, but the sound of Frost creeps in. . . .

The Psyche group consists of four love poems, and the poem for Masters is an elegy, which, though it brings Masters to the graveyard in Spoon River to lie among the familiar names from the "Anthology," is a perfectly fitting tribute. The whole design of the book is an interesting lesson in the dangers and possibilities of writing to or about writers.

> *John Holmes, "Of Time and Place and Versifiers," in* The New York Times Book Review, *August 3, 1952, p. 6.*

ANTHONY BOUCHER

There's nothing unconventional about August Derleth's **"Fell Purpose"** . . . , the first Judge Peck novel in many years. It's a pure old-fashioned whodunit of the bludgeoning of the social arbiters of a small Wisconsin town—quiet, plodding, mildly agreeable, rather like an American equivalent of John Rhode, with little to suggest the originality of the author in other fields or in his noble Solar Pons detective stories.

> *Anthony Boucher, in a review of "Fell Purpose,"*
> *in* The New York Times Book Review, *February 8, 1953, p. 31.*

RUSSELL MacFALL

"All things of live adventuring are kin" is the theme of [**"Country Poems"**], 30 poems about the birds and animals, cornfields and country church yards of his Wisconsin demesne. He is so much a part of it that he can "look about and see what beauty lies in simple things" and voice what he has seen and felt in lyrics that have the grace to be as simple and direct as the west wind and the chipmunk that he understands alike.

"Sirius: Midnight," with its clear sense of man's "kinship to eternity," is the most original and powerful poem of the book. **"Scent of Camomile"** is steeped in country living, and both **"Mushrooms,"** with its bold figure of speech, and **"The Moon on the Water"** are good examples of Derleth's skill in drawing a deep meaning from the small incident.

> *Russell MacFall, "Skillful Odes to Country Life in Wisconsin," in* Chicago Tribune, *February 10, 1957, p. 9.*

VICTOR P. HASS

[Mr. Derleth has written **"The House on the Mound"** as a sequel to **"Bright Journey"**] and if it lacks much of the dramatic impact of **"Bright Journey,"** it still is worth the long wait. Indeed, one understands why Mr. Derleth waited so long to write it, for it posed an exceedingly difficult problem: How to give middle-aged, generally eventless love and living the substance of drama.

He has solved the problem, in a measure at least, by telling it "plain." The simple truth is that not much *does* happen in this novel, and yet it is given stature by the goodness of the people involved. Dousman and his charming wife are persons you can love and respect. . . .

Mr. Derleth writes with deep love of his home state, from its admission to the Union in 1848 to Dousman's death twenty years later. His is a regional novel of a high order of excellence.

> *Victor P. Hass, "Midwest Millionaire," in* The New York Times Book Review, *June 22, 1958, p. 19.*

JAMES SANDOE

[**"The Return of Solar Pons"**] is an assembly of thirteen short stories about Sherlock Holmes, set forth with all his customary equipment (Watson, room, housekeeper) and in very much the mood and mode of Conan Doyle. Edgar W. Smith, "Buttons" of the Holmesian devotees (or addicts) in this country, finds Mr. Derleth the most consistently successful imitator in Holmesian history. One cannot after all quarrel with the judgment. But imitation is the operative word.

> *James Sandoe, in a review of "The Return of Solar Pons," in* New York Herald Tribune Book Review, *April 12, 1959, p. 11.*

VICTOR P. HASS

Few writers at work in America today have been able to register the heartbeat of a place with the fidelity, skill and warmth that August Derleth has brought to his beloved **"Sac Prairie."** . . .

With the exception of a small handful, mostly juveniles, I have read all of [Derleth's books], and I have never failed to find enjoyment in them. But much as I have admired his novels and his essays, **"Wisconsin in Their Bones"** . . . convinces me that his primary talent lies in the short story.

This, believe me, is a striking collection. Whether Derleth is telling a story of unrequited love, as in **"The Christmas Virgin,"** of savage father love, as in **"April Kinney,"** or of the distressing effects of indecision, as in **"The Telescope,"** he plays a penetrating light on the forces that often make a little town a serene pool one moment and a jungle the next.

Many of the stories here are very thin slices of life, it is true, but all make a point and make it wonderfully well. They make the point also, I think, that Derleth is a far more important writer than is generally granted. In him, regional writing has come to something very close to full flower.

> *Victor P. Hass, "A Writer at Home," in* Chicago Sunday Tribune Magazine of Books, *January 8, 1961, p. 3.*

JARED C. LOBDELL

Mr. Fairlie's Final Journey is the first Solar Pons novel, and one is driven to conclude (a view in which the author concurs) that the novel is not the best form for a Solar Pons adventure—any more than, with the exception of *The Hound of the Baskervilles*, it was the best form for a Sherlock Holmes adventure. (p. 758)

A Praed Street Dossier is an out-of-the-way sort of work, not a collection of adventures (except for the last 24 pages of the book, which contain two collaborative science-fiction detective stories, comprising what is surely one of the few attempts at this genre and even more surely one of the few successful attempts), but the raw material for a collection. Along with the section on the creation of Solar Pons, and the science-fiction detection, about half the book . . . is devoted to the journal of Dr. Lyndon Parker—the Pontine Watson—in the first year . . . of his association with Pons. Apart from the fact that it makes pleasant reading, the journal is worth noting for Mr. Derleth's strong defense of capital punishment.

The Adventure of the Unique Dickensians . . . is by way of being a double pastiche—a pastiche of Vincent Starrett's pastiche, "The Adventure of the Unique Hamlet." It is excellent fun. Nevertheless, one looks forward to the promised *Chronicles of Solar Pons*. The *Memoirs* are now out of print, but the other seven books are still available, and they are unquestionably the best substitute for Sherlock Holmes. That they may contain mistakes, inconsistencies, Americanisms, is no real weakness. The *Annotated Sherlock Holmes* devotes half its bulk to discussing the mistakes and inconsistencies in the original canon. Whether there will be Praed Street Irregulars along with Baker Street Irregulars at some future date I do not know: perhaps even now Pontine societies are meeting. The important thing is that as long as August Derleth is alive and writing in Sauk City, we need not unduly regret the death of Dr. Watson's literary agent in Sussex four decades ago. If not cut entirely from Holmesian cloth, Solar Pons is more than a patch on the old master. (pp. 758-59)

Jared C. Lobdell, "Addenda to the Canon," in National Review, *Vol. XXI, No. 29, July 29, 1969, pp. 758-59.*

BENNY GREEN

The Adventures of Solar Pons is utterly different, not only from the works of spoof scholarship, but also from most other works to do with Holmes, for it consists of short stories which candidly confess the intention to copy Doyle as closely as possible. Holmes and Watson in Baker Street become Pons and Parker of Praed Street, and, as Vincent Starrett says in his preface, it is a clear case of impersonation rather than of parody. The stories are mildly amusing, but as the power of the originals rests in their literary style, and as the creator of Pons doesn't have much of it, the appeal of the anthology rather depends on the degree of fanaticism of the collector.

Benny Green, "Rounding Up," in The Spectator, *Vol. 235, No. 7697, January 3, 1976, p. 14.**

Fumiko Enchi

1905-

Japanese novelist, short story writer, and dramatist.

Enchi is a significant contemporary Japanese novelist. Her fiction is characterized by subtle symbolism, precise use of language, and explorations of human psychology, specifically the complexities of female psychology. A scholar of classical Japanese literature, Enchi translated into modern Japanese the eleventh-century narrative *The Tale of Genji* and enriches her own fiction with allusions to classical works.

Enchi began her career as a playwright while in her twenties. She soon started to write fiction but did not become famous until the 1950s. Her best-known novel, *Onnazaka* (1957; *The Waiting Years*), which was awarded the Japanese Noma Literary Prize, and her novel *Onna-men* (1958?; *Masks*), are her only works to have been translated into English.

In probing the psychology of women, Enchi's fiction often touches on such subjects as repression, adultery, seduction, and eroticism. *The Waiting Years* concerns a nineteenth-century wife who must obey her husband's order to recruit a mistress for him. Though humiliated, the woman displays no emotion until she vents her anger in an outburst while on her deathbed. The novel explores the effects of her lifelong repression. *Masks* also exposes hidden dissatisfactions in human relationships. Like *The Waiting Years*, *Masks* revolves around an unspoken, insidious power struggle, but in this case the conflict occurs between a woman and her daughter-in-law. Both of Enchi's novels have been praised for their development of complex relationships and intricate characterizations.

Courtesy of The Yomiuri Shimbun

ANNE M. BURK

[*The Waiting Years*] is, in a sense, shocking, despite the fact that there are no explicit sex scenes and no coarse language. It is set in the Meiji period. A wealthy government official sends his wife to Tokyo to bring him back a mistress. The wife obeys because a woman always obeys her husband, no matter how much obedience may debase her. The result is an incredibly selfish man pitted against a woman with much bitterness walled up inside her icy exterior. The husband's further extramarital affairs (including one with his son's wife) deepen the gulf and turn their marriage into a contest of wills. In the end, everyone loses. The situation may not seem believable— yet how different is it from the role many women accept and live unquestioningly?

Anne M. Burk, in a review of "The Waiting Years," in Library Journal, *Vol. 97, No. 7, April 1, 1972, p. 1345.*

CHARLES G. BLEWITT

[*The Waiting Years*] is a positively beautiful yet depressing novel about the personal and cultural suppression of Japanese women after the turn of the century. . . . [It] is written with painstakingly heart-rending prose. Enchi creates a timeless mood of sadness and suppression. *The Waiting Years* literally bleeds. . . .

There are so many worthwhile things in *The Waiting Years*! For one thing, it was enlightening to understand and, thanks to Enchi, *feel* the sad state of affairs of the concubine. Sociologically speaking, the "Upstairs . . . Downstairs" view of upper middle class Japanese Society with many of the same contradictions and incongruities as our own society was well worth examining. Yet, it was Enchi's prose which made this book such a "tearful" joy.

Charles G. Blewitt, in a review of "The Waiting Years," in Best Sellers, *Vol. 41, No. 2, May, 1981, p. 45.*

EMIKO SAKURAI

The choice of the English title *The Waiting Years* in place of the original *Onnazaka*, the name of the long ascending road to the heroine's hilltop estate, is interesting. The sensitive and subtle author would not have used these words that so starkly define the oppressed wife's existence. She preferred the symbolism of the arduous path to describe her life. . . .

[*The Waiting Years*] is certainly one of the greatest works of the [Japanese] postwar era, subtle, sensitive, insightful and moving. The characters are palpably presented, and the unaffected prose resonates with carefully chosen images and

140

sounds. . . . *The Waiting Years* is an outstanding addition to the canon of Japanese literature in English translation.

Emiko Sakurai, in a review of "The Waiting Years," in World Literature Today, *Vol. 55, No. 4, Autumn, 1981, p. 728.*

KIRKUS REVIEWS

Subtle, challenging work from one of Japan's most respected (and oldest) female novelist/scholars: though [*Masks*] is quite short, a Western reader may feel at sea through much of it—what with learned references to Nō drama masks or an included-in-full essay written by one of the characters about female shamanism as a theme in *The Tale of Genji*. But, for the patient reader, the story will gradually become clear and powerful—as a tale of women's capacity for blackest revenge. Togano Meiko, a poet and mother of the recently killed Akio (and of Akio's retarded twin sister, Harume), toys with the emotional leash of Akio's young widow, Yasuko. Two potential suitors, Ibuki (who's married) and Mikame (single), vie for her—but Meiko orchestrates their affections to the point of manipulation. Finally, then, there'll be an intricate, hidden maneuver by which Yasuko becomes only the stand-in for the idiot Harume—who will be impregnated by one of the men in order that Meiko can have, by proxy, the child she always wanted most: Akio's. And it is Meiko's absolute amorality of revenge that Enchi makes so startling here, giving subtle tints to the explicit shamanism theme: "Just as there is an archetype of woman as object of man's eternal love," reads part of Meiko's essay, "so there must be an archetype of her as the object of his eternal fear, representing, perhaps, the shadows of his own evil actions." Fiction of feminine psychology/mythology, almost imperceptively woven—in a difficult but echoing pattern that is light-years away from the cruder approaches of writers like Angela Carter.

A review of "Masks," in Kirkus Reviews, *Vol. LI, No. 4, February 15, 1983, p. 196.*

PUBLISHERS WEEKLY

A stunning and subtle tale of women and envy, ["**Masks**"] follows the convoluted life of Togano Meiko, now a sophisticated mature woman in her 50s. Years ago Meiko, unhappily married, had a lover. She bore him twins, a daughter and a son. Now her husband, her lover and her son are dead, and her life revolves around her widowed daughter-in-law, Yasuko,

and her retarded daughter, Harume. Meiko's plan, a bizarre manipulation of the two women in her household, is exquisitely plotted and engineered, the product of a mind and heart embittered by loss. Fumiko Enchi writes of betrayal and sensuality, of the psychology of women, with astonishing insight and great beauty. Her allusions to the masks of *No* plays and to the classic "The Tale of the Genji," the brilliant way she layers and interweaves the ancient, the more recent past and the present are haunting and rich.

A review of "Masks," in Publishers Weekly, *Vol. 223, No. 9, March 4, 1983, p. 86.*

GEORGE KEARNS

[*Masks*] is an intense short novel set about a decade after the war. Enchi's characters are secularized, partly-Westernized intellectuals who maintain an antiquarian interest in traditional Japanese culture and amuse themselves by studying spirit-possession at a Madame Sosostris level of table-rapping. (The medium at a séance speaks in French.) In fact, their interest in spirit-possession and Nō masks is fairly unconvincing: they seem obliged to pursue their interests so that material will be at hand for the author's cloudy, ominous symbolism. *Masks* is faintly interesting for its glimpses of Japanese life in a post-MacArthur era of ball-point pens, Old Parr scotch, and private detectives who spy on adulterous husbands. The central character is Meiko, a respected poet and editor of a poetry journal, the most unpleasant literary Mother since *The Little Foxes*. Wronged by her husband in her youth, Meiko takes revenge on men with patience and precision, dominating her widowed daughter-in-law, Yasuko, and manipulating the two men who are in love with Yasuko, a professor of literature and a doctor-psychologist. Using Yasuko as bait for her trap, Meiko tricks one of the lovers into impregnating her retarded adult daughter in order to realize a twisted vision of matriarchy triumphant. . . . On [the] final page, Yasuko, caught in "helpless bewilderment," wonders that "the vast, mysterious depths within Meiko that had always so fascinated her seemed suddenly to become bottomless." And bottomless was my fascination with *Masks*—fascination with the spectacle of a gifted writer setting out determinedly to create so fetid a story. (pp. 251-52)

George Kearns, "World Well Lost," in The Hudson Review, *Vol. XXXVI, No. 3, Autumn, 1983, pp. 549-62.**

Michael Ende

1930?-

German novelist, author of children's books, and poet.

Ende's international bestseller *Unendliche geschichte* (1979; *The Neverending Story*) is a fantasy novel which appeals to adults as well as the traditional younger audience. This popular book is also the basis for a film of the same title. *The Neverending Story* is a "book within a book," with red and green ink used to differentiate between a book that the protagonist is reading and the fantasy in which he eventually finds himself involved. According to its publisher, *The Neverending Story* has become a symbol for the antinuclear movement in West Germany. Ende emigrated from that country more than twenty years ago and now lives in Italy.

LIBRARY JOURNAL

As in all good fairy tales, the protagonist [of *The Neverending Story*] undergoes various rites of passage, and Ende does an expert job of conveying a sense of magic in a traditional format. Imaginative readers know that the story doesn't end when the covers close; the magic to be found in books is eternal, and Ende's message comes through vividly.

> *A review of "The Neverending Story," in* Library Journal, *Vol. 108, No. 18, October 15, 1983, p. 1975.*

SOMTOW SUCHARITKUL

The Neverending Story seems destined, by dint of its advertising budget, for financial success. Since, in addition, it is an import from Germany and will therefore automatically be embraced by those who ride the bandwagon of reverse cultural chauvinism, I must confess to a certain initial prejudice, which redoubled when, on reading the first few pages, I found out that this was yet another book about an alienated person who falls into a fantasy universe. Any fantasy enthusiast will probably be able to rattle off a hundred titles of novels, from Lewis Carroll's all the way down to Stephen R. Donaldson's, which have made use of this plot. With competition like that, a novelist would have to be a consummate genius to bring it off completely.

That Michael Ende has taken this bewhiskered plot, endowed it with a certain amount of originality, populated it with characters who do not appear to be entirely stolen from the works of predecessors . . . is indeed an achievement to be proud of, and for this reason alone his novel is worth recommending. However, the reader will need perseverance because the book doesn't really get going until about page 160, and in general its pacing is not quite what Americans are used to.

What's more, the book's opening will seem to be dreary and cliché-ridden. We meet the young and preciously named Bastian Balthazar Bux, who is having soap-operatic father-relationship problems and has run away from school into a weird antique bookstore. The mundane root of his alienation is that of being too fat. Bastian steals a book (printed, like this book, in red and green ink) called *The Neverending Story*, sneaks off

© Jerry Bauer

to read it, and soon becomes engrossed. Slowly but surely he is sucked into Fantasiana, the magic kingdom in which the book is set.

While we wait for our hero to make an appearance in the fantasy universe, Ende marks time by parading before us a ragtag array of kobolds, elves, and other standard fantasy-world furnishings, who go off on a bunch of hackneyed adventures. The universe itself seems an annoying hodgepodge of other writers' universes. . . .

Now Fantasiana and its ruler the Childlike Empress are—you guessed it—in danger, and the only person who can save the universe is the one who's reading the book. For half the book we are treated to the exposition of these dire truths and of the ho-hum wonders of Fantasiana. Then, just about at the point when you're ready to fling *The Neverending Story* across the room, Bastian finally makes the crossing—and the novel makes an instantaneous leap from the mundane into the magical.

We discover that there's a reason why Fantasiana seems to be this goulash of random ransackings from myth and literature— that others, great writers among them, have visited the magic kingdom before and have in every case created the kingdom anew, for outside visitors have godlike powers. The more they create, however, the more memories of reality they lose, and when all is lost they lose not only their powers but their ability to return home. It is on this paradox that Bastian's journey toward self-knowledge hinges.

The second half of the book is as energetic, innovative, and perceptive as its first half is airheadedly uninventive. . . . Suddenly we understand the rightness of the book's initial trivialities; it is the very ordinariness of Bastian's origins that enables us to understand the triumph, anguish, and ultimate illumination of his kingship.

If there is a single subject with which all great fantasies deal, it must of necessity be the nature of reality. At its best, *The Neverending Story* is a profound examination of these unanswerable questions. Its ambition makes it—perhaps inevitably—a dramatically uneven work; its greatest flaw is the imbalance of interest between its two halves.

> *Somtow Sucharitkul, "Falling into Fantasiana," in* Book World—The Washington Post, *October 16, 1983, p. 11.*

DAN CRYER

Although **"The Neverending Story"** has been a best seller in Europe, it's hard to see why. The book's appeal seems limited to readers about Bastian's age. It is bereft of psychological insight or depth of characterization. It seems geared more to "Star Wars" viewers than Tolkien readers. Anyone over 12 who gushes over this book ought to be kept in at recess.

Michael Ende's problem, however, is certainly not plotting. The story begins in suspense and darts from adventure to adventure. Ferocious dragons, ancient seers, giant snakes, a wicked sorceress and a faithful dragon roam through these pages. Heroes must best their rivals, endure unspeakable trials, conquer their fears. . . .

Since the tale is fantasy and aimed at the junior-high mind, everything will turn out all right in the end. Courage, readers of this primer will learn, can work wonders for the most fainthearted; friendship is more nourishing than ambition; love is the highest good of all.

> *Dan Cryer, "Fantasy for Children Who Dream," in* Newsday, *October 20, 1983.*

DAVID QUAMMEN

["**The Neverending Story**"] is a fantasy epic with all the requisite elements of the genre: chimerical creatures, exotic forests and mountains, unpronounceable proper names, a picaresque plot predicated on a Great Quest, magical swords and amulets, chivalric protocol, high melodrama, a virtuous empress, a heroic little fat boy and a moral vision of Manichaean simplicity. The novel is splashed generously with literary color but, as though that weren't enough, it is also printed in alternate sections of red and green type. Over all, the effect is lighthearted and festive. This rather large book is full of small charms and seems admirably suited for reading aloud, in installments, at the bedside of a 7-year-old child.

But a curious thing about **"The Neverending Story"** is that certain adults are evidently inclined to take it quite seriously. According to its American publisher, the book was first published in Germany "rather quietly, as a children's book. It began to touch a wider and wider circle of readers, and was adopted as a symbol by the peace marchers." . . . All this over an ingenuous book, inventive in its frills, conventional in

its pieties, that combines some of the better features of Tolkien, "Peter Pan," "Puff, the Magic Dragon" and "The Little Engine That Could." But the fault is not Mr. Ende's. **"The Neverending Story,"** to its credit, does not seem to take *itself* very seriously. (pp. 39-41)

Throughout the first half of Mr. Ende's novel, Bastian remains placed in the outer narrative frame, as the Reader; over his shoulder we watch while another young boy, Atreyu, pursues a Great Quest to save the life of the Childlike Empress. . . . At the climax of that quest it becomes necessary for Bastian, the despised bookworm, to speak up himself and, in a moment of empathic transport, step across into the storybook world—Pirandello as played by the Muppets. The novel's second half follows Bastian through a course of challenges every bit as bizarre as those he had envied Atreyu, and eventually toward a lesson of growth and fulfillment he carries back into his mundane existence. It is all broad, innocent fun; nothing less, nothing more. (p. 41)

> *David Quammen, "Fantasy, Epic and Farce," in* The New York Times Book Review, *November 6, 1983, pp. 14, 39-41.**

PAMELA MARSH

Alas, it takes more than ballyhoo to make a book worthwhile. Just to open ["**The Neverending Story**"] is to suffer disappointment and be vividly reminded that it began its life in Germany as a child's book, for how can anyone take seriously a book published in colored ink? Worse, the first letter of every chapter is muddily illuminated. . . .

The contents match the packaging. The plot involves a small bookworm of a boy who starts to read a tale about an ever-changing quest through a strange dreamland, peopled with fantastic beings. . . .

There are moments when Michael Ende's imagination takes wing, and he tells us of the terrifying "nothingness" that devours the landscape, and the huge luckdragons, "as light as a summer cloud," which "swim in the air of heaven as fish swim in water." But that hardly atones for the author's expectation that we'll take seriously a creature called "cheesiewheezie."

"The Neverending Story" has been praised for the lessons it teaches, and certainly it lays down some praiseworthy morals. The transformation of this hero is designed to teach the importance of loving, and no one could quarrel with that, but it is hardly a startling revelation. More interesting are Ende's convictions that fantasy plays a vitally important role in the world and needs to be protected, lest it turn into propaganda, and that to recognize what one is wishing for is as difficult as it is important.

But morals, if they are to do their job properly, must be whipped up vigorously into the plot and not allowed to just lie there in undigested lumps.

> *Pamela Marsh, "Praiseworthy Morals, Unwieldy Fantasy," in* The Christian Science Monitor, *November 9, 1983, p. 26.*

ALEXANDER STILLE

Although Michael Ende wrote **"The Neverending Story"** as a children's book, it became a nationwide best seller in West

Germany and a bible of the peace movement there. Its success is particularly strange because the book travels to an imaginary land and has virtually no political content. It's as if "The Hobbit" had become the rallying cry of the SDS. . . . (p. 112)

In the first half of the book, Fantastica is a conventional, even saccharine fairyland with the usual cast of princesses, gnomes and dragons. But the book comes to life when Bastian enters the story, ingeniously playing on the relation between imagination and reality. Ende has attempted an ambitious, if not always successful, mix of modernism and children's literature: Pirandello turned loose in Disneyland.

What does this have to do with nuclear weapons? In Fantastica, what you wish happens. During the Vietnam War, Abbie Hoffman and the Yippies gathered around the Pentagon and attempted to levitate it by meditation. Similarly, Germany's peace demonstrators would like to make nuclear weapons disappear by force of will. Ende's book taps these utopian yearnings. (pp. 112, 114)

> *Alexander Stille, "A Movable Feast of Fiction: 'The Neverending Story','' in* Newsweek, *Vol. CII, No. 20, November 14, 1983, pp. 112, 114.*

RHODA KOENIG

[*The Neverending Story*] is a curious piece of work: A fantasy about a small, fat boy who enters into a book he is reading and becomes the hero of a magic quest. . . . The special effects may jazz things up, but the book, with a new magic creature on almost every page . . . , is about as lyrical as a German Walt Disney World. . . . [Periodically] throughout the quest we cut to descriptions of the boy marveling at the evocative writing, or sobbing and blowing his nose when the magic horse dies. This kind of bullying self-promotion only underscores the banality of the novel, as does another intrusion—the boy's muttering "Thank God" or having a stray thought about Jesus. Reminding us of the most powerful story of our age in the middle of a tale about clockwork gnomes is *really* asking for unfavorable comparisons.

> *Rhoda Koenig, in a review of "The Neverending Story," in* New York *Magazine, Vol. 16, No. 47, November 28, 1983, p. 103.*

TOM EASTON

[*The Neverending Story*] offers levels of meaning—pure wish-fulfillment, paradox and intrigue, a philosophy of fantastic creation. It is thoughtful and astonishing and—perhaps—above all—glowing with warmth and love. It deserves its status abroad, and it deserves as much again here. (p. 166)

> *Tom Easton, in a review of "The Neverending Story," in* Analog Science Fiction/Science Fact, *Vol. CIX, No. 2, February, 1984, pp. 165-66.*

EDMUND FULLER

["**The Neverending Story**"] is full of fresh, imaginative invention, although, like all such modern works, it owes honorable debts to our heritage of myth, legend and fable. Originality, in such matters, lies in variations upon themes, embellishing ancient motifs with new details.

"**The Neverending Story**" has the classic element of the unexpected entry of a human child into a wholly other world, crossovers from which are a tricky problem. It combines mission and quest, laying the burden of overcoming evil and destruction upon the shoulders of an initially reluctant, unprepossessing hero. . . .

Fantastica is threatened by Nothing. Vast holes of Nothing appear in the land, expanding, combining. Like a black hole, the Nothing sucks in anything that comes too close. Soon it will invade the very heart of the land, the Ivory Tower of the ruler of Fantastica, the Childlike Empress. . . .

The adventures, the terrors to be met and mastered, the bravery and wit, the fumbles and bad mistakes (you know Bastian is going to unsheath that sword sometime) are suspensefully varied. The book's themes are decidedly enigmatic and lend the story its adult dimension. . . .

I know people who are impervious or downright hostile to tales of this kind, who will rightly shun it. But if you like the genre, get your hands on the part of what we are assured is a Neverending Story beyond the covers of this or any other book.

> *Edmund Fuller, "Adventures in Fantastica," in* The Wall Street Journal, *February 14, 1984, p. 30.*

PAUL M. LLOYD

Ende has an eye for vivid colors and is fairly imaginative in the creation of adventures [in *The Neverending Story*]. However, these adventures are not all especially connected and one gets the impression that often enough he was simply adding adventures just to pad out the text. The book is clearly written for children, since the author rather ostentatiously talks down to his readers, something which even as a child I found annoying. I found the title amply descriptive: the book is unendingly tedious and didactic, but since it sold a million copies in Germany, it must have interested a good many readers. Unfortunately I was not one of them.

> *Paul M. Lloyd, in a review of "The Neverending Story," in* Fantasy Review, *Vol. 7, No. 4, May, 1984, p. 30.*

D(ennis) J(oseph) Enright

1920-

English poet, novelist, critic, and editor.

Enright is an important literary figure whose poetry and criticism exhibit a liberal, humanistic outlook. Underlying the witty, ironic, and sometimes irreverent tone of his writing is a sensitivity to the human suffering Enright has witnessed in England and during his many years of teaching abroad. Many of Enright's stylistic and thematic concerns are typical of those of The Movement, a literary group with which he is sometimes associated. As editor of the anthology *Poets of the 1950s* (1955), Enright is partially responsible for bringing what would become known as The Movement to the attention of readers and critics. The anthology includes poems by Kingsley Amis, Donald Davie, Philip Larkin, and Enright, among others. Enright is also well known as a literary critic whose reviews have appeared in the *New Statesman, Encounter,* and *London Magazine.*

Enright spent over twenty years teaching English literature in Egypt, Japan, West Germany, Thailand, and Singapore. Many of his works are informed by his experiences in these countries. Enright's first novel, *Academic Year* (1955), for example, concerns three expatriate Englishmen in Egypt with thematic emphasis on the conflict between Western and Eastern sensibilities.

The suffering and powerlessness of the individual which Enright observed in impoverished countries appears as a major theme in much of his poetry, most notably in his collection *Some Men Are Brothers* (1960). Political power and hypocrisy are themes which Enright develops through foreign settings but which he also applies to situations in England. *The Terrible Shears: Scenes from a Twenties Childhood* (1973) is an account of Enright's youth in a working-class family and his early recognition of human suffering. *Paradise Illustrated* (1978) and *A Faust Book* (1979) are tongue-in-cheek revisions of the biblical tale of the Garden of Eden and the Faust legend.

Enright's literary criticism displays the same mistrust of established authority as his poetry and fiction. In *The Apothecary's Shop: Essays on Literature* (1957) and *Conspirators and Poets* (1966) he examines classical and contemporary literature, questioning conventional interpretations of the works of numerous important authors. Similarly, in *Shakespeare and the Students* (1970) Enright questions traditional academic approaches to Shakespeare's plays and advocates more pragmatic interpretations based on character analysis.

(See also *CLC,* Vols. 4, 8; *Contemporary Authors,* Vols. 1-4, rev. ed.; *Contemporary Authors New Revision Series,* Vol. 1; *Dictionary of Literary Biography,* Vol. 27; and *Something about the Author,* Vol. 25.)

Courtesy of Chatto & Windus

ANTHONY THWAITE

The words *human* and *humane* ring briskly through [the essays in Mr. Enright's *The Apothecary's Shop*], as, indeed, do their implications through his poems. Mr. Enright is a moralist—undoctrinaire but (if one can rid the word of false and misleading accretions) committed. He is impatient with work which is not demonstrably *about* something, scornful of critics who obfuscate the something when it's there. . . .

'The greater part of current literary criticism resembles a game of skittles played with ivory chess pieces,' writes Mr. Enright. The danger of the other kind of literary critical game which has come into being since Mr. Enright wrote those words is that the equipment is deliberately crude and the players deliberately tough. . . . Mr. Enright is not really this sort of player, but there are a few distressing streaks, chiefly apparent in the dialogue on *The Cocktail Party* and, to a lesser extent, in 'The Use of Poetry.' What is painful is the slightly strained jauntiness of tone, a feeling that the poet is not just a man speaking to men but a chap chatting to chaps.

Healthy common sense is *not* enough. Mr. Enright's peculiar strength is his alliance of common sense with a wide range of reference: the general critical pieces are supported by essays on (among others) Shakespearian and Jacobean drama, Goethe, Thomas Mann, a useful juxtaposition of Auden and Rilke, and—as one might expect—a volley of praise for Forster at the expense of Virginia Woolf. Mr. Enright is already well known and appreciated as poet, traveller and entertainer: he is now available, in solid form, as a travelled and entertaining critic.

Anthony Thwaite, "Literary Games," in The Spectator, Vol. 199, No. 6752, November 22, 1957, p. 718.*

JOHN PETTIGREW

[*The Apothecary's Shop*] is an extremely lively, sensitive and sensible collection of critical essays, varying greatly in subject matter and in quantity. Some of the material—"On Not Teaching *The Cocktail Party*" and "The Use of Poetry" for example—was not really worth reprinting, but what remains reflects a vigorous and wide-ranging mind, and one which detests the vast amount of nonsense in much modern criticism. . . .

Mr. Enright's forthrightness and commonsense approach to literature and criticism come out nicely in the opening essay "Criticism for Criticism's Sake" and in "The Brain-washed Muse: Some Second Thoughts on Tradition" but, engaging as he is here, he is still better, because more positive, in such essays as those on *Coriolanus, Wilhelm Meister* and "To the Lighthouse or to India?". Personally, I find it refreshing to read a critic who refuses to elevate *Coriolanus* to the first rank of Shakespearean tragedies, who, while admiring Miss Woolf's technique, questions the value of her purpose, and who writes in a lucid and extremely witty style which makes his book a pleasure to read.

John Pettigrew, in a review of "The Apothecary's Shop," in The Canadian Forum, Vol. XXXVIII, No. 451, August, 1958, p. 119.

NORMAN MacCAIG

Thinking of D. J. Enright's poems, one feels no inclination to talk in terms of 'promise,' for they are already fully achieved things in themselves. They face up to whatever judgment one makes of them with no petitions in their hands, no defensive pleas based on age or inexperience or a broken home. [*Some Men are Brothers*] is divided into four sections—Siam, Berlin, Japan and Displaced—whose titles might suggest that its author is more of a foiled circuitous wanderer than he appears to be. For while he is strongly aware of the exile within him, and who is in all of us, he bridges the gap between him and the ferocious world of the strange, the starved and the brutal with a sympathetic irony which puts himself and it in their places. Sometimes, I guess more and more often, he closes that gap with an understanding compassion that has none of the distance in it that irony implies, and, though the ironic ones are charming and witty and not without a weight of meaning, it is these others that seem to me the most interesting poems in the book. He is not a man to quote in the small space of a review, for he is not notably a phrasemaker. It is the general tone of the poems, that is to say, fundamentally it is the quality of the mind and the sensibility behind them that give them their special flavour. That mind is interested in peasants and politicians, landscapes and loneliness, fans and furores, but always as they matter in everyday living. He recognises their involvement with each other and with him, and these poems therefore are about a real and complex world in which real and complex poems are still possible, as he shows.

Norman MacCaig, "Peering and Seeing," in The Spectator, Vol. 205, No. 6893, August 5, 1960, p. 223.*

P. N. FURBANK

[D. J. Enright] is out to make poetry from absolute, unambitious honesty. It is enough for him to be human and ordinary and to give exact rendering to the promptings of a humane consciousness. His role of professional and itinerant humanist is very sympathetic and one waits eagerly for the perfect Enright poem [in *Some Men are Brothers*], one in which the looseness of his verse justifies itself as flexibility, a freedom of approach allowing the subject to impose its own natural shape. (It would be the aesthetic counterpart of his tolerant and adaptable humanist ethic.) One has to do a lot of waiting; indeed, one gets into a mood of thinking the whole thing not poetry at all. When one remembers what Ezra Pound has done with free verse, Enright's often seems to have no more tension than a burst balloon. His great rambling octameters are not pulled into order by any tautness in the lines which follow them; indeed it seems a point of honour that no line should ever repeat the rhythm of the one that went before. And lacking any formal interest, what the poems have to say often seems scrappy and conventional too. However, the successes come at last, and they are worth waiting for. What really seizes and disturbs his humanism is the realization that there are some men who are outside its range; that there are human castaways so abject that it would be hypocrisy to think of them as human at all. Out of this thought springs a poem, **'Written Off'**, about Japanese vagrants, which is taut, poised, and most moving in its directness.

P. N. Furbank, in a review of "Some Men Are Brothers," in The Listener, Vol. LXIV, No. 1646, October 13, 1960, p. 651.

ROBERT TAUBMAN

The better part of *Figures of Speech,* or at least the more assimilable part, is a private view of Bangkok and Japan, with the author's comments on the East-West imbroglio and what Unesco calls the mutual appreciation of cultural values. It's Mr Enright's own voice one hears detailing the traps and vanities of university life, embassy parties and literary gatherings—and in his characters' observations on the equivocal scene. . . . [Mattie is a] Chinese typist on holiday from Singapore; voluble, Westernised, but baffling. The starting-point of her thoughts about anachronism is Chung Lu, a young writer from Hong Kong who quotes the sages and models himself on the Confucian 'superior man'—anachronism or not (Mr Enright seems to be saying yes and no), he's pretty baffling too. They conduct a strange courtship, and are left facing a marriage that I find unimaginable. Something about them, however, may be deduced from the English character, George: a teacher of English literature prone to misadventures, who after a night in jail is shipped home from Bangkok as one of the British Council's failures—to reappear in no time in another well-heeled cultural role, flashing an expense account. He, at least, is a familiar figure, in novels and indeed in life, and if I call him a stereotype it's only to make the point that Mattie and Chung Lu may be valid in their own way, and possibly Mr Enright's audience in the East will find them just as true to life. If so, I would still feel that *Figures of Speech* fails to communicate to the rest of us their peculiar aptness. (p. 456)

Robert Taubman, "Style-Spotting," in New Statesman, Vol. LXIX, No. 1775, March 19, 1965, pp. 456, 458.*

PETER VANSITTART

I have always respected D. J. Enright, a useful all-rounder; critic, poet, teacher, novelist. [In *Figures of Speech*] he has not greatly extended himself: alternatively, as they say, he is 'writing comfortably within his reach.'

I don't mean that the poet-critic is condescending to the wider public. He has achieved real comedy, entertaining, often witty, about intellectual life and love in Bangkok and Tokyo, while making things easy for himself with the sitting targets of cultural nannies, linguistic conferences, genial brothels, old-world diplomats worried by rising human rights, the usual farcical British Council lecture. . . . Occident and Orient rub noses and produce not sparks, but courteous solecisms, ornate misunderstandings.

The story links George, a casual English lecturer, with a priggish but teachable young Confucian and an attractive Chinese girl from Singapore. They fumble charmingly on the great divides of race, culture, sex, in a tinted atmosphere of well-bred unreality. On all sides are heard high-sounding exquisitely phrased moral principles whose actual practice must be avoided as pleasantly as possible. Like attending London PEN dinners without paying. Harrying the myth of the inscrutable and unchanging East, Enright has an adroit eye for the tender, absurd and gently disconcerting.

> *Peter Vansittart, "Strictly for Entertainment," in* The Spectator, *Vol. 214, No. 7135, March 26, 1965, p. 410.**

FRANCIS HOPE

The thesis that all liberals become defeatist reactionaries is one which D. J. Enright could see off wittily—has done so, indeed, in earlier poems. But [in *The Old Adam*] his pleas for the old Adam—private, disorganised, indecisive man—take him into strange waters, whose subtlety contains some less subtle fish. . . . He is nothing if not a civilised grumbler, detached even from his own detachment. It's a privileged position, whose cost, as he recognises, sometimes falls on others. . . .

[His] wispy but pointed observations certainly speak, or murmur, for the age. Poetically, they vary: they are never coarse or harsh but can sag a little, can become too restrained—even faded Japanese paintings are invoked:

> Soft pastels and stern primaries,
> A line which bears you where it will.
> The master at his most assured,
> Not one hair out of place.

But one still wishes that the master's assurance weren't so linked to understatement, that his line gave rather stronger evidence of its will; perhaps even that he would muss his hair up a bit. The ratio of stern primaries to soft pastels needs looking at. Not even jokes—and his can be excellent—will always do.

> *Francis Hope, "Pastels and Primaries," in* New Statesman, *Vol. LXIX, No. 1788, June 18, 1965, p. 972.**

DAN JACOBSON

Professor Enright apologetically suggests that some of the short articles and reviews he has collected in [*Conspirators and Poets*] could 'scarcely be called "literary criticism."' By the standard he himself set in the best essays in his previous collection, *The Apothecary's Shop*, that may be true. But the apology can be read in more ways than one. When he writes in one of these pieces that the symbolism in John Updike's novels is

> all very neat and contrived, as if some sophisticate is amusedly performing for a psychiatrist of low intelligence

—*that*, we can't help agreeing, is certainly not literary criticism of the kind we have become most familiar with. It is too swift, too witty, too decisive; it uses everyday experience to effect, in a manner carefully avoided by most writers on contemporary literature in the professional academic reviews. The fact is— to paraphrase the old joke about Shakespeare's comedies being better than other people's tragedies—that Mr Enright's journalism is often more to the point than other people's criticism. . . .

[With few exceptions] *Conspirators and Poets* deals entirely with 20th-century writers. The author fights or snipes on many fronts. In turn he tries to rescue literature from the academics, from the ideologists, from the fashion-mongers, from the moralists, from the sociologists *manqué;* and then, quite as spiritedly, repudiates the advances of the aesthetes, the dilettantes, the sub-Flaubertians, those who think of 'words as an end in themselves' and of art as a refuge from life's disorder and unseemliness.

If he is likely to displease critics and university teachers by attacking them for the 'mountainous molehills of criticism' which they are raising in every direction, he also makes pretty short shrift of some of our recent rebels and their causes. . . .

However, it would be quite wrong to give the impression that the book is entirely, or even mainly, deflationary in tone. The author is always ready to acknowledge the merits of the work he cares for least, and elsewhere in the book he writes gratefully and gracefully about the achievements of many other contemporary or near-contemporary figures: Thomas Mann, C. P. Cavafy, Dr Leavis, Italo Svevo, Mary McCarthy (though he excludes *The Group* from his approval), Robert Graves, Philip Larkin, D. H. Lawrence as a poet, Wilfred Owen, Gunther Grass. These writers' gifts are enormously different in kind and magnitude, but the praise Mr Enright gives to each of them never diminishes the value or meaning of that accorded to the others. One curious and paradoxical consequence of the journalistic origin of a few of the pieces, however, is that one feels them to be more allusive, more bookish, than a straight, formal critical essay might have been. We don't get Enright on Mann, for instance, but rather Enright on a book by Erich Heller about Mann . . . and so on. Which is a pity, especially as allusions and covert references to other writers abound in the essays anyway. 'Most of us,' Mr Enright says, in defence of literary journalism, 'don't have more than two thousand words' worth to say on most topics.' Here we have an exception propounding a rule—and then sticking to it. It is hard to decide, finally, whether he is to be applauded or chided for doing so.

> *Dan Jacobson, "Enright's Articles," in* New Statesman, *Vol. 73, No. 1856, October 7, 1966, p. 523.*

MALCOLM BRADBURY

Enright is so witty, cogent and right-minded a commentator on literary practice, and believes so energetically in culture in a straightforward sense—'people listening to music and composing it, reading books and writing them'—that [in *Conspir-*

ators and Poets] he offers a heartening view of what the endeavour is about. I would only say, *too* heartening. An inheritor of the *Scrutiny* tradition (one of the best pieces here is an unusually *genuine* appreciation of what *Scrutiny* gave us), he indicates that the distinguishing fiery spirit, the giant energy, of that magazine is not his. . . . One consequence of his geniality is that the old *Scrutiny* concern with the overall decline of culture gets played down. What remains is—along with a suspicion of criticism and literary fashion—a kind of 'man's unconquerable mind' theory of literary continuance. . . .

Enright's famous inaugural at the University of Singapore . . . praises Robert Graves for his literary 'soldiering on', ignoring fashion to answer to the dark gods prompting literary creation. The debate about whether a 'culture' or autonomous creation produces art is old; Enright is not unsophisticated or obscurantist; but even soldiering on depends on the culture's letting it happen.

The answer to a bad cultural environment—an essay on Dylan Thomas shows how literary culture can grow grotesque, a poet be ruined by idolatrous second-rate critics and frantically Bohemian friends—is hardly none at all, hardly a lone-wolf theory of art. Most of the cautions are proper; Enright shows, in a review of Irving Howe's *Politics and the Novel,* all the decent and necessary grounds for protesting against the current admiration for ideology, and 'the historical process', in letters— 'do we have to lick the hand that is suffocating us?' Yet we may have to fight in the arena for literate and *literary* culture in order to be able to go on saying that.

But it would be wrong to leave the impression that this is a severe or even schematized book, even though this thread of attention runs through it and produces notable pieces on several other English lone-wolf poets—Wilfred Owen, D. H. Lawrence, Philip Larkin. For the other striking tendency is its eclecticism; or rather cosmopolitanism. This comes out in the writers surveyed—in, say, the strong interest in German literature (filled out even more solidly in an earlier book) which in turn seems to assist in Enright's effective analyses of other modern ironists, from Svevo to the usually much underestimated Mary McCarthy, to whom he does fine justice. It also comes out as a tone, an appreciative if at times nicely ironic attentiveness to various neo-decadents (Durrell, Cavafy, etc.), the charms and oddities of eastern sex manuals, and the problems of English literature on foreign shores. The good thing is that the appreciation can stop short when it has to; one can only express a humble human and critical debt of gratitude for his answer to Simone de Beauvoir's question, Must we burn Sade? (He asks, why not?) Like all good occasional writing, it widens enjoyment and awareness and halts before excesses; and for the sake of mental vigour and general literary *concern* the culture surely needs not less but more of it.

Malcolm Bradbury, "Too Nice for a Statesman?" in The Listener, *Vol. LXXVII, No. 1974, January 26, 1967, p. 139.*

PHILIP GARDNER

In a wry little poem, **"The Fairies,"** D. J. Enright neatly sums up his response to the foreign countries in which he has worked: . . .

> and the closet door swings eagerly open
> And out falls a skeleton with a frightful crash.

Enright's inaugural lecture at the University of Singapore, on which this poem presumably comments, aroused governmental hostility by criticizing the banning of jukeboxes. Such a skeleton appears to an outsider comparatively small; it is his poems about Japan that display to the full his talent for dropping bricks, for X-raying through the public "face" of a country to the bones beneath.

The "humanism," the concern for individuals rather than governments, that conditions this response first made its appearance in **Academic Year,** a novel based on Enright's experience as a lecturer at the University of Alexandria. . . . Enright reiterates this problem in his preface to **Poets of the 1950's,** and says that "the poet's task . . . is to get beneath the mud"—a task which requires "a fairly tough intelligence and an unwillingness to be deceived."

These qualities are admirably in evidence in the Japan poems which make up his volume **Bread Rather than Blossoms** (1956) and comprise the largest "ethnic group" in **Some Men are Brothers** (1960). The tensions of a Japan in transition, in the years 1953 to 1956 when Enright was a visiting lecturer at Kōnan University near Kobe, seem to have bred an equivalent tension in the poems which makes them a significant microcosm of his verse: certainly the fact that they far outnumber his poems about any of the five other countries in which he has taught indicates how deeply Japan got under his skin, and the pointed observations of his prose commentary **The World of Dew** confirm this diagnosis.

One looks in vain among these poems for testimonials to the Japan of the tourist brochures, the Japan of cherry-blossom, Mount Fuji, Kyōto temples, Nōh, Tea Ceremony, Flower Arrangement, and Zen. All these aspects appear, but as a background against which Enright asserts the human beings and the human values which, for him, they negate. (pp. 100-01)

What he remarks, and remarks on, is a Japan of overpopulation, poverty, landslides, suicides, streetwalkers rather than geisha, and

> Concentration campuses, throbbing with ragged uniforms
> And consumptive faces, in a land where the literacy
> Rate is over 100%, and the magazines
> Read each other in the crowded subways.

For Enright, the enigma of the mysterious and inscrutable East is so much obscurantism manufactured by a national vanity to distract attention from inadequacies that, if pointed out, could perhaps be dealt with. . . . In **The World of Dew** he describes Japan as "the testing ground of humanism. An excess of man and an insufficiency of man's means: if your faith in man survives this test, it is impregnable." This "faith in man" is the positive pole which prevents Enright's poems from seeming to bite the hand that fed him, however much they may have embarrassed his Japanese hosts; and it is apparent that it emerged not too damaged: "If the Japanese can finally liberate themselves from the past and survive the present, they should do great things. There is an unused fund of virtue in them."

Slightly condescending as those final sentences of **The World of Dew** sound, they still convey the tenderness, the sense of human likeness, which underlies Enright's frequent criticisms of Japan; the condescension is perhaps a naturally irritated reaction to the "smug conviction [of 'certain Japanese'] that they and their country are so peculiarly unique and so unfathomably deep that no foreigner can hope to write successfully about them." For Enright "nothing is exotic if you understand," and his poetry attempts to correct the overbalance of interest in *Japonaiserie* by stressing that the Japanese are not "human dolls" but "real people, real people, real people." . . . This humanity, this "fund of virtue" Enright finds preeminently in the ordinary Japanese people, rather than in the upper classes with their constricting code of decorum and "expected" behavior. . . . (pp. 102-03)

Politics is one ivory tower which seems to Enright to be blind to the fate of individuals; the other is Japanese tradition and Japanese art, with their stylization and precise rules which are for him a denial of the merely human and an attempt to pretend that the real physical world and its inconveniences are only an illusion of the unpurified mind. In **"A Kyōto Garden"** Enright describes the neatly-planned miniature world of Japanese landscape-gardening where everything is designed to purify the viewer and bring him the peace of an aesthetic contemplation in which "the eye need never be averted, nor the nose." This viewer, however, refuses to be so purified, and asks, as usual, the awkward question: "What feeds this corpulent moss, whose emptied blood, / what demon mouths await?" Peace of mind, where so many are debarred from it, is too conscience-pricking a privilege, and the only aspect of the garden which brings Enright any satisfaction is the one which connects it to the disorganized world outside and to the common man. . . . (pp. 105-06)

Like the Tea Ceremony, the aloof, aristocratic Nōh drama, with its extreme stylization of gesture and austere use of stage properties, is an art-form for which Enright has only a frigid regard: "it is art-cum-religion, a mixture which always fills me with misgivings." But even Kabuki, which he clearly enjoys, feeling that it has "that right kind of stylization which has not lost touch with its human origins," does not always succeed in reinterpreting for its audiences the life to which they return when they leave the theatre; their pity is reserved for the daughter they have seen on the stage, "sold into a brothel with a modest groan," and is quickly forgotten in the flurried scramble for a taxi home. . . . It seems to Enright that, in Japan, value is attached not to how closely art approximates to life, but to how near man comes to being himself a "work of conscious art." Just as the government declares certain historic temples or gardens to be "National Treasures," and therefore subject to special protection, so, when a man has refined himself into a consummate artist, will it extend the same dubious honor to him. **"Psalm 72: Man Declared a Treasure"** broadly satirizes this strange tendency. (pp. 106-07)

Although Enright's humanism was already present in his Egyptian novel, Japan, by providing the contrasting friction of a traditional formalism, sharpened and defined it in his poetry; it is in *Bread Rather than Blossoms* that we first truly find his characteristic subject-matter: the inescapable involvement of the man of conscience with the lives and sufferings of his fellows. His dissatisfaction with Japanese poetry springs from its apparent lack of this kind of concern: "in no western literature of any period has the gap between art and ordinary life been so wide."

But whether this gap becomes either too wide or too narrow depends on the poet's vigilantly maintaining within himself the precarious equilibrium of man and poet. This double loyalty is not easy: just as the Japanese poet errs in the direction of art for its own sake, so "a sharp reaction" against this orientation in favor of truth to life "can throw one into a narrow preoccupation with the more obvious hardships and miseries of contemporary Japan and so lead to an inordinate amount of moralizing." A warning, "intended for myself," against undue moralizing is conveyed in the poem **"Busy Body under a Cherry Tree."** In one sense the cherry tree may stand for much in Japan that is shallowly pictorial, "a tree / Whose fruit is eaten only by the eyes"; but it is undeniably beautiful, and in another sense symbolizes the enviable perfection which only that kind of art which is free of propaganda may attain. . . . (pp. 107-08)

Asked, in 1962, "Do you see this as a good or bad period for writing poetry?" Enright replied that "in a scientific and technological age, many writers are bound to feel doubts about the usefulness of [their] writing." One can see that the humanist poet, with his particularly strong sense of the real, objective existence of human problems—and his feeling that, while as a poet he may be called upon only to describe them, as a man he is partially responsible for helping in their solution—would begin to have misgivings about his art *qua* art. Certainly Enright's Japan poems show that his occasional hankerings for poetic purity are outweighed by his doubts about poetry itself: for him, literature is subordinate to life. (p. 109)

[The] attitude expressed here has important repercussions in the kind of poetry Enright's is: it explains his lack of emphasis on "style." Not that his poems, particularly those of his Japan period, have *no* style; but it certainly consists far less in quotable passages of fine writing than in an habitual ironic stance and a system of careful and often punning cross-references which heightens by repetition the significance of key phrases. For Enright too much "appliqué" style is felt to be a betrayal of subject-matter. . . . Enright is no mere journalist; but he does feel that poetry should be "*about* something" and that the something should be "people, preferably other people."

This being so, the humanist poet has a special duty not to "tart up" experience but render it straightforwardly so that the reader's response will be less one of admiration for poetic skill than one of sympathy for the person or situation described. Even "humanism," in the wrong hands, can become a mere gimmick; the Japanese poet whom Enright advises, in **"Changing the Subject,"** to deal with human themes instead of "the moon, and flowers, and birds and temples, / and the bare hills of the once holy city" dresses up his portrayal of "those who sleep in the subway" with so much rhetoric that the real becomes the artificial:

"Are they miners from Kyushu?" Neither he nor I will
    ever dare to ask them.
For we know they are not really human, are as apt
    themes for verse as the moon and the bare hills.

(pp. 109-10)

Despite . . . Enright's scruples about the possible pitfalls of humanist poetry, one's final judgment is decidedly not that he falls into them. Rather one admires the unending effort to balance the respective claims of life and art, realizing that the emphasis placed on the former demands of the poet considerable artistic self-denial without bringing the man the compensating sense of having solved the problems of the world in which he lives. (p. 110)

> *Philip Gardner, "D. J. Enright Under the Cherry Tree," in* Contemporary Literature, *Vol. 9, No. 1, Winter, 1968, pp. 100-11.*

ALAN BROWNJOHN

[Enright's] personal commitment has been profound, and often courageous. But it has resulted in his verse becoming a sustained lament for the ineffectualness of art—'man's slight non-murderousness'—in a world controlled by politics and economics. It is hard to see how much more can be got out of this theme after the present volume [*Unlawful Assembly*], although the writing is as sensitive and likeable as ever. *Unlawful Assembly* repeats the topics and attitudes of several earlier books, with little new added and with rather less energy (the poems are less observant and pointed than they used to be). Enright continues to write appealing, but slightly tired, accounts of places and politics, casting wry glances at cultural foibles, shrugging off causes with sad, cultivated weariness. **'Writing Poetry in a Hotel Room'** ironically echoes the proud detachment of some Fifties poetry. . . . One trouble is that the irony has become an automatic response. No one writes on these things with a more compassionate perception, but it is sad to see an interesting talent standing still. (pp. 362-63)

> *Alan Brownjohn, "Repetitions," in* New Statesman, *Vol. 76, No. 1958, September 20, 1968, pp. 362-63.**

GAVIN EWART

[In *Unlawful Assembly* the] conversational, ironical tone of poems that are more like footnotes to experience than anything more ambitious, is immensely pleasing. . . . Commonsense and humour run through this whole collection ('ordinariness has much to be said for it'). Control is good, the effects are achieved—though sometimes with a certain amount of discursiveness (**'Processional'**) and sometimes with too much of the footnote's curtness (**'Cultural Freedom'**). Very enjoyable are **'After The Riots'**, **'Roman Reasons'** (about Enobarbus) and **'What became of What-was-his-name?'**, the miniature equivalent of a Graham Greene novel set in a Police State. Best of all, perhaps, is **'Map'**, where the material is compressed into a stricter form. Enright is not what anyone would call a 'soaring' poet, and his technical skill as a writer of verse is not dazzling (nor perhaps would he want it to be); but those critics who give him the brush-off have been reading too much pretentious nonsense. (pp. 94-5)

> *Gavin Ewart, "Old Scores," in* London Magazine, *Vol. 8, No. 9, December, 1968, pp. 92-5.**

MARTIN SEYMOUR-SMITH

The best . . . of this year's books on Shakespeare is D. J. Enright's *Shakespeare and the Students*. . . . It is relaxed and non-theoretical. It arises not only from teaching Shakespeare (as its author explains) but from an experience of life and poetry. There is no mystical pursuit of Shakespeare, no embarrassing attempt to expose a Christian or neo-Platonic "pattern": the approach is in the essentially human terms of psychology and poetry. It is truly eclectic (not in the now pejorative bibliographical sense), and almost unerring in its selection of what is most moving; its explanations stimulate where they provoke disagreement. There have been few commentaries so full of new insights. Perhaps this is because Mr. Enright is modest, has no theories, has not made up his mind about Shakespeare—is, in short, a true sceptic. (p. 63)

> *Martin Seymour-Smith, "Whose Shakespeare?" in* Encounter, *Vol. XXXIV, No. 6, June, 1970, pp. 56-8, 60-1, 63.**

ALAN BROWNJOHN

[Enright's *Daughters of Earth* is] a better volume than he has recently given us, more varied and less repetitive, more obliquely subtle yet also more trenchant. And the pictures of life in Singapore and Japan in his [*Foreign Devils*] . . . seem sharper than usual; and name names.

Enright is still writing with a despairing smile about a teacher's failure to communicate, about the pretensions of governments and the miseries of peoples in poor or 'developing' countries (**'Tourist Promotion'**, **'Board of Selection'**), and about hanging on, despite everything, to a faith in some humane western values. And no attitude, whether strenuously ideological, or high-minded, or just innocent, is ever right or untarnished. But in these two selections, the manner, the subjects and the treatment all seem to have gained a fresh lease of energy now that he has settled again in England after his long years teaching Eng. Lit. overseas. He is negative, pessimistic; yet by shunning false hopefulness his poetry manages to define an area of basic decency. His scope is wider in this latest work, partly so because of some personal poems which are both harder and more rewarding than the straight political satires. *Daughters of Earth* represents a good—and an enjoyable—shift of direction for a very talented writer who was getting bogged down. (p. 842)

> *Alan Brownjohn, "Change Direction," in* New Statesman, *Vol. 83, No. 2152, June 16, 1972, pp. 842-43.**

P. N. FURBANK

D. J. Enright is a poet preoccupied with responsibilities. He is an itinerant and committed, if lazy moralist, not positively seeking to squeeze out a moral from experience, but doggedly prepared to confront any moral that obtrudes itself on him—and thousands do. His sytle reflects this moral stance. The poems [in *Daughters of Earth*] spar about rather loosely to begin with, without especial finesse, before going in to deliver their upper-cut. This they deliver with great precision: the punches of this Forsterian 'connect' all right, sometimes with his own chin. Indeed he sticks his chin out on our behalf: in no egotistic spirit, but on the assumption that it might as well be his as another's—which is a good definition of humanism. 'Why are the faces here so lined?' he asks, in **'Public Bar'**, one of his most funny and telling poems. The faces' owners haven't, like critics and intellectuals, agonised over complex issues or tragic art. . . . Such single-moral poems, in forms so casual and in language so relaxed—as, relatively, it is even here—can only rise to a limited kind of beauty. You may wonder if they are poetry at all. But whatever the nature of their virtue, it is sterling and obvious. And, oddly, it is Enright's bringing the same trick off time and time again that, far from creating monotony, is his most convincing credential. (p. 375)

> *P. N. Furbank, "Knockabouts," in* The Listener, *Vol. 88, No. 2269, September 21, 1972, pp. 374-75.**

MYRA HINMAN

The four separate essays which comprise [*Shakespeare and the Students*] . . . will not be of great interest to serious critics of Shakespeare. Professor Enright presumably intends his leisurely discussions for students but does not indicate the level of sophistication of his audience, and his account of difficulties encountered by Singaporean students suggests that some of the misunderstanding he wishes to dispel has a cultural as well as a dramatic basis. Students at any level might well be confused by the many snippets of critical opinion used out of context and without adequate elaboration. . . . Moreover the critics cited, being almost exclusively British, lend a parochial flavor to the essays. (p. 337)

The emphasis on character analysis, in the tradition of A. C. Bradley's criticism, is obviously limiting here, but more serious is the divorce of these characters—in proving them "real people"—from their dramatic origins. He dismisses imagery, symbolism (which he goes out of his way, almost stubbornly, to condemn), and poetic effects as devices for realizing characters and their meanings within dramatic contexts of the individual plays, as well as a variety of dramatic conventions and Shakespeare's characteristic use of them that govern both the reliability and the significance of speeches. . . . Character analysis when too far extended beyond the normal artistic limits of a work becomes isolated from genuine aesthetic concerns, and can create problems, as these essays sometimes seem to do, that are not encountered when figures are seen as part of a complex dramatic whole.

It is hard to see how this work, though it sometimes provides useful insights, has any superiority over several better balanced guides already available to the student reader. The scene by scene organization, putting the reader at the mercy of "the author as conversationalist," sacrifices originality, a working hypothesis, and lacks the structure to direct expectation—the systematic presentation of an idea that invites new appreciation or understanding significant in scope or depth to merit a whole book. (pp. 337-38)

> *Myra Hinman, in a review of "Shakespeare and the Students," in* Shakespeare Quarterly, *Vol. XXIV, No. 3, Summer, 1973, pp. 337-38.*

WILLIAM WALSH

[D. J. Enright's] four novels, which appeared between 1955 and 1965, while they have had considerable critical acclaim, have received less than their due attention from the reading public. All these novels are set abroad, in Alexandria, the imaginary island of Velo, or Bangkok or Japan. No doubt this fits in with the simple biographical fact that Enright has spent a considerable part of his career abroad as a Professor of English Literature in various Far Eastern universities. He undoubtedly knows what he is talking about. But it is also in keeping with his reflective, poetically sensitive and coolly registering mind. He is a writer who believes that 'civilization consists in the diminution of human tears', and his response to Far Eastern life contains a quite unsentimental pity for the harsh life of the poor, a cool antagonism for affectation and power whether of academics or politicians, and the small and human virtue of hope, offered by Enright with a characteristic mischief—or flippancy, as some call it.

'The four novels I have published are all really travel books, I am afraid' is Enright's own comment on his fiction. This is an unduly modest dismissal of work in which the execution is finished, the writing light and elegant, the comedy smoothly evolved and the product of an individual point of view, the characters clearly projected, the values humane and coherent, the effect tartly different and original. And yet Enright's deprecating remark makes a point of substance about his first novel, *Academic Year* (1955). It is not so much that it has to do with travel as with a peculiar consequence of a certain kind of travel, that which makes a man an expatriate. Alexandria, the university, the academic year, the people well off or poor, that is, the place and its life, are seen through the eyes of three expatriates, Brett, a cultural officer destined for success though liable to bring disaster to others, Bacon, the long-serving university teacher, 'a rather unofficial kind of man', and another, younger university teacher, the spiritually youthful Packet. On each of the three the city makes its own impression. Brett sees it as *different*, sometimes horribly different, in its cruelty, violence, lawlessness, venality; Packet sees what is unique in it and mostly good; Bacon, the failure, the good man ruined, sees what is common or universal in it. Their separate views, wittily and sensitively articulated, together make a wholeness of vision and construct a place complete and human in its life, suffering and comedy.

The blend of sad and comic is something one is conscious of throughout *Academic Year,* as is the manner which never fudges the former or misses what is productive of the latter. The effect of the delirious Egyptian city on the three principals is seen with a kind of ironic sagacity or sardonic gentleness. The writer's personal tone is unmistakable throughout. It is one which works from the imagination not towards the document, but it never interferes with, its sensibility seems wholly in sympathy with, the accurate, sympathetic, unfussy registration of experience. (pp. 77-8)

Wit and then charity: this is the combination of qualities rare in the contemporary world, which marks Enright's work in the novel. It may be that it relaxes on occasion into witticism and sentiment, though not I think in *Academic Year,* but at its best, at its usual best, it is a most original marriage of intelligence and feeling. (p. 83)

Generosity of attitude, alertness to discrepancy, the insight of the poet, the knowledge of the inhabitant, the detachment of the expatriate—these things make Enright not only a fine observer of place and society but also a most capable fashioner of character. Character, the steady shape of the person in all his connections and relations, is something Enright's four novels are remarkably rich in. . . . [I am] aware in Enright's poetry, for all its spry contemporary spirit, of a traditional wholesomeness of feeling, and of a steadiness of moral centre. In the same traditional way he sees the individuality of the person in the stability of character, his universality in the nature he shares with others. Enright apprehends existence through its consistent shapes and particulars and he works towards a vision of human nature by means of specific forms and humble everyday instances. More modest than those who imitate Lawrence without his genius, Enright is concerned with hewing ordinary practical coal rather than with uncovering the mysterious substance of carbon, or he is concerned with the coal first and the carbon no more than indirectly.

Heaven Knows Where (1957) is Enright's *Utopia*. Packet, jobless after Egypt, answers an advertisement for a teacher of English Literature in the Far Eastern island of Velo. The King of the island is devoted to the *Anatomy of Melancholy* and he accompanies the action with a calculatedly ambiguous and Burtonian commentary upon the life of the community and in particular on the disaster which overtakes his rational and delightful society when it is subject to a managerially modern, political take-over. The inhabitants of Velo represent, or are, the quiet, the amused, the merely human, in contrast to the intellectuals and power maniacs who invade them. The only response the Velonians can make to the overwhelming military power of the Derthans is to fold them into a melting embrace—

and it does indeed melt their power away. This pointed parable or analogue of a situation daily to be seen in the newspaper—at least half of it is, the invasion part—confirms in one a sense one has of Enright as a writer with a peculiarly naked sense of actuality. He has the enviably unusual gift of being able to see what is there for his eyes to see. At the same time as he registers the fact he brings to bear upon it a richly orchestrated feeling for human value, at once tender, commonsensical, and ironic.

To be able to see, to evoke, to judge, to be able to let one's fantasy race, though within the limits of a deeper sanity, to have a wild appetite for the ridiculous checked only by an unpatronising generosity—these are certainly gifts helpful to a writer of an unschematic Utopian parable. If we add that the account of the imaginary island is conducted in a prose as well-bred and grave, as supple as Swift's, though without any of the intimations of loathing and disgust which his carries, we can understand how effective and shapely and entertaining *Heaven Knows Where* is. (pp. 83-4)

The sunniness and certainties of *Heaven Knows Where* give way in *Insufficient Poppy* (1960) to a bleaker and more troubled obscurity. There is the same fluent and lissom idiom but it draws on harsher sources. It is an effective—much less reflective than *Heaven Knows Where*—an effective, sad novel, closer in mood to Enright's poetry than the lighter *Academic Year* and *Heaven Knows Where*. The sadness which disturbs the even life of three friends in Bangkok, one, the narrator, Roderick, the manager of a family business dribbling away into nothing, who makes a little money by exporting live snakes, another a teacher of English, Harry, who is given the working-class, vaguely nonconformist, Trade Union background attributed to Packet in the first two novels, and another a weird ex-film-cowboy, Colorado Kid, a ruined, inexplicable hulk of a man, is not the small sadness we find every day in every breath, but a large and brutal sadness when one of the friends, Harry, is shot. This calamity shockingly ends the mild pleasures of the trio. . . . *Insufficient Poppy* is remarkable (as indeed *Academic Year* was in respect of Alexandria) for the tactful indirection with which the life of the place and its people is evoked. There are no set-pieces, no *longueurs*, no explicit descriptions, but we come to have, no doubt because it is refracted through human beings, the clearest vision of the life and the firmest feeling for its people. (p. 85)

Insufficient Poppy is a disturbing, painful book, at moments even, in the second and third parts, throbbing with intense personal anguish. But a certain blurring of the design and too explicit declaration of bitterness make it a less achieved and more fragmentary success than *Figures of Speech* (1965), which with *Academic Year* is, in my view, his best novel. *Figures of Speech* is decidedly more active as a story, the characters are more engaging, the fiction altogether more embodied and appealing. There are only three characters, in effect, another English university teacher, George Lester, Chung Lu, a high-minded young Chinese scholar, and Mattie, a crisp girl on vacation from Singapore, who displays both the elegance and the forcefulness characteristic of the educated young Chinese woman. The love affair of the two Chinese and the gorgeously comic adventures of George are plaited together with nimble and natural smoothness. There is also an abrasive treatment of George's relations with, and betrayal by, the British Council and the Embassy. The conduct of both towards their own nationals, especially when these are writers, poets and similar dandruffed types, shows unbridled cautiousness competing with

unabashed stupidity and composes a not very admirable if highly comic model of British diplomatic and cultural *moeurs*. In addition there is a characteristically sharp and perceptive account of the Japanese mode of entertaining foreigners, which is a marvellous piece of dancing humour and social analysis. It is hard to define the effect of this remarkable book in which an unaffected fastidiousness of spirit is accompanied by the most open and inclusive generosity of response, and in which both are conveyed in an idiom utterly personal and devastatingly witty.

It is the union of flippant and forgiving, wit and pity, in Enright's fiction which gives it its intensely personal flavour of blended tartness and kindness, or, given the Eastern provenance of so much of it, of its sweetness and sourness. We find this double savour throughout the narrative, in the tone, in the imagery, in the reflections which jink suddenly from melancholy to mordant. . . . And of course we sense this sweetness and sourness most in the characters. . . . Chung Lu's transformation as a result of his travels and of his feeling for the attractive and rational Mattie, from his cool state of Chinese superiority and his scholarly dedication to verse, calligraphy and correctness in thought and behaviour, into that of agitated and nervous lover, is shown with a balanced, unpatronising sympathy and a clear eye for every absurdity. Chung Lu is perhaps the most complete and satisfying, as he is the most graceful, character in Enright's fiction. Authentic and ancient in tradition, fine in quality, magnificently Chinese, he is also seen as instinct with a common and instant humanity. (pp. 87-8)

Enright's novels are, in a very special way, *intelligent*. By intelligence I mean that liveliness of faculty which combines a measure of wisdom with a sense for the concrete occasion and an intuition which effortlessly brings a cogently human standard to bear on the grasped situation, and it hardly seems necessary to stress why this capacity daily appears more rare and more desirable. This intelligence speaks in all the material of his fiction, just as it does in the actual writing, which joins a lithe, light-footed strength to sensitivity, and sardonic mockery to affectionate recognition. His account of the expatriate life of teachers, their friends, lovers and superiors in Bangkok, Singapore, Japan, is poetically evocative of the places, shrewd in its analysis of them, and at the same time quick with the sense of calamities, public and private, either waiting to trip us up or thronging to mob us. Enright is full of pity for others but wary about self-pity for himself. And he is always aware of the sanitary necessity of laughter. So often in official bad books himself, he feels for the victims of power, and who of us isn't one of those sometime? If intelligence is the principal character of—perhaps the principal character *in*—Enright's novels, the quality most marked in their method and presentation, their effect is to cherish and to foster in circumstances of brutal antagonism the remnants of humanity. (pp. 88-9)

William Walsh, in his D. J. Enright: Poet of Humanism, *Cambridge University Press, 1974, 107 p.*

NICHOLAS MOSLEY

D. J. Enright, in *Paradise Illustrated*, has written 34 short poems on the myth of the Fall of Man, and 20 more from a similar vein. They are wry, dry, succinct poems; often with a throw-away feel about them, leaving the reader wondering whether he has ducked, or has received, a punch line. Adam and Eve appear as a humorous, somewhat sexy couple who might be sharing, as it were, an apple in a pub. God is one of those omniscient landlords. . . .

These characters get through the opening-hours of sin, knowledge, alienation, labour; always ready with a quip, a self-defensive technique, a sort of Cockney or Jewish humour. As a model for enduring a fallen life, this is not a bad theology. There is no grandeur. This, too, seems reasonable—in the light of the one simple story.

What Adam and Eve seem to have learned from their eating of the tree of knowledge is a way not with things but with words: they have a penchant for punning, for double-entendres. . . .

This is a theology for a clever, self-conscious people who feel they do not have time for that more complex story about redemption, but who still are not going to be done down by a fall that has left them clever without much to be clever about. They have discovered a sort of karate technique of mockery to defend themselves: they can knock out with a funny kick a suggestion that there might be things to be solemn about. It is a theology for Don Juans having a good time in hell—away from all those stuffed-shirt angels.

> *Nicholas Mosley, "An Apple in a Pub," in* The Listener, *Vol. 100, No. 2567, July 6, 1978, p. 29.*

ALAN BROWNJOHN

Comic updatings of old tales rarely work well, whereas serious ones get away with it too often. D. J. Enright has made it clear that his intentions in *Paradise Illustrated* are at least fairly serious, but he is much too witty and clever a writer to let solemn truths about the Fall of Man drop too heavily from his typewriter. The result, in this long sequence about Adam and Eve, is an uncomfortable mixture: some of the jokes come off. . . . And some of them sink to depths of homeliness plumbed more often by Jewish comedians than poets. This is a surprising misadventure from a writer who redeems himself at the end of the book with some "Other Poems" which show him in top form: mordantly satirising authoritarianism in ex-colonial places, chastising modern biographers, detecting the dangers in the deification of "opinion". . . . (p. 67)

> *Alan Brownjohn, "Heads, Tongues & Spirits," in* Encounter, *Vol. LI, No. 5, November, 1978, pp. 63-9.**

PHILIP TOYNBEE

['**A Faust Book**'] is full of cunning literary allusions and learned puns (of which I probably missed as many as I recognised) and the perfect reader of Enright's book would be a widely read don with something of his own donnish turn of mind.

Considered only in these terms Enright's '**Faust**' is a very funny book. He has a great knack for sliding from the sixteenth century into our own and back again; and much of the humour comes from comic and pointed anachronisms. But this is plainly a book about 1979, and the trappings of the sixteenth century are really no more than a device for a sharp satirical glare at our own times. . . .

[A] careful reading of Enright's '**Faust**' shows that traditional morality is a scarlet thread running through the work from start to finish. Because the Faust legend is set as much in hell as on earth—wherever Mephistopheles is, he creates a hell all

around him—and partly, perhaps, because it is notoriously easier to describe hell than heaven, most of this poem is about the pains, follies and vices of mankind. . . .

Some of the jokes fall flat: sometimes Mr Enright is too keen for the applause of the Senior Common Room: but this is a good poem, and a serious one. The best of the jokes are serious which certainly doesn't mean that they are not the sort we laugh at. It seems to me that the message, however drily delivered, is that hope is a virtue, which should be practised in our own time as in every other.

> *Philip Toynbee, "A Faust for Our Time," in* The Observer, *October 7, 1979, p. 39.*

ALAN BROWNJOHN

It seemed well-trodden ground for D. J. Enright to cover in *Paradise Illustrated,* his sequence of poems updating the Fall; I thought the joke had been better done by other, less sophisticated, artists. Now, in *A Faust Book,* he has followed the exhortations of Heine and Valéry to do your own Faust, and come up with an altogether subtler, funnier and more sustained set of personal variations on the legend. His Faust and Mephistopheles are, for one thing, not put so relentlessly through all the latest hoops: the story seems to have compelled Enright to treat it a bit more on its own terms; perhaps a moral in that, about its more convincing relevance to our own times. . . . *A Faust Book* moves steadily through the Faust tale from beginning to end, getting most mileage out of its potential for modern academic and political satire; and using a considerable variety of forms. Enright perennially defines the boundaries of human achievement—of human decency and honesty—by outlining the cynical plausibility of the forces of darkness. In the past, he's rarely done the positive side with much conviction since his first two or three books; but his *Faust* comes much nearer to the scope and range of his best earlier work than "middle" Enright, which was always funny, and right, yet infallibly depressing and sometimes repetitive. (p. 67)

> *Alan Brownjohn, "An Unprovincial Province," in* Encounter, *Vol. LIV, No. 1, January, 1980, pp. 64-8, 70.**

DERWENT MAY

The earliest of [Enright's] *Collected Poems* go back more than 30 years, to the end of the 1940s; but already in them you find that absolutely characteristic move away from a feeling of his own to a thought about somebody else—and then another thought. . . .

Enright has lived abroad, teaching English literature, for much of his life, and he has written poems about Egyptians, Japanese, Germans, Thais, and the Malays and Chinese of Singapore. He has seen a lot of suffering and oppression; but he has always tried to picture it in individual terms, turning a situation from facet to facet to catch it in as many lights as possible.

He can write as well about an Asian prime minister, listing the names of students who are to be arrested that night and for a moment seeing his own past reflected in their lives, as he can about a 13-year-old Japanese bootblack who killed himself with rat poison because he had a headache. ('Kazuo—who found rat poison cheaper than aspirin,' Enright says in the last line of that poem—again remembering exactly what poverty means.)

It might seem that this is a very impersonal poetry, and indeed Enright has been admonished for that. . . . But of course the truth is that you feel his personal presence in all of his poems. It takes a very special art to put across such uncomfortable observations as Enright does without seeming priggish; and he does it precisely by his disarming personality, so funny, and so conscious of his own weaknesses, without ever losing sight of the point he wants to make. I spoke of his wit and his scrupulousness as though they were different things; but often they are one and the same, the humour lying in the very way in which he sees and reports some fresh implication. . . .

There is one [poem] I have always especially liked: the very Proustian **'Words',** where in a new country, where even the moon looks strange, this perpetual traveller begs: 'Words, tell me where I am!' I don't know if he feels his plea has ever been answered. But I don't think there is any English poet writing today whose words have done more to tell us where we are.

Derwent May, "Scrupulous Wit," in The Listener, *Vol. 106, No. 2728, September 24, 1981, p. 347.*

GAVIN EWART

Anybody at all interested in English poetry should read [D. J. Enright's *Collected Poems*]. It has in it the best autobiographical sequence written this century: **'The Terrible Shears.'** . . . It also contains, in the short pieces, some of the wittiest and wryest comment on the modern world to be found in the verse of our time. . . .

The intelligence, the irony and the wit are there from the first. . . . Puns appear throughout, good ('The hot iron of the railroad hisses in the air') and not so good ('The Metropolitan Water Bawd'). Yet the descriptions of Egypt and Japan often have a sensuous quality, and pathos is not beyond him. . . .

Enright isn't a lyrical writer, nor is he fluent as some poets are. He isn't strong on form, the rhymes happen when they want to. **'A Pleasant Walk'** is the one exception, where the stanzas stand like solid citizens and make one wish that this happened more often, though with him the truly free poems are often the most satisfying. Nursery rhymishness is common in the early verse. . . .

The tone is low-key, conversational, full of lightness and lack of optimism. . . . The judgment is only occasionally at fault. **'The Quagga,'** for example, is a fine doomful poem but its last line arrives with a terrific thump of expectedness. Verbalism sometimes gets the upper hand. . . .

From these minor faults **'The Terrible Shears'** (1973) don't suffer. They belonged in fact to his grandfather, a gardener in a public park. The 70 short poems are little cameos from Enright's early life, a working-class childhood in the Twenties and Thirties. Pathos occurs again here, a quality conspicuously lacking in contemporary verse of any intellectual standing, though attempted often in the poems on the deaths of budgies submitted for Poetry Competitions, and so does humour. . . . **'Paradise Illustrated'** (1978), the next sequence, lacks the personal emotional involvement (I feel). It relies of course heavily on knowledge of Milton, an extended academic *blague*—though many of the jokes are good, with some mickey-taking of Milton's style. . . . Is some of it slight, too easy an irony?

'A Faust Book' (1979), on the other hand, is sometimes laboured. The German Rustic of the peasants reminds me of

Benny Hill as a Swedish nymphomaniac. Theology was of absorbing interest to the Middle Ages; it's less interesting to us. Even the 'New Poems' that end the book are concerned with theology, the *causa causans*, etc.—**'The Retired Life Of The Demons'** is not a bad example. **'Guest'** and **'Explanation'** are actively good. The talent is alive and kicking and there are, for certain, many fine poems to come.

Gavin Ewart, "Very Much Alive and Kicking," in The Observer, *September 27, 1981, p. 32.*

ANDREW MOTION

The 'Movement' was doubtless a force in post-war poetry. But was it—as Robert Conquest, one of its leaders, claimed—unanimously empirical, ironical, and insular? Some of its members were incurably romantic, soft-hearted and keen on 'abroad'. Even D. J. Enright, who edited the Movement anthology *Poets of the 1950s*, was never absolutely faithful to the preferred neutral tone, and a reexamination which begins with him makes the Movement look rather a hotch-potch.

The bulk of his early poems are set in and around Egypt or the Far East, and respond to the exotic strangeness of those places with a good deal of flamboyance. . . . Equally, though, Enright's first two or three books [reprinted in *Collected Poems*] catch him in the act of developing an acute social conscience—and his view of the world becomes bleaker, his use of language becomes increasingly astringent. The suffering he encountered in Japan after the war had a particularly potent effect. Some cases of hardship were so appalling that to write about them at all seemed a kind of insult. . . . Others were more approachable, providing that the diction, form and attitude of his poems were kept scrupulously self-effacing. . . . The result was to turn him into a more typically Movement writer, and a more boring one, than he seems to have originally intended. . . .

Once his humane impulses had shaped a plain style, they hung on to it. There has never been any doubt his sensitivity to the sadness of the creatures, but neither has there been much chance of it being realised in terms other than the flatly colloquial or the wryly ironic. . . .

During the 1960s Enright seems to have felt increasingly frustrated by these self-imposed restrictions on tone and theme. In *Unlawful Assembly* (1968) he even admitted to having 'Nothing much to write about': 'Love and death' seemed impossibly 'grand and soporific themes'. In the '70s, though, he sought to solve his dilemma by making a virtue of the almost exclusively chatty, anecdotal mode he had allowed himself to develop.

The Terrible Shears (1973) retails incidents from his childhood with a dogged lack of drama; *Paradise Illustrated* (1978) tells the story of Adam and Eve as a series of quips, jokes and feeble satires; and *A Faust Book* (1979) recreates Faust and Mephistopheles as a couple of buffers pottering around refusing to deal adequately with the 'grand themes' that history thrusts upon them. All three sequences testify to a compassionate sense of the world's misery, without showing much inclination to make us feel it on our pulses. (p. 20)

Andrew Motion, "Limited Company," in New Statesman, *Vol. 102, No. 2638, October 9, 1981, pp. 20-1.*

PATRICK SWINDEN

[*Collected Poems*] is a severely pruned collection of poems written by Enright between 1953 and now. What picture of the poet emerges from them? Academic, humanist, traveller. (p. 85)

But most of all a single scene comes to mind. The poet is at his desk in some far-flung corner of south-east Asia. It is night, so the desk lamp is switched on. The poet continues to write, as insects gather under the lamp. Then the lizards come and eat the insects. The insects think the poet is punishing them by feeding them to a spring-jawed dragon. That is the scenario of **'The faithful'**. It ends:

> It isn't difficult to be a god.
> You hang your lantern out,
> Sink yourself in your own concerns
> And leave the rest to the faithful.
>
> (pp. 85-6)

And that is a large part of Enright's theme. It isn't difficult to be a god. But what about being a *just* god, with all the moral casuistries to try to make intelligible? After all, in the Western tradition, that's what a god is expected to do—which is something different from administering arbitrary punishment and rewards. In point of fact, Enright is not a god and his lamp is not a spring-jawed dragon. But he *has* hung his lantern out, he has sunk himself in his own concerns, and it can fairly be said that it's up to the faithful to interpret that as they please— or don't please. In other words, it's not difficult to have yourself taken for a god—by somebody. Prime Ministers do, cultural officials do, even the gulli-gulli man does—by his chicken. If he is not a god, he is at least 'the greatest of beings'. But there is an exception. And that is the poets. They are *not* gods. They have to work from the opposite end of the theological-cultural spectrum. As Enright says in **'Cultural freedom'**, 'You need defeat's sour / Fuel for poetry. / Its motive power / Is powerlessness.'

Powerlessness, for example, to prevent the deaths of children— which must be to the God in the sky what the deaths of ants are to the god at the typist's desk [in **'Hands off, foreign devil'**], or students to unscrupulous Oriental politicians [in **'Prime Minister'**]. Much of the *Collected Poems* reads like a gloss on the famous words Ivan Karamazov spoke to his brother Alyosha: 'If all must suffer to pay for the eternal harmony, what have the children to do with it?' (p. 86)

But it happens. Children die in their tens of thousands, and nowhere better to witness it than among the Asian poor. One of the very first poems in the book is entitled **'On the death of a child'**, followed by the better, because more tersely descriptive, poem from Enright's second volume, **'The short life of Kazuo Yamomoto'**. Kazuo, who 'wanted to die because of a headache', a headache shared, in the metaphorical sense (which makes all the difference) by 'the great ones', the politicians, the gods, grappling with notions of Sovereignty and Subjection. (pp. 86-7)

Unusual for a poet these days to have got his priorities right: gods, poets, the deaths of little children. In other words suffering, responsibility for suffering, and what is to be done about it, how one is to write about it. So far as the poet is concerned, the most important thing is not to confuse pity as a response to all this with pity as a subject to write about. . . . [Where poems] are good they are salutary reminders of the relativity of suffering, which can sound harsh, uncharitable. The poem from *The Terrible Shears,* for example, about a schoolgirl run over by a bus, having her leg amputated but passing her exams

and getting married. Not a bad life, in the poet's judgement. No secret police dragging you out of bed in the middle of the night, no children stabbed or having their brains dashed out, no one starving to death. (p. 87)

So it isn't difficult to be a god, but it's just as easy to be the victim of a god. Probably we are all both at once from time to time in our lives. The almost infinite gradation from ants to angels is bound to place us in the power of some strange being, and make us seem like some strange being to someone in our power. And when we drop out of the chain, we are soon replaced, our absence not noticed for long—as Enright reflects on leaving one of many houses he has occupied in Thailand or Singapore. . . .

In the earlier volumes, Enright places his insights in vividly realised, more highly coloured, circumstances. The Egyptian poems in particular make greater use of landscape and atmosphere than survives into the poems set in the Far East, which realise the scene more obliquely, more sketchily. Here the emphasis falls heavily in one sense, lightly in another, on the moral perception—tricked into life as much by teasing metrical games as by a fragment of a scene, or an object, or the tail-end of an event seen through the corner of the eye. (p. 88)

Later, we discover Enright making a great deal more use of literary reference and religious myth to sharpen his perceptions into pain, pity and suffering. In *Paradise Illustrated* and *A Faust Book* he reduces religious symbolism to a convenient method of stating the old questions in a way that allows new connections to be made between them. . . .

Enright remains what he calls 'a lurching humanist', but with a developed idea of how such a person, such a poet, might make use of the vantage points offered by the Creation story, or the Faust myth. What he is looking at from those vantage points is still the secular reality of human suffering. 'Thus Faust did good, as he wanted and / little good came of it'— the link between 'do-gooding' and 'good done' is clarified by the Marlovian and Goethean references. . . .

With Musil, then, Enright 'inclines to a chronic irony', but not one that he can flatter himself will lead to the downfall of anything so portentous as the Austro-Hungarian Empire (see **'Pains'**). Rather than cause, it comments on another kind of fall—what in Biblical terms he envisages as the Fall of man, into sin and death, pain and suffering, and finding that it isn't difficult to be a god, but that poets mustn't be. Poets must always be on the look-out for gods, both inside and outside themselves. For gods are really words, formed out of god knows what fears and apprehensions, and then masquerading as real—in useful stories, myths and legends. Now the stories must be used to return us to ourselves, to expose and disentangle the moral conundrums that words express, but conceal and distort too. (p. 89)

Patrick Swinden, in a review of "Collected Poems," in Critical Quarterly, *Vol. 24, No. 3, Autumn, 1982, pp. 85-90.*

JOHN GROSS

There is something to be said against collecting old book-reviews—but not when they are as good as D. J. Enright's. Flaubert and Heinrich Böll, 'Earthly Powers' and 'A Dictionary of Catch Phrases,' 'The Golden Lotus' and E. B. White: coming from most reviewers, the pieces assembled in **'A Mania for Sentences'** would simply represent so many fares picked up at the rank. But in Enright's case they cohere, bound together by a consistent (and consistently enlivening) approach and a distinctive tone of voice, and by the mixture of subtlety tempered by common sense (or *vice versa*) which makes him one of the most rewarding critics currently plying his trade.

He is also a master of the witty formulation, and the book would be worth reading for the jokes alone. . . .

Some of Enright's finest comic moments are at the expense of criticism (other people's criticism) which has lost touch with reality. His wit also serves as a teaching-aid, since he sees his own brand of criticism as 'practical'—by which he means that it is of the kind which attempts to be of practical use to readers 'by describing, drawing out, comparing, concurring or quarrelling with the work it discusses.' All of which he himself does to excellent effect. . . . On the other hand he does not seem to have any very strong urge to erect a large self-aggrandising theory of literature. . . .

What he does have is a keen sense of history, and more particularly of what history feels like at the receiving end. He warms to the Good Soldier Svejk; he writes amusingly about Chinese immigrants in cheap fiction (Fu Manchu and Charlie Chan) and thoughtfully about Chinese immigrants in complicated fact (the memoirs of Maxine Hong Kingston). He is also dedicated to the proposition that it takes more than one culture to make a world, while recognising just how tricky a business crossing a cultural boundary can be. . . .

A small bundle of essays, among the best in the collection, are concerned with language. A contentious subject just now, when usage has a much harder time battling against abusage than it did in the old hierarchical days (whose language is it anyway?), when idioms are unmanned in the name of sexual equality and students of 'verbal aggression' are pushing back the frontiers of four-letter scholarship. As you would expect, Enright takes a sensible undogmatic view of things. Not all change, he reminds us, is decay, and some decay turns into new life; but slovenly is slovenly, and illiterate is illiterate, and a good deal of what passes itself off as change is mere floundering around.

One opportunity which he does not fail to seize is presented by a dictionary of obscure and unusual words. . . .

There are many other miscellaneous pleasures in **'A Mania for Sentences'**—if I had to single out one, it would be the funny and touching account of the ways in which a group of American five-year-olds responded to the stories told them in kindergarten, a reminder (among other things) of how well Enright has written about his own childhood in his sequence of poems **'The Terrible Shears.'** Like everything else in the collection, it sets you thinking; like everything else it bears witness to the rival claims of fantasy and reality, and to the art through which they can sometimes be reconciled.

John Gross, "Mister Enlight," in The Observer, *July 24, 1983, p. 25.*

Nora Ephron

1941-

American journalist, essayist, novelist, scriptwriter, and editor.

Ephron is a commentator on popular culture who brings a fresh, iconoclastic approach to such contemporary topics as the feminist movement, the pains and absurdities of personal relationships, politics, journalism, Jewishness, and the New York vs. Washington mentality. She is not afraid to include herself in her wry observations and critics have praised her work for its frankness.

Ephron's first three books, *A Wallflower at the Orgy* (1970), *Crazy Salad* (1975), and *Scribble, Scribble* (1978), are collections of articles she wrote as a columnist for *Esquire* and *New York* magazine. These collections have drawn favorable critical commentary for her ironic view of contemporary life and are considered refreshingly humorous and enjoyable. *Heartburn* (1983), Ephron's first novel, describes her own experiences in the final days of her marriage to Carl Bernstein, a well-known journalist and author. The novel has received mixed critical appraisal. Some critics appreciate Ephron's candid, humorous portrayal of the dissolution of a marriage; others, however, find the novelistic aspects underdeveloped. Ephron's work with Alice Arden as coscriptwriter for the film *Silkwood* (1983) has also received some negative comment. Specifically, critics have accused them of taking an inordinate amount of literary license with a story purported to be factual.

(See also *CLC*, Vol. 17; *Contemporary Authors*, Vols. 65-68; and *Contemporary Authors New Revision Series*, Vol. 12.)

© 1984 Thomas Victor

CHRISTOPHER LEHMANN-HAUPT

[It's] a fairly pointless exercise to keep substituting real people and events for what goes on in the course of **"Heartburn."** After all, even the most scrupulous attempts to reproduce reality in prose always end up being violent distortions of the actual. And to compare Miss Ephron's story with reality, far from enhancing its effectiveness, is likely to distance the reader from the novel's modest virtues as a work of the imagination.

Besides, the major question that **"Heartburn"** raises really transcends the issue of the novel's resemblance to living people and events. That question is why any woman, real or imaginary, would attach herself and then reattach herself to a man who could cheat on her compulsively when she was carrying his child, then lie to her about it and promise to stop and then continue cheating on her when she was foolish enough to believe him. Obviously, there is something emotionally disturbed about this relationship, and it behooves Miss Ephron, whether the story she tells is real or imaginary, to try to get to the bottom of the characters involved.

For a while, she fends off the question with wit and comedy, and we collaborate happily in the evasion by laughing. . . .

But about two-thirds of the way through **"Heartburn,"** the gags and apothegms begin to pall. The comedy routines begin to seem less sprightly. And the plotting begins to seem farfetched. I think the reason for this is that we really want Rachel

to arrive somewhere beyond merely getting mad at her husband for mistreating her. We really want her to achieve a glimmer of self-understanding.

Rachel blames everything in sight for her dogged desire to hold on to her husband. She blames love, fear of loneliness, sentimentality, romance and the impossibility of her ever getting anyone better. "Let's face it," she complains to her therapist: "*everyone* is the one person on earth you shouldn't get involved with." Ultimately, she arrives at a theory that the reason she alienated her husband is that she got too involved with cooking. "I love to cook, so I cooked. And then the cooking became a way of saying I love you. And then the cooking became the easy way of saying I love you. And then the cooking became the only way of saying I love you. I was so busy perfecting the peach pie that I wasn't paying attention." . . .

One suspects that Rachel is right, that for her cooking did become a screen. But what it was hiding never does get revealed—to the detriment of what might have been an amusing dark little comedy.

> *Christopher Lehmann-Haupt, in a review of "Heartburn," in* The New York Times, *April 8, 1983, p. 25.*

STUART SCHOFFMAN

A pity Nora Ephron is so famous. A pity the grubby details of her divorce from muckraker Carl Bernstein have been trumpeted in the magazines and savored by millions in the Safeway checkout line. Full disclosure may be the great desideratum of journalism, but it threatens to distort appreciation of Ephron's surprisingly touching first novel ["**Heartburn**"].

For the first questions in many minds will be, where does she get her nerve? How could she publish a *roman* so shamelessly *a clef*, exposing the warts, peccadilloes and worse of her family, ex-husbands and friends? . . .

Fans of Ephron's articles have come to expect no less. For years she has written brazenly in the first person, letting fly some of the niftiest ad hominem barbs since Dorothy Parker. What is curious—and effective—is that in the present book her lance seems a bit blunted. Wit gives way to rueful wisdom; bitter jokes misfire; sentences ache with labor. "**Heartburn**," as its title announces, is about pain: Ephron's own. Camouflage and polish are less urgent than exorcism. (p. 2)

Is "**Heartburn**" a good novel? It is innocent, to be sure, of literary pretensions, resembling in style an endless but entertaining phone call from a college roommate not heard from in years. Rachel the narrator frequently intrudes on her story, not only to offer digressive anecdotes or observations—which are any novelist's glorious birthright, and Ephron's forte—but to apologize to the reader for, among other things, the thinness of plot or the use of cliches. Such amateurish insecurity can of course be dumped off on "Rachel," a cookbook writer attempting a first novel, who is not the author but the author's invention. Lit professors and coy novelists will tell you it is a dangerous mistake to confuse author and narrator. Here, such a caveat is laughable, and Ephron of course knows it. It is impossible to separate this novel from its own publicity. . . .

"**Heartburn**" contains more than a dozen recipes, ranging from *linguini alla cecca* to four-minute eggs, inserted almost randomly in the bittersweet confessional, as if to call time out and say: If you can't stand my kvetching—funny as I've tried to make it—I know you'll love my cooking. . . .

Few writers would have had the gall to write "**Heartburn**." Its genesis invites tongue-clucking, and that is too bad. For what makes this display of whining and dining so likable is precisely its disarming vulnerability—as honest as a belch at L'Orangerie. (p. 10)

Stuart Schoffman, "Marriage and Ephrontery: A New Woman Strikes Back," in Los Angeles Times Book Review, *April 17, 1983, pp. 2, 10.*

MARNI JACKSON

Heartburn is Ephron's first novel, and she was obviously nervous that her domestic tragedy would not translate well into comedy. She is eager to please, and her book begins with a flurry of extraneous characters, funny routines, useful aphorisms ("If pregnancy were a book, they would cut the last two chapters"). But as the writing settles down, Ephron succumbs to the tug of her own story. By the end, *Heartburn* is not just witty but ruefully honest and sad, as befits a novel about a family breaking up.

For a roman à clef about betrayal, her book is remarkably free of malice, cynicism or even bitterness. Rachel remains a hope-less, marriage-loving optimist, quick to trust and slow to learn. . . .

The more Ephron risks losing the quick laugh, the more satisfying the humor in *Heartburn* becomes.

Marni Jackson, "A Witty Woman's Revenge," in Maclean's Magazine, *Vol. 96, No. 19, May 9, 1983, p. 62.*

RHODA KOENIG

The most publicized aspect of *Heartburn*—the resemblance of the book's action and characters to those of Nora Ephron's life—is the least important thing about it: Novelists have always plundered their own and their friends' and enemies' lives, and art has no more obligation to be fair than life has. But a novelist does have an obligation to write a novel. Ephron could be taking as her model here the relentlessly note-taking writer in Randall Jarrell's *Pictures From an Institution*, who thinks "the novelist's greatest temptation is to create." In *Heartburn* she has simply regurgitated the contents of her diary onto the printed page without giving them any substance or grace. Yet, flimsy as *Heartburn* is, it's interesting as an example of a certain kind of women's fiction, the rather wan and stunted child of feminism, free love, and psychoanalysis.

In the past several months I've seen an increasing number of novels by young women in which the heroine is supposed to interest us not because of what she does but because of the awful things men do to her. . . .

These put-upon ladies moon and whine their way through their sufferings or, worst of all, toss off incessant wisecracks that are meant to show off their spunk but only display their masochistic tendency to turn their strongest feelings into cute little jokes. . . .

Rachel Samstat, the cookbook writer of *Heartburn* . . . , certainly deserves anyone's sympathy—she discovers, while seven months pregnant with her second child, that her husband is having an affair. . . .

Ephron has been widely praised for her wit, but the gag lines in *Heartburn* don't express more than a formula flippancy, a perky hostility. . . .

In *Heartburn,* as in other novels whose heroines have been battered by feminism and the sexual revolution, there's a half-formed anger about the state of the relations between men and women. The old, cute games won't work, but the women, not knowing what else to do, just go on playing them without any conviction. These women might make amusing minor characters, but as heroines they flounder around too much, alternately wistful and sour, dragging the books down with them. (p. 78)

Rachel keeps skittering away from what her story is ostensibly *about*—we never learn why Rachel and her husband got married, what their life together is like, why and how the affair began. Yet she whips up such contrived and irrelevant bits as the unbelievable robbery of her therapy group and the scene in which a drunken friend loudly proposes to her in Central Park and then falls into the sea-lion pool (if I can't believe that one, I have seen it; it's the climax of every third comedy about wonderfully wacky people in love).

While *Heartburn* solicits our sympathy, it's told in a very dictatorial way: Actions are stated rather than dramatized, characters are labeled rather than portrayed. Every image has been predigested for us—it's a monologue by a Venus's-flytrap. Her husband's analyst, Rachel tells us, "looks like Carmen Miranda," and she later calls the woman "that refried taco" and "Chiquita Banana." Ephron never shows us the analyst so that we can judge whether she's as foolish as Rachel thinks. . . . Like every therapy patient, Ephron has learned that if you keep talking you reveal the other person's side of the story; hence, she just clams up. Reading this novel is like walking through that art exhibit of the future Tom Wolfe imagined in *The Painted Word:* all captions and no pictures.

By the end of this self-serving monologue, you may feel that you're in the position of the analyst whom Rachel pays to be fascinated. . . .

Writing *Heartburn* must have been emotionally satisfying for Ephron, and reading it may be the same for women similarly placed. But books like this have nothing to do with art, or even entertainment. Nimble and breezy, *Heartburn* can be wolfed down without any effort, but the satisfaction it offers is no more than you get from any convenience food. (p. 81)

Rhoda Koenig, "Yakety Yak (Don't Talk Back)," in New York *Magazine, Vol. 16, No. 19, May 9, 1983, pp. 78, 81.*

PATRICIA BOSWORTH

Novelists have been drawing from their own lives since time immemorial. . . . But nobody has been quite as inspired by her own drama as Nora Ephron in her first novel, *Heartburn* . . . , which is as witty and malicious and personal as her journalism. In her widely read collected essays, *Crazy Salad* and *Scribble, Scribble,* Ephron revealed everything from her obsession with having small breasts to the secrets of her consciousness-raising "sisters." What makes her novel equally titillating (to people who care and even to some who don't) is that the story seems to be a thinly veiled version of the last weeks of Ephron's publicized marriage to reporter Carl Bernstein. . . .

Does drawing so brutally from one's own life make a novel less artful? Less worthy of being taken seriously? This may make it more documentary, less transcendent, but it still can be an entertaining read. Ephron presumably has improved on the boring parts, left out (one hopes) the really gruesome stuff and along the way striven for significance. *Heartburn* is dazzlingly well written. It has a nice plot, it moves swiftly and gracefully to its conclusion, and you can't put it down. And when the going gets tough, the story is punctuated with terrific recipes. . . .

What is best about *Heartburn,* with its wit and sparkle and genuine belief in fidelity, is the characters. They move in and out of situations worthy of a Marx brothers farce crossed with Steve Martin, Woody Allen and Elaine May. . . . Everybody in *Heartburn* is organically loony, and most are dealing with betrayals. They all deal with betrayal ineffectually, manically, pathetically, but how else can you deal with betrayal? (p. 124)

In her fiction, Ephron has documented a marriage in such a way that she has received an enormous amount of media attention. But when she writes about what it's like to have a baby wrenched from her womb, knowing her husband is in love with another woman, she rises above her vengeful phrases, her devastating asides . . . and touches a powerful human and moral level.

She's not only as vulnerable as everybody else, she has been hurt deeply. Humiliation and hurt more than dreams of celebrity and success, which she already had, compelled her to write about her "double-digit . . . terminal heartburn" so fiercely and so well. She should feel cleansed. (p. 126)

Patricia Bosworth, "Dazzling Double Takes from a Marriage," in Working Woman, *Vol. 8, No. 6, June, 1983, pp. 124, 126.*

FRANK TUOHY

'**Heartburn**' appears in England in a truncated form, and turns out to be nothing more surprising than 'Rhoda meets Henry Kissinger' (or, rather, she doesn't: he stays in the wings). Nicely written, funny in a sassy, downbeat, disabused way, about such well-known subjects as Jewish mothers, shrinks, group therapy, mugging, it shares the basic assumptions of such humour: everyone will recognise such things, everyone is basically the same. When you're single, Rachel Samstat tells us, 'you meet new men, you travel alone, you learn new tricks, you read Trollope, you try *sushi,* you buy nightgowns, you shave your legs.' Suppose you didn't do any of these things? You might become an individual, not a class-member, and that's where true novels used to begin.

Frank Tuohy, "Mediatized Offerings," in The Observer, *August 7, 1983, p. 25.**

RICHARD SCHICKEL

One rather imagines that the people who undertook [the task of relating Karen Silkwood's story in the film] *Silkwood* may now wish they had waited until later. For rarely has the desperation to square inspirational myth with provable, nonlibelous reportage been more apparent. And rarely has the failure to do so been more dismaying. All they can say without fear of litigious contradiction is that there were obvious defects in the way plutonium was handled in the Crescent, Okla., plant that employed Karen Silkwood; that this woman, whom they cannot show as anything but neurotically self-centered and very messy both in her private life and in her relationship with peers and superiors at work, for reasons of her own decided to take a leading role in her union's campaign to remedy these defects; that thereafter she began to suffer from radioactive contamination, which may have been caused by someone in the company, but could possibly have been self-induced; that on the night of Nov. 13, 1974, she lost control of her car and crashed into a wall (the only concrete object in this case) with instantly fatal results.

What they cannot say, however, is whether the working conditions under protest were the result of deliberate policy or middle-management bungling of an unmalicious kind. Nor can they identify a moment when Silkwood made a conscious commitment to a coherent program of opposition to the status quo, which would, naturally, have included a knowing (and thus heroic) acceptance of the risks she might possibly be taking. Shorn of the ability to make direct statements on these matters, the film, in its climactic accident, is robbed of its capacity either to instruct or to move. Unable to prove a corporate conspiracy against Silkwood, or even individual violence by someone whose job was threatened by investigations, the movie must content itself with showing, without comment, mysterious headlights appearing behind her car just before the crash. And then admit, on a concluding title card, that an autopsy revealed a large amount of tranquilizers as well as a small amount of alcohol in the system of this demonstrably unstable woman. This is the most significant set of contradictory implications in a movie that is a tissue of them. And they leave the viewer about where he began, free to consult his own paranoia, or lack of it, for an interpretation of her life and death.

If *Silkwood* aspired merely to documentary honesty, this approach would be entirely honorable, perhaps even praiseworthy. But it will not do for a film that feels a powerful obligation to politicized mythmaking and must, in any case, try to involve the audience at a more intense and immediate dramatic, emotional and intellectual level. The strategy, therefore, is to treat the particulars of its heroine's political activities and her death almost as irrelevancies. The important thing, we are supposed to believe, is that Silkwood somehow redeemed an inconsequential life, a life the film makers are at pains to treat disdainfully, by a miraculous, inexplicable focusing of her energies on a significant issue of social conscience in its final months. Again, this is not an interpretation proved by any of the facts the film can set forth. . . .

There is none of the affectionate respect for working-class life and values that marked the similar, and far superior, *Norma Rae,* nor any of that film's sense of felt reality either. One senses that [director Mike] Nichols and his colleagues [Nora Ephron and Alice Arlen] are reporting on a sociological field trip, that they made no instinctive emotional connections with Silkwood's milieu. . . .

The facts [the film] can lay its hands on do not support a politically alarming or dramatically compelling conclusion to the mysteries of this case. Nor do they lead to a very uplifting statement about the motives and character of its central figure. On the other hand, the passage of time has not yet burnished away the ambiguities surrounding this affair, which might have permitted a purely mythic, *Gandhi*-like approach. In short, the moviemakers are backed into a corner from which neither showbiz sophistry nor a resort to the kind of radical-chic attitudes Nichols has always favored, nor yet a hundred hymns, can lift them.

Richard Schickel, "A Tissue of Implications," in Time, *Vol. 122, No. 26, December 19, 1983, p. 73.*

STANLEY KAUFFMANN

[Dissatisfactions with *Silkwood* go past a number of problematical] matters of execution, bothersome as they are. The script by Nora Ephron and Alice Arlen is a compound of compromise,

alteration, and misleading implication—all serious matters in what purports to be a true story. (p. 24)

I am not remotely competent to sift all the evidence in this matter, but as far as I can make out, no irrefutable proof of murder or document theft has yet been produced although much time has been spent in trying to provide that proof. But this ambiguity has not deterred Ephron and Arlen—and of course Nichols and his producers—from implying heavily that Silkwood had incriminating evidence in the car and that another car came up behind hers on the road and forced her off. (In the film's worst sequence, Silkwood is "canonized" at the end. . . .) Also, some published accounts indicate that facts about Silkwood's private life have been altered to make her more popularly acceptable and that her experiences in the plant, with safety practices and with radiation tests, have been nudged a bit one way and another.

All these changes verge on the unethical, the deliberately misleading. E. L. Doctorow altered facts in the Rosenberg case for his novel *The Book of Daniel,* but he made no claim to be presenting that case factually. Quite the contrary: he was using elements of that case as he needed them for a work of art about the large themes involved. No such rationale applies in *Silkwood.* The film was made with the clear intent to tell us the truth about a conspiratorial crime, and it apparently does not. (pp. 24-5)

Part of the fact manipulation comes, I think, not so much from social or political sympathies as from dramaturgic need, the need to make a cogent script out of a life that is hard to organize dramatically. The end of Silkwood's life is shocking, but in the life itself it's difficult to clarify themes without leaning on facts. The film does indeed show her growing awareness of her social situation and its connection with the physical condition caused by her job, but this is not the same as making her something akin to a labor Joan of Arc.

One truth, however, the film does helpfully drive home: middle-class America is a middle-class myth. By millions of filmgoers, America is usually seen as a coast-to-coast suburb, each cozy house with multiple color TV sets and with offspring in college. *Silkwood* is about proletarians who live from paycheck to paycheck and who are vulnerable to brutalization much more direct than that of wall-to-wall-carpeted offices. The characters in *Silkwood* are just on the edge of the people we don't see off-screen, whom they may join from time to time, those people who—according to a plump and double-chinned White House spokesman—don't exist: the hungry. *Silkwood* flubs its main intent, but this side effect is salutary. (p. 25)

Stanley Kauffmann, "Death and Transfiguration," in The New Republic, *Vol. 190, No. 3, January 23, 1984, pp. 24-5.*

Eva Figes

1932-

(Born Eva Unger) German-born English novelist, nonfiction writer, autobiographer, editor, translator, author of books for children, and scriptwriter.

Figes is known both as an experimental novelist and as the author of the nonfiction work *Patriarchal Attitudes* (1970), a classic feminist text which traces the historical basis for male domination of society. Often compared with Virginia Woolf for her interest in female identity, Figes focuses in her works on psychological rather than social concerns. Fragmented in structure and often nightmarish in tone, these works are noted for their intense, lyrical precision of language. Throughout Figes's writings, alienation recurs as a prominent theme. Her experiences as a German-Jewish refugee in England during World War II are described in the autobiographical *Little Eden: A Child at War* (1978), and her struggle to come to terms with the Holocaust and with human cruelty is central to the novel *Konek Landing* (1969).

Figes employs a variety of experimental techniques in her novels. Her protagonists are often "fallible narrators" whose perceptions are abnormal in some way. Figes has stated that she was inspired to use this device by William Faulkner, who used a mentally retarded narrator in *The Sound and the Fury*. Thus, in *Winter Journey* (1968), her narrator is an ignorant, elderly deaf man, and *Nelly's Version* (1977) is told from the viewpoint of an amnesiac woman. The latter book explores confusion of identity, a theme which also appears in *B* (1972), an intricate metafictional work in which a writer and his character become intertwined, and in *Days* (1974), where the invalid narrator is a composite of three generations of women. Figes focuses on the issue of female identity again in *Waking* (1981), a short novel which relates seven morning awakenings in a woman's life from childhood through old age. In *Konek Landing*, Figes manipulates language to create a sound-texture rich in vowels with notable stylistic density. Figes has said of this book: "I'd adopted a style such that five hundred pages became two hundred pages with the same content." The central character, Konek, is a homeless refugee; this novel is Figes's most direct treatment of the sense of alienation engendered in Jews by the Holocaust.

Figes considers *Konek Landing* her most important novel, but critics generally found it overly difficult and pretentious. To a lesser degree, this charge has also been directed at many of her other experimental works, including *B* and *Days*. While critics respected the intelligence and inventiveness of these novels, many expressed frustration with the obscurity created by her experimental techniques. Edwin Morgan has said of *B* that the reader "may suspect that the pleasures of manipulation have outrun the idea of relevance to a theme," and Jonathan Raban has commented that *Konek's* "difficult surface seems unjustified by any fundamental complexity of conception." Figes's recent novel *Light* (1983) fictionally recreates a day in the life of the Impressionist painter Claude Monet and is one of her most highly praised works.

(See also *Contemporary Authors*, Vols. 53-56; *Contemporary Authors New Revision Series*, Vol. 4; and *Dictionary of Literary Biography*, Vol. 14.)

© Jerry Bauer

KENNETH ALLSOP

The opening of *Equinox*—'Air like mountain air, like mountain water which hardly seems to be there when you turn the tap on, soap lathering on a caress'—daunts. But after this first froth of ad-copy it becomes a remarkably fine novel. Microscopically introspective, a thirty-ish wife tirelessly prods the dying nerve of her marriage. Her scientist husband is a smart-alecky vulgarian whose boredom flares into occasional irritated antagonism or sexual rough-stuff. Liz, hurt by neglect, wavers between vicious resentment and craven fear of the void ahead. Difficult to tell how conscious she is of speeding the break-up by her frigidity and peevishness, but this is revealed with an unblinking accuracy that gives the impact of truth. (p. 114)

Kenneth Allsop, "Cockroaches and Kools," in The Spectator, *Vol. 216, No. 7179, January 28, 1966, pp. 113-14.*

B. A. YOUNG

[*Equinox*] probes into the mind of a mature woman with an emotional problem—a marriage wearing out, a faiblesse for another man—but [Figes] writes so affectedly it's hard to follow the story. Tiny pointilliste paragraphs proliferate, often with the names replaced by personal pronouns so that you have to re-read them to make sure who they refer to. There is a plethora of interior monologue. Behind all the camp is a rather sensitive story, but it's hardly worth the labour of digging it out.

B. A. Young, "First Novels," in Punch, Vol. 250, No. 6546, February 23, 1966, p. 289.*

ROBERT NYE

One of the more important jobs a novelist does—often to the useful discomfort of his readers—is surely to create the moment from inside, vividly, patiently, admitting every ounce of its current ambiguity, so that his sentences read like heart beats. Such a richness of life going on, actually being lived from one word to another, is well approached in **"Winter Journey."** This is Eva Figes's second novel; I missed the first, **"Equinox,"** but on the strength and sensitivity of her latest work I'd place her immediately as a writer to be watched. She goes beyond gesture to fix the most fugitive movements of existence in a pattern true to themselves. She allows nothing, in a very short book, to distract her attention from what she perceives to be essential. She is a real realist—and offers much that seems threatening to one's necessarily limited experience of "reality."

"Winter Journey" takes shape in the mind of an old man, Janus, living out the last days of his life in a London house. Janus is ignorant and bitter: "a dull head among windy spaces." Eliot's "Gerontion" makes a pertinent point of reference, as does that empathy for the impotence of extreme age found in some of Beckett's finest writing. Miss Figes gives us a man who has unearthed no peace in the accumulation of experience; his thoughts are stupid, his feelings flow in a cloudy stream of images inspired by needs he has never satisfied. . . . [All] the odds and sods of Janus's pointless existence are drawn together in a jerky, rambling style that is again reminiscent of Beckett in that it makes a kind of poetry of the inarticulate.

Yet **"Winter Journey"** does not rely, for its total effect, on the mere depiction of a sequence of psychological states designed to engender pity in the reader. Janus is rich in character because he is not a simple personality; his memories cancel each other out; his only abiding passion is the constantly re-iterated wish to "keep moving forever" because "if you could keep moving forever you would keep alive forever, it stands to reason." Out of the conflict between this ancient adolescent reduction of his existence to crazy going on, endurance, and the deathward drag of all his memories, Miss Figes has fashioned a detailed and compelling verbal substance. One feels in the presence of a person stripped to what he is and records gratitude for a 119-page experience that might otherwise have taken a lifetime.

Robert Nye, "A Dull Head among Windy Spaces," in Manchester Guardian Weekly, April 13, 1967, p. 10.*

CHARLES D. PIPES

[**Winter Journey,** an] "hors d'oeuvre" of a novel, may tempt those readers who prefer to feast on stream-of-consciousness or experimental works instead of on more conventional fare. Eva Figes chooses to create moods and thought processes rather than concise pictures; this is a confusing game for the reader and often leaves him stumbling over the pebbles of poetic prose scattered along a somewhat arid plot. . . . Gradually, the au-

thor conveys the feeling of hopelessness and frustration which is so often a part of being old. The main character is a believable old man lost in a callous, uncaring environment. Unfortunately, the reader wearies of the whole thing by the end. . . . Brief as it is, **Winter Journey** is tough sledding.

Charles D. Pipes, in a review of "Winter Journey," in Library Journal, Vol. 93, No. 5, March 1, 1968, p. 1019.

KENNETH GRAHAM

Eva Figes, **Konek Landing,** intense and clever, sparing with articles, pronouns, connectives: prefers deep visionary murmur, hard delphic spasms, very painful. Also archetypes: waves, pools, seeds, cupboard/womb, bonfire/orgasm, amputation, rats in the cellarage (yours and mine).

Konek, oppressed everyman, crawls ashore out of stinking sea-sludge. Then memories of persecuted childhood, twisted spine, escape from reformatory, retreat into various holes in ground, scribbles on the walls. . . . Crosses borders, escaping, seeking. Seeking? Ah, identity. . . .

Part Two, at sea again, visionary note stepped up, syntax shakier. Alas, your reviewer flags, loses track, recognises only familiar wastelandmarks. Then TRANSCENDENCE! swims ashore to tropic isle, drums throb, gourds of sweet drug, becomes a god. Anthropology *ex machina*. Floats off tranced on raft with white bird: ah, soul.

What can poor lifebound critic say, only that imagination pretty active here, in a protozoic way, but reductive style dissolves all separate things, moments, griefs to one glutinous gloomy mishmash. Seems private where not borrowed. Extreme jumps from hell to paradise leave out old middle-earth altogether. Suffers from overdose of *modernismo*: French-Irish-Czech. Settles the old scores, scratches the old sores. Daunts, bores.

Kenneth Graham, "Wastelandmarks," in The Listener, Vol. LXXXII, No. 2110, September 4, 1969, p. 319.*

JONATHAN RABAN

Konek Landing is a political novel . . . , a dun-coloured, 'serious', semi-experimental fiction which happens in an unnamed country, a Europe of frontier guards and barbed wire, of cheap boarding houses, police visits, borrowed clothes—a grim, rain-washed, industrial landscape. Stefan Konek, a stateless citizen and an orphan to boot, wanders through this world of Kafka crossed with Beckett in an endless series of interior monologues, fragmentary encounters and gloomy nightmares. I found it monotonous and often incomprehensible, a novel whose difficult surface seems unjustified by any fundamental complexity of conception. Even the language of the book appears to have died of undernourishment in this European wasteland.

Jonathan Raban, "Family Scrapbook," in New Statesman, Vol. 78, No. 2008, September 5, 1969, p. 315.*

KATHY MULHERIN

Patriarchal Attitudes] is an enlightening, entertaining and sensible historical survey of male supremacy. Eva Figes discusses both the real conditions of women through the ages, and also the ideologies (e.g. Judaism, Christianity, Romanticism, Puritanism, Freudianism) that justified those conditions. It is a convincing description of how all kinds of widely differing economic and social systems have been carefully organized by men to preserve their power over women.

The book is full of very interesting observations. She shows, for example, how taboos and social customs have largely replaced physical force in controlling women. . . .

Miss Figes shows also that men, recognizing sex as the main area in which they are vulnerable to women (that is, sex is the main leverage a woman has with a man) have created all sorts of rules designed to protect themselves. . . . She argues that the whole notion of sex in our culture as something unclean or base is an effort on the part of men to lessen the power of women in an area where men really need them.

My main criticism of the book is that the end does not live up to the rest. She ends up talking about the bad "habits" that the institution of marriage supports, but throughout she has always accepted that the relations between men and women are determined by the power of men and the powerlessness of women. She'd have done better to conclude by admitting that she didn't have any good ideas about how to change power relations. As it is the last chapter is muddled and empty. All the same it really is a good book. (p. 91)

> *Kathy Mulherin, "A Five-Foot Shelf for Women's Lib," in* Commonweal, *Vol. XCIV, No. 4, April 2, 1971, pp. 90-2.**

EDWIN MORGAN

[*B*] is in many ways compelling and distinctive, yet it manipulates the reader's uncertainties to the point where he may suspect that the pleasures of manipulation have outrun the idea of relevance to a theme. Not that the theme invites anything simplistic. A successful but unhappy and increasingly alienated writer called Beard is writing a book about an unsuccessful writer called B. whom he has apparently (though not certainly) known and who is now dead. The reader's initial suspicion is that B. is a projection or alter ego of Beard, and the book does not dismiss this suspicion, making Beard say indeed at one point: 'I seemed to be acquiring a remarkable resemblance to my own character, B.' Although B. is fictionalised as having his own way of life, quite different from that of Beard, and although they meet and talk together as separate persons, the reader's difficulty is that the evidence is presented by Beard himself. Furthermore, he is going through a nervous crisis—his first wife dies, his second wife leaves him, his son has no contact with him, and although he cannot stop writing he admits his 'vision had shrunk'—so that reality and fantasy, past and present, are shown as overlapping and sometimes mixing, and episodes are repeated in slightly different form as they might do in dream or nightmare.

> *Edwin Morgan, "Empty-Hearted Labyrinths," in* The Listener, *Vol. 87, No. 2243, March 23, 1972, p. 393.**

MARY BORG

Eva Figes already has a distinguished reputation. She extends her range again with *B* in which she assaults that most elusive of themes, the creative process itself: the relationship between experience and the art which it triggers. While admiring her intent and her talent, I have to confess to finding the book

more bleakly schematic and less palatable than, for instance, her earlier brilliant *Winter Journey,* which was a major triumph of sustained imaginative writing. . . .

The new work is far more intellectually ambitious, relying on intricacy of structure, a complicated sequence of trick mirrors, takes and retakes of scene and incident, more than on sustained imagery or verbal felicity. . . . The naked, stripped style sometimes hints of some lack of grip on the structure: invention and imagination are somehow not quite in tune. But the uncompromising intelligence of the whole is admirable.

> *Mary Borg, "Art of Money," in* New Statesman, *Vol. 84, No. 2140, March 24, 1972, p. 398.**

PADDY KITCHEN

Eva Figes in *Patriarchal Attitudes* . . . is concerned to demolish the false assumptions of the past which have made . . . [the drive for equality between the sexes] seem so necessary. . . . Only the last chapter of her book is devoted to the present, and here I think Eva Figes rather skimps the case for the future set up by her excellent historical swipe. I am all for equal pay, abolition of marriage (and therefore divorce and illegitimacy), love without economic strings, and more nursery schools. But if we are to introduce these changes we must also have a better understanding of what men and women in general really want and need in a free situation. (p. 501)

> *Paddy Kitchen, "How We Live," in* New Statesman, *Vol. 84, No. 2143, April 14, 1972, pp. 500-01.**

PETER ACKROYD

[The day I spent reading Eva Figes's *Days*] passed extremely slowly. But this was probably in unconscious sympathy with the heroine of the novel, who spends what little life she has in the private ward of a large hospital. Her meanderings, which set the pace let alone the content of the narrative, are couched in Beckett's perpetual present—deriving as they do from the I of a needle: "I merely think this. In actual fact I can only conjecture about what lies beyond the walls of this room. And in the last analysis it does not matter. I no longer allow it to concern me." Luckily for her, but not for us as she roams over her attenuated past like a fly over cold soup. . . .

It is only, of course, in the ruined choirs of Romanticism that a monologue can be found appealing. This happy fallacy has never stirred my particular stumps and a stream-of-consciousness retains its interest only for a very short time. It is also the case that a frayed or neurotic vision is that much less interesting than an average or healthy one. This offends against the canons of the School of Suicide and Worldly Despair, but it agrees with those of good taste. The masks and reminiscences of a "knot of nerve-ends," as the heroine engagingly calls herself, are not likely to amuse or convince unless they connect with something other than themselves. This is rarely the case in *Days*. . . .

I do not mean to be entirely condemnatory; the writing is always lyrical and often perceptive. The sadness of growth and age are lovingly detailed, and there is something to be said for a novel in which loneliness and dereliction, the perpetual favourites of the novelist, can be depicted without any overt commentary. The focus of *Days* is strong but narrow, and Miss Figes has wrapped her subject within a cocoon of false self-consciousness. I often find myself wishing for those days when the novel offered a rhetoric of moral community, carrying everywhere with it relationship and love. Nowadays we have to be grateful if characters so much as talk to one another.

Peter Ackroyd, "Salad Days," in The Spectator, *Vol. 232, No. 7594, January 12, 1974, p. 43.**

TIMOTHY MO

Discreetly under-pinned as it was by a wholly unexceptionable feminism, I felt a bit of a lout for disliking Eva Figes's *Days* as much as I did. For 113 leaden pages her narrator, an unnamed woman, lies sick in a hospital room commenting grumpily on her surroundings and reminiscing obscurely about the world outside. Her supremely trite reflections are pretentiously arranged in little paragraphs widely spaced. This sort of bashful mental lint-picking can't be remotely cathartic for the author nor is it kind to the reader. If Miss Figes wished to convey the texture of hospital monotony as rebarbatively as possible she has succeeded, but surely the point is to transform the experience imaginatively. One feels special exasperation because Miss Figes is capable of more. It takes discipline to force yourself to write as drably as this, but there are more efficacious courses of self-improvement. 'It is nice lying here. It is warm. I am being fed, I am being washed. The nurses are kind.' Miss Figes's spare, runic style was perfectly suited to *B,* her riddling thriller about character and creativity, but she ought to diversify the style and intelligence she is so perversely concealing.

Timothy Mo, "Sick Fantasy," in New Statesman, *Vol. 87, No. 2235, January 18, 1974, p. 86.**

VALENTINE CUNNINGHAM

[Eva Figes] dwells on the plight of a woman, but *Days* bids over-ambitiously to embrace the plight of all women, and its sympathies become rapidly too diffuse. A woman lies in a hospital bed, with memories of her own life, and thoughts about the men and women in it, sludging about in her mind. Her dribble—it's certainly less than a stream—of consciousness is least muddied when she focusses on the worthy females labouring about her. . . . [The] intrusive polemical moments are just condonable, I suppose, but a curiosity the novel fails to overcome is the merging of the first woman's thoughts with her daughter's. No warning is given of the switches back and forth and, confounding the confusion, the patterns of the two lives are identical. . . . We're intended to perceive an inextricable knitting of all womankind into a net of like dilemmas: instead, we're perplexed as to exactly what happens to any one woman. . . . But the strongest impression *Days* leaves is of unflagging rancour for the men who always win the prizes and the goodies, and who can't even spot what's wrong with the women. 'I hate men,' one of the women thinks. 'It was like a thought coming out of one's own head,' the other concurs.

Valentine Cunningham, "Woodman's Widow," in The Listener, *Vol. 91, No. 2339, January 24, 1974, p. 120.**

MARGARET COLE

Eva Figes does not pad out her slender book [*Tragedy and Social Evolution*] with extensive quotations, but this is because she only gives brief references to back up her own statements, some of which are quite astounding. (p. 20)

It must be conceded that the book is easy reading. Ms Figes writes fluently and in the earlier part, where she is reflecting upon some studies she has made in anthropology, particularly in the work of two writers on tribes of cannibals, she makes remarks which are worth considering. She draws attention, for instance, to the undoubted fact that what is called 'the moral order' in a society is really a network of beliefs and superstitions, images and associations: she suggests that the powers and functions of the god or gods in traditionally religious cultures have been taken over, in modern times, by police forces and the other apparatus of 'justice'; and she seems to think that the crime for which Oedipus suffered was not what we should call incest, but taking a wife from within his own tribe instead of an outsider. Her first chapter and the two which follow it, on 'Kingship' and 'The Dead', are also interesting; and one might well explore further the idea that the strength of the Tudor monarchy derived partly from the need the people of England felt to find a substitute for the father-figure of the Pope whom Henry VIII had dethroned. . . . She, like all her kin, puts a great deal of weight on interpretations of *Macbeth, Hamlet, Lear* and *Richard II* among Shakespeare's plays, and on Plato—the *Laws,* not the *Republic*—and on the *Agamemnon.* Shakespeare is, I suppose, fair game, though it is surely straining probability rather far to assert that in *Troilus & Cressida* Shakespeare is arguing with Machiavelli—whose *Prince* was not translated until 1640. . . .

But it is when we reach her fourth and longest chapter, which concerns itself with 'Women', that the author's casual way of treating evidence becomes painfully obvious. I could quote a great many instances but in mercy to the editor will content myself with the minimum. Eva Figes asserts categorically . . . that women who have made a mark in history were 'monsters'. . . . Granted that in a world largely man-made, women need to grow something of a tough skin, were all these women 'monsters'? And what about the Virgin herself? It will not do just to forget about them, or to say, as Eva Figes does in another connection, 'one can hardly count Cleopatra'.

Here is one absurdity; another is to equate the Medea of Euripides with Ibsen's Hedda Gabler. But Medea killed her own children? 'Yes', says our author, 'and Hedda killed a foetus and destroyed a manuscript, which comes to practically the same thing'! Just how silly can you get? It is a pity because she has brains and, as I said earlier, she can write. But the lack of ordinary common sense or respect for evidence vitiates much of what she has to say and throws, inevitably, some doubt on the remainder. (p. 21)

Margaret Cole, "Myths of Origin," in Books and Bookmen, *Vol. 22, No. 2, November, 1976, pp. 19-21.**

PADDY KITCHEN

Moral ambiguity . . . is usually set within a precise social context: you know where you are physically and historically, however much the characters' ethical bearings may fluctuate. With *Nelly's Version* the ambiguity is total. Nelly herself does not know who she is, where she is, or why, and nor do we. She signs a hotel register with an apparently false name, discovers with surprise that her suitcase is stuffed with banknotes, and makes forays into the strange town which turns out to have unidentifiably familiar undertones. Eva Figes has long been involved with developing the relevance and potential of contemporary fiction, just as I have long been described by my closest friends as one of nature's philistines, so my appreciation of her work (which early on was extremely enthusiastic) has tended to deflate as she advances and I get more entrenched.

What I feel about her and several other exploratory writers is that the evidence of their journeys is so wilfully arbitrary. The information imparted in their books seems to have no central intuitive, passionate motivation. It is like those visual art exhibits that profess either to be evidence, or not to be evidence, of travels which the artist may, or may not, have taken according to whichever viewpoint the spectator chooses to adopt.

As far as I can tell, Nelly is a middle-aged, gone-to-seed woman, out of touch with society's concept of sanity. . . . What some regard as the straitjacket of psychological or narrative logic is virtually absent. . . . The book is, I believe, making a serious statement about the inconsequentiality of life. (p. 95)

> *Paddy Kitchen, "Knowing Where You Are," in* The Listener, *Vol. 98, No. 2518, July 21, 1977, pp. 94-5.**

PETER ACKROYD

Nelly's Version, is, luckily, not feminine fiction. It may not even be female fiction. In fact, it's hardly fiction at all; its major purpose is to erase all of the properties of the male-dominated and bourgeois novel in an effort to be 'liberated' and modern. (p. 22)

[Nelly] evades all of the responsibilities of the male world—she is simply a recording device which details everything that happens to her, without any specific male or female identity. The heroine does not know who she is, where she is, or why she is. Neither do we. For the heroine this is some sort of advantage: to be a woman without female identity, it seems, is to know neither grief nor pain. For the reader there is a great deal of both.

Of course the narrative could be seen as an elaborate and partially successful analogy for the new liberated woman: Nelly has abandoned all of the social codes which had been foisted upon her but hasn't yet found a permanent substitute of her own. But there is nothing particularly novel about this condition: nineteenth century novelists used mad people for exactly the same effects. And, again, Eva Figes's bland and indefinite prose, which perfectly matches her bland and indefinite heroine, has been culled from very similar French novels which were actually all about men.

It's often said that the women's movement, like any political cause, can only produce rhetoric and not literature; in its pursuit of personal or social change it uses art as a loud-hailer. And so it turns out that Eva Figes's uneasy modernism, in part Lessing and in part Robbe-Grillet, is simply a way for her to harness 'modern' literature in order to make a limited and political point. (pp. 22-3)

[Believing] firmly as Eva Figes does in the liberation of the female character into her own imaginative world, what do you actually do when you sit down to write a novel? All you have left are a form (which Eva Figes unthinkingly adopts, forgetting that this itself is a variety of social determinism), and a language which cannot be easily 'liberated'. Despite the fact that Eva Figes tries very hard to turn Nelly's narrative into a miracle of clear-sighted, immediate analysis, she cannot free the language of its past. All kinds of connotation peep through, placing the novel firmly within an orthodox and, as Eva Figes

would say, male-dominated culture. And so the book turns out to be an uneasy hybrid—between realistic 'character' fiction and modernist writing, between conventional romance and political description, between disguised propaganda and old-fashioned story-telling.

In fact, it is the stories that save the book. By reducing the character of Nelly to a cipher, the whole weight of the novel falls upon her descriptions. *Nelly's Version* could be read by a casual reader as a tour around contemporary England. Eva Figes is best at documenting the sad paraphernalia of Britain: the schools, the inane hospitals, the little shops, the houses which coalesce into a prospect of grey, the skies always threatening rain. It is as if, when you remove character from the English novel, you are left with its enduring theme: the nature of English dampness.

This is the same as saying that, when you remove the conventional constraints of motive and of plot from the English novel and when you are not equipped like the French with a thread through the labyrinths of modernism, all that remains is melodrama and sentimentality. By removing all of the socially 'female' characteristics from Nelly, she simply becomes a prey to all the familiar angst and loneliness which have filled a thousand mysteries. She becomes, for this reason, simply an incompletely realised character—because the language of the book can't sustain its political intentions. It turns into a sentimental study of madness, a madness which has been hitched to the vehicle of Eva Figes's preoccupations. (p. 23)

> *Peter Ackroyd, "All about Eva," in* The Spectator, *Vol. 239, No. 7778, July 30, 1977, pp. 22-3.*

PETER LEWIS

[Figes's] artistic roots, like her personal ones, are Continental, and the influence of Expressionism is evident in her work, but it is also possible that she is one of the few English writers to have learned from the *nouveau roman. Nelly's Version* is an easier novel than [many of this type] . . . because it possesses a more coherent narrative structure, but by describing everything from the position of a middle-aged woman who is almost completely cut off from her own past and who is therefore without memories, Eva Figes sometimes renders her narrator's observation of the world with a cinematic objectivity not unlike that of the *nouveau roman.* In the two Notebooks that constitute the novel, the narrator, who calls herself Nelly Dean . . . , records scenes and events, including apparently insignificant details, with unusual precision, and the effect of this technique is to strip perceived reality of its habitual and conventional associations so as to make it alien and even menacing. Yet if there are affinities with the *nouveau roman,* there are more with Expressionism, as the quality of menace suggests. There is something decidedly Kafkaesque about this story of a woman who has apparently liberated herself from her previous life only to find that the past reasserts itself and that instead of escaping from it she remains trapped within it. At first only a few bubbles rise to the surface from her supposedly obliterated memory, but increasingly the grip of the past upon her life becomes evident, even though she tries to deny it or fails to recognise it. At the opening of the novel, Nelly is a kind of innocent who feels free to make her own choices and create her own life virtually ex nihilo, but is she in fact doing this or is she playing a role that has already been determined? She believes she is setting off on a voyage of discovery, but ironically discovers what she thought she had escaped from. Despite the tangible physicality of the places and people Nelly comes into contact with, the title reminds us that this is Nelly's version, not anybody else's, and Eva Figes is really exploring an inner landscape. She is concerned with the nature of and the quest for identity, the possibility or impossibility of human freedom, and the relationship between human experience and reality. The novel is not, however, as abstract as this may suggest, since the narrative proceeds by means of a sequence of dramatized incidents and concretely presented situations possessing thriller-like qualities of suspense, mystery and ambiguity. . . . The narrative is deliberately disorientating since Eva Figes refuses to tie up all the loose ends and provide thriller-like solutions. Is Nelly a chronic amnesiac, a possible interpretation of the First Notebook, or a schizophrenic, a possible interpretation of the Second Notebook? Is she an institutionalised patient constructing in her Notebooks an imaginary world based on people she knows? Is she a representative of modern middle-aged womanhood undergoing a crisis of identity, or a modern everyman, isolated and alienated? We can't answer such questions with any certainty. The only certainty is uncertainty. Instead of distinguishing between reality and delusion, Eva Figes seems to be making a delusion of reality and a reality of delusion. Some of those who meet Nelly diagnose her as paranoid, but from her point of view they are paranoid. This results in rendering the most ordinary and humdrum of experiences unusual, even bizarre. As in Pinter, harmless conversational remarks suddenly take on sinister implications, and Eva Figes obtains some Pinterish comedy out of verbal ambiguity. It was Schopenhauer who when asked, 'Who are you? What are you doing? Where are you going?', found he couldn't reply; Nelly is in the same state and so, by the end of the novel, is the reader. Although Eva Figes's preoccupations as a novelist are not as original as they may seem in an English context, she brings a highly individual gift to bear on them, and this ingenious, bewildering and mind-teasing novel, probably her best yet, should do much to enhance her reputation. (pp. 68-9)

> *Peter Lewis, in a review of "Nelly's Version," in*
> Stand, *Vol. 19, No. 1 (1977-78), pp. 68-9.*

THE ECONOMIST

[For Eva Figes, author of **Little Eden: A Child at War**], the garden of Eden was Cirencester in 1940 where, after escaping first from Berlin and then from the London bombs, she spent an idyllic year at a boarding school run by two eccentric spinster sisters. These enthusiastic and industrious ladies awakened in her an absorbed and eclectic interest in her surroundings and a nascent desire to be a writer. Her book is essentially a tribute to them.

Her own rather hazy memories of the period include the moment when her best friend told her that she could not pray because she was a Jew, the full implications of which she only grasped later, on being sent to see a newsreel film of Belsen. From back numbers of the local paper she pieces together a picture of wartime Cirencester very far removed from those horrors. . . .

Ms Figes provides in addition fascinating glimpses of the history of Cirencester, for centuries a rotten borough. . . . She deplores the paternalistic hauteur of the local gentry as much as she despairs of the latter-day development of the town, but the picture she paints of it is nevertheless redolent of the magical, silent-movie memories of childhood in a place where her

mother's continental method was enough to startle the knitting circle, and where, for a time, she could be unashamedly happy.

> *"Paradise Renamed," in* The Economist, *Vol. 267, No. 7033, June 17, 1978, p. 132.*

GERDA COHEN

Like a primrose which you must hold very near to find a frail, obstinate scent, this little autobiography [**Little Eden: A Child at War**] repays close reading. Without attention, you might miss its pale tearful charm altogether. After a start of phenomenal confusion, the author reveals that she spent 15 months in Cirencester, evacuated with her family to escape the blitz. . . .

[With the] delicate, gooseflesh misgiving which pervades the prose, the personal narrative has been bulked out by war-time data dug from the local papers. The intrusion is often laughable. War Weapons Week, Knitting for Victory, even Double Summer Time and the Gloucestershire Farmers' Union protest threat—all meander among budding nipples and anguish in the basement lavatory. . . .

Further padding is provided by local history. . . .

True feeling returns in 1941, when Eva became a boarder at Arkenside. Exuding the scent of lime flower and Victorian mildew, this diminutive prep school delighted her. . . . [The] predictably English prep school squalor did not seem to trouble the fastidious little refugee. Only when her best friend charged her with being a Jew, misery began. . . .

For the Unger parents, totally assimilated, being Jewish was merely the hated reason for exile. They kept it a shameful secret. So that although the grandparents left behind in Berlin, had been "deported," Eva still did not know what that really meant. The word Jew remained "a dark horror at the heart of the family which could not be spoken about." In 1945, as a schoolgirl, she finally learnt. "Go and see for yourself," Eva's mother gave her ninepence and sent her off to the cinema one spring afternoon, to watch the newsreel of Belsen, alone. . . .

This poignant episode, underwritten with exquisite pain, is almost impossible to believe. How *could* Mrs Unger have done it? How could she send a daughter, alone, to discover the piled Jew corpses of Belsen? Yet there is no hint of reproach. Only a frail, half-hearted perseverance of daughter reaching out for mother. The author is constantly pleading, between the lines, pity my mother. Pity them also, the dull-minded anti-semitic folk of Cirencester. Above all, pity me the author. . . .

By the end, one grows impatient.

> *Gerda Cohen, "A Double Exile," in* Manchester Guardian Weekly, *July 9, 1978, p. 22.*

LOUISE BARNDEN

> Tragedy in the theatre is the sad story of a central protagonist, who, either deliberately or by accident, offends against the most fundamental laws of his society, those laws which are so basic as to be considered divine.

Eva Figes uses this definition of tragedy in her book **Tragedy and Social Evolution,** where she takes a new approach to the much-vexed problems of the nature of tragic drama and of the relationship between such cultural phenomena and the society which produced them. Working on the basic assumption that specific historical and social conditions give rise to certain forms of artistic production, Ms. Figes looks at the way in which tragedy, in the past, has functioned as a ritual process through which societies ceremonially reaffirm their apparently universal values. In the times of the Greek tragedians and of Shakespeare, deeply-rooted beliefs about the hierarchy and order of society—for example, the status and role of the king or of woman—had to be upheld in order to prevent the disintegration of the social fabric. (p. 97)

Figes' description of the way in which tragic drama operates is based on the work of social anthropologists' studies of the totemic rituals of primitive tribes. She sees Greek and Shakespearean tragedy as a similar collective celebration of society's beliefs about the relationships between the living and the dead, the king and the commoner, the man and the woman, all of which can ultimately be understood in terms of the social hierarchy. . . . Ms. Figes suggests that with the advent of scientific rationalism the taboos finally break down altogether and tragedy can no longer exist.

This belief leads to the conclusion that after the seventeenth century the only truly tragic subject in Western literature is woman. Women are universally oppressed and if they seek to break the patriarchal law they will suffer for it. Figes draws an interesting parallel between Euripides' *Medea* and Ibsen's *Hedda Gabler,* and suggests that the reason that these two tragedies shocked contemporary audiences and still have the power to arouse hostility in men today, or at least lack of understanding, is that they present women who behave in a monstrous fashion and yet are still undeniably women. . . . This is a book which will be of value to all those interested in feminism and the way in which literature functions as an ideological force in stereotyping, or more rarely, in demythifying women, their 'nature' and their social roles.

More generally it is a book which will be stimulating for students of literature, literary criticism and social anthropology, and for all lovers of the theatre. Ms. Figes offers new insights into areas such as Hamlet's supposed Oedipus complex and the myth of Oedipus himself which are quite as convincing as the psychological psychoanalytical readings of Freudian interpreters. This book takes a sociological approach to the understanding of tragic drama which is a welcome addition to the more restricted and restrictive work of the traditional sociologists of literature. For Ms. Figes true tragic drama gives voice to the ideals and aspirations of a cross-section of society, gives form to a collective consciousness; for this reason she pays very little attention to French tragic drama in the seventeenth century. . . . However, within the terms of reference she sets herself, Ms. Figes' exploration of the implications of tragedy as popular culture and history as myth is a successful one. Critics who try to use either a rigidly Marxist sociological method of interpretation or the purist "textual" approach could do well to read this book. (pp. 97-8)

> *Louise Barnden, in a review of "Tragedy and Social Evolution," in* Gambit, *Vol. 9, No. 35, 1980, pp. 97-8.*

SUSAN BOLOTIN

Eva Figes demonstrates her intimacy with the dual promise and torment of time on nearly every page of her ambitious and unsettling new novel, **"Waking."** . . .

Given the novel's brevity and the unavoidable limitations of its innovative framework, it is amazing that we learn so much about the narrator. Though Miss Figes's prose occasionally sinks into sticky poeticism, her attention to detail never falters. She remembers how a child builds a secret house by drawing the bedclothes over her head and arching her spine. . . .

Even when the heat of a midlife affair dulls the narrator's usual cynicism, her litany of detail lets us see the lurking bitterness that she herself ignores. . . .

The ineluctability of time eventually devastates the narrator. The passing years and the thousands of awakenings to which we are not privy mark her, and she becomes sour. She yearns for the respect and privacy that her family denies her. She rails against the heaviness of pregnancy. She wills her aging body to move. Seconds seemed an eternity to her as a young girl; by her adulthood, years float by without notice.

The novel is not without false notes. When the narrator remarks, "I sleep so badly now," we suspect her of lying. How can we believe that this intensely depressed person has *ever* slept soundly? In fact, the book's title is a cheat, for Miss Figes has written a novel not about waking as most of us know it, but rather about hopeless wakefulness.

Furthermore, on first reading, the pattern of the narrator's life seems too pat. Does the all-too-brief love affair have to follow a misbegotten marriage, which comes after a miserable adolescence? Do her children have to loathe her lonely aging? Certainly, this woman's distress is as predictable as it is intense. But the narrator's very namelessness makes her less a character than a symbol of the patterns of a woman's helplessness, and the raw self-consciousness of her simple tale haunted me. . . .

The novel's political perspective is not surprising, coming from a writer best known here and in England for her work of feminist scholarship, **"Patriarchal Attitudes."** It is Miss Figes's application of her feminism to the drama of a woman's life that is daring. Viewed as a play performed in seven short acts, **"Waking"** makes good sense and good reading, though even readers who have known sleepless nights may find the notion of a sleepless life overly bleak.

> *Susan Bolotin, in a review of "Waking," in* The New York Times, *February 23, 1982, p. C13.*

D. M. THOMAS

A work of fiction defines a world of its own by excluding almost all of the real world. The writer sets limits to what he will deal with, as a painter decides the size of his canvas. Tolstoy gives us the illusion that the world of "War and Peace" and "Anna Karenina" is coextensive with the world we live in; in Jane Austen we are conscious of looking at a cameo, and much of our pleasure arises from our appreciation of her exquisite judgment in staking out the boundaries of her art. What a fictional work leaves out is as important as what it takes in.

In **"Waking"** Eva Figes has chosen to examine the life of a woman by revealing her thoughts in the quiet time between sleeping and waking, at different stages of her life. . . .

The exclusions imposed by the structure of this novel are formidable. It is difficult, if not impossible, for the author to create any living, interesting characters other than the woman herself. Action, the dramatic interplay of people, their squabbles, loving exchanges, humor, can be conveyed only by memories and reflections. . . . The exclusions necessary in the approach Miss Figes takes clear the way for the excitement of strict form. But she has narrowed the field more than she need have done. The woman, who is not named, gives no names to anyone in her life either. . . . I long to be told that her (perhaps understandably) withdrawn husband is called Fred.

The almost inevitable solipsism of the book is compounded by the woman's quite exceptional ability not to love or be loved. In puberty she loathes her parents, in pregnancy her husband; in middle age her teenage children treat her like poison. . . .

I can detect no signs of an ironic detachment. It would seem that we are expected to regard the heroine sympathetically. . . . I believe most readers, including most women, will find this woman's life exceptional in its sterility.

"Waking" has many fine qualities, however. Whether intentionally or not, the book is indeed an excellent study of a self-centered, solitary disposition. The atmosphere of silence; the relationship of a woman to her body, tender and wondering in youth, bitter in age; one's sense of the changing, darkening seasons of life—these are beautifully evoked. The first section is perhaps least successful, not because the author cannot relive childhood, but because she has a problem finding the right language to express those feelings and visions. (p. 9)

The finest writing is reserved for the last two sections, when the woman has drifted into her natural haunt, solitude. A Joycean echo in the last long sentence—she is a child again, by the shore, waiting for her mother to come for her—is no less beautiful and moving for that. . . .

Here, at last, the simple humanity of "mamma" restores the woman to the warmth of childhood and Miss Figes's narrative to the real world, as most people recognize it—"the gravitation and the filial bond"—a world in which other people are often more than mirrors. (p. 18)

> *D. M. Thomas, "A Life between Sleeping and Waking," in* The New York Times Book Review, *February 28, 1982, pp. 9, 18.*

A. ALVAREZ

Waking is a life distilled into a series of brief monologues . . . a kind of seven ages of woman. But the speaker is a woman who sleeps badly and finds relationships both difficult and unrewarding, so perhaps seven ages of loneliness is a more accurate description. . . .

The monologues are written in poetic prose: no plot to speak of, all mood and sensibility, a style Beckett brings off time and again, perhaps because even his most murmuring, far-off voices have a cranky individuality and wit that keep the whole tricky performance healthily objective. Miss Figes, however, is not much interested in wit and there seems little distance between her and her narrator. Instead, the monologues form a kind of rhapsody of the self: the narrator describes herself and her changes in detail—eyes, hair, mouth, coloring, body—and no one else is even given a name. Her primary responses to the world are distaste and, at every stage except the last, resentment.

She is presented as a woman diminished by intimacy, for whom everyone is an intruder. . . .

Her only relief from this evenhanded, relentless narcissism is when the world out there suddenly shifts and seems beautiful: the early light slides across the floor, a curtain moves in the breeze, the birds start up their hesitant dawn chorus. Miss Figes is moved by the world without people and writes of it tenderly, delicately. . . .

She is also strong on her narrator's manifold resentments: her sullen husband, the blind labor of motherhood, her own adolescent contempt for her parents' flabby bodies, her adolescent son's equal contempt for hers.

But there are moments—particularly in the opening monologues—when both her rhapsodies and her rage run on too slackly for a book so condensed and so apparently controlled. . . . If Miss Figes had been as ruthless with her adjectives and adverbs as her narrator is with her family, *Waking* would have been even shorter than it already is, but fiercer and more pure. (p. 23)

> *A. Alvarez, "Flushed with Ideas," in* The New York Review of Books, *Vol. XXIX, No. 8, May 13, 1982, pp. 22-3.**

KATHRYN SUTHERLAND

[*Sex and Subterfuge: Women Novelists to 1850*] is a book of fashion rather than of substance; . . . it is difficult to sympathise with its vague pioneering spirit and lack of critical direction. Ms Figes provides a roughly chronological survey of the novel written by and about women during a particularly fertile period of seventy or so years up to 1850, and she begins with a strong assertion: 'If there is such a thing as the classical novel in English literature, and I think there is, then women were responsible for defining and refining it'. . . . But when she comes to defend this bold thesis the thinness of her research is at once obvious, and her critical framework degenerates into a series of unhelpful and naive remarks. (p. 90)

These are not fresh ideas, and Ms Figes is content to follow them along well-trodden paths. There is no consideration of the many lesser known and forgotten women novelists whose works poured off the presses in the last thirty years of the eighteenth century. . . . Ms Figes is most assured in dealing with *Jane Eyre* and *Wuthering Heights*. Her readings of Jane Austen, particularly *Mansfield Park*, are humourless and over-schematised. Some large and potentially interesting statements are made . . . but, in the absence of a substantial context and rigorous specific analyses, they remain rather stale generalisations. The book in no way fulfils its ambitious claims. (p. 91)

> *Kathryn Sutherland, in a review of "Sex and Subterfuge: Women Novelists to 1850," in* Critical Quarterly, *Vol. 24, No. 3, Autumn, 1982, pp. 90-1.*

MIRANDA SEYMOUR

Light, Eva Figes's new novel, is her best piece of work yet. . . .

The idea behind the book is simple. The beauty is in its leisurely pacing and the harmony of its composition. Everything about it is orderly and reposeful. The author has married her language so closely to her subject as to leave the reader with the feeling that he has been present at the creation of one of the vast shimmering canvases to which Monet dedicated the last part of his life, and that the experience has been a remarkable one. (p. 24)

Miranda Seymour, "Shimmering," in The Spectator, Vol. 251, No. 8098, September 24, 1983, pp. 23-4.*

JOYCE CAROL OATES

Eva Figes's luminous prose poem of a novel, **"Light,"** like her earlier **"Waking,"** is clearly descended from [Virginia] Woolf's great experimental novels. Technique is all or nearly all in this fastidiously wrought narrative of a day in the life of Claude Monet in the summer of 1900. The reader is a witness to a remarkable variety of modulations of light—sunlight—beginning in the darkness preceding dawn and ending in night. . . .

"Light" is a stronger, more vivid and far more interesting work of fiction than **"Waking,"** which presented seven mornings in the life of an extraordinarily self-absorbed woman, whose musings on her experience as daughter, wife, lover, mother and elderly dying woman are resolutely impersonal, as if the species and not an individual were speaking. **"Waking"** was, in fact, very much about light, sunlight and darkness and a human being's all but unconscious passage through it. (p. 11)

While **"Light"** does not tell a story in any conventional style, it alludes to dramatic events beyond the immediate frame of the narrative itself. (p. 30)

Monet himself, however, is the novella's center, its focus of consciousness. He moves like a demigod through the human world, not precisely a tyrant but fully in control of his household and his art. Behind the shimmering surface of Monet's Impressionism is a clear, coherent, ambitious stratagem: Waterlilies, pond, bridge, trees, reflections, light itself are but the artist's quarry, his subject. . . .

Because of the novella's precise, friezelike structure, in which characters appear to inhabit different and not always overlapping planes of being, **"Light"** at times suggests slow-motion photography. Its prose is unhurried, richly descriptive, rarely ornamental or excessive—indeed, a kind of Impressionism in words. The parallel with "To the Lighthouse" and "The Waves" is instructive rather than distracting, for Miss Figes has applied Woolf's idiosyncratic vision to a subject as ambitious as Woolf's; that **"Light"** is self-consciously derivative in technique does not detract from the beauty of its images and prose. (p. 32)

Though experimental fiction has become a convention of its own in recent decades, no longer revolutionary or surprising and in the hands of some practitioners all too predictable, Eva Figes's prose poem suggests that the genre (if it can be called that) is far from exhausted. Each day, as Monet observes, is a new beginning; each day light plays, "defining and transforming what would otherwise be merely grey amorphous matter," inanimate or animate. Surely the same is true of the human imagination. (p. 33)

Joyce Carol Oates, "Monet, Summer, 1900," in The New York Times Book Review, October 16, 1983, pp. 11, 30, 32-3.

JASCHA KESSLER

[As] regards Monet, I have . . . just had my eyes opened a bit wider by a little novel, a mere 91-page novel, called **Light**. . . . Nothing could be simpler than the form of this book, which begins before dawn on what is to be an idyllic summer's day in 1900, and follows the artist, Claude Monet, through the hours of work, of eating and drinking with his family and guests, and into the evening, the late evening, when the world is once again dark.

There is no plot or story, in fact; one might call this little novel "impressionistic," although it doesn't resemble certain novels that could carry that description once upon a time. Instead, **Light** is what its title tells us: it represents Monet as a cunning hunter of light itself, . . . who has made his house and garden into a vast and intricate trap for light, which can be caught, or which he hopes to catch, moment by moment as it changes, from 4:00 a.m. through the blinding noon, and the warm, ever-changing shifting, slanting angles of heat and color through the long, calm day. The discipline of this painter . . . is offered by the writer as a study in what it means to be such an artist as Monet was. Not the least of its intensely-beautiful power is its calm and clear language, which is used to show us what we have looked at for 80 years when we looked at Monet's paintings. I am sure the author could have done nothing without the paintings themselves to show her what she puts into words, condensing so much of her own observations of the artist's life and works; yet her cunning lies in her ability to show us what the artist is seeing in some ways that we can only grasp by means of language, her language commenting not on the paintings but on what the paintings came from: the phenomenon of Monet's trying to see what he later painted. It is astonishing. But that is not all: Figes also tells us the story of Monet's wife and children on that day, summing up, as Impressionism itself sought to do, something more than the surface of the world as it is bathed in the light that changes, with time, moment by moment, and that something is the essence of people's lives which are to be seen, as the artist can see them, as moments that somehow contain everything and nothing at once. In other words, the vision of the moment, if seen deeply, can radiate in itself the vastness of meaning that flows outward from the point-source of the moment in all directions, just as light does. This novel is a beautiful, even extraordinary, little book that is simply not to be missed.

Jascha Kessler, "Eva Figes: 'Light: A Novel'," in a radio broadcast on KUSC-FM—Los Angeles, CA, December 7, 1983.

RONALD DeFEO

Since writers of fiction are creators themselves one would think that they could easily invent convincing portraits of artists. Yet this is hardly the case. Too frequently the writers, composers and painters depicted in fiction seem oddly removed from their work. Though they may spring to life as people and though their work may take on a certain reality, their actual involvement in the process of creation rarely comes across. (p. 706)

Eva Figes's short, carefully measured novel **Light** records one day in the life of Claude Monet at his beloved Giverny, and one of its chief virtues is that it makes believable the artist's immersion in his art. Here there is no question of distance; from the beginning of the book the artist and his cause are bound together. . . . During the course of the book Figes only briefly describes Monet in the actual process of painting. In fact, though his presence is always felt, Monet himself appears only intermittently. Much of the novel focuses on his family and friends, gently exploring their characters and moods and differing responses to their cloistered little world and its strange, revealing, almost oppressive light. . . . Although Monet is often offstage, Figes so firmly establishes his impressionistic, light-filled world, constantly and inventively noting the effects of light on rooms and objects, on the painter's precious gardens and lily pond, that we become party to his obsession: his subject is everywhere.

By concentrating on the play of light at various instances, Figes does in prose what Monet sought to do on canvas: capture fleeting images and colors, moments in time. This method of identifying with an artist's goal by rendering the world in his individual style seems to me a unique way for a writer to portray a painter. (pp. 706-07)

Figes's focus on the subtle transformations light works on objects and landscapes points to the general sense of change and passing time that affects, to various degrees, all the characters. She further links that process to the gradual passing of an era. Even in the quiet, removed Giverny of 1900, signs of the modern age are evident. . . .

Tightly structured and framed, meticulously following each character from dawn until dusk, *Light* is also virtually plotless. These features, along with its illumination of small moments of being, recall the late fiction of Virginia Woolf, though the book lacks Woolf's complexity, her quiet intensity and poetry. At times, *Light* seems too schematic and studied, with Figes straining to give symbolic weight to mundane matters. And at times I wondered whether the real Monet would have been as concise and academic in his observations about his art as is the fictional artist. (p. 707)

Taken as a whole, however, *Light* is convincing and effective, and in its closing moments surprisingly touching as well. The single star, the "pinprick of pure light" that appears in the darkening sky at the end of the book, recalls the star that Monet observed at the beginning. And as day fades into night and light dissolves, we feel, along with the characters, a growing solitude, an odd sense of loss, as if the world as well as the creative spirit were suffering a kind of temporary death. (pp. 707-08)

> *Ronald DeFeo, "Hail, Holy Light," in* The Nation, *Vol. 237, No. 22, December 31, 1983-January 7, 1984, pp. 706-08.*

MAUREEN HOWARD

[*Light*] is a likeable small book, but the spirit of [Virginia Woolf's] *To The Lighthouse* broods over it like a dark cloud, flattening the surfaces. Good heavens, we have the famous tyrannical *pater familias*, the dinner-table scene (great care taken with the food), the visitors (atheist and village priest), the unspoken passion, and so forth. But we do not have Mrs. Ramsay or anything like the tension of Virginia Woolf's prose, those paragraphs that find their own shape bravely, independently, and loop right into the whole cloth of the narrative. Nor does this story, though it takes place on the eve of the Great War, have the off-stage threat of war—that tragic slash across the canvas of comic village life—that Woolf makes a presence in *Between the Acts*. True, the French landscape is disturbed by a train, and Octave, the clever writer who has come to lunch, drives an amusing yellow motorcar. But this is too miniature, too softly lit. In an earlier work, *Waking,* . . . Figes has written about a woman waking up from youth to age—her *Jacob's Room*. She is like a copyist with her easel set up in the museum, and the work is remarkable in just that way. (pp. ix, xii)

> *Maureen Howard, in a review of "Light," in* The Yale Review, *Vol. 73, No. 2, January, 1984, pp. ix, xii.*

Michel Foucault

1926-1984

French philosopher, psychologist, nonfiction writer, and editor.

Foucault is considered one of the most important thinkers to have emerged from France since 1960. He is sometimes called a historian of ideas. Foucault's methodology, which he regarded as an archaeological examination of knowledge, is based on a combination of historical, philosophical, epistemological, and linguistic analyses. Language is of central importance to Foucault's theory, for it directly connects the formation and utilization of discourses with those who wield power in society. As James Mall has noted, "Foucault is especially preoccupied with the use of power: the ways in which the social order classifies, manipulates, and isolates certain elements of itself: madness, illness, criminality, sexuality, etc." While critics frequently link him with the structuralists or post-structuralists, Foucault himself rejected such classification.

Foucault's first major work, *Folie et déraison: Histoire de la folie à l'âge classique* (1961; *Madness and Civilization: A History of Insanity in the Age of Reason*), is a treatise on the definition and treatment of madness in seventeenth- and eighteenth-century Europe. R. D. Laing said that in this work "the madness of Europe is revealed not in the persons of the madmen of Europe, but in the actions of the self-validated sane ones, who wrote the books, sanctified, and authorised by State, Church, and the representatives of bourgeois morality." In this book, Foucault introduces two issues which are central to his next two works: the emergence of the medical profession and its privileged discourse, and the general essence of language as a power base from which the "sane" world operates. According to Jean Starobinski, *Naissance de la clinique: Une archéologie du regard médical* (1963; *The Birth of the Clinic: An Archaeology of Medical Perception*) and *Les mots et les choses* (1966; *The Order of Things: An Archaeology of the Human Sciences*), along with *Madness and Civilization*, "make up a trilogy in which the author is successively a historian of psychiatry and psychopathology, of medicine, of natural history, of economics, and of grammar."

Foucault's other important works include *Surveiller et punir: Naissance de la prison* (1975; *Discipline and Punish: The Birth of the Prison*) and *Histoire de la sexualité, Volume 1: La volonté de savoir* (1976; *The History of Sexuality, Volume 1: An Introduction*). *Discipline and Punish* is a study of the development of the French penal system in which Foucault reasserts a basic premise introduced in *Madness and Civilization*: that it is essential to the fortification of a social order that aberrant "others" be isolated. For many critics it is the most accessible of Foucault's arguments. In *The History of Sexuality* Foucault focuses on the progression of the discourse on sexuality. He is especially intrigued by the changes that occurred when this discourse became scientific with the emergence of Sigmund Freud's theories and the practice of psychoanalysis.

Because of the density of his prose and the complexity of his theories, Foucault is often charged with having written works which are inaccessible. Among academics, however, Foucault has a considerable following, and many critics agree that he

© Jerry Bauer

is a major influence on contemporary French thought. As Edith Kurzweil has written, "Foucault's own marginality, objectively assessing and 'transcending' all of philosophy and knowledge, turning back upon itself with irony, avoiding oversimplification and reduction, marks him as one of the giants of our time."

(See also *Contemporary Authors*, Vol. 105.)

ROLAND BARTHES

[*The collection from which this excerpt is taken was originally published in 1964 under the title* Essais critiques.]

[In *Folie et déraison: Histoire de la folie à l'âge classique*, Foucault] has not written the history of madness, as he says, in a style of positivity: from the start he has refused to consider madness as a nosographic reality which has always existed and to which the scientific approach has merely varied from century to century. Indeed Foucault never defines madness; madness is not the *object* of knowledge, whose history must be rediscovered; one might say instead that *madness is nothing but this knowledge itself*: madness is not a disease, it is a variable and perhaps heterogeneous *meaning*, according to the period; Foucault never treats madness except as a functional reality: for him it is the pure function of a couple formed by reason and unreason, observer and observed. And the observer (the man of reason) has no *objective* privilege over the observed (the madman). It would thus be futile to try to find the modern names for dementia under its old names.

Here is a first shock to our intellectual habits; Foucault's method partakes at once of an extreme scientific discretion and of an extreme distance with regard to "science"; for on the one hand, nothing happens in the book which is not nominally given by documents of the period; . . . and on the other hand, the historian here studies an object whose objective character he deliberately puts in parentheses; not only does he describe collective representations (still rarely done in history), but he even claims that without being mendacious these representations somehow exhaust their object; we cannot reach madness outside the notions of men of reason (which does not mean, moreover, that these notions are illusory); it is therefore neither on the side of (scientific) reality nor on the side of the (mythic) image that we shall find the historical reality of madness: it is on the level of the interconstituent dialogue of reason and unreason, though we must keep in mind that this dialogue is faked: it involves a great silence, that of the mad: for the mad possess no metalanguage in which to speak of reason. In short, Michel Foucault refuses to constitute madness either as a medical object or as a collective hallucination; his method is neither positivist nor mythological; he does not even shift, strictly speaking, the reality of madness from its nosographic content to the pure representation men have made of it; he keeps identifying the reality of madness with a reality at once extensive and homogeneous with madness: the couple formed by reason and unreason. Now this shift has important consequences, both historically and epistemologically.

The history of madness as a medical phenomenon had to be nosographic: a simple chapter in the general—and triumphant—history of medicine. The history of reason/unreason, on the other hand, is a complete history which brings into play all the data of a specific historical society; paradoxically, this "immaterial" history immediately satisfies our modern insistence on a total history, which materialistic historians or ideologists appeal to without always managing to honor it. For the constitutive observation of madness by men of reason is very quickly seen to be a simple element of their *praxis:* the fate of the mad is closely linked to the society's needs with regard to labor, to the economy as a whole; this link is not necessarily causal, in the crude sense of the word: *simultaneous* with these needs appear representations which establish them in nature, and among these representations, which for a long time were moral ones, there is the image of madness; the history of madness always follows a history of the ideas of labor, of poverty, of idleness, and of unproductivity. Michel Foucault has taken great care to describe *simultaneously* the images of madness and the economic conditions within the same society; this is doubtless in the best materialist tradition; but where this tradition is—happily—transcended is in the fact that madness is never offered as an effect: men produce in the one impulse both solutions and signs; economic accidents (unemployment, for example, and its various remedies) immediately take their place in a structure of significations, a structure which may well pre-exist them; we cannot say that the needs *create* values, that unemployment *creates* the image of labor-as-punishment: rather the two meet as the true units of a vast system of signifying relations: this is what Foucault's analyses of classical society unceasingly suggest: the link which unites the foundation of the Hôpital Général to the economic crisis of Europe (beginning of the seventeenth century), or on the contrary the

link which unites the disappearance of confinement to the more modern sentiment that massive internment cannot solve the new problems of unemployment (end of the eighteenth century)—these links are essentially signifying links.

This is why the history described by Michel Foucault is a structural history. . . . Without ever breaking the thread of a diachronic narrative, Foucault reveals, for each period, what we should elsewhere call *sense units*, whose combination defines this period and whose translation traces the very movement of history; animality, knowledge, vice, idleness, sexuality, blasphemy, libertinage—these historical components of the demential image thus form signifying complexes, according to a kind of historical syntax which varies from epoch to epoch. . . . A more formalistic mind might have exploited more intensely the discovery of these sense units: in the notion of structure to which he appeals, Foucault emphasizes the notion of functional totality more than that of component units; but this is a matter of discourse; the meaning of the procedure is the same, whether we attempt a history of madness (as Foucault has done) or a syntax of madness (as we can imagine it): the question is still one of making forms and contents vary *simultaneously*. (pp. 164-67)

[What] we can infer from Foucault's analyses (and this is the second way in which his history is structural) is that madness (always conceived, of course, as a pure function of reason) corresponds to a permanent, one might say to a transhistorical *form;* this form cannot be identified with the marks or signs of madness (in the scientific sense of the term), i.e., with the infinitely various signifiers of what is signified (itself diverse) which each society has invested in unreason, dementia, madness, or alienation; it is a question, rather, of a *form of forms,* i.e., of a specific structure; this form of forms, this structure, is suggested on each page of Foucault's book: it is a complementarity which opposes and unites, on the level of society as a whole, the excluded and the included. . . . Naturally, we must repeat, each term of the function is fulfilled differently according to period, place, society; exclusion (or as we sometimes say today: deviation) has different contents (meanings), here madness, there shamanism, elsewhere criminality, homosexuality, etc. But a serious paradox begins here: in our societies, at least, the relation of exclusion is determined, and in a sense objectified, by only one of the two humanities participating in it; thus it is the excluded humanity which is named (mad, insane, alienated, criminal, libertine, etc.), it is the act of exclusion, by its very nomination, which in a positive sense accounts for both excluded and "included" ("exile" of the mad in the Middle Ages, confinement in the classical period, internment in the modern age). Thus it is on the level of this general form that madness can be structured (not defined); and if this form is present in any society (but never outside of a society), the only discipline which could account for madness (as for all forms of exclusion) would be anthropology (in the "cultural" and no longer "natural" sense the word increasingly acquires for us). In this perspective, Foucault might have found it advantageous to give some ethnographic references, to suggest the example of societies "without madmen" (but not without "excluded groups"); but also, no doubt, he would regard this additional distance, this serene purview of all humanity as a kind of reassuring alibi, a distraction from what is newest about his project: its bewilderment, its vertigo.

For this book, as we realize when we read it, is different from a book of history, even if such history were audaciously conceived, even if such a book were written, as is the case, by a philosopher. What is it, then? Something like a cathartic question asked of knowledge, of all knowledge, and not only of that knowledge which speaks about madness. Knowledge is no longer that calm, proud, reassuring, reconciling act which Balzac opposed to the will which burns and to the power which destroys; in the couple constituted by reason and madness, by included and excluded, knowledge is a taking of sides; the very act which apprehends madness no longer as an object but as the other face which reason rejects, thereby proceeding to the extreme verge of intelligence, this act too is an act of darkness: casting a brilliant light on the couple constituted by madness and reason, *knowledge* thereby illuminates its own solitude and its own particularity: manifesting the very history of the division, it cannot escape it.

This misgiving . . . is inherent in Foucault's very project; once madness is no longer defined substantially (''a disease'') or functionally (''antisocial conduct''), but structurally on the level of society as a whole as the discourse of reason about unreason, an implacable dialectic is set up; its origin is an obvious paradox: for a long time men have accepted the idea of reason's historical relativity; the history of philosophy is invented, written, taught, it belongs, one may say, to a hygiene of our societies; but there has never been a corresponding history of *unreason;* in this couple, outside of which neither term can be constituted, one of the partners is historical, participates in the values of civilization, escapes the fatality of being, conquers the freedom of doing; the other partner is excluded from history, fastened to an essence, either supernatural, or moral, or medical; doubtless a fraction—tiny, moreover—of culture acknowledges madness as a respectable or even inspired object, at least through certain of its mediators, Hölderlin, Nietzsche, Van Gogh; but this observation is very recent and, above all, it admits of no exchange: in short it is a liberal observation, an observation of good will, unfortunately powerless to dissipate bad faith. (pp. 167-69)

Foucault shows very well that the Middle Ages were actually much more open to madness than our modernity, for madness then, far from being objectified in the form of a disease, was defined as a great passage toward the supernatural, in short as a communication (this is the theme of *The Ship of Fools*); and it is the very progressivism of the modern period which here seems to exert the densest form of bad faith. . . .

The history of madness could be ''true'' only if it were naïve, i.e., written by a madman; but then it could not be written in terms of history, so that we are left with the incoercible bad faith of knowledge. This is an inevitability which greatly exceeds the simple relations of madness and unreason; indeed, it affects all ''thought,'' or to be more exact, all recourse to a metalanguage, whatever it might be: each time men speak about the world, they enter into a relation of exclusion, even when they speak in order to denounce it: a metalanguage is always terrorist. This is an endless dialectic, which can seem sophistical only to minds possessed of a reason substantial as a nature or a right; the others will experience it dramatically, or generously, or stoically; in any case, they know that bewilderment, that vertigo of discourse on which Michel Foucault has just cast so much light, a vertigo which appears not only upon contact with madness, but indeed each time that man, taking his distances, observes the world as different, which is to say, each time he writes. (p. 170)

Roland Barthes, ''Taking Sides,'' in his Critical Essays, *translated by Richard Howard, Northwestern University Press, 1972, pp. 163-70.*

R. D. LAING

[*Madness and Civilization*] is a work of such distinction that it takes some time to accustom one's self to its sustained intensity and verbal momentum, before one can begin to come to terms with the measure of its truth, as total picture or in terms of its constituent elements.

Foucault's overall plan is to excavate the sane perception of madness (*la folie*) of the 17th and 18th century in Europe, and France in particular. He lays before us the archaeology, as he puts it, of the broken dialogue between reason and unreason: he reveals by a phenomenological method the history of how the theoretical, experiential and practical connotations of madness (as error, blindness, animal innocence and human culpability, derangement of reason and monstrous freedom) came at the beginning of the 19th century to be imprisoned in the medical theory and practice of pathology.

He shows clearly how, in the 17th century, a movement spread all over Europe to confine by a massive police operation what to us appear as a heterogeneous set of people, but who were perceived then in terms of some synthetic unity we can surmise without fully recapturing—the debauched, spendthrift fathers, prodigal sons, blasphemers, vagabonds, the poor and the mad. Within a few months one in a hundred of the inhabitants of Paris found themselves imprisoned thus. These people were a danger to the State, a threat to family life, exemplars of the fruit of sin. . . .

After Foucault the textbooks will have to be rewritten. . . . The separation of the 'insane' from the mass of the confined was, to a considerable extent, for the sake of the 'sane' population. Physical restraint was given up (and then only very partially) because 'moral' coercion was found to be an even more effective technique of terrorisation. No one ever dreamt of any other form of treatment than repression of one form or another. No one ever took what the mad were saying or doing with any other emotions than pity or horror.

It is not the account of the madness of the supposed madmen of the 17th century to the 19th century that is particularly terrifying about this book. We hardly hear their voices at all. What we do hear through these pages is how the men of reason experienced and treated the men of unreason. Victory belonged to those who could control the power structures of society. The other side of the story is possibly irretrievably lost. The madness of Europe is revealed not in the persons of the madmen of Europe, but in the actions of the self-validated sane ones, who wrote the books, sanctified, and authorised by State, Church, and the representatives of bourgeois morality. The history of madness documented here is the history of the projection into the few who were destroyed or forgotten, of the lunacy of the majority who won the day.

This book was first published in 1961, and it could not have been possible much before that. Until a few years ago, the collective definition of European man as sane by his own consent imposed such an iron vice on consciousness that hardly anyone was able to break out without breaking down. I do not know any other book which *see through* (that is *dia-gnoses*) what has been going on, in such a scholarly and systematic way. It remains itself fully within the idiom of sanity, while undermining the presuppositions of its own foundations. To define true madness—is to be nothing else but mad. . . .

Foucault's disenchanted illuminations reveal a desolate space occupied by the ruins of that classical age of reason which found it necessary to disavow all that threatened its formal purity. Madness epitomised the nightmare of being destroyed by what had been exiled from its elegant and ordered cosmic landscape. Foucault's intellect, style, and erudition would be impossible without the whole tradition that he both adorns and destroys. The intellectual structures of its ontological imperialism are rapidly crumbling, along with grosser material forms of dominion they once were used to justify, and perhaps sometimes also found justification within. . . .

Foucault sometimes whirls words into pirouettes which are more to be admired for their brilliance than trusted for their veracity. 'Madness designates the equinox between the vanity of night's hallucinations and the non-being of light's judgments.' He can be so daring as to begin the *closure* of an already long sentence with '. . . for tragedy is ultimately nothing but . . .' and tells us in 15 words!

Foucault does not 'take sides'. He simply brings into view a few turns of the amplifying spiral of one form of breakdown of communication between human beings in Europe, and by a classical dialectical reversal, the madness of the apparent sanity of 'reason'. More spirals of this vicious vortex have unfolded since the moment Foucault breaks off his narrative at the beginning of the 19th century, but he appears to have no axe to grind in contemporary psychiatric controversy.

His concluding chapter where he moves rapidly from Goya to Artaud is the weakest, leaving it unclear whether reticence, tact or lack of time may have deterred him from adding his own attributions about 'madness' to those of others he has so mercilessly displayed before us. Perhaps he was too clever to fall into a trap, he was not sufficiently wise fully to see. Nevertheless, we can surmise that if Foucault continues to survive the torrent of his own intellect he will be one of the writers to whom we shall in our life time continue to turn with a somewhat terrified delight, to be instructed when we are not too dazzled.

> R. D. Laing, "The Invention of Madness," in New Statesman, *Vol. 73, No. 1892, June 16, 1967, p. 843.*

GEORGE STEINER

[Foucault's] name carried a deepening, though esoteric, resonance throughout the early sixties. But it was with **"Les Mots et les Choses,"** published in Paris in 1966 and now published here as **"The Order of Things,"** that Foucault assumed his current eminence.

[An] honest first reading produces an almost intolerable sense of verbosity, arrogance and obscure platitude. Page after page could be the rhetoric of a somewhat weary sybil indulging in free association. Recourse to the French text shows that this is not a matter of awkward translation. The following is a crucial but also entirely representative example:

"Philology, biology, and political economy were established, not in the places formerly occupied by *general grammar, natural history,* and the *analysis of wealth,* but in an area where those forms of knowledge did not exist, in the space they left blank, in the deep gaps that separated their broad theoretical segments and that were filled with the murmur of the ontological continuum. The object of knowledge in the nineteenth century is formed in the very place where the Classical plenitude of being has fallen silent. Inversely, a new philosophical space was to emerge in the place where the objects of Classical

knowledge dissolved. The moment of attribution (as a form of judgment) and that of articulation (as a general patterning of beings) separated, and thus created the problem of the relations between a formal apophantics and a formal ontology. . . ."

Faced with almost four hundred pages in a similar vein, one must ask oneself, "Why bother?" Is this kind of thing to be taken seriously, or does it belong, with a good deal else that has come out of recent French "post-structuralism" and German "hermeneutics," to "the murmur of the ontological continuum"? Is anything being *said* here, which can be grasped and verified in any rational way? . . .

One asks these questions because Foucault's claims are sweeping, and because, one supposes, he would wish to be read seriously or not at all. His appeal, moreover, to contemporaries of exceptional intelligence both at home and in England . . . is undeniable. This is no confidence-trick. Something of originality and, perhaps, of very real importance, is being argued in these often rebarbative pages. Can it be hammered out, though necessarily in a simplified, abbreviated form? . . .

"Les Mots et les Choses"—the original title ("Words and Things") is much preferable—sets out to provide "an archaeology of the human sciences," or more simply, an account of how the organizing models of human perception and knowledge have altered between the Renaissance and the end of the 19th century. The particular models chosen by Foucault, who regards them as central and interrelated, are those of biology, linguistics and economics. In that they formulate and comprehend such vital notions as meaning, exchange and the critical discriminations between the organic and the man-made, these three disciplines are the "human sciences" par excellence. Understand their idiom and altering presuppositions, and you will obtain systematic insights into the ways in which Western culture has structured both its image of the personal self and of reality.

But why "archaeology"? The word has its aura of depth and genesis, outside its normal field, since Freud. Foucault uses it to establish the differences between his enterprise and that of intellectual history and phenomenology in the usual sense.

What concerns him, as he seeks to demonstrate in a long opening chapter on Velasquez's painting "Las Meninas," is the spatial mapping within which knowledge becomes knowledge rather than accidental array of facts and objects. We only perceive that which the conventions of significance lead us to see. A science, a philosophic doctrine, a linguistic and grammatical code can be regarded as "spaces of ordered and exploratory experience." The conventions of perspective and the stylizations of three-dimensionality in the graphic or plastic arts offer a rough analogy to what Foucault is after.

It is not, he argues, any autonomous logic inherent in a given body of knowledge, it is not the accident of individual genius in the thinker or scientist, which account for the true substance and history of "knowing" and, inferentially, of feeling. It is the available terrain and network of relations, some highly arbitrary, within which the sensibility of a given epoch and society will recognize a rational order.

The aggregate of significant spaces, the underlying stratigraphy of intellectual life, the whole set of the presuppositions of thought, is what Foucault calls an *episteme.* (p. 8)

Having formulated his methodological image—and one wonders whether "topology" would not have been more apt than "archaeology"—Foucault sets out to analyze the principal changes in the *episteme,* in the "knowing of knowledge," in Western thought since the Renaissance. At each stage of the argument, an all-inclusive philosophic and psychological framework is tested and made explicit by reference to the study of living forms, of speech and of economic relations. These are the three cardinal classifiers in the total set.

The thesis goes something like this. The *episteme* of the 16th century was founded on *similitude.* All phenomena and designative modes were based on a manifold mirroring and interplay of analogies and affinities. The Renaissance world was a kind of weave, folding upon itself, forming a chain of vital resemblances through which alone individual facts or objects could find a meaningful location. This principle of analogy made of the eye both a receptor and source of light, almost tangibly threaded to the object contemplated. It was thought that language works first because it is a system of autonomous signs and second because it is a kind of "organic mirror" in which every named or inferred thing has its exact counterpart. (pp. 8, 28)

The *episteme* of the 17th-18th century Classical period is radically different. It involved "an immense reorganization of culture," a literal re-orientation of the space in which Western consciousness perceived subject and object, reality and dream. The old kinships between knowledge and divination, the mirroring reciprocities of language and fact, break off. Now, instead of *similitude,* the crucial instrumentality is *representation.* Foucault seems to mean by this that words are now entirely transparent and arbitrary counters. Thus, to say things, to name them, is to put them in a kind of necessary order. The "necessity" seems to derive from the fact that Classical man now sees objects in a logical space or framework.

"The language of the Classical age is caught in the grid of thought, woven into the very fabric of its unrolling. It is not an exterior effect of thought, but thought itself." In other terms, knowing and speaking are interwoven. Every speech act, every mental proposition "down to the least of its molecules" becomes an exact way of naming. Grammar is a kind of tracing-paper laid across the ordered contours of the world. Hence the primary impulse of Classical thought and science toward taxonomy. The classificatory genius of the great botanist Linnaeus represents the true spirit of the age. . . .

The Classical *episteme* breaks down in turn. Henceforth, the central pulse of language and thought resides "outside representation . . . in a sort of behind-the-scenes world even deeper and more dense than representation itself." Pure knowledge becomes isolated and divorced from particular, empirical disciplines; these, however, become fatally enmeshed with problems of subjectivity, with the uncertainties that personal consciousness insinuates into every act of perception. Words cease to intersect with representation or to provide an immediate grid for the knowledge of things. They acquire an autonomous, enigmatic being of their own, interposing themselves, as it were, between self and object. (p. 28)

Dialectics, historicity and *energy* are the key terms of the new phase. They characterize the emergence of modern science after Cuvier, of modern economic theory after Ricardo, of the new linguistics first discernible in Bopp's celebrated studies of Sanskrit. "We speak because we act, and not because recognition is a means of cognition. Like action, language expresses a profound will to something." Foucault's choice of terms here

is deliberate: it reflects Nietzsche, in whom he sees one of the two principal witnesses of the new *episteme.* The other is Mallarmé, supreme experiencer of the opacity of words.

As to the future: "As the archaeology of our thought easily shows, man is an invention of recent date. And one perhaps nearing its end." The mode of individuation and "outside reality" which has dominated the past centuries of our civilization, especially in the West, may yield soon to new spaces of perception. If I understand Foucault, he is saying that "man" himself is a symbolic product of the ways in which certain men have, over a very short period of history, thought about themselves and human knowledge.

In a grossly abbreviated form (the style of this book is intensely repetitive), this is, I think, a fair outline of Foucault's "archaeology." What does it amount to?

The first point worth making is that similar ideas have been put forward as long ago as Lovejoy and Whitehead. In its gloss on the reciprocities and symbolic codes of the Renaissance, Foucault's account agrees largely with that given in the brilliant, pioneering works of Frances Yates. But Miss Yates's investigations of the 16th-century intellectual world are far more incisive and animate with a sense of magic. The notion of the *episteme* strikingly recalls Thomas Kuhn's well-known definition of "paradigms." . . . The close bracketing of linguistic communication and economic exchanges is, of course, the hallmark of Levi-Strauss. The choice of Nietzsche and Mallarmé as archetypal of the modernity of consciousness is, in current intellectual history, almost routine.

This is as it should be. A serious work of scholarship and intellectual analysis must draw, at many points, on the work of predecessors and contemporaries. The trouble is that Foucault speaks as if he were a solitary explorer, opening up silent seas. Where allusion is made to fellow-scholars or thinkers, it is usually anonymous and abusive. The unwary reader of **"The Order of Things"** will hardly realize how often Foucault's theses have been anticipated or been prepared for by detailed scholarly investigations elsewhere. In this lofty indifference, Foucault is, unfortunately, representative of the current French vein. Parisian intellectual movements have, over this past decade, "discovered" the legacies of Freud, of Roman Jakobson, of Malinowski, of Saussure, as if these epochal contributions had passed unnoticed in the rest of the world. The consequence is, at moments, a kind of breathless parochial grandeur.

As to the substance of Foucault's case, only detailed examination by scholars in the relevant fields will finally establish its strengths and defects. At decisive junctures, the choice of material looks very arbitrary. A glance at a standard work, such as H. Aarsleff's "The Study of Language in England 1780-1860," suggests that Foucault's readings of Locke and of the background to modern linguistics are, to put it mildly, wilful. In the light of editorial and analytic work now in progress, his observations on Newton and Voltaire seem slapdash. One can but wonder how much at home he is in the very intricate matter of the vocabulary of the exact and descriptive sciences in the 16th and 17th centuries. (pp. 28-9)

But this is not to say that there are not brilliant strains in this book. Foucault seems at his best not when asserting grand designs, but when working close to a defined text or focus. His interpretation of "Don Quixote" as a document in which we see language breaking off its old kinship with things—

"Don Quixote reads the world in order to prove his books"—is witty and penetrates deeply. Though, like much of the French intelligentsia, he greatly overrates the importance of de Sade, he has fresh observations to make on de Sade's role in the evolution of linguistic feeling. He is surely right when he sees in the insane loquacities of "Juliette" a desperate attempt by language to "name," and thus enact exhaustively, those finalities of desire and violence which always chide it.

The parallel discussions of the ways in which the dissolution of the classical notions of grammar and taxonomy can be traced in speech habits and the organic sciences, are richly stimulating. Though I am scarcely competent to judge, Foucault does seem to say acute and important things about Lamarck, a figure who plays a somewhat shadowy but fascinating part in modern biological thought. As not very many have before him, Foucault recognizes the sheer philosophic force and pivotal role of Ricardo's contribution to the theory of money. Indeed, time and again, a local observation in these pages will arrest one by its liveliness or suggestive paradox.

A thinner, more scrupulous book is struggling to emerge from this oracular corpus: a book that deals not with the allegedly dramatic metamorphoses of all Western consciousness from Francis Bacon to the surrealists, but with key moments in the history of language-studies and scientific logic during the 18th and early 19th centuries. Whether it be Spenglerian or "sociological," the whole idea of a visible "Consciousness" appearing on Monday mornings or at the start and end of centuries, is a fatal simplification. It is a part of the enormous but also indistinct task he has set for himself, that so many of Foucault's generalizations are too nebulous to be tested, while a good number of his particulars are too esoteric or devoid of context to be truly representative.

Foucault has better to offer. His previous work on the mythologies and practices of mental therapy is of undoubted stature. It shows a superb gift for intellectual mimesis. He is able to re-experience the idiom, the identifying reflexes of a past. He can master large masses of often recondite and technical documentation. He has a writer's eye for the incisive quote, for the nerve-center of a social attitude. He fixes on questions of intense interest.

"Les Mots et les Choses" opens with a discussion of one of the arcane, humorous fables of Borges. There is no finer craftsman of understatement and generous attribution. It is these one misses in Michel Foucault's enterprise. Yet even where its sybilline loftiness is damaging, one is left with a sense of real and original force. (pp. 30-1)

> George Steiner, "The Mandarin of the Hour: Michel Foucault," in The New York Times Book Review, February 28, 1971, pp. 8, 28-31.

RICHARD HOWARD

In 1965 I translated Foucault's earlier book **Madness & Civilization,** a work which presented me, my editor, and the reviewers . . . a great many problems of diction, phrasing and even, ultimately, sense. **The Order of Things,** which is an echo of Foucault's undertaking to write a history of madness in the Classical age, might be said not only to present but to absent (since no names are mentioned) a great many more such problems, for whereas in the history of madness Foucault was investigating the way in which a culture can determine the difference that limits it, he is concerned here to observe how a culture experiences the propinquity of things, how it establishes the *tabula* of their relationships and the order by which they must be considered. He is concerned, in short, with a history of resemblance. . . .

In his archeology of labor, language and the science of life which was not yet called biology, Foucault dramatizes man's existence, or rather man's invention, between two modes of discourse; that of the Classical period (post-Renaissance to Romantic) and that of our own. . . . I believe it is possible to read these many difficult pages to great advantage, though I do not want to pass over the difficulties without a sample, for . . . the difficulties are part of the way Foucault has found to free his mind of what is *not* difficult, of what is in fact easy and therefore, merely, known. A mind released from facility will produce, then, a prose like this:

> The methods of interpretation of modern thought are opposed by the techniques of formalization: the first claiming to make language speak as it were below itself, and as near as possible to what is being said in it, without it; the second claiming to control any language that may arise, and to impose upon it from above the law of what it is possible to say. Interpretation and formalization have become the two great forms of analysis of our time—in fact, we know no others. But do we know what the relations of exegesis and formalization are? Are we capable of mastering and controlling them? . . . It is true that the division between interpretation and formalization presses upon us and dominates us today. But it is not rigorous enough: the fork it forms has not been driven far enough down into our culture, its two branches are too contemporaneous for us to be able to say even that it is prescribing a simple option or that it is inviting us to choose between the past, which believed in meaning, and the present (the future) which has discovered signification. . . .

That is a sample of the difficulties, but it is also a sufficient hostage to fortune, defining the kind of rewards Foucault provides at any point. That I am not qualified, as I have admitted, to *receive* them at any point need not make against a reading of the book—even of the book as a whole. But I am qualified, in the two readings of the book I have made, in French and in English, to remark that on literature, a form of language recently codified, Foucault is quite central to our sense of where we are. After all, in our culture, even the isolation of a particular language whose special mode of being is "literary" is unexampled, is unexplored. And like the structuralists from whom he so rigorously separates himself . . . , Foucault is startling in his insistence upon, for literature, a radical intransitivity. In his archeology, or as a result of its findings, literature becomes detached from all the values which were able to keep it in general circulation during the Classical age (taste, pleasure, naturalness, truth), and creates within its own "space" everything which will insure a ludic—as opposed to legal—denial of them (the scandalous, the ugly, the impossible—Sade, Artaud, Bataille); for Foucault, literature breaks with the whole definition of genres as forms adapted to an order of representations and becomes merely a manifestation of a language with no other law than the law of affirming—in opposition to all other forms of discourse—its own precarious existence, "as if discourse could have no other content than the expression of its own form." It is at the end of his section on literature that I came, suddenly, to the realization that there was nothing— or almost nothing—freakish or parochial about Foucault after all; that he is carrying out, in the noblest way, the promiscuous aim of true culture, which is, as Matthew Arnold used to say, to do away with classes, or at least, as we would now append, with classifications. That when Foucault says that for us literature has become "a silent, cautious deposition of the word upon the whiteness of a piece of paper, where it can possess neither sound nor interlocutor, where it has nothing to say but itself, nothing to do but shine in the brightness of its being," he is speaking with the same eloquence we may hear in Northrop Frye . . . and in our own "formalist" critics, in Bloom and Hartman and. . . . The list is open, as is *The Order of Things,* which has taught me (has reminded me) of the essential and marvelous poverty of language, always brought back to itself where it is given its power of transformation: to say something else with the same words, to give the same words another meaning. (p. 22)

> Richard Howard, "*Our Sense of Where We Are,*" *in* The Nation, *Vol. 213, No. 1, July 5, 1971, pp. 21-2.*

PETER CAWS

Michel Foucault is one of a handful of French thinkers who have, in the last 10 years, given an entirely new direction to theoretical work in the so-called "human sciences," the study of language, literature, psychiatry, intellectual history and the like. He is best known for **"The Order of Things" ("Les Mots et les choses"),** a rich and controversial work in which he introduced an "archaeological" method of great originality and, I believe, importance. This method, or rather its presuppositions, is the subject of **"The Archaeology of Knowledge."**

It involves an attempt to decide just what it is about certain utterances or inscriptions—real objects in a real world which leave traces behind to be discovered, classified and related to one another—that qualifies them as "statements" (*énoncés*) belonging to various bodies of knowledge (biology, economics and so on). What is the reality of such bodies of knowledge? How do we arrive at them from the "statements"? How do these bodies of knowledge change over time? By Foucault's own admission his method is more an exploratory series of questions and reflections than a finished theory; its usefulness lies in its opening up a rather chaotic domain and in its implicit challenge to the neat but abstract categories of the history and economy of ideas.

This usefulness, however, is seriously damaged by a kind of conspiracy of unreadability between author and translator [A. M. Sheridan Smith]. . . . Never a man to use one word where five will do, or to say straightforwardly what can be said obliquely or figuratively, Foucault has, confronted with the genuinely difficult task he has set himself in **"The Archaeology of Knowledge,"** produced an extravagantly and self-indulgently rhetorical text, full of asides on his own development, other people's reactions to his work and so on, many of which I found downright embarrassing.

Now in French this is not so bad as I have made it seem. Almost everybody does it; stylistic showing-off, even of the most narcissistic kind, is something people get accustomed to,

so that it does not get in the way of the ideas that are being expressed. But in English it is thoroughly distracting and very hard to stomach. (p. 6)

[Foucault's] most baroque formulations are brought over inflexibly into English, and matters are made even worse by two tendencies of the translation: on the one hand to resort to awkward or archaic or recondite equivalents instead of plain circumlocutions, and on the other to make outright mistakes about the sense of what is said.

The result is often bewildering, and people who look for clarity in philosophical discourse will no doubt—and quite understandably—put the book down in large numbers as completely hopeless. . . . Foucault has a strong spatial imagination, and things are always happening behind or under the facade or the surface of discourse—for example, "an immense density of systematicities" lurks there. Working at such a disadvantage to begin with, he really does not need a translator who introduces spatial distortions of his own—yet consider "operates between the twin poles of totality and plethora" as a translation of "est placée sous le double signe de la totalité et de la pléthore."

All this is a great shame. Good ideas ought not to be encumbered with bad prose; readers ought not to have to endure such linguistic torture to get at them. Things are a little better in **"The Discourse on Language,"** Foucault's inaugural lecture at the Collège de France, printed here as an appendix. This is an extremely important work—much more so, in my opinion, than **"The Archaeology of Knowledge"**—which gives reason to hope that Foucault may have successfully survived his self-referential methodological turn and be opening a new line of inquiry even more interesting than the earlier ones—an investigation of the institutionalization and the politicization of discourse. (pp. 6, 22)

His hypothesis is "that in every society the production of discourse is at once controlled, selected, organized and redistributed according to a certain number of procedures, whose role is to avert its powers and its dangers."

His discussion of these procedures, which apart from obvious cases of censorship tend to be invisible to us, is penetrating and provocative. They include the more or less overt suppression of forms of discourse (especially those dealing too explicitly with sex or politics) that are considered to overstep acceptable boundaries; the dismissal of other forms as the product of insanity; the neutralization of others by commentators who inscribe them in "traditions" and "disciplines" (or dismiss them, again, because they refuse such pigeonholing); and the positive insistence that the speaker or writer should be properly certified as a competent authority. In these and other ways society manifests a kind of fear of the word, against which it seeks to protect itself by such strategies of exclusion and limitation. From now on, as a result of Foucault's perceptions, an analysis of these strategies in their historical development will have to complement any analysis of the bodies of discourse that have survived them. This is a new and potentially invaluable way of approaching the whole domain of intellectual history.

But here again Foucault is made to sound silly by careless translation. (p. 22)

A salient feature of Foucault's preoccupation with his own image continues to be his extraordinary sensitivity to any hint of a suggestion that he might be a structuralist, and by now one is inclined to concede the point: if he minds so much, other words can certainly be found. The term "structuralism," as Roland Barthes puts it, "has become uncertain," and while it has its place among the artifacts, we should allow Foucault to be the practitioner rather than the object of archaeological inquiry. But like so many practitioners he is really much better at doing it than at talking about it. (p. 24)

Peter Caws, "An Immense Density of Systematicities," in The New York Times Book Review, October 22, 1972, pp. 6, 22, 24.

MAURICE CRANSTON

Michel Foucault has for some years been the most prominent French practitioner of the history of ideas. . . .

Foucault, who is in his forties, has always wanted to make a break with the preceding generation of fashionable French intellectuals, led by men like Sartre and Merleau-Ponty, with their Germanic love of total metaphysics, and their austere rebarbative styles. Foucault has restored pleasure to French philosophy: what he has failed to restore is clarity. One thing, indeed, which he has never hitherto made clear is the nature of his own activity as a theorist. He does not like to be called a historian: and his own word for what he does is "archaeology." His latest book [*The Archaeology of Knowledge*], ably translated into English by Alan Sheridan Smith, is an attempt to explain what this peculiar kind of archaeology is.

It is a less interesting and attractive book than Foucault's earlier ones, if only because its subject matter, the methodology of history (or archaeology) is much more dry and technical than history (or archaeology) itself: and Foucault's virtuosity and panache is not much help to him in working over ground which has already been cultivated by such scholarly philosophers of history as Croce, Collingwood, Lovejoy and Oakeshott. Those philosophers have challenged the popular conception of history as a true record of the past, and each has offered an alternative interpretation of what historical understanding might be.

Foucault, on the other hand, takes the more extreme course of repudiating history altogether, and claiming to be doing something else: namely his archaeology. . . .

The only kind of history which he regards as philosophically respectable is a history conscious of itself as indistinguishable from the study of silent monuments and objects, indistinguishable, in effect, from archaeology.

However, the particular branch of history in which Foucault has specialized, cultural history or intellectual history, is the furthest removed from conventional archaeology, insofar as its raw materials are seldom silent monuments, but documents, books, works of art. It is perhaps the most difficult kind of history to write. What often passes for the history of ideas is highly suspect, and Foucault's own indictment of conventional history of ideas is a telling one.

Foucault does not care to be called a structuralist any more than he cares to be called a historian: but what has always been most effective in his analysis of the past has been his method of explaining cultural phenomena in the light of the dominant intellectual systems in terms of which past epochs conceived the world. As he puts it in his present book, the subject matter of his kind of archaeology is discourse—discourse not treated as a sign of something else, but discourse as a practice obeying

certain rules, not a "document" but a "monument." What Foucault seems still determined to deny is that this whole enterprise has more in common with structuralist anthropology than it has with anything that is ordinarily known as archaeology. The reader is tempted to persist in considering him, nevertheless, as an outstanding exponent of an explanatory method which the ethnologist Claude Levi-Strauss put on the map in France; together they have made the word structuralist almost as modish as the word existentialist 20 years ago.

Maurice Cranston, "Digging in the Junkyards of Our Past," in Book World—The Washington Post, October 29, 1972, p. 3.

JEAN STAROBINSKI

[*The Birth of the Clinic: An Archaeology of Medical Perception*] is a description of the changes in the language of medicine, particularly French medicine, between 1794 and 1820. It is therefore in the first place a work of history, concerned with a specific problem during a specific period. But it is also an experiment in a new way of writing the history of science, a testing ground for a radically redefined historical epistemology and methodology. Hence the double appeal of this book, which will be read not only by those who are interested in this seminal period of medical history but also by those who are dissatisfied with the traditional procedures of intellectual history and would like to see historians of ideas rethink their objectives and their methods.

The Birth of the Clinic, published in France in 1963, came after Foucault's *Histoire de la Folie* (*Madness and Civilization*, 1961) and preceded his *Les Mots et les Choses* (*The Order of Things*, 1966). Together these works make up a trilogy in which the author is successively a historian of psychiatry and psychopathology, of medicine, of natural history, of economics, and of grammar. This ambitious enterprise has not only yielded positive results of great value, it has also led to an important theoretical advance. Foucault's latest book, *L'Archéologie du Savoir (The Archaeology of Knowledge)*, may be seen as the methodological postscript to his trilogy on the history of science: in this work he sums up his position, clarifying his aims, freely criticizing certain aspects of his work, and proposing new goals for future research.

We cannot fully understand *The Birth of the Clinic* unless we are aware of its position in this series and take note of Foucault's subsequent declarations, in which he puts distance between himself and his preoccupations at the time when he wrote this book. In particular we need to know that the expression "*regard médical*" (medical perception), which figures in this book's subtitle and reflects much of Foucault's argument, now no longer seems to him "very well chosen," since it seems to "refer to *the* unifying or synthesizing function of a subject," i.e., of a thinker or a thinking mind. And there are indeed passages in *The Birth of the Clinic* which are genuine phenomenological analyses, where a subject (the doctor, the scientist, "medical perception" itself) is seen in the act of constituting the objects of its thoughts.

Since he wrote these pages Michel Foucault has completely transferred his emphasis to what he calls the "order of discourse," i.e., to discovering the laws that tacitly govern the intellectual discourse of a given period. He now emphasizes the "dispersion of the subject," i.e., the ways by which all thinking, no matter how individual or "creative" it may seem, is unconsciously but systematically constrained by the rules or codes that are embedded in the discourse of the times. . . . [Foucault] would prefer to leave out of *The Birth of the Clinic* those emotional terms which (however discreetly) suggest a psychology of scientific discovery.

Nevertheless Foucault is far from wishing to disown this book; it is an important element in the inquiry which is the basis of his current theorizing. . . . We could call this book a study of the styles of medical knowledge, or more precisely a study of the differences in such styles, an inquiry concerned with the mutations, discontinuities, incompatibilities, and displacements which make the medical discourse of the nineteenth century totally unlike that of preceding centuries. . . .

Michel Foucault's own style, as one might guess, is frequently polemical when he seeks to refute the old historiography. It has to be admitted that he handles his weapon well; his foil may draw blood occasionally, but at least it is not poisoned. Most of the time he simply omits to mention the previous studies on the subject as a sign of distrust for traditional scholarship. However, this polemic plays a secondary role in his book; the essential thing is his description of the different styles of medical knowledge, the social "space" in which these styles are practically deployed—at home or in a hospital for example—the objects they select or reject, the concepts they use, and the metaphors they favor. And this description is not done in the "scientific" language of contemporary linguistics or semiology; it is specifically philosophical in nature and is expressed in a splendidly literary language, full of figures, dramatic turns of phrase, metaphors, wordplay, allusions, and poetic inventions, all of which introduce an element of the unexpected into the treatment of such a subject. It should be added that Michel Foucault's prose, with all its bold playfulness and elegant originality, can be very attractive to the French reader.

Foucault may be difficult and occasionally irritating, but he is never obscure; he is disconcerting, but this is because his writing is so full of dazzling insights. The English translation by A. M. Sheridan Smith is both faithful and subtle, the translator teases out the meaning of Foucault's lapidary and sometimes cryptic formulations and performs veritable *tours de force* in the rendering of his metaphors. The reader is given the feeling of a style which is lively, original, and constantly thought-provoking.

Michel Foucault's starting point is the medical science that immediately preceded the rise, at the end of the eighteenth century, of the clinic, by which he means both clinical medicine and the teaching hospital. Eighteenth-century medicine, as he describes it, was concerned principally with classifying different forms of illness and setting them out in charts like those of the botanists. In practice the doctor's task was to recognize the species of illness of which the patient was a representative. . . .

This medicine preferred to let the ailment declare itself in its essential being and was afraid that this might be distorted by premature intervention; it therefore tended to favor biding one's time. Foucault—and this is a constant feature of his analysis—draws important conclusions from this concerning the social *space* where the illness was situated and the *place* occupied by medical practice. According to the "medicine of species" the patient should remain at home, while the doctor should give his assistance in "the natural environment of social life—the family."

This situation was to change radically when at the end of the eighteenth century hospitals were organized to receive a large number of patients and became the medical training ground par excellence. From then on medicine spoke a different language, creating for itself a new subject matter, basing itself on a different institutional organization, forming its concepts on the strength of new sorts of experience, and opening the way to different forms of medical practice. This change was in large part a consequence of the Revolution and the socio-political upheaval in French life. (p. 18)

Foucault demonstrates very clearly the interconnections between medicine as a science, medical activity as a social fact, and the university's role in transmitting "scientific learning." . . .

The French Revolution, as Foucault shows, reorganized the teaching of medicine, centralized it, subjected it to state control, and established new hierarchies. But before it did this, the Revolution went through a period of Utopian daydreaming: this was not the first time nor the last that people have dreamed of a just state sharing out prosperity equally among all its citizens and thus eliminating not only poverty but illness. Almshouses and hospitals thus became superfluous; they were the blemishes on the face of the old order. The new education would create nothing but healthy, virtuous people devoted to the revolutionary cause. . . .

After all these daydreams and myths what actually came into being was a new pedagogical and technical organization, in which teaching hospitals, "schools of health," and new categories of professionals were planned. The vision here was of a "transparent, undivided" medical domain that would be "exposed from top to bottom to a gaze armed nonetheless with its privileges and qualifications . . . : in liberty, disease was to formulate of itself an unchanging truth, offered, undisturbed, to the doctor's gaze; and society, medically invested, instructed, and supervised, would, by that very fact, free itself from disease."

But this vision too, according to Foucault, was itself "only one segment of the dialectic of the *Lumières* transported into the doctor's eye." In other words the revolutionary reorganization of the University was at first no more than a necessary condition for the rise of clinical medicine; while the revolutionary theme of the doctor liberating society from newly liberated disease was hardly an adequate conceptual basis for the practice of this medicine. What clinical medicine lacked and what it had to create was "a new, coherent, unitary model for the formation of medical objects, perceptions, and concepts."

At this point, writing of the same events, other historians bring in a series of factors whose combined effect they see as playing a determining role in the birth of clinical medicine. (p. 20)

["Traditional" history] invokes causal relations, none of which is presented as a sufficient cause, but all of which together make up a sociocultural pattern; in this way it defines the sum of conditions which made possible the rise of the new medicine. All of these facts are fleetingly mentioned by Foucault, but none of them is used to provide a causal explanation. He shows the same distrust of socioeconomic "causal attributions" as of expressive or psychological ones. He is as unwilling to admit a Freudian explanation of "scientific genius" as he is a Marxist interpretation of science as a superstructure. Instead, Foucault offers a theory of "formation systems," which he develops more elaborately in *The Archaeology of Knowledge*. Although they are produced by men, the "formation systems" constitute a world of their own. . . .

Having discarded all genetic interpretations, Foucault is determined to analyze what takes place "at the surface of discourse." To bring in the Industrial Revolution, the reunification of surgery and medicine, the surgical training of many clinicians as army doctors in the Napoleonic wars would for him be to get sidetracked into developments that teach us nothing about the specific characteristics of the new medical discourse. Foucault, in a more radical and more abstract way, is pointing to the same "revolutionary" phenomenon in science that has been described by T. S. Kuhn. He wants to deal with the appearance in medicine of (to use Kuhn's terms) "new paradigms", the "rules" he again and again refers to could best be defined as the patterns of thought which prevail in each dominant paradigm. Having rejected any belief in cumulative progress in medicine, Foucault's view of "scientific revolution" insists that the principal changes are, in the broadest sense, of a stylistic nature.

In chapter 9—"The Visible Invisible"—Foucault sums up the main rules which the new clinical medicine began to follow. They consist in a predominant role attributed to gaze (*"le regard"*) and in adopting "the point of view of death"—i.e., the point of view of a knowledge essentially based on what can be discovered through opening and observing corpses.

> Paradoxically, the presence of the corpse enables us to perceive it living—living with a life that is no longer that of either old sympathies or the combinative laws of complications, but one that has its own roles and its own laws.
>
> (p. 21)

Foucault then goes on to specify the rules themselves in five "principles" which he discerns in all the descriptions of organic lesions written by clinicians. There is first the "principle of tissual communication" by which each type of membrane had its own peculiar properties, and each therefore differed in its diseases. For example, the arachnoid membrane in the brain "may be affected by the same forms of dropsy as the pleura of the lung or the peritoneum, since there are serous membranes present in each case." The other principles Foucault finds in the clinical writings—e.g., "tissual impermeability" and "penetration by boring"—often complement or extend or modify the first, describing in advance the networks of possible paths that disease may follow.

These principles, of course, were not explicitly professed by the French clinicians: they are made explicit by Foucault, in a kind of phenomenological synthesis. The same can be said for the role of gaze, which had never been fully formulated as a theory by the clinicians themselves. It takes Foucault's virtuosity and verbal skill to describe its characteristics:

> The observing gaze manifests its virtues only in a double silence: the relative silence of theories, imaginings, and whatever serves as an obstacle to the sensible immediate; and the absolute silence of all language that is anterior to that of the visible.
>
> (pp. 21-2)

There is a striking parallel between what Foucault develops as his own method and the method he ascribes to, say, [M.F.X. Bichat, the great French anatomist]; in *The Archaeology of Knowledge*, Foucault does not want us to shift our attention

from what takes place on the "surface of discourse." In *The Birth of the Clinic* he shows us that "Bichat's eye is a clinician's eye, because he gives an absolute epistemological privilege to the *surface gaze*" (author's italics). . . .

Foucault declares that with . . . [the] "superficial gaze" death became "the lyrical core of man," and when one feels the truly lyrical appeal of so many pages of his book, one wonders whether the parallels may not go beyond Géricault and Baudelaire to Foucault himself. When he describes the break which separates the new clinical science from all preceding scientific discourse, Foucault is perhaps depicting in emblematic form his own undertaking, his own break with traditional intellectual history. Not the least of his book's attractions is that it repeatedly allows us to glimpse the face, the personal and distinctive features of a philosopher-historian whose declared aim is nevertheless to get rid of the subject and subjectivity, to disappear in his own discourse (perhaps to disappear from his discourse), and to leave the way open for a formulation of the anonymous rules which govern human knowledge and behavior. (p. 22)

> *Jean Starobinski, "Gazing at Death," in* The New York Review of Books, *Vol. XXII, Nos. 21 & 22, January 22, 1976, pp. 18, 20-2.*

FRANK McCONNELL

In *Discipline and Punish* [Foucault] is back asserting some by now familiar Foucaultisms. "Man" as an individualistic, psychological entity is an invention, and not a very good one, of the last two hundred years ("A meticulous observation of detail . . . a political awareness of these small things, for the control of men. . . . From such trifles, no doubt, the man of modern humanism is born"). Institutions, for all their rationalism, create what they pretend to perceive ("We must cease . . . to describe the effects of power in negative terms. . . . Power produces . . . domains of objects and rituals of truth"). And, most centrally, the modern, ritualized institutions of order are hazardous to your health ("At the heart of all disciplinary institutions functions a small penal mechanism"). But this time around the assertions sound, if anything, more ringingly convincing than before. Because this time he is writing about the most outside of outsiders, the most publicly reviled of exiles from the norm, the prisoner.

In fact, the birth of the *prisoner,* not the birth of the prison, is Foucault's real subject, and that is an important difference. Rather than deal primarily in the hard, statistical data of the rise and diffusion of penal institutions, Foucault here as usually relies on the ideas of institutions as articulated by the reformers, *philosophes,* and early liberals. Especially important for his argument is Jeremy Bentham's plan for a *Panopticon,* an unchained institution of perfect, and perfectly horrifying, surveillance. . . . Panopticism, for Foucault, is a cardinal moment. After an initial, economically motivated revulsion against public torture and execution . . . , the reformers first envision a "punitive city," an ideal(!) community where punishment will be constantly threatened, but reduced, meted out in a calculus of guilt to the measure of the crime that calls it forth. Bentham's plan, though, signals the abandonment of this utopia for a better repressive machine, the idea of the *delinquent.* The delinquent is not just an offender, but a psychic deformity from the social norm; he must be put away for private punishment, an example to us all, where society, become a massive police force, can claim with crocodile disingenuousness to be attempting his "reform." 1984, in other words, begins sometime around 1784.

At times, it looks as though Foucault is writing a dark counterpoint to the sociology of Max Weber. Instead of the "routinization of charisma," his chart for the history of modern institutions is the routinization of damnation. . . . [His] book is filled with metaphors describing incarceration and discipline as a "breaking" of the individuality of the delinquent, his subjection to an "apparatus" of thought control, etc. Torture in its most heinous aspect still survives, that is: but it survives subtilized, refined and concealed behind the humanist snow-storm of arguments for "leniency" and "pity." It is this technique of argument through allusion that allows him in his central chapter on "Discipline," to make his most powerful—and already most widely discussed—case: that the invention of the prison is the crucial, inclusive image for all those modes of brutalization, in industry, in education, in the very fabric of citizenship, which define the modern era of humanistic tyranny, the totalitarianism of the norm. Not even a history of the birth of the prisoner, *Discipline and Punish* at its most expansive and richest is about, quite simply, the birth of the blues.

It is a brilliant book, brilliantly written and plotted (Richard Poirier has recently observed that Foucault writes like a great novelist: to which the response—at least part of the time—is, alas, he does). But, one keeps wanting to ask, is this really news? He takes account of the fact that official criticism of the prison system begins almost simultaneously with the system itself. And, rather predictably, he dismisses this tradition of critique as another disingenuousness of the establishment, protecting its massive machinery of repression by earnestly pretending to be getting the last bugs out—what we might term the factory recall syndrome. But whether this is quite fair to the reformers . . . , it ignores another tradition of critique, the one to which Foucault really belongs. This tradition, of visionary radicalism, stretches from many of the most important novelists and poets of our century back to two figures conspicuously absent from this book. At the end of the eighteenth century, they both perceived as clearly as anyone has since the witch's brew of liberal ideology, social repression, and the mechanisms of guilt. One of them, the Marquis de Sade, madly dramatized its worst implications for the survival of civilization. The other, William Blake, madly devised ways to break the mind-forged manacles. Foucault, in the passionate, apocalyptic coldness of his argument, is the heir of both men.

His celebrated war with "humanism," indeed, simply continues the romantics' warfare against official, bloodless and therefore dangerous rationalisms: it is, that is, profoundly humanistic. And the closer he gets to his conclusion, the closer he approaches his lyrical colleagues. . . . [At] the end he finally approaches the rhetoric of his closest analogue, in both genius and bitterness, among prison poets: Jean Genet.

But if it isn't news, is *Discipline and Punish* at least, to continue the judicial image, the truth, whole and nothing but? Nothing is, of course: and that bitter knowledge is the chief heritage of the two hundred years of modern humanism whose history so obsesses Foucault. (pp. 32-4)

Foucault, like the other visionary outsiders in his tradition from Blake to Genet, matters. He matters because his work is a kind of front-line dispatch, from closer to the void beyond culture than the rest of us can or care to go. But because he does go

there, and often, he paradoxically enriches and complicates our life in the "norm" whose dangers and traps he explores. (p. 34)

Frank McConnell, in a review of "Discipline and Punish: The Birth of the Prison," in The New Republic, *Vol. 178, No. 13, April 1, 1978, pp. 32-4.*

MARK POSTER

[In *The History of Sexuality*] Foucault has attempted to redefine completely the question of sexuality by removing it from the paradigm of repression. Instead, sexuality for him must be considered in terms of concepts of knowledge and power. In this manner Foucault places sex in relation to the emergence of the administered society of the twentieth century. He challenges both Marx and Freud by shifting the grounds of the debate: the concepts of labor and repression no longer serve in the critical comprehension of history; the privileged places in social theory and social life are no longer the factory and the unconscious. Foucault suggests nothing less than a basic reconceptualization of the logic of history, one that promises to revitalize critical theory.

Before analyzing *The History of Sexuality* I shall situate Foucault's thought by suggesting some principles of interpretation that apply to all his main works. Foucault is first a critic of Marxism. In *The Order of Things* he diminishes the stature of Marx's thought by placing it in the context of an earlier paradigm. . . . Foucault's accomplishments undercut the privileged place of labor as developed by Marx. Foucault's books analyze spaces outside of labor—asylums, clinics, prisons, schoolrooms, and the arenas of sexuality. In these social loci Foucault finds sources of radicality that are not theorized by Marx and Marxists. Implicit in Foucault's work is an attack on the centrality of labor to an emancipatory politics. His thought proceeds from the assumption that the working class, through its place in the process of production, is not the vanguard of social change. Foucault may take this as a fact of life in advanced capitalism, or more interestingly, he may be suggesting that the working class is, in its practice and through its organizations (the Party and the union), an accomplice of capitalism and not its contradiction. Radical change may come instead from those who are and have been excluded from the system— the insane, criminals, perverts, and women.

The second general characteristic of Foucault's thought is that he looks at discourses/practices. Discourses are not simply texts but also patterns of action. Foucault has defined the principles that organize discourses at different times as *epistemes*. Epistemes are the unconscious rules through which words, things, and actions cohere. They are the grids which make possible discourse/practice. On the level of the episteme, Foucault maintains, Marx is not a radical. Indeed Marx does not provide a critique of the established rules of discourse, and his thought cannot offer a way out of the established system.

The third trait of Foucault's thought is the search for the Other. Without proclaiming it an explicit goal, in each of his studies Foucault defines what is different from the present. If it is true that Marxism is part of the present system and not its negation, if it has been incorporated in the order of society, contained and shorn of its negative potentials, then the goal of social thought must have been to set the limits of contemporary society. Theory must define the horizons, the boundaries of an order that is no longer captured by older positions. Marxism loses its grip on the present because it cannot define how the past was other than the present. . . . The insane of the Middle Ages, the criminal of *l'ancien régime,* the *ars erotica* of the East—these people, discourses, and practices are indeed different from ours. By analyzing them Foucault gives a definite shape to the present order. He undercuts the illusion generated by one-dimensional society: that everything has always been thus and must remain so.

Fourth, it can be argued that the place from which Foucault theorizes, the reference point of his work, is a world of which Marx knew little. Foucault is the social theorist of a society characterized by information. The late twentieth century is no longer the world of little factories with hard-working manual laburers. It is a world of science, information, computers . . . And this world is Foucault's world, the one whose history he implicitly seeks to trace and the shape of whose antecedents he attempts to define. Each volume he has written is a treatise on how it once was and how scientific, technological, informational discourse/practice arose and displaced what once was. As Marx theorized from the vantage point of the classic proletariat, so Foucault theorizes from the perspective of an emerging world of information processing.

The role of structuralism in Foucault's thought may now be clarified. Foucault is often lumped with Jacques Lacan and Jacques Derrida as a post-structuralist, but this designation hides as much as it reveals. Foucault has rejected the structuralist label, and properly so. He is not a formalist seeking only to plot the binary oppositions that form the logic of texts. He treats discourses *and* practices. Nevertheless, there are certain features associated with structuralist thought that are found throughout Foucault's works. There is the emphasis on the synchronic as opposed to the diachronic, the tendency to trace the intricate play within a discourse rather than focus on its origin. Foucault is more interested in how a given society organizes punishment, for example, than in how that practice arose and evolved. There is his stress on the discontinuity between social orders, on the absolute break or rupture separating one discourse from another, rather than on the dialectical or homogeneous development of one thing into another. Finally there is a decentered view of the totality in which no one place is privileged. In all these respects—decentered totality, discontinuity, synchrony—Foucault takes his lead from the structuralists. The consequence is the elaboration of a logic of history that is neither progressist nor evolutionist, neither Marxist nor Hegelian.

The History of Sexuality provides an arena in which my view of Foucault's work can be assessed. Foucault promised six volumes devoted to the topic. In 1976 the introductory first book appeared with the subtitle *The Will to Knowledge,* a transparent allusion to Nietzsche's *The Will to Power.* There have been rumors from Paris that Foucault has abandoned this project in favor of further studies of crime and punishment.

The History of Sexuality opens with an attack on the Freudo-Marxist position. The concept of repression, Foucault charges, is a false guide to the problem of sexuality. It suggests that sex disappears in the nineteenth century, that sex was pushed out of consciousness and out of practice as the bourgeoisie came to power. Even a superficial reading of history, Foucault counters, demonstrates the opposite: that sexuality flourished as never before in the nineteenth century. This surprising assertion refers not to erotic fulfillment but to the expansion of the discourse on sexuality. For Foucault sex cannot have been "repressed" and at the same time talked about so much. (pp. 155-57)

Foucault's main argument against [Freud's] doctrine of repression is that it is a false model of the relation between power and sex. Following Deleuze and Guattari in *Anti-Oedipus,* Foucault contends that the law does not act as a negative obstacle to the positive, natural drive of sex, as the doctrine of repression implies. Things happen quite differently. For Foucault power is positive: it creates the form of sexuality. In his words, "the law is what constitutes both desire and the lack on which it is predicated." This important shift in the argument requires elaboration. (p. 158)

According to Freud, children have natural erotic drives for their parents which become repressed. *Anti-Oedipus,* however, argues that the sexual attachments of children for parents is a coding initiated by the parents which elicits the desire and then prohibits it. There are thus no natural sex drives. All sexuality is "always already" coded by a law. . . . Without citing Deleuze and Guattari, Foucault takes this model as the essence of power. But if that is so, the project of a history of sexuality cannot proceed by searching for prohibitions against sex; it must look instead to power as the creator of sexuality. Foucault provides extensive examples of such a view of power taken from the history of medicine.

Rather than treat the history of sexuality as a documentation of acts of repression, Foucault directs his attention to the operations of power. At this point he introduces the notion of discourse. . . . Discourse for [Foucault] is not some idealist representation of ideas; it is, in materialist fashion, part of the power structure of society. Power relations must be understood in the structuralist manner as decentered, as a multiplicity of local situations. Discourses are important because they reveal the play of power in a given situation. They are not "ideological representations" of class positions but acts of power shaping actively the lives of the populace. The history of sexuality must study discourses on sexuality to uncover the shapes given to it. Foucault rejects the distinction, which derives from the episteme of representation, between ideas/discourses and action/sexuality. (pp. 158-59)

Foucault is in search of "true discourses." His definition of truth is not the philosopher's. He is not after the best-argued, the most logically coherent text. . . . The level he is after is much more mundane, much closer to the pulse of social life. His discourses are those of ordinary doctors; they are the files of clinics that treat sexual "disorders"; they are the letters of local priests; they are the dossiers housed in bureaucracies; they are grant proposals for the study of sexuality; they are the psychotherapist's file; they are the files of social welfare agencies. At these locations, in these discourses, the play of power and the question of sexuality reveal themselves. This is where "the political economy of a will to knowledge" of sexuality is constituted.

In the introductory volume of *The History of Sexuality* Foucault offers an outline of the history of sexuality that merits the attention of historians. The concept of discourse leads Foucault directly to the Christian confession as the locus of sexuality. Here he finds two phases. In the earlier period, before the seventeenth century, the priest was concerned with what people did. The faithful were asked in detail about their sexual *activities.* In that period sexuality concerned the body, which was allowed certain positions and denied others. The discourse of sexuality was rudimentary and crude; talk, in the society, was open and frank. (pp. 160-61)

With the Reformation and Counter Reformation the discourse on sexuality takes another form. In the confession the priest begins to inquire not only about actions, but also about intentions. Sexuality begins to be defined in terms of the mind as well as the body. The scope of the sexual expands to include the least thoughts and fantasies. A loquaciousness about sexuality emerges. Everything must be pored over and examined in great detail. A similar pattern of change is discovered by Foucault in his history of crime and punishment. Discourse intensifies from a concern with action and the body to a concern with the mind and its intentions. But the important change in the discourse of sexuality does not take place until later, during the capitalist period. At this time, although by no means because of the mode of production, the confession becomes scientific. Foucault offers as a hypothesis that the great alteration in sexuality occurred when the discourse on sex became a matter of science. Once that happened, sexuality became a major preoccupation and began to assume its current shape.

The major example of a modern discourse on sexuality, a new scientific confessional, is of course psychoanalysis. Perhaps Foucault's major accomplishment in *The History of Sexuality* is to treat Freud as part of history rather than to study the history of sex from a Freudian vantage point. The conceptual *point d'honneur* of the Freudo-Marxists—that Freud treats the instincts as outside society and therefore as a source of social criticism—is shorn of its scientific power. Freud's concept of the instincts becomes, in Foucault's hands, just another device to control and shape sexuality. The concept of the instincts is a power strategy by the new medical profession which allows them to inquire into sex, to explore it by the method of the "talking cure," to examine dreams and fantasies, the recesses of the mind, in a way never before contemplated. The Freudian view of the instincts does not provide a reservoir of resistance against the ruling class. It does not promise a sexual revolution. For sexuality, to Foucault, is not something outside society waiting to burst through the layers of repression. On the contrary, by positing a sexual instinct Freud opened up a new realm for the domination of science over sexuality.

Foucault's sexual liberation comes not with Freud but against him. To exult in sexuality is not to break with the ruling powers but rather to fulfill their prescription. Foucault charts the course of revolution not as the vanguard of sexuality against the ruling powers but as the insertion of the body against "sex" and power. (p. 161)

The heart of the matter for Foucault is that the history of sexuality amounts to a continuous increase, beginning in the seventeenth century, in the "mechanisms" and "technologies" of power. During the course of this history the locus of power shifts from the confessional to the research laboratories and clinics where sexuality is the subject of scientific investigation. Historians are directed by Foucault to explore in detail the "true discourses" on sex generated under the sign of science. In particular he calls attention to four "mechanisms of knowledge and power" on sex. These are: the hysteriazation of women's bodies, the pedagogization of children's sex, the socialization of procreative behavior, and the psychiatrization of perverse behavior. These mechanisms are directed at four "figures": hysterical women, masturbating children, Malthusian couples, and perverse adults. Taken together these "mechanisms" constitute the "production of sexuality" in the modern period.

Anyone familiar with the history of the nineteenth century will be impressed by Foucault's choice of subjects. The literature on sexuality is indeed concerned with these four figures to a very great extent. . . . One might question . . . Foucault's exclusion of the sexually diseased male, since some historians think that syphilis was epidemic in the nineteenth century. The aggressive female was another major concern of doctors and parents. . . . These topics would serve as well as those chosen by Foucault to examine discourses on sexuality, and Foucault's selection must therefore be regarded as somewhat arbitrary. (p. 162)

Attention to these "true discourses" on sexuality does not necessarily constitute a history of sexuality. It is doubtful that these figures could be generalized to serve as conceptual guides for a history of sexuality at any time other than the nineteenth century. Worse still, these figures and their attendant discourses only apply to one segment of the population in Europe and the United States. The bourgeoisie fits well into Foucault's categories; but the working class in the cities and perhaps the peasantry in the countryside do not. These latter groups were not subject to the knowledge/power of the medical and psychiatric professions, nor were they avid readers of discourses on hysterical women and perversions. Foucault might respond to the objection that his analysis does not account for class differences by pointing out that the spread of the discourse on sex through society took time to unfold. Yet the question remains how to account for class differences in the first place.

Foucault is cognizant of the importance of social class in the history of sexuality. He presents a fascinating discussion of the differences between the aristocracy and the bourgeoisie on the topic of the body. For the aristocracy the body meant blood. Lineage was the all-important consideration for them. For the bourgeoisie, however, the body was instead a question of life and health. (p. 163)

For Foucault the distinction between the aristocratic and bourgeois discourse on the body serves to strengthen his critique of the Freudo-Marxists. Far from repressing the body, he contends, the bourgeoisie devoted a great deal of attention to it. Nevertheless, while his argument is well taken, it does not really speak to the issue of sexuality. The bourgeois concern with the body was not an erotic one; good diet and hygiene are not the same as sensuality. The bourgeois body may have been cared for and tended better than that of the aristocracy, but it was far less a vessel of sexuality. One suspects in fact that the bourgeois attention to health was a utilitarian and economic quest. Energy for this social class was marshaled for the great battles of the market and the factory, not for the gentlemanly pursuit of a woman's favors. Although Foucault addresses the question of class and sex, he has not reached the heart of the problem.

The emphasis on knowledge/power leads Foucault against himself to a totalistic view of the history of sexuality. Although he asserts that there is no "unitary sexual politics," he does not offer a basis on which to comprehend sexuality in a given society in any way other than collectively. Discourses on sex may differ in a particular epoch, but they are the discourses of the society as a whole. Yet the history of sexuality cannot be pursued at the level of the total society. Social groups and regions differ too markedly in their sexuality to be considered together in one general framework. (pp. 163-64)

Foucault's account of the history of sexuality goes astray in overlooking the importance of the family. If the emotional structure of the family is taken into account, differences among classes regarding sexuality become intelligible. In the stifling air of the private bourgeois family of the nineteenth century, where the feelings of each family member have no outlet other than the family, the hysterical woman, the masturbating child, the pervert, and the Malthusian couple emerge with clarity. Although sexuality in the bourgeois family was open to the influences of medical discourses, the structure of everyday life in the family itself is of at least equal importance in the task of explanation. . . . Foucault's program for the history of sexuality deflects too much attention away from the family in favor of more distant agencies of power. (p. 164)

Commentaries on Foucault's earlier works have pointed out that his concept of power is vague and ambiguous. The power embodied in discourses on sex is not the clearly defined power of the state or even the discernible power of the "helping professions." Power, Foucault proclaims, is everywhere. In all the relations of society, power—especially the power of discourse—is exercised. Foucault is sensitive to the force of opinion on people's action. He sees clearly the way all practice is subject to the pressure of what he calls discourse. In everyday life no action is innocent; no project is carried out from the pure intention of the actor. Individual reason is not the power that determines what happens. Especially people who do not conform to dominant social values—the handicapped, racial minorities, those with unusual sexual preferences, the physically deformed—can feel the influence of what Foucault calls "force relations" or "technologies of power."

The irony of Foucault's position is that although he is acutely aware of "power relations" in society he pays little heed to the "power" of his own discourse. He does not pose the fundamental question, What is the role of his own discourse in the history of discourses on sexuality? If discourse is a mode of power that elicits sexuality and shapes it, will not the same fate befall Foucault's discourse? Foucault seeks to liberate society from the power of "true discourses" on sex and thereby to contribute to the "counterattack" of free "bodies and pleasures." Yet nothing prevents Foucault's project from becoming but another "true discourse." (pp. 164-65)

> *Mark Poster, "Foucault's True Discourses," in* Humanities in Society, *Vol. 2, No. 2, Spring, 1979, pp. 153-66.*

ALAN SHERIDAN

Foucault begins where all truly original minds begin, in the present. Such minds are not ahead of their times; it is the rest of us who are dragging our feet. His passion is to seek out the new, that which is coming to birth in the present—a present that most of us are unable to see because we see it through the eyes of the past, or through the eyes of a 'future' that is a projection of the past, which amounts to the same thing. Foucault's interest in the past is guided by that passion: there is nothing of the antiquarian about it. 'Why am I writing this history of the prison?', he asks in *Surveiller et punir.* 'Simply because I am interested in the past? No, if one means by that writing a history of the past in terms of the present. Yes, if one means writing the history of the present.' . . . [This] explains Foucault's early rejection of an academic career in philosophy, his exile and his silence. When *Histoire de la folie* was published in 1961, Foucault was thirty-five. He could

already have been the respected author of three or four works of philosophy. He chose silence until such time as he could hear the voice of the present. (pp. 195-96)

[His] life's work has been an attempt to catch what the present was telling him over the din of the past still echoing in his ears.

Such a position bears a superficial resemblance to that of the dominant philosophical movement of his youth. What may broadly be termed 'existentialism' and 'phenomenology' had a similar commitment to the present, a similar desire to escape the tyranny of history and the past. But the resemblance ends there. Existentialism sought to escape a restrictive ethical inheritance in the free 'authentic' exercise of individual choice. Phenomenology placed acquired knowledge 'in parenthesis' and tried to return to a pure, unprejudiced apprehension of the world by the individual consciousness. Both were philosophies of the subject, while rejecting a unitary notion of 'man'. For a French philosophy student of the late 1940s and early 1950s the only other system of thought with any pretension of speaking to present realities was Marxism, at the time almost exclusively in the hands of doctrinaire Communist Party ideologues. Most French intellectuals of the time managed to combine a general theoretical allegiance to existentialism/phenomenology, which precluded full acceptance of Marxism, with tacit support, in practice, of the Party. By the mid-fifties, Foucault had outgrown this particular combination of options; he had not yet worked out a coherent alternative. (pp. 196-97)

Foucault was in a position analogous with that of thinkers living around, say, 1650 or 1800. Philosophy and psychology did not possess truth because they possessed a history. The search for their origins led him . . . to a common source, the establishment of reason as sole, undisputed ruler of the mind. The way forward . . . was to go back. This meant a return to history. It would, of course, have to be a new kind of history. But how was such a history to be conducted? (p. 205)

It would ill behove an analyst of Foucault's thought to impose on the succession of his books any such notions as causal development, underlying unity, common origin. On the other hand, Foucault is not, despite the latest edition of the Petit Larousse, 'author of a philosophy of history based on discontinuity'. One's task is to recognize coherences and differences where they occur. The coherence of Foucault's works does not extend to a Foucault 'system'. . . . In a sense, each book arrives as a fresh start in a new world: methodology has to be adapted, new concepts forged. . . . But, above all, the deepest discontinuity occurs with *Histoire de la folie,* not only in relation to whatever Foucault had written previously, but also in relation to his own period. This book constitutes the first, essential stage in a radically new analysis of Western civilization since the Renaissance. Foucault's philosophical quest led him to psychology, the science of the mind, which led him to madness, the limit of the mind, which led him in turn to reason, to the will to knowledge and truth. To put it crudely—something Foucault himself never does—modern rationalism and science have the same ignoble origins as the lunatic asylum. (pp. 205-06)

[*Histoire de la folie*] provides the very foundations of Foucault's whole enterprise: the writing of the later books is inconceivable except by the author of *Histoire de la folie.* Similarly, the full extent of the book's originality can really only be measured retrospectively, in the light of the later work. It is quite clear, for example at so many points in the book, that Foucault knew exactly what his future achievement was to be. . . . [This] study was to be only the first, 'and no doubt easiest', of a long investigation carried out 'under the sun of Nietzsche's great search'.

Nietzsche may have provided the inspiration; he could not provide what is nowadays called the 'methodology'. There was no discipline, with its institutions, journals, internal controversies, conceptual apparatus, methods of work, within which Foucault could carry out the task he had set himself. Indeed, there was a sense in which, like Nietzsche's, his work would have to be carried on outside, even against, the existing academic frameworks. Not only would he have to create his own mode of analysis, his own operational concepts, even his own vocabulary; he would also have to create his own audience. His books would have to be addressed to the general educated public; it was a public of a kind that existed nowhere else in the world, but unlike a few thousand specialized students it was not a captive one. Foucault did conquer that audience and, through it, in the less rigid period after 1968, he was to win his academic audience as well. (pp. 207-08)

Foucault's relation to 'theory' is often misunderstood. Foucault does not have a theory of history, which he then sets about 'proving'. The mass of detailed analysis he brings to bear in his work is not material to support a theory, in the sense that this analysis would be 'invalidated' if the theory were proved 'false'. Foucault has always worked in quite the reverse way. In approaching a new area—and almost every book of his does this—he certainly has a number of prejudices and presuppositions deriving from his previous work and from the opinions of others in that field. However, he is not only on his guard against these 'given' theoretical notions, he subjects them, in the course of his detailed analysis, to the most rigorous scrutiny. What finally emerges is not theory, in the sense of a general statement of the truth as Foucault sees it, but rather a tentative hypothesis, an invitation to discussion, which, more often than not, is startlingly at odds with received opinion. For Foucault, theory does not enjoy the same status as detailed analysis, to which it is secondary, subservient. *Histoire de la folie* is not superseded or invalidated, therefore, when Foucault criticizes the conceptualization of 'madness' to be found in that book. Nor is the value of *Les mots et les choses* in any way diminished because it left a number of theoretical loose-ends and occasions of misunderstanding. However, Foucault regarded these shortcomings as sufficiently important to require full and detailed elucidation. *L'archéologie du savoir* reverses Foucault's usual practice: it is his only full-length book devoted primarily to theoretical and methodological problems—though even here, in the way it extends the concrete analyses of the previous book, it is not a matter of *pure* theory. (pp. 212-13)

[And] it was not until *Surveiller et punir,* which [Foucault] has called 'my first book', that his analysis of history really comes of age.

Foucault's 'political anatomy' constitutes a radical break with all previous conceptions of power, whether of the 'right' or of the 'left'. To begin with, power is not a possession, won by one class that strives to retain it against its acquisition by another. Power is not the prerogative of the 'bourgeoisie'; the 'working class' has no historical mission in acquiring it. Power, as such, does not exist, but in challenging existing notions of how societies operate, one is forced, in the first instance, to

employ the same word. Power is an effect of the operation of social relationships, between groups and between individuals. It is not unitary: it has no essence. There are as many forms of power as there are types of relationship. Every group and every individual exercises power and is subjected to it. There are certain categories of person—children, prisoners, the 'insane'—whose ability to exercise power is severely limited, but few members of these groups do not find some means of exercising power, if only on each other. Power is not, therefore, to be identified with the state, a central apparatus that can be seized. The state is rather an overall strategy and effect, a composite result made up of a multiplicity of centres and mechanisms, so many states within states with complex networks of common citizenship. Factories, housing estates, hospitals, schools, families, are among the more evident, more formalized of such 'micro-powers'. It is the task of a political anatomy to analyse the operation of these 'micro-powers', the relations that are made between them and their relations with the strategic aims of the state apparatus. (pp. 218-19)

Foucault's 'political anatomy' is the clearest and most fully developed version of a new political 'theory' and 'practice' that is just beginning to emerge from the discrediting of both Marxism and 'reformism'. (pp. 221-22)

Foucault shows that truth does not exist outside power, still less in opposition to it. Each society has its own régime of truth: the types of discourse accepted as true, the mechanisms that make it possible to distinguish between truth and error. In place of the 'universal' intellectual, Foucault places the 'specific' intellectual who, like everyone else, is competent to speak only of what he knows and experiences. His task is not to enlighten, but to work upon the particular régime of truth in which he operates. He is called upon neither to reveal the truth nor to represent others. The will to the power of truth is a pitiless tyrant: it requires a singular and total devotion. It is a service that has tempted the European mind since Plato. Nietzsche gave the first signs of its possible end: he also provided a way out, which he called genealogy. Genealogy was a 'grey' activity, but it was also a gay science, a science of the hypothetical. That gaiety, that love of hypothesis, pervades all Foucault's work. He is the reverse of a guru, a teacher, a subject who is supposed to know, though he would, in all modesty, be flattered if, without excessive seriousness, he were compared to a Zen master, who also knows nothing. For him uncertainty causes no anguish: his prose is punctuated by such words and expressions as 'perhaps', 'no doubt', 'it may be', 'it is as if'. He advances hypotheses with the delight that others reserve for the revelation of truth. His last two books have been explorations of hypotheses. 'Can one draw up the genealogy of modern morality on the basis of a political history of the body?' he asks on the dust-jacket of *Surveiller et punir*. The whole of *Volonté de savoir* is a hypothesis, which irritates or angers those for whom a 'truth', however banal or ill-founded, is of more value than a hypothesis, however illuminating. As he remarks in an interview published in *Ornicar?*, the uncertainty is genuine, not a rhetorical device. He compares his last book to a Gruyère cheese, with holes in which the reader can install himself. (pp. 222-23)

A love of hypothesis, of invention, is unashamedly, a love of the beautiful. What drew Foucault to the case of Pierre Rivière [which Foucault discusses in *Moi, Pierre Rivière, ayant égurgé ma mere, ma soeur et mon frère . . . (I, Pierre Rivière, Having Slaughtered My Mother, My Sister and My Brother . . .)*] was not the mass of official documentation, but 'the beauty of Rivière's memoir', a beauty that shamed the dreary prose of the educated experts who busied themselves around him. It was a daring, provocative remark, suggesting that beauty of expression is an indication that what is being said is worth listening to. The question of Foucault's own style is not insignificant. It is not so much that Foucault writes well—there are still academics who do that, though few contemporary writers of history, philosophy, or literary criticism give the pleasure of a Michelet, a Berkeley, or a Coleridge. It is rather that he writes with ostentatious brilliance: his writing betrays a quite shameless delight in its own skill that calls to mind the sumptuous prose of our own pre-Classical period, that of a John Donne or Thomas Browne. To write in this way is no affectation or self-indulgence. It is, if it requires justification, functional. Like all style, it is both natural and cultivated: a natural mode of expression for a writer striving to renew contact with a pre-rationalist world of communicating Reason and Folly and a conscious rejection of the language of Reason that seeks by its grey, measured, monotonous tones to give an impression of authority, objectivity, and truth. (pp. 223-24)

There is no 'Foucault system'. One cannot be a 'Foucaldian' in the way one can be a Marxist or a Freudian: Marx and Freud left coherent bodies of doctrine (or 'knowledge') and organizations which, whether one likes it or not (for some that is the attraction), enjoy uninterrupted apostolic succession from their founders. If Foucault is to have an 'influence' it will no doubt be as a slayer of dragons, a breaker of systems. Such a task should not be seen as negative; indeed it is the system-building that is the real negation. Its positive achievements may be measured by the range and variety of its effects, not by some massive uniformity. Nietzsche's 'influence' has been of this kind: Futurism, Dada, Surrealism; Freud, Mann, Hesse; Gide and Malraux; Shaw, Yeats, Wells, the two Lawrences; Ibsen and Strindberg—all acknowledge that influence. Nietzsche was felt, instinctively, to be part of the new age that was ushered in by the twentieth century—a new age that found its fullest expression, perhaps, in the 'modernist' movements in the arts. During several decades of total politics, Nietzsche suffered at the hands of his Fascist admirers, his Communist revilers, and 'liberals' who saw his books as a Pandora's box, better left unopened. Now that influence is once more at work in our thought. If it seems strongest in France, it is due in some measure to Foucault (and Deleuze). In England, where intellectual life so often appears to be in the grip of a narrow, smug, mentally lazy (il)liberal consensus, threatened on its fringes by a small band of Marxists, it is almost non-existent. Here, too, Foucault falls on the stoniest of grounds. The English reviewers' evident inability to read his books is seen, everywhere else, as a scandal. In America, which benefits from a more pluralist culture and the devotion of Walter Kaufmann, a German émigré, Nietzsche is widely read—so, too, is Foucault. To assimilate one to the other would help neither. Only those who know both can appreciate their profound kinship and differences, but their destinies do seem, in some subterranean way, to be entwined. It is difficult to conceive of any thinker having, in the last quarter of our century, the influence that Nietzsche exercised over its first quarter. Yet Foucault's achievement so far makes him a more likely candidate than any other. When one considers what is yet to come, one may well feel the ground stirring under one's feet. (pp. 225-26)

Alan Sheridan, in his Michel Foucault, *1980. Reprint by Tavistock Publications, 1981, 243 p.*

FLINT SCHIER

It's a pipe, a palpable pipe: not a painterly pipe, not an abstract pipe. Lord knows, it's not an Expressionist pipe; it isn't even a Freudian pipe. Beneath it in the obsequious copybook scrawl of a child, the subversive caption reads, "This is not a pipe." It is signed "Magritte." Here is paradox enough to sate the most perverse appetite. And in the French *philosophe* Michel Foucault, himself no mean practitioner of the oddball, Magritte's looking-glass pipe has found its Lewis Carroll, as the reader of [**"This Is Not a Pipe"**] will discover.

Doing a double take, one realizes that, of course, this is not a pipe; it's a picture of a pipe. Our *philosophe* is able to detect some significance in this precious banality, for does not Magritte's statement that the painting is not a pipe disturb the very illusion of presence that "realistic" representation pretends to effect? . . .

Anyone familiar with Mr. Foucault's influential work, especially **"Les Mots et les Choses"** . . . , will immediately see that Magritte's work has everything to recommend it to a writer of Mr. Foucault's sensibility. Throughout a lifetime of philosophical labor, Mr. Foucault has been engaged in "excavating" the shifting notions of representation in the history of Western culture. The very distinction between representation and world (a distinction that supplants the one between self and world for Mr. Foucault) has been given many different colorings. . . .

After Descartes the Idealists sought to subtract the absurdly meaningless material world. They argued that we are familiar only with appearances; the appearances signify a world outside us, but it is a world that may or may not really be as it appears to us. The gap opened up by Descartes between representation and world was closed up again by the Idealists, but only at the cost of our losing contact with the real world: The knowable world, nature, was simply the world of appearances, and the self, being the creator of its world, must of course stand outside of it; reality and self were jointly exiled from nature. (p. 8)

The interesting thing about Mr. Foucault is that he has reopened the radically sceptical case, but *his* Idealism says not that we know only appearances but that we know only the projections of our language. There is, for Mr. Foucault, no such thing as absolute knowledge; such knowledge would have to transcend its own representational resources, whether those resources are verbal or pictorial. Moreover, like the American philosophers of science Thomas Kuhn and Paul Feyerabend, Mr. Foucault thinks that different eras occupy different worlds, worlds that are created by the thought of the period and that determine the limits of what its thinkers can possibly conceive.

Nature, in Mr. Foucault's story, is simply the way each age represents the world to itself. The representational function must be outside nature since it produces nature. Thus there can be no natural science of man or thought. The appropriate stance for the mind in this predicament is to reject all pretensions to truth and to be available to the play of all possibilities, using each to cancel the claims of the others. And since different historical periods inhabit the diverse worlds of their own creation, and words and symbols can have no fixed reference across such distinct worlds, there is no possibility of understanding between periods. But Mr. Foucault is no solipsist: We're all in this predicament together, since our world is the projection of our common language.

What makes **"This Is Not a Pipe"** a book of such interest is that Magritte's art provides the perfect pretext for Mr. Foucault's sermon. Doesn't a picture that declares, "This is not a pipe," undercut our expectation that representation will give us the thing—in this case, the pipe—itself? The difficulty it presents is no accident. Magritte was perhaps unique among the visual artists of this century in the depth of his philosophical lore. . . .

From Mr. Foucault's reading Magritte emerges as a deeper Modernist than, say, Kandinsky. Magritte uses its own resources to undo realistic representation, unraveling the world in a series of visual puns, paradoxes and contradictions. His work proposes a critique not simply of depiction but of all "texts" that aim at the truth. In place of the sovereignty of truth, Mr. Foucault takes Magritte to recommend a free play of the imagination. But by what right Mr. Foucault can recommend this esthetic stance is a mystery to me. Although he may have a taste for the playful as against the authoritarian, what reason can he give to persuade others to accept his preference? None at all, since there can be no communication between worlds informed by different values: The advocate of any position either preaches to the converted or babbles meaninglessly. Thus does hyberbolic relativism induce conceptual claustrophobia. Mr. Foucault's is not an easy view to live with.

This essay not only proposes a new understanding of Magritte; it also constitutes a perfect illustration and introduction to the thought of the philosopher himself, France's great wizard of paradox. (p. 26)

Flint Schier, "Philosophical Paint," in The New York Times Book Review, *January 23, 1983, pp. 8, 26.*

Michael Frayn
1933-

English novelist, dramatist, journalist, and screenwriter.

In his humorous newspaper columns, novels, and plays, Frayn satirizes human foibles and contemporary society. Among his targets are middle-class values, the pitfalls of technology, and those aspects of popular culture which Frayn believes distort reality: mass media, public relations, and advertising. Frayn began exploring these topics as a columnist for the Manchester *Guardian* and the London *Observer*. The articles written for these newspapers are collected in his books *The Day of the Dog* (1962), *The Book of Fub* (1963), *On the Outskirts* (1964), and *At Bay in Gear Street* (1967).

In the 1960s Frayn began writing novels concerned with the subjects and themes developed in his journalistic pieces, and in the 1970s he also became known for his plays. In his novels Frayn often uses imaginative settings and plots to comment indirectly on contemporary social and political situations. His first novel, *The Tin Men* (1965), is set in a futuristic automated world where computers generate everything from organized sports to moral decisions. Also set in the future is Frayn's novel *A Very Private Life* (1968), which examines the insulating effect of a society's attempt to eliminate discomfort. Both of these works are sardonic indictments of irresponsible technological advancement. Another fantastical work is *Sweet Dreams* (1973), a novel which concerns a typical middle-class Londoner who goes to heaven and becomes one of God's right-hand men. Frayn depicts heaven as another busy place where one must struggle to succeed. Frayn's more conventional novels include *The Russian Interpreter* (1966), an espionage story set in Moscow, and *Towards the End of Morning* (1967), a satire set in a London newspaper office.

Satirical subjects and farcical situations also inform Frayn's dramas. In addition, the influence of Ludwig Wittgenstein, a twentieth-century philosopher whom Frayn has studied extensively, is evident in many of Frayn's plays. Beneath their satirical surfaces, the plays often reveal a Wittgensteinian concern with the relation between language, reality, and personal perception. For example, *Clouds* (1977), which centers on characters who tour Cuba, raises questions about the degree to which artifice influences fact. Similarly, *Noises Off* (1982) contrasts art with reality by chaotically presenting a farce about a farce. *Make and Break* (1980), a play involving movable walls, corpses, and corporate manners and mores, epitomizes Frayn's concern with illusion and reality and, in Leonie Caldicott's words, the "depressing world of rapid satisfactions" generated by modern technological society.

Although many critics suggest that Frayn's later novels overcome the weaknesses in character and plot frequently found in his earlier fiction, it is generally agreed that overall Frayn's novels have an uneven narrative quality and the characterizations in both his plays and his novels are underdeveloped. Frayn's most noted strengths are his wit and insight; he is widely praised for his ability to unite comedy with serious observation. As William Trevor notes, Frayn is "the only hatchet man of contemporary letters to combine a consistent attack with something that looks like a purpose."

Photograph by Mark Gerson

(See also *CLC*, Vols. 3, 7; *Contemporary Authors*, Vols. 5-8, rev. ed.; and *Dictionary of Literary Biography*, Vols. 13, 14.)

JEREMY BROOKS

It can't be easy to write even a weekly funny column. To be *constructively* funny—i.e., satirical—three times a week would seem an impossible task. Michael Frayn not only succeeded, he actually *got better*—a devoted follower could watch him exploring his way into a tricky form until he had the confidence to lash out with one of those superbly accurate pieces of social criticism for which one either loves or hates him. *The Day of the Dog* contains the best of these, and may come as a surprise to those who are not already with it, Fraynwise. Michael Frayn actually holds a handful of opinions, and doesn't care if people discover the shameful fact, nor whether his opinions are fashionable ones or not. Inevitably, one's hackles sometimes rise (dammit, a man who doesn't like *dogs* can't be good for much!), but even in the act of throwing the book out of the window one suddenly finds oneself chortling, and retrieving it for another shamefaced dip. (p. 826)

Jeremy Brooks, "Posh Funnies," in The Spectator, *Vol. 209, No. 7013, November 23, 1962, pp. 826-27.**

WILLIAM F. GAVIN

It has become impossible in the last few years to watch television, read a periodical or book, listen to records, or attend a show without being subjected to the latest outpourings of wrath from the angry young wit of the moment. Name a taboo and he'll break it; think of any possible subject and he'll harpoon it with a few well-chosen barbs. Usually unrestricted by taste, learning, talent or sense, he is applauded by the yahoos he insults, most of whom bear the double burden of being not only tasteless themselves, but proud to admit it. (Many of the young wits of a few years ago now sound only nasty and peevish, like an annoyed book reviewer.)

Well, Mr. Michael Frayn comes equipped with the proper credentials. . . . This collection of essays from his column in the *Guardian* [*Never Put Off to Gomorrah*] is full of funny names . . . , funny people . . . and—what you might expect from the wittiest man now writing in English—English wit. I wish him well and hope to read him again if the day comes when an Englishman can write without trying to be so terribly witty.

> *William F. Gavin, in a review of "Never Put Off to Gomorrah . . . ," in* America, *Vol. 111, No. 1, July 4, 1964, p. 18.*

ANTHONY THWAITE

The pieces in **On the Outskirts,** like its predecessors [**The Day of the Dog** and **The Book of Fub**], have the remarkable virtue, shared with some books of poems, of gaining strength from contiguity. A common tone comes through, and, more importantly, that firm point of view which earlier students of Mr Frayn were quick to notice. You can have your laugh at Wittgenstein, 'informal' television discussions, letters to *Radio Times,* and at the abiding nonsense of public relations and advertising; but you have to take, too, such a scorching piece of brilliant and humane contempt as 'From Each According to His Need', where the bland, thoughtless stock responses to the Welfare State are shown up in all their selfishness. Mr Frayn and his supporting cast of Rollo Swavely, Christopher Smoothe, Ken Nocker, the Crumbles, *et al.* are very funny; and when you laugh till it hurts, you know what has hurt you.

> *Anthony Thwaite, in a review of "On the Outskirts," in* The Listener, *Vol. LXXII, No. 1859, November 12, 1964, p. 773.*

WILLIAM TREVOR

Michael Frayn's first novel, **The Tin Men,** is a fast, swooping performance by one of our very few serious satirists. In the past he has exposed so brilliantly some of the many vulgarities of modern life—the insidious message of the advertisement, the creepy crookedness of our P.R. workers, the stupidities conceived daily in our boardrooms—that he has become the only hatchet man of contemporary letters to combine a consistent attack with something that looks like a purpose. In **The Tin Men** Mr Frayn satirizes and parodies, probes and pounces, with all his considerable skill. This is a funny book and delightful to read; but it doesn't quite work as a novel. It is more like a particularly good Frayn piece blown up to size, with extra bits added and a plot thrown in. The characters really *are* tin men—templates for thousands of others, representatives of this disorder or that. For all that, though, this is not a treat to miss. After all, who but Mr Frayn could arrange for a man

called Nunn to draw from his pocket a slim volume entitled *Prayers for the Rugby Field*?

> *William Trevor, in a review of "The Tin Men," in* The Listener, *Vol. LXXIII, No. 1869, January 21, 1965, p. 115.*

JULIAN GLOAG

There was every reason to look forward to Michael Frayn's first novel with the mouth already formed for laughter and wry smiles. . . . Mr. Frayn at his best is to my mind as penetrating as but perhaps gentler than Art Buchwald at revealing the sweet idiocies of our society.

And in his first novel, **The Tin Men** . . . , Mr. Frayn has hit upon a marvelous, if obvious, idea for a witty and devastating fable. His setting is a new school for automation research, his characters humorless men who see no reason why all things should not be automated, from football to the novel, from newspapers to prayer. Machines can substitute for every human activity, with the possible exception of the strictly animal functions. Mr. Frayn makes the case in detail, at times in completely deadpan and utterly hilarious fashion.

Yet there were far too many moments in this book when I found my smile, but not my attention, becoming fixed. The reason is simple: **The Tin Men** is repetitive. The two-dimensional characters do not change; they come on, go off, come on and perform exactly the same act all over again. And, unfortunately, too many of them are the old hacks of glib satire we saw a decade ago in the Ealing comedies. . . .

Despite flashes of Frayn verve, the thing is old hat, leaky old hat at that. It's too bad, and damn sad, to say that of Michael Frayn. Was it perhaps too easy? You'll smile all right at **The Tin Men,** but it'll be the smile you give to a good joke you've heard before, instead of the quick stab of laughter, or surprised assent, at the sharp truth mockingly presented, fresh and original. Meat and potatoes to the general, but from Frayn we expect caviar to the knowing ones.

> *Julian Gloag, "School for Robots," in* Saturday Review, *Vol. XLIX, No. 3, January 15, 1966, p. 40.*

ROBERT TAUBMAN

Maybe it won't be without effect on the Cold War itself that the entertainment media men have gone over in a big way to spoofing it. Michael Frayn stands rather apart, because he doesn't invent absurdities so much as respond to real ambiguities in the situation. **The Russian Interpreter** is a spy story about cross-purposes on both sides. His earnest hero Proctor-Gould—an Englishman so convinced by himself he's worth setting beside Mr Powell's Widmerpool—is engaged in Moscow on a mission in which good will shades into espionage. Russian motives are no less mixed; the counter-spy uses his network to bring in forbidden Western books, the girl professor of dialectical materialism turns into a nutty heroine of hotel-bedroom farce. Working for one's country is hardly distinct from working against it, or public duty from private enterprise.

Mr Frayn is as clever with these moot points as a one-man Ilf and Petrov; and since their day there haven't been many other novels about Russia so nicely poised between satire and sympathy. I only wonder if it isn't a bit too gentle, a bit droll merely. He deals with comparatively minor mishaps of the

Cold War that are nobody's fault. There's hardly a hint that anyone on either side could behave really badly.

Robert Taubman, "Comedians of the Cold War," in New Statesman, Vol. 71, No. 1829, April 1, 1966, p. 477.*

PAMELA MARSH

Michael Frayn has been compared to Evelyn Waugh. It is easy to see why. . . .

[In *The Russian Interpreter*] Mr. Frayn succeeds in a tricky job of juggling deceivers deceived, spies spied upon.

Unfortunately he needs wittier, lighter moments to come near Evelyn Waugh. The solemner a matter is, the funnier Mr. Frayn finds it. But neither his humor, nor the infrequent glimpses he gives of springtime Russia can dispel the atmosphere of self-righteous dullness he has deliberately created.

Pamela Marsh, in a review of "The Russian Interpreter," in The Christian Science Monitor, November 23, 1966, p. 15.

CHRISTOPHER KOCH

As a parody of the middle class's obsessive concern with privacy, Michael Frayn's new novel [*A Very Private Life*] begins auspiciously as a bourgeois children's story turned on its head: "Once upon a time there will be . . ." a land of utter privacy. Children's stories cope with exaggerated fears and hopes by explaining them in comforting homilies as part of a remote world. Frayn retains this style—but places his story in the future and thereby makes us its cause.

His futuristic world is based on McLuhan's aphorism that electronic technology extends our central nervous systems in a global embrace. His characters remain forever in their homes—windowless boxes connected to the outside world by tubes and wires. . . .

All this is well done, but as Frayn's heroine, Uncumber, questions the system we begin to have doubts. Her problem is ours: What outside her home permits this insulated existence? Her world is divided between rulers ("deciders") who live inside the homes and workers ("animals") who live outside and build the homes, repair the tubes and grow the food.

Uncumber, a decider's daughter, discovers an exit to the outside world in a fit of childish rebelliousness. Later she falls in love with [Noli], a worker she accidentally dials on holovision, and that motivates her to use the exit. . . .

Uncumber decides to leave [the outside world]. On the way home she is gassed, abducted by a gang that murders deciders, and finally captured by the police. She is eventually slotted back into the deciders' world, and we are told that "she will live happily forever after." A gratuitous coda suggests future rebelliousness, but by then it hardly matters.

The author is telling us that Uncumber—a representative of our future selves—must choose between utter privacy and communal bestiality. But those are not the real options, and Frayn manipulates his characters and technology in his attempt to prove they are. . . .

Still more seriously, Frayn ignores the political implications of his world. The deciders' private lives depend on a technology that denies privacy—two-way television sets in every room,

omnipresent police and drugs to penetrate the unconscious. Indeed, these are the stereotypes of totalitarianism. Yet his deciders live in a utopian democracy. Similarly, his workers are miserable, envious of deciders—and, in gangs, they can attack their homes. Yet as a class they are generally acquiescent and certainly not revolutionary.

Modern technology clearly requires a radical redefinition of privacy. . . . Frayn has ignored the fact that modern men must solve their problems communally, or there will be no future men, private or communal.

Christopher Koch, "Uncumber's Undoing," in The New York Times Book Review, September 15, 1968, p. 44.

BENEDICT NIGHTINGALE

Michael Frayn has long been concerned with what one might portentously call the nature of reality and, until now at least, he's always stood squarely opposed to those who've attempted to fob off the rest of us with alluring substitutes. Hence his rather puritanical obsession with pop culture and the mass media, with ignorant pundits, facile critics and, of course, the eternal PROs and admen. The novels, especially *The Tin Men*, have pushed the attack rather further than the journalistic pieces. Why not, he asks at one point, an eventual world in which computers play all the games, watch and appreciate each other playing the games and discuss the game afterwards on TV, watched by yet more computers? It's all very fanciful, and may seem frivolous to some, but there's a genuine anxiety somewhere behind it. What is happening, not just to people's ability to distinguish truth from pretence, but to their very capacity to feel? . . .

Frayn took his degree in moral sciences; and if anyone doubts that his interests are indeed essentially philosophic, he should closet himself with *A Very Private Life,* a novel that gnaws at the mind, like some maddening if nonmalevolent virus, and leaves it hot and irritated long afterwards; a subtle, rather difficult book, unusual by any criterion and easily the most original thing he, Frayn, has done.

Marshall McLuhan tells us we're living in a 'global village', and certainly the mass media force shared experience upon us; yet we don't seem markedly nearer achieving any brotherhood of man. Quite the contrary. Isn't it an observed sociological truth that urban, and especially suburban people are increasingly suspicious of and hostile to those outside their own tightly circumscribed group? In other words, is it altogether fanciful to imagine as Frayn does, a world where the privileged have retreated to hermetically sealed compartments into which machines pipe food, air and a hundred varieties of happiness? Indeed, such is the efficiency of the holovision, a TV-telephone more potent than Huxley's 'feelies', that physical contact with others is hardly necessary. You swallow your Libidin and Orgasmin, dial an agreeable girl, coyly remove the dark glasses from your one taboo area, your eyes, and spend a few days enjoying a multi-coloured, three-dimensional wet dream.

And what's so wrong with that? This time, I think, Frayn isn't simply pressing the case for his back-to-nature movement. 'Nature', after all, isn't so easily defined, any more than is 'reality'. His fable is more hesitant, more ambivalent than that. The heroine, futuristically called Uncumber, feels a vague dissatisfaction with the holovision. That sun, the mountains, those aromatic bushes aren't, she knows, the genuine article. So she takes a trip to the outer world, which turns out to be smelly, messy, intermittently brutal, and not very satisfactory in any sense. The man she falls for uses her in a desultory, offhand sort of way, as if he was masturbating. It is all very sad.

So which is to be preferred, life itself or a life of rapt hallucinations? It could be objected that Frayn has unfairly loaded his scales by presenting a peculiarly dispiriting picture of 'reality', or, again, that the choice itself is merely sportive. There's no such thing as holovision and not likely to be. Perhaps not; but that doesn't dispose of the questions Frayn raises. . . . After all, of what can we be absolutely sure except our private, subjective sensation? . . .

The subject is pregnant, as Frayn clearly knows. When one says, 'I love you', one means, roughly, I am experiencing a necessarily private complex of sensations which I find peculiarly satisfying and which, by a process of ratiocination, I conclude to be attributable to the sight, smell, sound and touch, indeed my own total sensory experience, of you. But if 'I' could achieve as satisfying a result more easily, 'you' would be redundant, because it is my private sensations, not you or 'love' or any other fuzzily-worded concept, that's the essence of the matter. Other people are necessary only as long as we lack an adequate substitute for them. In short, the material world as one knows it is a means to a private end, no more, and isn't of essential value in itself.

Where and how far Frayn would take this argument I don't know; but his book is very suggestive. It should appeal to anyone who wants to think more about, well, anything from the defects of existentialism to the Ian Brady case. And (no small matter) it's written with that elegant simplicity, that easy precision, of which Michael Frayn is so splendidly capable.

Benedict Nightingale, "Private Sensations," in New Statesman, *Vol. 76, No. 1960, October 4, 1968, p. 434.*

IRVING WARDLE

One's heart starts sinking from the first moment of Michael Frayn's play [*The Sandboy*] when Eleanor Bron drops an armload of cushions to stare at us aghast and go into her embarrassed hostess routine. It is one of those: the audience as uninvited guests. And not only that. We are also supposed to compose a huge television crew who have gate-crashed the house to film a day in the life of her celebrity husband.

I can think of no playwright who has pulled off this particular trick which produces a continuous collision of idioms when applied to naturalistic action. And the fact that Mr Frayn should have lumbered himself with a notoriously unworkable structure amounts also to an internal criticism of the play's content. His theme is the gap between what intellectuals say and how they live: the intellectual in this case being Phil, a city planner, happy as a sandboy translating the structural philosophies of [Noam] Chomsky and [Claude] Levi-Strauss into architecture, while blind to the surrounding debris of domestic collapse. Planning for doomsday, he feels himself immortal.

Comedies on this subject tend to be written by pragmatic outsiders. *The Sandboy* differs from them as it is the work of an intellectual who can arm his hero with any amount of plausible chat about the vocabulary of clip-on units and the need to give human life styles the flexibility of a biological structure. What Mr Frayn has failed to do is to place such speeches in comic perspective. The impression is that he is trapped in the same

bag with Phil, who might indeed have written the play himself. . . .

There are a handful of effective passages, as where . . . the workman lures Phil back into playing at army drill and almost gets him to lick his boots. But even this only drives home the unappealing point that superior people ought to assert their status. . . .

[There] is not much to laugh at in . . . [this] production: least of all the sight of an intelligent writer defaming his own best equipment.

Irving Wardle, in a review of "The Sandboy," in The Times, *London, September 17, 1971, p. 8.*

DAVE ROBINS

Michael Frayn is a clever humourist, a master of the witty phrase, the extended satirical anecdote. These talents . . . ensured that at least I laughed a great deal throughout *Clouds,* Frayn's new play. . . .

Clouds is set in Cuba—or at any rate an empty blue sky with beneath it just six chairs and a table. Into this void step Mara and Owen, two English writers come to report on life after the revolution. She . . . is a lady novelist of the Edna O'Brien type; he . . . , a jumpy, neurotic journalist. . . . Accompanying them on the tour of the country is Angel . . . , their slow-moving, slow-talking Cuban guide. . . . Also on the sightseeing tour is Ed . . . , an idealist academic from the wilds of Illinois, who, on visiting a new town site, manages to see future socialist worlds in piles of industrial sand. Finally there is Hilberto . . . , the party's happy-go-lucky, cigar-smoking driver. Is he the real Cuba? . . .

Clearly there are significant portents about human nature being suggested in all this. What do we *really* see when we try to report on things objectively? How *do* you tell 'illusion' from 'reality'? What is time and material progress? . . .

At the end of *Clouds,* the symbolic fivesome drive off into the Great Continuum. 'Pure light! Pure emptiness!' one exclaims. So many illusory stereotypes, so many real clichés, you can almost see through the seams in the characters.

Marcuse, Kolokowski—relax. As a 'thinker', Frayn is a minnow. He does little to strengthen Britain's second-rate philosopher squad. Nevertheless, *Clouds* is entertaining theatre. . . .

Dave Robins, in a review of "Clouds," in Plays and Players, *Vol. 24, No. 1, October, 1976, p. 27.*

LEONIE CALDICOTT

'And this is what the product is all about,' declares [John Garrard] at the end of *Make and Break,* swinging round the final section of his firm's wall system and revealing a corpse on the other side.

Death stalks Frayn's characters as they play out their good commercial roles against a lurid trade-fair background, punctuated by the faint menace of exploding terrorist bombs 'out there' in the city of Frankfurt. . . . At the centre of the frenzy is the managing director, John Garrard . . . , who unlike the rest of his staff, cannot shed his professional identity and the accompanying turn of mind, even for a moment. This is a brain attempting to work like a computer: absorb maximum data, process, place in order of priority, issue programme of action.

He questions his staff about their private lives (on the principle that if a man has two heads, why talk to only one), their religious views and their artistic preferences with the same all-consuming efficiency he applies to his business proper. Presumably he does the same to his wife, children, as they have all gone into headlong flight out of his life. The seduction of his partner's secretary . . . is carried out with an efficiency that is part idle curiosity and part single-mindedness (it certainly isn't rapacious lust), and culminates in a masterly piece of expressionistic theatre. (pp. 23-4)

[The secretary's] speech on the humble, moment-by-moment goals and pleasures of a lonely, underfilled life confirms the atmosphere of blighted quality that gives the play its power to move. Behind a depressing world of rapid satisfactions, the consolations of giant stuffed teddy bears and slick professionalism only just hold back the tide which threatens to engulf its ordered existence. . . .

Meanwhile, religion hovers everywhere, providing a counterpoint to the smash and grab ethos, but very little salvation. The youngest member of the sales team is a sweaty-palmed, born-again Christian, an attribute compatible with eager-beaver junior salesman role. . . . The secretary's interest in Buddhism is treated, though at greater length, with the same commodity-orientated attitude by Garrard. One gets the impression that Frayn might just be proposing the Four Noble Truths as a serious contender for getting these beleaguered human beings off their karmic wheels. On the other hand, they and other Buddhist principles are rattled off with the same ludicrous vacuity as the varieties of wood available for the wall-systems. I could not help feeling once again that Frayn should check his 'how to make anything seem ridiculous in three easy sentences' ability a little more than he does. Too many easy laughs put the drive of this type of play at risk, whilst at times unbalancing the tone beyond the point of credibility. . . . This may account for any longeurs in **Make and Break.**

Similar difficulties beset the character of Tom Olley . . . , Garrard's experienced but sympathetic Catholic second-in-command, who wields almost all the moral clout of the play, providing a foil to the emotional wasteland which Garrard has subjugated to his commercially utilitarian ethic. . . . These two men are supposed to be very close, yet over-emphatic characterisation gives rise to doubts about the credibility of the relationship. (p. 24)

> *Leonie Caldicott, in a review of "Make and Break," in* Plays and Players, *Vol. 27, No. 7, April, 1980, pp. 23-4.*

HAROLD HOBSON

[Mr Frayn's play **Make and Break**] is wretchedly constructed; old-fashioned in its views of women; relies on a surprise ending which would have suited a comedy thriller, but which left the Haymarket audience tittering and giggling with embarrassment, not being able to believe that Mr Frayn took it seriously; depends for an interminable time at the beginning on scenic tricks and *trucs* with characters rushing in and out of opening and shutting doors without a trace of the expertise which sometimes makes trap-door exploits in pantomimes acceptable. . . .

> *Harold Hobson, in a review of "Make and Break," in* Drama, *No. 137, July, 1980, p. 35.*

J. R. BROWN

Noises Off is a farce, the form of drama which is most difficult to read and most easy to dismiss from serious consideration. But such doubts should not deter any reader. Like Frayn's earlier comedies, this farce arises from a shrewd and, even, intellectual engagement in life and work in England today. Frayn is always aware of the expectations of his characters and comic disasters are so contrived that complacencies and hopes are constantly challenged and motivations defined. In this latest work Michael Frayn turns from journalism, travel, education and business, the subjects of earlier plays, and presents the world of theatre: this is a farce about the performance of a farce. Part of the joke is that *Noises Off* is about *Nothing On:* desperately the characters of Frayn's play strive to be the characters desperately involved in the play that Frayn has also written for them, and at the same time they strive to keep their own lives in some reasonable order. For most of the second act, the author has written his text in two columns, one for the on-stage action of *Nothing On* and the other for the off-stage action of *Noises Off.* That sounds complicated, and it is gloriously so in performance; the surprise is that in reading the text, the author's intentions become crystal clear without loss of wit or of the freedom of farcical fantasy. In a play where 'all round is strife and uncertainty'—as the burglar of *Nothing On* declaims just before final curtain—the characters speak improbable words with varying degrees of belief. The chaos that ensues is judged so nicely that their varying success gives great pleasure. A reader of the text has one advantage over a theatre audience in being able to take his own time to try to see how the trick worked.

> *J. R. Brown, in a review of "Noises Off," in* British Book News, *January, 1983, p. 54.*

FRANK RICH

It's strangely involving to watch actors struggle heroically in a ludicrous play. When absolutely everything goes wrong on stage, as when everything goes right, we're treated to drama that is urgent, spontaneous, unmistakably alive.

Yet whoever heard of a play in which both extremes of theatergoing pleasure occupy the same stage at the same time? That's what happens at Michael Frayn's **"Noises Off."** . . . All three acts of this play recycle the same theatrical catastrophe: We watch a half-dozen has-been and never-were British actors, at different stops on a provincial tour, as they perform the first act of a puerile, door-slamming sex farce titled "Nothing On." With a plot involving wayward plates of sardines, misplaced clothing and an Arab sheik, "Nothing On" is the silliest and most ineptly acted play one could ever hope to encounter. But out of its lunacies, Mr. Frayn has constructed the larger prank of **"Noises Off"**—which is as cleverly conceived and adroitly performed a farce as Broadway has seen in an age. . . .

It happens that Act I of **"Noises Off"** is the frantic final run-through of "Nothing On," on the eve of its premiere in the backwater of Weston-Super-Mare. As the run-through is mostly devoted to setting-up what follows, it's also the only sporadically mirthless stretch of Mr. Frayn's play: We're asked to study every ridiculous line and awful performance in "Nothing On" to appreciate the varied replays yet to come. Still, the lags are justified by the payoff: Having painstakingly built his house of cards in Act I, the author brings it crashing down with exponentially accelerating hilarity in Acts II and III.

Indeed, Act II of **"Noises Off"** . . . is one of the most sustained slapstick ballets I've ever seen. "Nothing On" is now a month into its tour, and we discover that its actors are carrying out a real-life sex farce that crudely parallels the fictional one they're appearing in. Mr. Frayn lets us see both farces at once, through the device of showing us a chaotic Wednesday matinee of "Nothing On" from the reverse angle of backstage. Everytime an actor playing an illicit lover in "Nothing On" exits through a slamming door, he lands smack in the middle of the illicit love triangles that are destroying the company in private.

Besides being an ingeniously synchronized piece of writing and performing—with daredevil pratfalls and overlapping lines that interlock in midair—Act II of **"Noises Off"** is also a forceful argument for farce's value as human comedy. Perhaps nothing could top it, and Act III doesn't always succeed. . . .

[But **"Noises Off"** is a] joyous and loving reminder that the theater really does go on even when the show falls apart. . . .

> *Frank Rich, " 'Noises Off', A British Farce by Frayn,"*
> *in* The New York Times, *December 12, 1983, p. C12.*

MICHAEL RATCLIFFE

[**'Benefactors'**] is a seriously amusing four-hander which takes Frayn away from the richer emotional resourcefulness of (in my opinion) his best play to date, **'Make and Break,'** and into the patterning of couples more familiar in Ayckbournland. It is, for him, an excessively neat, neoclassical sort of piece which draws on only a fraction of his imaginative range, and in which the four characters . . . speak both to one another and to the audience.

It is coloured throughout by the imagery of planning, destruction, rehabilitation and twilight zones as applied to areas of Victorian suburbia and the human refuse of liberal revolution alike, but Frayn seems to be both mocking the methods of Ibsen . . . and making use of them. Something quite delicate is being said about men, women and change—men believing they effect it, women knowing they cannot—but the real problem with the play is simply that the men remain shadows and only the women come to life.

> *Michael Ratcliffe, "Glenda's Marathon," in* The Observer, *April 8, 1984, p. 19.*

ROBERT BRUSTEIN

I hate to be a habitual dissenter regarding all these celebrated British imports—but I'm afraid *Noises Off* failed to get my pulse racing. . . . Watching this carefully manufactured laugh machine was like spending three hours staring into the works of a very expensive, very complicated Swiss clock—impressive workmanship, but for how long can one look at revolving wheels, moon disks, and star dials? . . .

I seem to remember that Lewis Mumford once declared the clock to be the key machine of the modern age, so maybe *Noises Off* represents the theatrical future—a time when instruments of stage precision will have replaced our more untidy dramatic endeavors. It is certainly more akin to engineering than to playwriting, directing, or acting; even the laughs issuing from the throats of the audience sounded mechanical to me. Ah, you may ask, why can't this sourpuss just sit back and enjoy an innocent little farce without injecting his morbid social generalizations? Well, the truth is I love farces—but ones that involve another dimension than efficiency, and more motor actions than slamming doors and falling down stairs. Farce may be a mechanism, but it is a mechanism rooted in behavior, however exaggerated. When Charlie Chaplin, in *Modern Times*, takes a break from the production line and continues to act like a machine, we laugh because of the contrast with his normal mode of being, just as Feydeau's indiscreet husbands amuse us by their convincingly agonized efforts to avoid exposure by their wives. But the characters in *Noises Off*—nincompoop actors from an incompetent British touring company—display little in the way of credible human reality. They are merely impulses in a laugh track. . . .

The backstage ambience of the play, where the company continues to rehearse and perform an inane English farce while engaged in fits of temperament, bouts of drunkenness, and tantrums of jealousy, is obviously appealing to audiences—people usually love plays about the theater. It would be unfair to compare Frayn's treatment with that of such superior works about theater as Pirandello's *Tonight We Improvise* . . . , Molnar's *The Play's the Thing* . . . , or Mamet's *A Life in the Theater* . . .—but I can't resist observing that in those plays relationships are formed and broken because something is at stake. In *Noises Off,* nothing is at stake except the comic payoff—and nothing truthful emerges except the fact that actors, no matter how awful they feel or how badly they behave, somehow still manage to perform. "Getting the sardines on—getting the sardines off," says the play's director, "that's farce—that's theater—that's life." That's certainly what passes for farce, life, and theater in *Noises Off.* (p. 26)

> *Robert Brustein, "Hard and Soft Machines," in* The New Republic, *Vol. 191, No. 3625, July 9, 1984, pp. 26-7.**

Gail Godwin

1937-

American novelist, short story writer, and essayist.

Godwin's main concern in her fiction is to create intelligent, thoughtful characters who try to rationalize the problems they encounter and who decide on the best ways to lead their lives. In her early novels, *The Perfectionists* (1970), *Glass People* (1972), *The Odd Woman* (1974), and *Violet Clay* (1978), Godwin's female protagonists often find their answers through artistic pursuits or by surrendering their independence to a man. Although some reviewers place Godwin within the feminist literary tradition, her themes are universal in scope, encompassing the relationship of art to life, the influence of the past on the present, and, most importantly, the struggle for freedom and self-fulfillment in a relationship with another person.

Godwin's novel *A Mother and Two Daughters* (1981) is a conscious broadening of her canvas. There are three central female characters instead of one, and her portrayals are more compassionate than in her previous novels. Critics have also noted that Godwin's male characters are more sympathetically drawn in *A Mother and Two Daughters* than in her other works. Some have found similarities with the Victorian novel, citing her large cast of characters and expansive format.

The stories in *Mr. Bedford and the Muses* (1983) are perhaps Godwin's most autobiographical works. They deal with the artist's relationship to her material and the conflict between wanting to gain experience in the world and having to adapt to a more dependent lifestyle. Critics have generally commended these genial, humorous stories.

(See also *CLC*, Vols. 5, 8, 22; *Contemporary Authors*, Vols. 29-32, rev. ed.; and *Dictionary of Literary Biography*, Vol. 6.)

© 1984 Thomas Victor

JONATHAN YARDLEY

A Mother and Two Daughters is a novel of genuine consequence, a spacious and generous book into which Gail Godwin has entrusted worlds of feeling and understanding. It has nothing to do with the cramped, narcissistic, self-indulgent novels now in favor among the literary elite; it is a populous, exuberant expansive novel in the Victorian tradition. It is everything that a novel should be: funny, sad, provocative, ironic, compassionate, knowing, *true*. It does what only the best fiction can do: it slows the reader down, insisting that he progress through it at the author's own pace. Making that journey is a remarkable experience.

It is a novel about that richest of all subjects, families, and it takes its inspiration from Montaigne: "To storm a breach, conduct an embassy, govern a people, these are brilliant actions; to scold, laugh . . . and deal gently and justly with one's family and oneself . . . that is something rarer, more difficult, and less noticed in the world." It is a novel about the death of a man to whom these words were precious, who made it his true life's work to live up to them, and about the emptiness his death leaves in the lives of the three women in his family. . . .

[The] daughters come home for the funeral, their friends and neighbors gather about them, and Leonard is buried. For his three women, it is an end and a beginning. Though Nell remains in the house where she and Leonard lived for most of their marriage, the old life is gone forever; for both of the daughters, their father's death coincides with moments of impending crisis in their own lives—and though there is no connection between his death and their crises, it serves to underscore the fragility and uncertainty that both of them feel. . . .

Godwin gives us each of these women as a discrete, distinct individual; she shifts with impressive facility from one voice to another. Cate is the central figure, no doubt because Godwin clearly identifies most strongly with her. Yet it is of the many strengths of this wonderful book that the central figure is by no means the most sympathetic. Cate's self-righteousness is infuriating, her rejections of love are bewildering, her self-pity is most unattractive. Yet precisely because she is so complex and articulate, she provokes strong reactions in others and leads them, as well as herself, to moments of illumination. It is, for example, when Cate whiningly tries to reject Nell's offer of aid and comfort in her time of trial that Nell suddenly, angrily, comes to a crucial understanding:

"'When you're alive, you do what you *can* do. That's the duty, that's the privilege of the living. I'm not sure the rest matters very much. If you love me, if you honor me at all, you will accept what I offer out of love—and because I *have* it to offer. Otherwise'—Nell spread her arms in an exasperated gesture—'what has it all been *for?*' "

Of the several major and minor themes that wind carefully through Godwin's narrative, this seems to me the one at the heart of the book: the joy of living and the obligation to try to do it well. Godwin describes the question Hawthorne asked in *The Scarlet Letter*—"Can the individual spirit survive the society in which it has to live?"—and answers it with a wry yet ringing affirmative. She poses death against life, and chooses life for every precious moment that it is granted.

There are nits to be picked—a couple of sentimentalized characters, some unnecessary foreshadowing, some awkward tidying up in the "Epilogue"—but I do not propose to pick them. Any flaws in this novel are those of daring and ambition, those committed by a writer trying, in Faulkner's memorable phrase, "to put all of the history of the human heart on the head of a pin." This Godwin is trying to do; in the extended family that in the end gathers to celebrate itself, she has given us nothing less than the family of humanity, in all its flawed and perfect glory.

She has also given us a novel of extraordinary range and detail. It moves at such a leisurely pace because the reader cannot stand to miss a word; everything is interesting or funny or perceptive or stunningly familiar—or all of those things and many others. She drops off provocative asides ("What were aristocrats but simply the barbarians who got there first?") with aplomb and insouciance. And she turns out—this was not really evident in her four previous books—to be a stunningly gifted novelist of manners. . . .

This quality of compassion is new to Godwin's novels, if not to the brilliant short stories that were collected in *Dream Children*. It was her missing ingredient, the one important quality that her fiction lacked. Now that she has put heart as well as intellect into a novel, she has moved to the high place among our novelists for which she has long seemed destined. *A Mother and Two Daughters* is a work of complete maturity and artistic control, one that I am fully confident will find a permanent and substantial place in our national literature.

> *Jonathan Yardley, "Gail Godwin: A Novelist at the Height of Her Powers," in* Book World—The Washington Post, *December 13, 1981, p. 3.*

BRIGITTE WEEKS

Gail Godwin's heroines have abandoned their soapboxes, and thank goodness for that. . . . Her complex and fascinating characters, like Jane Clifford in *The Odd Woman* and Violet in *Violet Clay,* have until now suffered from two crippling flaws: they have repeatedly indulged in long, often boring, interior monologues . . . and they have had no sense of humor whatsoever.

However, the news of Godwin's latest novel, *A Mother and Two Daughters,* is good, in fact, very good indeed. Nell, Cate, and Lydia Strickland, the three women who dominate the stage, are—like Violet Clay and Jane Clifford—thoughtful, well-educated, self-analytic people, but Godwin hustles them along at a brisk pace through this long, but definitely never tedious tale. They don't opine about the meaning of love or the perils of George Eliot, but do share with us their attempts to make a good job of an ordinary daily life familiar to us all. (p. 39)

Only a few times in this long novel does Godwin falter. A digression on contemporary fiction seems jarringly self-conscious. The requisite eccentrics are skillfully drawn, but show up right on cue: the overbearing, curious spinster aunt Theodora and the disfigured Uncle Osgood with his heart of gold and his redemptive role for latter-day sinners. The middle-class black couple seem plopped down in order to stir up a few thoughts on prejudice and change. All the characters take themselves very seriously, but it is part of their astonishing strength that they persuade us to do likewise.

Anyone from an average family will find themselves drawing a breath and muttering: "Yes, that's how *I* felt, that's how it always is." Godwin wrote of Jane Clifford in *The Odd Woman*: "Her profession was words and she believed in them deeply. The articulation, interpretation, and preservation of good words." She could have been describing herself. She pilots her cast of characters with infinite care, through turbulence, clouds, and sparkling skies. The smooth landing at the novel's end is deeply satisfying: not a neat tying up of loose ends, but a making sense of the past and a hint of the possibilities of the future. Gail Godwin is not just an established writer, she is a growing writer. (pp. 39, 41)

> *Brigitte Weeks, "Gail Godwin's Third Novel: The 'Odd Woman' Wises Up," in* Ms., *Vol. X, No. 7, January, 1982, pp. 39, 41.*

JOSEPHINE HENDIN

[The] tension between individual vision and the constricting power of circumstance finds a fresh and distinctive expression in Gail Godwin's **"A Mother and Two Daughters,"** a novel about three women who try to "renovate" their lives.

Here, as in her previous novels, Gail Godwin has drawn on the tradition of American individualism and adapted it to her concern with female lives. . . .

"A Mother and Two Daughters" extends this faith in the individual toward a vision of community, within the family, the town and, ultimately, the nation. In this novel, Gail Godwin's individualists are the female members of a family in crisis over the death of husband and father. The widowed mother and her two daughters have lost their first illusions; their bulwark is gone. Their necessity is to pull together. . . .

As each woman exerts her claims on the others, as each confronts the envy and anger the others can inspire, Gail Godwin orchestrates their entanglements with great skill. (p. 3)

As Lydia moves toward independence, as Cate strives toward a greater acceptance of others, and as their mother reconstructs her life, Miss Godwin achieves a richness of affirmations. In this generous novel, illness and age are enablers. And if time has taken the illusions and promises of youth from these women, it has also pressed them toward recognizing the serious courtesy due one another's pain. In one of the best-realized episodes of the novel Cate, whose face is temporarily paralyzed by Bell's palsy, reaches accord with a former high school friend whose leg was shattered in the Vietnam War. Anti-war activist and veteran—both battered by their choices—comfort each other with exquisite simplicity.

America is in flux as much as Americans are. The beauty of the small Southern mountain town in which the novel is set, the smug, traditional morality of the town's elite, even the mystery of Cate's favorite Thoreauvian old uncle, who chooses to live among his apple trees—all contribute to the bright American colors of the novel. Encroaching on these are darker shades: Skylab is about to fall, the Iranians hold American hostages, the town's appearance is marred by garish shopping malls, racial violence erupts. Although Miss Godwin does not entirely succeed in negotiating the distance between family and nation, between the personal and the political, she clearly hopes these distances can be narrowed. . . .

Ironically, the major flaw of "**A Mother and Two Daughters**" arises out of Gail Godwin's ability to modulate emotion. She is a thoughtful craftsman, countering her characters' excesses of emotion with excesses of mind, tempering their envy with concern, their disapproval with compassion—to the point where she neutralizes the force of her narrative. Perfectly balanced, the novel is imperfectly pitched. Its overmodulation produces a monotone of sweet reasonableness that seems inappropriate to the more painful aspects of her characters' experience: abortion, death, adultery.

"**A Mother and Two Daughters**" is nevertheless a remarkable novel. In this spacious, harmonious book—an expansive and imaginative celebration of American life—Gail Godwin retrieves her heroines from impasses. Through characters who are recognizable contemporaries, she takes us back to an Emersonian faith in the human capacity for good, for betterment. (p. 14)

> *Josephine Hendin, "Renovated Lives," in* The New York Times, *January 10, 1982, p. 3, 14.*

ANNE TYLER

[*A Mother and Two Daughters*] quotes Gail Godwin as saying that she's trying for

> a vision of America, where we've been and where we're going. . . . I see *A Mother and Two Daughters* as an attempt to penetrate, often humorously, the way a certain group of characters behave both as their stubborn unique selves, and as part of the interweaving, interacting system we call society.

She has succeeded, I believe. Certainly the three women represent three very different styles of coping with the modern world; and their individual histories reflect enough about their culture to interest an alert sociologist. (pp. 39-40)

A Mother and Two Daughters has much to say about modern society, but it speaks even more affectingly and more resonantly about the tiny, cataclysmic events that make up domestic life. A grown woman, long since proven competent and successful, still has a feeling of miserable inadequacy when confronting her older sister. A wife supposedly accustomed to widowhood experiences her grief all over again when she discovers the emerging crocuses planted by her husband over twenty years ago. And her grief is unsentimental, unglorifying, and therefore all the more poignant. . . .

The little world of Mountain City is as meticulously documented—the rituals of Christmas party and book club meeting; the maid who goes home to the slums every evening laden with hand-me-down clothes and leftover food, "everything in the world but the minimum wage"; the town heiress whose money comes from an ancestral energy tonic that doesn't freeze in winter. There's an observant, amused, but kindly eye at work here, and not a single cheap shot is taken at these people

who might so easily have been caricatures in someone else's hands. . . .

Best of all, *A Mother and Two Daughters* demonstrates, once again, Gail Godwin's uncommon generosity as a storyteller. She is openhanded—she's positively spendthrift—with her tales. The most insignificant character travels on a stream of absorbing histories, past love affairs, coincidences, recurring themes. Just look at the story of Nell's semi-seduction before her marriage; or of how old Uncle Osmond lost his nose in World War I; or of Lydia's cold-blooded pursuit of her husband-to-be. Any one of these plots could possibly have been a novel on its own, or at least a short story, but Gail Godwin doesn't measure things out so penuriously. When you read one of her novels, you have a feeling of abundance.

Is *A Mother and Two Daughters* as good as *The Odd Woman?*

Is that even a fair question to ask?

The Odd Woman remains one of my all-time favorites, perhaps partly because of the element of surprise—I read it before I knew how much one could expect of Gail Godwin. *A Mother and Two Daughters* lacks that element, of course, and it suffers too from what seems to me an unnecessary summary epilogue. . . .

There is one improvement, though. In *A Mother and Two Daughters,* the male characters have real depth and texture. Dear Leonard Strickland, and Cate's redneck millionaire suitor, and Lydia's sweetly stuffy husband and her earnest lover—all are solidly believable. For the first time, Gail Godwin's men are equal to her women. And that's saying something. (p. 40)

> *Anne Tyler, "All in the Family," in* The New Republic, *Vol. 186, No. 7, February 17, 1982, pp. 39-40.*

JOHN B. BRESLIN

[*A Mother and Two Daughters*] has its flaws, as annoying as they are unnecessary, but the complex pattern it weaves, the subtle analyses of motive and memory it sustains and the rich evocation of place and time it provides should render readers benevolent toward its stylistic lapses. Indeed, the book's strengths and weaknesses are bound together as inextricably as the lives of the title characters; and the title itself, provocative in its banality, promises neither more nor less than what the author delivers: a detailed portrayal of the interlocked crises that alternately unite and divide the lives of three contemporary women.

The novel begins and ends with a party. But where the first commemorates an old order dying and concludes with a fatal accident, the latter celebrates a wedding and a new order being born. It is a measure of Gail Godwin's skill as a novelist that these disparate notes harmonize rather than clash; the story is a comedy in the classic sense, moving from dispersion to reunion and, indeed, the final gathering on the lawn with minstrels playing could as easily be set in Illyria or the Forest of Arden as in rural North Carolina. But the specific questions under discussion and the circumstances of the women's lives are unmistakably late 20th-century American: mid-life identity crises, academic vagabondage, interracial permutations. Nell Strickland and her two daughters, Cate and Lydia, perform their family dance of estrangement and reconciliation to the music of a society so rapidly in transition that even massive physical landmarks have simply disappeared, like the hill in the middle of Mountain City, or been transformed beyond recognition, like the orchard of Nell's private school now part of a shopping mall. Fragile human constructs like marriage or civility or contractual obligations fare less well still. Left a widow early in the novel, Nell struggles both to remember and to go on living for her own sake and that of her daughters whose lives show the scars of the wider conflict. . . . The tension between the two sisters, never dormant for very long, grows more acute as Lydia's fortunes wax and Cate's wane, sexually as well as professionally; the result is, literally and figuratively, a conflagration whose scorch marks never fully heal.

Stated as boldly as that, the triangular structure of the novel could seem trite and contrived, especially when Lydia's two boys are presented as chiastic replicas of their mother and aunt. But that would be to see the skeleton and miss the body. Gail Godwin has fleshed out her story with a remarkable collection of secondary characters (mid-America's plenty) and a lavish display of sensuous and psychological detail. If every sentence does not certify its own inevitability, . . . still the sheer accumulation of incident and description, of psychological perception and social comment gives the novel a density that pulls the reader into this particular story while, at the same time, expanding awareness of cognate mysteries in his or her own life.

> *John B. Breslin, in a review of "A Mother and Two Daughters," in* America, *Vol. 146, No. 15, April 17, 1982, p. 305.*

CHRISTOPHER LEHMANN-HAUPT

In an author's note appended to the six delightful fictions in [**"Mr. Bedford and the Muses"**] Gail Godwin reflects on muses—on the need for them particularly when writer's block attacks in any of its unpleasant guises; on one muse in particular, a turtle named Mr. Bedford, who helped the author to finish the long story, really a novella, that is named after its boxy, slow-moving inspiration.

In the course of her reflection, Miss Godwin also indirectly acknowledges fashion as a spur to creation. . . .

This point set me to wondering whether Miss Godwin's appeal is a matter of fashion. Is it the conservative mood of the times that enhances one's enjoyment of her astonishingly vivid characters, who make their ways or founder in a world that is comfortably removed from absurdity? Or is it just that with each succeeding book . . . Miss Godwin keeps getting better? Actually, one could make a case for the culturally progressive attitudes that underlie her vision. But the form of these stories is classical and familiar, and readers of all tastes will find themselves at home in them. . . .

[All] the stories are about the relationship of artists to their material. In each of them the drama that unfolds with wonderful humor and variety is essentially the conflict between the writer's hunger to go forth into the world and acquire experience and the opposing pull to withdraw into passive dependency. . . .

There is also much about dreaming, telling lies, and feeling the lack of authenticity that artists so often suffer. There is also . . . much rich and humorous detail. . . . Still, the struggle that animates each of them is that of the artist trying to get outside of herself.

That is why Mr. Bedford, the pet turtle, makes an ideal muse for writers. Like a storyteller, what defined his existence was indistinguishably a part of him. When threatened, he tended to withdraw into himself, which could lead to loss of perspective and the risk of getting carried away (in Mr. Bedford's case by a dog, apparently). So determined was Mr. Bedford in following his owners from room to room . . . that when they gave parties, sometimes they "would fix a lighted candle to the back of Mr. Bedford's shell and he would come marching into the dark dining room all aglow and make the ladies scream." I hope that it will not seem too labored of me to point out that this bringing of light and making ladies scream has also been a practice of writers.

In short, it's a wonder that the turtle has not been heretofore universally celebrated as the muse of writers. I'm delighted that Gail Godwin has seen fit to do so now in this charming collection of stories about what moves artists to create.

> *Christopher Lehmann-Haupt, in a review of "Mr. Bedford and the Muses," in* The New York Times, *September 6, 1983, p. C14.*

JONATHAN YARDLEY

Mr. Bedford and the Muses is an unusually personal book, one that leaves the line between "fact" and "fiction" quite intentionally unclear. . . .

[The] most useful service Godwin has provided in **Mr. Bedford and the Muses**—quite apart from the pleasures she offers in the best of these stories—is to *admit* that the tales are to one degree or another autobiographical and then to show how they are, in the end, works of pure fiction. Taking a bow to her Muses, she acknowledges "this welcome band of inspirers who have appeared to me over the years in the most unpredictable disguises," but then leaves no doubt that "what Henry James called 'the virus of suggestion'" will come to nothing unless the imagination of the author seizes it and turns it into something quite different and unique.

The stories themselves focus, though not exclusively, on the origins and the process of creativity. The central mystery of **"Mr. Bedford"** is the dark secret of the enigmatic Eastons, but the real purpose of the story is to tell us what that relationship taught the aspiring young writer, Carrie Ames. . . . Carrie comes to learn that the artist, though sympathetic, must be merciless, plundering real life for the raw material of fiction.

Similar, or related, experiences await Constance LeFevre, in **"Amanuensis,"** and Charles St. John, in **"St. John."** . . .

Of the other stories, the most interesting is **"The Angry-Year,"** about a girl who has "transferred at last from the modest junior college in my hometown to the big, prestigious university with the good programs in English." She is bright, aggressive, "different," short on funds but long on aspiration, yet for reasons she cannot fully understand she finds herself hanging out with the fraternity and sorority crowd, "with people who demanded little of my mind." She is caught in that classic American dilemma: the outsider who holds the inside in contempt even as she desperately wishes to join it. She goes through much pain and bewilderment before she discovers "the real culprit, the crass conformist who'd been harboring inside the rebel all along"—a discovery that frees her to begin the literary career she desires above all else.

Mr. Bedford and the Muses is, by comparison with Godwin's previous novel, *A Mother and Two Daughters,* a slender book. But its size is deceptive. As in her longer and more ambitious works, Godwin takes on important themes while attaching them to appealing people in interesting situations. Her tone is genial, wry, pensive; it is as though she has stopped for a few moments to think things over, and has permitted the reader to listen in. In its modest way, *Mr. Bedford and the Muses* is a most appealing book.

> *Jonathan Yardley, "Gail Godwin: Autobiography into Art," in* Book World—The Washington Post, *September 11, 1983, p. 3.*

JUDITH GIES

Gail Godwin observed in a 1979 essay that "the most serious danger to my writing . . . is my predilection for shapeliness. How I love 'that nice circular Greek shape' . . . or a nice, neat conclusion, with all the edges tucked under." . . .

In general, Miss Godwin's gifts (like Margaret Drabble's) have been best served by the spacious dimensions of the conventional novel. Her talent lies in creating intelligent woman protagonists—usually middle-class and imaginative, often with artistic aspirations—who struggle to lead examined lives in the face of self-imposed as well as cultural constraints. Blessed with humor as well as perceptiveness, they are nearly always sympathetic, even when they behave badly. . . .

In any case, her reflective characters come to life slowly, emerging as much from thought as from action, and Miss Godwin's novels have generally accommodated them. I especially liked the edgy perversity of **"The Perfectionists"** (1970) and the irony and insight of **"The Odd Woman"** (1974), as well as the gentler but widening vision of **"A Mother and Two Daughters"** [1982].

I wish I could be as enthusiastic about **"Mr. Bedford and the Muses,"** a short novel and five stories. The stories have the more obvious problems, which are at least partly due to brevity and partly to their tucked-in edges. Shapeliness is deadly in short fiction. At best, it creates an excess of charm; at worst, it kills the story on the page. (p. 14)

There is a problematic tone, chatty and oddly schoolmarmish, that runs through the entire book and becomes most intrusive in the final Author's Note. We are told that **"Mr. Bedford,"** the title novella, was inspired by a story told to Miss Godwin years ago in London. "Now that I am putting his story together with some companions, all of whom had their respective Muses," she writes, "I feel compelled to acknowledge this welcome band of inspirers who have appeared to me over the years." She concludes: "I believe the air around us is thick with what Henry James called 'the virus of suggestion.' Sometimes it's enough just to keep your eyes and ears open, and answer the door; other times you might have to exert more energy and go digging into closets. But, 'Try to be one of those people on whom nothing is lost!' James advises, and, just as I've taken Mr. Bedford as my official Writing Mascot, I've made those words my motto."

This sort of academic self-congratulation, along with the constructed quality of the stories, makes the collection somewhat disappointing. Happily, the novella . . . has enough ragged edges to preserve it from shapeliness. And even when it threatens to slip into inconsequence, it is vastly entertaining.

The central characters in **"Mr. Bedford"** are an expatriate American couple who run a genteel boarding house for young people in London. The Eastons . . . enmesh the narrator, a young American boarder, in "a net composed of obligation, fascination and intrigue." . . . [Carrie Ames] has a sharp eye, and the Eastons assume nearly mythic proportions. Here is the quality we miss in the stories—a sense of the astonishing variousness of human beings. (pp. 14, 37)

On its own terms, which are not those of Miss Godwin's larger novels, **"Mr. Bedford"** is a memorable portrait of the kind of people who might have known Scott Fitzgerald during their "better days." It is wry, haunting and sharp.

There is a very short scene in **"The Odd Woman"** in which the heroine engages in a crushing power struggle with her stepfather over a jar of instant coffee. In the story **"A Cultural Exchange,"** the young American narrator is locked in similar psychic combat with Mr. Englegard, her autocratic old landlord in Copenhagen. Making coffee one night, she runs out of sugar and reaches for her host's package. On the box is a label: "Engelgard. Do not use!" "How small-minded could you get, I thought, outraged. I do not have to be a paying prisoner here." But she will not leave just yet because it is not quite convenient. This is Miss Godwin at her best, conveying the ways in which we are all at one time or another paying prisoners and the gallantry with which we measure out our rebellions—and our efforts at reconciliation—with coffee spoons. (p. 37)

> *Judith Gies, "Obligation, Fascination and Intrigue," in* The New York Times Book Review, *September 18, 1983, p. 14, 37.*

REBECCA RADNER

Gail Godwin's best is spectacular (if you haven't read *The Odd Woman,* you might wish to do so, instantly). Her latest book, *Mr. Bedford and the Muses,* is not her best. Say her fourth best—that's still not too bad.

One problem with *Mr. Bedford* is that Godwin's prose requires quite a bit of room, more than it gets in these five stories or even in the novella-length title piece. . . . Prose is fast and sharp these days, and Godwin is almost as slow and deliberate as a Victorian novelist. All very well, but not best suited to the compressed short story form.

Another difficulty is the nature of these pieces. Most writers fight the ever-present temptation to write about writing. Godwin has given us five authors out of six protagonists; three are women in their early twenties, first-person narrators. . . . This doesn't make for great variety of tone. "Revisionist autobiography," says Godwin unhelpfully. (pp. 25, 36)

"Desultory" exactly describes these stories at their weakest.

Yet at their strongest—well, somehow Godwin is a writer to trust. She says in this collection she was "re-interpreting and re-fashioning my own past." She does this with a cool, unsurprised tone. These young women are not treated with any particular tenderness. "There I was," she seems to say, "or someone like me, and it's strange, isn't it, what seemed to be happening back then."

Passion breaks through in only one of these stories—my favorite, **"The Angry-Year."** In 1957 Janie is a scholarship student, a junior at a famous university. She's fascinated by the wealthy, self-assured sorority girls. . . . She hates them, she satirizes them in the school paper and, of course, she longs to become them. Although this material is hardly fresh, in Godwin's hands it becomes powerful.

The title piece, **"Mr. Bedford,"** presents a young woman arriving in London in 1962. . . . This novella is full of unanticipated twists which never seem unlikely. Unfortunately, Godwin isn't terribly good at the kind of physical description which fixes a character's appearance in the reader's mind, although once in a while she succeeds with a minor character. . . .

In her quirky "Author's Note," Godwin quotes Henry James: " . . . the virus of suggestion," she says, is all around us. What she herself suggests particularly well are ideas, possibilities, pasts—the insubstantial, presented in unhurried, paradoxically substantial prose. (p. 36)

> Rebecca Radner, *"Reinterpreting Her Own Past,"* in Pacific Sun, *Vol. 21, No. 38, September 23-29, 1983, pp. 25, 36.*

H(ilda) D(oolittle)

1886-1961

American poet, novelist, dramatist, translator, memoirist, and editor.

H. D. is well known as an Imagist poet and her early free verse poems are credited with being the inspiration for Ezra Pound's formulation of Imagism. H. D.'s later poetry retained its clarity of image and free verse form but transcended the limitations of Imagism to include mythology, occult and religious themes, autobiographical material, psychoanalytic concepts, and symbolism. Her work in other genres also indicates that H. D. should be considered more than an Imagist poet. She is studied today not only because of the originality of her work, but also because much of it reflects her relationships with literary figures in England and America during the early part of the twentieth century.

Doolittle grew up near Philadelphia in an academic family with religious ties to the Moravian and Puritan faiths. She attended Bryn Mawr College and during this time met Marianne Moore and William Carlos Williams. At age nineteen she was briefly engaged to Pound and her intermittent involvement with him drew her to London in 1911. Although the marriage never occurred, Pound did establish her as "H. D. Imagiste" and helped get her poetry published in Harriet Monroe's *Poetry* magazine. Among the poets H. D. met in London literary circles was Richard Aldington, whom she married in 1913. Together they edited *The Egoist*, a literary forum for Imagist writers. Among the friends of the Aldingtons were D. H. Lawrence and his wife, Freida, an association which inspired novelizations by Aldington, Lawrence, and H. D. A series of tragic events, including the death of her brother, a miscarriage during her first pregnancy, and her own serious illness, led to the collapse of her marriage in 1919.

After her separation from Aldington, H. D. developed a relationship with the heiress and writer, Winnifred Ellerman, known as Bryher, which lasted until 1946. After travelling through Greece and other countries, H. D. and Bryher settled in Switzerland in 1924. In 1933 and 1934 H. D. underwent psychoanalysis with Sigmund Freud; this experience had an important influence on her work. H. D. returned to England during the Second World War and spent her last years putting her papers together and writing *Hermetic Definition* (1972). In 1960 she became the first woman to receive the Award of Merit Medal from the American Academy of Arts and Letters.

Sea Garden (1916), H. D.'s first book of verse, exemplifies her stark, specific use of imagery and the musical rhythm of her early poems. Another characteristic evident here and in H. D.'s other work is the classical Greek influence derived from her lifelong interest in Greek poetry and drama. "Oread" and "Heat" are two of her most celebrated Imagist poems. Two other volumes, *Hymen* (1921) and *Heliodora* (1924), were added to *Sea Garden* and published as *Collected Poems* (1924), a volume which established a firm foundation for H. D.'s reputation as the "perfect Imagist."

H. D. wrote two books based on her relationship with Pound: *End to Torment* (1979) and *HERmione* (1981). The first is a memoir of particular interest to Pound scholars for its inclu-

The Bettmann Archive, Inc.

sion of "Hilda's Book," a collection of poems Pound wrote for H. D. *HERmione* is a novelization of their early courtship which indicates that H. D. may have been bisexual. *Bid Me to Live* (1960) is a *roman à clef* about H. D.'s marriage to Aldington, his affair with Dorothy Yorke, and the platonic attachment H. D. formed with Lawrence. One of H. D.'s best prose works is *Tribute to Freud* (1956), variously termed a "prose love poem," a "psychobiography," and a novel. It describes the impact of the famous analyst on the young feminine protagonist's artistic and emotional development.

H. D.'s poetic work during the interwar period included *Red Roses for Bronze* (1929). This volume was faulted for its failure to fuse idea and emotion and for its lack of the brilliant images abundant in her early work. Two of the novels she wrote during this time, however, gained attention as experimental narratives. *Palimpsest* (1926) superimposes cultures and historical periods to present the parallel lives of three intellectual women in Rome, Egypt, and London. Each is seen as a "facet of H. D.'s total personality." The other experimental novel, *Hedylus* (1928), traces a young male artist's attempt to gain selfhood. Many commentators find the quest for self-identity a common theme throughout H. D.'s writings.

After returning to war-torn England from Switzerland, H. D. produced her major poetic work of the war years: *Trilogy*, comprising *The Walls Do Not Fall* (1944), *Tribute to Angels* (1945), and *Flowering of the Rod* (1946). Here H. D. combines autobiographical material and Egyptian mythology with the historic particulars of the destruction of London. After the war she wrote her long poem *Helen in Egypt* (1961). Perhaps because it is an epic quest which centers on a woman, the poem has received much attention, especially from scholars of women's writing. Helen is a persona for H. D. and other mythological figures have been identified as having their counterparts in H. D.'s life. While H. D. may be best remembered as an Imagist poet, such later works as *Helen in Egypt* have earned her a broader classification.

(See also *CLC*, Vols. 3, 8, 14; *Contemporary Authors*, Vols. 97-100; and *Dictionary of Literary Biography*, Vol. 4.)

HARRIET MONROE

The amazing thing about H. D.'s poetry is the wildness of it—that trait strikes me as I read her whole record in the *Collected Poems*. . . . She is as wild as deer on the mountain, as hepaticas under the wet mulsh of spring, as a dryad racing nude through the wood. . . . She is, in a sense, one of the most civilized, most ultra-refined, of poets; and yet never was a poet more unaware of civilization, more independent of its thralls. She doesn't talk about nature, doesn't praise or patronize or condescend to it; but she is, quite unconsciously, a lithe, hard, bright-winged spirit of nature to whom humanity is but an incident.

Thus she carries English poetry back to the Greeks more instinctively than any other poet who has ever written in our language. Studying Greek poetry, she finds herself at home there, and quite simply expresses the kinship in her art. (p. 268)

It would be an interesting speculation to consider how much H. D. owes to the pioneers whom all Americans descend from more or less. The pioneers took a shut-in race out of doors, exposed it to nature's harsh activities, and thus restored a certain lost fibre to its very blood and bones. H. D., eastern born and bred as she was, has inherited from them rather than from the barons and earls of England's past. And her poetry is more akin to that of our aborigines than it is to the Elizabethans or Victorians, or any of the classicists or romanticists between them. . . .

Her technique, like her spiritual motive, is lithe and nude. The free-verse forms she chooses are not even clothing, so innocent are they of any trace of artificiality; they are as much a part of her spirit, they complete it as essentially, as harmoniously, as the skin which encloses and outlines the flesh of a human body.

One may follow her flight from worldliness in all her poems, but perhaps it is most explicit in two of them. *Sheltered Garden* is a protest—observe that even her protests are uttered out-of-doors. . . . (p. 269)

There is a bold and trained athleticism in such poetry. . . . H. D.'s art has not the unstudied spontaneity of folk-lore, often so beautiful in its naiveté; it is shaped by an artist, carefully wrought to an effect of seeming improvisation. Its lines are simple in their strict firmness, but their simplicity is the result, not of instinct alone, but of right instinct sternly educated and disciplined. The keen rhythms of her poems respond with lyric magic to a spirit ever accepting nature's rhythms, a spirit growing with the grass, circling with the sun, racing with the wind, resting with the rocks on the slow beating-out of seasons.

In a certain sense she is inhuman, or perhaps superhuman. Her art is above and beyond little individual loves and hates; these, if they appear at all, merely serve to emphasize passions more ascetic in their indestructible hardihood. One feels that she has lived through and left behind the fierce surge of emotion which drowns so many souls. . . . Indeed, her intercourse is with gods. Her poetry is familiar with them, like that of the Greeks, and she claims them under their familiar Hellenic names as the natural companions of her spirit.

Perhaps, in the last analysis, the much abused word mystic should be invoked to describe the super-sensuous significance of her poetry. Her real subject is the experience and aspiration of the human soul—the flowers and trees she writes about, the rocks and winds and mountains, are symbols of the soul's adventures, of a soul which discards and transcends and sublimates the daily events and emotions of ordinary life. (pp. 271-73)

There is in this poet's work a cool hardness—indeed, the parallel is with sculpture in bronze or marble. *Hymen* carves a marble frieze, stained with clear colors in the old Greek or Chinese fashion. . . . The mood, and the April-of-life freshness of it, are sustained by an art singularly serene and sure.

The later poems, *Heliodora* and the rest, are further testimonies to this poet's quality, enriching her fame though scarcely advancing it. She has rarely done a lovelier thing than *Fragment Thirty-six,* her variations on a Sapphic theme. And we may reasonably hope that her work is not yet half done, for her firm and practiced art is no mere passing impulse of youthful talent.

H. D. has been called "the most imagistic of the Imagists." When some of her poems first appeared in the fourth number of *Poetry* (January, 1913), following Richard Aldington's beautiful *Charicos* in the second, it was evident that a new spirit was in the air, a spirit demanding for the art precision, economy of word and phrase, rhythm personal and not metronomic or derived, and direct presentation of the image, stripped of superfluous ornament. Her own stern instinct had been verified and strengthened by Ezra Pound's harsh discipline, and reticence had saved her from exposing immature work to the world. Thus there are no juvenilia in her record—she was a finished product when she began. (pp. 274-75)

Harriet Monroe, "H. D.," in Poetry, *Vol. XXVI, No. 5, August, 1925, pp. 268-75.*

STANLEY KUNITZ

The publication of *The Flowering of the Rod* brings to a close H. D.'s war trilogy, which has received less attention than it merits. "**War trilogy**" . . . requires some qualification. It is true that the poem, which will be considered here *in toto*, begins amid the ruins of London, in the flaming terror of the Blitz, but it is equally true that it ends in an ox-stall in Bethlehem. The war was the occasion, it is not the subject-matter of the poem. Neither is "trilogy" wholly satisfactory, since it implies more of temporal continuity and progressive narrative line than the three parts possess. The relation between the parts seems to me more that of a triptych than of a trilogy, each book being a compositional unit, though conceptually and emotionally enriched by association with its companion units; each composition, furthermore, embodying a dream or vision. This formal arrangement is particularly suited to H. D., whose art has unmistakable affinities with the pictorial.

Pursuing the triptych analogy, we find the second book, **"Tribute to the Angels"** . . . , falling naturally into place as the central composition; in the background "a half-burnt-out apple-tree blossoming," in the foreground the luminous figure of the Lady, who carries, under her drift of veils, a book. (pp. 36-7)

The left side-panel, titled **"The Walls Do Not Fall"** . . . , shows the ruins of bombed-out London. They have an Egyptian desolation, like the ruins of the Temple of Luxor. The ascendant Dream-figure is Amen, not as the local deity of Thebes, ram-headed god of life and reproduction, nor even in his greater manifestation as Amen-Ra, when he joined with the sun-god to become a supreme divinity incorporating the other gods into his members, but the Amen of Revelation . . . with the face and bearing of the Christos. . . . The background figure recording the scene is Thoth . . . , scribe of the gods, in whose ibis-head magic and art married and flourished.

The interior of an Arab merchant's booth is represented in the foreground of the right side-panel **"The Flowering of the Rod."** Half-turned towards the door stands a woman, frail and slender, wearing no bracelet or other ornament, with her scarf slipping from her head, revealing the light on her hair. . . . The noble merchant with the alabaster jar is Kaspar, youngest and wisest of the Three Wise Men, transfixed in the moment of recognition, of prophetic vision, before he will present her with the jar containing the [costly myrrh]. . . . In the background he is seen again, making his earlier gift, also a jar, to the other Mary of the manger.

Much has been omitted in this simplified presentation, but enough has been given at least to suggest the materials of the poem and its psychological extensions out of the modern world into pre-history, religion, legend, and myth. . . . No hint of staleness or weariness, however, blemishes the page. On the contrary, the poem radiates a kind of spiritual enthusiasm. . . . What H. D. is seeking for, what she has obviously found, is a faith: . . . faith that even to the bitter, flawed Mary is given the gift of grace, the Genius of the jar; faith in the survival of values, however the world shakes; faith in the blossoming, the resurrection, of the half-dead tree. (pp. 37-9)

Each of the three parts comprises a sequence of forty-three poems, and all the hundred and twenty-nine poems, except for the very first, are written in (basically) unrhymed couplets. The modulations and variety of effects that H. D. achieves within this limited pattern are a tribute to her technical resourcefulness and to her almost infallible ear. Her primary reliance, orally, is on the breath-unit; aurally, on assonance, with an occasional admixture . . . of slant or imperfect rhyme. . . . (p. 39)

Like Yeats, though with a different set of disciplines, founded on her Imagist beginnings, H. D. has learned how to contain the short line, to keep it from spilling over into the margins. For straight narrative or exposition she usually employs a longer, more casual line that approaches prose without becoming, in context, fuzzy or spineless. . . .

The lyric passages have, at once, purity and tension, delicacy and strength, seeming to rejoice in the uncorrupted innocence of the worshiping eye. . . . (p. 40)

One of H. D.'s innovations is a form of word-play that might be called associational semantics. . . . To a large extent her poem develops spontaneously out of her quest for the ultimate distillations of meaning sealed in the jars of language. . . .

She takes, for example, the Hebrew word "marah," meaning "bitter," fuses it with "a word bitterer still, *mar*," and emerges triumphantly with "mer, mere, mère, mater, Maia, Mary, / Star of the Sea, Mother." . . . [Such] passages impress me as being too self-conscious, too "literary," in the bad sense, though I recognize their catalytic function.

Although the significant fusion, the mutation into a new kind of experience, a new large meaning, does not take place in the body of the poem, it would be wrong to say that this ingenious, admirably sustained, and moving work fails because it does not achieve monumentality. H. D.'s is not a monumental art. Her poem remains as precise as it is ambitious. (pp. 41-2)

Stanley Kunitz, "A Tale of a Jar," in Poetry, Vol. LXX, No. 1, April, 1947, pp. 36-42.

DAVID DAICHES

["**By Avon River**"] has a charm and delicacy not often found among the tougher ironies of our modern poets and critics. It is in two parts: the first a series of lyrics evoked by the contemplation of Shakespeare's "Tempest" and of certain aspects of his world and art and their sources in earlier currents of thought. These poems have a clear, yet slightly muted, tone, pleasing though occasionally slightly monotonous to the ear; they show a restrained, classical skill.

The second part, which occupies the bulk of the book, is a prose essay on Elizabethan poets, in which quotation of their lyrics falls naturally. The essay works up to a discussion of Shakespeare himself. H. D. thinks of him sitting on that last convivial evening with Drayton and Ben Jonson . . . and follows his imagined reminiscences on this occasion to present aspects of his life and thought.

It is a strange and interesting essay. H. D. chats and speculates in an almost dreamlike wandering among men and ideas of the period, with a fine delicacy of phrase and a slightly distracted air. There lies scattered in these impressions of years of wandering among earlier English poets a new and subtle theory of the relation between the themes and images of the great Elizabethan writers on the one hand and the medieval world of religion and courtly love on the other. The essay is a fascinating text for meditation and discussion.

David Daiches, "Shakespeare's World," in New York Herald Tribune Weekly Book Review, September 11, 1949, p. 3.

HORACE GREGORY

The following notes on the poems of H. D. are written to pay tribute to an American poet whose writings have yet to receive full measure of critical attention in the United States. . . .

Today, and in view of her later poems, it seems somewhat strange that most people still associate her writings only with the cause of "free verse" and "imagism," "the School of Images," that Ezra Pound in 1912 so cheerfully announced held the future "in their keeping." In 1956 H. D. remarked, "One writes the kind of poetry one likes. Other people put labels on it. Imagism was something that was important for poets learning their craft early in this century. But after learning his craft, the poet will find his true direction." Although she learned much from Pound, who included her among *Les Imagistes*, H. D.'s lyric gift, even in her early poems, soon found its own voice, its own themes and measures—all of which were clearly unlike those of her contemporaries. This individual voice is evident throughout her recently published *Selected Poems.*

The kind of poetry the early H. D. liked and wrote was of a classic purity of diction and imagery. No poet since Walter Savage Landor in his "Ianthe" and "Rose Aylmer" moved more surely in the direction of classic lyricism than did H. D. This is not to say that H. D. emulated or imitated Landor, but her economies of statement, her precise choice of rhythms and colors, her sense of the dramatic incident revealed in lyric forms brought her closer to the best of Landor than any American poet of her times.

H. D.'s choice of Greek themes and incidents had been inspired by epigrams from the Greek Anthology, lines of Meleager on Heliodora, the epigram of Plato which recited a prayer offered up to Aphrodite. Through these inspirations and others of their kind H. D. wrote her own lyrics on Lais, on Heliodora, on Helen of Troy, on Penelope at Ithaca. These were re-creations in modern verse of enduring passions and situations—"the showing-forth" of the timeless moment in situations that are as true today as they were three thousand years ago. (p. 82)

[The great] majority of H. D.'s critics have been so preoccupied by the presence of her imagery that several of her better known poems seem to have been unheard. The way toward a renewed understanding of her poems is not to strain the eyes, but to hear the poems clearly.

So much then for the early sources of H. D.'s inspiration and her particular revival of pure melody in English verse. What of the content of her poems? (pp. 82-3)

During the years of World War II which H. D. spent in London, she wrote a trilogy of poems, *The Walls Do Not Fall, Tribute to the Angels, The Flowering of the Rod,* all in celebration of the spirit in time of war. . . .

It should be remembered that the trilogy of H. D.'s devotional poems had been written at least ten years before the present decade of poets has turned to a revaluation of religious verse. H. D. in her perceptions of timelessness, and in her search for the "real," has always seemed to be writing in advance of her times. In that respect the present generation might well regard her as "a poets' poet."

To be "a poets' poet" has few tangible rewards, for this means that the poet who holds that title must often wait upon the future for true recognition. Yet the poems of H. D. have acquired a life, a being of their own; at this date one need not argue that they should be read. Of contemporary poets H. D. is among the few whose writings are likely to endure. (p. 83)

Horace Gregory, "A Poet's Poet," in Commonweal, Vol. LXVIII, No. 3, April 18, 1958, pp. 82-3.

HARRY T. MOORE

["Bid Me to Live"] evokes the England of the Imagists and of World War I, those times when, as she says, "Jocasta danced with Philoctetes." H. D.'s central character, Julia Ashton, is a poet whose marriage to another poet is disintegrating. Her husband Rafe, home on leave from the Western Front, becomes involved with a girl who lives in a room above the Ashtons' Bloomsbury flat: "I love you, I desire *l'autre,*" Rafe tells Julia, who drifts into a love affair with a musician. But all the while she is magnetized by a writer named Frederick (Rico),

who cannot easily be magnetized away from his "great Prussian wife."

Rico is very plainly D. H. Lawrence (Lorenzo), and his physical as well as his spiritual-artistic resemblance to Van Gogh is one of the leitmotifs of this novel, which among other accomplishments adds some interesting bits to the Lawrence legend. The curious will find much else here that can be tagged, for the people, episodes and atmospheres in the story share a cousinship with many of those in novels by Lawrence ("Aaron's Rod," "Kangaroo") and Richard Aldington ("Death of a Hero"), in the London poems of Ezra Pound, in the autobiographies of Aldington, John Cournos, Cecil Gray and others, and in the books about Amy Lowell by S. Foster Damon and Horace Gregory. The fun the reader has in discovering who's who in the masquerade is, of course, of secondary importance, though in the case of others besides Lawrence the material provides some bizarre if minor contributions to literary history.

The London scenes in the story are balanced by West Country interludes, and the main pattern of the action is symbolically repeated in charades the characters perform and in quoted samples from Julia's work in progress, "Orpheus." In method and tone, particularly in its use of interior monologue, H. D.'s book often seems to be a period piece, a product of yesterday's avant-garde. Poetic without being a prose poem, it looks fairly thin beside the chunkier novels that are so common today, but its cool nuances have a vitality that carries it along. And **"Bid Me to Live"** has a consistent clarity of vision as it probes the delicate tissues of human relationships while revealing so much of the complex structures of a woman's consciousness.

Harry T. Moore, "The Faces Are Familiar," in The New York Times Book Review, May 1, 1960, p. 4.

KATHRYN GIBBS GIBBONS

Perhaps this is a time not so much for an evaluation of H. D.'s art as it is an appropriate time to acquaint ourselves with just what H. D.'s art is. (p. 152)

The most common adverse criticism of H. D.'s early poetry was that it made no social protest and that it was not journalism. . . . Keeping the elements of style for which she was praised early, H. D. has developed a poetic structure that is clearly unique and yet one could say that it is in the tradition of the best meditative lyricists (Herbert, Donne, Dickinson), and of the best elegists (Milton, Wordsworth, Whitman). For H. D. writes directly to the hugest problem of our time, that of life against destruction. Her answer may not be new in all its facets, but the elaboration is poignant. (pp. 154-55)

[A close examination of] *The Walls Do Not Fall* reveals the simultaneous complexity and simplicity of the answer to the problem which exists between man's intellectual seeking for spiritual reality and the historical fact of the destruction of civilizations. Internal evidence proves that the impact of destruction from a particular war does not occasion the whole poem. For other civilizations, particularly the Egyptian, are cited, and other gods than Christian are invoked. This poem's answer is that a spiritual regeneration has arisen from the destruction of previous cultures and can survive any possible destruction of our own. A spiritual reality has survived for man through both the written word, that tells of past cultures, and through the recurrent manifestation of the Logos, the Word born as man. Through enchantment, the poem states, rather than through sentiment, that spiritual reality may be ours. In the poem there is an affirmation of faith that through enchantment with the idea of regeneration, which is in the mystery of the Logos, a man may find the spiritual reality he seeks and turn from destruction.

"Enchantment" is the word that is the philosopher's stone to our understanding of the poem. Enchantment is both the attitude of the poet in the poem and the resulting effect of the poem upon the reader, i.e., the tone. "Magic" is a synonym for enchantment which is reminiscent of the Persian Magi, those mighty prophets and interpreters of dreams of whom three were said to have found their way to Bethlehem; whereby the poet declares that she has found a new master over love. . . . There is enchantment, in the sense of delight to a high degree, in the poet's attitude toward the words themselves. This is particularly true because of the etymological feeling H. D. has for words. . . . In this poem the historical sensitivity toward words, together with the selection of kinds of words—words which are as distant in space from each other as a star is from sea coral, as distant in time as is Osiris from a Moravian in Pennsylvania—combine the far away and long ago, the minute and the immense with a perilous immediacy, and the spell is cast. "Enchantment" is from the Old French verb *enchanter* that means to sing against. The poem itself is a long lyric, singing against destruction—an incantation in which the words are so accurately chosen that the spell is upon us. . . . Words in H. D.'s poetry have an emotional effect as well as an intellectual content. (pp. 155-57)

There is also in *The Walls Do Not Fall* a respect for passion and a conquering of passion by reason's limits—or by the poet's classic sensitivity. (p. 157)

H. D.'s images are not all visual or even kinesthetic. Sound is intricate in her poetry, sound is repeated, and, as we can hear, the repetition of sound adds to the effect of enchantment. As Horace Gregory suggests [see excerpt above], "The way toward a renewed understanding of her poems is not to strain the eyes, but to hear the poems clearly." Any selection from H. D.'s poetry would bear examination for this effect; that is what one would expect of a poet who in the words of her own epitaph was following "intricate song's lost measure." (p. 158)

H. D. wrote, after the death of Freud, a book that is a free verse poem in the best elegiac tradition, titled *Tribute to Freud*. . . . To indicate something of the elegiac structure of the book, I refer you to the 4th section of it in which H. D. explains that she wanted to send gardenias to "the Professor" but could not find them. By her request, a friend sent orchids to him instead. . . . The flower motif, the theme of the death of the young Dutch flier, the excursion into the dimension of death or immortality, the dreams and the visions, the ruined cities and the broken idols, the affirmation—these are all indicative of the elegiac structure of the book. The poetic prose form was not new in *Tribute to Freud,* although it startled some uninitiated readers of H. D. She had been developing it at least since her early novel *Palimpsest* in 1926.

Among other books she has written there is *By Avon River* in which lyric prose and elegiac structure are again employed. After the lyric prose section that enlarges a myth about Shakespeare, H. D. has written a metrical poem, *Good Frend (sic).* In this poem she imagines herself the Claribel of *The Tempest.* . . . (pp. 159-60)

H. D.'s last book, *Helen in Egypt,* is a long psychological meditative lyric which represents the height of her art. It is

actually a series of lyrics with transitional and introductory prose passages, the whole containing a clear narrative that carries the enchanted reader quickly from the first to the final line. It is the culmination of long years of poetic experimentation and refinement. As we would have expected, the writing does not lack depth or intricacy in its examination of the relation of the personal problem of guilt to the social problem of war. . . .

We who believe in the enchantment that language contains may find in H. D.'s songs of affirmation something that is significant, not only for our small and important literary circles, but for our young scholars we may find something more in poetry of this day than a protest, an irritation, or a lost world. (p. 160)

Kathryn Gibbs Gibbons, "The Art of H. D.," in The Mississippi Quarterly, *Vol. 15, No. 4, Fall, 1962, pp. 152-60.*

HUGH KENNER

The poems in ["**Hermetic Definition**"] date from circa 1960, when [H. D.] was 74. She had been inserted into literary history at 26, when Ezra Pound invented "Imagism" to supply a context for five poems of hers. . . .

Unhappily the invented movement that was meant to float her reputation encapsulated it, and though she lived many more decades and extended her self-definition through many volumes, she has remained totally identified with the very little she had done when she was first heard of. . . .

The first section of "**Hermetic Definition**" addresses a comer who is partly angel, partly several remembered men, partly the head of the Paris Bureau of Newsweek, who catalyzed the poem by stopping by for an interview. . . . His eyes compelled her, and he took her mind to Paris, where the statues on Notre Dame make an anthology of secret gods. . . .

Anyone's eyes, the cadence of any voice, might bring a clue to the invisible sacred host whose thronging presences commanded her devotion and whose integration into the Eternal Lover seemed the goal of her sleepless vigils. So the presented actual . . . dissolved into lore, into allusions, riddles. Drifting apart, it encountered her sharp exact arrays of hermetic terminology, and was fixed on an elusive plane where one no longer says what a poem is "about." These poems are "about" her phantasmagoric self, in part her sense of having become a myth prematurely. . . . Unlike most ghosts, she had the guts to keep coming back; and her hour may be here at last. In psychedelic times, there are new tastes abroad for her work to gratify.

Hugh Kenner, "Two Letters Were More than Two Names," in The New York Times Book Review, *December 10, 1972, p. 55.*

SUSAN STANFORD FRIEDMAN

[The essay from which this excerpt is taken originally appeared in College English, *March 1975.]*

Why is [H. D.'s] poetry not read? H. D. is part of the same literary tradition that produced the mature work of the "established" artists—T. S. Eliot, Ezra Pound, William Carlos Williams, D. H. Lawrence. . . . Like these artists, H. D. began writing in the aestheticism and fascination for pure form characteristic of the imagists; and like them, she turned to epic form and to myth, religious tradition, and the dream as a way of giving meaning to the cataclysms and fragmentation of the twentieth century. Her epic poetry should be compared to the *Cantos, Paterson,* the *Four Quartets,* and *The Bridge,* for like these poems, her work is the kind of "cosmic poetry" the imagists swore they would never write.

The pattern of her poetic development not only paralleled that of more famous artists, but it was also permeated by major intellectual currents of the century. . . . Her growth into a poet exploring the psyche or soul of humanity and reaching out to confront the questions of history, tradition, and myth places her squarely in the mainstream of "established" modern literature. But still, outside of a few poets like Denise Levertov, who wrote "An Appreciation" of H. D., Robert Duncan, and the aficionados who circulate a pirated edition of *Hermetic Definition,* few people read her poetry. Once again, why?

Is her poetry just plain "bad," however serious the philosophic and human issues she embodies in image and epic narration? . . . From my single, necessarily subjective perspective, there is no doubt that her poetry is magnificent. But I have no intention here of raising the thorny questions of what makes literature "great." . . . I do insist, however, that H. D. was a serious prolific poet exploring the same questions as her famous counterparts and thus inviting comparison with them. . . . And so I am still asking why H. D.'s work is buried under a scattered knowledge of **"Oread"** or **"Heat."**

The answer is simple enough, I think. It lies biographically and factually right in front of our critical noses—too close perhaps to be seen easily. It lies in what makes H. D. and her work different from a long string of studied poets like Eliot, Pound, Crane, Williams, and Yeats. And it lies in the response of her critics. She was a woman, she wrote about women, and all the ever-questioning, artistic, intellectual heroes of her epic poetry and novels were women. In the quest poetry and fiction of the established literary tradition (particularly the poetic tradition), women as active, thinking, individual human beings rarely exist. . . . They are [instead] the static, symbolic objects of quest, not the questors; they are "feminine principles," both threatening and life-giving, and not particularized human beings. . . . As a woman writing about women, H. D. explored the untold half of the human story, and by that act she set herself outside of the established tradition. (pp. 93-5)

What she has to say about women and men in her poetry should be as much a part of any class as what Pound or Eliot have to say about men and women. If the elite of acceptable literature will have explored the experience of only half the human race (at best), with this incompleteness, this subjectivity, it will have lost a profound understanding of its own humanity. (p. 109)

> *Susan Stanford Friedman, "Who Buried H. D.? A Poet, Her Critics, and Her Place in 'The Literary Tradition'," in* Feminist Criticism: Essays on Theory, Poetry and Prose, *edited by Cheryl L. Brown and Karen Olson, The Scarecrow Press, Inc., 1978, pp. 92-110.*

EMILY STIPES WATTS

Among Imagist poems, the verse of H. D. stands apart. Although she has been called "the perfect Imagist," she was never really an Imagist, as Pound defined that term anyway. Although she is credited with being one of the formulators of the three Imagist principles, she was hardly any more a "follower" of them than Guiney, Cather, or Reese. (p. 152)

If we examine the three original principles of Imagism as stated by F. S. Flint in the March 1913 issue of *Poetry,* we find that H. D.'s verse is related to, undoubtedly should stand as the original inspiration of, Imagism, but is in fact something else besides. The first principle is "1. Direct treatment of the 'thing,' whether subjective or objective." In a general sense, this principle in fact reflects much of women's verse in the nineteenth century. If taken literally, for example, it describes much of Dickinson's verse. Flint means, however, "direct" in the sense of being without the poet's presence or personal interjection, an impersonal poetry, such as Pound achieved in "In a Station of the Metro" or William Carlos Williams in "Poem" or "The Locust Tree in Flower." However, even in one of the first "Imagist" poems ever published, H. D.'s **"Orchard"** (originally titled **"Priapus"**) in the January 1913 issue of *Poetry,* H. D. did not even try to achieve such an "impersonal" or "scientific" distance. . . . (pp. 152-53)

"2. To use absolutely no word that [does] not contribute to the presentation." This is a rule of good poetry in general and can be applied to anyone from Shakespeare to Alexander Pope. Flint meant, however, no "ornaments" or "decorations," only the "necessary" words. Pound could write this kind of poetry, as could Williams. H. D., however, could not: her parallel syntactical constructions and her careful alliterations in *Sea Garden* and *Hymen* are a different kind of word economy from that which Pound intended and which he himself practiced at this time.

"3. As regarding rhythm: to compose in sequence of the musical phrase, not in sequence of a metronome." Regardless of what Flint (and Pound) meant—and the meaning is debatable—H. D.'s prosody is more "traditional" than this principle might suggest. H. D.'s meters are based roughly on Greek meters . . . but, more specifically in the very early poems, her "free verse" is simply consecutive lines of different meters. . . . (p. 153)

However, if we assume that such critics as William Pratt and Hugh Kenner are even partially correct, then an American woman poet, H. D., was the inspiration for and an active collaborator in the formation of a major movement in American poetry [Imagism], which affected male poets. On the other hand, it is also apparent that H. D.'s verse is a culmination of certain aspects of previous American women's verse. Thus, for example, her early verse especially is permeated with female figures from classical mythology. What was a new and exciting source of poetic images for Pound, Eliot, Yeats, and other men in the early twentieth century was, in fact, for H. D., a natural and traditional source of images. Moreover, like earlier American women poets, H. D. reinterpreted the classical figures in her own way. Unlike the male poets, she did not use myth as an expression of traditional (or even archetypal) values or as a vehicle for cosmic transcendence. (pp. 153-54)

One major difference, however, between H. D.'s treatment of mythological characters and their use by earlier American women poets is the complex, layered texture of H. D.'s poetry. Indeed, the major problem for the modern reader of H. D.'s verse is that we are not familiar with classical mythology and its vocabulary. In her early verse, I think that H. D. expected her reader to respond much as the ancient Athenians responded to the tragedies of Aeschylus. For the Greek tragedians and their audience, the "story" was not important (everyone knew the story of Orestes and Electra), but the method of presentation was the significant creative factor. Thus, when one reads H. D.'s *Hymen,* the presentation and nuances are striking, but only to one who has a firm understanding of the myths. It is possible that H. D. misjudged her audience; after all, women poets in America had been using mythological figures as personal images since 1800. On the other hand, H. D., like Pound and Eliot, may have intended to write arrogantly esoteric verse.

Unlike her fellow American women poets from 1800 to her own day, H. D. did not deal exclusively with the major female mythological characters (some are minor), nor was she careful to provide the backgrounds of their stories, as preceding women poets had. On the basis of her late poetry, it appears that H. D. originally made the mistake of assuming that many of her readers understood the classical myths as fully as she did. In her *War Trilogy* (1944-1946), she shifted to the better-known Christian myth of the Virgin Mary; in her final major work, *Helen in Egypt* (1961), she meticulously explained the entire myth, with all its various implications.

With her return to the classical myths in *Helen in Egypt,* H. D. continued a symbolic exploration evident throughout much of her career. Even in her earliest poetry, she had symbolically juxtaposed the values of Greece (male, rational principles) and Egypt (female, passionate principles). . . .

One of the few long poems written by an American woman in the twentieth century, *Helen in Egypt* is a mixture of poetry and prose. . . . H. D.'s story is based in obscure classical mythology. . . . (p. 155)

The poem is an attempt by H. D. to explore abstract and complex concepts; her intent is didactic. H. D., as narrator, explains what is happening or what the characters are thinking in prose, in declarative sentences, and then poetically describes the same event or thought, with a heavy reliance upon image patterns. An example of the modern poetic sequence, *Helen in Egypt* is the climax of H. D.'s career, both intellectually and poetically.

Not only did H. D. anticipate Modern (male and female) poetry in the various ways we have already discussed, her early attempts to incorporate techniques from the plastic arts into her verse seem also to have been innovative and seminal. In certain early poems, H. D. was working as close as she could to a mingling of the art forms. She seems to have tried to "see," to represent the visual poetic image with reference to or by means of techniques of paintings she had viewed in Europe. Such a means of expanding the visual presentation of either poetry or prose was to become more and more common in the twentieth century, both for expatriate Americans and for those who stayed in the United States.

H. D.'s early verse seems to be the first modern American verse to display such an interdisciplinary tendency. (pp. 156-57)

Thus, in several ways, H. D.'s verse represents the very earliest expression of those tendencies by which we identify poetry as Modern. Nevertheless, with her interest in mythological women, her "international" and broad humanistic tendencies, her type of prosodic experimentation, her sense of the visual image, and her refusal to be "cosmic"—her verse represents a development from many poems written by American women throughout the nineteenth century, with, as I have shown, a basis especially in the late nineteenth and early twentieth centuries. That H. D.'s verse does not completely correspond to Pound's three dicta [for Imagism] is evidence of her independence and originality—a poetic individualism which continued until her death. (p. 158)

Emily Stipes Watts, "1900-1945: 'A Rose Is a Rose with Thorns'," in her The Poetry of American Women *from 1632 to 1945, University of Texas Press, 1977, pp. 149-76.**

L. M. FREIBERT

While one might hesitate to classify Hilda Doolittle with the great poets, even though she is the best of the Imagists, one could hardly deny the radical transformation and new direction she has given to the genre by creating the neo-epic *Helen in Egypt* (1961), which explores the evolution of woman as person and as artist. The poem adheres to the epic conventions in that it is basically a quest which carries its protagonist into war, through the gates of ecstasy, into an underworld experience which includes a meeting with parent figures, and eventually into a new life. The poem departs from the genre pattern in two ways, as do its twentieth-century counterparts *The Waste Land, The Bridge, Paterson,* the *Cantos,* and the *Maximus Poems:* first, its quest is not public but is a private search for self . . . ; second, its questor is not a political, military, or folk hero but is rather an artist and a prophet, exhibiting close ties with the author of the work. In addition to these deviations, *Helen in Egypt* strays radically from the tradition in that its protagonist is a woman and that her search is for an understanding of her changing status.

The evolution which H. D. traces, and that which will be explicated in this paper, is fourfold. Caught in the fixed mobility of timeless-time, like the symbols of the Zodiac and the mythological characters with which she identifies herself, Helen changes (1) from ideal to real, (2) from artifact to artist, (3) from vision to voice, and (4) from semblance to selfhood, all the while examining and articulating her own psychic and emotive actions. As a result, the poem becomes the epic of woman evolving from the traditional passive image into the contemporary active person.

Because of the ontological instability of the persona and the rapid temporal and spatial shifts in the subject matter, some critics of *Helen in Egypt* have found the work structurally and philosophically shaky. . . . [What these critics] fail to perceive is that the instability of the persona and the elliptical structure of the work are essential evidence of the precarious condition which the female, particularly the female artist, has experienced within the context of Western society, a condition to which H. D. was especially sensitive.

In creating her protagonist, H. D. brings together two images of Helen: one, that of the passive Helen of Troy, who, like her mother Leda, was subject to the whims of the gods; the other, the active, real Helen who appears in the *Pallinode* of the Greek poet Stesichorus. Stesichorus claims that Helen never reached Troy but was spirited by the gods to Egypt, where she remained throughout the war. He holds, therefore, that only a phantom accompanied Paris to Troy and that it was for this illusion that the Greeks and Trojans died.

Using Stesichorus' *Pallinode* as a base, H. D. fashions her Helen according to the pattern of the twentieth-century woman. This Helen perceives herself as the equal of her male counterpart, but constantly reminded of her past, she recognizes the difficulty of maintaining her newly achieved status vis-à-vis the persisting tradition. . . . H. D. brings the new Helen into a relationship with Achilles, the classical hero, who has passed through war and death because of the phantom Helen but who has now become "the new Mortal." The confrontation between the two is mirrored through Helen's consciousness, the primary focus being on her search to understand herself and her new relationship to the representative man.

In addition to creating a new consciousness for her persona, H. D. also devises a contemporary structure for her work. She chooses the objectivist style, espoused by so many former Imagists, combining prose and verse in an alternating pattern. She organizes the poem into three parts: **"Pallinode,"** **"Leuké,"** and **"Eidolon,"** each of which is divided into books, subdivided into short passages. The basic narrative is carried in the prose headnotes which open each segment. (pp. 165-67)

In the **"Pallinode"** section Helen had recognized her reality and received the approbation of Thetis; in **"Leuké"** she assumed the role of creator and prophet. In **"Eidolon,"** integrating all these characteristics, she reaches selfhood. (p. 173)

What H. D. has done . . . in *Helen in Egypt* is to employ a variation of the mythical method, to stop time so that the real Helen can, in that finite moment, come to grips with the passive victim-image of the past, take stock of her potential, and stabilize and strengthen her identity as the creator of her own future. The kaleidoscoping of time and space and the fusion of characters and images, instead of weakening the poem, serve rather to illustrate H. D.'s perception of the precarious nature of the history of woman's evolution in Western culture and bring the texture of the neo-epic into clear focus. (p. 175)

> *L. M. Freibert, "From Semblance to Selfhood: The Evolution of Woman in H. D.'s Neo-Epic 'Helen in Egypt',"* in Arizona Quarterly, *Vol. 36, No. 2, Summer, 1980, pp. 165-75.*

BERNARD DUFFEY

H. D.'s "memoir" of Ezra Pound [*End to Torment*] is somewhat mistitled since written late in her life, it is more an exploration of her feelings about Pound, and about others, than a detailed recollection of the poet. Their relationship had originated in a youthful and ardently romanticized love affair during Pound's graduate year at the University of Pennsylvania, albeit one strictly supervised by H. D.'s father. By the time H. D. betook herself to London in 1911 the romance was over, and she was quickly drawn to Richard Aldington and to others in the London international set.

Students of H. D. should find more of interest in the work than students of Pound. The latter, perhaps, will be most gratified by . . . the text of "Hilda's Book," a small volume of poems Pound wrote for H. D. during their romance, which now appears for the first time in print.

> *Bernard Duffey, in a review of "End to Torment: A Memoir of Ezra Pound,"* in American Literature, *Vol. 53, No. 2, May, 1981, p. 324.*

JUDY COOKE

[*Hedylus*] is a poet's novel, rich in metaphor and meaning.

Set in the classical world, the story explores the predicament of Hedylus, the young son of the beautiful Hedyle and, indeed, her mirror image; he is dazzled by her presence, yet longs to find his own identity. She stands for the intellect and Athens; he is for the imagination, Alexandria, India. The psychological tension between the pair can be resolved only by their separation, deathly though this will be to Hedyle. Inevitably, events

are precipitated by a young girl (in some ways, the theme parallels *Sons and Lovers*) but the mother's antagonism seems certain to blight the match. Enter a stranger, Demion—a god, a lost father, perhaps simply a free man—who gives Hedylus the courage to take his independence.

A stylish piece of prose, the writing achieves that clarity and precision so prized by H. D. and her fellow Imagists, Pound and Aldington. Its weak point is dialogue. Its strength is a sure sense of colour and form.

> *Judy Cooke, "The Voyage In,"* in New Statesman, *Vol. 101, No. 2620, June 5, 1981, p. 23.**

SUSAN STANFORD FRIEDMAN

Hilda Doolittle's emergence on the pages of *Poetry* magazine in 1913 as "H. D., Imagiste" heralded the beginnings of a writer whose canon spans half a century and the genres of poetry, fiction, memoir, essay, drama, and translation. This achievement was firmly rooted in H. D.'s central participation in the imagist movement, a short-lived moment in literary history, but one whose experiments changed the course of modern poetry with its concept of the "image" and its advocacy of vers libre. (p. 1)

Sea Garden, published in 1916, was the poet's culmination of her early apprenticeship in London, and it won for her the reputation of being the best of the imagist poets. Her poems avoided the vague moralizing and sentimental mythologizing that the imagists deplored in much of the "cosmic" poetry of the late nineteenth century. They were crisp, precise, and absolutely without excess. The imagist emphasis on hard, classical lines, however, did not mean that the poems were without emotion. Most imagist poems rely heavily on precisely delineated objects from nature to embody subjective experience. But as poems like **"Heat"** and **"Oread"** demonstrate vividly, H. D.'s imagist poetry was not a form of nature poetry adapted to the modern world. The essence of the imagist task was to locate the "image" that incarnated an "intellectual and emotional complex in an instant of time"—or, to use T. S. Eliot's later term, the "objective correlative" of subjective experience. In *Sea Garden,* H. D. fulfilled that task by rendering intense passions and perceptions in images that originated in her visits to Cornwall and her American childhood. . . . The mythological personae that appear in many of her poems did not represent an escapist attempt to return to ancient Greece, but rather served as personal metaphors or masks that allowed her to distance intense emotion sufficiently for artistic expression.

H. D.'s ability to fulfill the aesthetic demands of imagist doctrine has been well recognized. Less frequently understood, her contribution to the major shift in modern poetry was organizational as well as aesthetic. She, along with Amy Lowell, helped to insure the continuation of the imagist community after Pound's efforts to retain sole editorial power split the original group in 1915. As editor of *The Egoist* from 1915-1917, H. D. encouraged poets to write and helped them find an audience during the difficult war years. But H. D.'s efforts to keep alive the poetic visions of her soldier-husband, Richard Aldington, and the other members of their artistic community were doomed by the violence and meaninglessness of the First World War. (pp. 2-3)

Bid Me to Live (A Madrigal), her roman à clef, tells the story of the intersecting personal and cultural catastrophes that ended her "specialized" success. Aldington's affair with Dorothy Yorke and the dissolution of her marriage, the deaths of her brother and father, the loss of D. H. Lawrence's friendship, and her own grave illness during the last stage of her pregnancy merged with the general destruction of war to break apart the relatively secure world of imagist compatriots. The war did more than strain personal relationships, however. It produced the historical conditions that made the intensely aesthetic world of imagism inadequate and gave enormous impetus to the growth of modernism. The hysteria of mindless patriotism and the omnipresence of death in a trench war for inches and feet of blasted territory created the necessity for a different kind of art, one that could record the fragmentation of culture and begin the quest for new meanings. (p. 3)

The dissolution of symbolic systems unveiled as grand illusions impelled a literature centered on quest, art whose forms and themes were consistent with the search for new patterns of meaning. The bitter events of history forced H. D. and her writing companions to emerge from the limited perfection of imagism. With its emphasis on the poem as the instantaneous visual incarnation of an "emotional and intellectual complex," imagism could not explain the violence of war and the fragmentation of belief systems. . . . Imagism had begun as a philosophy of art, but it evolved into a craft that could be incorporated into the larger explorations of modernist literature. H. D.'s reflections in an interview with the *New Haven Register* in 1956 are a perceptive commentary on the significance of imagism in the development of modern poetry. She emphasized to the reporter that "the term [imagist] cannot be applied to describe her work since World War I." . . . H. D. described "her early work as 'a little sapling,' which in the intervening years, 'has grown down into the depths and upwards in many directions.' (pp. 3-4)

In the postwar years, artists went beyond the earlier imagist breakthrough and turned increasingly to the archetypes of quest in mythological and literary traditions for models of search. . . . H. D.'s development from imagist to epic art places her squarely in the center of this modernist mainstream. Her work shares with [such writers as Ezra Pound, T. S. Eliot, William Carlos Williams, James Joyce, W. B. Yeats, and Hart Crane] the fundamental spirit of quest given shape by myth and mythic consciousness, by religious vision or experience, and by a new synthesis of fragmented traditions.

H. D. did not, however, find the direction that led to her mature art with the immediacy of compatriots like Pound and Williams. While *The Cantos* and *Paterson* began to take shape in the twenties, H. D.'s route to a modernist perspective and aesthetic was more indirect and included considerable experimentations with a variety of genres and even art forms as she attempted to find her "true direction." (pp. 4-5)

H. D.'s artistic efforts during the twenties were extensive although the results were uneven and often left in draft form. . . . H. D. experimented with her own technique of interior monologue in her two published novels, *Palimpsest* (1926) and *Hedylus* (1928) and a number of shorter prose works like "Moose Island" and "Narthex." All of them prose masks for her own life, primarily her marriage to Aldington, these autobiographical fictions disturbed many of the readers who had admired "H. D., Imagiste." Her "specialized" success as an imagist created narrow expectations for her new work that inhibited her desire to expand into new forms and subjects. . . . In actuality, her desire to develop a new "H. D." involved fiction to a greater extent than her critics imagined. She left in manu-

script form three thinly disguised autobiographical novels. . . . (p. 6)

Interest in fiction did not lead H. D. to abandon poetry, however. In *Hymen* (1922) and *Heliodora* (1924) she expanded the imagist gems of *Sea Garden* into more diffuse, exploratory correlatives for emotion. Her *Collected Poems* (1924) presented an overview of the poetic achievement begun in 1913, and, at the end of the decade, she brought out *Red Roses for Bronze* (1931). Her work on translations from Greek lyrics and verse drama in *Hippolytus Temporizes* (1927) as a source of influence on her own poetry paralleled the pattern of Pound's work. By the end of the twenties, H. D. did not appear to be in search of her "true direction." She had worked enormously hard at a variety of manuscripts. Some two decades of writing and publication had established H. D. in the public domain of literature. But this achievement reached an aesthetic dead end in the thirties. With the rise of fascism and the imminence of a second catastrophic war, H. D. wrote far less regularly and published little in any genre. She did translate and publish Euripides' *Ion* with her own commentary (1937), work that Pearson said was very important to her later development. She did write a few short stories and a group of nine loosely connected poems, apparently intended for a small volume called *The Dead Priestess Speaks*. But none of the short stories were published, and only parts of a few poems appeared in little magazines such as *Life and Letters Today*. The unfinished volume, with its multiple drafts and various tables of contents, testifies that H. D. seemed to have lost that certain sense of direction, that sure inner knowledge of "WHO H. D. is" or should be. (pp. 6-7)

The violence of war jolted H. D. out of a decade of relative latency. . . . The Second World War functioned for her much as the First World War had for writers like Pound. Her sense of destiny as poet-prophet in the modernist apocalypse was certain and took on various forms of quest in *The Gift, Tribute to Freud,* and most importantly in her epic, *Trilogy,* composed of three volumes published as she wrote them: *The Walls Do Not Fall* (1944), *Tribute to the Angels* (1945), and *The Flowering of the Rod* (1946). In the *Trilogy,* which can serve as both primer and profound expression of the modernist spirit, H. D. sought to discover or create through the "Word" some ordering pattern that could redeem the surrounding ruin. . . . The *Trilogy* is a record of quest, a search deep within the unconscious and throughout many mythological traditions for the knowledge of unity beneath division and destruction. In short, H. D. began to write the kind of "cosmic poetry" the imagists had sworn to abandon. . . . Her "rebirth" as a revitalized poet during the war gave her a sense of her "true direction" that led her with steady inspiration to produce the mature work written in the late forties and fifties: *By Avon River* (1949); *Helen in Egypt* (1961); *Winter Love* (1973); *Sagesse* (1973); *End to Torment* (1979); and *Hermetic Definition* (1973).

Cosmic quest did not, however, lead H. D. to abandon imagist craft. Her later work bears a strong resemblance to imagist technique in the continued clarity and simplicity of her poetic line and the precise shape of her images. She continued to anchor the poem in the concrete world with images of flowers, rocks, insects, birds, and the seashore. The continuities between her imagist and epic work recall the way Pound's "superpositions" survived as small units within *The Cantos*. Similarly, the intensely personal emotion masked by mythological personae in poems like *Helen in Egypt* and *Winter Love* was present in her imagist lyric. Conversely, the seeds of later growth existed in the nearly animistic apprehension of nature in her imagist poetry. . . . But her growth ''into the depths and upwards'' fundamentally transformed the function of both myth and subjective experience in her poetry. In the *Trilogy* and in all the poetry she wrote thereafter, the personal and mythological are made to serve the needs of a religious and philosophical quest to explore basic humanistic questions about women and men, life and death, love and hate, destruction and renewal, war and peace, time and eternity.

With the benefit of hindsight made possible by the explosion of H. D.'s writing in the early forties, it is clear that the extensive experimentation of the twenties and the relative latency of the thirties were a sort of ''incubation'' period out of which the new H. D. emerged. Why did it take her twenty years to develop her own modernist voice when her writing companions of the First World War made the shift so much earlier? What, in fact, were the conditions of H. D.'s gradual metamorphosis? The clues to her development lie in her own images of self-exploration in *Tribute to Freud.*

Although this memoir revolves structurally around Freud, it reveals the framework of her search in the thirties for a regenerated and redirected artistic identity. As she had done even in her earliest imagist poetry, H. D. identified herself with a figure from mythological tradition to stimulate the unfolding reflections of memory and myth. For her persona, she chose Psyche, the mortal woman whose search for Eros has frequently been interpreted as the soul's quest for divine immortality. The name ''Psyche'' comes for the Greek word for ''soul,'' often portrayed in Greek art as a butterfly that leaves the body at death. (pp. 7-9)

H. D. wove together these fragments of myth and imagery to create her own ''legend'' of metamorphosis, as she called it. . . . The First World War and its subsequent personal and cultural consequences had constituted a kind of death for H. D., a descent to the underworld from which she had to emerge in a process of spiritual rebirth that was decades in the making. Repeatedly, she used imagery based on the life cycle of the butterfly to describe the journey of her soul from death to life. . . . After a period of living death, the soul begins its emergence as butterfly. In her autobiographical novel *Her,* H. D. recalled such a period in her life. Hermione is her persona, and ''Her'' is her nickname as she images her emergence from breakdown in the correlative of the butterfly leaving the cocoon. . . . (p. 9)

In the *Trilogy,* H. D. announced the rebirth of Psyche, the butterfly who emerges from the cocoon of near-death. (p. 10)

Psyche's ''gestation'' was gradual, unlike the transformations that produced *The Cantos, Paterson,* and *The Waste Land* in the twenties. *Tribute to Freud* once again points to a possible explanation for this. A pervasive undercurrent in the book is the theme of her ''difference'': her recognition of, desire for, and pride in multiple forms of ''difference.'' What set H. D. apart most profoundly, however, was her status as a woman writing in a predominantly male literary tradition. . . . Even as a woman in the male circle of imagists and artists in London, H. D. was alone. Sappho's influence on imagists no doubt helped to validate H. D.'s leadership role in the development of the modern lyric. But as historical forces fostered a poetry of quest that borrowed from epic and heroic tradition, H. D. became even more of an anomaly. Few women poets have ventured into the masculine domain of quest literature. . . .

Archetypes of questors in both literary and mythological tradition are overwhelmingly male: figures like Perseus, Hercules, Jason, Theseus, Lancelot, Percival, and Beowulf overshadow the travels and trials of Demeter, Isis, and Psyche. Indeed, cultural definitions of the heroic presume masculinity while the complementary assumptions about the nature of the heroine frequently presuppose feminine passivity and helplessness. Patriarchal tradition held out little encouragement for H. D. to develop a woman-centered epic in which woman was the seeker and doer instead of the angelic or evil object of male quest. From this perspective, it is not so amazing that H. D.'s growth was more gradual than that of her fellow modernists. Rather, it is extraordinary that she ultimately managed to defy the dominant tradition entirely by creating woman heroes whose search for meaning bears so little resemblance to the stereotyped female figures in the quest poetry written by men. . . . H. D.'s woman-identified questors spun a different web of meanings, ones that resurrected the life-giving female symbols and values which J. J. Bachofen had identified with the goddesses of ancient matriarchies.

The roots of H. D.'s emergence from the cocoon of the thirties lay in two sources of inspiration that seem antithetical, but which she experienced as parallel forms of spiritual quest. Broadly defined, those inveterate foes science and religion took her ''down into the depths and upwards in many directions,'' to quote from her own definition of growth. Her experience with psychoanalysis, highlighted by her sessions with Freud in 1933 and 1934, led her down into the depths of unconscious memory and dream. As modern ''Door-Keeper'' of the human psyche, Freud appeared to her like the Egyptian god Thoth, the ''infinitely old symbol, weighing the soul, Psyche, in the Balance.'' . . . Psychoanalysis took H. D. inward in a way that systematized and expanded on her early fascination for intense, subjective experience. In the unconscious decoded with Freud's help, H. D. found the wellsprings of inspiration. At the same time, this journey inward taught her to relate the personal to the universal. (pp. 10-11)

Esoteric tradition, including the many shapes of the occult, contained the ''tribal myths'' that reproduced her personal dreams on a cultural level. Complementing the impact of psychoanalysis, syncretist religious traditions led her out of her moment in history, took her through many cultures and eras, and revealed universal patterns underlying the shape-shifting forms of all experience. . . . With Freud's help in decoding her dreams and visions, H. D. found the spiritual and philosophical underpinnings of a chaotic and violent world.

With the war as her catalyst, H. D. wove the science and religion of the psyche together to produce an art that was both deeply personal and broadly based in religious traditions that are the legacy of time. The impact of Freud and of esoteric religion was enormous, both personally and aesthetically. Both influences permeate her mature work and form the context in which it can be most fully comprehended.

To research the parallels in H. D.'s work with psychoanalytic or occult tradition, however, would result in a superficial understanding of their significance for her development. . . . Whether or not we accept Harold Bloom's hypothesis that the anxiety of influence reenacts the Oedipal family romance, the process of influence must surely be recognized as fluid and personal, dialectical and never static. It operates as a creative collaboration in which the artist interacts with her or his sources and ultimately transforms them to serve the requirement of individual vision. This dynamic quality in the process of influence is clearly delineated in H. D.'s case, particularly in her interactions with Freud. Their relationship was a complex emotional and intellectual dialogue in which their disagreements did as much as their agreements to focus Psyche's quest. Especially because she left a record of that dialogue, their collaboration serves as a virtual paradigm of working influence. Because Freud's impact on twentieth-century art has been so enormous, H. D.'s creative transformation of his theories can serve as a superbly outlined case study of his influence on literary artists.

The interplay of their creative minds, however, points to the paradoxical nature of Freud's influence on H. D. and other modern artists. She described Freud as the "guardian of all beginnings," but she also reminded herself repeatedly that "the Professor was not always right." . . . . His impact on H. D. and other artists was dependent upon their ability to revise fundamental assumptions in his work. . . . [Freud] celebrated reason over passion and belief, and looked forward to a future when the infantile consolations of religion would be replaced by the rational power of "logos." . . . In contrast, H. D. and others influenced by Freud were disillusioned with the limited truths of rationalism and the destructive horrors of technological progress. They celebrated intuition, the vision of dreams, and the "primitive" myths still living in the human psyche and recorded in tradition.

On another level, H. D.'s very survival as a woman artist required her to confront Freud's misogyny if she were to continue in the traditionally male roles of questor and poet. . . . His theories of psychosexual development became "scientific" arguments for the inferiority of women and therefore rationalizations for inequality. H. D. sought inspiration from one of the greatest legitimizers of patriarchy. Her success as a woman depended upon conflict.

Mutual warmth and respect characterized their relationship, as both their letters and *Tribute to Freud* attest. But in another sense, their sessions together represent a prototypical confrontation between the polarities that permeate the modern world: man against woman, science versus religion, fact versus faith, objective versus subjective reality, reason versus intuition, the rational versus the irrational. H. D. and Freud dramatically personified the intellectual opposition of the age. Their "argument," played out in his office at Berggasse 19 and in the pages of H. D.'s memoir, is a microcosm of vital twentieth-century debate.

H. D.'s response to the confrontation was fundamentally dialectical. To serve the needs of spiritual quest, she developed aspects of Freud's thought until they became antithetical to his own perspectives. Freud, she wrote, was "midwife to the soul." . . . But, once reborn, Psyche emerged with a voice distinctly her own. Once having clarified the poles of opposition, her search for synthesis led to a transcendence of their differences in a vision that incorporated the whole. This transformation of Freudian theory simultaneously served as the basis of her mature art and as a brilliant reevaluation of Freud's significance for the twentieth century. Long before theorists like Norman O. Brown and Herbert Marcuse reinterpreted Freud's thought, H. D. reflected on the man who survived in her memories and in his books until she found the artist within the scientist, a prophet within the apostate, and the woman within the man. (pp. 11-14)

Susan Stanford Friedman, in her Psyche Reborn: The Emergence of H. D., *Indiana University Press, 1981, 332 p.*

LUCY M. FREIBERT

[*HERmione*] is remarkably engaging. Completed in 1927 at the height of the modernist period, the novel has a surprisingly contemporary ring. Its vitality, arising in part from H. D.'s experience, depends upon the bisexual nature of the relationships involved and the emergence of the protagonist as an artist. (pp. 93-4)

[The] sensitive nature of the novel's content prevented its publication during the lifetime of the principals. . . . Though all of H. D.'s work contains deeply personal material, careful encoding and a willingness to risk exposure allowed her to publish much of it during her lifetime. Not so with *HERmione*. . . .

By its very nature H. D.'s poetry, especially the later mythical works, allowed privacy, but her prose, even the most guarded, created something of a problem. Much of the early prose remains in manuscript form. However, she released two novels soon after finishing them: *Palimpsest* (1926), the story of three women of different historical periods who lived virtually the same life, closely parallel to H. D.'s; and *Hedylus* (1928), the account of a young male poet's struggle to attain selfhood and independence—a struggle much like the one which occurs in *HERmione*. (p. 94)

HERmione treats a particularly distressing period of H. D.'s life from which she emerged aware of her sexual proclivities and artistic potential and aware also of the near impossibility of a woman's becoming independent in the patriarchal society. While H. D. may not have been aware earlier of the full implications of her experiences, in writing the novel she overlooked none of the psychological ramifications.

The narrative covers the summer after Her Gart failed "conic sections" at Bryn Mawr. She feels that she has failed her parents completely, has let down her brother, and has lost a sense of herself: "I am Hermione Gart, a failure."

During this period of confusion, Her becomes involved simultaneously with two exciting young people: George Lowndes, a wild young poet just back from Europe [modeled after Ezra Pound], and Fayne Rabb, a young woman "fey with the same sort of wildness" as Her, herself. At first Her's parents oppose her meeting Lowndes. . . . When Her announces her engagement to George, they are appalled. However, learning that his family has some wealth and that his mother is a literary person, they withdraw their objections, and Her's mother actually looks forward to the marriage. Although the heterosexual romance seems to be progressing, it is in fact declining, for Her has become infatuated with Fayne. Both Her's parents and George strongly object to Her's attachment to the psychologically intense young woman. . . .

The intimacies of the two relationships contrast sharply. Her enjoys the excitement of her forest walks with George, but she resents his ambivalence toward her poetry, his harlequin stance toward life, and especially his attitude toward her. He would want her to be a traditional wife, to be "decorative," to be the subject of his poems. Furthermore, Her is repulsed by George's sexual advances, which she thinks violent and humiliating. . . . (p. 95)

Ultimately, both relationships, through an ironic turn, disintegrate. Her regrets not at all the loss of George, as she had already rejected him. . . . But she is greatly distressed at the loss of Fayne. Her tenuous state worsens to a complete collapse which lasts for months. When she comes out of her illness, she accepts her vocation as a writer and sets out to develop her gift.

The simple recounting of major events only hints at the complex levels of understanding H. D. reaches in **HERmione**. Stream of consciousness precisely reflects Her's mental state. The discontinuity of the story line allows changes in Her's perceptions of herself and others to deepen toward sophistication, and the interior monologues replicate the confusion, frustration, and anxiety on which Her's life turns. The pervasive use of forest imagery emphasizes the extent to which Her (woman) is immersed in nature, and it also reveals George's (man's) inability to respect and value nature. (pp. 95-6)

Chapter 6 of Part One emphasizes H. D.'s thesis that as a woman artist struggles to achieve selfhood and independence of the male-dominated society, she may find her greatest support in another woman. . . .

In writing **HERmione** H. D. committed a daring act, the harbinger of her daringly unconventional life and a lifetime of unconventional works which would have to wait years for a receptive climate. **HERmione** places the rest in perspective. (p. 96)

> Lucy M. Freibert, in a review of "HERmione," in Arizona Quarterly, Vol. 38, No. 1, Spring, 1982, pp. 93-6.

ALBERT GELPI

H. D. always wrote her own personal and psychological dilemma against and within the political turmoil of the twentieth century, the toils of love enmeshed in the convulsions of war. Her marriage to and separation from Richard Aldington turn on World War I, and that concatenation of private and public trauma stands behind the poems of **Sea Garden**, which sum up the Imagist concision of her first phase. The sequences of **Trilogy**, written through the London blitzes of World War II, usher in the longer, multivalent and more associative poems of her later years. The travail of aging and illness in her last years did not issue in the stoic silence which made Pound leave incomplete his life's work in the **Cantos**, but instead, as with William Carlos Williams, made for a final and climactic efflorescence of creative energy. The results were **Helen in Egypt**, published in 1961 almost concurrently with her death, and **Hermetic Definition**, published posthumously in 1972.

Even the reviewers who shied away from dealing with **Helen in Egypt** as a poem by detaching particular lyrics from the whole for dutiful praise (as though they were still Imagist pieces) recognized dimly that **Helen** was the culmination of a life in poetry. But it is an event even more culturally signal than that: it is the most ambitious and successful long poem ever written by a woman poet, certainly in English. It is so often observed as to take on a kind of fatality that no woman has ever written an epic, that women poets seem constrained to the minor note and the confabulations of the heart. H. D. confounds that complacent dictum by assuming and redefining the grounds of the epic. . . . H. D. repossessed the Trojan materials that have inspired the Western epic from Homer to Pound and converted them into an anti-epic centered not on heroes like Achilles and Hector but on a heroine, none other than the woman who, male poets have told us, roused men to Love, and so to War. (pp. 233-34)

Helen in Egypt draws Greek and Egyptian myths, epic and psychoanalysis and occult gnosticism into an "odyssey" of consciousness enacted as a series of lyrics written in irregular free-verse tercets of varying length and linked by prose commentaries sometimes longer than the lyrics. (p. 234)

Helen is, of course, H. D.'s persona as she writes her epic of consciousness. If this strategy seems more archly literary and aesthetically distanced than Whitman's stance in "Song of Myself," we need only remember that the "I" who spoke in **Leaves of Grass** as "Walt Whitman, a kosmos," is a fiction in some ways more deceptive than "Helen" because it pretends not to be a fiction. Moreover, in **Helen in Egypt** the configuration of the three male figures around Helen's central consciousness presents H. D. re-creating mythicized and fantasized versions of Richard Aldington in Achilles, of Freud in Theseus, and, in the figure of Paris, a recapitulation of her romantic passions from Ezra Pound to Dr. Erich Heydt, the analyst and doctor at the Klinik Brunner. (pp. 234-35)

[Achilles] begins the poem in the aggressive male posture adopted by Aldington during World War I and dramatized by H. D. as Rafe in **Bid Me to Live:** the swaggeringly blunt warrior used to using his women. Like Freud, who served H. D. during the thirties as wise old man, surrounded in his office by ancient Greek figurines, and applying his reason to help her sort out the confusion of her life and feelings, Theseus is for Helen the wise man and paternal authority. . . .

The associations with Paris are more complicated and more inclusive; they span all H. D.'s adult life up to the time of her writing of the poem. (p. 235)

The point of these autobiographical connections is not that the characters portray real people accurately . . . but rather that they are psychological fantasies or fictions which represent areas of psychological experience of the masculine on which H. D.'s selfhood turned. Where in her previous poetry she had sought to project her autobiography into myth, here at the end she sought to assimilate and validate myth within herself. (p. 236)

[The] mythic psychological status which Helen attains in the poem is not merely that of daughter-maiden; she becomes mother before daughter, encompassing the whole feminine archetype: Demeter-Persephone-Kore in one. In writing her own Helen-text, H. D. arrived at a reading of identity which resumed and surpassed the past. That moment—between time and eternity and participating in both—is the "final illumination" of the poem, and it is the moment of death. Through the mother-goddess she has conceived and come full term, dying and rising to herself. . . . Under the name of Helen, H. D. spelled out her hermetic definition. Though **Helen in Egypt** is a death-hymn, H. D. told her journal: "I am alive in the **Helen** sequence" because "there I had found myself"; those poems "gave me everything."

Early in the poem Helen asks: "is it only the true immortals / who partake of mortality?" The poem's response inverts the proposition: true partakers of mortality achieve immortality. (p. 245)

To many readers the "final illumination" to which **Helen in Egypt** builds is at best impenetrably gnomic and at worst hypnotic nonsense, and this explication of the poem admittedly leaves many matters unaddressed and many questions unanswered. But the vision of the eternal moment, with time concentered individually and cosmically in eternity, is H. D.'s occult version of Eliot's Christian "still point of the turning world." (p. 246)

No resumé or excerpting of passages can indicate how subtly the images and leitmotifs of *Helen in Egypt* are woven into the design. Some reviewers found the prose passages distracting intrusions among the lyrics, but H. D. wanted . . . a counterpoint of lyric expression and reflective commentary. In identification with the mother-goddess, assimilating Greek and Egyptian, Christian and gnostic wisdom, H. D. came to read the scribble of her life as hieroglyph. Nothing need be forgotten; nothing could be denied; everything was caught up in the resolution. (p. 247)

The poem links Helen's recovery of the mother with a shift in her relation to the masculine, dramatized by the progression from Paris as sexual lover to Achilles as filial-fraternal partner, and the shift signals a re-imagining of woman's unhappy lot, which has been the theme of H. D.'s fiction and verse. (p. 248)

In the long, tortuous, fragmented history of women writing about their womanhood, the supreme distinction of *Helen in Egypt,* with all its idiosyncracies, is that it transforms the male epic into the woman's lyric sustained at a peak of intensity for an epic's length, and the woman's myth it evolves posits the supremacy of the mother: Helen self-born in Thetis, Hilda self-born in Helen. (p. 250)

Albert Gelpi, "Hilda in Egypt," in The Southern Review, *Vol. 18, No. 2, April, 1982, pp. 233-50.*

CAROL CAMPER

As the title suggests, *HERmione* is about a young woman divided against herself (Her and Hermione Gart are the same person) and against a certain perception of the world. Although this is the autobiographical narrative of a future poet, the handling of these divisions is unlike anything you will encounter in other portraits of young artists. An intensely personal narrative voice demands that you follow her on her terms and in her language only. The voice confides her universe of desire, drawn with emblems of a troubled, idealized beauty. . . . The voice is "overwrought" . . . and the symbolism extravagant, even a little too self-consciously Jungian. Hermione is engaged in a war with precise, sane, emotionally expurgated language, the language of her father, a science professor, and of her brother, a biologist of sorts. Her Gart retreats from the aloof, instrumental world of her father even while convinced that her retreat (her failure in science at Bryn Mawr) brands her a failure in life.

All the basic elements seem to be assembled for yet another dip into the Oedipus complex, as Hermione calls it, for a plunge into that "emotional bog and intellectual lagoon" psychologists attempt to chart. If you dislike this kind of exploration, take heart, H. D. is not about to offer you a familiar version. Science, Hermione confesses, is a perception that has eluded her. H. D. charts her way around the character George Lowndes (Ezra Pound, H. D.'s former fiancé and life-long obsession). Lowndes, a promising poet, mesmerizes Hermione with his eloquence and erudition; she uneasily competes with him for the distinction of having the most original mind. His self-confidence irritates and overwhelms her, his sexual attentions alarm her, and his clowning infuriates—she wonders always whether she is being trifled with. She can't quite make him out. Thirty-one years after completing *HERmione,* H. D. will still be puzzling him out in *An End to Torment* where she compares his imaginative influence to "the crater of an extinct volcano." (pp. 378-79)

HERmione is an irritating book with many flaws. Effusive, indulgent, repetitious, rhetorically inflated, it also has a narrative that advances by fits and starts. It is, nonetheless, a very good introduction to the mythologizing impulse behind H. D.'s poetry, to the way in which she seeks out symbolic analogues for personal values. Beyond that, those who have the patience to hear Hermione out will catch the vivid voice of a woman whose alienation profiles patriarchy's most blighting effects. Hermione delivers platitudes at the conclusion of this novel and prepares to travel to Europe. This was, evidently, the note on which Hilda Doolittle left Pennsylvania for Europe. Fortunately, this was not H. D.'s final farewell to Pennsylvania. (p. 380)

Carol Camper, "The Autobiography of a Future Poet from Pennsylvania," in Contemporary Literature, *Vol. 23, No. 3, Summer, 1982, pp. 377-80.*

ALISON TARTT

[*The Gift,* a] previously unpublished work, written in 1941 and 1943, re-creates fragments of H. D.'s childhood in Bethlehem and Upper Darby. Each chapter develops a mosaic of incidents . . . associated in the author's remembrance by the logic of the subconscious. Combining symbols, images, remembered words and phrases, and bits of family history into patterns of highly rhythmic prose, H. D. evokes the impressionism of childhood and the amalgam of memory. The final chapter brings the reader back to the present time and place—London under seige during World War II—and unifies many of the earlier motifs in a tour de force that shows H. D.'s control of her material. A moving and engrossing piece of autobiography.

Alison Tartt, in a review of "The Gift," in Library Journal, *Vol. 107, No. 15, September 1, 1982, p. 1660.*

JANICE S. ROBINSON

In her early poems H. D. expressed a particularly feminine viewpoint in relation to the poetic tradition. As time went on this stance became more and more clearly defined; today we would call it feminist. It is important to understand how H. D.'s particular poetic sensibility, which she expresses in a metaphorical or palimpsest way of thinking and writing, differs from the more masculine poetic thrust.

What we must first come to understand in H. D.'s poetry is what we might call a figural or allegorical interpretation of nature. Every natural occurrence, in all its everyday reality, is correspondingly a part of a spiritual world order, which is also experiential and in which every event is related to every other event. In the western literary tradition, nature has traditionally been understood to be feminine and mute; H. D. makes nature speak. Because her perspective is feminine rather than masculine, she interprets events in terms of the timeless natural world rather than in terms of the historical process. This perspective is immediately recognizable as one of psychological or spiritual realism. Once events occur, they occur for all eternity and persist into the future as a portion of our inherited body of fate. The Greek dramatists, whom H. D. studied, knew full well the tragic personal and political consequences of being unaware of (or forgetting) one's fate. It is important to understand that H. D.'s poems are not poems of desire; neither are they prophecies of historical occurrences or poems of social protest. Rather, they are presentations of a situation.

Pound had presented H. D. with a situation in which she lost either way: she could either go back home to America with her parents or submit to Pound outside of the context of marriage. Both alternatives were unacceptable to her in the sense that they were inconsistent and incompatible with the person she had become. Her response was to *present* the situation as she had experienced it. That presentation turned out to be poetry. . . . When confronted with two equally unacceptable alternatives it is important to choose a third; that is, it is important to create one's own alternative. This is the feminist basis of H. D.'s poetic stance. (pp. 56-7)

H. D. expresses a good deal of defensiveness and resistance as well as sadness and a sense of loss in her early poetry. The loneliness, vulnerability, and sense of estrangement and uprootedness that come with a decision to defy the masculine impulse and create one's own space is expressed in **"Hermonax,"** published in *Poetry* magazine in February 1914. (p. 57)

H. D.'s poems had been written according to Hulme's principles as a process of disentanglement. But the manner in which Pound appropriated them and acted as though they were written for him simply shocked her. By his manner he made them his own—his to edit, his to publish, his to interpret. . . . If H. D. had not been in shock, she might have reclaimed her own work, published her poems in her own way, in her own good time, and in her own interpretive context. But once Pound had defined a context for her poetry, it was important for her to redefine that context, so she had to keep writing in order to do so. . . .

In a sense H. D.'s poems came out of the tension of a situation in which two men, Pound and Aldington, were fighting for her. (p. 58)

Another factor to take into account in understanding H. D.'s emergence as a poet is that she certainly did not know what it meant for a woman to publish poetry in the extremely patriarchal world of 1913. In the very act in which H. D. was attempting to recover herself—the act of writing the poem—she was, through the action of men, throwing herself into the center of a man's world as a muse (that is, a woman who is other than a wife; a woman who is considered by men to be in the category of hetaera). Ironically then, the very act by which she is attempting to recover herself as her mother's child can result in a separation from her mother forever. . . .

What is clear is that [H. D.] did not cross the line from the world dominated by feminine values into the world dominated by masculine ones with no way back. In some sense she crossed that line in her imagination—she had some sense of what it

meant to be in the milieu of the masculine wisdom. But instead of being either in the matriarchal or the patriarchal world, she became an artist and created a world of her own—a world in which her mind was in control of her experience. (p. 59)

H. D. came to understand the poem not as an assertion of phallic desire, but as presentation, an act of birth, a means of disentanglement from the burden of the inseminating thought, and a way to recovery of primal integrity. (p. 61)

Janice S. Robinson, in her H. D.: The Life and Work of an American Poet, *Houghton Mifflin Company, 1982, 490 p.*

LUCY M. FREIBERT

[*The Gift*] is a novelistic memoir of H. D.'s childhood. Like her epic trilogy, it issued from H. D.'s creative burst during the period of chaos (1941-1943) following the Battle of Britain. The final chapter of *The Gift*, in fact, dramatizes Hilda's efforts, between air raids, to write the memoir.

H. D. casts *The Gift* in a haunting, mystical, yet childlike, voice which matures as the memoir unfolds. She employs the mythical method throughout the work, overlaying fact with religious, literary, and cultural parallels. In the opening chapter, **"Dark Room,"** Hilda charts her Moravian ancestry. She begins with the death by fire of a young girl at the Moravian seminary in Bethlehem, Pennsylvania . . . , but she focuses on her own inheritance of the mystical, artistic gift from her maternal grandmother. Re-creating the familial context of her youth, she shows how her mother nurtured "the gift," seeking fulfillment of a fortune teller's promise that she would have "a child who was gifted." Hilda broods over whether "a gift" can be transferred from one branch of the family to another and thus lost to the person who should have it, whether only men can be artists, and how works can evolve from one genre to another. (p. 90)

The brilliance of *The Gift* comes from H. D.'s ability to recall unique moments which illustrate the growth of the artist and to deepen them through the use of the mythical method. Her probing into words, ideas, and actions with the mystical intuition of the child and her formulating resultant insights with the genius of her art fashion the memoir into a beauty which literally takes one's breath away. (p. 91)

Lucy M. Freibert, in a review of "The Gift," in Arizona Quarterly, *Vol. 39, No. 1, Spring, 1983, pp. 89-91.*

Edward Hirsch

1950-

American poet, short story writer, and critic.

Hirsch has been praised as a sophisticated and promising young poet. The poems of his first collection, *For the Sleepwalkers* (1981), have received acclaim for their disciplined structure and their imaginative play with words and images. Hirsch's indebtedness to such major poets as Rainer Maria Rilke, Marianne Moore, and Federico García Lorca, as well as to such visual artists as Henri Matisse and Paul Klee, is evident throughout *For the Sleepwalkers*. While a few critics have found this volume uneven, exaggerated, or pretentious, most consider it remarkably polished for a first collection, noting especially the strikingly precise images and the strong, convincing metaphors. Jay Parini describes one poem as "vivid, musical, and richly allusive," and Phoebe Pettingell notes that while the poems in *For the Sleepwalkers* vary in quality, Hirsch's "failures suggest promise, and at his best he speaks with authority."

(See also *Contemporary Authors*, Vol. 104.)

PUBLISHERS WEEKLY

The poems in this fine collection ["**For the Sleepwalkers**"] have the unusual quality of being at once intellectual and deeply heartfelt. Hirsch's strong, highly original metaphors combine gracefully with detailed observations and phrases from everyday speech. His subject matter ranges from art and perception (subtle distinctions between life and still life, for example) to eroticism, death, fantastical fairy tales and the meaning of regret. . . .

> *A review of "For the Sleepwalkers," in* Publishers Weekly, *Vol. 219, No. 22, May 29, 1981, p. 35.*

HUGH SEIDMAN

In the very first poem of "**For the Sleepwalkers**," Edward Hirsch reveals a major conflict:

> . . . yet we manage, we survive
> so that losing itself becomes a kind
> of song, our song, our only witness
> to the way we die, one day at a time . . .

But if this is a poetry of survival, it is also a poetry of narcissistic invention employing exaggerated tone and metaphor. . . . As Mr. Hirsch notes in "**Cocks**," "The guardian / Angel of poetry" endlessly tries "to astonish . . . and to offend."

"**Poets, Children, Soldiers**" can paradoxically contain a striking image of insomnia—"I'm tired / of living like a broken yellow oar / awash in the blue waters of nightfall"—immediately followed by the trite implication that *only* poets, children and soldiers "know about the black / trenches of moonlight on the ceiling." . . .

Personae appear, some famous (Rilke, Rimbaud, Nerval, Vallejo, Smart, Lorca). At his best, Mr. Hirsch confirms our

expectations of these people, but often his approach is pretentious. . . .

In general, Mr. Hirsch presents us with the seductive inventive excess that has come to typify much contemporary American poetry. (p. 34)

> *Hugh Seidman, "Four Poets," in* The New York Times Book Review, *September 13, 1981, pp. 14, 32, 34.**

PHOEBE PETTINGELL

[Young] poets who are too careful sometimes dry up. Edward Hirsch is not cautious, and his first book, *For the Sleepwalkers* . . . , is uneven. Nevertheless, his failures suggest promise, and at his best he speaks with authority.

The brave opening, "**Song Against Natural Selection**," proclaims that "The weak survive!"—a sentiment in keeping with Hirsch's willingness to face up to failure. This poem, though, happens to be a complete success. . . . The formal structure, making the reader only belatedly aware of rhyme, complements the wry acceptance of loss.

I suspect that Hirsch is fond of the French "Homage" (those elegies written at somebody's tomb) because of the chance it gives him to indulge his mimetic gifts, not merely out of an admiration of Baudelaire and Verlaine. He is a good imitator, and some of these poems—transposing Lorca to the Upper West Side of Manhattan, or Vallejo to a soup kitchen in Paris—are wonderfully effective. Still, it is easy to sound inept mimicking dead poets. Hirsch's **"At the Grave of Marianne Moore"** is prefaced with her famous dictum: "Whatever it is, let it be without affectation." Although he copies Moore's quirky style without trouble, since it is not native to him he *does* sound affected. He also stoops to an occasional bad pun unworthy of Moore. . . . And when Hirsch praises Moore because "her scrupulous method / in verse bequeathed us a heritage / the honesty of her intelligence," he cannot mean this to sound as prosy and patronizing as it does. These lapses notwithstanding, it is obvious that Moore's precise eye has influenced Hirsch in the better poems than this one.

Hirsch's tributes to great poets are merely one manifestation of his preoccupation with the artist's role. In **"The Acrobat,"** he uses the training of a young circus performer as a metaphor for the disciplines required in mastering any art. . . .

Following the motions of its protagonist, **"The Acrobat"** revolves in a spiral: from the outsider's admiration of the graceful contortions, to the apprentice's disgust at the ugliness of some of the tricks of the trade, then full circle to an appreciation of the "dignity and great courage" required to perfect one's control. Finally, the acrobat swings out to merge with his art. . . . I admire Edward Hirsch for his mystical vision, for the mastery he has already attained—and for his daring (p. 15)

> *Phoebe Pettingell, "Taking Chances in Verse," in The New Leader, Vol. LXV, No. 5, March 8, 1982, pp. 14-15.**

JAY PARINI

Edward Hirsch writes in *For the Sleepwalkers* with a slight, somewhat self-conscious, formality, as if he wishes to hold his material in place by distancing himself from it. He achieves this formality—and it is an achievement—by following regular stanza patterns and metering stresses in a given line; in addition, he elevates his diction so that his poetry becomes, in the words of Gerard Manley Hopkins, "the common language heightened." Thus, he opens **"Dusk"**:

> The sun is going down tonight
> like a wounded stag staggering through the brush
> with an enormous spike in its heart
> and a single moan in its lungs. There
>
> is a light the color of tarnished metal
> galloping at its side, and fresh blood
> is steaming through its throat. Listen!
> The waves, too, sound like the plunging
>
> of hooves, or a wild hart simply
> crumpling on the ground.

He ends this lovely poem:

> And now here is the night
> with its false promise of sleep, its wind
> leafing through the grass, its vacant
>
> spaces between stars, its endless memory
> of a world going down like a stag.

Hirsch might well have avoided the unfortunate "stag staggering," but one can forgive such a small lapse of taste in a poem so vivid, musical, and richly allusive. The reference to Pascal's terrifying, infinite spaces between the stars at the close is typical of Hirsch's learning, which he wears lightly. If you don't "get" the allusions in his work, it doesn't really matter: the poem will still be an experience worth having; if you do catch them, a whole string of bells will go off in your head.

For the Sleepwalkers traces the poet's descent into the dark, that nether region of the imagination where "We have to learn the desperate faith of sleep- / walkers who rise out of their calm beds / and walk through the skin of another life." That, from the title poem, provides a key to this book, in which Hirsch inhabits, poem by poem, dozens of other skins. He can become Rimbaud, Rilke, Paul Klee, or Matisse, in each case convincingly. Or he can speak as a diner waitress in Arkansas. . . . Whatever guises Hirsch takes on, he does so with gusto, and his poems easily fulfill Auden's request that poems be, above all else, "memorable language." (p. 39)

> *Jay Parini, "A New Generation of Poets," in The New Republic, Vol. 186, No. 15, April 14, 1982, pp. 37-9.**

PETER STITT

Edward Hirsch's *For the Sleepwalkers* is [a] surprising first book—surprising not just for its quality but for its literary sophistication as well. Hirsch's poems fall into that vague, hard to define category of the post-modern; he has read the American surrealists, he has learned from John Ashbery. Poets in this tradition generally value technique at least as much as they do content, a fact evident just in the large amount of verbal experimentation they engage in. As Ashbery did as a young writer, Hirsch here tries his hand against the rigorous limitations of such forms as the sestina. (All poets do this kind of thing now and then, but the technical play involved is important enough to the likes of Ashbery and Hirsch that they print the results.) The immediate payoff from this experimentation is a tightness of imagery in many of Hirsch's poems; that is, rather than accumulate many images in a given poem, he will set up a few rather complex ones and then repeat and modulate them throughout the work.

Hirsch regularly offers the unexpected. The first several poems in his book are amusing, playful, outrageous, as when a buzzard delivers this **"Apologia"** for his kind: "A violent muscle is / pumping blood through a few scattered clouds / until a violent color sizzles up in the ground. / I, too, have a heart and wings, and I / say that a single pulse animates the world." (p. 444)

[The] literature of post-modernism—prose and poetry—is often less interested in truth, meaning, and content than in the pleasures of pure technique, making it a sort of latter-day art for art's sake. But again the poems of Edward Hirsch turn out to be exceptional. As this book progresses, a sense of elegiac tenderness begins to emerge more and more clearly. (p. 445)

Most impressive of all is a four-part elegy [in the fifth section of this book] entitled **"The Dark Sun."** Its concluding section is called **"Dusk: Elegy for the Dark Sun"**:

> A sword is bandaged in the clouds.
> Call it the sun, though others
> May think it's an anchor
> Sunk in the sky, or a knife
> Carved into the leaves.

But call it the sun. And call
The hands pressed to its face
The clouds, though others may think
They're a blanket containing heat
Or four shoes clapped onto a horse.
That horse can run. And call the field
Where it runs the sky, and the stable
Where it rests the sea. And the hay
That it eats is blue and yellow.
Call it the rain and the wind.
These imaginings make it possible
To survive, to endure the hard light,
Though darkness is floating in.
And that thing breaking in my chest
Is more than a heart; it is also
The sun bandaged in a sheath of clouds
And thrown up over the waves
Like a lifebuoy, like a hand
Trying to call its fellow men.

The profusion of metaphor here is astonishing, though all of the figures coalesce around and add meaning to a few central images—sun, hands, heart—conveying a strong impression of wounding, of degeneration, of decay, of time passing all too relentlessly. The arbitrary quality of the imagery ("Call it the sun, though others / May think") emphasizes the central fact that individual perception determines reality in this century. . . . Central to this poem, of course, is the ultimate justification for this kind of poetry, pulling Hirsch's work well out of the art-for-art's-sake category: "These imaginings make it possible / To survive, to endure the hard light, / Though darkness is floating in." . . . Hirsch's is not a solipsistic art—these poems of wonder and consolation are not dedicated to his own precious soul, but comment on the world, lovely and rapacious by turns, that we all inhabit. (pp. 445-46)

Peter Stitt, "The Objective Mode in Contemporary Lyric Poetry," in The Georgia Review, *Vol. XXXVI, No. 2, Summer, 1982, pp. 438-48.**

J. D. McCLATCHY

Hirsch comes to poetry as to a wind-up toy. He plays with it, turns it inside out, breaks and mends it, plays. Sometimes it ticks like Gertrude Stein. . . . Sometimes it spins on the axis of its own silliness. . . . [A] kind of slapstick abounds. When he can restrain himself, Hirsch is better. He prefers the expressionist portrait (**"The Enigma: Rilke,"** or the sweet **"Matisse"**) or a stew of dissolves and associations (**"Cocks," "Reminiscence of Carousels and Civil War"**). This poet has talent, but it is vitiated by a coy or dizzy self-indulgence: updated Dada. As a result, the poems [in *For the Sleepwalkers*] aren't memorable. But from scattered hints, from a colorful diction and a rhythmic surety, it may be predicted that he can—and will—write a more substantial book than this: one for the wide-awake.

J. D. McClatchy, in a review of "For the Sleepwalkers," in Poetry, *Vol. CXL, No. 6, September, 1982, p. 347.*

Evan Hunter

1926-

(Born S. A. Lombino; also writes under pseudonym of Ed McBain; has also written under pseudonyms of Curt Cannon, Hunt Collins, and Richard Marsten) American novelist, scriptwriter, short story writer, dramatist, and critic.

Hunter's works of popular fiction explore such family-oriented topics as parent-child relationships, love, and individual responsibility and such social issues as drug abuse, gang violence, and war. Under the pseudonym Ed McBain, Hunter is widely known for his realistic crime novels that center on a fictional urban police precinct. Although Hunter has maintained a large and faithful readership throughout his career, his work has yet to receive much serious critical attention.

Hunter published many short stories and science fiction works early in his career, but *The Blackboard Jungle* (1954) earned him his initial critical attention. This novel is based on Hunter's own experiences as an English teacher in a New York City vocational high school. The protagonist is a young, idealistic teacher whose enthusiasm is nearly turned to apathy by the indifferent attitude and lack of motivation of his students. The popular success of *The Blackboard Jungle*, still considered by some critics to be Hunter's finest work, helped foster greater understanding of the problems of teenage delinquency. The novel was adapted for film in 1955. In *Sons* (1969), another critically acclaimed novel, both world wars and the Vietnam conflict affect three generations of a midwestern American family. Critics contend that Hunter's depiction of America's rise to power—and the consequences of obtaining such power—evokes a poignant sense of history. In *Streets of Gold* (1974), another multi-generational novel, Hunter's narrative is focused on an Italian immigrant family and their search for the American dream at the expense of their old-world values. Although some critics noted an abundance of clichés and stock situations in this work, others found *Streets of Gold* rich in moralistic themes and praised Hunter's ironic depiction of happiness and prosperity in America.

Some critics maintain that Hunter has written his best fiction as Ed McBain. His series of detective novels, collectively titled *The 87th Precinct Series*, are commended for their authentic portrayal of urban crime prevention. Although there are recurring characters in these novels, most critics consider the precinct itself to be the most recognizable feature of the series. Another notable aspect of these books is the absence of the stereotyped detective common in crime fiction; unlike most other detectives, Hunter's investigators exhibit basic human traits and frailties. Although some critics view the later McBain novels as marginal in comparison to the earlier works, chiefly because they revolve around sensational sex crimes and grisly murders, Hunter is considered one of the most creative and original writers in the genre.

(See also *CLC*, Vol. 11; *Contemporary Authors*, Vols. 5-8, rev. ed.; *Contemporary Authors New Revision Series*, Vol. 5; *Something about the Author*, Vol. 25; and *Dictionary of Literary Biography Yearbook: 1982*.)

NATHAN ROTHMAN

Evan Hunter's **"The Blackboard Jungle"** is the most realistic account I have ever read of life in a New York City vocational

high school. I can testify to its accuracy, having had some years of experience in one of them, as has Mr. Hunter. His novel more than matches the sensations in some of the stories we have seen recently, in newspapers that have become happily school-conscious. But it is free of their distortions and dishonesty; it makes no easy moral assumptions nor does it arrive at righteous judgments. Mr. Hunter's North Manual Trades High—it is fairly typical—is a complex organism, the resultant of many forces, economic facts, social emotions, hostilities, suspicions. It can, if it is not to be considered irreparable, be handled only with understanding, courage, in the last analysis, humanity. Nothing else will work. You won't find that in the newspaper accounts, but it is here, implicitly stated in Mr. Hunter's story, and Richard Dadier, the young teacher, is a human and spirited embodiment of that statement.

Dadier's history as we read it covers one term, five months, of teaching in his new job at North Trades. It should be said at once that Mr. Hunter has telescoped a vast body of material into that five months. Nobody ever experienced so much, learned so much in one term of teaching. The alternative, of course, would be a longer and less integrated document, and I am willing to accept this telescoping as a necessary device. Otherwise Dadier's history is incontrovertible. If you have been teaching in a vocational high school for four years, all of this has happened to you, or your neighbor. You have been greeted with, "Hey, teach'!'' You have set down some requirements and been told, "Dig that cat, he's playin' it hard,'' or "Teach', you ever try to fight thirty-five guys at once?'' You have faced the cold war in the classroom, and sometimes the hot war in the stairwells or outside the school on a dark night. You have seen the offerings you made riotously rejected—the phonograph records broken, the pictures delaced, the windows and blackboards cracked. And you have had to face a boy with a knife. (pp. 16-17)

There is no happy ending. This very lesson is followed by a vicious experience with Artie West, the blind antagonist, the kid with the knife that you read about. But the whole picture is here, every element of it. Mr. Hunter has been particularly good with his portraits of the faculty and, even more, the pupils. Most memorable is the Negro boy, Gregory Miller, himself so complex a figure. (p. 17)

Nathan Rothman, "Cold-War Class," in The Saturday Review, *New York, Vol. XXXVII, No. 41, October 9, 1954, pp. 16-17.*

BARBARA KLAW

"**The Blackboard Jungle**" is that rare combination—a problem novel in which both the problem and the novel are intensely interesting and in which both elements are blended so skillfully as to be inseparable.

Evan Hunter's problem is New York vocational schools, where, as he presents it, all the students who are not intelligent enough to qualify for academic high schools are shunted by the city. The author, who has himself taught in one of these schools, gives a shocking picture of dullness, profanity, disrespect and violence among both the students and the faculty. "This is the garbage can of the educational system," one of the older teachers told Richard Dadier during his first day's work as an English teacher at the North Manual Trades High School. "And you want to know what our job is? Our job is to sit on the lid of the garbage can and see that none of the filth overflows into the streets."

Dadier didn't believe him. He wanted to teach. . . .

The novel concerns his first term, his testing period, and what it did to him, his wife and his students. Before the term is over he has been able to evaluate the cynicism of the faculty expressed daily in the lunchroom. He has been beaten, tricked, badgered. He has played the buffoon, the actor, the taskmaster in an effort to reach his students. He has despaired and seen his friends give up and quit. He has hated the boys and has had a deadly fight with a student who pulled a knife on him. He has had the satisfaction of working with eager students in a school play and the bafflement of seeing the same students become his adversaries again in class. He has seen one student emerge from the "garbage can," and, at last, in one period with one class he has penetrated the children's indifference, and won their participation.

These undramatic victories, more than the violence, more than Dadier's moving relationship with his pregnant wife, are the climax of the story. That the reader is intensely moved by a high school English class' response to their teacher is a tribute to Evan Hunter's skill as a writer. For the author has not used his shocking material merely to appall. With a superb ear for conversation, with competence as a storyteller, and with a tolerant and tough-minded sympathy for his subject, he has built an extremely good novel!

Barbara Klaw, "Garbage Can of the Schools," in New York Herald Tribune Book Review, *October 17, 1954, p. 4.*

STANLEY COOPERMAN

The good surface realism of "**The Blackboard Jungle**" hides its lack of depth. Hunter lays to rest for all time the notion that high-school teaching is simply a white-collar job with "short hours and long vacations." Education, for thousands of boys in New York City, is often a violent hypocrisy, prime examples of which are the "trade schools" set up as depositories for the unmanageables of the academic school system.

The original reason for establishing these schools was sound enough: adolescents who could not, for a variety of psychological and social reasons, profit from academic education should be given the opportunity to learn useful skills. But the schools swiftly degenerated. Relegated to the oldest buildings and poorest neighborhoods, they became the Siberia of the educational system for teachers and students alike, and the inevitable result was self-perpetuating violence and cynicism.

Evan Hunter breaks through the verbiage which has long clouded the facts of vocational teaching with his story of a young man who tries to extract meaning and hope from this educational underworld. It is true that he makes only cursory attempts to probe the well-springs of the action he photographs so well, but he succeeds in dramatizing an area heretofore neglected in fiction. (pp. 493-94)

Stanley Cooperman, "Violence in Harlem," in The Nation, *Vol. 179, No. 23, December 4, 1954, pp. 493-94.**

JAMES KELLY

In its simplest terms, "**Second Ending**" covers the step-by-step disintegration of a trumpet player named Andy Silvera who has become a hopeless hophead. The theme is what happened and how, not the why. Now in his last days, Andy is full of promises to kick the habit and get back in shape for a job audition. Alternating between exultation and despair, emotional anguish and abnormal lucidity, his is a tortured soul. . . .

Any reader whose personal experience has touched the arena where drugs and music come together will soon accept the clinical, fascinating truth of Mr. Hunter's details. This truth extends beyond the authentic jargon of jive talk or addict talk to the overwhelming human tragedy looming high above. And it is heightened by the author's compassion for these victims of too much love of living who still register upon each other as accountable human beings long after society has filed them away as problems. At the closing brutal scene, one is reminded again that individuals can climb or they can sink, with freedom of choice sometimes lost to circumstances: "When you are dead, there is nothing but heroin. There's a big H written across the sky, and that's all there is. H, and it doesn't stand for heroin, it stands for Hell."

"**Second Ending**" (like Mr. Hunter's earlier, hotly debated novel, "**The Blackboard Jungle**") could be called a tour de force, since its significance does not interfere with its impact as entertainment. . . . If Mr. Hunter sometimes shows a notable lack of restraint in his use of bravissimo and florid periods, most onlookers will still agree that this second novel was very much worth doing and that he did it well.

James Kelly, "H Stands for Hell," in The New York Times Book Review, *January 8, 1956, p. 27.*

WILDER HOBSON

[In **"Second Ending"** there] is nothing stereotyped or simply sensational in Hunter's portrait of the trumpet player Andy Sivera. It is a very human and moving achievement. When he comes for aid to the apartment of his old jazz band associate Bud Donato, who is now boning up for examinations at the College of the City of New York, the trumpeter talks of curing himself by the agonizing method he knows as "cold turkey" (stopping at once, no tapering off). Hunter almost immediately manages to suggest that this is very unlikely in Silvera's case. It proves all of that, despite the efforts of that harassed college boy and of two young women, one of whom has herself conquered heroin. The account of Sivera's final descent is extremely dramatic, and Hunter intersperses long flashbacks revealing the past history of his characters.

His success with his chilling themes is all the more remarkable because he is in many ways an awkward and overblown writer. But he has a great deal of rude power, a sensitive feeling for such matters as adolescent love in the drab streets and neighborhood social clubs of Brooklyn, and a galvanic way with passages in which people oppose each other at the pitch of mutual desperation. The reader is not likely to forget such scenes as that in which Donato chases Silvera, re-equipped with a hypodermic, through the streets of New York, or the book's most searing episode when the all-demanding addict turns on Donato and accuses him of failure in the deepest obligations of old friendship. The wretched Donato is made to feel guilty for his own struggles toward stability and education.

Wilder Hobson, "Hot Music and Cold Turkey," in New York Herald Tribune Book Review, *January 15, 1956, p. 8.*

ROBERT C. HEALEY

With an abundance of compassion and clinical detail, [Hunter, in **"Strangers When We Meet"**,] . . . has traced a year of tragic adultery by Larry Cole, thirty-one, free-lance architect, and Maggie Gault, twenty-seven, free-lance housewife. . . .

Doggedly realistic most of the way, Hunter gives the whole book an oddly moralistic tone by plunging into a cloudy compound of philosophy and symbolism for his climactic sequence. Finally forced to decide between Maggie and his wife, Larry drives wildly through a shrieking tropical storm lashing New York. He broods on the meaning of his moments with Maggie. Was sex just "a sure thing in a world of uncertainties, an accomplishment in the world of unrealized dreams and frustrated goals?" Or was this affair an escape into a glamorous adolescent concept of romance?

This is the man's story, Larry's story. It is his undoing, his tragedy in his first and last experiment in infidelity. For Maggie, life must go on, but it cannot go on with her husband alone.

Robert C. Healey, "An Infidelity in Suburbia," in New York Herald Tribune Book Review, *July 20, 1958, p. 5.*

RILEY HUGHES

It was inevitable that Evan Hunter would turn his attention to the suburban development jungle. In his earlier novels problem and background were given equal attention—one seemed to grow out of the other. [In **Strangers When We Meet**] background is merely backdrop; the problem is everything. The predicament of the unfaithful husband occupies these 375 pages of shrill insistence. Perhaps a tract against lust is indeed intended. Still, there is such a ruthless portrayal of the stark realities of the problem that the moral fulcrum is lacking. The best indication of the spiritual poverty in the world Mr. Hunter displays here is that only a *deus ex machina* . . . solves the protagonist's dilemma. . . .

Mr. Hunter is serious, strident, and terribly flat in an intended case history which, this time, does not at all come off.

Riley Hughes, in a review of "Strangers When We Meet," in Catholic World, *Vol. 187, No. 1121, August, 1958, p. 391.*

ANTHONY BOUCHER

["**A Matter of Conviction**" seems] intended, by both author and publisher, as a serious mainstream novel; and I hate to report that Hunter's commercial and pseudonymous paperbacks, especially those by "Ed McBain," are more satisfactory by any serious standards. The present book starts off well with a blunt account of a teen-gang killing in Harlem; but most of the novel is devoted to the agonizing of Harlem-born assistant D.A. Henry Bell, who must prosecute the case. The coincidences and improbabilities which arise to torment him might be tolerated in soap operas and the subtlety, validity and originality of his social thinking might just about do for that medium. But even the most credulous television audience, trained by now in court procedure, should find the climactic trial scene absurd.

Anthony Boucher, in a review of "A Matter of Conviction," in The New York Times Book Review, *June 7, 1959, p. 27.*

JAMES SANDOE

["**Til Death**" is] the ninth of Ed McBain's 87th Precinct stories and as good as any of them. Its perturbation for Steve Carella is a threat sent to his brother-in-law on the day of his wedding. McBain's manipulation of a split-narrative mode in tracing the subsequent excitements is nimble, and although he has taken an easy-chancey way out plotwise to justify the multiple thrills, they seem genuine enough at the time and to a lot of people he has made us suitably worried about.

James Sandoe, in a review of "Til Death," in New York Herald Tribune Book Review, *September 20, 1959, p. 15.*

ANTHONY BOUCHER

Ed McBain's **"Til Death"** . . . nobly upholds the traditions of the 87th Precinct: it is a fresh, human, humorous, exciting novel about a vivid and unusual situation—in this case a series of attempts to erase the bridegroom during a wedding and the following reception. . . . McBain tells a fine suspense story (despite one coincidence too many for purists) while giving an almost anthropological report on an American folk institution.

Anthony Boucher, in a review of "Til Death," in The New York Times Book Review, October 4, 1959, p. 26.

ANTHONY BOUCHER

[In **"King's Ransom"**] here am I once more saying, "McBain has done it again."

Praise of a consistently admirable performer must get monotonous and even boring. If you're tired of reading here about McBain, the best remedy is simply to drop this paper and start in reading the book itself. This one's about a kidnaping, with quite a number of fresh variations on the Big Snatch theme. It's as immediate and convincing as any of the 87th Precinct tales, and a little more (in the best sense) theatrical than most. The book is powerful and compelling; and one looks forward to a dramatic version that might be even more so.

Anthony Boucher, in a review of "King's Ransom," in The New York Times Book Review, December 6, 1959, p. 42.

JAMES SANDOE

In Ed McBain's 87th Precinct when you **"Give the Boys a Great Big Hand"** . . . it's human, of course, and turns up in a small suitcase without the rest of the body. The inquiry that follows makes for as good a tale as any McBain has spun in his lively, lengthening series. The mode is procedural and the company includes, of course, a number of old acquaintances including Steve Carella and Cotton Hawes. . . . The precinct, the city, some curiously contradictory evidence about a stripteaser, an episode in a crowded men's shop, a garrulous landlady are all elements in a muscular, laconic tale, the tenth item in a valuable account.

James Sandoe, in a review of "Give the Boys a Great Big Hand," in New York Herald Tribune Book Review, March 27, 1960, p. 11.

ANTHONY BOUCHER

[**"The Heckler"** tells] how the boys of the Eighty-seventh Precinct worked vigorously and valiantly—and failed to prevent or to punish a singularly daring crime which laid waste a large part of the city. . . . Despite a number of promising leads, the precinct cops never quite reached [the criminal] (our good friend Steve Carella getting himself nearly killed in the final flight and pursuit.) . . . Fortunately, the Eighty-seventh is so warmly established in our affections by now that we can find an account of such frustration as fascinating as any of their triumphs, especially when it is told with all McBain's gift for easy naturalism and vivid color.

Anthony Boucher, in a review of "The Heckler," in The New York Times Book Review, July 31, 1960, p. 23.

ANTHONY BOUCHER

McBain, fortunately, is not concerned with writing according to the McBain formula, and can sometimes depart from it almost entirely. This latest [**"See Them Die"**] is not a detective exploit of the 87th Precinct, but something close to a straight novel about life in the precinct, in which the police are among the characters. A bigtime Puerto Rican hood, half-despised,

half-idolized by his compatriots, is hiding out from the law. The spectacular police siege of his hideaway serves as dramatic focus for a number of other plots, including an oddly realistic love story and an attempted teen-age killing. The action is tight-packed into a couple of sharply illuminating hours.

Anthony Boucher, in a review of "See Them Die," in The New York Times Book Review, December 11, 1960, p. 40.

AL MORGAN

Evan Hunter is a man of many talents and many names. As Ed McBain, he is writing the most authentic squad-room thrillers since Sidney Kingsley researched "Detective Story." You may have read him as Richard Marsten. A couple of other aliases tag his science-fiction and paperback and pulp output. Under the parent name, Evan Hunter, he has written what he must consider his serious novels . . . **"The Blackboard Jungle," "Second Ending," "Strangers When We Meet"** and **"A Matter of Conviction."**

Whether he is writing the whodunit, the potboiler, the pulp or the serious novel, he is a thoroughly professional writer: a "pro." His style has drive, pace, tempo and authenticity.

All of these virtues are apparent in his newest, **"Mothers and Daughters."** There is, however, something more. **"Mothers and Daughters"** is a panoramic novel, covering a span of slightly more than ten years and a multiple cast of characters. The two pivotal characters are Amanda and Gillian, roommates at a Connecticut college. . . .

The recurring theme of the novel is the difficulty of one generation to communicate with and understand the other. The specifics include a long and candid description of a love affair in a cold-water tenement on the fringes of Greenwich Village: the adulterous romance of a Connecticut matron and an Italian soldier in Rome: the clinical details of insanity: the suicide of a man who discovers his wife's infidelity, and always—the gulf between mothers and daughters, fathers and sons.

If there is an occasional touch of melodrama and predictability about the book, life itself is not immune from the same failing.

"Mothers and Daughters" is in the best sense of the phrase, a women's book. It is a book basically about women, told with insight, understanding and compassion. The people of Evan Hunter's novel are three-dimensional human beings, fighting that most vital of all battles, the battle to know, see, touch, and understand each other.

It is a first-rate piece of fiction.

Al Morgan, "Gulf Between Generations," in Lively Arts and Book Review, May 21, 1961, p. 28.

VICTOR P. HASS

Mothers and daughters who manage to speak to each other without the urge to kill are going to love this novel because it will make them feel so good.

If you can believe Evan Hunter, there can't be many mothers and daughters who enjoy what we like to think of as a normal, happy relationship. Indeed, he wasn't able to find any, and [**"Mothers and Daughters"**] is a ghastly parade of intolerably messed up people with tormented psyches and quivering ids.

Incidentally, the title is woefully incomplete. It would have been closer to the mark if it had been "Mothers and Daughters and Sons and Husbands and Assorted Slobs," or something of the sort. . . .

The novel covers 20 years up to about the present, and after three evenings of wallowing in it I was beginning to fear it would take me 20 years to finish it. Hunter goes into the television rat race, and the Broadway theater rat race, and the Hollywood rat race, and the rat race period.

He runs in some fine background stuff on World War II and the decade following it, but most of it is lost in the purgatory of his story.

One of these days Hunter is going to have to crawl out of that hole in which he has been operating. If the shock of seeing sunlight doesn't undo him, I think he is going to write a novel that doesn't leave you in need of a hot bath.

> Victor P. Hass, "Tormented Psyches and Quivering Ids," in Chicago Sunday Tribune Magazine of Books, May 28, 1961, p. 3.

ANNE KEEHAN

Although it gets off to a slow start, "Paper Dragon" does develop into a quite interesting story of a five-day plagiarism trial. As a novel, though, there are shortcomings which do not permit me to give unqualified praise, although the author is consistent within his own style of presentation. Evan Hunter is an extremely prolific writer who has turned out six novels under his own name, as well as many pseudonymous works and short stories. Perhaps the best known of these is the "Blackboard Jungle." As is perhaps typical with a consistent producer of fiction, acclaim has been spotty. Hunter's books have been appraised alternately as authentically powerful, melodramatic, cliché ridden. "Paper Dragon" has elements of the three.

Set in the New York pre-Christmas season, the direct action takes place in a courtroom on Foley Square. But in the manner of many other courtroom dramas, the character development takes place through flashback and, as the book develops, out of court. Particularly at first, the flashbacks are onerous and irritating; the author seems to be begging the question of creating three-dimensional characters by amassing mere detail. . . . Much of this is almost insufferably banal. Yet at the final analysis, the bombardment of verbiage has given "roots" to the principals. Some of the stream of consciousness work is excellent.

Although the plot appears at first to have predictable knights and villains, there is a skillful deepening of character and concomitant plot ambivalence. Arthur Constantine is the plaintiff, a man driven to fight the spectre which threatens his creative self. He has brought suit against James Driscoll who has published the lauded novel "Paper Dragon" which Arthur is fully convinced has been substantially pirated from his earlier play "Catchpole." The author has tackled a demanding theme for in a certain sense this is a novel about a novel. The "Paper Dragon" is at the same time Driscoll's (Constantine's?) creation, and Evan Hunter's. Throughout most of the book, the sense of artistic involvement is most keenly felt through Arthur Constantine. (pp. 259-60)

As the trial progresses, what might have been a matter of black and white takes on many hues of gray. Doubts and suspicions gather on all sides, as plaintiff and defendant seesaw back and forth on every aspect of the two works. The protagonists are all creatures of fate—as much so as Arthur Constantine. Sidney Brackman is the not so successful lawyer whose origins are a Lower East Side childhood and Harvard, who now waits anxiously on the answer of Chickie Brown, travel agent, fourteen years his junior, to a proposal of marriage. Jonah Willow, lawyer for the defense, whose very perfect marriage to Christie Dunseath has ended in failure, is weary of successful cases. There is James Driscoll, and his wife Ebie, whose tortured past holds the key to the resolution of the trial. In the web of these tangled lives lies a cross-section of the whole 20th century American experience. It is a frank, brutal, dog-eat-dog world. Unfortunately, passion has taken second place to sex in that world—and, particularly in the flashbacks, there are descriptions of sexual awareness which are nothing less than crude. But others are nothing less than poetic. . . .

Before Judge McIntyre produces his written decision, which comprises a sort of appendix to the book, the skeins of evidence and counterevidence have been disentangled. But, unlike an earlier book of his about a trial, "Matter of Conviction," Hunter has not tamely adjusted the plot to reach a happy ending. It ends bitterly as Arthur Constantine, beleaguered on all sides by script writers and directors, and faced with a fairly inevitable judicial decision, compromises his new play, and his fiercely defended artistic selfhood. (p. 260)

> Anne Keehan, in a review of "Paper Dragon," in Best Sellers, Vol. 26, No. 14, October 15, 1966, pp. 259-60.

KIRKUS SERVICE

Grant that the designation is ours rather than the author's or publisher's—[A Horse's Head] is a light comedy of male menopause. It would make a fine movie vehicle, motor-governed to Jack Lemmon's speed and it's lots lighter and brighter than Hunter's big sellers that went to Hollywood—The Blackboard Jungle and Strangers When We Meet. It's all about the killingly scheduled hours in the life of Mullaney who was standing on the corner of 14th Street down to his last few cents, with a hot tip on a horse called Jawbone and no place to raise the money for a bet, when along comes this limousine . . . Mullaney had been abducted by a Mafia-esque mob that needed a stand-in for a corpse. From there on it's hairsbreadth chase and escape through Manhattan and environs for over 48 hours. . . . [Mullaney] gets chased right into middle-age. You kind of hate to see him go.

> A review of "A Horse's Head," in Kirkus Service, Vol. XXXV, No. 8, April 15, 1967, p. 524.

FRANK N. JONES

[A Horse's Head] is a lively, fast-moving tale of big-time robbery in New York City recounted by the innocent victim of an abortive plot to spirit the loot out of the country with a genuine corpse. Instead of becoming the corpse, the narrator has two days of whirlwind chases and hair-breadth escapes from Newark to the lower East Side to the Bronx to the Aqueduct race track. . . . In the end, when the harassed narrator, who is in fact a book salesman on a year's gambling junket, gets trapped by the crooks, he tosses in his chips and goes back to the loving wife he deserted to make a killing with the big-time gamblers. He is a sort of poor man's James Bond character, and Mr.

Hunter combines features of O. Henry, James Thurber, James Joyce, and "The Man from U.N.C.L.E." This book has unusual literary quality for a light-hearted thriller.

*Frank N. Jones, in a review of "A Horse's Head,"
in* Library Journal, *Vol. 92, No. 16, September 15,
1967, p. 3056.*

KATHERINE GAUSS JACKSON

[*Last Summer* is a] slow-building but compelling story that begins innocently enough with an idyll involving three bright and funny young people—two teenage boys and a girl just turned sixteen—and a seagull on a summer-resort seashore island. The shocking end of that episode should prepare one a little, though not entirely, for what comes later when a new girl joins the three. It is an unforgettable—and highly sophisticated—story, for all its apparent simplicity, of young love and explosive violence, which tells as much about the moderately rich, pleasure-seeking, middle-class adult life that shaped them as it does about the young themselves. It's not a pretty story but once started on it I don't think anyone will leave it unfinished.

Katherine Gauss Jackson, in a review of "Last Summer," in Harper's Magazine, *Vol. 236, No. 1417, June, 1968, p. 94.*

JOHN D. FOREMAN

Novels of any real significance are rare these days. The role of the artist, or the poet, or the novelist as a social commentator doesn't seem to be appreciated. The most effective and the most trenchant comment has often been the least "acceptable" to the "establishment". "**Sons**" can be an important exception to this observation since it is a powerful novel that says something about the chronic problems that retard the pursuit of the American Dream. Evan Hunter, who has previously enlightened darkened corners of our society in such novels as "**The Blackboard Jungle,**" has now put together an outstanding new work that examines some of our problems as they have appeared to three generations of an American family. (pp. 185-86)

What we actually have in "**Sons**" is a panorama of major events of three decades of the 20th century as seen through the eyes of the young. Bert, the grandfather, faces the horrors of World War I, the hardships of post-war readjustment, the joys and trials of love, the injustice of the "Red Scare," and racial hatred. Will, the father, sees the glories, the fun-and-games, the pressures, the fears of a combat pilot in World War II, starts a race riot in Chicago while on leave, is strangely depressed when he leaves the challenge of combat and in a terrible moment of self-confrontation comes to the realization that he misses war. Wat, the son, goes to Yale, to Mississippi to try to assist voter registration, meets and falls in love with Dana Castelli in one of the most touching love stories of the year (told primarily through her letters), quits school and ends up in Vietnam.

Throughout this impressionistic mini-history of 20th century America the author catches the speech and character of the three generations of this century with great subtlety and captures the ethic and the ethos of the 'Teens, the Forties, and the Sixties with great skill.

Hunter does not try to solve the problems facing the three generations that his characters represent. What he does is to show the dilemmas of American life are viewed by one family with different experiences of the same problem. Like the proverbial blind men with the elephant, things seem much different to each. To be able, as Hunter does, to give us a look at both the blind men and the elephant is a major accomplishment. . . .

"**Sons**" is an excellent novel-essay for our times. Let us hope that it helps stay its own dire view of the future. (p. 186)

John D. Foreman, in a review of "Sons," in Best Sellers, *Vol. 29, No. 10, April 15, 1969, pp. 185-86.*

RICHARD P. BRICKNER

To read "**Sons**" is to read the just-published work of a serious novelist in a Joan Crawford movie. It covers thousands of miles and more than 60 years while unfolding the story of a 20th-century American family over three generations. But it is no mere rugged epic. It has an intellectual frame, like horn-rimmed glasses. Wat, Will and Bert Tyler take turns narrating the novel in the continuously repeated sequence of son, father, grandfather. This is meant to expose ironic twistings in the family line—and, or so one would have thought, differences between the narrators' voices. But the voices are one voice, and it belongs to one thousand writers. Its timbre is no less glib for being earnest as hell. . . .

The Tylers' qualities are glued onto them because Evan Hunter wishes to show us what he supposes to be "typical" representatives of this century's generations in America. But for the typical to be convincing, they must first be specific. Hunter's types are designed for symmetry, not humanity.

Evan Hunter has an industrious research-eye. He knows what a Wisconsin town looked like early in the century, or a Mississippi Air Force base in 1944. He knows how many different kinds of things work, and the names and locations of many kinds of institutions.

As if it were also the result of diligent geographical research, his heart, too, is in the right place, which is to say on virtually everybody's moral map. An occasional scene in "**Sons**" is peculiar or intense, and thus absorbing, but for the most part there is so little to ponder in the behavior of Hunter's types, and so little mood in the film-clips of their environments, that the book moves at a steadily swift clip right up to the typewriter-bell of its painlessly tragic ending. The Story of Twentieth Century America from the Woods of Wisconsin to the Jungles of Vietnam is too small a subject for a novel without characters or ideas.

Richard P. Brickner, "From the Woods of Wisconsin to the Jungles of Vietnam," in The New York Times Book Review, *September 28, 1969, p. 54.*

WILLIAM B. HILL, S. J.

Evan Hunter has a good sense of structure, he can write a lively scene with realistic dialogue, and he can keep a plot in motion; nevertheless, his "**Nobody Knew They Were There**" is curiously out of focus. It is a futuristic sort of book with only contemporary relevance and very poor projection, a realistic sort of parable that fails in realism though it has its moments of strength as a parable.

It starts off with a man about to blow up a bridge. He manages to project the image of fearless, practical secret agent but it is a fragile image. His co-conspirators, amateurish though they are, find him out rather quickly. They merely wanted him, in the time of the novel which is some few years from now, to kill the president and thus end oppression and war—the president is narrow, strong, and effective. The assassin thinks that the only practical way to kill the president will be to blow up his train at a point just outside the town where the plot is laid. Eventually, the blundering plotters discover that their soldier is not a professional killer but a lawyer who is using his partner's name, who knows nothing about dynamite or any other form of murder, but who wants revenge for the son he has lost in war. . . .

Nobody has very much significance in this story and the wildly improbable plot is annoying. The America of the time is supposedly almost a police state and still, nobody knew they were there. Mr. Hunter has many failings, though he writes better than many novelists who have used more promising materials.

> *William B. Hill, S. J., in a review of "Nobody Knew They Were There," in* Best Sellers, *Vol. 30, No. 24, March 15, 1971, p. 536.*

LOUIS D. MITCHELL

"Streets of Gold," by Evan Hunter, is a novel which encircles the character Ignazio Silvio di Palermo who is also called Iggie, Ike, Blind Ike, and Dwight Jamison. This blind pianist was born in Harlem in 1926, one fourth of a century after his Italian grandfather emigrated from a little southern Italian village. He came, like so many others, in order to make his way on and over New York City's "gold paved" streets. The grandfather of this briefly idolized pianist wanted to return home; but Grandfather never managed to journey home to his beloved and often-dreamed-of Italy. He married Teresa and what with the many years and all the babies—along with her family that naturally became his own—La Vicinanza evolved into a close-knit neighborhood in New York City.

Ike, born blind, grew up in a tight and lusty world. The old man's love, Ike's mother with all of her volatility, the large number of relatives, huge eating bouts weekly, the discovery of women, the excitement of music along with his natural talent, help dot the book with some interesting asides and pictures.

It is some while later that Ike discovers jazz, and somehow—by doggedness and a burning desire to play that art form—he forces his career onto the very famous 52nd street. A career with some good fortune and an appreciable amount of brilliance move Ike up among the greats of his time.

[The] "great American Dream" comes true beyond all of the most extensive dreams or expectations of his grandfather. It is all much too American and much too sentimental to take seriously, even for the author himself. It is, however, reported with as much sincerity as one who is faced with relating such a sugary plot can muster.

Yet the work suffers from other frailties than these very few. One supposes that with a bit of polishing of the language and the elimination of some of the raunchy details, one might get the entire soapy story onto a mid-afternoon serial with some detergent as a willing sponsor. . . .

Evan Hunter, who manages to use the novel form with more freedom than skill, belabors not only a somewhat fictitious tale but a sketchily biographical one. His style is crude rather than candid, harsh rather than honest, loose rather than lyrical. Upon declaring his own blindness the author skirts by many opportunities to observe some most profound states of being. He understates some of the attitudes towards blindness from both the sighted man's point of view as well as from his own. He does not seem to be able to handle the many ironies of blindness, the metaphysical twists, the double levels of meaning, the slanted truths and the imposing myths, the distant awkwardness of those who see and fear blindness, and the tender understanding that often intrudes into the somewhat remote state. He misinterprets—often misleads the reader concerning—the anxieties and the social intercourse that result from the condition of blindness when it comes face to face with the world which sees most and thinks little. Somehow he fails to investigate the loss of perception and the gain of insight that must accompany the transcendental nature of blindness.

I find the book arduous to read. It suffers from its inadequate message and a frightening delight in trying to titillate. I fear that the sexy sections are not even amusing to say nothing of their lack of attraction. Perhaps this book will sell, but so did Edgar Guest.

> *Louis D. Mitchell, in a review of "Streets of Gold," in* Best Sellers, *Vol. 34, No. 16, November 15, 1974, p. 369.*

JEAN M. WHITE

McBain's forte is his ability to evoke the atmosphere of big-city streets and the workaday world of a police squadroom. In *Bread* . . . , the familiar faces of the 87th Precinct are investigating arson in a fire that gutted a warehouse jammed with a half-million dollars worth of miniature wooden animals. This lilliputian menagerie leads to a tale of greed, double-dealing, a real estate firm and love nest in the black ghetto, and some very unpleasant characters and facts. . . . McBain not only solves an exciting case but, as always, captures a feeling for the problems of everyday law enforcement on the streets.

> *Jean M. White, "The Case of the Cornflake Crunch," in* Book World—The Washington Post, *November 17, 1974, p. 4.**

THE NEW YORKER

["**Streets of Gold**" is a] pop epic that takes the form of a family history and autobiography by Iggie Di Palermo—in later years known as Dwight Jamison—a blind jazz pianist who rises from a New York slum and attains stardom briefly in the fifties and sixties. . . . At times, Iggie speaks of the confusion of someone who has exchanged his ethnic past for an Anglicized "American" illusion; since Mr. Hunter is also of Italian blood, the book can be read as a disguised search for the author's own roots. The scenes of tenement life are warm, witty, and accurate-sounding, yet tend toward coarseness and violence. . . . When we come to Iggie's decline, which hinges on a bit of standard adultery, the familiarity of his story becomes really depressing. Yet much of the book has a definite personal stamp, and its evocations of jazz—of a "jump into water that's icy cold and deep"—are pleasant.

> *A review of "Streets of Gold," in* The New Yorker, *Vol. L, No. 47, January 13, 1975, pp. 90, 93.*

JAMES R. FRAKES

The country may not be exactly drooling with hunger for another novel about "Westering," but Evan Hunter, in his 17th book ["**The Chisholms**"], evokes some freshness from the tritest materials and focuses our concern on complex, often perverse, human beings rather than on the vacuous panoramic vista that too often dominates this genre. When the Chisholm family pull out of barren Virginia in 1844 and head doggedly for the promised land, they do not automatically become archetypes, rendered featureless by the author's grim determination to make some Big Statement about the pioneering spirit of our hardy forefathers or how Noble Women Helped to Win the West. (p. 42)

This family may be the center of the action, but the action itself is familiar if not hackneyed by now. "**The Chisholms**" contains just about every standard ingredient of frontier narrative: a buffalo stampede, river crossings, Indian raids, saloon whores, horse theft, hanging of horse thief, scalping, childbirth, gang rape, seductions, murder, tongue removal by knife. But Mr. Hunter still plays fair by judicious proportioning: the buffalo gallop for only a few paragraphs, the gang rape occupies only four sentences, the saloon whores are only local-color bits. The stripped narrative line is one of Hunter's prime virtues, so that when he decides *not* to cut short an action—the harrowing Indian raid on the isolated family, the tonal mixture of comedy and horror when the rather charming horse thief is hanged—he has truly earned his license. (p. 43)

> *James R. Frakes, in a review of "The Chisholms,"*
> *in* The New York Times Book Review, *September*
> *19, 1976, pp. 42-3.*

JULIAN SYMONS

The first of Ed McBain's 87th Precinct stories, "**Cop Hater**," appeared in 1956, and for a while he published two or three tales about the Precinct each year. . . . Mr. McBain did not invent the police procedural story, in which the investigation of a crime is shown as it is handled by a police department, but his books are among the best in the field.

This is chiefly because Mr. McBain has succeeded in making his detectives distinct individuals. Steve Carella, who appears most frequently, marries the beautiful deaf and mute Teddy in "**Cop Hater**." Cotton Hawes, who has a white streak in his hair and was named for Cotton Mather, plays the feminine field; Meyer Meyer had a father who thought the double name would be a good Jewish joke; Arthur Brown is that color; Bert Kling is young and impressionable. The author skillfully avoids making them stereotypes, and he avoids also the pietism about the police that marred John Creasey's Gideon books by introducing some rogue cops like the sadistic Roger Havilland (killed off in an early book), Andy Parker and the fat, unsavory Ollie Weeks of the 83rd Precinct.

Though Mr. McBain offers a reasonably balanced view of what policemen are like, he is an entertainer, not a sociologist or social reformer. Any idea that these stories approach realistic accounts of police activity is well off the mark. One hopes that no detective's wife is as often in danger as beautiful Teddy Carella, and Mr. McBain feels the need to bring the private lives of several detectives rather intrusively into the books. No doubt as an entertainer he is perfectly right. . . .

The 87th Precinct stories also offer the pleasures of much crisp, credible dialogue that is never too smart for its own good or

our enjoyment, and some alert observation about the contemporary scene. "**Calypso**" exemplifies this aspect of the saga. A calypso singer is shot to death after a concert, a hooker is shot to death on the same night in another part of the city. . . . We know that the two crimes are connected, but Carella and Meyer are ignorant of it until they get this information from Ballistics. Perhaps half the McBain books offer a detective problem to be solved, but in this story we know all the things that Carella and Meyer are trying to find out.

We also understand early on that the plot's basic concern will be with sadomasochistic pornography, and its expression in actual rather than make-believe violence. . . . [Without] explicit moralizing, [McBain] shows what appalling things can happen when sadomasochistic games go wrong.

"**Calypso**" is admirable in its concision, in the sharpness of some images, in its awareness of contemporary language and attitudes. . . . This is a story that will not suit those who want a cozy read, and the plot has improbabilities that put it into the second class of 87th Precinct books, but the narrative grip and storytelling zest are still there. To have maintained those qualities through a series of more than 30 books, so that we are still eager to read a new story about Carella and his colleagues, is Ed McBain's principal achievement.

> *Julian Symons, "Procedure at the 87th Precinct,"*
> *in* The New York Times Book Review, *May 6, 1979,*
> *p. 12.*

JEAN M. WHITE

[*Ghosts*], Ed McBain's latest 87th Precinct mystery (the 34th), has a new twist for the many fans of this long-running police procedural series. Can you imagine Steve Carella, the hard-nosed cop experienced in the routine of tracking down criminals in a grimy big city, going off with a psychic to a New England haunted house? . . .

The spooky scene in an abandoned summer cottage (yes, Carella does see ghosts) is scary enough. Yet, it's a strange interlude. Carella and McBain are much more convincing on their big-city turf. In the end, it's slogging police work that turns up to the clues to the killer. *Ghosts* is middle-grade McBain but far superior to last year's *Calypso* with its kinky sadism.

> *Jean M. White, in a review of "Ghosts," in* Book
> World—The Washington Post, *May 18, 1980, p. 6.*

STANLEY ELLIN

There's a high degree of magic in a novel when you now and then find yourself so acutely frustrated by the self-destructive behavior of a character in it that you want to grab him by the shoulders and shake sense into him. Or her. Nor is the frustration eased by your awareness that of course this behavior stems from the very nature of the character and has a terrible inevitability.

Evan Hunter's *Love, Dad* has that magic. A long book but never a dull one, it deals with a segment of comparatively recent social history—the upsurge of youth against the parental Establishment under the impetus of the Vietnam conflict—which even in retrospect has the power to hit a good many nerves.

The focus throughout is split between two members of a single family, the Crofts: father Jamie and teen-age daughter Lissie.

The period covered extends from 1968 through 1971, but the final chapter carries us in one leap to the present and provides us with a marvelously ironic epiphany toward which the story has been moving from its opening lines. . . .

The novel's title is very much part of the story. Jamie Croft, an attractive and talented young man, quintessentially middle-class with an eye toward upward mobility, marries a girl just out of school. She envisions a partnership where each will move into successful careers and, when the logical time comes, will share in the bringing up of a family. She conceives a child almost immediately however, and that, to all intents and purposes, destroys her dream, turns her into a resentful housewife who never forgives her husband for this betrayal and for the huge success he does eventually achieve as a photographer-journalist. . . .

Jamie, however, with a fund of affection to offer, finds an outlet for it in daughter Lissie. Is there a suggestion of incest here as the girl emerges into her late teens? Hunter touches on this Freudian cliche and wisely moves on, choosing to deal only with what Jamie knows about himself, never mind the unverifiable unconscious. As for golden girl Lissie, we first come to know her in depth and breadth in that troubled year 1968 when she's about to graduate from one of those traditionalist boarding schools which, rowing hard against the prevailing current, is still trying to maintain some semblance of scholastic and moral standards.

From there on, through alternating views of father and daughter, we watch Jamie more and more futilely struggle to impose on his daughter his concern for her, while Lissie inches her way into the disorderly ranks of that youthful host now raising its psychedelic banners on the far side of the generation gap. The transition from golden girl to hippie, partly accidental, partly wilful, is very soon complete, and what Jamie finds himself contending with is a daughter on the verge of maturity who is totally immature, self-righteous, disingenuously exploitative and, like the company she keeps, stoned more often than not. Sliding out of daddy's reach, she makes the requisite hegira from Amsterdam southeast through Europe and Asia to India, promised land of cheap and plentiful pot and hash, circles back to her homeland—Jamie's money paying her way—to take up with male company that brutally exploits her, all the while followed by her father's pathetic letters making frightened inquiries, assuring unshakable love.

That love, turned against him, becomes her ultimate weapon in her undeclared war on him; her ultimate triumph comes when Jamie, having at last found the right woman to share life with, divorces his wife, and Lissie can now impale him with the charge that he has cruelly betrayed her mother.

So in wholly human terms we have here a microcosm of a whole period of social history now fast receding into the distance, as Hunter's last chapter sharply reminds us. It all adds up to an exceptionally rewarding and entertaining novel.

Stanley Ellin, "*Daughter of the Revolution*," in Book World—The Washington Post, *March 29, 1981, p. 5.*

IVAN GOLD

Born "Lombino" in New York City in 1926, Evan Hunter, under that pseudonym and the further *noms de plume* of Hunt Collins, Richard Marsten and Ed McBain, has published upward of 60 books of fiction since 1952, which should make him one of America's most prolific authors over the past 30 years. Lately, without greatly affecting production, Marsten and Collins have dropped from the picture. But in the banner year of 1956, all four were represented, McBain weighing in with three thrillers and Hunter contributing a collection of stories as well as a novel, for a total of seven full-length works.

One could more easily accept this kind of productivity from pornographers or pulp writers, but Mr. Hunter is neither. A number of his books, notably **"Last Summer"** (1968), have been well received, and his 1954 novel, **"The Blackboard Jungle,"** was turned into what has become something of a film classic. (A master of swift, smart dialogue, Mr. Hunter himself penned the screenplay for Hitchcock's 1963 movie, "The Birds.") While his fiction has been called "aggressively topical," he has also been praised over the years for his professionalism and versatility, and Ed McBain's **"87th Precinct Series"** of gory detective novels has a loyal following. It does not appear, therefore, that awesome speed of composition *necessarily* entails a sacrifice in quality; and (here to let the matter rest) the judgment that some of his books are better than others can also be passed on the perpetrator of only 10 novels, or a mere five, or a pair.

In **"Love, Dad,"** however, something seems to have come loose at the seams. As the story opens, professional photographer and doting father Jamie Croft is mounting a retrospective of his daughter Lissie's life, in his own living room, in celebration of her 17th birthday. . . . Melissa (or Lissie) discovers him at the task, is touched, and they have a tearful loving scene. The year is 1968; the family has moved recently to a converted sawmill in Connecticut, largely to satisfy Jamie's wife, Connie. It soon becomes apparent that Jamie is not overly fond of Connie, in part because she speaks in a "Vassar voice," and uses obscenities without much élan. But there are more substantial difficulties—their conjugal relations are in a poor way, and in one of the many bits of sexual business Mr. Hunter is adept at rendering, Jamie brings himself imaginatively to climax, following a longish scene in which his wife seems to offer, then withdraws, her favors.

By the time 1971 rolls around, Jamie has abandoned Connie for a beautiful young flutist named Joanna Berkowitz who appears to be afflicted, or blessed, with multiple personalities (one, for example, is "Jewish," another is "musical"), and who seems to want to talk interminably about her various lives, or about, less charitably, the sundry elements of her character the author has failed to knit together. Also by 1971 Jamie will have finally renounced Melissa, his beloved and only child, who has grown into a creature of consummate obnoxiousness: liar, fishwife, thief, addict, a will-o'-the-wisp moral cipher (self-described as a "hippie"). Mr. Hunter appears to want us to hold "the sixties" responsible for her behavior, rather than her upbringing or character. . . .

Along the way, Mr. Hunter, through Jamie, shares his thoughts on literary cocktail parties on the Vineyard, takes swipes at shrinks, digs away at the flabbiness of suburban living; none of the observations seem particularly off the mark, but they're like items crammed into an overflowing portmanteau. There is, as the title implies, an epistolary novel, and a good one, scattered through the book; there is a short book (if we need yet another) analyzing "the sixties"; a thoughtful novella on a jaded marriage; an essay (perhaps to be called "So It Goes") on the odd inequities of the literary life in America; there is an Asian travelogue . . . ; even a still-born detective novel.

"Love, Dad," in sum, is thin gruel, a never-boring hybrid of genres. Mr. Hunter is a serious and honorable writer trying to entertain us, and also trying to tell us, now and again, some useful things about our lives. If his enterprise has here sprung a leak, we should not, on the evidence, have to wait long for repairs.

Ivan Gold, "Family Relations," in The New York Times Book Review, *May 10, 1981, p. 14.*

JEAN M. WHITE

[*Heat*] demonstrates why McBain, even when he is not at the top of his form, still writes the best American police procedurals.

The McBain hallmarks are there: dogged police leg-work, crisp dialogue, Q. and A. transcripts with the ring of authenticity, detectives who have become human beings with personal lives, victims and murderers lifted full-bodied from big-city streets, and sinewy, taut prose.

In *Heat,* Steve Carella, the quiet, steady man of the 87th Precinct regulars, investigates the apparent suicide of an alcoholic commercial artist. But Carella is bothered by some nagging questions. Why did the victim turn off the air-conditioner in the midst of a sweltering heat wave? Why did a man who had a phobia against swallowing pills decide to end his life by downing sleeping pills?. . .

Carella's case is intriguing with an odd coupling of two unlikely suspects. But the ex-con ploy seems thrown in for contrived suspense. Never mind. McBain still is fresh with his observations, and his prose is as sturdy as ever. He knows that a good police-procedural novel is more than a hodgepodge of cases lifted from the police blotter.

Jean M. White, in a review of "Heat," in Book World—The Washington Post, *December 20, 1981, p. 8.*

BILL GREENWELL

A maudlin score of violins has maundered down the scale. 'Well then,' admits the officer in charge, 'the airplanes got him.' But our hero has another theory: 'Ohhh no. It wasn't the airplanes. It was Beauty killed the Beast.' And thus the last, melancholy seconds of *King Kong* surrender to the credits. Ed McBain, effortless progenitor of so many mutilations, amputations, and general spiller of the common corpuscles, is up to the third in his new sequence of novels [with *Beauty and the Beast*]. They are 'based' upon fairytales (the last two were *Goldilocks* and *Rumpelstiltskin*), although most of the original plot is cheerily jettisoned. . . . But if the Beast unfairly cops it in *King Kong,* Beauty is given shorter shrift in the McBain— she's bound hand and foot with wire hangers, doused in gasoline on a deserted beach, and burned to a quick crisp.

Beauty and the Beast pushes me to the miserable conclusion that McBain has lost his touch. To my astonishment, more than 50 of the maestro's efforts are spilling off my shelves. But his shift away from the 87th precinct has led him out of the whydunnits into the whodunnits. In particular, it has brought in a new hero, the vapid Matthew Hope, an attorney whose innermost secrets we are forced to share because he's our narrator. Carella of the 87th had the advantage of being one among many. Here, Ed McBain is squandering his energy, and that wry commentary, always just the right side of parody, is a shadow of its former self.

Bill Greenwell, "Tall Tales," in New Statesman, *Vol. 103, No. 2674, June 25, 1982, p. 23.**

HELEN ROGAN

Evan Hunter writes the kind of reliable engrossing novel that is a welcome sight in the paperback racks at airports and bus stations. The police procedurals he's written under the name of Ed McBain, and his popular novels, which include *The Blackboard Jungle, Strangers When We Meet,* and *Love, Dad,* are sometimes slick or overwritten, but always readable. In *Far From the Sea,* he's done it again, but he's chosen to work with a most dismal set of circumstances. . . .

Hunter's interest is primarily in his characters—their reflexes, preoccupations, foibles. Instead of dumping stereotypes into a situation, he shows how the small details animate people: the relatives gathered every day outside the intensive care unit obsessively discussing soap operas; the dying man worrying about his tax return; and, most poignantly, David Weber, struggling to be frank with his wife despite the distance and her answering machine, reliving his randy youth as he feeds his father ice chips, and wearily negotiating with non-English-speaking room service for a whiskey and soda. By the end, when David begins to shed the cynicism with which he's protected himself for years, the reader wishes him well, and that's to Mr. Hunter's credit.

Helen Rogan, in a review of "Far from the Sea," in Harper's, *Vol. 26, No. 1592, January, 1983, p. 76.*

RICHARD FREEDMAN

Hooked into a cat's cradle of life-sustaining apparatus, few of us today can hope, with Keats, for an "easeful Death" in which we "cease upon the midnight with no pain"—to say nothing of the humiliation of having tubes jammed into every available orifice. So thanks to the marvels of modern medical science, it takes Morris Weber, the moribund central figure of Evan Hunter's 17th novel ["**Far From the Sea**"], a full Monday-to-Friday workweek in which to die, following a colostomy. And thanks to Evan Hunter's keen reportorial eye, we're with him all the way, or at least with his son, David, who has flown down to Miami from his New York law practice to be at his father's bedside.

Approaching 50, David himself is nearly tired to death. He has just lost an important case. Relations with his wife, Molly, have been strained ever since their 15-year-old son was killed in a car crash on the great Bicentennial Fourth of July weekend.

Even the 600-room Miami Beach hotel he checks into is practically at death's door. Few of the rooms are occupied; the air conditioning has conked out, and the incompetent staff lives in the wan hope of a transfusion of South American tourists.

But the 82-year-old Morris Weber, inveterate punster, perennial business failure, Bronx Lothario—in short, the classic Jewish *luftmensch*—is literally dying. He is simply not rallying properly after his operation, and the doctors don't quite know what to do about it.

Although it's no "Death of Ivan Ilyich," "**Far From the Sea**" is very eloquent about the way in which we leave this world. Always a joker, old Morris keeps making dreadful puns to the last; he hallucinates that the hospital can't wait to sell his effects at a tidy profit; and conveniently, maddeningly, but mercifully, he forgets that his grandson was killed five years ago. David in turn alternates between profound love for his father and a heartfelt desire that if he is going to die, he should get it over with as soon as possible.

The novel is at its best, in short, when it deals with the conflicting emotions and harrowing duties of the soon to be bereaved: tracking down an elusive doctor to get a straight prognosis, wondering if the nurse will see fit to admit him a few minutes before official visiting hours, feeling guilty about cravings for food, drink, sex and sun on what is, in its morbid way, really an unexpected vacation for him from everyday cares and commitments.

Although father and son are close to the sea that languidly licks at Miami Beach in this torrid June, both are far from the mythic sea of David's remembered boyhood, when the family would journey by subway to Coney Island. Soon his father will lie "full fathom five." But not much that is rich and strange by way of transformation can be expected to emerge from this unsparing and personally felt novel of how we go about the business of dying in the late 20th century.

> Richard Freedman, "Father and Son," in The New York Times Book Review, January 16, 1983, p. 12.

JONATHAN COLEMAN

I must be one of the unfortunate few who have never read Ed McBain before. He has written more than 60 novels—including those under his real name, Evan Hunter—and that is clearly impressive in itself. But more important is the fact that his work is good and entertaining—something I am pleased finally to discover for myself. . . .

[In "Ice"], "the Eight-Seven" must solve the murders of Sally Anderson, a dancer in a hit musical; Paco Lopez, a teen-age cocaine dealer; and Marvin Edelman, a precious-gems dealer, among other things. There is only one common link in these cases: A .38 Smith & Wesson is the murder weapon. As Detectives Carella, Meyer, Kling et al. begin looking for other connections, one is impressed by their diligence in tracking down leads and asking tough questions. Equally impressive is the crash course one receives about the procedures, minutiae and language of police work. . . .

There are some things in the book that are too obvious, like the connection between Sally and Paco. But what the novel occasionally lacks in mystery is more than compensated for by its razor-sharp dialogue and its exciting climax, as well as the many things one learns about the drug trade and its practitioners, the theater business ("ice" refers to a lucrative ticket scam) and the importance of informers.

> Jonathan Coleman, "Assorted Murders," in The New York Times Book Review, May 1, 1983, pp. 14, 19.*

ROBIN W. WINKS

[Ice] is grim stuff, as McBain usually is. By now McBain has the 87th Precinct down pat: he could probably write in his sleep. But then Arnold Bennett wrote a good bit of his prose in his sleep too, and if a writer really knows his craft, there surely comes a time when it is possible to coast. Ice begins with a seemingly senseless killing on a New York City street— not a novel idea—and moves through the underworlds of drugs, diamond smuggling, and a scam involving theater tickets, with the usual patented McBain ease, in which real people sound like real people. In the classic mystery every detail counts, or may be assumed to count; with McBain, as with real life, there is an enormous amount of what proves to be truly irrelevant detail, and none of it seems like padding. . . . We are told that Ice is a major work that transcends the genre of crime fiction, doing for crime novels what John Le Carré has done for espionage fiction. This is nonsense: the gap between Ice and The Little Drummer Girl, Le Carré's truly transcendent novel, is enormous. But taken on its own terms, Ice is just fine. . . .

> Robin W. Winks, in a review of "Ice," in The New Republic, Vol. 188, No. 23, June 13, 1983, p. 36.

DAVID LEHMAN

Ed McBain is an acknowledged master of the detective subgenre known as the police procedural, and in "Ice" he returns us to the Detective Division of the 87th Precinct in Isola. That imaginary metropolis bears more than a passing resemblance to New York City, McBain's hometown. Like its more than two dozen predecessors in the 87th Precinct series, "Ice" features a conglomerate hero—in this case, officers Carella, Meyer, Kling and Brown. Their ethnic identities correspond, in one of McBain's many comic asides, to the sandwiches they eat for lunch: sausage and peppers on a roll, hot pastrami on rye, tuna on white and ham on toasted whole wheat, respectively.

Three apparently unrelated homicides put this quartet's sleuthing to the test. A dancer in a hit musical, a cocaine-pushing punk and a middle-aged diamond merchant have all been "iced" the same gruesome way, with the same weapon. Searching for the missing links, the cops fan out through a variety of urban enclaves, from the ghetto to the theater district, from high-rent high-rises to "Ramsey University," en route to a denouement that gratifies our desire for plausible surprises. McBain aims, he has said, at "a tone of clinical verity." With his adroit handling of police routine—ballistics reports, laboratory analyses, bureaucratic snags—he has little trouble getting us to suspend our disbelief.

McBain's razor-sharp prose creates some stunning effects. Consider the multiple meanings of "ice" that he brings into play. Besides the murders, there is the ice of winter, the "ice" of ill-gotten jewelry, hidden in a tray of ice cubes, and of actors "doing ice," a particularly profitable form of ticket scalping. ("A hot show *always* generates ice," a producer explains.) With the proceeds, they indulge an appetite for "snow," or cocaine. In the precinct of McBain's imagination, winter kills. Where there's ice, there's gunfire as well.

Readers spoiled by "Ice" are likely to find McBain's other new novel, "Beauty and the Beast," something of a letdown. Attorney Matthew Hope, whose previous exploits are told in "Goldilocks" and "Rumpelstiltskin," seems destined to solve murderous puzzles that spring from sinister, modern-dress versions of fairy tales. Beauty makes a quick exit from the script. Shortly after she files assault-and-battery charges against her husband, the charred remains of Michelle Harper's "carved from alabaster" body turn up on Whisper Key beach. George Harper, the most obvious suspect, is an ugly hulk of a man. He is also "the color of coal, the color of midnight, the color of mourning," and Hope's footwork on Harper's behalf leads to a clandestine black and white social organization that calls itself The Oreo. The writing here is solidly competent rather than inspired—perhaps because Florida's Gulf Coast, where

Hope operates, seems insufficiently congenial to McBain's urban sensibility. (pp. 70-1)

David Lehman, "Murder Most Entertaining," in Newsweek, Vol. CII, No. 2, July 11, 1983, pp. 70-1.*

PUBLISHERS WEEKLY

[In **"The McBain Brief"**] the creator of the famed 87th Precinct gives us eight stories with policemen. . . . Also included are an amusing story about a con man who gets conned (**"Hot Cars"**), a private eye mini-whodunit (**"Death Flight"**) and a miscellany of other amusements, including a case of infanticide and one of fratricide. Mostly, the violence is *by* men *against* women, but there's one ruthless female here. The stories vary in merit—a few are too predictable—but all entertain. The reader is drawn in from the start, and the pages seem to turn themselves.

A review of "The McBain Brief," in Publishers Weekly, Vol. 224, No. 3, July 15, 1983, p. 43.

JOHN L. STUBING

Through the years, Evan Hunter has written stories under a number of pseudonyms, including those of Richard Marsten and Hunt Collins. His most familiar *nom de plume,* is, however, that of Ed McBain. *The McBain Brief* is a collection of his short stories which were published at various times under other names. . . .

This book isn't just an excuse for McBain to clean out his closets, though; it is a museum of an author in transition. Arranged in no apparent order, the stories reveal a writer in search of his style. . . .

Occasionally, the rough edges show. As with any compilation, there is trash lurking among the treasure. . . . Some experiments simply don't work, while others display flashes of brilliance which eventually were translated to a commercially successful technique.

Through these experiments, McBain evolved into the master of the police procedural. With these tales, he developed his art. It was in these stories his characters lost their innocence, and no fan of McBain's will be satisfied without reading the **Brief**.

John L. Stubing, in a review of "The McBain Brief," in Best Sellers, Vol. 43, No. 8, November, 1983, p. 289.

PUBLISHERS WEEKLY

McBain's new mystery [*Jack and the Beanstalk*] is another in the series featuring Florida lawyer Matthew Hope, a strong rival of the author's popular 87th precinct police series. Based on another macabre fairy tale burlesque, it is the story of Hope's young client, slain Jack McKinney, and his stolen fortune. And it's racy, intricate, well-crafted suspense.

A review of "Jack and the Beanstalk," in Publishers Weekly, Vol. 225, No. 5, February 3, 1984, p. 398.

PUBLISHERS WEEKLY

[In *Lizzie*] Hunter has . . . produced a hybrid work that is not successful as a novel and only partially convincing as a detective story. Using the actual transcripts of the inquest and Lizzie Borden's trial in August 1892, he intersperses fictional flashbacks to Lizzie's trip to Europe two years previously, and comes up with a provocative theory to explain both the motivations and circumstances under which the murders were committed. The contrast between the actual and the invented material is so acute, however, that it is almost like reading two different books that do not fuse. Hunter's account of Lizzie's trip abroad amounts to a travelogue of London, Paris and the Riviera, full of local color and period details but written in the style of a campy gothic novel. This florid prose jars with the flat, factual nature of the inquest and trial testimony, retarding dramatic tension until the very last scenes. Hunter's theory does explain why the actual murder weapon and blood-spattered clothes were not found, but this in itself is not enough to infuse life into a tepid narrative. (p. 66)

A review of "Lizzie," in Publishers Weekly, Vol. 225, No. 12, March 23, 1984, pp. 65-6.

EUGENE A. DOOLEY, O.M.I.

[*Lizzie*] is a retelling of the famous murder trial of a spinster girl of New England whose name has become immortalized in the four-line bit,

> Lizzie Borden took an ax,
> And gave her mother forty whacks.
> When she saw what she had done
> She gave her father forty-one.

It would be wise to read the very last chapter of this bulky novel before embarking on page one, because Hunter admits he has mixed facts with lots of fiction. A reader may easily become befuddled at the way the story is told. The novel cleverly alternates the whole story between Fall River, Massachusetts (where the two murders were perpetrated in the year 1892) and several swanky European cities where Lizzie is supposed to have sojourned. It was there, Hunter opines, that she became sexually involved with a pretty lesbian girl whose bedroom exploits and hedonistic philosophy are graphically narrated. Hunter has splendid skill at portraying people, times and events. In the questioning of witnesses for the trial, he has used even some of the original court documents. (pp. 88-9)

Eugene A. Dooley, O.M.I., in a review of "Lizzie," in Best Sellers, Vol. 44, No. 3, June, 1984, pp. 88-9.

D. V. O'BRIEN

The mystery novel has changed in many ways since 1900, and this Matthew Hope adventure [*Jack and the Beanstalk*] is a *tour de force* of the new genre. Hope, who has appeared in three earlier novels, is a long way from the omniscient Sherlock, and even from the suave, self-assured sleuths of the Forties. He is a lawyer with apparently an indifferent practice, and his former wife despises him. . . . He can't fight too well, and even an old country lawyer with diploma-mill credentials outfoxes him. Worst of all, he can't determine whodunnit without turning to the detective who also has to teach him that Marquis of Queensbury rules of pugilism are as archaic as his professional and romantic methods. Indeed, the conflict in the book is between theory and practice, between the world as he was told it would be and the way, to his discomfiture, he now finds it. . . .

There's a murder or two, and we don't know the perpetrator or the purpose. That's certainly standard fare, but in the context of the author's artful dodges from the stereotypes of the genre, even these elements tend to unsettle us, so that we share the narrator's sense of irony and cynicism. Yet, where there's Hope, there's hope.

> *D. V. O'Brien, in a review of "Jack and the Beanstalk," in* Best Sellers, *Vol. 44, No. 3, June, 1984, p. 93.*

CHARLES MICHAUD

[In *Lizzie*] Hunter presents his case in chapters that alternate between the imagined story of Lizzie's seduction by a hedonistic English lady during an 1890 European tour and the almost verbatim court record of her 1893 murder trial. This approach is not always satisfying and at times seems a curious cross between a court stenographer's emotionally uninvolving transcript and a sexed-up version of Henry James. Yet the portrait of Lizzie that emerges is fascinating, ultimately sympathetic: a murderess yes, but the victim of the repression and sexual exploitation of her time.

> *Charles Michaud, in a review of "Lizzie," in* Library Journal, *Vol. 109, No. 11, June 15, 1984, p. 1252.*

JOHN HOUSE

[The case of Lizzie Borden] has inspired more than a dozen books, several plays, two television treatments, even a ballet. Like many of those before him who have been fascinated by the case, Evan Hunter [in **"Lizzie"**] comes away from his research with a theory, a handful of facts rounded out with supposition and the zealous conviction of the amateur sleuth who's cracked an elusive nut. Widely known for the police novels he has written as Ed McBain, Mr. Hunter is a keen analyst of criminal motive, and his reconstruction in the last chapter of Lizzie Borden's actions on the day her parents were slain is an intriguing piece of speculative history that makes for the best reading in the book. Unfortunately, the platform on which that final scenario is played seems rather wobbly at times. . . . The fictional chapters, which alternate with the factual, send Lizzie on a trip to Europe, where she is seduced into a lesbian affair by a woman she meets in London. Curiously, these episodes, based entirely on conjecture, are more important than those rooted in fact when it comes to shoring up Mr. Hunter's ultimate argument. He has a good punch line, but the way to it is long and murky. **"Lizzie"** is less a well-built suspense novel than a provocative speculation on one of America's most notorious crimes.

> *John House, in a review of "Lizzie," in* The New York Times Book Review, *June 17, 1984, p. 20.*

Molly Keane

1904-

(Born Mary Nesta Skrine; has also written under pseudonym of M. J. Farrell) Irish novelist and dramatist.

Keane's strongly atmospheric novels recreate the Anglo-Irish world of family estates and fox-hunts in which she grew up. Her attitude toward this world has been described as one of "affectionate malice." She does not hesitate to reveal the foibles of the squabbling families she portrays in a style which sometimes verges on black comedy, but she does so with compassion, usually succeeding in eliciting sympathy even for her unattractive characters. Keane's love of Ireland is revealed in her enthusiastic descriptions of the Irish countryside, especially in the novel *Mad Puppetstown* (1932), in which two cousins choose to leave a comfortable life in England to return to their decaying childhood home in Ireland. Critics note that although Keane rarely varies her setting from the Irish country estate and repeatedly uses the popular theme of the decline of the landed gentry, she makes her novels appear fresh and original.

Keane's writing career, which began in the late 1920s, was interrupted by a long hiatus following the death of her husband. Her early works, which include the plays *Spring Meeting* (1938) and *Treasure Hunt* (1950) as well as several novels, were published under a pseudonym. Keane's return to writing in the 1980s with *Good Behaviour* (1981) and *Time after Time* (1983) marked her first publications under her own name.

(See also *Contemporary Authors*, Vol. 108.)

Courtesy of André Deutsch

THE TIMES LITERARY SUPPLEMENT

M. J. Farrell's *Young Entry* . . . , presumably a first novel, has just those qualities that are more often found in books written by novelists of long experience. The characters, in the first place, are allowed to explain themselves instead of being explained by a process of *oratio recta* on the author's part; and, secondly, the dialogue springs naturally from the action and is not merely a decorative appendage of it. Miss Farrell has two admirable backgrounds, Ireland and the hunting-field, for her book, which is, in the last analysis, a character study of two "country girls," Prudence and Peter. Both are modern, but sanely and not tiresomely so; and one of Miss Farrell's greatest triumphs is the way she manages to give a vivid sense of their characters through stray snatches of their conversation. The dialogue of modern young people has been a great trial to novelists, who in their efforts to reproduce it have either over-elaborated or else reduced it to a series of more or less improper monosyllables. Miss Farrell has caught the exact tone of it—laconic, abrupt, illuminating, occasionally obscure owing to the quick, unheralded jump from subject to subject, and occasionally affectionate. In this cunningly shaped mirror the movements and features of Peter and Prudence are perfectly reflected. The reader can, as it were, sit back in his chair and understand without effort the similarity and the difference between them. . . .

Because Peter and Prudence are so lovable and interesting the reader will the more resent Miss Farrell's unnecessary attempt to drag a supernatural element into the book. The suicide of the cook and haunting of the house are out of key with the rest of the novel—Miss Farrell's one lapse into amateurism—and he can be assured that in her descriptions of hunting, in her dialogue and, above all, in Prudence and Peter she has provided more excellence than anyone has the right to expect in three average first novels put together.

A review of 'Young Entry," in The Times Literary Supplement, No. 1364, March 22, 1928, p. 213.

MARGERY LATIMER

You just can't be horrid and superior about [*Young Entry*] even though salmon fishing and fox shooting mean nothing in your life—and never will. The spirit of the young author is in every sentence, in the stiff phrasing, in the clichés and stock characters and the rough, eager form of the novel. You can't help liking her aliveness, which is neither deep nor lyrical but a surface quality of health and sturdiness. You smell good things all through the story; you smell the people and their excellent clothes and the clean, cool air. . . .

All the time the two girls, Prudence and Peter, are not very different from the healthy girls who used to be in "The Youth's Companion," always making trouble for their elders and then saving the day in some fashion at the very end. But you have to like these girls anyway, you like the way they talk to their dogs and horses. . . . The eyes of all the characters are turned outward on the land, the hounds, rabbit holes, a good chunk of cake, foxes. Affection is not inhibited and can be expressed by swearing airily, eating a good meal together, riding hard, calling each other Puppy. . . .

But you cannot read this book without thinking of all people as innocent manifestations of their backgrounds, no matter how amused and enlivened Miss Farrell intends you to be. Her intention is to write a simple story from the outside. Her main interest is the friendship between Prudence and Peter, their engagements, the separation, and then the return to their old gay manner. These people are all practical, all happy in their small world. They express themselves completely and joyfully in hunting and fishing and eating. . . .

The author is usually bad when she tries to write about her characters—this for example: "Her very ordinary, jade-green frock set off to perfection the creamy thickness of her skin." But when she lets them talk it is always amusing: "I hate that cloth, Puppy—all flecks; looks as if the hens had been peckin' it." Or Lady Mavis: "My dear, when I think how different things were in my day! They [men] literally crawled. Yes, with boxes of chocolate, like worms."

> *Margery Latimer, "Young Folks," in* New York Herald Tribune Books, *March 10, 1929, p. 18.*

THE TIMES LITERARY SUPPLEMENT

The modern novel of sex and cocktails grafted on to the old-fashioned Irish tale of foxhunting and country-house life is a curious combination. That, however, is a not unfair description of [**Taking Chances**]. . . . Miss Farrell has, it appears, determined to go a little deeper and to attack more important problems than in her previous light hearted books. In this there is a vein of tragedy all through, and the end is tragedy unadulterated. On the whole she has been successful. Her personages, with one exception, are perhaps only types, but they are true types. Her machinery is excellent, and the sporting and humorous accessories as good as before. Yet there is something unpleasant, not in her subject, but in her handling of it—a treatment of the sensual which becomes sickly after a while. And how tiresome the girls' oaths and slang, quite genuine though they be, their "Come on, chaps!" their "crashings" and "terriblys," are when administered in large doses!

The book has five characters who count: the three Sorriers of Sorristown, the brothers Roguey and Gerald and their sister Maeve; their neighbour Rowland Fountain of Castle Fountain, who at the beginning of the story is about to marry Maeve; and the English girl Mary Fuller, who arrives as Maeve's bridesmaid, and stays to become Rowland's mistress (first) and Roguey's wife. As we have hinted, the first four are conventional enough. . . . It is the Saxon visitor Mary, who spoils every one's life, including her own, that is her creator's best achievement. One may call her *grande amoureuse* or born harlot according to one's views and standard of politeness; in either case one cannot deny that she is not only disturbing and dangerously attractive but quite convincing. Miss Farrell might go farther if she would use a blue pencil, not in the interests of morality, but in those of good taste.

> *A review of "Taking Chances," in* The Times Literary Supplement, *No. 1434, July 25, 1929, p. 590.*

THE NEW YORK TIMES BOOK REVIEW

Occasionally there appears a book which disarms criticism. "**Taking Chances**" is one of these, perhaps because Ireland gives enchantment always, and Miss Farrell had laid her scene there. To most people there is something much dearer and even much more exciting about familiar things than unfamiliar. Recognition can be more wildly rapturous than discovery. Everything in this book is delightfully familiar to any one who has read any good Irish novel before: the bog, the hunting, the weeping skies, the charming people, the innumerable dogs and horses—all are here.

Apparently modern Ireland is as good a place as the old Ireland; and, by Miss Farrell's convincing interpretation, even cigarettes and cocktails become part of the most romantic equipment of love. Of fox-hunting one might imagine that everything had been said, but Miss Farrell makes it afresh the most glorious experience that can fall to the lot of man. Whatever quality this is that she possesses of making the ordinary exciting, the dull brilliant, the foolish very engaging, is put most to the test and is most successful in her relation of the passionate love of Mary and Rowley. Mary is an enchanting character, vindicating all that is foolish, helpless, rash, unvirtuous and entirely modern in any woman. (pp. 6-7)

It makes a very good story. (p. 7)

> *"'The Love of Jeanne Ney' and Other Recent Fiction: Enchanting Ireland," in* The New York Times Book Review, *February 16, 1930, pp. 6-7.*

THE TIMES LITERARY SUPPLEMENT

Miss M. J. Farrell has already written two or three novels with an Irish setting which are lively and amusing in their way, but nothing nearly so good as **Mad Puppetstown**. . . . It, too, is light and amusing, but it has its serious side also and the observation displayed in it is acute. Above all, the three chief characters, Easter Chevington and her twin cousins Basil and Evelyn Curtis, are delightful creations. The author's heart is evidently in Ireland, and she has weighed down the scales in Ireland's favour when contrasting life in an Irish and in an English country house. One cannot say, however, that she has exaggerated the charm of the former. . . .

Puppetstown is the Irish mansion of fiction, but none the less real for that. The scene opens some seven years before the War, when Easter is eight and her cousins a year older. Miss Farrell certainly understands Irish children, and has made these three as amusing as they are true to type. Then comes the War. . . . A little later there is a flight from Puppetstown. The soldier who has come to pay his court to Mrs. Curtis is murdered on his way home; she dashes off to England with the children; and the house is left to the care of the old gardening Great-Aunt Dicksie.

Then we are transported to Oxford, whence the boys have gone on from Eton and where Easter, now of age, is visiting them. The rest of the book is taken up with the struggle of the three against their new surroundings. Handsome, princely Evelyn succumbs, but Basil and Easter, suddenly and without warning, dash across to Ireland to find Puppetstown in a state of filth and Aunt Dicksie living alone in the house but for Patsy the pantry-boy, her sole domestic staff. We leave them there putting things in order, probably going to marry when Aunt Dicksie dies. Basil, Easter and Puppetstown itself are all so charming that we should like to hear more of them.

A review of "Mad Puppetstown," in The Times Literary Supplement, No. 1545, September 10, 1931, p. 680.

THE NEW YORK TIMES BOOK REVIEW

["**Mad Puppetstown**"] follows a more or less familiar pattern, but it is written with so much beauty and freshness that it seems, while one is reading it, to be alone of its kind. It is primarily a novel of locale, and nothing in it is so important as the feeling of a particular place that it conveys—the atmosphere, the color and activity, the sights and sounds of an Irish home. The considerations of plot and character are secondary—though the plot, what there is of it, is quite adequate, and the characters are ably and unmistakably drawn. Puppetstown, the seat of the Chevingtons, dominates the book.

In those mellow and prosperous years before the war and before the turbulent outbreak of the Irish rebellion, Puppetstown had been the centre of life for the Chevingtons. . . . Above all, Puppetstown was Irish to the core—there was something that set it apart from a similar country place in England, a hint of savagery or romantic wildness that responded perfectly to the romantic wildness in the blood of the Irish Chevingtons.

M. J. Farrell succeeds admirably in evoking this characteristic atmosphere as it grew into the consciousness of three children—Easter Chevington and her two cousins, Basil and Evelyn. . . .

[After being removed to England] . . . Basil and Easter return to Puppetstown—but to a Puppetstown that is changed, to a house fallen into decay from neglect and disuse under the jealous and miserly care of Aunt Dicksie. There is a double tragedy in the conflict of their homecoming—tragedy on the part of the young people who find the place spiritually closed against them and on the part of Aunt Dicksie, who sees it about to be taken from her. . . .

To reveal the fashion of the tragedy's resolving would do as much injustice to the beauty of Miss Farrell's writing, as to the tact and appropriateness of her conception. Suffice it to say that "**Mad Puppetstown** " is a novel superb in its kind, and that there will be few who can read it unsympathetically.

> *"'Mad Puppetstown' and Other New Works of Fiction: 'Mad Puppetstown'," in* The New York Times Book Review, *June 19, 1932, p. 7.*

THE NEW YORK TIMES BOOK REVIEW

"**Point-to-Point**" [published in England as "**Conversation Piece**"] is a sporting novel, from the opening pages in which a certain Captain Pulleyns arrives at Pullinstown by his cousin's invitation to attend the point-to-point meeting of the Springwell Harriers, to the closing pages, which are partly concerned with Willow Pulleyns's misguided little romance, but more with a cub hunt, and some thrilling out-of-season riding. To the casual observer it must have seemed that Willow and her brother Dick lived solely for sport. . . .

Even their romances—or what threatened to become their romances, for there existed between brother and sister a sympathy and likeness of mind which outsiders found difficult to cope with—were partly governed by their preoccupation with sport. . . .

These slender episodes comprise about all the book has to offer in the way of plot. For the rest, it contains a succession of vividly described sporting events, fox hunts, horse shows, and point-to-point races. . . . It is difficult to do justice to the quality of the book, to the beauty and economy of Miss Farrell's style, or to the contagious enthusiasm with which she writes. It is equally difficult to convey an impression of the life and habits of her Irish sportsmen, and the amazing combination of civilized formality and simple savagery which she attributes to them. It is enough to say that the book is thoroughly delightful and a worthy successor to "**Mad Puppetstown**."

> *"'The Men of Ness' and Some Other Recent Works of Fiction: A Sporting Novel," in* The New York Times Book Review, *April 9, 1933, p. 7.*

MARGARET WALLACE

Miss M. J. Farrell, who has entertained us in the past with stories of fox hunting and horse racing in Ireland, has chosen for her latest novel a quite different background and a set of characters hitherto foreign to her pen. Excellent and full flavored as her hunting tales are, one does not regret the change. It is probable that "**Devoted Ladies**" is Miss Farrell's best novel to date. Certainly she finds in it an opportunity for the exercise of a stinging wit and an extraordinarily acute and vital faculty of observation. This, together with the graceful and luminous prose style which readers of her previous novels will remember, forms an irresistible combination.

The novel opens in London, at a party given by Sylvester Browne for a group of his pseudo-literary and artistic friends and acquaintances. Sylvester, a successful playwright and novelist, takes a somewhat ghoulish delight in prying into the private lives and motives of other people, and studiously surrounds himself with persons most likely to afford him amusement of this kind. Although the story, and most of its incidents, are seen through his eyes, Sylvester himself is by no means immune to the shafts of the author's wit. Foppish and self-indulgent, alternately kindly and malicious, victimized by an unflinchingly acute and realistic turn of mind, Sylvester is one of the most amusing of this whole gallery of amusing and pungently delineated characters. . . .

["**Devoted Ladies**" is] an extremely neat and witty tale—a tale which, for its sparkle and vitality, really deserves that abused adjective, brilliant.

> *Margaret Wallace, "'Devoted Ladies' and Other Recent Works of Fiction: 'Devoted Ladies'," in* The New York Times Book Review, *June 10, 1934, p. 7.*

JANE SPENCE SOUTHRON

[In *Full House*, M. J. Farrell] has deserted her Irish fox-hunting and fishing for satirical characterization blended with a psychopathic and exceedingly sympathetic study of inherited insanity. For a comparatively young writer this was undoubtedly an ambitious and hazardous undertaking, and one can understand why she elected to make a clean sweep of her former literary stock-in-trade. She has kept Ireland as the scene of her drama, but she treats it as a somewhat negligible background, instead of as the breath and life of the book.

It is true that some of the most satisfyingly beautiful passages are scenic . . . but they are subordinated to the moods and tragedies of the characters, with which they are usually made to correspond. . . .

Has M. J. Farrell justified her desertion? In venturing satire she necessarily challenges comparison with older writers who have made the same sort of ineptitude, selfishness and silliness their targets. Her score is by no means a contemptible one; which she can easily better by a more remorseless use of her quite considerable talent in this direction.

In its deeper aspects the work suffers from limitations deriving from what are, apparently, the author's personal predilections. Sir Julian and Lady Bird and the self-centred, sport-obsessed society that flutters in and out of Silverue, their lovely Georgian Irish home, are fit subjects for satire. The tragedy haunting the lives of John and Sheena, the grown-up children, and of 7-year-old Mark is real and terrible and is presented convincingly to our imagination; but it does not grip us as it should and as it might were the victims not hedged in and protected from the ordinary buffets of circumstances by the sanctity of their caste.

Little Miss Parker, the pitifully eager, hopelessly bearded governess, for whom Lady Bird is perpetually devising time-consuming tasks, does get under our skins and her unavailing, one-night revolt strikes a note of genuine pathos. But John and Sheena, modern people in the Ireland of today, living oblivious to any interests but those pertaining to themselves or to their own privileged set, leave us cold. They have beauty, physical health, charm, money, leisure, everything but an ancestry untainted by madness; which of itself would be tragedy enough to hold us were they not insulated by the assumption of class superiority.

In most other respects the book is worthy only of praise. . . .

A good deal of the satire is aimed at society functions, such as Lady Bird's charity garden fête, or saccharine conversational inanities. After hearing ''sweet,'' ''sweet one,'' ''poor sweet'' and ''darling'' ad nauseam, from men and women alike and quite irrespective of applicability, young Mark's verbal vulgarities, wholly and delightfully boylike, sound refreshingly sincere. Had the satiric dialogue, however, been considerably curtailed a much stronger effect would have been produced and the reader spared the possibility of surfeit.

> *Jane Spence Southron, 'Valiant Is the Word for Carrie' and other Recent Works of Fiction: Shadow of Madness,'' in* The New York Times Book Review, *October 27, 1935, p. 7.*

CHARLOTTE MOODY

[*The Rising Tide*] is an extremely interesting and absorbing novel. . . . It is as much a story of a place and a period as of people; the place is Garonlea, an Irish estate, the period 1900 to the first years after the war, the people are the family of French-McGrath. Despite its setting and period, the war and the Irish Troubles are not important to the story, which concerns itself entirely with personality and environment. . . .

It is difficult to give an accurate idea of this book without falling into phrases about Periods of Transition and the Spirit of the Times, which would be unfair, because the book is too human for that, some of its scenes too indelible. It is written with considerable beauty and sensitivity. If it has a flaw it is that feminine one of over-sensitivity, a too-great absorption in flower forms, a too-frequent use of the word ''sleek.'' But a too-precise delicacy does not seem to matter here, where there

are humor, perception, detachment, and penetration in a novel which is true of its period.

> *Charlotte Moody, ''Irish Edwardians,'' in* The Saturday Review, *London, Vol. XVII, No. 16, February 12, 1938, p. 10.*

GARRETT EPPS

I read *Good Behaviour* in one sitting, and, when I'd finished, shook the book like a greedy child hoping one more goody would fall out.

Keane's characters are the impecunious Anglo-Irish gentry between the wars, and her central character is Aroon St. Charles, one of those poisonous unmarried female relations who infest every extended family. . . .

But as Aroon recounts her path to manipulative spinsterhood, Keane performs the difficult trick of getting us inside this unattractive, overweight woman to see the naive but appealing girl she once was. Aroon is betrayed by her adored brother Hubert. . . . She is betrayed by her mother, who regards her from birth as a rival for the love of the unfaithful Major St. Charles. She is betrayed by the father himself, who loves her but can never quite take seriously her hopes for love. When, at last, Aroon has her sticky revenge, the reader has come round to her side, and sadly agrees that she has made the very best of a bad bargain. . . .

Keane is working the same social and literary territory that inspired Evelyn Waugh. Indeed, several characters in *Good Behaviour* might have wandered, in an absent-minded daze, out of *Vile Bodies*. But her formidable skills let her stay in the ring with an established master like Waugh, taking the jumps with ease. (p. 39)

> *Garrett Epps, ''Three First Novels,'' in* The New Republic, *Vol. 184, No. 23, June 6, 1981, pp. 38-40.**

SALLY EMERSON

The opening of Molly Keane's *Good Behaviour* is chillingly unforgettable. The narrator, 65-year-old Aroon St. Charles, relates the death of her mother in the small Gothic folly where they have moved, with one maid, surrounded by mementos of their past. . . . Aroon then takes us back to her childhood and we see the distance between the harsh woman she is now—as her mother used to be—and the affectionate girl she was then. We see where life has let her down.

The eccentricities of Aroon's mother and father as they pass their days at their ancestral home, Temple Alice, make the reader forget the macabre opening for a while. . . . This novel incorporates something of the sparkling, irresponsible mood of the 20s and 30s celebrated in her novels *Conversation Piece* (1932) and *Devoted Ladies* (1934). The language revels in the details of life in a grandish country house. Occasionally, when Aroon is at spectacular parties, looked after by her loving father and brother, or when she is mooning over her brother's handsome friend Richard, the reader is transported into a simple, romantic world. But always these moments are undercut by the dark reality seeping up between the floorboards of Temple Alice, whispering at the edges of Molly Keane's prose, because nothing is as it seems, nothing is simple and romantic.

When a governess, Mrs Brock, commits suicide and little Aroon does not know why, we do know (Aroon's philandering father has broken off his affair with her). When her brother forms a close friendship with Richard we know why their father is anxious, although Aroon never realizes. We are aware of the mother's frigidity, aware that Richard whom she loves will never love her. Homosexuality, drunkenness, cruelty of many kinds—they are all here, although never mentioned. Molly Keane's skill in letting us work out what is going on beyond the narrator's gaze is masterful.

> *Sally Emerson, in a review of "Good Behaviour,"*
> *in* The Illustrated London News, *Vol. 269, No. 6998,*
> *September, 1981, p. 70.*

A. N. JEFFARES

[*Good Behaviour* is an] atmospheric novel . . . ruthless in its black humour, irony, clarity of conception and execution. It is also profoundly sad. To tell the plot would spoil its effect, for there is a very real intellectual pleasure in store for the reader who gradually begins to realize the different planes upon which the story moves: there is the illusion of Anglo-Irish life with its well-brought-up silences, its refusal to face the facts of life. These include money, politics, religion and sex. And so the characters move in a world of faded elegance and damp decay, of luxury and extreme discomfort, taking their horses very seriously indeed. This is the world of the big house in decline and disintegration. It has a long literary history. . . . [And] now Molly Keane has joined the tradition. . . . [*Good Behaviour*] captures the impish quality of the humour of the Anglo-Irish and takes a detached view of their way of life, both enjoying its absurdities and appreciating its strengths and failures. It is written with a dash and *brio* that bring the characters and period vividly to life.

> *A. N. Jeffares, in a review of "Good Behaviour,"*
> *in* British Book News, *January, 1982, p. 56.*

QUENTIN CRISP

Time After Time is an interesting and funny tale full of grim, accurate observations, but to me it does not possess the stylish, classical form of [*Good Behaviour*] . . . nor has it that masterpiece's almost Lillian Hellman-like inevitability. Furthermore, instead of tracing a single heroine's decline from innocence to obese self-indulgence, it scatters our attention among five characters almost equally detestable from the start.

As ever in Keane's world, we find ourselves hobnobbing with the gentry in southern Ireland. The action and inaction take place mainly in a dilapidated house where once three sisters and a brother lived with their parents in heedless opulence. The narrative swims backward and forward from the wounding memories of a mysteriously troubled past to the petty anticlimaxes of the present.

By the time we meet these exiles from happiness, the Swifts are all disfigured in one way or another. The old man has only one eye, the other having been shot out by his youngest, dyslexic sister. Of the other two siblings, one has a maimed hand and the other is deaf. These physical deformities are accompanied by, or possibly represent, innumerable diseases of the soul—dishonesty, vindictiveness, and an appalling meanness. . . .

If we might read this story as a joke—a sort of Charles Addams illustration transcribed into literature—our laughter could be unrestrained, but it is not easy to do this. The bleakness of these people's lives is too graphic for that, and their decline into poverty and old age is too detailed. . . .

Keane's view of life seems to be that time does not ripen us but, rather, that each passing year renders us more cantankerous and bitter. In some instances this may be true, but the nastiness of the characters in this book is so persistent as to become a universal law. A novel written with nothing but contempt for its subject is like a banquet in which every course is steeped in vinegar. It could be made palatable only if it were served with the utmost elegance. Here this is not the case. Several passages have to be read more than once—not to be savored but merely to be understood. . . . Along with such wonderful phrases as "the inconsolable age of fifteen" are others of extreme awkwardness—"her words *wasting* into the silent room."

Time After Time has fascinating if repulsive characters involved in an elaborate plot full of surprises, but even if it were clothed in prose of Swiftian grace, the novel would remain a flawed gem. We may all be physically repulsive, we may all be spiritually stunted, but a book that evinces no pity for our weakness is ultimately unacceptable.

> *Quentin Crisp, "Castle Rackrent," in* New York
> Magazine, *Vol. 17, No. 3, January 16, 1984, p. 60.*

ANNE TYLER

Good Behaviour was a dark, subtle, savagely amusing study of the decline of a well-born Irish family after the First World War.

The members of that family destroyed each other, and that they did so with all due courtesy made the destruction no less cruel. But compared to the Swifts in *Time After Time,* the St. Charleses of *Good Behaviour* were angels of kindness.

Time After Time describes a family already ruined. . . . They more or less dislike each other, and yet they remain together, sniping and bickering and scratching out some shabby kind of life for themselves. . . .

The novel's pacing is perfect. Roughly the first one-third of the story sets us within the routine at Duraghglass as it has been practiced without change for years. . . . Each person has a particular interest, and each (it is hinted) a shameful secret.

There's a point at which the family's stasis becomes so vivid that the reader himself experiences a kind of claustrophobia. It's here that the perfect pacing comes in; for precisely when we feel we have to get out of this book for a breath of air, the tempo changes. Enter Cousin Leda, who was last seen as a flirtatious young girl. . . . [She is] a catalyst if ever there was one, restless and probing and intuitive and more than a little malicious.

The irony is that Leda, who was always coldheartedly curious about Jasper's maimed eye and May's maimed hand, is now maimed herself. She is blind. Unaware of the signs of her own aging—her wrinkles and obesity, her utterly faded charms—she is also unaware of any alterations in her cousins. . . .

Does all this sound a little grim? Does it strike you as a story to avoid if you're struggling through a winter depression? Well, it is. The Swifts are grotesque and often unlikeable. Leda is so consistently, uniformly the villain that she might have stepped out of an old silent movie.

On the other hand, the novel also happens to be exceptionally funny. . . . [Observe] the shattering breakfast at which Leda stages a confrontation. It's a genuine, old-fashioned climax, the kind we used to diagram in English class, and all the more effective because the Swifts, true to character, manage somehow to sail above a large part of it.

Time After Time is a shade overstated. It is less believable and less sympathetic, if more humorous, than *Good Behaviour.* But there's no denying Molly Keane's skill. She's as sharp-eyed as Barbara Pym, as battily comic as Beryl Bainbridge, as mordant as Jean Rhys. Bundle up warmly before you start reading this cold little dagger of a book.

> Anne Tyler, *"The War between the Swifts," in* The New York Times Book Review, *January 22, 1984, p. 6.*

ANN HULBERT

Keane directs [the] symmetrical and suspenseful plot [of *Time After Time*] with a dexterous hand. Staging a drama of revelation, she plants hints . . . and plays agilely with her characters' distorted perspectives. Keane proved herself a master of unreliable narration in *Good Behaviour,* letting deluded Aroon tell the story, at the same time betraying to us the true, even sadder, tale of her family's fate. This time Keane multiplies the myopia and shifts, artfully and comically, from one solipsistic Swift to the next. . . . Keane's feat is not only to make us correct for their skewed vision but also, improbably enough, to prompt us to care about their cantankerous views and fates. The brittle caricatures are still capable of surprising themselves, Keane convinces us—and curiosity thus roused can lead unexpectedly near to sympathy.

Keane depends on curiosity to spin out her old-fashioned fiction. So does cousin Leda to ensnare the Swifts. In fact, Keane seems to mirror in Leda the manipulative imagination that is at work in her own art. When Leda arrives halfway through the novel, hers becomes the crucial perspective, as she sets the Swifts against one another and treacherously teases out their secrets. (p. 40)

Despite her insinuating gifts, Leda couldn't write a book about the Swifts if she wanted to—and in fact even fails to enthrall them in the end. A genius at manipulation, she, unlike Keane, has no inkling of the moral imagination that must complement and complicate it: she knows all about the possibilities of power, but not about the limitations of knowledge. Keane, however, is an expert on delusion, which tends to triumph in her fiction—usually for the best in the darkly comic world she creates. At the close of *Time After Time,* it's all-knowing Leda who is trapped, and the blinkered Swifts who are enlightened—but only a little, just enough to exert their waning powers in purposeful, instead of perverse, directions. (p. 41)

> Ann Hulbert, *"Visitations," in* The New Republic, *Vol. 190, No. 4, January 30, 1984, pp. 40-1.**

V. S. PRITCHETT

As one who knew something of the period of Molly Keane's *Good Behaviour* I was astonished to find there no hint of the Irish "Troubles," the Rising of 1916, the later civil war, or the toll of burned-down houses. Was this an instance of the Anglo-Irish, indeed of the general Irish habit of euphemism and evasion? What, of course, is most real to Molly Keane is the game of manners, the instinctive desire to keep boring reality at bay yet to be stoical about the cost.

The Victorian and Edwardian codes stayed on far longer in southern Ireland than in England. *Good Behaviour* . . . is less a novel than a novelized autobiography which exposes the case of Anglo-Irish women, especially in the person of the narrator, a shy, large, ungainly, horsy girl. . . .

Molly Keane's real novel, substantial and ingeniously organized, is the more recent *Time After Time.* . . . Now good behavior is in abeyance, although its shadow is there. We are now in a period closer to the present day. Still no politics, though there is a horrified glance at a political crime abroad, the Holocaust.

For the rest, the Irish imbroglio tells its own tale. (p. 7)

[*Time After Time* is a] thoroughly well-organized traditional study of intrigue, malice, and roguery. It is rich, and remarkable for the intertwining of portraits and events. It is spirited, without tears. The ingenious narrative is always on the move and has that extraordinary clean athletic animation that one finds in Anglo-Irish prose. Mrs. Keane has a delicate sense of landscape; she is robust about sinful human nature and the intrigues of the heart, a moralist well weathered in the realism and the evasions of Irish life. No Celtic twilight here! Detached as her comedy is, it is also deeply sympathetic and admiring of the stoicism, the *incurable* quality of her people. . . . [Irish] . . . realism, with the solace of its intrigues, dominates this very imaginative and laughing study of the anger that lies at the heart of the isolated and the old, and their will to live. (p. 8)

> V. S. Pritchett, *"The Solace of Intrigue," in* The New York Review of Books, *Vol. XXXI, No. 6, April 12, 1984, pp. 7-8.*

MARGOT JEFFERSON

Good Behaviour is a tale of appetites, pursued and thwarted, written in a style that lusts after the lethal aims tucked into civilized exchange, yokes mournful, sensuous description with analytic dismemberment, and sifts a high-handed 18th century rhythm through 1920s speediness. *Time After Time* gives us the same world, moved from the '20s to the present—aged, sour, full of cracks and grudges. Keane's writing seems tainted by the woes of her world: there's too much expositional clutter and fuss; stage directions dwarf the moments they're supposed to set up. It's a domestic drama of manners (Keane is scathingly funny, but rarely comic) into which a World War II thriller intrudes, unsettling the writer's balance nearly as much as it unsettles her characters' lives. . . .

It's Leda who tears wounds open and sets moral consequence whirling in a house where dust is "heavy as fur" and each worn chair cover glistens "like an unhealthy skin." There's something irritating about this—too many British writers have depended on Jewish ancestry plus temperamental ruthlessness to rattle the family skeletons. Keane tries to do more than that: she wants to trace the shapes that wrongs, public and private, take in people's lives, changing meaning, changing proportion, changing everything but emotional needs and limits. But she manages to do this only intermittently. Leda's private cruelties to the Swifts are as real as spit in the eye, but the public, political ones, when revealed, seem strained and not quite believable, like a creaky deus ex machina. Keane captures the Swifts' embarrassed, inadequate discomfort, but seems somewhat helpless before it, relieved as they settle back into a routine where ''in the present, as in the past, each morning advanced briskly toward its difficulties,'' and each difficulty knows its place.

Now in her second writing life, Molly Keane has produced a perfect first novel and an uneven second one that's well worth reading. I hope she's at work on her third, in full command once more of a writing self that's part elegist, part gravedigger, and part changeling. Her world is like those zoos in which animals roam through fascimile natural habitats; Keane lets us watch, from a safe distance, creatures who are subtle and also primitive, who possess all the reflexes and few of the realities of power.

Margot Jefferson, ''Every Other Inch a Lady,'' in The Village Voice, *Vol. XXIX, No. 16, April 17, 1984, p. 42.*

Charles R(aymond) Larson

1938-

American critic, essayist, novelist, and editor.

Larson is a foremost scholar of Third World and minority literature. In his first critical work, *The Emergence of African Fiction* (1972), Larson examined what he considered representative examples of the best African writing. The works of Chinua Achebe, Camara Laye, Wole Soyinka, and others are discussed in terms of plot and characterization, and then related to African literature as a whole. Larson's next critical work, *The Novel in the Third World* (1976), is a comparative study of novels from various Third World countries. As he did in *The Emergence of African Fiction*, Larson analyzes individual works and then attempts to define them in a larger context. He notes, in particular, the way in which African writers reflect their country's attempt to assert a national character in the face of Western cultural domination. *American Indian Fiction* (1978) has been called "the first critical and historical account of novels by American Indians." Much of this work focuses on the difficulty of determining authentic "Indianness." Despite objections concerning Larson's premises and conclusions in this work and in his commentaries on African literature, his scholarly efforts are important contributions to studies of world literature.

In addition to his critical studies, Larson has also written three novels: *Academia Nuts* (1977), a satire on university life; *The Insect Colony* (1978), which explores the confrontation between African and European cultures; and *Arthur Dimmesdale* (1982), a retelling of Nathaniel Hawthorne's novel *The Scarlet Letter* from the perspective of Arthur Dimmesdale.

(See also *Contemporary Authors*, Vols. 53-56 and *Contemporary Authors New Revision Series*, Vol. 4.)

Photograph by Roberta Rubenstein; courtesy of Charles R. Larson

THE TIMES LITERARY SUPPLEMENT

[The] steady superiority of Professor Larson [in *The Emergence of African Fiction*] is a reflection of his real familiarity with both classical and contemporary fiction, and of his finer critical judgment. The former prevents him from applying some strict and inappropriate notion of the "proper" novel to the material before him, while the latter enables him to look carefully at what is actually present in the work under review. Thus he makes some really interesting observations on the relative "plotlessness" of the first part of *Things Fall Apart*, on Achebe's preference for exhibiting character in action rather than through description or extensive dialogue or monologue, and on his use of short conte-like sequences within his novel to create a density of background for the principal action.

Professor Larson is also at least adequate in his discussion of [Wole Soyinka's] *The Interpreters*, and correctly identifies it as belonging with the later work of Armah rather than with the more situational novels of the first generation of African writers. But he goes badly adrift in failing to recognize the intensely African nature of Soyinka's approach to tragic action and fulfilment. This probably results from his failure to look at Soyinka's work as a whole; for an intensive reading of his plays and poems is essential to a full understanding of what is hap-

pening in *The Interpreters* and to a grasp of mythological structure in that novel. Likewise, Professor Larson fails to see that Armah's *Fragments*, while registering the distance that the contemporary Ghanian bourgeoisie has travelled from African tradition, is not seeking to bury that tradition with the dying Naana, but (like Soyinka) to provoke a search for new ways of articulating it in modern life.

Thus he devotes far too much space to an attempt to untangle what "happens" in each chapter of the novel, but totally ignores the importance of a number of crucial incidents within it. . . .

The Emergence of African Fiction suggests that breadth of reading, open-mindedness and adequate critical skills will carry any author a long way, regardless of his ethnic origins; but there is no substitute for a bit of preliminary work on African oral tradition, mythology, religious ritual and symbolism if the critic is to avoid the danger of missing a number of important clues and connexions.

> *"Through the Drum," in* The Times Literary Supplement, *No. 3695, December 29, 1972, p. 1573.**

OMOLARA LESLIE

[With] some thought, the sources of irritation [in Charles Larson's book] become manifold. First, there is the title itself—

The Emergence of African Fiction—which indicates a scope not attempted. African fiction is not merely African prose literature since World War II, because fictional arts existed in Africa since traditional times. Neither did African fiction in European languages emerge only after World War II; such fiction goes back to the 1880's in Portuguese Africa. . . . Mr. Larson's study is as generally weak on history as it is on non-Anglophone African fiction as a whole.

It appears that "emergence" is used, not in an etymological but in a figurative and personal sense of "emerging into the mainstream of Western tradition," the note on which the study's last chapter ends. (pp. 91-2)

[The] authorial personality in *The Emergence of African Fiction* obtrudes, moving further and further away, as the chapters progress, from careful consideration and scholarly statements to *ex-cathedra dicta,* exhibitionism, hearsay and personal prejudice. . . .

African scholars such as Irele, Nwoga, Echeruo, Ogunba and Wali, among others, demonstrate more humility before their subject matter than Mr. Larson, who ascribes to himself the right to appoint deans of African letters, to challenge Amos Tutuola about his writing habits, to throw aside African culture as passing anthropology, to pretend to inside knowledge of Africa for having taught some time there, to claim knowledge of "the African reader," to intimate to this "African reader" what his aesthetic and literary preferences should be, and to speak for him regarding reasons for his likes and dislikes—which in summary are that the "average" African reader (who is never identified) cannot appreciate the lyrical, the subtle, the complex, or the cerebral. . . .

In the opening chapter, "Critical Approaches to African Fiction," which is a fitting start to such a work and a potentially interesting study in itself, Mr. Larson does not accomplish the required scholarly task of collecting the major critical ideas or critical approaches regarding African fiction and discussing them in some depth. Rather, this first chapter skims the surface of critical thought and excludes the theoretical ideas of practising African critics. (p. 92)

Unfortunately, Mr. Larson is guilty of all the faults he self-righteously condemns. His main points are: 1. the reception of African literature by the West has, for the most part, been sympathetic (Who needs sympathy?); 2. anthropologists have been favorable to African literature because they have been interested in African cultures *per se,* and not literature itself; and 3. literary critics have been unsympathetic simply because they have attempted to force the African writer into a Western literary tradition to which he does not always belong. Mr. Larson thinks "The African writer has relied on his own traditional African aesthetic. It is therefore unrewarding to the non-African reader and critic to look at any of the major genres in contemporary African writing—the novel, poetry, and drama—solely from the perspective of Western literary criteria and terminology." In his view, this is too much like "trying to force a glove with three fingers on to a hand with five. Instead we must look at African writing not only for whatever its similarities with Western literary forms may be, but also—once we have identified these—for what is different, and therefore African."

But the last conclusion does not follow. Distilling the Western from the African does not leave an exclusively indigenous residue. Contemporary African writers do not write wholly from their traditional aesthetics, nor would Mr. Larson be ca-

pable of identifying those aesthetics, even if the writers did. Culture is not separable from literature if literature is the imaginative rendering of life in words, the image of an individual or collective cognition of reality. (pp. 92-3)

In the second chapter, he discusses *Things Fall Apart,* which is called the "archetypal" African novel—the archetype being the "situation" identified as the conflict resulting from the European's arrival in Africa and the subsequent cultural stress created in all African societies. An insightful point, since, indeed, African writers appear preoccupied with this drama. Mr. Larson also does a careful step-by-step analysis of *Things Fall Apart* which deserves emulation, just as he gives an interesting, original analysis of the integration of oral material and devices into the novel's mode.

Unfortunately, the chapter is weakened by a poor knowledge of the sociology and history of the African novel, as the whole work is weakened by insufficient information about the sociology of Africa. . . . (p. 93)

Notably absent in this chapter are references to forerunning serious and sustained essays on *Things Fall Apart;* strikingly present are unverified critical statements and unverifiable allusions to unknown students and informants, something continual in the study. . . .

In trying to limit his area of discussion to sub-Saharan Africa, he creates a straw man of the possibility of a "typical" African fictional form and proceeds to battle it throughout the study. The reasoning in the whole paragraph concerning *why there cannot be a "typical" African fictional form because of French fiction* is mysterious. He overstates ethnic differences while he shows a lack of information regarding French African literature and criticism. (p. 94)

[In the chapter on Amos Tutuola] Mr. Larson's discussion of Time, Space and Description is at times brilliant and always ingenious. It is clear however, that he cannot deal with the ontological gap or with Yoruba cultural symbols, such as the Thumb Child. It is, in fact, striking that Mr. Larson makes no use of Yoruba sources and authorities, nor does he use the most important literary studies which have been made on Tutuola apart from Harold Collins. (pp. 95-6)

In the final chapter, Mr. Larson declares the fiction of Soyinka and Ayi Kwei Armah to be the novels of the future because their authors ignore the past(!) to solve "present day social and political problems"; and because they treat Western themes, such as individualism and the alienation of the artist, using modern Western techniques and modes of experimentation. When Mr. Larson's study ends . . . : "How surprising we might conclude that with Wole Soyinka and Ayi Kwei Armah, the African novel as a literary genre now moves into the mainstream of Western tradition, yet how even more surprising, we might think, that this did not happen long before now"—the irritants crystallize. The facets declare a belief in a literature in *vacuo;* the myth of a necessary evolutionary progress from a different traditional literature to the mainstream of Western tradition; the movement from a mindless African past to a "civilized" thinking present. And at the heart of the crystal is the shining faith that we are all, if equal, Americans under the skin; that given time, Western education and the inevitable erasure of cultural aberrations, we shall all walk into our Anglo-American inheritance: of individualism, monogamy and the atomic family; free enterprise and free competition; the collapse of emotional order and a superficial challenge of all forms of authority; masculinity neurosis and the loss of most human moorings—all of which, of course, are not culturally determined. (p. 97)

Omolara Leslie, in a review of "The Emergence of African Fiction," in Black World, *Vol. XXIII, No. 10, August, 1974, pp. 91-7.*

BUD FOOTE

[On a reading of] *Academia Nuts,* I am forced to the critical conclusion that Charles R. Larson . . . has been drinking coffee laced with rum. He needs to be warned away from that stuff; it is dangerous. . . .

[This] is a very funny book that will get handed around every English department in the country with chortles and snickers and the occasional howl of glee. What I hope is that its public is not that limited, that everyone who has ever had to write An Interpretation of a Literary Work, or everyone who has ever shaken his head, bemused, at the number of academically certified readings that can be hauled out of a book by Freudians, Jungians, Marxists, and Structuralists will find joy in watching Professor Larson avenge them.

Bud Foote, "The Sole in Oedipean Tragedy: Laughing Through English Lit," in The National Observer, *June 6, 1977, p. 19.*

PETER S. PRESCOTT

["**The Insect Colony**"] is about useless Americans scratching at each other in West Africa. . . . [The] characters are afflicted by irresponsibility and a sense of alienation; . . . illicit sex is the spring that propels the narrative. . . .

[Larson] conveys the illegitimacy of his characters' presence in a landscape that has no need of them, that they cannot even profitably exploit. It occurs to Hunter Schuld, toward the end of his sojourn in a remote village of Cameroon, that he and generations of white interlopers had been blind to the reality of Africa; callous and inefficient predators, they gave nothing in return. Poor Hunter: a lonely entomologist who might have been content had he been left to study his African spiders, he awoke to only half the truth, the other half being that he is himself a victim, caught in a web set for him by a devouring woman. Hunter is vulnerable because he is innocent. He stands 4 feet 7 inches tall and has never been to bed with a white woman. Myrna Jeffers changes that: the wife of a defeated USIS official and a pathological liar, she seduces Hunter handily. Too late, Hunter tries an act of atonement but he fails, and that failure, it is hinted, precipitates his own abrupt demise.

This is a remorseless story strongly told. The sex fairly steams and the symbols are painted with the kind of bold brush that eases the lives of freshman English instructors. I particularly like the use to which Larson has put that most troublesome of structural devices, the split narration. Myrna tells much of the story; her husband, some; the wretched Hunter, being so early dead, must rely on the author to carry his part of the tale. There is a point to this diversity: because of his need for Myrna, Hunter must accept the fantasy she offers. The reader will not know for a long time that it is a fantasy, and Hunter never finds out. At the book's end, Myrna is still spinning her self-deception, confirming with every strand what her former lover feared was true about the white man in the black man's continent.

Peter S. Prescott, "Hot Tickets," in Newsweek, *Vol. 92, No. 14, October 2, 1978, p. 94.**

PETER NAZARETH

Surprisingly—because we tend to dismiss critics turned novelist—*The Insect Colony* is a fine novel. Larson has a novelist's sensibility. He uses various novelistic techniques such as split narration, varying levels of perception, movement through time zones and the ending of every chapter with a startling revelation or question. Hunter Schuld, an entomologist, has returned to West Africa to study spiders. Metaphorically, everybody gets caught in a web of connections—an image Larson may have picked up from West African writers like Wole Soyinka, but one which works both because of the details of web construction and because we are made to see connections between people, sensibilities and histories.

The Insect Colony is not an African novel, nor does the author claim it to be such. On the contrary: explicit references are made to Graham Greene's African novels and Conrad's *Heart of Darkness*. Like its literary antecedents, Larson's is a novel about Europeans pursuing their own interests in Africa. However, Africa exists on the edge of Hunter's consciousness; and it assumes an increasing reality. . . . (pp. 292-93)

[Larson, the critic, is] a fine novelist who, from a clearly identified Western perspective, reaches out to the same kind of statement as that made by [Ayi Kwei Armah] in his great novel *Two Thousand Seasons*. (p. 293)

Peter Nazareth, in a review of "The Insect Colony," in World Literature Today, *Vol. 53, No. 2, Spring, 1979, pp. 292-93.*

JACK L. DAVIS

The title of [Charles Larson's] pioneering study [*American Indian Fiction*] is somewhat misleading, for Larson intends a discussion of novels only, not shorter fiction as well. One suspects this restriction owes to the author's self-admittedly brief acquaintance with imaginative literature written by Native Americans. Unfortunately, the limitation leads the author into generalizations based upon but 16 works, from Simon Pokagon's *Queen of the Woods* (1899) to Leslie Silko's *Ceremony* (1977). If Larson had consulted, for example, Kenneth Rosen's collection of contemporary Indian stories, *The Man to Send Rain Clouds,* he would have found a dozen and half examples of how many gifted young Southwestern Indians approach the craft of fiction. The nihilism and despair which are overemphasized in this study could have been tempered by the affirmative notes struck in these other stories.

Not that Larson's critical study is superficial or unworthy of serious consideration. . . . On the positive side, *American Indian Fiction* is the first attempt to deal critically with all the known Indian novels of the past 80 years, and the study is in many ways surprisingly creditable for an author with relatively little knowledge of traditional or modern Indian life.

Some students of contemporary Indian fiction will not be entirely satisfied with Larson's criteria for an Indian novel. One requires that the writer be an enrolled tribal member, a useful distinction but like all a two-edged sword. What if such a person writes a novel having nothing to do with Indian life? The result may be interesting, but is it what most of us think is an Indian novel? . . . Clearly, the issue of authentic Indianness is difficult and Larson's solution a possibility, but a more sophisticated set of criteria seems necessary.

Beyond the matters of tribal affiliation, blood, and subject matter lies the problem of audience. Unlike virtually all Euro-American novels, which are addressed to the writer's culture, many Indian novels are directed to an alien culture. Only fairly recently does one find fiction which includes native people in the intended audience. The question of two radically different audiences deserves more attention than it receives here. It may, in fact, require native critics to interpret works written primarily to the Indians.

On the basis of 16 novels, Larson discovers a developmental pattern of four phases: assimilationist, rejectionist, revisionist, and "no all-encompassing pattern." This is somewhat less than helpful. The difficulty here derives both from the limited sample consulted and from imposing a developmental model upon writers who probably were little concerned about, or even aware of, some of the earlier novels cited in this study. This is an instance where wider experience with Indian short fiction and poetry would have helped Larson fill out a fuller and more representative picture of the themes and perspectives of modern native authors. (pp. 192-94)

> Jack L. Davis, in a review of "American Indian Fiction," in American Indian Quarterly, Vol. 5, No. 2, May, 1979, pp. 192-94.

LARRY EVERS

[*American Indian Fiction*] is the first book-length study of fiction written by American Indians. Larson treats novels by twelve authors: Simon Pokagon, John M. Okison, John J. Mathews, D'Arcy McNickle, N. Scott Momaday, Dallas Chief Eagle, Hyemeyohsts Storm, Denton Bedford, George Pierre, James Welch, Leslie Marmon Silko, and Nasnaga. Though the book is titled *American Indian Fiction,* Larson discusses only novels, ignoring the fine short fiction of Simon Ortiz, Leslie Silko, and others for plodding discussions of the third-rate novels of Nasnaga, Pierre, Bedford, and Eagle. Larson gives some interesting readings of individual novels, but the study is marred by a curious and often imprecise conceptual frame.

This is nowhere more evident than in the introductory chapter in which the limits of the study are defined. The single criterion for inclusion of an author is whether he is "genuinely a Native American." This of course is a question which has plagued administrators, scholars, and Indian people themselves for well over a century, and it is one that has never been answered satisfactorily. Larson does no better. He looks first to tribal rolls which imply "a kind of kinship with fellow tribesmen"; then to biography and documentary information about the authors "that attests to their general acceptance by their own people"; and finally settles on the author's "Indianness" as the final criterion. Nowhere is Larson able to tell us what "Indianness" is. On the one hand, his discussions suggest that the quality is somehow related to the way in which the author and his work are received by Indian communities. Thus Pokagon possesses "Indianness" because he was a Pottawatomie "chief," Mathews because he served on the Osage Tribal Council, and others because their work has been included in anthologies edited by American Indians. On the other, we are given the impression that "Indianness" is a quality the aware reader can intuit: "*Seven Arrows* in many ways seems to be more 'Indian' than any of the others." Throughout, the working definition seems to be that a person is an Indian if he chooses

to be identified as an Indian, though that is nowhere made explicit.

After all this discussion of who is an Indian and who is not, Larson's first critical chapter is not devoted to fiction written by American Indians, but rather to the countless fictional versions of the Pocahontas story written by non-Indians. When Larson finally makes the connection to his subject matter, we get this: "Like Pocahontas, the Native American has rarely been able to tell his own story." Thus allusion to the Pocahontas story becomes an artificial organizing thread for the rest of the study, pulling Larson into some contrived and astonishingly naïve critical statements. (pp. 287-88)

Even when Larson stays with close readings of individual novels and eschews these Pocahontas connections, I have trouble with his interpretations. His reading of *House Made of Dawn,* for example, is misinformed on many significant points, and the interpretations it offers unconvincing as a result. . . .

The best that can be said of this study finally is that it is the first of its kind. For that reason, it will be read, and, perhaps, it will provoke others into more considered critical responses to an important part of American literature that has too long been ignored. (p. 288)

> Larry Evers, in a review of "American Indian Fiction," in Arizona Quarterly, Vol. 35, No. 3, Autumn, 1979, pp. 287-88.

RICHARD BJORNSON

[In *The Novel in the Third World,* a] collection of essays on ten representative novels from Africa, India, the Caribbean, Papua New Guinea, and the Black and Native American communities in the United States, Larson proposes an evolutionary schema according to which third-world fiction can be defined in terms of its common characteristics, and not in terms of its relationship to Western literary models. Based primarily on narrative content, this schema distinguishes various stages in a process which has presumably repeated itself each time an European-American culture has sought to dominate non-Western peoples whose value systems are rooted in communal consciousness, a holistic view of history as cyclical recurrence, an inflexible attachment to traditional forms of behavior, and a propensity toward oral modes of story-telling.

The first stage in this process reflects an apparent death of the indigenous culture, a phenomenon that Larson considers pervasive in Maran's *Batouala* . . . , Ouologuem's *Bound to Violence* . . . , and Eri's *The Crocodile.* . . . The second stage—illustrated solely by Storm's *Seven Arrows* . . .—develops out of the conviction that the suppressed culture deserves to survive, even if it must be redefined within a context that remains implacably hostile to it. Accompanied by the growth of individualistic self-consciousness, a third stage emerges when the victims of colonialist oppression recognize the need to confront and assimilate their own past in order to exorcise its power over them. The attempt to accomplish this goal may ultimately result in evasion, as in Toomer's *Cane* . . . , or it may culminate in a heightened awareness of potential solidarity with others who have been similarly deprived of their roots, as in Lamming's *In the Castle of My Skin.* . . . Larson's final stage occurs during or after a successful revolt against the colonizing power, and it offers the promise of a dynamic new synthesis between the traditional values of indigenous culture and the intense awareness of self that characterizes Western thought.

Rao's *Kanthapura* . . . forms a transitional link between the third and fourth stages, whereas Narayan's *Grateful to Life and Death* . . . , Markandaya's *Two Virgins* . . . , and Head's *Question of Power* . . . are used as examples of the fourth stage. (p. 70)

Larson's enterprise is a bold one, and he offers numerous provocative insights into important but little known texts, yet the principal thesis of his *Novel in the Third World* remains unproven because he has failed to substantiate the assumptions on which his approach is based. The term "third-world" is never clearly defined. If it is synonymous with "formerly colonized" or "developing" countries, as he intimates in his introduction, his exclusion of Latin American and Asian fiction becomes indefensible, and his omission of all works not written in English or French severely limits the overall validity of his findings. In his concluding paragraph, for example, he remarks that most third-world writers become estranged from the cultures that nourished them, but his justification for making such a contention rests on the fact that he selected writers who had assimilated Western modes of thought and expression far more fully than most of their compatriots. Furthermore, close textual analyses of ten arbitrarily chosen novels cannot provide adequate information on which to elaborate a theoretical model for a heterogeneous and highly complex literary development in various parts of the world. Larson's evolutionary schema is seriously weakened by his disregard for historical chronology and cultural diversity. Some of the most recent novels are relegated to the first stage of development; some of the older ones are placed in the final stage. Such a procedure might be justifiable if Larson could prove that the societies involved reached different stages of evolution at different times, but that does not appear to be the case since fiction from the same culture is indiscriminately employed to illustrate earlier or later stages in the same process. Finally, the traditional cultures of all non-Westerners are not the same, and Larson inadvertently falls victim to ethnocentrism by overlooking distinctions between traditional cultures as diverse as those of India and West Africa.

Yet *The Novel in the Third World* has a significance which transcends its flaws. It draws attention to a large body of Anglophone and Francophone literature that has until recently been unfairly neglected. It also articulates a potentially fruitful paradigm for further investigation by suggesting that indigenous societies have an internal dynamic that enables them to overcome the menace of annihilation by an intrusive Western culture. Larson's contribution resides in his attempt to show how this dynamic has shaped and influenced the literature of those societies. . . . From a different perspective, Larson's book serves a useful function in the theory-dominated critical climate of comparative scholarship in the Western world, for

it is imperative that theoretical speculations be tested not only on a small sample of European-American texts, but also on the broad spectrum of non-Western literature such as that discussed by Larson in his *Novel in the Third World*. (p. 71)

Richard Bjornson, "Reviews of Professional Works: 'The Novel in the Third World'," in Yearbook of Comparative General Literature, No. 28, *Horst Frenze, General Editor, Indiana University, 1979, pp. 70-1.*

KIRKUS REVIEWS

[*Arthur Dimmesdale* is] Hawthorne's *Scarlet Letter* revisited— to no apparent purpose. Dimmesdale, you'll remember, is the Puritan minister tortured by his association with the sin for which Hester Prynne wears the scarlet letter "A" on her breast. Larson's Dimmesdale, however, is an explicit adulterer who gets Hester with child and damns both; his suffering afterwards is mental (a Puritan conscience and hell-fire fear inflamed beyond balm) and physical (stigmata—an "A", naturally—that appears on the skin of his chest). Indeed, Dimmesdale appears about to be consumed alive with guilt when Roger Chillingworth intervenes, offering Indian shaman cures and hypnosis. And the ordeal ends only when Hester, in secret forest meetings, reveals to Dimmesdale that she'd actually been married (chastely) to Chillingworth in England—where he was a magician, an evil shaman who is now devilishly bent upon prompting Dimmesdale's destruction under the guise of ministering to him. Larson . . . , seemingly aware of this re-telling's pointlessness, occasionally studs it with academic, self-conscious jokes. (Dimmesdale, digesting the significance of the "A": "Accouchement or amblosis? He was afraid to ask . . . *Agenbite of inwit* about their allogamous affair?") But such arch asides only tend to highlight the thinness of this inert exercise.

A *review of "Arthur Dimmesdale," in* Kirkus Reviews, *Vol. L, No. 15, August 1, 1982, p. 893.*

PUBLISHERS WEEKLY

["**Arthur Dimmesdale**," a] recasting of Hawthorne's "The Scarlet Letter," from the viewpoint of the pusillanimous young minister, gets high marks for vision. However, so overwhelming is the convoluted psychic landscape of Minister Dimmesdale that the reader wilts under his vacillations and can only marvel that Hester aroused passion in such a one. Larson's version of the sin that Puritan Boston deemed a crime is forthright, differing from the studied ambiguity of the original. . . . [Larson] gives some unique Gothic touches to a classic.

A *review of "Arthur Dimmesdale," in* Publishers Weekly, *Vol. 222, No. 6, August 6, 1982, p. 58.*

J(ean) M(arie) G(ustave) Le Clézio
1940-

French novelist, short story writer, essayist, and critic.

With the publication of his first work, *La procès-verbal* (1963; *The Interrogation*), Le Clézio emerged as one of the most provocative and promising young writers of contemporary French literature. Sometimes considered a descendant of such writers of the "Nouveau Roman" ("New Novel") as Nathalie Sarraute and Alain Robbe-Grillet, Le Clézio shares with these authors an interest in experimenting with literary form. Disordered narrative sequences, a repetitive, hypnotic attention to minute details, and a surreal montage of sensory perceptions characterize Le Clézio's fictional experiments. With little emphasis on plot or character development, Le Clézio's novels and short stories primarily recreate a feverish sense of anguish and alienation which he blames on the spiritual emptiness of contemporary society.

Critical reception to Le Clézio's work has been mixed. Although the publication of *Le procès-verbal* caused a stir in Parisian literary circles, many critics contend that Le Clézio's subsequent works have failed to fulfill the potential of his first novel. Critics commonly cite the repetitive themes, the obscure technical experiments, and the underdeveloped characters as elements which detract from the success of his fiction. However, he has been highly praised for his imaginative and impressionistic portraits of modern cityscapes.

© *Jerry Bauer*

THE VIRGINIA QUARTERLY REVIEW

"The Interrogation" brilliantly explores human experience beyond the pales of conventional human relations and reason. Mr. Le Clezio subjects his cool protagonist to the trials of solitude and the quest for ontological fulfillment. . . . This abstrusely metaphysical quest in the French manner comes vividly alive through Mr. Le Clezio's artistry. His novel proves that extremism in the exercise of the imagination can be a virtue with an artist whose vision is deep and precise. Such qualities are indeed rare and in one of Mr. Le Clezio's age and experience something truly remarkable.

> *A review of "The Interrogation," in* The Virginia Quarterly Review, *Vol. 41, No. 1 (Winter, 1965), p. x.*

STANLEY KAUFFMANN

[*The Interrogation*] deals with a young man named Adam Pollo who lives alone in a house near the sea in southern France, walks, does not walk, talks to people, visits and is visited by a girl, but is in essence as solitary as the Crusoe who supplies the epigraph for his story. The novel traces his mental decline after his release "out of a mental home or out of the army"— much of it in interior monologues. But his retrogression is presented as contemporary heroic myth, not pathology, in a manner that implies the superiority of his withdrawals and distortions to the facts of life around him, that these withdrawals are indeed caused by the drabness and terror of the facts.

This of course is neither a new field for fiction nor a fresh view of contemporary society. The highhandedness of the young about the stupidities of the world they inherit is an ancient strophe, and the private purities of schizophrenia and paranoia are a latter-day mode of expressing it. LeClezio burdens himself with superficial trickeries—lines crossed out in the printed text, newspaper pages—but he has some gift of vision and an imagination that flies at the touch of a certain light, a view, a voice. If over-reaction were not the very tonality of his book, one could indict him for over-reacting. As it is, his novel— easily readable and sometimes poignant—fails simply by being insufficiently relevant to large concerns, a youthful paw at the universe instead of the intended tragic embrace. The tragedy soon wears away into self-consciousness and we are left with a series of attitudes substantiated, partly, by a vivid talent. (p. 21)

> *Stanley Kauffmann, "Novels from Abroad," in* The New York Review of Books, *Vol. III, No. 2, January 14, 1965, pp. 20-1.**

RICHARD MAYNE

J. M. G. Le Clézio's first book, *The Interrogation,* was likened to *La Nausée;* and his work is clearly influenced by Sartre, as well as by Camus's *L'Etranger* and some of the so-called 'new novelists'. That's to say that he focuses with hypnotic intentness on objects, like the director of a Thirties documentary: by accumulating small, vivid, indifferent facts he induces a sense of daze and emptiness, turning us into sleepwalkers or drunks for whom visual trivia dwarf the world. In the nine stories collected in *Fever,* this mood often has objective pretexts—sunstroke, toothache, old age, oppressiveness of various sorts. But pretexts are what they are, excuses for the deployment of Le Clézio's special aptitude, for the imposition of his vision with its sad metaphysical (or anti-metaphysical) overtones. Brilliant, powerful, joyless, but not lacking a kind of alert humour in its sour juxtapositions, this isn't a book that opens new questions, as did those it derives from; but . . . it certainly grips.

Richard Mayne, "Forbidden Fruit," in New Statesman, *Vol. 71, No. 1833, April 29, 1966, p. 622.**

KLÉBER HAEDENS

[The following excerpt is from a translated essay, the original of which appeared in Le Nouveau Candide.]

It's certain that right now J. M. G. Le Clézio has no intention of striking out on a different path. His new novel, *Le Déluge* [translated into English as *The Flood*], repeats his favorite theme without let-up: loneliness in the crowd and the constant threat of death.

Up to page 46 a somber verbal flood carries everything along with it in a tide of bad days. "Men and women were no longer alone very much; they formed a crowd. And in that barbaric chaos you were lost." Yes, we are lost in this barbaric chaos where a confusion of images replaces style and thought. We glimpse the features of a city: its buildings, streets, advertising, cars. Maybe we are already dead. Somebody is getting hell ready for us.

But there is a faint glimmer of light amidst these shadows. On a January 25th, at 3:30, without any visible reason, a siren goes off. At the same moment we see a young girl appear on a motorbike. The girl rides off, disappears between two rows of houses. Immediately, the siren stops. "There was nothing left but silence. And nothing, nothing, not even a vivid memory will remain in our minds. Ever since that day everything has been rotting. I, François Besson, see death everywhere."

Why does the sight of a young girl accompanied by the whine of a siren suddenly cause the world to rot, why does her disappearance plant death in the brain of a young man twenty-seven years old? That is J. M. G. Le Clézio's secret. . . .

As for the novel's characters, François Besson is not much better than an animal. He seems to be deficient in both will and reason. . . . This silly and feeble individual gives rise to such boredom that to follow him in his activities is real torture. The landscape he traverses and the people he meets are cut to his measure. (pp. 378-79)

Le Clézio seems to lose himself in his dramatis personae and wallow in their unfathomable blues. "No one is sick longer than he wants to be," said Montaigne. The author of *Le Déluge* and his heroes have decided to be sick day and night until death overtakes them. The weak spark of existence that animates them gets lost in the crowd, and they sink into the verbal dough in which the novel holds them captive. The deluge that destroys them consists of words. . . .

Failure, despair, suicide, death: Le Clézio doesn't seem capable of talking about anything else. Even though I felt there was a generous portion of the literary in all this, it began to bother me. . . .

[What] life is to Le Clézio [is] a zero, and the whole book is just a morose translation of this nothingness. (p. 379)

What to do about it? To walk for hours in the rain, sit on benches, wander in the night, drink water from public fountains and wait. Le Clézio shows himself at his best in delineating this program. He hasn't lost the gift of making us see things: the street at dawn, the shopwindows, women shopping, the wind, the rain, the big yellow dog that gets killed at the crossroads. But all this was already present in *Le Procès-Verbal*, and with much more energy, more spontaneous richness. *Le Déluge* is an unnecessary repetition. (pp. 378-79)

Kléber Haedens, "A Flood of Words," in Atlas, *Vol. 11, No. 6, June, 1966, pp. 378-80.*

LEO BERSANI

Le Clézio is an appealingly tedious writer; he has a knack for making you like him while he bores you. . . . What I admire in him is, in fact, what makes him rather tedious: his stubborn, solemn, and, until now, generally unsuccessful attempt to find the medium that will help him express (and discover) where his interest and talent as a writer lie.

This search for a form, a tone, a literary mode is only too visible in the nine stories of *Fever*. . . . (p. 4)

There is . . . something very unfeverish about the dogged, cerebral density of Le Clézio's descriptive writing. I find his descriptions generally far less suggestive of the immediacy of sensation than of an astonishing verbal virtuosity which Le Clézio either can't or won't direct and control. Images are confusedly piled up with what seems like the relentless, ponderous application of a schoolboy trying to outwrite the rest of the class. (pp. 4, 16)

But the main trouble with most of these stories is . . . that they set out to be stories and don't quite make it. . . . What's missing, in a variety of ways, is the *distance* that would make conflict—that is, drama—possible. For one thing, Le Clézio is apparently having trouble deciding what distance he himself should take from his stories. He occasionally substitutes himself for characters (as in **"A Day of Old Age,"** when he addresses a fairly painful reminder of mortality to the reader), or, more frequently, he tries weakly to be casual about them by pretending not to be sure what's happening to them. He also gives us only the briefest glimpses into the psychological distances separating characters from one another; not one story has at its center an interesting relationship. Finally, the moment of fever often has no history. What provoked it is either obscure or unconvincing, and characters have almost no reality outside their hallucinations, in spite of Le Clézio's scrupulously naming everyone who appears and even dropping hints (which will interest you as little as they do Le Clézio) about the rest of his characters' lives. . . .

There are, however, some successes in this collection. I liked especially the first half of **"Fever"** (the vagueness of the wife's role spoils the rest of the story), the impressionistic portrait of nature in **"The World Is Alive,"** and **"The Day That Beaumont Became Acquainted With His Pain."** **"Beaumont"** is by far the best story in *Fever,* and this is largely because the metaphorical extravagances never become completely detached from the very clear, located reality of a toothache. . . . [In] conclusion I should say that a certain talent for dialogue appears each time we have someone nagging someone else. Beaumont's call to Paule, Adam Pollo trying to make Michèle talk about the time he raped her in *Le Procès-Verbal,* and Joseph's stubborn curiosity about what the old woman is seeing as she sits dying are all effectively uncomfortable scenes of characters hammering away at the resistance of others. The stubbornness is awful but oddly appealing, and it dramatizes, in a human relationship, the less appealing obstinacy of the descriptive passages in which Le Clézio mauls a scene metaphorically until he becomes what he sees. Characters occasionally provide the resistance and the discipline lacking when Le Clézio is, so to speak, on his own. I don't know how bright a future such a limited talent promises. For the moment, Le Clézio himself is nagging away at a literary medium in search of an answer, and this makes for a touching if not an always absorbing spectacle. (p. 16)

> Leo Bersani, *"Inside Tales," in* Book Week—The Washington Post, *July 10, 1966, pp. 4, 16.*

PAGE STEGNER

In many ways ["**Fever**"] is a disappointing sequel to [J.M.G. Le Clézio's] first novel, "**The Interrogation**" . . . ; disappointing because it *is* (intentionally or not) a sequel, and some of its inclusions strike one as rejected chapters from that earlier work. Variation on a theme is one thing. Repetition of form, language, point of view, character and so on is another. Eventually, even a talent as considerable as Le Clézio's can bore when its performance so seldom changes.

In a brief introduction to this book, Le Clézio calls his collection "nine tales of little madness." Actually, they are not tales at all; they are nine impressionistic renderings of the landscape of the imagination. They are concerned with a variety of sensations (fever, pain, fatigue, etc.) and with the ability of these sensations to transport the mind into ecstatic states of hyper-consciousness. At their best ("**The Day That Beaumont Became Acquainted With His Pain**," for example), they achieve a complete fusion of the psychological and the physiological aspects of sensory experience. At their worst ("**Then I Shall Be Able to Find Peace and Slumber**"), they remind one of a "consciousness-expanding experience" reported in The Psychedelic Review.

It is not external reality that Le Clézio explores. Rather, it is the internal reality of a free-floating consciousness, traveling through a timeless, spaceless universe of impressions. His characters are merely transformers for sensations produced by the tactile world. . . .

Often Le Clézio's narrators attempt to transcend time and space and achieve a union with the infinite reality, God, by merging themselves with the animal, vegetable, mineral objects of their contemplation. Like Renaissance men in reverse, they descend the great chain of being. In so doing, they produce some fantastic transformations of their physical surroundings; but ultimately, after the fourth or fifth story, this all becomes too much, too relentless, too repetitious. . . .

In spite of these objects there is much in Le Clézio's collection that is arresting and absorbing. . . .

In all of the stories, the author's verbal felicity is amazing. Even if wearied by the repetition, we come away awed by his skill in manipulating language and dazzled by his ability to create with words vividly impressionistic paintings. His greatest achievements are rhetorical. He deserves to be read for this reason, if for no other.

> Page Stegner, *"A Little Madness," in* The New York Times Book Review, *July 31, 1966, p. 5.*

JOHN WEIGHTMAN

The French "New Novel," although still an amorphous entity very difficult to define, is now old enough to have produced a second generation of exponents, among whom I would place [J.M.G. Le Clézio and Monique Wittig], who have been the most widely acclaimed young writers to appear during the last two or three years. *La Fièvre,* a collection of short stories written in the "New Novel" manner, is Le Clézio's second book. . . .

M. Le Clézio and Mlle. Wittig are, temperamentally, very different from each other, the former being very neurotic and, indeed, perhaps too overtly anguished to fit entirely into the "New Novel" pattern, the latter robust and commonsensical, in so far as a writer of this kind can believe in commonsense. Neither, however, tries to any extent to achieve objectification in created "characters"; both occasionally seem to be describing named people from the outside, but this is merely a way of avoiding the monotony or inaccuracy of saying "I" all the time. Their theme is the fluctuation of their own inner awareness, the mystery of identity, the impossibility of coinciding with being and, in this respect, they derive, of course, like a good part of the "New Novel," from Existentialist psychology. Each consciousness is, at once or successively, subject and object; it can only know itself as subject by turning itself into object; and then again, when an object is contemplated intensively, it surges back into, and swamps, the subject. . . . Le Clézio is so convinced that the drama of the consciousness's relationship with itself is the central problem for the writer that he looks upon the traditional literary genres as out-of-date devices corresponding to mistaken concepts. . . .

Literature becomes, then, the meandering monologue, or internal dialogue, of the subjective-objective consciousness. (p. 24)

[Le Clézio tries], with naive honesty, to extend the description of the alienated consciousness that was already carried a long way in Sartre's *La Nausée* and Camus's *L'Etranger.* His "New Novel" aspect is that he disregards all social and political problems and fills a good deal of space with dogged enumerations of physical details, as if the only thing the consciousness can do in certain moments of stress is to relieve the ache of its anonymous void by close attention to the discrete particulars of the external world. . . . By "fever," Le Clézio means more or less the same thing as Sartre's "nausea," i.e., contingency sickness, the vertigo which arises from persistent contemplation of the central point of non-comprehension. Now and again, there are hints that the vertigo might suddenly turn into ecstasy, as if the nothingness of the creature might be unexpectedly transformed into fullness through communion with God. But these mystic intimations are slight and, in any case, are not accompanied by any metaphysical comment. . . . [However, Le Clézio's] writing is, as yet, on the verge of the clinical, as if he were just managing to hold in check some serious psychic disturbance which may have more to it than Existentialist nausea. Hence, as one reads him, a strong impression of claustrophobia, which combines with the usual, oppressive solipsism of the "New Novel." But he is undoubtedly a talent with remarkable possibilities. (pp. 25-6)

> *John Weightman, "The Indeterminate I," in* The New York Review of Books, *Vol. VII, No. 9, December 1, 1966, pp. 24-6.*

J. MITCHELL MORSE

Le Clézio is a phony, an imitator of second-rate and third-rate fashionable novels that once were avant-garde, a vendor of old experiments to the new generation. His pretentious incompetence [in *Fever*] offers nothing to compare with Roquentin's black root, much less with Malte's cannister lid. His foreword is embarrassing in its stale naiveté. Writing a book like *Fever* and sending it to a publisher is the literary equivalent of nailing two pieces of scrap lumber hastily together, spilling some paint on them, and sending them to an art gallery.

> *J. Mitchell Morse, in a review of "Fever," in* The Hudson Review, *Vol. XIX, No. 4, Winter, 1966-67, p. 676.*

HUGH KENNER

In a time of permissive publishing, to end the world takes only ink and paper. Novel writing is the least expensive of handicrafts. Thus it costs next to nothing to bring before the reader's mind a giant affirmation of queer menace:

"Somewhere between earth and sky there oscillates a large, flattish object, its surface daubed with blood, apparently made of riveted and interlapping steel plates, sliding to and fro with each compression or expansion of their over-all mass, and yet very much all of a piece, easily liftable on some gigantic bar, like a curtain."

If you were making a film, and had to budget a few thousand dollars for Special Effects to fabricate one of these, you would think several times about its rhetorical necessity before writing the order. But if you're covering pages with words, you can conjure it up amidst 3,000 words about odd meteorological goings-on without taking thought at all.

Though **"The Flood"** exhibits considerable talent for metaphor, it is difficult to locate a passage that doesn't suffer, in this way, from encountering too little resistance. The budgetary resistance against which the film maker tests his notions isn't the only kind, of course, and has never been the operative kind for the writer unless his ambitions are defined by best-sellerdom. It's relevant to invoke it here because **"The Flood"** is more like a French film—Godard's "Alphaville," say—than it is like a novel.

It's film that has created the fashions on which J.M.G. Le Clézio relies for his effects: apartment-house facades, loudspeakers, graffiti; squeal of tires, uproar of jet engines; a boy obsessed with a pinball machine; a man listening to a tape-recorded suicide; a man waking next to a woman and examining her sleeping body with detached intentness.

The continuity—12 days in the life of François Besson—is preceded by an equivocal apocalypse that delivers the urban world into a universe of non-meaning, and followed by an equivocal eternity of blackness in which the ordinary carries on. . . . The literal cause of the blackness is that Besson has burned out his retinas by staring at the sun. A thousand verbal curlicues admonish us, however, not to be so square as to focus on the literal. . . .

[Has Besson been attempting to] live a meaningful life, presumably? But, if so, it's no surprise that he can't. He's been acting, we can only believe, at the whim of the writer, in the course of this protracted fictional doodle. For what metaphysic can we extract from a doodle? Only that the pencil seeks its own amusement, in pursuit of little local virtuosities.

The authority of the camera, that's what's lacking: the stubborn resistance of the real, of faces and bodies asserting their identity through whatever arbitrariness of scripting and editing. Dimly at Mr. Le Clézio's shoulder stands some such wraith as the Godard of "My Life to Live," a film whose 12 episodes triumph over such dialogue as "Life is . . . life" and "I wish I were someone else" and "The more you talk, the less it means." Godard's episodes are even better served by such dialogue than they would be by more resonating language, precisely because we can see bodies, faces, clothes, movements, rooms, cars, a city: all real. In **"The Flood,"** because it is a book, all reality is dissolved into words, words. (p. 4)

The arc of a man's passion, exactly that, is what we miss in **"The Flood."** Through the words, as in Beckett, we discern the airless humdrum. But behind the words, as not in Beckett, we detect not a disciplined sensibility, with a point of view about the airless humdrum and about the nature of the obligation to describe it, but simply a young Midas, a Midas enabled by syntax and by the dictionary to create fashionable vistas inexpensively, at the touch of the pen. Feats of creation, feats of annihilation, ought to be harder than he makes them look. (p. 40)

> *Hugh Kenner, "Twelve Days to Despair," in* The New York Times Book Review, *January 28, 1968, pp. 4, 40.*

BARRY COLE

Terra Amata's author is described as 'one of the most promising French writers of fiction to emerge since Camus,' and his earlier novels have been enthusiastically praised. Le Clézio's new novel, however, seems more like a product of despair, a sort of 'where do I go from here? *Can* I go from here?'

Chancelade is a small boy apparently determined to take from life all he can. His author uses the boy's projected life as a peg to which he can attach his own games and experiments. What we get, unfortunately, are incidents without purpose or sense. . . . In an attempt to fill the pages, Le Clézio ranges from chapters of sign language, Morse and straight incomprehensibility to theology, and questions (arbitrary and unoriginal): 'Do you like money? What will it be like a million years from now? Where is God? How will it all end?' He lists the human contents of a beach (twenty-nine names). Science fiction interrupts and we are treated to variations on a theme by Asimov and Clarke which evolve into mathematics. . . .

[We] get a wooden dialogue. The narrative includes such felicities as butterflies which 'dart madly,' centipedes which have 'a thousand feet,' trees which stand 'peacefully,' nightingales with 'artificial cries' and potato bugs which make 'vain' excursions. And, despite his SF interest, Le Clézio can still write of the 'four corners of the sky.' Or was St Jerome playing tricks again? The book as a whole seems to be the work of a fine and talented writer desperately trying to make up for a false start. Unfortunately, he rarely gets beyond second gear.

Barry Cole, "Jerome at Work," in The Spectator, *Vol. 222, No. 7336, January 31, 1969, p. 142.**

Geoffrey Wolff, "1969—A Rich Year for the Novel," in Newsweek, *Vol. LXXIV, No. 25, December 22, 1969, pp. 97-8, 99A, 99B.**

JOHN HEMMINGS

Le Clézio's heroes have been described before now as the heirs of Meursault and Antoine Roquentin, and this is very plausible. The beaches of the Riviera correspond closely to those of Algiers, and all Camus's feeling for the poignant evanescence of natural beauty seems to have passed into Le Clézio, who first came into prominence just about the same time the elder writer was killed. The comparison with Sartre's first novel is justified by Le Clézio's characteristic preoccupation with the endless multiplicity and yet separateness of everything, the world being presented as full and over-full, a 'furious labyrinth, a great living, palpitating mass, like a giant body sprawling on the ground and living its thousand blended lives'. But whereas for Roquentin there was nothing but nausea in this cram-full earth, for Chancelade [the protagonist of *Terra Amata*] such plenitude induces easy ecstasies. Formally, *Terra Amata* is another womb-to-tomb history. It has its gimmicks—a love-letter in morse, a poem in Polish, the table of contents turning up in the last chapter but one. Most people would not recognise it for a novel, not even a 'new novel', unless the definition of that term be stretched to cover any writing which undertakes to divorce the novel from its bossy helpmate, social history, and remarry it to art.

John Hemmings, "Butyric Whiffs," in The Listener, *Vol. 81, No. 2081, February 13, 1969, p. 216.**

THOMAS LASK

"**Terra Amata**" carries its character, Chancelade, from cradle to the grave. Steps in this progress are marked by lyrical essays, punctuated with vapid conversation, Whitmanesque lists of names, words, events and cosmic ruminations. For the burden of the book is that man is born, lives and dies, and that his life is meaningless. He is pushed out by the generation that comes after him, he leaves no impress on the world; he ages before his life is fulfilled. Better not to have been born, etc.

These adolescent outpourings sound like cries of woe between bites of eclair. There is nothing in the novel to indicate that Chancelade is worth listening to. He has done nothing, suffered nothing, experienced nothing to make him worth our regard. Sure, life is bitter, brutish, short. It needs no simpering hero come from France to tell us this. But it is how he responds to this fact that gives us a measure of a man. With Chancelade you feel not so much that the world has failed him as that the salesman has not been able to get him the right color for his car.

Thomas Lask, "Man and His Woes," in The New York Times, *April 3, 1969, p. 41.**

GEOFFREY WOLFF

"**Terra Amata**" is a short novel with epic ambitions. It is about man's genesis, flowering, erosion and destruction. It is at once fastidiously intelligent, cool and moving. . . . [Le Clézio's] landscapes live—literally. The earth twitches, grimaces and weeps, and Le Clézio, with craft and cunning, manages to make such immoderate conceits acceptable to us. (p. 98)

J. R. FRAKES

Some books deliberately set themselves up as targets for critics bound by traditional "rules" of fiction and weary (often justifiably) of show-off experimentation with form, narrative line, characterization, denouement, resolution, etc. For these critics, "experimental" novels are usually messy, spiteful splurges of sophomorism masquerading as radical iconoclasm. Despite the acclaim for Le Clézio's earlier works (*The Interrogation, The Flood, Terra Amata*), *The Book of Flights* is such a target. Apparently shapeless, a hodge-podge of pseudo-lyrical meditations, typographical eccentricities, catalogues, guidebook descriptions, rhetorical questions, assertions of a snotty self, this "adventure story" is a model of skippability. . . .

All this guff is easy to dismiss. Too easy, for *The Book of Flights* is not dismissable as faddish self-indulgence. Rather it is a horrifying vision of the unending war between system and chaos, of man fleeing from nihilism into ultra-nihilism, of motion itself as the only human action capable of sustaining life on this rotten planet—even if that life remains meaningless. Technically, the book will remind you of Baudelaire's *Little Prose Poems* and Rudolph Wurlitzer's threatening 1970 novel *Flats*. The extended sequences in the desert and in the leper-colony are much more than tours de force; they are masterful conceits that contribute to a stunning metaphor—"these pure, clear lines, this wordless transparency, this truth transmuted into landscape."

J. R. Frakes, in a review of "The Book of Flights: An Adventure Story," in Book World—The Washington Post, *January 9, 1972, p. 2.*

PETER BROOKS

"**The Book of Flights**" continues, with increased daring, to deconstruct the novel within itself. Notably, it is interspersed with chapters called "Self-Criticism" in which the author calls into question his procedures, casts suspicion on his enterprise, points up the various sleights-of-hand and falsification of the act of writing.

Yet Le Clézio is a curious mixture of the new sensibility, with its intense self-awareness about the fiction-making process, and an older quest for a literature of presence, significance, plenitude and even innocence. At heart, he is a romantic, obsessed by "writing's abandonment of reality, loss of meaning, logical madness"—by the loss of a language having a full grasp on things.

Really, I think, he writes out of protest against the state of affairs recognized and accepted by Robbe-Grillet or John Barth, whose works insist upon the fictionality of fictions, their inherent inadequacy to the phenomenal world, their status as a supreme game where the reader's engagement with the text is the true act of significance. Le Clézio recognizes the game, indeed he plays it with talent, but he wants it to lead him through to an esthetic of presence. He wants to have his self-criticism and his innocence both, to deconstruct literature and to make it, in full romantic fashion, serve as salvation. And this, I think, accounts for the smugness and moral stridency that sometimes characterize his work. (p. 6)

Le Clézio sometimes reminds one of Godard in his creation of a certain poetry of the banal from the overwhelming clutter of the contemporary landscape, including the static of a zapped-out language. At his best, Le Clézio is ever the master at rendering existence at the level of sensation with a daring and admirable freshness of language. He conveys in many strong passages a feeling of "material ecstasy" (**"L'Exstase Matérielle,"** he called his book of essays), a joyful penetration into the heart of things. But he lacks Godard's cool. There is too portentous an insistence that we must see, must react. We have become somewhat jaded about alienating cityscapes, hallucinatory highways and the daily apocalypses of contemporary consciousness. Le Clézio's mode is in fact perhaps too insistently the apocalyptic, which points once again to an unacknowledged disjuncture between his sophisticated suspicion of literature and his essentially romantic commitment. (pp. 6, 34)

[There] are parts of this book that are very moving.

Yet I find something ultimately self-deceptive about his writing. For all his elaborate self-consciousness about the novel, literature and language, he is not finally searching for a further expansion in our awareness of the fiction-making process—in the manner of Borges—but for a para-literature and para-language which would be adequate to the immediacy of experience and would restore our freshness of vision and response. He proclaims the futility and terminal illness of literature—only to make, surreptitiously, the highest claims for his form of it. This comes close to self-righteousness. (p. 34)

> Peter Brooks, "Para-Literature, Para-Language, Para-Novel," in *The New York Times Book Review, January 30, 1972, pp. 6, 34.*

JAMES P. DEGNAN

J. M. G. Le Clezio's *The Book of Flights*—novel? anti-novel? oh well, to quote the blurb (by far the most interesting, and the *only* coherent part of *Flights*), "*flight* . . . not merely from the conventions of the novel" but "flight in time and space . . . from reality and the prison of self" and, well, you get the idea—is one of those awful collections of pretentious trash—e.g., of "free ranging meditations, exclamations," and so forth—that remind one of William Burroughs and Grove Press and the worst (not to mention some of the best) of Lawrence Durrell. . . .

Flights concerns the flights—real? imaginary? what, after all, does it matter?—of Young Man Hogan, not John Hogan or Ben or Bill, just Young Man or "*the* person called Hogan." Anyway, Young Man does and says things in the course of *Flights* . . . which obviously constitute what the extraordinarily imaginative blurbist calls "metaphysical lyricism of great beauty." Once, for instance, "planting himself on his two feet," Young-Man-*the*-person called-Hogan, "tries to bend his shadow upward" (not downward, mind) "in the direction of the sun." Once, addressing the reader in a postscript to a chapter—a chapter that has absolutely nothing to do with water or glasses or bottles—Young Man says: "Nothing easier than pouring a little water from a bottle into a glass. Go on. Try it. You'll see." But, ultimately, it is in the "metaphysical lyricism" of his remarks on the nature of writing and of literature that Mr. (Young-Man-the-person) Le Clézio hits that thing you dread to see him hit—his stride. Writing a book, he informs us, is the *same* thing—not a thing analogous to—but the *same* thing as "contemplating the slow sprouting of a dried bean in an earth filled jam jar" or of brushing your teeth. Had he chosen to do either of these, he tells us, he would not have had to write *Flights,* since he would have been doing exactly the *same* thing as writing *Flights.* One can only wonder: why didn't he?

> James P. Degnan, in a review of, "The Book of Flights," in *The Hudson Review, Vol. XXV, No. 2, Summer, 1972, p. 334.*

BARBARA PROBST SOLOMON

In his earlier novels **"Terra Amata"** and **"The Book of Flights,"** Le Clézio developed a highly original brand of the plotless, characterless novel. In **"War"** he has a young female heroine, Bea B., wander through a maze of peace, war and the mess of modern cities. As we read Bea B.'s wonderful wide-eyed internal babble and her scraps of poetry, jottings and letters in a diary she carries in her air-travel tote bag, Bea B. becomes the perfect foil for the modern apocalypse she stumbles through. . . . Le Clézio is one of those Frenchmen who has spent much time, young, outside France (in Bangkok and Mexico City) and this experience may have helped him succeed in his central narrative device: as Bea B. wanders through a territory that is presumably Vietnam—and a permanent legacy of ten thousand years of war—at the same time she is emotionally walking through France and Europe. Le Clézio is marvelously agile in this fusion of France and the Third World.

Le Clézio's psychological perceptions of the emotional state one undergoes during a war—how people actually experience war—is extremely accurate and is, indeed, the true theme of this novel. What Le Clézio does is literally to smash the landscape around Bea B. in order to create an effect of total visual disorientation. Thus Bea B. herself is not fragmented, words are not fragmented, but everything around Bea B. is in disorder and what she sees and the way she sees it is what is happening. The one thing Bea B. holds on to—with an almost fanatic desperation, as though it is her last possession on earth—is the specificity of words, the exact naming of places and objects.

The visual distortions created by modern war are quite literally overwhelming and Le Clézio is both right and stylistically brilliant when he has Bea B. madly search for signposts in her efforts to locate herself. (p. 5)

Le Clézio's real strength lies ultimately in his lyrical descriptions of Bea B.'s thought processes and the world she moves through. . . .

When, toward the end of the novel, after the world has entered into a state of total war, Bea B. utters her plaintive final cry—"I myself am not really sure I am born"—we believe in her enough to wish Le Clézio had not resorted to the use of names as cold as Bea B. or Monsieur X. For Le Clézio appears to be somewhat afraid of his emotions and his own humanity. At those moments he speeds the novel up so much—backing off into film and collage effects—that he loses the reader unnecessarily. Yet if Le Clézio lacks the sober total vision of Claude Simon or the ultimate power to move of Jorge Semprun, he is still one of the most powerful and daring of the young French writers. By the end of the novel, he has managed to create a new Fourth World that combines the shiny airport look of American Europe with the wreckage of Third World battlefields throughout the centuries. Bea B. has become the victim of a life lived in the bruised landscape of permanent modernity and permanent warfare. And we can see that despite the occasional flaws of his book Le Clézio has altered the form of the novel for traditional and authentic reasons: the old forms no longer serve to express his modern experience. (p. 34)

Barbara Probst Solomon, "Only the Words Intact," in The New York Times Book Review, *July 15, 1973, pp. 4-5, 34.*

REINHARD KUHN

On first glance the constant interspersal of non-literary elements among the extensive fragments of a narrative might seem revolutionary; a closer reading [of **Les Géants,** published in English as **The Giants,**] destroys the illusion created by leafing through the book at random and leads to the sobering realization that Le Clézio has actually up-dated Orwell's *1984* by writing a pop version of Zola's *Au Bonheur des dames*. There is even a coherent plot of sorts to be extracted from among the jumble of public-relations slogans, there is a traditional exploitation of symbols, and a familiar and reassuring unity exists underneath the apparent chaos. For everything revolves around the department store of Hyperpolis, the scene for the futile efforts of Tranquillité to find an acquaintance who works at the Information Desk. While her quest fails, she does succeed in distracting another habitué of the emporium, Machines, from his fascination with shopping carts and escalators. Aroused from his torpor, he is tempted to set fire to the shopping center. This laudable enterprise results in his interrogation (Kafkaesque, as is fitting) by the ever-vigilant authorities (either the giants of the title or their servitors). All this time a third major figure, a wayward boy who goes by the name of Bogo le Muet, steadfastly refuses to speak, because he is afraid that by opening his mouth he will do like the others and give orders. Even the style of the novel has its old-fashioned aspects which emerge like vestiges of a past cultural tradition so strong that despite his efforts the author cannot divest himself of its ruins. . . . Every feature of this book, whether literary or extra-literary, is an assault on the intelligence and the senses designed to force the reader to carry out the author's design. The fundamental flaw is that the propagandistic techniques which the author employs to urge the reader to incinerate Hyperpolis are the ones which were used to create it. The author neglected to imitate the exemplary behavior of Bogo le Muet, with the result that he does give orders. It is as if an opponent of brain-washing were to try to eliminate it by brain-washing its potential victims. So, in a very profound sense, this book is not a novel but an advertisement. The medium is the message and at the same time a contradiction of the message. For this reviewer, who does not like to have his mind manipulated in the service of any cause, be it for the conflagration of a department store or for fire prevention, there is the temptation of the simple response: *il faut brûler "Les Géants,"* but by proffering such advice he would be emulating Le Clézio rather than Bogo. (pp. 799-800)

Reinhard Kuhn, in a review of "Les Géants," in The French Review, *Vol. XLVIII, No. 4, March, 1975, pp. 799-800.*

JOHN STURROCK

["**The Giants**"] is thoroughly benign, an undeniably stylish but overlong and glib exhortation to the world to wake up and Be Free. It seems that those superannuated ogres, the hidden persuaders, are still at work, and they reappear here as the Masters of Thought or the Masters of Words, keeping us all down by thinking our thoughts for us. Le Clézio's call to arms

against them has the form of a parable, though not much crystallizes from his indefatigable prose by way of a location or a narrative. We are in, or around, a brightly-lit cement dystopia called Hyperpolis, something like a giant supermarket full of shambling, zombie-like consumers. The few characters are so underdeveloped they are almost translucent and have whimsically parabolic names like Tranquility, Machines and Dumb Bogo, an urchin who is a kind of hero because he either can't or won't talk.

Not to talk in Hyperpolis is to be free, because it means you are no longer mouthing the thoughts fed into you by the omnipotent corporations and their advertising agents. But Le Clézio . . . writes too richly or blandly to endow Hyperpolis with the necessary unpleasantness, and his human figures are far too dim to be sympathetic. Actually, Hyperpolis hardly seems worth running away from. The translation, it so happens, is extraordinarily good—rather wasted on a lazy book such as this.

John Sturrock, in a review of "The Giants," in The New York Times Book Review, *November 23, 1975, p. 22.*

VALENTINE CUNNINGHAM

Scrabbling forlornly about on the outside of **The Giants**—a novel whose truculent bloatedness is the result of over-doses of *anti-roman* steroids—is a clearer, thinner, and much more recognisably simple-minded fiction. Called, say, *The Unhidden Persuaders,* its thesis, that the human race is being bombarded by advertisements propagated by industrial giants and their agency hacks, who don't care that they're killing language, doesn't sound too original—it *isn't*—so it's not allowed to interfere too much with Le Clézio's inflationary restatement of Vance Packard's familiar threnody. Instead, we're shoved inside Hyperpolis and its Supermarket, a world of invading vocables, a landscape of signs, invented by the commercial and political Masters, in which a girl called Tranquillity and a trolley-supervisor called Machines vainly struggle (à la Orwell, you might venture to suggest) for personality and relationship. Naturally, when Machines lights a fire in the Supermarket (a damp squib of a try at burning down Hyperpolis) he's arrested. His hapless struggle against the Masters much resembles the fiction's own forlorn tussle with the modish appurtenances (slogans, computer programmes, poems for machines) that in this novel trample old-fashioned stuff like plot and character into submission. The 'hero' is Dumb Bogo, a youth who, depressed at what the Masters are doing to human speech, has given up words for the language of pebbles and suchlike dazzling communicators. It does make an odd shift, however, this blaming all human speech, and urging the virtues of word-smashing dictionary-burning, and pebble-fancying just for the iniquities of some of language's practitioners.

Valentine Cunningham, "Native Daughter," in New Statesman, *Vol. 90, No. 2332, November 28, 1975, p. 686.**

JENNIFER R. WAELTI-WALTERS

[It] has become abundantly clear that Le Clézio's writings to date function as a cohesive whole. There are constant reflections, echos, and even direct references from book to book as well as within each volume, and successive works take up themes that have already been treated in order to develop them further or offer an alternative statement. (p. 159)

[The] works tend to go in pairs. *The Interrogation* and *The Flood* offer the poles of heat and cold, light and darkness while telling the same story of bewilderment, refusal, and flight from society by symbolic annihilation of man's faculties of comprehension. *The Ecstasy of Matter* and *Terra Amata* are the theory and practice of human life in Western Europe and hence complement each other totally. The attitudes and preoccupations of the first three novels come together in *The Book of Flights,* with its tale of repeated turning away, whereas the contrast between village and city established in this book provides the division and parallel which have marked the pairs since 1969. *War* shows the struggle against modern city life; and its parallel was to have been found in *In Iwa's Country*—the story of life with the Panamanian Indians. Similarly, *The Giants* has its partner in *Journeys to the Other Side* in which the overwhelming accumulation of consumer goods is exchanged for the seething possibilities of the natural world. And in both the mind leaves the ordinary thinking plane. In the first case under the influence of the subliminal messages broadcast in Hyperpolis the movement is induced by others. In the second case NajaNaja teaches her friends to control their own minds in such a way that they can escape the restrictions of reality for a more universal plane whenever they wish. Simultaneously, *Journeys to the Other Side* provides the missing complement to *The Book of Flights*. The latter showed physical and geographical flight while the former explores mental and cosmic escape through the power of the imagination—a solution used tentatively at the beginning of Le Clézio's career in *The Interrogation* and *The Ecstasy of Matter.*

Throughout the work the protagonists are dominated by two major influences: the sun and the sea—or occasionally water in some other form. The sun brings understanding, an understanding of things which are sometimes too painful to withstand; thus man tries to escape what the light forces him to see. But everything is focused on the sun; for Le Clézio all man's thought and hence the structures he establishes are created around it, for it is the source of revelation. It is reality. (pp. 159-60)

The complementary influence is water, and it is not surprising to find that the women in Le Clézio's books are often found close to water. Chancelade and Adam both make advances to girls on the beach, and both fail to understand them. In *The Book of Flights* a woman is identified with a river; in *The Giants* Tranquilité and her friend drown; and finally NajaNaja walks on the water into the sunset, thus linking both images and providing an absolute contrast to François Besson crawling out to the end of the breakwater at the height of the storm. Besson seems to be trying to escape from his life and from the sort of relations with women where his security is constantly threatened; indeed, he is attempting to return to the womb. NajaNaja is the total opposite to the struggling image of rejection offered by Besson. She controls her environment; she has mystery, youth, beauty, flexibility, competence; she commands love and allegiance and seems to have power over all of life and death. Le Clézio gives her the attributes of the archetypal woman. (p. 161)

Solitude, alienation from society, its people and values, and travel in Asia and South and Central America where alternative philosophies can be found have brought Le Clézio along a path very similar to the one he traced in the work of Henri Michaux at the time when his own body of work was embryonic. The

cohesion that exists between Le Clézio's critical work and his creative writing is striking. Everywhere we find the same choice, war or flight, imposed by a fundamental isolation rooted in fear; this is shared by Lautréamont, Artaud, and Michaux, to whom . . . Le Clézio is drawn. For all of them writing is a safety valve protecting them more or less effectively from madness. Drugs and travel are used as means of escape and revelation. Each writer is concerned with the expression of his own deep feelings and his need to communicate them to others. This need for communication creates a profound struggle in the writers, owing to each one's alienation from his fellows, and produces a language of unusual violence coupled with a certain hermeticism. (p. 162)

That Le Clézio's struggle is a personal one manifests itself, in the early novels at least, by the fact that his characters are very alike and that each of the young men is similar in a number of respects to Le Clézio himself. They are all alternative statements of the same thing. Indeed, the juxtaposition of alternatives is a technique the author uses at all levels and, in particular, . . . [there is] the instability of his subject pronouns at all times. Narration moves frequently from "I" to "you" to "he" without any apparent motivation—a technique which both alienates the reader and forces him to share the alienation of narrator and protagonist very intimately. The novels have little or no plot, and in many cases the sections within a book have no apparent order. Usually they are made up of a series of situations which illustrate a given theme from different angles. These can be complementary or contradictory, developing the theme further or offering another possibility, a different interpretation. The effect is that of a number of tableaux rather than of continuous narration. Each book is complete in itself and yet is linked to the other works by a system of recurrent detail, repetition of images, new or further treatment of themes and problems. Hence all Le Clézio's writings are woven together into a single growing structure in which each strand reinforces the others, and adds to their combined impact and power. (pp. 165-66)

Against society Le Clézio pits the forces of the natural world, and, above all, the elements. He is a relentless observer of the world around him, with the patience to record minute details, long sequences of phenomena, actions, and the gift to transpose what he has seen into words with extraordinary realism. It has been suggested that his evocations of heat are the most telling in the whole of French literature, and it is certainly true that he excels in the creation of "set-piece" descriptions: a storm at sea, a rainy night, and so on. His books are permeated by atmospheric conditions, overwhelmed by consumer goods and modern building. This is his universe. The only objection that can be made is that sometimes the author seems to be fascinated by the flow of his own sentences, and his effects then lack a conciseness which would increase their force.

In his personal explorations he has pushed beyond the usually accepted bounds of the novel into a realm of lyric reflection in which fiction, philosophy, and poetry are combined. It is no wonder that frequent references are found in Le Clézio's writing and that of his critics. Like them Le Clézio is trying to describe the universe, and his cosmic prefaces and epilogues are but the more extreme of his attempts.

In many ways he reminds us of Jean-Jacques Rousseau. Both are intensely personal writers, consummate stylists, mystics making pertinent social criticisms, observers of nature in all its forms. Both reveal acute problems in their personal relations with other people and with women in particular. It is partly the result of each one's need to be accepted that they write copiously.

Given these resemblances, it would seem proper to end this study with two well-known quotations from Rousseau. Le Clézio's treatment of these statements is very different from that of his predecessor, but the criticisms contained in them sum up his attitude very well: "Man is born free and everywhere he is in chains." "Everything is good when it comes from the hands of the author of all things; everything degenerates in the hands of man." Le Clézio indicts modern society, its growth and values, and shares with us his attempts to resist its pressures. He sees life as a period of uncertainty, movement, change between birth and death which both lead out into darkness. His is a totally relative universe where particles swirl, combining and dividing in a constant shift, and where matter may assemble in the shape of man for a short time—this is the result of modern science. Simultaneously, Le Clézio is a humanist of sorts. He believes that man, thus formed, should take responsibility for his context. He should remain as closely tied as possible to the other natural formations around him, for through them he can come to know himself perhaps. The man-made elements of the modern world prevent him from doing this—they alienate him from matter and therefore from himself, who is matter also. Le Clézio's work is one long attempt to deal with alienation and the accompanying diminution of the individual. By his way of writing he forces us to share and come to grips with his situation and therefore our own. He is a man of our time, and his writing is a valuable addition to the corpus of available experience. (pp. 166-67)

Jennifer R. Waelti-Walters, in her J.M.G. Le Clézio, *Twayne Publishers, 1977, 180 p.*

EMILE J. TALBOT

Unlike Pascal, the characters in J.M.G. Le Clézio's second collection of short stories [*Mondo et autres histoires*] are not frightened by the silence of infinite spaces. Rather, they seek it in the sea and the sky and find in it a cosmic freedom, a sense of belonging to the universe that is unfettered by the constraints of civilization. Jon, the boy of **"La montagne du dieu vivant,"** who experiences the infinite most intensely atop a mountain in the company of a mysterious shepherd boy, feels only limitless solitude on his return to the world of men. For Le Clézio, man has regrettably narrowed the universe to fit his own needs and desires. His major characters, all of whom are children in this collection, feel the need to escape from such a limiting and confining world, and this forms the unifying theme of these stories (as well as an important theme of Le Clézio's entire fiction). . . .

Intimacy with the universe has provided [Le Clézio's young characters] with their salvation, . . . [but] their reintegration into the world of men can never be complete. As young mystics among men, they will continue to be the link between the human race and the universe.

Emile J. Talbot, in a review of "Mondo et autres histoires," in World Literature Today, *Vol. 53, No. 2, Spring, 1979, p. 249.*

PATRICIA J. JOHNSON

Composed simultaneously, Le Clézio's volume of essays, *L'Inconnu sur la terre,* and his volume of short stories [*Mondo et*

autres histoires] are facets of the same wish to lead the reader through words, into a parallel, wordless, primitive universe of spontaneous perception. The essays delineate these themes with clarity, the short stories create worlds in which these themes are immediately perceptible. (pp. 153-54)

[In *L'Inconnu,* Le Clézio's] point of view is that of a child, perhaps the child within all of us, who sees the universe surrounding him directly, without the interference of previous prejudices, of human knowledge. The world into which he leads the reader is a primitive one, forgotten by civilized man, but still the province not only of the child but of the poor and the very old, the timeless representatives of a humanity that expects nothing, that is simply there, open to the universe.

This deliberate choice of point of view causes Le Clézio to glorify the perceptions linked to primitive man: the world is a series of cycles, of unending repetition of day and night, where simple gestures (the making of bread, for example) and animal ruse are glorified at the expense of more civilized perceptions. He sees the philosophy and logic of contemporary civilization as opaque screens which prevent man from being really present in the world. Language, too, becomes divided between the primitive and the civilized: musicality of language is linked to the child (Le Clézio quotes, approvingly, the Spanish song "Golondrinas," which consists of only one repeated word, the Spanish word for "swallows"), whereas he rejects as part of the encumbering civilization logical communication by words. . . .

In his attempt to include language within the world of spontaneous perception while removing it from the world of adult civilization, Le Clézio makes words into animate entities. They become in several essays insects which burrow and hide, animals, and even children. . . . Non-verbal communication is glorified, the smile becomes a primeval means of contact, and the glance of another person (preferably that of a woman, child, or old man) conveys a wordless secret which surpasses any possible linguistic interaction.

Searching for the basic life source within the human being (most often symbolized by light or the sun), Le Clézio frequently reverts to the Romantic theme of *évasion*. Both essays and short stories reveal . . . a yearning for experience and communication on a non-rational level. Roads, busses, clouds, the sea with its cargo ships, all become suggestions of the urge to become united with the "azur" of the sky, the "bleu libre de la mer." At the end of this quest is the elemental silence, the ultimate unification with the universe. . . . (p. 154)

The volume of short stories, containing seven stories in addition to the title story, recreates this quest with, for the most part, children as central figures. Their names are deliberately non-realistic—Mondo, Lullaby, Jon, Juba—and the location of the stories seems equally indeterminate. One has vaguely the feeling that some stories may be taking place in Africa, some in the south of France, and some seem clearly linked with Mexico or elsewhere in Latin America. Le Clézio's favorite locations for communication with the universe form the background for many of these *nouvelles*: abandoned houses and gardens, *casemates* returning to nature, rocks overlooking the sea, and the primitive world of desert and pastures. At one with this universe, his child-heroes (he calls them "enfants-fées") know spontaneously the secret of communication with the natural world, a secret lost to the world of adults.

Obviously, the use of words to communicate non-verbal feeling and non-logic, to glorify primitive life forces over civilization, creates a tension in both volumes, a tension which Le Clézio sometimes exploits to his advantage . . . , but which can lead to both repetition and wordiness. Each of the children in the short stories describes what he has just seen as the most beautiful thing he has ever seen; each natural element becomes in its turn the only god. The essays seem to circumvent this problem successfully, whereas one has the distinct feeling that one is reading the same short story over and over, with only incidental changes of names and scenery. What is most noticeably missing here is the humor of much of Le Clézio's early work. In these volumes, Le Clézio appears dead serious about his child-heroes; the reader may find it somewhat difficult to share this viewpoint. (pp. 154-55)

> *Patricia J. Johnson, in a review of "L'Inconnu sur la terre" and "Mondo et autres histoires," in* The French Review, *Vol. LIII, No. 1, October, 1979, pp. 153-55.*

EMILE J. TALBOT

Since . . . *Le procès-verbal,* J. M. G. Le Clézio has continued, through a dozen impressive works, to reaffirm his stature as one of France's great living novelists. *Désert,* lexically rich in its evocation of nomadic and desert life, yet clear and classical in its syntax, is certain to figure among his major novels and to enhance his reputation further.

Désert consists of two narratives which interrupt each other and which take place some seven decades apart. One is situated around 1910, when nomadic desert tribes were making a final attempt to resist colonial conquest. It is a tale of courage and honor which, given the inequality of the forces engaged, could end only in tragedy. . . . This narrative, which both opens and closes the novel, serves as a kind of epic *Vorgeschichte* to the other narrative, which is centered on the descendant of one of these proud, defiant soldiers.

Lalla's story is itself divided into two parts, the first of which, entitled "Le bonheur," relates aspects of her life as an orphan in a slum village on the edge of the desert. . . . The second part of her story, "La vie chez les esclaves," relates the degradation of her life in Marseilles, where she works as a cleaning woman in a seedy hotel. . . . In this young woman there lives

enough of the pride and strength of her forefathers to flee enslavement, whatever its guise, for the freedom of the desert.

The refusal of subjugation in *Désert* is part of a desire to live in reverent contact with nature in spite of the hardship it sometimes brings. . . . *Désert,* which postulates the greatness of primitive peoples, not because they are good in a naïve Rousseauistic sense but because they are close to nature and its elements, may also be considered as a poetic inquiry into man's relationship with the cosmos.

> *Emile J. Talbot, in a review of "Désert," in* World Literature Today, *Vol. 55, No. 2, Spring, 1981, p. 270.*

STEPHEN SMITH

Le Clézio's *Désert* joins that very limited number of contemporary French fictions that deal in a significant way with the relations between France and her former North African colonies. His first novel since *Voyages de l'autre cote* (1975), it represents a major addition to his already impressive literary production and is quite possibly his most esthetically satisfying achievement to date. The prolixity of his style has been reduced, and there remain virtually none of the self-consciously ingenuous passages that have previously marred some of his finest pages. (pp. 898-99)

Trois Villes saintes, published simultaneously with *Désert,* resembles the author's earlier *Haï* in being a lyrical meditation on certain aspects of various native cultures of the Americas. (p. 899)

Désert and *Trois Villes saintes* both provide striking new illustrations of many of the themes that have long characterized Le Clézio's writings: the contrast between modern civilization, with its dehumanizing and enslaving artifices, and those societies that are in closer accord with the natural order; silence and solitude, in both their positive and negative aspects; waiting, watching, and the mystical power of "le regard"; "la parole" and the evocative poetry of names; liberty and the rebellion by which it might be achieved. (p. 900)

> *Stephen Smith, in a review of "Désert" and "Trois villes saintes," in* The French Review, *Vol. LIV, No. 6, May, 1981, pp. 898-900.*

Bernard Mac Laverty

1942-

Irish novelist, short story writer, and scriptwriter.

Mac Laverty has gained considerable attention as an important new author. His novels and short stories deal perceptively with a wide range of human conflicts, from the difficulties of growing up to the ordeals of growing old. His most successful work, the novel *Cal* (1983), has been particularly recognized for its insightful depiction of the effects on individuals of the hostilities between Catholics and Protestants in Northern Ireland.

Mac Laverty made his literary debut with *Secrets and Other Stories* (1977), a collection in which the process of growing up is a prominent theme. While critics enjoyed Mac Laverty's wryly comic tone, they also noted the underlying seriousness of stories that portray young protagonists who confront the reality of death for the first time or undergo other emotional trauma. Mac Laverty's first novel, *Lamb* (1980), was widely praised as a compelling and tragic story of pure love in an impure world. *A Time to Dance* (1982), Mac Laverty's second collection of short stories, expands his range to include examinations of growing old along with stories of young people coming of age.

Cal is Mac Laverty's first work to concentrate fully on wartorn Northern Ireland. Nineteen-year-old Cal and his father are the only Catholic family in a Protestant neighborhood, a highly volatile situation. Yielding to various pressures, Cal becomes involved with the Irish Republican Army and drives the getaway car in the assassination of a Protestant police officer. This is Cal's first and last exercise as an accomplice to terrorism. Later, he meets and falls in love with the murdered man's widow, and through their relationship he attempts to overcome his sense of guilt and find redemption. Critics admired Mac Laverty's depiction of the violence of Ulster life, which is conveyed forcefully without sensationalism. However, the novel has also been faulted for not developing the larger social and political issues it introduces and for ultimately remaining a conventional love story. Despite these criticisms, reaction to *Cal* has been generally favorable, and it is primarily this work which has established Mac Laverty's present importance among contemporary Irish fiction writers.

PATRICIA CRAIG

[The stories in *Secrets and Other Stories* are] completely without affectation or self-indulgence. The themes are simple—loyalty and its failures, compromise, apprehensions of one kind or another. Apart from the boy whose excessive holiness sometimes causes involuntary levitation, the central characters are all unremarkable, but they are presented with that kind of dispassionate authority that makes them stay in the reader's mind.

The settings in time are the 1950s and the present, but the current abnormality of life in Belfast is not stressed. Soldiers in the streets make no more dramatic statement than 'Wot?' when a drunken layabout assures them that they are doing a

© Jerry Bauer

grand job. Yet their presence has ominous implications and these are summed up in single observation. In **'Between Two Shores'**, young girls giggling at soldiers are ignored: 'Soldiers before them had chased it and ended up dead or maimed for life'. (p. 49)

Patricia Craig, "Stories of Ulster," in Books and Bookmen, *Vol. 23, No. 8, May, 1978, pp. 48-9.**

WILLIAM DeMERITT

[In] the world of Bernard MacLaverty . . . the loss of innocent illusions is usually comically ironic—not at all as the characters imagined—yet . . . the loss seems to matter less than the innocence itself.

Several of the better stories in *Secrets and Other Stories* deal with a boy's loss of innocence or his initiation into a corrupted adult world. Yet in MacLaverty's stories these transitional steps do not destroy the former, innocent world. Indeed, those worlds seem to take on new depths of tenderness and reality by exposure to the new. In **"The Exercise,"** a story reminiscent of Stephen Dedalus' disciplining in *A Portrait of the Artist*, a boy is caned by his Latin teacher for daring to suggest that his homework must be right because it was done by his father—a mere barman. Both father and teacher warn that henceforth

Kevin will have to work Latin problems out for himself. At the story's conclusion, the boy hasn't yet faced telling his father that his assertion, "'Son, your Da's a genius,'" no longer applies to Latin. Yet characteristic of MacLaverty, and in marked contrast to Joyce, this beginning of disillusionment produces no alienation between father and son. . . . (pp. 130-31)

Several of MacLaverty's comic situations seem material for raucous one-liners, not the stuff which a grant-winning academic dropping allusions to Joyce, Hopkins, and Forster (and Mr. MacLaverty is also one of these) would find satisfyingly complex. . . .

But darkness intrudes into MacLaverty's predominantly comic world, and his darkened tones are perhaps more convincing because not so stridently insisted upon. Death confronts a number of MacLaverty's children, and death is simply an event to be acknowledged or evaded, not understood. The young boy who sees a drowning in a public pool, in **"The Deep End,"** can find solace in his mother's arms. But the young boys out hunting, in **"Where the Tides Meet,"** are isolated and silenced when their dog is killed: "On the way back to the car in darkness, we string out, a single file, about ten yards between each of us, coming together only to help one another over the fences." The protagonist of the title story, **"Secrets,"** has been caught poring over his maiden aunt's private love letters. Cursed as "dirt" by the aunt, who swore she would remember his desecration till her death, the boy faces her death ambiguously. His crying silently for forgiveness is touchingly juxtaposed against the remarks of his mother, innocently and busily burning the letters, that "'the poor thing was far too gone'" to speak or to remember anything. (p. 131)

Bernard MacLaverty's short stories have appeared in numerous publications, including *New Irish Writing* and *Scottish Short Stories 1977*. *Secrets and Other Stories,* his first collection, reveals a writer of considerable range and ability. As a stylist, MacLaverty is comfortably traditional. His Northern Ireland settings are memorable and distinct; his characters are recognizable and presented so that readers can easily "identify" with them. His comic plots are carefully constructed, and their ironic twists continue to surprise and delight even when anticipated. Some of the tales are self-consciously "literary," and contain first-person narrators who pore over every word of Joyce, teach literature, write fiction, and carry their Hemingway down to the bar when meeting young ladies. But there's been so much of this going around for the last decade that MacLaverty can't be singled out for too much criticism. Besides, two of the "literary" stories produce some of his finest humor, **"Anodyne"** and **"A Pornographer Woos."** And despite all this "literary" stuff, *Secrets and Other Stories* indicates what Bernard MacLaverty's wide-ranging and substantial abilities may contribute to the traditions of Irish short fiction. (p. 132)

> *William DeMeritt, in a review of "Secrets and Other Stories," in* Éire-Ireland, *Vol. XIII, No. 2, Summer, 1978, pp. 130-32.*

JOHN NAUGHTON

Lamb is Bernard MacLaverty's first novel, and an impressive début it is too. The central characters are a man and a boy—the former a Christian Brother who works in an Irish borstal, the latter one of his wayward charges. The story opens in a windswept reformatory on the west coast of Ireland, where a community of Christian Brothers strives to inject a comprehensive fear of both God and man into kids who are either too young for jail or too much for their parents.

The casual, almost cheerful, brutality of the place is well evoked. In particular, there is an economical portrait of one Brother Benedict, the chief disciplinarian of the establishment, which will bring out the weals on any former client of the Brothers who chances to read it. The regime proves, in the end, too much for Michael Lamb, alias Brother Sebastian, who decides to quit the Order after his father dies and leaves him a little money. In departing, however, he takes with him a young epileptic called Owen with whom he has built up an affectionate relationship over two years. . . .

The novel traces the development of their relationship under the pressures of flight, and chronicles the gradual closing of their options with sympathy and skill. It's a story which could easily have degenerated into schmaltz, but Mr MacLaverty keeps his nerve all the way, and brings off an ending which, though predictably tragic and moving, is in no way sentimental.

> *John Naughton, "Hitler in the Amazon," in* The Listener, *Vol. 103, No. 2656, July 3, 1980, p. 25.**

JULIA O'FAOLAIN

"Lamb" reads like one of Aesop's fables. Plain, suspense-filled, streamlined, whittled down, it has the nerve to ignore verisimilitude in the interest of reminding us that reality is often more innocent and desperate than we think. Dostoyevsky was good at doing this, children's stories sometimes come close to it, and the aplomb with which Bernard Mac Laverty pulls off the trick in this first novel makes it look as easy as kite-flying. . . .

[Owen and Michael] are two of a kind: innocent—Michael's love for the boy is not sexual but Christlike, and it is significant that his job at the Home was teaching carpentry—wary, but incapable of foresight, and the wavering growth of trust between them is tactfully and movingly graphed. (p. 13)

Some English reviewers of this novel were unconvinced by Michael's innocence about money—he is shocked to see how fast it goes—and they thought it flawed the narrative. This ignores the blend of canniness and simplicity common among monks, and Mr. Mac Laverty's persuasive implication that the flaw lies in the way things are. Though the events are seen through Michael's unsophisticated eyes, the author manages to convey parabolic resonances. For instance, the false name under which Michael checks into their first hotel is Mr. Abraham, and when he tries to give Owen a reading lesson, the story he happens on is that of Icarus. The reader feels menace before either lamb has a whiff of it. Intent on immediate problems—Owen's wetting hotel beds and having an epileptic fit at a football match—Michael takes a while to see the greater fatality pressing upon them. When it overtakes him in the dark passion of the final page, the reader is drawn into an emotional affinity rarely achieved by serious writing in our time. "He had started with a pure loving simple ideal but it had gone foul on him, turned inevitably into something evil. It had been like this all his life, with the Brothers, with the very country he came from." The country Mr. Mac Laverty comes from is Northern Ireland, and although the political allusion is unobtrusive, it is enriching. Simple ideals are indeed perilous; the rings of resonance widen to engulf us all. This is an impressive book. (pp. 13, 22)

Julia O'Faolain, "Irish Innocence," in The New York Times Book Review, *November 2, 1980, pp. 13, 22.**

THOMAS KELLY

The tales [in *Secrets and Other Stories*] are recognizably Irish for setting and wit—here with the bite of a Belfast accent—and usually display that ease of language peculiar to the Irish writer and exasperating to the American or British. MacLaverty has obvious talent and discipline, but he often lacks the consciousness of the tradition and techniques with which he is working to achieve successfully the modern voice within anecdotal structures.

The opening story, **"The Exercise,"** is endearing, the sort that usually promises a good collection. A young boy thinks his father, a publican, can do no wrong; he gets the man's help on a Latin lesson; next day, the boy is chosen to read his answers in class, and all of them are wrong. . . . There are no traumatic re-evaluations, no tarnishing of the world. He still loves his father very much, but now with a bit more wisdom from the lesson he has learned. Were the volume to continue in such a vein, it would be enjoyable and commendable. The second story, **"A Rat and Some Renovations,"** shows MacLaverty's ability in a different mode: farce. It is a terse and very amusing anecdote, the kind of reminiscence a friend might tell over a drink. What follows, however, demonstrates MacLaverty's lack of control when combining the anecdotal framework with the desire for modern restraint.

"St. Paul Could Hit the Nail on the Head" does not begin with the warmth of childhood memory or the bite of wit. Its more sombre tone, even pace, and strain of silence between the characters—a housewife and a distant cousin she hardly knows, a priest on his yearly visit en route to stay with a friend—all alert in the reader that appetite ignorant of the anecdote. We expect some insight, some touching or exposure of souls, something to come of the care taken in creating the atmosphere. This is almost given: we learn that the old priest's friend has died. . . . The well-crafted ending retains its pace, is terse and objective, and touches the reader's emotions. Seemingly, it is a deeply felt story, even deeply written, but what has really been offered, what given? We receive another anecdote, this time pathetic rather than amusing. All that is said is that it is hard to make new friends in old age. Most details are wasted—her being married to a Protestant whose job is wrecking buildings, the emphasis on an epistle of St. Paul. There are certainly the beginnings of characterization, but they are all invested, or dissipated, in the anticlimactic ending, in the anecdote. The characters have little flesh, little pulse.

There is nothing wrong with that in itself. The problem lies in what is offered. The author's tone and craft are harmonized for intimacy with the reader, for insight of some degree, but the materials on which he goes to work are unsuitable. The story suffers from the author's not being fully aware of, or decisive about, his purpose and his tools. It suffers, especially, from anecdote. This is not to say that the remainder of *Secrets* is given over to such failures. There are several well-conceived stories executed with control. **"Anodyne,"** another story of making friends in old age, develops character more successfully than does **"St. Paul,"** though it, too, is unsure of direction at the end. **"Between Two Shores"** attempts to concentrate almost wholly on character, and is better than most of the stories, but fails for lack of purpose, for lack of a specific point of view

by which to direct the reader: it is more an overwrought character sketch. Still, it exhibits MacLaverty's strengths; when he concentrates on characterization, he is more in control, more conscious of his craft. (pp. 156-57)

Though some of the other stories are good, and all are at least tolerable, the failures and the awkward mixture detract from such a fine story as **"Secrets."** The worst story is **"Hugo,"** and I suspect that the author favors it. This tale, again, relies on anecdote to carry the significance implied in the self-conscious voice and the several regrettable direct asides to remind the reader that something important is intended. There is nothing important in the story. Yet, MacLaverty is not to be dismissed. The trial-and-error search for a voice, the uncertainty and unevenness of *Secrets* do not obscure MacLaverty's talent. (p. 158)

Thomas Kelly, in a review of "Secrets and Other Stories," in Éire-Ireland, *Vol. XVI, No. 1, Spring, 1981, pp. 155-58.*

JAMES CAMPBELL

[MacLaverty's prose is] vivid and virtually faultless. He has the knack of breathing life into a character in the time it takes to say a simple sentence and he never loses his awareness that the first duty of the writer of fiction is to tell a story. Following his recent first novel, *Lamb, A Time to Dance* is a splendid collection of short stories. The longest of the ten is undoubtedly the best: '**My Dear Palestrina**' is about the relationship between a gifted, if reluctant, boy pupil and his flamboyant music teacher, Miss Schwartz. The boy strolls through whatever piece his teacher happens to set him, and as she stands by the piano week after week in only a black silk dressing gown while he tries to keep his mind off something he has never seen, there develops a curious love affair, platonic but in some ways deeply passionate. . . .

MacLaverty's favourite subject is childhood, but it is never the sexless innocence of the worst kind of romanticism. His children are usually misfits of one sort or another and their struggle to function against the more powerful adult authority is what gives impetus to these stories. But MacLaverty's imaginative range is not limited to the pre-pubescent: a cleaning-woman, used to being beaten by her husband, succumbs to the lure of her employer's wallet and lies thinking about the shopping list while he sniffs her bruises; a cultured 83-year-old man at a Day Centre meets a former pupil whom he had once caned for nothing, and keeps his fitness but loses his mind. The author is an Ulsterman resident in Scotland, and some of the stories have a Scots setting; but the mind jumps most smartly to attention when Belfast bombs can be heard exploding in the background. Perhaps the stirrings of a novel are audible in there too. However, I would never presume that his stories were mere throat-clearings: MacLaverty is one of the best practitioners of the genre we have.

James Campbell, "The Twain Meet," in New Statesman, *Vol. 103, No. 2667, April 30, 1982, p. 23.**

ALISON WEIR

Short stories are fashionable and none more welcome than [*A Time to Dance and Other Stories*] by Bernard Mac Laverty. His tone is sombre, his material human. Without resorting to those Gothic pieces of description that point up the moral in many a story written by his contemporaries, he shows us how tragically cruel we are to one another. Yet Bernard Mac Laverty observes the human race with love and heaps loving detail on each story. Mild though they are, there is infinite satisfaction in the carefully drawn settings and the formation of the characters. Each movement is recorded, from the old men and their aluminium frames (one the unwavering pourer of illicit malt whisky at the old people's day centre to celebrate his eighty-third birthday) to the daily woman's humdrum cleaning of the bathroom, watched obsessively by her employer. . . .

The richness of these stories has much to do with Mac Laverty's skill in hanging together events, detail and meaning: the son in **'Life Drawing',** for example, sketching the face of his moribund father who had smashed his boyhood efforts and disowned him for going to art school. There are many, many more; all excellent.

> *Alison Weir, in a review of "A Time to Dance and Other Stories," in* British Book News, *October, 1982, p. 641.*

DEIRDRE DONAHUE

In his second book of short stories, *A Time to Dance,* Bernard Mac Laverty recalls the fears of childhood and imagines the indignities of old age. This Ulster-born writer, now living on the Isle of Islay, explores the world of the very young and the very old, the innocent and the helpless. His best stories map out a frightening terrain where the inhabitants smash up against reality.

The collection's best story, **"The Beginnings of a Sin,"** traces the disenchantment of a fatherless Irish altar boy named Colum. Called a "creeping Jesus" by his older brothers, the child has the ardor of a very young and very earnest soul. He idolizes an old priest, failing to see, as every villager knows, that the man is a sot. . . .

[The] theme of knowledge blasting innocence runs throughout Mac Laverty's work. His first novel, *Lamb,* chronicles the warping of a pure love between a Dublin slum child and a teaching brother. The motif reappears in **"A Time to Dance,"** the title story of the collection.

Set in a Scottish strip joint, the tale recounts a fateful noon. We wait with a small boy locked up in a broom closet. Outside his mother peels off her pasties to the accompaniment of a hooting crowd quaffing its liquid lunch. The boy gleans his mother's true occupation by peering over a crate onto the strobelit runway. He realizes he will never again see her in the same way. . . .

Mac Laverty's compassion extends to the aged as well. In **"No Joke,"** we encounter an old man as he arises on his 83rd birthday. Watching the dawn, he tries to recall some snippet of Baudelaire's poetry he once committed to memory. The retired headmaster of a parochial school, Frank Stringer valiantly attempts to stave off mortality.

Like most short story collections, *A Time to Dance* offers a mixed grill. Mac Laverty is best when he writes of masculine youth or old age. The three stories told from a feminine viewpoint lack a clear tone. The reader does not experience a twinge of recognition.

The best stories, **"A Time to Dance," "The Beginning of a Sin,"** and **"No Joke,"** though, erase the memory of a few false notes.

> *Deirdre Donahue, "Innocence and Experience," in* Book World—The Washington Post, *October 3, 1982, p. 9.*

JOHN WALSH

"Give me a big enough wedge and I'll split the world" says young Cal McCrystal [the protagonist of *Cal*] in an uncharacteristic burst of rhetoric. But all around him the world is already split beyond the powers of healing—he lives with his father under a kind of siege, in the last Catholic household on a Protestant estate. . . . He is beset alike by the Protestant toughs who beat him up on the way home and set his house ablaze, and by the implacable Republicans—the murderously clodlike Crilly and the smoothly rational Skeffington—who try to elicit his support on IRA missions.

Above all he is beset by guilt—the memory of a killing in which he drove the get-away car, and the memory of a voice crying a name, "Marcella!". When he meets Marcella again, the worst possible thing happens—he falls in love with her. As their lives pull together—he moves into the cottage next door, she lends him her books, they go brambling—it is clear that a localised cataclysm is imminent amidst all the soldiers, the guns and the neighbourhood threats.

MacLaverty spins his tale with the minimum of fuss and as a thriller it works extremely well. It's given an additional dimension, though, by the flexibility of his style, which accommodates both the banalities of dance halls and teenage hard men, and the quirkily poetic neologisms of the Northern Irish soul. . . . We are in Seamus Heaney country here, immaculately wedded to a Jennifer Johnston tone of urban pathos. It works extremely well, lifting this story of modern Ulster life into something quite out of the ordinary.

> *John Walsh, in a review of "Cal," in* Books and Bookmen, *No. 328, January, 1983, p. 32.*

VALENTINE CUNNINGHAM

Marinaded in legend, memorialised in endless song, televised nightly, no politics are more self-consciously alert to the way they appear on stage than the Irish sort. And Bernard Mac Laverty's gripping new political thriller, **'Cal',** grips not least because of its attentiveness to how things look, and to how people obsessively watch themselves, within the Ulster frame. Mac Laverty's people keep wanting to take snapshots of, as well as potshots at, each other. Eager voyeurs, they peer continually through windows, through lenses, through camera shutters. What they, and we, see are beauties and terrors awesomely mingling.

Telling moments are stilled, with daunting indiscriminateness, into the illuminated clarities of poetic vision and into chilling pauses for deadliness or death. 'Freeze,' scream the blacked-up soldiery as they burst into young Cal's derelict rural hideaway. Life stands still, filled only with the onion pongs of fear from the arm-pits, as Cal revs up the getaway car outside the off-licence that brutish Crilly is robbing on behalf of the Provos. Cal never forgets his glimpse through yet another getaway car window of the reservist policeman being blasted out of life on his own doorstep. And, in-between, Cal's farmwork focuses the sights, sounds and smells of Ulster fields as magically as in a Seamus Heaney poem (the 'slabbery' dung of cows, the 'tink' of sledgehammer on woodchopper's wedge, the 'withered buff potato tops lying flat on the ground'), while his wistful passion celebrates the beauties of sultry Marcella—Marcella clothed, unclothed, with her child, at her desk in the public library.

Try as they might, of course, Marcella and Cal can't prevent the Troubles spoiling the radiant glories of their love and the rural idyll that they briefly construct. For whoever you are in Mac Laverty's Ulster—whether yahoo Prods burning down Cal's father's house, pale revolutionaries with 1916 in their holsters compelling Cal into the cause, or haunted priests unburdening their bleak sin-mindedness onto captivated children like Cal—you end up seeing through a glass darkly. For Marcella is the wife of the policeman in whose killing Cal assisted.

It's a lover's dilemma fraught with peculiarly Irish manifestations—no novel that I've read about the Ulster of our times seems so inward with the terrible plight of Northern Irishness as 'Cal' is. But it expands also into still more powerful fictional dimensions, with Cal and Marcella as characters with a Shakespearian largeness of moral scope, the Romeo and Juliet *de nos jours*. In its tense amalgam of historical particulars and mythic universals 'Cal' achieves a formidable fictional triumph. Mac Laverty's second novel shows him a man to be watched.

> *Valentine Cunningham, "An Ulster Tragedy," in* The Observer, *January 16, 1983, p. 47.**

FRANCIS KING

Significantly, Bernard MacLaverty's [*Cal*] opens with the words: 'He stood at the back gateway of the abattoir . . .' The North Ireland here depicted is itself a giant abattoir; and just as the hero, the eponymous Cal, has given up his job as an animal slaughterer, so too he wants to opt out of the human slaughter in which, press-ganged by a former school-friend, he has ineluctably become involved. Unfortunately, it is easier to quit the abattoir than to quit the Cause. As one of his associates ominously tells him: 'If you're not part of the solution, then you become part of the problem.' . . .

Mr MacLaverty describes the sad, straitened, passionate lives of his characters with tremendously moving skill. The image of animals brutally maimed or slaughtered persists throughout the book. A mine, intended for humans, blows a cow in two, spattering with blood the rest of the herd, which, wholly unconcerned, continues with its grazing. Wishing to hurt the woman whom he loves, Cal insists, after she has cooked him a meal of *costelette di vitello*, on telling her how vets deal with unborn calves: 'They cut them up with cheese-wire. The vet puts cheese-wire inside the cow and cuts them up before they are born. Then they get born in bits.' Similarly, the passage implies, anyone born in Northern Ireland is also 'born in bits'. Wholeness is impossible. This terrible sense of predestination—merely by being a Roman Catholic, Cal can no more escape from his fate than an ox from the killing pen in the abattoir—persists throughout the novel. Yet co-existent with this world of bombing, shooting, fire-raising and knee-capping, there is the banale world of public-library, dance-hall and boozer, just as the slaughterers in the abattoir, among them Cal's father, smoke cigarettes and chat to each other while carrying out their grisly tasks.

> *Francis King, "Born in Bits," in* The Spectator, *Vol. 250, No. 8066, February 12, 1983, p. 21.**

ANATOLE BROYARD

How strange it is to read about a religious war in an English-speaking country in our time. Yet that's essentially what Bernard MacLaverty's **"Cal"** is about—the undeclared war between Irish Catholics and Protestants in Ulster.

It seems almost surrealistic to hear a Protestant in **"Cal"** talk of being "ruled from Rome," or living "under the yoke of Roman Catholicism." We wonder how much of this fear is real and how much imaginary. If it weren't so bloody, we might be glad to see people quarreling about spiritual matters for a change, actually arguing about the fate of the soul. . . .

Cal himself is a rather empty young man, not yet beyond redemption, but poised between good and evil. . . .

In spite of his idleness and lack of resolve, Cal is appealing in the way that simple humanity, eloquently caught, always is. When he goes to church, the source of so much trouble, Cal feels the sermon as "a time of comfort, of hearing but not listening." When he and his father are threatened by the hooligans who will eventually burn down their house, they fill the bathtub as a precaution against the flames. Don't put the blankets in this time, the father says. They're too hard to dry. The everyday matter-of-factness of their attitude—the bathtub, the blankets—makes us realize how domesticated violence has become in our time. . . .

Because this is a nonpartisan novel, Mr. MacLaverty has captured the pathos and the madness of both sides. One of his best images is of a cow that is blown up "by mistake." The innocence of the cow is everybody's innocence, and the guilt for the killing is everybody's too. When Cal drives the assassin's car, the ridges of the steering wheel remind him of the ridges in the roof of his mouth. When he goes to work for the murdered man's mother and is given the man's leftover clothes to wear, Cal is finally all dressed up in his confusion.

Though **"Cal"** is a bleak novel, there is a flicker of lyricism running through it, like the sun shining through the shattered windows of a ruined church. At one point, Cal reflects that Protestants are called "staunch," while Catholics are "fervent." Mr. MacLaverty's novel is both, and something more.

> *Anatole Broyard, "Domesticated Violence," in* The New York Times, *August 20, 1983, p. 12.*

JACK BEATTY

Political hopelessness hangs thick over *Cal*, a novel of love and guilt set against the backdrop of the Troubles. More, it seems to have infected the author, a well-regarded Scotch-Irish writer, with a lethargy of spirit. For despite many admirable touches, *Cal* lacks that energy of language, invention, or plot through which art transcends tragedy while depicting it. (p. 3)

The very terms of its story limit the novel's range of representation and meaning. Cal is a 19-year-old Catholic youth lured into a loose affiliation with "the Movement," the euphemism Mac Laverty uses for the Provisional IRA. A year before the novel opens, Cal sat behind the wheel of a getaway car while a Provo gunman shot an Ulster police reservist dead in the doorway of his home. The story begins with Cal glimpsing the reservist's widow in the town library and goes on to record his guilt-ridden, convincingly rendered, eventually reciprocated passion for her. Now if this woman, Marcella, were a Protestant, the love story could be a fine vehicle for exploring Ulster's sectarian psychology, the prime source of the hate and violence that have inflamed the province. But no, Marcella is a Catholic; not only that, she is of Italian descent! And instead of being a round character, equipped with an individual as well as social identity of credible thickness, she is a thin projection of that stock romance novel fantasy—the lonely widow hungry for a man's saving touch. Several British reviewers have praised Mac Laverty for throwing light on the Ulster condition, but they are embarrassingly wrong as regards the love story at the center of this novel. An affair between an Irish Catholic and an Irish-Italian Catholic reveals nothing of Ulster's dominant reality. If Mac Laverty skirts the Protestant/Catholic conflict by making Marcella Catholic, he also misses the chance to depict the terrorist mentality as love breaks the grip of hate upon it by making Cal a passive youth who is used by the terrorists, not the type of the hard cases who set off the bombs. And since he is essentially apolitical, the conflict within Cal is the familiar one of love against guilt, not the really interesting conflict of love against political fanaticism.

Still, the British reviewers are not altogether wrong. Mac Laverty captures the impotent fury of the Catholic minority toward the British soldiers who have been reinforcing the Ulster police for more than a decade now, and the Protestant majority, whose fear of someday finding themselves in a minority in a united Ireland wears the mask of a bristling bigotry. Mac Laverty also offers a chill portrait of an IRA intellectual, a fastidious Mephisto who bedaubs his threats to Cal with justifications of political murder: "In Cyprus the dead hardly ran to three fingers. That's cheap for freedom," and instructions to "Think of the issues, not the people." (Now if only *he* had been the one to fall in love with Marcella!).

Above all, Mac Laverty catches the sin-haunted consciousness of Catholic Ireland. Young Cal is possessed by distinctly Catholic fantasies of punishment for helping kill Marcella's husband. This is the deepest level of his character and perhaps of the Irish character as well. The Irish Catholic psyche, as those of us who have one know, cannot live with guilt but is driven to purge it in punishment. This comes, as Mac Laverty's religious imagery suggests, from the Irish absorption with the dark rhetoric and symbols of their faith—with sermons extolling martyrs to mutilate themselves for the love of God, for example, with the idea of inviting suffering in order to "offer it up," and with the Crucifixion as the abiding symbol of the human lot.

I have never seen the masochistic side of the Irish Catholic imagination so fully delineated. Yet Mac Laverty's objective, no-comment narrative leaves me in doubt as to how far he shares this world view himself. . . . I wanted Mac Laverty to show some Joycean wrath at all this. Instead, the novel ends with the police surrounding Cal and him looking forward to a cleansing beating.

Ulster has had enough of that. It needs forgiveness, not more punishment. . . . If Mac Laverty had chosen to make Cal confess his crime to Marcella, then he would have had to face the question of forgiveness and so might have offered his countrymen a symbol of hope. This was to me his most disappointing failure. Since the Irish cannot forget the Christ crucified who haunts their tragic history, they badly need symbols to remind them of the God-man who urged his puissant father to

"forgive them for they know not what they do," even as a Roman spear pierced his side. (pp. 3, 6)

Jack Beatty, "Catholic Guilt and Irish Troubles," in Book World—The Washington Post, *August 21, 1983, pp. 3, 6.*

MICHAEL GORRA

With "Cal," one feels again the "terrible beauty," in Yeats's phrase, born of Ireland's torments. Its power is all the more impressive because nothing in Bernard Mac Laverty's first novel, "Lamb" (1980), quite prepares one for the beauty of this novel, for the delicacy and poise of its account of a teenage boy's futile attempt to stay clear of the Troubles in Northern Ireland. "Lamb" was the expertly told but unbearably claustrophobic story of an Irish Christian Brother who flees from a reform school with a student he loves and eventually murders. "Cal"'s world is as harsh as its predecessor's, but whereas "Lamb" could only shock its readers, this novel has the capacity to move them.

The novel is filled with an unassuming knowledge of the way people act and puts its knowledge tellingly at odds with the violence of its subject. It is both completely of its times in its description of Northern Ireland and completely outside them in its suggestion, as Graham Greene wrote in an essay on François Mauriac, "of another world against which the actions of its characters are thrown into relief." Mr. Mac Laverty, who was born in Belfast, takes no sides in Ulster's political battles. His viewpoint is Christian without being either Catholic or Protestant. "Cal" begins in the conscience, where ideology ends, and its meditation on human suffering and responsibility carries the complexity and amplitude of the very finest novels. (p. 1)

Mr. Mac Laverty makes no false steps in this novel, yet "Cal" is anything but a tiny marvel of technical perfection. It opens into a world larger than itself with a confidence that makes one take that world on the novel's terms. Every page carries a longing for the quiet life that its characters can never take for granted—Cal doing dishes; Marcella teaching him "not to be polite" when eating spaghetti but "to bite off mouthfuls and let them fall back on the plate." The sense of joy at moments stolen from the Troubles gives the novel a sad, expansive beauty and calls into question the efficacy of all sectarian violence.

Mr. Mac Laverty suggests that Cal's situation embodies that of Ulster as a whole: that behind the Troubles lies the attempt to avoid guilt in a world whose problems can only be solved by an acceptance of that guilt and the penance that follows it. "Cal" is finally a most moving novel whose emotional impact is grounded in a complete avoidance of sentimentality. One hesitates and then risks a prediction. In its full imaginative consideration of an apparently intractable political problem, "Cal" will become the "Passage to India" of the Troubles. (p. 17)

Michael Gorra "Guilt and Penance in Northern Ireland," in The New York Times Book Review, *August 21, 1983, pp. 1, 17.*

Czesław Miłosz

1911-

(Has also written under pseudonym of J. Syruc) Polish poet, essayist, novelist, translator, and editor.

Miłosz, the winner of the 1980 Nobel Prize in literature, is often called Poland's greatest living poet, although for political reasons his work has not been published in Poland for over forty years and he has been in exile since 1951. He writes nearly all of his poetry in Polish, saying that "poetry can only be written in the language one spoke in his childhood." In his essays, Miłosz emphasizes the important role that he believes history must play in poetry, and in his own work can be seen the effects of his exposure to the political and military turbulence which characterized Eastern Europe during the first half of the twentieth century.

Miłosz was born and educated in Lithuania, a small Baltic country which has been under the control of Poland or Russia for most of its existence. While studying law at the University of Vilnius, Miłosz wrote poetry and was a founder of a leftist literary group, the "Catastrophists," which prophesied a cataclysmic global war. Miłosz spent World War II in Warsaw, writing, editing, and translating for the Polish resistance. After the war, he served Stalinist Poland as a diplomat for several years but left his country in 1951 because he objected to compulsory "Socialist Realism" and felt that the regimentation of cultural life under the totalitarian regime made it impossible for him to continue there as an author. He went first to France, and since 1961 he has lived in the United States, teaching Slavic literature at the University of California at Berkeley.

In his collection of essays *The Witness of Poetry* (1983), Miłosz contends that the most meaningful poetry fuses the individual with a particular historical circumstance. Referring to the radical upheavals which have plagued Eastern Europe, Miłosz views poetry as "a witness and a participant in one of mankind's major transformations." He contrasts the poetry of Eastern Europe, tied to history and universalized by the magnitude of such tragedies as the Nazi blitzkrieg, the Holocaust, and the oppression of Soviet domination, with Western poetry, which tends to emphasize the individual and to be introspective and confessional. Miłosz considers Western poetry a statement of personal alienation, while Eastern European poetry gains strength "when an entire community is struck by misfortune." In the aftermath of World War II atrocities, Miłosz believes that one of poetry's most important functions is to bear witness to the reality of tragic events. In a 1945 poem he asks, "What is poetry which does not save / Nations or people?" and in his Nobel Prize acceptance speech he stated: "Those who are alive receive a mandate from those who are silent forever. They can fulfill their duties only by trying to reconstruct precisely things as they were and by wresting the past from fictions and legends."

Miłosz's early poetry, most of which has not been translated, was apocalyptic. In the early 1940s, when the predictions of Miłosz and the other Catastrophists had been realized, Miłosz began writing anti-Nazi poetry which was published clandestinely. His war poems are his best known in the United States and many critics say they are his most powerful. Some of these

poems express the guilt of the Holocaust survivor. Critics note Miłosz's restraint and most agree that he effectively communicates the horror and anguish of the time. Miłosz commented in *The History of Polish Literature* (1969): "When a poet is overwhelmed by strong emotions, his form tends to become more simple and more direct." Even in his recent work, Miłosz has for the most part avoided the experimentation with language that characterizes much modern poetry, concentrating more on the clear expression of ideas. His later poetry sometimes verges on rhythmical prose and contains many classical elements, including a respect for balance and form and an economical style. However, much of his work is also strongly emotional and acknowledges a transcendent spirituality. Critics have commented on the influence of Miłosz's Roman Catholic background and his Manichean fascination with good and evil both in his poetry and his prose. A humanistic outrage at the evil in the world, whether it is Nazism in Europe or corruption in California, is a hallmark of his work. English language collections of Miłosz's poetry include *Selected Poems* (1973; revised 1981), *Bells in Winter* (1978), and *The Separate Notebooks* (1984).

Although Miłosz considers himself primarily a poet, he has also treated the historical events of twentieth-century Eastern Europe in a variety of respected prose works. His first American publication, *Zniewolony umysl* (1953; *The Captive Mind*), is a study of the effects of communism on creativity which he wrote to explain his defection from Poland. It is a stridently antitotalitarian work in which Miłosz tells the true stories of four unidentified writers under a totalitarian regime. *Dolina Issy* (1955; *The Issa Valley*), about Miłosz's youth in Lithuania, has been variously described as an autobiographical novel, a lyric novel, and a long prose poem. Miłosz said in his Nobel Lecture that "the landscape and perhaps the spirits of Lithuania have never abandoned me"; these are most apparent in *Issa Valley,* which reveals his strong feeling for the ancestry and history of Lithuania as well as his love of nature. *Rodzinna Europa* (1959; *Native Realm: A Search for Self-Definition*) is a more expository, autobiographical work which incorporates historical events of Europe with the story of the growth of an intellectual. As in *The Captive Mind* and *The Witness of Poetry,* Miłosz deals with the effects of social and political upheaval in Eastern Europe on its intellectuals and distinguishes between intellectual life in Eastern Europe and in Western societies. Miłosz's later works, both his poetry and a collection of essays, *Widzenia nad Zatoka San Francisco* (1969; *Visions from San Francisco Bay*), often touch on his feelings of loss associated with living in exile. Miłosz feels that exile is a universal state in the twentieth century, and the committee which awarded him the Nobel Prize called him "an exiled writer—a stranger for whom the physical exile is really a reflection of a metaphysical . . . exile applying to humanity in general." Miłosz has also written several scholarly works dealing with Slavic literature and numerous philosophical essays.

While Miłosz has always elicited interest among academics, his reputation grew significantly after he was awarded the Nobel Prize. Many of his works were then reprinted or printed for the first time in English; more importantly, Miłosz received his first officially sanctioned publication in Poland since 1936. In 1981, he visited his country for the first time since his exile and was hailed as a symbol of the resurgence of freedom in Poland. Criticism of Miłosz's work has tended to focus first on his stimulating political and moral ideas and his historical content, and only secondarily on the literary merits of the work; negative criticism on either count has been scant. The exiled Russian poet Joseph Brodsky called Miłosz "one of the greatest poets of our time, perhaps the greatest."

(See also *CLC,* Vols. 5, 11, 22 and *Contemporary Authors,* Vols. 81-84.)

BURTON RAFFEL

Czeslaw Milosz is one of those rare writers who survives transplantation. Forced into exile, most writers, even so well-established as Thomas Mann, even so heralded and carefully tended as Joseph Brodsky, tend to slowly atrophy. Cut off from the root of all style, the *praktik* of a language, their work becomes increasingly disoriented. . . . But Milosz has managed to hold on to his inner world. . . . Kenneth Rexroth notes, in his brief introduction [to *Selected Poems*], that Milosz's own poetry has now "crossed the borders of language and stands in translation as amongst the very small body of truly important poetry being written in English and French today." Whatever posterity may think, the statement seems to me pretty much indisputable. (pp. 145-46)

Milosz' noblest and truest voice [can be heard in the poem **"Dedication"**]. Something has been lost in translation, but even without the music of the original this can, as Rexroth says, cross the borders of language and speak to us, reach us. Nor does the voice suffer from age and/or transplantation. . . .

[**"Throughout Our Lands"**] is not simply European, it seems to me specifically Polish. The hard exterior crust, lightly and transparently stretched over the softer and gentler interior spaces, strikes me as typical of Zbigniew Herbert, or Antoni Slonimski, or Tadeus Rozewicz, or Adam Wazyk—or Czeslaw Milosz. It is attractive to many American poets: some have successfully incorporated at least some of this complex, subtle mixture of stances and evasions and confessions and truths and lies into their poetry. But the whole thing is peculiarly Polish property; it is Milosz's birthright, and no matter how he has managed to bring it across the Atlantic to us, undimmed, undiminished, we need to be grateful. . . .

[Even] in Warsaw, even in 1944, Milosz could begin his **"A Song On the End of the World"** with wry tenderness. . . . (p. 146)

We may be reminded of Auden's "Musée des Beaux Arts," but there is no need to write an urgent letter to Milosz, in Berkeley, to ask if he had been reading Auden, in English or in translation. The intensity and duration, the *sympathy,* of the poet's vision is something Auden (and no English poet after Hopkins) could achieve. The fierce and yet gentle power of "as it should always be" is, again, both European and specifically Polish European.

So too is this entire book, even the one poem written directly in English. . . . A life's work is here beautifully on display: an extraordinarily fine book. (p. 147)

> *Burton Raffel, in a review of "Selected Poems," in* The Denver Quarterly, *Vol. 11, No. 2, Summer, 1976, pp. 145-47.*

HARLOW ROBINSON

Milosz's poetry and prose is political only in the higher sense of the word. The seemingly irresolvable plight of modern industrialized man—his loss of identity (national and personal), and especially his "refusal to remember"—disturbs and inspires Milosz's work. One has the feeling that Milosz has been dragged into the political arena reluctantly, that he would have been content to sit at his desk behind volumes of classics and foreign dictionaries. The times into which he was born, however, determined otherwise: neutrality and detachment, especially for a Lithuanian-Pole who was 28 when the Nazi blitzkrieg rolled into Warsaw, became an impossibility. . . .

By nature an artist who demands a cold distance from his material, Milosz has been pushed by the circumstances of his (and his country's) history to immediately confront cruelty, death and destruction.

This combination of control and passion is one that Milosz shares with other great poets of the twentieth century: Osip Mandelstam in Russia, T. S. Eliot in England. (In Milosz's words: "The voice of passion is better than the voice of reason. / The passionless cannot change history.") Never romantic or maudlin, Milosz has rejected nothing of his long odyssey from the pagan green valleys of Lithuania to the emptying cafés of wartime Europe to the desolate concrete freeways of California. (p. 737)

A sense of this geographical and moral dislocation informs the poetry collected in [*Selected Poems*]. . . . Some of the most powerful and successful [poems] are from the wartime years, when he worked as an editor and writer for Resistance publications in besieged and ruined Warsaw. "**Café**," dated 1944, contrasts present reality with history in a way that is characteristic of much of his poetry. . . .

In all the poems collected here one senses the weight of the culture that lies behind the words: Latin theological training in Catholic Vilnius, a legal education, café afternoons in Paris, where Milosz spent much time in the 1930s and later in the 1950s. Milosz is the first to admit that his poetry is not easy, that it is not written for the masses. . . .

Another theme that runs through all of Milosz's writing is nationality—actually, the relativity of nationality. As the child of a landowning family in Lithuania, a pagan country until 1386, Milosz grew up surrounded by a weird clash of languages, religions and traditions that gave him first-hand knowledge of how language is both identity and the means of oppression. . . . "The landscapes and perhaps the spirits of Lithuania have never abandoned me," he remarked in accepting the Nobel Prize.

It is with these landscapes and spirits that *The Issa Valley*, first published in Polish in 1955 and now translated into English for the first time, is populated. This charming, lyrical prose poem is a nostalgic return to the poet's youth in Lithuania, an attempt to recapture and understand the springs of his creativity. Though touted as a novel, it is not really a work of fiction. Indeed, Milosz has said that "I do not consider myself a fiction writer at all. . . ." (p. 738)

Thomas, the boy protagonist of the book, is a sensitive, wise-beyond-his-years observer, fascinated by the strange tribal rites and small romantic tragedies that surround him. There is no plot in the traditional sense; rather, this is a Lithuanian, bucolic *Portrait of the Artist* told in a restrained, almost timid tone. We learn less about Thomas's feelings and psychology than about the strange creatures—both human and animal—that he watches with such bemused intensity. Milosz is an intensely private writer. He looks out at the world, absorbed with other beings and with history rather than with himself. After the nearly sickening self-absorption of so many modern writers, it is a relief and pleasure to read a poet with a sense of propriety.

As in the poems, ancestry and history are major concerns in *The Issa Valley*. . . . The sense of place is strong and sure; it establishes a first innocent point of reference for the tumult of war and nationality that would follow. Cataclysmic events in the outside world—even World War I—are only distant echoes in this isolated fairy tale world.

Russian writers—especially Turgenev and Gogol—seem to stand behind this boyhood chronicle. . . . From Gogol come the kindly—and evil—forest spirits that torment and tantalize Thomas's friends and relatives. (pp. 738-39)

Thomas accepts these phantoms—even loves them. They are all part of the wonderful communion of nature that surrounds and nurtures him; he prefers them to the uncertain and tedious attentions of alternately attentive and uninterested relations. One feels that these benign and enigmatic Lithuanian forest spirits are profoundly important to Milosz's poetic identity, to the quietly sensuous music of some of his lines.

The Issa Valley is not a sensational book. It is not an especially profound one. The mood is Chekhovian, autumnal, of small and subtle changes in a late November sunset. But in our age of loud superlatives, such an assuredly quiet voice sounds with refreshing and welcome authority. (p. 739)

> Harlow Robinson, "Passion Is Better than Reason,"
> in The Nation, *Vol. 232, No. 23, June 13, 1981, pp.*
> *737-39.*

JOHN BAYLEY

[*The Issa Valley*] is an idyll of immense charm and poetic depth, a story without much conventional plot about a boy growing up in the Lithuanian countryside and raised largely by grandparents proud of their Polish background. . . .

The portraits in this novel will remind readers of those classic figures drawn from Tolstoy in *Childhood and Boyhood*, and by Aksakov in his family memoirs. But Milosz is more humane than Tolstoy and less "creamy" (in literary historian Prince Minsky's word) than Aksakov. The child of *The Issa Valley* accepts his elders with unconscious and uncomprehending love, but the pattern of their days and their being is created with a great poet's unobtrusively vivid power. As the book progresses we understand more and more of the nature and outlook of the hero's grandfather, who is at first a painting in words, like Ghirlandaio's *Old Man*. The hero's grandmothers are similarly memorable. (p. 29)

Meantime he's growing up, hunting and dreaming, taking in portents both from nature and from the age-old accessibility of the human consciousness around him. He communes, too, with lives that form subplots to the novel; the mistress of the priest who killed herself with rat poison when he sent her away; the forester haunted by the Russian soldier he has stalked and killed in the forest; a Polish small landowner who teaches the hero to shoot, and whose Lithuanian housekeeper—primitive, contemptuous, and bewitching—leads her own mysterious life in a corner of the narrative. (pp. 29-30)

It takes a masterpiece to reveal the sheer unreality of our modern creative modes and poses, and Milosz's novel is such a masterpiece. Its account of childhood in a valley inhabited by an "unusually large number of devils" has no obvious originality, nor is it in any sense a strikingly distinctive work; but, strangely enough, even the fact that it is a translation only appears to accentuate its closeness to real things, for it seems to be about those things and not about the author's invention of them, odd or novel. It makes us realize the extent to which an American masterpiece tends to be about itself only, and has to be. . . . Such comparisons are not wholly invidious: it is a fact that a writer like Milosz is effortlessly master of a primeval world, of which the art of the West no longer has any conception, and can only reconstitute in solipsistic magic, the supermarket gothicism of Edna O'Brien or Joyce Carol Oates. . . .

Of course there is a strong element of pastiche in *Dr. Zhivago*, an element of *fin-de-siècle* fantasy, and *The Issa Valley* is not free from pastiche either. It could hardly be otherwise with a book written today about a boy growing up in the small valley, the countryside of the author's childhood. But both Pasternak and Milosz are poets, poets of the first class though of very different kinds, and this difference is shown in the texture of their prose. In the case of Milosz experience emerges as a quality that overrides the impossibilities of translation. A poet so good that he can be translated is a supreme paradox, one which many poets today, and readers of poetry, would refuse to recognize, so strong is the tendency now for poetry only to congeal and inhere in the carefully exploited accuracies and idiosyncrasies of a language. (p. 30)

The fact that what Milosz says comes across with such primary force and impact is itself an indication that, as a poet in the largest sense, he is an ideal kind of recipient of the Nobel Prize. It is possible that there are real differences here, though of a wholly indefinable kind, in the nature of languages themselves: some are more amenable than others to moving sideways, to acquiring a kind of international potential. (pp. 30-1)

Even more striking than the fact that this poetry remains poetry in another language—with the advantage, it is true, of having been translated in collaboration with the poet himself—is the sense of a shared experience that Milosz manages to give, a limpid repose upon the way things are that is no less than our sense of wonder at them. (p. 31)

There is in a way nothing personal about them. Milosz's world is collective—a place for everything and everything in its place. He is one of the few poets who do not give the impression of seeing something in his own special way. The self in his poetry is not impersonal but effortlessly manifold, like the emotions and sensations in its records. . . . We become our relations, our moments, each other, even our graves; at least we do so if we live in the kind of dense and populous relation with the world which Milosz records and celebrates. The relation to the past moment in his poem is the same as that to his grandmother's grave in *The Issa Valley*. In *The Issa Valley* too we see the beginnings of the poem **"Diary of a Naturalist,"** however much later on that poem was written, in an experience of the young boy. . . . Milosz does not sentimentalize the adolescent's worship of nature, as predatory as the beasts it moves among. *The Issa Valley* is full of hunting and hunting expeditions, as memorable as those in *Pan Tadeusz,* or Aksakov and Turgenev. (pp. 31-2)

The characters in *The Issa Valley*—grandfather, grandmothers, neighbors, the local forester, are all members of a household, even though the Lithuanian peasant shows at moments an atavistic hostility to the Polish *pan,* or local gentry. As in Tolstoy, the more closely integrated the members of a family, the more peculiarly individual they appear. In this pre-American melting pot the racial and social mix produces not uniformity but a matured exactness of distinction, of the kind found in nature itself and worshipped by Milosz when he writes as a botanist and ornithologist.

That habit of exactness explains the twin paradox of Milosz's distinction as a poet: his sense of things as they are, and yet his power—almost a conscious power it sometimes seems—of projecting what he writes out of the absolute linguistic form which poetry usually demands. His own poetic temperament and upbringing again offer a clue. He has a sense of a poet as "not just one person," an instinct akin to Keats's perception of the poet as a man in whom personality has been exorcised in the intensities of negative capability. But Keats's poetry, in all its richness, its vulnerability as language, is held down to the very words in which it was first uttered. Milosz's seems to aspire to some ideal language, almost to Wordsworth's "ghostly language of the ancient earth," and not the earth only—the sky too, the steady rationale of a sentient universe.

It is the same with the novel. Despite its immensely local subject and setting there is nothing in the least provincial about it. (p. 32)

He was conscious always of the precarious and provisional nature of the country in which he grew up, and how complete would be its extinction when the moment came. France, he points out, survived a German invasion and conquest without undue discomfort, and would have done so even if the Germans had remained the winning side. For Poland—the new nation—defeat would mean calamity and extinction. The young Milosz got the nickname of "catastrophist" from the tone of the poems he wrote in the years before the war, but, though history was to prove him altogether too accurate a prophet, his own survival during the time of apocalypse chastened him. He was too honest not to see that survival is its own form of humiliation, one that subdues not only the pride of the ideological visionary—and Milosz then was a believing Marxist and revolutionary—but the impulse to denunciation of such ideology, a counter-attitude.

Life itself, and the reverence for it, becomes then the precious thing to be explored and celebrated. It is this lucid humility which sets Milosz apart from Solzhenitsyn, a self-martyred soul who inhabits a country where conviction is more important than reflection, where the vowels are deeper, the shapes of speech more minatory. Solzhenitsyn's power as a writer demands that life should be intensified, directed, and organized in the Russian style; Milosz's provenance makes him conservative and freedom-loving in a wholly different sense. In his novels and poetry, life and time are caught in an unending study of awareness. . . . (p. 33)

John Bayley, "Return of the Native," in The New York Review of Books, *Vol. XXVIII, No. 11, June 25, 1981, pp. 29-33.*

JOSEPH C. THACKERY

[In] the modern poetry of the West there has been an almost exclusive concentration on perception for perception's sake, ignoring both myth and history. For years one would not have known from the pages of American poetry magazines that there were dangers from fallout, war in Vietnam, starvation abroad, or nations striving for freedom while immersed in bondage. (p. 2)

However, to poets like Milosz, Tadeusz Rozewicz, and Zbigniew Herbert, all of whom saw the Warsaw ghetto gutted and later beheld Warsaw itself leveled and then throttled by a new authoritarianism, philosophy became an imperative of spiritual survival. As Milosz himself points out in his **History of Polish Literature,** 1969, the imperative centered on poetry for the very pragmatic reason that poetry took up less physical space in the Underground. Its adventures and its explorations thrived. Nevertheless, as Milosz has written: "Nazi rule did not spur clear thinking about the future. Literature registered emotional reflexes ranging from pain, hatred of the occupier, through horror, pity, sarcasm, and irony." The Occupation had revealed society not as an entity in itself, but as a dilating and fragile shell in which human relationships could be molded at will. The writer was well fed, but held to account for every word.

Between 1945 and 1949, the censors became more quiescent; there were few forbidden subjects and debate centered on what literature should "be" under socialism. But from 1949 to 1955, the new ruling class thoroughly suffocated free expression. Soviet models, forced upon writers in the interest of "modernization'' of the state, drew a sterile pall over literature. (pp. 2-3)

From 1956 to the present, however, a broad new realism has intervened. . . . Poets have dared the censors in order to produce unconventional and adventuresome work. . . . However, the earlier spiritual affliction suffered by the experimenters in reconstituting their philosophy is poignantly illustrated by Milosz in his *History:* "The act of writing a poem is an act of faith, yet if the screams of the tortured are audible in the poet's room, is not his activity an offense to human suffering?''

The work of the three Catastrophists, . . . Rozewicz, Herbert and Milosz himself, exemplifies this dilemma. Each sought spiritual survival in a different way. . . .

All three Catastrophists blend history and myth. But it is preeminently Milosz who fixes on history as backdrop, with man as an absurd social phenomenon, thrust into the *mise en scène* as if at the hands of some ironic and impersonal god. Although analogies to Eliot's ''Four Quartets'' are observable in Milosz's conceptions of time past, time future and time merging, he has refused to examine the world, as did Eliot and Lowell, in terms of his own anxiety. Instead, the authority of poetry is to be tested by a journey through history, the response to the pilgrimage being a rejuvenating sense of wonder. (p. 3)

Wonder and philosophical absolution . . . inform Milosz's **"A Song on the End of the World,"** in which Armageddon is always *in esse,* but an old man, knowing that ''the whole of the world is greater than its horror'' (*Selected Poems* . . .), goes on tying up his tomato plants. Appreciation of how this poet has been able to synthesize history and a sense of its horror with survival and absolution may be gained by a discussion of his syntactic intentions. These aims are powerfully illustrated by six poems in a section of his major *oeuvre, Bells in Winter.* They are **"The Unveiling," "Diary of a Naturalist," "Over Cities," "A Short Recess," "The Accuser,"** and the apotheosis poem, **"Bells in Winter.''** Together they search for a poetry that will be at once harsh and mollifying, that will enable men to understand, if not to rationalize, the debasement of the human spirit by warfare and psychic dismemberment, while simultaneously establishing a personal *modus vivendi* and a psychology of aesthetic necessity.

Three concerns appear to influence the poet's approach: (1) his sense of the betrayal of speech, (2) his conception of Heraclitean change, and (3) his belief in *apokatastasis* or restitution and restoration, *versus katastasis* or establishment and fixity. A fourth phenomenon, which may arise only in subliminal consciousness of the reader, is what might be called ''the third language,'' deriving from unexpected shifts of meaning in the transitions from one vocabulary to another. We consider these categories in order. Thus, in **"The Unveiling,"** the poet suggests the fallibility of the tools of literary creation—words. . . . **"Over Cities"** expands the scope of betrayal; it deals with the dangers of reason itself and the trivialization of art by ''intelligence'': ''Yet while we hear everyone advising us to understand clearly causes and effects, let us beware of those perfectly logical though somewhat too eager arguments.'' . . .

"The Accuser" is in effect a trial at law in which a generalized Other, perhaps God (though certainly an impersonal God), acts as the poet's prosecutor, judge and jury. He charges that the optimism of creativity cannot gloss over horror and that there is never either time enough or a *locus poenitentiae* when all

are guilty. Words fail in the end and leave only the life impulse: ''—Yet I have learned how to live with my grief. / —As if putting words together has been of help.''

The title poem, **"Bells in Winter,"** sets forth the poet's belief in restoration and recovery—the conviction that form is eternal—the cut oak, the sacrificed lamb are ''annihilated'' but their forms ''exist forever.'' It is the vehicle of the form—the word—that is inadequate. . . . (p. 4)

Milosz's second major semantic trend is toward the full apprehension of Heraclitean change. In this mode, evidence of the influence of Eliot, the Bergsonian *élan vital* and the Symbolists echo through his conception of ''reality.'' It is as though he had pulled together the remotest philosophical insights into a pragmatism that is both the rock in the river and the water that flows over the rock. (pp. 4-5)

The form of **"The Unveiling"** itself suggests a time past merging into time present and future, as in Eliot's ''Burnt Norton.'' Thus, the poet repeatedly shifts back and forth from his early life to his San Francisco refuge. Interpersed are ''choruses'' like those in Greek drama, half-accusatory, half-grieving, as if the poet were keeping a sharp eye on himself that he might not betray his aesthetic responsibility. But, as **"Diary of a Naturalist"** implies, permanence is not to be achieved in mere survival: ''That boy, does he already suspect / That beauty is always elsewhere and always delusive?'' . . .

Though it is not the most powerful of the six poems (in this writer's opinion, **"Over Cities"** has that distinction), **"A Short Recess"** comes closest to the poet's insight that man is an absurd ''occurrence'' in the immensity of time and history and that evanescence overhangs every artistic effort. . . . (p. 5)

"A Short Recess" teems with an action imagery in the manner of Shakespeare's *Tempest.* The subjunctive mood suggests time lost, squandered, never to come again. . . . In this poem, and indeed, in the generality of Milosz's work, we are cast against a four-dimensional landscape of sky, mountain, plain, horizon and time—primordial and indeterminate. Man cowers in the foreground, indistinguishable in his own perspective. Let him begin to concentrate on detail, on the putatively definite, and meaning becomes progressively indefinite. The same displacement occurs at the other end of the reality scale: in the world of the quark, the neutrino, the particle, man is as absurd and inconsequential as when he is pasted like a wafer against the universe. (pp. 5-6)

Milosz's third preoccupation is with the tensions between *katastasis* (fixity) and *apokatastasis* (restoration). In these opposing conceptions, set forth in **"Bells in Winter,"** the poet struggles with his hatred and unwillingness to forgive. . . . He wonders if his sense of the immortality of form coupled with the promise of restitution in the Christian Bible is sufficient to stem the anxiety of never measuring up to self-image. Similar doubt occurs in **"The Unveiling"**: ''When will that shore appear from which at last we see / How all this came to pass and for what reason?''

In **"Diary of a Naturalist"** a schoolroom lecture by a Doctor Catchfly suggests that because of his learning, man wrongly sees himself as the center of all importance; he must therefore account for his waste of nature and his insensitivity to the agony of non-human life. The drive of the intellect toward science fails as salvation, but religious awakening may be no adequate substitute because it contains its own denial and the hope for peaceful stasis is vain. . . . (p. 6)

The poet's impulse toward renewal wilts under the impact of savagery, but under the principle of *apokatastasis,* it cannot be killed. He submerges himself in the creative process so that the muse, the "other," may take over the task for which he feels inadequate. Though this release to subconscious powers creates anxiety, there is always a new vision, hard-won, but uplifting, as in **"The Unveiling"**. . . .

A kind of distorted salvation arises just because humanity is so vulnerable. In **"Bells in Winter"** the poet dreams that his double, a Greek youth, is relating the story of this condemnation by St. Paul in Corinth for having committed incest. . . .

This dream releases the poet from anxiety. He can once again picture the writing room of his youth. His imagination restores his one-time servant Lisabeth to her rightful human importance. The city is roofed with a canopy of bells as she, the personification of all persecuted womankind—tortured witch, outcast wench, mourning wife, mother of felon—attends mass and lines out her missal with her dirty fingernail. The memory saves the poet from hatred and confirms that form is eternal and therefore aesthetics, its vehicle, is timeless. (p. 8)

Milosz adventures far beyond metaphor to plunge the reader into the sense of double existence, inside and outside time; indeed into the "cosmogonic moment of creation" in which there is in effect no time, only the creative *élan* and its reverberations in the soul. . . .

Analysis of Milosz's poetry leads one to the opinion that no other poet in the world could have written it in quite the way it exists. This statement is not a tautology; nor is it self-evident; it is the product of an empathy that moves the reader to elect this great man as spokesman of the millions of dead of the Holocaust, the Gulags, the Polish and Czech uprisings, and the added millions of those who will go on dying in an imperfect world. The former captive of authoritarianism is the living analogue of the double metaphor—the outsider released by virtue of his alienation from the obligation to follow the crowd. The Catastrophists, and especially Milosz, have expanded their reach precisely because they have achieved freedom from the self-absorption that inhibits the poetry of western democracies: the you-under-this-tree-sensing-me-under-that-tree syndrome. Their holistic sweep of expression is comparable to the shared necessity of micro- and macro-physics to hypothesize in metaphor: "neutrino," "helix," "black holes," "googol." It suggests that when mankind's bus stops extend to the stars, poetry may once again, as in primordial times, become a part of everyday life. (p. 10)

> *Joseph C. Thackery, "Czeslaw Milosz: The Uses of a Philosophy of Poetry," in* The Hollins Critic, *Vol. XIX, No. 2, April, 1982, pp. 1-10.*

P. J. KAVANAGH

Ever since his publication of *The Captive Mind* in the 1950's Czeslaw Milosz, born a Lithuanian, a famous poet in Polish, has been a man worth listening to. In that book he almost lovingly charts the subtle entrapments by which a totalitarian regime can gain the support of intellectuals. . . . In another splendid book, *Native Realm,* he also marks the slow degrees

of his disenchantment which led, in the end, to his arrival in the West, which he is by no means enamoured of either. . . .

What he has to offer [in *Visions from San Francisco Bay*] is a foreign and valuable scintillation. He comes from a Central European culture where 'intellectuals'—and apparently poets there fall into that category—are expected to use their intellects; to discuss, in a manner we would foolishly find embarrassing, large matters; to arrive at conclusions and to publish them. . . .

Now, winner of the Nobel Prize for Literature, settled in California, he shows no signs of changing his Central European ways. *Visions from San Francisco Bay* is a collection of essays whose inviting titles remind us how caught we are in a set of belle lettrist evasions. What English poet, for example, would risk 'A short digression on Woman as Representative of Nature', 'On Catholicism', 'On Censorship', 'On Virtue'? And say what he really thought on these topics, without looking over his shoulder?

Perhaps Milosz is able to do this because he has known of so many real knocks on the door in the small hours of the morning. He has worked in the interests of Moscow, has been a refugee, has starved, has survived the Warsaw Uprising by hiding in a boiler and, above all, has seen the political and physical destruction of his native Lithuanian culture. He could be called the quintessential European man of our time, who has experienced in his own person the history we, thankfully, have only known at several removes.

So, what does he make of us, and of 'the illegitimate child of Europe' as he calls the United States, from his perch in the most extreme manifestation of it, California? The answer is disconcerting. We are used to dire warnings; we are even accustomed to careful cheerfulness. What we do not often come across is a kind of detached glee—at awfulness; an ungloomy recognition that we cannot go on as we are—in any direction. He holds up a mirror and shows us ourselves, without blame and with no suggestions either, and in the mirror he himself is also reflected.

American writers seem to detest their country, they go on and on about its soulessness, and so forth. What they detest Milosz seems to like. . . . He has little time for America's well-heeled rebels. Of course he also knows about the 'alienation' of so much American life. Well, so be it. (This is what I meant by 'glee':) 'If so, then it is truly a privilege to live in California and every day to drink the elixir of perfect alienation. . . .' (p. 23)

He is like a brilliant talker at a café table and we willingly join him, entranced, because he knows what he is talking about, he has been there. . . . [In the last essay of the collection, Milosz] gives the key to the energy behind these pieces; perhaps 'glee' is not the right word after all: 'I am certain only of my amazement. Amazement that something like America exists, and that humanity still exists, though it should have exterminated itself long ago. . . . [Whenever I take up my pen] I treat that act only as the exorcism of the evil spirits of the present.' (pp. 23-4)

> *P. J. Kavanagh, "Exorcist," in* The Spectator, *Vol. 249, No. 8056, December 4, 1982, pp. 23-4.*

TOM ALESSANDRI

[In *Visions from San Francisco Bay*] Milosz gives us the underpinnings of those bleak themes (*The Captive Mind, Native*

Realm, The Issa Valley) that the Stockholm judges awarded so highly. And Milosz is nothing but honest with us. He variously searches, gets lost, theorizes and struggles to manage the hodgepodge that is his own life and the life of polymorphic Berkeley. He is the exile on the pavement, amid all the wanderers stoned on cannabis, religion, politics and ecology. . . .

This artistic honesty and variety is not, however, without its shortcomings. The prose can be intense and thick, so painfully personal that it nearly forbids admittance, particularly in sections of rather esoteric philosophizing. But when Milosz focuses on particular persons or places, his essays move with excitement. . . .

Milosz is marvelous at the abutment of *all* the world and its history with 1969 Berkeley (year of the original publication in Polish). The America of self-denial and Puritan repression is dying and is being replaced by the individualistic "condensed virtue" of technology. The West agonizes over its rootlessness, turns philosophic eyes East and concludes by marketing a super micro-chip to digest the *Vedas*.

Visions from San Francisco Bay is a series of opaque meanderings—honest and honestly tortured. It requires courage to write and just as much courage to read.

> Tom Alessandri, in a review of *"Visions from San Francisco Bay,"* in America, Vol. 147, No. 20, December 18, 1982, p. 399.

HUGO WILLIAMS

[*Visions from San Francisco Bay*] is a course of bromides on The American Way of Life And Where It Is All Heading: intellectual tummy rumblings. Like Polonius, Milosz is full of Philosophy. . . . The datedness of everything he says is always camouflaged by [its] wooden latin abstractedness. 'I do not number myself', he informs us, 'among those who seek unusual landscapes, nor do I take photographs of Nature's panoramas'. We are to understand that he has weightier matters to contend with, but he sounds more like a pantomime dame than a poet. (p. 44)

For Milosz, society is a board game for the senile, with easy-to-spot trends and tendencies boldly outlined in black and white: 'The police ban on marijuana is causing the whites to draw nearer the blacks because of the similarity of their situations.' This is pretty keen. But he has the benefit of 20 years' hindsight, remember. Self-evident truths have a way of disintegrating in his hands, which is always useful. . . .

Milosz didn't take kindly to the hippies he found lying about everywhere in his adoptive country. He accuses them of all manner of nonsense once his blood is up. . . . The concept of him defending lumberjacks and others from the 'scorn' of this rabble provides a rare laugh in his book. For Milosz is your typical East European Nobel-Prize-winning New American Capitalist, randy with respectability. He is terribly grateful to America for putting him up and he can't forgive these whippersnappers (who must be grandfathers by now) for not seeing it his way.

He is even funnier about the French: 'During all the years I lived in Western Europe, I did not have a single offer from any institution concerned with propagating knowledge,' he explodes. . . . I must say, his conceit, which blinds him to all self-knowledge is genuinely international. Perhaps the French noted the hollow at the heart of this academic jet-setter's particular brand of intellectual Esperanto and steered him discreetly westward, into the setting sun. (p. 45)

> Hugo Williams, *"Bromides,"* in New Statesman, Vol. 104, No. 5, 2700 & 2701, December 17 & 24, 1982, pp. 44-5.

ALFRED KAZIN

[In **"The Witness of Poetry"**, Mr. Milosz] constantly reminds us of a West-East axis in poetry drawn from contrasting human experiences; if he thinks ours more fortunate, he also, like his hero Dostoyevsky, thinks our writers pitiable.

He draws fervently on the terrible experiences of Polish poets in our time. But far from apologizing for poetry that may well be thought too extreme in the West, he just as fervently believes that the elemental strength of poetry, its ancient ritual quality, is realized "when an entire community is struck by misfortune, for instance the Nazi occupation of Poland." . . .

What Mr. Milosz presents is obviously the great divide in his mind between West and East—between our "alienated" poetry, full of introspective anxiety, and a poetry emerging under constant tyranny where "a peculiar fusion of the individual and the historical took place, which means that events burdening a whole community are perceived by a poet as touching him in a most personal manner. Then poetry is no longer alienated." This may sound like a formula, and in fact it is a traditional one in Eastern Europe, where a more "social" sense of literature (not necessarily *engagé* but less self-celebrating than ours) has long operated. Mr. Milosz on the subject of American mass media reminds me of many a Russian, then and now, scornful of Western culture. . . .

Mr. Milosz speaks not only from the Polish experience of atrocity but from independent religious zeal. He lovingly recalls what Polish culture owes to Latin and the cultural unity with the West inspired by the Catholic Church. . . .

Mr. Milosz's own strength as poet and critic owes much to his tacit spirituality. Years ago, when I discovered him at Berkeley, I made a particular note of his saying, "Nothing could stifle my inner certainty that a shining point exists where all lines intersect." . . .

Mr. Milosz is scornful of everything that is trivial and trivializing in contemporary poetry. No one concerned with the survival of poetry in our own culture can miss what a Polish poet resident in California means when he says: "When poets discover that their words refer only to words and not to a reality which must be described as faithfully as possible, they despair." . . . Poetry to Mr. Milosz is profoundly a recall, not a mere impression of present experience. It more resembles—or should—"the cries of Job" than the endless defenses of the ego in our society. . . .

The spiritual aloneness that Mr. Milosz celebrates in the teeth of Nazi-Communist despotism is not what we Americans call a "failure in interpersonal relationships." If ever there was proof of the great divide between West and East, between a worried civilization and a tormented one, **"The Witness of Poetry"** furnishes it. Writing out of the Polish agony, Mr. Milosz sighs that left-wing Latin American writers are not on his wavelength.

What Mr. Milosz's Harvard audience made of his brilliant but scattered observations is anybody's guess. There is not only a great divide between East and West, but in Mr. Milosz's orphic rambling style a divide between one sentence and another. When he writes, ''What can poetry be in the twentieth century? It seems to me that there is a search for the line beyond which only a zone of silence exists, and that on the borderline we encounter Polish poetry,'' I thought of how much ''silence'' is actually present in Mr. Milosz's lectures, as in his poetry. The ''discontinuity'' in European civilization that he feels to be the effect of war and occupation operates in his own style to a marked degree. In one sense this is the famous elusiveness of modernist poetry, forever making its way up and down ''the stairway of surprise.'' Where successive lines do not continue an image or thought, silence seems to intervene. In Czeslaw Milosz's lectures the sense of ''silence'' between thought and thought is poignant. It expresses all that a Polish poet returned from hell *cannot* say to an American audience. (p. 20)

> *Alfred Kazin, ''Writing Out of the Polish Agony,'' in* The New York Times Book Review, *May 1, 1983, pp. 1, 20.*

ADAM GUSSOW

Defenses of poetry have been around almost as long as poetry itself. Both rarely have much effect on the real world—the world outside of poems, in which wars are fought, people die, and ideals are tarnished. Perhaps, suggests Milosz, the blame lies partly with the poets themselves. Perhaps they and those who defend their craft have grown afraid of reality, afraid to see it clearly and speak about it in words we can all comprehend. (pp. 58-9)

[Milosz] speaks in *The Witness of Poetry* with the sort of quiet, preeminent brilliance that makes his defense . . . a classic for our time. . . . Milosz works outward from the facts of his life— his provincial origins, his classical and Catholic education, his experience in Poland during the catastrophic years of World War II—to explain why true poetry is and always has been ''the passionate pursuit of the Real.''

Milosz's chief target in these pages is the French symbolist poets, those lonely *fin de siècle* souls who retreated from society into art for art's sake, and took most of modern literature along with them. Such cultivated alienation, insists Milosz, was a luxury possible only in societies with relatively stable social structures. Today's unsettled world demands poets who, like Homer, Dante, and Shakespeare, will speak for rather than against the enduring values of their communities. Profound and accessible, passionate without a trace of sentimentality, *The Witness of Poetry* glows like the sun in a late autumn sky. (p. 59)

> *Adam Gussow, in a review of ''The Witness of Poetry,'' in* Saturday Review, *Vol. 9, No. 8, May-June, 1983, pp. 58-9.*

LEON WIESELTIER

''Is non-eschatological poetry possible?'' A smart shudder of embarrassment passed through the crowd at Harvard University when Czeslaw Milosz asked this question. It seemed to put the burden of proof upon the enemies of the eschaton. It was surely not a proper question of poetics. The occasion was the Charles Eliot Norton Lectures, which were not set up as a spiritual exercise. But Czeslaw Milosz's were. . . .

The Witness of Poetry, the text of his Norton Lectures, is the credo of a great poet. It reveals that Milosz is really a religious thinker. His religiousness is not ''tacit,'' as a critic recently claimed; it is explicit, as it has been in his poems for many years. What is tacit, in this book, is his politics. The politics, to be sure, are anti-Communist; and the authority of Milosz's anticommunism is pretty much absolute. He is angry at universalism and utopianism. . . . Milosz reveres, instead, human custom. And he reveres the Roman patrimony of his country. . . . (p. 32)

Milosz brandishes a belief in miracles. ''The desire for the miraculous . . . the universal human longing for liberation from what is cold as two times two is four'' is what he defends against all forms of determinism. It is like Simone Weil's defense of grace against gravity, which Milosz admires. (He was one of the earliest partisans of her work.) By the miraculous, however, he does not mean the epiphanous. He wants not a disruption of the natural order, but a more strenuous relationship with it. His subject—in his poetry and in his prose— is the proper interpretation of appearances. He calls poetry ''the passionate pursuit of the Real''; the capital R refers to something more than ordinary cognition, but not quite to mysticism. Milosz is a poet of the subject-object relationship. He never quits the senses. He trusts them more than the mind. Their relationship to reality is immediate, and they offer a kind of certainty; this certainty is quietly celebrated in *The World (A Naive Poem),* a cycle of poems that may be the most beautiful Milosz has written. His literary and spiritual style, in fact, can be characterized as *vrai naif.*

The Norton Lectures begin with the observation that ''both individuals and human societies are constantly discovering new dimensions accessible only to direct experience.'' Directness is Milosz's criterion of spiritual significance. His book is an attack on all forms of indirection, on all the interceptions of experience by ideas. This master of form and historian of literature speaks sternly against the contrivances of classicism, because they clutter the elementary connections between the writer and the world, and even close them off; ''a quarrel exists between classicism and realism,'' he writes ruefully, between aestheticism and a really ambitious art. Milosz's poetry is written, therefore, from a principled plainness. In this respect he is like George Herbert: ''Is all good structure in a winding stair? / May no lines passe, except they do their dutie / Not to a true, but painted chair?'' Art's traffic is with things, which are an avenue of access to truth; and truth is simple, and comes sometimes in small sizes. Many of his lyrics are tranquil studies of telling details. (**''Mittelbergheim,''** an early poem, is a deeply affecting prayer for this poetic project.) In Milosz's hands, metaphysics are modest.

If this were all, however, Milosz would be only the heir of Rilke. It is not all. The experience of history accompanies the experience of nature. The thesis of *The Witness of Poetry* is that these experiences are epistemologically similar. ''The historical dimension,'' Milosz hastened to add in his first lecture, is also directly discovered. And, later: ''The twentieth century has given us a most simple touchstone for reality: physical pain.'' Pain, too, is immediate—so immediate that contemporary philosophers have worried that it is not possible to know another person's. It, too, is certain. It, too, when it comes from tyrants and torturers, is a form of the subject-object relationship—a rather pure form. And nothing is more naive than pain. There is a reason, therefore, that Milosz's acquaintance with terror reminds him of his acquaintance with trees. Both are revealed; and the consequence of revelation, of the feeling that forces from outside have intruded, is a sense of situation, of what is above and what is below. When Milosz writes that "all reality is hierarchical," this is not the usual sentimentality for order, or love for law. It is the lesson of a life that has consisted in the constant learning of its own limits, which have been taught by gardens as well as by prisons. The pursuer of the Real pursued by the real—that is Milosz's full plot.

Milosz's book is very concerned with the pessimistic tone of modern poetry. His concluding lecture "On Hope" offers optimism on the basis of what Milosz takes to be a new need for the past that the spread of knowledge and the reproduction of art are purveying across the planet. It is not terribly persuasive—certainly not as persuasive as his own pessimism, which he has not successfully shed. He still sounds a bit like a "catastrophist," as his literary circle in Wilno in the 1930s was called; and catastrophism is rather right in a world that may be wrecked by nuclear war or wrecked by totalitarian rule. As Milosz himself admits, there is a high price to be paid for "the human family" to which the poet Oskar Milosz, a millenarian cousin who died in 1939, aspired. "If we must choose the poetry of such an unfortunate country as Poland to learn that the great schism . . . is curable, then the knowledge brings no comfort." Yet there is comfort elsewhere. *The World (A Naive Poem)* includes a poem called **"Hope,"** which provides a rather different prescription against pessimism than the one he gave at Harvard. . . . (pp. 33-4)

> Leon Wieseltier, "The Real and the Revealed," in The New Republic, *Vol. 189, No. 5, August 1, 1983, pp. 32-4.*

REGINALD GIBBONS

Milosz calls one of his chapters [in *The Witness of Poetry*] "Poets and the Human Family," and it is that bond, which he explores both historically and critically, that marks the best work, in Poland or anywhere. Milosz does not call for poems *about* political situations. Rather, he seems to wonder how good work can be written, no matter how private its subject matter, without the poet having been aware of the pain and threat of the human predicament, so tormented in so many ways and places—including our own neighborhoods and courtrooms and bedrooms, in our own history both social and familial. Milosz describes a poetic style that is apparently not very adaptable to American life—the characteristically laconic, bitter, ironic style of many Eastern European poets, whose distrust of language comes not out of semiological distaste for blatant reference to the tangible world, but out of having been lied to, and having had to lie, in situations where life was trampled by oppressive institutions and lawless men. Milosz's book can be read as a polemic, but to do so would be to regard it too warily, too defensively. It is rather a tender and sorrowful account of what it is that poetry has been called to witness in our time, and how poetry has tried to answer that call. (p. 192)

This is . . . a book of the rarest and most valuable kind of criticism, and an example of the very best of that kind. It creates a perspective from which to view poems, and while Milosz's point of view may have limits or blind spots, or may see sometimes only what is harshly illuminated, he offers a profound corrective to many of the current assumptions not so much of criticism but of poetry itself. (p. 193)

> Reginald Gibbons, in a review of "The Witness of Poetry," in TriQuarterly 58, *No. 58, Fall, 1983, pp. 191-94.*

THOMAS H. TROEGER

[*The Witness of Poetry*] is not a remote essay on poetics, requiring an intimate knowledge of contemporary verse, but is accessible to any thoughtful reader. Many great issues of twentieth century faith echo in the fresh, clear voice of a poet who is free of our usual theological jargon and therefore able to help us look anew at the nature of hope, the necessity of eschatology, and the importance of being related to some larger domain of image and myth than the subjective world of the individual. (p. 491)

Milosz believes that the future of poetry is dependent on more than literary fashion and the genius of independent artists. The Zeitgeist must ultimately affirm some perspective of hope. . . .

[Milosz traces] the increasing isolation of the artist, the impact of science, a kind of "mandatory" hopelessness that arose with realism, and the devastations of modern war. Thus his literary reflections become a journey into the contemporary soul, not simply the individual's but the corporate soul of our shared humanity.

This does not mean that Milosz denies the importance of the individual or puts down our peculiar experience—all charges which I believe a cursory reading of him might awaken from our jealously privatistic age. Quite the opposite, he eloquently affirms the acuity of the particular. . . . Like all poets, Milosz understands incarnational dynamics, but he is concerned about the greater pattern and perspective that poets embody in their verse. Does poetry witness only to the inner experience of the artist or to some grander constellation of meaning?

Drawing on the work of an earlier, distant relative, Oscar Milosz, the author traces how poetry "withdrew from the domain common to all people into the closed circle of subjectivism". . . . The result has been a breakdown between the "Poets and the Human Family" (the title of chapter 2) so that twentieth century verse has become more and more an enclosed aesthetic sphere inaccessible to all except the literati who understand the complexities of its isolated self-expression. Both Oscar and Czeslaw consider this phenomenon to be a tragic rending in the spiritual fabric of our culture and its literary expression.

Oscar, writing in the 1930s saw poetry as "'a passionate pursuit of the Real'". . . . Mark the capital R—not just what is personally real, but what is Real in a larger, transcendent sense. (p. 492)

Czeslaw then suggests that poetry can only be reconnected to that greater "'soul of the people'" by moving beyond an exclusive concern with the self to eschatological poetry concerned with "Salvation and Damnation, Judgment, the Kingdom of God, the goal of History—in other words, to everything that connects the time assigned to one human life with the time of all humanity". . . .

Milosz's literary discussion suggests that two of our culture's most popular values—authentic experience and the primacy of the individual—may be at odds with each other. We tend to assume that the more idiosyncratic our experience, the more genuine it is. But in fact, this is to limit the sources of experience and expression to what Oscar Milosz called the "'paltry ego,'" the "'often empty and always cramped ego'". . . .

The poets—and I would add all of us—must rediscover the world larger than our own private little world, the truth greater than our own private little truth, the reality that is not constricted to the dimensions of our mind and imagination, no matter how lively they may be. . . .

Milosz does see redeeming possibilities for the future. His vision is not rooted in some return to the past but in a pattern of liberation that he believes is the developing salient characteristic of our age. (p. 493)

Milosz helps us to hear how some of the major issues that have occupied twentieth century theology resonate in the experience of a significant poet. He elucidates how important it is that the individual creative act be related to a larger realm of meaning. . . .

Milosz's ''passionate pursuit of the Real'' is an inspiring witness to what it means to see and hear and say the truth with precision and power.

Finally, but most importantly, here is an affirmation of hope that springs from insights into the soul, from an awareness of the pain and devastation of our age, from a broad historical and literary perspective that points to this good news: humanity is redeemable. (p. 494)

> *Thomas H. Troeger, in a review of ''The Witness of Poetry,'' in* Theology Today, *Vol. XL, No. 4, January, 1984, pp. 491-94.*

JASCHA KESSLER

In his magnificent collection of poems, *The Bells in Winter,* published at the time when [Milosz] won the Nobel Prize for Literature a few years ago, we could see the full flowering of his poetic art, which, like his autobiographical writings, always expresses in poignant, visionary lyrics a world that sees the historical past and the personal past as present, living memories, and thus juxtaposes the richness of the present with the ever-present and richly-remembered, richly-evoked past.

Now we have a new collection of poems that epitomizes Milosz's career as a poet. It is called *The Separate Notebooks.* I think that is an appropriate title for a work that gathers poems from Milosz's whole life, as well as trenchant, mysterious, lovely prose passages from his journals. This is, then, a composite work, not even arranged chronologically; rather it's put together in mosaic fashion, so that many experiences and many themes are explored and rendered brilliant by mutual reflection. And yet it is not a coherent whole, not in the usual sense, even as a mosaic; instead it projects the sense of a whole because in fact Milosz's lifelong effort is the attempt to integrate what cannot be integrated: the constant experience of disruption, dislocation and terror, for that was his fate as a man who was always at the center of events, both in politics and in art, yet who managed to escape from all those disasters alive, though doomed never to be whole. And yet, that sense we get of a whole, from this book, if not of wholeness, is no accident, because Milosz, now in his old age, though hardly decayed, casts his mind back and forth over his life, wondering how he has managed to survive and what he can make of things. Furthermore, by offering his early poems, we can understand the profound pathos of a poet who can remember and recall in words those times and places and people who have vanished utterly and forever. . . .

[Everywhere] in these poems Milosz sees and marvels at the naked pathos of created beings—trees, animals, waters, men and women; everywhere the mark of the historian and humanist is deeply impressed, so that the uniqueness of mere existence, so fragile and vulnerable to time and evil, is always his subject. Yet, Milosz also believes that somehow the truth of the forms that were and are and perished survives, and is everlasting.

> *Jascha Kessler, ''Czeslaw Milosz: 'The Separate Notebooks','' in a radio broadcast on KUSC-FM— Los Angeles, CA, February 29, 1984.*

HELEN VENDLER

[The works in **''Selected Poems''** have] been, in the wake of the Nobel, reviewed less as poems than as the work of a thinker and political figure; the poems tend to be considered en masse, in relation either to the condition of Poland, or to the suppression of dissident literature under Communist rule, or to the larger topic of European intellectual history. . . . [The new collection, **''The Separate Notebooks,''** contains] poems written as early as 1934 and as late as 1980. Its appearance offers an occasion for a consideration of Milosz's work as a modern poet. . . .

Apparently, there takes place frequently in Milosz's poetry that rise in temperature which comes when two words that have never before lived side by side suddenly mingle—provoking what we feel in English when we read of Marvell's ''green thought,'' Traherne's ''orient and immortal wheat,'' Donne's ''unruly Sun,'' or Keats' ''sylvan historian.'' This breaking down of ''natural'' compartments is one of the most powerful effects of poetry, which by its concision and free play can represent better than most prose the fluid access of a daring and unhampered mind to its own several regions. Such linguistic versatility—combining words that have never been combined before, but doing it with a sublime justice and propriety, so that the effect is not a jolt but a confirmation of rightness—gives perhaps the highest pleasure that poetry exists to confer. But in reading Milosz we are barred, as foreigners, from knowing that pure bliss of the newly created linguistic object as a reader of the mother tongue knows it. We are also barred from hearing the indispensable falls of sound and cadence.

If we cannot hear Milosz's native euphonies, and if we miss many of the surprising and (we are told) immensely touching effects of his diction as he searches into long-forgotten or darkened corners of the Polish past and brings them, by a word, into an alignment with the present, what can we bear away from a reading of the poems? We find in them, first of all, a truncated autobiography (to be read against the autobiographical essays of **''Native Realm''**). The poetic autobiographer, like the prose one, is reticent. . . . He is not a ''confessional'' poet; his voice is, one might say, disinterestedly personal. For Milosz, the person is irrevocably a person in history, and the interchange between external event and the individual life is the matrix of poetry. Like most lyric poets, Milosz was probably not by nature very much a social being, but, given the situation of his life, he cannot help being a historical one. There is an eerie solitude in Milosz; it sometimes seems that he has suffered the twentieth century all alone, vividly aware of historical cataclysms—those he saw in person (the war, the Nazi occupation of Warsaw, the subsequent Russian occupation, and Communist rule in Poland) and those of Europe in general—yet living in catastrophe as a hermit. . . . (p. 138)

There are two convictions, both of them mentioned in Milosz's introduction to **"Native Realm,"** that are important for his poems. The first is that "one can get at man only obliquely, only through the constant masquerade that is the extension of himself at a given moment, through his historical existence." All of Milosz's poetry has, even if sometimes unwillingly, this historical grounding: through circumstance humanity is made visible. At the same time, it is the second conviction that seems to me the more important in isolating Milosz's idiosyncrasy as a poet: he says that if the "chaotic richness" of "the particulars of our fate" did not exist "we would not constantly be aspiring to form achieved by a process of elimination." Milosz offers this as an axiom, and for him it is: form is the achievement, by the poet, of a paring away, of a refinement of original multiplicity into elemental leanness. . . . Milosz is a stern poet; forbidding and austere lines appear in most of the poems. But they rarely occur alone; they are accompanied by a relenting, a thawing mildness. And it is in this peculiar balance between a juridical, frowning severity and a lyrical, melting attachment that Milosz's power to unsettle us lies. Of course, there are other characteristic aspects of his writing; the one most often remarked on is a gift for classical aphorisms. The aphoristic, or gnomic, sentence offers a linguistic form for Milosz's historical irony—an irony that sees, by virtue of historical length and breadth, beyond the individual case, even if that case is one's own. Poets with a tendency to universalize become (at their worst) deprived of an individual voice; poets who forget that their own fate is part of the common lot fall into self-pity. Milosz's grimness has not blunted the antennae of his painful sensibility; and, conversely, his own exposed nerves have not fatally distracted him from the historical events he has recorded almost involuntarily.

Milosz is more intellectually conscious of his own aesthetic than many poets are. He says, for example:

> Particular existence keeps us from the light
> (That sentence can be read in reverse as well).

The struggle between a clarifying, if inhuman, light and the darkness of particular fate underlies everything that he writes, and provides, in fact, an endlessly fertile resource for invention, as particulars and light dispute each other for room in his work.

From the start, Milosz was a natural ecstatic, destined for intense and radiant perception. (One of the aphorisms reads, "From childhood till old age ecstasy at sunrise.") But everything in his life after his childhood was a scourging of his natural temper. (pp. 138-39)

Milosz reads like a soul who has received a wound from which he has never recovered: an air of doom now hangs over every moment of joy, so that the simplest happiness appears always as a reprieve or furlough from an evil sure to reassert itself. The precariousness of life and writing is always felt in Milosz; his contemporaries who died or were killed or were silenced (not only in Poland but in all of Europe) contribute to the voice he has become—a voice almost necessarily that of a generation rather than (or as well as) that of a single man. The "I" who speaks many of the poems speaks for all who witnessed the dissolution of Europe. . . . Milosz finds transparently simple ways of expressing the evaporation of materiality and spirituality alike. As bombs render one's native streets unrecognizable, and as all codes of ethics fall at once, space swarms and letters flicker and vanish: Milosz's free pillaging of all historical eras opens out his canvas. It is only by such an oblique treatment of the destruction of Warsaw that Milosz succeeds in treating it at all.

As [Stanislaw] Baranczak points out, Milosz rejects symbols in favor of metonymy and synecdoche, those figures of speech which represent a whole by a thing allied to it or by a part of it. The originality with which Milosz finds the briefest of words for inner events is one of the reasons to read him. "The years have transformed my blood," he says, "and thousands of planetary systems have been born and died in my flesh." As in the best poets, we feel this account to be not figurative at all but the most literally truthful way of saying what has happened. What is this changing set of interplanetary relations but a concise history of a Polish intellectual's inner life from the forties to the sixties? The sort of change Milosz wants to describe can only, for him, be described in those terms usually reserved for the life and death of immensely long cycles; what we gain from his language is a sense of indecent speeding up, as one inner galaxy after another is conceived, brought to being, and annihilated.

His own compulsion to write sometimes drives Milosz to bitterness and anger. . . . He finds himself condemned to "odious rhythmic speech / Which grooms itself and, of its own accord, moves on." If such passages testify to the guilt of the survivor, they testify as well to the tormenting distance every poet feels between the miraculous Aaron's rod of art and this world "where men sit and hear each other groan." (pp. 139-40)

In the surpassingly beautiful **"The World: A Naïve Poem,"** a sequence of twenty poems written in 1943, Milosz renders a past of depth and profound feeling in the simplest measures and the simplest words available to a poet, as though only the first syllables of the mother tongue could be words deep-rooted enough for the deepest of primal experiences. **"The World"** is the most opalescent of Milosz's sequences; it exists as pure light against a background of abysmal darkness, preserving that doubleness of perspective—extreme joy recalled in extreme despair—which is Milosz's unique discovery in the art of poetry. . . .

All of **"The World"** is written in primer style. It is a style in which, one feels, it is impossible to lie, or even to shade the truth. Blake, one of Milosz's masters, knew this when he wrote his songs.

In **"The World,"** the sweetness of Milosz's recollection passes from the visual and the personal to the religious, with three childlike poems on the three highest, or "theological," virtues—faith, hope, and love—which make up the thirteenth, fourteenth, and fifteenth poems of the sequence. After that, the child goes abroad to the forest and sees the skies, the kingdom of the birds, who live in a "free, high, shining place;" here he first grasps the possibility of far voyaging. In the single frightening poem, the child becomes Blake's little boy lost in the forest, but, as in Blake, he is found by his ever-watchful and kind father. The security and beauty of the world as it should be, and as we all feel it could be if it were governed by faith, hope, and love, is the theme of the father's rescue of the trembling child. This poem, the most radiant and sacred of the sequence, is called **"Recovery;"** it must be remembered that it was written in the devastated landscape of Warsaw in 1943. The father speaks:

> Here I am—why this senseless fear?
> Soon now the day will come, and night will fade. . . .

To imagine this steady parental reassurance in the most simple and fundamental words of the mother tongue, in the metres immemorially present in hymn and nursery rhyme, is to remind oneself of what this father's voice must sound like in its original Polish, as it embodies the oldest dream of all, underlying our most primitive infant memories—that the universe is, as Carlyle said, not a charnel house but godlike, and our father's. Since this dream is the mythical projection of a faith in being, of a hope for reality, and of a reciprocal love, the poem stands firmly as an essay in archetypal forms, as a predication of the deepest values, and as an anguished personal memory of an incinerated culture. (p. 140)

It is clear . . . that Milosz has a powerful inner investment in antagonism. In his poetry, cultures are set in opposition; world views clash; existence struggles with annihilation; learning vanquishes, and is vanquished by, ignorance; laughter and weeping succeed each other; contempt vies with grief. Milosz is not a writer of one chief emotion (as we might think of Blake as chiefly a poet of indignant vision, or of Crane as supremely a poet of Platonic longing). It seems sometimes that Milosz's poems should split open from the sheer internal pressure of their confined contents. What is confined is often at the same time both mysterious and intelligible, if hard to acknowledge. The sequence **"Album of Dreams"** is a striking group exhibiting this pressure. The dreams retold are dated, as if to give them the force of testimony:

NOVEMBER 23

A long train is standing in the
    station and the platform is
    empty.
Winter, night, the frozen sky is
    flooded with red.
Only a woman's weeping is
    heard. She is pleading for
    something
from an officer in a stone coat.

In this brief glimpse, there is both a general emptiness of landscape and a fullness in the tableau of suppliant and officer; there is both purpose (the long train) and negation of intent (the empty platform); there is darkness and yet a suffusion of blood suggested in the red sky; there is the original, silent scene and the shocking intrusion of weeping and pleading; there is the abject humiliation of the woman and the adamant implacability of the stony officer. Such antagonisms are sensually, aesthetically, ethically, and intellectually unbearable. A more sentimental poet might have represented the hopeless woman and the inhuman officer as a tableau of social protest, but in Milosz's dream logic the woman and the officer represent, philosophically speaking, the irresistible force and the immovable object, and it is that conjunction (philosophically inconceivable) which the aesthetic of the poem must mirror, and does, in its irreconcilable items of presence and absence, reality and surrealism, flesh and stone, silence and the sound of agony. In little, this is the pattern of the best of Milosz's work. To read it is to feel that one's interior being will crack from incorporating such incompatible pressures.

A strong-minded poet of this sort risks an almost vicious power if he permits one force-field to dominate, unmitigated by another; and Milosz's poems of lethal scorn, though memorable, sin perhaps in allowing no shelter from their commination. (p. 143)

Milosz's later poems—those collected in **"Bells in Winter"** and **"The Separate Notebooks"**—incorporate long ruminations on self, body, language, the past, good and evil. They can seem less pure and less corrosive than the earlier poems, though any true comparative judgment could be made only by a Polish-speaking reader. Milosz's dark spirit of mockery lives in them side by side with his racked religious yearning. His gibes and his prayers vie with each other for room, his macabre visual caprices co-existing with his ineffable simplicity of recollection. It is almost impossible to convey the turbulence of mind produced in a reader by such a succession of mental and visual leaps; that turbulence is the aesthetic on which Milosz stakes his claim. (p. 144)

Milosz's elaborate inner system of grids is in one sense the common possession of any European intellectual—the grid of history, the grid of class structure, the grids of manifold visual experience, the grid of plural ethnic and religious allegiances. But in Milosz the grids are curiously permeable to each other, and the mobile flickering of language darts from one to the next, impelled by a rapid and nearly inhuman intelligence keeping a violent welter of feeling just barely in subjection. Milosz speaks both from within the Heraclitean flux and from above it. (p. 145)

There are no direct lessons that American poets can learn from Milosz. Those who have never seen modern war on their own soil cannot adopt his tone; the sights that scarred his eyes cannot be seen by the children of a young provincial empire. A thousand years of history do not exist in American bones, and a culture secular from birth cannot feel the dissolution of the European religious synthesis, on which Milosz dwelt in **"The Witness of Poetry,"** his recent Charles Eliot Norton lectures at Harvard. But the work of Milosz reminds us of the great power that poetry gains from bearing within itself an unforced, natural, and long-ranging memory of past customs; a sense of the strata of ancient and modern history; wide visual experience; and a knowledge of many languages and literatures. Not, as in Pound, the self-conscious allusiveness of the autodidact, returning obsessively to the books of his formative years, but, rather, the living and tormented revoicing of the past makes Milosz a historical poet of bleak illumination. (p. 146)

Helen Vendler, "From Fragments a World Perfect at Last," in The New Yorker, *Vol. LX, No. 5, March 19, 1984, pp. 138-40, 143-46.*

NORMAN DAVIES

"The Land of Ulro," first published in Polish in 1977, examines Milosz's state of mind and intellectual preoccupations in the last phase before he achieved international fame. Its preoccupation is the decline of European civilization since the 18th century, but it is an extremely personal book, written largely for the author's own purposes and possibly for a handful of fellow Polish literati. In the end, one has to accept that Milosz is engaged here in nothing more than "a personal adventure," recording his private impressions. The chosen means are consciously inadequate for the scope of the theme. One learns much about Milosz himself—his nostalgia, love of the esoteric, delight in ideas as wonderful playthings and self-indulgent distress as an "external alien" in a bad world growing worse. But one would look in vain—since Milosz had no such intention—for a comprehensive analysis of the alleged decline of civilization. In this sense, **"The Land of Ulro"** is a minor work in the Milosz repertory, less focused than **"The Captive Mind,"** less compelling than **"Dolina Issy."** It is an intimate *divertissement*, peppered nonetheless with stimulating insights and packed with food for thought about our drift toward disaster.

Like Milosz himself, one has to be intrigued by the "elaboration of intricacies." In the course of this ramble through his memories and literary experiences, he inevitably leaves a trail of clues about the salient features of a complex personality. The pleasure is in the traveling rather than in the arrival.

First and foremost, Milosz is a Polish *inteligent*—not just an intellectual in the Western sense, but a member of a social caste whose traditional function is to nourish the nation's cultural and spiritual values in opposition to the demands of an alien and repressive state. (pp. 1, 16)

[Milosz] was obliged to emigrate; but his inner eye is firmly fixed on that cultural homeland far away to which he belongs. Like all exiles, he protests against the pain produced by the physical separation from his roots, especially since fate has condemned him to live in the materialistic and "puerile" civilization of the United States; but it is also clear that he has no regrets, and in the stimulating contact with his pupils at the University of California, a number of valued consolations. . . .

Second, Milosz is an anti-Nationalist, or rather an adherent of Poland's older and more respectable multi-national tradition. People forget that the Polish society into which Milosz was born was an amalgam of many nationalities, languages and religions, united not by any common ethnic origins but rather by experiences and values shared over the centuries. . . .

Milosz, like his idol [the 19th-century poet Adam] Mickiewicz, thinks of himself primarily as a Lithuanian, with his home beside the waters of the Niewiaza, although he freely admits that Polish is the only language in which he can properly communicate. . . .

It is in this context that one must examine Milosz's self-confessed rebellion against his Polishness. On the one hand, he was driven to exaggerate his Lithuanian identity. . . . On the other hand, he was also driven at an early stage of his career into a skeptical stance toward Roman Catholicism. . . . However, one suspects that his religious rebellion had always been more superficial than real. Precisely in view of his lasting doubts and frictions, Milosz remained a profoundly religious person, gamely baring his "Roman Catholic soul" which he had once judged unbecoming for an avant-garde poet.

The central theme of **"The Land of Ulro"** is the steady decline of European civilization thanks to the growth of scientific thought and the resultant divorce of spiritual and secular values. All the intellectual guides Milosz chooses to consult at length—Mickiewicz, Dostoyevsky, Swedenborg, Blake and Oskar Milosz—were preoccupied with religion. True enough, they were all eccentrics and heretics. . . . [All] of them were religious rebels who rejected conventional religious thinking in their search for a more worthy religion. Czeslaw Milosz hankers to be the same.

Third, and by extension of his anti-Nationalism, Milosz is a devout European. There are few words here of politics in the narrow sense, and no mention of a European ideal. But the assumption that European civilization is, or rather was and ought to be, a coherent whole informs the entire work. (Apropos, see Milosz's earlier volume of memoirs, **"Rodzinna Europa"**—**"Native Realm"**—of 1957.) **"The Land of Ulro"** is saturated with allusions to the European classics, the ancients and English and French authors, to Goethe repeatedly, and tellingly to Dante, in whose "Divine Comedy" Milosz clearly venerates that long lost unity of religious and secular thought. Equally, there is immense respect for the Russian masters whose literature, though not their country, Milosz counts as a brief but integral element of European civilization. . . .

It is not difficult to make play with some of the author's foibles. One can see, for example, why Oskar Milosz loomed so large in his nephew's estimation, but it is problematical for most non-nephews to accept him as an authority on a par with Dostoyevsky or Mickiewicz. If the arcana of Milosz the uncle may be inspiring to the few, they are likely to be confusing to the many. A poet who cultivated "deliberate obscurity" is destined to remain fairly obscure. At times, reading **"The Land of Ulro"** is reminiscent of Milosz's own reading of Swedenborg—"to wander through a hall of mirrors arousing a range of conflicting emotions," from mockery and boredom to awe and assent.

Yet the language is lucid, even where the subject matter is opaque. The book makes no pretense at structured argument, and the reader has to meander round Milosz's 41 chapters which include numerous digressions and a series of set-piece lectures—on Dostoyevsky and the religious imagination of the West, on Mickiewicz's Romanticism, on Blake's Prophetic Books, and on Oskar Milosz's "Les Arcanes," all with extensive textual quotations. . . .

"The Land of Ulro," it turns out, is Blake's name for "that realm of spiritual pain such as is borne and must be borne by the crippled man," where men "rage like wild beasts in the forests of affliction" and in their dreams "repent of their human kindness." At first, when Milosz is writing eloquently about his own sense of alienation both from the Polish national ethos and from his decadent Western refuge, it appears that he is an Ulrian exile par excellence. But then, although he confesses enigmatically to having submitted to the fashions of the contemporary world, he seems to suggest that spiritual growth and repentance have given him a sufficient degree of strength and certainty to stand apart. (p. 16)

One half of him reminds us that his esteemed and tormented masters, not least the schizophrenic Swedenborg, often bordered on madness. But the other half wants to stay in their company. He cannot bring himself to forecast the advent of a "Third Era," an "Age of the Spirit," in the manner of the Polish Romantics. But he still wants to dream of "a civilization in which man will be freed from the servitude of Ulro" and of a renewed "human environment" where the lies and oppressions of modern life will be recognized in their spiritual, not merely their socioeconomic and behavioral, dimensions.

The reader, in fact, never gets a full view of Milosz's target area. The topography of Ulro is not adequately mapped out. Blake's triad of English villains—Bacon, Newton and Locke—evidently spreads the initial confusion, but who exactly was it that widened and extended their false trails? The modern social sciences, especially psychiatry and sociology, are curtly rejected. Freud and Marx are briefly denounced for their "pseudoreligions," but Jung is treated seriously. H. G. Wells is cited, together with the science fiction genre as a whole, for work of "perfect despair." These subjects, particularly Marxism, of which Milosz can speak brilliantly and from hard experience, merit greater exposition. . . .

Milosz's theme, the decline of European civilization since the 18th century, is hardly a modest one, and the range of erudite references, from A to Z—Akhmatova to Zdziechowski—is suitably impressive. Many of the byways of the book, such as the Jewish Cabala, the Polish Socinians or the French Albigensians, are revealing. Yet the overall approach is curiously idiosyncratic and unsystematic. Each of Milosz's five main figures are discussed at length in relation to each other—Blake's debt to Swedenborg, Dostoyevsky's parallels in Mickiewicz, Oskar Milosz's latent sympathy for the others, had he been familiar with them all—but none are examined in the context of their times. There's nothing much, for example, about the philosophers of the Anti-Enlightenment. Although 19th-century concepts of progress and scientific humanism, and the conflict between religion and science, are central to the argument, Darwin is not mentioned. Among the moderns, there are tributes to Simone Weil and Samuel Beckett, but almost nothing on the Existentialists, who may not be entirely irrelevant. . . .

Milosz eventually apologizes for the shortcomings, and craves tolerance for a book "both childish and adult, earthbound and ethereal." But one's tolerance is repaid. Obstinate in his private beliefs, highly individualistic, skeptical of all authority, fearful of coercion, a messianist *manqué,* Milosz is more Polish than he cares to admit. He could never aspire to the mass appeal of Walesa or to the inspirational charisma of John Paul II. But in his chosen field of literature he exudes the defiant stance, the freedom of spirit and the depth of cultural commitment of his homeland, which more than any other is truly a **"Land of Ulro"** on earth. (p. 17)

Norman Davies, "The Making of His Mind," in The New York Times Book Review, *September 2, 1984, pp. 1, 16-17.*

Edwin (George) Morgan

1920-

Scottish poet, essayist, and translator.

Morgan's poetry is characterized by broad experimentation with language, form, and subject matter. He often borrows the rhythms of Scots verse and sometimes writes in the vernacular. Also prominent in his poetry is the unconventional usage of typography and phonetics. Concerned with the visual impact of his work, Morgan has written concrete poems, found poems, and poems partially typeset by computer, while his interest in sound has resulted in the use of music, dialogue, and repetition. One critic has referred to Morgan's work as a "Joycean romp through language." Morgan's subjects are diverse; he has written love sonnets, science fiction fantasies, and poems about social problems. Underlying most of his work is his belief in the improvability of humankind and his reverence for ordinary life. Morgan has been compared to the Scottish poet Hugh MacDiarmid for his wit and his socialist political attitudes.

Morgan's first major collection of poems, *The Second Life* (1968), received praise for its direct and simple language. These poems build meaning through the compilation of concrete images written in a free verse style similar to that of Walt Whitman. A later work, *Instamatic Poems* (1972), attempts to capture events objectively. In these poems Morgan uses newspaper stories and other reported incidents as sources for his subject matter. The collection was considered innovative but linguistically unsuccessful. In his next major volume, *From Glasgow to Saturn* (1973), Morgan combines themes by including his previously published *Glasgow Sonnets* (1972) together with concrete poems and poems concerning space travel. Some critics concluded that Morgan's experiments with different styles and themes contributed to the unevenness of the collection.

The New Divan (1977) was Morgan's next important collection. The title poem is based on the poetry of the fourteenth-century Persian poet Hafiz; the volume also includes experimental wordplay poems, science fiction poems, and love lyrics. With *The New Divan,* most critics accepted Morgan's broad poetic spectrum as an attempt at universality and agreed that his concrete and wordplay poems had transcended mere cleverness.

The publication of Morgan's retrospective *Poems of Thirty Years* (1982) has brought new attention to his career. Though his variety and his use of unconventional techniques are sometimes dismissed as eclectic and trendy, Morgan is considered by many critics among the more daring and imaginative of contemporary poets.

(See also *Contemporary Authors,* Vols. 5-8, rev. ed.; *Contemporary Authors New Revision Series,* Vol. 3; and *Dictionary of Literary Biography,* Vol. 27.)

JULIAN SYMONS

[*The Second Life*] contains straightforward verse and (printed on differently-coloured paper) concrete poems. [Morgan] is certainly the wittiest and least pretentious practitioner of con-

Photograph by: Jessie Ann Mathew: Courtesy of Edwin Morgan

crete poetry, in which his range extends from the charming piece that plays variations on the word 'pomander' to social comments like *Starryveldt,* in which this word changes gradually to Sharpeville and shriekvolley, then to smashverwoerd and spadevow, sunvast, survive and SO:VAEVICTIS. I still feel that this sort of trickiness is not the right form in which to comment on the South African situation, but Mr Morgan goes a long way to justifying concrete poetry as something more than a joke, although he has some good jokes too like *French Persian Cats Having a Ball.*

The poems that lack the support of typographical devices sometimes tend, like those of E. E. Cummings, to drop into sentimentality. The best of them are those in which fantasy has a fairly free rein, like one that begins 'The white rhinoceros was eating phosphorus!' and a poem about a Canadian timber-wolf hunted through Hertfordshire by planes and helicopters, which is finally shot and bludgeoned to death. There are good poems about the deaths of Hemingway and Marilyn Monroe, and throughout the book Mr Morgan shows a dash and romantic bravura that are welcome elements in our present thoroughly mud-coloured poetic scene. (p. 179)

Julian Symons, "Versions," in The New Statesman & Nation, *Vol. 75, No. 1926, February 9, 1968, pp. 178-79.**

MARTIN DODSWORTH

[Morgan's semi-concrete] poems must be taken in their entirety or not at all. They will not be fragmented (which is, I take it, the justification for their existence). They are among the best things in his varied book, *The Second Life*. There are more conventional poems, equally intelligent, but they seem embarrassed by the nakedness of the emotions expressed, which are too often dour and dreary. A lot of the poems are about looking back and feeling miserable. . . .

The Second Life is worth reading, though. It is a book without consistency, but the successes are real and memorable, in the anti-semantic manner. There are some excellent SF poems—like the one about primitive people sensing the presence among them of invisible time-travellers. (p. 414)

> *Martin Dodsworth, "Modified Smiles," in* The Listener, *Vol. LXXIX, No. 2035, March 28, 1968, pp. 413-15.**

THOMAS E. LUDDY

Edwin Morgan's prodigious talent has [in *The Second Life*] produced one of the most refreshing collections of poems I have read. They range in tone from light to serious, and from the real to fantasy. The book includes groups of experimental poems: some concrete poetry and some permutations on sounds and letters which produce fascinating results. . . . Included are some powerful poems in memory of Hemingway, Marilyn Monroe, and Edith Piaf. But the major group of poems is linked to the title poem, and is mostly nightmare-fantasy or science fiction in which the author suddenly finds himself alive again, but with *déjà vu*. The theme here is renewal. . . . But this is renewal in a grotesquely possible world that makes this real one seem paradisical.

> *Thomas E. Luddy, in a review of "The Second Life," in* Library Journal, *Vol. 93, No. 14, August, 1968, p. 2882.*

ANNE CLUYSENAAR

Perhaps because pity is the predominant sentiment of *Glasgow Sonnets,* as I read them, run a close second by indignation, the poor of that city appear as if at a distance, much as Larkin observed Whitsun weddings though the animating sentiments are so different, so sympathetic. Life in the run-down area of Glasgow is characterized (in sociologically relevant terms) rather than described. One is more moved, ultimately, by the poet's attitudes than by his subject. Which is to say that the sonnets fail by what is, I am sure, their own standard. The privileged outsider's eye turns realities into props.

> Under the darkness of a twisted pram
> a cat's eyes glitter. Glittering stars press
> between the silent chimney-cowls . . .

These images are selected for aesthetic effect. As the same poem laments, there is no substitute for the deliverer who has never risen 'from these stone tombs to get the hell they made / unmade' and whose eye would be accurate in a different sense. Similarly, the sonnet-form seems unadaptable to this subject-matter, bringing with it an 'artist's humour'—and Morgan handles the form in a relatively conventional way, if one compares his structures with Keats' experiments with the genre. Another aspect of the problem is brought out by the absence of the abstracter facts of poverty, as of the daily indignities of social

interrelationship (Department of Health and Social Security, rent collector, local shop), which prose reporting and television are so well-adapted to handle in a moving way. . . . Poetry has very great problems in standing up to such competition, and *Glasgow Sonnets* has not solved them, though it may help others to. (pp. 70-1)

> *Anne Cluysenaar, in a review of "Glasgow Sonnets," in* Stand, *Vol. 14, No. 3 (1973), pp. 70-3.*

ALAN BROWNJOHN

From Glasgow to Saturn collects, interestingly, most of the many facets of Morgan's poetic personality: one gets for the first time some sense of the whole *oeuvre*, not just glimpses of his work as a writer of lyrical love poems, or sci-fi fantasies, or slightly loaded whimsicalities in 'concrete', or excursions into horror which suggest a George MacBeth without the fastidiousness or the zany charisma. All that said, it's an uneven book. The love lyrics derive only too plainly from the pop songs to which he pays tribute. Wilful—and, one suspects, clumsy—mystification rubs shoulders with beautifully constructed and entertaining collages, like **'Soho'**. . . . Where Morgan doesn't contrive, he is ineffective; where he does, he gives the impression of a magnificently fertile, highly intelligent and intensely self-aware poet who is still failing to decide what he really wants to do, and doing it well. One wants to be moved, as well as to admire his facility and range. (p. 94)

> *Alan Brownjohn, "Identity Parade," in* The New Statesman & Nation, *Vol. 86, No. 2209, July 20, 1973, pp. 93-4.**

DABNEY STUART

Most of [*From Glasgow to Saturn*] is graduate school diddling with all kinds of neat-o stuff: science fiction, American westerns, typographic calisthenics, computer creation, voice inversion. Some of it is coffee-break cute, much of it simply silly. Remarkable are a few love lyrics scattered at the beginning of the book, two prose poems near its middle, and especially the series of ten **"Glasgow Sonnets"** that close it. It's a shame that such substantial achievement has been dumped in a playground as if it were no different from the seesaws.

> *Dabney Stuart, in a review of "From Glasgow to Saturn," in* Library Journal, *Vol. 98, No. 20, November 15, 1973, p. 3381.*

JOHN MATTHIAS

Morgan's range is wide. Wide enough, in fact, to touch both of the antagonistic poles of Scottish poetry—Ian Hamilton Finlay and Hugh MacDiarmid—and an amazingly large number of points along the way between them. The trouble with being versatile and working in many forms is that readers (and especially critics) will want one thing or another, this sort of poem or that. Even though the possibility exists that a book manifesting widely divergent techniques can achieve a shape and identity as its parts combine to form a whole, this is not very often admitted, and poets who don't stick pretty much to one mode are likely to be abused for not doing so. All the more reason I should apologize for feeling that [*From Glasgow to Saturn*] doesn't manage to cohere. Morgan's propensity for trying to pull off strange virtuoso pieces is partly responsible for this. These tend to be overcharged with his admirable energy; they fuse out or explode. And I'm not persuaded by the science fiction poems, the computer assisted poems, or the poems written partially or wholly in made-up words or noises. But the excitement of a poet delighting in language and willing to play with it, and to take risks, is engaging even in poems which are seriously flawed. The book ends with a series of monologues having to do with a particularly grisly abortion, and with ten well made and moving sonnets about the Glasgow poor. There are probably five or six good poets in Edwin Morgan. But a fatal triple-headed muse—trivial, typographical, and trendy—has a few of them in thrall. (pp. 51-2)

> John Matthias, "Travellers," in Poetry, *Vol. CXXIV,*
> *No. 1, April, 1974, pp. 45-55.**

DESMOND GRAHAM

Whether in the individual poem, the sequence or the collection, Edwin Morgan makes a plurality of styles into a thoroughgoing eclecticism. At once unpretentious and daring his range of production over the past twenty-five years is almost worryingly wide. His wit has done as much as anything to make the "Concrete" and "Sound" poem respectable and accessible. His refusal to decry the contemporary or to set barriers between modes has led to poems using, for example, the terms of space-fiction. He is a tireless translator or adapter. . . . Theoretically, his work could be seen as the inevitable inheritance of the movements of this century's art—pragmatic, multiformed and experimental in technique. Yet the very judgement and tact which protects each element of his enterprise from the least smear of opportunism can seem to limit, even to tame, its impact. Free of what Robert Lowell has described as his American generation's vice of seeking a unique voice in one's poetry, he can seem voiceless, welcome in every style because he brings little of himself to trouble it. It is easy and understandable to thus misrepresent Morgan's work, and it has taken his most sustained effort so far, the title sequence of one hundred poems in *The New Divan,* to dislodge my own doubts. But first, the other half of this packed collection. Here we have Morgan the impersonator, extending the idea of the persona or mask to include the voices of creatures from another planet, or those of inanimate objects—a streak of lightning or a shattered windscreen, or in his series of **'Ten Theatre Poems'** the voice of a drum, a fan-dancer's fan or a cod-piece. Such roles for the poet Morgan are not masks for himself but attempts to enter the quiddity of a world which is not ego-centred. When he does write directly of human situations his characteristic position is that of someone—foreign correspondent or tragedian's messenger—sending interim despatches from a world viewed as eye-witness: a collection of physical impressions, words, half-understood connections. There will be consequences; there are causes; but here, in mid-stream, the patterns are half-known, always provisional. (pp. 76-7)

Reading through the poems of this second half, a consistency, more in an area of preoccupation than in a distinct line of thought, gradually impresses itself. You realise that the provisional place of the poet in each poem is in fact a way of truly reflecting a view of time, of language, of experience. The words of a Concrete poem can fracture to a beautiful pattern (as a windscreen fractures) or they can discompose to a stuttering fear. That either can happen, and a score of other things, shows us it is not just his style that is eclectic but the world itself. . . . In the space-fiction poem at the collection's centre, **'Memories of Earth'**, it is made clear that such an outlook is not disregarding of the human consequences of such disorder.

Here visitors from another planet report from Earth to their world of pure science. They are the perfect, immune witnesses of a world of disparate phenomena. But what they encounter—beauty, inconsequence and man's inhumanity—discomposes their calm. Their planet's rules for scientific observation break down as they observe the whole sequence of events in which a body of people arrive and are killed at a Nazi extermination camp. The evident humanity of the victims denies the onlookers a scientific impartiality and they return to their planet variously deranged by the impress of human feeling. This perspective makes so much deeper sense of Morgan's own depersonalizing of man's activities. From it we see his impersonating art as a testing of the limits of the non-human.

In the title sequence of this collection it is to a direct engagement with the human that he turns. Here, in one hundred poems of between six and twenty lines Morgan's imagination finds an ideal environment: the Middle East—where the bizarre and exotic co-exist with the pungently mundane, the ancient and historical so closely overlap with the present that they are indistinguishable from it. The east, its philosophy and history brought to him by his source poet Hafiz, accepts multiplicity and a time-scale permanently concerned with the presentness of things. In such a world he can be outsider: traveller, tourist, Second World War soldier; but one who carries a poet's freedom to offer the voices of others.

The poem is packed with physical evocations, of meals and meetings, random encounters and sights, the desert, the towns and bazaars, and so often, the sea. Moods, forms and styles all change but it is this physical, sensory perception which is constant and central. (pp. 77-8)

Acceptance of diversity, quiescence and delighted curiosity are the bearings Morgan takes as he guides his poem through a thoughtfully timed diversity of styles and moods. The hard, fragmentary world of *The Waste Land*'s questing (and this reference comes to mind as Morgan directly alludes to Eliot's poem) is re-explored, and this time with love. It is not the lack of purpose or order which troubles the poet, only the human consequences of change and death and lost opportunity. He doesn't doubt his love of the world, for he feels this in his senses: suffering, he knows, is human suffering.

My knowledge of Morgan's main source, Hafiz's *Divan,* is second-hand and thin, but I do know that much ink has been split debating whether Hafiz's poem is sensual and materialistic or mystic and philosophic. It is just this convergence of ostensibly opposed levels that Morgan's tenderness towards the physical world maintains. Above the lovers, dancers or desert-war soldiers there is a sky whose daily changes of colour and tone acts out the paradox of permanence of change; desert and sea alter with equal randomness.

> The dead climb with us like the living to the edge.
> The clouds sail and the air's washed blue. For you
> and me, the life beyond that sages mention
> is this life on a crag above
> a line of breakers. Oh I can't speak
> of that eternal break of white, only of
> memories crowding in from human kind,
> stealthily, brazenly, thankfully, stonily
> into that other sea-cave
> of my head.

The warmth of this, from the last of the sequence's poems, makes the quoted terms with which my review opened look cruelly ungiving—hard, stripped, bare, stark, naked. Certainly

Morgan has learnt from Pound and the Imagists, but what he achieves here and throughout his sequence he achieves through his sureness of context: a context not only of craft but of feeling. (pp. 78-9)

Desmond Graham, "Notwithstanding Imagism; or, The Limits of Austerity," in Stand, *Vol. 19, No. 1 (1977-78), pp. 74-80.**

MICHAEL SCHMIDT

Poetry, Edwin Morgan says, should 'acknowledge its environment'. It can do this in the development of its themes, in its imagery—drawing from particulars of place and time—or in its approach to language, reproducing in the word order or in the word itself specific processes of the environment. In a sequence of poems called **'Interferences'**, for instance, the failure of language in various extreme circumstances is expressed in the deformation of certain words at the climax of the experience; in the **'Glasgow Sonnets'** the references are drawn directly from the city, its history and the present; and in the Science Fiction poems the themes relate to actual human ambitions and actions, with analogies to actual experience, but carried into other spheres—'imaginative poetry exploring time and space'. . . . The poems are memorable as plots and occasionally as rhythms, but phrases and lines seldom stay in the mind, except from the lyrics. Morgan is drawn towards 'directness' and 'realism', though he recognizes the danger in over-directness. (p. 314)

[Morgan] has come to prefer the poetry that emerges from newspaper stories, small incidents, 'what time barely kept', to poetry that built on earlier verse, and to poetry of subjective experience and observation. Hence he has written 'instamatic' poems and other incidental pieces to capture, and in captivity to explore, 'what actually happens'. The long series of *Instamatic Poems* (1972) attempt a photographic immediacy. They are unfortunately thin linguistically, neither particularly accurate nor evocative. The language, coldly used, aspires to be a lens. In the best of them—**'Mougins Provence September 1971'**, for instance—he achieves an almost surreal effect by suspending the real moment, without its cause or aftermath, in a perpetual present. It is the surrealism of photography. But few of these experiments are successful.

Morgan's concrete poems take the immediate 'happening' into language, or treat words as themselves images capable of surrendering multiple significance. This is best illustrated in **'Message Clear'**. In a sense Morgan's work is all translation, translating 'the real' into language, not modulating it through language. His is not a poetry of metamorphosis or even process. He attempts to evoke what *is* in a real or an imagined world.

His first extended collection of poems was *The Second Life* (1968). On the contents page each poem carries the date of composition or of the incident to which it refers. Each witnesses to a particular experience in time, whether in the poet's life or the planet's history. He is wary lest the poems slip anchor from their specific temporal origins. (pp. 315-16)

The range of reference throughout Morgan's work is wide—to history, literature, travel. The variety of detailed allusion characterizes the best of his work. Often, too, there is an engaging whimsy, comedy, and wit. But in his first collection the memorable poems are the sober ones, particularly the animal poems which stress man's inhumanity to the animal world and introduce the theme of innocence that dominates the later

work. He cautions the beasts, 'O wild things, wild things / take care, beware of him.'

His documentary technique is most successful in the love sequence, opening with **'The Second Life'**. . . . These lyrics are at times unabashedly sentimental. Their veracity, down to the details, cannot be doubted. Nothing has been rearranged: the poems bear witness. In other documentary poems Morgan tends to moralize implicitly or explicitly. The images become fixedly emblematic in rhythms altogether too rhapsodic for the subject matter and the moral burden. (pp. 316-17)

In *From Glasgow to Saturn* (1973) the moralizing is more contained. In the documentary **'Stobhill'** he explores, in a sequence of dramatic monologues, an incident: the disposal of a living foetus in a hospital. No judgements are passed. The sequence has the authority of his lyric poems, a number of which are included in this second extended collection. . . . Most of the lyrics lament elegiacally the impossibility of fantasy, the thwarted romantic impulse. Temperamentally Morgan is a romantic, but unwilling to let himself be carried away. . . . Even the love poems are elegiac, with little of the happy incredulity of the earlier sequence. The burning of the letters in **'For Bonfires'** brings to an end the sequence begun in *The Second Life*.

Another of Morgan's forms is the free ballad—**'Blue Toboggans'**, **'Song of a Child'**, and **'Flakes'**, for example—which with innocent rhythms effect subtle tone changes. The freedom from punctuation produces a suggestive, fluid line-to-line syntax. Morgan calls many of his poems 'songs' and the effect—a lightness of language, a strong rhythmic emphasis—is in quality song-like. There is a thematic and formal analogy with Blake's 'Songs'. Frequently Morgan confronts human and natural innocence with experience, often technological. But the experienced men who use technology often become its victims, especially in the astronaut poems, and the innocents are more sensible and active than in Blake, often exacting—almost without meaning to—revenges on their oppressors, as in **'The Mill'**. A moral warning, gentle but insistent, comes from Morgan's world, a caution to observe and experience the moment, as in **'London'**. . . . Morgan's romanticism finds vent in social optimism, a belief—even in the debris of the Glasgow slums—in the possibility of a better world. The political message is cast in Biblical terms in **'The Fifth Gospel'**, where he rewrites the parables, reversing their moral burden. Christ becomes a Michael Foot figure, urging industry, cooperation and community. The **'Glasgow Sonnets'** are less apparently optimistic, but they are documentary, evocative, and socially critical, implying his basic humane optimism in the terms of their criticism.

Some of Morgan's poems are simply entertainments, short stories with mysterious unresolved tensions, as in **'Christmas Eve'**. There are, too, imaginary conversations—Morgan has a good ear for dialogue. This form is taken to great lengths in the sequence **'The Whittrick'**.

If Morgan has never 'found his own voice', as some of his critics claim when confronted by his versatility and facility, he has created an extensive and varied body of poetry which, from various angles, explores certain central themes. For a poet so committed to the 'real' and the 'moment', it is strange that many of his poems exist finally only within the tensions of language, without analogy in the wider environment they should—in his belief—be witnessing to. Yet this is Morgan's achievement: exploring tensions in language, whether the single word, the verse paragraph, or pure sound, showing how language can be renewed from an understanding of its inherent qualities and how these qualities can at times engage intractable subject matter. (pp. 317-20)

Michael Schmidt, "Edwin Morgan," in his A Reader's Guide to Fifty Modern British Poets, *Barnes & Noble, 1979, pp. 314-20.*

ALAN YOUNG

Edwin Morgan is a Scottish poet who has achieved original and interesting results by employing experimental methods which dislocate conventional poetic vocabulary and syntax. . . . At a technical level, however, Morgan is also rooted firmly in traditional modes of writing. His poetry ranges, therefore, from original work in English and Scots (including translation from several European languages) to linguistic games of chance, many of which are certainly more anarchically neo-modernist than anything by [Ian Hamilton] Finlay. (p. 118)

As the title indicates, the poems of [*From Glasgow to Saturn*] include both local, sometimes most moving, social commentary and space-age science-fiction narratives and episodes. There are traditional English and Scots poems, including an effective sequence of ten **'Glasgow sonnets'**, and **'Stobhill'**, a set of five strongly ironic but ultimately compassionate monologues revealing a dramatic gift which Morgan has developed only rarely. His exploration of effects which can be achieved through gradual shifts of sound and meaning produces several delightful poems for performance, including a sci-fi black comedy **'The First Men on Mercury'** and the sequence **'Interferences'**. But some of Morgan's experiments fail to ignite, it seems to me, because he sets up games with rules which are too mechanical and limited in potential linguistic outcomes ever to achieve those effects of surprise and wonder for which he aims. The 'Computer' poems in *From Glasgow to Saturn* fail to recapture the humour of Morgan's earlier **'The Computer's first Christmas card'**. On the other hand, **'The Loch Ness Monster's Song'**— a dada-style phonic poem—does come over well in performance by the poet. . . . (pp. 119-20)

The same criticism may be levelled at most of the experimental poems in *The New Divan* (1977). There is something tedious and predictably dull about poems such as **'Space Sonnet & Polyfilla', 'Lévi-Strauss at the Lie-detector',** and **'Wittgenstein on Egdon Heath'**. . . . [These] particular experiments [are] mere games, duller by far than ludo. (pp. 120-21)

Alan Young, "Three 'Neo-Moderns': Ian Hamilton Finlay, Edwin Morgan, Christopher Middleton," in British Poetry Since 1970: A Critical Survey, *edited by Peter Jones and Michael Schmidt, Persea Books, Inc., 1980, pp. 112-24.**

DICK DAVIS

Edwin Morgan's *Poems of Thirty Years* is a curate's egg of a book. Large stretches of it are only intermittently comprehensible (e.g. **'The New Divan'**), it contains a great deal of versified sci-fi which can be of interest only to aficionados of that genre, and a lot of the earlier verse verges on the worst kind of 1940s apocalyptic twaddle (it was I think a mistake to include the hitherto unpublished **'Dies Irae'** of 1952). On the other hand, many of the poems display passion, wit and a desperately inventive verve which is very persuasive; Morgan is at his most impressive in parody and invective, as in the early **'Vision of Cathkin Braes'** or the later **'Five Poems on Film Directors'**,

and despite the omnivorous range of subjects he treats, this rather suggests a talent in search of a theme.

The last poem, **'Cinquevalli'**, is about a juggler, a man of 'balance, of strength, of delights and marvels', and there is more than a hint that this is how Morgan sees the poet. His book has its share of delights and marvels, and, like Cinquevalli, Morgan takes immense risks that dazzle when they come off; but even if he intends the air of circus tawdriness that clings to much of his verse, it is an air that can seem smothering if breathed for too long. (p. 23)

Dick Davis, "Private Poems," in The Listener, *Vol. 108, No. 2791, December 16, 1982, pp. 23-4.**

JOHN LUCAS

[*Poems of Thirty Years*] brings together a vast amount of original work remarkable for its variety and skill. The skill is sometimes frittered away on sound and concrete poems, which may be fun to write and to utter but are not much fun to read. There are also elegies which feel merely dutiful and love poems notable for their lack of any intense feeling at all; yet these failures do not greatly matter. Morgan's imagination is not much stirred by the purely personal, but against that is the fact that he is an exuberantly inventive poet. *Poems of Thirty Years* is thoroughly entertaining, because although you never know quite what will come next you know that sooner or later you will come upon a poem that takes hold.

This is particularly true of his handling of that most unpromising of genres, the science fiction poem. Most sci-fi poems are either dull or plain silly or both; and I suspect they are written by poets who, to adapt a remark by Schoenberg, are incapable of writing well in the key of C Major. Not Morgan's, however. His long sequence **'The New Divan'** may owe something of its form to Lowell's *Notebook*, but its subject-matter is very different. A kind of space-traveller's diary of stopovers in odd nooks and moments of our world, it is sometimes a pre-Martian poem, sometimes impenetrably obscure, always surprising and often delighting by its imaginative jumps and turns. The same is true of **'Memories of Earth'**, which uses the gimmick of a space-traveller's record of various aspects of the history of our own century (including some of the worst) to imply serious moral and political judgements. These are less successfully, because less imaginatively, invoked in the **'Glasgow Sonnets'**.

John Lucas, "Ignorant Eyes," in The New Statesman & Nation, *Vol. 104, Nos. 2700 & 2701, December 17-24, 1982, p. 45.**

ALASDAIR D.F. MACRAE

The thirty years in the title of [*Poems of Thirty Years*] run from 1952 to 1982 and over this period Edwin Morgan has been remarkably productive. . . . Abroad he is perhaps best known for his concrete poems, poems such as **'The Computer's First Christmas Card'** and **'The Loch Ness Monster's Song'** where he plays with permutations of sounds, words and shapes on the page. Play, improvisation, surprise discoveries are central to his idea of poetry. Although he often writes in conventional metres, he obviously believes that many poems present themselves to the vigilant observer; thus, his *Instamatic Poems* (1972) catch the poetic moments as they are offered. The dangers in this notion of the found poem are that what is striking to one observer may not be so interesting to other readers, and that the immediately striking often seems, in retrospect, flashy or narrowly topical. Some of Morgan's poems are decidedly slight and inconsequential.

This collection includes a group of previously unpublished early poems and some uncollected later poems but the strongest section of his work probably remains *The Second Life* (1968). Throughout this large retrospective volume there are excellent poems in different modes and Edwin Morgan's example constitutes, in its constant experimenting and willingness to take risks, a challenge to younger poets. Unlike so many poets, he glories in technical advances and tries to write a poetry appropriate to space travel, the sensationalist tactics of the media, and the discrepancies between the glamour of Hollywood publicity and the abject misery of ordinary life for many. Morgan demands to be read by anyone interested in contemporary poetry. (pp. 51-2)

Alasdair D.F. Macrae, in a review of "Poems of Thirty Years," in British Book News, *January, 1983, pp. 51-2.*

JOHN WAIN

[Morgan] makes statements, lots of them, and his poems are not ingenious but deeply intelligent. Since the death of Auden, who brought a tremendous range of speculation and knowledge into his poetry, Morgan seems to me to stand out almost unchallenged as a poet of ideas.

In case I seem to be saying that Morgan is a poet like Auden, let me add at once that he has nothing like the same gift for the felicitous phrase and is altogether a heavier, more viscous writer. He resembles Auden only insofar as the two of them are natural intellectuals. (p. 75)

Morgan, for his part, is a poet of amplitude. He is interested in so many things, the beam of his vision flashes round so widely, that he needs space to work in. People who like neat, epigrammatic poetry will not often like his longer poems, where a certain torrential eloquence, even at the risk of saying the same thing in too many ways, is his chosen manner. An example would be **'The Cape of Good Hope'**, a poem from the mid-fifties, which takes the metaphor of a sea-voyage (I suppose, an actual voyage to South Africa which the poet made, perhaps during the war) and uses it as a framework for the poet's reaching out to life through his art, and for man's reaching out generally. It is, like most of Morgan's poetry, personal and discursive at the same time: a poem about himself and his own situation but always with that window open on the world, both the natural world and what man has made of life in that world. So we get powerful, even prodigal, descriptions of the unrestrained mighty force of the ocean itself, and also a section consisting of verse essays on certain speculative thinkers and artists who have engaged Morgan's attention—Leonardo da Vinci, Michelangelo, Newton, Beethoven, Melville, Mayakovsky. The purely descriptive passages, evoking the vastness and uncontrollability of the sea, remind one that the young Morgan was a contemporary of Dylan Thomas . . . and also that he must have come under some of the same influences as a fellow-Scot like W. S. Graham, though the voice I hear most strongly behind Morgan's is that of Hart Crane. Pitting his gift for words against the sea's immensity, Morgan pulls out all the stops in some splendidly uninhibited writing. . . . (p. 76)

A poet as wide-ranging as Morgan, as keen to try his hand at every new thing that comes up, will inevitably have times when he goes beyond the range of the individual reader. Personally I don't get much out of the science-fiction poems, though some of them are witty; and the long poem **'The New Divan'** was just too much for me, I sank under its weight. But there was still an enormous amount that interested and held me. I think, after establishing preliminary agreement that Morgan is an energetic, interesting and valuable poet, the setting up of an order of preference becomes very much a matter of individual choice. (pp. 76-7)

Because Morgan is an ambitious poet, in agreeable contrast to those hedge-hoppers who stay entirely within their range, he is rewarded now and then with the power to break through his own barriers. For instance, he has, on the whole, not a very good ear; one rarely finds a line, let alone a whole poem, that has much lyrical quality. But because he does not give up, does not cease *trying* to write a lyrical poem, he is now and then rewarded by achieving one. (p. 77)

Most of Morgan's poems use very loose form—looser as the years go by and the collective literary mind forgets poetic form more and more completely—but he has kept himself alive to the possibilities of form, the advantages that can come from an ability to master it, and the result can be seen in the excellent **'Glasgow Sonnets'** (1973), where the tightness and elegance of the sonnet form is itself an ironic comment on the disordered, sprawling dilapidation of the city.

In his variety, range, restlessness of mind and large output, the poet Morgan most reminds me of is Browning, and I intend that as a compliment. Browning's stock is not very high these days, compared with what it was in his own time, and yet he is not in danger of being forgotten; and neither, if people still know a good thing when they see one, is Edwin Morgan. (pp. 77-8)

John Wain, "Celts," in London Magazine, *Vol. 23, No. 4, July, 1983, pp. 74-8.**

Manuel Mujica Láinez

1910-1984

Argentine novelist, short story writer, biographer, poet, critic, journalist, and essayist.

A prize-winning Argentine author, Mujica Láinez is noted for his elaborate, often fantastic narratives written in a richly elegant prose style. *Bomarzo* (1962), the novel for which he is best known to English-language readers, is a representative work: the life story of a sixteenth-century Italian duke is recounted several centuries later when he is "reincarnated" as the modern-day author Mujica Láinez. Although he has not attained the critical status of such Latin American writers as Gabriel García Márquez and Julio Cortázar, Mujica Láinez is praised as the author of unusual and striking works which achieve a high order of literary entertainment.

Mujica Láinez began his writing career with short stories, poems, historical romances, and biographies focusing on the history and people of Buenos Aires. The four novels of his "saga of Buenos Aires"—*Los ídolos* (1953), *La casa* (1954), *Los viajeros* (1955), and *Invitados en El Paraíso* (1957)—established him as an important Argentine author. Taken together, these works chronicle the decay of Argentina's wealthy elite as their society dissolves following the upheaval of the Second World War. The theme of decay is common to the novels of both Mujica Láinez and García Márquez. As George Schanzer has found, Mujica Láinez's *De milagros y de melancholías* (1968), the history of a fictional South American city, is similar to García Márquez's *One Hundred Years of Solitude* in that both works follow a city into decay and in both works the characters and events are a combination of the realistic and the fantastic. A crucial difference between them, according to Schanzer, is that while *One Hundred Years of Solitude* is a work of serious social and political comment, Mujica Láinez's novel "is a parody of Latin American reality." Throughout Mujica Láinez's fiction, humor and irony play a central role.

Mujica Láinez's most popular and acclaimed novel, *Bomarzo,* is the fictional autobiography of a vengeful, alienated hunchback who was a member of the Italian nobility during the Renaissance. From the vantage point of the twentieth century, and with the benefit of such modern systems of knowledge as psychoanalysis, the duke is able to understand why a historical era that glorified human achievement, and that associated physical imperfections with spiritual flaws, rejected him. Critics have described the prose style of this work as colorful and brilliant. But while many applauded Mujica Láinez's evocation of the past and the skill with which he exposed the tensions and paradoxes of Renaissance thought, some charged that *Bomarzo* was not supported by any larger or more serious aim than that of telling a fascinating story.

Like *Bomarzo,* the recently translated *El unicorno* (1965; *The Wandering Unicorn*) features a twentieth-century narrator who recounts a story from the distant past, in this instance twelfth-century France, where magical powers and supernatural creatures are a reality. Critics were divided in their reception of this work. Some thought the book enjoyable and have described it in terms of fantasy or escapist literature. One re-

Photograph courtesy of Taplinger Publishing Company and Lester & Orper Dennys Publishers.

viewer has observed that in this work Mujica Láinez neglected to confront the social and political themes which have distinguished much of contemporary Latin American fiction. Others found the book to be built solidly on eternal themes of love, death, and human isolation, praising its author once again for his writing skill and his ability to tell an engaging story.

Two more recent novels, *Cecil* (1972) and *Sergio* (1976), have entirely modern settings, though they are no less exemplary of Mujica Láinez's idiosyncratic subjects and techniques. *Cecil* is an autobiographical rendering of a period in Mujica Láinez's life. The title character is the author's English whippet, and the novel is told through a perspective that is a fusion of man and animal. *Sergio* is the story of a young boy whose great beauty makes him prey to both men and women. Throughout the narrative the author speaks directly to the reader, commenting on the conflict between pure beauty and a corrupt society. These two novels have been especially praised for their subtlety and ironic humor.

(See also *Contemporary Authors,* Vols. 81-84, Vol. 112 [obituary].)

ROBERT EVETT

[The Opera Society of Washington] climaxed a season distinguished by productions of virtually unknown Haydn and Massenet operas with the world premier of *Bomarzo,* a product of the Argentine composer Alberto Ginastera and the Argentine poet and novelist Manuel Mujica Lainez.

Both text and music reflect a number of strong influences which have been assimilated with varying degrees of success. (p. 28)

The principal characters themselves are drawn from history. The dukes of Bomarzo were members of the house of Orsini—which, during the high Renaissance, was in fairly constant competition with the Medici, the Farnese and the Borgia for the papacy. During a couple of centuries, the Orsini contributed their fair share of saints to the Roman canon, but these people do not figure in the opera. The "Bomarzo" of the title, Pier Francesco Orsini, succeeded to the dukedom against considerable odds. . . . The opera endows the duke with formidable sexual problems, exacerbated by his hideous personal appearance and his poisonous involvement with his grandmother. The acting out of his fantasies involves an encounter with a nude courtesan who figures in orgiastic ballets so uninhibited that, a few days before the premiere, some of the ballerinas refused to dance. In the end, the duke dies, poisoned by his own astrologer, at the base of a statue called "The Mouth of Hell."

In spite of the historical basis of the material, it must have taken a great deal of effort on the part of Sr. Mujica Lainez to convert it into acceptable adult theatre. His technique has been to divide the literary drama into a set of short episodes, presented like movie flashbacks, in which the events are seen from the point of view of the Duke, and the symbols are drawn from the sculptures of the Bomarzo estate. What emerges is a disagreeable interior journey, a series of fifteen humiliating defeats in fifteen scenes, in which symbol and metaphor combine to convey the kind of existential horror and nausea one finds in an opera like Berg's *Wozzeck. Bomarzo* becomes the libretto of an Italian opera by an author who has read Freud, studied the best operas since *Pelléas,* and presumably seen a lot of Swedish movies. (pp. 28-9)

Robert Evett, " 'Bomarzo', Si, 'Rigoletto', No," in
The New Republic, *Vol. 156, No. 23, June 10, 1967,*
*pp. 28-9.**

TIME

The figures chiseled out of Etruscan boulders include a 19-ft.-high elephant crushing a warrior in its trunk, a giant dismembering a man, a goddess with each pubic hair clearly delineated, and a 20-ft. satanic head whose mouth opens into a large chamber. These overwhelming creations are 50 miles north of Rome. It is known only that they were carved between 1555 and 1585 at the command of Duke Pier Francesco Orsini.

But are they part of a kinky Renaissance Disneyland for a bored nobleman or projections of a tortured soul? When he visited Bomarzo, Argentine Art Critic and Writer Manuel Mujica-Lainez opted for the latter. He had moreover, an odd feeling of having been there before—perhaps in another life.

Combining a scholar's passion for detail with a novelist's fertile imagination, Mujica-Lainez set about constructing from the few known facts a sumptuous fictional Doge's Palace of the mind. Like that famous seat of the Venetian Republic, whose ceiling, walls, and floors constitute a convulsion of visual splendor, *Bomarzo*'s pages glitter with descriptions of processions, land and naval battles, landscapes, and courtesan's sultry rec room and a cabalist's murky study.

Mujica-Lainez conveys not only the well-known creative energies of the Renaissance but its less understood anxieties as well. . . .

Mujica-Lainez focuses this aesthetic and religious conflict in the mind and body of *Bomarzo*'s Duke Orsini. He recreates him as a hunchback who tells the story of his life as an omniscient observer not only aware of his own time but of events from the time of his death until the present. Mujica-Lainez's implication is clear: Orsini's true immortality resides not in the few historical facts and artifacts we know but in his re-creation as a fictional character.

Bomarzo's Orsini combines Gothic deformity with a beautiful refined face and a graceful pair of Tintoretto hands. Yet it is Orsini's genetic baggage, "the rucksack of my misfortune," that shapes his soul. In his childhood, the hump fostered his father's disdain and his brother's malice. When he was a youth, it caused impotence and self-disgust as Orsini had to view it multiplied in a harlot's mirrored chamber.

Like Philoctetes' stinking wound a classical symbol of the relationship between art and abnormality—Orsini's back is the burden of his genius. It compels him to refine everything into art, including cruelty and murder. . . .

But procreation, high fashion, and grand frescoes prove too ephemeral for Orsini. Only the stone of Bomarzo could preserve his suffering and redeem his miserable existence. "Love, art, war, friendship, hope, and despair—everything would burst out of those rocks in which my predecessors had seen nothing but the disorder of nature." It is an outcry that invites both admiration and pity, a strong but unstable mixture that Mujica-Lainez keeps bubbling with an alchemist's patient intensity.

Like alchemy *Bomarzo* is based upon a richly human and dramatic scheme of symbolism and metaphor. It does not create any real gold, but fine fiction has always been essentially a ritual of appearance.

"Long Live the Duke," in Time, *Vol. 94, No. 24,*
December 12, 1969, p. 104.

DAVID GALLAGHER

Although the hero of "**Bomarzo**" is some 450 years old, the story he offers us is one, relatively speaking, of his youth, in the Renaissance as the hunchbacked Prince Pier Francesco Orsini, Duke of Bomarzo, who, having sustained a long, heroic and sometimes successful battle against impotence through two marriages, fought without distinction in the battle of Lepanto. The tone of the novel recalls Italo Svevo's "Confessions of Zeno." Mujica-Lainez shares Svevo's candidly endearing irony, and like Zeno, Bomarzo is able to bring to bear on his complexed Renaissance life the lessons of psychoanalysis that he has learnt, centuries later, in Buenos Aires. (p. 40)

The Freudian lessons acquired in Buenos Aires are not lost: the hero has killed his father in order to become him—to become the Duke of Bomarzo—but his life is tormented by the guilt his action has inspired. The fantasy of the hero's remarkable age is indeed a useful device to combine a contemporary account of a Renaissance life with the improving perspectives of a 20th-century education in psychoanalysis. Bomarzo is even aware, in retrospect, that the erect swords flourished at his wedding ceremony were boldly flamboyant, though useless, phallic symbols.

"Bomarzo" has been a best seller in Argentina, and it has earned extravagant praise from perhaps the finest Latin American writer, Jorge Luis Borges. It is as easy to speculate on its appeal as it is to imagine the sour reception it will have from many quarters. Is it not impudent, after all, that a writer from an underdeveloped country should be engaged in a reconstruction of the Italian Renaissance aristocracy instead of tackling the problems of his own people? Those who entertain such reactions should remember that Buenos Aires is a wholly cosmopolitan city, in which the Italian Renaissance is as real to many of its vast proportion of immigrants as the poetry of the pampas and the gauchos.

The novel is, nevertheless, perhaps objectionable on other grounds, for it flaunts the ingredients of a best seller too obviously. Like many best sellers, it presents an irresistibly forbidden exotic world of princes, palaces and jewels. The reader is flattered into sharing the impressive confidence of the narrator's friends: Catherine of Medici, the innumerable Orsinis, Benvenuto Cellini, Michelangelo Buonarroti, lascivious popes, scheming cardinals, and the Emperor Charles himself. Spiced with a story of sexual impotence conveyed with careful suspense (will he make it on the wedding night or not?) and the decadent elegance of the narrator's palaces, what more could a reader of popular fiction ask?

"Bomarzo" is a skillful novel. It has been rendered into English by the most talented of all translators of Latin-American fiction, Gregory Rabassa. But among a generation of Latin-American writers of such vigorous linguistic and imaginative talent as Alejo Carpentier, Julio Cortázar, Gabriel García Márquez, Mario Vargas Llosa, and Guillermo Cabrera Infante, to name but a few, Mujica Lainez's achievement is indeed a slender one. In the 19th century, under the Romantic aura of elegant historical novels, it would have passed. Indeed, the names dropped (cultural name-dropping is a notorious Argentinian literary habit) have a distinct 19th-century flavor about them: the novelist's heroes are Victor Hugo and Gérald de Nerval, two poets who greatly influenced Latin America's most self-consciously and objectionably exquisite literary school— the modernist movement that flourished in the 1890's. In many ways "Bomarzo" is a modernist novel 80 years late.

In fairness, we may perhaps ask ourselves what it is that allows us to accept a given type of writing if we know it was written at a particular time in the past when we reject it if it is deployed by a writer now. . . . The sometimes humorous fantasy involved in Bomarzo's great age and the modern perspective that his psychoanalytical bent brings to bear on his subject are lost in nearly 600 pages of sublimely anachronistic narrative. The fact that Svevo is a contemporary of Zeno's makes "The Confessions of Zeno" an incomparably more vigorous novel. The same is true of Lampedusa's "The Leopard." The difference between them is the difference between women's magazine history and literature. (pp. 40-1)

David Gallagher, "Hunchback Methuselah from the Renaissance," in The New York Times Book Review, *January 11, 1970, pp. 40-1.*

DAVID WILLIAM FOSTER

Although unlikely ever to be considered a great novel, Manuel Mujica Láinez's *Bomarzo* . . . has certainly been one of the most memorable—and unusual—works of Argentine fiction in recent years. . . . Through some feat of necromancy Orsini is able to tell his tale, complete with all the appropriate period accoutrements, while ensconced in his twentieth century study beneath his own gaze as painted by Lorenzo Lotto four hundred years before.

The painting is undoubtedly one of the central keys to the novel. The narrator comments ironically on the idealized Renaissance perfection the portrait exudes, a perfection of body that bore scant resemblance to the man's true physique. Orsini, in frank admissions, describes his physical deformities and the excruciating psychological suffering occasioned him by it through his "central" existence during an age that ill tolerated physical imperfection, believing it to be a sign of inner weaknesses. (p. 33)

Pursuing his central conceit of inverting Renaissance values and infusing them with the black humor of contemporary civilization, Mujica Láinez has Orsini (who may claim to be a faithful figure of the author himself as he would care to be remembered) find himself as a black magician. Not the Renaissance *magus* who would decipher God's universe, but the necromancer who would plumb the black hell of his own soul. The final result, with much human suffering along the way, is the famous Park of Bomarzo. Intended to clash sardonically on one level with the immense Renaissance murals of the palace detailing the hollow public frame of the master, the Park is an embodiment in horrendous and Gargantuan stone figures of the baroque images of the Duke's inner consciousness. The figures are literally a panoramic representation of the horror, despair and evil of his intensely private human existence, an existence that is incomprehensible to his own contemporaries and, one supposes, only really consciously meaningful to Orsini himself four hundred years later.

Why the Renaissance? Certainly the novel does have something of an aura of falseness about it, although Mujica is too sensitive and dynamic a writer to serve up to the reader unassimilated literary archaeology. My own guess is that many of us in the West still labor under that paradigmatic Burckhardtian-Nietzschean myth of the Renaissance, and one of its most potent legacies, that man is the measure of all things, primarily since he is made in the image of the Divine Being. One need not insist too much that the modern intellectual finds such a cheery if well-worn belief unacceptable. By having Orsini portray himself in the awesome dimensions of contemporary Everyman while still an integrated partipant in the pageant of the Renaissance, Mujica Láinez not only reinforces the validity of the Duke's tortured being, but he offers as well a telling denunciation of the positive man-centered values that we cherish as our Renaissance inheritance. The portrait is magnificent, but the Park of Bomarzo is what brings man to the stark contemplation of his own inner abyss, and for that reason—the elaborate backdrop of the novel aside—it remains, as the title, the more potent of the two metaphors. Orsini's value as a witness is not so much in his self-realization, but in the clinical, detached manner in which he expresses it, as the inescapable and therefore only necessary drama that must preoccupy man. The novel's central conceit and its ironic anachronism become in the end effective devices in support of this original perspective on what is virtually a contemporary psychological— or psychoanalytic—truism. The Park of Bomarzo with its weird and immense figures of stone is Orsini's only true immortality that had been forecast for him by the stars. It is an immortality of his misshapen soul, which is far more tangible than that of his surviving twisted physical form.

To a great extent, *Bomarzo* deserves to be called autobiographical, not because its details are in any sense a key to Mujica

Láinez' personal life, but to the very extent that the author-narrator considers himself, in his artistic perception, the immortal embodiment of the Duke. The novel itself is a reenactment, so to speak, of the latent drama of the immobile figures of the Park, and in attempting to recreate their prehistory, the novelist offers his own equally immortal version of the Garden, its mirror-image as well as its horrifying interpretation as a metaphor of the human soul. (pp. 33-4)

> David William Foster, "The Monstrous in Two Argentine Novels," in Américas, Vol. 24, No. 2, February, 1972, pp. 33-6.*

GEORGE O. SCHANZER

Since 1965, when Peñuelas noted "la ausencia de nombres hispanos en la extensa bibliografía del mito" [the absence of Spanish surnames in the extensive bibliography of myth], the subject of myths has been explored by Hispanic scholars, and comments on their use by Spanish American writers have become quite frequent. Usually such studies or remarks refer to the born narrators among the novelists of the "boom" who do not emphasize self-reflective structure in their works. The use of myths has been noted and studied in Carpentier and García Márquez, among others. This use has been largely overlooked in Manuel Mujica Láinez, especially in *De milagros y de melancolías [Of Miracles and Melancholies]*, which has received meagre attention, since its publication, late in 1968.

De milagros is the work of a famous writer, who has more than a dozen books to his credit as well as six or more literary prizes, both national and international. . . . Mujica Láinez, six years younger than Carpentier, but eighteen years older than García Márquez, has been labeled part of the anti-Perón establishment in Argentine literature. Why, then, did this recent work of Mujica Láinez, which represents a thematic homecoming, not score as well as the earlier ones?

The circumstances of publication of *De milagros y de melancolías* provide a major but not the only clue for the relative neglect of the book: the would-be chronicle of the mythical city of San Francisco de Apricotina del Milagro was launched by Editorial Sudamericana of Buenos Aires, the same press which eighteen months earlier had published *Cien años de soledad [One Hundred Years of Solitude]*. The reviews of Mujica Láinez' novel thus far available, do not refer to it in relation to the work of García Márquez, whose "escandaloso éxito" [scandalous success] (to quote Rodríguez Monegal) completely eclipsed *De milagros*. . . . Suppposedly written by an exile from the prodigious city between December 1967 and July 1968, *De milagros* could have been inspired by *Cien años*. Therefore the possibility of a parodistic or imitative relationship exists and ought to be explored.

A review by Ghiano, which traced the use of myths in Mujica Láinez' earlier works, did not specifically link *De milagros* to the author's *Crónicas reales [Royal Chronicles]*, written in the same vein in 1966 and therefore definitely prior to *Cien años*. . . . While the earlier ironic work presents vignettes from the history of an imaginary European dynasty, *De milagros* pretends to be a documented history of a South American city. Neither book contains the motif of a quest for the cue of magic documents, whose decoding coincides with the fatal ending of the novel, which we know from García Márquez. But it does appear already in Mujica Láinez' *Bomarzo*, years before *Cien años*.

In view of obvious parallels, it is surprising that the two authors have not been linked more often. . . . The patent similarities, as well as the dissimilarities, of the latter and *Cien años* call for a comparison and an examination of Mujica Láinez as a myth-maker.

Unlike the saga of Macondo, the chronicle of San Francisco de Apricotina does not avoid the appearance of history and bases itself on a two-page apocryphal bibliography, divided by periods, poking fun at erudition of all sorts. This documentary nature, rather than a "new novel" feature, . . . seems a take-off on documentary narratives. While we sense a relationship of the mythical Macondo with the area familiar to García Márquez . . . , "la ciudad del Milagro" [the city of the Miracle] is a synthetic Spanish American provincial capital, in a mountainous region south of Northern South America, not too far from the sea, near a remaining Inca stronghold, whose warrior horsemen are the "panchos" and long-haired Indians, called "jipis." Now that we know—or rather do not know—the place, Mujica Láinez leaves no doubt about time and the sequence of events. They begin in the period of Philip II; they end with the assassination of the proletarian líder of the city, four hundred years later, in the nineteen sixties, which necessitates the exile of the would-be chronicler. There follows an "Epílogo espiritista" ["Spiritist Epilogue"], which provides an open-end conclusion by means of a reportage on a timeless vision, supposedly having taken place earlier at the voodoo brothel of the demagogue-governor, who somewhat resembles Perón. It is interesting to note that at the end of both *Cien años* and *De milagros* the city is in ruins. While García Márquez' novel is subdivided yet gives the impression of rambling along, its underlying structure . . . can be constructed by the reader. Mujica Láinez, on the other hand, leaves no doubt that we are studying the highlights of a linear sequence, which is divided into chapters dealing with the mythical heroes of San Francisco: El Fundador, Gobernadores que tuvo . . . hasta su Independencia, El Liberador, El Caudillo, El Civilizador y El Líder [The Founder, Governors Until Independence, The Liberator, The Caudillo, The Civilizer, and The Leader]. A further, invisible, structuring is afforded by the technique of presenting history as a sequence of slides or verbal pictures (obviously modernist cuadros [tableaux]), which evoke real or synthetic historical canvasses. Indeed, in a letter—in excellent English—Mujica Láinez referred to his technique of using a "historical framework to build a succession of scenes (tableaux) of constant irony" (9/25/72).

Unlike *Cien años*, the Argentine novel makes no pretense of being a family saga, although *los próceres* [the leaders] of the prodigious city are often interrelated, in both conventional and unconventional ways. Both books would benefit from appending a genealogical-dynastic chart of the protagonists, such as the one prepared recently for *Cien años* for didactic purposes. As the successive or simultaneous Buendías share characteristics, the chief executives of San Francisco are all variations of "The Hero of a Thousand Faces" (in this case six plus), but they are all *tuertos* [one-eyed] whether they are one-eyed congenitally or as the result of violence. Whereas the protagonists of both novels act rather irresponsibly, the incongruous and selfish actions of Mujica Láinez creations somehow lead to the common good and progress of the city. Both Macondo and San Francisco are founded after prolonged wanderings through the wilderness, but it is Mujica's opening chapter which parodies a deliberate quest, the Hispanic colonizing pattern, and the celebrated "utopía-epopeya" [Utopia-Epopee] myth. Of course, the establishment of a shipyard in the mountains inland by the apricotinos clearly outdoes the discovery of a Spanish galleon miles from the sea, in *Cien años*. Likewise, while the sexual prowess of García Márquez's characters is as mythical as the dimensions of certain of their organs, Mujica Láinez, with greater sophistication, shows considerable interest in sexual deviation, as he has effectively done in previous works. Nevertheless, he also includes sexual initiation scenes, an aunt-nephew relationship, and San Francisco's mythical warrior, the caudillo Bravaverga, leaves not seventeen but fifty-seven spurious sons who later form a legion of shock-troopers (with purple capes, not green berets), the ''Vergas Bravas'' [Fearless Penises]. Sex is somewhat grotesque in *De milagros,* and avoids the excessive endogamy of *Cien años*. Both works ridicule legal issues, but San Francisco's famous trial, in which the firm of Martíncz Kafka represents both parties who are the same person, tops them all. Literary allusions abound in the two novels and especially those to works by Cortázar and Fuentes treated as reality by García Márquez are known. Mujica Láinez incorporates whole lines from famous writers and blends them together. He also uses parody extensively, and perhaps excessively, by providing fake neoclassical, romantic and even gaucho poetic inserts in his prose.

While the immortality of the omniscient first-person narrator in *Bomarzo* and *El unicornio* is an effective literary device and the extraordinary longevity of Ursula together with the timeless quality of Melquíades affirm the mythical nature of García Márquez' creations, the survival of the Duchess of Arpona, in *De milagros,* from Chapter I to Chapter V (three hundred years), on a prescription of nightly intercourse, appears a gag, even if we associate it with the Phoenix myth.

We have come to the fundamental differences between the two novels: In spite of its Rabelaisian features . . . , *Cien años* never leaves any doubt that it is a serious work; the same quality, in Mujica Láinez advertised even on the back cover, makes his book a humorous one. ''. . . vuelve la narrativa argentina a los rasgos del humorismo crítico . . .'' [the Argentine narrative returns to the characteristics of critical humorism] is Ghiano's appropriate comment. Also, the repetitions in García Márquez' saga come to a conclusion with the end of the clan, of Macondo and of the book; yet San Francisco de Apricotina del Milagro may be founded again and again. While in Macondo, a transfiguration of Aracataca, according to Mejía Duque ''los hechos se magnifican y sacralizan'' [events are magnified and sanctified], the legends, anecdotes, and traditions of the synthetic San Francisco are festively debunked. Whereas García Márquez ''no deja traslucir . . . que haya diversidad de sustancia entre lo prodigioso y lo diario'' [does not permit the conjecture that there is a real difference between the prodigious and the routine], according to Gullón, Mujica Láinez insists on showing us how natural events become prodigious and indicative of divine intervention. Only for two miracles does he fail to offer an explanation, therefore making them even funnier: one concerns the survival of the Duchess of Arpona, the other the instant arrival of persons and things, including a temporary Wall of China, merely by mentally concentrating on the image.

Both works make use of the age-old myths of the heroic leader, unlimited virility, defeat of death and eternal recurrence, but it is Mujica Láinez who shows them as collective necessities in a Jungian sense. The archetypical ''jefe tuerto'' [one-eyed leader] of San Francisco is needed to galvanize community action. In *De milagros* eternal recurrence is ''plot vehicle, unity device, and canceller of time.'' Other characteristics, not yet

mentioned which the two novels share and which Meehan, in a recent review of a third novel conveniently listed as ''identifiable elements traceable to the Colombian artist'' are: ''the extensive use of enumeration and exaggeration . . . , the employment of epithets or 'tags' to identify characters . . . frequent images of age, decay, and destruction; strong female characters and weak male personages obsessed with their extravagant enterprises.''

Further traits, typical especially of Mujica Láinez, are seen in *Crónicas reales* and *De milagros* as well as in earlier novels: A penchant for the recreation of the past—quite unlike Rodríguez Larreta's, despite the use of verbal paintings mentioned above; constant links between the past and the present; e.g. the characters dream of devices which later would become part of modern life; the use—and perhaps overuse—of comical names; last but not least an extraordinary linguistic creativity. It is regrettable, indeed, that the limitations of this paper do not permit the reading of samples of the grotesque humor, fanciful enumerations, and picaresque situations of *De milagros y de melancolías,* a book which deserves to be better known.

In a letter dated August 22, 1972, Mujica Láinez confirms the composition of *De milagros,* prior to his own reading of *Cien años,* which he greatly admires. Linking his novel with the preceding *Crónicas reales* he writes: ''Juntos forman una especie de anti-historia del mundo occidental, compuesta por un escritor que se vengó así, alegremente, de las torturas que le habían impuesto la celosa Historia y su hijo bastardo el Anacronismo cuando escribía novelas como *El unicornio, Bomarzo,* etc.'' [Together they make up a sort of anti-history of the Western world, composed by a writer who thus took revenge, good-humoredly, for the tortures which jealous History and her bastard-son Anachronism made him suffer when he wrote novels like *The Unicorn* and *Bomarzo*]. In a subsequent letter (9/25/72) the novelist refers to a new work which will form a ''tríptico'' [triptych] with *Crónicas* and *De milagros.* Mujica Láinez' remarks place the latter clearly in line with his other creations. While this excludes a parodistic or imitative link to *Cien años* it leaves no doubt that *De milagros* is a parody of Latin American reality. It satirizes the history of Spanish American ''personalismo''; it lampoons both foibles and traditions and, even if it accomplishes it in a delightful, intelligently and artistically humorous way, it may hurt, especially coming from a member of the Argentine Literary Academy, an establishment almost totally devoid of a colonial past and cultural ''subdesarrollo'' [underdevelopment]. Perhaps Latin Americans do not easily laugh about themselves and this may account, in addition to poor timing of its publication, for the meagre success of a novel which disguises itself as a chronicle. The myth of the eternal recurrence of the one-eyed strongman, in an ambient fraught with credulity, is not fashioned by Mujica Láinez (This would be impossible, if we accept the concept of myths as psychological reality.) It is explored by the author and deflated. He is not a mythmaker, but a delightful destroyer of myths. (pp. 65-71)

George O. Schanzer, ''The Four Hundred Years of Myths and Melancholies of Mujica Láinez,'' in Latin American Literary Review, *Vol. 1, No. 2, Spring, 1973, pp. 65-71.*

KESSEL SCHWARTZ

Manuel Mujica Láinez, Argentine essayist, journalist, short story writer, and novelist, like Gabriel García Márquez, Julio

Cortázar and other giants of contemporary Spanish American fiction, evokes a magic world of fantasy, managing to fuse the abstract with the real and to concretize the ephemeral and the absurd.

Mujica defines [*Cecil*] . . . , replete with picaresque humor and French and English interpolations, as "autobiografía novelesca." It takes place near Córdoba in a world partly peopled by ghosts and is narrated by his faithful companion, the English whippet Cecil. Through his love for his master, Cecil, who indulges in his own autobiographical recall, fuses with the writer's mind, observing with his thoughts and seeing with his eyes. We learn of Mujica's need to withdraw from Buenos Aires in order to see clearly within himself. (p. 186)

The villa in which the author lives with his wife, an eighty-eight year old mother, two maiden aunts, and a one-eyed cat is loaded with photographs, drawings, statuary, a 13,000 volume library, and numerous paintings, including one of the fairy Melusina of *El unicornio* done in the likeness of his wife and one of Heliogabalus, a Roman emperor, Etruscan relics, and a host of other archeological wonders, each with its own memory, literary allusion, or history. The objects have a temporal quality which allows them to live in two worlds at once.

On their walks to visit friends like the septuagenarian French Madame Pamelá or the fortyish Günter, both of whom, along with Mujica, believe in the supernatural, Cecil's master projects imaginary creatures so vividly that they acquire an ephemeral life. Cecil encounters the ghost of Mr. Littlemore, whose legend, love life, and death by poisoning, the writer reconstructs. Cecil tells us the house's history, a composite of truth and legend, and about the people who lived there, fusing relatives, ghosts, and literary images so that it is difficult to separate the limits of one world from another, existence from non-existence.

In addition to recalling his own past, such as his sojourn in Nazi Germany, Mujica, through objects and incidents, creates a new reality. The bust of Jean Rotrou, an almost forgotten seventeenth-century poet, helps him recreate a former owner's life in novelistic terms. While listening to a Renaissance song, the writer recalls Boabdil and Juana la Loca. The painting of Heliogabalus becomes an obsession for Mujica who, after reading countless books on Roman history and antiquities, writes a biography of that third century emperor, transcribed in thirty-five intercalated pages by Cecil. While in the process of creating this work, Mujica is distracted by the impending arrival of a statue of Achilles, which triggers in his mind associations with the French Opera, "Achille et Deidamie" and fragments from the Greek hero's life and times. When the statue finally arrives, the author gives the role of Achilles, in his mental lyrical drama, to Leonardo, a young architecture student with whom he becomes fast friends but who deserts him for the young girl who is writing a study of Mujica's works. Finally, a visit to see some cave drawings sets in motion, in the writer's mind, the phantoms and the real people who have visited the villa, all of whom are overshadowed by his association with Cecil, the final vision of his novel, the one we are now reading. (pp. 186-87)

> *Kessel Schwartz, in a review of "Cecil," in* Hispania, *Vol. 57, No. 1, March, 1974, pp. 186-87.*

RICHARD A. VALDÉS

Manuel Mujica Lainez is a very prolific Argentine author, perhaps best known for his novel *Bomarzo*. . . . *Sergio* is his fourteenth work published by Editorial Sudamericana. It is the story of a young man's introduction to love and the sexual life. Sergio, the protagonist, has the curse/blessing of being beautiful. His unusual attractiveness makes him prey for several men and women who try to force their affection on him. . . . The subtlety with which [the author] treats erotic subjects and motifs blends well with the humorous and sometimes satiric tone of the novel.

Throughout the novel the author speaks directly to the reader. In so doing he creates the atmosphere of a tale being told to the reader, creates a literary distance between the audience and the characters which adds verisimilitude to coincidences and situations that might not otherwise be acceptable to the reader, and subtly presents the main theme. The reader becomes increasingly aware of how a society which ostensibly esteems beauty persecutes someone cursed with it. The subtlety of this theme is such that it may escape some readers.

The story is well written, often humorous and has a picaresque plot somewhat reminiscent of Tom Jones's trip to London in Henry Fielding's novel. Sergio, like Tom, does not always escape the assaults upon his virtue from those enamored of him. The tragic ending to the story is necessary, given the plot and the theme. The foreshadowing in the seance and Sergio's imaginary trip through *Las Meniñas* while in a self-induced trance weaken the novel, however. Up to this penultimate chapter the events of the novel have been acceptable within the inner dialectic which the author has established. There are many coincidences, but they do not break the logic established in the work. The presages of Sergio's death debilitate an ending which would have been ironically integrated into the story and would have given a logical and inevitable resolution to the situation.

While the novel is not a literary masterpiece, it is skillfully written, enjoyable, and it presents an interesting view of a society that exploits and destroys beauty. (pp. 593-94)

> *Richard A. Valdés, in a review of "Sergio," in* World Literature Today, *Vol. 51, No. 4, Autumn, 1977, pp. 593-94.*

ANNE COLLINS

One way to judge *The Wandering Unicorn* is as a 322-page-long evasion. Here is an Argentinian writer, Manuel Mujica Lainez, still living in Argentina under the military regime that invented that particularly 20th-century crime, the disappearance. But in this novel he is not accounting for the missing, or risking his neck in a land where storytellers are the only ones with half a chance of getting unreal reality across. Instead, Mujica Lainez is playing, wishing himself into the Middle Ages, among fairies and dragons, devils and angels, holy hermits and knights in the death throes of courtly love. We could judge him harshly, but we won't. In Mujica Lainez' case, wishful thinking is not so much an evasion as a recognition of all those fictional things that can make us happy.

His allegory is not about tyranny but violent love: unrequited or forbidden, incorporeal or very much of the body. His narrator, the most breathless of lovers, is the immortal fairy Melusine, part dragon, part woman, passionate and benighted. Melusine loses her sense of duty and most of her fairy powers when she is smitten with love for a 15-year-old boy. . . .

Mujica Lainez is obsessed with illuminating the confusions of love. His knight, Aiol, is crucified by them—the Christ-like or devilish unicorn of myth hunted down in "a murderous wood."

Melusine helplessly watches and recounts every chapter of lovelorn and lost tragedy: Aiol and his sister, Aiol and the lady Seramonde, Aiol and the lord Aymé, Aiol and the whore Pascua. . . .

It is her undignified predicament ("he doesn't even know I exist") that begins to have the most meaning. . . . When she asks her wicked fairy mother for a young, beautiful body, her mother gives her what she asks for—Melusine becomes young and beautiful indeed, but male. Melusine/Melusin's frustrations are legion and never soothed.

When a holy oxcart carries Aiol heavenward for his eternal reunion with his true lovers, Melusine the fairy cannot fly that high—she is the hardest hit because she is the only one who cannot die. As Jorge Luis Borges writes in the foreword, Mujica Lainez is in no danger of drowning us in the escapist "music of nostalgia." He is saved by the unhappy ending of his own fairy tale.

> Anne Collins, "Wishful Ways of Escape," in Maclean's Magazine, Vol. 95, No. 13, March 29, 1982, p. 65.

PAUL STUEWE

The Wandering Unicorn is a myth-based fantasy of picaresque adventure in medieval Europe, and it is simply delightful: complexly delightful, actually, given the detailed tapestry of love, enchantment, and chivalric valour the author has so beautifully woven around the figure of the serpent-woman Melusine. I particularly enjoyed the tone of the narration, which manages to be simultaneously chatty, suggestive, and gnomic in a way that very few writers—Borges of course among them—can consistently control. It's a marvellous piece of work, and just the thing for anyone who finds Tolkien entertaining but less than adept at the delineation of character.

> Paul Stuewe, in a review of "The Wandering Unicorn," in Books in Canada, Vol. 11, No. 5, May, 1982, p. 29.

JOHN WALKER

To describe Manuel Mujica Lainez as a South American writer, as the dust jacket of *The Wandering Unicorn* does, is a misnomer which hardly does justice to Argentine literature or to Mujica Lainez. There was of course something of a boom in the fiction of that continent in the 1960s and 1970s, and names like Borges, García Márquez, Carlos Fuentes, Vargas Llosa, and Julio Cortázar became, if not exactly household names, at least well-known enough to figure in the book pages of the *New York Times* and other reputable publications. However, the only thing they have in common is geography, since a Colombian novel like García Márquez's *One Hundred Years of Solitude* has little in common with Carlos Fuentes' treatment of the Mexican Revolution in *The Death of Artemio Cruz,* or Cortázar's monumental blockbuster *Hopscotch,* or Vargas Llosa's indictment of Peruvian society in *Time of the Hero.* As an "anachronistic" Argentine writer, Mujica Lainez would appear to have little in common with any of the above, although *The Wandering Unicorn* was published in 1965, right in the middle of the boom.

Argentine literature has, not surprisingly, reflected something of the development of that country. . . . As one of the "white" republics which sought the panaceas of education and immigration (especially Anglo-Saxon), Argentina, in its rootlessness, has spent the twentieth century questing for its identity, looking back nostalgically to the nineteenth century (gaucho and country) while trying to cope with the realities of Europeanization, the city and a whole existentialist strain which is characteristic of contemporary River Plate literature.

Perhaps because of this very rootlessness, the existentialist concerns and the eternal search for *la argentinidad* (the essence of Argentine-ness), there has also grown up in the Plate region literature a "fantastic" current, as manifested in some of the work of the aforementioned Cortázar, Bioy Casares and perhaps the best known of all Latin American writers, Jorge Luis Borges, who in his *ficciones* has created a world of the imagination difficult to distinguish from the "real" world, whatever that might be, Borges would surely add. (pp. 1224-25)

In introducing Mujica Lainez I used the word "anachronistic," since in a sense he is not of this world or of this century. By style, temperament and cultural awareness, Mujica Lainez belongs to the Europeanized, cosmopolitan aristocracy of the nineteenth century. As a poet-magician he makes use of the qualities of magic and fantasy and has recourse to the world of the supernatural, mythology and legend, not so much to reconstruct the past but to offer us what Borges calls "a glowing dream set in the past." When one reads *The Wandering Unicorn* one forgets the mythological trappings and is convinced by the verisimilitude and credibility of these legendary but real characters.

The Wandering Unicorn . . . was published three years after the appearance of perhaps [Mujica Lainez's] best known and most successful novel, *Bomarzo* . . . , an imaginary recreation of the life of the little known Italian Renaissance duke Pier Francesco Orsini. As in *Bomarzo,* the narrator of *The Wandering Unicorn* relates (from her favorite bell tower) what happened to her centuries before. The fairy Melusine, as legend tells us, was cursed by her wicked mother, and thus turns into a serpent-woman every Saturday. She is forbidden to reveal her terrible secret to her husband, who nevertheless finds out. Thus Melusine is fated to remain trapped half-woman, half-serpent for all time. (p. 1225)

There is so much to admire in *The Wandering Unicorn*—the language is rich, colorful, brilliant, and expressive. Through the medium of his fairy narrator he informs, educates, entertains, surprises, and shocks us with his matter-of-fact but humorous and telling instruction, nay correction, about life in the Middle Ages—for example, the alleged lack of hygiene. "Whatever they tell you, we liked bathing in the Middle Ages. I was there, and I know. . . . Dirt came in later, with the Puritans." How deliciously ironic and illuminating. But one must not think of the medieval period in such prosaic and mundane terms. After all, Melusine is a fairy: "There are angels too. You may be sure that angels and fairies exist, as they did in the Middle Ages. Angel and fairy—they were the Middle Ages. And the Devil, of course." But although Melusine is a fairy, her ambition is to be a nice, peaceful, ordinary housewife. With just a little tongue in cheek, Mujica Lainez links the past and present with a satirical explanation of her condition: "I had to wait for Sigmund Freud to illustrate the motives behind my mother's excessive reaction, and to show that she was in fact frustrated and revenging herself on me."

The Wandering Unicorn is a fascinating, thought-provoking, challenging novel which, for all its fantasy, is never mere escapism, although it does restore to contemporary fiction what Borges calls "the sense of destiny, of adventure with its hopes and fears." In the life of the protagonist Melusine, one sees the theme of immortality, not just in its religious sense, although in the spiritual world of the Middle Ages this is an obvious concern, as we see in the climactic ascension to heaven of Aiol and the Leper-King. . . . Melusine, who is already inflicted with the curse of immortality, an earthly immortality, cannot aspire to that kind of glory. She sinks earthwards once more, companionless forever, to suffer the fate of alienation, the incommunicability of the sexes—the existentialist themes of other Argentine writers, which brings us and Mujica Lainez back to Earth and our own time, alongside other great contemporary writers of the River Plate region like Mallea, Sábato, Onetti, and Cortázar.

Manuel Mujica Lainez, the aristocratic dandy and exemplar of nineteenth-century Argentina, appears to be an anachronism in the crassly materialistic philistine world of the 1980s of cosmopolitan Buenos Aires—and North America. *The Wandering Unicorn* appears to be just a brilliant and imaginative exercise in the recreation of places and times of far away and long ago. However, by his treatment of the eternal themes of life and death, love and hate, mortality and immortality, and the search for values and ideals, Mujica Lainez transcends the geographical and chronological barriers to penetrate to the heart of the human condition. With such metaphysical concerns he raises himself to the level of the universal writer. To have achieved all this with a fine prose (well translated by Mary Fitton) that corresponds to the profound themes treated, Mujica Lainez reveals himself to be a great artist. (pp. 1225-26)

> *John Walker, in a review of "The Wandering Unicorn," in* Queen's Quarterly, *Vol. 90, No. 4, Winter, 1983, pp. 1224-26.*

ANTHONY BURGESS

Manuel Mujica Lainez's [*The Wandering Unicorn*] comes with an accolade from Borges. The great experimentalist is happy to see here a return to "the sense of destiny, of adventure with its hopes and fears, the tradition of Stevenson, Hugo and—why not?—Ariosto." The old magician has unerringly picked on the essential elements of this strange tale of a twelfth-century knight preparing to help rescue Jerusalem from the hordes of Saladin. It is a good read, like the two romantic spell-binders he mentions, and it has the frank magic of *Orlando Furioso*, as well as some of its wit and sexual candour. The heroine is a monster, half-human, half-serpent, immortal and no fool, who conceives an immortal lust for the young knight. It is no pastiche of the past but a very contemporary book, ironically baroque, and a reminder that Spanish American fiction is not just *A Hundred Years of Solitude*.

But Lainez will never get the Nobel: he writes too well and there is no political protest in him. The same could be said of Borges. (p. 77)

> *Anthony Burgess, "Tokyo Roses," in* Punch, *Vol. 284, No. 7431, April 27, 1983, pp. 76-7.**

(Jean) Iris Murdoch

1919-

Irish-born English novelist, dramatist, poet, essayist, nonfiction writer, and scriptwriter.

In addition to producing a lengthy novel almost yearly, Murdoch, a former teacher of philosophy at Oxford, is also known for such scholarly works as *Sartre: Romantic Rationalist* (1953) and *The Fire and the Sun* (1977), a study of Plato's aesthetics. Her background in philosophy is evident in her fiction, which often deals with complex moral, religious, and ethical issues. Her novels are also noted for their wit, intricate plots, and precise descriptive detail. Murdoch won the James Tait Black Memorial Prize for *The Black Prince* (1973) and the Booker McConnell Prize for *The Sea, the Sea* (1978).

Murdoch's first novel, *Under the Net* (1954), is regarded as one of her best and is characteristic of her career's work in its treatment of moral problems. The central character, a writer named Jake Donoghue, is initially concerned with establishing a pattern for his life and insulating himself from the impact of "contingency," random happenings which are not a part of his design. In the course of the novel, Jake comes to accept contingency as a part of life and particularly to accept the reality of other people and their influence on him, which frees him to love. The changes which Jake undergoes in *Under the Net* are representative of what critics have identified as some of Murdoch's recurring thematic concerns: the relationship between love and freedom; the conflict between contingency and design; and the necessity of looking beyond one's self to discover truth.

Some of Murdoch's novels have been categorized as bittersweet comedies and others as ironic tragedies. Her subject matter is usually the various conflicts involved in love relationships, and complicated love triangles often occur in the novels. While most of Murdoch's novels are set in modern times, elements of magic and mystery and sudden, bizarre twists of plot invite comparison with the eighteenth- and nineteenth-century Gothic novels. Often a modern-day "enchanter" figure, such as Mischa Fox in *The Flight from tthe Enchanter* (1956), the psychologist in *A Severed Head* (1961), or the philosopher in *The Philosopher's Pupil* (1983), influences the behavior of other characters and manipulates events in Murdoch's novels. Her imagistic prose aids her creation of the fantastic, symbolic quality of her works. As she explained in an interview with Harold Hobson, "In real life the fantastic and the ordinary, the plain and the symbolic, are often indissolubly joined together, and I think the best novels explore and exhibit life without disjoining them." Murdoch's works have also been compared to those of the nineteenth-century Russian novelists whom she admires, particularly Fedor Dostoevski, for they are often voluminous texts which involve numerous characters in complex interrelationships, rather than focusing exclusively on the viewpoints of one or two central figures in the manner more common to contemporary Anglo-American fiction.

Critical assessment of Murdoch's importance in contemporary literature is divided. Critics say that in her best novels she maintains a delicate balance between artful storytelling and abstract moralizing without allowing either to dominate. One

Photograph by Mark Gerson

of her expressed fictional tenets is that characters should have a degree of freedom from their creator; she hopes that in her novels "a lot of people who are not me are going to come into existence in some wonderful way." However, her characters sometimes appear to be puppets, illustrating moral and ethical issues in her intricately machinated plots. Moreover, while the fantastic elements in her fiction add variety and narrative richness to her work, it has been suggested that Murdoch's use of symbolism and melodrama can become heavy-handed and that her adherence to the conventions of the English novel make her work predictable. Nevertheless, although some critics attribute her popularity to what George Stade called her "Harlequin romances for highbrows," many place her among the major English post-World War II fiction writers.

(See also *CLC*, Vols. 1, 2, 3, 4, 6, 8, 11, 15, 22; *Contemporary Authors*, Vols. 13-16, rev. ed.; *Contemporary Authors New Revision Series*, Vol. 8; and *Dictionary of Literary Biography*, Vol. 14.)

STEVEN COHAN

Of her twenty novels, Iris Murdoch has written six in the first person, each one using a male narrator. . . . [One] cannot help wondering if her continual use of a male narrator amounts to another woman writer's surrendering her pen to the authority of the male novelist.

As far as Murdoch herself is concerned this would seem to be the case. While she has declared that she does not find "much difference between men and women," she also claims a male viewpoint for much the same reason that Marian Evans chose a male pseudonym:

> I think perhaps I identify with men more than with women, because the ordinary human condition still seems to belong more to a man than to a woman.
>
> (p. 222)

Murdoch's preference "to be male" is in many ways central to her art. Her choice of male narrators allows for a playful act of male impersonation as an ironic commentary on the paradox of fiction writing. She uses the male voice to articulate a sense of lived experience unique to another self, while making sure that her narrators themselves remain bound to the limitations of their own identities. While she seems to be eliminating any signs of her own female personality, since she speaks through a voice that is obviously not hers, her narrators write their stories out of the conviction that no one else can possibly understand what they have felt, why they have acted. At one point in *A Severed Head* the narrator, Martin Lynch-Gibbon, exclaims to his mistress, "I can't expect you to understand all this. You'd have to be me." That Murdoch, a woman, can assume their voices to do exactly what Martin wants, becoming them, implies a position on her part at once objective and sympathetic to her narrators' experiences as men. (p. 223)

Always under the spell of some elusive woman, her narrators initially strike us as literate, intelligent men who use their narrations to examine their feelings with candor. Their own power over women is emphasized, in their minds, by their ability to tell their own stories; but such power ultimately proves illusory, for Murdoch undercuts their authority as narrators, sometimes rather chillingly, always for a satiric effect quite devastating to their self-esteem. In making these men the narrators of their own stories, Murdoch is merely giving them the opportunity to reveal in their own voices the surprising extent of their egoism and its potential for destruction, which their narrations try to explain, if not justify, as a celebration of love.

That this kind of ironic narration ends up working to satirize a male fantasy of woman, however, has only emerged as the explicit focus of Murdoch's irony in her most recent first-person novel, *The Sea, the Sea,* where Charles Arrowby's narration highlights a satiric indictment of the male's brutal manipulation of women. With this particular satire of the male in mind, the other narrators can all be seen pointing to the characterization of Charles, whose narration, in turn, can be read as a commentary on the earlier books. *The Sea, the Sea* is a significant novel in Murdoch's career because it puts into focus the psychological material of her other first-person novels to satirize its narrator, not as a representation of the human condition, but specifically as a male voice. If the male rules "the ordinary human condition" as Murdoch repeatedly sees it through her narrators, with *The Sea, the Sea* she brings to bear on this voice what has previously been only the indirect target of her irony: the aggression against woman that the male celebrates as love.

In all of her books what Murdoch finds most appealing—and comic—about her male characters, narrators or not, is that they do fall in love so wholeheartedly and so disastrously. Such emotional dunderheads appear as her protagonists in novel after novel because the tangled relations between men and women resonate the tensions Murdoch makes central to her ideological understanding of what it means to be emotionally and imaginatively alive. As anyone familiar with her novels quickly comes to realize, the typical Murdoch plot begins with three or four couples living in the environs of London, to turn on Jane Austen's own formula for a similar comedy of manners, but with this twist: each partner becomes somehow entangled in the sexual lives of all the others. The round-robin configurations formed by this network of marriages, affairs, and friendships call to mind the spellbound lovers in *A Midsummer's Night Dream,* Murdoch's favorite Shakespearean source. The conceit of love as a dream appears repeatedly in her work to underscore both the follies and the illusions that envelop lovers when they try to make out of a transient passion something absolute and timeless: romantic love. (pp. 223-24)

Like Austen, Murdoch has discovered from the start of her career a comic framework that serves her imagination well because it coordinates the dramatic activity of her plots with the themes that have not ceased to preoccupy her intellectually. Early in her career she wrote an essay prescribing directions for the future of the novel, and her comments have provided her readers with a valuable understanding of the intellectual frame she imposes on her own novels. In this essay ["Against Dryness: A Polemical Sketch"] she called for "a renewed sense of the difficulty and complexity of the moral life and the opacity of persons." As opposed to form, "which is an aspect of our desire for consolation" through fantasy or fiction making, she wanted "a respect for the contingent," which she associated with "the destructive power of the now so unfashionable naturalistic idea of character." To put the matter simply, she had in mind E. M. Forster's notion of round characters who are capable of surprising a reader to reveal their complexity and opacity, their essential mystery as an individuated self. By virtue of being able to surprise they challenge the principle of form, which fiction relies on, Murdoch's not excepted, but which is so imaginatively powerful that it works to seduce us into mistakenly imposing form onto life as well; this mistake Murdoch calls "fantasy." Her characters expose their "destructive power" by falling in love. Then they intrude upon each other's fantasies to force everyone to adjust his or her scripting of emotions to contingency. The value of this volatile confrontation, the germ of any Murdoch plot, is that it can lead to an awareness of the inherent instability and randomness of human action. (p. 225)

Of all her books, Murdoch's first-person novels offer the clearest illustration of the form/contingency frame. Composing his own story into a narrative is the male's most audacious and self-deceptive attempt to impose form onto contingent experience. The very act of narration demands that he find a principle of causality and structure for his story. But his story itself recounts how he, as much as he wants to, cannot be a director of events. In the story he is narrating, in other words, he tries to order events, but other people end up disrupting his sense of causality to reveal his own egoism. His egoism, too, has so befuddled his vision that it has not occurred to him, as an actor in his story, that other people are actually opaque, resistant to his understanding, antagonistic to his direction. (p. 226)

The opening episode of *The Black Prince* epitomizes this quandary for the narrator. Bradley is drawn into a marital rift between his best friends Rachel and Arnold, an action that ultimately leads into all of this book's complications. Yet Bradley discovers that even when literally invited into the bedroom of a married couple he cannot get more than a confusing glimpse of another's private self. As Rachel tells him toward the end of the novel, although her marriage has entangled him, even exploited him, it is finally always impervious to his understanding.

In narrating his story Bradley must therefore take into account his limitations both as an egoist and a fantasist. . . . Without the omniscience of a third-person narrator the characters other than Bradley remain ''definite but hidden'' personalities, which we as readers can penetrate no more fully than he can. In fact, to emphasize the inescapable subjectivity of Bradley's version of events, Murdoch ends *The Black Prince* with postscripts written by the other characters, each refuting what Bradley has had to say. The events themselves cannot be disputed. . . . What can vary, on the other hand, is the interpretation of events, the form placed over them. Rachel, for instance, assumes that Bradley has acted out of a passion for her, not Julian. Because she sees him as a self-deceived egoist, all she can conclude is that in *his* version, which makes up the novel proper, he ''seems to be invincibly wrapped up in his own fantastic conceptions of what happened and of what he himself is like.'' . . . (pp. 226-27)

Taken on its own terms Rachel's suspicion of Bradley's egoism serves her own egoism. It also explains why Murdoch's narrators are male. First, as a narrator the male enacts the process of reconciling form (the act of narrating) with contingency (the lived experience he is narrating), a problem Murdoch indentifies with the male, since as a cultural figure he embodies the authority of form and yet, as a lover of women, he must either respond to the pressure of contingency—or lose his vitality. Second, as a narrator, the male cannot escape the egoism with which he tries to effect that compromise between form and contingency. ''Wrapped up in his own fantastic conceptions'' of what he is narrating, each narrator allows Murdoch to satirize how the male's egoism affects the way he perceives woman in order to place a symbolic value on her. Such a reading of woman in symbolic relation to the male's understanding of his experience is another manifestation of his need to find form in his emotional life, which woman has stimulated into chaos by disrupting the stability that seemed to exist prior to his falling in love with her. As a composer ''of what happened and of what he himself is like,'' each narrator tries to impose a sense of form onto the muddle of emotions he feels for the female. (pp. 227-28)

Both *A Severed Head* and *The Italian Girl,* written early in her career, give an oedipal reading of their narrator's attraction to woman. As each narrator moves toward an acceptance of woman as the epitome of contingency, he still sees her figure in terms of his oedipal feelings, which therefore call into question his understanding of contingency. Since he is her narrator, the woman herself has no independent character of her own to resist his deeply rooted oedipal fantasy and help clarify Murdoch's attitude toward his point of view. And because Murdoch uses this fantasy in both novels to characterize her narrators psychologically, as well as to satirize the innocence with which they face contingency through their sexuality, she cannot easily keep the fantasy from obscuring the impact of what they are meant to learn about woman ideologically. (pp. 229-30)

[The later first-person novels] expand the form/contingency frame to begin focusing their irony more directly at the male's absorption of woman into his fantasy life. Though it contains the tension between Hilary's compulsion for order and his destructiveness in terms of the form/contingency frame, *A Word Child* begins to link the male's quest for form to his sexual fantasies, and with this connection made, to suggest the brutality that such fantasies manifest. The male in the later books lets fantasy, an expression of his need for form, stand between his self and the woman's, thus intensifying the volatile impact of contingency. Her identity as a woman remaining forever beyond the grasp of his understanding, he ends up trying to destroy her identity in order to keep his fantasy intact. (p. 231)

These men can love a woman to death! From *A Severed Head* to *A Word Child,* Murdoch's male narrators have been bringing closer to the surface of narration a satiric criticism of the fantasy of innocence that propels the male's preoccupation with love. This satire, however, has not been made the central focus of her fiction until *The Sea, the Sea,* which crystallizes into a dense and, for Murdoch, innovative narrative pattern what the psychologies of the earlier narrators have only implied as a subtext to the form/contingency frame.

The narrator of *The Sea, the Sea* is Charles Arrowby, a famous man of the theater—director, playwright, actor—who has retired to Shruff End, an antiquated house by the sea. Now into his sixties, Charles is ''wifeless, childless, brotherless, sisterless.'' Obsessed with order, particularly when it comes to the rituals of cooking and eating, he hates ''mess''. . . . He has therefore chosen a solitary life at Shruff End determined ''never [to] be anxious any more about personal relations; such anxiety is too often a form of vanity''. . . .

Charles's retirement seems genuinely connected to his past, because he discovers living in the nearby village his childhood sweetheart, Hartley, who jilted him forty years before, disappearing from his life without a trace or an explanation. *The Sea, the Sea* recounts Charles's destructive attempt to rekindle this old love. Pursuing Hartley . . . , Charles only ends up revealing how brutally he has treated women, how egocentrically he has seen them. His obsessive love for Hartley . . . merely expresses a fantasy of woman's innocence which he uses to envision his own innocence. (p. 234)

More so than Murdoch's other first-person novels, *The Sea, the Sea* develops out of the form/contingency frame to show how the narrator's egocentric attempt to impose form onto experience through his fantasy of love actually manifests a predatory attack on woman. But what is it about this particular novel that allows Murdoch, finally, to examine her narrator as she has not quite done before, seeing him critically as a man whose fantasy of love works to undermine the very idea of woman that his love means to celebrate?

The explanation has to do with Murdoch's dense texturing of Charles's narration. Unlike her other first-person narrations, *The Sea, the Sea* is a novel of memory, with Charles using his internalized narration to sift through his impressions of the past for a glimpse of his lost ''better self.'' (p. 236)

The more Charles concentrates on Hartley, the more obvious it becomes that there are actually two competing plots to his narration. The pursuit of Hartley, Charles treats as the primary plot of his ''novelistic memoir,'' which seems natural, at first reading, because she focuses for Charles much of what happens to him at Shruff End. But as it turns out, if he sincerely hopes to connect his end with his beginning, then his narration has pursued a false scent, leading him away from the actual plot of his life's story. The Hartley plot is not a conclusion but an evasion. Though he records events in the present as they occur, he is merely trying to do with lived experience what he can easily do with narrated experience: turn contingency into form. To do this he has to dismiss the importance of forty years of his life, widening the disparity between the Hartley of his imagination and the woman of present reality. That important gap in time exposes the illusion behind his love for her to reveal, as well, why he so readily discounts everything in his life that does not concern Hartley. She allows him to orchestrate a fantasy memoir of his life, which he desperately tries to make real once he sees her again. (pp. 236-37)

Murdoch's accomplishment in *The Sea, the Sea* comes from her rich, complex texturing of Charles's narration. I have actually looked at only a portion of what she is doing. The displacing of plots, the use of other characters as critical voices, allow her to use Charles's voice as an articulation of fantasy, as a narrator of a dream text about woman. She thus achieves the objectivity of third-person narration without lessening the singularity of her narrator's vision. The layered plots of this novel, moreover, allow her to work the narrative out of the contingency/form tension so that it does frame, rather than obscure, the critical vision of men that has become progressively dominant in her fiction: a commentary on their unconscious "sickening casual brutality" passing under the name of love.

The Sea, the Sea, then, marks an important breakthrough for Murdoch. Where she is heading after this or how far she will go is not yet clear. Her current novel, *Nuns and Soldiers* (1980), shows a new interest in female consciousness, with its focus on two female protagonists surrounded by kind, gentle, timid men. Being a prolific writer, Murdoch cannot avoid repetition and even reversals in her books, but her yearly novels do allow us to watch her slowly working through the concerns at the center of her art, with one novel's success evolving out of an earlier novel's problems. It will therefore be revealing to see what she will next do with first-person narration, whether she will move beyond Charles's voice, perhaps to a female narrator, or fall back, as she has sometimes done in the past, to old familiar patterns. (p. 241)

Steven Cohan, "From Subtext to Dream Text: The Brutal Egoism of Iris Murdoch's Male Narrators," in Men by Women, edited by Janet Todd, Holmes & Meier Publishers, Inc., 1981, pp. 222-42.

ELIZABETH DIPPLE

Although Murdoch argues against Plato on several points, it is nevertheless clear that her sense of the integrity of art reflects his injunction that fantasy and sophist lies be avoided: the world Murdoch knows best is always her subject, and if this means a proliferation of civil servants and middle-class types, her uncanny achievement shows how little the contours of an original and varied series of novels are limited by such necessities.

A patient study of Murdoch's work reveals how deceptive the bourgeois surface in fact is, and how ironic her deployment of its materials. Although she operates structurally from situation and character, the process of her best books involves a subtle peeling-off of layers of bourgeois complacency and prejudice. Her primary tools are a devastating accuracy in the detail of human character and an enormous allusive frame which pushes the reader toward a willingness to see how large her intentions are. When the allusions fail, as they tend to in early novels like *A Severed Head* and *The Italian Girl,* the result is overplotted, tricksy books where the profound laws of causality

central to Murdoch's thought are lost in clever satire. When these allusions to mythology, art and religion are functioning at a high level of imaginative power, however, their syncretic force is such that they become images assisting the novel towards profound and unnerving ends. These ends are religious in impact, but the novels never succumb to the warm fuzziness of consoling or salvational piety. (pp. 2-3)

The fact that ultimate reality, even the cosmos itself, lies behind the drifting and often frenetic bourgeois surface is the vast secret of Murdoch's best fiction, and the sheer nerve and ambition required in the projection of such a stage on which to place traditional realism make her fictions risky in the extreme. There can be no doubt, for example, that it is correct to read *A Fairly Honourable Defeat* as an oblique commentary on the combat of good and evil and the defeat of the Christian Trinity, and yet its psychological verisimilitude deflects the allegorical loftiness of its conception. (p. 3)

Ostensibly a realist who has been criticized nervously by some British critics for continuing boringly in a bourgeois mode as opposed to following American, French and East European experimentalism, Murdoch has soldiered on through twenty novels from 1954 to 1980, the limit of this study. In the process of writing these twenty novels her style has changed and her authority grown. Her extensive achievement in radical thinking about the novel as a genre as well as in her use of it as a vehicle for those ideas has involved a participation in subtle and difficult ways with an oblique method of experimentation. . . . Murdoch palpably believes in texts and a novelistic tradition, and sees the form as she does all art as having an important function within human experience and knowledge. (p. 4)

In the novels, her artist characters are almost always negative and opposed by firm realists or spiritual beings whose hold on external reality is in sharp contrast to the vagaries and idealism of the artist, and her fictions constantly reflect on their own impossibility. One of the most frequently used, dangerous words in Murdoch is magic; she associates it not only with human misuse of theories, ideology and religious materials, but also with the chimerical delights of the surfaces of art. The novelist is bound to use magical devices to enchant the reader and produce form, and Murdoch is no mean practitioner, but for her this is all a subservience to the patina and not reflective of the deep uses of fiction. Her irony about her materials separates her from most of her British contemporaries but does not quite manage to align her with American experimentalists. In spite of her radical distance from them, her nearest relatives are Saul Bellow, Isaac Bashevis Singer and, in a small way, British writers fundamentally interested in magic—John Fowles and Muriel Spark. The difference lies in the fact that for Murdoch, as for Singer, magic is a tool which must be used ironically and not believed in; the real area of significant fiction, and the one that relates to its primary task, is for Murdoch unmagical realism as it was practised by Shakespeare and the great nineteenth-century novelists, and towards them she aims.

Much has been written and conjectured about the contemporary British novel, where experimentalism is limited by strong realism and good storytelling, where in fact pure experimentalism is shunned. Murdoch would seem to be aligned with this current tendency, but her work does not reflect the same weariness within the tradition and failure of nerve which characterize her compatriots. She makes it clear that her realism reflects a conviction about the uses of art, and in opposing it to her necessary 'magical' materials—both technical and ideological—she forges a distinctive product which tries to steer clear of the mediocre art produced when devices are foremost as they are in most contemporary experimentalism and in some British realism.

Murdoch's strongest area of experiment lies in the fact that she is a writer with enormous content, and no one can read many novels without being haunted by the need to uncover that content. No simple tale-spinner, she plays the role of the invisible writer teasing her reader into thought and thereby engaging him in the deeper purposes of an all too often frivolous genre. The quality of thought in Murdoch has produced alienation in some readers, but it is the most tantalizingly serious aspect of her novels and must be examined as such. There is complete consistency of idea in Murdoch; once the thought patterns are worked out the reader can watch the technical expertise with which she plays them, yet each novel is entirely new and in a sense a continuation and elaboration of elements one thought one knew. Thus each novel presents a new milieu with new problems in depicting progress towards human consciousness and change. Denying the conventional solaces of the novel as a genre, Murdoch never presents the ideal end but concentrates rather on a real and stringent depiction of the errors and resultant causality which rule human affairs under the general aegis of chance. Inhibiting herself as much as possible from becoming the kind of realist that uses the novel as a forum for moral argument, she nevertheless makes it clear that art itself has a moral base and that its real function, apart from enjoyment, is truth-telling. (pp. 5-6)

One can gather from Murdoch's essays and novels that she is above all interested in the degree and sort of knowledge attainable by humankind, and that she believes the knowledge available must be treated as experience and not as abstract intellectualism. The experiential base of literary realism is therefore an ideal vehicle, not because it can include preaching which Murdoch abhors, but because it is centred on the particular and on detail. For Murdoch, knowledge is a process of particularizing, of making experience more and more explicit rather than abstracting it into theory. The particularity of description and event which the novel as a genre allows gives her the breadth she needs, and her work can be seen as a progressive illustration of a life the reader shares with his fellows and contemporaries. The natural mode for such particularization is expansion and amplification, and as Murdoch's style develops, this is certainly her direction. . . . The urge towards particularization also defines many of Murdoch's strengths, for in detail, allusion and moment-by-moment richness, her later style is unequalled by her contemporaries. Her concentration on the inner life and experience of her characters keeps her mature novels far from the utilitarian subservience to plot which characterizes some of the early ones, and the Murdoch of her serious twentieth-century reputation will be the Murdoch of these rich extended fictions.

Intrinsic to her study of the particular is the contrasting temptation so many of her characters have towards gnostic breakthroughs and towards the kind of knowledge that demands theories to explain it. This desire for knowledge is aligned to her persistent presentation of all characters in a state of metaxy and longing where they despairingly contrast their limited and all too particular present with various grand ideals towards which they aspire—innocence, romantic love, God. (p. 7)

All Murdoch's characters are world-immanent beings who, in spite of an inclination towards ideals and knowledge, are forced to concentrate on ordinary action in a realistic world where muddle reigns. It is evident that for Murdoch the transcendent is too easily deceptive and distracts human beings from focusing on the truth of the particular and immediate, the truth that is available without tricks or game-playing or magic and that is so well served by realism. However, realism as strict reportage is not what Murdoch is after. . . . Murdoch's characters are not allowed transcendence and their seeking of an ideal end is always brutally smashed, but they do know about virtue or holiness, and the best way of describing this is through the Platonic idea of the good. This religious apprehension lies at the core of Murdoch's work and removes it from simple realism into a more serious realm where an external other presents the reader with an idea against which the fiction can profitably be placed. Refusing manifestations of the divine, Murdoch nevertheless operates ironically within a limited idea of a theurgic universe where the idea of the good, which must be sought in a stringent way without hope of reward, is seen as the basic human access to the spiritual life. . . . [Murdoch] extends the novel form to include a teaching which is beyond the bounds of the genre as practised by her contemporaries. (p. 8)

Elizabeth Dipple, in her Iris Murdoch: Work for the Spirit, *University of Chicago Press, 1982, 356 p.*

NICHOLAS MOSLEY

Iris Murdoch is a professional philosopher, and it has been interesting (though perhaps hitherto somewhat unprofitable) to speculate on what might be the relation between her philosophy and her brilliantly skilful though sometimes weirdly anarchic novelist's art. However in [*The Philosopher's Pupil*] . . . she has as her central character a renowned philosopher called Rozanov, and there are deliberate, though still enigmatic, connections made between philosophy and art.

Rozanov returns in his old age to his home town of Ennistone— a spa in the south of England noted for its hot water springs. Rozanov has lost his faith in the efficacy of philosophy, as a priest might have lost his belief in God. (There is in fact such a priest in the novel, Father Bernard, who ends up preaching to the birds about the non-existence of God.) . . .

Rozanov tries to organise the world around him by will: he has a hypnotic effect on people just because, perhaps, he believes there is nothing to be trusted except will. Around him circulate typical Iris Murdoch characters in various states of exaltation or despair: there are the McCaffrey family of a mother and three sons; their wives, servants and girlfriends; all are more or less under the guru-like spell of Rozanov. From their almost arbitrary circuits, like those of electrons, there from time to time appear emanations, or portents, such as also there often are in Iris Murdoch novels. . . . Citizens realise that the town is going through one of its 'funny times': it is as if Tunbridge Wells had been transported to the edge of an animistic rain-forest.

The various stories of passion and hopeless attempts at manipulation whirl fascinatingly enough, even if there is not quite the concentrated, gripping narrative of the same author's *The Black Prince* or *A Word Child*. At the beginning, George McCaffrey tries to murder his wife and at once dramatically rescues her; at the end he tries to find liberation by murdering Rozanov but Rozanov happens to be already dead. . . . Most of the characters end up in a trance-like state not very different from that in which they began. Father Bernard at least survives: Rozanov does not. But the chief interest of the novel remains in the question—what is a philosopher making of all this? (p. 19)

In *The Philosopher's Pupil* Rozanov says he agrees with Plato ('art is certainly the devil's work') but does not move on from this. He sees that 'the holy must try to know the demonic, must at some point frame the riddle and thirst for the answer'; but nevertheless, he decides that this 'longing is the perfect contradiction of the love of God'. Rozanov's God is a philosopher's god; it cannot live with contradictions.

At some stage in most Iris Murdoch novels there is apt to come to a reader the thought: 'But surely human beings are not like this: we do not really, do we, spend our time whirled around by such portent-laden passions imagining we find meanings where there are none?' But on the heels of this comes the feeling: 'Perhaps this is just what human beings are in fact like, and it is precisely our delusion to imagine that we are not.' But still there is the further question: 'What then is this luminously meaningful business of Iris Murdoch writing such intelligent novels, and ourselves getting such pleasure in being informed by them?'

The story of *The Philosopher's Pupil* is told by a mysterious narrator, N, who pops up every now and then like one of the portents such as the fox who sits in the front seat of Rolls-Royces. N describes himself as 'an observer, a student of human nature, a moralist, a man'; it is his 'role in life to listen to stories'. He adds: 'I also had the assistance of a certain lady.' The lady is, it seems, Iris Murdoch. As far as the business of making 'a formal utterance of a perceived truth' goes, it is the philosopher, Rozanov, who, striving for order on a rational and human level, fails; and it is the artist (the philosopher's pupil?) who, by making out of human disorderliness something orderly on what Father Bernard would call a religious level, succeeds. The artist's business is, paradoxically, through listening and observing, the framing of riddles. (pp. 19-20)

> *Nicholas Mosley, "The Philosopher Fails—The Artist Succeeds," in* The Listener, *Vol. 109, No. 2806, April 28, 1983, pp. 19-20.*

ROBERT TAUBMAN

George [is the title character of *The Philosopher's Pupil*], and a somewhat hypothetical figure, a product of the ideas in the novel. He has a reputation for being 'beyond good and evil' and 'closer to awful aspects of the world' than other people. He is ambiguously involved in the near-drowning of his wife at the beginning, and in the attempted murder of the philosopher Rozanov at the end. . . .

The need to try to explain George is widely felt in Ennistone. In his own voice, he comes on like Edgar on the heath, uttering snatches of quotations that are mostly nonsense but signify a soul in torment. Rozanov, the elderly philosopher who is the object of George's obsession, is for his part obsessed with his granddaughter's virginity. Rozanov is much the more believable character, though this involves believing in a very abstruse thinker at a time of crisis and despair. He has his own murderous impulses, which is doubtless what makes Althusser spring to mind. But Rozanov isn't mad; nor is he, like George, 'beyond good and evil'. What indeed makes him credible is simply that he is a puritan and a moralist. He is now 'tired of his mind' and tired of philosophy, in which 'everything went wrong since Aristotle.' But he is still a moralist, and what he fears most is 'to find out that morality is unreal'. Evidently (there's some guesswork to be done) this is what he does find out at the crisis of his relations with his granddaughter. He has already taken poison before George tips him into the bathwater.

It's hardly as effective as Dostoevsky—whose one image of eternity as a spider in a Russian bathhouse conveys more than all the Xanadu-like elaboration of Ennistone. The two principals are the less conspicuous for being surrounded by other strange creatures who might have stepped out of other Murdoch novels. . . . Lots of women—this is bafflingly typical of Iris Murdoch—are in love with George and Rozanov: as ever, the least attractive of her men get the most devotion. The supernatural has its usual place among the mere contingencies of existence. Marvels and portents occur and are simply noted, as if by the unsurprised eyes of a child. . . .

Power is a keyword: all the characters exercise powers over each other, which are less like natural powers than a kind of enchantment. And it would all be fun—our own English brand of magic realism—if it were neatly self-sufficient and the pattern of reversals quite harmonious. But not so. Far from being merely playful, *The Philosopher's Pupil* reaches out after meaning, and undertakes to deal with such issues as evil, innocence and salvation. So it borrows suggestively from literature: George is one of a trio of brothers with a family resemblance to the Karamazovs (the narrator with his talk of 'our town' and 'our citizens' also seems to be out of Dostoevsky). Another line of interpretation is offered: Rozanov as Prospero and George as Caliban. Interpretation isn't just a possible strategy for dealing with a Murdoch novel: it is imposed by the novel itself.

But it's also opposed from within the novel, for the great obstacle to interpretation is the ambiguity of the styles in which it is written. One can 'place' the narrator's style—and even guess his identity, though the novel doesn't disclose this. His is a 'cool' style, if quaintly mannered . . . and well-suited to the narrative function, though suspect as a mirror of the inner life. But readers of Iris Murdoch are already familiar with a 'hot' style which seems to come unbidden to her characters at important moments. It is one of Rozanov's ways of talking philosophy. . . . But mainly it's the language of emotional stress arising from 'spiritual devastation, inward wreck'—as in Rozanov's love-scenes with Hattie, or in George acting out his idea of redemption. . . .

It remains a moot point, after many Murdoch novels, whether these moments of excess are meant to convince the reader or not. Some think so, like a hostile critic of her last novel, *Nuns and Soldiers:* 'Writing this bad cannot be faked.' But it's also possible that they're simply due to the use of a convention: a somewhat theatrical convention, and in doubtful taste, but just one of the possibilities of 'as if' that the novel deals in. Acting is what her characters often do, entering the novel as if it were a proscenium stage and giving a performance: and the staginess of it—not the authenticity—is of the essence.

But to admit the use of theatrical conventions doesn't get one far enough. Obviously they deter one from being too literal and serious-minded in pursuit of deeper meanings, and they don't explain why the presence of meaning and the need for interpretation are so coercively suggested at almost every moment. But we may accept them as theatrical conventions, and still find something wrong here. And the trouble isn't in the bizarre effects they achieve, but in what these are set against: the implied norms of natural behaviour. The oddities and excesses are what we notice, in character as well as in style.

Nearly everyone here is like George, 'significantly at odds with reality'. . . . Spiritual devastation, secret passions and symptoms of madness appear with all Iris Murdoch's usual profusion. But lurking in the bizarre, and largely contributing to its effect, are the novel's assumptions about normality: the accepted view of mistresses or of homosexuals, the sacrament of marriage, the philosophic life, the Church of England. It is to all this, and 'affection, happiness and wisdom', that the characters supposedly return in the coda of the novel. Yet reality is just what these norms lack: they are only another kind of convention, and mostly of a most vapid, stereotyped kind. It is the norms underlying the fantasy which, in their significant silence, produce that sinking feeling, the debilitating effect of reading Iris Murdoch.

What good anyway comes of this play of opposites, her great divide between the noumenal and the norm, or fantasy and reality? Without the tension between opposites her novel wouldn't exist: but does it do enough to justify the novel's existence? It often seems only to polarise what would be better left unpolarised. Here is sex, for instance, in some of its wilder manifestations: but nothing about it as a fully human experience. At one extreme, it vanishes into the noumenal, or gives rise to a fit of the horrors, as in Rozanov's passion for his grandchild ('Oh wicked, wicked, the pain of it'). On the other hand, sex in the ordinary course of events is dismissed with an indifference that goes to another extreme: 'She had some small messy love affairs . . .' 'After messing about with human sexual adventures . . .' 'After a few unpleasant little adventures he had decided to give up sex.' Either way, sex is devalued—like so much else in this apparently commodious novel. It's not a novel that values the experience it's made of. It will be objected, of course, that novels aren't made of experience but of words, and one grants Iris Murdoch a great deal of cleverness with words.

Robert Taubman, "Double Life," in London Review of Books, *May 19 to June 1, 1983, p. 23.*

ROBERTSON DAVIES

It is not easy for a reviewer to know where to catch hold of a novel by Iris Murdoch, when he has to make up his mind about it. [*The Philosopher's Pupil*] is the most difficult of all. Has it a story? Yes. A good one? Yes, but not one of your neat plots; wambling and discursive, like life itself, rather than smartly turned by a fabulist's invention. Is the style distinguished, then? There are several styles, and all are right for what they have to carry. Is it innovative? (This is the voice of eager youth.) Well, yes, you might say so. Is it a good read? (This is the voice of slippered age.) That depends on how alert you are to what is being said. What influences are apparent in it? (This is a professor, hot for the long chain of succession in what he calls The Art of the Novel.) Well, sometimes it reminds me of the 19th century novel in its leisurely pace and heaping-up of significant detail, and its pleasure in description of natural surroundings; but at other times it is a novel which could only be written now. Would you know it for a philosopher's novel? (This is someone who knows that at one time the author plied that demanding trade.) No, or at least not to the point where it hurts. Do you recommend it, then? Oh, indeed I do, but don't come whining to me if it is not your sort of book.

Not an easy book to write about, as you see. There were moments when I wished that it could be infinitely extended. There were other moments (such as the 4,000 words that in-

tervened between a character reaching a door and crossing the threshold) when I found myself mentally shouting Get on with it! The author has a fine profusion of imagination, but her complexities do not always justify themselves; she delights in parentheses and conditions, so that if we are not always alert we may miss something important; she cares nothing about putting the reader at ease, and likes to tease us by calling a woman Alex and a man Emma. She assumes that her reader has a strong visual imagination, and delights in her power of painting with words. . . .

She has many voices, and to me the most astonishing is the Dialogue Voice; the talk among her characters whips along rapidly, pushing the plot well beyond the speed limit, and giving us insights and illuminations that we must catch on the fly; a dramatist might envy her skill. She cannot wholly discard the Philosophical Voice, and once—just once—she allows herself to set up a clergyman as stooge for her philosopher, who wipes the floor with him in a fashion just a little too easy. (p. 1)

Her philosopher is her principal character, though perhaps she meant the pupil named in the title to have that place. It is difficult to make a philosopher credible in fiction, because to carry complete conviction he would have to talk sometimes in a way that would leave us nonphilosophers baffled. But John Robert Rozanov convinces us because he is clearly a man of powerful intellect, and at the same time a victim of that overwhelming silliness that may overcome a man who has lived most of his life in his mind, and does not know what to do with emotion when it tosses and gores him. (pp. 1-2)

All the people in her book are in muddles of one sort or another, but they are not the tedious muddles of stupid people of whose fate we soon weary. They are the muddles of people who, either because they think more than they feel, or feel more than they think, cannot gain any serenity, however fleeting. But they all possess some distinction that makes them worth caring about, and they all behave in ways that we believe, even if we do not fully understand. When the philosopher, supposedly a man of wisdom but really just a man of broad knowledge, gets into a fantod about an affront to his granddaughter, we know why he does it, and how truly angry he is, and we feel for him as we wish to shake him into a better frame of mind.

Indeed, this may well be the real power of the book, which has many sources of energy. The author does what old-fashioned novelists did when they could; she makes us gods, observing, weighing, rebuking, forgiving, and happy with our omniscience. To professors who talk about The Art of the Novel this has been abhorrent for many decades, but it is one of the most difficult and rewarding things a novelist can do for us. It is an age-old attribute of the real storyteller, and Iris Murdoch possesses it in high degree. (p. 2)

Robertson Davies, "Iris Murdoch's Crowded Canvas," in Book World—The Washington Post, *June 26, 1983, pp. 1-2.*

RICHARD EDER

Iris Murdoch is a conjuring kind of novelist. Her characters are upper middle class, mostly, with a sprinkling of intellectuals, artists and assorted Bohemians. Their language, tastes and habits are at the very blunted edge of contemporary Western civility.

And they are infested with passion; unpredictable and primitive and with lashings of pagan magic. Under the leather brogues the feet are cloven; under the tweed jacket is a fell. The cultivated English countenances have their fundament in a mermaid's tail or a centaur's haunches; the countryside and country towns are haunted.

The ostensible form of the Murdoch novel—she has written 21 by now—is the comedy or tragicomedy of manners. Each detail is precise, each social nuance is just so. The pleasures, pursuits, meals, anguishes and silly walks of her assorted English intelligentsia could not be more engagingly and dryly set down.

All this is carriage work and scenery. The engine that makes her books go—high-powered, tricky and sometimes, as in [**"The Philosopher's Pupil"**], with a tendency to stall—is the whiff of supernatural force. Her characters press along with reasonable purposes, but they are like people making their way against a high and shifty wind; sometimes their purposes blow off or reverse. The Pan-like hauntings and acts of possession, without quite winning out, bring about sudden violence and sometimes an equally violent and arbitrary happiness.

At her best Murdoch has made a unique blend of the realistic novel and the magical tale. Not all conjuring conjures magic, though. It is always fun to see a water-diviner at work; it doesn't always produce water. **"The Philosopher's Pupil"** has been accused of unwieldy bulk and confused purposes. These are certainly there; on the other hand, there is quite a lot of fun in it. (p. 2)

There are many . . . characters, and the plot is [complex]. . . . There are events and pseudo-events, an attempted murder, a suicide, a town celebration that takes on hints of a pagan orgy. Above all there is pain, which is perhaps the book's main subject: Rozanov's pain at exhausting his philosophy and finding himself subject to his own grossness and decrepitude; George's Lucifer-like pain at being rejected by his god; and assorted pains for the book's galaxy of assorted personages.

Murdoch lets her characters go. There is excess in **"The Philosopher's Pupil"**: too many characters are described too completely in all their baroque convolutions; and they all talk much too long. Even a pet dog is given his point of view. Each character has an exhaustive life-history, and each anguish produces rages approaching sheer ranting.

The confrontations are deliberately melodramatic, and the melodrama tires. Still, the author has her purpose, and it is a quite individual one. Her tone is fundamentally cool and ironic, though not truly detached; she is dealing with people's demons and to do so she lets them run and rage. And at her best she finds disconcerting lines of sense in the chaos of human feelings. Of George's long-suffering wife, who is also, in her passive way, a manipulator, she writes:

"People who thought that Stella lived in hell were not wrong; but like all those who do not, they failed to understand that hell is a large place wherein there are familiar refuges and corners."

The refuges and corners of hell are, increasingly, Murdoch's territory. She writes about them subtly and with a disconcerting gaiety. (pp. 2, 8)

Richard Eder, "The Conjuring Magic of Murdoch,"
in Los Angeles Times Book Review, July 3, 1983,
pp. 2, 8.

JOYCE CAROL OATES

In Iris Murdoch's ambitious, unique and ingeniously plotted novels—**"The Philosopher's Pupil"** is the 21st—men and women are blinded by the dance of illusions. They fall in love, often violently and senselessly; they fall under the spell of individuals who appear to be special or extraordinarily powerful. A representative Murdoch novel—this one, for instance—is so densely populated and its dazed characters kept in such frenetic motion that it is sometimes difficult to remember what has happened to whom and why, which is perhaps the author's intention. For most people, life is a matter of sequential enchantments, a harlequinade in which many seek salvation but few find it, because they are captivated by mere shadows and blind to the true source of light. (p. 1)

From the start of her writing career, Miss Murdoch has chosen to associate, often with a wonderfully savage wit, the dance of shadows with that congeries of emotion called romantic or erotic love. In novel after novel she has mercilessly anatomized the delusions of love, returning often to familiar combinations (overly cerebral male in pursuit of ordinary female, for instance) and insights: "A human being hardly ever thinks about other people," a character says in **"Bruno's Dream."** "He contemplates fantasms which resemble them and which he has decked out for his own purposes." Most of the action of **"The Philosopher's Pupil"** consists of chasing about after these "fantasms." . . .

For readers familiar with Miss Murdoch's other novels (consider simply the early titles **"Under the Net"** and **"The Flight from the Enchanter"**), Rozanov will provoke a sensation of *déjà vu*. He is one of Miss Murdoch's magicians, a wizard, an enchanter—an emperor without any clothes—lacking the power to save himself but possessing the power, even if accidentally, to manipulate other lives. . . .

The difficulty here lies in the reader's willingness to suspend disbelief. Since Rozanov is rarely heard saying anything philosophical in a strict professional sense—since he is rarely heard saying anything original or profound, in fact—why do so many people flock around him and think obsessively of him? Even the *faux mauvais* George, the failure, the "dull dog" ("What made you bad at philosophy makes you bad at being bad," Rozanov says), has his circle of worshipful females, including the most beautiful woman in Ennistone. Can all this be seen in terms of human beings' endless capacity for delusion? Is life really to be so flippantly explained? "We would all be comic characters if we were in novels," the anonymous narrator of **"The Philosopher's Pupil,"** N, casually observes.

Where Miss Murdoch's celebrated early novels were brisk, polished, sardonic and highly original, rather like Restoration comedies in prose fiction form, her recent novels—from approximately **"A Fairly Honourable Defeat"** onward—are far more whimsically structured, freer, chattier, by turns funnier and more ponderous. The early novels seem quintessentially English, the later self-consciously "Russian." Here the narrative voice is likely to be breathless, plunging, unedited. . . . And defiantly overwritten. . . . (p. 20)

Allusions to Dostoyevsky are explicit in **"The Philosopher's Pupil,"** where the potential murderer George hallucinates a hammer-carrying double and insists on discussing with Rozanov such matters as good and evil, God and Satan, and whether there is a point beyond morality at which "everything is permitted." Where such passionate discussions spring to life in Dostoyevsky, especially in "The Brothers Karamazov," they strike a rather odd, dated note here. In any case, it is fully realized characters who debate in Dostoyevsky, not merely ideas. When George taunts Rozanov with the notion that they are both demons and that he is a caricature of Rozanov, hence Rozanov's hatred of him, he is purposely echoing Pyotr Verkhovensky's remarks to his idol, Nikolai Stavrogin, in "The Possessed"—but the echo, as well as other pointed parallels between the novels, only suggests the relative thinness, the *willed* quality, of "The Philosopher's Pupil."

Perhaps the very term novel of ideas is tautological, for what novel is barren of ideas, unshaped by ideas? One never thinks of D. H. Lawrence's "Women in Love" as a novel of ideas, for instance, because it is clearly so much more. As for Dostoyevsky's great novels and Thomas Mann's, ideas can assuredly be found in them and may in fact have generated them but are not finally equivalent to the rich narratives that sustain those ideas. Among Miss Murdoch's long novels, it is "**A Word Child**" and the splendid "**Henry and Cato**" that rise above the limitations of the novel of ideas. These are marvelous works, at once deeply moving and entertaining.

"**The Philosopher's Pupil**" is strongest, perhaps, when it does not labor to be gnomic and profound. (pp. 20-1)

> *Joyce Carol Oates, "Love and Other Illusions," in* The New York Times Book Review, *July 17, 1983, pp. 1, 20-1.*

JOHN UPDIKE

[If we] long for what James called "the palpable present *intimate* that throbs responsive," we can turn to no more reliable purveyor of intimacy than Iris Murdoch, whose latest novel, "**The Philosopher's Pupil**" . . . , is one of her biggest and best. It opens with a whirlwind of an argument between husband and wife, and its first paragraph is the best description of driving a car in the rain—a "palpable present" sensation par excellence—that I have ever read: . . .

> The malignant rain rattled on the car like shot. Propelled in oblique flurries, it assaulted the windscreen, obliterating in a second the frenetic strivings of the windscreen wipers. Little demonic faces composed of racing raindrops appeared and vanished. The intermittent yellow light of the street lamps, illuminating the grey atoms of the storm, fractured in sudden stars upon the rain-swarmed glass. Bumping on cobbles the car hummed and drummed.

Let this evocation stand as typical of Miss Murdoch's magic when it works: the blunt successive sentences, with scarcely a dependent clause among them, yield up the superb "little demonic faces composed of racing raindrops" to remind us that not all is as simple and declarative and breathless as it seems—that a highly symbol-prone intelligence presides behind this hurrying actuality. In twenty-one unstinting novels now, this writer has mined her imagination and the world around her for philosopher's gold. With rare concern and knowing, she writes, in a post-religious age, about spiritual activity, as it sparks along that interface where human perception breeds demons out of raindrops.

The quarrelling couple is George and Stella McCaffrey. . . . [The McCaffrey family is at] the center of the saga, which has so many other characters they seem to constitute the entire population of Ennistone, the small English city, "not exceed-

ingly far from London," where the action takes place in a busy period of about three months. The compressed time span, the device of a disappearing and reappearing first-person narrator who knows impossibly much, and the emphasis upon a certain family and a provincial community feel reminiscent of Dostoyevski's later novels. If Miss Murdoch has deliberately refreshed her reading of these, it is a happy move; the Russian's theatricality, wild humor, and troubled spiritual urgency are all up her alley. Like Dostoyevski, she is interested in people's influence over one another—their *sway,* the bogies we make in one another's minds, the gravitational permutations as spiritual bodies plunge on in their self-centered orbits. (pp. 197-98)

The peekaboo narrator calls himself N and names the town after himself—N's town, Ennistone. He is, we gradually learn, middle-aged, unmarried, something of a voyeur, and Jewish. Jewish also are Stella McCaffrey, Father Jacoby, and, one surmises, Steve Glatz. Enough plot, surely. There is plenty more of it, all sumptuously cloaked in Miss Murdoch's unfailing and seemingly effortless provision of faces and costumes and hairdos, of furnished rooms and architectural façades, of histories personal and local, of delightfully individual toads in botanically specific gardens. She is the happiest imaginer in the English-speaking world, fearless and fresh whether she displays a night of homosexual initiation or a music lesson, a Quaker meeting or a murderer's exalted frenzy, a dog's impression of a fox or an old woman's dream of dispossession.

This reviewer found "**The Philosopher's Pupil**" more involving and satisfying than the previous, equally energetic and knowledgeable novels by Miss Murdoch that he has read lately—"**The Sacred and Profane Love Machine**" and "**Nuns and Soldiers.**" Why? For one thing, love has been given something of a vacation here, or at least romantic infatuation shares with other sorts of steam the propulsion of the characters. A certain friendly grit coats this little industrial town, with its "strong and longstanding puritan and non-conformist tradition." Away from the dreaming spires of Oxford and the verdant squares of London, Miss Murdoch shows a bracing grasp of plain unpleasantness. In George McCaffrey she has created a fascinatingly nasty man—conceited, disappointed, muddled, and outrageous and destructive with a smugness that perhaps only an Englishman could muster. . . . Unless we call love George's mad desire to impress Rozanov, or Stella's aloof loyalty to her cruel and slovenly mate, erotic passion scarcely enters the plot until halfway through, and then in the ironic form of a knightly quest openly allegorized. Until then, and throughout, we are in the grip of a type of murder mystery, in which the question is not "Whodunnit?" but "What did he do?" Did George try to kill Stella? And the psychological mystery the author has set herself to examine is not that of amorous affect but that of human destructiveness, bilious and incorrigible. Miss Murdoch, in short, has given her darker side some rein and her broad and shrewd perceptions of human nature some breathing space away from the doctrine of omnipotent Eros. "The Triumph of Aphrodite" is a masque rehearsed in the novel, but the reader is excused from seeing it performed.

Also, in the so thoroughly and affectionately constructed setting of Ennistone she has given her volatile spiritual dramas a solid stage. The town is distinguished by the presence of famous and ancient hot springs. The waters, dating back to Roman times and rumored to have medicinal and aphrodisiac qualities, are housed in a set of pools and Victorian structures called The Bath Institute. Almost all the citizens of Ennistone swim the year round, and the gatherings and encounters of the characters at this watery forum as they stand about in the near-nude like figures on one of Dante's penitential terraces make a recurrently resonant image—souls, and not bodies, seem to be assembled. Miss Murdoch, with her painterly eye and theatrical sense, is a deviser of tableaux, of meaningful environments. . . . The Ennistone baths, with their constant steam and rumble issuing from an unfathomable underground source—the earth's subconscious, as it were—afford the novel's vapors and machinations a hot center that yet is quaintly, sturdily actual. . . . Water has often figured in Miss Murdoch's work as the outward emblem of the amorous power that suffuses and overwhelms us; by enhousing it at the center of her city she has tamed and channelled and strengthened the symbol. Things fit; the novel's furniture is irradiated by feeling, and functions as thing and sign both. When, toward the end, a UFO swoops low and blinds a character, we are not put off as by whimsy; we know by now what is meant, and in what sense such things do happen. (pp. 199-200, 203)

Of course, fault can be found, as with any free and generous production. In a field of characters so immensely extended, not all ripen as perhaps was intended. Adam and his dog Zed rather fade away; Ennistone's crowd of "bright young things" do little more than swell the scene. . . . [Father Bernard is] flimsy, and a victim of the author's tendency to hit and run, to fling scarecrows into her gardens. . . . The novel's evident moral haphazardly falls to the priest to pronounce, in a letter penned from Greek exile: "Metaphysics and the human sciences are made impossible by the *penetration of morality into the moment to moment conduct of ordinary life:* the understanding of this fact is *religion*."

Miss Murdoch has long been trying to rescue religion from an intellectually embarrassing theism. A headless chicken may flap about for a while, but it does not lay eggs; a Godless Christianity is scarcely more feasible. Yet she continues to give us atheistic priests and nuns and patiently to record the subtle shades of disbelief and lapsedness—John Robert Rozanov is an unrepentedly lapsed Methodist, Diane Sedleigh a churchgoing but incredulous Anglican, Brian McCaffrey a Quaker in the same condition, and so on. There is something dilute and wavering and flirtatious in all this that has enraged stout post-Christian critics. But her rendering of these dim religious halftones is realistic, it seems to me. . . . (pp. 203-04)

"The Philosopher's Pupil" considerably resembles an early Murdoch novel, "The Flight from the Enchanter." There the philosopher is in the dedication (to Elias Canetti) rather than the title; but both deal with teen-age females awakening to love, and with the spell exerted upon a circle of characters by a charismatic shaman- or father-figure. The plots share small things in common: gypsies, carved netsukes, foxes—the Enchanter is named Mischa Fox, and Alexandra McCaffrey's grounds are haunted by a beautifully actualized family of foxes. Reading these two books, with their affinities, one is struck by the glittering edge possessed by the younger writer, a jaunty farcicalness reminding us that Miss Murdoch came of age in

the day of Waugh and Huxley and Rose Macaulay and Nancy Mitford, that she cut her teeth on a novelistic style of savage brightness and heedless nihilistic romp. One misses, in the later Murdoch, that unbaggy feminine sharpness—feminist, indeed: "**The Flight from the Enchanter**" is really about female uprisings—and the nontheoretical, "palpable present" bite to the heroines' amours. Hattie Meynell, in "**The Philosopher's Pupil**," is vivid in quarrel but almost wordless in love, the inert object of a quest rather than a quester herself. Men have taken over the center of Miss Murdoch's novels—the opposite of what happened in the oeuvre of Henry James—and a certain stale scent of after-dinner cigars flavors the less dazzling pages. But, all in all, the earlier novel is greatly surpassed by the later, a book that seems as large as life, so large and various that no two people will read the same story in it. (pp. 204-05)

> *John Updike, "Baggy Monsters," in* The New Yorker,
> *Vol. LIX, No. 39, November 14, 1983, pp. 188-205.**

WILLIAM H. PRITCHARD

[In *The Philosopher's Pupil*], as always with reading Iris Murdoch, there is much that is entertaining, things which—like the discussion of a Mallarmé poem between a homosexual priest and Rozanov's young female ward—would be beyond the abilities of most novelists. She has lost none of her ability to describe places and houses and the physics of things generally. But the human aspect of it all seems woefully absent, even as compared with *A Severed Head,* which in its focused concentration on the first-person narrator, Martin Lynch-Gibbon, had cumulative force even if it didn't go very deep. *The Philosopher's Pupil* has neither depth nor cumulative power; it diffuses itself rather, wandering among endlessly proliferating details. As just one instance of this, what does one do when, after 340 hefty pages have been traversed, we are taken on a picnic attended by the major characters at which the food and drink are described in detail—who brought what and what kind of Yugoslav Riesling or Double Gloucester cheese it was. All this information is presented in sentences which open in parallel manner: "The drinks before lunch had been as follows . . ." "The food at lunch had been as follows . . ." Why should we know these things, and why should they be enumerated to us by a faceless narrator who strives for no distinction of language in the rendering? The Murdoch operation, so hugely professional in one sense, is also (as the students now say) quite impossible to suspend disbelief in, and as the August days rolled by, with me still reading, troubled thoughts surfaced about the worth of it all. What, other than finishing the novel, *was* the purpose of continuing? For all her intelligence as a critic and theorist of fiction, this writer seems quite passive and unthoughtful about the accumulation of words, of novels—increasingly automatic and self-propelled—that is her literary career. A very strange case indeed. (pp. 748-49)

> *William H. Pritchard, in a review of "The Philosopher's Pupil," in* The Hudson Review, *Vol. XXXVI, No. 4, Winter, 1983-84, pp. 748-49.*

Craig Nova
1945-

American novelist.

Reviews of Nova's first two novels, *Turkey Hash* (1972) and *The Geek* (1975), were mixed. Set on the seamy side of Los Angeles and on a barbaric Greek island, respectively, the two books focus on the lurid and vulgar aspects of life while maintaining a lighthearted manner. Critics called Nova's writing style technically proficient and witty, but some contended that his characters were not sufficiently developed. *Incandescence* (1979) elicited similar comments. Again the focus is on a down-and-out protagonist who participates in a series of bizarre incidents but does not change or grow over the course of the novel. Critics agreed that Nova did not assist the reader in understanding his characters and used imagery and metaphors which were irrelevant to his themes and story line.

Nova's novel *The Good Son* (1982) is a departure from his earlier works both stylistically and in subject matter. Critics have unreservedly praised this work for its fully developed characters and engaging story. An upper-class family estate is the setting for a father-son power struggle which parallels the thematic conflict between passion and discipline. The novel is narrated by eight different characters and critics concluded that Nova handled this difficult technique well.

(See also *CLC*, Vol. 7; *Contemporary Authors*, Vols. 45-48; and *Contemporary Authors New Revision Series*, Vol. 2.)

Photograph by Ken T. Ohara

MICHAEL WOOD

[*The Geek*] belongs to a distinct but elusive Anglo-American genre, which includes a lot of Hemingway, Lowry's *Under the Volcano*, and a good deal of John Hawkes: that form of fiction which pits a solitary Anglo-Saxon against an ancient, alien, and violent culture. . . .

There is something too cryptic about a lot of the novel's transactions, a suggestion of dialogue out of Henry James shifted to a dusty taverna, and, as I say, the writing keeps reaching for effects that are more than a little lurid. But the blending of emblematic and literal truth . . . is remarkable. The specificity of the island landscape, the clear characters and past history of the individual islanders, the careful tracing of Boot's reactions to separate events, all help to pitch *The Geek* somewhere between reality and nightmare, as if it were a dream that had found its own geography in the material world, or a familiar piece of geography that had toppled into a dream. Boot, the double exile, drunk and alien, fills out his fiction . . . and his Greek island will stand for many places where men of honor, beaten down by craftier antagonists and their own fatigue, have given up the ghost and subsided into humiliation. (p. 11)

Michael Wood, "Crying for Attention," in The New York Review of Books, *Vol. XXIII, No. 10, June 10, 1976, pp. 8, 10-11.**

JOHN MELLORS

The bizarre happenings in *The Geek* are set on a Greek island in a Gothick atmosphere of unexplained death, unmotivated violence and heavily charged sex. A sandy-haired American called Boot drinks immense quantities of beer and ouzo and finds a dead girl on a beach. A patchy-bearded monk called Lukas dreams 'of a hymen tearing with the sound of a ripping sheet'. An opium-smuggler seduces a 14-year-old girl who gives off a 'crystalline' smell. The sea is 'glassine'. Craig Nova has a feel for heat and sweat and blood and dust, but clarity and character are lost in an un-Aegean fog. On the last page, Boot bites off the head of a live chicken and thinks: 'I'm not even curious whether it was a matter of loss or victory.' By then, my own curiosity had evaporated, too.

John Mellors, "Stern Stuff," in The Listener, *Vol. 96, No. 2485, November 25, 1976, p. 688.**

JOHN DOMINI

Mr. Nova's men are out solo; they stumble along grim coastlines against which they seek nothing but to destroy themselves brightly—which seems only natural, amid the stench of hydrocarbons.

The world of **"Incandescence,"** however, is considerably more hospitable than that of Mr. Nova's earlier novels, **"The Geek"** . . . and **"Turkey Hash."** Most of the action takes place in "the dark furrows of New York." . . .

Mr. Nova has never been unfunny, but **"Incandescence"** displays a sure grasp of the absurd. Much of the humor resides in metaphors that enliven the drab. . . . And Stargell himself actually gives evidence of having hope, of wanting, in his own queer way, to live and prosper. Not that the odds aren't against him. Formerly one of the whiz kids in a think tank, he now finds himself unemployed and, soon enough, heavily in debt to a loan shark.

Stargell's descent takes place mostly over one terrible night, during which he is led along by a weepy blind derelict; the next morning, we discover, is Easter. By these touches of allegory it would seem that Mr. Nova wants to establish a tangible bond between his protagonist's self-destructiveness and his nobility, between the burn-out of oblivion and "that incandescence . . . when you'd know your skin was filled with magic"; but I'm not sure he entirely succeeds. Although the episodes of that night are marvelous in themselves—notably, a scene in which derelicts sleep standing up, their arms, their arms slung over clotheslines strung across a flophouse room— their cumulative effect is diffused.

Still, in the charged scene where Stargell visits his father for the last time, Mr. Nova does convey a paradoxical impression of serenity at the edge of catastrophe. Though we cannot be sure the protagonist's skid has ended, we can have no doubts that his run of bad luck has made a special novel. Craig Nova has proved that nothing gives off sparks like hard living struck against surfaces even harder: the passing of time and our relentless struggle to make it stop.

John Domini, "Dark Furrows in New York," in The New York Times Book Review, February 11, 1979, p. 15.

TIM O'BRIEN

Stargell, the 29-year-old narrator of Craig Nova's *Incandescence,* is a man of intelligence. Perhaps even genius. He once worked as an inventor at one of those high-powered think tanks but was fired after spending half a million dollars on a project to extract oil from the wing joints of moths. . . .

So when the story opens, we find Stargell a down-and-out taxi hack in New York. He's broke. He's on the skids. He lives— survives—in a dingy three-room apartment. . . . A long, dizzying fall from the think-tank heights. And, in the course of this novel, a sad predicament gets even sadder. Partly in horror, partly in puzzlement, we watch as Stargell makes some zany but essentially halfhearted efforts to pull himself out of this mess. Alas, he only manages to descend deeper into darkness.

What are we to make of this inventor, one who seemingly can't invent solutions to the most ordinary of human problems?

We look for clues. On the second page of *Incandescence,* a single sentence stands alone amid two inches of white space: "My name is Stargell." We never learn his first name. Clearly, then, the name Stargell must be important. Why else would the author maroon that sentence as he does, inviting the reader to ponder meanings? Why, as if to buttress the point, would the author call the company for which Stargell works the Star Garage? Stargell: star, light, brilliance, Day-Glo, incandesc-

ence. The associations are plentiful, and Nova uses all of them. Indeed, either by coincidence or design, this star business inevitably leads us to the word "nova" and from there to the author's own surname, Nova. Question is, how does all this hook up with the story? It isn't enough, after all, to display constellations of associated images and metaphors. The function of imagery and metaphor is to expand and, so to speak, illumine the dramatic events of a story, heightening but not imposing meaning on those events. The feeling, after reading this novel, is that the plot—the tracing of a falling star—hasn't the strength to support the heavy imagery, or the even heavier metaphor. In the end, the general outweighs the particular.

There is, however, much to admire in this, Nova's third novel. The writing is brisk and often funny. Stargell's hip cynicism, though grating after a time, produces some very witty lines. And why not? His, after all, is an incandescent wit. Studded throughout the book, in counterpoint to the comic aspects, there are several entirely uncomic and even tragic scenes that convey the terrors that can befall a man who can neither understand nor escape his own disintegration.

The plot of *Incandescence* is difficult to summarize. Events are linked by the flimsiest and most coincidental of circumstances; characters pop in for brief appearances and then disappear entirely. Incandescence: the quick, bright flicker of people and places. Incandescence: the random burning of flames, or stars, in the black world of urban New York City. (p. 53)

Stargell auditions for a job as a gorilla at an amusement park. The scene has funny moments and a semitragic outcome, but it runs much too long and makes us wonder what the point is. Black humor for its own sake can become boring. . . . The characters begin to seem like links on a chain, identical in their tough-guy fatalism, their world-weary lingo, their antic behavior. This sense of repetition also infects the events of the novel, which become variations on the same slapstick joke.

One interpretation for all this might be that Craig Nova wanted to take us on a tour through the concentric circles of hell, New York-style. But concentric circles imply a tightening of the screw, an increasing of tension, a multiplication of horror. In *Incandescence* each ring seems identical to the last. There is in the book no sense of change.

Beyond this, though, Stargell's peculiar ambivalence to his plight is never resolved. He accepts, with a few cynical asides, the terrible things that happen to him, and we never find out why. Why, in fact, doesn't he bite the bullet and find himself a decent job and start cleaning up his act? Despite all the "falling star" stuff, human beings are *not* stars. Human beings— Stargell especially—have brains, and human beings have the potential for reform and understanding and adaptation. The reader can't help wondering why Stargell doesn't start exercising some willpower. We want to know more about what makes Stargell behave as he does. We want, and never really get, psychological insight. What we get instead is a metaphor, and it isn't sufficient. (p. 54)

Tim O'Brien, "Falling Star," in Saturday Review, Vol. 6, No. 4, February 17, 1979, pp. 53-4.

RANDALL ROTHENBERG

[*Incandescence*] has a striking profusion of tantalizing baseball references: The narrator's name is Stargell, and he is joined by a host of tangential characters called Munson, Carew, Lee MacPhail, The Georgia Peach, Concepcion, and Al Hrabosky.

One searches in vain, however, for the baseball metaphors these names promise. Their use is, in fact, nothing but an idle literary device that serves no larger purpose—not surprising, really, since there *is* no larger purpose, not to mention theme, discernible in *Incandescence.*

Nova's characters do not grow in the course of the story; they stand still, reveling (as does the author) in their own quirkiness. . . . Yet not only does Nova give his characters unexplained eccentricities; he senselessly maims them as well, chopping off the legs of one, blinding another.

As for the story itself—well, there isn't much of that either. The author has merely strung together a series of throwaway vignettes—apparently believing them to be relevant, funny and poignant—in the hope that their very novelty will justify their creation. . . .

Finally, the book has no significant climax. The scene where Stargell rouses himself to audition for the job of gorilla at an amusement park should be the cathartic height of the novel; after all, Stargell is here tapping the sum of his intellectual and emotional energy in a way he had not since his days at the Tank. Moreover, Nova seems to be trying to achieve in this section something similar to what John Guare achieved in *The House of Blue Leaves.* In a scene of that play, a devout Catholic's son acts out the tragicomic incident in his life that has warped him, leading him to a murder attempt on the Pope. The son's frantic role-playing, complete with feats of athletic prowess, tells you a great deal about the character and his motivations. Unfortunately, Nova's portrayal of Stargell's monkeyshines accomplishes nothing near this.

Although the absence of growth in a character is itself a cause for pity or sadness, in the case of this novel it merely signifies the author's failure to pick up where his literary devices leave off. In the future, Craig Nova should try to come to terms with his incandescent ideas before asking us to do so.

> Randall Rothenberg, *"Batting in the Dark," in* The New Leader, *Vol. LXII, No. 9, April 23, 1979, p. 20.*

THOMAS R. EDWARDS

Incandescence is one of those novels that confront an awful world by generating brisk, tough, comic patter about sharply observed details of an incorrigibly vulgar culture. The suggestion is always that the absurd or horrifying is in fact perfectly normal, quite what one had been expecting, without power to hurt, depress, or anger. Nova is quite good at it, and the novel has its fine moments. . . .

Like some other pleasures, writing like Nova's makes you long for ever more subtle and complicated versions of what you've just had, and the occasional miscalculation, however slight, encourages a suspicion—perhaps unfair—that rhetoric, not experience and understanding, is doing most of the work here. (p. 40)

> Thomas R. Edwards, *"Feeding on Fantasy," in* The New York Review of Books, *Vol. XXVI, No. 12, July 19, 1979, pp. 41-2.*

JOHN IRVING

Pop Mackinnon—"a coarse, charming man, a lawyer, and a good one"—wants his sons to follow his path: to be lawyers who know how to hunt and marry well; to be gentlemen who join that unassailable aristocracy which is earned by tough, nononsense cleverness and is protected by money. Son John disappoints Pop; he is killed in World War II. So son Chip—a fighter pilot who was shot down in the war but survived as a P.O.W.—becomes the title character of **"The Good Son,"** Craig Nova's fourth novel. In this dark, deep story of a father and son who love (and love to fight) each other, the good son is the one who will defeat, or even kill, his father with the father's own weapons.

I've read no better, no more bitter and ironic understanding of professional cunning and ambition since Joseph Heller's "Something Happened." I've read no fuller mixture of human frailties, no more deft revelation of the chinks in moral armor since Robertson Davies's "Leaven of Malice." I've read no more comic and painful exploration of the disasters of loneliness since Nabokov's "Laughter in the Dark." As a virtuoso handling of first-person narration, **"The Good Son"** is as marvelous as André Brink's recent "A Chain of Voices."

In this exquisitely delineated battle between father and son, both men are consumed and changed; each gets his own way but both victors pay a price. . . .

The good son, Chip, does everything *de jure*—that is, according to Pop's law—until a passionate affair with a woman beneath his class wrests him from his father's grasp. Finished with college, finished with the war, finishing law school, Chip is engaged to a woman Pop approves of when he meets a solitary runaway from Ohio. Jean Cooper is a young woman who inspires such perilous longing that she has had to flee her hometown, where the menfolk were destroying themselves over her. Although Pop detests Jean for interrupting his plans for Chip, he too desires her, to the point of courting their mutual destruction. While Pop fights to break up Chip and Jean, he fights to free himself from wanting her; Jean's hunger for a life of her own has such a visible force that it seems to create a hunger for her in others.

Jean's vulnerability to insult is what finally forces her to leave Chip, allowing him to return to his father's path. Chip would not have had the strength to leave her; both father and son are chastened by encountering her. For Mr. Nova, Jean Cooper represents a vision of the world in which passion is terrifying, by nature short-lived and outside society—although its pressures and disruptions are beautiful. Chip is made the stronger for having felt such passion, and is sensitive to its demands, one of which is to allow its leavetaking. This same confrontation with passion makes Pop weaker (probably because his passion for Jean is never realized). It is not so much that passion dies as that Jean takes it with her. Her departure from the novel is an amputation; it leaves an ache.

Jean occupies the middle of this novel, like a heart; when we last see her, she's still moving on—away from Chip and from Pop. . . .

We are at once relieved and disappointed to see Chip marry his jilted fiancée, to become wedded at last to the safety of a relationship suitable to his life's professional course. Pop may win the fight for returning his son to the straight and narrow, but the fight has cost him. When Jean leaves, it is Chip who seizes control of Pop. . . .

Between chapters recording the battling of father and son are excerpts from "Mrs. Mackinnon's Book of Animals, Reptiles, Plants, Trees, Birds, Bugs, and Flowers"; Mrs. Mackinnon is Pop's lonely and dominated wife, Chip's sensitive mother, who in her journal of minute observations of nature reveals the isolation of life with Pop and her acute perception of the war between her husband and her son. (p. 3)

So much of the excellent tension in "The Good Son" is provided by a male struggle for a male kind of power; it is both lovely and astonishing that often the keenest understanding of this power struggle is Mrs. Mackinnon's and Jean Cooper's. In a novel so focused on a father and his son, Mr. Nova never neglects the female point of view.

The narration of the novel is entirely in the first person, but the narrators change. Chip tells about learning to drive with his father's chauffeur, a loner and ex-convict named Wade. . . . Wade's understanding of loneliness and of regret makes him the right narrator for Jean's meeting with Chip. Pop narrates Chip's wedding—fittingly, because he has worked so relentlessly to orchestrate it. . . . Our introduction to Jean, in her confining Ohio town, is voiced by her younger sister, Annie; it is perfect that a woman whose effect on men is so devastating (and so devastating to her) should first be seen and loved by the one person who can admire her unselfishly (and not sexually).

But the appropriateness of the narrative voice for each of this novel's big scenes is only one aspect of the novel's near-perfect form. (pp. 3, 25)

The structure and the language of this novel are almost without fault. Despite the ambition of having so many narrators speak uniformly well, yet differently, Mr. Nova makes only a few mistakes in voice. . . . But this is such a big, complex novel to be written with such consistent grace; it is a narrative of momentum and of linear clarity; it has characters of great, outward bravery and of heartbreaking inner need—indeed the characters are as vivid with suffering and with spirit as recurring dreams.

Mr. Nova's previous novels—"The Geek," "Turkey Hash," "Incandescence"—were insufficiently praised and little read; they are good books, but none of them prepared me for the broad scope and pitch-perfect performance of "The Good Son." It is not only Mr. Nova's best novel; it is the richest and most expert novel in my recent reading by any writer now under 40. (pp. 25-6)

John Irving, "Desire, Ambition and Father," in The New York Times Book Review, *October 3, 1982, pp. 3, 25-6.*

CHARLES TRUEHEART

Plenty of grownups spend their lives locked in mortal combat with their mothers and fathers, psychological shadow-boxing, flailing at specters and apparitions that linger from childhood conflicts long since irrelevant. For others, of course, the conflicts are real, and whether this is better or worse, more tractable or less, is hard to say.

Craig Nova's "The Good Son" is a story about just such a struggle, a real one between a father and his grown son. If there is something writ too large about their collision—their stubbornness one with the other, the contending passions each feels for making and having his own way—then perhaps the author is toying with allegory. He has tried to give flesh and substance to struggles that usually remain imprisoned in the psyche. By and large, his effort is successful. . . .

Nova, who is the author of three earlier novels, is a thoughtful and canny storyteller, if a trifle brooding in tone and labored in method. The novel is narrated through the 1940s and early '50s by a number of characters, central and peripheral. Their separate histories and preoccupations are sideshows, echoes and variations suggesting the larger world that Pop and Chip have shut out in their consuming obsession.

"The Good Son" is a dark and affecting exploration of how families inexorably transform love into pain and self-esteem into self-destruction—and somehow survive to endure the wreckage.

Charles Trueheart, "Love, Pain and Family Conflict," in Los Angeles Times Book Review, *October 31, 1982, p. 5.*

DAVE SMITH

The Good Son is a portrait of unending combat between passion and discipline. Nova's first three novels, **Turkey Hash, The Geek,** and **Incandescence** were energetic, eccentric, exquisitely written tales of people who were on the whole, well, just not like us. As readable and demanding as any of them, *The Good Son* differs in that its people are like us except that they have a lot more money. Their difference seems to have little to do with the passed-on effects of corrosive passion and everything to do with the dignity of the self. . . . For Pop Mackinnon a man's importance and character may be found in how he does things, whether it be driving a car, hunting a deer, preparing and consuming a mint julep, or facing up to the responsibilities of his class. He understands the world to operate according to precise codes of discipline in law, society, or family. He intends to keep order in a disorderly universe and to that end trains his sons John and Chip. (pp. 130-31)

The very order of behavior which is Pop's passion is also, however, his blinding constriction, for it removes him from love, rapture, and even the most ordinary tenderness. . . .

Mackinnon's instruction is predicated on his conviction that verbal abuse, physical violence, money, shame, whatever-will-work is acceptable if it reveals "that delineated center, the place in the heart or mind or fears which you need only mention to a man to make him flinch." Mackinnon's tutelage is long on intimidation and short of affection, but it arises from an excessive love. (p. 131)

The Good Son concludes with painful accommodation. Chip Mackinnon and Carolyn Cooke marry in an outdoor ceremony on Pop Mackinnon's farm, and the house of civilization is reaffirmed. It is a funny, violent, and deftly symbolic scene which provides a figure for both unrestrained desire and civil restraint which disciplines desire. A powerful ram which Pop had allowed to roam loose over his ground while he was preoccupied with his lost son appears suddenly and charges the wedding party. Battering booze, food, minister, servants, guests, and Miss Cooke, the ram traumatizes the ceremony of union until Chip fetches the rare Männlicher rifle, with which his father had taught him to hunt. Chip's execution of the ram is a brilliant image of his grudging acceptance of social responsibility, and it evokes in us a hard sadness at the yielding up of the heart's wildest fury. We cannot manage the beast of utter and brutal desire, but neither can we well deny it or escape it. Insofar as Craig Nova's novel carries implicit meaning, it would seem to be that we must discipline ourselves but we must also keep near us that rampant disorder of passion, else all postures of stability are so much sheep piss on the wedding cake.

There are times when one wants to be restrained in one's enthusiasm for a book, mostly because one suspects a changed opinion is possible. Yet I cannot imagine a reader who would find **The Good Son** anything less than a totally satisfying piece of work. Its prose is as intensely beautiful as a fine poem, and its structure is as precise as a Bach fugue. Yet it is mostly the power with which Nova is able to engage and set free the myth of love that impresses. His is a severe, inflexible, and hurting world. I think that he believes, however, as Conrad did, that there is no impossibility of its being made good—not morally right or ever free of our ordinary, predictable hemorrhages—but good in our knowing, good in our possession. . . . **The Good Son** is a portrait of ourselves, rich and poor, and a good one. (pp. 133-34)

Dave Smith, "Myths of Love: New American Fiction," in The Kenyon Review, *Vol. VI, No. 1, Winter, 1984, pp. 121-34.**

Julia (Mood) Peterkin

1880-1961

American novelist and short story writer.

Peterkin is known primarily for her humane and realistic depiction of the Gullahs, black Americans who lived and worked on South Carolina plantations during the first decades of the twentieth century. Peterkin, the wife of a plantation manager, used her experiences with the Gullahs to fashion stories that are often violent or macabre. She has been praised for her accurate rendering of the Gullah dialect and folklore. Peterkin was initially recognized for her portrayal of the Gullahs as complete, meaningful characters, which undermined the stereotypical view of blacks during the 1920s and 1930s. Her reputation waned, however, when increasing awareness and understanding of black culture made her works seem to degrade the Gullahs as inferior or primitive. Several scholars recently have defended Peterkin, claiming that her works have been unfairly treated and that they are valuable as a record of a transitional period in American race relations.

Peterkin's first book, *Green Thursday* (1924), is a series of sketches and stories tied together by a narrative that centers on a black plantation family. As in all of Peterkin's works, the major characters of *Green Thursday* are blacks who have virtually no contact with white society. Much of the action is violent and the situations sordid: one child dies, a second is maimed, and the father's sexual interest in an adopted daughter finally splits the family. Critics applauded this work, praising Peterkin for her poignant portrayal of the Gullahs. In later years, however, some have pointed to *Green Thursday* as evidence of the way in which Peterkin depicted blacks as uncivilized and self-destructive. *Black April* (1927), her next work, is the story of the plantation foreman, a heroic figure who is brought to ruin by a combination of physical illness and social circumstances. Critics considered this work more unified than *Green Thursday* and praised Peterkin's blend of picaresque detail with tragic elements. *Scarlet Sister Mary* (1928) was Peterkin's greatest success. This novel relates the story of Mary Pinsett from the dissolution of her marriage and her many subsequent love affairs through her resolve to follow spiritual rather than physical yearnings. *Scarlet Sister Mary* was awarded the Pulitzer Prize in fiction. Some recent critics have faulted this novel for suggesting that black families are basically unstable.

Collected Short Stories of Julia Peterkin (1970) renewed critical debate on Peterkin's importance. Some critics maintain that, in addition to her often demeaning portrayal of blacks, Peterkin unrealistically avoided racist themes by describing a world that was filled entirely with black characters. Others suggested that Peterkin should be considered an important social historian and regional writer.

(See also *Contemporary Authors,* Vol. 102 and *Dictionary of Literary Biography,* Vol. 9.)

THE NEW YORK TIMES BOOK REVIEW

Mrs. Peterkin of South Carolina is one of the first to write a book unaffectedly about negroes, without conscious or uncon-

Courtesy of Bobbs-Merrill Company, Inc.

scious belittling mockery in view of superior white advancement.

"Green Thursday" is a collection of short narratives—sketches almost, so slight is the thread of action—dealing with the vicissitudes of the family of a negro husbandman on a small South Carolina farm. With sincerity, simplicity, delicacy and sympathy the author reveals glimpses of the life of Kildee, his wife Rose, his children, the little maid-servant . . . , and the life of the negro community. . . . [A] constant thread of toil emerges in Kildee's manful struggle with the soil. There are broad splashes of color; a house that burns, the time that Baby Rose is burned to death, the time the red rooster picks out the eye of another child. Tragedies conceived of simple elements, yet poignant and deep as nature itself. Dialect, thought, action is perfectly convincing and charming. Nothing is hidden—anti-kink lotion, outlandish costumes, superstition, emotion, poverty, ignorance, seasoned with fragments of negro lore as sound and earthy as the loam from which they spring.

The book is neither a novel nor a series of short stories. They are brief descriptive pieces that might answer to the description of sketches were it not for the fact that together they form an integral whole that paints a picture of negro peasant life in the South, as exemplified on one small farm in one small community. Mrs. Peterkin has shown herself in **"Green Thursday"** as a literary artist, without any prejudice except the saving artistic predilection for unity and coherent form. Into the mold of the graceful form she has chosen she pours the distillation of a rich, human observation of the secret life of a people who have not yet been understood by the whites, because the whites have always found it easier to laugh at it than to attempt to comprehend it.

"Again a Serious Study of Negroes in Fiction: 'Green Thursday'," in The New York Times Book Review, *September 28, 1924, p. 8.*

JOHN W. CRAWFORD

["**Black April**"], concerning life among the negroes on an isolated South Carolina coastlands plantation, at first sight seems to fall into the category of the traditional modification of a picaresque novel—picaresque, that is, not only for its treatment of a man outside the ordinary laws, but for its structure of thinly connected episodes. Certainly the figure of black April, the foreman of Blue Brook plantation, who gives the book its title, is of the heroic, almost grandiose, mold of the legendary protagonists of fiction. Mrs. Peterkin's story flares with some of the incidents into a compellingly vivid intensity, too high-pitched to be sustained; succeeding passages all but falter into a complete break of the mood. . . .

Mrs. Peterkin is treating of the darkies variously called "Gullah" or blue-gum, who inflect the English language as if it were a tribal dialect of Africa. While Mrs. Peterkin has not transcribed the speech of these negroes with . . . [scholarly accuracy], she has by no means distorted it to a purely literary artifice. What she has accomplished is a lucid, yet idiomatic, racy speech for the mouths of her negroes, retaining the full-bodied integrity of the original without divorcing it from the comprehension of those unfamiliar with the source. . . .

There are, thus, three factors which might well contribute to an alienation of the reader's sympathies from Mrs. Peterkin's story. She is writing of negroes in a strange and special social mode of being, whose erotic impulses move freely and untrammeled within the customarily forbidden confines of consanguineal relationship, and whose speech is almost unknown outside the rice lands of South Carolina. It is a signal triumph for Mrs. Peterkin that none of these count against "**Black April.**" She has made a world of her own. It is true that her impersonal attitude toward the vagaries beyond the pale of these men, Old Breeze and April, disarms any feeling of revolt, but it is also true that her intention embraces a retribution for them, equally outside convention, and still further absolves the reader. . . .

This ethical sternness contributes toward a cleansing horror rather than a shuddering and soiled disgust. It does not, however, grant the reader immunity from the fascinated contemplation of the world which Mrs. Peterkin has created. Part of the power of this world depends upon Mrs. Peterkin's implication of another, contrasting world, the society of ante-bellum days. . . .

[Mrs. Peterkin appears] to have fulfilled the apparently irreconcilable conditions of maintaining a single character in appropriate surroundings, developing him in dramatic incident, and of subordinating that same character to the larger vision of some major aspect of American life. The conflict between the world and the Church, or religion, has been fruitful, world without end, of literature. Sigrid Undset based her powerful trilogy of Norwegian life in the fourteenth century, "Kristin Lavransdatter," upon that identical theme. Mrs. Peterkin has translated it to the inevitable conditions of the United States, in its manifestations among the Southern plantation negroes. Her abstractions are organically related to her specific instances, and the story is so fluid that it is impossible to stop it at a single point and say here is the kernel, this is what she means. . . .

This is a fine and beautifully conceived book. It is not too much to call it a big book. It is not, however, perfect. Mrs. Peterkin invests her characters at times with an ill-advised sensibility. At the moment when April quarrels with his unacknowledged son, Sherry, while another unrecognized son, Little Breeze, stands by, Mrs. Peterkin seriously mars the noble austerity which the scene requires by refracting the scene through Little Breeze and by making him suffer extraordinary shivers and quavers of emotional disturbance, and by reflecting thereupon in the birds and the sky and the very ground underfoot the sorrow that wrings the heart of Little Breeze. That sort of overwrought receptivity and reactiveness is repeated elsewhere in the novel sufficiently often to flaw the work, yet not bulking large enough to overshadow the excellence of the book as a whole.

John W. Crawford, "Hound-Dogs and Bible Shouting," in The New York Times Book Review, *March 6, 1927, p. 5.*

CHARLES McD. PUCKETTE

In many respects [*Black April*], Mrs. Peterkin's second published volume of fiction dealing with the negroes in the South, must stand as the most genuinely successful attempt yet made to capture the soul of these people. This book is put down with the feeling that one stands nearer to truth than one has stood before, in a field of fiction the surface of which has been often scratched, and the rich depths seldom upturned.

Mrs. Peterkin makes one singularly happy stroke. There are no white people in this book. From first to last it is the story of the negroes' lives in relation to each other. That is quite a different thing from negro life in its relation to another race, or even with the presence of white people and the existing social system as a background constantly present. It is a device which assists in Mrs. Peterkin's search for truth. Nor does she contrive this setting for her story mechanically. The black people of her pages are the hands on an isolated South Carolina plantation on the coast, visited by its owners only in the shooting season. April, the foreman, is a negro; and though the "big house" is there, the story is of the plantation quarters, a community of the black people, indeed isolated. . . .

Mrs. Peterkin's rich store of understanding knowledge of the negro shows itself on every page. But this insight is not more remarkable than the honest art with which she tells her story. It is the reality of simple truth. One is not conscious of the art, nor of the writer. The story flows from life itself, and not from one to be observed observing life. The negro's superstitions, morals, humor, mind, customs are what they are. Mrs. Peterkin throws them into no relief against anything or anyone else. Other fiction of negro life seems false in the light of Mrs. Peterkin's achievement.

Charles McD. Puckette, "On a Carolina Plantation," in The Saturday Review of Literature, *Vol. III, No. 34, March 19, 1927, p. 660.*

JOHN R. CHAMBERLAIN

["**Scarlet Sister Mary**"] all but cries with color, scent, sound. It has the rich fragrance of a hot candied yam. Mrs. Peterkin rings all the changes of season and weather to build up the world of Scarlet Sister Mary, and she does it in a style that is a happy combination of solidity, brilliance and pure beauty. Sometimes her story sags with too much beauty, but to err in that manner is superhuman and quite easily forgiven.

So real, so arresting to the five senses, is the sub-tropical world of the Blue Brook plantation—a fruitful sector in the sea-island country of the South Carolina lowlands—that Mary's lusty, fertile habit of taking up with any man who suits her fancy seems native to a place where "the earth's richness and the sun's warmth make living an easy thing." This black incarnation of the goddess of fertility is jilted by her lawful husband [July], but she remains even-up with life by filling her house with children, the only two of which by the same man happen to be twins.

As was the case in "**Black April,**" this book is crammed with the doings and superstitions of the Gullah folk. . . . Here, in her second novel, Mrs. Peterkin relates everything to the central character; she has made her story more intense by a process of narrowing down.

Mary's character is simple and elemental. It takes color from the world about her. . . .

What impresses one about Mary is her direct whole-heartedness. If July hadn't been conjured by another woman, Mary would have remained a faithful wife all her black life. . . .

There are two occasions upon which "**Scarlet Sister Mary**" seems to verge upon the factitiousness of farce. One is when Unexpected [Mary's first child], true to his name, returns from up north, carrying a child in his arms. "Whoa," the reader is inclined to say, "this is too much." The second comes when July marches home from the outland after some twenty years. Mary shakes with an inward desire to take him in again, but she steels herself to dismiss the wretch. It is only when July glimpses eight illegitimate children that he is willing to give up and say farewell. These two touches make an otherwise sound book seem untrue for the moment.

> *John R. Chamberlain, "Julia Peterkin Writes Again of the Gullah Negroes," in* The New York Times Book Review, *October 21, 1928, p. 4.*

HERSCHEL BRICKELL

["**Scarlet Sister Mary**"] represents a very definite advance in the technical handling of rarely interesting material, without any sacrifice of the notable qualities of honesty, sincerity, sympathy, and keen observation that made "**Black April**" and "**Green Thursday**" landmarks of first importance in the south's current literary revival.

"**Green Thursday,**" a collection of short stories, left behind it an impression of freshness; it sounded a new note in the handling of rich race material by a Southern author. The stories in the volume were wholly free from the several *clichés* that have attached themselves to the treatment of the negro in fiction. They had a primal vigor, a direct and at times shocking brutality, prompted, however, by nothing except the author's unmistakable desire to set down the life about her wholly and without mitigation. . . .

"**Black April,**" among its other striking qualities, showed Mrs. Peterkin's ability to create living characters, and at the same time to give them universality. It furnished, too, a picture of life on a remote Southern plantation that is the finest thing of its kind in American literature.

"**Black April**" suffered from overcrowding. Mrs. Peterkin was over-lavish with incident, with folk-lore, with characters. The book seemed to be born of an overpowering inner urge, and to have eluded the shaping power that would have given it more sharply realized form, made it a more admirable work of art. As in "**Green Thursday**" there was emphasis upon the physically disagreeable, which, while wholly honest on the part of Mrs. Peterkin, troubled a good many readers.

In "**Scarlet Sister Mary**" Mrs. Peterkin seems calmer and surer of herself. The book has a direct simplicity that is perfectly suited to the subject. It has, besides, the deeply felt and felicitously expressed beauty of the plantation that is its setting, an occasional loveliness of picture that is never tinged with artificiality. Mrs. Peterkin has sacrificed nothing of consequence to write more easily and more happily.

Mary is introduced to us as a slim and handsome girl of fifteen, well brought up, and good. She marries July. . . . When he leaves, Mary is broken-hearted. She grieves until at last the hard lesson is learned that no man is worth a drop of water from a woman's eye, and then she embarks upon the career that is to earn for her the characterization of Scarlet Sister. . . .

Without straining in the least, Mrs. Peterkin has made a pagan figure of Mary with something closely akin to magnificence about her; a reincarnation of the Bona Dea, the Great Mother, whose worship has endured so long in the world because it is so profoundly and surely rooted in a fundamental human emotion. Mary thrives because she is able to realize to the fullest the physical completion of motherhood; she is not concerned with the moral scruples of the community, neither is she disturbed by economic difficulties. . . .

Mrs. Peterkin has managed in "**Scarlet Sister Mary**" to keep the dialect at a minimum. What is left is skilfully handled, and there is sufficient to give the narrative the needed flavor. "**Scarlet Sister Mary**" should find an even wider audience than "**Black April.**" It very firmly establishes its author as an interpreter of negro character; but more than this, it leaves no room for doubt that she is a novelist whose work has enduring quality.

> *Herschel Brickell, "Pagan Heroine," in* The Saturday Review of Literature, *Vol. V, No. 15, November 3, 1928, p. 318.*

ROBERT HERRICK

"**Black April**" was a remarkable book, possibly the most convincing presentation of the Negro that has yet been made by a white person. More than that, it was a considerable work of art. With a mastery of dialect and folk-lore unequalled and with a pervasive sense of the plantation background from which the black figures emerged, Mrs. Peterkin so completely dramatized all her material that it was almost impossible to tell whether the writer was an alien observer or a Negro become wholly conscious and expressive. That sense of strangeness of the looker-on, which the most sympathetic treatment of the Negro by the white has always betrayed, as if the "superior" were trying in vain to comprehend the "inferior" across the racial barrier, was never once present. In "**Black April**" Mrs.

Peterkin did not explain or exploit: she created the black world in its own terms. . . .

In this second book, **"Scarlet Sister Mary,"** Mrs. Peterkin has failed, at least in the first part, to merge herself fully with her material. These introductory chapters are told as the white observer might see them, descriptively, and not especially well told: the story wanders, scatters. Rich as is the background and firmly drawn as are the few characters, the story does not move of itself and sweep the reader at once into its own atmosphere, as did **"Black April."** This failure to dramatize becomes less apparent as the story passes from the girl's to the woman's life of Si May-e. Something of the inevitability which made **"Black April"** such a remarkable first novel takes the place of the earlier fumbling. The profound change in Si May-e's character wrought by July's abandonment is told rather than presented: it seems more due to the author's wilful desire than to the black woman's own nature, as does her triumphant rejection of the returned husband. Nevertheless, Si May-e holds firmly together as a human being and comes into her own, with a brood of a dozen children, more or less, no two of them being by the same father. In her fecundity, kindness, health and happiness, as well as in her indifference to social stigma, she embodies many essential qualities of all strong women, more frankly because more primitively than would be possible for her sophisticated white sisters. (p. 172)

There is more concentration upon the one character in **"Scarlet Sister Mary"** than in **"Black April,"** less crowding of folk material, and an even richer atmosphere of the plantation. . . . And yet this second book, like the first, remains less a story than a series of pictures. . . . There are so many of these, they are so rich in atmosphere and so true in detail, that the book becomes something more than a novel—the revelation of a race, which has lived with the whites for hundreds of years, without becoming known beneath the skin. One feels that Mrs. Peterkin has much more to reveal, and to create. (pp. 172-73)

> *Robert Herrick, "A Study in Black," in* The New Republic, *Vol. LVII, No. 734, December 26, 1928, pp. 172-73.*

ARCHER WINSTEN

[The isolated world of *Bright Skin*], for most of us necessarily exotic, has authentic beauty and more than a touch of nobility. Mrs. Peterkin's simplicity of style matches with perfect art a subject equally devoid of complication. But readers who are familiar with her previous work will note that *Black April* and *Scarlet Sister Mary* had the same subject and are not improved upon. Details may vary, but the essence is the same. And it happens to be an all-pervading essence which is expressed in similar phraseology and incident. Moreover, the characters, nicely individualized within a single book, are to some extent repeated under different names in each subsequent book. For instance, Blue in *Bright Skin* and Breeze in *Black April* might be the same small boy.

Instead of starting out to write a tetralogy or a *Forsyte Saga* and setting up a time sequence, genealogies and the devices of that sort of work, Mrs. Peterkin has begun anew with each book. She has apparently thought that a different plot and some variation of character would constitute another novel. For some writers this would be true, but not for her. The graphic incident is the brick of her novel-building. And there seems to be a natural limit to significant character variation among her simple

people. Either that, or she as a white woman is not able to delve deeply into the secret places of another race.

Mrs. Peterkin has written four volumes, but they are only one novel. She must now decide whether to start a new novel or add another volume to her already masterful creation of Negro life. In the latter case she must remember that her stage is fully set. The heroic figure of April begging to be buried "in a man-size box" though his legs have been amputated, and the marvellous, ever-sinning Si' May'e lend to their stories a crowning quality which is lacking in *Bright Skin*. For in the end Cricket has eluded us; she has gone where the author cannot follow, and her going confirms our suspicion that we have learned little which was not said in the earlier volumes. Luckily the stuff of Mrs. Peterkin's novels bears repeating uncommonly well. (pp. 107-08)

> *Archer Winsten, in a review of "Bright Skin," in* The Bookman, *New York, Vol. LXXV, No. I, April, 1932, pp. 107-08.*

JOHN CHAMBERLAIN

In **"Bright Skin"** Mrs. Peterkin has made an attempt to repeat the episodic pattern of **"Black April,"** though on a diminished scale, and the book will suffer, perhaps unjustly, from the inevitable comparison with the earlier work. Yet for all the similarity of pattern, there is a difference in intention between the two books. **"Black April"** depended less upon intimate characterization than upon a mass effect; its hero, the gigantic plantation foreman, April, being of heroic proportions, was also of the heroic generality; and the background of hog-killings, duck hunts, dancing and cotton picking, against which April's generalized figure was projected, usurped the book and made it the work of enduring beauty that it is.

The present work, too, makes much of the background of the sea-island country of Carolina. . . . [This tends] to give the work the cyclic, episodic effect of **"Black April."** But there is more of an attempt at intimacy here; the heroic note has gone. And because the nature of Mrs. Peterkin's talent is what it is, the loss is genuine.

The truth is that Mrs. Peterkin's ability is not a dramatic ability; it is descriptive. . . . But in **"Bright Skin"** Mrs. Peterkin has attempted to reconcile her descriptive talent with an intimate record of the crises of young Blue, who grows up in what was once the Carolina rice country. Blue comes to manhood, marries Cricket, his "bright skin" cousin, under peculiar circumstances; is deserted by her; lives with another woman, attempts to get Cricket back, and ultimately lets her get a divorce so that she can live in Harlem with Man Jay. But we never feel that Blue has grown up; to the last, Mrs. Peterkin treats him as a boy, sentimentally. . . .

In the early stages of the book, before Blue has definitely fallen in love with Cricket, the writing is easier, events drop into place with a sureness of touch, and the general atmosphere of the mixed Christian and pagan life of the Negro community is brought to a glowing life. As always, Mrs. Peterkin writes of the four seasons with a sensitivity that is a joy to read. . . . The easy morals of a community that is certainly not Christian in the Pauline sense are handled by Mrs. Peterkin with a delicacy that makes them the more natural to their setting; the Negroes simply do things a certain way, and that is all there is to it. It is only when Blue has let Cricket know that he wants her in spite of her being a contrarious "no-nation" girl (a mixture of black and white blood), that Mrs. Peterkin gets into deep water; then, forced to abandon the description, she becomes a secondhand writer, getting at problems of miscegenation, illegitimacy, migration from the South to Harlem, and so on, by what she has been led to believe, through looking on, is the way her people would act. Her real forte is a re-creation of natural beauty, passed through her own sensitive mind; it is too bad that she has seen fit to attempt a drama which she cannot wholly feel, or at least does not wholly communicate on paper.

> *John Chamberlain, "Mrs. Peterkin's New Novel of Negro Life," in* The New York Times Book Review, *April 10, 1932, p. 7.*

WELBOURN KELLEY

All good South Carolinians have three salient characteristics: they believe that theirs is the last home of true Southern chivalry and aristocracy, they think that Ambrose Gonzales was the greatest writer of regional literature who ever lived, and they love and respect Julia Peterkin. (p. 377)

In her latest book ["**Roll, Jordon, Roll**"], a romantic ethnology of the Gullah Negro . . . , Mrs. Peterkin bids for a place beside Gonzales in the critical esteem of her own State. . . . Mrs. Peterkin has softened her Gullah dialect in order that people not fortunate enough to have been born in the State could understand her stories. (pp. 377, 382)

In "**Roll, Jordan, Roll**," Mrs. Peterkin uses little dialect, yet her artistry is such that the Gullah Negro's lazy chatter, rhythmic movement, low-down blues, or hysterical prayer is on every page. Her method is this: she knows the Negro men, women, and children who live about her, and she tells their stories for them with such sympathy and understanding that one often forgets the presence of the author and believes he is hearing the stories from the Negroes' own lips. . . .

[The] chapters flow on, each one adding to the ethnological pattern of how a Gullah Negro is born, what he eats, drinks, and thinks, how he lives, loves, marries, works, and dies. (p. 382)

> *Welbourn Kelley, "Plantation Lore," in* The Saturday Review of Literature, *Vol. X, No. 24, December 30, 1933, pp. 377, 382.*

HARLAN HATCHER

Julia Peterkin's work offers an entertaining ethnology of the Gullah Negroes who live by the hundreds on the Peterkin cotton plantation near Fort Motte in the center of South Carolina. As seen by "Cap'ns wife," it is a romantic survival into the modern age of an old and exotic group of Negroes. They are untouched by the mechanized and changing world; they belong somewhere in the golden days of happy servitude before the Slavery War.

In complete contrast with T. S. Stribling's point of view, Julia Peterkin has remained thoroughly objective, with the interest of a painter rather than of a moralist or sociologist. Instead of exclaiming, How unjust! How cruel!, she has observed, How quaint the Gullah Negroes are! and has proceeded to exhibit them in the spirit of a Southern hostess on a large plantation showing her northern guests her unique collection. She has lived intimately among these people, she has doctored and judged and cared for them, and she knows them in all their

moods. . . . There is no spirit of criticism or reform, there are no social problems which extend beyond the plantation. The people, for the most part, are reasonably happy and content, and at the farthest remove from the "new," educated, assertive Negro of T. S. Stribling and New York. The mode is realistic, and the structure of the novels is just tight enough to make a narrative of separate episodes which she has taken directly from the life. She simplifies the dialect so that it can be understood but without actually falsifying it, and she catches the easy, relaxed pace of the life she describes. The Julia Peterkin novels, particularly **Black April,** are a definite part of American fiction. (pp. 146-47)

> *Harlan Hatcher, "Exploiting the Negro," in his* Creating the Modern American Novel, *Farrar & Rinehart Incorporated, 1935, pp. 140-54.**

VERNON LOGGINS

[There] have been in America many negro writers of exceptional skill and talent. . . . But as yet no negro writer has been able to detach himself from the problem of the color line and stand out boldly as an artist and nothing else. Racial discrimination has been his bar. When that bar is removed, he will write about his people as no white could possibly write about them. Of all the whites who have made the attempt, Julia Peterkin is the truest and the finest—not excepting Joel Chandler Harris, whose Uncle Remus tales are established classics, nor Dubose Heyward, whose *Porgy* ought to become a classic, nor Roark Bradford, who is the real creator of America's greatest folk-play, *The Green Pastures* (Marc Connelly's part in the authorship of this play was mere transcription). It was indignation at the way these writers and others dealt with the negro that spurred Mrs. Peterkin to write. She began with the passion to be sincere and fair and just, and she has retained it. (pp. 216-17)

Mrs. Peterkin created in *Scarlet Sister Mary* an important social document and a tale of the greatest charm. The book maintains throughout that closeness to reality and that unhesitating verity of detail which must characterize all valid regional writing. But the quiet mellowness of the language and the byplay of picturesque embellishment lift the book to the level of the highly imaginative poetic. (pp. 218-19)

While the three books she has published since *Scarlet Sister Mary* do not quite attain its full folk-epic scope, not one of them contains a dull or tedious page. The Gullah speaks in her every phrase—and the Gullah is always different, always interesting. (p. 219)

> *Vernon Loggins, "Regional Variations," in his* I Hear America . . . Literature in the United States Since 1900, *Thomas Y. Crowell Company, Publishers, 1937, pp. 195-224.**

IRENE YATES

[Conjure lore] is interesting, and in Mrs. Peterkin's novels it becomes important in the characterization of the Negro as well. Mrs. Peterkin's Negroes are unreasoning and inconsistent. They may go to church and shout with fine frenzy, and leave to procure a conjure that will cast a spell. . . .

This conjure lore is important, too, in Mrs. Peterkin's plots. An episode in **Bright Skin** centers about the use of a conjure and its evil effects. In this instance the conjure is sought as a help in time of trouble in the love affairs of the married. Wes, Aun Missie's husband, had taken to staying away from home at night. Aun Missie, who obviously was a believer in conjure, betook herself to Big Pa, who obligingly made a charm that would measure up to Missie's specifications. . . .

The conjure worked, but not as Big Pa or Missie hoped it would. Wes did stop his night-roaming, but he stopped roaming altogether, for not long after the conjure was used on him, Wes got into a fight and was stuck with an ice-pick. His condition became serious. When he discovered the bags under his pillow, he attributed his condition to them and complained resentfully, showing real fear of the magic that was operating in his fate. . . . (p. 140)

Throughout . . . Mrs. Peterkin makes the Negro's faith in conjures useful to her plot. It is natural for people to seek causes, and it is easy for the Negro to point out false reasons as he, in his ignorance, attempts to reconcile cause and effect. He seeks no proof by testing. An occurrence or two, such as the preceding, establishes a law. Big Pa is confident that his conjure was indeed a powerful one; the other Negroes regard the whole episode with fear and with an increased faith in conjures. Mrs. Peterkin uses the belief just as it would exist in the life of the Negro. The razor or ice-pick fight is common; the use of the conjure is common; and the belief that the result, death, is brought about by the cause, conjure, is perfectly natural. The conjuring as a background for the incident heightens interest and colors the entire episode. (p. 141)

Probably in *Black April* more than in any other story does the black magic of the conjure become one with a tragic fate. The ultimate catastrophe is brought about by two curses and two conjures. From the uttering of the first curse to the denouement, the reader feels that bitter tragedy is the only possibility. (pp. 142-43)

In *Bright Skin, Scarlet Sister Mary,* and *Black April,* not only does the use of conjuring serve in making a true representation of the Negro character, but it becomes important to the artistry of plot development. Wes could have died from the ice-pick fight without Missie's charm, but the charm increases the effectiveness of the episode. Mary could have been the same Mary without the love conjure, but the situation would have lost interest thereby. Black April's fate could have been the same without the curses, but with them the entire situation becomes more powerful, more humanly interesting, more dramatic. The conjure provides the element of fear, suspense, impending danger, and the reader shares the character's emotion, which is rooted in belief in the conjure.

From the conjure to the folk cure is but a step. In fact, some of the cures are nothing more than a kind of black magic involving hocus-pocus that anyone might practice without the help of the conjure doctor. (p. 144)

The Negro knows and uses a multitude of such cures, some of them revolting, some amusing, and most of them pathetically useless. . . .

Much of this matter is more or less incidental; however, it serves to show the Negro with his everyday problems and his solutions for them. Such cures are part of the daily life of the Negro, and they are introduced into the story just as they would occur any day or every day. (p. 145)

It is clear from this brief examination of Julia Peterkin's novels that she has skilfully woven into her stories a mass of folklore dealing with conjures and cures. This lore is interesting in itself.

And . . . in Mrs. Peterkin's hands it becomes a means of enriching her art especially in the characterization of the Negro and in the development of the plot. (p. 149)

Irene Yates, "Conjures and Cures in the Novels of Julia Peterkin," in Southern Folklore Quarterly, *Vol. X, No. 2, June, 1946, pp. 137-49.*

FRANK DURHAM

Most people think of Julia Peterkin's literary career as beginning with the publication, in September, 1924, of her first book, *Green Thursday,* a collection of twelve short stories and sketches of plantation life. *Green Thursday* did bring her both national and international attention and led to her becoming a novelist, but, in fact, for three years before the book appeared, she had been publishing starkly realistic short stories, sometimes grim and terrible in their anticipation of what has been called the Southern Gothic school, but tempered by an abiding compassion and by an understanding of the life of the South Carolina Gullah Negro. In such stories as **"Over the River," "A Baby's Mouth," "Missy's Twins,"** and **"The Foreman,"** she reached a level of achievement not often matched by her work in *Green Thursday* and her novels. Throughout her career as a novelist she continued to publish short fiction. And in the novels themselves—*Black April, Scarlet Sister Mary,* and *Bright Skin*—the hand of the author of the short story is frequently evident; for her novels, notably *Black April,* are often episodic, relying for their effectiveness on the rounded incident rather than on a rigidly architectured structure.

As a writer in the short story form Mrs. Peterkin deserves to be remembered, for several of her stories are worthy to stand beside pieces by William Faulkner, Eudora Welty, Flannery O'Connor, and other Southern practitioners in the form. Until [the publication of *Collected Short Stories of Julia Peterkin*], most of her works of short fiction have lain unavailable in the pages of long-deceased magazines or out-of-print anthologies. Only her Pulitzer Prize-winning novel, *Scarlet Sister Mary,* remains on the bookstands. Such neglect is unfortunate and improper. One of the purposes of the present volume is to remedy this situation.

Not only as an artist but also as a keen observer of and commenter on the Southern Negro, Julia Peterkin has much to say to us today. She was one of the first Americans to write of the Negro truthfully, sympathetically, without bias, without an axe to grind, or a proclamation to proclaim. Shearing away most of the sentimental distortions of the plantation tradition and equally avoiding the shrill astigmatism of the propagandists, in her best short stories Julia Peterkin sees the Negro plain, and she sees him as a human being with dignity and with stature. She leaves far behind the misty-eyed paternalism of Thomas Nelson Page, and she feels no temptation to depict the educated cardboard Negro in confrontations with the biased whites as did T. S. Stribling in *Birthright* (1922) and Walter White in *The Fire in the Flint* (1924). In some ways her work is comparable to Jean Toomer's *Cane* (1923) in its emphasis on the Negro's "Negritude" and his closeness to the life-giving earth—but it is also different from *Cane* in that it seeks less the lyrical style of Toomer and more the direct and unadorned presentation of truth. (pp. 1-2)

Frank Durham, in an introduction to Collected Short Stories of Julia Peterkin *by Julia Peterkin, edited by Frank Durham, University of South Carolina Press, 1970, pp. 1-2.*

ELIZABETH BOATWRIGHT COKER

[It] would be hard to think of any writer in America in the twenties and early thirties more original and unusual than Julia Mood Peterkin. Obviously she wanted recognition, indeed fame; she worked toward that end with a dedicated seriousness. In her place and time the subjects she chose and the candor with which she approached them were considered outrageous. . . .

Julia was the first American writer to tell stories of blacks who itched, laughed, tilled the soil, ate, lusted, grieved and died just like whites. People they were, among whom she walked every day. (p. 3)

Though the stories [gathered for *The Collected Short Stories of Julia Peterkin*] are largely episodic and anecdotal and told in dialect, a rereading of them today, by an eye accustomed to the new realism, shows that they take precedence in the realm of the explicit over the fashionable stream-of-conscious and writer-tells-all techniques of such deliberate shockers as *The Love Machine* and *The Valley of the Dolls*.

Julia constantly used her own vivid personal nature, her ability to record what went on around her, but there is nowhere any hint of the autobiographical except in the short **"Seeing Things,"** published in *The Century,* telling of her bride-days on the plantation. There is no self-exposure. No self-gratification is necessary for dramatic tension and effect. She does not rely on the lurid details of sex to let you know what is going on in the dark. (p. 6)

She makes no personal claims on our sympathy and acceptance. Satisfied to tell of the things and happenings that concerned and fascinated her, she cried not of the woes of the world; only the woes and wonders that at a certain moment actually happened to her people. Nor does she attempt to impersonate the soul of her characters. She contents herself with their conversations and reactions to their fate. (pp. 6-7)

Only in her last—*Roll Jordan Roll*—is the stark adjectiveless prose of the early days deliberately enriched with more sophisticated treatment. The reader sighs, disappointed. The wine has been watered. The effervescence has fizzled out. She has succumbed to popularity. Even in her own state! (p. 7)

> *Elizabeth Boatwright Coker, "An Appreciation of Julia Peterkin and 'The Collected Short Stories of Julia Peterkin',"* in The South Carolina Review, *Vol. 3, No. 2, June, 1971, pp. 3-7.*

BRAINARD CHENEY

Forty years after they were written, what can the negro stories of the late Julia Peterkin, a white South Carolina plantation mistress, say to the black man today? How can they speak to the present situation in this country? to the issue of race? What can these forgotten tales possibly tell us? (p. 173)

It was in 1924 that the publication of *Green Thursday,* her first collection of short stories, arrested national and even international attention. The negro community on "Blue Brook" plantation presented a fresh literary scene. But what was essentially new in Julia Peterkin's projection of her characters was the terms of their responsibility. Then prevailing in the South was the threadbare and incomplete myth of the irresponsible negro, whom the responsible white man had to take care of. In the North, little Eva still came over the broken ice on the river to escape a Southern Simon Legree, and into the alms of a Republican public welfare, but remained at a safe literary distance.

In *Green Thursday,* the white man wasn't on the stage at all, and, to the literate world, Julia Peterkin's negroes showed themselves to be astonishingly human, in their generosities and their cruelties, their virtues and their sins. In her simple primitive rural community, in its material poverty, there was a compensating richness of humanity. Her negroes supplemented their diet of corn pone and fatback with the warm blood of family and feud, and the reality of religion and superstition. To an even then decaying great society these direct dramas of love and labor, of hate and fear, at times of heroism before a grim reality, and, through them all, a pervasive compassion and endurance—these simple tales were, to an oversophisticated world, indeed refreshing. (pp. 174-75)

To an urban sophisticate, to many sophisticated negroes, even back in the 'twenties, the people of her stories must have seemed but little removed from their aboriginal African culture. And to today's Blacks, aside from furnishing appalling proof of the recentness of plantation peonage, they may seem even closer to Africa. But the similarities are deceptive. If one reflects upon the matter in the light of history, the impressive thing about Julia Peterkin's blacks on Blue Brook plantation is not so much the persistence of their superstition as the reality of their Christianity. This is a deep and a wide gap. If anywhere in the United States negroes have a valid claim to blackness— at least, perhaps, to black skins—it is on the South Carolina coastal plantations. But this fact does not establish them as Africans. And this does not establish Africa with them, either.

A revival of Julia Peterkin's stories may not be helpful to the "Afro" myth. But it should prove wholesome for the negro leadership's sense of reality—sense of history, too. And a sense of history isn't easy to come by in the midst of an emotional partisan conflict. What negro leaders need to perceive (if they claim the fatherhood of Abraham, or even a statesmanlike responsibility to their race) is that History will not see the negro's servitude, in the American bondage of his forebears, as the thing of lasting importance to the negro. Nor is their suffering, nor the injustice done them, nor even the inhumanity shown them, the lasting importance. The lasting importance of 250 years of slavery in what is now the United States is that through this experience, the negro has had modern civilization inculcated in him. Blue Brook plantation is the nether proof of it. I think it is equally important for some white men in this country to realize this, too. We may not be identical twins. But we are brothers in the bondage of this small earth's evolving civilization—evolving with many aches and pains and fevers, evolving despite widespread rot and crumbling.

But there is more in Julia Peterkin's old stories for the modern negro, or the post-modern negro, if you will, than the evidence of his sharing in the Western Christian tradition. . . . I think *Scarlet Sister Mary,* her most famous work, is a good novel; but her finest and most powerful pieces are in short-story form. Take for example that gem of understatement **"A Baby's Mouth"**. It isn't easy to make physical deformity, a baby born without a mouth, an heroic subject. But Julia Peterkin's brief tale has the awesomeness, the dignity, and the power of Greek tragedy.

There are thirty-three pieces of fiction in [*The Collected Short Stories of Julia Peterkin*] which Mr. Durham selected as "representative of the several facets of the author's talents". Roughly in chronological order, they also trace "the development of

[Mrs. Peterkin's] skill in the short form''. He has arranged them as stories and sketches coming before *Green Thursday,* then the twelve related stories that comprise the volume of that title. There are in addition seven of the best of her stories that came afterward. (pp. 175-76)

I would agree with Mr. Durham [see excerpt above] that, though they came early in her writing career, **"Missy's Twins"**, **"The Foreman"**, and **"Over the River"**, in addition to **"A Baby's Mouth"**, reached a level of achievement not often matched by her later work. I share his opinion, too, that **"Over the River"**, a deaf-mute girl's pilgrimage in search of the father of her unborn child, anticipating a similar journey in William Faulkner's *Light in August,* is, if grimmer, ''more artistically complete with the death of the child and [the prospect] of the mother's return to her home''. (pp. 176-77)

But I would single out at least three of the stories from *Green Thursday* as signal achievements, also. There is **"Ashes"**, in which an ancient negro woman, about to be evicted from her cabin by a ''Snopes'' who has built his house in her front yard, burns down the almost completed building and is protected in her arson by a white sheriff of the old order. It is one of the few stories in which Julia Peterkin deals directly with race relations in terms of the old sentimental myth. But nowhere else in fiction have I seen this handled with more realism and tact.

In **"Meeting"**, little Missy's first prayer-meeting is led by ''Daddy'' Cato, who has suffered paralysis on one side of his face and tells the congregation that he has been kissed by ''the Stranger'' (Death). . . . Mrs. Peterkin's brief narrative achieves . . . [hearty humor] without descending into farce, and it embodies, too, the mystery of the supernatural. . . .

Finally, **"Plum Blossoms"** (the incident in which Kildee realizes that he has fallen in love with Missy, the waif whom his wife brought into the house to wait on her and who has now grown up) is, in its quiet realism, one of the most elevated, beautiful, and compassionate handlings of the triangle theme I have ever encountered. But the title story, **"Green Thursday"**, and a half-dozen others are equally good, if less conspicuous. (p. 177)

> Brainard Cheney, ''Can Julia Peterkin's 'Genius' Be Revived for Today's Black Myth-Making?'' in The Sewanee Review, Vol. LXXX, No. 1, Winter, 1972, pp. 173-79.

THOMAS H. LANDESS

[Julia Peterkin] deserves a greater measure of critical attention than she has received. She was, after all, a Pulitzer Prize winner during a time when many intellectuals still were agreeing with Mencken that the South was the ''Sahara of the Bozart.'' In the late 1920's and early 1930's she was acclaimed in Eastern literary circles and in the black intellectual community as the Southerner who best understood the black experience, who portrayed without prejudice or condescension black characters in a black world.

To be sure, the Pulitzer Prize is no absolute measure of lasting literary fame, nor should a preoccupation with matters racial command automatic attention; yet there is still more to be said for her. At her best she is a consummate artist and almost without exception her narratives are powerful, even shocking in their spare intensity. No one has probed the potential horrors of rural life with greater candor than she. To a generation

charmed by an old lady's necrophilia or the theft of a girl's wooden leg, Mrs. Peterkin has much to offer. (p. 221)

[With] one or two early exceptions, the sordid, grotesque element in her work is thematically functional; and the subtlety with which she weaves archetype and allusion into the fabric of her primitive narratives sometimes tricks the casual or skeptical reader into a sleepy assent to something less than the full aesthetic experience.

In order to understand and accept these generalizations, one must first *read* Mrs. Peterkin—as I suspect several of her more prominent detractors have not—and the place to begin is the *Reviewer* sketches; for they provide valuable insight into her gradual development as a prose stylist and ''builder'' of fiction. The earliest—as she herself maintained—were fragmentary and crude. (p. 222)

An example of such a story is **"A Baby's Mouth,"** published in May of 1922. In this tale of horror Maum Hannah (a character who appears in all Mrs. Peterkin's major works) is acting as a midwife at the birth of a child, and after the delivery she discovers that the infant is deformed—born without a mouth. Because there is no doctor nearby, she borrows a razor from a squeamish neighbor and slices a mouth so that the child may suckle at the mother's breast. The scene ends in a tranquility that can hardly be shared by the reader.

A second sketch [**"Missy's Twins"**] even elicited a cautionary note from H. L. Mencken, who called the piece ''effective but terrible.'' The anecdote is a fragmentary account of members of a white family who leave for the North worrying about a black girl's pregnancy. When they return, they find that the girl has given birth to twins, both of whom have died. But this is not the ultimate tragedy, for the graves of the babies have been plundered by the dogs, and thus the dead are denied even the consolation of a peaceful repose. At this stage one can sympathize with Mrs. Peterkin's critics, for these incidents do seem unjustifiably sordid. Had they been rendered more fully, invested with significant human dimensions, they might have been self-redeeming.

By July of 1925, however, she had begun to realize the larger potential of her subject matter, as evidenced by her final contribution to the *Reviewer,* a narrative entitled **"Manners."** Far from being a fragmentary sketch, **"Manners"** is a full-blown short story, one of the best of Mrs. Peterkin's efforts in this genre. . . . With its careful and confident exploration of consciousness, **"Manners"** signalled Mrs. Peterkin's graduation to a wider range of artistic possibilities than one journal could contain. (pp. 222-23)

[*Green Thursday* is] a collection of twelve sketches and stories involving Maum Hannah, Killdee, Rose, and Missie—a black family whose struggles with the land, the elements, and their individual consciences provide the subject matter for what can best be described as a loose plot highlighted by moments of primitive power. The book has as its chief virtues the same qualities which characterize the best of the *Reviewer* sketches. For one thing, the ancient and basic conflict of man with nature is presented as a stark drama, filled with danger and cosmic terror.

Another virtue of the book is its faithful depiction of the special Gullah culture found in the South Carolina Low Country. Aside from her accurate rendition of the strange dialect, she also explores the practices and doctrines of the primitive black church, a subject which contemporary historians have left largely untouched. This exploration is thematically linked with the more basic life struggle, because it is the church which is the primary enemy of the "natural man" who must survive in the face of taboos and strictures which limit his ability to cope with elemental forces. (p. 224)

[Mrs. Peterkin has stated that many of the incidents in her books are based on fact. In *Black April,* the] story she chose "out of her experience" was that of a beloved foreman whose terrible ordeal and death had first driven her to writing, almost as a form of therapy.

Yet she was either naive or shrewd when she suggested that she had not attempted to improve on reality. A comparison between *Black April* and her earlier treatment in the *Reviewer* of the foreman's trouble suggests just how much she had learned in her years of apprenticeship. While there are some structural difficulties in the novel, her "blending of incidents" lifts the climactic episode to new heights and informs it with a thematic complexity that approaches the highest level of literary sophistication.

For one thing, she combines with her narrative of the hero's downfall an "initiation story" which is thematically significant itself and at the same time adds a new dimension to the primary plot. (p. 225)

The ending . . . unites the two narrative strands and to some extent justifies Mrs. Peterkin's lengthy catalogue of religious beliefs and superstitions, which at times seems little more than interpolated folklore.

The basic design of *Black April*—the tragedy of a great man as viewed through the eyes of a lesser figure—is a familiar structure in literature. One immediately thinks of *Moby Dick, The Great Gatsby, All the King's Men,* as well as the best works of Joseph Conrad, Mrs. Peterkin's favorite novelist.

The presence of the focal character Breeze—as in these other works—provides the aesthetic distance so necessary to the operation of what Northrop Frye calls the "high mimetic mode," the rendition of a hero who resembles Aristotle's magnanimous man. It is this hero who provides the terror of tragedy, while in the lesser figure one sees the active operation of pity. It is interesting to note that in portions of her novel Mrs. Peterkin deliberately echoes Aristotle's language.

If *Black April* is Mrs. Peterkin's tragedy then *Scarlet Sister Mary* is her comedy. This novel . . . is concerned with the adult life of a remarkably vital woman from her excommunication at the age of fifteen for sexual indiscretions to her "rebaptism" into the church after years of scandalous cohabitation with a series of well-satisfied men. (pp. 226-27)

The chief virtue of *Scarlet Sister Mary,* aside from its careful craftsmanship, is the portrayal of the main character—as spirited a heroine as almost any in modern American literature. As Mrs. Peterkin depicts her she is the embodiment of *joie de vivre,* an earthy woman who takes her pleasure where she can find it, rejoices in giving life to her nine children (eight illegitimate), and embodies the Christian virtues of charity and kindness to a fault. . . . Yet with all her amiability she is never a benign idiot. She has her hatreds, and they are as positive and passionate as her affections. For these reasons Mrs. Peterkin was more pleased with Mary than any of her other characters; and both readers and critics agreed. (p. 228)

The only thing that distinguishes [the novel *Bright Skin*] from the others is its initial preoccupation with questions of race and class as they are understood by the Gullah community. As soon as Blue, the hero of the novel, arrives at the plantation, he is introduced to the girl Cricket, his mulatto cousin. . . . Because the child has sprung from a relationship regarded as taboo, she is something of a pariah in the community. . . . (pp. 228-29)

For a while it seems as if Mrs. Peterkin will stick to her theme of racial bias and show Cricket combating the prejudices of a black community that is almost as fearful of "mongrelization" as the white community. . . .

However, after a tragic love affair and a brief, unsatisfactory marriage to Blue, she leaves the plantation for the bright lights of New York and eventually seeks a divorce. Significantly, her flight is not into the world of the white man but to Harlem; and this action is prompted by her allegiance to her grandfather, a black nationalist who preaches racial supremacy. The reader is left at home with Blue to repeat experiences which are explored in the other novels and to view Cricket from afar with regret and bemusement.

Bright Skin was not a critical success and marked the end of Mrs. Peterkin's career as a writer of fiction. . . . [Perhaps] she realized that she had exhausted her literary resources and could not break through the barrier of her own experience to create a fictional world of broader significance. (p. 229)

Like Pindar, however, she still had some arrows left in her quiver; and she published one significant book of non-fiction after *Bright Skin.* It was a collection of twenty-one sketches and essays entitled *Roll, Jordan, Roll,* and in this volume Mrs. Peterkin abandoned all pretense of overall unity and returned to the short portraits and anecdotes with which she had begun her literary career in the *Reviewer.* Indeed a number of the pieces are slightly revised versions of those earlier sketches— modified, improved, but in essence the same material. . . .

But in addition to the old material, there are some new and important narratives, as well as expository and even polemical essays which have little of the sentimentality or zealous rage that are found in most discussions of the race issue by her contemporaries. Much of the material is unique, since it is derived from firsthand experience. Some of it is relevant only to the Gullahs—to their peculiar customs, superstitions, and folkways; but from the study a good deal can be predicated about the Southern black culture in general since the plantation world was the common heritage of virtually all descendants of slaves. Among the important questions which Mrs. Peterkin discusses are the origins and nature of the plantation, relationships between the sexes, the church and religion, beliefs and superstitions, the family burial customs, and the perennial cycle of plantation life.

In *Roll, Jordan, Roll* Mrs. Peterkin has not averted her eyes from the hardships of the world in which these simple Gullahs live, but neither has she emphasized those hardships at the expense of the joys which were just as present in their community and just as real. She is honest in her vision, serving no social ideology and no political creed. There is no hint of the reformer in her, nor is she attacking the idea of reform. As in her novels, she is as close to the pure analyst as any modern commentator on black life has ever been. These sketches, essays, and vignettes are important social documents which embody essential lessons for a society embroiled in fierce racial conflicts which threaten to destroy its very fabric.

At present *Roll, Jordan, Roll,* and the four works of fiction, have been largely forgotten by those who write books and articles on Southern literature, and anyone who has read Mrs. Peterkin's minor masterpieces must wonder why. The truth of the matter may be that she has fallen into disrepute for some of the same reasons that she enjoyed her former popularity. She is still being read as a social historian. In the late 1920's and early 1930's she was regarded by many responsible critics as the finest contemporary portrayer of black life and culture. W.E.B. Du Bois, Walter White, Joel Spingarn, Paul Robeson—all ratified her credentials as sociologist because at that time blacks in literature were too often hidden behind the masks of popular stereotypes: the Happy-go-lucky Minstrel, the Faithful Retainer, the Shiftless Scoundrel. Later, however, after the masks had been stripped away by Realists like Mrs. Peterkin, the battlers for social justice began to endorse new stereotypes: the Noble Martyr, the Sadistic Landowner, the Crusading Liberal. And so the tide of critical opinion changed. (pp. 230-31)

[Many critics now dismiss Mrs. Peterkin] largely, I suspect, because they cannot read a work like *Scarlet Sister Mary* without worrying about the current political orthodoxy. Thus literature which deals with black characters is, by definition, obsolescent in a dynamic society. . . .

[There] is little sign that she will be understood in the near future as anything more than a bad sociologist, a writer of the kind she despised and categorically denounced on more than one occasion. Yet she is a genuine literary talent whose works embody fictional values which have little or nothing to do with the blackness of her characters. Indeed that blackness is so absorbed by the human dimensions of her narratives that the reader all but forgets about it once he has adjusted to the peculiar fictional world that Mrs. Peterkin creates. The questions her work poses for the critics are finally literary rather than social or political, however valuable her observations and lore concerning the Gullahs she knew. Unfortunately, we are living in a time when non-fiction has replaced fiction as the staple of the intelligentsia and novelists are abandoning their craft to pursue careers in journalism or else to run for public office. Under such conditions, one can hardly expect Julia Peterkin to receive the reading she deserves. (p. 232)

> *Thomas H. Landess, "The Achievement of Julia Peterkin," in* The Mississippi Quarterly, *Vol. XXIX, No. 2, Spring, 1976, pp. 221-32.*

KIT VAN CLEAVE

One of the early writers on American blacks was Julia Peterkin. . . . Peterkin's literary oblivion after mid-century has been found a puzzle by the few readers who have attempted to understand it. . . .

Long before her death in 1961, Peterkin's works (*Green Thursday, Black April, Scarlet Sister Mary, Bright Skin*) had been largely ignored. . . .

Julia Peterkin's serious face can be found peering out of the pages of *The New York Times* or *Saturday Review* during the 1920's. A reading of her books further defines her obvious sincerity in presenting a close description of the lifestyle of "gullah" blacks on a South Carolina plantation. Regardless of her intent to gain sympathy for her black characters, however, this white southern woman could not identify her sufficiently with her resources to write a completely realistic portrait of their lives.

While some critics of Peterkin's own time understood that she was trying to be objective without directly referring to racism,

these white critics could only discuss her writing in their own frame of reference. One anonymous *New York Times* critic gave Peterkin credit for writing unaffectedly about blacks "without conscious or unconscious belittling mockery in view of superior white achievement" [see excerpt above]. But he also delighted that in *Green Thursday* she had seasoned her story with "anti-kink lotion, ornate costumes, superstition, emotion, poverty, ignorance." (p. 235)

No one who has read Peterkin's works could establish that she was a racial bigot. But there is no doubt that her white perspective created a "hidden racism," and distorted her readers' perspective of the actual suffering of South Carolina blacks. Her omissions of basic and daily realities in the lives of her prototypes eliminated from all her major works the racial tension that is an inherent characteristic of southern history and literature.

First of all, Peterkin, in each of her four books, almost totally omits the white frame around her black characters. There are two white men and a sheriff in *Green Thursday,* and a white shopkeeper/postman in *Black April;* these four comprise the total white personnel in the books. While Charles McD. Puckette attempts to explain this as a "singularly happy stroke" because it emphasizes further "the story of the Negroes' lives in relation to each other" [see excerpt above], elimination of whites from any important position in the lives of American blacks in the 1920s is at best unrealistic. At worst, it perpetuates many of the stereotypes in southern literature, and substantiates folkloric myths about black people in America.

Nancy M. Tischler [in her *Black Masks, Negro Characters in Modern Southern Fiction*] outlines these stereotypes as (1) faithful and faithless retainers, (2) the black Ulysses, (3) black sirens, (4) maladjusted mulattos, (5) the black Christ, (6) the black proletarian, and (7) the new southern black. . . . All of these character-types are included in Peterkin's books. Moreover, she has given her people all the archetypical talents and vices of the mythicized black: musical talent, love of dancing, bright clothing, sexual prowess and promiscuity, male irresponsibility with regard to the nuclear family unit, bloodlust, stupidity, long-suffering, and a host of other such familiar syndromes.

While the reader is saved from descriptions of pickaninnies eating watermelons, Peterkin has included enough blackeyed peas, cornbread, collard greens, hog parts, and hominy grits to satisfy the most fanatic soul-food devotee.

Basically, Peterkin's value lies in her ability to set down the lifestyle of black Americans to whom she was in some way close. (*Green Thursday* is dedicated to the memory of "Maum" Lavinia Berry.) At least she was interested enough to try writing about blacks. Her worthwhile material about voodoo, camp and church meetings, and black social life could not have been imagined and indicates close and caring research.

Still, there is no statement, implicit or explicit, in her novels about ways to improve South Carolina blacks' difficult lives. By avoiding any mention of white people and *their* lifestyle, Peterkin could conveniently sidestep the racial violence, job discrimination, despair and oppression which certainly touched southern blacks in those days. (pp. 235-36)

Certainly no character in any of Peterkin's books is interested in the slightest in doing anything about civil rights, voting power, better education, or protest against white racism; she has not included these conflicts in her work. Her characters are apparently content to have a number of illegitimate children, "pleasure" themselves, work from the light of the early star until night tilling the soil and picking cotton, losing their relatives due to inferior or no medical care, and losing an arm or leg because of too much curiosity about farm machinery.

Because of Peterkin's deletion of the reality of black-white interaction, she becomes a purveyor of a myth that supports one held today by many white Southerners, of a "basic savagery" of black people that Hamilton Basso summed up in *Cinnamon Seed:* "Niggers do just three things—fight, fornicate, and fry fish." (p. 236)

Peterkin's characters are past the years of slavery. Other than the fact that the blacks still live on her fictional Blue Brook Plantation (and a few older characters remember their parents in Africa), no specific mention of slavery is made. The agonies endured by slaves, and the white slavemaster attitudes still around today, are conveniently not brought out.

The past, for Peterkin's blacks, lies in Africa, not America; they have no connection with the "cavalier tradition" W. J. Cash outlines as traditional for Southerners in *The Mind of the South.* Their religion is an emotional, superstitious Protestantism with an underlying synthesis of black-magic and voodoo-charm culture.

The family unit in these four novels is constantly broken up as the men and women both seek new sexual partners, with only a cursory glance at the marriage contract. While black men are shown as generally self-reliant and hard workers, they suffer by comparison with the white male individualism and chivalric code portrayed in southern literature of the 1920s.

And Peterkin herself, in some difficulty with her peers for dealing sympathetically with blacks in her books, avoided the topic of interracial sexual attraction, perhaps the biggest source of tension between black and white Southerners. The closest to such a reference comes in *Bright Skin,* when the mulatto Cricket and her inamorato Man Jay return wealthy from Harlem to Blue Brook. (pp. 236-37)

Here is a prime example of Julia Peterkin's hidden racism. Instead of discussing the situation openly, rather than dealing with the reality of biracial sex attraction, she solved the problem by a twist of fiction. The idea that an illiterate country black man could have all the white women he wanted in a Harlem night club would have been an issue too scorchingly hot to handle, whether or not it was true; Peterkin simply had her character prefer black women. . . .

Peterkin also does not deal in the slightest with any lingering shadows from the Civil War, and no comment is made about the emancipation of blacks. . . .

No criminal elements are seen in any of the Peterkin works, despite the statistical evidence that during the time of her peak blacks made up 31.3 per cent of the prison population in the South. . . . The gap between reality and fiction is readily apparent, and the validity of her Pulitzer Prize more doubtful.

A final reason for Peterkin's decline from the status of a nationally-popular novelist is the loose construction of her plots. (p. 237)

Peterkin came closest to black writers of the period in grasping the element of chance accident and imminent death that pervaded the lives of those who lived close to the primitive in an agrarian society. She does have some inspired moments in her descriptions of the helplessness felt by a simple people whose voodoo conjure did not often work to heal or to cure serious illness. . . .

Peterkin can also wax lush on occasion about the identity of the black man in relation to his simple farming existence; the life of Killdee in *Green Thursday* is a constant effort to keep the crops alive. Peterkin does a fine job in describing Killdee's life. . . .

[In such descriptions] Peterkin could get close to the black experience, but she was always outside it. . . .

Peterkin's avoidance of reality in many themes affecting black Americans of her day . . . helped her to gain a popularity among whites who knew nothing about black people, and probably among black people who had nothing else to read largely sympathetic to black life. . . .

With the growing awareness of conditions of life among U.S. black people, the publishing of American black writers, and a more objective reading of all American works by the public *and* prize committees, Julia Peterkin's kind of subtle, sensitive, status-quo-keeping literature has not held up. While many of her early readers thought she had captured the style of American blacks in their own communities and homes, more likely she had seen the most common mechanism of moving away from white oppressors: a codified, simplistic, impervious mask of passive acquiescence and "happiness" blacks have put on for years when confronted by whites. (p. 238)

> *Kit Van Cleave, "Julia Peterkin: Lost, and Good Riddance," in* The Crisis, *Vol. 83, No. 7, August-September, 1976, pp. 235-38.*

THOMAS H. LANDESS

At the moment Mrs. Peterkin is all but forgotten; and her fiction, when it is discussed at all, is usually dismissed as either malicious or trivial. . . .

The earliest rebirth of interest in her work, however, may come in the fields of sociology, folklore, and history, where she has much to offer the serious scholar. Certainly her portrayal of plantation life has a ring of authenticity that is lacking in most modern fiction on the subject; and since she was often more reporter than literary artist, she is all the more valuable as a primary source for historical research.

Both *Black April* and *Roll, Jordan, Roll* are priceless collections of black folklore and contain much material that bears close examination. Once again her artistic failures become positive virtues to serious students in the field. The tedious initiation of Breeze into plantation life is, at the same time, a compendious catalogue of Gullah attitudes on a variety of subjects; and the loose structure of her last major work allows for a more overt examination of black folkways than would otherwise have been possible. To be sure, these books are not, in and of themselves, examples of good scholarship; but they are certainly the raw material for more thoughtful investigation.

And one can envision a day—far in the future, to be sure— when historians will be able to look at the South dispassionately enough to see its essential complexity. To such excellent sages, Mrs. Peterkin will surely be a more reliable authority than Thomas Nelson Page on the one hand, or Erskine Caldwell on the other; for she lived in the interregnum between the tyrannies of two mythologies; and for a moment in time, with the scales of opinion perfectly balanced, she wrote honestly and clearly of what she knew to be true. (p. 150)

Thomas H. Landess, in his Julia Peterkin, *Twayne Publishers*, 1976, 160 p.

WILLIAM A. SESSIONS

It may be that certain literary works are written just at the moment when the society that each work describes is actually dissolving. Reading Plato or Dante or Faulkner, for example, we are conscious of a tenuous moment that the artist is holding for us. We sense the vitality of a fixed work of art, but within it we also sense communal values that are vanishing, even, we suspect, for readers in the writer's own time. In the work, structures of language embody moments in time that are changing into some larger and freer, or less free, or simply quite different, reality. The South Carolina novelist, Julia Peterkin, with an almost miraculous objectivity of scene and language, describes one such moment for a society of readers that has disappeared, like her subject. Peterkin's range was small and her work not major (despite her 1928 Pulitzer Prize), but what remains valid in her fiction and worth reconsideration, as a careful reading will show, is her rendering of a moment of transformation in southern life and American culture. (p. 736)

What was remarkable . . . was her courage, worthy of the teaching of her character Maum Hannah, in breaking out of a silence as profound as any described by recent feminists and daring to write in the 1920s on blacks and their habits of life, especially from the vantage point of their universality, their essential nature as human beings. This courage, taken with an obvious zest and delight (as the pace of all her letters, novels, and stories proves), clearly sustained Julia Peterkin amid social and communal pressures that few writers today can adequately understand. What especially called for courage from this middle-aged plantation mistress was that she had to face the subject matter itself, clearly and honestly, and then, more frighteningly, her own limitations as a writer, both in relationship to this subject matter and to her own isolated situation.

We can easily misunderstand these latter concerns because we dismiss her subject matter in our world popularly influenced by the theories of W. J. Cash and television spectacles like *Roots*. Peterkin's work seems so much romanticizing of black life in a South that was a fiction itself. This was not the critical attitude of her time toward her work. One of the canonized figures of Black Marxism, W.E.B. Dubois, along with Joel Spingarn, a founder of the NAACP, Paul Robeson, and H. L. Mencken, praised the achievement of Julia Peterkin in presenting characters truly human. Her blacks were recognized in a very special, even exotic setting as universal human beings, objectively invented: the kind of perennial figures that appear when we move beyond accidentals in time and history.

Of course, Peterkin's very sympathetic observation and transmission of Gullah customs and dialect, remarkably enriched by a sharpness of eye specially trained by her physician-father and a modulation of ear disciplined by years of studying music,

produced local color of a high level of artistry. Yet what gave Julia Peterkin's image of human life, black and Gullah, its universal cast is an aspect that transcends the special exotic world of Low Country South Carolina blacks. It is, I believe, the philosophic basis of her work that gives Julia Peterkin a special place in American letters, that is, not only her probing into the perennial dilemmas of human existence, but also her formal projections of these insights into the texts of her work.

Nowhere is this essential nature of her literary art more revealed than in her evocation of landscape—a specific world that I call here the land of Chicora simply because that is the name given by the Indians. . . . As the works themselves reveal, this landscape of Chicora acts as a positive emblem—an "objective correlative" if one wants—of the permanence of reality within the fictional world Peterkin invented. It reflects, through the fiction, a permanence within the social order of Julia Peterkin's South that was itself changing in her lifetime as rapidly as theories of the universe. In other words, the thesis I am offering is that at the center of Peterkin's work there is a *topos*, an invented landscape rising from an actual landscape, that explains the structural basis of the Peterkin canon. . . . [This] landscape involves both character and setting and determines the very nature of the Peterkin plot. It also offers, I might add, one more aspect to our larger view of landscape as central motif in American literature. (pp. 736-38)

Julia Peterkin is, after all, in the mainstream of American writing. She is one of the very last who can evoke with magnificent precision the natural landscape that surrounded American life for two centuries or more. Furthermore, in her work the American innocent, depicted in what appears on the surface as an exotic primitive, confronts a nature revealing to the character not only its own forces of beauty and death, creation and destruction, but the very meaning of existence itself. The terrible cosmic emptiness and alienation that follow the initial revelation may almost overwhelm Breeze, Mary, or Blue. The very landscape, however, in which each remains offers a certitude. The courage Maum Hannah had called for will be enough to survive, if one lives and suffers within the rituals both of community and of nature itself. In this sense the central characters do not act, as has been suggested about Breeze in **Black April**, as Ishmael to some Ahab or Jack Burden to some Willie Stark, that is, as devices to show larger heroic effects in the novels. Rather each is like Huckleberry Finn facing the River itself, maneuvering down its treacherous stream and, in most cases, surviving and heading out for a new landscape. In her own moralized landscape, invented with a generally unrecognized artistry out of the land called Chicora, Julia Peterkin offers, in a special microcosm, this same sense of the tragic, perpetually incomplete, nature of human existence. (pp. 747-48)

William A. Sessions, "The Land Called Chicora," in The Southern Review, *Vol. 19, No. 4, Autumn, 1983, pp. 736-48.*

Anthony (Dymoke) Powell

1905-

English novelist, dramatist, journalist, and scriptwriter.

After writing five urbane and humorous novels during the 1930s, Powell solidified his reputation as a major literary figure with his twelve-volume novel, *A Dance to the Music of Time* (1951-1971). In this work, as in his pre-World War II novels, Powell chronicles the insular world of the English upper class with a mixture of sharp satire and shrewd insight.

A Dance to the Music of Time follows a group of characters whose lives mirror social changes from pre-World War I to the 1970s. These people pass through the narrative in what appears to be a drifting, almost inconsequential manner, but this randomness ultimately evolves into a final pattern, that of "dancers" whose lives are controlled by a certain fate and by the passage of time. In describing this "dance of life," Powell evokes the image of the dancers in the Nicholas Poussin painting that gives the novel its name: "Human being, facing outward . . . , moving hand in hand in intricate measure: stepping slowly, methodically, sometimes a trifle awkwardly, in evolutions that take recognisable shape: or breaking into seemingly meaningless gyrations, while partners disappear only to reappear again, once more giving pattern to the spectacle: unable to control the melody, unable, perhaps, to control the steps of the dance." The pattern is observed and interpreted by the narrator Nicholas Jenkins, a novelist whose life is similar to Powell's in many respects. The central tension in *A Dance to the Music of Time* is between Jenkins, who is sensitive and loyal to his own values, and Kenneth Widmerpool, a self-serving materialist who unscrupulously pursues financial gain and social status.

Literary authorities have praised *A Dance to the Music of Time*, some suggesting that it stands as the greatest English novel since World War II. Critics have applauded the skill with which Powell drew from his extensive knowledge of the arts. Powell's complex, often convoluted prose style is refreshed by his subtle, ironic humor, and his deftness in capturing the essence of his characters has also been commended. However, some critics have objected to the fact that Powell studied only the upper classes in this novel. Others have contended that Powell failed to examine certain aspects of human behavior, most notably the passion of sexual relationships, thus making many of the affairs seem superficial or improbably simple.

Powell's reticence is also a characteristic noted by critics of his four-volume memoirs, collectively titled *To Keep the Ball Rolling*. Comprising *Infants of Spring* (1976), *Messengers of Day* (1978), *Faces in My Time* (1980), and *The Strangers All Are Gone* (1982), these memoirs are less autobiographical than they are evocations of an era, with Powell acting as observer and recorder. Each book is loosely ordered, developing as Powell muses on events from his life and recalls his many friendships. Some critics assert that the character descriptions of Powell's famous friends are the most interesting part of these volumes, perhaps because of the intriguing parallels between those people and the fictional characters of *A Dance to the Music of Time*. Reviewers of the memoirs have expressed regret that Powell never discusses his own life in detail. None-

theless, *To Keep the Ball Rolling* provides valuable insight into Powell's creative technique by revealing the processes through which he created art out of everyday life.

(See also *CLC*, Vols. 1, 3, 7, 9, 10; *Contemporary Authors*, Vols. 1-4, rev. ed.; *Contemporary Authors New Revision Series*, Vol. 1; and *Dictionary of Literary Biography*, Vol. 15.)

SIMON RAVEN

Anthony Powell was born on 21 December, 1905, with a silver-plated spoon in his mouth, his father being a regular officer in a dim regiment of the line and his mother a Wells-Dymoke (of the Lincolnshire family which supplies the new Monarch's Champion at coronations). From the time when he was first old enough to assess these circumstances Mr Powell has accepted them, as he has accepted all others of his life, with quiet, well informed and ironic amusement, unperturbed by envy on the one hand or guilt on the other. What is given is given, in this world as in Euclid's, and it is very silly and perverse to fret oneself about it.

This is one message of *Infants of the Spring*. The second is that such uncomplaining acceptance does not amount to passivity. Civilised acceptance implies civilised understanding, the latter of which teaches one, not indeed to attempt to change the given circumstances (for this, though sometimes possible, is a messy, time-consuming and pleasure-spoiling business), but to change or modify one's position in regard to them. It is all a question of angles and attitudes. . . .

But all this is to anticipate. Before further examination of Mr Powell's philosophy as revealed, or hinted at, in *Infants of the Spring,* I should state that this book is the first volume of Anthony Powell's memoirs, *To Keep the Ball Rolling;* that it comprehends some foggy Welsh genealogy (going back to the ap Howels of the sixteenth century and even to the ap Gruffydds of the twelfth), some diverting sketches of the author's more immediate forebears, and an account of his first twenty odd years from birth to leaving Oxford with a Third in History— an account distinguished by that sly and mocking brand of common sense which has already been illustrated above.

This operates, first, at the expense of institutions and is instructively exemplified in Mr Powell's loving elaboration of his own formulae for surviving in them. Nowhere, of course, is there the faintest advocacy of change or amelioration, for the great points to remember are these: if institutions *were* sanely and happily run, then, firstly, there would be nothing left in them to tease or satirise, which would make them deucedly boring, and secondly there would be no excuse for shifts and evasions, the devising of which gives Mr Powell (and his readers) so much pleasure. It is, perhaps, unfortunate if boys are whipped for things they haven't done: but doubtless they deserve whipping for something else (undiscovered) which they have; it is, furthermore, salutary for boys to be early acquainted with injustice (which is, at bottom, what their parents are paying for). In any case, when the first and the last has been said on the topic, it will never be Master Anthony Dymoke Powell who is undergoing the whip. . . .

This is grossly unfair to Mr Powell; I fear I have gone much too far. But I have, I think, conveyed an idea—albeit crude and exaggerated—of Mr Powell's technique for coping with the given realities of institutions and of the manner in which he himself describes the process. Let us now consider how he applies this shrewd, compliant and elusive *nous* of his to dealing with people.

People, like institutions, are given. It is not one's business to reform or deplore them, but to put up with and if possible enjoy them. This is best done by responding to the worst which they may say with a light and well-bred laugh, and to the worst which they may do with disapproval so civilly modulated as almost to pass for approbation. They will then do and say a lot more things even worse than before, from all of which one may make entertaining calculations about what finally makes them tick. This method not only elicits such incidental gems as Robert Byron's remark that he would love to be, of all things, an incredibly beautiful male prostitute with a sharp sting in his bottom; it also leads to Mr Powell's profound conclusion on the character of Cyril Connolly, that he suffered, not from the common disease of mere egotism (or selfish desire to push his own fortunes) but from that rare and horrifying condition, a passionate interest in, and even love of, himself as such.

Having noted Mr Powell's diagnosis of Connolly, one should add that, from time to time, Mr Powell comes perilously near to making, or rather unconsciously disclosing the same diagnosis of himself. . . . What saves him from the infatuated interest in himself of which he accuses Connolly is this: Mr Powell, who can never resist deflating other people's preten-

sions, is in the end far too fair, too decent, too modest a man not to deflate his own.

Simon Raven, "On the Margin," in The Spectator, Vol. 237, No. 7737, October 9, 1976, p. 19.*

C. DAVID BENSON

Anthony Powell may enjoy the most peculiar reputation of any novelist writing in English. Although many well-read Americans have apparently never heard of him, for others his recently completed 12-novel series, *A Dance to the Music of Time,* is the most sophisticated chronicle of modern life we have. Both admirer and uninitiate will be disappointed if they go to this first volume of memoirs [*Infants of the Spring*] expecting to learn anything directly about Powell the man or the writer. They will find instead a puzzling volume as artful as any of his fictions and employing many of the same devices—a vastly clever and informative narrative that deliberately plays with and perhaps even mocks its readers.

Powell belongs to the great generation of British writers who came to maturity just after World War I. Many, including Waugh, Betjeman, Connolly, Orwell and Muggeridge, were Powell's friends and as a group they have been especially attracted to autobiography. . . . This entire generation was marked by having experienced the extinction of the privileged England of their childhoods which was replaced by a completely different post-war world. (p. 29)

Powell is less forthcoming about himself than about his ancestors and adopts many strategies to avoid self-revelation. His elegant sentences are not the tools for inner probing; he maintains in his prose the cool exterior we see in the book's photographs and willingly confesses nothing. Yet there are frustrating clues of a more turbulent inner life. Powell clearly has no warm feeling for his emotional father (who may be the cause of his own extreme detachment), but all he will allow himself are indirect judgments, harsh in their brevity: "He was never able to make up his mind whether success or failure in a son was the more inimical." Likewise, near the end of his section on Oxford, Powell admits that although he has recorded mostly colorful activities, "a great deal of my time was spent in a state of deep melancholy." Was this simply a fashionable adolescent pose or does it reveal something essential about the man? Powell will not say. And yet, as these examples suggest, Powell is often frank about his secretiveness. He mentions a chance meeting sometime in the late 1950s with Henry Yorke (the novelist Henry Green), with whom he was once close. After recalling events from their now-cooled friendship, Yorke, almost in tears, declared that he was not well and insisted that he would soon die. Powell then observes: "I felt rather upset after this encounter. It was the last time I saw him. He died in 1974." Which is the more amazing: the flat refusal to explore still-powerful emotions or the disjunctive style which demands that the reader recognize that refusal?

Powell sees his function as observing the actions of others— a stance perhaps more successful in a novel than in memoirs. *Infants of the Spring* could be the autobiography of Nicholas Jenkins, the reticent, almost emotionless narrator of the *Music of Time.* In both books the narrator remains hidden behind a literary structure of great skill and wit. Throughout these memoirs Powell self-consciously plays with the reader like the novelist he is. He gives us a warning of what he is doing by recalling one of the favorite practical jokes of his paternal grandfather, who liked to "thrust a walking-stick suddenly between the shins of the companion strolling beside him; safely catching the victim, as he heeled over, just before reaching the ground.'' Powell himself is more intellectual, but no less upsetting in his jokes. He decries at length the tendency of novel-readers to suppose that a fictional character is ever an accurate portrait of any real person, but later boasts that he once met ''in the flesh'' the model for the most famous character in Waugh's *Decline and Fall,* Captain Grimes. (pp. 29-30)

Given his intricacies of style and multi-volumed novels, Powell might be thought a throwback to the Victorians, but *Infants of the Spring* makes clear that his true literary ancestors are to be found in the 17th century: especially John Aubrey, the author of the *Brief Lives* and the subject of Powell's one nonfiction book. He shares Aubrey's taste for the odd and quirky and his intricate, witty style. . . . In further imitation of Aubrey, Powell's accounts of his time at Eton and Oxford quickly become a series of brief lives. The full-length portraits of Yorke and George Orwell, good friends of his youth and middle age respectively, are curiously the most distant and belittling. Although he clearly admires Orwell and was a stout friend during his last years, Powell's long assessment remains annoyingly condescending. (p. 30)

Powell's accounts of more casual acquaintances, where there is no question of strong emotion, are completely successful, as if the added distance had improved his perspective. . . . *Infants of the Spring* certainly fails as a conventional autobiography, but succeeds as a sort of anti-autobiography: an entertaining puzzle full of good stories about others. As the book ends, Powell is preparing to leave Oxford for London, his marriage and first novels still before him. We have to wait for the next volume to discover if he can conceal his maturity as interestingly as he has his youth. (pp. 30-1)

> *C. David Benson, in a review of "Infants of the Spring," in* The New Republic, *Vol. 176, No. 4, June 11, 1977, pp. 29-31.*

MARTIN GREEN

My old teacher, F. R. Leavis, would spend critical time only on novelists who reach the level of ''significant fiction''; and the ''insignificant'' category turned out to include Trollope and even Thackeray. Recently I've rejected that criterion, and preferred a vertical slicing of writers into different kinds or *qualities* of significance, instead of his horizontal slicing between adequate and inadequate *quantity*. But Anthony Powell reawakens the old idea in me; his is such a clear case of insufficiency—of a lack of intensity of being. . . .

[*Infants of the Spring*] is not a novel but an autobiography—but much more about other people than about himself—so like his novels. So the same reaction seems appropriate. He spends some pages instructing us in the differences between art and life, but I remain unconvinced that that matters, as far as my interest in Anthony Powell goes. He was an intelligent bystander in the literary England of the '20s and '30s, which was an interesting case of the kind of dandyism which can come to power when a society loses faith in its models of mature manhood, as England did after 1918. That is what he wrote his novels about, and that is what he writes his autobiography about. Powell saw everything that was going on, in the sense that he was more centrally placed than most other observers, in terms of class and family ties, and in terms of temperament. He was as passionately curious about the scene as, say, Evelyn Waugh and Cyril Connolly; but his vision suffered, and suffers,

fewer of the limitations and distortions caused by self-dramatization. . . .

It may seem a mere paradox to talk of his dramatizing himself as undramatic, for his is not a case of tense and mysterious anonymity, like early Hemingway. But I think there is a good likelihood that some of the energy missing from his experience went into damping down his capacity for experience. For if, when we compare him with Waugh and Connolly, his vision is unblinkered, it is also comparatively dim. And one can see why.

His father was an intelligent but eccentric soldier, who became very cantankerous as he grew older; and his mother spent her energies soothing her husband. Anthony, an only child, developed defensive habits of aloofness. . . .

Socially, however, he was very active. He spent a lot of time with eccentric and colorful friends like Maurice Bowra, the don who became Warden of Wadham, and Hubert Duggan and Robert Byron and other figures from the world of Evelyn Waugh. To be with them was to be aloof from his father's world, while he was also aloof from them, in the sense of being average and anonymous.

The keynote of that world was bad behavior: outrageousness of some kind—dandified, roguish, brutal, or whatever. But of course there were well-behaved people in that world—they were perhaps its social cement—and Powell was one of them. ''Well-behaved'' is in fact one of his categories in this book, and a very characteristic one.

The trouble is that that category is interesting only as a polar opposite to ''badly behaved,'' and Powell is always defusing that polarity. He will not allow us any real outrage at the bad boys—will not allow that they were bad. It comes as a shock to *hear,* for instance, Bowra and a rival salon-holder: ''Bowra always referring to Kolkhorst as 'Kunthorse'; Kolkhorst, to 'that fly in the ointment on the seats of the mighty.'''

And it is clear that it was just that element of violence which attracted Powell to them. But he admits to nothing comparable in himself. His own tone is this, about another friend: ''He was one of the nicest of men, in certain moods content to live a quiet even humdrum existence; at other times behaving with a minimum of discretion, altogether disregarding the traditional recommendation that, if you can't be good, be careful.''

One is tempted to suggest that Powell's whole career has been conducted according to that traditional recommendation. . . .

Who should be recommended to read this? Of course lovers of Powell; beyond them, I'd say it all depends on how interested you already are in English dandyism. He won't get you interested. He has told us so often that there is nothing remarkable about him that it has started to be true.

> *Martin Green, ''An Intelligent Bystander,'' in* Book World—The Washington Post, *October 9, 1977, p. E3.*

THE VIRGINIA QUARTERLY REVIEW

Most that is memorable [in *Infants of the Spring*] is derived: other men's witticisms, other men's adventures, the force of other men's characters. The portraits of Orwell and Connolly stand out, Bowra and Henry Green disappoint. But far from a tale told by an idiot savant, here are reminiscences of a seasoned novelist, full of years and clear memories, surrounded by the ghosts of famous friends, speaking over port beside a wood fire. Let me suggest that there are much worse ways to spend an evening. (p. 48)

A review of "Infants of the Spring," in The Virginia Quarterly Review, *Vol. 54, No. 2 (Spring, 1978), pp. 47-8.*

PHILIP TERZIAN

It is astonishing how an epoch can grow cold. All it takes, or so it would seem, is a sufficient number of memoirs mixed with the requisite stories and nicknames, all repeated and confused by whatever rendition is at hand. It has happened before and, undoubtedly, will happen again. . . .

Now, in the second volume of Anthony Powell's memoirs [*Messengers of Day*], the cast of London in the '20s is brought forth for one more turn at the footlights, a cast wearily familiar by now: He-Evelyn and She-Evelyn (Waugh), Osbert and Dame Edith, Brian on the beach and Tallulah on the floor. Somewhere between Balliol and Dunkirk the British intelligentsia must have conspired to get sick on the same oysters and champagne, for as surely as our hero leaves one dinner party we know before he tells us where he's going.

This is disappointing because Anthony Powell, now 73 and apparently well into his anecdotage, could have written a very skillful memoir, although it may be argued he has written it already. His 12-volume series, *A Dance to the Music of Time,* is one of the masterpieces of fiction in this century and, as he acknowledges, much of it was drawn from material that composes *Messengers of Day*. This book is a good lesson in understanding the fine hand of the novelist, for the sensibility that turned these tiresome and commonplace episodes into art knew at one time where its vocation lay. . . .

Powell has always had two particular strengths as a novelist. One is his ability to discern the subtle distinctions within personalities: the small quirks and tics and offhand phrases that turn, in time, into masquerades. The other is his understanding of the role coincidence tends to play in life: how people and places and events tend to mingle capriciously, at odd moments and with consistency, as variations without a theme.

It cannot be said that these skills are much in evidence here. The portraits are flat and drawn so cursorily that the reader neither learns to know the subjects nor cares to. Powell is either ambivalent about telling "the whole story"—which can be forgiven—or is an ungifted historian outside the realm of fiction. . . .

His friend Evelyn Waugh once said that autobiographies ought to be written by those with no interest in the future; in Powell's case it would seem that his recollections were defeated before they were begun, for he seems to have no interest in the past. The short, isolated vignettes are both languid and dry, having about them a stale flavor of age and repetition. . . .

Powell's recollections are clearly in order and cross-indexed, but there simply is something missing in them—perhaps it is the element of curiosity. He has used his characters for what they could have offered him as a storyteller; having observed and recorded, he leaves the outer shell, which promptly flops onto the pavement.

I imagine this is to some extent a matter of what one expects from autobiography about which, of course, there is no consensus nor are there any hard and fast rules. It is all very well

to draw scenes and tell tales and repeat phrases, but by inviting the reader into the realm of his memories the writer, mindful of his vanity, has certain responsibilities. There should be some evidence of an interior life, an illumination as well as an explanation. We don't care how Powell did things so much as *why*.

One continuing theme is the years Powell spent as a publisher's assistant in London, a Dickensian sort of existence, years of torpor and uncertainty, punctuated by some brilliant characters and some wild interludes. Why, the reader yearns to know, did he stay on and on? Powell prefers to cast his eye around the room rather than focus on himself. . . . That is fair enough, in its way, but by merely exhibiting a jaundiced detachment Powell fails to deliver the sort of insight a reader may expect from the memoirs of a literary man. Nor is such an omission redeemed by the funny stories and good lines in which the book abounds. Wit is not so much a substitute for wisdom as it is its companion, and one unrelieved by the other can grow intolerable.

There are a few things worth mentioning. Enthusiasts of Evelyn Waugh will be interested to learn that Powell was acquainted with all the parties to the failure of Waugh's first marriage. He was, in fact, witness to several episodes in what has been, in Waugh's life, a decidedly mysterious interlude. Unfortunately, Powell raises nearly as many questions as he answers and, in fact, is sometimes garrulous where it need hardly matter. Several pages, for instance, are devoted to proving how Powell saw through the slimy characters of Donald Maclean and Guy Burgess—years, indeed decades before his opinion was confirmed by the facts. So what? Anyone's career is full of as many good judgments as bad; this presumably was included to bear out the notion that novelists frequently see what politicians do not. Powell's powers of analysis may have been acute in that instance, but elsewhere he is as devoted to deplorable people who didn't happen to be double agents. All of which means that, in the end, we are in the realm of memory and interpretation, very perilous waters, and *A Dance to the Music of Time* is a safer vessel than these haphazard recollections.

Philip Terzian, "Anthony Powell and His Crowd," in Book World—The Washington Post, *September 17, 1978, p. E6.*

ROBERT MURRAY DAVIS

It is difficult to determine whether Anthony Powell's stance as a completely unremarkable man is the result of art or nature. Occasional passages [in *Infants of Spring* and *Messengers of Day*] seem to contain irony so subtle as to be almost invisible, but for the most part his portraits of contemporaries are neither vivid nor searching, and his literary judgments, including those of his own work completed or in progress, are commonplace. (pp. 511-12)

Others have conveyed more vividly the atmosphere of Eton, Oxford and London in the 1920s, and Powell alludes to and frequently comments on the reminiscences of such contemporaries as Henry Yorke (the novelist Henry Green), Cyril Connolly, George Orwell and—the writer to whom he is inevitably compared—Evelyn Waugh. These writers convey impressions through vivid phrases; Powell deals in sober facts. For instance, he is aware that not everyone will know the composition of Pop at Eton or the full membership and later achievements of the original Eton Society of Arts. His explanations of these and other English institutions are always helpful, for he explains rules, speculates on the more obvious motives and delineates the lines of force in the power struggles. In dealing with the lively eccentrics who make this generation attractive to people who would rather read about them than read their works, others have portrayed Waugh more acutely, but none that I know of has noted or described Waugh's "curious little high-pitched affirmative sound, a mannerism that always remained with him." Powell adds many other details, some of them—notably the history of composition of Waugh's *Decline and Fall*—questionable but too complex to examine here.

However, Powell does take pains to be precise in his substance. The style is another matter, for in these volumes Powell shows himself to be perhaps the clumsiest professional writer ever to emerge from Eton and Balliol. (p. 512)

> *Robert Murray Davis, in a review of "Infants of Spring" and "Messengers of Day," in* World Literature Today, *Vol. 53, No. 3, Summer, 1979, pp. 511-12.*

SIMON BLOW

At the close of the second volume of Anthony Powell's memoirs, *To Keep the Ball Rolling,* Powell had published his first three novels; at the opening of this new volume [*Faces in My Time*] he continues to work part-time for the publisher, Duckworth's. The major event of the early chapters is his marriage; Eton and Oxford friends are less in his life than formerly as he tries his hand in the more lucrative Grub Street of scriptwriting. This existence has its hazards but Powell's setbacks are well concealed beneath his now highly developed restrained narrative manner. . . .

What's Become of Waring, Powell's fifth novel, was published early in 1939, and when war broke Powell joined the Welsh Regiment. Part of the training took place in Wales, which Powell was afterwards to transpose into *The Valley of Bones.* Later he was posted to Military Intelligence in Whitehall, and Powell covers factually much of the ground he treated fictionally in *The Military Philosophers.* But whereas in fiction Powell is able to tease officialdom, when reminiscing he gives it a respect that deadens. His character portraits have a hollow echo too, and his account has none of the humorous warmth and melancholy that inhabit the war trilogy of *The Music of Time.* In that one remark of Stringham's, 'Awfully chic to be killed', there is more of the war than in these pallid, rekindled events.

How, though, can a writer of Powell's sensibilities make the telling of his life such a dull matter? Of course it is a drawback to have already written a version of it in *A Dance to the Music of Time.* Often, for a fuller description of event or character, we are referred back to the corresponding novel while the narrative is delivered in the abbreviated tongue of retired colonels. A wartime instructor is 'a charming old boy with a V.C.', and Powell's best man for his wedding, 'an old friend, reliable for such an occasion'.

Fear of stepping out of line is evident also in Powell's attitude towards sexual behaviour. Powell's views on homosexuality remain those of the entrenched heterosexual. . . .

But Powell is far more sympathetic, because reserve and convention are dropped, when discussing the problems of writing fiction—or 'creative fantasy' as he has called it. Towards the end of the present volume he gives an explanation of his de-

cision to embark on *The Music of Time.* The explanation is of interest since it shows how some writing talents were stimulated by the crisis of war and others not. Powell was one who found his energies cut short by the gathering menace of the late Thirties and, when war came, his inspiration ran dry. Unlike other non-political writers such as Elizabeth Bowen, Henry Green and William Sansom, whose imaginations were braced by the crisis, Powell had nothing to say. It took until the late Forties for Powell's inventive faculties to recover, but the freshness of invention that had inspired the early novels had gone. Thus the idea that germinated with *A Question of Upbringing* he planned to span over a number of volumes at least. The result we know, and it has won him wide admiration, but it is also arguable that the war killed off a talent which many have missed.

It is sad that there should be such a noticeable falling away in Powell's memoirs, and one looks for what the reason can be. Twenty-five years of writing *The Music of Time* proved an exhausting exercise. The revelations on life that came to Proust did not come to Powell, and although he dislikes the comparison, I suspect that at the outset he hoped they might. Proust developed his eccentric vision that led to hitherto unrealised conclusions by remaining an outsider; and perhaps as a homosexual and partly Jewish, he had much that enabled him to resist the threat of conformity. But Powell has determinedly remained a gentleman, and a gentleman's life has become his smokescreen against revealing a complex character. But it is a smokescreen that is confining his memoirs, just as it prevented *The Music of Time* from being the life-changing monument it ought to be.

> *Simon Blow, "Gentleman's Reflections," in* New Statesman, *Vol. 99, No. 2564, May 9, 1980, p. 719.*

ANATOLE BROYARD

For those who don't know him, Anthony Powell is an English writer who put out five very good novels in the 30's and a dozen not quite as good, collectively called **"A Dance to the Music of Time,"** between then and now. . . .

Now Mr. Powell is writing his memoirs, and he has every reason to. England is a small country and it appears, from **"Faces in My Time,"** the third volume of another projected series, that the author knew almost everyone worth knowing in his day. He tells us, for example, that Elizabeth Bowen was blind to cockroaches in her kitchen, that Dylan Thomas fell asleep under a bed in which two women were unsuccessfully trying to make love, that Somerset Maugham prided himself on a rather inadequate knowledge of British social protocol, that F. Scott Fitzgerald was surprised that Lord Donegall should be surprised when he used the word "cinquecento." . . .

Sometimes **"Faces in My Time"** gets a little more ruminative than some readers might wish. Mr. Powell asks himself whether George Orwell was influenced by Charles Péguy, whether Joseph Conrad was affected by Henri-Frédérique Amiel. He goes into considerable detail about the favorite reading of a fellow officer during the war.

Mr. Powell is also the author of **"John Aubrey and His Friends,"** a critical biography of a 17th-century writer who published a wonderfully pithy book of short portraits called, "Brief Lives." Aubrey's book was in the form of notes that he never found time to finish and these have a lively, staccato shorthand quality. Mr. Powell also uses a "Brief Lives" approach in **"Faces** in My Time,'' but his shorthand, curiously enough, is not pithy or staccato but verbose and circumlocutory. He is capable of writing phrases like ''recognizing the expediency of not contemplating too analytically the metamorphosis.'' Or ''my immediately post-war dentist.''

Literary historians may be concerned to know how Mr. Powell's fictional soldiers correspond to the gentleman he based them on. I was not, but these portraits are enjoyable in their own right. It is interesting to hear Mr. Powell say that reviewing anonymously in The Times Literary Supplement, speaking as the voice of the paper, as it were, tends to inhibit both praise and blame.

When Mr. Powell returned from Hollywood, where he was briefly employed in writing a film about messenger boys, he found the pocket of his dinner jacket filled with swizzle sticks. That's what **"Faces in My Time"** reminds me of: a dinner-jacket pocket filled with swizzle sticks.

Anatole Broyard, in a review of "Faces in My Time," in The New York Times, *Section III, February 4, 1981, p. C21.*

HAROLD ACTON

Readers of [Powell's] autobiographical series will be able to trace the origins of some of his characters, a veritable goldmine for future thesis-writers. In his third volume, *Faces in My Time,* he introduces us to more friends and acquaintances in the course of his literary career and service as a military intelligence officer during the last world war, explaining how some of these contributed to his fictional narrative. Certain figures, like Constant Lambert and his own brother-in-law Henry Lamb, recur as in his novels, and we are delighted to meet them again. How refreshing it is to read of his marriage that ''after nearer fifty than forty years'' he has ''never wished to be married to another woman''. Lady Violet, his wife, shares the literary talents of the prodigious Pakenham family to an exceptional degree.

Powell's happy marriage, however, may account for the scarcity of feminine faces among the heterogeneous males in this book. Apparently he is one of the last of our polite authors, far too polite to unbutton himself or others in public. If Powell does not lay bare his inner soul, he allows us glimpses through the interstices of his social contacts. Never sensational, he keeps his cool, to borrow a colloquialism. His tone is that of civilized conversation, gathering momentum here and there in a comical anecdote, one of the funniest concerning Queen Victoria's first cousin, the venerable Duke of Cambridge. Hearing of an outbreak of venereal disease at Sandhurst, ''he set off for the Royal Military College at once, *en civil*, carrying as ever a rolled umbrella, to deliver a rebuke. When the cadets were all assembled, the Duke of Cambridge waved the umbrella above his head. He thundered: 'I hear you boys have been putting your private parts where I wouldn't put this umbrella!' ''

Since we were contemporaries at Eton and Oxford I have known a sizable proportion of the personalities in these pages and can vouch for the accuracy of Powell's portrayals.

Harold Acton, "Anthony Powell: Meat and Drink," in Manchester Guardian Weekly, *March 8, 1981, p. 18.*

MAGGIE LEWIS

''Faces in My Time'' is a delight to read and hard to review, because it is full of things I wanted to know, but it is also the third volume of Anthony Powell's autobiography, following his elegant and magically funny 12-volume novel, ''A Dance to the Music of Time.'' . . . Though there is a lot in ''Faces in My Time'' for anyone interested in the life of the mind, it's very tempting to be a Powell snob and tell general readers they can't have this until they've read the rest.

They can, though. Powell is very well read, very intelligent, and very private, but even that won't keep you away. Here he is refusing to tell us much about falling in love with his wife while recounting a visit to her family's castle in Ireland and their marriage after they'd known each other for three weeks: ''I shall not attempt to describe how my personal problem was (to borrow a favoured Jamesian idiom) beautifully solved, when Violet Pakenham arrived at the house. . . . She herself has in any case touched on that in her own autobiographical volume 'Within the Family Circle' (1976).'' The essentials are there (together with a typically Powellian reference to further reading), and he withholds the rest so gracefully that that in itself has a certain romance. . . .

Powell doesn't spare us the miserable gloominess of wartime London. If you have never been in a war, this aura is more affecting than dramatic battle scenes, because more easily imaginable. The war means tedium and discomfort. The blitz causes insomnia. Mrs. Powell leaves, having just found out she is pregnant, for the country. ''It was a sad and upsetting moment when the train steamed out at Paddington, and one I don't care to dwell on,'' writes Powell.

When his own train steamed out for his regiment, ''No one talked much so far as I can remember. It was a long journey, one leading not only to a new life, but entirely out of an old one. Nothing was ever the same again.''

It's as if the anonymity of being in uniform has liberated Powell's writing from its shyness in this volume. More often than in the earlier works, we know how he feels. And he is suddenly forthcoming about which acquaintances went together to make certain characters in ''A Dance to the Music of Time.'' . . .

This book is really an account of how Powell stayed himself through the war, a heroic task for anyone. In his case it resulted in writing ''A Dance to the Music of Time.''

Even though the world seemed to be ending, or at least changing fearfully, Powell looked after his cats, enjoyed France, and kept on thinking about Welshmen, Kierkegaard, and John Aubrey. It is this relentless, humorous mind that invigorates the reader all through all 12 volumes of ''A Dance to the Music of Time.'' This book should encourage anyone living through a catastrophe.

Maggie Lewis, "An Anglophile's Delight," in The Christian Science Monitor, *March 9, 1981, p. B3.*

MELVIN MADDOCKS

After twelve volumes of his justly celebrated sequence, *A Dance to the Music of Time,* Anthony Powell, 75, has established himself as the reigning novelist of British understatement. In this third volume of his autobiography [*Faces in My Time*], the master whisperer so thoroughly muffles the barbarous yawps of the mid-20th century—from Dylan Thomas to World War

II—that they emerge as discreetly as the sound of one teacup cracking.

As this most seemly of chronicles begins, Powell, 28, is about to marry Violet Pakenham, 22. An opportunity, surely, for a passing brushfire of emotion, recollected in tranquillity? Not at all. Whatever might be hot or sweet is buried in the cool shade of 13 pages devoted to Violet's family tree. . . .

Pain, as Powell readers know, gets registered no more sharply than pleasure. There is, however, a good deal of subliminal throb. While his wife is writing for the press "on horses and equitation," Powell's career as a largely unread novelist goes nowhere. He works for Warner Bros. near London, hacking out scripts about messenger boys and Victorian philanthropists. None are produced. . . .

Faces in My Time can be read as one humiliation after another, swallowed with barely a twitch. When his fifth novel, *What's Become of Waring,* sells exactly 999 copies, Powell records the figure in the tone of a conscientious bookkeeper. When World War II comes and his colleague Evelyn Waugh flies off to serve as a commando in Greece, Powell goes to the War Office, enlists—and gets assigned to posts in England and Wales, where there is little to do but read Kierkegaard. When George Orwell dies, Powell is left to choose the hymns. In every Powell book somebody has to play the misfit schoolboy who wears the wrong kind of overcoat. In *Faces* the author takes the role. (p. 72)

> Melvin Maddocks, "Muted Memoir," in Time, Vol. 117, No. 10, March 9, 1981, pp. 72-3.

MICHAEL GORRA

[The first three volumes of *To Keep the Ball Rolling* confirm] what one has always suspected: that Powell's sensibility and that given to Nicholas Jenkins, the narrator of his twelve-volume novel, *A Dance to the Music of Time,* are virtually indistinguishable. This similarity becomes evident in looking at the attitude struck by either Powell or his character toward his own gaffes. . . . Look . . . at a sketch of Maurice Bowra in *Infants of the Spring:*

> One evening, dining tête-à-tête with Bowra in his rooms, I spoke of how little I liked being at Oxford, and how I longed to get it over and go down. The lack of finesse in voicing such sentiments in the particular circumstances was, of course, altogether inexcusable. . . . One learns in due course (without ever achieving the aim in practice) that, more often than not, it is better to keep deeply felt views about one-self to oneself. In any case a little good sense—a little good manners even—might have warned me that such a confession was not one to make to a slightly older friend, who, even then, was rapidly becoming one of the ever brightening stars of the Oxford firmament.

(p. 595)

I pause . . . [at this quotation], at the idea of Powell unburdening himself to anyone. Certainly he does not often allow Jenkins to indulge himself in that, in particular with regard to his marriage. Powell shares that reticence to such a degree that he offers no reason beyond the possibility of embarrassment for his casual statement about those "deeply felt views." Given that statement, one might wonder that he has been able to

commit an act of autobiography. But in fact he has not. These three books, dealing with Powell's life up to 1951, when he published *A Question of Upbringing,* the *Dance*'s first part, are carefully labelled "memoirs"; the generic distinction is important. Autobiographies trumpet the self, concern themselves with the fashioning of a consciousness, an "I" to which the external world is subordinated. Memoirs, however, look outward, dealing not so much with their "I" as with the world in which he lives. . . . Autobiographies are always ambitious in intention and appearance; memoirs, however grandly conceived, have the appearance of modesty in two senses of the word. First, in that they seem to make no claim for themselves other than to tell a few anecdotes about one's life and times. Second, because their focus upon the external world provides the opportunity for self-effacement. The achievement of a memoir need not, however, be modest—it can achieve more to the degree that it finds a subject which allows it to be something other than a string of loosely connected stories.

In practice, the two forms are almost always mixed, as in Yeats's *Autobiography.* *To Keep the Ball Rolling,* however, provides as pure an example as I know of memoir, books in which Powell follows his own advice about confession nearly without exception. The basic facts are of course all there, most of them corresponding to the outline of the life Powell has given to Jenkins: born in 1905, his father an army officer, educated at Eton, then Balliol. *Messengers of Day* covers his life in London after leaving Oxford—working for Duckworth's, the publishers, and then the start of his career as a novelist, with *Afternoon Men* in 1931. *Faces in My Time* begins with his marriage to Lady Violet Pakenham in 1934, and then moves through the war, ending with his plans for the *Dance.* Beyond that, Powell says little about his writing, except to bemoan attempts at an identification of his friends and relatives with his characters; still less about his emotional life as a young man, except to hint that he had one and that it's not particularly interesting.

Self-revelation enters indirectly when it does at all, stray sentences in a description of someone else. Powell writes, for example, that he was not sure he would accept an invitation to meet George Orwell, because "I was at first unwilling to involve myself in so much frugal living and high thinking." . . . My point about Powell's statement, however, is that his reticence can't be confused with personal austerity. Since he rarely mentions what he does—observation aside—at the parties described either in his novel or his memoirs, it's hard at first to realize that Powell is not just a connoisseur of raffish characters, but a bit of one himself, drawn to the "seedy chic" of the demi-monde by something more than voyeurism.

Yet it would be equally wrong to mistake that raffishness for a mannered frivolity. . . . Powell's interest lies in the arts themselves rather than in being "artsy." One need not live frugally. A fastidious reluctance to use one's habits, tastes, and talents as social weapons, vulgar tools with which to provoke or offend, will be enough. As with so much else in Powell, it is a matter of taste.

Modesty too is a matter of taste, and for Powell a virtue. In these books he has seized the appearance of modesty that memoir affords—its self-effacement, its air of conversation. *A Dance to the Music of Time* also has that feel of memoir. Yet in its scope the novel is anything but the product of modest ambitions, nor is the final integration of its anecdotes a modest achievement. That integration takes place through Jenkins' imposition of a controlling metaphor upon his experience, and in the style through which he observes and comprehends that experience. The standard comparisons are with Proust and Waugh, the first because the *Dance* takes the form of memory, the second because Powell and Waugh were friends, and because much of the *Dance* takes place, like Waugh's novels, at parties and in country houses. Both comparisons strike me as inappropriate. Powell is not interested in memory for its own sake, and he does not turn his London into Waugh's Metroland. A more fruitful comparison is with Meredith. Both novelists set their work within a system, a frame to which action within the novel can be referred; in Meredith's case, his ideas about Comedy; in Powell's, the conception of the Dance. Both view the incidents they describe as essentially funny. Meredith reduces his characters to counters in some grand game, with which to illustrate, albeit ironically, the aphorisms with which his novels are studded. Powell's comedy works by regarding his characters not as counters or things, but as invididuals, in accordance with Nietzsche's observation, quoted in *Faces in My Time,* that "the individual when closely examined is always comic." (pp. 596-98)

Jenkins expects nothing of Powell's other characters in both senses of the phrase: he finds their actions random, unpredictable, but also has no faith that those actions will ever take an unambiguously positive turn. This results in a sense of comic resignation similar to that of Meredith's narrators, in which laughter lies not so much in the practical jokes of daily life themselves—the tennis match between Messieurs Orn and Lundquist in *A Question of Upbringing* is a good example—as in Jenkins' *post facto* comprehension of an incident, his way of treating all characters as if they were Uncle Giles. In *A Buyer's Market,* however, Nick wonders, "Was it possible to take Uncle Giles seriously? And yet he was, no doubt, serious enough to himself." That realization forces Powell to substitute sympathy for Meredith's derision. Jenkins never loses his sense of detached amusement at the other characters' grotesqueries, but combines that with an attempt to understand their motivations and self-conceptions, to take all circumstances into account.

Yet in expecting nothing of those around him, Jenkins above all does not expect them to share his style of perception. . . . Jenkins' style, because it expects nothing, not of himself but for himself, is an act of pure generosity. This suggests another comparison—the Jean Renoir of *The Rules of the Game,* to which Powell's early novel *From a View to a Death* (1933) bears a surface resemblance, although its poker-faced narration lacks the movie's, or the *Dance*'s warmth. This generosity requires that both Powell and Jenkins refuse to speak with authority about others, about the ways in which Uncle Giles may be serious to himself. Hence the clouds of speculation, of circumstances taken into account, which are responsible for the *Dance*'s peculiar flavor, but also for its main weakness, the way in which, as James Tucker says, "Jokes may be stilted by their own fat."

Yet if Powell will not impose a meaning or judgment upon individual action, he will—almost in compensation—impose a principle of order upon experience in its larger, external motions. And that principle, the Dance, is not simply a comic one. At Eton, Powell was considered moody; the action of his novel possesses an air of somber inevitability, of melancholia—something brought home by the quotation from Robert Burton with which the whole sequence concludes. Isn't the fact that the closely examined individual is always comic essentially a sad one, a suggestion of human limitation and frailty more than

anything else? The conclusion to Meredith's *The Egoist* leaves me drained, disturbed, confused; similarly the end of *A Dance to the Music of Time*.

Yet hopeful as well. That sense grows from Nick's style, which I find both valuable and wise. Kenneth Widmerpool, with whose death in *Hearing Secret Harmonies* the novel ends, is commonly taken to be the Dance's focus. Yet though the novel is built around him, it is not about him. He is an organizing principle, a means, not an end, and serves primarily to establish a system of judgment within the novel. For Widmerpool, sweeping all before his insistent I, before his will to dominate, ignores precisely what one finds in Nicholas Jenkins—the willingness, the understanding, required to see things as being more complex than one can fully understand. And that failure on Widmerpool's part makes us value Nick's style, turns it into the novel's final good, a process delicately realized largely because Nick never takes an explicit stand against Widmerpool, never blames him for what he cannot help, for being, even more than Uncle Giles, a man from whom nothing can be expected. *A Dance to the Music of Time* is finally a quiet affirmation of the value of Nick's, or Powell's, style. This is not a modest claim for him to make; neither, I think, is it a false one.

His three volumes of memoirs, however, persist in their modesty. In his novel, Powell turned a temperamental inability to talk about himself to an advantage; he doesn't repeat that here. One needs a subject; given that Powell will not take himself as one, as an autobiographer does, he must find one external to himself. I have never been so fascinated by Widmerpool in his own right as most readers, yet Widmerpool is what the memoirs lack, inasmuch as the character gave Powell a subject upon which to exercise his style. He doesn't have that here—or, rather, he has a series of subjects, each providing the occasion for a well-wrought two or three pages. But there's very little to connect those short scenes to each other, and this gives the memoirs a fragmentary quality that makes reading them an exercise in frustration. At times, in *Infants of the Spring* especially, Powell does pursue a single subject for a dozen pages, as he does with Orwell or Bowra. This concentration upon a single subject at length produces a formal intensity altogether lacking in these books as a whole, and one wishes that instead of letting his memoirs take their present form, Powell had produced a volume of similar portraits along the lines of David Garnett's *Great Friends*. These books are always lively, engaging, and important as sources for those interested in the period. But they are modest in every sense of the word.

Yet for all that, valuable. The ways in which Powell withholds personal information finally present something more useful and interesting than frankness—some insight, however fleeting, into the psychology behind the *Dance*. This is true above all of the title he has chosen for the series (one presumes there will be at least one more volume): *To Keep the Ball Rolling,* a title taken, along with the first volume's epigraph, from Conrad's *Chance:*

> To keep the ball rolling I asked Marlow if this Powell was remarkable in any way.
>
> "He was not exactly remarkable," Marlow answered with his usual nonchalance. "In a general way it's very difficult to become remarkable. People won't take sufficient notice of one, don't you know."

Powell has made a career out of that quotation—from remarking, or taking sufficient notice, of others, and from not, some would say, taking sufficient notice of himself. But a character not worth remarking? No; that modesty is simply the attitude Powell has found essential to the production of his fiction, something more than a pose yet less than the truth. The pedestrian don't have so many interesting friends and aren't snapped up as undergraduates by talent scouts like Maurice Bowra. And they don't write novels like the *Dance,* a work that even its critics must account in some way remarkable. This epigraph is Powell's ironic acknowledgement of that fact; these memoirs—tantalizing, for all their faults, in the occasional glimpse they offer of those deeply felt views—a way to keep his own ball rolling, just outside the reader's grasp. (pp. 598-600)

> *Michael Gorra, "The Modesty of Anthony Powell,"*
> *in* The Hudson Review, *Vol. XXXIV, No. 4, Winter,*
> *1981-82, pp. 595-600.*

STEPHEN BROOK

The Strangers All Are Gone displays the same desultory qualities as the preceding three volumes [of Powell's memoirs]: reticence, arbitrariness, sketchiness. No one would guess from these memoirs that Powell is a novelist of considerable grace and humour. This book is not so much poorly organised as not organised at all. Episode follows vignette follows reflection seemingly at random. It is not simply that the book has no shape but that it suggests a life the author is too lazy to shape for the reader. . . . The self-effacement is almost total, and an opinion or prejudice, when volunteered, is invariably conventional. Powell writes, as he has always done, about Time and Death, but has nothing to say about either.

Perhaps a clue to why these memoirs are so dispiriting can be found in the following apologia:

> I have chosen to make a kind of album of odds
> and ends in themselves at times trivial enough.

This has the complacency, and the weary arrogance, of the writer who has given up.

> *Stephen Brook, in a review of "The Strangers All*
> *Are Gone," in* New Statesman, *Vol. 103, No. 2670,*
> *May 21, 1982, p. 23.*

ALLAN MASSIE

Anthony Powell has always tended to puzzle even while he delights. Wodehouse once said: 'It's extraordinary how interesting his stuff is, you know. And it just goes on and on, with nothing much in the way of scenes or anything'. Not perhaps a fair judgment on *A Dance to the Music of Time*—think of the party given by Mrs Foxe for Moreland's symphony or of the dinner at Stourwater at which the Seven Deadly Sins were enacted for Sir Magnus Donners's camera—the words might well be applied to Powell's four volumes of memoirs, though here it is not perhaps so much scenes that are lacking as the narrative impetus expected from the conventional autobiography.

That is reasonable enough; Powell has always been concerned with the distorting effects produced by memory. Now, in this final volume [*The Strangers All Are Gone*] which begins more or less in 1952 at the time when *The Buyer's Market* was published, he finds that 'as one picks one's way between the trees of Dante's dark wood of middle life, its configuration

becomes ever less discernible. . . . All the time a perspective that once gave at least the illusion of order to the past diminishes. . . .'

So one need not look for 'sustained chronological narrative' here. Nor will Powell readers—and these volumes of autobiography obviously offer their ripest interest to us fortunate addicts of his fiction—expect to find revelations about his private life. . . .

[The] laconic objectivity with which he treats his material is well-judged. What, after all, is a writer's life? It is a matter of sitting at a desk writing words. Nothing in a public sense happens to him; nothing too private for his novels properly matters to the public. It is fair, therefore, that the summing-up should offer 'an album of odds and ends in themselves at times trivial enough', especially since Powell 'has often found the trivial to be more acceptable, even in the long run more instructive, than attempts at being profound.'

Yet the relationship between life and letters, hardly trivial to any writer, is one that has always fascinated Powell in his awareness of the 'uncertainties . . . regarding what is true, what worth writing about.' And this relationship is exposed here when he comes to write about people who served, to some extent at least, as models for characters in his fiction. We can observe with a quickening of interest the contrast between the vital completeness of a character in a novel, who has no proper existence beyond those lines of fiction which serve to delineate him, and the original breathing man. The paradox of course is that it is the fictional character who seems to take on autonomous life such as can hardly be claimed by the man described in a biography or memoirs. . . .

The portraits of friends and acquaintances have been the liveliest part of Powell's memoirs, as indeed they tend to be in any consistently readable autobiography. . . .

Interest of another sort is provided by a chapter called 'Fit for Eros' in which, by way of Erich von Stroheim and the Chatterley trial, Powell takes a look at the battle for 'uninhibited treatment of sex in art', the outcome of which has certainly been the most remarkable development in literary manners this century. Powell's objections to Lady Chatterley, and indeed to Lawrence as a novelist, seem pretty just, and he finds 'a certain justice in the rights and wrongs of Lady Chatterley being hammered out without a vestige of humour on either side', not something that could be said of his own treatment of that absurd case. Characteristically, this chapter says nothing about the remarkable development of Powell's own handling of erotic themes that took place over the quarter century of *The Music of Time*'s composition. (p. 23)

These volumes of memoirs stand in fascinating and splendidly entertaining relation to his fiction, while at the same time sketching, with the economy of a great artist who can bring a drawing into life with what seem to the onlooker absurdly few strokes of the pencil, *la vie littéraire* of the last half-century. They recall, in their mixture of portrait sketches always individual, not perhaps wholly reliable, with ruminations on the difficult business of writing and forging a career as a writer and some penetrating maxims, drawn from experience and observation of literary work, those other masterpieces of casual reminiscence, Ford Madox Ford's *Memories and Impressions*. (p. 24)

> *Allan Massie, "An Album of Odds and Ends," in*
> The Spectator, *Vol. 248, No. 8030, June 5, 1982,*
> *pp. 23-4.*

PAUL DELANY

The action of *A Dance to the Music of Time* comes to the reader by courtesy of Nick Jenkins, that non-participant observer whose presence never seems to make any impact on the endless round of social gatherings he attends. When Powell began to publish his memoirs, fans of *Dance* hoped that the mystery of what Jenkins was *really* like might be revealed; now that the memoirs are completed, it is clear that these hopes will never be satisfied. 'Scratch an invisible narrator, get an invisible narrator'—to borrow the old joke about actors. Sometimes Powell's memoirs appear to be mere piffle ('Once more the food was good, though not up to Air France'), sometimes acute, sometimes one suspects an elaborate joke is being played on the reader. Hardly ever, though, does the author present himself as a figure of substance: it is not Jenkins's creator we meet, but Jenkins's ghost. . . .

[It] comes as a surprise to learn from the *Memoirs* that Powell's exemplary novelist is Dostoevsky, and that he considers *The Devils* the greatest novel ever written. One can see hints of the Dostoevskian mode in Powell's novels, particularly in his brilliant scenes of the eruption of egotism and disorder into conventional social functions. But these incongruities never manifest any substantial principle of evil, as they would in Dostoevsky. Evil usually is expressed in either politics or personal morality: Powell has managed to become a considerable novelist without showing more than a token interest in these two subjects. For him, personal actions first show themselves as just *happening,* the products of random encounters on London streets; behind chance there is an endless cycle of re-enactments of a few myths; behind the myths perhaps an occult significance—though Powell's use of occult themes remains entirely enigmatic.

In all these traits, Powell remains a traditional kind of British novelist, interested in *society* (in the older sense) rather than either the individual or the state. Above the social realm politics loom—treated by Powell either satirically or dismissively. Beneath society lies domestic life, whose passions and commitments he reveals only obliquely, as they might be inferred by a curious outsider. Powell's first novel, *Afternoon Men,* marks out his favourite ground: the hours between four and six when people have a freedom to manoeuvre in the transition from the demands of a career to those of family. His heroes [in *Dance*]—Stringham, Bagshaw, Trapnel etc—try to extend the drinking hours into a whole way of life, having failed to strike any deeper roots in the world. His anti-hero—Lord (Ken) Widmerpool—moves ponderously through this world of grasshoppers, stubbornly insistent on being an ant.

Widmerpool's success as a comic figure stems directly from Powell's deliberate omission of any recognisable motivation for his antics: neither his inner life, nor the prizes at which he aims, are given any visibility in the novels. The social round is bathed in a clear light, while everything else is left hazy. Indeed, Powell's mode of composition is predominantly visual; and it is in character for him to claim that the human race can be divided into 'voyeurs and exhibitionists'. He defines himself as one of the former—the right class, presumably, for the novelist who strives both to appreciate the performances of those he meets, and to speculate on their hidden compulsions. Voyeurism also implies, for Powell, a lust for control of others: sublimated in the novelist's art, indulged directly by *Dance*'s exemplars of worldly power, Lord Widmerpool and Sir Magnus Donners.

But if voyeurism is a master-concept in Powell's novels, what role can it claim in his memoirs? Here, caution and even prudery seem to have drawn the thickest of curtains across the secret life of Powell and his peers. His concept of autobiography is reflexive: draw the portraits of a man's friends, and let the man himself appear in the various sides of his nature that are implicitly revealed. But Powell's friends serve mainly as a source of 'copy': wandering through this gallery of eccentrics, it is more apparent what he saw in them than what they saw in him. He offers some shrewd comments on how a friend might be transformed, or absorbed, into a novelistic character: but he withholds the crucial revelations that might allow us to compare the imagined personality with the raw material that contributed to his or her making. . . .

Inevitably, Powell's determined reticence makes one wonder if the voyeur has any intrinsic interest, once dissociated from what he has looked upon. *The strangers all are gone* offers hardly any revelation of its author not already available from reading between the lines of *Dance*. Its very title, with its hint that strangers and friends are ultimately synonymous, seems to leave a last word that we cannot really expect to know others—nor even, probably, ourselves.

Paul Delany, "Voyeur," in London Review of Books, *May 5 to May 18, 1983, p. 19.*

MICHIKO KAKUTANI

Like Nick Jenkins, the amiable narrator of his *roman-fleuve,* **"A Dance to the Music of Time,"** Mr. Powell tends to be self-effacing and reserved when it comes to talking about himself. He eschews glimpses "into the person crater, with its scene of Hieronymus Bosch activities taking place in the depths," preferring the role of observer; like another famous narrator named Nick—Nick Carraway of "The Great Gatsby"—he remains a sympathetic but somewhat distant guest at the carnival by the sea. And yet if Mr. Powell's own life seems less than remarkable on the surface, his memoirs still promise a special fascination, for the author belongs to and has chronicled that remarkable generation of English writers who came of age between the wars—a generation that includes Evelyn Waugh, Graham Greene, George Orwell, Cyril Connolly, Henry Green, Harold Acton and Malcolm Muggeridge. (p. 9)

More discursive than the previous three volumes, **"The Strangers All Are Gone"** is, in Mr. Powell's words, "a kind of album of odds and ends in themselves at times trivial enough." In addition to the portraits of Mr. Muggeridge, Kingsley Amis and V. S. Naipaul, there are ruminative digressions about the 1960 obscenity trial of "Lady Chatterley's Lover" and the differences between America and England, as well as lots of color about the author's family and friends.

"Hitherto a comparatively sustained chronological narrative has been achieved," he explains. "But the last 20 or 30 years are not always tractable to continuity of design. As one picks one's way between the trees of Dante's dark wood of middle life its configuration becomes ever less discernible. . . . Books are published; professional schemes take shape or fade away; journeys are made; new persons met. All the time a perspective that once gave at least the illusion of order to the past diminishes. The outlines of individuals and events, perhaps clear enough in themselves, grow ever more blurred in relation to each other."

This difficulty with "continuity of design" is not peculiar to middle age, however. Whereas fictional events may be orchestrated and shaped into a pleasing pattern, real events tend to be messy and resistant to the tidy, idealized designs favored by the imagination. As a character in **"Dance"** says at one point, "Human beings aren't subtle enough to play their part. That's where art comes in." It is an observation that underlines the different effects of Mr. Powell's otherwise remarkably parallel novels and memoirs.

Both the memoirs and the novels, after all, detail what happened to those young people who grew up during the 20's—that hectic decade in which parties and easy flirtations provided an escape from the memories of the Great War—and the uneasy, politized decade of the 30's. Both deal with the close-knit world bound on one end by bohemian Soho and on the other by aristocratic Mayfair, a world in which nearly everyone has attended public school and Oxbridge and knows everyone else. And both chronicle the gradual decline of the upper middle class and announce the noisy advent of the brash new world ushered in by World War II, which "drew a hard line across the story of one's days after which nothing was ever quite the same again."

The language Mr. Powell employs in both his fiction and nonfiction is elegant and poised; it achieves irony by understatement rather than exaggeration. In both too Mr. Powell's penchant for long, intricate sentences reflects his books' expansive, anecdotal form. A Proustian density results from the accumulation of details, and physical descriptions and personal mannerisms—from the absence of an accent to the presence of a mustache—are used to illuminate people's inner lives, whether they are Orwell and Connolly in the memoirs of X. Trapnel and Pamela Flitton in **"Dance."** Interested readers can also trace correspondences between the fictional and real characters—between, say, Sillery and the warden of Oxford's Wadham College, Maurice Bowra; between Stringham and an Etonian named Hubert Duggan; between the Tollands and the author's in-laws, the Pakenhams.

The difference, of course, is that the memoirs record events and personalities, while **"Dance"** transforms them into myth. That myth, in turn, illuminates Mr. Powell's vision of life as a dance, in which human beings move "hand in hand in intricate measure: stepping slowly, methodically, sometimes a trifle awkwardly, in evolutions that take recognizable shape: or breaking into seemingly meaningless gyrations, while partners disappear only to reappear again, once more giving pattern to the spectacle."

Because **"Dance"** is fiction, Mr. Powell can attach a moral to the story, find a parable in his characters' fates. The New Man, Widmerpool, who stands for everything that is rude and ungainly, acquires more and more social and political power as the decades pass, while Stringham and Templer—those charming exemplars of all the old public school virtues—are killed in the war.

The weakest sections of **"Dance,"** in fact, are those least transfigured by the imagination. (pp. 9, 19)

Mr. Powell seems well aware of the limitations of writing about firsthand experience. Lamenting his inability to sum up the quality of post-Oxford life, he tells us in his memoirs, "Since there was not much pattern to these early years in London, I can introduce some of those who played a part only in a rather disjointed manner; though perhaps the chain of acquaintance that led to certain byroads in itself illustrates the sort of life I was leading." Or again, "The images that present themselves to the mind of any novelist of more than amateur talent take an entirely different form when the same writer attempts to describe 'real people' known to him, the former altogether more complex, free-wheeling, wide-ranging. . . . The 'real person' who sets going the idea of a major 'character' in a novelist's mind always requires change, addition, modification, development, before he (or she) can acquire enough substance to exist as a convincing fictional figure. . . . The smallest deliberate change made by a novelist to suit the story's convenience means, in truth, that all genuine dependence on the original model ceases—in contrast with traits (possibly inconvenient from a fictional point of view) that must unavoidably be chronicled about a 'real person' in Memoirs or Autobiography."

Clearly, gifted memoirists are able to transcend these limitations, but more often than not they are not accomplished novelists. In Mr. Powell's own generation, it was Cyril Connolly, Peter Quennell and Harold Acton—authors who never produced major works of fiction—who succeeded in writing the most resonant autobiographies. On the other hand, Mr. Powell's memoirs, like those of Evelyn Waugh, Graham Greene and Henry Green, tend to read like an etiolated version of his fiction. (pp. 19-20)

Michiko Kakutani, "The Novelist As Memoirist," in The New York Times Book Review, *June 26, 1983, pp. 9, 19-20.*

Yannis Ritsos

1909-

(Also transliterated as Gïannes) Greek poet, novelist, translator, dramatist, and essayist.

Ritsos is one of the outstanding contemporary poets of Greece. A national hero to many in his country, Ritsos writes of cultural and historical concerns important to the Greek populace. Ritsos's reputation was firmly established with the publication of *Epitaphios* (1936), still considered one of his most important works. Some of his other poems have been collected and translated in *Selected Poems* (1974), *The Fourth Dimension* (1977), and *Ritsos in Parentheses* (1980).

Ritsos demonstrates considerable versatility in his poetic style. His poems range from short, imagistic lyrics to long narratives and dramatic monologues. His themes and subject matter are intensely focused on issues of human rights. An artist with leftist interests, Ritsos was imprisoned and exiled by the various military regimes which governed Greece from the mid-1930s to the late 1960s. Some of Ritsos's poetry which was considered especially subversive was publicly burned. One of his most famous poems, "Romaiosyni," was set to music by the Greek composer Mikis Theodorakis and is the national anthem of the political left in Greece.

(See also *CLC*, Vols. 6, 13 and *Contemporary Authors*, Vols. 77-80.)

KIMON FRIAR

Yánnis Rítsos published, in 1934, his first poems of social content in a book belligerently entitled *Tractor*. Although influenced by Palamás' interest in machines and written in traditional meter, stanza and rhyme, they retain some of the sarcastic pessimism of Kariotákis, are harsh, violent, almost barbaric in tone, with such revealing titles as **"To Marx," "To the Soviet Union," "To Christ,"** and with individual portraits and caricatures such as **"The Individualist," "The Intellectual," "The Undecided," "Revolutionaries."** (p. 89)

In his early career, Rítsos may be considered to be the heir of Várnalis, whose proletarian books of poems, *The Burning Light* and *Slaves Besieged,* it will be recalled, had been published in 1922 and 1927, during and after the Asia Minor Disaster. Like Várnalis, and like Kazantzákis after him, Rítsos also places Christ among the revolutionary heroes of the world. . . . Haunted by death, driven at times to the edge of madness and suicide, Rítsos throughout his life has been upheld by an obstinate faith in poetry as redemption, and in the revolutionary ideal. *Tractor* and his next two books comprise his first period during which his humanitarian poems of social concern and those of rhetorical inspiration . . . were nonetheless written in strict meter and rhyme, most of them in quatrains, couplets, or in the traditional fifteen-syllable line. *Epitáphios*, published in July of 1936, written in the rhymed couplets of the folk *mirolói,* is a long revolutionary lament of a mother over the death of her son killed in a street riot during the breaking of a strike by army and police. (pp. 89-90)

As though to announce and repeat the orientation of his second period, ushering in a dichotomy that was to follow him throughout his life, all the titles of Rítsos' next four books are firmly musical: *The Song of My Sister* (1937), *Spring Symphony* (1938), *The Ocean's Musical March* (1940), and *Old Mazurka to the Rhythm of Rain* (1943). In these poems he broke forever from the shackles of meter and rhyme, wrote in free verse of short, staccato lines and, in a riot of color, sound and imagery, turned to themes that express the pain and endeavor of man to overcome his fate, the nostalgia of adolescence, the durability of the Greek landscape. His titles in shorter poems during the same period express now some of the delicacy, nuance and impressionism of a Wallace Stevens or an Odysseus Elýtis: **"Rhapsody of Naked Light," "A Glowworm Illuminates the Night," "Small Brother of the Sea Gulls," "Weekend in the Neighborhood of Summer," "Winds in the Western Suburbs."** In the last of these books, his free verse took the form of long, undulating lines reminiscent of Walt Whitman's versification, a cadence he has used ever since in the writing of long poems. Although each of these four books consists of one long poem, the various parts are not arranged in a hierarchical or compositional order, for often one section may be interchanged with another without harm to the general structure. They are rather musical movements of various tonalities, speeds or colors in an over-all symphonic arrangement, a rise and fall from one mood to another rather than an arrangement of musical motifs such as may be found, for instance, in Eliot's *Four Quartets.* Perhaps a more fruitful analogy may be found in the poems of John Gould Fletcher.

At about the same time, however, between 1938 and 1941, Rítsos was also writing extremely short free-verse poems which are terse, hard, concrete, objective, imagistic and symbolistic, with laconic titles such as **"Duty," "Punishment," "Myth"** and **"The Hill."** All his subsequent poetry was to hover between the two extremes of long and brief poems; in the general total of his many works the poems of average length are few. To fulfill these dual aspects of his nature, Rítsos needs, on the one hand, the long discursive poem in which he can ramble almost to loquacious length, to ruminate, to amplify, to digress, to indulge in mood and musical movement; and, on the other hand, he needs equally the brief, almost epigrammatic poem that is sharp, cryptic and symbolistic, almost surrealistic. . . . In the long poems, he orchestrates primarily with strings and woodwinds; in the short poems he raps out his Morse code with percussions. Trumpets and bugles are sparse or muted, for his general tone is low-keyed, tender in lamentation, lyrical in exultation, smoldering in anger.

The Second World War and the Occupation plunged Rítsos into his third period, wherein the lyrical element deepened into hardness to express the tragedy of those years, the civil war, the heroism of the Resistance. . . . His involvement in personal and communal suffering turned his proletarian poetry away from theoretical themes to those of a more concrete nature, to more humanitarian and less doctrinaire concerns. Like most poets of this nature, Rítsos is an idealist and romanticist, a man who identifies himself in empathy with the suffering of his fellow men, who espouses whatever movement promises best to alleviate mankind's slavery and injustice. (pp. 90-1)

With the publication of *Moonlight Sonata* in 1956, Rítsos entered into his fourth period. His long poems become more structural in composition, the esoteric and thematic movements are better planned, the diction is stripped to more naked expression, the idioms are more colloquial, the themes shift from purely humanitarian concerns to existentialist problems of wider range expressed with clarity and precision as though the dark abysses of an inner world have been cleansed in the light of an ultimate certainty. Loneliness, death and decay are now among his basic themes, the dynasty of chance, the tyranny of necessity, the acceptance of the totality of life in all its incomprehensibility. The problem of loneliness, as in *Moonlight Sonata,* is seen in the larger context of decaying civilization, symbolized by the house in which the woman in black unravels her "terrible strength for resignation." This poem bears curious analogies to another Rítsos has never read, Eliot's "Portrait of a Lady," for both express the agonized loneliness, the sense of withering, the confession of an older woman to a younger man against a musical background, that of Chopin in the one and that of Beethoven in the other. Rítsos no longer draws conclusions from a priori standards, philosophical, political, or aesthetic. Although to reach heights of personal inner consciousness, or to lose oneself in larger humanitarian struggles may in some ways alleviate loneliness, these in themselves become a new, though more expansive, solitude. (p. 92)

In his later, longer poems, Rítsos perfected the technique of the dramatic monologue, somewhat as in Browning. The poems open with descriptive stage settings; usually two or three persons are involved, but there is no dialogue between them, only the dramatic projection of one mind restlessly exploring an obsession, monologues that strive in vain to become dialogues. These poems are small scenes of introspection from untheatrical plays that have no ending. In all these poems Rítsos hides behind the third person singular, not so much in an attempt to divert personal confession or preoccupation as to penetrate into the heart and mind of others, of existential problems seen from the outside, an endeavor to derive universal spiritual truth from some person, object or scene. This also holds true of his shorter poems, "Testimonies," as he now calls them, with their deep problematical and symbolic character, their esoteric theatricality, their reliance on objects, their sharp depiction of slices of life, their almost surrealistic overtones. Like the couple in **"Honest Confrontation,"** the poet has now confronted the dual aspects of his nature, has stripped and offered himself—but always behind the veil of the third person singular—without proofs, justifications or guarantees, indulging in "the cruel pride of action." And yet, for Rítsos, no amount of whitewash—that healthy, new, classical simplicity of the modern Greeks—can wash away or dare cover up the black widow weeds of a peasant mother in her lamentation.

In his last period Rítsos has returned to classical myth, in such long poems as **"Orestes"** and **"Philoctetes,"** in which ancient situations are seen to be problematically modern—the struggle of man with his fate, the clash of personal freedom with necessity, the themes of ancient tragedians given an existential projection into modern times. The Greek echo in Rítsos, as in **"Ancient Amphitheater,"** does not imitate or repeat, but continues, to an immeasurable height, "the eternal cry of the dithyramb." (pp. 92-3)

Kimon Friar, "Introduction: The Social Poets," in Modern Greek Poetry, *edited and translated by Kimon Friar, Simon & Schuster, Inc., 1973, pp. 88-97.**

PETER LEVI

Yannis Ritsos is the old-fashioned kind of great poet. His output has been enormous, his life heroic and eventful, his voice is an embodiment of national courage, his mind is tirelessly active. In a sense he belongs to the modern movement, but he is closer to Neruda, or even to Vallejo, and to Brecht, than he is to Seferis or to Yeats or Laforgue. The modernism of the left in poetry is a special behaviour of language; in it the socialism of poets insists on the details of the real world, nothing is left ignoble or merely disorientated, and modern techniques of poetry cry out with the same passion for detailed realities. Ritsos is one of the greatest poets now living; in French he has been well served by Dominique Grandmont but until recently he has hardly been available at all in England. Nikos Stangos produced the first small selection a few years ago. He has now widened his scope greatly in *Selected Poems,* and for the first time it will be possible for English readers to have some notion of the breadth and depth of this humane and enigmatic writer. . . .

And yet it is not possible for a collection like this to be truly representative. There are almost none of the longer poems, the long pages of long lines. The exception is *The Dead House* (1959) which is also by several years the earliest poem we are given. . . . What most people in England know about Ritsos, if they know anything, is that he wrote **"Romaiosyni"** [also **"Romiosini"**], that astonishing sequence set to music by Mikis Theodorakis, which has become the national anthem of the left in Greece. Stripped of its music, in fact, the poems of that sequence are even stronger, more rigorous, more direct and more terrible. If he had written nothing else Ritsos would still be an important and even a great poet. It is a pity it has never been properly translated. [Translator Nikos] Stangos's first selection [*Gestures and Other Poems*] covered only the years 1968-70, this time he ranges from 1963 to 1972, with the one very strong, long poem of 1959; grateful as we ought to be, Ritsos has a wider range and deserves fuller selection.

This poetry is bound up with Greek history and social history since the war. **"Romaiosyni"** is a commemoration of the dead in the resistance and the civil war. It is the same kind of frightening history that is so present you could touch it in *The Dead House.* The poems of 1963 are as disturbed and as disturbing, there is a sense that surrealism has got into the bloodstream of Greece, but they are more about social than about public history, and some of them are unexpectedly moving and lyrical, at least for a few lines at a time. . . . In 1967 democracy was abolished in Greece; from that time onwards Ritsos wrote the poetry of imprisonment, exile and suffering. There is a bitterness nothing can or should sweeten; what was positive in his poetry at that time was a sort of despairing courage. . . .

One of the most brilliant gifts of this poet is the sheer abundance, the striking force and consequential rhetoric of his imagination. It is difficult for a foreigner to make the finest judgments about language, nor is it reasonable to attempt this for Greekless readers. But it can be said in general that his Greek is warm, lively, demotic and his rhythms are like those of a subtly controlled dialogue. It seldom occurs to you to try to scan a line by Ritsos, there are no two ways of pronouncing it, it imposes itself as poetry, and its rhythmic unit is rather the whole short poem than the single lines. Each line modifies the rhythms of the others. Even in the depressing sadness and, one ought to admit, the claustrophobic frustration of poems written under the last years of the colonels, the mature technical strength of these rhythms goes on increasing. Even the old, imaginative abundance never quite dries up. As a monument of human persistence and of intellectual survival, the poetry of Ritsos has been a remarkable achievement. . . .

Last year there was some talk of a Nobel Prize for Ritsos. He is not the same kind of writer as Seferis or as Pasternak, nor is it ever possible to compete with the dead. But Ritsos is a fine poet and he repays study. His poetry is more substantial perhaps than it seems in this collection; these poems are some of the cleverest, but he has a broader strength that these shorter poems are not always long enough to reveal. They read so well in English one is tempted to think they were chosen because this kind of poem translated so well, but I have been looking at the originals and that is not true, or not the whole truth. They have a subtlety and a power which once it is apprehended one can hardly exorcize. They occupy and haunt the mind with no excess of violence, in the same way as Cavafy, almost to the same degree. They seem to be casual jottings, and yet there are no rhythms that beat the air, no wasted words, no loose colours. There is an imagism about them sometimes that seems to preclude any development, but the images are ominously powerful, deeply rooted in life and experience, weighed down with a simple meaning and with resonance. They are supple, they are not "aesthetic". How can such a freshness and vividness not have withered? At times the presence of the poet seems to be that of a boy of twenty-one.

The Dead House has a special importance because it does allow of development and a cumulative, epic or tragic blackness. As social history this is an intensely truthful poem. It has some

of the qualities of a novel or one of those films which used to change our lives in the 1950s. The themes it touches have been important to Ritsos and they occur elsewhere in his work; one builds on another. Line by line, it has the swift sharpness that he isolates in shorter poems. . . .

There is something Chekhovian about the Greek provinces, and Ritsos can catch it, though other parts of the same poem have the atmosphere of Isaac Babel. Still, in the end there is a calmness about Ritsos which belongs only to those poets who are at home with realities, who love them and will not be satisfied with anything else.

Peter Levi, "At Home with Realities," in The Times Literary Supplement, *No. 3827, July 18, 1975, p. 809.*

SAMUEL HAZO

[*The Fourth Dimension*] is the most complete gathering of Ritsos's work yet published in English. . . .

Although Ritsos shares with a poet like Francis Ponge a concern with the universal in the minuscule and with Kazantzakis and Rilke a sure sense of the cosmos, his poems have about them the coherence of dreams. As in dreams, his images swim and evolve into their own order, and his capacity to word the "daily nightmare" is as present in his early work as in his most recent. (p. 347)

As a dramatic poet, Ritsos's lyrical talents are subsumed into what Eliot interestingly called the third voice of poetry—the one that speaks not from *I* to *you* but for *them.* This is the voice of the four monologues in *The Fourth Dimension.* Perhaps the most moving of these monologues is **"Ismene."** Ritsos expands on the Sophoclean story by portraying Ismene as a figure whose only reward in life is living on. Besides the fulfillment of Antigone's brief life, Ismene comments on her own longevity until we see that her only prize is the loneliness of mere survival. Even her final quest for love is made too late and with too much prudence. The only victor is the ticking clock, the symbol of death in the poem.

For a man whose political sensitivities and convictions are as pronounced and significant as Ritsos's have been and still are, the political dimension figures into only one of the longer poems in this book, **"The Blackened Pot."** . . . Ritsos is not a propagandistic poet of the Left. Nor is he a versifying ideologue. When wedded with the music of Mikis Theodorakis, Ritsos's words have the force of anthems, expressing the deepest aspirations of the Greek people. This is especially evident in his most popular poem, **"Romiosini,"** which is referred to and quoted from but not included in this book. It should have been included since its conclusion is one of the most memorable crescendos in all modern Greek poetry: "The hour has come, every hour is our hour. Be prepared. / This earth is theirs and ours / no one can take it from us." This kind of poetry (most poets in England and the United States are simply incapable of it) is the poetry of the blood in the spiritual and not the genetic sense. You can find it in the poetry of Alberti, Pasternak and Paz. Ritsos is correct in calling it more than "virtuosity and inventiveness," and the work of legions of poets in America and elsewhere who have reduced poetry to prosody or the mere penning of erudite valentines to one another seems not only anemic in comparison but, quite frankly, insignificant.

If good poetry is derivative of how well a poem works in itself and if great poetry depends on what universalities are at work in the poem, Ritsos's poems qualify on both counts. It is not surprising that he has been twice nominated for the Nobel Prize nor that he has been regarded as a major poet of this century by Neruda, Aragon, Sartre and Ehrenburg. Ritsos needs no further apologists on this score.

All he needs is to have his poems more widely known, particularly in the United States, and Rae Dalven's translations have now made that possible. The poems will do the rest. (pp. 347-48)

Samuel Hazo, "Wording the Daily Nightmare," in The Nation, *Vol. 224, No. 11, March 19, 1977, pp. 347-48.*

PHILIP SHERRARD

[In *The Fourth Dimension,*] Dalven's translations convey the style and verve of the poetry with considerable success. . . .

[But here] it must be said that, in view of the considerable claims often made for it, Ritsos's poetry is disappointing. This is not great poetry. Too much of it is merely episodic, a matter of sensation, of a piling-up of endless accidental details not fused by any overriding imaginative or intellectual vision. Great poetry is written within a tradition shaped by master after master and learned in deliberate study and detachment. Modern Greek poets like Solomos, Sikelianos or Seferis belong to such a tradition. Ritsos does not. Nor, in spite of the fact that Theodorakis has set some of his poems to music is his poetry that of the people, of ballads and songs handed on from generation to generation.

Ritsos's poetry belongs to an in-between world, to a disinherited, materialist world that has broken with the unwritten tradition and has not yet learned the written one. It is the poetry of the commonplace, of sentiment and pathos—a poetry, consequently, that makes but the barest challenge to, or demand upon, the imagination or intellect of the reader. It can be swallowed, more or less effortlessly, in a single draught, and forgotten as easily. In fact, its world is not the world of the imagination at all but that of fantasy and illusion, optical and acoustic. Statues demolish themselves, empty coats close doors, statements with an air of gravity turn out to be merely banal: "Sometimes I ask myself whether we aren't born solely / to acknowledge simply that we die . . . Nobody can take away from us any longer what does not exist." Even from a short poem one can extract impressionistic images, or juggle with them, without the poem gaining or losing. The long monologues (which are simply not dramatic) lack internal sequence, are but a kind of anecdotal pastiche in which no section is either related to, or more—or less—significant than, any other. One can see why, in an age that esteems so highly what it calls realism or what a mirror moving down a city's street can capture, this poetry is so popular.

All this is not to say that Ritsos's poetry has no value. Certain poems, and individual lines within poems, in their directness and with their sense of anguish, are moving, and testify to the courage of at least one human soul in conditions which few of us have faced or would have triumphed over had we faced them. That alone is rare enough. But, whether one likes it or not, sincerity, suffering and courage, and even an eye and ear for striking images, do not in themselves make great poetry. When we are told that it is these things, or things like them, that make Ritsos's poetry great, then we need to recall the criteria which any art must satisfy before it can merit that exalted title.

Philip Sherrard, "Poet of the People," in Book World—The Washington Post, *May 8, 1977, p. E17.*

KIMON FRIAR

Ritsos himself has written about his urge since early childhood in Laconia to write laconic poems, recognizing that this is no simple play on words but a temperamental necessity. *Corridor and Stairs* is such a book of short poems—which since 1963 have gone under the general title of *Testimonies*—and is of particular interest because they were written during the years of the dictatorship and because all of them deal, either specifically or indirectly, with the tragedies and traumas of that period. Basically, all of Ritsos's short poems are testimonies and witnesses to fleeting moments of life to which he may respond with lightning speed by pinning them down under his microscope to examine them minutely and thus magnify them into life's awareness. They are compact and concrete, lacking abstraction, crammed with objects and things. Even persons are seen objectively, unsentimentally, with an almost cruel detachment, as though they were themselves objects and their emotions and reactions little different than the movements of wind or waves. Human beings are seen at a dramatist's distance, almost impersonally, unrhetorically, disinterestedly; yet beneath this seeming detachment the arteries bleed, the heart is lacerated, the mind is torn, the body is bruised.

These "objects" play dual roles. On the one hand, they are simple, tangible, irrational concretions, things in themselves as they really are; but on the other hand, they are the small and innocent accumulators of human emotion and thought which lave them daily and make them the unwilling though innocent pawns in a drama which really does not concern them. . . . Within them resides the indefinite, the inexplicable, the irresponsible elements of life. They remain incomprehensible; they contain the enchantment of ambiguity; they raise questions to which there may be no answers. These common, everyday, humble objects are steeped in the storehouse of subconscious memory. . . . Ultimately they accumulate a myth of their own, shifting, changing and evoking within us unfathomable accretions.

Presented in simple sentence structures, wherein each object is given an undivided attention of utmost clarity, they are nonetheless not related to one another by any surface logic of continuity or plot but are juxtaposed one against the other so abruptly, so unexpectedly, so surprisingly that the reader is forced to wonder in what way they are related to one another and what the drama is which they are playing. They possess both the precision and yet the blurred and symbolical suggestivity of objects seen in dream. They seem to be surrealist in origin but are only so in impact. Beneath their seemingly illogical disconnections the reader-interpreter senses that a logic of the imagination is at play, that beneath the absurdity of their irrational existence and their deeds lies the luminous rationale of their creator—luminous because Ritsos, like Kazantzakis, has accepted the ultimate absurdity of life but has pushed far beyond it in gratitude for life's teeming multiplicity in order to embrace all phenomena in a fierce, almost savage love and affirmation. (pp. 483-84)

Kimon Friar, in a review of "Corridor and Stairs," in World Literature Today, *Vol. 51, No. 3, Summer, 1977, pp. 483-84.*

GEORGE ECONOMOU

"The Fourth Dimension" offers a representative cross section of [Ritsos's] work from 1938 to 1974, and contains a liberal selection of short poems, a few long poems . . . and the superb sequence "Twelve Poems for Cavafy."

In the short poems, most of which are not overtly political, Ritsos is full of surprises. He records, at times celebrates, the enigmatic, the irrational, the mysterious and invisible qualities of experience: Our senses are impressed as much, if not more, by the random and accidental as they are by the deliberate and institutional. If his perceptions, which stress paradox rather than irony, can be disturbing, they also define a major source of his inspiration, for it is the inexplicable and uncertain that Ritsos finds worthy of poetry. . . . (p. 14)

The first long poem in the book, "The Blackened Pot," written in a concentration camp in 1948-49, represents the period of Ritsos's career that produced his most important political poem, "Romiosini," unfortunately not included in this volume. . . . There follow four of Ritsos's many dramatic monologues, long poems ranging from 10 to over 20 pages. These poems do not in the least resemble American and English instances of the genre: For one thing, Ritsos frames them with beginning and ending paragraphs in which he describes setting and narrates actions, if only minimally. One of the effects of this technique is to obliterate the conventional distinctions among story, poem and play. In the poems based on ancient myths, he innovates with a spare yet precise use of anachronistic detail not just in order to make their settings and characters contemporary but also to imply universality.

"Twelve Poems for Cavafy" . . . "bring the poet back to life," says the translator [Rae Dalven] in her introduction, "with an intensity that suggests he had known him personally for years." It is likely Ritsos's intentions, like Cavafy's, are a little more complex. As the third person narrator of these poems says, in number 8, "Surely he is out to involve us in his own complication." As the last poem in the series reveals, the Cavafy poems articulate and demonstrate the legacy of the Alexandrian poet to Greece and the contemporary world in general and to poet Yannis Ritsos in particular. . . . (pp. 14, 37)

> *George Economou, "Deliberately Random," in* The New York Times Book Review, *July 10, 1977, pp. 14, 37.*

EDMUND KEELEY

The title [*Ritsos in Parentheses*] I have given this selection of translations is not as playful as it may seem. Two of the three groups of poems by Ritsos from which the selection is made actually carry the title "Parentheses," the one written in 1946-47 and first published in volume two of the 1961 collected edition, the other covering poems written from 1950 to 1961 and still to be published in Greek. The third source, a volume called *The Distant*, written in 1975 and published in March 1977, was chosen by the poet to accompany these versions from the two "Parentheses" groups, presumably because he considers the poems from this recent volume to be in the same general mode as the earlier "parenthetical" works. (p. xiii)

In what sense are these three groups of poems from different periods "in parentheses"? They are not really an interlude between those longer works that were primarily responsible for shaping Ritsos's reputation in Greece—for example, "Epitaphios," "Romiosini," and "Moonlight Sonata"—because

shorter poems of the kind found in these three groups have been important from the beginning and have now come to dominate Ritsos's oeuvre. One might call them parenthetical to those poems—early poems, on the whole—that promoted political themes directly and that helped to establish Ritsos as a leading Communist poet; but to regard them as an "aside" in this sense is to give too much weight to the ideological aspect of Ritsos's work and too much credit to his more blatantly political, rhetorical, and sometimes loquacious exercises. In my opinion, each of the three groups considered here reveals subtleties that are not found in more famous works, and though each group is uneven, the three combine to make a statement at least as important as that of any of the longer poems which served most to create Ritsos's reputation in his home country, in particular those that were assisted by the musical settings of Mikis Theodorakis.

My use of "parentheses" has more to do with metaphor than with judgment in any case. I am not sure what Ritsos himself has in mind when he offers the term, but certain metaphoric possibilities suggest themselves if "parentheses" are seen in the context of mathematics and symbolic logic, that is, as a way of designating separate groupings of symbols that form a unit or collective entity. The analogy underlines one aspect of these three groups of poems: a unity of symbolic vision or sensibility, both within the individual groups and progressively linking the three. Each shapes its own parenthesis, enclosing a particular way of viewing reality at a particular moment in the poet's career. At the same time, the three groupings, the three parentheses, are part of a developing vision that distinguishes these poems in terms of stance, mode, and perspective from other works—especially the longer ones—that make up Ritsos's vast oeuvre. The developing vision can be seen as an expansion of the space within the parenthesis representing each of the separate groups. In the case of each, the two signs of the parenthesis are like cupped hands facing each other across a distance, hands that are straining to come together, to achieve a meeting that would serve to reaffirm human contact between isolated presences; but though there are obvious gestures toward closing the gap between the hands, the gestures seem inevitably to fail, and the meeting never quite occurs. In terms of the poet's development, the distance within the parenthesis is shorter in each of the two earlier volumes. By the time we reach *The Distant* (the title especially significant in this context), the space between the cupped hands has become almost infinite, seemingly too vast for any ordinary human gesture that might try to bridge the parenthetical gap. (pp. xiii-xiv)

The poet's thirty-year journey from *Parentheses, 1946-47* to *The Distant* has been one of bitter catharsis, a progress from his focus on so-called simple things and more or less abortive gestures to a focus on bare—not to say barren—essentials and primitive rituals performed by those whose deity appears to be an infinitely distant, absolutely white, unapproachable and silent ambiguity. The starkness of this late vision, with its desiccated landscape and haunting presence of death, is paralleled by an aesthetic absoluteness that replaces the earlier grammatical complexity with an uncomplicated syntax consisting largely of declarative sentences and a purified style that leaves no room for figures of speech, no coloring other than basic adjectives, no images that have not been drained of overt sentiment. It has been a movement from masked simplicity to an attempt at the real thing. The earlier mode produced poems of subtlety and warmth, and it also produced poems marred by sentimentality; the later mode precludes sentimentality, but it does not always preclude an excess of stylistic dryness and a degree of obscurity. Yet the effect of the long catharsis in those late poems that work well is to provide a sense of reality that transcends the merely representational, a sense of the deeper psychic meanings—the hidden threats and nightmare memories—that lie below the surface of things. The poet's development has served to promote symbolic richness at the expense of decorative coloring and tragic vision at the expense of ideological rhetoric.

The development starts much earlier than has been generally acknowledged in Greek literary circles—. . . at least as early as the best of *Parentheses, 1946-47*. Beginning with that volume, Ritsos appears to have moved in much the same direction as that chosen by his strongest predecessors in this century, Cavafy, Sikelianos, and Seferis. Each abandoned rhetorical self-indulgence or subjective lyricism at some point in his career in favor of the dramatic and symbolic expression of a tragic sense of life that came to each with a mature vision of the human predicament and that discovered its profoundest form in the kind of simplicity which emerges from catharsis, personal and stylistic. These three groups of poems "in parentheses" can be taken as testimony of both the pain and the wisdom of Ritsos's progress toward a like discovery. (pp. xv-xvi)

> *Edmund Keeley, in an introduction to* Ritsos in Parentheses *by Yannis Ritsos, edited and translated by Edmund Keeley, Princeton University Press, 1979, pp. xiii-xvi.*

VERNON YOUNG

Ritsos' poetry is filled with invisible guests, wilfully invisible to one another at times, if merely inscrutable to the poet. And this partial visibility becomes more tantalizing, to the limits of the grotesque, in poems written under the pressure of dictatorship and resistance in Greece. (Among the ironies that crowd: Communism, the Abominable Snowman of Mandelstam and Milosz, has been for Ritsos the deferred Messiah!) From a landscape which has been perennially a subject for poetry since Homer, Ritsos' copious verses have assembled a landscape of their own which, if it resembles the illogical scenography of surrealist paintings, should not be termed unconditionally surreal. . . . [The] disjunctures in Ritsos' poems, becoming sharper and less amenable to deft interpretation over the years, were derived first from the intrinsic isolation and perplexity which Ritsos saw (oppugnant, surely, to a belief in Communism!) as man's condition. Later they were intensified by the treasons and concealments of civil war, in which equivocation becomes a principal mode of discourse; the significance of every gesture is a compound riddle.

Among the earlier poems . . . [those in *Ritsos in Parentheses*] nonhuman (even impalpable) phenomena are as sentient and transitive as human beings. "The night went by with its mouth full of speechless water. . . . And / the mountains / grew larger and sharper like the teeth of one who hungered." . . . Fewer of these pathetic fallacies appear in the later poems but long before the poet's arrest by the Papadopalos regime in 1967, which spurred some of his most vitriolic output, the dominating ambience of the Ritsos poem—this would return in another, more oppressed context—was that remarkable gift he has for suggesting the sound and color of silence, the impending instant, the transfixed hush. (pp. 624-25)

[Translator Edmund Keeley] interprets the poet's thirty-year journey from *Parentheses, 1946-1947* to *The Distant, 1975,* as "a progress from his focus on so-called simple things and more or less abortive gestures to a focus on bare . . . essentials and primitive rituals performed by those whose deity appears to be an infinitely distant, absolutely white, unapproachable and silent ambiguity" [see excerpt above]. After 1972 this description is drastically modified by many of the poems translated by Kimon Friar as *Scripture of the Blind*. Friar places a welcome emphasis, in his exhaustive introduction, on the extent to which Ritsos' sardonic vision, acrid and contemporary, is yet imbued with the ancient Greek sensibility and reminds us, apropos the title, that "All Greek literature, from ancient to modern times, is haunted by the shades of its three great Blind Men: Homer, Tiresias, and Oedipus. . . . All but one of these poems," he tells us further, were written ". . . at white heat, sometimes two or three in a day, in a concentrated two-month period . . . at the height of the junta years, when it seemed that tyranny, oppression, torture and degradation were to be the fate of Greece for many more years to come." While there are among these poems the always characteristic ones arising from "that deep inaction where music reigns," the majority are peopled with monstrous characters, deformed relationships, armless statues and headless dolls, the dead in refrigerators, "guards, prisons, flashlights, and old women, old women, old women"—all the horror, the betrayals, the fatigue, and the corruption that accompany a war against tyranny which has gone on too long and bred its own maggots. (pp. 625-26)

> *Vernon Young, "No One Said It Would Be Easy," in* The Hudson Review, *Vol. XXXII, No. 4, Winter, 1979-80, pp. 621-34.**

JOHN SIMON

The poems of *Ritsos in Parentheses* were culled from three sources: a volume titled *Parentheses, 1946-47;* a second collection, *Parentheses, 1950-61,* still unpublished in Greek; and *The Distant* (1977), containing verse written in 1975. In the succinct, incisive Introduction, [Edmund] Keeley identifies the themes of Ritsos' poetry—the progression from greater to lesser sharing, from stouter to slenderer hope [see excerpt above]. . . . (p. 239)

What I find remarkable about Ritsos' poetry is its ability to make extraordinary constructs out of the most unforcedly ordinary ingredients—surreality out of reality. And seem not even to make it, just find it. Footling details are taken out of context and seen either strictly for themselves or in some dizzyingly vast framework. Sensory experiences are detoured through some other than the obvious sense, yet without any showy, programmatic synaesthesia. Colors are expressionistically heightened or nudged in a direction they might have only hoped or feared to take. The actions of dreamers, eccentrics, or creatures impaled on despair are viewed with the alert amorality of a child. (pp. 239-40)

Yet sometimes the images leave reality virtually unchanged and still manage to get at something inscrutable or ineffable. . . . And sometimes there is no imagery at all, only an insistently resonant situation or incident, as in the three-line poem **"Spring"**: "They sat down in the field facing each other, / took their shoes off, and bare like that, their soles / touched in the tall grass. And they stayed." Are these two creatures lovers turning into friends or friends changing into lovers? Or are they either or both communing with something bigger? (p. 240)

Ritsos, on the evidence of these poems, is also a great bard of loneliness, but of loneliness ennobled and overcome. Poem after poem, image upon image, suffuses aloneness with a gallows humor that begins to mitigate its ravages and makes the person in the poem a Pyrrhic winner. (p. 242)

*John Simon, '"Traduttore, Traditore' or the Tradition of Traducing, II,"' in Poetry, Vol. CXXXVII, No. 4, January, 1981, pp. 220-42.**

RACHEL HADAS

Aristotle says in the *Poetics* that no work of art or nature can be beautiful if it is too big to be seen all at once. Because of the quantity of Ritsos' output, any one selection of his poems risks imbalance or incoherence, not to mention incompleteness. (p. 342)

To some extent, this confusion is inherent in Ritsos' productivity and scope; it should not be blamed on an editor who is faced with the imposing task of choosing representative work. Nevertheless, it ought to be possible to read Ritsos at a less punishing pace. Taking him in one poem at a time allows us to pause and admire details or subtleties if they are there at all, rather than forcing us to crane in order to see the whole monumental mural at a glance. In *Ritsos in Parentheses* Keeley . . . has given us a chance to do just that. Probably the longest poem in this collection ("Rainy") is 21 lines long, and most are shorter, many only five or six lines. Almost without exception (though generalizations about Ritsos are fraught with peril), the poems take place on a scale where intimacy and bleakness, loneliness and domesticity, intersect. (pp. 342-43)

The book is composed of selections from two groups of poems both called *Parentheses* . . . and from a third source, *The Distant*. . . . The notion of distance . . . seems especially significant in the spatial context suggested by the image of parentheses. "By the time we reach *The Distant* . . . the space between the cupped hands has become almost infinite, seemingly too vast for any ordinary human gesture that might try to bridge the parenthetical gap."

However we choose to read *Ritsos in Parentheses,* remote distance is rarely separated from smallness and constriction. Sometimes the poems depict tiny-seeming scenes in their entirety, as through the wrong end of a telescope. It is not just a matter of static visual imagery; there are often sounds and movement also, but over the whole frequently hangs a sense of nightmarish removal which serves to enhance the sense of enclosure. . . . Several details, either unremarkable or quietly incongruous . . . , are [often] combined in a flat, unemphatic language that gradually acquires tension. Sometimes Ritsos uses a succession of short sentences whose causal relation to one another is puzzling . . . ; elsewhere, as if to abjure causality, there may be a string of nouns and participles but almost no main verb. . . . (pp. 343-44)

Trimming rhetorical excesses and narrative borders off the scenes he depicts in his poems, Ritsos always manages to leave room for two kinds of activity, object, or image: the humdrum and the sinister. Think of the paintings celebrated by Auden's "Musée des Beaux Arts" in which the Old Masters, never wrong about suffering, concentrated on the torturer's horse scratching its innocent behind on a tree, or on the farmer who sturdily keeps ploughing while Icarus falls out of the sky. Shrunken versions of this device, Ritsos' poems focus on an alarm clock, a suitcase, a teacup, while off to one side (or in the all-important

last line) we hear of an explosion, a tank, a scaffold. The fact that throughout this volume Ritsos' imagery hews to the humble and everyday only serves to emphasize the sordid horror which so often rescues (or is supposed to rescue) the slicing of bread or the gathering of greens from banality.

This combination of awfulness and ordinariness is probably the single most striking device in *Ritsos in Parentheses,* and it surely provides one reading of the book's title. Are the everyday things of life sandwiched into the allotted spaces of a brief interlude while the tanks rumble on outside? Or is it—one hopes—horror that fits into the parentheses while life continues, as in the wonderful line of the *Iliad* which tells us that when Niobe was tired of tears she thought of eating? One could easily imagine Niobe frying herself an egg and listening to the radio in one of these poems. Ritsos is deft, in the best Modern Greek tradition, at interweaving myth and contemporary reality, or rather juxtaposing them in such a way as to show us they never differed much anyway.

> "Eurydice," he called. He ran down the stairs.
> There was no light in the entrance hall. He searched the
>   mirror with his hands.
> At the far end the woman with the yellow umbrella was
>   leaving.
> The second woman in the basement called out to him:
>   "She's dead."
> The three airmen emerged from the elevator with a
>   huge suitcase—
> inside it were her two severed hands and my
>   manuscripts.
>
> **("Descent")**

This brief, hard-hitting poem bears out my point about the horrible and the quotidian, the reality and the myth. The last line could easily have been lifted from a gruesome 1979 *New York Times* article . . . about the wholesale kidnapping, murdering, and mutilation of "dissidents" by the secret police in Argentina. One woman persisted in demanding proof that her daughter, who had vanished months before, was indeed dead. She was eventually shown (or sent? I forget which) her daughter's chopped-off hands.

Of course Ritsos is hardly alone in deliberately juxtaposing the homely and the hideous. Although Ritsos is not a particularly literary poet in the sense of overt references to other writers, a few of the names that come to mind when I consider his work are Sartre, Beckett, Simenon, Donald Barthelme, and deChirico, as well as Ritsos' notable Modern Greek predecessors, Cavafy and especially Seferis. . . . The flat unemphatic surface, the colloquial diction, the omnipresent, almost automatic irony, the sense of looming menace, and the mythological and historical dimension reduced to a domestic scale that one finds among these writers all mark the poems in *Ritsos in Parentheses.* deChirico's half-Fascist, half-classical nightmare landscapes and Barthelme's neat straddling of the line between writing and draughtsmanship recall some of Ritsos' visual vividness. Indeed, many of the smaller poems in this book are as bare and suggestive as cartoons. Is it relevant, in this connection, that John Ashbery's self-consciously reflexive style has been compared to that of the artist (and cartoonist) Saul Steinberg? Ritsos' is a less self-regarding art than Ashbery's, but many of his poems, far more easily than the American's, could be translated into line drawings without losing their quiddity. . . . (pp. 347-49)

Despite their modest dimensions many are packed with detail and provide the pleasures of recognition that some paintings do. Their potential range is as flexible as the imaginative sympathy of the reader. . . . (p. 349)

It is surely no coincidence that the first and last poems in *Ritsos in Parentheses* both seem to touch on the nature of Ritsos' poetic. In "**The Meaning of Simplicity,**" Ritsos makes rare and possibly disingenuous use of the first person singular:

> I hide behind simple things so you'll find me;
> if you don't find me, you'll find the things,
> you'll touch what my hand has touched,
> our hand-prints will merge. . . .
>
> Every word is a doorway
> to a meeting, one often cancelled,
> and that's when a word is true: when it insists on the
>   meeting.

Placed at the beginning of the volume, this looks directive, programmatic. In a more oblique way the last poem in this selection, "**The Distant,**" has the air of summing up what has been, and what can never be, said. With its long singing lines and unabashed use of apostrophe, the poem is as lofty and melodic as Ritsos cares to be in his parentheses. . . . The impulse to invoke peaceful negation [in "**The Distant**"] closes the volume on a grateful note of stillness. Inaction seems to be finally more desirable than all the busy sights and sounds that have come before, no matter how unapproachable and ungrantable such peace, or the wish for it, may be. If the sentiment looks nihilistic or defeatist, the music of this poem . . . does something to soften the effect of negation.

Since "**The Distant**" closes out the volume, I feel entitled to see in the old jester in the middle of the poem an image of the tired author, composing himself to the sincerity of stillness once the audience has gone home. One can see Ritsos both in the painted mountebank and in the unadorned weeper: the former because of his inexhaustibly prolific energy and variety, the latter because of the stubborn core of painful truths around which his poetry has developed. A great deal of Ritsos' variegated output, after all, results from the impulse to protest, lament, or at least bear witness to enormities.

Scripture of the Blind serves up a concentrated dose of enormities. Unlike either *Ritsos in Parentheses* or *The Fourth Dimension,* this is a translation of a single volume of Ritsos' work. Although the poems in *Scripture of the Blind* have never before been published in either Greek or English . . . , they were written in 1972—to be precise, between September 28 and November 28, 1972, and to be *very* precise, often at the rate of three or four poems a day during those two months. As the blurb reminds us, 1972 was "the height of the junta years, when it seemed that tyranny, oppression, torture, and degradation were to characterize Greek political life for many years to come."

Predictably, the grotesquerie and bleakness in this volume are nearly unremitting; the collection has less stylistic and thematic range than Keeley's or Dalven's selections. But *Scripture of the Blind* is a valuable book. It is one thing to be told that Ritsos is prolific, to be assured that any given selection of poems can hardly represent his eighty-odd volumes of work. It is quite another thing to see, as this book permits one to do, that on September 28, 1972, Ritsos wrote two poems, on the 29th one, on the 30th three, on October 2nd three, and so on. . . . The place-names and dates at the bottom of each poem compose, if read in sequence, a poignant poem, at once urgent

and monotonous, mosaic and monolithic, all by themselves. (pp. 349-51)

According to the dates of composition provided, only one poem in *Scripture of the Blind* took more than a day to write. Not that November 19, 1972, was an idle day; Ritsos seems to have been en route from Kálamos to Athens and had apparently already completed two shorter poems before starting "**The Statue in the Café.**" The long lines and leisurely pace of this poem, especially in the context of this book, make the discovery that it is only the length of a sonnet a startling one. It is not only the size of "**The Statue in the Café**" that distinguishes this poem; one could also cite its clear title, firmly articulated beginning, middle, and end, its relaxed pace, and its consistent imagery. Because of these features, the poem is somewhat out of harmony with the urgency, bordering on incoherence, that is the predominant note in *Scripture of the Blind.* But uneasy as it my seem in this volume, "**The Statue in the Café**" presents renewed evidence of the variety and subtlety of Ritsos' gifts—and of the kind of thing he can accomplish, perhaps, when he gives himself two whole days. (p. 353)

As a figure Ritsos is heroic. . . . But a critic has to try to distinguish between the life and the work even as she acknowledges and salutes heroism. Despite the power and scope of Ritsos' oeuvre as shown in these two books, I find it hard to forget a couple of facts which, be they niggling or damning, are negative. First, Ritsos' is not an extremely original voice. Second, it is not a voice which loses a great deal in translation. . . . But Ritsos is just not one of those poets who causes translators to tear their hair in desperation at the task of rendering into another language a distinctive cadence, a verbal witticism, the inimitable blend of music and meaning that has always been one measure of poetic excellence.

Ritsos writes in the poetic lingua franca of the twentieth century. True, the poems have Mediterranean details, but there are times when I could easily imagine them to be Spanish or Portuguese, Argentine or El Salvadorian poems competently rendered into English. For if Ritsos lacks the untranslatable melody and manner of a Pushkin, Valéry, or Yeats, neither does he usually seem to have the devotion to his own tongue and tradition that is so crucial in the work of Cavafy, Sikelianos, or Seferis—a devotion that gets lost in translation but that in Greek unmistakably stamps the voices of these Greek poets. Ritsos' language is an international vernacular which he deploys with skill and, within its limits, variety; but there is no use denying that the effect can become as monotonous and unmemorable as the kind of architecture that now covers most of Attica.

But if Ritsos does not challenge a translator's highest powers, his output is awesome enough to terrify any anthologist or editor. *Ritsos in Parentheses* and *Scripture of the Blind* both succeed wonderfully well in their complementary aims. We can choose to see Ritsos steadily over a period of two months, day by day, poem by poem; or, within reasonable limits, we can see at least a part of him whole. No one who is seriously interested in this remarkable writer can afford to ignore either view. (pp. 354-55)

> *Rachel Hadas, "Two Worlds According to Ritsos,"*
> in Parnassus: Poetry in Review, *Vol. 9, No. 1, Spring-*
> *Summer, 1981, pp. 342-55.*

CHOICE

In all his vast output of verse, Yánnis Rítsos has seldom published any love poetry. . . . For so verbally sensuous a poet this was odd. Now, unpredictable as ever, Rítsos, nearly half a century later, has brought out a triad of long poems [*Erotica*]—"**Small Suite in Red Major**," "**Naked Body**," and "**Carnal Word**"—that constitute an exultant hallelujah to physical love. He moves from the objectivism of "he" and "she" in the first poem through the involved, yet still surreal and dislocated "you" of the second, to a full, splendid, sensuous diapason in the third. "The poems I lived on your body in silence / will ask me one day for their voices, when you have gone." They will not be disappointed. . . . Rítsos has, in addition to his many other achievements, now written some of the finest, most deeply felt, most vividly expressed love poetry of this century—and at an age when poets generally have quite different things on their minds. Yeats, of course, was another exception; and Rítsos will stand comparison with Yeats.

A review of "Erotica," in Choice, *Vol. 20, No. 9, May, 1983, p. 1297.*

Philip (Milton) Roth

1933-

American novelist, short story writer, and critic.

A prominent contemporary author, Roth often draws on his Jewish background to present his recurring thematic concerns: an individual's search for identity, the effect of American culture on self-realization, and the relationship of art to life, among others. Roth's humorous, often outrageous satires of American life have inspired a considerable amount of critical debate, often centering on the irreverence toward Jewish life perceived to permeate his fiction. In interviews, essays, and even in his fiction Roth has defended and explained his work. He has both enthusiastic supporters and vehement detractors among critics, as well as a large, appreciative audience of readers. In defense of Roth's fictional treatment of Jewish life, Alfred Kazin stated that Roth portrays the "Jew as an individual and not the individual as a Jew." Irving Howe, one of the major challengers of the value of Roth's work, declared that "the talent that went into *Portnoy's Complaint* and portions of *Goodbye, Columbus* is real enough, but it has been put to the service of a creative vision deeply marred by vulgarity." Nevertheless, most commentators agree on Roth's exceptional skill in rendering Jewish dialect and evoking place and praise his exuberant inventiveness and his stylistic talent.

Roth introduces one of his major thematic concerns, the individual's search for identity, in his first book, *Goodbye, Columbus, and Five Short Stories* (1959). In the title novella, Neil Klugman, a poor boy from Newark, falls in love with nouveau riche Brenda Patimkin. Roth examines the conflicting emotions of Neil, who struggles to fit into an "alien culture." By contrasting the backgrounds of these two young people, Roth is also able to satirize the American dream of financial success. Gabe Wallach of *Letting Go* (1962), Roth's first novel, also experiences conflicts of identity in his various relationships.

Roth's most flamboyant portrayal of a character in search of himself is Alexander Portnoy. The best-selling *Portnoy's Complaint* (1969) vaulted Roth into widespread public and critical scrutiny. Some critics called it the funniest "serious" literature they had ever read and reacted sympathetically to the hero's machinations to free himself from the suffocating restrictions of his Jewish background. Others objected to the sexual explicitness and what they considered Roth's degrading treatment of Jewish life, claiming that the novel led nowhere. *The Breast* (1972) fantasizes the transformation of a professor into a six-foot mammary gland. Those who were drawn into the fantasy claimed that the determination of David Kepesh to come to terms with his "reality" demonstrated the human will to survive with dignity.

Particularizing his theme in order to focus on how literature affects an individual's self-realization, Roth, in *My Life As a Man* (1974), depicts himself as an author writing about a novelist, who is also writing about a novelist. Many critics suggest that this is Roth's best novel. The Roth-Tarnopol-Zuckerman character reappears in Roth's recent Zuckerman trilogy, a satiric view of artistic recognition in America. In the first of the novels, *The Ghost Writer* (1978), Zuckerman is a young author who recalls Roth himself. Once again, the hero is trying

© Nancy Crampton

to establish his identity and Roth uses the situation to pose some provocative questions about the relationship of life to literature. The subsequent volumes, *Zuckerman Unbound* (1981) and *The Anatomy Lesson* (1983), trace Zuckerman as he experiences the joys and disadvantages of fame and then eventually succumbs to the terrors of writer's block. Many critics faulted the self-preoccupation of the narrator but did appreciate some of the hilarious and imaginative entanglements in which Roth's hero finds himself.

Three other novels exemplify the versatility of Roth: *Our Gang* (1971), specifically a political satire of President Nixon, but also a critical view of political logic and doubletalk; *The Great American Novel* (1973), a parody on the mythology of both baseball and the idea of "the great American novel"; and *When She Was Good* (1967), Roth's only novel to feature a female character and to be set in a protestant, midwestern milieu. As usual, these three works met with sharply divided response.

The gamut of negative criticism to Roth's work ranges from charges of anti-Semitism, degrading depictions of women, obscenity bordering on pornography, repetitiveness of theme, lack of humanity toward characters other than his alter-ego hero, and the joylessness of his humor. But the positive response to his work is equally strong and maintains that Roth

is a deeply moral writer, that his books are fantastically humorous, even if darkly so, and that his satires, although written from a Jewish perspective, offer insight into the foibles of
American life. The quality and variety of critical opinion that
greets each new book by Roth indicates that he is a novelist
to be taken seriously. Although he may not please everyone,
he is, in the words of John Gardner, "on good terms with the
hunchbacked muse of the outrageous."

(See also *CLC,* Vols. 1, 2, 3, 4, 6, 9, 15, 22; *Contemporary
Authors,* Vols. 1-4, rev. ed.; *Contemporary Authors New Revision Series,* Vol. 1; *Dictionary of Literary Biography,* Vols.
2, 28; and *Dictionary of Literary Biography Yearbook: 1982.*)

JOHN N. McDANIEL

Philip Roth is a singular figure in recent American fiction: he
is a social realist who adamantly refuses to withdraw from the
field, even though he sees around him no smiling aspects of
American life. Taking as his domain the recognizable present,
Roth has been the most prolific—and the most controversial—
writer in America in the last decade and a half. His immense
popularity in the universities and the marketplace has raised
appreciative eyebrows and elicited cries of outrage, in some
cases both at the same time. Irving Howe reveals the ambivalence that Roth's fiction typically generates when he says,
"His reputation has steadily grown these past few years, he
now stands close to the center of our culture (if that is anything
for him to be pleased about)," and "we are in the presence
not only of an interesting writer but also of a cultural 'case'"
[see *CLC,* Vol. 2].

Roth's wonderfully rich and varied works—the sharp-edged
and well-crafted stories in the *Goodbye, Columbus* collection
(1959), the gloomily realistic *Letting Go* (1962) and *When She
Was Good* (1967), the serio-comic *Portnoy's Complaint* (1969),
the fabulistic *The Breast* (1972), the satiric *Our Gang* (1971)
and *The Great American Novel* (1973), the candidly autobiographical *My Life As a Man* (1974)—illustrate important insights into America's cultural predicament as Roth sees it from
his own vantage point: up close and personal, as the television
commentators say. No other living writer has so rigorously
and actively attempted to describe the destructive element of
experience in American life—the absurdities and banalities that
impinge upon self-realization in this "The Land of Opportunity
and the Age of Self-Fulfillment" (as David Kepesh in *The
Breast* says). And no other writer so clearly bridges the buoyant
optimism of Jewish-American writers of the fifties and the
dark, despairing world view of such recent writers as John
Hawkes, Thomas Pynchon, Joseph Heller, Ken Kesey, Anthony Burgess and Jerzy Kosinski. Yet Roth is more often than
not dismissed as a cultural "case," as if that explained away
the variety and vision of his fiction or mitigated the acute
embarrassment that accompanies the spectacle of brash young
soldiers obstinately continuing in losing battles.

But of course Howe is right: Roth *is* a cultural "case" in that
he has been both attracted to and repelled by the shaping forces
of society—and who of us has not? Here, perhaps, is a key to
the popularity that Roth enjoys as a spokesman for a growing
sense of disgust, outrage and impotence felt by so many Americans who view the Vietnam War, the Watergate affair, the
sensationalism of the press, the fatuousness of popular novels,
television sit-coms, broadway shows, indeed the entire phenomenon of American society, with fascination and repulsion.
As Norman Podhoretz says in taking issue with Howe, "Roth

is now central not because he has sold out . . . but because in
the course of his literary career more and more people have
come along who are exactly in tune with the sense of things
he has always expressed in his work and who have accordingly
and in increasing numbers come to recognize him as their
own." (pp. 3-4)

Roth's struggle with American culture has developed along
two fronts, one religious and the other artistic. By far the more
important of the two has been the artistic battle, one that calls
upon the artist to confront American society, "the real thing,"
head-on. This, Roth feels, is a confrontation that is essential
to the writing of fiction and to the writer of fiction. It is, then,
with some regret that Roth discovers how uncommon his artistic stance is—and how alone he seems to be in his fight. In
a seminal essay entitled "Writing American Fiction" Roth
charges that there has been "a voluntary withdrawal of interest
by the writer of fiction from some of the grander social and
political phenomena of our times." (p. 5)

[Roth] believes it is the writer's task to make an imaginative
assault on "the corruptions and vulgarities and treacheries of
American public life." . . . Roth's complaint, like Portnoy's
is a sweeping observation about the cultural predicament facing
the sensitive, creative individual: American reality, Roth concludes, "stupefies, it sickens, it infuriates, and finally it is
even a kind of embarrassment to one's own meager imagination," . . . and hence it is understandable, perhaps, that many
modern writers continue in the romantic strategy of evasion,
which involves, as Walter Allen notes, the "opting out of
society." (p. 6)

It is difficult to overestimate the importance of the hard core
of social realism at the center of Roth's artistic creed: it qualifies the most romantic of Roth's early stories and explains his
most recent ventures into social and political satire (*Our Gang,
The Great American Novel*) and fantasy (*The Breast*); it gives
credence to Roth's exploration of stereotypes and stereotypic
attitudes promulgated by mass media and accepted by some
segments of the American public; and, perhaps most importantly, it generates the central conflicts and basic themes found
in Roth's fiction. (pp. 6-7)

In emphasizing the predicament that the modern writer faces,
Roth suggests a broader predicament, one that is faced, he
feels, by many people. Although he has the writer specifically
in mind, there is no doubt that the problem he describes is
cultural. Making note of Benjamin DeMott's observation that
there seems to be today a kind of "universal descent into
unreality," Roth goes on to observe that he too is often overwhelmed by the "unreality" of the world that he wants to
describe in his fiction. . . . (p. 7)

"What the hell," exclaimed John Barth recently, as if confirming Roth's observation, "reality is a nice place to visit but
you wouldn't want to live there, and literature never did, very
long. . . . Reality is a drag." Yet it is precisely this predicament that fascinates Roth, captivating his imagination and
feeding his creative impulse. He will *not* be defeated; he will
not turn to other matters, other worlds. Like Kafka before him
he will turn the familial, communal, and cultural pressures
facing him into the very substance of his art. The problems
facing the artist become, in Roth's fiction, human problems to
be faced by the hero; the "unreality" of American public life
exercises a brutal power which the hero can attempt to conquer
but cannot evade. Like the hero of Ellison's *Invisible Man,*
whom Roth so admires, the Rothian hero must go out into the

world—even if it is only to discover that he is a man without a country, invisible, homeless, a stranger to himself and his deepest beliefs—before he can go underground to wait for a new spring and the promise of hope. (p. 8)

The religious issues raised by Roth's fiction have precipitated a battle of a different sort, yet one that Roth has entered aggressively. Jewish readers and literary critics alike have taken stands on the "Jewishness" of Roth's fiction. . . . Praised as a Jewish moralist and condemned as a self-hating Jew, Roth has been offered, as David Baroff says, as a "kind of shibboleth for American Jews; they define themselves and other people in terms of how they react to Philip Roth." . . . The controversies that swirl around the "Jewishness" of Roth's fiction have clouded, in most cases, the more essential questions of Roth's artistry: his affinities with social realism, his vision of human potential, his assault on American reality. It seems, however, that Roth has been called, ironically enough, to bear the standard in a dubious battle, while more fundamentally Jewish writers like Bernard Malamud and Saul Bellow have been allowed a graceful retreat behind university walls. (p. 21)

The complaints most often made against Roth's fiction by the Jewish community do not legitimately come under the heading of literary criticism in that such complaints do not derive from an analysis of the fiction. It is true, however, that the values that emerge from Roth's fiction often serve as a point of departure for charges of anti-semitism. After *Goodbye, Columbus* was published, many rabbis and other members of the Jewish community responded with letters and sermons denouncing Roth's fiction. (p. 22)

The charge of anti-semitism against a Jewish writer is not, of course, new. . . . In Roth's case, however, charges of anti-semitism have extended beyond the stage of initial reaction, and the question of his Jewishness continues to occupy not only the Jewish community but also serious literary critics—both Jewish and non-Jewish.

If anything is clear about the controversies surrounding Roth's depiction of Jewish life, it is that there is no agreement among respected critics on just how traditionally Jewish Roth's values are. (pp. 23-4)

Roth and his fiction do not yield easily to Jewish-oriented theses about Jewish-American writers and their fiction, primarily because Roth is the most "marginal" of Jews. His reliance on Jewish materials and Jewish values is qualified by an essentially secular and skeptical perspective, a perspective that he has defended vigorously, even in the camp of the supposed enemy—in, that is, Jewish magazines like *Commentary* and Jewish symposia like the one held in Tel Aviv in 1963. His defense of himself is occasionally acerbic, in large part because of the intense and often heated attacks directed at him and his fiction by critics both inside and outside the Jewish community; his own point of view is, however, both consistent and illuminating, and thus serves as a helpful context for understanding his intentions and achievements as a Jewish-American writer.

Perhaps the most obvious and necessary observation that can be made is that Roth is very tentative about his relation to Judaism. He said in a recent symposium held by *Commentary* that "there does not seem to me a complex of values or aspirations or beliefs that continue to connect one Jew to another in our country"; rather, Jews are held together by a disbelief in Jesus as Christ. Such a relationship is "enervating and unviable," for any religious, social, or moral community "springs not from disbelief, but faith and conviction." Roth feels that

"neither reverence toward the tradition, nor reverent feelings about the Jewish past seem . . . sufficient to bind American Jews together today," and he himself "cannot find a true and honest place in the history of believers that begins with Abraham, Isaac, and Jacob." (pp. 29-30)

This is not to say that Roth does not regard himself as a Jew. . . . Roth feels, however, that the American Jew does not inherit a body of law and learning, but rather a psychological shell without clear historical, cultural or moral substance. Thus, Roth believes, "one had to, then, I think, as one grew up in America, begin to create a moral character for oneself. That is, one had to invent a Jew. . . . There was a sense of specialness and from then on it was up to you to invent your specialness." . . . This challenge to invent moral responses and attitudes is for Roth both a blessing and a burden, for it provides one with unique obligations and a special perspective. He concludes, "If I can make any sense about my Jewishness and of my desire to continue to call myself a Jew, it is in terms of my outsideness in the general assumptions of American culture." (pp. 30-1)

It is, of course, precisely this "outsideness in the general assumptions of American culture" that supplies much of the impetus to the satire found in Roth's fiction. Roth does not, however, bring a strong sense of Judaistic heritage to either his fiction or his view of himself as a writer. He makes a fine, but important, distinction when he says, "I am not a Jewish writer; I am a writer who is a Jew. The biggest concern and passion in my life is to write fiction, not to be a Jew." (p. 31)

Roth insists . . . that as a writer and as a thinker his arena of interest is in no sense strictly Jewish, a point that is emphasized, to some degree, by the lack of attention to Jewish characters and to the Jewish milieu in **"Novotny's Pain,"** *When She Was Good, Our Gang,* and *The Great American Novel.* He is, if anything, a humanist whose concerns are broadly moral and social, and whose artistic vision, though rooted in the particularities of Jewish life, extends outward to the common humanity shared by all men. (p. 32)

So much is Roth interested in the "human situation," in fact, that he feels no particular empathy for the Jewish characters in his first full-length novel, *Letting Go;* rather, the "distinction between Jewish characters and Gentiles was not always present in my mind. They existed as individuals, as people." (p. 33)

Roth has repeatedly answered his critics from the Jewish community by insisting that as a writer he has no obligation to write Jewish "propaganda." . . . [He has said,] "I cannot help but believe that there is a higher moral purpose for the Jewish writer, and the Jewish people, than the improvement of public relations." In regard to his own fiction, Roth strikes a similar note in responding to his critics. When, for example, Jews objected to Roth's depiction of a Jewish adulterer in one of his stories, Roth was quick to point out that adultery is not a uniquely Jewish but rather a human possibility; and when Jews objected to his depiction of a malingering Jewish soldier, Sheldon Grossbart in **"Defender of the Faith,"** Roth responded, "He is not meant to represent The Jew or Jewry. . . . Grossbart is depicted as a single blundering human being." . . . Jewish critics, Roth maintains, confuse the purpose of the writer with the purpose of a public relations man. Jews feel that Roth is "informing" on Jews when he should be providing a picture of the positive aspects of Jewish life; Roth argues that he is indeed an informer, but all that he has told the gentiles is that "the perils of human nature afflict the members of our minority." (pp. 33-4)

It is perhaps one of those interesting ironies that Roth, like Kafka, is the most marginal of Jews who, nonetheless, must fight the hardest against religious and communal pressures to deliver himself from his past into his future. If it is true that as a social realist Roth keeps his eye steadily on human character and heroic potential as it is developed in or defeated by communal life in America, it is equally true that his own potential and his own character have been tested by the community—and Roth has responded to the challenge openly and directly, not only in interviews and nonfictional essays but in his fiction as well. Clearly, however, if we would understand Roth's intentions and achievements as a writer of fiction, we must look at his central characters not as Jews in an ideological, traditional, or metaphorical sense, but as men yearning to discover themselves by swimming into dangerous waters beyond social and familial strictures: beyond the last rope. Only by so approaching Roth's fiction are we likely to see what it is that the stories are really about. (pp. 35-6)

In examining the "circumstances of ordinary life," Roth has employed a wide range of artistic techniques resulting in a fictional canon notable for its variety. In fact, the diversity of Roth's fiction has generated evident difficulty in assessing Roth's intention and achievement as a writer of fiction. Certainly most critics acknowledge Philip Roth as a major talent, as one who has been keenly responsive to the human condition as it is revealed in contemporary American experience. . . . Despite such acknowledgment, however, the critical community has been divided in its response to Roth as a significant contemporary author. Critics have taken stances toward his achievement that are as diverse as the fiction itself: he has been called an anti-semitic and a Jewish moralist, a romantic writer and a realistic writer, a polemicist, a satirist, a mannerist, a sentimentalist, and a liar; he has been praised for having "a clear and critical social vision," condemned for having a "distorted" view of society, and accused of entertaining an "exclusively personal" vision of life that does not include society at all. Whereas Alfred Kazin recently spoke so confidently of what he calls Saul Bellow's "signature," it seems that from the collective viewpoint of the critical community Roth's mark has been something of an indecipherable scrawl. (pp. 199-200)

The uniqueness of Roth's "signature" is intimately associated with his commitment to social realism, to a willingness to confront the community—its manners and its mores—as subject for his art. The confrontation between the hero (activist or victim) and world, between private and public realms, between "un-isolated" individuals and the shaping forces of general life, is the confrontation that is central to the realistic mode—and the fiction of Philip Roth. Certainly many critics have detected in Roth's fiction a noticeable attention to manners, to moral issues, and to literary realism; too often, however, Roth's most characteristic mode has been dismissed. . . . It is my contention that we can best assess Roth's artistry by viewing him, rather broadly, as a writer whose artistic intentions are "moral," whose method is realistic, and whose subject is the self in society.

Given Solotaroff's contention that Roth's sensibility is embedded in a Jamesian concern for motives and for what Trilling calls "moral realism," it is altogether possible to think that Roth writes, in part, to fill a void that Trilling pointed out in 1948 [in "Manners, Morals and the Novel"]:

Perhaps at no other time has the enterprise of moral realism ever been so much needed, for at no other time have so many people committed themselves to moral righteousness. We have the books that point out the bad conditions, that praise us for taking progressive attitudes. We have no books that raise questions in our minds not only about conditions but about ourselves, that lead us to refine our motives and ask what might lie behind our good impulses.

As our examination of Roth's fiction has shown, the question of what lies behind "good impulses" is one that virtually every major character in his fiction asks. The crises depicted in Roth's fiction are not so much ontological as they are moral, for although the character may begin with the question of identity and selfhood, he is likely to conclude with the questions of Neil Klugman, Gabe Wallach, and Peter Tarnopol: what do I owe to my fellow man, and how do I explain my actions toward him? What is my relation to society, and what are the dangers of the moral life? To what extent have I been victimized by false ideals and self-deceptions grounded in the society of which I am an ineluctable part?

Inevitably, when we hear such questions we think immediately of Tolstoy, Conrad, Dostoevski, Gogol—the great European novelists—and Henry James, America's most prominent novelist of manners and moral realism; nor is it surprising that allusions to these novelists and their works appear frequently in Roth's fiction. . . . The burdens of responsibility, the clash between the actual world and the "invented reality" that grows out of what one "sees and feels," the moral difficulties of "letting go" (a phrase that Roth borrowed from Mrs. Gereth in *The Spoils of Poynton*, who tells Fleda Vetch, "Only let yourself go, darling—only let yourself go!")—all these are concerns that Roth has in common not only with James but with other European novelists of manners and moral realism as well. (pp. 202-04)

Perhaps the most significant aspect of Roth's moral interests is that they extend clearly into his conception of art (and here the affinity between Roth and such writers as Henry James is at its strongest). (p. 205)

For Roth, as for James, fiction not only treats moral issues, but has the purpose of elevating and liberating the reader's social and moral consciousness through realistic examination of "man's condition." Just as "those of us who are willing to be taught, and who needed to be, have been made by *Invisible Man* less stupid than we were about Negro lives," so can the stereotypes of Jewish malingerers, Jewish mothers, Jewish family life, and Protestant Midwestern fathers, mothers, sons and daughters be put into new perspectives—for "the stereotype as often arises from ignorance as from malice." (pp. 206-07)

A strong social and moral consciousness, coupled with a readily evident persuasion toward a realistic portrayal of man in society, points toward Roth's distinctiveness as a contemporary American author, for it is the prevailing opinion that such concerns have never been central to the American literary tradition. In 1948 Lionel Trilling asserted, "The fact is that American writers of genius have not turned their minds to society. . . . In America in the nineteenth century, Henry James was alone in knowing that to scale the moral and aesthetic heights in the novel one had to use the ladder of social observation." Trilling's contention that "Americans have a kind of resistance to looking closely at society'' is not a startling observation, most critics of the American novel would agree. (p. 207)

Certainly Roth is not a proponent of the documentary social novel or a novel of manners in the European sense of the term (for, as Trilling persuasively argues in ''Art and Fortune,'' such a novel is not possible in America); nonetheless, Roth's relation to his contemporaries is more sharply defined if we consider him as a social realist—as a writer, that is, who does not yield to the romantic impulse as defined by Chase, Allen, Lewis, and others. Roth has been characteristically associated with such Jewish-American writers as Mailer, Salinger, Bellow, Malamud, and Gold, when in fact his closest associates among American authors are Sinclair Lewis, F. Scott Fitzgerald, John O'Hara, John P. Marquand—writers who, as James Tuttleton demonstrates, are primarily ''concerned with social conventions as they impinge upon character.'' (p. 208)

In Roth's view, Salinger and Malamud are two of America's best authors, yet their works seem to be curiously out of touch with the actual world. Neither writer ''has managed to put his finger on what is most significant in the struggle going on today between the self (all selves, not just the writer's) and the culture.'' . . . In the fiction of Saul Bellow and William Styron Roth finds a similar inability or unwillingness to confront the social world in all of its recognizable aspects. In Roth's opinion, the fiction of Bellow and Styron, peopled by heroes who affirm life in foreign and unrealistic climes, is further evidence that our best writers have avoided examining American public life. . . . Roth's objection to the novelistic strategies of Bellow and Styron certainly places his own attitudes clearly in front of us: the author must confront the social world squarely if he is to describe human character faithfully, and affirmation achieved through geographic displacement or metaphoric evasion is, finally, no affirmation at all. (p. 211)

Roth's assault on the American experience—his exploration of moral fantasy, his concern for moral consciousness, his willingness to confront the grander social and political phenomena of our time—is, I think, the most significant aspect of his art. Despite the diversity of Roth's fiction, despite the variety of themes, values, and characters that emerge from his novels and short stories, we see an abiding faith beneath Roth's pessimism. . . . Roth has demonstrated a willingness to explore the limits of his artistic creed with a deeply felt concern for man and society, a concern that is detectable beneath his ponderous realistic novels and his most vitriolic satire. (p. 214)

> *John N. McDaniel, in his* The Fiction of Philip Roth, *Haddonfield House, 1974, 243 p.*

SANFORD PINSKER

Prometheus remains the quintessential rebel-hero, the mythological figure who defied Zeus, stole the secret of fire from Hephaestus, and gave it to mankind. For that liberating act, he was punished—chained to a rock where an eagle pecked away at his liver. Nathan Zuckerman is a paler post-Modernist version. He defied the American Jewish community, exposed its dirty little secrets and then blabbed the whole business in public—i.e. Gentile—print. For that liberating (?) aesthetic act, he became Rich and Famous, Remorseful and Troubled. Zuckerman's portrait of the assimilated American Jew specialized in warts. No wonder his readers cried ''Foul!'' when they saw the mirror he held up to their nature.

Nathan Zuckerman is, of course, Philip Roth's fictionized extension, his way of paying off old debts, of exorcizing old guilts, at the same time that he can, and does, insist that one keep author and character forever separated. In large measure the device worked in *My Life as a Man* (1974) and it was brilliantly effective in *The Ghost Writer* (1979), but, this time, even True Believers will have trouble swallowing the latest installment of Nathan Zuckerman's ''complaints.''

Zuckerman Unbound is about the surprises that success brings. Like Woody Allen's *Stardust Memories*, it is an exercise in biting the hands that have fed them, at the same time that it aspires toward confession. In earlier, simpler times, a writer like F. Scott Fitzgerald could believe that ''The rich are different from you and me'' and set about writing fiction that would convince his countrymen that the mystique was true. . . . Poor Zuckerman lives in a tougher-skinned, less romantic decade. Nobody is interested in hearing about how hard life in the fast lane can be because, as Nathan points out, ''a poor misunderstood millionaire is not really a topic that intelligent people can discuss for very long.''

Nonetheless, Nathan Zuckerman cannot *not* discuss his put-upon, beleaguered life, and Philip Roth cannot resist *any* chance to play ''defender of the [aesthetic] faith.'' . . . But Zuckerman protests too much about highmindedness. He is yet another of Roth's Temper Tantrum Kids, this time with the Harvard Classics at his fingertips and the Modernist Giants firmly in his handgrasp. When Zuckerman yells, he insists on good literary company: ''What would Joseph Conrad do? Leo Tolstoy? Anton Chekhov? When first starting out as a young writer in college he was always putting things to himself that way. . . .'' The rub, of course, is that none of *those* writers grew up Jewish in Newark. . . . Out of the nearly equal measures of attraction and repulsion, of frustration and self-righteousness, about American Jewish life, Nathan Zuckerman's art is made.

By now, all of this has a familiar look—not only in terms of Roth's canon . . . , but also in terms of the longer tradition of American Jewish letters. Zuckerman is uncomfortable—yea, guilt-ridden—about the money that crashes in as copies of *Carnovsky* roll off the presses. . . . In Abraham Cahan's scathing portrait of the *alrightnik, The Rise of David Levinsky* (1917), success is synonymous with an ashy taste. Despite his millions (or, more correctly, because of them), Levinsky tries desperately to reestablish contact with his earlier, authentic (read: Jewish) self. Roth is perhaps the first American Jewish writer to give the scenario a literary twist; now High Art, rather than the garment industry, can make one wealthy and estranged.

Roth has specialized in this corner of the American Jewish saga. He writes about Jewish *kitsch* as if that alone constituted the cultural whole. His *voice*—half wise-guy, half Jeremiah—is still his greatest resource. And yet, it is when Roth waxes poignant, as he does when describing his father's death and its aftermath, that he can generate passages that move us in ways that his broad assaults on Jewish motherhood, however funny, never quite do. *Zuckerman Unbound* ends with a symphony to fatherhood we have not heard so powerfully since the last pages of *The Professor of Desire* (1977).

Given Roth's penchant for self-analysis, it is fitting that the last words about *Zuckerman Unbound* come from one of Roth's own characters. For some time Roth has been writing with his head arched over his shoulder, as if his reviewers and critics might be gaining on him. . . . Nonetheless, in *The Ghost Writer*, a much younger Nathan Zuckerman sought out an established writer to act as his mentor, father-figure, and role model. In *Zuckerman Unbound,* his secret-sharer is Alvin Pepler, the wacky know-it-all who can match Zuckerman paranoia for paranoia, self-righteousness for self-righteousness. In his unfinished review of *Carnovsky,* Pepler/Roth makes a very savvy point:

> Fiction is not autobiography, yet all fiction, I am convinced, is in some sense rooted in autobiography, though the connection to actual events may be tenuous indeed, even nonexistent . . . yet there are dangers in writing so closely to the heels of one's own immediate experience: a lack of toughness, perhaps; a tendency to indulge; an urge to justify the author's ways to men.

The same things could be said, in spades, about *Zuckerman Unbound.* (pp. 53-4)

> Sanford Pinsker, "Zuckerman's Success," in Midstream, Vol. XXVII, No. 10, December, 1981, pp. 53-4.

PATRICK O'DONNELL

Interpretative fantasies, from *Clarissa* and *Tristram Shandy* to *Finnegans Wake, Pale Fire,* and *Gravity's Rainbow,* have traditionally concerned themselves with such problems as "validity," "discursivity," and "reality" vs. "textuality," particularly with the status of fictional texts, their origins, ends, and authoritative power. Philip Roth's recent novel, *The Ghost Writer,* is part of this tradition: it is about origins, and the problems of originality that any serious writer eventually comes to face. It is the kind of novel that forces us to reflect upon the act of writing, in a traditional sense, as an embodiment of "selfhood," and less traditionally, as the place where the "self" may be lost in the warp and woof of the text. In this first-person narration of writer Nathan Zuckerman's quest for a spiritual and aesthetic father, Roth presents us with a parodic reflection upon the notion of "textuality," or language in search of its source of power and authority, orphaned by the very contingencies that make it come into being. Yet the parody here is paradoxical and serious; the novel is a kind of "deconstruction" that mimes both customary and revolutionary notions of inspiration, influence, interpretation, authority and literary production. That this comes from one of our finest parodists, whose greatest success thus far is a send-up of the autobiography or confession in *Portnoy's Complaint,* where ideas of "self" and "generation" are comically considered, is unsurprising. In *The Ghost Writer,* Roth renews his essential concern with the limits of writing and fiction.

One first notices that *The Ghost Writer* is filled with "texts." Among these are the forgotten stories of E. I. Lonoff, a Jewish writer who, years ago, escaped civilization for the Thoreauvian respite of his country home in the Berkshires. Lonoff's response to the tedious question, "how do you write?" is a wearying parody of the writing process: "'I turn sentences around. That's my life. I write a sentence and then I turn it around. Then I look at it and I turn it around again. Then I have lunch. Then I come back in and write another sentence.'" There is the text of *The Ghost Writer* itself, narrated by Nathan Zuckerman, a novelist who bears a ghostly resemblance to *the* Philip Roth, and who recounts his two-day stay with Lonoff "more than twenty years ago—I was twenty-three, writing and publishing my first short stories, and like many a *Bildungs-*

roman hero before me, already contemplating my own massive *Bildungsroman.*" . . . Within this double textual inversion— Zuckerman the hero of the fiction he will one day write—we are given Zuckerman's reading of Henry James's "The Middle Years" late at night as he examines the riches of Lonoff's study: James's story tells how an author, reading his own latest novel, is led through an encounter with a young admirer to assess the value of his life and art. His imagination stirred by James, by Lonoff, and by a vigorously overheard encounter between Lonoff and the surrogate daughter/lover who lives in the house as a "research assistant," Zuckerman produces another text. He recounts an internalized fiction in which the girl, Amy Bellette, is revealed to be Anne Frank, now in America, in disguise, anguished over the fact that she has had to disown yet another text, her famous diary, so that it might not lose its effectiveness as a dispossessed portrayal of dispossession. And, within this infinite regress of texts, there are dozens of references to other writers—James, Kafka, Hemingway, I. B. Singer, Isaac Babel, Poe, Joyce, Mann, Felix Abravanel (a thinly disguised combination of Norman Mailer and Saul Bellow)—as well as a barrage of fragmentary marginal discourses in *The Ghost Writer,* including letters, recorded conversations, and Lonoff's underlinings of everything from James to articles on the television industry.

Summary alone of the flurry of texts in the novel creates a kind of fictive vertigo. We are compelled to wonder if Roth is not attempting to write what Roland Barthes has referred to as an "ideal," infinite text, wherein "the networks are many and interact, without any one of them being able to surpass the rest; this text . . . has no beginning; it is reversible; we gain access to it by several entrances, none of which can be authoritatively declared to be the main one." Such attempts, Barthes avers, must fail, but the Chinese-box effect of receding texts in *The Ghost Writer,* like the labyrinthine intertextuality of John Barth's LETTERS or the fragmented textual archaeology of Thomas Pynchon's *Gravity's Rainbow* suggests, by implication, the possibility of an "infinite" text. Roth's novel may be seen as a vortex in which "texts," kinds of discourse— Roth's, Zuckerman's, Lonoff's, James's, Anne Frank's—whirl about disconnectedly, collide, and vanish, their "authority" and literalness subverted.

Roth is an unusually economic writer, and the spare fiction *The Ghost Writer* is may seem too frail, indeed too "ghostly," to support the weight of entangled discussions of textuality. Yet this slight narrative is laden with references to, and inversions of, acts of perception and interpretation that cause us to question the critical act of making, and reading, fictions. We know, for example, of Roth's debt here to Henry James, who established for modern fiction the relative, changeable relationship between the viewer and the view, the reader and the text. James's "The Middle Years" is quoted and summarized in *The Ghost Writer,* and the narrative "framing" of Roth's novel, in its inverted complexity, resembles that of James's classic ghost story, *The Turn of the Screw.* There, we never know what the "true story" is, but if we approach the narrative from the outside moving in, we listen to a series of narrators as we make our way through a maze of texts that allows us to approach, though never to uncover, the "real" events at Bly. (pp. 365-67)

So too, in *The Ghost Writer,* a phantom double, in many respects, of James's tale, there are a series of narrative inversions. A diagram of the narrative frames in Roth's novel reveals a spare fiction with a highly complex structure. . . . (p. 368)

The consequences of the narrative structure in Roth's novel are similar to those elicited by *The Turn of the Screw,* but with some interesting differences. By the time we get to the last false bottom of *The Ghost Writer,* the events of a diary contained within a story imagined by the younger version of the narrator to whom we are listening, the sense of "story" has been entirely destroyed for us, and what the novel seems to be about is the parallel lives different kinds and levels of discourse lead. The encounter between Zuckerman and Lonoff, which might be termed the subject of the former's recollection, takes up only part of our attention: a dinner with Lonoff and his wife, Hope, a halting after-dinner conversation, and a brief meeting between master and epigone the next morning amidst a chaos of departures is all there is to the "story." The bulk of the novel is given over to preamble, reflection, transcription, interpretation—to the many other "texts'" of *The Ghost Writer.*

Unlike *The Turn of the Screw, The Ghost Writer* does not encourage us to traverse a series of narrative screens in order to reach a central, if unrelatable text. Rather, the texts of Roth's novel seem ghostly, orphaned repetitions of each other, leading nowhere, resonating with the false notes of self-conscious, dispossessed "fictions." (p. 369)

The textual inversions and displacements . . . are complicated and deepened by the metaphorical search for self and parent that comprises nearly the entire "plot" of *The Ghost Writer.* The quest for or questioning of parental authority parallels the fictional pursuit or denial of origin, source, and authority, those qualities that confer upon the "word" of the novel its value and validity, its reflective authenticity. (p. 370)

The refusal of parenthood and the lack of generation in *The Ghost Writer* is almost parodically self-evident. While Zuckerman is having difficulties establishing a relationship with his spiritual father, he has already, through his art, alienated his real father. His most recent story, "Higher Education," is a humorous portrayal of an aunt's determination to put her twin sons through medical school by selling roof shingles and siding. . . . Zuckerman's tale of his relative's moxie enrages his father, who declares that it represents only the partial truth about "Jewish family life," a story that the *goyim* will hold up as proof of stereotypical greed, stubbornness, and family in-fighting. . . . The partial, treacherous words of the story parallel the shattering of the bond between father and son, the thwarted passing on of life and "truth."

Other texts in *The Ghost Writer* reflect a similar pattern. (pp. 371-72)

The separation that texts engender is revealed with the greatest complexity in Zuckerman's "story" about Amy Bellette, née Anne Frank. Anne's *Diary* is the most dramatically orphaned text in *The Ghost Writer,* its author denying her existence as she lives under a pseudonym in America, refusing her father, Otto, the knowledge that his daughter is still alive: the denial of parentage to the text concurs with the denial of the biological parent. Anne's self-abnegation as the originator and author of the *Diary* occurs for good reasons. She feels it will lose impact if the dead girl who is its heroine reappears, a live ghost. But the power of textuality has been purchased at a great price, for Amy wonders if "having outlived the death camps, if masquerading here in New England as somebody other than herself did not make something very suspect—and a little mad—of this seething passion to 'come back' as the avenging ghost." . . . That is, she has had to make herself ghostly, like the dead girl in the *Diary,* in order for the memoir to survive; authorial

suicide is committed in the generation of the text as its creator vanishes, reappearing only as the phantom avenger behind the text who pursues revenge upon the criminals who have "killed" her. (pp. 372-73)

In essence, Zuckerman's narration of the writing of the *Diary* and the fate of its author exhibits the vertiginous prospect of a live girl pretending to be dead, reflecting upon a text she wrote when she was "alive," talking to a phantom about the fact of her own emotional ghostliness in relation to her parents, embodied in her continual nightmare of being orphaned. In a double negation, she disinherits her text while orphaning herself from her real father. Zuckerman's fiction about Amy (itself authorless, since Zuckerman quickly denies its validity to himself the next morning) is a textual hall of mirrors in which authors are reflected only as ghostly progenitors of texts that, themselves, threaten to vanish if authorship or parenthood is put under question. (pp. 373-74)

Of all the authors in *The Ghost Writer,* Zuckerman plays the dead man's game most avidly. He is a marvel of self-effacement as he takes on the role of humble supplicant before the "master," Lonoff. . . . Through his fiction, Zuckerman has established his filial relation to Lonoff, but it is one in which the strong will of the son, his word, is subsumed by a spurious parental authority. The disparity between the psychological importance Zuckerman detects in his relationship with Lonoff and the "reality" of the situation is comic (we hardly need Roth's nudging pun) but it also reflects the complex sexual aspect of the problem of authority and textuality the novel pursues. Zuckerman can "write" his fiction about Amy because he revels in his voyeuristic vision of Lonoff ("Dad-da") consoling his "little girl," Amy, on his knee while Zuckerman stands on a book (James's "The Middle Years") so that he can overhear their conversation in the room above him. The psychological reversion of this comically Oedipal scene matches the byzantine textual complexity of the novel. It is an allegorical rendering of the son's, Zuckerman's, accession to a ludicrous and impotent patrimony, a relation in which self-effacement and masturbation—Zuckerman's response to Amy's late night entry into her bedroom—are the exercises through which the text is generated. Distancing, effacement, submission, all seem to be activities that Zuckerman must partake of in order to become the literary son who will one day, himself, become a full-fledged author.

But all of these serious considerations are travestied when we think about the form of *The Ghost Writer.* In a novel that uses the concept of narrative framing to undermine the accepted relationship between text and author, text and text, text and "reality," the final irony comes with our realization that *The Ghost Writer* is itself "framed" by its formal function as a parody. . . . *The Ghost Writer* parodies the formal constraints of many different "texts." It is a *Künstlerroman* in which Zuckerman seriously portrays his quest for artistic maturity, but the novel is more apparently an imitation of the "growth of the artist" that ridicules the entire notion of an artistic son searching for an artistic father, whether he be an individual figure, literary tradition, or some historic *geist* to which the apprentice submits himself even while he rebels. The birth of the artist portrayed in *The Ghost Writer* is hilariously incongruent, especially when we consider the principals involved: Zuckerman, supplicating before the inconsequential Lonoff, or lusting after the "femme fatale" Amy, really an intelligent but uninspiring co-ed from the local educational institution, Athene College. The novel is also a parody of James's *The Turn of the Screw* as well as of Roth's own *Portnoy's Complaint:* it burlesques the narrative inversions and ghosts of the former while parroting the confessionalism, psychological confusions, and "Jewish life" of the latter. (The fact that *Portnoy's Complaint* is, itself, a parody of the autobiography seems more than appropriate.) Within the novel, there is the presentation and parodying of Anne's *Diary,* and of the process of excerpting, revising, and commenting upon texts—the act and art of interpretation. This parodying of several texts is yet another manifestation of the novel's concern with "textuality." Parody is usually defined as an imitation of an original for the purposes of ridicule, burlesque, criticism, or reinvention. The thoroughly parodic nature of *The Ghost Writer* defines its lack of "originality," its status as imitation, ever removed from its literary sources in the *Künstlerroman,* the confession, or the autobiography. The novel is a text made of texts that mimic and duplicate other texts. It lacks the definitive text that would authorize all the others and ground them in some version of the "true" or "real" from which their variation would suggest some traditionally interpretable source of meaning.

We may then see Roth's novel as a kind of deconstructive fantasy in which some important relations, those between artistic fathers and sons, authors and texts, texts and meanings, are questioned and parodied. But the textual problems and inversions that the novel raises might also be seen as parodic: Roth could be ridiculing here the oftimes spurious and overly intricate complications promoted by some recent theoretical considerations of textuality, reading, and interpretation. Opposed to the present-day critical Byzantium, Roth could be offering a return to "reality" that contrasts with the prodigiously self-conscious fictionalizing that takes place in the novel. (pp. 374-77)

But the "reality" of *The Ghost Writer* is also questioned and parodied, so that if Roth is offering any alternatives to the intricacies of *écriture,* they are ambiguous and, themselves, undermined. Hope may seem some figure out of medieval allegory who will lead Everyman to the bliss of concreteness, but she is "in reality" a carping woman whose world is confined to the task of piecing together domestic fragments. . . . Amy is childish and petulant, and seems in person only a ghostly, immature reflection of the Amy/Anne whom Zuckerman creates. The "real" Lonoff is fussy and pedantic, as Hope describes him, a petty domestic tyrant. . . . [The] fictions of the novel, no matter how unrestrained, invalidated, uncalled for, and unreliable, no matter how "unreal," seem much more satisfying and inspired, certainly more "original," than these portrayals of the novel's "real" characters. Amidst the flurry of disappearing texts that *The Ghost Writer* embodies, Roth engages the old conflict between fiction and reality without attempting to resolve it; clearly, his reduction of "reality" in the novel to merely one level of discourse among many, through the use of parody, suggests this. The effect of *The Ghost Writer*'s parodies, inversions, and refractions is to make us question the search for "validity" and "reality" in literary texts, that critical discovery of certain origins, grounds, and meanings which, traditionally, comprises the act of interpretation and from which Roth's labyrinthine discourse disinherits us. He thus creates a fiction whose "meaning" is embodied in the unravellings of its constructions and in the wake of its vanishings. The novel thereby generates the anxiety and doubt of the reader confronting a text, or the author confronting "life," forging scandalously out of that uncertain relation the unreliable, unfounded fictions produced by reading and writing. Analogically, Zuckerman's confession stands as a parodic

attempt to deny the artistic and "real" fathers in whom reside the origins of self, life, inspiration, authority, and the seminality of meaning. Ultimately, *The Ghost Writer* unmoors us from certainty, and convinces us to agree with James's Dencombe that "'Our doubt is our passion and our passion is our task,'" to accept the doubt about the nature of "reality" that inspires the "task" of art. If so, then Roth has conceived a most passionate portrayal of our doubt, as we observe the ghostly productions of the imagination. (pp. 377-78)

Patrick O'Donnell, "The Disappearing Text: Philip Roth's 'The Ghost Writer'," in Contemporary Literature, *Vol. 24, No. 3, Fall, 1983, pp. 365-78.*

CHRISTOPHER LEHMANN-HAUPT

In **"The Anatomy Lesson"**—Philip Roth's rich, satisfyingly complex conclusion to his **Zuckerman trilogy,** of which **"The Ghost Writer"** and **"Zuckerman Unbound"** formed the first two parts—the writer Nathan Zuckerman has a pain. . . .

It is a pain that has forced Zuckerman to give up writing and spend most of his time lying on the floor in his apartment on a play mat. . . .

Does Zuckerman learn anything from his mysterious ailment, as Tolstoy's Ivan Ilyich did from his? Do the cemetery and hospital settings of the final scenes of **"The Anatomy Lesson"** suggest that Zuckerman has come to terms with death and suffering like the protagonist in "The Death of Ivan Ilyich"? It's difficult to say.

Zuckerman is not Philip Roth of course; art is not to be confused with reality. . . . Moreover, there is a perceptible distance between the narrator of **"The Anatomy Lesson"** and its protagonist, most distinctly at the end, where Zuckerman's determination to escape his separateness as an artist becomes just strained and ridiculous enough to suggest that Mr. Roth is treating it ironically, if not with outright ridicule.

Still, we do get an awful lot of Zuckerman in **"The Anatomy Lesson."** He can be passionately articulate in his rage against his tormenters, and he can be a wildly funny-black comedian in his role as Milton Appel the purveyor of sex. But he can also be a little tedious in his endless self-absorption and scab-picking.

Moreover, as with the two great precursors Mr. Roth's trilogy so consciously evokes, "The Portrait of the Artist as a Young Man" and "The Magic Mountain," there is sufficient ambiguity of tone to make it difficult to judge exactly how much distance lies between the self that created the book and the self that the book creates. In the case of Joyce and Mann, it helps to know that they went on to write books in which the selves that dominated the earlier works were reduced to relatively insignificant characters. One cannot be so sure that Philip Roth will do the same thing. Clearly enough, he would like to. But it remains to be seen whether his next book will prove **"The Anatomy Lesson"** to be the last installment of the Bildungsroman his body of fiction has seemed so far.

Christopher Lehmann-Haupt, in a review of "The Anatomy Lesson," in The New York Times, *October 19, 1983, p. C26.*

ROBERT KIELY

Philip Roth, recalling a visit to Prague in 1971, said he was struck by the contrasting situation of writers in a country that is not free and in the United States. Here, it seemed to him, "everything goes and nothing matters"; there, "nothing goes and everything matters." It is this concern that seems to underline the trilogy that Roth began with **"The Ghost Writer,"** continued with **"Zuckerman Unbound"** and now concludes with **"The Anatomy Lesson."**

Certainly, Roth's fictitious novelist, Nathan Zuckerman, faces neither censorship nor imprisonment in his rapid journey up the freeway of American literary notoriety. What Zuckerman does face is an ambitious and egocentric self, strong on nerve and stomach, weak in empathy—an impoverished self that is at once his only resource and his major stumbling block. In **"The Ghost Writer,"** Zuckerman is a young beginner who tastes critical approval without the popularity that is the dream of artists no less than of politicians and other performers. A few years later, in **"Zuckerman Unbound,"** Zuckerman attains fame with the publication of "Carnovsky," a novel not unlike Roth's own **"Portnoy's Complaint."** But Zuckerman gains his renown at the expense of his family, who feel betrayed by his apparent caricatures of them in "Carnovsky," and despite the critics, who consider the novel sensational and shallow.

If it is difficult to feel sorry for Zuckerman, his family or his critics, it may be because they all indeed inhabit a country in which "everything goes and nothing matters." But the country inhabited by Zuckerman is not so much a political or geographical entity as it is a state of mind. Self-indulgence and moral vacuity do not characterize the fiction of all American writers by any means. . . .

It is not clear that Zuckerman has it in him to create serious fiction, though he proves beyond a shadow of a doubt that he can disturb, or to use Roth's words, he can be a "pain in the neck" to himself and to all who come near him. The trouble with **"The Anatomy Lesson"** is that it illustrates the pain and the pointlessness of Zuckerman's plight all too well. Like its central figure, the novel is a collection of symptoms, a host of problems.

Through long dramatic monologues, Roth explores the mind of an author who is the personification of chronic irritation as artistic stance. In **"The Anatomy Lesson,"** Zuckerman is depicted as middle-aged, out of ideas, emotionally exhausted and living in a state of perpetual physical pain. . . .

This contemporary Job does not fall into his suffering from a previously lofty position of righteousness, and he cannot be described as patriarchal, except in the pejorative sense in which the word is used today by feminists. Nonetheless, he has comforters—four women who perform various clerical, domestic and sexual services. . . .

Zuckerman's comforters provide temporary diversion, but they cannot cure him. Like massage, acupuncture, hypnosis, special collars, pillows, braces and particularly drugs and alcohol, the women become indistinguishable from the ailment. Zuckerman dissolves and absorbs them until they become symptomatic variants. (p. 1)

[As] the novel ends, Zuckerman is . . . wandering around the hospital "as though he still believed that he could unchain himself from a future as a man apart and escape the corpus that was his."

The play on the word "corpus" as body and collected writings, in combination with the irony of that last sentence, suggests that there *is* supposed to be a lesson in **"The Anatomy Lesson."** In contrast with more conventional didactic fiction, however, it is the writer (and only incidentally the reader) for whom the moral seems to be intended. Roth has written, not a contemporary defense of fiction or poetry, but of the writer as bankrupt. Bereft of ideas, subject matter and self-confidence, the writer is nonetheless bound to his profession as he is to his own body. . . .

Where this leaves the reader is an interesting question, and one that Roth does not ignore. Like much contemporary fiction, **"The Anatomy Lesson"** contains its own varieties of reader response. There is the reader-as-adoring-mother, for whom Zuckerman can do no wrong. There are readers-as-the-four-women-comforters who bring their own problems to the book and think that rubbing them together with those of the author will bring on mild temporary relief all around. Then there is Milton Appel, the reader-as-arch-critic, self-righteous, learned, accusatory, looking for "War and Peace" in every new novel and never finding it.

Finally, there is the reader-as-female-limousine-driver in Chicago, trying to get on with her work while Zuckerman rants and raves from the back seat. . . . For her, the talkative passenger is a nuisance, a "pain in the neck." With her, the reader of this book can too easily identify:

"This is my car and I do what I like. I work for myself. . . . I don't want to be under contract to you."

"Because you are a . . . feminist."

"No, because that partition between you and me in this car is there for me as well. Because the truth is I'm not interested *at all* in your life."

Given the insight with which he anticipates the reaction of readers, there is no doubt that Roth sees the problem with fiction that has no subject other than its lack of a subject. . . . If Roth's writer must endure what Samuel Beckett calls "the long anguish of vagrancy and freedom," its source seems to lie deep within himself. The author-narrator-character does not merely occupy stage center; he insists on being stage, cast, director and audience all in one. Few could survive such exposure. The humor, abuse and verbal fireworks are not brilliant enough to make the vacuum bearable. (p. 23)

> Robert Kiely, "Roth's Writer and His Stumbling Block," in The New York Times Book Review, October 30, 1983, pp. 1, 22-3.

GARY GIDDINS

When *Zuckerman Unbound* appeared two years ago, it was widely assumed to be Nathan's farewell to his past and Philip Roth's farewell to his alter ego Nathan. But Roth had a trilogy in mind.

As *The Anatomy Lesson* demonstrates, Nathan's problems were just beginning. During the next four years, his self-esteem withered under one assault after another until he no longer knew if his talent was still intact. The death of his mother left him mourning over unfinished business; his brother blamed him for both parents' deaths and stopped speaking to him; a hugely respected critic—once a supporter—published a savage attack, legitimizing middlebrow accusations that had been leveled against him earlier. . . .

Add to this a confluence of psychosomatic ailments which has altered Nathan's calling to that of a full-time patient. . . . After four . . . years of inactivity, however, Nathan takes action.

He decides, at 40, to go for the road not taken, and flies to his alma mater, the University of Chicago, with the intention of entering medical school. . . .

[A broad] outline tells very little about the substance and richness—the satiric bravura—of *The Anatomy Lesson,* but it brings up a couple of preliminary matters that have become almost inescapable in discussing the gripes of Roth: can the book stand alone without reference to, first, Roth's other work, and, second, Roth himself? The answer in the first instance is a resounding no, in the second an apologetic yes. Anyone who resents Roth for demanding of his readers as much devotion as, say, John Jakes demands of his will derive little pleasure from the latest installment. Indeed, early readers of *The Anatomy Lesson* have already echoed those reviewers of *Zuckerman Unbound* who were piqued by Roth's presumption of familiarity with his previous work. This type of reader is impatient for Roth to get to his big novel (his great American novel?), and will continue to miss the impressive scope—perhaps even the inspired japery—of the **Zuckerman trilogy** until it appears between one set of hard covers.

The Anatomy Lesson isn't necessarily dependent on the earlier novels for plot elements; it can be read—if not fully savored—on its own. Yet the trilogy gains irony and gravity from the manifold ways in which the three volumes interlock. In *Zuckerman Unbound,* Roth succumbed to Walter Brennan Syndrome and gave the best and funniest part to a supporting character, the former TV quiz kid, Alvin Pepler; Nathan's plight paled by comparison. *The Anatomy Lesson* redeems its predecessor, putting the middle volume and Nathan in perspective, and highlighting themes only sketched the first and second times around. It clarifies Roth's ambivalence about Nathan.

Roth is a deeply moral writer for all the exuberance of his wise-guy wit, and the **Zuckerman trilogy** approaches the decorous imperatives of an exemplary novel. Nathan was made, transformed, undone, and revived by literature, and our interest in him is as much sustained by the lessons he seems to learn (but, in fact, incompletely grasps) as by Roth's comic brilliance. (p. 43)

Make what you will of Zuckerman's various manifestations, and suffice it to say that familiarity with, at the very least, *Portnoy's Complaint, My Life As a Man,* and the trilogy is necessary to relish Roth's gamesmanship about what literature is and does to American readers and writers. It might be argued that too much depends on the reader's memories of Alex Portnoy and the furor over his complaint. The trilogy doesn't tell us what kind of writer Zuckerman is; we know nothing about the content of *Carnovsky* other than a few clues that make it indistinguishable from *Portnoy's Complaint*—this in a work which insists, page after page, that a writer is not his characters, that an imaginative process transforms life into something else. If you don't know Portnoy, you can barely imagine Carnovsky, and if you don't recall the impact *Portnoy/Carnovsky* had in 1969 (there's been nothing like it since), you might feel impatient with the entire conceit.

Roth gets away with it partly because Portnoy *is* so well remembered. (pp. 43-4)

[The] Portnoy experience prepared [Roth] for a new subject, an expansion of his corpus. Roth's stunning, if belatedly recognized, return to form with *My Life As a Man* (he's been on a roll ever since) established, among other signs of a dazzling increase in powers, his willingness to aim at a particular kind

of reader—one who shares with Roth a nearly collegiate enthusiasm for literature's gods and ghosts. He strikes a special chord with the peculiarly American—even peculiarly Jewish American—version of first-generation intellectuals, who, like Roth, discovered literature in school, used it to rebel against their bourgeois backgrounds, and were left to ponder its political and medicinal uses. . . .

The critic Milton Appel [Roth's fictional version of Irving Howe; see Howe's essay in *CLC,* Vol. 2] is the source of some of the most riotous passages Roth has written. . . . Appel is always offstage—his only dialogue is heard over the phone, during which conversation he sounds "wearyingly intelligent," as Wilfred Sheed once said of Howe. Otherwise, we know him by what he writes—or by what Zuckerman chooses to tell us about what he writes; he is the critic as ogre, a comfort to the philistines and a probable source of Zuckerman's mysterious pain. . . .

As fictional invention, Appel is an inspired foil. Nathan rails at him with dialectic, occasionally fatuous, branding him as an aesthete suddenly sympathetic to "the ghetto world of their traditional fathers now that the traditional fathers are filed for safekeeping in Beth Moses Memorial Park." . . .

Appel and Zuckerman represent two generations of apostasy from the Jewish bourgeoisie (which, needless to say, doesn't differ much from any other bourgeoisie)—both feel less pride in their own bookishness than shame at their parents' lack of it. Nathan is outraged at Appel's hypocrisy as an intellectual mandarin who suddenly pretends solidarity with the Catskills culture that is the butt of Zuckerman's satire. But he's also plain wounded by the devastating attack from a writer he once admired. . . . (p. 44)

Clearly, Zuckerman is learning something about the consequences of literature. Diminished to a blathering Beckettian mouth while prostrate on his mat before a harem of willing mother-substitutes, he finds himself turning into his fictional stand-in Carnovsky, "smothered with mothers and shouting at Jews." He blames his "whammied" muscles on Appel's "Jewish evil eye," and when he finally confronts Appel on the phone, Nathan sounds disconcertingly like a Jewish father defending himself against the superiority of his over-educated son. . . . [When] his impotent rage is exacerbated by a plea from Appel on behalf of Israel, he's tempted to repeat what Carnovsky/Portnoy shouted at 14—that the world can take its concern for the good of the Jews and shove it. Roth, anticipating his readers as usual, restrains Nathan, who is thereby "demonstrating to himself if to no one else the difference between character and author . . ."

Zuckerman's revenge—his intricate, "burning" improvisation on the idea of Appel as porn tycoon—is a splendidly deranged metaphor for the practical uses of art. Roth's revenge, on the other hand, raises questions of propriety. He has waited 10 years to respond to Howe, and for all the textual validity of his conceit, there is blood on the page. Previous literary feuds on the order of the Lewis-De Voto and Wilson-Nabokov exchanges were relative models of decorum. Because Roth has scrupulously adhered to verifiable facts regarding Appel's attacks and positions (they are unmistakably Howe's), the reader must wonder how much of the less easily verified information also relates to Howe. (pp. 44-5)

Even in the age of the true-life novel, Roth would appear to be treading on precarious ground. But, of course, Kafka-disciple that he is, he practically begs for the critical abuse he earns. It's the wise guy in him, laughing all the way through the gauntlet, comforted by the knowledge that he is offending all the wrong people for all the right reasons—fulfilling the admonishment of his favorite "sit-down comic" Kafka to do more harm to your contemporaries than they do you. Still, in many respects he is quite fair to Appel. Howe's essay doesn't stand up against *Portnoy's Complaint* because it fails to comprehend its intentions or appreciate its comic extravagance. . . . But Howe does real damage to *Goodbye Columbus* when he argues that "even a philistine character has certain rights, if not as a philistine then at least as a character in whose 'reality' we are being asked to believe." . . .

Roth, after all, has long since become too good a novelist to cheat a character—philistine or critic—of his integrity, and when Appel is finally heard from (on the phone), he is sufficiently convincing and sensible to enfeeble Zuckerman's rage and turn it back on him. Nathan is riddled with doubt: "What if twenty years of writing has just been so much helplessness before a compulsion—submission to a lowly, inconsequential compulsion that I've dignified with all my principles, a compulsion probably not all that different from what made my mother clean the house for five hours every day." Who would have thought that the shifty and prolific Philip Roth would become the poet of literary terrors, the bard of block?

For most of *The Anatomy Lesson,* Roth's narrative hand is wonderfully sure, his comic timing worthy of the Ritz brothers, with whom Zuckerman compares himself, his voice unencumbered by the typographical screaming of *Portnoy's Complaint.* Not since Henry Miller has anyone learned to be as funny and compassionate and brutal and plaintive in the space of a paragraph. Juggling elegiac passages with broad lampoon, Roth frequently keeps the reader off balance.

Roth is frequently accused of having turned his back on Judaic culture, and, to be sure, there is nothing in his writing to suggest much interest in the covenant with Moses. . . . But Judaic culture is also the secular world in which American Jews find themselves living, and far from turning his back on it, Roth has given a texture and shape to that experience unmatched in the work of his contemporaries. Far from ignoring his birthright, he celebrates its cultural resonance in his diction and themes. In refusing to demand special dispensation for Jews, he's been able to engender a howl that is quintessentially American, though infused with a Jewish accent and energy. Roth is one of those rare writers whose books are keenly awaited for the sense they might make of insensible times. Because he writes with a firm and gentle hand on the tillers—literary and personal—of the past, and delineates the spleen of urban isolation with a steadier mixture of exuberance and intelligence than anyone else around, he's in the enviable position, at 50, of still being promising. (p. 45)

Gary Giddins, "Zuckerman Fights Back: Philip Roth with a Vengeance," in The Village Voice, *Vol. XXVIII, No. 44, November 1, 1983, pp. 43-5.*

JOSEPH EPSTEIN

There is, as the folks in the head trades might say, a lot of rage in Philip Roth. What, one wonders, is he so angry about? As a writer, he seems to have had a pretty good roll of the dice. His first book, the collection of stories entitled *Goodbye, Columbus,* published when he was twenty-six, was a very great critical success; in brilliance, his literary debut was second in modern America perhaps only to that of Delmore Schwartz. . . .

After two further novels, *Letting Go* (1962) and *When She Was Good* (1967), he wrote *Portnoy's Complaint* (1969), a *succès fou,* a tremendous hit both critically . . . and commercially (it was a bestseller of a kind that removes a writer permanently from the financial wars). One recalls the protagonist of Saul Bellow's *Henderson the Rain King,* regularly muttering, "I want! I want! I want!" Philip Roth, who at an early age had critical attention, wealth, and celebrity, continues to mutter, "It isn't enough. It isn't enough. It isn't enough."

What does Philip Roth want? For one thing, he wishes to be recognized as a great writer, the natural successor to Gogol and Chekhov and Kafka. He wishes also to have the right to strike out against the bourgeoisie—particularly the Jewish bourgeoisie—and to be adored for his acute perceptions of it. And he wishes to have appreciated what he takes to be the universal application of his own experience as it has been transformed by the imagination in his several novels. Recognition, adoration, appreciation—all this would be his if people would only understand what his work is really about. Or so he believes, and so he would have us believe. But thus far all too few people do understand. In fact, they don't seem to understand at all.

Not that Philip Roth, in his many interviews about his work, has neglected to enlighten them. The Roth *modus operandi* is to publish an interview around the time each of his new books appears, or shortly thereafter, and in these interviews meticulously explain what the book is about, what the influences behind it have been, and what its place is in the Roth canon. . . . One thing is clear: Philip Roth is far and away the most generous critic we have of the writings of Philip Roth.

It may be useful to keep this in mind because when reading the novels of Philip Roth one discovers that he is not all that generous to anyone else. Make no mistake, he is an immensely talented writer. He is always very readable. He has a fine eye for the detail and texture of social scenery. He has a splendid ear and an accompanying gift of mimicry, which allows him to do the Jews in a thousand voices. He is famously funny, dangerously funny, as Mel Brooks once characterized the kind of humor that can cause strokes from laughter. He has a most solid literary education. Philip Roth has in fact everything but one thing: a generous spirit. Reading through his work, however, one begins to wonder if, in the case of a novelist, this one thing may not perhaps be the main thing.

Randall Jarrell once wittily defined a novel as "a prose narrative of some length that has something wrong with it," and there has certainly been no shortage of critics ready to declare various things wrong with Philip Roth's novels. Many a rabbi took to his pulpit to denounce the treatment of Jews in *Goodbye, Columbus. Letting Go* was in more than one quarter found sententious. . . .

Philip Roth, then, has taken his critical lumps. But the deepest and unkindest cut of all came from Irving Howe, who, in an essay in COMMENTARY entitled "Philip Roth Reconsidered" . . . [see *CLC,* Vol. 2], quite consummately eviscerated all Roth's work. (p. 62)

This essay, as we shall see, has left Philip Roth in the spiritual equivalent of intensive care for the more than a decade since it was written.

I have said that Philip Roth is always very readable, but I have recently learned that (as Howe pointed out) he is not very rereadable. Trial by rereading is a tough test for a novelist, and I am not sure exactly what it proves, except of course that it is obviously better to write books that can be reread with pleasure than not. . . . Roth, on a second reading, begins to seem smaller; one starts to notice glancing and low blows. In *Goodbye, Columbus,* for example, a cheap point is scored off Mrs. Patimkin, the mother of the family of rich and vulgar Jews who it is fair to say are the target of the novella, because she has never heard of Martin Buber. "Is he *reformed*?" she asks. The assumption here is that people who do not know the name of Martin Buber are swine, like people who listen to the recordings of Kostelanetz and Mantovani. The term for the thinking behind this assumption is intellectual snobbery, and of a fairly low order. . . .

Or, again, in rereading *When She Was Good* I discovered myself feeling an unexpected rush of sympathy for that novel's main character, the moralizing and man-destroying Lucy Nelson. For all that Lucy Nelson is mean-spirited and endlessly judgmental, throughout the novel there is someone meaner and even more judgmental on her tail—her creator, the author. The novel is relentless, ending with Lucy Nelson's death in the cold, a chilling performance in every sense. Mighty is the wrath of the Lord; but the wrath of Roth, for those of his characters on whom he spews it—from the Patimkins to Lucy Nelson, to Jack and Sophie Portnoy, to assorted lady friends in various of the novels, to the critic Milton Appel in the recent *The Anatomy Lesson*—is not so easily borne either.

A highly self-conscious writer, the early Philip Roth no doubt felt the weight of his own crushing moralizing. True, in his first book he was moralizing against moralizing—yet it was still moralizing. . . . What may have caused Roth to modify his sense of moral earnestness was the unrelieved gloom in which it issued in such novels as *Letting Go* and *When She Was Good.* Roth's early fiction was about what he construed to be the coercive forces in life—family, religion, culture. At some point he decided that among those coercive forces he had to add another: his own literary moral seriousness.

Near the end of the 1960's, that time of many liberations, Philip Roth achieved his own with the publication of *Portnoy's Complaint.* . . . It was meant to cause the squeamish to squirm, the righteous to rave—and by and large succeeded in doing so. If Berkeley was what happened to the university during the 60's, Andy Warhol what happened to contemporary art, *Portnoy's Complaint* was what happened to American Jewish fiction.

For Philip Roth, *Portnoy's Complaint* was evidently, in one of the cant phrases of the day, a breakthrough. Suddenly, the sexual subject, with all its taboos shattered, was now fully his to command; suddenly, in his use of material and language, he was little boy blue. He had also developed a new tone, a detached intimacy such as a practiced analysand might adopt with his therapist. Psychoanalysts—variously called Spielvogel, Klinger, and other German names—will henceforth appear in Roth's novels, while Roth himself will come to view the psychoanalytic as an important mode of apprehending reality. (p. 63)

The later Roth has, I believe, shed his true-believer views of psychoanalysis; in his most recent novel, *The Anatomy Lesson,* he seems to have shucked them off nearly altogether. But he has retained certain of the habits of the analysand—classically conceived, as they say down at the Institute—not the least of which is an unshakable belief in the importance of sex and an

implacable confidence in the significance of one's own splendid self.

Although I have not taken an exact count, it strikes me that, along with John Updike and Norman Mailer, Philip Roth is a hot entry in the sweepstakes for the most fornication described within the pages of a single body of serious work. . . . By now a practiced hand, Roth can describe sex as easily as Dickens could describe London, though the views Dickens offers are more interesting. Roth has mastered his technique to the point where he can advance his plots through dialogue while keeping his characters *in flagrante.* . . .

Yet it isn't the sheer volume of sex in Roth's novels that is troubling; one feels, rather, that sex is one of the few subjects left to him, and that it has now begun to qualify as an uninteresting obsession. . . .

Philip Roth has lived for some while pretty close to the autobiographical bone. The relationship between fictional representation and autobiographical sources is endlessly complicated, and can usually only be properly understood by a literary biographer willing to spend decades with his subject. . . .

This is a touchy point for Philip Roth, who again and again has accused his critics and readers of confusing his life and his work. . . .

Time and again, in interviews and essays and now even in his fiction, Roth has gone on insisting that he is not, in his novels, writing about Philip Roth, except through the transmutations of art. "That writing is an act of imagination," says Nathan Zuckerman in *The Anatomy Lesson,* "seems to perplex and infuriate everyone." Roth has spoken of readers getting a "voyeuristic kick" from reading his autobiography into his books. I think "voyeuristic kick" is exactly the correct phrase, and my first response to it is that, if a writer doesn't wish to supply such kicks, perhaps he would do better not to undress before windows opening onto thoroughfares.

Yet one wonders if voyeuristic kicks are not precisely at the heart of Roth's recent novels (as well as those of other contemporary novelists). (p. 64)

In short, it is the novelists who make this gossip, these voyeuristic kicks, possible in the first place. If they don't wish so to be read, the way out is through invention, imagination, fresh creation, greater subtlety. Another prospect, however, is simply to give way, to write about oneself almost straight-out, to cultivate the idiosyncratic vision, to plow away at one's own obsessions, becoming a bit of a crank, something of a crackpot, and risk being a minor writer indeed. Alas, I think this is the path that Philip Roth has set himself upon. . . .

Roth's fictional works, like runny cooked vegetables on a plate, begin to bleed into one another. Three Roth protagonists come on the scene: Nathan Zuckerman, Peter Tarnopol, and, not yet breastified, David Kepesh. A Chinese-box effect sets in. . . . By now, Philip Roth has written three books about this Nathan Zuckerman character. All that remains to complete the circle is for Peter Tarnopol to write a novel in which David Kepesh is teaching a year-long honors seminar on the novels of Philip Roth.

These characters have a number of qualities in common: they are bookish (two are writers, one a teacher of writing), Jewish, single, past or current analysands and hence mightily self-regarding, great prizers of their personal freedom (two have had disastrous first marriages, one, Nathan Zuckerman, has had three marriages about two of which not much is said), fearful of a great deal but above all of personal entrapment. Their characteristic condition is to feel put upon; their characteristic response is to whine and complain. Much of their time on the page is spent in the effort of self-analysis through which they hope to arrive at self-justification. Oh, yes, one other thing: for the above-mentioned reasons, none is in any way easy to sympathize with.

Reading these novels, one begins to sense with what pleasure a psychoanalyst must look forward to knocking off at the end of the day. It's a small world, that of the patient—it has, really, only one person of importance in it. So, too, with Roth's novels which feel so terribly underpopulated, confined, claustral. One admires their sentences, picks up on their jokes, notes the craft that went into their making, and finishes reading them with a slight headache and a sour taste in the mouth. (p. 65)

More and more of Roth's subject is falling away from him, like the hair on Nathan Zuckerman's head in *The Anatomy Lesson*. In *My Life as a Man* this same Zuckerman is said to have written a novel, filled with "moral indignation," entitled *A Jewish Father*. Roth himself, in such portraits as those of Mrs. Patimkin, Aunt Gladys, Sophie Portnoy, and others has been putting together a bitter volume that might be entitled *World of Our Mothers*. Now, however, that generation, in whose rage for order Roth read repression and perhaps unintended but nonetheless real malevolence, is old and dying and hardly any longer worth railing against. Even Roth appears to have recognized this, and some of the few touching moments in his later fiction—the scenes with David Kepesh's widowed father in *My Life as a Man,* memories of Nathan Zuckerman's mother in *Zuckerman Unbound* and *The Anatomy Lesson*—are tributes to the generation of his own parents.

When a writer has used up all other subjects within the realm of his experience, one subject remains—that of writing itself. Philip Roth's last three novels—the **Zuckerman trilogy**—are about precisely this subject. The first, *The Ghost Writer,* much of which takes place at the home of the ascetic writer E. I. Lonoff, is about the toll in loneliness and self-abnegation that the writing life exacts. Being a Roth novel, *The Ghost Writer* is not without its comic touches, or without its attempts to *épater les juifs.* (p. 66)

Zuckerman Unbound, the second Zuckerman novel, is about the wages paid for large-scale success in America. . . . Here again one begins to feel many autobiographical teases. Did Roth's parents react to *Portnoy* as Zuckerman's did to *Carnovsky*? Does Roth feel the same petulance about publicity as Zuckerman? "Never trust the artist. Trust the tale," pronounced D. H. Lawrence. Yet the more it becomes apparent that there is little to choose between tale and teller, the more one ends up trusting neither. Part of the burden of *The Anatomy Lesson,* it seems to me, is that Roth may no longer trust either himself.

A long while ago Philip Roth removed the fig leaf; now, in *The Anatomy Lesson,* off—or nearly off—comes the mask. In this novel Nathan Zuckerman is suffering a great unexplained pain in his back and neck. So great is the pain that he cannot write. He can, though, while settled on his back upon a rubber mat on his living-room floor, carry on love affairs with four different women. But these affairs do not absorb him nearly so deeply as does an attack written on his work by a Jewish intellectual critic he once admired by the name of Milton Appel that appeared in the magazine *Inquiry.* Not many people will

need to know this, but Milton Appel is another name for Irving Howe and *Inquiry* is intended to be COMMENTARY. . . . I am sure a number of characters are invented, touches and twists are added, nothing is quite as it was in life, but at its center this is a *roman à clef*—one that is being used, through gross caricature and straight insult, to repay an old wound.

It is also a *roman* of clay. The only points of interest have to do with the sense it conveys that Philip Roth himself may feel he can go no further in this vein. He has written himself into a corner and up a wall. "There's nothing more wearying," Zuckerman tells a friend, "than having to go around pretending to be the author of one's own books—except pretending not to be." Elsewhere he remarks: "If you get out of yourself you can't be a writer because the personal ingredient is what gets you going, and if you hang on to the personal ingredient any longer you'll disappear right up your [orifice deleted]." And later he adds: "Chained to my dwarf drama till I die. Stories now about Milton Appel? Fiction about losing my hair? I can't face it." Neither, for much longer, I suspect, can we.

When, with *Portnoy's Complaint,* Philip Roth's career took its turn toward investigating the inner life, Roth must have thought he was on his way to becoming the Jewish Gogol, the American Kafka. But it has not worked out. Roth's fictional figures lack the requisite weight; they aren't clown-heroes out of Kafka or Gogol who have somehow been tricked by life, the butt of some towering cosmic joke. A character who is having love affairs with four women and wishes to get his own back at a literary critic—this is not, as Philip Roth the teacher of literature himself must know, exactly a figure of universal significance. No, it has not worked out. *Portnoy's Complaint* ended on the couch, with the psychiatrist remarking to Alex Portnoy, "Now vee may perhaps to begin. Yes?" *The Anatomy Lesson* ends with Nathan Zuckerman, determined to give up writing for a career in medicine, helping the interns in the hospital in which he himself is a patient. I should have preferred to see it, too, end in a psychoanalyst's office, with the analyst announcing to Portnoy-Tarnopol-Kepesh-Zuckerman-Roth: "Now, vee are concluded. Vee haf gone as far as vee can go. Yes?" (pp. 66-7)

> *Joseph Epstein, "What Does Philip Roth Want?" in* Commentary, *Vol. 77, No. 1, January, 1984, pp. 62-7.*

MERVYN JONES

It's remarkable that Bellow, Styron, Malamud and Roth have all written novels in which the central character is a writer, more or less closely identifiable with the author whose name appears on the title-page. It's also rather interesting, to my mind, that all these writers are men; while they write about their problems as writers, women writers write about their problems as women. The American public, undeniably, receives these confessions with fascinated appetite, but it isn't axiomatic that a writer's life is of richer significance than the lives of the whaling captains or tobacco farmers chronicled in earlier American novels. In [*The Anatomy Lesson*], Zuckerman remarks: 'Other people. Somebody should have told me about them a long time ago.' It's slipped in as a casual, wry wisecrack, but it brings home with unintended sharpness the first serious limitation of this kind of novel.

There are other limitations, no less grave. Whereas a writer can observe a tobacco farmer with detachment, the primary condition of truth, he can't bring the same detachment to writing about himself—nor, it must be added sadly, to writing about rival novelists, editors or critics, who are described here with a malicious vengefulness that reduces long passages to the level of the snide gossip column. While Roth appears to be portraying Zuckerman with devastating frankness, the thoughtful reader is far from convinced that Zuckerman-Roth really is like this. He may be a better man or a worse, but the writer himself isn't the one to know. (pp. 27-8)

In fact, the crippling vice of the self-absorbed novel is its tone of unjustified self-importance. Roth's big commercial success was *Portnoy's Complaint,* an amusing novel which has dated considerably since it achieved a *succès de scandale* in 1968. Thousands of words in *Zuckerman Unbound,* and more thousands of words in *The Anatomy Lesson,* are taken up with the question of whether this book could be considered anti-Semitic. One might imagine that we are talking about *The Merchant of Venice.*

But, because of Roth's indifference to 'other people', what stands out isn't his (debatable) inaccuracy about Jews so much as his assumption that Jews of his class and generation are the only people with whom he need concern himself. He goes on and on in these books about the way in which the Newark in which he grew up has been ruined since it became a predominantly black town. It doesn't occur to him that the blacks might have their own community structure, their own values and pleasures, which at least contribute to the diversity of American urban life. Nor does it occur to him that the people of older American stock who predominated in Newark earlier in this century may have thought that it was ruined, or changed in a way that nostalgia inclined them to regret, by the Jews. I don't say this because I have any particular views on the matter. . . . I say it because respect for the outlook of those who are different from oneself, and indeed simple curiosity, are qualities of which no writer should divest himself.

Like Roth's other novels, *The Anatomy Lesson* is an easily readable book. Here and there, it is very funny. Although there are no real characters except Zuckerman himself (the women are presented only as satisfying or unsatisfying from his angle), there are several sharp and witty vignettes. The writing is practised and skilful. The last 30 pages—worth persisting for— are a successful exercise in Grand Guignol horror. Yet the enjoyments that it provides are radically different from the satisfaction to be derived from the work of a writer like Kundera, who aims not at effect but at exploration. The lack of such a purpose means that self-absorption, instead of rising to self-analysis, merely descends to self-pity, which is as tedious in literature as in life. This, ultimately, is what makes *The Anatomy Lesson* a boring book despite the periodic infusions of vitality. I was glad to get to the end. (p. 28)

Mervyn Jones, "Roth on Roth," in The Listener, *Vol. 111, No. 2846, February 23, 1984, pp. 27-8.*

JOHN MELLORS

Zuckerman in *The Anatomy Lesson* is a pugnacious rebel and one can well imagine his railing at God and waving a banner saying 'Unfair to Zuckerman!'. Indeed, the polemics in Philip Roth's third Zuckerman book are among its most effective passages. . . .

Roth is at his best complaining, as he has shown in *Portnoy's Complaint* and, indeed, in most of his fiction. He—and one cannot help thinking of the 'he' as a composite character, Philip

Nathan Roth Zuckerman—rants and raves against all his enemies, especially 'those sentimental, chauvinist, philistine Jews' who regard his satires as treachery. The most hated of them is a critic, Milton Appel, who had referred to Zuckerman's 'mean, joyless, patronizing little novels'. Zuckerman has it in for others, too. There are those who pay only lip-service to the idea of freedom. There are moralists who profess to consider pain 'significant'. There are feminists who read a hatred of all women into his books. Whenever Roth gets steamed up, whenever Zuckerman gets hot under his surgical collar, the result is riveting. (p. 106)

Everything Roth wants to say comes through loud and clear. Some will think him too shrill and too verbose. However, like all Roth's fiction *The Anatomy Lesson* offers savage satire, shrewd self-analysis, albeit tainted with self-pity, and vivid pictures of slices of American life. It is also very funny, as well as perceptive, about the nature of a novelist. (p. 107)

John Mellors, "Unfair to Life!" in London Magazine, *Vol. 23, No. 12, March, 1984, pp. 105-08.**

JULIAN WEBB

[*The Anatomy Lesson*] is the finest, boldest and funniest piece of fiction which Philip Roth has yet produced—and that is quite something to say about the author of *Portnoy's Complaint, Goodbye, Columbus* and *Letting Go.* Perhaps because of the 'personal' nature of most of his work—and also perhaps simply because he is one of the half-dozen writers alive who make you laugh aloud—readers and some critics in this country have tended to underestimate the scale and nature of Roth's gifts. He has been treated as a Jewish-American *farceur* who took advantage of a good education to hoist his emotional confusions on a public eager to read about sex—so long as it was wrapped in the severe packing of ideas, and literary ideas, at that. My own guess is that his extraordinary combination of careful observation, unfettered fantasy and elegant discussion of a multitude of themes, make him unclassifiable as a writer, and this makes people nervous of overpraising him.

Though how much and for how long he has been compared to other writers, living and dead! Salinger and Mann, Kafka and Bellow, Chekov and Malamud have all been brought into service at one time or another in the attempt to pin him and cut him down. Because Roth has the skill to incorporate literary criticism within the body of his narratives, he is accused of intellectualising. The variety of his eloquence has told against him. It is a sad fact that well articulated imagination should elicit the kind of abuse which is usually reserved for objects of fear.

It was precisely this theme which was central to *Zuckerman Unbound.* Nathan has produced *Carnovsky* (a novel which it is impossible not to equate with *Portnoy's Complaint*) and with its enormous success come gross threats and accusations. Zuckerman is charged with a multiple betrayal: he has sacrificed his race, his family and even himself on the altar of his sexual anxiety. Zuckerman fights off his paranoia by indulgence on the one hand, and on the other, by a heady discussion, mostly interior, of what he was trying to do and say in *Carnovsky.* In *The Anatomy Lesson,* Zuckerman is bound again, this time with an intolerable pain which stretches from his neck through his shoulders down to his arms. The reader meets Zuckerman when he is beginning to recognise that the pain has no attributable physical cause. He is the centre of a complex revenge plot instigated, it seems, by himself. . . .

He has no less than four active girl friends, each wonderfully realised by Mr Roth, to tend to his almost every need. . . . One of them, Jaga, drinks large quantities of red wine to drown her expatriate sorrows. She also asks to borrow a book each time she visits Nathan, and each time she leaves the volume on the corner of his desk. When Nathan confides in her that he wants to be a doctor (precisely, an obstetrician), as he sees this as the only practical way to stop wanting to write, to do something useful and to come to terms with his suffering, Jaga is not impressed. 'You want to have fine feelings like the middle class. You want to be a doctor the way some people admit to uncommitted crimes. Hello Dostoyevsky. Don't be so banal,' she admonishes him.

But he does not heed her, nor anyone else. He leaves New York for Chicago. The realism of the first part of the book is gradually, subtly abandoned. For all the high fantasy of thought and feeling which fills the first sections of the book, it is rooted in everyday experience as expressed in a slightly heightened vernacular. Once on the plane to Windy City, overdosed on Percodan and vodka and his own mad researches into obstetrics, he is released into a language and a style which might be called the rhetoric of pain, the solemn crazy oratory of an obsessive. . . .

What had been largely reverie and speculation becomes externalised. Zuckerman talks aloud to everyone around him—to his old college buddy, to his female driver. Milton Appel, it should be explained, is the name of a highly respected Jewish writer and critic who has taken Zuckerman to task for his irresponsibility as a Jew. It is this attack, and a contemptuous second-hand letter saying that Zuckerman could at least write something about Israel—the date is 1973—which gives Zuckerman the final push off his trolley.

The last scenes of the novel take place in the hospital where he had hoped to take up his new profession in medicine, but he is admitted as a patient after a climactic scene in a cemetery. The hyperbole of his invention and anguish is silenced; his tongue is so grotesquely swollen that he cannot speak.

The triumph of *The Anatomy Lesson* is that it transcends the symbolic, the fabulous and the metaphorical. Even at its most wild, Roth convinces the reader of the urgent reality of what is happening. Every incident and personality is seen with such clarity, and Zuckerman's reaction recorded with such honesty and comic acuteness, that the frontiers of fiction have been extended. And this masterpiece is created without once descending into the murky world of stylistic experiment.

> *Julian Webb, "Nathan Agonistes," in* The Spectator,
> *Vol. 252, No. 8121, March 3, 1984, p. 23.*

W. CLARK HENDLEY

The Ghost Writer must be initially examined from the context of the *Bildungsroman* because Roth has so deliberately placed it in this context. After focusing on the novel as a work of fiction within a clearly defined tradition, then the critic can look to the narrative for parallels to the author's life and insights into his growth and development. In comparing the novel with its predecessors we can not only evaluate its departures from that tradition but also assess Roth's implications about the viability of this form in late twentieth-century fiction. . . . Roth's late twentieth-century *Bildungsroman* protagonist typically searches for a father and simultaneously flees both a father and all the suitable father substitutes, a fashion that bears

the mark of the late twentieth-century fragmentation which has eroded family ties and given rise to homelessness. Thus in a pattern that is repeated throughout *The Ghost Writer,* the tradition of the *Bildungsroman* is both utilized and corrupted, adopted and rejected. (pp. 88-9)

[The] neglect of Nathan's childhood in *The Ghost Writer* may initially appear inconsistent in a *Bildungsroman,* for, aside from short reminiscences of family Sundays, the place where he copped his first feel, the sting of a mother's slap, and the memory of a father relegated to "Doc" in the neighborhood because he was a podiatrist and not a physician, Nathan spends little time reflecting on his childhood. Yet the other central concerns of the *Bildungsroman* are very much the stuff of which *The Ghost Writer* is made—provinciality, alienation, the larger society, ordeal by love, and the search for a vocation and a working philosophy. Even, however, when Roth's themes are traditional, his treatment can be personal and idiosyncratic, and herein lie the vitality and viability of the form which lends itself to adaptation and hence to different cultural contexts.

The typical *Bildungsroman* usually begins with its child hero somewhere in the country . . . and follows him to the city and maturity. The myth of growth recognizes that the postulant must undergo a trial, and the foreign environment of the city is the most likely place for this important step. Roth accepts the movement, the clash of lifestyles, and the trial, but it is clearly not possible to take a boy brought up in Newark and educated in Chicago and send him off to the city. So for Nathan the situation needs to be reversed. *Vir urbi* must go off to the country, and Roth insures that Lonoff's world is as different from Nathan's as it can be. In fact, Lonoff's pastoral retreat is all that Nathan ever thought he wanted. There a writer, surrounded by natural beauty, can indulge himself throughout the day in all of the cerebral pleasures he ever dreamed of. The house has books, magazines, records, typewriters, and quiet. At night there is conjugal bliss and there are admirers—both male and female—to stroke the delicate artistic ego. Lonoff has all of this—all that Nathan aspires to—and he is miserable.

Even though the movement of *The Ghost Writer* contradicts the traditional town-country formula, the novel nevertheless retains the provincial environment that the incipient artist must escape. Newark's Jewish society is clannish, narrow, and suspicious of outside ideas. The best Jewish Newark has to offer is Judge Leopold Wapter, a man idolized by Doc Zuckerman and his generation. Wapter represents the Jew who has gained position and esteem in the Gentile world. . . . The stifling environment that Nathan must repudiate is well represented in Judge Wapter's reaction to one of Nathan's short stories. The judge responds to the manuscript of the story with a letter to its author which is a rhetorical masterpiece of manipulation. . . . Clearly this environment is hostile to art, to creativity, and to imagination; the only ideas it will tolerate are those which do not threaten complacency or conformity. The artist must leave his provincial home or repudiate his art, for significant fiction cannot flourish in the sterile soil of Newark.

If Roth manipulates the urban-rural conflict to suit the demands of his age and his own purposes as well, he treats the artistic questions of *The Ghost Writer* as seriously and traditionally as Joyce did in *A Portrait of the Artist as a Young Man.* More than any other work, it is this novel which Roth invites us to have in mind as we read *The Ghost Writer,* and more than any other literary predecessor, it is Stephen who provides inspiration for Nathan. In fact the important second chapter is called

"Nathan Dedalus" in case the reader misses Roth's implied comparison of the two. Like Stephen, Nathan aspires to become a serious writer. Like Stephen, he comes from an environment that neither understands nor encourages artistic achievement. Both young artists are sensitive souls who are frequently insensitive to those around them, and both are alienated from their backgrounds. Significantly, both protagonists eventually say "no." . . . Ultimately, then, just as *Portrait* is about art and its relationship to the artist as well as to society, so too is *The Ghost Writer*. A part of the achievement of this book comes from the amount of material on this subject Roth can work into a short novel without sounding preachy or polemical. Both books agree that the artist is inevitably a misunderstood man, condemned to insoluble conflicts, confusion, and solitude. (pp. 89-92)

The Ghost Writer presents a variety of attitudes about art for Nathan and the reader to consider. Nathan, himself, appears initially as the unashamed lover of art. . . . Lonoff is a realist. He knows that art is not glamorous. His art consists in pushing sentences across a page and turning them around. Lonoff is wholly dedicated to his work, yet it is a merciless master that holds him in thrall. (pp. 92-3)

Roth presents the two main women of the novel as also holding views of art which contrast dramatically with those of the idealistic Nathan. Like her husband, Hope, too, has no illusions after thirty-five years of ascetic existence. The husband who refuses dinner invitations and tyrannizes the members of his household rejects life. "*Not* living is what he makes . . . fiction *out* of," she screams, and in a colossal effort of will, she rejects his living death. . . . Amy, on the other hand, is a pragmatist; art for her is a means. At age sixteen she presented herself to Lonoff as a "highly intelligent, creative, and charming" refugee who wanted a new start in life. She became his student, his editor, his accomplice, and yearned to become his mistress and muse. (p. 93)

Roth uses Felix Abravanel to represent the most calculated approach to art in *The Ghost Writer*. . . . Abravanel in his five-hundred-dollar shantung suit accompanied by his young, "juicy" mistress, Andrea, soon proved to be the artist very much in the world and of the world. . . . [The] full irony of Nathan's rejection of Abravanel and embracing of Lonoff appears only in [*Zuckerman Unbound*], the sequel to *The Ghost Writer,* where we find Zuckerman the successful and worldly novelist, pursuing a career much more like that of the celebrated Abravanel than that of the reclusive Lonoff.

The alienation of son from father is a familiar theme in the *Bildungsroman,* from the hatred felt by Henry in Stendhal's *La Vie de Henri Brulard* to the haughty disdainfulness of Stephen smirking when his father calls him a bitch. No alienation is so important or so potentially permanent as the repudiation of the faith of one's fathers. . . . Nathan's father is more involved in his son's life and writing than the elder Dedalus, and he senses Nathan's apostasy even before his visit to upstate New York. The cause for his alarm is Nathan's story "Higher Education," based directly on recent family history. . . . Doc Zuckerman's pride for the son written up in *Saturday Review* is dampened by the shame he feels for a family incident best forgotten. How can his naive son know how such a story will be perceived in the world? "It's not your fault that you don't know what Gentiles think when they read something like this. But I can tell you. They don't think about how it's a great work of art—they read about *people*. And they judge them as such. And how do you think they will judge the people in your

story, what conclusions do you think they will reach?" . . . Nathan's inexperience leaves him ill-prepared for the world outside Newark. . . . Nathan flees from his father, from Newark, from his heritage, and from his past to the writers' retreat at Quahsay, and he is thus prepared for the visit to Lonoff which will conclude his conversion.

In the evening spent at the Lonoffs, Nathan exchanges Judaism for art, his new religion, a process which may have begun at the University of Chicago. Every minute in the presence of the man he histrionically calls the "chief rabbi, the archdeacon, the magisterial high priest of perpetual sorrows" confirms him in his decision. . . . Nathan's narrative is informed throughout by the language of religion. (pp. 93-5)

What is this new religion for which Nathan sacrifices the Judaism of his fathers? It is a faith with some hope but with even greater elements of frustration, misunderstanding, and disappointment. (p. 95)

[Nathan] shares another important characteristic with the earlier *Bildungsroman* artist: both he and Stephen are often not very likeable. . . . But when Nathan's self-absorption irritates the reader who shares the despair of the spurned Hope and the grieving parents who helplessly watch their son rejecting family and religion, he is redeemed much as the headstrong Emma and stubborn Stephen by the sustained internal view the narrative provides. (p. 96)

Likewise, both Stephen and Nathan are redeemed by the paucity of choice offered the reader. If we must choose between the narrow xenophobic world of Newark's elderly Jewish community and Nathan's art, our sympathies will surely rest with the hope of youth as certainly as the tradition of Latin comedy ensures that the audience will sympathize with young lovers and scoff at aged fathers who only obstruct. Stephen's family does not understand him any more than Nathan's parents understand their son, but rather than view the family schism as tragic, both novels treat this subject in the broad perspective of comedy. (p. 97)

Nathan's spontaneity, artlessness, and honesty humanize him in a way that guarantees the reader's sympathy.

Nathan's honesty has its limits, however. He can evaluate his own shortcomings, he can deprecate his literary endeavors and even acknowledge his immaturity to the reader. In remembering his relationship with Betsy he frankly recounts his infidelities. . . . In a cloud of penitential gloom he abandoned Betsy and their relationship, and in *The Ghost Writer* the youthful heart is ready to be re-engaged. Thus it is that Nathan allows himself to be totally beguiled by the mysterious Amy. For Nathan she becomes Anne Frank so completely that it is only with difficulty that he can call her by her own name. Amy-Anne represents for Nathan a chance to live a life of romance and adventure rather than imagining it. The illusion he conjures offers Nathan an opportunity to gain the respect of his family and to humiliate the self-righteous Wapters who have accused him of disloyalty. What an impression he could make in Newark with the reincarnated modern Jewish saint as his bride!

Nathan's love ordeal is as real and as painful as that of Pip's in *Great Expectations*. Unlike Pip, Nathan has not been manipulated by others to hope for and expect a relationship that the reader knows to be impossible; like Pip, however, Nathan participates fully in his own deception. . . . [The] ordeal Nathan puts himself through because of the beautiful immigrant in the Lonoffs' home reveals to Nathan and the reader his uncertainties and insecurities. What the reader suspects all along becomes quite clear: Nathan does care about his heritage, and he yearns to accommodate both his family and his own artistic aspirations. With Anne Frank as his wife, Nathan would not have to defend his commitment to his Jewish heritage to anyone, and he would be free to write even about family members who strike the young author as amusing. The reality he slowly and painfully has to accept is that Amy is not Anne Frank, and that no one can magically legitimize Nathan's fiction to a suspicious Jewish society. If the Nathan of the final page of *The Ghost Writer* is more mature and more experienced, he is also sadder and wiser. He came to Lonoff's house to learn the secrets of the great writer. Instead he found that his idol had feet of mud, not porcelain, and the main secrets he learns are discoveries about himself.

The Ghost Writer has been read as if it is several different books; in fact, the variety of comment it provoked upon publication may qualify the novel as Roth's most misunderstood work. Reviewers saw it as a roman à clef and dutifully identified the characters and places for readers unfamiliar with the landscape of contemporary American fiction. The book was described as being in the manner of authors as different as Chekhov, Tolstoy, and James; it was termed "an anecdote with interruptions" and "fiction once removed." It was critiqued as if it were really the story of Amy, not Nathan, and it was accused of the basest kind of irreverence for exhuming "that little pile of bones on Belsen heath" for use in a Holocaust romance. What *The Ghost Writer* has not been read for

is Roth's contemporary treatment of the *Bildungsroman*, yet in many respects this novel is his most traditional work. In adapting the *Bildungsroman* to the mid-twentieth century, Roth simultaneously shows the viability of the form and the archaic aspects of the form as well. Ultimately, the importance of the *Bildungsroman* as a genre of fiction may be primarily historical, and the type may have had its greatest significance in the context of the development of modernism from the mid-nineteenth century through the first quarter of the twentieth century. But *The Ghost Writer,* by following many of the conventions of the *Bildungsroman,* demonstrates conclusively that the form is not moribund in the right hands; it may, perhaps, be now in the process of change. We are unlikely to see late twentieth-century *Bildungsromanen* following a young man from the innocent provinces to the worldly city where he encounters challenges and disappointments which mold him into manhood. But the search for self during the agonizing period of growth, accompanied by the strong personal commitment of the novelist to his subject, are likely to be legitimate concerns of serious fiction-to-come, just as they were in novels in the past. *The Ghost Writer* fulfills enough of the criteria of the nineteenth-century *Bildungsroman* to qualify as a part of that tradition; more importantly, however, by shifting some of the emphases of the genre, it may serve as a useful bridge to refinement and further development of the form in the future. (pp. 98-100)

W. Clark Hendley, "An Old Form Revitalized: Philip Roth's 'Ghost Writer' and the 'Bildungsroman'," in Studies in the Novel, *Vol. XVI, No. 1, Spring, 1984, pp. 87-100.*

Bernice Rubens

192?-

Welsh novelist and filmmaker.

A distinguished writer who has experimented with style in many of her novels, Rubens has maintained compassion for victims of emotional suffering throughout her fiction. Among the issues Rubens examines are the conflicts in personal relationships and the destructiveness of loneliness. Although most of her themes are pessimistic, Rubens infuses her best works with humor and irony.

In her first four novels Rubens drew on her ethnic background to delineate the inner struggles of Jewish family life. *Set on Edge* (1960), Rubens's first novel, details the ways in which the members of the Sperber family exploit and hurt each other. Many of the concerns of her early fiction are integrated in *The Elected Member* (1969; published in the United States as *Chosen People*), often called Rubens's most accomplished novel. In this work, a Jewish family disintegrates under the pressure of its various problems. Although the themes of these novels are of universal import, the significance of Rubens's families lies in the closeness of her characters and in the compassion she shows toward their plight. Critics find especially praiseworthy Rubens's realistic protagonists and her use of black humor, which balances the pervading bleakness of her work. Rubens won the Booker Prize for *The Elected Member*.

Sunday Best (1971) was Rubens's first novel not primarily concerned with Jewish characters. It is the story of a transvestite forced by a series of scandals to face his unpleasant childhood. In this work, as in all of her fiction during the 1970s, Rubens experimented with perspective. Her darkest novel, *Spring Sonata* (1979), centers on a four-year-old child who refuses to be born; when he becomes aware of the pain in the exterior world, he cuts his umbilical cord. *Birds of Passage* (1981), the story of a group of passengers on a cruise ship, was praised for its insights into the lives of its lonely, disaffected protagonists. Although some critics faulted the novel for its inadequate development of character, most agreed that Rubens was skillful in her selection of detail.

In her recent novel *Brothers* (1983) Rubens again focuses on the Jewish family. In this work she traces the fortunes of several generations of brothers from 1835 to the present. Also included are historical accounts of European anti-Semitism.

(See also *CLC*, Vol. 19; *Contemporary Authors*, Vols. 25-28, rev. ed.; and *Dictionary of Literary Biography*, Vol. 14.)

JOHN COLEMAN

Stripped of the heavy riddles, which it quickly is, [*Set on Edge*] turns out to be the story of a love-hate relationship between a Jewish mother and daughter somewhere in the provinces and down the years. Long-suffering Gladys is finally found a husband, but he dies on their honeymoon. Eccentric brothers and sisters-in-law nip in and out of the central tangle. No one is endearing in this packed, sharply written novel; in places, the spleen almost bursts its deft stitching. It leaves a bad taste in the head and the question: 'Why?' But several incidents of

Photograph by Mark Gerson

cruel, precise observation promise one that Miss Rubens will write a better, possibly a very good, book now this one's out.

> John Coleman, "Murals and Miniatures," in The Spectator, *Vol. 205, No. 6913, December 23, 1960, p. 1022.**

R.G.G. PRICE

Madame Sousatzka has received a warm welcome that I wish I could join in. But I found the story of the child pianist with his cannibal mother, his devoted, autocratic teacher and the smooth impresario too sugary. The supporting eccentrics did not convince me that they were anything except properties and neither little Marcus's pianistic brilliance nor the melancholy insight of his teacher seemed to me to have much to do with music or human relations. Jewish warmth and humour and colour and passion for the arts come through too winningly.

> R.G.G. Price, in a review of "Madame Sousatzka," in Punch, *Vol. CCXLIII, No. 6378, December 5, 1962, p. 835.*

PETER KEMP

When it comes to raising the reader's eyebrows in incredulity, . . . Bernice Rubens takes some beating. *Spring Sonata* is the edited journal of Buster, a foetal genius who refuses to be born, evades detection during a Caesarian operation, and lurks in his mother's womb for over three years. While she is accused of indulging in a phantom pregnancy, he makes use of materials sneaked into the womb during the Caesarian—a prescription pad on which to write his thoughts and a violin to express his musical talent. Bach wells out of the proud mother. And her relatives, finally convinced that she has a child, greedily plan a profitable concert tour for the odd duo. Whereupon, realising that the world will only exploit and harass him, Buster commits suicide by sawing through the umbilical cord with his violin bow.

Presumably making some sort of statement about creativity—those who refuse to believe the mother are castigated for lack of imagination—the book, despite its central oddity, relies heavily on stereotyped material. This is most apparent in its characters, familiar inhabitants of the Jewish Novel: a smothering mother of the 'With such good news, who needs the bad?' variety; an even more ethnic grandmother keening out 'Oi, veh is mir'; and a predictably prodigal son. In *Spring Sonata,* the clichéd and the bizarre grate discordantly against each other.

> Peter Kemp, "Topless and Hopeless," in The Listener, *Vol. 102, No. 2636, November 8, 1979, p. 642.**

ANGELA HUTH

Miss Rubens, no new literary figure, has written ten novels; she won the Booker Prize in 1970, and was short-listed for it in 1978. You would think, then, she was bound to be a household name like Bainbridge or Murdoch. For some unfathomable reason she is not. As Miss Rubens's most active fan I have been conducting a one-woman promotion service on her behalf for many years—converting, I like to think, dozens of readers to her entire works. I even wrote a panegyric on her for the World Service, calling her book, **The Elected Member,** 'The Electric Member' in my enthusiasm.

Why is she such a heroine to me? **Birds of Passage,** Miss Rubens's new novel, contains many of the answers. For a start she is funny and that, among women novelists, is a rare quality indeed. Her humour is gentle, poignant, never hilarious. It contains confusions: the possibility of tears beneath the smiles. She is never earnest. Her characters may search for themselves, but she spares us the embarrassment of making any such vulgar declarations, grants us the intelligence to discover for ourselves what they are up to.

Birds of Passage is the story of two elderly widows, Ellen Walsh and Alice Pickering. Neighbours for many years, brave of heart and hopeful of Something, they set off on a luxury cruise. The adventure they encounter would not have entered their wildest widows' dreams.

The shipping line employs a waiter who is also a long-time rapist. His victims for this trip are Ellen and Alice. Alice falls in love with him, Ellen loathes him. They both suffer their private agonies in silence, not confessing their plight even to each other. Meantime, by day, their affections are dallied with by lone gentlemen passengers. They get to know another lonely lady, Mrs Dove, and her aggressive half-lesbian daughter—a fine portrait of younger despair. All needing each other, their lives intertwine to the background hum of shipboard life (Miss Rubens, like William Trevor, is superb at maintaining the jostling of her subsidiary characters). Shadowing everything are

the nightmare nights. Perhaps credulity is strained a fraction—surely after all these years someone would have reported the rapist? And at moments Miss Rubens glides towards farce, though never topples over. Always beneath the humour we are aware of the serious helplessness of these wretched people on their desperate cruise. (p. 793)

> Angela Huth, "Electric Rubens," in The Listener, *Vol. 106, No. 2740, December 17 & 24, 1981, p. 793-94.**

EDITH MILTON

["**Birds of Passage''**] almost works as comedy: Bernice Rubens is quite funny, for instance, in her description of the Walsh and Pickering ménages when she describes their sexual and social lives in terms of the ritual care and trimming of the hedge between the two households. She also offers some poignant insights into the heart: "It had been years since anyone had held her, and it frightened her," she says of Mrs. Dove as she is embraced by her daughter. "She thought she might erupt like a long-dormant volcano, and her lava would rage with longings."

But the novel's comic and serious dimensions do not complement each other. Nor does Bernice Rubens's subject matter coordinate well with the distance of her perspective. I am willing, reluctantly, to admit that there may be women, like Mrs. Pickering, who are so dedicated to self-denigration that they would find violation thrilling. I know that others, like Mrs. Walsh, can be bullied and blackmailed into going along with almost anything; and I can see that an apparently ordinary man with a wife and two children might be in the grips of a compulsion to rape the middle-aged passengers of a ship's cruise. But both the man's need and the women's response to it fall into the category of pathological behavior. It is the sort of thing that might do nicely either as outright farce or as a serious, psychological novel; but it is quite wrong for Bernice Rubens's brisk, ironic approach, which serves to belittle her characters. She does not seem to like them much, or even to find them very interesting; and in the end they look not only silly and small but also as though they had been manipulated by the author to serve her own frame of mind rather than their fictional necessities. Despite its many good moments, **"Birds of Passage"** leaves the reader unsatisfied. (p. 25)

> Edith Milton, "Worlds in Miniature," in The New York Times Book Review, *June 20, 1982, pp. 11, 25.**

THE NEW YORKER

["**Madame Sousatzka"** is a] strange little story, set in London, about an eccentric piano teacher (famous for her Method) who polishes an amiable eleven-year-old prodigy's technique (he spends weekends at her Hyde Park house, which, despite its stylish address, is decaying) and then finds herself (along with her odd batch of boarders) loath to surrender him to success in the form of a crass, tin-eared impresario. This second novel by Bernice Rubens was first published in England in 1962; some of the nine novels that she has written since then—**"Sunday Best,"** for example, and her most recent, **"Birds of Passage"**—are slier and more self-assured. Nevertheless, here are most of Miss Rubens' admirable hallmarks: a small cast, mostly of curious and quirky loners who know that silence is a form of speech. . . ; regular reports on the daydreams into which they tend to drift; and a plot that starts out simple and then, twisted and split to make way for these digressions, proves to be full of surprises.

A review of "Madame Sousatzka," in The New Yorker, *Vol. LVIII, No. 28, August 30, 1982, p. 90.*

RICHARD DEVESON

It is 1835. Reuben and Benjamin, both aged ten, uncle and nephew though they have been brought up as brothers, are in peril of forcible 25-year conscription into the Russian army. Jakob Bindel, their father and grandfather, tells them how they must try to live: 'There is no cause on earth worth dying for, no God . . . no country . . . no principle . . . Only in the name of love is Death worthy. And friendship.' They must survive, he says. And, as generation of brothers succeeds generation, the Bindels survive, or try to survive. Five hundred pages' worth of accidents of history (though also of contrivances of plot) visit upon them a pogrom in Odessa in 1871, a Welsh mining disaster in 1908, incarceration at Buchenwald—where a Bindel brother is driven to assist in murder so that he himself can survive—death in Auschwitz, and torture at the hand of Soviet 'psychiatrists' in the 1970s. Yet each generation manages to pass on to the next the original life-preserving injunction of Jakob Bindel. And Bindel brothers continue to survive.

Bernice Rubens's *Brothers,* a different sort of novel from any she has written before, is a brave, almost defiant statement of the philosophy that protecting oneself and those one loves is more virtuous than defending principles or beliefs; the latter she sees as a kind of baptism. Yet survival is surely only one aspect of the Jewish inheritance, which has also seen its martyrs, idealists and fighters. And in any case, isn't Jakob Bindel's injunction too vague to offer real guidance? What *are* 'love' and 'friendship', and what counts, or doesn't count, as defending them? Historical accident ensures that no Bindel brother is conscripted into the Allied armies to fight against Hitler: would *that* risk of death have been justified in the name of 'love', or would it too have been a kind of baptism?

This book is written with passion—rather depressingly, all the marriages of Jews with non-Jews are made to come to grief—and its subject-matter cannot help, as always, being both unbearable and stirring at once. Yet is also remains curiously colourless, as though it has been translated from another language. Conversations and situations often either seem anachronistic or belong to no particular time or place. If the effect sought is the simplicity of epic, the price (for all the considerable research) is a loss of historical authenticity—which isn't, anyway, helped by things like a reference to 'Leningrad' in the 1870s or reports of talk about Auschwitz among German Jews as early as mid-1940. And what Jewish tailor, in South Wales in 1903, would speak of teaching as a 'prestigious profession', however much he meant it? One is left wondering: would the book's passion, and its wholesale defence of the Bindel principle, themselves have entirely survived a profounder application of the historical and novelistic imagination?

Richard Deveson, "Loyalties," in New Statesman, *Vol. 106, No. 2738, September 2, 1983, p. 24.**

PUBLISHERS WEEKLY

The scope of [**Brothers**] is encompassing, impressive, daunting: 150 years of European Jewish history refracted through the experiences of six generations of one Russian family as it undergoes agonies and vicissitudes (exile, pogrom, holocaust) and—for the surviving remnant—the final triumph of diaspora. . . . Rubens tells the complex tale with persuasive authority, no small feat given the scale and the intricacy of detail, and may be forgiven her occasional lapses into excessive use of archival material and sometimes burdening narrative movement with plodding prose. (pp. 64-5)

A review of "Brothers," in Publishers Weekly, *Vol. 225, No. 4, January 27, 1984, pp. 64-5.*

ROBERT GREENFIELD

In her 12th novel, Bernice Rubens has abandoned the small canvas for the large. Discarding the relatively modest yet always human situations that previously have been her subject matter, in **"Brothers"** the English novelist follows six generations of a Jewish family as they suffer through 150 years of unrelenting European oppression. The awful guilt that accompanies survival is a price nearly every character in this novel pays, over and over again. . . .

Throughout, we are presented not so much with real characters as with names to whom action and lines of wooden dialogue are attributed. One after another, Bindels are born, bar mitzvahed (if they are male) and married, often in the space of a few pages. They then have children (two sons, usually) and begin their marionettelike march toward death. Miss Rubens seems determined to let nothing get in the way of the long span of recorded history she has set out to cover. Unfortunately, the first casualty of her intent is the quality of the writing.

At times, **"Brothers"** reads as though it had been written in a foreign language and awkwardly translated into English. . . .

Miss Rubens uses phrases like "Bindeldom" and "Bindelhood" as though they referred to states of being. She creates compounds that have never before been introduced to one another, as in "the Jew-fear" and "The mighty Czar would brook no Christ-refusal." Certain incidents of plot challenge all laws of probability, as when one Bindel daughter, a Welsh-Jewish suffragette who has served time in jail for sabotage, just happens to meet an American naval officer wandering the streets of Cardiff before World War I. The officer is not only looking for her father, a tailor, but is named Saul Weinberger. Naturally, they soon marry and move to America.

The few vivid sections of this novel are overshadowed by long and barren stretches of writing that numb even the most patient reader long before the end. Miss Rubens's fourth novel, **"The Elected Member,"** about a Jewish family in the East End of London, was awarded Britain's prestigious Booker Prize in 1970. . . . Perhaps Miss Rubens will soon return to the smaller frame she has proved herself better able to fill, leaving this sort of novel to those who regularly grind out such soap operas.

Robert Greenfield, "The Suffering Bindels," in The New York Times Book Review, *March 25, 1984, p. 25.*

(Ahmed) Salman Rushdie

1947-

Indian-born English novelist and critic.

Rushdie is best known for his second novel, *Midnight's Children* (1981), which was awarded both the Booker McConnell Prize and the James Tait Black Memorial Prize. This work established Rushdie as an innovative and accomplished young novelist.

Although his first novel, *Grimus* (1975), did not draw wide attention, several critics appraised Rushdie as a promising literary talent. *Grimus* relates a quest for the meaning of life undertaken by Flapping Eagle, an immortal American Indian. Flapping Eagle's encounters with supernatural events and bizarre characters and Rushdie's witty observations on the ways human beings rely on myth were particularly appreciated.

Midnight's Children chronicles the recent history of India, beginning in 1947 when India became independent from British rule. The protagonist, Saleem Sinai, one of a thousand and one babies born during the first hour of India's independence, is presented as a man in his early thirties who has aged prematurely and become impotent. The novel has been widely read as an allegory, with Saleem and the other thousand babies, many of whom died at birth, representing the hopes and aspirations as well as the frustrating realities of independent India. *Midnight's Children* is rich in allusions to Indian history, literature, and mythology. For this and other reasons, the novel is widely viewed as a stylistic tour de force. Rushdie introduces fantastic and comically absurd events into socially realistic settings, a technique known as "magic realism." Rushdie's use of magic realism and his exuberant prose, which features extensive use of symbolism and hyperbole, led many critics to compare his style with that of Gabriel García Márquez. Critics were also impressed with the multiple narrative perspectives employed by Rushdie to expand the scope of *Midnight's Children*. Several critics have placed Rushdie among the great chroniclers of India's political, social, and cultural history.

Rushdie's recent novel *Shame* (1983) presents a fabulistic account of events in an unnamed country that strongly resembles Pakistan. He examines the related themes of honor and shame, shame and shamelessness, as cultural influences that affect the personalities and actions of individuals in Pakistan. A number of characters in this novel embody various forms of shame and honor. While *Shame* lacks the sweeping scope of *Midnight's Children,* Rushdie's stylistic techniques are similar in both books, and in *Shame* he weaves an elaborate, multilayered plot that many critics found rich and intriguing. However, several critics objected to Rushdie's presentation of actual events, and some asserted that he was more interested in constructing an intricately complex story than in providing a serious examination of contemporary Pakistan. Nevertheless, *Shame* was generally received enthusiastically, and many found it a poignant artistic analysis of Pakistani culture and society.

(See also, *CLC*, Vol. 23 and *Contemporary Authors,* Vols. 108, 111.)

BLAKE MORRISON

'Shame' begins deceptively, not as a political allegory but with a miraculous birth, as if we were to have the fabulism of 'Midnight's Children' all over again, only more so. Three sisters, Chhunni, Munnee and Bunny, give birth jointly to a child of prodigious gifts called (no relation) Omar Khayyam. Locked away in the upper storeys of a mansion, Omar, who sleeps a mere 40 minutes a night, teaches himself Arabic, Persian, Latin and voyeurism. Aged 12, he descends by dumb waiter to the outside world and impregnates a girl whom he has put under hypnosis. . . .

Omar promptly disappears to the fringes of a narrative dominated by the rivalry of two men. One is Iskander Harappa, devotee of stud poker, horse-race fixing, French food, opium and women, who, at 40, goes serious and becomes leader of the Popular Front and then Prime Minister. He is based unmistakably on another playboy-turned-politician, Zulfikar Ali Bhutto. His antagonist is Raza Hyder, pouch-eyed general, who restores the morale of his army by losing wrestling matches against his under-officers and becomes Iskander's right-hand man and later his executioner—the General Zia figure.

This 'masculine saga' of 'power, patronage, betrayal, death, revenge,' factually based if scarcely documentary realism, is balanced by a more obviously fantastic 'feminine' plot involving Bilquis, neurotic wife of Raza, Rani, long-suffering Penelope-like wife of Iskander (she embroiders shawls depicting her husband's fateful progress) and Sufiya Zinobia, brainsick daughter of Raza and wife to Omar. . . .

'I'm only telling a fairy story,' Rushdie reminds us, and apologises that he has to use goblinish means to bring down Raza/Zia ('*You* try and get rid of a dictator sometime'). Self-conscious asides like these are part of the novel's fabric. Where **'Midnight's Children'** was narrated by the hero, Saleem, the narrator of **'Shame'** is Rushdie in person, who breaks in to have his word on the Islamic revival, or to make Kundera-like jokes about regimes ('you can get anywhere in Pakistan if you know people, even into jail'), or to concede that he knows Pakistan only as an outsider: 'I must reconcile myself to the inevitability of the missing bits.'

The missing bits include the generous and authentic detail, the sights, smells and sounds, that made **'Midnight's Children'** so compelling. Instead of the super-sensory Saleem we have what Rushdie calls a 'peripheral hero' (a dignified way of handling the fact that Omar never took off as his author hoped?) and a plot so frenziedly eventful as to make one hanker at times for a long cold bath of Proust or Henry James. Against this, one can say that **'Shame'** is more economically written than its predecessor, more confident (though never didactic) in its political allegorising, and no less funny: Rushdie can be a wry, waggish, almost facetious writer, much more so than his solemn advocates admit. . . .

Whether or not he repeats his earlier success, Salman Rushdie has earned the right to be called one of our great story-tellers, a magical realist in the tradition of Grass, Calvino, Borges, above all Garcia Marquez. How far his magical family chronicle can be about the 'real' Pakistan is a question many will ask and which he keeps teasingly coming back to. But the answer he intends is there in a sentence from **'Midnight's Children'** 'Sometimes legends make reality and become more useful than the facts.'

> *Blake Morrison, "On a Magic Carpet," in* The Observer, *September 11, 1983, p. 31.*

TIMOTHY HYMAN

Shame stands to *Midnight's Children* very much as Pakistan to India; a smaller book for a meaner world. To embody a nation in a book, yes; but the kind of book called forth by India, the ultimate 'loose and baggy monster', can hardly be repeated for India's angry appendage, that sad artificial afterbirth of Independence. Entering a world less known, and less loved, Rushdie discovers a wasteland. *Midnight's Children* may have been triggered by the shame of India's emergency, yet India remained throughout the book a magnificent possibility. Pakistan, the Land of the Pure, was in Rushdie's account a mistake from the start, 'a failure of the dreaming mind'. Its shame engulfs all. (p. 93)

Rushdie begins in fairytale, more or less beguiling; but as the book continues, the invented characters are elbowed more and more out of centre, and History hogs the floor.

It was Brecht who best articulated the need some artists have felt, in the face of political disorder, to sacrifice their talent, to speak less seductively. Some such conflict seems here to be at work in Rushdie, and one wonders if he sometimes sees his story-telling, world-creating gifts merely as useful sweetener, to sell the political denunciation. In the earlier book the tale

was often fractured by the narrator, but this narrator was himself part of the fiction, and it was even possible to read it all as his marvellous, unreliable yarn. But in *Shame* the authorial presence is Rushdie himself, suddenly interposing in his everyday rôle as enlightened, sharply-commenting man of the world. From the fairy-tale we shift jarringly into a kind of *Time-Out* Agitprop. . . . Somehow, meanwhile, the substance of the novel—the brilliant dialogue, the rich sense of place, the warm characterization, all that fertile invention one knows Rushdie is capable of—seems to slip away, or is never allowed to surface. . . . Rushdie can be, by turns, arch, convoluted, journalistic and tedious; and because he lacks sympathy his acrobatic style here conveys only a cold-hearted cleverness. Yet there are moments when this voice still rises to an eloquence few contemporaries can rival: the sustained elaborate invention of the shawls knitted by Harappa's wife; or earlier, the child Omar's exploration of the dreamlike mansion in which he's been all his life immured. But the stilled tableaux, the empty rooms, tell the same tale. Until Rushdie's allegorical gifts are once again conjoined with a population that speaks and feels, we are left with the bitter taste of his arid conceits. (pp. 93-4)

> *Timothy Hyman, "Fairy-Tale Agitprop," in* London Magazine, *Vol. 23, No. 7, October, 1983, pp. 93-4.*

MARGO JEFFERSON

Rushdie, born in India, moved first to Pakistan and then to England. In life he is a migrant and exile, in fiction a fantasist and historian. He's a wonderful writer. *Midnight's Children,* published in 1981, is dense with passion, intelligence, excitement, and every vocal and literary effect conceivable. *Shame,* his new novel, is also brilliant and risky—not so steadily dazzling, more raw in parts, but just as daring. The rawness is there because Rushdie is always testing the tenets of history, politics, and art; for him, composition is inseparable from intellectual improvisation.

He was born, like Saleem Sinai, narrator of *Midnight's Children,* in 1947, the year India gained independence from the British and emerged as a new myth—"a collective fiction in which anything was possible, a fable rivaled only by the other mighty fantasies: money and God." Pakistan, Land of the Pure, was born the same year, from religious obsession and political chicanery, its name invented by a group of Muslim intellectuals in England. "To build Pakistan," Rushdie writes in *Shame,* "it was necessary to cover up Indian history, to deny that Indian centuries lay just beneath the surface of Pakistani Standard Time." This post-colonial world strains the limits of historical reality. Politics mingles with the occult; old feuds and loyalties join new ones. Facts are screened by hopes or lies; spiritualism is draped over ideology. Myths, screens, veils abound in Rushdie's work. The women are continually shrouded in burqas, sheet, dupattas, chadars, garments of womanly honor meant to preserve manly pride. . . .

Certain themes and obsessions dominate, you could even say ignite, Rushdie's work. He takes psychoanalytic insights into children—their solipsism, their craving for love and approval, their boundless capacity for guilt, the literalism that makes them believe thoughts are equivalent to deeds—and combines them with the determinism spawned by religion, ideology, and the occult. The result is an endless chain of factual and metaphorical links between individuals, sexes, families, and societies.

Primal myths about women (fear of their sexual and maternal potency rises in proportion to the limits placed on their political and economic power), paternity (fathers are always being lost, sought for, and wrongly identified), and the fragile boundaries between physical and psychic needs are played out: as mythology, history, tragedy, farce. What we call miraculous can be taken as both fact and metaphor (a marriage of science, magic, and literature). This kind of writing is called magic realism at the moment; it might be seen as a taut balance between the excesses of imagination and the unconscious (fantasy) and those of history and politics. . . .

Metaphor becomes literal in Rushdie—thoughts poison the air people breathe or the food they eat; blushes don't just look like flame, they burn like flame. Analysts of fairy tales have been describing these links for years, but Rushdie doesn't veil the symbol or let the metaphor (a word whose root means to transfer, to bear) carry the whole weight of the message. This amounts to a code of aesthetic ethics, or maybe ethical aesthetics. Rushdie has much in common with the Delhi street magicians of *Midnight's Children*: Marxists and illusionists, their "hold on reality was absolute; they gripped it so powerfully that they could bend it every which way in the service of their arts, but they never forgot what it was."

His code is bound up with politics in the broadest sense, with being an outsider, an exile at the mercy of unmerciful powers. . . .

Rushdie is immersed in fiction's intricacies, in writing as a process of excavation and innovation. But there's none of that insistence, so bellicose, so dreary, so common to criticism and literature now, on writing as the supreme reality. You can have a wonderful time playing trace-the-echoes-and-influences in his novels. (Among those which especially please me, for mingling so vividly and sometimes improbably: Sterne, Musil, Borges, Márquez, Poe, Ellison, Pynchon; the parental or romantic identity mixups found in Mozart operas or Gilbert and Sullivan; a gallery of characters speaking a mix of high and low Anglo-Indian, British, black and late '60s white American dialects.) But influences are transmuted, not imposed. Refuse to trace them and the books are still resonant and exhilarating. . . .

"Not so long ago, in the East End of London," writes Rushdie in *Shame*, "a Pakistani father murdered his only child, a daughter, because by making love to a white boy she had brought such dishonour upon her family that only her blood could wash away the stain. The tragedy was intensified by the father's enormous and obvious love for his butchered child, and by the beleaguered reluctance of his friends and relatives (all 'Asians,' to use the confusing term of these trying days) to condemn his actions. Sorrowing, they told radio microphones and television cameras that they understood the man's point of view, and went on supporting him even when it turned out that the girl had never actually 'gone all the way' with her boyfriend."

Rushdie, a father and "Asian," was appalled because, among other things, he understood the father's point of view. "We who have grown up on a diet of honour and shame can still grasp what must seem unthinkable to peoples living in the aftermath of the death of God and of tragedy: that men will sacrifice their dearest love on the implacable altars of their pride." . . .

Rushdie goes on. "Wanting to write about shame, I was at first haunted by the imagined spectre of the dead body, its throat slit like a halal chicken . . . I even went so far as to give the dead girl a name: Anahita Muhammad, known as Anna. . . . But finally she eluded me, she became a ghost, and I realized that to write about her, about shame, I would have to go back East, to let the idea breathe its favourite air. Anna, deported, repatriated to a country she had never seen, caught brain-fever and turned into a sort of idiot.

"Why did I do that to her? . . . All stories are haunted by the ghosts of the stories they might have been. . . . These ghosts, like Anna, inhabit a country that is entirely unghostly." . . . (p. 14)

Rushdie's ghosts become the heroine, or rather the victim and the scourge (what else are heroines?) of *Shame*. She is born to a Pakistani couple who crave a son and acknowledge her with rage and resignation: what better source of original shame? By the age of two she has contracted brain-fever and become retarded ("I did it to her, I think, to make her pure," Rushdie-the-author confesses). "Sufiya Zinobia Hyder blushed uncontrollably whenever her presence in the world was noticed by others. But she also, I believe, blushed for the world." By the age of 28, she has become a virgin wife, a streetwalker, a murderess, and an animal.

Sufiya is one of many who practice purity and bestiality in various forms. With nothing akin to linear narrative, Rushdie tells the story of two Pakistani families, the Hyders and the Harappas, whose patriarchs become heads of state, collaborators, and competitors in "the mutually advantageous relationship between the country's establishment and its armed forces." *Shame*'s hero, such as he is, the man who marries Sufiya, is a hypnotist, autodidact, and immunologist. His mother was one of three sisters raised in wealth and ignorance in a remote Indian border town. Isolated and devoted, they swore to share whatever children any of them might have. When their dictatorial father died, they found that he had left them nearly penniless, and threw a scandalous party. They served liquor, forced local musicians to play Western dances, neglected Indian guests in favor of English sahibs and their gloved begums, "raucous-voiced and glittering with condescension."

One of the sisters became pregnant that night, and all three promptly retired to their mansion, ordering food and supplies through a specially constructed dumbwaiter. They delivered a son in perfect synchronicity—nobody ever discovered which one actually bore him. He was named Omar Khayyam, for a poet unloved in his own land, and known largely in translation. . . . Scorned by the townspeople for his shameful origins, he developed a defensive shamelessness which served him well in his friendship with Harappa and his courtship of Hyder's daughter.

Scattering asides on literature and politics as he goes, tucking small stories into larger ones, Rushdie wends his way through the histories of Omar and Sufiya, Pakistan and its ruling families. Isky Harappa is a philanderer; his wife Rani stays alone on their estate, seemingly dutiful, but passing the years of humiliation by weaving shawls that document his political crimes. (Rushdie's description of her handiwork brilliantly joins a "J'accuse" indictment with a stream-of-consciousness soliloquy.) Raza Hyder puts piety at the service of military coups; his wife Bilquis spends her girlhood in movieland dreams of glamour, her old age in a kind of madness, sewing shrouds and uttering gnomic, futile pronouncements. Sufiya has her counterpart in Arjumand, called "The Virgin Ironpants" because she is ambitious, smart, and rebellious. (" 'This woman's body,' she tells her father, 'it brings a person nothing but babies, pinches and shame.' ") Regimes rise and fall, the one constant being exploitation of the ruled. Marriages wither and rot, comedy mingles with horror and farce, personal and societal shame fester until the means of purification become sub- or supernatural.

I started to write "sub- and superhuman," then stopped myself, because calling foul deeds subhuman lets the human perpetrators off the hook. But the words do describe views men and women have of each other, and Rushdie is increasingly complex on the subject. . . .

Rushdie describes women with all the ingenuity that love, fear, and obsession can bestow. Some are monstrous, some ordinary, some gifted and willful. All have lives forced into the striking but narrow grooves made when tyranny presses itself onto individual temperaments. Propriety and convention suddenly crack open and give way to anarchic impulses. Every archetype/ stereotype of the East and West makes its way into Rushdie's pages, to be embraced, lingered over nostalgically, or rejected. . . .

But once the women have made their way to the center of *Shame,* Rushdie must go further. The basic repertoire of conception and copulation horrors is here. . . . Rushdie must show "life within the veil" (the phrase is W.E.B. Du Bois's), must show how these women, born into a family of men who ignored them and abused each other, take revenge on their sons, who take revenge on someone else's daughters. He must slip past the sanctioned images of Greek legend (Pandora flinging open the box of worldly ills, faithful Penelope at her loom), and explode the false dualities of fairy tales like "Beauty and the Beast."

This is a quest worthy of anyone wanting to be a hero in fact or fiction these days. It's woven into the story's texture; it's stated baldly, even doggedly at times, as we all state newfound insights to keep our courage up. (p. 15)

> *Margo Jefferson, "A Magician for Our Times," in*
> VLS, *No. 21, November, 1983, pp. 14-15.*

CHRISTOPHER LEHMANN-HAUPT

If Mr. Rushdie had followed [the logic of realistic psychology] in **"Shame,"** he would have robbed his novel of its spectral magic, its breakdown of narrative logic that allows time to rush suddenly forward and reveal the end of things, or permits characters to be reincarnated in each other. He would have robbed his novel of its truth—not precisely the truth of parable or allegory or myth, but the truth of a narrative that describes a world apart and is a system accurate and logical only unto itself.

Most damaging of all, an adherence to realism would have robbed **"Shame"** of the character of Sufiya Zinobia Hyder. . . . Sufiya Zinobia is the tiny girl whose gender so enraged her father, Raza Hyder, the future military dictator of his country, that even at her birth she blushed in shame. The heat of that shame incubates a beast inside of Sufiya Zinobia, a beast that grows and takes possession of the tiny girl until as an adult she must be immured in an attic to be kept from wandering out at night, seducing strange men and tearing off their heads. When she escapes that attic, she leaves "a hole in the bricked-up window. It had a head, arms, legs." At the end she will return in the form of a white panther to topple her father's regime and destroy her shameless husband with the heat of her rage. I am not giving anything away. The suspense of the story lies in its fabulous illogic.

The story of Sufiya Zinobia is just one the the threads in a pattern so rich and various that it rivals the 18 shawls embroidered by Rani Harappa to depict "The Shamelessness of Iskander the Great," Rani's husband and Raza Hyder's rival for the dictatorship of the country the author calls P. Follow any one of the threads and it leads to a conclusion equally phantasmagoric. Still, a reader steeped in Western rationalism wants to know what seeds Mr. Rushdie's country has sewn to reap such a terrifying whirlwind. Is it a sin of geographical presumption she has committed—of being "a palimpsest" obscuring what lies beneath? . . .

Or does the ultimate responsibility lie in the character of the novel's picaresque "shameless" hero, Omar Khayyam Shakil, who bears the name of an Eastern poet famous only in the West, who has a phobia about being on the edge of things (he grows dizzy whenever he approaches the border of his country), who embraces Western logic by becoming a medical doctor, and who ends up marrying a Jonah in the belly of Pakistan?

Each of these answers has a truth; the tragedy of **"Shame"** lies both in the evasion of historical destiny and in embracing that destiny too violently. Yet this doesn't begin to account for the extravagantly tragicomic nightmare evoked by **"Shame,"** which does for Pakistan what Mr. Rushdie's equally remarkable first novel, **"Midnight Children,"** did for India. The narrative voice of **"Shame,"** creates its own irresistible logic. In a postscript to his story, the author acknowledges having quoted Milan Kundera, Franz Kafka, Nikolai Erdmann and Georg Büchner. Here and there in the text, one can't help thinking of Gabriel García Márquez. These are extraordinary writers with whom to be associated, but it's company that Salman Rushdie deserves.

> *Christopher Lehmann-Haupt, in a review of "Shame,"*
> in The New York Times, *November 2, 1983, p. C27.*

SALMAN RUSHDIE (INTERVIEW WITH MICHAEL T. KAUFMAN)

[Michael T. Kaufman]: *How would you characterize the political position, or rather, the political lament, of your novels about India and Pakistan?*

[Salman Rushdie]: Well, I think it's very difficult for a writer in the 20th century to look at the world and avoid a tragic view.

Yet your villians, if that's what they are, don't really come across as monstrous.

No, they are too small for that. I think the great characteristic of our age is that we don't have great despots, we have very low-grade people. This is not exclusive to the East. I would include many governments in the West. One of my central ideas during the writing of **"Shame,"** though it is stated nowhere in the book, is that what you have in Pakistan is a tragedy on a very large scale. But the protagonists are not tragic actors. It's as if you had "Macbeth" and you cast a group of second-rate vaudeville clowns in it, and you have clowns trying to speak those great lines.

Why did you choose **"Shame"** *as the title?*

It seemed to me that the opposite of shame is shamelessness, but it is also honor. There are two axes—honor and shame, which is the conventional axis, the one along which the culture moves, and this other axis of shame and shamelessness, which deals with morality and the lack of morality. **"Shame"** is at the hub of both axes. You have the politicians, representing shamelessness, acting without honor, but also without shame. And then you have a girl who is the incarnation of shame. But the book is also full of manifestations of honor.

Do you see a relationship between **"Shame,"** *and your earlier novel,* **"Midnight's Children"?**

Yes, I do. There's no connection in terms of story, but the two novels, put together with a half-dozen stories I wrote at the same time, seem to me to represent a kind of statement, in a way that **"Midnight's Children,"** on its own, did not. (p. 3)

Were you aware in writing these India books that the clearing you were making was in such virgin territory? I mean that no one had mined they myths of contemporary India.

Yes. It was amazing. It seemed to me that if you had to choose a form for that part of the world, the form you would choose would be the comic epic. It seemed like the obvious, the most natural form. And it seemed amazing to me that when you looked at the literature that had been produced about India, it seemed dated and delicate, and I wondered why these dainty, delicate books were being written about this massive, elephantine place? It was as if you'd seen an area of cultivable land and the richest soil in it had never been cultivated. You know that everybody is trying to grow crops in the stony ground around the edges and this wonderful prime soil is just left there.

Are you, like the hero of **"Shame,"** *a child of three mothers?*

When I wrote the book, it was an unconscious allegory, but since then, well yes, I think that is true. In the sense that there are these three places that have more or less equal claim on me—India, Pakistan and England—in which I have spent roughly equal amounts of time. England is the country where I live, India is the country where I was born, and Pakistan is the country where my family lives.

But the three mothers in **"Shame"** were not used consciously for that reason. I was thinking about the connections between various kinds of repression. The political repression in Pakistan is, in a way, permitted by the existence of a social code that is in itself repressive, and the people who feel that mostly are the women. So it seems that when women are kept down in such a society, they form all kinds of very interesting and important networks of support and solidarity among themselves.

In **"Shame,"** for instance, there is a telephone link between two of the characters that is like an umbilical cord through which they nourish each other; sometimes one character is stronger than the other so the nourishment flows in different directions at different times. In the beginning the three girls who become the mother were kept locked away by their father and what I was trying to do, at the time, was achieve an intensified metaphor for that kind of drawing together, that kind of closing ranks against the world, that many women achieve in that kind of circumstance. (pp. 3, 22)

If modern literature is largely a literature of alienated man, written by Western cosmopolites and émigrés, do you think that with books like yours and those of Gabriel García Márquez, Wole Soyinka, Chinua Achebe, V. S. Naipaul, alienation is being increasingly expressed within third-world contexts?

I think that's almost right. It seems to me that the idea of rootlessness has certain problems. I know it is something that explains a kind of Western intelligentsia. But I don't think that migration, the process of being uprooted, necessarily leads to rootlessness. What it can lead to is a kind of multiple rooting. It's not the traditional identity crisis of not knowing where you came from. The problem is that you come from too many places. The problems are of excess rather than of absence. That's certainly the feeling I have.

I've often been asked about my identity crisis and as far as I'm aware I've never had one, never had a feeling of unknowing about myself. What I have had is a feeling of overcrowding. It's not that there are pulls in too many different directions so much as too many voices speaking at the same time. There are some odd effects of this. When I go to India or Pakistan, I stop dreaming in English and start dreaming in Urdu. Once you change language you also change who you are—self alters when language alters. I've become familiar with these shifts. They cause a certain dizziness for a few days but no pain.

I have a fear that it may, at some point, become necessary to make choices among these three countries, and that it would be very painful. (p. 23)

> *Salman Rushdie, in an interview with Michael T. Kaufman, in* The New York Times Book Review, *November 3, 1983, pp. 3 22-3*

UNA CHAUDHURI

Shame has as vast and exotic a cast of characters as *Midnight's Children,* and it is as rich in incident, yet it is a wholly different sort of book. History here is a collective fantasy clinging to the dusty deserts and dilapidated cities of reality, not emanating from the wild imagination of a single, terribly self-conscious narrator. The laughter it provokes is consequently edged with a familiar pain and the marvels it contains are never free of palpable horror.

Most appalling of these is the novel's heroine, Hyder's daughter-who-should-have-been-a-son. Brainless, bestial, immeasurably violent, she is the embodiment of shame itself, and though she prowls around the edges of the story for most of the time, she is the monstrous referent and ultimate ground of all its dark visions. Into this image Rushdie has packed a wealth of psychological insight, for Sufiya Zinobia is the utterly convincing and terrifying product of a culture lost in falsehood and corruption.

Shame is a profoundly disturbing book. Courageously, Rushdie has resisted the temptation to write another exuberant epic. Instead, he has created a concentrated and dark masterpiece, an answer to those who may claim that certain evils of modern history are beyond either representation or translation. Rushdie is intensely aware of such claims, and begins his journey into these evils with a refusal to submit to that which causes them—peripherality and shame. . . . With *Shame,* Rushdie vindicates the claim staked in *Midnight's Children* to a place in the company of such writers as Gunter Grass, Milan Kundera, and V.S. Naipaul, who are giving modern history a forceful voice. (p. 591)

> *Una Chaudhuri, in a review of "Shame," in* Commonweal, *Vol. CX, No. 19, November 4, 1983, pp. 590-91.*

LEON WIESELTIER

When *Midnight's Children* appeared a few years ago, Salman Rushdie was "admitted to the ranks," as critics say, of the world's great writers, and those who did the admitting wrote as if a South American writer was suddenly born in the subcontinent. Rushdie seemed condemned to be always compared to García Márquez, and more generally to that kind of inflammation of the imagination, that tropical expressionism, to which a lot of literary taste has surrendered. Magic realism is its latest label. Rushdie surely shares its phantasmagoric ways, its interest in the knowledge that is turned up by delirium, its visionary violence, its appetite for epic and for epic exaggeration. This new novel will show, however, that the acclaim was only approximate. The shock of *Shame* lies in its fidelity to reality. It is a moderately distorted report on a world that is already deranged. This great English novel of Pakistan asks to be admired not for the richness of its invention, though admiration is plainly deserved, but for the truth of its judgments. It is a reckoning with a whole country and a whole culture; which requires not only language, but courage. Rushdie, then, is a different sort of fantasist. He is not that free. There is more pain than play. The extravagance is an emergency. The novel is more closely stuck to things than its style makes it seem; and it is punctuated with personal and political commentary in which all fictional pretension is dropped. When he calls his manner of writing "off-centering," he is not falsely modest. That is all, alas for those who live in "not quite Pakistan," that it is. For this reason Rushdie recalls Kundera, rather, though he lacks Kundera's metaphysical concentration and his sublime silences. This fairy tale is not the invention of a world but the completion of a world. Here the miraculous is a tool of analysis.

Shame is the story of Pakistan. . . . The story is wildly comic and wildly cruel, because of the disparity between the scale of Pakistan's history and the scale of the people who determine it. The people, in Rushdie's telling, are small squalid little creatures, "God-absorbed" and perfectly profane, unbecoming to the sacred history of a society. The history, however, is large; indeed, it is too large. Pakistan is "a palimpsest" that leaves Pakistanis with the problem of "what to retain, what to dump." (pp. 32-3)

Hanging over it, too, is the sentiment that gives the novel its name, and for his exploration of the emotional economy of his culture Rushdie deserves its (and not only its) gratitude. The emotional life he describes is extreme, and in an advanced state of excitement; it is madly disciplined or madly dissolute; it is fearfully pre-psychological. According to Rushdie, it swings between shame and shamelessness, and every swing leaves wounds. Rushdie is withering about what he calls "the stink of honor." He gives in detail its destructive consequences. A swimmer botches a dive "so completely that he preferred to drown rather than emerge from the waters of his shame," and up from there all the way to the affairs of state, where all kinds of physical and political outrages are owed to this horror of humiliation. It is not far from mortification to murder. (p. 33)

The most moving figure in the novel is Raza Hyder's idiot daughter Sufiya Zinobia, who should have been a son. She is a kind of infernal incarnation of a whole people's shame; cursed by an uncanny consciousness of the inner ignominies of everyone around her, she is seized by a state of burning ("blushing is slow burning") and turns to slaughter, tearing the heads of men from their necks with her helpless evil hands.

Whence all this shame? Rushdie does not say. There is a clue, though, in the novel's constant noise. This is the picture of a society in which the soul has no corners in which to hide. All is public. The people in this story offer no resistance to the judgments of others. (It is as if the social sense has skipped the superego and lodged deep in the ego.) When they do resist, lives are lost. Shame makes them feel like dying, or it makes them feel like killing.

You read this book with a flushed feeling of repugnance, with what Dickens called "the attraction of repulsion." It is an original study of the dark side of the species. Still, it is not hard to read. It is, in the first place, hilarious; the tawdriness of third world politics, for example, has rarely been so well captured. . . .

It is, moreover, written with tenderness, which not even the sexual and scatological grotesqueries can mask. Rushdie is brilliant, but he is not like the heartless Naipaul.

Indeed, compared to Naipaul the unsentimental Rushdie is a sentimental fool. There is a good reason. He is not a man without a place. He is a man with a place that is hard to bear. The difference matters. Rushdie calls this "a novel of leave-taking," which is a familiar kind of modern novel, but he writes affectingly, a little even to his own surprise, of the young polity's hopes. He writes most affectingly of their women. They are twisted and they are abandoned, but they are not insulted; it is the men who insult them who are insulted. Rushdie's women are the custodians of his meanings, and not just the terrible Sufiya. We meet Bilquis, who is doomed to marry Hyder and bear Sufiya, in the years of parition, in the middle of a religious riot, her clothes torn off in a crazed crowd that has gathered outside the ruins of her father's movie theater. (He blew it up with himself inside, satisfied that he had insulted the Hindus by screening a Randolph Scott cattle Western.) . . .

There is compassion behind Rushdie's cruelty. The mannerisms of the marvelous do not interest him, and neither does the glamor of the homeless. I wonder how Pakistani readers will read his book. Bringing the bad news is a brave thing to do if you intend to stay. "Realism," as Rushdie observes, "can break a writer's heart," and a reader's heart, too. Still, happy is the man who can see so clearly. (p. 34)

> Leon Wieseltier, "*Midnight's Other Children*," *in* The New Republic, *Vol. 189, No. 3594, December 5, 1983, pp. 32-4.*

D. J. ENRIGHT

[*Shame* has] all the welcomed virtues of *Midnight's Children*, and most of the vices (peculiarly hard though these are, in a work whose "logic" is partly that of the fairy tale, partly that of the nightmare, to separate from the virtues), and it possesses an extra virtue. It is considerably shorter—which, in a writer whose riches are embarrassing, can well indicate a firmer control. *Shame* is often exasperating, in the way of Günter Grass's best novels, but never (or so I found) to the point of blinding one for long to its sheer power—in horror, humor, slapstick, shrewd wit, and even pathos. . . .

While the story owes much to Salman Rushdie's imagination, Rushdie owes much to Pakistan, to the reality afforded by a real Pakistan, even while his dealings with that reality are (to say the least) highhanded. Or, as some would protest, below the belt. Of course we shall agree with the author that he is not writing "only" about Pakistan. He is writing about sexual rivalry, ambition, power, betrayal, and so forth—matters found everywhere and always—and about politics and religion and history and ghosts. Pakistan happens to provide these in abundant and striking forms.

The core of the story consists in the protracted and intensifying feud between Rushdie's prime minister Iskander Harappa, a clever and debauched civilian, and his president, Raza Hyder, a grim, none-too-bright warrior; Harappa dies at the hands of Hyder, and Hyder at the hands of fate, in the shape of three crazy old women. The parallel with actual personages, the late Zulfikar Ali Bhutto, once prime minister of Pakistan, and the present president, Zia ul-Haq (whose government executed Bhutto in 1979), is obvious enough—yet equally obvious is it that the fictitious characters exist at a more than slight angle to the real people. Harappa and Hyder are Bhutto and Zia as they might appear, centuries later, in some *Thousand and One Nights*—magnified, transmogrified, distorted. We may ask, Can an author rightly do this to real persons? Well, think of what these real persons have done or caused to be done to so many other real persons. Is no one sacred? Not until human life is sacred. Should novelists be allowed to exaggerate? We should congratulate them if they manage to.

The narrative of *Shame* is hardly less difficult to summarize than that of *Midnight's Children*. It helps somewhat if we see two of the characters, nominal hero and nominal heroine, as the book's symbolic poles: Omar Khayyam Shakil, literally (it would seem) fatherless and brought up by his three mothers not to know the meaning of the word "shame," and Sufiya Zinobia, Hyder's first daughter, who is shame incarnate, carrying within her the unfelt shame of others. Sufiya Zinobia was born blushing—she was meant to be the son Hyder never had—and at first looks much like the traditional holy idiot. The shame-less one, we can see, is going to marry the shame-full one—and the inevitable explosion is bound to ensue.

Without Rushdie's linguistic verve, the novel would never get off the ground. Hence—and even if he has his mother tongue in his cheek—it is sad to see him selling his adopted language short: "this Angrezi in which I am forced to write." He may consider "shame" a "paltry" word—he didn't grow up with it—and "a wholly inadequate translation" of *sharam*, which (he says) contains "encyclopaedias of nuance" and "dialects of emotion for which English has no counterparts." But it serves well as the title of his book, a book which, were he in Pakistan, would earn for him a fate worse than shame, or even *sharam*. I am not suggesting that he doesn't have the right to carry on so shockingly while living in safety, out of range of reprisals. . . .

No, my point has to do with Rushdie's Nabokov-like complaints against the language that has brought him both renown and cash. And related to it is his interpretation of the true story . . . of the Pakistani father in London who killed his only child because she had brought dishonor on her family by making love with a white boy. . . . (p. 26)

By the supposedly flaccid standards of Western morality, that Pakistani father was a murderer. And it would be interesting, though less than decent, to speculate on what in the man drove him to leave the land, the society, in which his act would have been something nobler than murder and settle in one where it wasn't. Rushdie is biting the hand of both the language and the society that are feeding him. The thought is one for such as Rushdie to bear in mind. In others' minds it is merely grudging and mean (quite aside from the declared fact that the poor London-Pakistani girl was, however indirectly, the inspiration for Sufiya Zinobia). Such writers are more than welcome for their additions to literature and their modifications to language; if England can't always quite take them, then English can, that remarkable language which, incidentally, quite a few

remarkable Americans have used, abused, exploited, and enriched.

Shame is more a "dramatic poem" than a naturalistic fiction, and Rushdie's diction is correspondingly rich and varied, including "straight" English, "Asian" English (once called "babu"), idioms translated out of Urdu, and crossbreeds between all these, such as (Anglo-Hindi) "snack-wallahs." The conventional grandeur of "the moon-faced, almond-eyed types so beloved of poets" collapses into the colloquialism (originally US) "in that neck of the woods"—the resultant effect of jauntiness being perhaps one of the author's devices for keeping the reader on his toes. A homely allusion to "the famous forty winks" chimes nicely with "the forty thieves," not those of *The Thousand and One Nights*, as it happens, but the forty husbands who sidle into a women's dormitory to visit their wives at night. (pp. 26-7)

It is not the mingling of reality and fantasy that disquiets, but the degree of reality in the fantasy. Compared with *Midnight's Children, Shame* is more tightly constructed, yet some of its strands are too lurid for the most willing suspension of disbelief. The four-times repeated reference to the umbilical cord that strangles Hyder's only son as prefiguring the hangman's noose in which Harappa will die is merely a heavy-handed gimmick whereby a raconteur renews his grip on the audience. But the anecdote about a team of scientists and engineers sent in patriotic fervor to develop newly discovered gas fields on the southwest frontier goes over the top: the "tribals" rape every one of them "eighteen point six six times on average (of which thirteen point nine seven assaults were from the rear and only four point six nine in the mouth) before slitting one hundred per cent of the expert gullets." Likewise the arithmetical progression of Good News's babies: first twins, and then, at yearly intervals, triplets, quadruplets, quintuplets, sextuplets, septuplets. And also perhaps, comical though it is, the account of Harappa persecuting the representatives of foreign governments by opening diplomatic bags and interpolating scandalous misinformation, so that the US ambassador apparently confesses to a strong and longstanding sexual attraction toward Secretary Kissinger. Like everything else, extremes can go too far, fertility turn into excess, the unbelievable sometimes fail to convince.

The dividing line between what works and what "goes too far" is impossible to locate, but as we read we can tell which side of the border the author is operating on. Among many successes are a macabre incident in which Harappa's long-suffering wife embroiders eighteen pictorial shawls. . . . Even the sensational transformation of the blushful Sufiya Zinobia into a magical beast given to wrenching poeple's heads off and pulling out their guts—even this comes off, because we recognize and accept the allegorical sense: one's sins will find one out, Nemesis will eventually catch up with Shamelessness.

Rushdie isn't writing realism, but he is acting coy when he says, at least twice, that he is only telling a fairy story and so "nobody need get upset." The horrific ways in which, one by one, his characters meet their ends belong to neither realism nor fairy story, but are nearer to the Jacobean revenge plays, the stage left littered with corpses; and the suggestion is that those who live by atrocity can be cast out only by the most extreme means. (pp. 27-8)

It is the author's too-frequent interventions and personal appearances that are truly tiresome. Not when he introduces the nonfictitious Pakistani girl sacrificed to family pride or defends his right to his subject—this is highly pertinent—but when he complains about his characters seeing into the future less clearly than he does himself, or confides in Shandean fashion that he has "idled away too many paragraphs in the company of gossips," or frivolously accuses his "so-called hero" Shakil of giving him "the most Godawful headache."

Such behavior led a critic in the *London Review of Books* to rebuke Rushdie for his "self-regarding tricksiness." With tricksiness and self-regard too, it is a question of degree. Writers deal in tricks, and—though it is an emotion we do well to conceal—this writer has considerable reason for feeling pleased with himself. For the greater part of *Shame,* linguistic extravagances, imaginative inventions, and sinuous intricacies of plot march—or scamper—together, seemingly about their own multifarious businesses and yet progressing in one ordained direction, moving through terror (though evoking little pity) toward the nasty death of a couple of mortal gods. (p. 28)

> D. J. Enright, "Forked Tongue," *in* The New York Review of Books, *Vol. XXX, No. 19, December 8, 1983, pp. 26-8.*

MICHAEL GORRA

Shame is in some small degree a *roman à clef* about the relationship between Pakistan's last two dictators, Zulfikar Ali Bhutto and General Zia ul-Haq, but any *clef* is strictly secondary to Rushdie's consideration of Pakistan itself as a failed act of the imagination. The country's very name is an acronym, he writes, meant to denote the peoples and regions of its western portion—while ignoring the Bengalis who comprised the bulk of its population until the founding of Bangladesh. That irony makes the country's history grotesque from the start, and yet Rushdie hesitates before assaulting it. . . . "Is history," he asks, in one of the many passages in his own voice interpolated into, and commenting on, *Shame's* narrative line, "to be considered the property of the participants solely?" Well, perhaps—but if so, Rushdie can take certain liberties with it, can avoid "the real-life material" that would otherwise "become compulsory," in favor of a symbolic version. Rushdie's compromise with history is to write about a country that is "not quite" Pakistan, one that occupies the "same space" but exists at "a slight angle to reality," an angle that gives him the freedom upon which this "modern fairy tale" is predicated. . . . His prose prances, a declaration of freedom, an assertion that *Shame* can be whatever he wants it to be, coy and teasing an ironic and brutal all at once. He's been compared to Sterne, but the eighteenth-century novelist who comes to my mind is Fielding. To read Rushdie is to re-experience the novel as novel, as new, to recapture Fielding's claim, in *Tom Jones,* to be "the founder of a new province of writing [in which] I am at liberty to make what laws I please." *Shame* is, like *Tom Jones,* full of narrative games, a fiction about fiction that is nevertheless crammed, and finally most concerned with, the vibrant stuff of life.

Shame, like its predecessor *Midnight's Children,* hangs on the knife edge between comedy and horror. . . . If Rushdie never falls off the edge of the knife, the events he describes nearly always do, existing first on one side of it, now on the other. What begins as a joke develops into nightmare. General Hy-

der's mentally retarded daughter, Sufiya Zinobia, blushes at birth for shame at not having been the boy her parents wanted, and that blush looses the devouring Beast of Shame within her. Shame is for Rushdie a perversion of honor, calls honor's sense of self-worth into question, and attempts to re-assert it through violence. Shame turns Sufiya Zinobia into a more clearly seen version of *Midnight's Children*'s Major Shiva, into a juggernaut, a destroyer. . . . And as the Beast grows within her, a sense of horror begins, with a Fordian *progression d'effet,* to supplant the comedy in which Sufiya Zinobia, and the novel as a whole, were born. Pakistan's botched name becomes, in the glow of such destruction, something other than a joke.

Earlier reviewers of Rushdie's work have compared it to that of Grass, Kundera, and García Márquez. That conjunction of names suggests to me that perhaps one can finally begin to isolate a fictional mode that is to the late twentieth century what realism was to the nineteenth. Realism is or was an attempt to enact the belief that the way of the world is rational and sensible. It depends, as George Levine has argued [in *The Realistic Imagination*], upon "the quietly dishonest assumption that the real world is not rife with extremes of action and feeling," and attempts to transform that world into "a subtly disguised version" of the form's own dreams and desires. It is a form inextricable from liberalism, and as such has persisted in England and America. In the works of the writers I've named, among others, one can begin to see the outlines of a similar transformation, one springing from the fact that, as Joseph Epstein said in [*The Hudson Review*] a year ago, "the great sad central experience of our century has been to live under one or another tyranny." Such tyranny seems to me far more responsible than any Joycean revolution for realism's decline internationally, and perhaps for its loss of confidence and amplitude in those countries where it is still the norm. For realism is impossible in such a world. . . . [Rushdie's work] is responsive to the world rather than removed from it, and it is because of this responsiveness that the mode in which he works represents the continued life of the novel. That mode— and one wants something better to describe it that the term "magical realism"—is an assertion of individual freedom in a world where freedom is strangled, a proclamation of the imagination's ability to reshape from within the lives upon which brute force is imposed from without.

One learns, almost as the foundation of the liberal arts education whose historical roots are the same as realism's, that such imaginative resourcefulness can save, if not your life, at least your sanity. Most of us don't quite manage to believe in that foundation, however much we profess it. Rushdie's work reveals the essential truth beneath the truism, and suggests as well the kind of world in which one must, sadly, live before one can feel the importance and urgency of such resourcefulness as something other than an intellectual platitude. What remains alive in the world of Sufiya Zinobia is Rushdie's style, a style whose flexibility is not a luxury but a necessity, a way of surviving in a world split between laughter and bloodshed without falling into pieces oneself. *Shame* restores one's faith in the novel's ability to matter. (pp. 162-64)

> Michael Gorra, "Laughter and Bloodshed," *in* The Hudson Review, *Vol. XXXVII, No. 1, Spring, 1984, pp. 151-64.*

Frank Sargeson

1903-1982

New Zealand novelist, short story writer, nonfiction writer, and dramatist.

Sargeson's fiction focuses on alienation and isolation among New Zealand's lower classes. His characters are often uneducated, inarticulate, and frustrated male drifters and deviants who cannot conform to the standards and expectations of society. Many of his protagonists seek comfort in "mateship," a relationship in which they are dependent upon other men for support and affection. Sargeson usually portrays his heterosexual characters as discontented, having found females to be either insensitive or inconsequential. Sargeson's works that concern homosexuality include the highly acclaimed long story "That Summer" (1943) and the novellas "A Game of Hide and Seek" and "I for One," collected with the title story in *Man of England Now* (1972). Other works which promote the idea of male primacy are the narcissistic tales of Michael Newhouse, a latter-day Casanova recounted in *Memoirs of a Peon* (1965), and *Joy of the Worm* (1969), a novel in which the Reverend James Bohun and his son Jeremy discard a succession of submissive women in order to reserve their true admiration for themselves.

Sargeson began to comment on society in the stories of his first collection, *Conversation with My Uncle and Other Sketches* (1936), which are restricted in their focus upon certain people in certain circumstances. Later, though Sargeson continued his social criticism, his tone and approach became more relaxed. He began to inject humor and tolerance into his work and, though he continued to use New Zealand life as its basis he began to broaden his themes. Among the more prominent themes in Sargeson's fiction is the individual's search for freedom in a repressive, puritanical society. Sargeson's own renunciation of unnatural, guilt-producing tenets is reflected in his autobiographical novel *When the Wind Blows* (1945) and its sequel, *I Saw in My Dream* (1949). Repression often finds an outlet in violence, as in the short story "Sale Day" and in the novel *The Hangover* (1967), in which the protagonist cannot reconcile with reality the messages of inflexible Puritan ideology.

Because of the inability of his narrators to express themselves in any but elementary terms, Sargeson's stories are sometimes limited in character development, point of view, and language. Many of them are episodic or anecdotal; as a result, much commentary has been devoted to the brevity of Sargeson's work. Most critics consider his writing to be exceptionally realistic, in part because of his ability to assume "masks," or the personae of his narrators. Many caution that his is still an artistic interpretation, however, and should not be taken as representative of the people and conditions in New Zealand.

In addition to his stories and novels, Sargeson also wrote two plays, *A Time for Sowing* (1961) and *The Cradle and the Egg* (1962), and three highly praised volumes of memoirs: *Once Is Enough* (1972), *More than Enough* (1975), and *Never Enough!* (1977).

(See also *Contemporary Authors*, Vols. 25-28, rev. ed., Vol. 106 [obituary].)

Photograph by Michael King

H. WINSTON RHODES

[This excerpt is part of an essay which was originally published in Landfall *in 1955.]*

New Zealand criticism has been chiefly concerned with the vain and unrewarding attempt to discover signs of national characteristics and the influence of local environment in our literature, rather than with the search for meaning and the examination of the moral climate which may be related more to Western man than to the accident of locality. It has fastened its attention on problems connected with the mental and geographical isolation of New Zealanders, on the literary consequences of the struggle to break in a new country, and the implications of a high level of material prosperity; but it has less frequently occupied itself with the way in which the loss of social meaning and religious faith in Western society has produced a climate of opinion that has been having profound effects on writers whether they live in London or New York, in Dublin or in Auckland.

And yet it is this moral climate which is of primary importance in the writing of Frank Sargeson. It is this rather than the treatment of local character, scene, or idiom that provides a solid core of meaning to his work and gives it cohesion. It is this that determines his angle of approach to the life around him, that dictates much of the form in which his stories are cast, and the strict economy he has cultivated in the use of words. Plot and personality, background and dialogue are important only in so far as they contribute to his theme, to his whole meaning, to the figure in the carpet—the morality which is implicit in his work. His craftsmanship is not an end in itself, but a means. Consciously or unconsciously he has organized his material and selected fragments of human experience in order to form a pattern, the outlines of which begin to emerge immediately his stories are examined together and attention paid to the 'value' judgments implied in them.

The world of Sargeson's stories is one inhabited by casual workers and rouseabouts, by station hands and street loungers, by the misfits, the dispirited and the lonely. Because of their mental attitudes and habits they are isolated from the smug conventionalities of the garden suburb. They are separated from social groups and organized communities by their anarchic behaviour, by their inability to accept the recognized prescriptions for achieving respectability and a comfortable bank balance. (pp. 413-14)

The subtleties of human relationships in a sophisticated society with its aesthetic teas and cultured prattling have no place in Sargeson's stories. 'I've only got a sort of polite interest in Jack's missus and those friends of hers' the narrator of **'The Hole That Jack Dug'** comments. 'They're always talking about books and writers, but never any I know anything about.' His characters are uninterested in such matters not only because the cultivated social life of a Jamesian novel is not well developed in New Zealand, but also because their creator is bent on exploring that primitive moral code which is all that remains after the veneer of respectability and conventional behaviour has been stripped off. They live outside the domestic circle, outside the social group, either of which, by its traditional customs, its established laws and regulations, may provide for its members a temporary substitute for life's meaning. In Sargeson's writing, however, it is a substitute destructive to those natural instincts, those primitive feelings and ideas which are the residue left to us by chaos.

Both women and men, . . . the toughs and the unsuccessful on farm and racecourse and waterfront, in the bar-room and dingy lodging-house, are separated from human society because there is no human society capable of giving meaning to their lives. Their loneliness has nothing to do with the physical isolation of the back country or with the geographical isolation of New Zealand. It is a loneliness that is bred in the soul when both social meaning and religious meaning have been lost. . . . (p. 415)

The pattern that weaves its way through Sargeson's stories is one of the pathos of isolation. It is something more profound than the misery of solitary confinement which may lead to despair; something that is not merely the result of a frustrated life made empty by lost opportunities. . . . On a different social level and in a different social environment it is the same isolation that led Virginia Woolf to ponder on the darkness at the core of the human personality and the darkness of a civilization in which men and women have 'dispersed', unsustained by any robust faith that their lives are part of a social organism or that their actions contribute to the whole meaning of life. It is the same isolation that led Ernest Hemingway to describe man as a fighting, lusting animal, only vaguely aware that the exercise of his primitive instincts could not provide any permanent satisfaction or offer more than a temporary relief from the gnawing pain of an existence without hope or meaning. (p. 416)

Where [the characters] live and where they go are unimportant except in relation to Sargeson's ability to describe a local scene. What is important is the world in which they live; and the reader is soon made aware that however the sun may shine, whatever the degree of physical satisfaction that can be obtained from the mere fact of existence, it is a world of poverty and hunger, cruelty and oppression, loneliness and death. Neither traditional religious belief nor any coherent political philosophy gives meaning to the lives of his forgotten men and women, his voluntary or involuntary outcasts from society. . . . It is a world in which the 'Good Samaritan' has become an anachronism, and Jones can do the right thing only by doing the wrong thing, and the boy who never wanted to be a good boy is condemned because he has an attack of righteousness 'just like father and mother'. Sex is either Lawrence's 'dirty little secret' as it is in *When the Wind Blows* or a casual encounter after the flicks. Social and religious convention have bred cruelty and sadism, the twisted and the sullen life. Miserable or happy, victims or outcasts, . . . without faith to sustain them, and only a primitive instinct for survival and affection to guide them, they live their lives, failing even to give complete utterance to what is truest in themselves. (pp. 417-18)

And yet chaotic as it is, the world that emerges from, rather than is described in, Sargeson's stories has vivid patches of sunlight in the midst of the surrounding gloom. When the worst has been said, when the cruelty, the lust, the poverty, the sordidness have been acknowledged, when conventional social behaviour has been seen for what it is, when religious hypocrisy has been unmasked, and the accumulation of rags and tatters and false finery has been stripped from the moral life of man, there is still a residue. That residue, that irreducible minimum, without which man would cease to be man and become one of the lower animals, can be detected and revealed more readily, Sargeson seems to suggest, among the failures, the rejects, the forgotten men and women, among the toughs and the wanderers and those who cannot conform. Isolated from civilized society though they may be, unaccustomed to the exchange of ideas and unable to do more than hint at the emotional life within them, unanchored by any creed or accepted code of conduct, they yet retain something that under happier circumstances might be the beginning of a rich and satisfying existence. They have their moments of beauty; they have a 'natural' understanding and appreciation of the possibilities of life even in the chaos they inhabit.

They live through their senses and their human associations. There is more than an occasional glimpse of the pride of achievement, the peacefulness of solitude, the happiness of physical well-being, and the satisfaction derived from common human pleasures. Although their appetites are those of adults, few of them outgrow the instinctive behaviour of children; and they look back to their childhood on the farms and beaches of New Zealand, wistfully recalling the time when life was less complicated and more innocent. It is not at all surprising, therefore, that some of the most moving descriptions of human loneliness in Sargeson's stories are given through the minds and emotions of children. . . . And in each of the three stories **'Boy'** and **'Granma'** and **'Cowpats'** it is a child who responds so instinctively and naturally to the affection that banishes loneliness or to the pathos of loneliness without affection.

Like the children, the adults act by instinct rather than by reason; they follow the promptings of the heart. From beneath their rough exteriors, through the midst of their halting words, there often emerges something that is truer and more funda-mental than can be found in the polished phrases of the charm-ing and the intelligent. (pp. 418-19)

The moral climate in which . . . [Sargeson's] characters live is one from which nearly everything has been taken away except the sense of isolation and the need for fellowship, the instinctive urge to find some object for affection. As in 'A Man and His Wife' it may be a dog or a canary; it may be a child or a cobber; it is never a wife. It is because Sargeson finds the material for most of his stories among the forgotten men and women, because he is concerned with the problems of hunger and love in a setting of human isolation, that he avoids the happier sides of domesticity. The satisfying human companionship and sexual relationship that can exist between a man and a woman is evidently not a theme which interests him. (pp. 420-21)

In *When the Wind Blows* his treatment of family life helps to reveal rather than it blurs the outlines of the 'figure in the carpet'. He finds in the smug respectability, the narrow reli-gious beliefs, and the protective care of the domestic circle an artificial hothouse atmosphere in which unhealthy seeds of sexual maladjustment can germinate. Henry Griffiths passes from babyhood through adolescence to early manhood gath-ering vague impressions of cruelty and violence, obscenity and lust, of the secrets of physical life and the mysteries of con-ception and birth. Filled with a sense of guilt, tormented by his ignorance, he finds a refuge in the studious achievement of respectability and the unctuous platitudes of an orthodox creed; but he cannot resist the continual assaults made by life on his ignorance, and at every crisis seeks to return to the blissful and protective comfort of the womb. Henry's loneliness is far more terrifying than the loneliness of the social outcasts, because it is thrust upon him by the conventions of society. His expanding consciousness is darkened by fears and inhi-bitions which isolate him from normal human companionship.

If *When the Wind Blows* reveals the loneliness of man in terms of an abnormal sexual attitude and the destructive influence of an abnormal family life, 'That Summer' presents a predomi-nantly male world in terms of homosexuality and mateship. There were hints in such stories as 'A Pair of Socks' and 'I've Lost My Pal' to prepare Sargeson's readers for this preoccu-pation with an exclusively masculine situation, but in 'That Summer' there would seem to be the deliberate intention of exploring both a normal and an abnormal hunger for compan-ionship, each of which exists among such undomesticated wan-derers and outcasts as Sargeson chooses to describe. It is no-ticeable that although the dramatic significance of 'That Summer' depends on the homosexual theme, its human significance de-pends on the relationship between Bill and Terry, a relationship which, on Bill's side at any rate, is the expression of an urgent need to find an outlet for his affection. His casual sex expe-riences fail to satisfy his vague longing for human intimacy, and it is only in the idea of mateship that he can discover anything to give stability or meaning to his life. (pp. 421-22)

This compelling but inarticulate desire for close companionship with a cobber is a theme which occurs again and again in the shorter stories. 'That Summer' is extraordinary not only be-cause the homosexual episodes help to stress Bill's normality, but also because in the scene beside Terry's deathbed the terror of loneliness gives place to a selfless and pathetic devotion which is all the more impressive because it is only implied. . . . (p. 422)

Thus it is that in Sargeson's stories there arises a conception of male companionship that has certain resemblances to the ideal of mateship in early Australian writers like Tom Collins. This is something that may be regarded as a natural develop-ment during the pioneering period of a young country, but in Sargeson it has little to do with the masculine isolation of a pioneering life and a great deal to do with his rejection of a normal sex relationship as an adequate basis for the pattern that he is drawn to observe. The perversions and maladjust-ments which he frequently describes are, as it were, merely an attempt to stress his main theme from a particular point of view. (p. 423)

The brotherhood of man is the hazy but positive ideal that is present in the minds of some of Sargeson's characters. It is referred to by implication in the 'Conversation with My Un-cle'. . . . [It] gives point to the theme of 'The Good Samaritan' and also to that of 'The Making of a New Zealander', but most of the characters in the other stories are too inarticulate to give expression to an abstract ideal and too anti-social to concern themselves with any social objective. Their conception of ma-teship is presented in personal terms. It is concrete and real. It is the human embodiment of their unconscious search for a free, equal relationship with their fellows, and has little to do with religion or politics, but much to do with an instinctive urge to crouch down and hold on tight. Human companionship can make this more tolerable. Their loneliness can become more endurable, and a temporary meaning and significance can thus be given to their casual experiences. (pp. 423-24)

Sargeson's version of the doctrine of brotherly love is closely linked to his variations on the theme of the Noble Savage. His preoccupation with the inarticulate toughs and loungers whose instinctive goodness and sensitivity are barely concealed by their inability to think, suggests that he has not entirely escaped the influence of the modern cult of the primitive. (p. 424)

[Sargeson] was attracted to the doctrine of the Noble Savage in the shape of the casual worker, not necessarily because he was influenced by English or American writers, but because he was sensitive to the moral climate of a sophisticated and urban civilization which has emphasized the importance of efficiency and standardization at the expense of human spon-taneity and freedom. (p. 425)

It is the presence of so many of nature's gentlemen in the stories of Sargeson that probably accounts for the impression he has made on a considerable number of readers. Many of them have felt uneasily that the Bills and Bobs and Freds and Jacks and Teds are by no means typical or even individual New Zealand figures, that neither their characteristics, nor their behaviour, nor their idiom can be as closely associated with the New Zealand scene as some of his admirers affirm. They feel, however vaguely, that their creator is observing life around him from an angle that is not common to most of his readers; and they are quite right. Like most artists, Sargeson has con-centrated his attention on the pattern which his individual qual-ities and experiences have moved him to describe, and has been encouraged by what he has seen to impose this pattern still further on life. His art is deceptive in that it might lead his readers to think that he is engaged in reporting the lives of representative New Zealanders in a series of vivid snapshots of character and episode, but, again like any artist, he is con-cerned with a private vision that touches external reality only at a number of points. As has been suggested, this private vision is related far more closely to what has been called the moral climate of the twentieth century than to typical New

Zealand attitudes. It is the personal response of a creative writer to the social morality of an age of disintegration.

Sargeson is not primarily interested in a dramatic situation because of its dramatic possibilities, but because it may be used to reveal the primitive moral code that is associated with instinctive behaviour. . . . In his stories, 'natural' goodness and 'natural' evil are always being opposed to the conventional goodness and evil of an unnatural society where cruelty, rapaciousness and lust receive official sanction. Sargeson explores his limited portion of life with the mind of a moralist and the technique of an objective recorder. The superficial toughness of his style and theme emphasizes rather than it conceals his preoccupation with the hungry hearts of lonely people who are desperately seeking the values which could give meaning to their lives. These values are described only in terms of the instinctive behaviour of child-like people who cannot become accustomed to a civilization in which social habits conflict with the promptings of the heart and who, therefore, refuse to adjust themselves to abnormality.

Sargeson has not succeeded in avoiding all the dangers that dance attendance on the heretic. . . . If he is not guilty of expressing an open contempt for the things of the intellect, his emphasis on a primitive morality is such that few readers would be able to derive from his stories even a moderate faith in the power of human beings to change the conditions under which men live or to make any substantial progress towards the ideal of the brotherhood of man. His characters do little but crouch down and hold on tight. Their solitude is relieved only by the presence of others in a like predicament. They are the displaced persons whose fate it is to remain for ever rootless, but tormented by vague desires that can never be satisfied. (pp. 427-29)

> *H. Winston Rhodes, "The Moral Climate of Sargeson's Stories," in* Landfall Country: Work from "Landfall," 1947-61, *edited by Charles Brasch, The Caxton Press, 1962, pp. 412-29.*

E. H. McCORMICK

If one speaks of art in reference to contemporary New Zealand fiction, that is largely due to the achievement of Frank Sargeson. More than two decades have now passed since there appeared in [the periodical] *Tomorrow* a series of sketches later collected in *Conversation with my Uncle* (1936). The contents of that small pamphlet bore the clear imprint of their time and first place of publication: superficially they were 'radical' in their purport, attacking or questioning the assumptions of bourgeois society. But where *Tomorrow's* contributors usually made a frontal assault on war or capitalist economics or middle-class morality, Sargeson approached them by a method of indirection. An issue was reduced to the simplest terms and set forth in a kind of dramatic monologue; in the title sketch, for instance, monopoly capitalism was presented through the homely image of bananas at a picnic. Besides the moral and political fables, there were two sketches more closely resembling normal 'stories', **'Sketch from Life'** (later retitled **'A Good Boy'**) and **'I've Lost my Pal'**. The first introduced one of Sargeson's recurring characters, the 'good', well brought up boy who breaks away from his respectable parents; the second entered the society of rural workers and shearers, the 'proletariat', here bearing little resemblance to the noble abstraction of intellectual debate. . . . As a medium for his deceptively naïve approach, he used a simple, colloquial English based on New Zealand speech and adapted in each sketch to the character of the monologist. He was not the first writer to employ the local idiom, but none of his predecessors had shown so sensitive an ear for the rhythms and vocabulary of everyday speech, and none had learned so much from the American masters.

The sketches and stories collected in *A Man and his Wife* (1940) disclosed a notable advance in technique. The colloquial monologue, still the predominant form, had now been shaped into a far more flexible medium, working at its best with the allusive economy of poetry. This subtle art had been developed not, of course, as an end in itself but as a means for expressing a wider and profounder view of life. The new collection included sensitive studies of childhood and in **'Three Women'** of young womanhood; the settings ranged from small town to rural slum, while on one notable occasion the scene was European; the characters numbered factory-workers, struggling farmers, minor public servants, racecourse hands. Sargeson's world at this period was largely that of the social underling, his chief preoccupations the lusts and fancies and strange affections that lie hidden in obscure recesses of the human heart. This phase of his work, finely expressed in such stories as **'The Making of a New Zealander'** and **'An Affair of the Heart'**, culminated in *That Summer* (1946), a collection which drew its title from a *nouvelle*. **'That Summer'** remains Sargeson's most satisfying story, beautifully proportioned and nearly always convincing: the down-at-heel urban *milieu* is superbly evoked, and through the eyes of the hero-narrator the characters take shape with a Defoe-like actuality. Occasionally the prose is opaque with esoteric slang, and the homosexual sub-plot is clumsily devised; but these flaws apart, skill is here triumphantly united with understanding.

I Saw in my Dream (1949) elaborated to novel length the subject of an early sketch: Sargeson took the son of middle-class, church-going parents and traced his moral pilgrimage through childhood and youth to the point of emancipation. The work is rich in incidentals. A whole era of history passes before the reader's eyes, the minutiae of life in New Zealand town and country during the early decades of this century. Alas, the strength of a novel does not lie in its incidentals, nor in its contribution to social history. *I Saw in my Dream* lacks any unifying theme except the groping struggle of the hero, Henry-Dave, who is too negative a figure to excite interest, much less compassion. Periodic failure—and the failure of this novel is qualified and only relative—is one of the hazards that beset a writer who works without the support of tradition, who is indeed the forger of tradition. Sargeson has since returned to the *nouvelle* form and opened up new territory with *I for One* (1954). This comic and corrosive study of the realities lying behind the suburban façade does not differ greatly in intention from the sketches which . . . enlivened the pages of *Tomorrow*. But to compare the qualities of those stiff little fables with the multiple complexities and subtle ironies of the later work is to measure the extent of Sargeson's artistic growth in the intervening years. It is to recognize, moreover, that he has been consistently true to his personal vision and has cultivated to the full his native talent. Of no writer can more be expected. (pp. 132-34)

> *E. H. McCormick, "The Thirties," in his* New Zealand Literature: A Survey, *Oxford University Press, London, 1959, pp. 108-35.**

WILLIAM TREVOR

Frank Sargeson's *Collected Stories* really are worth reading. Unlike so many of his Australian neighbours, Mr Sargeson, a

New Zealander, eschews the Wild West figures of the anti-podean past, and substitutes for the cracker-barrel philosophy of the outback a rare and welcome gentleness. With the speed of the real short-story man, and with unpretentious efficiency, he can snap his characters into life in the sort of introduction that doesn't let you go: 'Mrs Clegg was quite a decent sort, but she had a glass eye that was cracked right down the middle, and it was funny the way she sort of looked out at you through the crack'. Though writing in a contemporary manner, Mr Sargeson belongs with the traditional mainstream of the short story. He tries no modish tricks: he is far too good for that. Mr E. M. Forster remarks in his introduction to this volume: 'I like him because he believes in the unsmart, the unregulated and the affectionate, and can believe in them without advertising them'. One need hardly say more, except to register enthusiastic agreement.

> *William Trevor, in a review of "Collected Stories," in* The Listener, *Vol. LXXIII, No. 1879, April 1, 1965, p. 497.*

EDWIN MORGAN

Frank Sargeson's *Collected Stories* are perhaps dangerously recommended if one calls them distinctive sketches of New Zealand life and character. But these extremely accomplished pieces, mostly very short and wry, one of them long and picaresque, are neither provincial nor exotic but simply human. They are mostly told as first-person narratives, and are adept at evoking character through voice and turn of phrase. Maoris and immigrants, farmers and layabouts, beaches and baches, betting and beer-drinking and trotting sheilas, going crook or feeling like a box of birds—the subjects and the language build up a whole way of life complete with beliefs and attitudes ('good cobbers' being better than 'good people'). The weaker stories tend to make their comments too explicit, but in the best of them, like **"Toothache', 'Three Men', 'In the Department', 'A Man and his Wife',** or **'The Hole that Jack Dug',** the human relationships speak for themselves in an almost Chekhovian sort of way. (p. 538)

> *Edwin Morgan, "West Coast Scottish," in* New Statesman, *Vol. LXIX, No. 1777, April 2, 1965, pp. 538-39.*

NORMAN LEVINE

Sargeson's material is that of growing-up in the depression years in New Zealand. He writes in a colloquial style that, despite its simplicity, I found mannered, and with a tendency to be monotonous. . . .

The shorter pieces [in his *Collected Stories*] are often just sketches of particular individuals who were part of his growing-up. . . . It is interesting to see that from his earliest stories to his last the style doesn't change. And that he relies almost entirely on the inventiveness existing in life for him to tell his stories. When he tries to write one in the more conventional way like **'A Great Day'** . . . he is not very effective. But these are small criticisms. He has made something recognisable as Sargeson from his material—which is about all one can ask of a writer.

His best story is **'An Attempt at an Explanation.'** How when he was hungry his mother tried to pawn the family Bible. Not being able to, they go to the park, sit on a bench, take in the sun. Then they see their Methodist minister coming along looking at the flowers; he says a few words to them and goes away.

And the boy watches birds looking for worms. Then people come into the park to eat their sandwiches, and throw away the crusts in their bags. The boy retrieves and shares the crusts with his mother. Then he does somersaults on the grass and his mother laughs. From this material Sargeson not only makes something very poignant, but he concentrates an intensity of feeling which is absent in most of his other stories.

> *Norman Levine, "Places and People," in* The Spectator, *Vol. 214, No. 7139, April 23, 1965, p. 538.**

DAVID CRAIG

Memoirs of a Peon, set in New Zealand early this century, works by creating a character in the first person through a highly idiosyncratic style. The reader is apt to concern himself with how cunningly the style is kept up, regardless of what it is meant to express. Here it is an absurdly pompous Latinate diction, long-winded and devious, and presumably it is meant to create the persona of a man who has taken refuge from the squalors, embarrassments and rebuffs of everyday life . . . in a pose of pedantic detachment. It is clearly a serious effort of literary art that is being made; but it fails, it is generally not different enough from quite inadvertent longwindedness, because little means is found of suggesting what the 'hero' would have been like objectively.

> *David Craig, "American Families," in* New Statesman, *Vol. LXX, No. 1802, September 24, 1965, pp. 448, 450.**

MALCOLM BRADBURY

Memoirs of a Peon is a frank and a literary re-creation of the traditional picaresque novel. . . .

Frank Sargeson lives in and writes about New Zealand, and perhaps this in part explains the strange sense of survival one has in reading this carefully structured narrative of a young innocent who sets out on intellectual and sexual adventures, covering a fair amount of his society in the process. Sargeson, in his earlier work in English periodicals, has shown himself a sharp social commentator and a sophisticated literary craftsman; and his adaptation of the eighteenth-century picaresque manner, of the *Tom Jones* and *Candide* conventions, to present-day New Zealand is done with the greatest literary assurance, as if this were the ideal form for an essentially provincial and raw society. And so it works out. The old principle of procrastinated rape sustains the main structural interest, which is appropriate enough in a society dubious about its sexual ethics, suspended between bourgeois and proletarian values. It is an essentially episodic novel, but since Sargeson is not only a sharp social observer but a writer with an eye for the witty, revealing scene this works superbly. Michael Newhouse, too educated and aristocratic to be at home in New Zealand life, makes a valuable innocent, and gives the book its most striking quality—it is intellectually lively and convincing.

> *Malcolm Bradbury, "A Farewell to Fiction," in* Punch, *Vol. CCXLIX, No. 6525, September 29, 1965, p. 475.**

IAN REID

As in much of his work, Frank Sargeson [in *The Hangover*] directs his unblinking but not uncompassionate eye towards an adolescent struggling to reconcile the disturbing facts of his widening experience with the assumptions derived from a narrow religious upbringing. It is a matter of special interest in *The Hangover* that this familiarity of the subject-matter is offset by the novelty of its narrative technique. Previously Mr. Sargeson has either written in the first person or adopted a limited third person stance which still keeps within one character's experience; but here the narrative perspective shifts, and although much that happens is refracted through the consciousness of the central figure, we often leave him to follow some other person's thoughts or doings. I'm not happy with this way of telling the story. Its scale and basic structure seem to me to call for the concentrated narrative method which he has used to such effect in earlier work. As it is, this novel lacks for me the coherence of *Memoirs of a Peon,* say, or *That Summer.*

Having stated these reservations I must redress the balance by saying that nevertheless *The Hangover* is a piquant story told with sensitivity. I recommend it; but I point out that in some respects it is untypical of Sargeson so that if you read it and are dissatisfied you won't dismiss his work without sampling further. (pp. 110-11)

> Ian Reid, *"New Zealand Allsorts," in* Australian Book Review, *Vol. 7, No. 6, April, 1968, pp. 110-11.*

JONATHAN RABAN

While the Great War goes on, and wives desert and die, a father and son, deep in the New Zealand 'backblocks,' exchange letters in the style of Gibbon, Hooker and Sir Thomas Browne on the advisability of investment in the cinema business, on the decay of the English language, on Love (17th-century style) and on the intricacies of theology. The Reverend Bohun makes small-hours trips in his nightgown to the bedrooms of successive housekeepers, while his son Jeremy pilfers the petty cash from the local council office where he is employed as County Clerk and assaults his frigid wife with lyrical hymns on the poetry of true love. Lapped in the luxury of a literary style they can't afford, the two central characters in Frank Sargeson's new novel *Joy of the Worm,* become so possessed by their pretensions that they entirely blot out the scrawny realities of the external world. Provinciality becomes a mode of consciousness; a counterfeit style and surface supplant the dismal details of an arid civic and domestic life. *Joy of the Worm* is an idiosyncratic masterpiece; elegant, formal, deliciously ironic.

The Bohuns' favourite tag, lovingly exchanged in their correspondence, is 'cucullus non facit monachum'; but for both of them the hood does indeed make the monk, style makes the man. At the beginning of the novel Jeremy Bohun timidly moves away from his father's domination to find a job and a wife and to ponder the meaning of the phrase which starts the book, 'I am Jeremy Bohun'. The direction of the novel is inevitable: the separate identity does not exist and Jeremy, ordained at the end of the book after his father's death, has taken on his parent's persona, even down to the portentous 'Post Scriptum' of his father's letters. The Reverend is dead; long live The Reverend. Yet what an extraordinary identity he has acquired—he has become an eccentric English country parson of, perhaps, the early 18th century, utterly oblivious of the colonial 20th century world which he only technically inhabits.

External events—the war, Jeremy's marriage, the death of his mother, the arrival of his children, even the death of his fa-

ther—happen invisibly in the gaps between chapters, or, at most, are given as cursory facts, irritating contingencies which impinge on the real life of the novel, the growth of a style. The men's letters to one another, splendidly orotund, are ironically counterpointed by the letters of their womenfolk, full of unpunctuated trivia and reminders about chamber pots and winter woollies. The narration of the book weaves alternately amongst all the styles used by the characters; for pages it rides grandiloquently along on a tide of high euphuism, then abruptly and bathetically it stumbles over some bare fact or physical detail. Again and again the novel deftly sabotages the bubble of its own rhetoric. But though much of the delight in reading *Joy of the Worm* stems from its switchback, baroque prose, from its subtlety as a stylistic maze, one is left finally with a marvellous portrait of Jeremy Bohun, the model of the provincial consciousness, whose glittering carapace of finely-worked words merely exposes the trembling, prematurely wizened, incompetent creature within. 'Style' becomes a metaphor for all the delusions and dreams with which we insulate ourselves from the gaucheries and disorders of the world we live in—a brilliant and sardonic inversion of Wittgenstein's famous proposition. (pp. 186-87)

> Jonathan Raban, *"Growth of a Style," in* New Statesman, *Vol. 78, No. 2004, August 8, 1969, pp. 186-87.* *

IAN REID

I do think that because of its attenuated quality—whether deliberate or not—*Joy of the Worm* falls between two stools. Material that might have made a fine sketch has been inflated . . . without acquiring real amplitude in the process. The author has attempted something very difficult: to sustain our interest in two bores, the Rev. James Bohun and his son Jeremy. Bohun senior is a bookworm whose chief joy is savouring Gibbon and Hooker—and reproducing their cadences in flatulent discourse of his own. . . . Bohun junior is a nonentity. There is something inert about the narrative: the inner action is as uneventful as the external. The relationship between father and son and the marital relationships of each are examined at some length without anything very noteworthy being elicited. . . . In a recent interview, Sargeson said he intended the book to be "a celebration of the Bohun vitality"; but this quality doesn't come through dramatically enough to convince me. In case I appear to be dismissing the novel as wholly tedious, let me add that there is much in it to enjoy: Sargeson's mimic gift is amusingly displayed in the numerous letters, from various hands, that carry much of the story, and the reader who knows his Catullus and Vergil will relish some incidental allusions. But such things only thicken the texture of the narrative slightly without giving it a full-bodied flavour. (p. 337)

> Ian Reid, *"The Pattern of New Zealand Fiction," in* Australian Book Review, *Vol. 9, No. 12, October, 1970, pp. 337-38.* *

H. WINSTON RHODES

['Man of England now'] consists of three short novels, each of which is more involved and more suggestive than a bare summary of its episodic plot would indicate. 'Man of England now' is a tragi-comedy of migration, a foreshortened historical study of social change from the early twenties to the emergence of the so-called affluent society, a condensed account of vicissitudes in the life of a young English migrant whose sturdy endeavours and sunny disposition do not lead to more than an insecure foothold in the little Eden of the South Pacific. From scrub-cutter to suburban dustman does not provide the formula for the usual success-story, but Sargeson's ironic contemplation of life and progress in New Zealand destroys more than it fosters illusions. (p. 260)

Unlike so many of Sargeson's stories **'Man of England now'** is not told in the first person, nor has it an identifiable narrator, and yet there is a running commentary implied by the language, the manner of narration and sometimes by the intrusion of an unknown voice. It is the title of the third story in the present volume **'A Game of Hide and Seek'**, that draws attention to one of the characteristic qualities of Sargeson, for no New Zealand writer is more fascinated by the literary game of hide and seek, that is to say the game of 'find the author'. He has always been a man of many masks who conceals himself behind his varied personae, who is never quite there however often the first personal pronoun is employed, and whose personality and attitudes can be discovered only by a process of detection through the whole of his work. Who tells the story of the fresh-cheeked, equable but lively Johnny? The voice is not one of the voices used in *I Saw in My Dream,* in *The Hangover* or in *Joy of the Worm.* Here it is affectionate, sympathetic and understanding, even slightly arch and sentimental. It is ironically flippant and at times regretful, as though the success-story is not becoming quite such a triumphant record of achievement as intended; but the voice is determined to make the best of it. . . . This cheerfully ironic voice adds a further dimension to a tragi-comedy of migration. . . . (pp. 260-61)

In contrast to **'Man of England now'** [**'I for One'**] presents in diary-form the emotional disturbances of a sheltered young school-mistress as she passes through a series of traumatic experiences during a period of little more than three months. Here, any authorial voice is completely absent and we listen to the private musings of Katherine Sheppard as, Pamela-wise, she rushes to confide to her journal her confusions and half-acknowledged ignorance of her relations with other people and the dilemmas in which she is involved. As a penetrating study of the illusions and disillusionment of the female mind caught in the entanglements of a resolutely puritanical environment, **'I for One'** has for too long been almost inaccessible to those who value the best of New Zealand writing. In this short novel the twists and turns of the plot which in itself would seem to require more space and time for satisfactory resolution may be easily forgiven because, as so often in Sargeson's fictions, the gains are considerably more significant than the losses. The feminine voice is so authentic, her misapprehensions and uncertainties so naturally expressed that it is almost with a shock that one realises that the whole story, the series of diary entries, has been skilfully arranged and provided, as it were, with cross-references for the reader, so that he soon suspects and becomes increasingly confident that he knows much more than Katherine Sheppard herself of what is happening and why she seems 'to see all these things with the eyes of a stranger, of one set apart.'

The final story is **'A Game of Hide and Seek'**, the personal account of an intellectual and sexual deviant among other deviants in a contemporary city environment. Perhaps it should not be taken too seriously, if only because it is mainly a game, both a word-game and a sex-game. . . . The revelations . . . as well as the behaviour patterns of the bizarre characters within the story are all parts of the game of hide and seek. . . . [The narrator] is insufferable because he bears a resemblance to the

hero of Sargeson's earlier novel, **Memoirs of a Peon,** certainly not sexually, but in his estimate of his own intellectual superiority and artistic taste, and expresses himself in a language not quite as dated or pedantic as that affected by Michael Newhouse, but no less mannered. (pp. 261-62)

[If] this short novel avoids any kind of social realism, beneath its preposterous sexual jests, its outrageous matter and equally outrageous manner there is more than an occasional hint of a serious theme that comes to the surface in stray comments on the human predicament as well as in the tragi-comic fortunes of some of the seemingly bizarre characters. (p. 263)

> *H. Winston Rhodes, in a review of "Man of England Now," in* Landfall, *No. 103, September, 1972, pp.259-63.*

H. WINSTON RHODES

[Apart] from its intrinsic merits and continued relevance to enduring human habits, *I Saw in My Dream* has considerable historical value for those who wish to trace the contours of social behaviour.

Sargeson's 'dream' of a twentieth century, New Zealand pilgrim's progress is no allegory and is less a visionary search for a heavenly goal than a curiously patterned but dramatic portrayal of adolescent deprivation culminating in the pursuit of wholeness and the quest for fulfilment. Christian left the City of Destruction behind him, and at the end of the first part of *I Saw in My Dream* so does Henry; but neither the destructiveness of the City nor the reason for departure bears much resemblance to *The Pilgrim's Progress.* They have slightly more relationship to Stephen's leave-taking from Dublin in *A Portrait of the Artist as a Young Man.* Stephen became aware that 'when the soul of a man is born in this country there are nets flung at it to hold it back from flight' and soon escaped to Paris. Henry/Dave [Sargeson's protagonist] also recognizes the existence of nets, but they are the nets woven and cast by self-righteous conformers to a secular rather than a spiritual creed of prohibitions, bent on holding their victims in protective custody and enclosing the mental traveller in a prison of their own devising. Henry/Dave seeks and finds both a temporary refuge and the prospect of regeneration, not abroad but in the hill-country of his own land so that, whereas *I Saw in My Dream* begins with a menacing series of denials, restraints, and suppressions, it ends with a repeated affirmation and the partial release of the spirit into the freedom of creation and harmonious development.

The literature of escape (not to be confounded with escapist literature) has a long and interesting history that provides an ironic commentary on human progress. It goes back at least to the early pastorals and the town-versus-country themes of the Elizabethans. In more recent times E. M. Forster in England or Mark Twain in America, writers with whom Sargeson has some affinities, have expressed in fictional form the need to break loose from conventional restraints imposed by a puritanical middle-class and, through intimate contact with more primitive modes of being, recover some of the lost pagan virtues. In his short stories Sargeson had shown a preference for the warm-hearted, urban outcasts who, unaffected by the shibboleths of conformity, sought the freedom of the roads and the casual life of fringe-dwellers; but in *I Saw in My Dream* he concerned himself with the ambiguities and paradoxes of what might be called rather pretentiously the philosophy of escape. It is the Dave-half of the divided self of Henry/Dave who, in the unexpected and abruptly impressionistic climax to the first part, is at last able to escape from the mental prison that has nearly enclosed him for ever. His emergence from the long dream of trying 'to walk through miles and miles of dry sand carrying a heavy sort of swag on his back' is accomplished through the accidental discovery of the fallibility of his parents and the hollowness of their assumptions about life. . . . He himself had become divided between his obsession with 'the pilgrim's role' and his unrecognized aspirations for a completely human pilgrimage that would take him not through dry sand with a 'heavy sort of swag on his back' but through a mysterious world of burgeoning, sentient life. He has learnt the important lesson that ignorance is not innocence and, before entering a new world of experience, has reached a position in which it is possible to say 'I don't know a thing'. . . . Sargeson, of course, was not seeking a simple answer [to the problem of escape]; he was writing a fictional account of a young man's search for integration in a disintegrated world where the separation of man from nature, body from spirit, and sense from intellect, hampers any attempt to achieve an organic relationship between the human being and his mental and physical environment. Alienation is neither averted nor avoided by a flight to the wilderness, and the only solution for Henry/Dave is similar to that expressed by Molly Bloom at the conclusion of Joyce's *Ulysses*—an affirmation of life. (p. xii-xv)

Readers accustomed to the biographical novel of dramatic incident and closely-knitted plot, to an array of characters all of whom are essential to the development of the narrative, to a smooth progression from scene to scene and a unified structure based on the realistic portrayal of life may find in *I Saw in My Dream* much to disconcert them. They are wise if they keep its title in mind, but wiser still if they perceive that the language structure is more significant and revealing than the plot structure. Although episode, dialogue, and description of background are convincingly rendered, Sargeson is not strictly representational in his method. He rejects the naturalistic mode of writing and his approach to the novel is poetic in the sense that a theme stimulates his imagination to create a linguistic and unifying pattern. . . . [Sargeson's] vision of life is not restricted to a more or less faithful reproduction of external or experienced events. He allows himself the freedom of interpretation and by verbal suggestion gives increased meaning to common reality. Thus the texture of *I Saw in My Dream* is threaded with incidents and images of enclosure. . . . (p. xv)

The main theme of enclosure and escape controlling the first part of *I Saw in My Dream* is continued in the longer and later addition, the afterthought, that completes the novel. Sub-themes appear and proliferate and although they succeed in enriching the texture and increase its density, they also disturb the even flow of the narrative. The subtleties of innocence and experience are counterposed and illustrated in a number of ways; attitudes of Maori and pakeha considered; rival influences of nature and nurture examined; different concepts of purity and impurity, ignorance and sophistication are contrasted. No one could seriously suggest, however, that Sargeson's novel is a thinly disguised moral fable, that it is didactic or dominated by an abstract 'thesis'; nor that it becomes episodic in the way *That Summer* has been described. If an element of contrivance sometimes reduces the impact made by memorable scenes, the scenes still remain memorable. If the relation of the parts to the whole is occasionally obscured, the significance both of parts and whole is not greatly impaired. Such minor defects may be regarded as the almost unavoidable results of the attempt to achieve an imaginative unity. (pp. xvi-xvii)

It is probable that some will insist on treating *I Saw in My Dream* as a psychological case-history or, perhaps, a fictional study by a psychological realist, and thereby fail to appreciate its imaginative strength or come to terms with its literary mode. They may seize on the climax to the first part, and complain of the remarkable speed with which the victim of fancied guilt and unwarranted fears recovers from his long illness. They may plead that cause and effect are insufficiently related, that adequate detail is lacking, that this is not realism at all, but some kind of literary hoax. In a sense they are right, but only if no place can be found for impressionism in the writing of the imaginative realist. Sargeson needed a suitable climax that would relate back to the hero's early experiences, one that would suggest the duplicity of a strict sectarian's life and release the mental invalid from the guilt-ridden fears that oppressed him. For the reader willing and able to accept an impressionistic technique, it serves its purpose, but is quite unsatisfactory either for the determined realist or for the collector of case-histories.

The frequent use of italicized passages indicating an interior monologue may irritate those who usually resist any atttempt to conventionalize reality. To reproduce the stream of consciousness is impossible without some form of artifice, for the reader must be placed in possession of the key that will unlock the meaning of disjointed words and phrases. The writer must give the illusion of the processes of thought, but at the same time can indicate only those portions of experience that have already been communicated to the reader. The increasingly frenzied and incoherent thought of Henry imaginatively reveals the chaos within, and refers back to smaller and larger crises with which he has been unable to cope or failed to understand. Although Sargeson counterpoints his theme with considerable skill, introducing into the interior monologues the words and phrases that suggest past and present anxieties, the method is seldom satisfactory. . . . It is not without interest to note that Sargeson has found it unnecessary to return to the method employed in *I Saw in My Dream*.

By any estimate, however, this early novel remains a remarkable if not flawless achievement. It has been an exciting experience to . . . discover that, despite any real or fancied shortcomings, it retains a life of its own. It still has something to say to us today, and says it in a manner that can hardly fail to impress. (pp. xviii-xix)

> *H. Winston Rhodes, in an introduction to* I Saw in My Dream *by Frank Sargeson, edited by H. Winston Rhodes, Auckland University Press, 1974, pp. vii-xix.*

RAY COPLAND

This exploration of his own formative years [*Once is Enough*] is conducted by Sargeson with a smiling ease made possible not only by his complete assimilation of the material he deals with but by the mastery of his prose medium. Having throughout his career as a narrator practised the impersonation of his characters, he appears here to come 'down again' to his own personal voice. This is not to say, however, that either the tale he tells or the manner in which he tells it is to be taken as 'perfectly true' or 'perfectly natural', if indeed such things can ever be. This 'memoir' must be regarded as a portrait *of* the artist *by* the same artist as has fashioned the stories and the novels. (p. 70)

The second half of the book has been fully prepared for. Sargeson's story passes by the lightest of movements from accounts of life on his uncle's farm to descriptions of his relations and other personalities he has met. He provides searching and sometimes highly diverting portraits, the one which emerges most memorably being that of his appalling paternal grandmother. . . . None of the grandparents displays the puritanism and narrow propriety that his parents imposed upon the author. It was, perhaps by necessity, the parents' business 'to become well and respectably established in a growing and pushing community'. They perfectly represent their time and place; and Sargeson's deep attention to his own origins and his assessment of his own dissenting needs have thus an importance for the social historians of this country. It is evident, and interesting, that he remains his parents' son because of, not despite, his complete rejection of their values.

With a vocation at least as rigorous in its non-conformity as that of his parents, Sargeson has made, and here recorded, his long pilgrimage back to those humane values which in their largeness he once called 'Chaucerian'. Yet, from the beginning there remained in his stories much moral simplicity. . . . And no one in New Zealand has brought to literature so strongly scriptural and doctrinal a scepticism. Without being aware that his talent was unusual he had made his own way into the literature of theological controversy and acquired the habit of scriptural allusion which has always been a mark of his thinking. Both his early satire and his late comedy have sprung from the same Christian sources as had nourished his parents' piety. (pp. 70-1)

As this book closes, the writer's imagination circles back again to the centre, 'the crisis of emotion' which occurred long ago on his uncle's farm. The return to the theme is rendered by a physical return, and the young man wanders from room to room of the farm-house: 'Back again in the kitchen I knew when I felt the stove that my uncle could not be very far away . . .'. Throughout the book there is this masterly correspondence between scene and theme. Moreover the tone of the writing always moves sensitively into harmony with the widely varied subject matter. These closing pages have an appropriately elegiac character as the writer's recollections come to rest in a long-ago moment 'of withdrawn concentrated quietude [when] time, space and circumstances ceased to be of any importance'.

This book is far from being the mere record of a life. It is one of the most accomplished works of imagination that Sargeson has ever written. In this self-portrait he has realised with cool and sometimes comic fidelity not only the figure of the artist but the physical and social landscape against which he has moved for more than seventy years. The title perfectly strikes Sargeson's mature note: the journey has had its rewards and delights, but *Once is Enough*. (pp. 71-2)

> *Ray Copland, in a review of "Once is Enough," in* Landfall, *Vol. 29, No. 1, March, 1975, pp. 69-72.*

PATRICK EVANS

It is hard to know where to begin praising this little memoir [*More Than Enough*]. I think it will be read for two important reasons—for its accounts of the many people Sargeson knew well, such as Rex Fairburn and D'Arcy Cresswell, and for its depiction of the growth of Sargeson's art in the inhospitable environment of New Zealand. This second theme is one which could stand for every New Zealand artist's struggle—against

frequent ill health (luridly described), undying poverty (a *Catch-22* situation, Sargeson having to earn money by writing on a typewriter which was all too often in the pawnshop to earn money) and the friendship of such people as a Cockney named Jock, whose monumental indecisiveness itself became a sort of art form. And above all there was the indifference or enmity of the Right-Thinking Public, nowhere better represented than within his own family. . . . Out of all this, and against what he claims to be a natural inability in writing, Sargeson teased the stories and short novels which marked the first twenty years of his career, usually at the rate of a page a day.

His recollections of personalities of our literary past are entertaining and important as a record. (pp. 159-60)

The most moving account in *More Than Enough* is of the author's friendship with the distinguished German poet, Karl Wolfskehl, whom Thomas Mann called 'the last European'. Wolfskehl became a refugee from Nazi Germany, living lost and unrecognized in a cultural wasteland. Sargeson describes him with a technique which he uses often in this memoir—he shows the old poet to be vast and heavy with a thousand years of civilization and wisdom, a bulk which makes him a ridiculous figure in the streets of Auckland where shopgirls and typistes giggle at him, and which sinks him ankle-deep in Sargeson's vegetable-garden. The account of the near-blind Wolfskehl's solo journey one wet winter night from the centre of Auckland to Sargeson's lonely bach, to arrive sodden, lost, and muddy, is beyond pathos. It is a tragic image of the best of our European heritage lost in an Antipodean storm—to show so much so innocently is not simply fine autobiographical writing, it is superb literature in its own right, and Sargeson manages it constantly. (pp. 160-61)

> *Patrick Evans, "Sargeson's Life, Part Two," in* Landfall, *Vol. 30, No. 2, June, 1976, pp. 159-61.*

LYDIA WEVERS

Reading *Sunset Village* I was reminded of D'Arcy Cresswell's reaction to Sargeson's first book *Conversation With My Uncle* when it appeared in the mid-thirties: 'it was as though the first wasp had arrived, a bright aggressive little thing with a new and menacing buzz'. Sargeson has retained the wasp quality (no pun intended) in *Sunset Village* but oh what a delicate sting it now possesses. How tenderly he explores the idiosyncrasies of his characters, how elegantly makes manifest their foibles. (p. 316)

Loosely speaking *Sunset Village* is a murder story, a thriller, but to leave it at that would be very loose speaking indeed. Although it contains the essential ingredients: a murder, an intrigue, a faded but glamorous corpse, two painstaking detectives, plenty of suspects and even (a master stroke) the piquancy of an event involving a macabre and mysterious doll, these do not add up to a dish which would satisfy the aficionado of crime fiction. The murder, or at least the long trail towards the solution of the murder, staple diet of any true addict, is simply not of all-absorbing interest. It is a convenient narrative locus in which Sargeson places his characters: although discussion about the murder involves much of the novel there is no breathtaking dash to the finish, no lengthy explanation of the brilliant deductive powers of the hero, not even an apprehension of the murderer. Poor stuff, if one were expecting a thriller. However, fortunately for the avid pursuer of sex, crime and violence, *Sunset Village* makes no pretence at providing such a diet: it is in fact some way into the novel before one becomes aware that anything as dramatic as a murder is the stuff on which dreams are made.

A pensioners' village might seem unpromising material for entertainment, especially as entertainment is a rare enough thing in New Zealand novels . . . but it is the most immediate pleasure afforded by *Sunset Village*. What we are treated to is a wry, often compassionate view of people with time on their hands to speculate, gossip, meddle, remember and engage in liaisons sexual and otherwise, who are suddenly transfixed and engrossed by an event of nearly tragic proportion. Sargeson does not, however, let anything in *Sunset Village* assume heroic stature. The intrinsic irony of the dramatis locus, always containing its latent implication of a zoo for the elderly, is offset by the bland undulating narrative style which insists on our recognition of the whimsical and humane face of decay. People do not lose passion, sex, fear or an unhealthy interest in their neighbours simply because they are old. Nor does the narrator feel obliged to offer social comment, make any deferential concessions to age, or crucify human vanities on the crosstree of senility. (p. 317)

[*Sunset Village*] has, I suppose, a soft heart, an essential kindness that precludes judgments while demonstrating the ironies and eccentricities involved in the way people handle their predicaments. No obvious stalking horses are to be found. . . . Nor are there any easy moral codes to follow; morality, like other social virtues, is governed by inclination. . . . Nevertheless the tender insouciant irony that informs *Sunset Village* does not dismiss the perennial human affirmations and it is this that not only keeps it one step from comedy, but also almost allows the possibility of tragedy. (p. 318)

[Although] the vulgarities of murder, adultery and homosexuality indicate the twentieth century, there is more than an accidental resemblance between Jane Austen and Sargeson in this novel, unlikely as the comparison seems. It is partly that this small village with all its petty intense concerns, its sense and sensibility, is a footnote for mankind; it is, more importantly, an atmosphere of affectionate irony, a recognition that life, even in its more dramatic murderous moments, is seldom grand and heroic but nevertheless absorbing and important, and that our judgments can never be more than critical opinions. . . .

Sunset Village is the kind of elegant self-contained novel that makes no claims for itself and indulges in no pretensions. To subject it to the sort of critical archaeology that digs for levels of meaning hoping to find the real Troy would be to unjoint and destroy it. (p. 319)

Lydia Wevers, "'Just Plain Affection',' in Landfall, Vol. 30, No. 4, December, 1976, pp. 316-19.

R. A. COPLAND

A very high proportion of Sargeson's [earliest] stories are told in the first person. The degree to which the narrator is aware of the implication of what he tells varies widely from story to story: thus the tone may lie anywhere between the extremes of puzzled uneasiness and full consciousness. The physical elements of a story, however, are usually carefully contrived to enable the reader himself to contribute the appropriate response—compassion, a sense of irony, or of shock.

In 'Chaucerian' these elements provide a severely simple contrast between a humane physicality (as found in *The Canterbury Tales*) and a pinched moralism (as found in certain religious

sects). . . . Through surprise . . . the implications of the story are widened and the sense of consciousness *behind* the narrator increased. In 'Chaucerian' these effects are substantiated, for the narrator's own horizons do become larger, and his own mature consciousness of the moral burden of his tale is precisely the point of the story. . . . (p. 11)

Elsewhere, however, this 'knowingness' in the narrator is an irreparable flaw. In another story, **'In the Midst of Life'**, . . . the usual 'I' can remain an acceptable person (and hence earn the reader's endorsement of his values) only so long as he writes in innocence of his superiority over 'Frances'. But in sentence after sentence he reports on the narrowness of her ways and the triviality of her mind. . . . Throughout this story the narrator consciously supplies the value system that a good story should silently construct (as indeed the majority of Sargeson's own stories do). We cannot maintain that the character of the narrator is meant to be as defective as that of 'Frances', because he voices sentiments that carry unmistakably the authorial impress. . . .

The artistic possibilities of such short prose pieces are fully revealed in **'Miss Briggs'**. Here we are able to find that both character and narrator are flawed: both are victims of the same social ills. A descriptive account . . . is given of the title character, and almost every line adds to her presence. Stroke by stroke a portrait is built up of this skimpy and dogged spinster who sells things, dragging her two heavy cases from street to street. Around her Sargeson sketches an environment of decrepitude and misery. . . . The narrator seems always to be more puzzled than pitying, and we discover that he too is cramped by his poverty and his own brand of pride. . . . Sargeson swiftly touches on happier mortals, who can buy grandstand tickets or take tea in the croquet pavilion, but these contrasts are allowed to carry their own meanings. If the narrator 'enters' his story at all it is with a misplaced humour suggesting that he, being poor himself, finds nothing here for tears. (p. 12)

Both the drama of character and the crucial event are brought together in some of the most memorable of Sargeson's early stories. No one having read **'Sale Day'** will forget the increasing sexual tension between Victor, the farmer's son, and Elsie the kitchen maid, or the shocking symbolic event (Victor dropping the randy tomcat into the kitchen stove) with which the story is resolved. Another story in which a shocking action brings resolution to emotional tensions is **A Great Day'**. The ending of '**A Great Day'** is especially sinister in a Sargeson collection because the two men involved appear to be in the normal relationship of his working-class men. The words 'mate', 'pal', 'cobber' recur just as they do, for instance, in **'The Making of a New Zealander'**. . . . The reliance of a man upon his mate forms a vital part of the larger moral scheme in Sargeson's world. But when, in **'A Great Day'**, a man criminally abandons his mate the treachery is even more shocking than it might seem in the world of another writer. A realistic fidelity to the New Zealand scene being an essential part of these stories, the horror that they contain is sharpened by the normality of the setting. (p. 13)

Both ["**Cow-Pats**" and "**The Hole That Jack Dug**"] display the gift that uniquely identifies their author—the gift of symbolism. In the sixty lines of '**Cow-Pats**' Sargeson seems to summarize both the Dickensian sense of childhood's suffering and the Shakespearian sense of despised old age. The children in the country whose boots weren't 'any too good' and who discovered the bliss of standing in winter time in newly-dropped cow-pats, and the old man on the city street who stopped to soak his hands in a cleaner's bucket of warm suds, seem to symbolize all human pain between them. The narrator, tight-lipped with social comment, concludes that such things were 'somehow a bit too much for me'. 'The Hole That Jack Dug' has too many diverse implications for them all to be treated here. But especially interesting is the ambiguity of Jack's motives as he toils away at an enormous hole in his back garden. . . . But central to the story, amounting indeed to something proverbial in its aptness, is the symbol of the working man and the absurd heroism of his misapplied strength as he digs his vast hole only to fill it in again. . . . (pp. 14-15)

The symbolism of these stories has special force because it is based on such a realistic presentation of New Zealand life. So strong is Sargeson's representation of the probable gesture, the probable scene, the probable dialogue, that the reader is apt to regard a given story as no more than a pen and ink sketch of local activities; and sometimes it is the anecdotal value of a story he has heard that impels Sargeson to retell it. . . . But usually it is the symbolic power of the story which has seized the author and which comes through to the reader.

These short stories convey truths about New Zealand life and character that are for the greater part suggestively implicit rather than explained: emulating the reticence of the characters he normally chooses (the lowly, tough, silent, secretive, and lonely), Sargeson reduces to a minimum his own explication. The stories are characteristically very short indeed. They isolate situations which will speak, as it were, in silence. The language used by the characters is authentic even in its emotional evasiveness; and the language of the narrator commonly proceeds from just such a hypothetical personage as the characters might be supposed to fraternize with. There is thus a sustained harmony between the characters and the language through which they are given their existence. (p. 15)

> *R. A. Copland, in his* Frank Sargeson, *Oxford University Press, Wellington, 1976, 47 p.*

PETER CAMPBELL

Frank Sargeson's third volume of memoirs [*Never Enough!*] is subtitled 'Places and People Mainly'—but the choice is in no way random. Looking back over more than 70 years, he wants us to understand his life, see the justification of it. At the centre, as he describes it, there is a paradox—that he was never likely to become the sort of writer who would be much read by the New Zealanders he most liked. . . .

A romantic feeling for the land, and for people who work it, which he, better than other New Zealand writers, got into his fiction, appears in this book as something existing in a compartment. The never-realised dream of living in some sort of rural co-operative would perhaps have been a reconciliation of the two sorts of living—the natural and the intellectual. . . .

In his life as a writer, he never gave up hope that the intractable ground of New Zealand society would thaw enough for him to flourish. It is one of the pleasures of this book that he is able to record something of this sort happening in the Sixties when, after a rather bleak decade, *Memoirs of a Peon* was published and plays produced. His decision to stay at home, not to try to build something in London on the reputation he gained [with the publication of] . . . *That Summer* and *I Saw in My Dream,* was a recognition of his need for New Zealand.

What New Zealand had for him, if it stopped short of financial reward on any scale, was, of course, more than subject mat-

ter. . . . In a small country, one skill is not enough, and a literary world will never be big enough to be self-contained. This book gives a view of a life given over, primarily to the disciplines of writing in a society that has not much time for them. It is a situation which, in Sargeson's case, concentrated and sharpened the mind. . . .

Sargeson writes of New Zealand in a way that it is, so far as one can see, no longer possible for anyone to write of England—and while the view is more complete because the subject is more limited, the view of a whole organism gives something microscope sections of a more complex creature cannot give.

> *Peter Campbell, "Frozen South," in* The Listener, *Vol. 99, No. 2557, April 27, 1978, p. 555.*

BRUCE KING

In a colonial situation where English middle-class social values are inappropriate, the first really believable characters in fiction are usually the eccentrics and outcasts. It was Frank Sargeson who made such types representative of an authentic New Zealand. . . . Sargeson follows a pattern often noticeable in Commonwealth writers: rebellion against a stodgy middle-class background, expatriation, discovery abroad that one is not British, return to the native land both as a critic of its colonial bourgeoisie and with a new awareness of it as home.

During the 1930s and '40s Sargeson worked towards creating a fictional style appropriate for his country. The result was a small body of sketches and short stories, in which language, subject, attitude, characters and form capture representative qualities of New Zealand life. Drawing upon the depression concern with the down-and-out, the out-of-work, the poor, he wrote realistically of the attitudes and world of the social underdog, the disappointed immigrant, the drifters, wanderers and rootless. While the stories imply sympathy and compassion, the tone is flat, objective and tinged with irony in comparison to the idealising of the poor often found in 'protest' writing. The stories often indirectly attack the middle class and capitalism by quietly bringing into prominence callousness, exploitation and social conformity.

Sargeson showed how realism could be used to portray colonial culture. He looked directly at the society around him, refused to idealise it, and attempted to describe it accurately. The social disorder resulting from an underpopulated, underprivileged settler society was reflected in the episodic lives of his fictional characters and in the anecdotal nature of his stories. He captured the then often remarked upon isolated, improvised quality of local life, especially among the labourers, in the small towns and on the farms. It is a society in which men are equal but without communal bonds, an atomised society in which the 'mate', a companion of the same sex, temporarily becomes what equivalent there is of family. To create a representative, seemingly authentic quality, Sargeson often pared the short story form to dramatic monologues or dialogues of three hundred to five hundred words, narrated seemingly objectively in a colloquial but toneless voice by someone outside the middle class. As in the European tradition of realism, the suppression of the author as narrator requires that values be implied by irony, symbols and other means of 'placing' characters and events. The language of the stories is idiomatic, the vocabulary has many local words, and the rhythms of speech and sentence patterns give the impression of typical New Zealand talk. (pp. 141-43)

Sargeson's stories are similar to V. S. Naipaul's early fiction in recording, where there was no literary tradition upon which to build, the nature and quality of a society undergoing change, and where colonial myths were not relevant to actual life.

The models for Sargeson's art are recognisable, if subtly transformed to fit New Zealand: Mark Twain, Sherwood Anderson, Ernest Hemingway, James Joyce, and perhaps the Australian Henry Lawson. Each of these writers worked within the realist tradition of fiction and each was concerned with matters of the narrator's voice, objectivity, and implied ironies, especially towards middle-class and conventional values. The colloquial voice, laconic dialogue and apparent naiveté of Sargeson's narrators are within the tradition of Twain, while the extreme understatement and economy show study of Hemingway and Joyce. Like many other Commonwealth writers, Sargeson has availed himself of the lessons learned by American and Irish authors concerning the techniques by which a local society can be treated seriously in literature without falling into idealisation or condescension. (pp. 144-45)

The limitations for a writer who sees society from the perspective of its wanderers, outcasts and impoverished are shown by Sargeson's difficulty in expanding his fiction to larger forms. The episode, anecdote and sketch cannot be fused into a sustained long narrative. . . . ['**That Summer**'] is an attempt at capturing within the apparently casual joining up of two 'mates' an analogous relationship to that more often associated with an intense, shattering, doomed love affair between a man and a woman. It would be unnecessary to comment upon the homosexual foundation of the story, as Sargeson has elsewhere written about his friendships, were it not so often implied that women, marriage and domesticity are dangerous traps for the kind of person the author admires, and if such male relationships were not often conspicuous in other new English literatures. Exploration, the frontier, pioneer society, and a life of wandering on the road create a culture for men which women threaten. The responsibilities of marriage, children, steady jobs, mortgages and staying in one place no more appeal to Sargeson's heroes than they would to Walt Whitman, Twain's Huckleberry Finn, Melville's Ishmael, or J. F. Cooper's Deerslayer. The frontier and vagabond themes found in some new national literatures reflect anti-bourgeois attitudes and a rebellion against a local middle-class society which, along with its other sins of gentility, hypocrisy and injustice, the author usually sees as a relic of European colonialism. (pp. 145-46)

It is paradoxical that in a supposedly puritan, conformist, conventional society Sargeson's homosexual stories should be seen as the quintessence of New Zealandism. A possible explanation might be seen in the transformation he made of a cultural ideal. Nationalism often identifies authenticity with rural areas and the poor—the land and the people. In contrast high culture is seen as foreign, metropolitan, cosmopolitan, snobbish, elitist, a form of imperialism. The writer rebelling against his middle-class background usually either heads towards London, Paris or New York, with their international and metropolitan values, or identifies himself with the land and the people. Sargeson, like Mark Twain or Synge, creates a folk tradition from those on the fringes of society.

But the imitation of the 'people' does not offer sufficient material and technical interest to make an artistic tradition. . . . Sargeson was aware that his own art had to progress beyond the short story to the novel and from focus on the outsider to a more personal exploration of problems of individual and national identity. While '**That Summer**' is an attempt at such

progress, it is an interesting dead-end. . . . His later narratives include some of his best and worst work, but in either case the increase in length, range of subject-matter and style shows his awareness that he must go beyond the anecdotal realism of the short stories. (pp. 148-49)

[With *I Saw in My Dream*] Sargeson has modified the realistic method of his earlier stories for a larger, more thematic, associative way of writing fiction. The flatly stated, objectively presented events are counterpointed by memories and emotions revealed in the italicised passages. Puritanism, conventionality, enclosure and middle-class comfort are contrasted to sexual desire, individuality, freedom, the working class and economic insecurity. The life Henry lives is oppressive, contrary to his inner emotions, and causes his breakdown. That he collapses when a detective appears at the office shows Henry can no longer bear his feelings of guilt, guilt expressed by his compulsive enclosure of two uninhibited women. After a cleansing dive into the river that concludes Part I, which symbolically washes away his inhibited, colonial, middle-class behaviour, he is reborn not to a new identity but to an awareness that he must define himself in relationship to his environment. The search is personal but can be seen as representative of the nation. Part I ends with Henry lying naked on a grassy river bank. He must begin again.

In Part II Henry uses the name Dave while working on a farm in the hills. The change of name corresponds to his awareness of the problem of his own identity. . . . In Part II the detail and texture of the story are more filled in, the episodes longer, and there is more continuity. If the fragmentary style of Part I implied a dazed, inhibited, enclosed, sketchy, unresponding relationship to life, the more novelistic feel of Part II shows a growth in awareness, of others and of reality. Form reflects content; genre imitates psychology. In Part II Dave puts up with discomfort, has friends, is more relaxed and in touch with nature, and is open to experience. The landscape itself is a new world awaiting fulfilment. . . . The hill is not Eden. It is a change from the constrictions of puritan suburbia. It is a chance to begin again, a chance to discover one's authentic self. But it is also lonely, isolated and dangerous. It is New Zealand itself from which the middle class flees into the constriction and snobbery of colonial suburbs. Two motifs are of particular importance in this quest: the presence of the Maoris, and Cedric's escape from being imprisoned by his family. (pp. 152-53)

The seemingly instinctive and mysterious ways of the Maoris contrast to those of the Europeans, and are more suitable for the landscape, but the Maoris have been dominated and pushed to the outer fringes of colonial society. The Maoris represent to Dave the physical, sensual and natural which his family has repressed. This cannot be his own identity, but he must accept it as part of himself and the land.

The mysterious Cedric Macgregor, who is spoken about but never actually appears in the novel, found his freedom through the Maoris. Raised in the hills 'with only those dirty Maoris down the road for nearest neighbours' he stays away from school and spends his time with the Maoris and their women. Cedric is 'wild', a 'child of nature', contrary to a well-brought-up middle-class child, the opposite of Henry in Part I. The Macgregors decide Cedric is out of his mind and convert a cave into a prison where they intend to keep him. . . . Apparently with the aid of the Maoris, Cedric flees. The Macgregors pretend he is living a conventional life in the city, but he has disappeared. . . . The Macgregors' attempted imprisonment of Cedric should probably be understood as similar to family pressures to force Henry into a law office. Cedric's mysterious escape cannot, however, be Dave's freedom: *'it's all right for Cedric. Cedric's Cedric . . . Cedric never had a Henry to forget . . . I've been Henry, now I'm Dave. But I'm only TRYING to be Dave.'* The rural hills and farms are not the end of Dave's journey. They also could be a trap, a false home. (p. 154)

It is because Henry has lived as Dave that he can, in the brief concluding Part III of the novel, think of marrying Marge, think of travelling around the world, or assume he can 'do something special . . . something nobody else can do except me'. The final 'yes, yes' of the novel is an affirmation of life, creativity, the individuality and selfhood Henry lacked. It is Sargeson autobiographically celebrating his decision to become a writer.

I Saw in My Dream is a remarkable book. It is a blend of symbolist experimental techniques with a kind of realism common to regional literature; but it is from the dialectic between *avant-garde* and nationalist currents that the best works of the new literature have resulted. Unfortunately Sargeson did not have the skill to create another *Portrait of the Artist*. The realism and mental associations in *I Saw in My Dream* are imperfectly integrated; the italicised passages are often crude attempts at symbolism; and Part III, the conclusion, is unconvincing. *I Saw in My Dream* was a necessary attempt at liberation from the limitations of a local realism, but Sargeson's skills remained principally those of his early stories. His later attempt, in *Memoirs of a Peon* . . . , to write a sophisticated satire on both the New Zealand middle-class establishment and on those who pretended to rebel against it fails because the style lacks the subtlety to be convincing. Influenced by his reading of European literature, especially Casanova, the narrator describes his sexual and social conquests in an imported literary fashion. The comedy results from the discrepancy between the literary models and both the unromantic reality of New Zealand life and the narrator's own lack of energy and ambition. The experiment of *I Saw in My Dream* had, however, broadened Sargeson's palette; several good novellas followed which, while avoiding *avant-garde* symbolism, are more extended and cover a greater social and emotional canvas than the short stories. (pp. 155-56)

> *Bruce King, "New Zealand: Frank Sargeson and Colloquial Realism," in his* The New English Literatures: Cultural Nationalism in a Changing World, *St. Martin's Press, 1980, pp. 140-56.*

MURRAY S. MARTIN

[Frank Sargeson] shows a refined sensitivity of ear and a careful precision in writing, qualities that enhance his ability to portray the society he knows. No biography, however, can show the impact of Sargeson both as a writer and as a man upon New Zealanders. The story of the impact, which this article endeavors to demonstrate, carries with it a moral to all critics, a moral of which Sargeson himself was conscious: one must not allow one's image of a writer to conceal the real writer. (p. 123)

The lasting themes of [Sargeson's] writing are the same as appeared in his earliest stories. One of his recurrent themes is isolation, the lack of communication among people. . . . [One] may sense, from the reiteration of the phrase "It's difficult to have a talk with my uncle," in the sketch **"Conversation With My Uncle,"** that the reader is being forced to face the irony of isolation in what should be a context for sharing. Talking with someone who can't imagine or "suppose," and who doesn't like risky subjects, is unproductive. . . . A person with imagination, without intellectual speculation, without the ability to share ideas, is a "dead man" even if he continues to walk around and wear his bowler hat. The theme is reiterated in **"In the Midst of Life,"** where the narrator is unable to penetrate his cousin Frances' closed world, a strange world created by her excessive reading of the romantic novels of Ethel M. Dell. . . . In these stories one can recognize the burden of isolation, both implicit and explicit, in a world with narrow bounds. The question of how one can, or should, share the good things of life is posed. And, finally, the stories point out how clearly all the unsavory aspects of life are rejected from consideration by this self-consciously respectable society. These are the themes that Sargeson has used in multiple settings in all his writings. (p. 124)

[Within Sargeson's stories there is] a remarkable consistency of method and a unity of view. The unity was not at once appreciated by critics who hankered after the "real Sargeson," but gradually they came to realize that all these seemingly disparate visions were part of the same world, their themes enunciated in the earliest writing but now fuller, sometimes even inverted, and all shared in the process of finding out, of becoming whole, even in a lame, unsatisfying world. As early as 1947, Sargeson had set out his own test for a writer's achievement.

> The writer should have capacity to hear, see, feel, think, imagine, invent and arrange; second . . . capacity for using words . . . to make the reader feel he has received an important communication . . . both moving and entertaining . . . truthful above all other things and third . . . he should reveal an attitude.

Clearly this ideal produces literature, not a realistic image of "life," and clearly this ideal does not bind the writer to one format or style alone.

Because much of Sargeson's work was written in the first person, he had a double problem to solve: first, how to reconcile this technique with his own authorial moral stand—his "attitude"; second, how to reconcile the needs of the narrative with the actual literary capacity of the supposed narrator. This is Yvor Winters's "almost insoluble problem," the reconciling of the narrative with the subject. If by raising the level of the narrative one risks falsifying the personality of the subjective narrator, then by lowering the level of the narrative one risks the loss of literary power. It is here, if anywhere, that Sargeson might be judged to fall short of his literary ideal, since it is difficult to give readers the feeling of receiving an important message (his second criterion) while still retaining stylistic truthfulness to the petty world of the characters. His skill in writing and his devotion to the truth about the world he himself knew best help him towards overcoming this problem. (pp. 125-26)

Sargeson himself talks of *masks*, which he regards as necessary since life would otherwise be intolerable. He agrees that there was a limit on how long he could continue writing in the masks he assumed in his early stories. "There is a constricting factor in using the first person, more particularly when I have assumed the mask of a person who is non-literate." That choice was, however, made deliberately, because the limitation of language matches the moral limitation of his early characters, thus embodying his attitude of "unjudging pity" for those whose isolation inevitably mutilates them emotionally. Any attempt at reproducing the world familiar to Sargeson would have to be accompanied by linguistic approximation: not coy attempts to dialect, but deep attention to actual idiom and rhythm. The critics and other authors were quickly aware of Sargeson's "perfect ear," though Sargeson saw himself as needing to search for the "appropriate language" to describe the world he knew. The innovation that came later to be seen as the Sargeson style was "the very articulation of a hitherto inaudible vernacular." . . .

The fringe nature of New Zealand as a whole is explored through its own fringe world of the unsuccessful, the drifters and the rootless people, those who have not won their right to a share in the economic feast. . . . Sargeson's awareness of the centrality of isolation—not cultural or geographic isolation only, but personal, emotional isolation—is central to his handling of language and theme. . . . He also stresses that personal and social loneliness, and private aberrations, are inextricably linked. . . . (p. 127)

The restrictions of the society bottle up the emotional side of mankind, with the inevitable result of violence, both moral and physical, as recurs so frequently in Sargeson's writing. But at the same time the leavening of emotional catharsis is excluded, as is represented at once by the unwillingness to admit difference and the fierce retention of the standards that are threatened by the outsider. This combination helps explain Sargeson's preoccupation with that "outsider" as the person most able to show the dilemma of the tightly-knit New Zealand social scene. . . .

Although the majority of Sargeson's characters are clearly incomplete as people, and the settings in which they play out their frustrated lives also appear to be unfulfilled and unfulfilling, it is important to note that some, at least, do overcome their deficiencies. Overcoming is usually a result of love, sympathy, and selflessness, as shown by the grandmother in "Toothache." But it is equally true of the protagonist in "Man of England Now," who retains his integrity even though he is three times a loser. The lesson that should perhaps be drawn from the rarity of such successes is the difficulty of maintaining one's wholeness in the face of societal unconcern. Moreover, even though readers are clearly drawn to approval of these characters, Sargeson is careful never to ask for such approval. One is expected to draw one's own conclusions and to recognize that all men are a strange mixture of good and bad, so that certain actions . . . are inevitable and proceed not from a depraved nature, but from the combination of environmental, social, and personal pressures that shape an individual's response to moral crises.

Although Sargeson's early stories are held to demonstrate most clearly his complete linkage of theme and language, because they create a coherent whole, his later works can be seen as the donning of a further series of masks. The characters of the early stories are prevented by their inarticulateness from making a moral choice; indeed, they do not even grasp that there is a problem of choosing. In contrast, the characters of his later novels are not inarticulate in the sense of being unable to express themselves, but they are inarticulate in a still worse way, in that their possession and control of language does not render them any freer morally. Indeed, despite their loquacity they speak to one another no more than did their predecessors. (pp. 128-29)

Critics have usually focused on the changes in style and vocabulary between the stories and the novels, without seeing that the same theme is being expressed. The later works differ only in showing that the achievement of universal literacy is nothing in the absence of any core of belief or conviction. That core has held no more for the intellectual than it has for the common man. The surface is intact and the interior is hollow, but because the intellectual has more words at his disposal, he can play games and indulge in self-deceit in a way that is not accessible to those without the words. (p. 129)

In first-person writing, it is tempting to seek autobiography. In [*Joy of the Worm*] there appears to be reference to Sargeson's own experience. Jeremy's earliest feelings are close to those expressed in Sargeson's early stories—an appreciation for the natural man—and Jeremy's later retreat to literature appears to parallel Sargeson's later use of a more complex vocabulary. One must, however, remember Sargeson's own warning that these feelings are "related to" the writer, but are not "life," not his own sentiments. They do, nevertheless, express the same dilemma facing the intellectual in an unsympathetic world.

In another novel, whose very title *A Game of Hide and Seek* suggests the ambiguity so prevalent in his work, Sargeson presents the reader with a neatly-contrived conundrum.

> What I intend to put down on paper is fiction, that is to say dreams, make believe, fancy. There is no question about it, but one has to insist, because what one writes, and the more especially the more it convinces, will be supposed to have happened. It is strange and contradictory—everyone tells lies and most of us readily; but it is only with reluctance that we bring ourselves to credit people with imagination, which is in any case often thought to be some *dis*credit, perhaps a reluctantly-approved form of lying.

There are layers of meaning here to be uncovered, but which of them is "true" is impossible to determine. The very uncertainty, however, is yet another mask, one more way of stating the isolation of the individual. It is also a way of reinforcing the lesson that indirectness may be the only method available for a writer intensely moved to address his central cares in an alienated and alienating society—certainly a society in which the narrator could not have openly admitted his homosexuality, for example, and survived. . . . For [Sargeson] and for Jeremy the end is the inevitable return to the father, literally for the one, allegorically for the other. In order, however, to disguise this inevitability, they each weave a web of words.

The fear of inevitability is particularly acute for the intellectual. Michael, in *Memoirs of a Peon,* senses the terrible appeal of the ordinary, humdrum world. . . . Yet he deceives himself by thinking that he can maintain detachment from the world and still attain his own goals, because these goals lie within that world.

Alienation is the central theme of these works, together with the violence, both physical and moral, that alienation brings in its train. In perhaps his most devastating denunciation of isolation, Sargeson presents the picture of a youth rendered defenseless by his inability to wear a mask. *The Hangover* is a brief excursion into the fringe world of the hippies, during which the lad Alan loses both his innocence and his sense of belonging. . . . But disillusionment with the new world of values follows that with the old and, now having nothing to sustain him, Alan falls prey to the violence that meaninglessness engenders. For a moment, during a night spent outdoors in a childhood bower, he hopes to recover the innocence of childhood—"to survive the night it had been necessary to re-enter that lost world. It isn't possible, of course. There never is any second childhood. To pretend, then—at the very least to touch upon the fringes." With nowhere to return to and no one in whom to believe, the only recourse is to seek one's pleasure, a course of action that again leads to isolation and eventually to violence as a way of removing the reminders of one's own inabilities.

Although this is the most explicitly violent tale, violence has a symbolic value through all Sargeson's work. It is the symbol of a "change in mental attitudes, that, altering the eye, alters all that it sees." In a claustrophobic society, such a change is only too likely to lead to violence because the society's limitations inhibit less-drastic forms of change. Alan's violence in murdering his mother and friends is not greatly different from that of another character, Fred, who, unable by blandishment or personal ability to recover his girlfriend from Ken, simply leaves him to drown on a reef, thus removing a problem beyond his power either to describe or to resolve. Perhaps this inaction represents the final triumph of the inarticulate. It is a triumph that Sargeson understands and refrains from judging, because he sees it as only a more startling example of the typical failure of a materialistic society to provide any escape from individual isolation. In its effect it is not too different from the heedless cruelty of the rich "who often mention money, but not pay," and whose callousness towards others is simply a way of denying their existence. They too are found wanting by the writer, yet pitied as well, because they are also alone. In this way he fulfills his own requirement that the writer should show an attitude. Sargeson's attitude is one of pity for people who destroy their own capacity for life. (pp. 130-32)

Murray S. Martin, "Speaking through the Inarticulate: The art of Frank Sargeson," in The Journal of General Education, *published by the Pennsylvania State University Press, University Park, Pennsylvania, Vol. XXXIII, No. 2, September, 1981, pp. 123-34.*

Nathalie Sarraute

1902-

Russian-born French novelist, essayist, critic, and dramatist.

Sarraute is often named as one of the originators of a French literary movement which began in the mid-1950s known as the "Nouveau Roman," or the "New Novel." *L'ère du soupçon* (1956; *The Age of Suspicion*), a collection of critical essays in which Sarraute announced a break with the traditional form of the novel, is regarded as one of the classic texts of the movement; its publication coincided with a similar announcement by Alain Robbe-Grillet, the best known of the New Novelists. Although Sarraute shares with the New Novelists a rejection of traditional plot structures, identifiable characters, and other realistic conventions of the novel, she and some of her critics have pointed out that many of her connections with the New Novelists are superficial. Sarraute's primary interest is in human beings and their psychological states, while other New Novelists emphasize visual description of the external world, something which is almost completely absent from Sarraute's work. The New Novelists' fascination with language apart from any point of reference in the real world is also anathema to Sarraute, who uses language to explore the real, albeit unseen, inner world of her characters. In an essay, she asks, "What is a work of art if not a break through appearances toward an unknown reality?" Sarraute initiated many of the innovations associated with the New Novel in *Tropismes* (1939; *Tropisms*) and *Portrait d'un inconnu* (1948; *Portrait of a Man Unknown*), works which significantly predate the movement. But it was not until its tenets had been formulated and gained recognition that these early works became widely read. This fact reinforces the perception of Sarraute as part of the New Novel movement.

One of Sarraute's major contributions to contemporary literature is the concept of the "tropism." As one critic explained, Sarraute borrowed this term from biology to describe "the almost imperceptible movements concealed behind the social facade of gestures, actions and language, the authentic, constantly moving realm of instinctive reactions." The technique which Sarraute devised as a medium for expression of tropisms is "subconversation." Subconversation consists not of unspoken dialogue, but of half-formed thoughts and feelings which are conveyed to the reader impressionistically through metaphor, imagery, sound, and rhythm. These elements give Sarraute's work a poetic quality. In his book *Style and Temper*, W. M. Frohock defines Sarraute's innovation as the use of imagery which "operates on the level of the first recognition of phenomena, rather than on the level of evaluation, and thus identifies a kind of psychic activity very rare in earlier fiction." Sarraute's writing is often difficult to understand because of her almost complete lack of exposition, her use of ellipses in place of standard punctuation, and her refusal to distinguish between different speakers, between spoken and unspoken thoughts, and between real and imaginary events.

Sarraute has said of her first work, *Tropisms*, that "it contains *in nuce* all the raw material that I have continued to develop in my later works." In the twenty-four short sketches which comprise the work, Sarraute explores not only the form of the tropism, which is the basis of all of her work, but also the

thematic concerns which recur in her novels. These include the compulsive and often nameless fears which plague everyone, the ignorance and intolerance of bourgeois society, and humanity's "terrible desire to establish contact," a theme which reflects the influence of Fedor Dostoevski on Sarraute's work. Sarraute's first two novels, *Portrait of a Man Unknown* and *Martereau* (1960), utilize a narrator and a story line to unify tropisms. In both works, the narrator is a sensitive young man who is obsessed with unraveling the mysteries of other people's lives; he is largely outside what little action there is in the story, yet the novels are primarily concerned with his tropisms. A central theme of both books, which parallels the author's struggle to create a work, is the narrator's effort to construct a reality from disparate, often random pieces of information. Many of Sarraute's works are concerned with the process by which fiction is created. Sarraute's next three novels are explicitly concerned with literature. *Le planétarium* (1961; *The Planetarium*), one of Sarraute's most conventional novels, is a comedy of manners that satirizes the literary world. A sensitive young man also appears in this novel, but Sarraute has done away with the narrator figure entirely and relies solely on fragments of dialogue and subconversation. *Les fruits d'or* (1964; *The Golden Fruits*), which again satirizes the lack of relationship between literary merit and literary reputation, has neither narrator, identifiable characters, nor plot. The subject of *The Golden Fruits* is the critical and popular reception of a book of that name, and Sarraute demonstrates, through disembodied voices, the rise and fall of its reputation while revealing nothing of the nature of the book or the character of the critics or author. In *Entre la vie et la mort* (1968; *Between Life and Death*) Sarraute attempts to reflect the creative process through an "everyman"-type author. Again, there are no traditional characters, no setting, and no plot.

In recent years Sarraute has published several collections of radio plays. Critics observe that her literary theories and style lend themselves well to this genre; like her novels, the plays do not depend on narration for their development and feature dialogue by unidentifiable characters. One critic has likened reading Sarraute's work to listening through a motel wall to the conversation of people one has never seen. In *L'usage de parole* (1982; *The Use of Speech*) Sarraute returned to the sketch form she used in *Tropisms* to explore the dramatic substructures of commonly used banal phrases, which she uses as epigraphs at the beginning of each sketch. Her subject matter throughout the book, which is unified by the commentary of a narrator, is the significance of language and the superficial way that it is often used.

Critical opinion of the New Novel has often been negative, especially on the part of English and American scholars. The New Novelists are often accused of abolishing many staples of the traditional novel without offering the reader anything of value in their place. Because Sarraute shares with the New Novelists a rejection of such novelistic conventions as plot and character, she has often been the target of similar objections. Critics frequently complain that nothing in Sarraute's work justifies the difficulty of understanding it. For example, Henri Peyre, one of her most prominent detractors, contends that Sarraute's refusal to give names to most of her characters "erects a hurdle of dubious value between the book and the reader." While critics admire Sarraute's use of tropisms to take the psychological novel a step beyond the work of Dostoevski or Virginia Woolf, many contend that the psychological elements of Sarraute's work cannot stand without an ordering of the many details of sensibility which she relates. Another common appraisal of Sarraute's work is that it has duplicated the tedium and boredom of the real world so faithfully that the books themselves are tedious. Despite the opinion of some critics that Sarraute's novels are too inaccessible to merit wide readership, her concept of the tropism and her technique of the subconversation are considered among the few major innovations in contemporary fiction. As Claude Mauriac has stated, "What [Sarraute] says corresponds to what our experience has taught us, but nobody has expressed it before her"; he also calls her "the only living author who has created anything new after Proust."

(See also *CLC*, Vols. 1, 2, 4, 8, 10 and *Contemporary Authors*, Vols. 9-12, rev. ed.)

ANNE KOSTELANETZ [LATER ANNE K. MELLOR]

[*The essay from which this excerpt is taken originally appeared in* The Massachusetts Review *in Autumn, 1963.*]

Not since Henry James have the acumen of the critic and the psychological sensitivity of the accomplished novelist been so well fused as in Nathalie Sarraute. This is particularly evident in her essays, collected as *The Age of Suspicion* [1963] (originally published in 1956 as *L'Ère du Soupçon*), which reveal her awareness of the novel both as an artistic craft and as a means of communicating "psychological reality." Here she traces the development of the psychological novel from Dostoyevsky to the present, defines her own original approach to the form and describes the fictional techniques necessary to realize this new kind of fiction. Thus these essays serve two functions: they provide a lucid analysis of the nature and practice of the psychological novel since Dostoyevsky and they also, like Henry James' *Prefaces,* contain the most illuminating critical discussions we have of Mme. Sarraute's own novels. (p. 544)

In her earliest novel, *Tropisms* (1939; reissued, 1957), Mme. Sarraute probes the psychic lives of those *nouveaux bourgeoise* women who have moved from the country to a Paris apartment. Since she confines herself to a single social class, she can treat the psychology of all these women as one mind and show how the innermost thoughts of each reflect the notions of all. Flickering from one mind to another, she grasps those "tropismes" (a biological term meaning the response, usually an orientation, of a plant or animal to the influence of external stimuli) which characterize these women's response to their daily routines. Although Mme. Sarraute's fictional concern wavers between lyrical description and psychological probing, although she has not yet discovered the means or the material to construct an effective fictional vision, she has already defined the direction in which her work will move—the definition of psychological depths beneath the objective surface of situation and character.

Her next novel, *Portrait of a Man Unknown* (1947), continues to test the hard surfaces of appearance for signs of underlying realities. The narrator, an anonymous "I," tries desperately to penetrate the motivations and characters of the alternately rough and charming father and his "hypersensitive" daughter who live in his apartment-house. Despite repeated encounters and surreptitious spyings, the narrator is unable to crack their external masks—what he thinks are moments of insight are actually nothing more than imaginative projections. Ironically, it is the narrator's own acute sensibilities, as they play over these two figures, which suggest that kind of perceptive introspection which becomes the mark of her best fiction.

Martereau (1953) is a crude attempt to define that area of psychology her later novel grasps so surely. The narrator poses his own affectionate responses to Martereau against his uncle's suspicions and his aunt's concern (perhaps adulterous) in an attempt to define the essence of this man. He succeeds only in destroying his own relationship with Martereau without ever discovering the truth of the man's character. But already we find Mme. Sarraute capturing the unspoken nuance of social encounters, for it is the barely hinted suggestions, the delicate plots and counter-plots, the constant awareness of the listener's reaction to one's statements, and the eternal anxiousness to please and satisfy which make up the real matter of this novel. Here, however, it is her sluggish words—heavy, static, defined—which keep the novel from moving forward. Only in the most recent novel are these words metamorphosed into movements which generate the form of the novel from their own energy.

The "characters" in *The Planetarium* [1959] are only named consciousnesses, each speaking in the first person, each rotating in his own orbit until a sudden collision throws him into contact with another and stirs his submerged thoughts and feelings into rapid turmoil. Nathalie Sarraute skillfully expands these isolated collisions in time and in relevance until the universal conflict of rebellious youth and parental authority is constructed. The basic pattern of collision is the archetype of initiation into or rejection from a defined social group. The "groups" presented vary from the writers' clique commanded by Germaine Lemaire, which the young critic Alain hopes to enter, to the familial communion which their parents wish to reestablish with Alain and Gisèle after their marriage, to the "special place" in Alain's heart which his Aunt Berthe must maintain even if it means sacrificing her apartment, to the perfect marriage which Alain and Gisèle are incapable of achieving.

It is not these social situations which make up the novel's texture, however, but the sensations aroused within the characters when they collide. Their spoken words flow smoothly, but beneath are hidden depths of half-grasped, often inarticulate, desires and fears. Mme. Sarraute suggests these barely conscious movements with a slight nuance, a fleeting metaphor, an undeveloped suggestion and, very rarely, an image as developed as the surrealist description of natives stalking their victims in the jungle which evokes the sensation of terror with which Berthe awaits the loss of her apartment. (pp. 548-50)

With *The Planetarium,* Nathalie Sarraute achieved that new kind of psychological novel which her critical essays describe, a novel which captures those movements which cannot be seen directly and clearly by the conscious mind, those movements which form and disintegrate with utmost rapidity "on the extreme edge of consciousness." She has internalized character, plot and description and has discarded from her form all the antiquated conventions of the traditional novel which impede the flow of these movements beneath and around the levels of spoken dialogue. She has subtly evoked complex and varied personalities and diverse social situations with which we can identify (perhaps more easily than with James' limited "drawing-room" situations). She has articulated the very real sensations which we all feel whenever we are intensely involved in an uncertain situation, the numerous and complex movements that give meaning to our actions and our words. She has taken from Dostoyevsky his sensitivity to the complicated and contradictory feelings which are never revealed in conventional dialogue and developed a new instrument—nothing more nor less than her style—to present them to the reader. But her style so deftly captures the dimly perceived pattern of our innermost lives that we, too, echo the final communion between Alain and Germaine . . . "I think we're all of us, really, a bit like that." (p. 552)

Anne Kostelanetz [later Anne K. Mellor], "Manifesto for a New New French Novel," in On Contemporary Literature, *edited by Richard Kostelanetz, revised edition, Avon Books, 1969, pp. 544-54.*

VICTOR BROMBERT

The figure of the writer seems to occupy the center of Nathalie Sarraute's latest novel. The opening paragraph projects the image of a man typing, tearing out the page, throwing it away, taking another sheet, continuing to pound on his typewriter. **"Between Life and Death"** is however not so much about the writer as about the act of writing. Words are here the true protagonists. (p. 4)

Can one even say that this is a novel? No, if one looks for definable characters, dramatic situations, psychological developments in the habitual sense. Yes, if one believes that it is the prerogative of the novelist to blend levels of reality, to

telescope time, to project fears into the as yet unlived moment, to transform even the pettiest of obsessions into a poetic experience.

Perhaps it would be fairer to say that this is a dramatic prose poem about words. "Words" might indeed have been a fitting title, had not Sartre used it recently for his remarkable autobiography. In fact, there are some clear points of contact between these two otherwise very dissimilar works. Both Sartre and Sarraute view words as realities that determine, as well as forces that can liberate. Words oppress, protect, hurt, transform, immobilize—and, above all, survive. They preside over our lives and can become an alibi for not living. Literary creation may well be such an alibi. (pp. 4-5)

[In **"Between Life and Death"** we] come across sentences such as these: ". . . I'm alone in the enemy camp . . . defenseless . . . protect me." "But she resists, she clutches him, she clings to him, hems him in, he stands up to her, they are fighting, they are locked in struggle." Yet all this talk about enemies, tactical tricks, blocking of roads, fatal encirclement, corresponds neither to the presence of Amazons nor to the excitement of actual battles. Whatever is epic here remains at the purely verbal level. But that is the point of the novel. Words are our enemies, our allies, our traitors. They lock us in, they choke us—and they lead us to a manner of freedom.

Viewed in this light, **"Between Life and Death"** does tell a story. At the beginning, there is sheer sensitivity to words. . . . Next comes the awareness that words are not merely vague threats, but sharp weapons. . . .

The cruel games people play with each other (in part, to hide their sense of vacuity and despair) create a relentless nostalgia for a magic order. Words, this time, become the instruments of clarity, composition, a superior calm. But this order has its own limits: this peace resembles inertia, it resembles death. Between life and death: the title of the book clearly defines the problem, not merely in temporal terms, but in terms of the survival of all art, caught between life-giving formlessness and sterilizing formalism. Ultimately, the answer—and the salvation—may well depend on the degree of complicity between the artist and his public. Appropriately, the novel ends with a question: ". . . Let's look together . . . does it emit, deposit . . . as on the hand glass held up to the mouth of the dying . . . a fine mist?"

The tragic undertones are obvious: the sense of separation and exclusion, the solipsistic urge, the fear of life, the puritanical longing for an absolute. But all this remains subdued. What is so remarkable in the work of Nathalie Sarraute is that she can make so much of what appears to be so very little. It turns out, of course, that it is not so little after all, that her novel illustrates a double paradox. It is fear of life (not fear of death) that produces art, and the production of art in turn generates new terrors.

This climate of seemingly petty anxieties, wounded pride, tormented perfectionism, and yearnings for a protective shell, comes across, with almost total directness. . . . One question, however, occurs to some faithful readers. How many more novels can one, or should one, write in this vein? (p. 5)

Victor Brombert, "Is It a Novel? Yes, but Also a Poem about Words," in The New York Times Book Review, *May 18, 1969, pp. 4-5.*

DAVID J. DWYER

[The central character of Nathalie Sarraute's *Between Life and Death*] is a writer and her central concern is the "mere complexities, the fury and the mire" of his creative life—the whole thing smacks not of autobiography (too little occurs to justify that word) but of alteregoism. And, as the young Turkish poet Murad Osman-Talaat has written:

> . . . nothing strikes an alteregoist with more horror than the prospect that someone may be converted to his way of seeing. . . .

Miss Sarraute rattles the reader around in this writer's head for nearly two hundred pages without a "conversion," without a coincidence of understanding between reader and character. This is partly the fault of the book's hyperintellectuality, even more of its prose.

Maria Jolas' translation is extraordinarily good, in the somewhat extraordinary sense that it accurately reflects a falling-off in Miss Sarraute's style. Her previous work, especially *The Golden Fruits,* had a witty consistency of tone that now seems shattered; large stretches of *Between Life and Death* could have been written by a dyspeptic machinegun.

The book's dustjacket, quoting *Le Monde,* tells us this style is "new, simple in its means but bold in form." It is certainly "bold," if not audacious, in some of its elements—I cannot recall another book in any language wherein so many pronouns do (or attempt) the work of so few appositives. But is there anything original in such writing as this:

> Perhaps it's better to wait a little longer, continue to postpone the moment . . . that it's really no longer possible to resist, that that forces your hand. . . . That. What's that, after all? Everybody out here keeps on saying it, keeps shouting it from the rooftops: there's no 'that' that matters. [dots and spacing in original]

or this:

> The fall of day. Poor human glory. Not the pain of trying. Or again, when our material interest is involved in it. As in Inga's case. Yes, her. She owes it to herself. Oh, I'd be proud and happy.

The second passage quoted seems to me as representative of Miss Sarraute's "new" style as the first—despite the fact it was written by Valery Larbaud in 1921, in self-confessed if unsuccessful imitation of Joyce.

> *David J. Dwyer, in a review of "Between Life and Death," in* Commonweal, *Vol. XC, No. 19, August 22, 1969, p. 523.*

MADELEINE WRIGHT

[Nathalie Sarraute's intention] seems to be to rule out—not arbitrarily but necessarily—most of the technical props which traditionally helped bridge the gap between the world of the writer and the world of the reader. The goal she has set herself not only is extraneous to those props, but is contrary to them. In two cases, nevertheless, modified versions of the traditional props reappear in Sarraute's novels. Her quest for reality leads her to demystify those fictions which conceal the real. The plot is no longer for her the indispensable ingredient of a fictive work; and the adventures of the tropisms she projects constitute

an action that takes place within a single consciousness, but on two distinct levels: the tropisms either confront one another; or, when they are caught in the nets of verbal consciousness, they confront the external, social, and collective world.

Sarraute's modified versions of fiction and action, however, exclude all concern other than what is required by her initial goal: to intercept inner reality. The game is therefore played between the writer and his double, not between the writer and his public. She is engaged in a creative act that goes far beyond the definition of literature as a universally recognizable art form. Literature for Nathalie Sarraute becomes a strictly personal pursuit, a quest for identity which revolves entirely around the subject's psyche. From inspiration through form to the author's ultimate reincarnation, a loop is looped.

Nathalie Sarraute sets up for herself two very stringent criteria of success: the work must come alive, and some kind of contact must be made. But two questions immediately arise: for whom should the work come alive? and with whom is the contact made? The life of the work is subordinated to tropisms which must remain intact throughout their verbal translation. Tropisms are transferred from the subconscious to the conscious with the help of language. This means that any man for whom an articulate awareness of his deeper self is vital engages in a literary quest of his own. This literary pursuit then becomes a matter of "life or death" for the writer, the life or death of the work being equivalent to the life or death of his own psyche. But in itself the content of a psyche has no meaning for another psyche. It is too shapeless and too erratic; it offers no essential point of reference, no basis for analysis and interpretation. As a result, the more accurate, the more faithful, the more literal even its verbal, or literary translation happens to be, the more opaque that translation becomes to a consciousness other than the subject's. The very qualities of a literary technique aiming at the linguistic expression of a preverbal state consequently become directly responsible for the probable hermetism of the finished product. A second argument reinforces the first: only the author can evaluate the life of a work that sets out to reproduce an experience known to the author alone. Only Sarraute possesses the frame of reference against which the life of her novels can be measured: the initial tropisms that are her models and her inspiration, the personal impulse that gave birth to the literary form. As a result, no one but Nathalie Sarraute can fully evaluate the life or death status of her production.

Contact is established mainly between the writer and her work for very similar reasons. Such contact can come about only within a very closed circuit. The literary form best capable of capturing tropisms does not include universal frames of reference and does not yield to universal recognition and understanding. For Sarraute, tropisms are privileged means of communication, not with the outside world, but with her double, with her many doubles. The consciousness at work in Sarraute's novels is that of a character looking for an author. The contact takes place and the work comes alive when there is a fusion between both.

This does not necessarily mean that contact between work and reader is totally out of the question. But the nature of tropisms makes any subjective form of interpretation hazardous, if not preposterous. . . . Sarraute entrusts the translation of tropisms into words almost exclusively to images; but Bachelard's intense faith in the communicative power of images is of no avail in Sarraute's case: her brand of "rêverie" does not purport to transcend reality, but rather to grasp and possess it in its entirety. In other words, the deeper the reality which she tries to express, the more subjective the form she adopts in order to do so. The decoding of such images may be rich in possibilities for the outsider; but there can be no guarantee whatsoever that the result will coincide with the reality behind the image itself. The opacity of Sarraute's images is the by-product of a self-contained psyche which must block out all outside interferences in order to communicate with itself.

For the critic, therefore, only one avenue of investigation perhaps remains open: the linguistic, semantic and formal analysis of the work. The reader confronts what is, in fact, an individual language within a code language. The code language consists of very common words, about which Sarraute herself wrote: "I had to create . . . an unreal dialogue made up of usual words to express what is not ordinarily spoken about. The most ordinary words are used, but what is said is not what is being talked about. . . ." This code language, which is immediately accessible to the reader, does not reveal the writer's inner truth; to the contrary, it constitutes the fictive portion of the work. It relies largely on humor, which Sarraute manipulates in order to denounce the collective myths—mostly verbal—which blur our vision of reality. The techniques that preside over the writing at this level can be analyzed systematically, but such an elucidation leads only to the negative aspect of the work: a void is created, which tropisms will fill once the clichés have been swept away. In contrast, Sarraute's individual language, which is immediately accessible to her, is not immediately accessible to the reader; and its deciphering is an exercise in hermeneutics. Sarraute's literary techniques seem to rest on the double postulate that the usual semantic content of words is deeply misleading, and that reality is best expressed through whatever escapes the linguistic conventions of symbolic meaning. (pp. 32-5)

Sarraute's novels come the closer to the truths she wishes to express as their form breaks more sharply away from accepted formal codes. There is a definite progression in her literary production, a progression that goes from her relatively accessible works like *Tropismes* and *Le Planetarium* to her latest (and more obscure) novels, *Entre la vie et la mort* and *Vous les entendez?* The earlier works include, if not characters, at least occasional proper names and the embryo of a story; but the expression of tropisms in these novels remains somewhat ambiguous; it owes too much to psychology, to introspection, to the form of introspection which reasons, argues, discusses—i.e., analyzes. It stems from the writer's intellect. The role of the intellect, in her latest works, is much more strictly delineated: as a professional writer, she uses it to choose her techniques and control the structure of her works; she is definitely highly conscious of her goals, of her efforts and of the results obtained. But she no longer allows her intellect to tamper with the raw material she starts from. It is quite possible that the closer she gets to her goal, the greater will be the distance between novel and reader. The reader approaches the novel through the formal deciphering of a work that rejects formalism: a certain discrepancy seems unavoidable. Yet, formalism may well be the most valid approach for the reader or critic anxious to break through the deceptive layer of her code language in order to reach the inner core of her private world. Her work, which sets itself over and beyond style, is nevertheless at the mercy of stylistic analysis. The public is likely to feel somewhat alienated from novels written not only *by* but mostly *for* the author herself. (p. 36)

> Madeleine Wright, "Nathalie Sarraute: Alienated or Alienator?" in Bucknell Review, *Vol. 22, No. 1, April, 1976, pp. 29-36.*

A. OTTEN

Finally [in *Théâtre*] all of Nathalie Sarraute's plays—even the most recent—are available in one volume. . . . Together they form a dramatized version of some of the ideas set forth in the author's prose fiction. There is, for instance, the uneasiness of a group of people in the presence of a young man who remains entirely silent. Another gathering is disturbed by a young woman's obvious lie about her past. The third play deals with a character's habit of pronouncing the suffix -*isma* instead of -*isme*. What is beautiful comes to be seen as being simply what is "normally" accepted.

As in Nathalie Sarraute's prose fiction, a dissenting voice says that reality is a network of habitual patterns of group behavior in which the "I" confronts "them" in a thousand guises, to triumph for a moment or to be swallowed by the opaque communal pool that her *tropismes* inhabit. As in her fiction, each depends on the other; in their minute interplay beats the very pulse of Nathalie Sarraute's art.

> A. Otten, in a review of "Théâtre," in World Literature Today, *Vol. 53, No. 3, Summer, 1979, p. 479.*

GRETCHEN ROUS BESSER

Although Nathalie Sarraute may have been a precursor of the New Novel in many of its aims and methods, she has always held herself aloof from identification with any literary movement or school. She refuses the application of any labels to her work, just as she rejects all delimiting classifications. . . .

When Robbe-Grillet asked her, in 1972, if she belonged to the group of writers (loosely comprised of himself, Pinget, Ricardou, and Simon) who were then being designated as exponents of a "New New Novel," she firmly disclaimed her adherence. Most of these novelists, she pointed out, had experienced an abrupt rupture in their work about 1960, after which their fiction assumed a new orientation; instead of continuing to "represent" the world, either subjectively or objectively, they tended now to concentrate on questions of language and textuality *per se,* with a consequent subversion of literary and social structures. In her own case, she acknowledges no rupture of this kind. . . . (p. 169)

Even at an early period in her writing, Sarraute recognized a distinction between her own position and the tendency of other New Novelists, particularly with respect to objective description. The New Novelists are acutely attuned to the presence of physical objects, endlessly catalogued and recorded in their minute manifestations. While Robbe-Grillet may depict in microscopic detail the movements of a fly on a ceiling (in *Jealousy*) or the flotsam clinging to the bow of a ferryboat (in *The Voyeur*), Sarraute keeps external description to a minimum. Where she indulges in descriptive passages (more prevalent in her earlier books, like *Portrait* and *Martereau*), these are not related to the outside world, but serve to externalize the inner sensations of tropisms. Sarraute clearly distinguishes between the divergent aspects of reality that she and Robbe-Grillet present. Whereas he shows the exterior of things, objects, places, and people, she concentrates on interior movements and psychological states. His universe is static, immobile, transfixed; hers is in a process of perpetual movement and transformation. They are almost opposite in temperament and vision. (p. 170)

Sarraute has always been a loner, plying her craft on the sidelines of popularity. When her writing happened to coincide with the tendencies of her contemporaries, she was willing to accept a modicum of kinship. When her former colleagues veered off in other directions, she was satisfied to continue along the track she had outlined for herself. Because she has allowed others to assume the role of spokesmen for the New Novel and has restricted herself to discussing her own work and intentions, her pioneering position in the vanguard of modern literature has often been overlooked. The breath of vitality she has infused into the concept of fiction, the strength of her conviction in the restorative powers of the novel, have yet to be adequately acknowledged, even by those who, wittingly or unwittingly, follow the directions and recommendations she was the first to call for. (pp. 170-71)

Once having appropriated to herself the tiny domain of tropisms, Sarraute has persevered in exploring it inch by inch, in all her works, novels and plays alike. By exposing these hidden, unbidden fragments of feeling that underlie human discourse and behavior, she has isolated a timeless quality common to all human beings, of whatever background, nationality, or social stratum. The critics who accuse her of depicting a "bourgeois" milieu or a middle-class mentality have failed—like many of her own characters—to transcend appearances, to discover the kernel of eternal truth concealed beneath a semblance of momentary circumstance.

From the initial observation of tropisms as they *exist* and as they precondition behavior in the restricted areas of the family, Nathalie Sarraute has expanded the terrain in which tropisms flourish to include every conceivable area of human relationships. But if she were merely repeating the evidence of the earlier books in a broader field, her works would be repetitious and, eventually, stagnant. It is because she has used the medium of tropisms as a lens through which to view fundamental issues of human concern that Sarraute's work has attained a panoramic dimension. Never deviating from the very particularized tropistic response, Sarraute manages to call into question problems of both individual and universal scope. From the dilemma of "knowing" another person, she progresses to the concept of "knowledge" about literature, art, and ideas; from everyday clichés of speech, she proceeds to the totalitarian possibilities inherent in the misuse of language generally; from a concern with standards of aesthetic judgment, she advances to the broader consideration of ethical values and conduct. Her earliest novels unmasked the dangers and conflicts menacing members of the same family; her latest works hint at the far more dangerous threat that collective ignorance, fearfulness, and intolerance pose to individual members of society. It is the recapitulation of certain universal themes—their unifying resonance from book to book—that welds the self-contained entities of the individual novels and plays into a cohesive *oeuvre*. It is the unlimited human implications of these evanescent impulses that turn the minuscule domain of tropisms into a microcosm of the world. (pp. 171-72)

> *Gretchen Rous Besser, in her* Nathalie Sarraute, *Twayne Publishers, 1979, 192 p.*

GRETCHEN ROUS BESSER

The gathering of Nathalie Sarraute's plays into a single volume [*Théâtre*] allows the reader to note the emergence of certain patterns and themes. The action of each play begins *in medias res*. As in her novels, where the reader must make his way unaided by the accustomed props of characterization and plot, the background exposition of conventional drama is withheld.

The reader/spectator is plunged into the heart of an ongoing conversation, into a maelstrom of swirling tropisms. Since all of Sarraute's plays were originally conceived of as plays for radio, the clash among opposing attitudes and feelings is revealed uniquely in the cross-patter of voices. In each play there is a hypersensitive recipient of tropisms, who is attuned to emotional repercussions imperceptible to the "others." Often, like H.1 in *Le Silence,* like Pierre in *Le Mensonge,* like the husband and wife in *Isma* and H.2 in *Elle est là,* this character is torn between the ambivalent need to convince others of his perspicacity, gain their adherence, associate himself with the group, and the contrary need to remain a loner, reinforce his isolation, and maintain his individuality. Invariably, this person becomes the catalyst whereby buried tropisms come to light. Thanks to his nagging persistency, hidden impulses rise to the surface, arouse an assortment of unacknowledged emotions—jealousy, rage, frustration, envy, even violent impulses to torment and kill—before they subside into oblivion.

Language has always been of primary concern to Sarraute—language as a means of perverting meaning, preventing communication, congealing feelings, breeding intolerance. Language and its inadequacies are at the heart of her earlier plays. In the total picture of her theater, a progression can now be discerned. From a concentration on the power of language—the ominous ambiguity of non-communication in *Le Silence,* the inextricable intertwining of truth and falsehood in *Le Mensonge,* even the irritating effects of speech mannerisms in *Isma* and of certain pat formulae in *C'est beau*—Sarraute has arrived at a concentration on the power of thought itself. By exploring dogmatism as a form of moral coercion—not on a grandiose politico-philosophical scale, but in its tiny, unnoticed, and insidious emotional repercussions on quite ordinary human beings—she opens a door onto profoundly disturbing vistas. In her diffident, circuitous way, Nathalie Sarraute has become a moralist for our time. (p. 498)

> *Gretchen Rous Besser, in a review of "Théâtre," in* The French Review, *Vol. LIII, No. 3, February, 1980, pp. 497-98.*

JOHN STURROCK

[*L'Usage de la parole*] is a delectably austere, beady-eyed book, short and with no word *roman* or *récits* on the cover to say that it is fiction. *Roman* it is not, *récits* hardly; but fiction yes, and, as always with Mme. Sarraute, of the rarest, most moral kind. There are ten brief sections, each with its own epigraph of some commonplace phrase or group of words.

The first of these is in German, "Ich sterbe", the German for "I am dying" and the last words spoken by Chekhov on his deathbed at Badenweiler, the spa to which he had despairingly gone for the sake of his health. They have the pathos of all recorded last words, but made keener by the fact that for Chekhov they were a literal alienation of his thoughts, since he spoke them in German not his native Russian. From this Sarraute argues, touchingly, to the dramatist's heroic modesty *in extremis,* but it is rather the harrowing discrepancy between the bare form of words—as if he were setting out to conjugate a verb not easily used in the first person singular—and the foreknowledge they contain of his own approaching extinction, which gives Chekhov's historical "Ich sterbe" its rightful precedence in *L'Usage de la parole.* It is a sombre, humane opening to what is elsewhere a mordant and unforgiving book.

The phrases which give rise to the remaining nine scenes or episodes are French ones: "A très bientôt", "Et pourquoi pas?", "Ton père. Ta soeur", and so on, ordinary enough until Sarraute imagines for them a context which turns them from bland civilities into weapons of psychological warfare. Friends meet and converse, in a café or in the street, and are all sociability; except underneath, where the best of friends can at moments be the most savage of opponents, Sarraute resorts sardonically to metaphor to indicate what words will not capture: the shameful and ineffable animosities that constantly imperil our urbanity.

This is a party-game for grownups; to allow the imagination to play around the vacuous and paltry remarks which daily meet the ear. It is a game which Sarraute invites her readers, ironically, to play with her; for the otherwise random scenes of *L'Usage de la parole* are unified by the artful commentary of a narrator, asking for our trust and forbearance as each scene opens, and ultimately for our cooperation, since the scenes are meant as specimens, as object-lessons in the interpretation of human motives. Sarraute's are micro-dramas of evasiveness and anxious conformism, of our will to live by the prevailing rules and also to see our friends as consoling alter egos. Each variation on what is really the one scene records a profound, disorienting intrusion by one person on another, a violation of the superficialities we live by. The two speakers have roles, never names, because the fateful anonymity of language is both a refuge and a curse, it makes conversation at once easier and less authentic.

Sarraute has no equal at imagining the form of these secret contests.

> *John Sturrock, "De profundis," in* The Times Literary Supplement, *No. 4019, April 4, 1980, p. 391.*

GRETCHEN ROUS BESSER

Almost reminiscent of the format of *Tropismes,* the individual pieces composing *L'Usage de la parole* are more abstract and more profound, less anchored to a particular individual or group, than the sketches contained in Nathalie Sarraute's earlier work. Here the author is delving into the significance of language itself, often deflected from its original meaning by continual usage and habit. In each case she takes as her point of departure some commonplace word or expression, which she then subjects to microscopic scrutiny. It is too much to say that Sarraute dissects language. Rather, like a sensitive turning fork, she picks up echoes and reverberations and transmits them to her reader. . . .

Like the writer in *Entre la vie et la mort,* Sarraute is fascinated by words. They are, of course, the writer's stock-in-trade. But how often words are misunderstood, even when they are intended to persuade and convince. The more banal the expression, Sarraute seems to say, the further removed it is from its original import and the more susceptible it becomes to misinterpretation. And misinterpretation—the slight misalignment of two speakers, their divergent perspectives, their unexpected reactions—is the basis for half the world's ills. Sarraute never says as much, of course. She never dots her *i*'s or crosses her *t*'s, preferring the ubiquitous *points de suspension*, which leave conclusions—even the endings of sentences—up to the reader.

This reader finds Sarraute to be a tacit moralist in the lineage of La Rochefoucauld and La Bruyère. Her instantaneous *portraits,* sketched in and rubbed out in the same twinkling gesture,

capture the essence of human relationships. She re-creates *en passant* the torment of incomprehension, the magic of love, the fear of abandonment, the anguish of betrayal, even the unthinkable act of dying. There is almost always a victim tyrannized by a victor. The oppressor and the oppressed, the strong and the weak, the bold and the timorous are joined in a linguistic struggle, where words are the ultimate weapon. (p. 625)

Once again—as in *Le Silence* and *Le Mensonge*—Sarraute notes the power of language and the perils of misunderstanding, as well as the fear and distrust of direct communication. (If a subject is disagreeable, who interrupts to say, "Ne me parlez pas de ça"? If an argument is dense, how many speak up with, "Je ne comprends pas"?) But Sarraute refuses to dictate behavior or make value judgments. It appears that she is merely describing what is, not suggesting what ought to be. In fact, her manner is so mild, her weapons so disguised, that we are barely aware of hearing a soft-voiced call to arms. (p. 626)

> *Gretchen Rous Besser, in a review of "L'usage de la parole," in* The French Review, *Vol. LIV, No. 4, March, 1981, pp. 625-26.*

A. OTTEN

Like *Tropisms,* [*L'usage de la parole*] is a collection of prose pieces and reconfirms that the "primary subject of writing" has been the object of [Nathalie Sarraute's] search. Language is the author's powerful tool, and the word is the true "hero" of this book. Endowed with microscopic vision, she examines the word's reactions to the forces that surround it. Various "voices"—words such as *love, family, hypocrisy, friendship, fatherhood, laughter* and *silences*—create minuscule dramas. Spanning the entire spectrum of human experience, these short pieces condense the essence of what Sarraute has sketched elsewhere on a larger canvas. There is the "institution" of the family, in which every member is fixed within established relationships; the word *love* is associated with God but also with hypocrisy and boredom; acquaintances in a chance encounter would much rather pretend not to see each other, yet they convey meaning to their void with banalities. Again, solid order and walls crack to reveal that nothing is stable. Discrepancies between façade and authenticity become evident in a constantly shifting present. Again Nathalie Sarraute has proven herself a master of French prose and a keen observer of the human mind.

> *A. Otten, in a review of "L'usage de la parole," in* World Literature Today, *Vol. 55, No. 2, Spring, 1981, p. 279.*

VALERIE MINOGUE

A glance at a page of Nathalie Sarraute's, with its quotation-marks, dashes, trails of dots, broken sentences, clusters of groping quasi-synonyms, and incomplete syntax, is sufficient to indicate that we are in the realm of the undefined. Reading her novels confirms that we are not in pursuit of definition. On the contrary, we move not from the indefinite to the security of definition, but to an open-ended interrogation. The processes of this prose do not dissolve in paraphrase or summary. They are not 'doing' something, they are 'being' something. They are not talking *about* something, which can be summed up beyond and without them: they are talking *to* the reader, and saying the something which they are.

In this poetic enterprise, *Tropismes* at once establishes the poetic tone, and initiates the reader into the dramas of preverbal experience. The first two novels induct the reader into the new modes, using a rather nebulous first-person narrator to question and undermine the distinctions and categorisations we are accustomed to in the novel. They introduce us to a reality whose mobility is attested by proliferation of versions, a reality whose emotive features are mixed, and constantly changing. The categorisations of character-portrayal are experienced, rather than shown, as inadequate and false. Psychological classifications are experienced as unreal: the psychiatrist's advice to N in [*Portrait d'un inconnu*] has neither strength nor validity against the intensity of gaze of the blurred, unfinished, anonymous portrait, nor, ultimately, against the vitality of N's apparently defeated narrative. The categorisations adduced by, and attributed to, Martereau and his wife, in their self-portraiture, and the narrator's transient efforts at stable characterisations of them, are as false as the arranged smiles and postures of an old family photograph.

In the third novel, where the narrator himself is deposed and narrated, we cannot trust a narrative that reduces Berthe to 'une vieille maniaque' to amuse a social gathering, or interest Germaine Lemaire, when we have, in the course of the novel, *been* that 'vieille maniaque', and know that she is like us, and that we are like everybody. All three novels disarticulate the narrator and systematically undermine narrative authority. They also take us into the inner pulsations of experience with their repetitive rhythms and dynamic patterns. The repetition indeed reasserts the primacy of experience, and the inadequacy of language: the reality of experience is communicated in the gaps between the quasi-synonyms, in the fumbling and self-correcting, in the palpable rhythms of hesitant or self-assertive voices.

The fourth novel, *Les Fruits d'or,* is an orchestration of many such voices. It is not a satire of Parisian intellectual life (though it has elements of that). It is an elaborate deconstruction of literary definitions and a reassertion, in the face of the competent and learned, the articulate and arrogant, of the primitive but inalienable rights of the stumbling, the inarticulate, and the timed. It vividly reaffirms the primacy of what lies before and under the words, and this reaffirmation is made *with* words, and *of* words. Elaborate rhetoric is deployed but undermined by wit, by humour, and equally elaborate contradiction. If humour and irony perturb and disrupt, they are not allowed to *destroy:* we are not, in the Sarrautean novel, in the mode of the 'purely comic'. Disrupted images may be disturbed and scattered, but they are not totally dismissed. On the contrary, their richness and the strands that connect them to an inner core of human feelings make them precisely a mobile, discontinuous, and poetic reflection of human reality. When the noise of the sometimes deafening voices and their clashing words—breaking over heads like truncheons, stilling resistance with the force of water-hoses—dies down, we hear, briefly but insistently, the quiet uncertain voice of one neither declaiming nor denouncing, but pursuing his own solitary search for truth, groping at words, turning them over cautiously, thinking, feeling, pondering his experience of a work he loves—impregnable, in his timidity, against the mockeries of fashion.

Entre la vie et la mort takes us to the centre of the artistic struggle to defeat words with words, as the writer, tempted by postures of sovereignty and authority, 'unwrites' the siren-songs of his temptations, and maintains his humility. The novel persuades ultimately that the authentic writer is, after all, a Holy Fool, despite his contradictions and his shortcomings. He embodies the heroism of humility, when he continues and endures, despite multiple rejections, caricatures, and mockery, strong in his faith that his stumbling pursuit of reality is after all worthwhile. (pp. 182-84)

The title of Nathalie Sarraute's most recent work is . . . *L'Usage de la parole* . . . , and here, abandoning the novel-structure, she has collected ten short essay/sketches each exploring as abstractly and generally as possible, the dramatic sub-structure of certain precise locutions. *L'Usage de la parole* seems to mark an extreme point in Nathalie Sarraute's artistic evolution. Having, in the novels, explored the possibilities of the continuous narrative, she returns to the greater freedom of construction found in the prose-poems of *Tropismes*. Indeed, centring her concerns on a few banal locutions, she has, here, even more space for exploration in depth than was available there. No characters (save, in a very limited sense, Tchekhov, who appears in the first text—but it is not his character that is at issue), no décors, no specific situations distract the reader from the 'play' of the words. I use 'play' here, in the widest sense, to indicate range, possibilities, purposes, effects, manner of making or losing points, and latent drama. . . . (p. 189)

In **'Ton père. Ta soeur',** the phrase already met in *Entre la vie et la mort* . . . : 'Si tu continues, Armand, ton père va préférer ta soeur' (If you go on, Armand, your father will end up preferring your sister) reappears, stripped this time of its status as focus for the preoccupations of a central figure. It is also further stripped of the potentially distracting plot-value of the parental threat it enfolds. Our attention is here securely focused on 'Ton père, Ta soeur' and the characterisations and distances these words create, the tone of voice which they produce—'sa voix résonne comme ces voix anonymes, venant on ne sait d'où, qui dans les lieux publics diffusent les informations' . . . (her voice resounds like those anonymous voices which, coming from who knows where, relay information in public places).

There is no imaginary narrator in this work, save a Diderot-like authorial first-person, and the 'play' of pronouns is ever more intensely questioned. . . . If, in *Les Fruits d'or,* to borrow Ann Jefferson's phrase . . . , 'Address resolves the impossible problems of definition' for the one reader who silently apostrophises the work itself, in *L'Usage de la parole,* the work itself addresses us the readers from the very first page.

The first appearance of the first-person pronoun is artfully prepared—first it is the German 'Ich', in the phrase 'Ich sterbe', then it is a purely linguistic 'I' in the phrase which translates it: '*Ich sterbe*. Qu'est-ce que c'est? Ce sont des mots allemands. Ils signifient je meurs' (*Ich sterbe*. What's that? They are German words. They mean I am dying). The 'I' so far has no referent, and therefore provokes the question: 'Mais d'où, mais pourquoi tout à coup?' (But from where, and why, all of a sudden?) The 'person' that now clearly emerges in the narrative is the second-person, the 'you' of the reader directly addressed: 'Vous allez voir, prenez patience' (You will see, have patience). The next significant pronoun that arises is again first-person, but this time it is plural—text and reader joined in an intimate 'nous': 'ne nous hâtons pas, allons au plus près d'abord' . . . (don't let's hurry, let's get as close as we can first). This is a 'nous' that recalls the *we* of the writer and judge, joined in creation at the end of *Entre la vie et la mort,* a union in which the reader is also enclosed. The introductory page of 'Ich sterbe'—a profoundly moving meditation that follows the spoken word to the ultimate point, the point of expiration and death—sets the tone for the texts that follow. They unite writer and reader in a common quest for the reality beneath the words—the shock-waves emanating from the word 'esthétique' (aesthetic), incautiously placed in a banal conversation, the volcanic eruption produced by 'Eh bien quoi, c'est un dingue' (Oh well, after all, he's an oaf), the death-ray of 'Ne me parlez pas de ça' (Don't speak to me about that), the sudden sting of 'Mon petit' (My boy, *or* Sonny) and the almost imperceptible aeration of the most banal words that communicates the shimmer of feeling far better than 'Le mot Amour' (the word Love), and its derivatives. The aggressive questioning provoked by the failure to find adequate words: 'Comment appelez-vous ça?—je ne vois pas, je ne trouve aucun mot qui le désigne.—Aucun mot? Mais vous savez bien que rien ici-bas ne peut prétendre à l'existence tant que ça n'a pas reçu de nom . . .' . . . (What do you call that?—I can't see, I can't find any word that applies to it.—No word? But you know perfectly well that nothing on this earth can claim existence until it has been given a name . . .)—finds a convincing answer in these successfully exploring texts.

Nathalie Sarraute is not explicitly concerned to moralise. Yet there is clear moral concern and effect in all [her] works. She teaches implicitly that the humble pursuit of truth is always worthwhile, whatever we are doing, creating, or saying; that authority is no substitute for argument; and words, no matter how loaded, no substitute for thought. She persuades that superiorities are transitory, for 'nous sommes bien tous un peu comme ça' (we are all really a bit like that), and have more in common than we are usually prepared to recognise, whatever our class, sex, race, creed, or colour. All [her] works testify to the conviction that reality is always on the underside of language, and humility the natural and only mode of pursuing truth.

The war of the words is never decisively won, but is always worth waging. The works of Nathalie Sarraute reassert the reality that engenders words, but that words, once fixed, deny. It is a reality which necessitates the breaking of the moulds, and the creation of new forms. Such an endeavour generates not rhetoric but poetry, for it is a matter of articulating the virtualities of what is neither spoken nor even formulated, a matter of giving voice to human silence. (pp. 190-92)

> *Valerie Minogue, in her* Nathalie Sarraute and the War of the Words: A Study of Five Novels, *Edinburgh University Press, 1981, 230 p.*

ROGER SHATTUCK

Essentially Mme. Sarraute seeks out the first tender shoots of our mental life—more evolved than the undifferentiated static that fluctuates during every living moment, but not yet so conscious that it gets caught and stifled in the rough net of conventional language. As a result, all her novels alternate between clumsy pregnant silences and the impasse of freeze-dried clichés.

This alternation also characterizes the mood and style of **"Childhood"** and shapes its vignettes. Time after time a section hinges on a commonplace expression that crashes into a young girl's consciousness and becomes the burden of her existence. . . .

Several sections begin with such an arresting expression and patiently try to worm their way around the verbal-mental block it created in the child. Others open in an intermediate realm of the child's floating perceptions and suddenly come aground on the shoal of unfeeling words thoughtlessly uttered by adults. Sometimes these scenes carry a wistfully comic flavor, or at least a glimpse of precocious gallows humor. Mme. Sarraute's consistent and sensitive attitude toward language lends a strong unity to her work and approaches that of a troubled poet like Rilke or Mallarmé—speech as both essential and unbearable.

The comic in these unassuming memories almost disappears behind the gradual crescendo of sorrow and self-protection. Nathalie Sarraute's earliest memories of herself as Natasha Tcherniak concerned her awkward, often painful shuttlings between the domiciles of her Russian parents, divorced soon after her birth and both remarried. . . .

From an early age Natasha has been aware of the inappropriate singularity of what she calls "my ideas"—tremors that grow from a low muttering in her mind into uncontrollable eruptions of word or deed. . . . An infantile form of the demonic seems to drive her, like a character out of Dostoyevsky. But Natasha tries hard to master her demon and sometimes believes she has succeeded. **"Childhood"** can be read as the story of the formation of a will, though I cannot recall the word being mentioned.

Next to the sorrows of separation and the vagaries of a young will, the third and late-arriving element in these memories is Natasha's shift from racial innocence as a good little French child like all others in school to an awareness of her Slavic Jewish ancestry. It comes as a quiet revelation, not as an immediate social problem, after she goes to mass with her governess and then listens to her free-thinking father. . . .

The low-keyed form of **"Childhood"** affords it the double quality of directness and reflectiveness. Mme. Sarraute accepts without distress the fragmentary nature of her memories. She has probably made some adjustments; any probe disturbs the circumstances being probed. Events follow a loosely chronological order with enough cross-references to keep us alert. These short sections move at an almost respiratory pace that may be in part attributable to the steady weaving of the verb tenses between present and past. That oscillation springs directly from another feature of the form.

By an evidently careful decision, Mme. Sarraute has created for herself and out of herself in **"Childhood"** an interlocutor, an alter ego who addresses her as *tu,* questions her motives and her credibility, supplies alternative explanations and goads her to undertake the project. The opening pages present a playful dialogue between one voice for Natasha-Nathalie, child protagonist grafted onto adult narrator, and another voice for the interlocutor-author who doubts and coaxes and also tends to push her literary effects too hard. . . .

It sounds like a gentle mocking of her own novels. We are in good hands, a long way from the spectacular intellectual surfing of Sartre's autobiography, "Words," traversing large expanses of time organized by *le passé simple,* and also a long way from the poised, self-deprecation of "Barthes on Barthes," another contemporary French autobiography.

I have not yet put my finger on the particular quality I find in **"Childhood."** In Antonioni's film "Blow-Up" the photographer enlarges his cryptic pictures in order to discover clues in the shrubbery. But blown up beyond a critical point of graininess, the photographs no longer yield any visual content that can be assembled and recognized as reality. This paradox of magnification relates to the writer's dilemma. The scale on which **"Childhood"** is written brings the reader miraculously close to the texture of life the way a child, precariously balanced between two parents, two countries, might experience it. But when you approach so close, language no longer serves adequately to record the observations; it seems to obliterate the very thing it is meant to designate. Still tiny, sitting on a park bench between her father and an alluring young woman of uncertain status, Natasha Tcherniak has just heard a tale from Hans Christian Andersen. Nathalie Sarraute, remembering the moment and operating inside the same "I" as the child Natasha, cannot accept the terms "happiness" or "ecstasy" to describe Natasha's feelings, not even the simple word "joy." Such words "cannot gather up what fills me, brims over in me, disperses, dissolves, melts into the pink bricks, the blossom-covered espaliers, the lawn, the pink and white petals, the air vibrating with barely perceptible tremors, with waves . . . waves of life, quite simply of life, what other word? . . . I am inside them with nothing else, nothing that does not belong to them, nothing that belongs to me."

The passage, like all of "**Childhood**," records a prolonged probing toward language whose full realization would bring everything to a standstill. Some say the French novel will never recover its greatness without finding great subjects. Nathalie Sarraute says in her quiet voice that a form of greatness lurks in remote twinges, in interior moments where we rarely look for it. (p. 31)

> Roger Shattuck, "*Life Before Language,*" *in* The New York Times Book Review, *April 1, 1984, pp. 1, 31.*

STEPHEN KOCH

Sarraute has survived. Among other things, she has survived becoming outmoded, ever since the absolute, irremediable, and final obliteration of the *nouveau roman* (a phenomenon of the '50s and '60s to which her name, as to a bit of overused flypaper, remains rather irritatingly stuck) from the agenda of fashionable French literary life. No matter: Sarraute was writing before the "new novel" had its name, and these memoirs were among the largish successes of last year's French publishing season. (p. 1)

Yet Sarraute has survived to bring her method to bear on her own past. What united the new novelists was a common trick: They embedded strictly real (that is, possible) events in an irreal and strictly subjective time. To be sure, each worked differently. Robbe-Grillet is all eyes, addicted to a seen continuous present. Sarraute is a listener, and her aim is not the voyeur's ecstasy but satire. She has kept her water glass pressed, always, against the paper-thin wall of life's small talk. ("Small talk": I know of no French expression equivalent to this delicious phrase, but it might have been invented for Nathalie Sarraute.) Listening to small talk, she strains to catch the false notes of inauthenticity. She is forever listening for the lie, the revelatory catch and quaver of falsehood. That giveaway tremor is her truth.

So it is in *Childhood.* Once again, Sarraute is gathering evidence. . . . Her childhood was unhappy, and the little girl had every reason to learn to listen for the lie. . . . The little cosmopolite—a mixture of French, Russian, and Jewish heritage—was torn between an increasingly indifferent mother in Russia and a cold but constant father in Paris. . . . Retrieving the small talk of these large betrayals, Sarraute repeatedly moved me with her lawyer-like precision, finding the locus of a little girl's double-binds. . . .

No accident that the grown-up Sarraute came to call one of her books *The Age of Suspicion.* Her art of mistrust had been earned. *Childhood* is composed in two voices. The first is that of a sensuous, energetic, wistful, remembering, slightly (but only slightly) sentimental self. This is what remains of the child's voice. The other—commenting—voice is a none-too-generous, punitive, intelligent, superegotistical, irritable "adult" counter-voice. It seems reluctant to permit Sarraute to write at all.

Though informed by truth and an uncompromising intelligence, *Childhood* does not seem to me destined for a place among the best memoirs of childhood in modern literature. . . . It is too thin, too reticent, and its anger is too unresolved. Too much that is too important is not said. *Show, don't tell:* Here the tiresome, exhausted modernist bromide reaches a kind of *reductio.* Sarraute's method, based in reticence, resists the idea, I know. But I cannot help believing that Sarraute should be telling more, much, *much* more, about her betrayals. We are shown the manipulations of 70-some years ago. But what the manipulated child has to tell the adult, and vice versa, is the whole interest of the memoir as a form. Sarraute understands this, she makes it central to her book. Unfortunately the adult intelligence here is neither compassionate nor supple. It is irritable, reprimanding, snobbish. "The past is not dead," Faulkner wrote. "It is not even past." Every memoirist tests the power of this absorbing half-truth. Listening for her childhood's lies, the artist of suspicion has come up with an old, and very familiar one—that parental love can be trusted. *I knew it,* she seems to say, *I always knew it.* But then she lifts the angry stepmotherly forefinger of her mistrust, and will not let it speak. (p. 14)

> Stephen Koch, "*The Early Years of Nathalie Sarraute,*" *in* Book World—The Washington Post, *May 20, 1984, pp. 1, 14.*

ERIKA MUNK

The astonishing thing about Nathalie Sarraute's *Childhood* is that it takes a style which for 30 years has been associated with the dissolution of character and narrative, unites it with a subject that readers inevitably sense as real, chronological, human, and psychological—just like the subjects of those conventional books that all Sarraute's work opposes—and through this opposition creates an autobiography which seems true through and through. Not just factual and emotionally straightforward, but true to the processes of memory and of writing. As an avant-garde autobiography, *Childhood* makes a persuasive case for the claim that antinaturalistic writing is the most realistic writing. . . .

After 50 years of developing the means to catch, clarify, and reproduce the inner movements of others, Sarraute has used her enormous resources to pin down the precise movements in her inner and outer life as a child that impelled her to write, and to write in her particular way. (p. 41)

Sarraute could not have written her memoir as a flat-out narrative of memory, however subtle or complex, without committing a "minor crime" against her perception of life as we know it from her other works, against the style she has evolved, against everyone's recognition that your own childhood is inevitably mythologized, revised, ahistorical. She solves this by telling her story to a questioning Other, who opens the book with the words, "Then you really are going to do that? 'Evoke your childhood memories' . . . how these words embarrass you," and meanly adds, "it could be that your forces are declining." (p. 42)

The partner in *Childhood* sometimes speaks like a friend, sometimes like an analyst (or a well-analyzed friend), a conscientious editor, or, purely, the promptings of an honest superego.

The second voice can also become a mechanical device, tsk-tsk-tsking disingenuously away: "You haven't been able to resist introducing something a little prefabricated . . . it's so tempting, you've inserted a pretty little piece . . ." The narrator defends herself, or, when nagged, admits that because she actually had a wicked stepmother, she's afraid of veering into fiction. Such lessons in conscience and technique are a little tricky and unnecessary, condescending to the reader.

On the other hand, the questioner's presence keeps us from sinking so deeply into Nathalie—wonderful child—or into Sarraute's gorgeous imagism that we forget the struggle, not just of writing the book but of thinking through any childhood. We are forced to suspend belief; the voice creates, parallel to the autobiographical narrative, an essay on the effort of memory we are all constantly making. By starting with this secondary voice, Sarraute mildly sabotages herself, only ultimately to strengthen the sense of truth, in the same way that her lack of vengefulness or whining serves to strengthen the shocking sadness of so much that happens. Most important, the technique prevents Sarraute from recreating in the relationship between writer and reader the kind of lies, bad faith, and miscommunication she is describing between parents and child—though this paradoxically creates such an extreme consciousness of style that manipulation becomes a subject of a different sort.

The use of the second speaker, the way "characters" shift and mutate, the need for connection also place this book in a formal context that recreates the flow and tone typical of most of her work, with its constant internal revisions and extenuations, its ceaseless editing of consciousness. Recreates quite directly indeed: it's easy to find, and then be overwhelmed by, the links between what is presented in this factual and "accessible" work, and everything else, however fictive and difficult, Sarraute has written.

Childhood is almost shockingly connected, as if after years of gazing at a tree, you saw its roots, its seed, as if you were suddenly granted X-ray eyes. Some of these connections are banal, almost amusing: Nathalie began without suspicion of her parents; she learned better; Sarraute's collected literary essays are *The Age of Suspicion.* Nathalie had "her ideas"; *It*

Is There is a play entirely about the intellectual and emotional havoc caused among some male intellectuals by a woman with "ideas." (pp. 42-3)

Large chunks of Sarraute's later subject matter can thus be traced to the most quotidian moments of her recollection, and so, on top of its other achievements, *Childhood* has gracefully, almost surreptitiously, made a hundred dissertations redundant. . . .

Yet this book is extremely different from Sarraute's others and not because—precisely not because—it is about herself. Indeed, writing about her self, and her small, long-gone childhood world, has expanded her horizons. In *Childhood,* the malice and claustrophobia of her novels disappear. Sarraute has seized on a reality which can withstand her scrutiny of language and character.

Childhood is not more realistic because it is, as its publishers keep urging, "accessible" in the sense of easy to read. It is no less "difficult" than *Tropisms* or *The Use of Speech* or, granted you know the milieu, *The Golden Fruits.* While *Childhood*'s sharply imagistic scenes and rather clear divisions between one speaker and the other make it, page by page, far from the "existential puzzle" of *"Fools Say,"* and the kind of people who inhabit *Childhood* make it much less of a chore to read than *The Planetarium,* it lacks those works' saving, acid humor. The broadening of her realism comes simply from the way a subject of widest meaning—the relationship of lies and power, rooted in a child's developing relationship to words and authority—is presented through a technique which can replicate this development as no ostensibly "naturalistic" style could. . . .

Sarraute in *The Age of Suspicion* described with contempt those modern writers who make their characters commit "unwonted, monstrous acts" which the reader, who has committed no such acts, "quietly thrusts aside . . . without the heavy shadow that submerges his own dark places having lifted for a second." Her scrupulous book lifts that shadow, and while what's bared is of all things a bourgeois family, that family's deceptions, affections, and most fleeting transitions have correspondences for most of us, and are the starting point as well as the mirror of our society as well as hers. (p. 43)

Erika Munk, "A Suspension of Belief: Nathalie Sarraute's Unsentimental Education," in The Village Voice, *Vol. XXIX, No. 31, July 31, 1984, pp. 41-3.*

Lynne Sharon Schwartz

1939-

American novelist, short story writer, and critic.

Schwartz's novels, which portray marriage and family in contemporary America, have attracted considerable critical attention. Her first novel, *Rough Strife* (1980), follows a married couple through the ups and downs of their twenty years together, ultimately presenting a positive view of the institution of marriage. Some critics asserted that Schwartz's characterizations and the quality of her prose were not sufficiently developed to sustain interest in a novel of such limited focus. However, most critics agreed that the novel revealed a notable perceptiveness and sensitivity to the nuances of love and marriage.

Like *Rough Strife, Disturbances in the Field* (1983) revolves around a married couple, Lydia and Victor, but in this later novel Schwartz's scope is much broader. The family tragedy that occurs midway through the novel adds a serious perspective to the dailiness of life. In addition, Schwartz writes about Lydia's friends, her childhood, and her profession, and includes discussions of philosophy. *Balancing Acts* (1981) deviates from Schwartz's other novels in subject matter, concentrating on a rebellious teenage girl and an equally rebellious elderly widower, whose interaction allows Schwartz to examine the experiences and problems of adolescence and old age.

(See also *Contemporary Authors*, Vol. 103.)

© 1984 Thomas Victor

LORE DICKSTEIN

In the last few years, in lives outside novels, things have slowly begun to change. Women have turned to men not as supports for weak egos and empty wallets, but as partners, equals, friends. Many found a life devoid of men and children lonely. The biological clock, which many women had turned to the wall, was running out; the revolutionaries were in their thirties and feeling panic.

In this context, it should come as no surprise that . . . [*Rough Strife*] should be touted as "deeply typical . . . the private history of a generation." Schwartz has written an American "Scenes from a Marriage." Without sentimentality or bitterness, the author traces the slow and subtle changes of a 20-year union between Caroline and Ivan, and it all rings true: the crises and dull spells, the falling in and out of love with the same person, the struggle of creating an enduring partnership. . . .

While [Caroline] and Ivan *like* being together, . . . they are weighed down by the idea of marriage, by society's expectations, and by their own "vague constraint, like behaving well in school." (p. 37)

[They] conceive their first child after years of trying, just when the seams of the marriage are about to unravel. This fortuitous timing seems rather forced, exposing, I suspect, a splicing of the author's prizewinning, original short story, **"Rough Strife"** . . . with the novel she has constructed around it.

Slightly revised, the short story is a brilliant chapter on Caroline's first pregnancy. "No matter what I suffer," she thinks as she is rushed into delivery, "soon I will be thin again." You want to cheer and cry at the same time. But the following years of family life, and the birth of a second child, are boringly familiar and unfortunately uninspired. (Art mocks life here.)

Ivan settles into a peaceful domestic routine, working successfully, reading *Wuthering Heights* to their two daughters, cooking meals. But Caroline's life becomes more frenetic as she rushes from the university to the nursery school, to the kitchen, and to quickly consummated liaisons—she has no time. She is becoming Super Mom, and then collapses in anger and frustration into feminism. Ivan becomes her oppressor, "a natural enemy." (Her reaction is too sudden and extreme; he doesn't deserve it.) (pp. 37-8)

Caroline's feminism is the only false note in this otherwise sensitively written novel; it is shallow and shortlived, quickly done in by love. (The author writes better on love than on politics.) "The cause *was* just," Caroline bitterly comments, "but were their lives not their own, and a cause more just?"

What is one to make of this? Caroline's dilemma mirrors that of many women who see marriage and feminism as opposite, conflicting polarities; commitment to one means betrayal of the other. This thinking is based on two false premises: that

387

feminism can cure all the problems of marriage and that a happy marriage obviates the need for feminism. In the best of all possible worlds, a peaceful, if uneasy, coexistence may be possible; but there are no easy solutions, in either marriage or politics. (p. 38)

Lore Dickstein, "A 20-Year Marriage In and Out of Love," in Ms., Vol. VIII, No. 12, June, 1980, pp. 37-8.

KATHA POLLITT

For the upper-middle classes, it has been said, marriage is the only adventure left. This is a charming notion—a brave little bank of explorers set off two by two for the mysterious and uncharted coasts of intimacy, while friends and relations cheer and toss in the air their copies of Psychology Today—but it's also a little sad. Are there really no new worlds to conquer except the ones in the bedroom and the kitchen? Must one's energies be focused relentlessly inward, as though society at large had no use for them?

For Caroline and Ivan, whose 20-year marriage is the subject of this flawed but talented first novel ["**Rough Strife**"], the answer is yes. When we meet them, at 45 and 50, their lives are outwardly smooth, comfortable, conventional. . . .

To each other, though, they are anything but ordinary. They are mythic figures, fated lovers like Catherine and Heathcliff: "There had been a quiver of recognition when they first met . . . not love at first sight, but bowing to destiny." And ever since destiny swept them to the altar, their marriage in all its parts—good, bad and indifferent—has been the one absorbing drama of their lives.

The irony behind the idea of marriage as middle-class adventure, though, is that everyone's adventure turns out to be the same—at least in novels. Caroline and Ivan see themselves as forging a new and original relationship, but they follow the broad cultural pattern of the last two-and-a-half decades as though it were a train schedule. . . .

Lynne Sharon Schwartz registers the fluctuations of marital feeling with the fidelity of a Geiger counter. She understands the permanent resentments that can be mixed with love (Caroline thinks Ivan is arrogant, which he is; he thinks she is soppily emotional, which she is) and the alternating currents of weakness and strength that pass between two people whose lives are joined together. (p. 14)

About halfway through, though, my admiration for Miss Schwartz's gifts as a reporter of emotional weather turned to irritation at her lack of interest in anything else. Caroline and Ivan have no friends who count, just cardboard couples whose function is to demonstrate the varieties of marital failure. Caroline's lovers are cardboard too: sexual conveniences to her, narrative conveniences to us. Although we know she leads a full, busy life, we never see her in front of a classroom, on a demonstration, having lunch with her daughters, or buying a dress; and except for the occasional paragraph about math, all we overhear her thinking about is her marriage, her feelings, Ivan. After a while, this relentless focus begins to seem claustrophobic.

The problem is, the emotional dynamics of Caroline's marriage are not interesting enough to bear the close inspection Miss Schwartz bestows. In order to keep us reading, which she does, she is driven to blow every domestic event—a quarrel, a child's

illness—into a full-scale melodrama and to inflate her language beyond proportion. Caroline doesn't just fall in love, she is "pierced by the cruel, mocking shafts of love." And 20 years later, the same overly heightened language is being lavished on trivia: "All winter through the grease fire in the oven, and the breakdown of the plumbing, through Greta's broken arm, her own bitter fight for the Women's Studies program, the theft of the Volvo—through all the abominations they had dreamed of a time alone." Abominations? A grease fire in the oven? It's enough to make one wonder if marriage is an adventure after all. (pp. 14, 22)

Katha Pollitt, "Twenty Years of Marriage," in The New York Times Book Review, June 15, 1980, pp. 14, 22.

GEORGIA A. BROWN

[In evaluating the literary merits of **Rough Strife**] I would submit the novel's first paragraph:

> Wasn't it miraculous, that she could feel this way after so long? Desire, she meant, and its fulfillment. Ivan lay collapsed on her, slipping out in a protracted slowness. She made no effort to keep him. In a moment she would open her eyes to the bedroom ceiling, an off-white marked by grainy, old imperfections on the surface. She would repossess identity, a structure chiseled by circumstance. Till then she would yield to this larger existence: the breadth of oceans, the reach of continents! A dupe, of course, yet what a fine geographical extravaganza, sponsored by Ivan. Caroline smiled.

If the reader admires such prose the reader may well admire this novel. The reader may even find such writing spare, exacting, or gifted. I find it astonishing that a publisher might let such a paragraph go without copyediting.

Desire is not a *way* of feeling, nor is *fulfillment*. A *dupe* is a deceived person, not, as the construction indicates, a deception. Moreover, the second sentence indicates (*she meant*) that this rhetorical questioning is Caroline's; how then can she not yet be returned to her "identity"? . . . There are certain assumptions too that one might wish to question. For example, in what way has Ivan paid for—that is, *sponsored*—her seagoing voyage? Why should simple desire "after so long" be *miraculous*? When does "a slowness" become *a protracted slowness*? The definition slipped in of *identity* as a "structure chiseled by circumstance" is certainly disputable. None of these questions is answered in what follows, for none is intentional. (pp. 281-82)

As a portrait of a marriage **Rough Strife** is (not surprisingly) neither clearer nor more illuminating than the prose that renders it. A good deal is made of the opposing qualities, talents, and predilections of the partners. But I found myself continually trying to remember which qualities were supposed to be attributed to which, even at times referring to the dust jacket for the answer. (p. 282)

The marriage is presented as surviving for all of twenty years, despite the sort of differences in personality which the author finds consequential but I find negligible. (After all, they are not the same person—or are they?) The union weathers such crises as the birth of two children, a child's operation, one child's rather disruptive personality, numerous casual affairs (no confrontations, however, since none of these is revealed or discovered), the women's liberation movement, a few job changes, a few moves. Hardly rough strife. Instead, what we see is playful horsing around, the usual misunderstandings, evasions, and a good deal of what Caroline refers to as "lust." That they are so compatible sexually seems as reasonable a bond as any.

Ivan claims there is a "wildness" about Caroline that attracts and holds him. The quality, however, is never convincing. Characterization in this novel consists mostly of assertion. Caroline's favorite pastime seems to be reflecting on their varying personalities. The reason for this rehearsing may be that she has trouble (as I do) getting things straight. At the very end of the novel she congratulates herself on being "luckier" than Isabel Archer. (Caroline reads "Henry James and his more fey contemporaries," it is said, because they are "the perfect mental nourishment: pungent but safely digestible.") "The self-absorbed aesthete she had married was good, not evil." Yet the Ivan we have seen seems not particularly self-absorbed (he is much more attentive to the children than she is), and by no means an "aesthete." Caroline's problem seems to be that she thinks of fiction as a comment on her life.

There is no evidence that the author has a more comprehensive view of fiction. This is fiction as reportage; "safely digestible" it probably is. (pp. 282-83)

> *Georgia A. Brown, in a review of "Rough Strife," in* The Yale Review, *Vol. 70, No. 2, Winter, 1981, pp. 281-83.*

JUDITH GIES

In this extremely likable novel [*Balancing Acts*] a retired acrobat captures the imagination and affections of a 13-year-old girl. During the uneven course of their relationship one of them learns to accept life and the other to relinquish it. . . . Each is looking for transcendence, a way to escape the law of gravity. What they find, as they jostle each other's lives, is a precarious sense of balance.

The novel is well-written, artfully constructed, and peopled with engaging characters, but it suffers from an excess of symmetry. Schwartz's first novel, *Rough Strife*—a fine anatomy of a marriage—was also about a kind of balance, but the author left the edges a bit rough, like marriage itself. In *Balancing Acts,* perhaps because the protagonists are more vulnerable, the effect is less abrasive, and the central metaphor is polished to an insistent shine. Like the grown man in the riddle of the sphinx, the book walks very nicely on two legs, but unlike the author's first novel, it seldom soars.

> *Judith Gies, in a review of "Balancing Acts," in* Saturday Review, *Vol. 8, No. 6, June, 1981, p. 54.*

ANGELA HUTH

Rough Strife is Lynne Sharon Schwartz's first book, and you can understand her thinking: enough of all the downbeat stuff, I'll have a go at the good news. But unaccompanied by zest and witty insight, marital contentment is full of dangers.

Miss Schwartz tells the long, dull story of the years of happy marriage between Ivan and Caroline. . . . They have their dreary downs and drearier ups, and still go on loving, wanting and needing each other. Which is fortunate, because it is unlikely anyone else would put up with either of them—a more deadly couple I've rarely met in fiction.

Indeed, there is only one lesson to be learned from their tale: if you want a happy marriage, call your loved one by his or her name *constantly*. Caroline and Ivan do so all the time, like characters in a Mike Leigh play gone mad—even when they are alone and could not possibly be addressing any other happily married character. . . . Miss Schwartz is apparently considered 'brainy' and 'deeply moving' by her American critics. I fail to agree with them: to me the only memorable part of the book was the shock of finding 'diaper' had become a verb. The dreadful Ivan 'diapered' the baby, thus becoming a 'true father'.

> *Angela Huth, "Marriage Matters," in* The Listener, *Vol. 106, No. 2721, August 6, 1981, p. 120.**

BILL GREENWELL

Not to beat about the bush, *Balancing Acts* is the best book through which I've browsed and burrowed for a long time. It has that beguiling simplicity of style which lets the reader rummage innocently in its pages, until, by some invisible and subtle act of stealth, it reaches in to give the heart a quick twist. Thereafter, the pages turn themselves, oblivious of fingers.

The plot pits its protagonists quickly together. Widower Max, a circus veteran in his seventies, has a rumpus with the rules in a respectable residence for the elderly. But his real war is waged upon the happy memories of his marriage, which threaten to overwhelm him. He volunteers his acrobatic skills to a local school, where his energetic antics enliven the schoolkids, amongst whom is Alison. Alison, thirteen, is lonely and rebellious like Max, frustrated by her friends and family, whose humdrum aspirations she despises. . . .

For Alison, Max is like 'a messenger in a play who bursts in with news of the outside world', and he unwittingly catapults her fantasies into the circus's whirling world. She besieges her unwilling idol. But Max is treading a different tightrope, and his grudging admission of Alison to his privacy at 'Pleasure Knolls' is only because of Lettie, an ageing former chorus-girl with whom he has an unforeseen romance at the home. From warm, generous Lettie he is learning the lessons of old age; he has little time to teach a gauche young girl the tricks of his trade.

Lynne Sharon Schwartz handles the clash of Max and Alison beautifully, with one thumbing her nose at the conventions of adolescence, the other snubbing a senility into which he seems expected to lapse. The suburban American setting might offer a weaker writer the option of easy caricature; the story might easily succumb to sentiment. Both temptations, however, are wonderfully shrugged aside in *Balancing Acts,* and the result is a novel of impressive charm and friendly intelligence.

It comes as no surprise to find Alison reading *The Member of the Wedding*, since she is herself a modern Frankie, just as Lynne Sharon Schwartz has the skill of a Carson McCullers. (p. 22)

> *Bill Greenwell, "All the Fun of the Fair," in* New Statesman, *Vol. 103, No. 2660, March 12, 1982, pp. 22-3.**

KIRKUS REVIEWS

Like Schwartz's fiction debut, *Rough Strife*, [*Disturbances in the Field*] is a model of emotional richness and pliability, with sunniness clouded by shared history . . . yet still surviving. And here once more (in contrast to her slight, disappointing second book, *Balancing Acts*), Schwartz is paying close attention to the subject-matter she illuminates so well, with such generosity: a marriage and a family. Victor Rowe, a painter, lives with wife Lydia and four children on New York's Upper West Side. We are drawn into their daily life, their recalled courtship at Columbia/Barnard in the 1950s, who their friends were and are. (Schwartz gives Lydia a nucleus of women friends who, over the years, have met to discuss Greek philosophy—as their lives, married or single, have become less and less hypothetical; it's a risky, lovely touch.) . . . Then, suddenly, there's a fracture. The two youngest children are killed in a ski-trip bus accident—and all comes tumbling down. . . . Schwartz gives Lydia's grief a texture of dailiness so well-modulated, within a society of sympathy (her friends gather around yet all are deficient), that it feels like the way people truly do mourn—through living it out, with the mind and the sorrow as two distinct reflections of the soul, moving side by side through time, each at its own pace. (For instance, Lydia thinks about the dead children only obliquely, just as a wound still seeping can't be directly prodded.) And if the reconciliative ending here, much like the one in *Rough Strife,* seems a bit willful, everything else in this novel comes across as the utterly honest weaving-together of natural serious feelings. Strangely comforting, solid and resonant: a quiet masterwork of late-20th-century American realism, fulfilling the great promise of *Rough Strife.*

A review of *"Disturbances in the Field,"* in Kirkus Reviews, *Vol. LI, No. 13, July 1, 1983, p. 729.*

CAROL STERNHELL

The triumph of *Disturbances in the Field,* Lynne Sharon Schwartz's luminous third novel, is that it faces the most relentless loss without sacrificing its humanity. Where our pain is beyond language, and perhaps beyond literature, Schwartz turns to music; the resulting symphony—like Schubert's "Trout" Quintet, the piece that more than any other reverberates through the book—offers "a sense of loss and nostalgia amid plenty, of death in the midst of fertility." . . . *Disturbances in the Field* creates . . . a balance, a harmony of ideas, despairing in order to affirm. . . .

In many ways, the first half of *Disturbances in the Field* is a portrait of the good life as it might be lived by a certain kind of fortyish Upper West Side woman: a prefeminist intellectual who prefers philosophy to politics, introspective, talented, secure in a marriage so rewarding that she guards its secrets even from her closest friends. Lydia and her artist husband Victor, together since the days of college Chaucer, "felt born from the same soil, our cells interchangeable, and our love had the heady tingle of incest. Even to say I love you was a semantic error, too great a separation."

The college friendships with Gabrielle, Nina, and Esther . . . ripen and endure, though in middle age the passion for ideas gives way to other loves. . . . Images of Lydia's parents, who "carried so many heavy things in their arms" but "in time weakened and died"; of her ethereal sister Evelyn, who once loved to climb the dunes and now lives far away in the Swiss

Alps; of the perfect rightness of one summer by the beach, weave in an intricate pattern through the scenes of adult life. . . .

By the time Lydia has been married for 20 years, she is enveloped in a haze of peaceful permanence; her life seems "fulfilled and, in a way, over." . . . [Life], like that one summer by the beach, has achieved a condition of harmony "which though it partook so thoroughly of the natural cycles seemed utterly static and safe."

Nothing is ever static, of course; perhaps nothing is ever safe. . . . Alan and Vivian, those radiant children, are killed in a school-bus accident, an icy skid and a burst of flames. The bereaved and unbelieving parents begin a long—probably endless—process of reconciliation, an agonized obsessive scrutiny of the details of their lives, these deaths. . . . The perfectly harmonious marriage, cells interchangeable, begins to disintegrate, in fire and in ice.

The death of a child may be our most terrible loss, the most difficult to accept. . . . It's a tribute to Schwartz's skill that she tells this story without melodrama or excess, that she never forgets the exuberance at the heart of poignancy. Nevertheless, the second half of *Disturbances in the Field* is weaker than the first, as if some of its light has been extinguished with the children's deaths. . . .

What distinguishes *Disturbances in the Field* for me is the quality of its ideas, its insistence, as Lydia would say, on living the examined life. The power of the story is undeniable, but what makes this novel more than cathartic is its intellectual range and depth. Like the strains of Schubert's "Trout" or the music of the spheres, philosophical speculation informs Schwartz's work, providing counterpoint to the dailiness of life. Unlike Schwartz's critically acclaimed novel *Rough Strife,* which I found rather claustrophobic in its dissection of one long-standing marriage, *Disturbances in the Field* opens far beyond the story of Lydia and Victor Rowe. Even the long waiting for that possible day when "ordinary things would resume their rightful proportions and places in a universe of ordinary things"—that future when Lydia will "be able to look at a chartered bus without feeling sick"—takes a lesson from Thales, who measured the height of a pyramid by waiting "until that time of day when a man's shadow became equal to his height." The wonder, for Lydia, is in the waiting—and in the human figure as the measure of the universe.

If Schubert offers "death in the midst of fertility," this impressive novel celebrates fertility in the midst of death. "The unexamined life is not worth living," Victor would murmur to Lydia in the early days of their romance. "Impressive," she remarks years later, after fire and ice. "But is the examined one?"

That it is, and that we believe it, is Schwartz's simple gift to us.

Carol Sternhell, *"Emotional Rescue: Simple Gifts from Lynne Sharon Schwartz,"* in VLS, *No. 20, October, 1983, p. 10.*

ANATOLE BROYARD

It takes a long time to get to the good part in Lynne Sharon Schwartz's third novel, **"Disturbances in the Field."** One has to slog through a lot of adolescent talk, which led me to wonder whether anyone but the parents or peers of adolescents could find them consistently interesting. They try so very hard: even their ideas seem to be choked with hormonal changes, to have poor complexions. . . .

In every college, there's a certain kind of student who insists on writing "lyrical" or "personal" term papers, trying to mix memory and desire with the curriculum. When this happens, the instructor is almost always embarrassed or frustrated, and this is how I felt much of the time while listening to Lydia, Nina, Gaby and Esther. All through the book I came across sentences beginning "Heraclitus was right," "The Greek atomist Leucippus believed," "I thought again of Empedocles" or "Grief, Aristotle wrote . . ."

There's a fortune-cookie quality to many of these quotations, a strenuous and uninspired reaching for analogy or metaphor. Even when the parallel works, it seemed to me like the undigested lessons of an intellectual nouveau riche. It's hard enough to keep the rather ordinary lives of these four women clear in one's mind without the intervention of Schopenhauer, Abelard and Heisenberg. In a true novel of ideas, all of these doctrines would have been implicit, for no character comes alive through a reading list. The very title of the book is a labored physics metaphor for human vicissitudes, which does nothing to explain or elevate them. . . .

Twice we hear about the unexamined life's not being worth living, and I was reminded of Joseph Epstein's remark, in his recent book, "Middle of My Tether," that he's not so sure about the examined life either. What we need in novels is *lived* life, examined or unexamined. Miss Schwartz would do well to leave some of the philosophical correlations to the reader. Readers go to school, too.

But there are two sides to Miss Schwartz's book, two voices. Though Lydia ironically refers to the movement from "the cosmic to the personal" as a falling off, she is, like Antaeus, strongest when her feet are on the ground. When the two youngest children of Lydia and Victor are killed in a bus crash while on a skiing trip, she becomes a woman, wife and mother and puts off, at least part of the time, her perennial student persona.

At the end of **"Disturbances in the Field,"** Lydia's voice comes from the center of herself. It goes beyond literature and philosophy to a tough, battered truth. Perhaps it is only when the truth of a situation is simple that the people involved in it are permitted to have complex responses. It's as if their feelings dance around the brute dilemma instead of expatiating on it. . . .

The last part of **"Disturbances in the Field"** is so well written that it balances all the rest. Unfortunately, what that leaves us with is a dead heat.

> *Anatole Broyard, in a review of "Disturbances in the Field," in* The New York Times, *October 28, 1983, p. C28.*

CAROLE COOK

Disturbances in the Field is just such a novel as Henry James would have approved, being not so much a story, moral or otherwise, as the execution of an entire, unique world out of a generous accumulation of detail, character, and incident. In its size and its freedom, it achieves the "immense and exquisite correspondence with life" that James maintained was the stuff and soul of fiction. It has the total quality of reality, in all its untidiness and muddlement and mulish resistance to logic and

formula. It is a novel in which an intensely rich and complex scene radiates out from the hub of its subjective center.

It begins, like [James's *Portrait of a Lady*], from the premise that ordinariness is far more interesting than the exotic. Lydia Rowe introduces herself on the first page like this: "I was nearly forty-two and still seeking to understand." Presumptuous indeed, Lydia is not content merely to live—she wants to understand as well, and it is ultimately as a seeker of wisdom that she constitutes herself as a worthy Subject.

At forty-two, Lydia has it all, that is to say, everything the average middle-class American girl aspires to: a devoted husband, a rising career as a chamber musician, four beautiful children, and a close-knit group of loving friends. Her best friends—Nina, Gaby, and the formidable Esther—date from her Barnard years, where they first tasted the fruit of knowledge together in a philosophy survey course. (p. 601)

Schwartz traces the respective fates of the four friends from their undergraduate aspirations through the vicissitudes of young adulthood, as they marry, or don't, or survive divorce, take up careers or drop them, quarrel or make peace with aging parents, have or don't have children more by accident than by choice. Four well-delineated and familiar representatives of the restless sixties and confused seventies, they are distinguished primarily by their talk (for this is a novel full of good talk) and their collective inquiry into what any of this—career, marriage, maternity—has to do with philosophy.

They couldn't be further from the tired sensibility of Ann Beattie's emotional drifters, but they share the winter of her discontent. (pp. 601-02)

At the same time, if none of them is entirely content with her lot, their lives proceed out of their respective "essences," and The Philosophy Study Group sustains them, particularly by its Aristotelian article of faith that "a friend is another self." It's what they have, we expect them to say, instead. And up to a point, the novel functions partly as a Socratic disquisition, in that the characters within their dialogues can answer as well as ask questions about knowledge and ethics.

But then Schwartz tosses her heroine the ultimate question— the hard one by which Ivan Karamazov's cynicism prevails over his brother Alyosha's faith. In a freak accident, Lydia's two youngest, and most beloved, children are killed.

When Ivan presents his question—Why do the innocent suffer? Why do children die?—it is a splendid, fiery, awesome moment in fiction, such terrifying high tragedy that we end with a certain satisfied pride in our own intellect and humanity. . . .

Schwartz underplays the situation, and brutally so. Already off-center in a chaotic, unsatisfactory world, Lydia now withdraws from feeling, becomes a frigid observer of the events around her. She cannot respond to her own tragedy, except by spraining an ankle, so she can relish the small physical pain that substitutes for the other one. She indicts her friends, accusing them of abandoning her in her hour of need. She loses her husband along with her will to live, and finally regains both by clinging tenaciously to the ancient, somewhat ragged shards of Philosophy 101. By the time we leave her, everything, and nothing, has happened to the presumptuous girl who sought the truth in philosophy and found her destiny in the lives, and deaths, of other people. If she has learned anything, it is only that no one has permission to go under, and seeking is its own business.

The triumph, if we want one, belongs not to her heroine but to the novelist herself, who transforms the life of her character and her bootless search for truth into the truth of that search. (p. 602)

It is precisely in all the "ado" of *Disturbances in the Field*—the swirl of events surrounding this one passionate, vital, intelligent but altogether ordinary individual and her insistence, to paraphrase James again, on mattering—that the novel finds its justification. If the novel cannot explain reality, it can nonetheless embody its frustrations and limitations. This is the beautiful neo-Platonic lie of fiction: like Lydia Rowe, we understand our lives only dimly and we despair, but through her, we know our condition. (pp. 602-03)

Carole Cook, in a review of "Disturbances in the Field," in Commonweal, *Vol. CX, No. 19, November 4, 1983, pp. 590, 601-03.*

MICHAEL GORRA

[*Disturbances in the Field*] is this quarter's entrant in the Domestic Realism Sweepstakes, Upper West Side Division, a long and messy book told in the first person by one Lydia Rowe, who at forty-two has four lovely children, a talented and successful husband, her own increasingly satisfying career as a chamber pianist, and a Volvo. She keeps up with her college friends, thinks about the pre-Socratic philosophers she read as a freshman at Barnard, and has settled comfortably into a present in which she believes she has attained the "placidity that comes with the relief of growing up and believing that nothing wonderful or terrible will ever happen to you again." So guess what happens in the next chapter? No, it's not as macabre as it was in *The World According to Garp*. The accident happens offstage, only two of her children are involved, and they even get to die instantly and presumably without pain. In the aftermath Lydia becomes cold and competent and inhuman. . . . No wonder Victor leaves her for "the embrace of some fat old mama." Schwartz's narrator is so would-be-ironical about fashionable "lifestyles"—and so completely a sucker for them. Lydia's college friend George, now a therapist, provides the novel's title. "Disturbances in the field" take place when "something gets between the expressed need on the one hand and the response on the other. So the need doesn't receive the proper response and the transaction remains unfinished." One part of life gets in the way of another. The death of her children interferes with her relationship with her husband.

Well, of course! But for Lydia the inescapable dangers of social life, not just in the extremity of a child's death but on an everyday basis as well, are shrouded by a vocabulary that is meant to express them but instead anesthetizes them. How do you "act out" your feelings about the death of a child? Lydia tries to be ironic about the psycho-babble, but really, what does Victor's sexiness have to do with his feelings about the death of his children? And Schwartz's own irony fails as well; she too is a prisoner of George's terminology. Her fundamental problem, which she shares with most American novelists-of-manners, is that her work is born of a psychological comfort that it never quite manages to criticize. It comes from a world in which people assume that self-fulfillment is a right rather than the product of luck and privilege, assume that life should work the way in which they want it to, and look to terms like George's to fix things up when it doesn't. That world is so fundamentally safe that, once having accepted its terms in the slightest degree, a writer has to become sensational in order to evoke a situation for which those terms are patently inadequate. I'd rather read Barbara Pym. (pp. 159-60)

Michael Gorra, "Laughter and Bloodshed," in The Hudson Review, *Vol. XXXVII, No. 1, Spring, 1984, pp. 151-64.*

(Marvin) Neil Simon

1927-

American dramatist and scriptwriter.

Simon is among the most commercially successful playwrights in the history of American theater. While some critics share Jack Kroll's opinion that a Simon work is an "anthology of gags disguised as a play," audiences have consistently applauded such comedies as *Barefoot in the Park* (1963), *The Odd Couple* (1965), *The Sunshine Boys* (1972), and *California Suite* (1976). Several of Simon's plays have been made into popular films, and he has also written a number of original screenplays as well as the books for several musicals.

Much of Simon's comedy is a reflection of his own values and experiences. *Come Blow Your Horn* (1961), for example, is based on the adventures of Neil and his brother, Danny Simon, after they left home for the first time. *Chapter Two* (1977) deals with the death of Simon's first wife and the agonies and joys of his subsequent courtship and remarriage. In *Brighton Beach Memoirs* (1983) Simon contemplates his childhood and examines the implications of growing up Jewish in New York City in the 1930s.

Relationships are at the heart of Simon's plays. Many of them revolve around the more turbulent aspects of family life: sibling rivalry, infidelity, divorce, the gender and generation gaps, selfishness, insecurity. According to prevailing critical views, Simon's message is that a relationship need not be destroyed simply because it needs some work. A theme which recurs throughout his plays is the emptiness of a life without commitment. Other subjects examined by Simon within the context of relationships are the benefits of choosing moderation over extremes and the value of compromise (*Barefoot in the Park*); lack of communication, and expectations versus realities (*Last of the Red Hot Lovers*, 1969); the decay of modern society and the threat of aging to one's sense of worth (*The Prisoner of Second Avenue*, 1971); and the problems of old age (*The Sunshine Boys*).

Most critics believe that Simon's strength lies in his witty, unpretentious approach to everyday incidents in middle-class, urban life, things familiar to the majority of his audiences. While some have admitted to being mystified by the popularity of Simon's humor, which they perceive as simplistic and sometimes directionless, others recognize his ability to touch and hold his audience in play after play. His proponents contend that all his works contain serious themes within a humorous framework; his detractors claim that he buries his serious themes in an overabundance of gags and one-liners. Despite such critical controversy, Simon's works have enjoyed consistent audience appeal.

(See also *CLC*, Vols. 6, 11; *Contemporary Authors*, Vols. 21-24, rev. ed.; and *Dictionary of Literary Biography*, Vol. 7.)

RICHARD WATTS, JR.

Neil Simon has developed a notable gift for light and amusing comedies that possess a kind of ingratiating charm of their own. His latest play, "The Star-Spangled Girl," . . . lacks

© Jay Thompson

something of the brilliantly expert artifice that marked "Barefoot in the Park" and "The Odd Couple," but it is brightened by enough of his humorous and often witty inventiveness to provide an engagingly entertaining theatrical evening.

Here he has gone in for the basic situation of two young men and a desirable girl. The men are two youthfully ardent rebels living in penury in a duplex studio apartment in San Francisco, and hopefully trying to get out a protest magazine called Fall-Out. The girl is a scatterbrained Olympic swimmer, who is recovering from her humiliation over having been defeated by a contestant from a desert country. A somewhat elementary patriot, she disapproves of them violently because she is convinced that they are editing a dangerously subversive publication.

But don't think Mr. Simon is deeply preoccupied with issues of a free press and the right of youth to protest. Actually, he takes the approval of both subjects for granted, and, eventually, the girl concurs. What disturbs her at first is that one of the young men is making excessive gestures of romantic love in her direction. Later, she discovers to her alarm that she really is angered because the other youth is showing no signs of a similar attitude toward her.

All this merely provides the playwright with his springboard. Mr. Simon has a fine way with a freshly amusing line relevant or irrelevant, and for humorous observation of character and situation, but **"The Star-Spangled Girl"** is by no means just a succession of jokes or comic business. His plot structure may not be sturdy and there are certainly no big surprises in the development of his narrative, but his people are always likeable and essentially believable as well as amusing, and you are likely to be interested in what happens to them.

Despite the fun and ingenuity, the slightness of his story occasionally takes its toll, and there are moments when one begins to worry lest the delicate structure collapse and tumble in on him. And once or twice he has to resort to fairly obvious mechanics to prevent it. But almost unfailingly the charm, brightness, deft inventiveness and capacity for good, honest hilarity rush immediately to the rescue, something genuinely fresh and delightful pops up, and his play proceeds on its cheerful and unpretentious path happily. . . .

"The Star-Spangled Girl" is a deftly likeable comedy.

> *Richard Watts, Jr., "The Girl Patriot and the Rebels," in* New York Post, *December 22, 1966. Reprinted in* New York Theatre Critics' Reviews, Vol. XXVII, No. 20, December 26, 1966-January 1, 1967, p. 194.

NORMAN NADEL

[If] one boisterously clever first act could make a hit, then the term would apply to Neil Simon's **"The Star-Spangled Girl."** . . . But for a hit you need a strong second act and a zinger of a third act, and Simon hasn't come forth with either.

I don't mean that he lets his audience down entirely; there are laughs intermittently to the finish, and you could do far worse for a light evening out. What we miss is new material after that first act. We want the three characters to change somehow—to develop, deteriorate, reverse themselves, go out of their minds, do something. What they do is essentially what they were doing earlier in the play. We hope for a surprise and nothing very surprising happens. The play runs a predictable course.

> *Norman Nadel, "'Star-Spangled Girl': Funny—For One Act," in* World Journal Tribune, *December 22, 1966. Reprinted in* New York Theatre Critics' Reviews, Vol. XXVII, No. 20, December 26, 1966-January 1, 1967, p. 196.

CLIVE BARNES

[The Neil Simon and Burt Bacharach musical **"Promises, Promises"** proved to be] the kind of show where you feel more in the mood to send it a congratulatory telegram than write a review. . . .

The hero is not a nice man. In fact he is a kind of mousefink, who decides to sleep his way to the top of business without really lying. The sleeping is done—in a manner of speaking—not by him but by the senior executives in the life insurance firm in which he works. He gives them the key to his apartment and they give him the key to the executive washroom. They find a haven for their girls, and he finds a haven for his aspirations. . . .

Then he falls in love. He falls in love with a girl who is on visiting terms with his apartment but not with him. Guess what happens? You are right the first time.

Mr. Simon's play (and revealingly I find myself thinking of it as much as a play with music as a musical) crackles with wit. The jokes cling supplely to human speech so that they never seem contrived. The whole piece has a sad and wry humanity to it, to which the waspishly accurate wise cracks are only a background.

It is also interesting to see how Mr. Simon wins our sympathy, even our empathy, for his morally derelict hero. In a dramatic trick half as old as time, or at least half as old as Pirandello, he has this dubious young man address the audience direct. The same dubious young man—he must have been great at selling life insurance—takes us so far into his lack of confidence that we feel sorry for him. We even forgive his halfbaked way of talking to invisible audiences. Mr. Simon, you see, is a very resourceful man, and persuasive. He wouldn't even have to sell you the Brooklyn Bridge; you would be prepared to rent it.

> *Clive Barnes, "Simon-Bacharach 'Promises, Promises' Begins Run at the Shubert," in* The New York Times, *December 2, 1968, p. 57.*

RICHARD WATTS

[Neil Simon's **"The Prisoner of Second Avenue"**] is full of the humor and intelligence characteristic of this brilliant comic playwright. . . .

Here he is wryly contemplating the misfortune of a Manhattan family. The husband has lost his job, is fighting pollution and his neighbors, and faces the problems of living in a violent city. In fact, he is about to undergo a nervous breakdown. His wise and understanding wife is for a while the pillar of the family, but, after her job has gone and their apartment has been stripped by robbers, she, too, has a breakdown. It's a hard world, and the Edisons are soon aware of it.

This is surely the material for a serious drama, but Mr. Simon has a gift for taking a grave subject and, without losing sight of its basic seriousness, treating it with hearty but sympathetic humor. Because he has a talent for writing a wonderfully funny line, his capacity for insight and compassion is sometimes overlooked and he is thought of as merely a skillful gag writer, but this ignores the quality that has made him our most important writer of stage comedy.

The most hilarious part of **"The Prisoner of Second Avenue"** is the incidental broadcasting of some local television news. It offers a number of hot items. You learn, for instance, that Gov. Rockefeller is in the hospital after being mugged in front of his New York home, that the Police Commissioner has been kidnapped, and a Polish ship has crashed into the Statue of Liberty. This certainly helps to establish the background of Mr. Simon's frenetic Manhattan.

There is a good scene in which the husband's relatives foregather to make idiotic plans to support him after his illness and the flow of humor is quite steady. But there are stretches wherein the comedy is slightly less than in his major vein. There is never a time, however, when it can be forgotten that Neil Simon, even when he is a bit under his peak, can write rings around all the other American dramatists specializing in humor. He demonstrates the fact again here.

> *Richard Watts, "The New York of Neil Simon," in* New York Post, *November 12, 1971. Reprinted in* New York Theatre Critics' Reviews, Vol. XXXII, No. 19, November 22-28, 1971, p. 191.

MARTIN GOTTFRIED

["**The Prisoner of Second Avenue**"] is a comedy about the breakdown of the system in New York. Superficially, it is similar to Simon's screenplay, "**The Out-of-Towners**," though the main events in the movie—the rapes, the muggings, the burglaries, the endless strikes—are just the background for the play. (In the play, they are described through the deadly technique of a television news announcer in the dark between scenes.)

The foreground of the play shows the breakdown of the system as it relates to the individual. It is about a 47-year-old man who has lived by the rules and achieved success by the rules, as indicated by the home, the possessions and the way of life demanded by the rules. . . .

Suddenly, the system breaks down for him. The burglarizing junkies who have been terrorizing the city strip his apartment. The unemployment that has been raging through New York's publishing and advertising businesses reaches out and takes his job away. Stripped of these signs of achievement in which he so devoutly believes, he cannot handle the loss and so, finally, he breaks down.

Now the way I have put this, "**The Prisoner of Second Avenue**" would seem an indictment of the material system, a criticism of its values and a compassionately bitter example of what can happen to the foolish man who allows himself to live by it. . . .

But Simon chooses to turn 180 degrees and make the exactly opposite point. The system is fine and what's wrong are the junkies, the strikers, the rapists, blaming the symptoms for the disease. He fears that without the system, everything will go: That relaxing the rules for the sake of humanity will be paid for in the collapse of family, marriage and sanity. This fear is strangling his impulses and his work, and it must be overcome if he is to fulfill his impressive potential.

I have been talking about the play in its most serious terms because they—Simon's problem and his possibilities—are what is most interesting about it. In fact, "**The Prisoner of Second Avenue**" has been written and staged as if it were mainly a comedy, and it has been neither written nor staged well in that respect. . . .

[The result is that] instead of being the story of a man being a prisoner of the New York East Side system, it becomes five or six signposts of plot along a road crammed full of jokes. Nor are the jokes as funny as Simon can be (which is hysterical). More than ever he has shied away from the abstraction and eccentricity that is his wildest comic talent. . . .

Simon, who opens the play with the problem of materialism and ends it with a materialistic solution, is . . . troubled. But he has come so close to the surface of his struggle that if he just takes it from here, he can be tremendous.

> *Martin Gottfried, in a review of "The Prisoner of Second Avenue," in* Women's Wear Daily, *November 15, 1971. Reprinted in* New York Theatre Critics' Review, *Vol. XXXII, No. 19, November 22-28, 1971, p. 192.*

CLIFFORD A. RIDLEY

As *The Prisoner of Second Avenue* begins to unfold, it's clear that Mel Edison . . . is your prototypical middle-class New Yorker. A 46-year-old account executive who has lived six years in his 14th floor apartment . . . , he is beset by all the existential woes of the urban condition. . . .

Mel Edison, in brief, is quite literally losing his sanity; and in establishing this condition, Neil Simon has done his best work to date. . . . If it is not a wholly successful play, it is a wholly admirable one.

In those opening moments, Simon catches the feel of New York existence, the sense of raw nerve ends rubbing crazily against each other, about as well as anyone ever has. If art consists in appropriating the stuff of everyday existence and stripping it down to essentials, he has made a mad, dissonant art form out of ordinary urban clay. His concern is reminiscent of *Little Murders,* but where Jules Feiffer saw the urban world in terms of surreal, unseen, almost Godlike forces at play, Simon sees it as a congeries of tangible, petty irritations. Feiffer's Alfred has been deadened by the city, stripped of all his responses. Simon's Mel still greets each successive indignity with a wisecrack, although he knows it does no good. He has only to turn on his television . . . to hear of an endless parade of strikes, muggings, abductions, and other catastrophes that make his circumstances pale by comparison.

Still, those circumstances grow worse. His apartment is robbed—denuded of money, clothing, liquor, and TV set. . . . And in an economy move, he is fired from his job.

At this point Mel's predicament begins to seem a good deal less laughable than it looked at the outset, and Simon wisely cools the play down, forcing your sympathy for a man who is in fact at the brink of mental collapse. Simon has attempted this tragicomic blend before—notably in the first playlet of *Plaza Suite,* the first act of *Last of the Red Hot Lovers,* and almost all of *The Gingerbread Lady*—but he is singularly successful here because he has set you up so well. His evocation of the daily harassments in urban life has been so meticulous, so concrete, that you know the battered condition of Mel Edison's mind as you have known little else in the Simon canon.

And then Simon does an unfortunate thing. As Mel stands on his balcony during a shouting match with an upstairs neighbor, he gets a bucket of water dumped on him. Actually, it's not a bad metaphor—the crowning insult, all that—but in this context, in this play by this playwright, it shatters the mood. It's okay, Mabel; we can start laughing again. Curtain.

The second and last act is a mixed assortment. At the outset, Mel has been out of work seven weeks and his wife . . . has gone to work to support the two of them. It is a devastating, funny portrait of a bored and useless man that Simon paints here, shading slowly toward Mel's total mental collapse. Yet the collapse itself is overdrawn and improbable, and again the playwright draws laughs where he needs them least.

Did he perhaps *intend* to create a laughable breakdown? I don't think so, for he follows it with a break-the-ice sort of family conference at which Mel's brother and sisters agree to furnish him X amount of dollars toward his recovery—so long as X is very small. Another devastating scene, this, and matters proceed briskly to the final curtain, at which—you may have guessed it—Mel is doused for a second time. And by this point, Neil Simon is sounding very much like Jules Feiffer, for Mel and Edna—like Alfred—ultimately conclude that if you can't beat urban insanity, you might as well join it. At the final curtain they stare out from their tastefully upholstered sofa, as alone and indomitable as the couple in *American Gothic,* awaiting their revenge.

This is a different Neil Simon than the one who used to laugh just for the hell of it; if you want to know *how* different, I refer you to *The Comedy of Neil Simon,* an anthology of work from *Come Blow Your Horn* to *Last of the Red Hot Lovers.* Yet in another sense he's not so different; in a sense Neil Simon's journey is the journey of many of us over the past several years.

There's a clear connection, after all, between the 6th floor, walk up love nest of *Barefoot in the Park,* and the 14th-floor express elevator strait jacket of *The Prisoner of Second Avenue.* Mel and Edna Edison could be the Corie and Paul Bratter of that 1963 comedy grown up, but the timing is wrong. Mel and Edna have children in college. Wait, however. Suppose we assume that Corie and Paul didn't move into their loft in 1963, but in 1953? Then it all works out.

And they did, you know, for the fact is that comedy in 1963 dealt with a world that had stopped existing for almost everyone but newlyweds and comedy writers. Simon and his comperes had their details right, but the mood was wrong, their characters still believed in the perfectibility of man and his works, although many people in real life did not. Today, however, the message reaches us a hundred times a day. And so the toilet that was cute in *Barefoot in the Park,* flushing only if you pulled the handle up, has become a gurgling monster in *The Prisoner of Second Avenue,* refusing to *stop* flushing until the handle is jiggled.

This is the key to the change in Neil Simon along with the change in many of us. In eight years, that damned toilet has been fixed tens of times, and it still doesn't work. Nothing works. Or as Edna Edison puts it: "Is the whole world going out of business?"

Yet there are still people who choose to ignore all this, who visit a Neil Simon play in the expectation of recapturing the world of *Barefoot in the Park,* of guffawing mindlessly at unreal and untroubled people. That is why the twin dousings in *The Prisoner of Second Avenue* are so unfortunate: Coming from Neil Simon, the old boffmeister, they trigger an avalanche of brainless and cruel laughter that I'm convinced Simon did not intend. I must ask you to forgive the cliche here, but at these moments, and during Mel's crackup as well, Simon is asking us to laugh because it hurts too much to cry. But that's not the kind of laughter he's getting.

It's a shame. Directed . . . and performed to near perfection . . . *The Prisoner of Second Avenue* is a much better play than it likely will receive credit for being.

> *Clifford A. Ridley, "Neil Simon, Boffmeister," in The National Observer, November 20, 1971, p. 24.*

GERALD M. BERKOWITZ

Neil Simon is a critical embarrassment. It is bad enough that he is commercially the most successful dramatic writer of the past decade, but to make matters worse no one is quite sure why his comedies are such triumphs. It is very easy to point out the qualities that Simon's writing lacks; indeed, when placed up against any conventional checklist of "characteristics of great comedy," his plays are likely to fail on every count. Every count but one, that is; the fact is indisputable that a Neil Simon comedy makes the audiences laugh, and this laughter is louder, longer and more constant than that produced by any other modern dramatist. I propose to offer a partial explanation for Simon's success: that the secret of his special comic talent is a matter of pure technique; that it is not the content of his plays, but the manner in which that content is presented that

generates most of the laughter; and that the specific technique in question is so simple and automatic as to turn his plays into virtual laugh machines, producng a product—laughter—with foolproof ease and accuracy.

To double back for a moment to what Simon's plays do *not* do, however—it is universally agreed that they offer no specific insights into the human condition. And one might secretly be thankful for that, for this is certainly not where Simon's talent lies. On the rare occasions that he attempts some more-than-surface characterization or philosophising, the result is either bathetic (as in Barney Cashman's long autobiographical speech in Act I of *Last of the Red Hot Lovers* or almost any moment in *The Gingerbread Lady*) or just cliched, as in the moment of great discovery in **"Visitor from Forest Hills,"** the final playlet of *Plaza Suite:*

> *ROY:* She's afraid of what they're going to become.
>
> *NORMA:* I don't understand.
>
> *ROY:* Think about it.
>
> *NORMA:* What's there to think about? What are they going to become? They love each other, they'll get married, they'll have children, they'll grow older, they'll become like us . . . I never thought about that.

No, Simon is at his best, and safest, when he sticks to the surface. The characters, events and dialogue of his plays are there to produce laughter, and they rarely get more complex or sharply drawn than is necessary to that end. Certainly Simon never seems overly concerned about realism of characterization. Almost every play has its resident caricature—Victor Velasco in *Barefoot in the Park,* Jesse Kiplinger in **"Visitor from Hollywood,"** the never seen but often described Mrs. Mackininee in *The Star-Spangled Girl,* and so on—and even the more "realistic" characters frequently sacrifice their depth or consistency for the sake of a joke: milquetoast Felix Ungar turns and browbeats a chastened Oscar Madison . . . , inept would-be lecher Barney Cashman has brief moments of surprising effectiveness . . . , intelligent Andy Hobart becomes inexplicably dense. . . . (pp. 110-11)

And it is equally clear that Simon's special secret is not the inventiveness of his plots. None of the plays, with the possible exception of *The Odd Couple,* has a particularly original premise, and none carries its plot into particularly surprising twists: the aging playboy of *Come Blow Your Horn,* the innocent young lovers of *Barefoot in the Park* and *The Star-Spangled Girl,* and the middle-aged couples of *Plaza Suite* are all staples of television and B-movie comedy, and what happens to them is thoroughly predictable. . . .

So what is left but the jokes themselves? Seemingly it is the verbal humor that is Simon's secret weapon, since everything else in the plays is subjugated to it. But even that isn't the answer; how many funny lines do we remember when we leave the theatre after seeing a Simon play? Very few, I suggest, and not merely because there were so many jokes that few stick with us. This experience—not being quite sure what it was that was so funny—is even more pronounced when we read the plays, and go through page after page without finding something to laugh at. . . . How [do the gags], so dead on the printed page, work so well in the theatre?

I suggest that Simon's success stems more from the form of his jokes than from their content, that he doesn't write funny lines as much as lines that *sound* funny. There are certain rhythms and manners of speaking—certain linguistic structures, if you will—that we associate with jokes and that we have been conditioned to respond to as jokes, and Simon's dialogue is full of such structures. Thus we laugh, or at least are primed to laugh, regardless of how clever the lines actually are. This is one key to the secret of Simon's theatricality; this explains in part, at least, why we laugh in the theatre but are unable to remember afterwards, even with the text before us, just what was so funny. In many cases nothing was so funny; Simon just made us think it was at the time.

Of course, the fact that there are certain patterns of structure and delivery that almost generate laughs by themselves is well established. When a night club comic leads into a line with an emphasized "BUT . . ." or "AND SO . . . ," or when he follows it with a quick "But seriously . . ." or a clash of cymbals, he is as much as telling us "This is the joke, folks; this is where you're supposed to laugh." And we usually do. When Simon writes an exchange like this one.

> *ANDY:* We really wouldn't have to worry about money if you would let me do what I suggested.
>
> *NORMAN:* What was that?
>
> *ANDY:* Selling you to a medical school. . . .

we *know* that Andy's answer is going to be a joke even before it comes, because this kind of three-liner is as old as burlesque. And so we laugh, more because our expectations have been fulfilled than because the line is particularly funny. . . . The typical Neil Simon comedy is essentially a string of such sequences, that don't necessarily telegraph the punch line itself, but do announce that a punch line is coming. Some of the jokes are funny, even when read rather than heard, but many are not, and the amount of laughter generated does not seem to depend on that factor. (p. 111)

Those jokes that Simon doesn't telegraph in advance he punctuates and underlines on arrival, again with the effect of stimulating laughter more because the occasion seems to call for it than for any other reason. His favorite means of announcing "This is a joke" is an increase in volume:

> *SOPHIE:* Do you know what he's doing now?
>
> *ANDY:* He's mopping your kitchen floor.
>
> *SOPHIE:* He is mopping *mah kitchen floor!*
>
> *ANDY:* And you don't want your kitchen floor mopped.
>
> *SOPHIE: (Screams)* Ah don't want it mopped 'cause Ah waxed it last night and now *he's moppin' up all the wax!* . . .

Every one of Simon's comedies includes at least one character who spends most of his time shouting in exasperation: the Father in *Come Blow Your Horn,* Oscar in *The Odd Couple,* Roy Hubley in **"Visitor from Forest Hills,"** etc. And there is nothing wrong with this; exaggerated rage and frustration is legitimately comic behavior and its dramatic use goes back at least as far as the Magistrate in *Lysistrata.* Simon's particular twist is to use this kind of delivery to make otherwise uncomic lines seem funny. . . . In every case the effect is the same: we laugh at what *seem to be* jokes, because they are delivered in a manner that makes them *sound like* jokes, and we never notice when the Emperor has no clothes on. (pp. 112-13)

Another punctuating device that Simon likes is simple repetition, apparently on the premise that we might miss an occasional modest joke if the play weren't stopped dead for a moment to call it to our attention. . . .

> *BUDDY:* The most important thing to her is peace in the family.
>
> *ALAN: And* a clean apartment.
>
> *BUDDY:* And a clean apartment. . . .

By underlining his jokes in this way, Simon accomplishes the same things that the "APPLAUSE" sign in a television studio does: he calls our attention to the fact that a joke has just gone by, gives us our cue to laugh, and implies by the momentary pause in the action that he's not going to go on until we do laugh. And, being polite and well-trained, we laugh, much more than the jokes themselves deserve.

There is one more technical trick that Simon employs extensively to produce more laughter than his jokes actually warrant. Adopting the technique of the lightweight boxer who knows that a one-two-three combination can do as much damage as the really solid punch that he doesn't have, Simon exploits the power of the multiple gag, the rapid-fire string of small jokes whose snowballing effect is greater than that of a single first-rate comic line. Consider this exchange from *The Odd Couple:*

> *OSCAR:* They broke up! The entire marriage is through . . .
>
> *SPEED:* After twelve years?
>
> *VINNIE:* They were such a happy couple.
>
> *MURRAY:* Twelve years doesn't mean you're a *happy* couple. It just means you're a *long* couple. . . .

The basic joke here lies in Vinnie's speech, and the incongruity of its sentiment. It's not a very good joke, and wouldn't be worth much on its own. But Simon doesn't leave it on its own. The first sentence of Murray's response serves as punctuation and emphasis, like the repetitions discussed earlier; the weak little joke is now given the status of a big Pow-Socko gag. Then Murray's final line, with its new twist also punctuated, this time by volume and exasperation, climaxes the sequence and signals the audience to release the laugh that has been carefully built up. This device recurs as often in Simon's plays as the other tricks already noted, and with the same consistency of structure; two small jokes, neither of them particularly good, gain in effect through the speed with which one follows the other, and are finally underlined by that sure-fire cue to laughter, the shout of rage. . . .

This analysis has, of course, been unfair to Neil Simon; his plays do contain much legitimately comic material, and many of his jokes are funny. But funny jokes alone do not a Neil Simon laugh riot make. It's the Amazing Laugh Machine—the combination of Pavlovian conditioning, relentless pounding, and simple *chutzpah*—that is Simon's secret weapon. And unless he unilaterally disarms, which is unlikely, the audiences of the world will continue to be at his mercy. (p. 113)

Gerald M. Berkowitz, "Neil Simon and His Amazing Laugh Machine," in Players Magazine, *Vol. 47, No. 3, February-March, 1972, pp. 110-13.*

JACK KROLL

Neil Simon's relentless fertility is a real esthetic virtue. Clearly he can write a play about anything: it would be fun to set him up officially as America's playwright laureate, perhaps in the theater on Broadway that he owns, where he could create a continuous theatrical obbligato to the events of the day, dashing off a play on Billy Carter, or Lee Marvin's nonmarital problem or even a fast funny musical about the OPEC countries. And on the side he could run a more private service, whipping out personalized plays for ordinary people, say a one-acter on your kid's bar mitzvah or a gag epithalamium on your impending marriage. Something like this is what Simon has done in **"They're Playing Our Song,"** apparently based on the real-life relationship between composer Marvin Hamlisch and lyricist Carole Bayer Sager, and which includes songs by Marvin Hamlisch and Carole Bayer Sager. I enjoyed it.

This kind of thing is Neil Simon at his best. He's grasped the essential truth about life today—that no matter how serious the details may be, it's a joke, Mac, a series of routines turned out by the Great Gag Writer in the Sky. When the President of the United States makes a crack about "Montezuma's Revenge" to the President of Mexico, you know we've reached the moment in history when everyone wants to be a stand-up comic. In Simon's world, everyone is. His hero, Vernon Gersch . . . , is a neurotic, arrogant but lovable writer of hit tunes, and his heroine, Sonia Walsk . . . , is a neurotic, vulnerable but lovable writer of hit lyrics. They come together to collaborate on some songs, and their musical chords lead to romantic discords, the cutest upsy-downsy romance played out in a rippling rhythm of thirteen scenes, 173 gags and nine songs.

It's an unassuming but stylish piece of work, amiable, amusing, warm, winning and like that. And in its own quiet way it's something of a breakthrough in Broadway's current musical dilemma, whose horns are the zillion-dollar extravaganza like "Ballroom" and the pocket-size, "bookless" musical like "Ain't Misbehavin'." **"They're Playing Our Song"** steps intelligently in between these extremes.

Jack Kroll, "Simon Sings," in Newsweek, Vol. XCIII, *No. 9, February 26, 1979, p. 76.*

DOUGLAS WATT

Is Neil Simon going soft? Or is the prodigiously industrious playwright tapped out? One hopes not, but his latest effort, **"I Ought to Be in Pictures,"** an oddly muted comedy . . . , is, when all is said and done by its three characters, an empty and labored evening. "Shaky confidence" is ascribed to the middle-aged hero by his middle-aged mistress, and it also seems to be Simon's problem here. Teetering on the edge of sentimentality, this play about a father and daughter rediscovering—or discovering, really—one another after a long separation worries its subject all evening long, never daring to be either too funny or too caring.

It has been written and directed . . . and is acted with painstaking attention to detail and an almost solemn air of sincerity. But there is little evidence of enthusiasm in the writing, so that in the end we are only aware of contrivance and of characters who vanish from our consciousness like puffs of smoke.

Herb Tucker is a down-on-his-luck screenwriter living in a bright, cheerless horror of a cracked-stucco, tiled-roof West Hollywood bungalow with a single bedroom and a small plot of ground on which he has proudly grown an orange tree and a lemon tree, objects to which Simon glancingly attaches symbolic significance. Sixteen years earlier, Herb simply up and left his wife and two small children, a boy and girl, in Brooklyn (he offers two seemingly contradictory reasons for his action, but no matter), and within a month was settled in movieland.

For two years now, and after a couple of short-lived Hollywood marriages, he has been having a comfortable affair (on Tuesday nights only; in between, he sees other women) with a divorcee named Steffy Blondell, who has a good job as a movie makeup woman and two kids of her own. Steffy would like Herb to give up his ratty dwelling and move in with her, but there's that "shaky confidence."

Enter Libby Tucker, Herb's 19-year-old daughter (the orange tree), who has bused and hitchhiked her way west with the avowed intention of becoming a movie star, but actually to get to know and receive a sign of love from her dad, whom she has neither seen nor heard from since she was three. A spunky, plain-looking girl, she gets her wish and heads back to Brooklyn after a two-week stay.

We leave Herb at the typewriter, ready for action once more, as Steffy slips off to prepare a Chinese dinner at her presumably more livable house. Maybe there's hope for Herb after all. . . .

The first half ends, by the way, with Libby reading from "The Belle of Amherst," Emily Dickinson's description of the loss of her father, a brief passage so moving that it doesn't belong in the same theater with **"I Ought to Be in Pictures."** . . .

One can sense the tone Simon is striving for in **"I Ought to Be in Pictures,"** but it has eluded him along with any suggestion of genuine feeling, the result being a dead play.

Douglas Watt, "New Simon Empty, Labored," in Daily News, New York, April 4, 1980. Reprinted in New York Theatre Critics' Reviews, Vol. XLI, No. 6, March 24-30, 1980, p. 293.

HOWARD KISSEL

In many ways Neil Simon's **"I Ought to Be in Pictures"** . . . is a fantasy play. It presumes that a daughter who was abandoned by her father at the age of 3 can establish a close relationship with him, speak more candidly, manage to convey all the inner warmth daughters who have lived with their fathers all their lives cannot. But the theater, after all, is a place where wishes are fulfilled, and the play is set in Los Angeles, which everyone knows is not a real place—so it is not at all hard to suspend disbelief and accept the play for what it is, the most genuinely touching play Simon has written, one in which laughs stem from character, one in which the master yocksmith is not afraid to trust his emotions.

"I Ought to Be in Pictures" is as full of tenderness as it is of humor, and Simon never seems to feel he has to compensate for honest sentiment by throwing in cheap, quick laughs as he did in **"Chapter Two."** For my money it is his best play since **"The Odd Couple."** . . .

"I Ought to Be in Pictures" represents a new side of Simon, and an extremely welcome one.

Howard Kissel, in a review of "I Ought to Be in Pictures," in Women's Wear Daily, April 4, 1980. Reprinted in New York Theatre Critics' Reviews, Vol. XXXXI, No. 6, March 24-30, 1980, p. 294.

JACK KROLL

Everybody has to make a separate peace with Neil Simon. Mine came when I decided he was really an abstract artist who used gags the way Mondrian used little cells of color—a good Simon play was a formal construct in which the gags were in pleasing tension with one another. The subjects—odd couples, red-hot lovers, sunshine boys—were really only different ways of arranging the Mondrian gag-colors into different patterns. Since having this momentous insight into the Simon gestalt, I can enjoy his plays like any other Simon fan. As a good American, I want to *be* a Simon fan and this is the way that works for me. At least it did until **"I Ought to Be in Pictures"** came to Broadway.

This play can't be Mondrianized. It's got little gag-dabs running through it, but not nearly enough to make a true Simondrian. It looks, God help us, as if Simon MAY NOT WANT TO BE FUNNY ANYMORE! He may just want to be serious first, and funny second. But as a scholar of comedy, Simon should know that funny men can only be serious if they're funny first. At least it's got to be a dead heat, as it was in **"Chapter Two,"** where funny and serious met on equal terms like that old Chinese vaudeville team Yin and Yang.

Another of my momentous theories is that great popular comic talents, like Chaplin and W. C. Fields, use comedy as a means of embracing, yet transcending, sentimentality. This is a suspenseful process, as watching Chaplin arm-wrestle sentimentality in "City Lights" makes clear. In **"I Ought to Be in Pictures,"** Simon arm-wrestles sentimentality and you can hear his humerus crack. And Simon with a cracked humerus is a sad spectacle.

Simon's theme of a 19-year-old girl who barges in on the father who hasn't seen her in sixteen years could have been funny and touching as hell. At times it *is* funny and touching—but very few times and never as hell. The father, Herb, has been a Hollywood scriptwriter since walking out on his family. But he can't hack the scripts anymore and even his understanding girlfriend, Steffy, is getting fed up with their part-time relationship. Libby, the daughter, pops up in Herb's Spanish omelet of a house, fixes the house, fixes his car, fixes Herb and in the process fixes the gap in her life which she's temporarily filled by talking to her dead but still wise grandmother.

With material like this you have to work against it: bite it and make it bite back. Sometimes Simon finds a gag that's funny because it draws a drop of blood, as when Herb, frazzled by his long-neglected daughter's invasion, wails, "I don't even know how she found me. It took them twenty years to find Eichmann." But mostly Simon simply milks his scenes for their bottom-line emotion, which comes out as the mawkish camouflaged by the raucous. (pp. 106-07)

> *Jack Kroll, "Cracked Humerus," in* Newsweek, *Vol. XCV, No. 15, April 14, 1980, pp. 106-07.*

DOUGLAS WATT

The last time Neil Simon fooled around with Russia, in **"The Good Doctor,"** he engaged himself in an uneasy partnership with Chekhov. Now in **"Fools,"** . . . he has contented himself with a comic fairy-tale romance that should prove mildly diverting to adults and even more so to schoolchildren.

Once upon a time, according to Simon's fable, a new schoolmaster arrived at a Ukrainian village whose inhabitants had been struck dumb—or rather, stupid—200 years before by a curse which has afflicted all their descendants. Following in the footsteps of countless other schoolteachers, all of whom evidently had the good sense to back off before it was too late, Leon Tolchinsky must deliver the people from the curse within 24 hours or, if he fails and does not leave before the time is up, turn stupid himself.

The situation would appear at first glance to be a promising one for a writer of Simon's comic talents, but on closer inspection it becomes obvious that only so many changes can be rung on it. In a shifting interior-exterior storybook setting . . . , it takes the author less than an hour-and-a-half, not counting an intermission, to work things out. The solution, after a few close calls, is a bit sloppy, as if Simon had exhausted his invention, but all ends happily.

The odd and rather disarming thing about **"Fools"** is the gentleness of most of Simon's humor. Not that there isn't a plenitude of typical Simon gags. One of them (Doctor: "You'll live to be 80." Patient: "I'm 79 now." Doctor: "You have a wonderful year ahead.") might even have been left over from **"The Sunshine Boys."** But true love, of all things, is uppermost in our playwright's mind. And Tolchinsky's adored little fool of a Sophia, whose loveliness keeps him there in the village of Kolyenchikov till the clock strikes the fateful hour, has a wisdom surpassing his textbook knowledge. . . .

"Fools" is low-keyed and even slight Simon, but it is also surprisingly warmhearted Simon, and it passes the time amiably enough.

> *Douglas Watt, "'Fools' from Simon: The Younger, the Better," in* Daily News, *New York, April 7, 1981. Reprinted in* New York Theatre Critics' Reviews, *Vol. XLII, No. 7, April 6-12, 1981, p. 294.*

CLIVE BARNES

To say that I am at a loss for words is merely to put a cliche where my heart should be.

But I truly am at a loss for words. I probably admire Neil Simon more than most of my colleagues. He is a major playwright, a comedian who survives fashion through the honesty of his comic agony.

But here I am at a loss for words. *Fools* . . . is simply terrible. I am not only at a loss for words, I am even at a loss for a cliche. Unfortunately, Simon is here not at a loss for either.

It is a one-joke play. And Simon tells the same joke over and over and over—and much moreover—again. It is a Russian village. In the Ukraine. Scarcely Russia, but near enough. The village is cursed, it is cursed with stupidity.

Everyone—except a schoolmaster who unexpectedly arrives to give this strange concept some kind of conceivable purpose—is stupid. "How stupid are they?" you ask. Think of stupidity at its most obvious and least amusing, and that, so horribly precisely that, is how stupid they are. . . .

This is not a play, but a premise for a play. Everything is based on stupidity. Why? What the hell? What is so interesting about stupidity? . . .

[But] one must remember that this is Simon's 19th play, and he is entitled to the occasional dash of drivel for the record.

> *Clive Barnes, "'Fools' Die—Or Should," in* New York Post, *April 7, 1981. Reprinted in* New York

Theatre Critics' Reviews, *Vol. XLII, No. 7, April 6-12, 1981, p. 295.*

FRANK RICH

Say what you will about Neil Simon, but there's no denying that he has a real nose for jokes; he doesn't go looking for laughs where they can't be found. So how can one account for **"Fools,"** [an] almost total misfire . . . ? This peculiar endeavor was destined to be fruitless from the moment the playwright dreamed it up. Why the shrewd Mr. Simon plunged ahead anyway is one of the minor mysteries of the Broadway season.

"Fools" is about Kulyenchikov, a mythical Ukrainian village of "long ago" whose residents all live under an evil curse of stupidity. It's a one-gag premise that might make for a dandy 10-minute Sid Caeser-Imogene Coca sketch or a throwaway anecdote in a Mel Brooks-Carl Reiner "2,000-Year-Old Man" routine. But a two-hour play? As one watches Mr. Simon, the director Mike Nichols and a topflight cast struggle to puff up this show, a feeling of unreality sets in. It's as if a team of brilliant high-priced surgeons has been assembled to operate on a splinter.

While Mr. Simon has come up with a few funny moments, there are only so many jokes that *anyone* can make about stupidity. Once we learn that the town peddler sells flowers as whitefish, that the town doctor can't read his own eye chart and that the town shepherd can't find his sheep, there's an inevitability about every punch line. . . .

To stitch them all together, the playwright has come up with a story of sorts. The hero is a teacher named Leon—is he the lost offstage Leon of Mr. Simon's **"They're Playing Our Song"**?—who has come to Kulyenchikov to chase the curse away. Leon . . . quickly falls in love with the stupidest girl in town . . .—thus allowing Mr. Simon to hit us with a few more by the final curtain. We learn that love and self-respect can conquer ignorance, and, rather contradictorily, that ignorance can at times be bliss. This is not big news, and, even so, Mr. Simon must strain to deliver it. By Act II, the playwright is adding so many arbitrary last-minute secret clauses to the village's curse that the actors all but apologize for having to explain them to us.

Running about this ersatz fairybook land are seasoned comic actors who deserve a full-fledged Simon comedy. . . . But there's a limit to how much any of them can accomplish. Because virtually every character manifests the same stupidity—an inability to remember names, for instance—every actor seems to be playing the same role. . . .

[What] we really have here is a formula for silliness, not comedy—and surely no one knows that better than Neil Simon. Maybe **"Fools"** is just an April fools' prank that somehow ran berserk.

Frank Rich, "'Fools' by Simon," in The New York Times, *April 7, 1981, p. C11.*

JACK KROLL

"Fools" is Neil Simon's nineteenth play in twenty years—and his weakest. It's a fable about a Ukrainian village whose inhabitants are under a curse of stupidity. Apparently Simon is trying to say something about how society can wrongly label some of its groups; maybe this is his allegory on race and IQ.

If so, he's wrecked an important subject by trying to be a folk artist, forgetting that he *is* a folk artist in his real plays like **"The Odd Couple"** and **"The Sunshine Boys."** **"Fools"** is so cute it commits cutecide. Wait till next year.

Jack Kroll, "Simple Simon," in Newsweek, *Vol. XCVII, No. 16, April 20, 1981, p. 104.*

CLIVE BARNES

Imagine Eugene O'Neill with a soft streak down his back. Imagine Tennessee Williams in a memory play just slightly cuter than it needed to be.

This is Neil Simon's *Brighton Beach Memoirs*—it is effortlessly his best play yet, it is in its way the best play of the season so far, and it is strangely a slight disappointment.

Simon is one of the significant English-speaking playwrights of the century. His position is as secure as the Statue of Liberty. And *Brighton Beach Memoirs* . . . was clearly intended as his run for the final touchdown.

It made it. But in a perverse way it showed Simon's limitations almost as clearly as his virtues. It didn't have the honesty of his earlier *The Gingerbread Lady*—particularly that first version of the play that was excised in Boston—and it was merely better written.

I enjoyed it a lot—I laughed and I cried, although dangerously I enjoyed it more when I was laughing than when I was crying. This was a proportion neither Williams nor O'Neill would ever have permitted us.

Simon here is returning to his past. The play has something in common with his very first adventure for our multiple familial recollections, *Come Blow Your Horn*. It is, not unexpectedly, a lot brighter. . . .

[The humor] is typical Simon. He has a reputation for being a gag-writer who one bright day strayed on to Broadway and cleaned up a lucky fortune. Unfair.

The man in fact is a wonder at using words that sting the ordinary into the marmoreally memorable, of suddenly revealing to our collective unconscious a moment of recognition, a point of identification.

He is always brooding on the littleness of life and that wryly comic aspect of the domestic mini-tragedy. He is the poet of all our forgotten yesterdays—even if we grew up far from Brooklyn on other beaches and even, I suspect, at other times. His jokes cling to the air like iridescent, Proustian bubbles of times past.

The small things count. Listen to this girl—she is [the protagonist] Eugene's cousin and along with her ailing sister and widowed mother, has been given shelter by their uncle, Eugene's father. Now she is talking about her late father—he died at 36—describing him to her younger sister. She describes the wonderment of his pockets—a soft cave of surprises, its voluminous folds of dust and candies.

One day, soon after her father's death, she finds his old overcoat in a closet. Plunging her hand into its once familiar pocket she finds—nothing. Her mother had sent the coat to the cleaners. For the first time she comprehends and accepts the fact of his death.

Now this is just about as good a piece of dramatic writing as you are going to find. It is in no way innovative, but it nudges our perceptions and makes us understand ourselves. Some family conversations here—father to son, brother to brother, sister to sister—have just the right ring. The voice is different, but it does, I submit, have the same note of authority you gratefully hear in O'Neill or Williams.

But Simon always pulls back from the jugular. He never pushes beyond pain. He always shrugs deprecatingly, makes a slight Jewish joke and hides his heart behind his well-tailored sleeve. A pity. A great playwright must be prepared for the final plunge even if it kills him and he sinks without trace.

Brighton Beach Memoirs settles too easily for anecdotes. This is going to be unfair, but unfair in the right direction. Simon too readily confuses the Reader's Digest with literature, Norman Rockwell with Rembrandt, and Norman Lear with *King Lear*.

But—having got that aria off my chest—let me stress what a very lovely play this is. I am certain—if the kids of our academic establishment can get off their pinnacles and start taking Simon as seriously as he deserves—*Brighton Beach Memoirs* will become a standard part of American dramatic literature.

> Clive Barnes, "'Memoirs' Is Simon's Best Play," in New York Post, *March 28, 1983. Reprinted in* New York Theatre Critics' Reviews, *Vol. XLIV, No. 4, March 21-28, 1983, p. 345.*

FRANK RICH

[In the autobiographical memory play "**Brighton Beach Memoirs**"] Mr. Simon makes real progress toward an elusive long-time goal: he mixes comedy and drama without, for the most part, either force-feeding the jokes or milking the tears. It's happy news that one of our theater's slickest playwrights is growing beyond the well-worn formulas of his past.

The other likable aspect of Mr. Simon's writing here is its openness and charity of spirit. Far more than most Simon plays, "**Brighton Beach Memoirs**" deals explicitly with the Jewishness of its people. While one might fear that this development could lead to caricature, it generally does not. Mr. Simon's characters—the seven members of the extended Jerome family of Brighton Beach—are, for all their archetypal manners, appealing. Even though Mr. Simon is trying to come to terms with his less-than-rosy Depression adolescence, he looks back not with anger but with an affection that is too warm to be fake.

Thanks to these attributes, "**Brighton Beach Memoirs**" offers more surprises than any Simon play since "**The Sunshine Boys.**" It is also, disappointingly, not nearly so good as one keeps expecting it to be. Oddly enough, Mr. Simon's kindness eventually extends so far that it has a boomerang effect: even as it makes us like the man who wrote this play, it softens the play itself. "**Brighton Beach Memoirs**" boasts some big laughs (in Act I) and some genuinely tender speeches, but it never quite stops being nice and starts being either consistently involving or entertaining. It's a pleasant evening, blessed with a handsome and highly energetic production, that lacks emotional and theatrical bite.

The makings of a more forceful play are certainly in evidence. Eugene, the 15-year-old hero . . . , lives in crowded, lower-middle-class circumstances. His household not only contains his father . . . , mother . . . , and older brother . . . , but also the mother's widowed sister . . . , and her two daughters. "If you didn't have a problem, you wouldn't live in this house," says the father—and that's no joke. Two of the characters have heart disease, and one has asthma; two at least temporarily lose jobs needed to keep the straitened family afloat. There is an offstage car accident; two of the children contemplate running away from home.

Mr. Simon uses the family's miseries to raise such enduring issues as sibling resentments, guilt-ridden parent-child relationships and the hunger for dignity in a poverty-stricken world. When the mother and her sister air a lifetime's pent-up angers or when the bone-weary father, a garment-district cutter, plods home from work as wearily as Willy Loman, we find real, eloquently stated pain.

But the author doesn't fully trust his material. He leans on Eugene's narration to spoon feed us his messages and, eventually, he sweeps both the play's crises and promise of dramatic tension under the rug. In Act II, most of the family's problems, moral dilemmas and conflicts are neatly resolved; by the end, Mr. Simon even reaches over to Europe to rescue some unseen Polish cousins from the coming Holocaust. Perhaps life can be this benign, but these happy endings are paraded so patly that they push an affectionate play over the line into unconvincing Pollyannaism.

In this context, the author's handling of his on-stage alter ego is highly revealing. No matter how miserable the goings-on around him, Eugene is usually ready with a wisecrack—and he records those gags in the composition book that is the repository of his first literary effort, his "memoirs." After a while, Eugene's good-natured brand of storytelling all too glaringly points up the deficiencies of Mr. Simon's own writing in "**Brighton Beach Memoirs.**" We feel that a brisk, superficial glibness is papering over the rough edges of the lives in view—especially the hero's.

Eugene, in the end, proves less a character than a master of ceremonies. Unlike the others, this boy has few personality flaws—some slight selfishness and a rampant lustfulness for his 16-year-old cousin excepted. He is, as his brother says, "a terrific kid," and however preoccupied he may be with sex or the Yankees, he still gets nearly straight A's in school.

As in "**Chapter Two,**" Mr. Simon's autobiographical stand-in is finally so saintly and resilient he becomes elusive and opaque—a vacuum where the play's sensitive center should be. At one point Eugene asks, "How can I be a writer if I don't learn how to suffer?"—yet we never really see him suffer. Eugene has most of the jokes, and they're not the bleeding kind: they obscure rather than reveal his true feelings.

If the play's undercurrents don't run deep, its surface mostly gleams. Mr. Simon wittily captures the texture of the Jeromes' milieu—where all gentiles are malevolent "cossacks" and where a contentious family dinner can, in Eugene's words, begin like "a murder mystery in Blenheim Castle." Though some of the Jewish mother, puberty and food gags are overdone, others are dead-on. Trust Mr. Simon to explain, hilariously, how Eugene's first wet dreams resemble "The 39 Steps" or to demonstrate how certain words must always be whispered in a Jewish home. . . .

One hopes there will be a chapter two to "**Brighton Beach Memoirs**," in which Mr. Simon . . . [builds on his] often-endearing work by, paradoxically, trying a little less hard to please.

Frank Rich, "Neil Simon's 'Brighton Beach'," in
The New York Times, *March 28, 1983, p. C9.*

WALTER KERR

Whenever a writer gets around to presenting us with his own
portrait of the artist as a young man, he invariably does two
things. He makes his young man sensitive, very sensitive. A
blossom on the vine that will wither and die unless it is promptly
given succor. And he makes his young man a victim, a stranger
in the household who is not going to be properly nurtured
because he is so blatantly misunderstood; he must escape the
obtuseness about him at all costs. You know how it goes.

Now, . . . we have Neil Simon's portrait of the artist as a
young man, and Mr. Simon, as generous a man as ever was,
has done three things. In **"Brighton Beach Memoirs"** he has
made his 14-year-old hero, whose stage name is Eugene but
who is plainly the playwright's remembered alter ego, sensitive
enough, I'd say. . . .

He is also a victim. He can walk into a room—a room in
Brooklyn during the Depression year 1937—and without having heard a word of the conversation until now, fully expect
to hear the expression "Eugene will do it." And he will do
it, too, whatever it is, because he has no choice. He is the
unelected slave, the permanent gofer, the knickerbocker kid
on call for two Jewish families, living in overcrowded quarters,
and if each day demands 16 trips to the grocer's—well, so be
it. . . .

The third thing Mr. Simon has done? He has made the artist
as a young man funny—oh, Lord, he has made him funny—
and I have repeated the word "artist" here to a purpose. The
shrewdest of Mr. Simon's ploys, and very probably the best,
is not simply to have made the boy hilarious in his likes and
dislikes, his comings and goings, his sexual gropings. He has
made him funny in the very perceptions that are going to turn
him into a writer of some kind, some day. He has created a
character, believably young and attractively innocent, whose
habit of mind is to seize upon the discomfort of the moment—
his or anyone else's—and to see that discomfort as lunatic. In
effect, Mr. Simon lets us watch the comic mind growing up. . . .

Though **"Brighton Beach Memoirs"** is probably Neil Simon's
most serious play, as you may well have heard by this time,
we are invited to watch its resentments grow and its angers
flare through the eyes of a canny adolescent who has already
learned how to translate trouble into high humor. It's an ingenious device and, given Mr. Simon's own special equipment,
no doubt a wise and honest one. During the long, lovely first
act, it leads to an extended scene between two brothers that
embraces their counterpointed moods perfectly: Eugene's desperate eagerness to learn a little something about sex, older
brother Stanley's restless preoccupation with matters more
mundane and much more urgent. The give-and-take between
them is warm, edgy, exasperated and stunned in about equal
proportions and a masterfully engaging variant on what is, after
all, very familiar material.

I confess that I am nowhere near so enamored of the play's
second half, but—given the immense care that has gone into
its crafting on all levels—I'm still not prepared to surrender
"Brighton Beach Memoirs" as a whole. What happens, not
too long after intermission, is that we tend to lose Eugene.
The boy seems to have been retired to the wings, or possibly
to the kitchen in search of oatmeal cookies, and instead of

following the evening's new sorrows through his specially ground
distorting lens, we now see and hear them in their resolutely
ugly ordinariness. We become neighbors who have dropped in
at exactly the wrong moment. (p. 3)

What is troublesome here is not that the recriminations are
serious, though there is some feeling that "serious" and "unpleasant" mean approximately the same thing. The problem
is really structural. There are simply too many donnybrooks
in a row, too many venomous two-scenes back to back, too
many couples determined to get into the act. The fight-card
needs some pruning. Or it needs Eugene whispering his kind
of comment from the sidelines. After all, there ought to be
something funny to be said about one brawl giving birth directly
to another. The play wants its gently comic vision back.

It gets it, before . . . dismissal-time; it gets it a bit sentimentally, but at least shapeliness returns. Meantime, Mr. Simon
has at least twice done what I think he must very much have
wanted to do; touched us. The emotion surfaces in odd places,
not in obvious ones. . . .

My own favorite brief passage comes as brother Stanley, in
disgrace, prepares to leave home. . . .

He is, as he should be, self-absorbed, and we're not really
certain how well he understands his younger brother. Packed
and ready to go, he hesitates for a moment in the doorway of
their room, then murmurs reflectively that he supposes Eugene
will probably turn out to be the writer he wants to be. "If you
ever write a story about me," he says on impulse, "call me
Hank, I've always liked that name Hank." Of course, that
isn't precisely what the moment is saying. It is saying that he
has been more aware of Eugene, and of Eugene's qualities than
we'd supposed. It also says something about himself. Under
another name, he might be better.

You may or may not mind the threat of derailing that overtakes
"Brighton Beach Memoirs" during the hammer-and-tongs ha-
rangues that use up so much of the second act. I assure you
you'll like the youngster who is going to grow up to write
comedy. (p. 13)

Walter Kerr, "Seeing a Comic Mind Emerge," in
The New York Times, *April 3, 1983, pp. 3, 13.*

JOHN SIMON

Brighton Beach Memoirs is Neil Simon's *Long Day's Journey
Into Night*. Simon is the world's richest playwright and he even
owns the Eugene O'Neill Theater, but though you can buy the
name, you cannot buy the genius. Actually, rather than into
one night, the play takes us into two consecutive Wednesday
evenings in 1937 (when Simon was ten rather than, as in the
play, fifteen), but the pseudo-autobiographical hero is actually
called Eugene, and there is an ostensible scraping off of layers
of patina to get at the alleged truth; if no one takes dope, there
are plenty of dopes around, not least the author, who, like all
those comedians wanting to play Hamlet, imagines that he can
write a serious play.

The first problem with *Memoirs* is that it has no intention of
being truthful. . . .

Then why, you ask, the comparison to O'Neill's play? Because
Eugene is a budding playwright with problems (not TB, to be
sure, only puberty and lust for his cousin), there is a serious
money shortage, there is near tragedy in the house across the
street, there is the Depression and the threat of Hitler to Jewish

relatives in Europe, there is Father's losing one of his jobs and getting a minor heart attack, there is everyone's hurting everyone else's feelings and apologizing profusely and making up. What there isn't, though, is honesty. The first act is typical Simon farce cum sentimentality, and the better for it; the second, in which ostensibly grave themes and conflicts are hauled out, is fraught with earnest speechifying, ponderous and platitudinous moralizing, and heartwarming uplift oozing all over the place, with everybody's soul putting on Adler Elevator shoes and ending up closer to heaven. The dramaturgy itself becomes woefully schematic: Every character gets his tête-à-tête with every other character who has taken umbrage, and all ends in sunshine—even for the endangered relatives in Europe.

If all this were presented as farce, it might work. If it were honestly and painfully told, it might work. But Simon, who has also filled the play with those odious clean dirty jokes, wants to have his pain and let everybody eat cake, too. So everyone is funny and noble and ends happily. . . . Simon is a reverse Antaeus: The closer his feet get to touching the ground of reality, the weaker his writing becomes. And, as a final dishonesty, his Jewish family talks and looks as un-Jewish as possible (through the writing, casting, and directing), so that Wasps should not feel excluded, let alone offended. In fact, the Irish family across the way—though drowning in drink and filth—are, we are sanctimoniously informed, very nice people indeed. . . .

Still, the man behind me was convulsed with laughter; if you like commercial theater at its most mercenary, you should love this one. (p. 55)

> *John Simon, "Journeys into Night," in* New York Magazine, *Vol. 16, No. 15, April 11, 1983, pp. 55-8.**

ROBERT K. JOHNSON

Simon's mature theater work combines comedy with moments of poignance and insight. Examples abound. In *The Odd Couple*, Oscar Madison and Felix Ungar, although hilarious to see and listen to, demonstrate how destructive a selfish person can be. *Promises, Promises* dramatizes how Chuck Baxter and Fran Kubelik, who think they can manipulate people at no cost to themselves, learn that others, more shrewd and calculating, manipulate them and make them pay heavily for their proud schemes. The exchanges between Bill and Hannah Warren in *California Suite* reveal how easy it is to misjudge who is the strong person and who is the weak, and to fail to perceive that although two people talk at length about one topic, their views on that topic merely reflect thoughts and feelings rooted in more fundamental aspects of their lives. *Plaza Suite, The Sunshine Boys,* and *Chapter Two* also do a superb job of fusing the comic and the insightful.

Another recurring feature in Simon's plays is the humor itself. It might seem facetious to state that Simon's plays are consistently—at times, dazzlingly—funny. But much too often this primary component of his work is taken for granted. It is not true that all of Simon's hit shows consist of clusters of funny one-liners. Yet even if it were true, it would be no small accomplishment. Precious few people can write any kind of funny lines. . . . In the 1961-1981 period, Simon's success in creating page after page of laugh-provoking dialogue is unmatched by any other playwright's efforts. Indeed, very few playwrights have matched his achievement during any twenty-year period.

Simon admitted that early in his playwriting career he was guilty on occasion of stuffing a one-liner into some character's mouth. Quickly, though, he weeded out such lines from the drafts of his newer plays; and, soon, all the humorous conversation emanated from the plot and characters. If, then, while discussing Simon's work chronologically, one gradually stops quoting funny lines, it is not because they dwindle in number. There are as many funny lines in the conversations between Diana and Sidney Nichols as there are in those between Corie and Paul Bratter in *Barefoot in the Park*. In the best later plays, however, the richness of character delineations and related matters demands that a discussion of these works concentrate on quotations pertaining to character and theme.

Simon does, on the other hand, sometimes have problems with his plays' structure. *Fools,* which gives little attention to characterizations and, instead, focuses on its fairy-tale story, is woefully weak in structure. The plot barely moves forward in the first part of the play; in the remainder, it has far too many twists and turns. *Come Blow Your Horn* is repetitious in construction and too contrived at times. *Barefoot in the Park* dramatizes a tension between Corie and her mother, then suddenly drops the whole matter. Happy endings that are not entirely convincing occur in several plays, including *The Odd Couple, I Ought to Be in Pictures,* and, most clearly of all, *The Gingerbread Lady*. A few plays, however, are exceptionally sound in structure. For example, *Chapter Two* deftly intertwines its complicated major and minor plots. In *California Suite,* the lurking fundamental problem in the relationship between Diana and Sidney Nichols is adroitly set up step by step until it finally declares itself—a declaration causing a major crisis in the Nicholses' marriage. *The Sunshine Boys* has an airtight structure.

With regard to character delineation, Simon has no peers among contemporary comedy playwrights. Other writers have created vivid characters—but not in the sheer abundance Simon has. Even if one leaves aside the captivating broad comedy characters found in such plays as *The Good Doctor, Plaza Suite,* and *California Suite,* plus the liveliest characters in all the musicals, there are still numerous compelling characters, major and minor, in the more realistic comedies. To cite only one play's excellently sketched minor characters, there are the feckless musician Lou Tanner and the homosexual actor Jimmy Perry in *The Gingerbread Lady*. . . . (pp. 139-41)

Another dominant feature of Simon's work is his outlook on life. As is true for all other outstanding writers of comedy, Simon humorously dramatizes his serious basic beliefs. Through his characters, he suggests that the individual should choose to remain within the social network. No Simon hero or heroine makes the ultimate Romantic gesture of thumbing his or her nose at society. . . . Simon's emphasis in [his] early plays on the desirability of working within society remains undiminished in his later works. In *Last of the Red-Hot Lovers,* for instance, Barney Cashman's attempts to break free of society's conventions render him comic, not heroic. In all his plays from *Come Blow Your Horn* to his most recent work, Simon honors the ultimate symbol of the social network: the family unit. (pp. 141-42)

This stress not on the primacy of the individual, but on the primary importance of society has triggered negative reactions in several critics. Some critics, assuming that Simon's "old-fashioned" beliefs constitute no beliefs at all, declare his work flimsy and superficial. Most members of the audience, however, are delighted to find Simon upholding their own beliefs. Simon's point of view, though, does not arise simply out of a desire to pander to the beliefs of the "moral majority." Simon opts for society because he sincerely believes that human beings are frail creatures who will be less vulnerable to attack and more likely to thrive if they seek the nourishment society provides.

By no coincidence, then, two virtues Simon stresses are moderation and fidelity. To function well within society, one must compromise. To compromise, one must be mature enough willingly to embody moderation. Too much ego or self-love, found in Oscar Madison and Felix Ungar, for example, is destructive. . . . Rarely, if ever, do those who pursue sexual infidelity gain happiness. . . .

[And, in] Simon's eyes, divorce is never a victory. (p. 142)

Although the moral beliefs that Simon advocates are "old-fashioned" ones, his view of human experience is not blithely sentimental. The happy endings in his best plays are often only minimally happy. Chuck Baxter and Fran Kubelik finally get their lives on the right track, but they have been deeply scarred in the effort and are more than a little gun-shy emotionally. Equally scarred are the Nicholses and George Schneider and his wife, Jennie. . . .

Simon also acknowledges the complexity of human experience. *Last of the Red-Hot Lovers* shows that guilt feelings can lead to moral conduct that, in turn, brings happiness and a sense of relief. But both *Chapter Two* and *Fools* demonstrate that guilt feelings can be negative, destructive forces. Simon celebrates love and tenderness in *Promises, Promises,* yet in that same play points out that people must be tough in order to defend the love they feel and share. The meetings between Muriel Tate and Jesse Kiplinger in *Plaza Suite* and between the Warrens in *California Suite* portray how a simple course of action can be ladened with a bewildering complexity of conflicting motivations. Furthermore, Simon reveals in play after play how greatly the fear of aging and dying complicates every human being's life.

Simon emphasizes the need for honesty, yet he demonstrates that honesty does not always provide a solution to troubles. Honesty can be more destructive than creative. Karen and Sam Nash's discussion "clears the air" between them, but their frankness renders a formerly difficult marital situation impossible. (p. 143)

Finally, however, Simon does suggest that, if risked, honesty can ultimately prove constructive. Corie and Paul, Diana and Sidney, Jennie and George—many of Simon's couples—engage in bluntly honest exchanges and, as a result, pave the way toward better, stronger relationships. Both Barney Cashman and Faye Medwick feel relieved and legitimately optimistic after they admit to themselves that they are simply not cut out to be "swingers." Willie Clark gains at least a modicum of peace when he accepts the fact he is now an old man.

Walter Kerr has stated, "Whenever a playwright manages to be hilariously funny all night long . . . he is in immediate danger of being condescended to." Because Americans have always tended to underrate writers who make them laugh, Neil Simon's accomplishments have not gained as much serious critical praise as they deserve. His best comedies contain not only a host of funny lines, but numerous memorable characters and an incisively dramatized set of beliefs that are not without merit. Simon is, in fact, one of the finest writers of comedy in American literary history. (p. 144)

Robert K. Johnson, in his Neil Simon, *Twayne Publishers, 1983, 154 p.*

Susan Sontag

1933-

American essayist, critic, novelist, short story writer, editor, screenwriter, and film director.

Sontag is among the most influential contemporary American critics. Her numerous essays concentrate on utilizing a new sensibility in evaluating a work of art. Early in her career, Sontag proposed an end to standard methods of critical analysis that rely on content and various levels of meaning. She asserted that the function of criticism is to show "how it is what it is, even that it is what it is, rather than to show what it means." Sontag is credited with making the works of such writers as Antonin Artaud, Roland Barthes, and Walter Benjamin more accessible to American audiences, and she has also earned the reputation among critics as an advocate of popular culture.

Sontag established her precepts for evaluating art in *Against Interpretation and Other Essays* (1966). In the title essay she contends that critical interpretation "depletes and impoverishes" creative works, arguing that art should be received with the senses—evoking pleasure and excitement—and not the intellect. Included in this volume is the famous essay "Notes on 'Camp,'" in which Sontag defends "camp" as a legitimate art form that is "serious about the frivolous, frivolous about the serious." She also proposed that style is the essence of "camp," asserting that "there exists a good taste of bad taste." Although most critics dubbed her the "Queen of Camp," some acknowledge the essay's importance in introducing avant-garde works into the cultural mainstream. "Trip to Hanoi" (1968) is a journalistic essay that recounts Sontag's visit to North Vietnam. Several critics commended her for not resorting to political rhetoric. Sontag instead concentrates on the personal growth and enlightenment realized through her interaction with the North Vietnamese. *Styles of Radical Will* (1969) contains the essays "The Pornographic Imagination," in which Sontag argues that pornography is a valid literary genre, and "The Aesthetics of Silence," an analysis of the intentionally noncommunicative qualities in works by John Cage, Samuel Beckett, and others. Also included are several pieces on the cinema.

Illness As Metaphor (1978), written after Sontag's own fight with cancer, discusses the ways in which society conceptualizes illness. She draws a parallel between the nineteenth-century tendency to equate tuberculosis with romanticism and the twentieth-century perception of cancer as an isolating, passionless disease. In both cases she contends that such attitudes have hindered scientific research into the causes of the two diseases. *Illness As Metaphor* is regarded as an attempt to remove these obstacles and advance the research and cure of cancer. The essays in *Under the Sign of Saturn* (1981) focus on European art and philosophy. Critics generally agree that the essays on German filmmakers Leni Riefenstahl and Hans-Jurgen Syberberg are the best in this volume.

While Sontag is best known as a critic, she has published two novels, *The Benefactor* (1963) and *Death Kit* (1967), and a collection of short stories, *I, etcetera* (1978). She has also directed and written the screenplays for the films *Duet for Can-*

nibals (1968), *Brother Carl* (1972), and *Promised Lands* (1974), a documentary on the Yom Kippur War of 1973. These works have not received the same serious recognition as Sontag's expository writings, yet the experimental nature of her fiction follows Sontag's conception of art as an immediate and sensuous experience. *A Susan Sontag Reader* (1982) is a selection of previously published works, including excerpts from the two novels.

(See also *CLC*, Vols. 1, 2, 10, 13; *Contemporary Authors*, Vols. 17-20, rev. ed.; and *Dictionary of Literary Biography*, Vol. 2.)

ALICIA OSTRIKER

The chief commodity of Susan Sontag's *Against Interpretation*, according to its author and her reviewers, is a modern sensibility. Stress the modernity here, since she is distinguished less by a decided or passionate point of view . . . than by an eagerness to explore anything new. At times this eagerness lapses deliberately into inarticulateness, as in her celebrated essay on Camp, which will probably be unintelligible in ten years. At its best—for example in the essay on Happenings—it reports immediate emotions unpretentiously and sensitively. But sensitive people are a dime a dozen. The rarer gift Miss Sontag has to offer is brains. The theoretical portions of her book are delightful to read because she can argue so well. Even when she fudges her argument with standby ploys like name-calling, the shifted definition, the straw man, or the historical distortion, she does it with the skill of an expert. Her literary and philosophical references are broad and applied with originality. Her ideas are consistently stimulating, particularly when they do not get in the way of her major theoretical premise—as in the little essay "Piety Without Content," where she uses the analogy of political fellow-traveling to destroy, beautifully, the rosy idea of common-denominator religiousness.

For all that, however, her major premise is that brains are bankrupt. This is explicit in the snide comments about "philistinism" and about the bad effects on culture of "people with minds," in the vague asides about "magic" in art, in the preferences for non-verbal over verbal art, in the insistence that we need more feeling and less thought. It is implicit everywhere in her refusal to carry any line of reasoning through to the end. Finally, it cripples her attempt to develop "case studies for an aesthetic" (her own description of her intention) because an aesthetic is an intellectual thing.

What Miss Sontag wants to encourage, in art and criticism, is respect for sensuous surfaces, for feeling, for form, for style. What she apparently wants to encourage in real life is respect for the unconventional, the amoral, the extreme sensation, be it sensuous gratification or madness. So far so good. Anybody who does Freudian criticism or looks for morals in art, or whose vision is directed only toward what is happy, healthy and prudent, needs this book. But it is not enough to offer a corrective to such people.

Miss Sontag, seems to think it is enough, perhaps because she has despaired of the possibility that artists, critics, or the public can use their minds to create new syntheses of matter and manner, good and evil, health and insanity. She shares, perhaps, in a popular and anti-rationalist superstition according to which intelligence has not only failed to solve the problems of mankind, but is also indirectly responsible for getting us into our contemporary fix with the Gog and Magog of alienation and the bomb. (p. 83)

The sensuous bias of such criticism has severe limitations. It is so preoccupied with what we presumably need that it is ready to throw out a lot of what we can get. It asserts that we don't need "content"; but "content" is precisely what most verbal and much visual art, and even much music, from Buxtehude to Beethoven to the blues, ultimately depends on. Such criticism cautions that some arts are too prone to interpretation; of course they are: so is anything interesting. Because pedants flourish, shall we have no more cakes and ale? Reminding us to remember that *Hamlet* is about Hamlet, Miss Sontag omits the fact that Hamlet is importantly distinguished from Joe Schmoe because he "contains" a pattern of human behavior which is both permanent and significant. Jeering at psychoanalytical, religious, and sociological interpretations of Kafka because they can't all be right, she neglects to observe that they all may be relevant, and that Kafka's genius may lie precisely in his ability to perform a psychoanalytic study *and* a study of bureaucracy *and* a religious manifesto in a single fantastic fable.

Obviously it makes a difference what writers say. It makes a difference what painters say, whether they choose to paint "about" virgins and children, the disasters of war, or the harmonies and cacophonies of colors. Miss Sontag's kind of criticism fails to understand that great artists may want to change our lives by changing our vision. . . . (pp. 83-4)

Another problem of sensuous modern criticism is that it gives minor artists too much credit. Many of the styles and authors Miss Sontag admires, like Surrealism, Pop, Happenings, Genet, Peter Weiss in *Marat/Sade,* can be classified as representing what Coleridge called Secondary Imagination, or Fancy, as opposed to the Primary Imagination. That is, they are works of combination and juxtaposition, not of synthesis. In dripping watches in the desert, in Campbell's soup cans in the Modern Museum, in baby dolls glued to machine parts, in black people playing white people, in "discussions of the deepest issues of contemporary morality and history" used as "decor, props, sensuous material," we see artists having ironic fun, fooling around with things. There is nothing wrong with this, until fooling tries to impose itself on all other possibilities. Miss Sontag declares that "the most interesting works of contemporary art are adventures in sensation, new 'sensory mixes.'" Well, maybe so. In that case, our era resembles the latter half of the 18th century, which Coleridge found unsatisfactory because it contained no first-rate unifying, synthesizing imagination. In retrospect, it seems that most late 18th-century artists were trying to escape from a classical aesthetic that no longer compelled belief, but didn't know where they wanted to get to. Hence the proliferation of sentimental junk about graves and peasants and mountain landscapes; hence also, perhaps, second-rate pornography like *Fanny Hill.* There may be more similarity than meets the eye between 18th-century picturesque, and 20th-century grotesque, adventures in sensation.

In her final essay, "One Culture and the New Sensibility," Miss Sontag claims that this art is experimental in the same sense that science is: cool, rational, etc. But scientific experiment has as its assumption the real existence of facts and laws, and as its object the synthesis of principles or "models" which will resolve old paradoxes, which will incorporate all that is known, which will be simpler and more inclusive than anything thought earlier. So does some art; we are deceived if we sell our birthright to it for the mess of pottage in some new sensuous mix. (pp. 83-4)

    Alicia Ostriker, "Anti-Critic," in Commentary, Vol. 41, No. 5, June, 1966, pp. 83-4.

RICHARD GILMAN

[*The following excerpt is taken from an essay originally published in* The New Republic, *May 3, 1969.*]

That Susan Sontag is philosophically oriented and has something of a metaphysical impulse to her thinking . . . is among the reasons why I think her one of the most interesting and valuable critics we possess, a writer from whom it's continually possible to learn, even when you're most dissatisfied with what she's saying, or perhaps especially at those times. For the past several years she has been the chief voice in America of one main tradition of French criticism, which is one of the reasons, I'm convinced, why she is disliked, where she's disliked, with such ferocity and xenophobic scorn. (p. 30)

When she said in the preface to her first book of essays and reviews [*Against Interpretation*] that "what I have been writing is not criticism at all, strictly speaking, but case studies for an aesthetic, a theory of my own sensibility," the remark was thrown out as an afterthought, a footnote, whereas it ought to be front and center, the motto for everything she has done.

And that would include the journal of her recent visit to North Vietnam, reprinted in this new collection, *Styles of Radical Will.*

The point isn't that there is criticism, neat, familiar, unquestionable as a procedure, and then there is what Miss Sontag does, odd, peripheral although maybe useful; but that what she has been doing, or attempting, is more interesting and more relevant to what is going on than is most traditional criticism. (At least, on a pragmatic test, I don't know of any critic more interesting or more relevant.)

Her sensibility departs from that of the traditional literary critic in that she is very little interested in, or at least in writing about, fiction (except as it enters extreme modes, as in pornography) and seems to care nothing at all about poetry. . . . But she differs, too, from the traditional critic of general culture in that she is deeply involved in aesthetic awareness. We might call her a critic of ideas, except that she has always wished to treat ideas sensuously, aesthetically; or decide that she is a philosopher of cultural forms, except that philosophy for her has always been a drama rather than a method. (pp. 30-1)

The alarm that many people feel at the approach of Susan Sontag, the distaste, resentment and even fury she causes, has, it seems to me, two bases. . . . The cruder one is moral and "humanistic." She has been accused of being inhuman or antihuman for ignoring moral and spiritual elements in art, or rather for sanctioning and encouraging the immoral, pornography or camp, for example, violence or extravagance. To this the only answer is that no material or data or subject or, for that matter, mood in the aesthetic realm has anything to do with being sanctioned or deplored, needs validation or, in short, lies in the moral universe at all. . . . The moral charge against Miss Sontag, which is mainly a charge against the kinds of art she has been interested in, issues from the same morale such charges always do: apprehension in the face of new consciousness.

Beyond this Miss Sontag has marched, aggressively and with her great bristling apparatus of learning . . . , pointing every which way but most dangerously at certain processes of literary erudition itself, into some sacred realms, to the consternation of their guardians. At the least newcomers are expected to observe the rules. And one of the chief rules is that criticism is a province of the dispassionate (and fact-finding) intellect, which it is designed to serve and, so to speak, to fill out.

But Miss Sontag, it seems, would like to fill out the body or at any rate the whole man, to return the intellectual side—especially the hermeneutic side—of aesthetic experience to a subordinate place. When she wrote, as the coda to one of her most famous essays ["Against Interpretation"], that "in place of hermeneutics, we need an erotics of art," she drove many persons nearly wild with misapprehension that what she meant amounted to a new barbarism, a new species of self-indulgence, a relinquishment of the hard-won rationality through which we have steadily mastered art and myth in order to put them into the service of civilized being, of "culture." What she meant, of course, was a new appreciation, a new agreement on mystery, a new delight.

She hasn't always meant it convincingly, it's true, or, to speak more plainly, she hasn't always demonstrated that mystery and delight are what she herself experiences. It is surely a notable fact about Miss Sontag's sensibility—her "subject" and the principle of her shift in critical method—that it so often strikes you cold, even icy. This is the irony, detected by many, of her demand for an erotics of art. But to be caught in an irony of this kind has nothing to do with being inhuman; writers, more than most humans, are situated between what they are and what they hope it's possible to be. Nor is it a matter of any classical inability to "feel," and attempts to discredit her on this ground . . . are obtuse and unjust.

For the problem of her sensibility is also the generating power of its interest and importance for us as she exemplifies and tests and expounds and shapes it into form in her writing. It is precisely classical ability to feel, which, as it works itself out in our shibboleths and humanistic myths, means to feel *the way others have,* to feel certain emotions (in certain ways) that have been sanctified as properly human and necessary, that has come into question. (pp. 33-5)

Susan Sontag has been engaged in trying to plot the course of her new feelings, which is to say her responses as a representative advanced consciousness. . . . In doing this she has indicated all the debilities and irresolutions and compensatory aggressions and contradictions that are inevitable in consciousness in transition. The chief content of that transition now is the challenge to Western literary culture, or rather to the supremacy of literature *as* culture; the growing breakdown of the erstwhile separation between art and audience, or more strictly between art as object for contemplation and as material for reabsorption into total experience; the claim of bodily experience to a place in aesthetics; the more insistent relationship between politics and sensibility. These are Miss Sontag's themes; and she is the victim of their assaults, in their status as realities, upon our preparation, training, inheritance and need for continuity—on *what we were like before*—as much as she is their elucidator and master in awareness.

What we were like before, which is to say what our models were like for the fullest, most exemplary, victoriously sentient civilized beings, was learned, complex, ironic, intellectually armored, central, balanced, full of explanation and the wisdom of the abstract. Miss Sontag is still many of these things, and the discrepancy between them and wanting to be something else, something spontaneous, concrete, sensual, ready for extremes and wise through physicality, is the failure and the fruitfulness of her writing.

To take an important essay from the new volume, "The Pornographic Imagination." In this long, dazzlingly learned, risky piece of advocacy and interrogation, she illustrates the perennial problem of how to argue for the rights of the body and the more dangerous passions without having to rely on the intellect. . . . (pp. 35-6)

One way of dealing with this problem is to write sensually, to evoke rather than rest on analysis, and this is characteristic of the French writers Miss Sontag admires for their writing on the erotic—Bataille is chief among them—although I don't mean to suggest that they are pure lyricists in whom analysis plays no part. But what they can do, as she has so far been unable to, is offer the feeling of the erotic, as actuality and consciousness, in all its ardor, despair, questionableness, contradiction and urgency, instead of merely a learned process of thinking about it.

But Miss Sontag is of course not French, and if this essay suffers from her coldness of temperament and almost complete lack of any lyric impulse, what's in its favor is the fact that lyrical writing about the erotic so rarely in this country is saved by intelligence from being sheer sentiment, romantic asseveration or rhetorical wish-fulfillment. Her piece is full of an extraordinary intelligence, which sets as its tasks first the establishment of the theoretical possibility that pornography may indeed be literature and second that there are certain pornographic works that actually are.

She is rather better on the first task than the second, but she's continually interesting on both. To argue, cleanly and decisively as she does, that the main sophisticated counts against pornography as literature have to do with retrograde and obtuse identifications of fiction with verisimilitude, psychological realism and narrative logic is to say what needs saying—about fiction as well as pornography that uses the form. Here is Miss Sontag with her strong, complex intelligence focused on the new as it has to do with altered conceptions of fiction. She insists, with absolute rightness, that fiction is not to be defined by considerations of character-building, psychological complexity or centrality of theme, so that in its narrowness, obsession, extremity of theme and refusal of ordinary characterization, pornographic writing may still qualify as literature.

She then goes on to discuss a number of what she calls pornographic works, chiefly *The Story of O, The Image* by the pseudonymous Jan de Berg, and Bataille's *The Story of the Eye*. She is very good on them, even if she rates *The Image* much too highly, but the strength is analytic and very little is conveyed of how these erotic writings actually reach and move the imagination or why they should have a place there. And something else very curious emerges. I have been going along with her in calling a whole class of books "pornography," but a distinction should really be made, and Miss Sontag inadvertently provides one.

The books mentioned above and others she cites are distinguished from what we ordinarily call pornography precisely by their relative lack of explicit sexual scenes, certainly by their lack of sexual scenes composed as hermetic and single-minded substitutions for any other kind of experience, and by their correspondingly greater content of writing of an imaginatively freer and more complex kind. It isn't that they are less erotic; if anything, the books she admires have greater erotic power than ordinary pornography, but this is because of their greater literary power.

The result of all this is that they cannot be taken as representative of pornographic writing, which remains, as long as it *is* pornography, bad writing. What Miss Sontag fails to see is that she ends by defending not pornography but only such examples of writing with a sexual theme or even a sexual purpose (she defends, with much justice, the legitimacy of "arousing" through writing) as have shaken loose from the undifferentiated mass of such writing precisely through the greater literary strength and concern of their authors. I think it useful to retain "pornography" as a term (without moral condemnation) to denote sexual writing that fails as literature; that which succeeds doesn't need a defense, except perhaps against the kinds of minds Miss Sontag so admirably takes on in her remarks on the petrifaction of definitions of fiction.

"I have been writing . . . a theory of my own sensibility." With this avowal as justification, I would like to point out that from both the new essay on pornography and Miss Sontag's earlier famous one on Camp there rises an aura of will, or willfulness, a wish that something be true, an unavowed prescriptive desire. There is nothing wrong with this, there is even I suspect something extremely useful in it, but it hasn't been seen. For all the brilliance of these pieces and their true extensions of our awareness, they reveal, as most of her other writing does, how beneath the clean-functioning, superbly armed processes of her thought exists a confused, importunate, scarcely acknowledged desire that culture, the culture she knows so much about, be other than it is in order for her to be other than she is.

When she writes that Camp is "loving" and "tender," the wish she is trying to fulfill is for the sophistication that Camp possesses and denotes to be redeemed from its quality as modern sophistication: hard, snobbish, ugly, ungenerous, a means of establishing superiority over the past and over simplicity. When she writes about pornography without attention to its narrowing and unliberating effects, she reveals how her authentic and justifiable longing for bodily liberation, her longing to lighten her own burden of consciousness, mistakes the statement for the thing. One can say that pornography is always wish-fulfillment (nothing inherently wrong with that), but the important thing about this, in her usage, is that it is not so much a wish for erotic experience as a negative desire for eroticism—as subject and atmosphere—to overcome the imbalance of a heavy, weighted, complex, abstract history, the history of the mind as it has offered itself to us as identical with life itself.

I think Miss Sontag is representative in this, and that her own so impressive qualities of mind make her more representative rather than less. And I also think, after reading *Styles of Radical Will,* that she is moving into areas where the "problem" of her sensibility, its transitional quality and status as an arena where new movements are seen and tested at least partly from old perspectives and where culture is being redirected from contemplation to action, will have even more usefulness than it has had. (pp. 36-9)

While Miss Sontag has never been apolitical, she has admitted that she hasn't been able to find the way for her political passions and awarenesses to enter her work on culture and aesthetics. The account of her trip to North Vietnam last year, "Trip to Hanoi," the major piece in her new book, seems to me to be a sign of a new-found ability to do just that as well as being a remarkable document in its own right.

Miss Sontag went on her journey, as a guest of the North Vietnamese, convinced that "unless I could effect in myself some change of awareness, of consciousness, it would scarcely matter that I'd actually been in Vietnam." At first she found the country and the culture alien, impenetrable, marked by what she regarded as a boring and "fairy-tale" simplicity. Her whole weight of Western complexity and psychological subtlety militated against her understanding and possible affection for the North Vietnamese. How she was able to effect the change in consciousness she knew she had to have, so that she emerged with the sense of different possibilities of life, a potential way out of self-consciousness, guilt, moral ambiguity and the ironic stance that has been the Western intellectuals' chief weapon of both aggression and defense—all this is what the essay is about. And by being about these things, it is more centrally, refulgently and authentically about mind, consciousness, sensibility—and what is new in them—than any of the technical, analytic pieces whose bravura and cold knowledge-ability have gained her her reputation. (pp. 40-1)

Richard Gilman, "Susan Sontag and the Question of the New," in his The Confusion of Realms, *Random House, 1969, pp. 29-41.*

VERNON YOUNG

In that ideal Republic which is invoked by anyone who writes a criticism of life, Susan Sontag would have no status, since her mind is nourished solely on products of decomposition. Her opportunity depends absolutely on there being a condition of latent anarchy to sanction the impudence with which she defines the condition as admirable. . . . Miss Sontag has many of the secondary attributes of a professional revolutionary: an irreparable want of humor, a sweeping disregard of the nuances of history, a hatred of elites over which she does not personally preside, a faculty for translating all data into propaganda—and underneath it all, barely concealed, a private thirst to be devoured by something bigger, more forceful and simpler than herself: in her case, an Apocalypse which would nullify forever her compulsive quarrel with the Word.

From first to last, in [*Styles of Radical Will*], she is preoccupied with the familiar sequence of modern agony: the problematic nature of art; the burden of language and the urge to "destroy" it; the elimination of the subject, the object, the image; silence and "self-transcendence" as the ultimate other-worldly gesture of the artist. Every essay is a *ruse de guerre*, an ordering of her little circle of friends, a strenuously argued attempt to hold an untenable position. Always one senses that the proposition going forward is what Freud called a memory screen: the real battle is going on somewhere else and the arrangements she has chosen are provisional, designed to consolidate her foothold of the hour. . . . (p. 513)

[Sontag] has no passion, only resentment, which may well be a major source of her anxiety. Her convictions have been inhibited by too many academic reservations, by the milieux in which she has, I gather, been conditioned (Southern California and the Parisian Left), by the frigidity of her sympathies (her mind seems to cherish no content of affection or rooted memory) and by the temptations of Madison Avenue. (It is hard to maintain a nostalgia for the abyss or to remain a sleeping Trotskyite when you're *chic*-photographed by *Vogue*!). Her typical mode of discourse is neither altruistic nor inflamed; solipsistic, rather. Her aesthetic principles are up-to-date and bleak—like Swedish Modern. . . . Her repeated effort to impose herself as an apostle of the multiple point of view scarcely attains the stature of a deception, for she is rarely able to pay attention to an alternative point of view of any subject she takes up. Her preferences and her method are alike *exclusive;* her strategy is that of the post-graduate seminar: from the matter at hand eliminate all normative, "moral" considerations and concentrate on its linguistic and structural components. (p. 514)

"Trip to Hanoi" chronicles the fall of valor. Her subject: not What is Happening in Vietnam but What is Happening in Susan Sontag. No blinding conversion, evidently; on the other hand, few amendments to her obtuse but strained partisanship: her visit is an extended exercise in ideological temperature-taking. She is constantly dismayed, like a sophomore, at the vacillations of her spirit under fire. Disoriented by harrowing transitions in space and time, she is understandably confused by almost everything. . . . (p. 518)

Understandably confused. But not sufficiently to enlarge her rudimentary political doctrine or to dispense with the simplistic Commy slogans she finds herself accepting in lieu of any more plausible; insufficiently to restrain herself from quoting those God-awful gems of Ho Chi Minh, such as "There are no bad people; there are only bad governments." Not the least unbelievable feature of her account is that nowhere does she in so many substantial words recognize that *the North Vietnamese were fighting the South Vietnamese*. There was only *North* Vietnam, a peace-loving but embattled little country fighting off an imperialist aggressor. She swallowed whole the verdict

of that rigged Stockholm tribunal and the official line of Ho Chi Minh which every uninformed liberal seems to have accepted since 1965. What took place in 1954 she never broaches. I can understand why, since this *is* a complex question; all the same, when legality, moral outrage and U.S. bombing tactics have been enlisted to condemn the duration of the war, it is pertinent to remember that it was Ho Chi Minh who chose to resume hostilities in order to impose Communism on the South and that the South pleaded for American assistance. . . . [In] her eye (she couldn't have used both) the North Vietnamese are altogether innocent, noble and altruistic (those she met may have been), doing no more than defend their homeland against a colossus seeking to crush them (for no reason except Imperialism with which she never comes to grips) while hopefully preparing the *peaceful reconciliation* of the peninsula. Never a hint of the 50,000 village headmen murdered in the Collective preparation of 1954; of prostitutes who had their breasts cut off for fraternizing with the French; of 1200 Laotian tribesmen, women and children among them, battered to death with clubs and guns (this is a mere incident in the history of Viet Cong atrocities).

Her gullibility is often comical. I resist—against my susceptibility to the exotic anecdote—her straight-faced retailing of the restoration of North Vietnamese prostitutes to a condition of primal innocence. "Fairy tales were read to them; they were taught children's games and sent out to play." There is also room for reasonable doubt of her amazed, and I don't think very approving, impression that men and women worked, fought and slept together "without raising any issue of sexual temptation." How does she *know* there wasn't, for certain? I'm skeptical because her inference is not verified by Robert Shaplen's amusing observation on the thousands of cadre-women utilized by the Viet Cong in their Underground Village Committees throughout South Vietnam. "While women are hard workers, the Communists acknowledge that 'they are credulous and cannot resist love'; they need special indoctrination on revolutionary concepts toward sex relations.'" Be that as it may, Little Miss Muffet was otherwise seriously upset by the spider of empiricism which, in North Vietnam, sat down beside her. At one perilous moment, she abandons herself completely to the duplicity and banality of language, with no semantic provision for escape.

> If some of what I've written evokes the very cliché of the Western left-wing intellectual idealizing an agrarian revolution that I was so set on not being, I must reply that a cliché is a cliché, truth is truth, and direct experience is—well—something one repudiates at one's peril.

A temporary convulsion. If the brunt of reality had intruded as painfully as she would have us believe, then, upon returning to the West (i.e. Sweden, the ultimate boneyard towards which she has long been travelling) she would have torn up the scenario of that film [*Duet for Cannibals*] she had prepared as being, from the point of view of life, an affront to the spirit of authentic suffering. Faced with acknowledging the irreconcilable or maintaining her previous profile, she chose the profile. (pp. 518-20)

Vernon Young, "Socialist Camp: A Style of Radical Wistfulness," in The Hudson Review, *Vol. XXII, No. 3, Autumn, 1969, pp. 513-20.*

WILLIAM PHILLIPS

More than any other writer today, Susan Sontag has suffered from bad criticism and good publicity. If she could be rescued from all her culture-hungry interpreters, it might be possible to find the writer who has been made into a symbol. This is no longer easy because a popular conception of her has been rigged before a natural one could develop—like a premature legend. . . . The standard picture now in circulation is that of the up-to-date radical, a stand-in for everything advanced, extreme and outrageous, for artistic revolt, political disaffection, perversity and that peculiar combination of moral responsibility and moral irresponsibility associated with revolutionary movements—a fusion of Che and Genet. Middle-aged liberals are shocked by her politics and her aesthetics, and loudmouthed moral conservationsists have been accusing her of trying to undermine the good old sexual establishment. On the other hand, a recent adulatory review endowed her with the kind of subversive wisdom only a great revolutionary prophet could have. And then there is the tintype of the smart rebel promoted a few years ago by the fashionable magazines and the commercial media with their cultural thermometers looking for the hottest things going in intellectual life. Naturally, they have struck gold in the Camp and the Hanoi pieces, and have ignored the rest of her writing. (p. 388)

[Since] she is taken as a spokesman for The New, she is thought of as someone to take a stand for or against. Hence, as with so many of the younger writers, the reactions to her have fallen into the stereotypes of polarization. But because she is so articulate and takes all questions as her theoretical province, because her writing has political as well as literary implications, the polarization is both sharper and more distorting. (p. 389)

Susan Sontag is both an exponent and a victim of the new polarization: an exponent in that she doesn't go in for modulation and adjustment, a victim because her concern with speculative and literary problems often falls outside the prevailing left-right fashions. Hence she is not radical enough for the footloose generation and the new crop of militants who think with their feet, and she is too wild for those who get scared when they discover that the new movements do not look like the old ones. She is particularly frightening to those who do not like either their art or their politics to be open, fluid, uncertain, unbridled and youthful. She is too much a child of her time and too intelligent to accommodate to the placid thinking of an earlier period, yet she is too much addicted to theorizing and too much aware of complexities to be satisfied with a purely activist politics and aesthetics. All Susan Sontag's writing has these two sides: a skeptical mind steeped in the unsolved problems that make up the history of thought and a strong, almost willed, feeling for change and discovery, and for new ideas that are attractive because they cannot be insured by history. (p. 390)

The three best and most typical pieces [in *Styles of Radical Will*], on Pornography, on Silence and on Vietnam, are essentially reexaminations of accepted ideas about art and politics. In all three—as in the other essays too—the point of view from which the accepted rules and definitions are revised is the malleable sense of literature and society that shapes writing and thinking today. But the language is the accepted language of criticism; and the assumption throughout is that the way to understand the current rejections of the past is through the continuities of criticism, and history. This has been the traditional role of criticism. And if at times her tone is apocalyptic and oracular, there are precedents in the essays of Ortega y Gasset, and the manifestos of the Futurists and the Surrealists.

Yet it is this self-assured and condensed style that offends most academic critics, this mode of assertion and speculation that

disdains an orderly argument, that repeats old ideas with the same verve with which it explores new ones, that bypasses contemporary American criticism as though it didn't exist. Hence some of her criticism is thought to be homemade and half-baked by academicians brought up to be orderly. My own feeling, however, is that while rigorous analysis will reveal many such failings, it doesn't do justice to one of the few bold and original minds to be found among the younger critics. And anyway, the so-called order of most academic criticism comes from playing it safe. The usual run of criticism is devoted to the application and refinement of some accepted views of literature and society. . . . Susan Sontag's shortcomings, on the contrary, are usually of her own making. Thus it can be said that the essay on Silence never really overcomes the ambiguities of the term, and it confuses the deflation of the human claims of art talked about by Ortega and exemplified in earlier abstract and experimental painting and writing with the deflation of art itself, in pop, rock, ephemeral theater and movies that write off the medium. Nevertheless, it is an unusually sophisticated exploration of the theoretical implications of contemporary styles. Similarly, her discussion of pornography, though it doesn't sufficiently explain the difference between potboilers and literature, takes us out of the cozy limits that have kept literature safe for academic criticism. Her idea of a "pornographic imagination" goes beyond the liberal tolerance of a subject; it legitimizes a repressed faculty.

Actually, some of the implications of Susan Sontag's argument are more far-reaching than the flamboyant views with which she is associated. Despite the fact that she is an elitist, she suggests a way out of the predicament of elitism. For in pressing for the liberation of the arts from their history, Susan Sontag opens them up to popular exploitation, thus breaking with the elitist tradition which assumed serious art to be alienated from middle-class society and hence from the political and commercial manipulations of the mass mind. But it is also a break with the kind of adaptation to popular taste in the last few decades that made literature so conventional in form and in subject. The effect is to rescue the experimental tradition from its loss of power and the exhaustion of its subject, from its unbearable isolation as it struggled to remain both pure and advanced. In a sense, this is a formal solution to a social problem, the problem of the social role of art and its relation to an audience, for the loosening of style has made it possible to be at the same time popular and unconventional. . . . [One] of the striking things in Susan Sontag's essays is her recognition that the last few decades have been a kind of interlude during which avant-garde writing lost its elan, while most academic criticism went into the business of educating readers or talking vaguely about the relation of literature to society. This is why most of Miss Sontag's critical references are to an earlier period and to the French who are often saved from banality by their aloofness from reality.

The essay on Silence is a good example of Susan Sontag's method. The idea of silence actually is used as a metaphor for the opposite of talkiness in art, talkiness being too full of subject matter, too directly aimed at an audience, too bustly in its language, too neatly constructed—all suggesting a closed, stale view of existence. Art that babbles thinks of itself as finished, with an audience out there, an inert, voyeuristic mass. Only a silent medium can properly engage an audience, because it is not performing but completing itself. . . . Throughout all her essays, she attacks the idea of the separation of form and content as the main source of the illegitimate moral and social demands on art, particularly since the dichotomy, she says, leads to the primacy of content. This is not exactly a new idea for academic criticism, though her insistence that despite all disclaimers the separation of theme from form is rooted in our cultural habits goes beyond the usual analysis. Nor is she able to solve the problem, which, I suspect, is not soluble today because the terms in which it is put preclude a solution. But the most suggestive approaches have been taken by younger critics like Susan Sontag and Richard Poirier who argue that style is the shape and meaning of the "content"; and that an examination of the style is an examination of the "subject." . . . The trouble with this view is that so long as we are locked into the old language and the old categories it leads less gifted critics to exalt any kind of formal innovation and to downgrade thematic innovation. But, then, the critics who ride a new approach always run it into the ground.

Miss Sontag has also been taken down for not displaying in her own work the abandon and playfulness her aesthetic calls for. There is, of course, a quality of intense dedication in her writing, suggesting a generational gap between her intelligence and her sensibility. And sometimes there is an elevation of tone which endows "art" with the very sanctity she is constantly questioning. Nor is she a witty writer. But the play of her mind is to be found in her speculative sensibility, expressed more in the texture of her thinking than in her writing.

Another familiar charge is that Miss Sontag's aesthetic comes down to a celebration of novelty. Usually, this indictment takes the crudest form and is proved by ignoring what she actually has said. Whatever basis there is for the accusation is to be found in her observation that contemporary art is less concerned with the quality of a finished work than with the process and the idea of making it. Nor does she dissociate herself from this attitude; on the contrary, she regards it as basic to the entire modern tradition. She points out, correctly, I think, the sources in such figures as Joyce, Picasso and Beckett of the tendency today to break down the formal structures of art through irony, self-parody and the free play of the medium that calls into question its very existence. This does not mean the end of critical judgment, which is what Susan Sontag is accused of by critics with a large stake in the past. All that can be said is that she has failed to reconcile the new deflation of art with the old merit system. But Miss Sontag can't be held responsible for a dilemma all modern criticism has failed to resolve: the dilemma of how to judge—or relate—new works that defy the old criteria. (pp. 391-94)

The collection also includes Susan Sontag's long essay on her trip to Hanoi and a short reply to a political questionnaire in *PR*. So far as I can recall they are her first excursions into politics, and though both are spirited and sophisticated they lack the depth and the daring of the best of her criticism, not the daring to oppose the system, but to question *all* assumptions. (p. 395)

The tortured honesty and clarity of Susan Sontag's analysis is quite impressive, and I am scarcely doing justice in this quick summary to the awareness that makes her self-examination an important document of radical thought. But I am more concerned at the moment with what I think is its exemplification of the dilemma of the Left. What I mean is that Susan Sontag's discussion of the aims of the North Vietnamese and the role of the United States has great moral and emotional force but fails to put them in any new or large perspective. It reduces the combat to the good guys vs. the bad guys. And this is one of the reasons why Miss Sontag has trouble squaring all the complexities of thought and social vision that have come

out of the West, including its radical ideas, with the villainy of the Americans. Obviously, the policies of the United States make no sense morally, politically, militarily, not even in its own terms, in terms, that is, of "anti-communism" or the "national interest." But it should be clear by now that opposition to the war—or to America—is scarcely enough on which to build new socialist policies or theories. Nor is it any reason to romanticize all revolutionary or militant movements, or to fail to distinguish, say, between the advanced consciousness of the revolutionary Czechs and the tragic limitations of the North Vietnamese, who, after all, were forced to support the Russian invasion of Czechoslovakia. My own feeling is that the brightest revolutionary hopes have been sustained by the Czechs, who brought to socialism a glimpse of its human possibilities. And I suspect it is an awareness of these distinctions, not the intellectual baggage of the West, that kept Susan Sontag from identifying with the Vietnamese, despite all her good will.

But whether or not one agrees with her analysis, her speculations are so wide-ranging that one is led to think about many of the questions occupying the Left. (pp. 395-96)

And if there are no answers to many of [the questions raised by Susan Sontag's new book], it might be because this is a time not for rigor and caution in politics and criticism but for boldness in disgarding stale ideas and trying out untested ones. This, it seems to me, is one of her main achievements. Miss Sontag has given some shape and will to a new sensibility in art and politics, but, appropriately, without systems or programs. Hence she has been able to speculate about many of the contradictions facing those who are both aware of the past and open to new literary and political experience. Isn't this enough?—even if she can't satisfy her conservative critics or keep up with the latest styles in radicalism. (p. 400)

> *William Phillips, "Radical Styles," in* Partisan Review, *Vol. XXXVI, No. 3, 1969, pp. 388-400.*

WALTER KENDRICK

[*Under the Sign of Saturn*] contains seven examples of the form in which Sontag first made her popular reputation and in which she still does her best work—the supple, graceful genre that used to be called the occasional essay. The pieces reprinted here were published at odd intervals between 1972 and 1980; two are brief personal memoirs (of Paul Goodman and Roland Barthes), two are mainly concerned with film (Leni Riefenstahl and Hans-Jurgen Syberberg), and the remaining three (on Antonin Artaud, Walter Benjamin, and Elias Canetti) belong to a venerable subgenre that the 19th century excelled in but the 20th has neglected, the "literary portrait."

For much of the past decade, Sontag worked in other forms: short fiction (*I, etcetera*), and full-length nonfiction (*On Photography* and *Illness as Metaphor*). She also directed a film (*Promised Lands*). . . .

I have . . . [followed Sontag's] criticism with interest and respect, and I think I do her no injustice by saying that in *Under the Sign of Saturn* she returns to her *metier*, in which it's a quite sufficient accomplishment to have, as she does, no living American equal.

It may be that, by defining her as primarily an essayist, I'm exercising what she calls in her memoir of Paul Goodman the "terrible, mean American resentment toward someone who tries to do a lot of things." I'm not sure that the resentment exists, or that Goodman suffered from it; but Sontag's remark, true or not, illustrates the intriguing doubleness of her critical writings, a doubleness surely missing from her "creative" work. The remark applies to Goodman, but any reader familiar with Sontag knows that it applies to her, too. So it's an intersection, a double illumination. Indeed, the doubleness may be triple, since the intersection of Goodman and Sontag casts light on "America," which Sontag has been characterizing, piece by ambivalent piece, since her career began.

This multiplicity of response is aided by the fact that *Under the Sign of Saturn* pretends to no overriding unity of form. . . .

The unity of *Under the Sign of Saturn* is not formal. It derives only from the "modernity" of its subjects and what Sontag would call the "sensibility" of its author. These two terms tend steadily toward identity, since as the foremost diagnostician (or pathologist) of our modernity, Sontag has defined our idea of the modern by what she has written about it. Yet doubleness persists. Deeply involved in modernity, she still stands outside it, bringing to bear on its writhings a set of standards so extremely old-fashioned that they look radically new. She sees modernity, as it were, from behind, judging it always in terms of the 19th century, off which, even now, it persistently and helplessly rebounds.

That Sontag's distinctively modern sensibility should also be firmly Victorian isn't quite the paradox it seems. The desperate search for new forms, new styles, and new subjects her essays have chronicled gets its impetus and its desperation from the modern sense that the old forms are glutted, old styles worn blunt from overuse, old subjects drained and dead. It was the 19th century that despoiled all these things, and a principal constituent of what she calls "the modernist agony" has continued to be the maddening awareness that, though the 19th century invented the terms by which we still understand it, the 20th must always be taking the 19th into account. Sontag's stalwart Victorianism is probably the most modern thing about her.

She maintains in these essays, as she has always done, a chaste decorum of style. Artaud may babble of semen and shit, but Sontag, riding high above such mean specifications, speaks rather of his "disavowal of all forms of mediation." This has been her consistent tactic in dealing with the deliberate shock effects of modernism—the critic is never shocked, or if she was, she's fully recovered by the time she writes her essay. Those essays never ape their subjects. Instead the subjects get absorbed into the smooth, steady flow of a style that deserves to be called classical. . . .

This distinction, or discrepancy, between Sontag's style and subjects suggests another old-fashioned feature of her criticism—its confident sense of the function, even the duty, of the critic in relation to both the artist and the general public. Artists have long been thought of as the antennae of their societies, but insects can give but a poor account of what they do; and the public was and is a vulgar herd. The professional critic, as the 19th century knew him, belonged to neither the artistic nor the popular camp, though he had access to both. His proper place was between and beyond them, explaining each to the other while placing artist and audience alike in the larger context of "culture."

This has always been Sontag's critical project. She has been for two decades the foremost interpreter of the European avant-garde to American readers. . . . She continues that project in *Under the Sign of Saturn,* turning her attention now toward

Germany, with essays on Riefenstahl, Benjamin, and Canetti. . . . (p. 44)

In her devastating debunking of Leni Riefenstahl (part one of "Fascinating Fascism"), Sontag demonstrates how, from Riefenstahl's earliest work as an actress in 1920s silents to her posh picture-book *The Last of the Nuba* (1974), she has adhered without deviation to the code of what Sontag calls "fascist aesthetics." Its manifestations have been various and might easily be thought to mark a course of creative growth: cloudy-headed "Alpinism" in the '20s; glorification of physical splendor in her two famous "documentaries" of the '30s, *Triumph of the Will* and *Olympia;* melancholy adulation of a dying African tribe in the '70s.

Since the end of the war, Riefenstahl and her apologists have been fashioning for her the image of a lifelong searcher after beauty who believed for a while, mistakenly and forgivably, that the Third Reich embodied what she sought. But Sontag corrects the record: Nazism was not a detour in Riefenstahl's artistic journey; she always had been, and still is, thoroughly in harmony with its values. Sontag adduces plenty of documentary evidence to show that Riefenstahl worked hand-in-hand with Hitler and his henchmen. . . . Even more telling is Sontag's classic exposition of the absolute consistency in Riefenstahl's work from first to last. Riefenstahl never grew, never changed; she was aesthetically fascist in 1926, and she is so now.

Riefenstahl's campaign to purify her image by rewriting history would be reason enough to debunk her. Even more outrageous for Sontag, however, is Riefenstahl's reiterated claim that in her best-known film, *Triumph of the Will,* "Everything is genuine. It is *history—pure history.*" This, of course, is nonsense—dangerous nonsense. The 1934 Nuremberg rally that Riefenstahl's film records was deliberately designed to be filmed. It was not an innocent historical event at which a beauty-seeking filmmaker happened to be present; it was reality planned as an image, falsified by the knowledge that future generations would take the image for reality. As Sontag writes, "the document (the image) not only is the record of reality but is one reason for which the reality has been constructed, and must eventually supersede it."

Here the case of Leni Riefenstahl, small enough in its own right, intersects one of Sontag's continuing concerns. *On Photography* and *Illness as Metaphor* express this concern most vehemently, but it is present to some degree in all her work—the nervous worry that, in modern culture at large, the real thing and its image are getting progressively more involved, and confused, with each other. The threat of photography and metaphorized cancer is the same as that of *Triumph of the Will* unwisely viewed: The image, feeding back on the real, pollutes it, so that reality, even in the making, turns self-conscious, distanced, and false.

The antidote to this modern poison is exemplified by another German subject treated in *Under the Sign of Saturn,* Hans-Jurgen Syberberg's *Hitler, a Film from Germany.* . . . The best thing about Syberberg's film, for Sontag, is that it presents images as images, hoodwinking neither itself nor its audience by blurring the line between the imaged and the real. Its scene is a stage that looks like one, its actors are clearly actors, and its Hitler is a doll. Syberberg has no truck with "realism" (his and Sontag's 19th-century *bete noire*); he calls his art "a continuation of reality by other means," and this for Sontag is just what all art should be.

When she feels free to track the strategies of images, Sontag is unfailingly brilliant. But when she gets anxious about reality, she gets muddled. *On Photography, Illness as Metaphor,* and to a less severe degree "Fascinating Fascism," shipwreck on the paradox that reality for Sontag must be full, immediate, alive—innocent in its spontaneity and in need of no defense—while at the same time images, those pale copies of the real, are capable of draining it, dulling it, and forcing it to call in defenders. She has never come close to resolving this paradox, and one sometimes gets the feeling that she simply doesn't understand it. But so long as she sticks to what she does best, the interpretation of cultural surfaces, and steers clear of the murky metaphysical depths, perhaps she doesn't need to understand what lurks beneath.

The interpreter of one culture to another can belong wholeheartedly to neither, and it has been a mingled release and burden for Sontag that, though she's emphatically American, her critical project has led her to take up a position between Europe and America from which she can see both cultures whole. The anguish of this position was at its most acute in the late '60s, when, in her famous "Trip to Hanoi," she tried to think of herself as a "citizen of the American empire," and complicatedly failed. In the post-imperial world of *Under the Sign of Saturn,* her transcultural isolation reflects itself mostly in a resigned but slightly bitter contempt for the American madhouse, a confirmed elitism that's thoroughly justified but must be rather lonely.

From the start, Sontag was an elitist, writing about the enthusiasms of her own clique in the correct expectation that what her friends had already embraced the general public would eventually latch onto. The interesting interplay of elite and mass culture was the fruitful source of such essays as the famous "Notes on Camp" (1964) and "The Pornographic Imagination" (1967). But in the '70s her elitism turned a bit sour—lending to *On Photography,* for example, the ungraceful, monitory tone of one who has seen the awful truth while the rest of us stumble in the dark. Elitism is stronger than ever in *Under the Sign of Saturn*—but it is also calmer and even somewhat academic, as if Sontag had given up playing the harbinger of things to come and were content to be the preserver of things past.

At one point, elitism turns explicit. "The hard truth is," she writes in "Fascinating Fascism," "that what may be acceptable in elite culture may not be acceptable in mass culture, that tastes which pose only innocuous ethical issues as the property of a minority become corrupting when they become more established. Taste is context, and the context has changed." Overlooking the platitude in the last sentence—Sontag's fondness for platitudinous aphorisms remains as strong as ever—the worst thing about this statement is not that it's true (it very likely is), but that it suggests Sontag's retreat from a problem she once attacked with an urgency and energy and that produced some of her finest writing. (pp. 45-6)

"Approaching Artaud" is a brilliant exercise in the venerable critical function of making an off-putting writer palatable, and it's also the finest example we've had in decades of what I called at the start of this review the "literary portrait." . . . "Approaching Artaud" is Sontag's most ambitious effort in this form, but in retrospect one sees that she's had an affinity for it all along.

The greatest advantage to the literary portrait is that, neither purely critical nor purely creative, it allows its writer to comment on another writer's work while producing at the same time art of his or her own. It therefore has the power of bridging the tiresome old gap between the creative and the critical, between writing about "life" and writing about other writing. All the great 19th century literary portraitists suffered from some version of this malaise . . . and in the 20th century the gap has come to seem unbridgeable, splitting writers off into discrete parties of book reviewers, academic critics, and artists who drive themselves mad trying to be constantly "creative."

Sontag, too, one assumes, has worried about the split between criticism and creation, and the disproportionate success of her own two kinds of writing has no doubt afflicted her with the well-known critic's guilt for inhabiting a cave yet darker than Plato's, making images of images instead of images of life. Ever since her essays in the early '60s, however, . . . Sontag has been at her best when situating herself not only between cultures and between classes, but also between genres, reflecting on the ambiguous relation of an artist's life to his work, of that work to its audience, and of the critic to both and to himself. These reflections are, in the fullest sense of both terms, artistic and critical at once.

It might seem perverse to find Sontag's roots in the 19th century when she has so clearly been influenced by all the fashionable forces of the 20th. If one listened to her on this matter, one might see her primary precursor in Walter Benjamin. . . . Or one might choose Michel Foucault, whose unacknowledged, largely mishandled influence is particularly visible in *Illness as Metaphor.* Or Roland Barthes, to whom she remains, as she says in her remembrance of him, "toujours fidèle."

But these European influences are red herrings, excrescences on a body of work that belongs squarely in the mainstream of the Anglo-American tradition of the genteel essay. Note how often "philistinism," both the word and the concept, appears in Sontag's essays from early to late, and you'll see Matthew Arnold everywhere in her. Consider how enrichingly ambivalent her mingling of cultures has been, how her double perspective on America and Europe has informed her best writing, and you'll recognize the ghost of Henry James. Her weaknesses, too, are part of this tradition—her inability to sustain an extended argument, her frequent sacrifice of sense to euphony of phrase, her snobbery—but her strengths from the same source far outweigh them. *Under the Sign of Saturn* confirms that Susan Sontag is, without a doubt, our greatest living Victorian writer. (p. 46)

Walter Kendrick, "Eminent Victorian," *in* The Village Voice, *Vol. XXV, No. 42, October 15-21, 1980, pp. 44-6.*

FRANK KERMODE

Susan Sontag is a good deal more than a mere explainer. Her strong, idiosyncratic sense of the contours of her own culture makes her sensitive to the cultural difference of the alien sage. She may think veneration an appropriate response to some subjects, but not, usually, at the expense of her own judgment. It is therefore not surprising that in this collection of essays [*Under the Sign of Saturn*], nearly all of which are about alien sages, there are some that one could confidently propose as models of what such introductory studies ought to be, though there are others in which the cult corrupts the exposition, and we are asked to wonder at the Hercules under discussion rather than to understand his labors.

The long essay on Artaud seems to me the finest in this collection. It was written as an introduction to a selection of Artaud's works, and since it isn't difficult to imagine a perfectly satisfactory, workmanlike piece doing just that job, one has a measure of the much greater achievement of Sontag; fully engaged, urgent, bold, she strives to hand over an image of Artaud as a whole—a whole conceived by her and not assembled from scraps of prevailing wisdom on the subject. Her Gnostic Artaud may not be yours, but he is credible, and belongs to a credible history of ideas. . . .

The characteristic strength of this piece lies in the author's awareness that to explain Artaud (or any other hero) is, in part, to domesticate him, to make him useful, to make it possible for his work to be understood as other literature is understood; while at the same time she knows that this kind of writing . . . cannot, without betrayal, be subjected to the ordinary forms of exposition. And it is precisely this exasperated sense of the near impossibility of the project that causes some expository defects—overheated language, an occasional uncertainty in the progress of the argument—that are more in evidence in other, less majestically conceived, essays, when there seems less reason, the subject being less extreme, for resort to rhetorical extremes.

Artaud is "modern literature's most didactic and most uncompromising hero of self-exacerbation"—Sontag often sounds like that, even when the occasion is less pressing. It is the style of hero worship, but also of the need to coerce the reader into hero worship. It tries to satisfy the need to account, to one's own intellectual satisfaction, for the greatness of the subject, but it also tries to inflame a possibly ignorant, possibly skeptical readership with the same enthusiasm. By having opinions of her own, and letting them show (on movies, on political anarchism) this writer mostly keeps her balance. But she does have difficulty assessing her audience. . . .

The other heroes expounded in this book are Paul Goodman, Walter Benjamin, Hans-Jürgen Syberberg, Roland Barthes, and Elias Canetti. (There is only one villain, Leni Riefenstahl.) The Goodman piece is an obituary notice. . . . Neatly turned, and a little self-regarding, the piece dwells on the shyness that muted the author's personal relations with Goodman; goes on to express devotion; complains that other obituarists had wrongly dismissed Goodman as a maverick, a writer who spread himself too thin. It praises a distinctive voice, a distinctive courage. Perhaps because it was written for an audience that might be expected to know Goodman's work already, it is unspecific; it focuses on a hero (and on hero worship) rather than on the hero's labors.

Much the same might be said of the longer piece on the death of Barthes, though she knew Barthes better, less shyly, and catches the personality in a way that is at once expert and endearing. Yet again, however, the man seems more important to her than his books. It is a familiar modern paradox that the Death of the Author, so powerfully demanded by theory, seems slow to occur in practice; Barthes, who had seemed alarmingly rigorous in his adherence to the new Inhumanism, let it be seen more and more clearly that he was in many respects an old-fashioned *littérateur* and extremely charming to boot.

Sontag, very much alive to the charm, wants to correct any wrong impressions we might have about this hero. When he first became well known outside France it was as a polemicist and a formidable one. . . . But Sontag is right to say that his personality is not so much polemical as celebratory—though

to call him a "taxonomist of jubilation" may be rather more resonant than accurate. (p. 42)

The peculiar heroism of Walter Benjamin proves more resistant than Barthes's, and there is a special misfortune in the blurb writer's singling out Benjamin as, of all her subjects, the one Sontag herself most closely resembles. She does have some things in common with him—curiosity, an openness to oddly angled pieces of information, a willingness to pursue a notion wherever it goes, to find out if it will eventually pay off. And perhaps, like Benjamin, she has the advantage of loosely adhering to a guiding faith or set of principles. But of the penetration and accuracy of Benjamin's notations on specific texts, his power suddenly to transform with his intelligence a paragraph of Kafka, Proust, Goethe, Baudelaire, she has little (nobody has much). I think she may exaggerate the relative value, among Benjamin's works, of the book on the Baroque *Trauerspiel*, seduced by its strangeness and its parody of erudition; but I am not sure about this—the thoughtful accuracy of her caption for Benjamin's style ("freeze-frame Baroque") is a warning that one might lose the argument.

Benjamin's version of the saturnine temperament is the origin of the title of this book; he didn't know all that is now known about Renaissance and Baroque theories of melancholia and its creative aspects, but in his eccentric way he devised variants of them, and Sontag reasonably enough thinks of all her heroes as under the same sign: "Melencolia I" broods over every desk, all those strange but very concrete objects held in stillness by the saturnine glare. . . .

Elias Canetti, though a lesser figure than Benjamin, has something of the same appeal to Sontag. Another Middle European Jew, only a little younger than Benjamin, he is also celebrated as an exotic, a polymath who would like to live forever in order to become wise and good, in order also sometimes to pause, to breathe. Canetti is restless and misogynistic, but Sontag will overlook these defects, and, though restless herself, ends her book with an exhortation to "talented admirers" (including, presumably, herself) to "give themselves permission to breathe . . . to go beyond avidity," and so "identify with something beyond achievement, beyond the gathering of power." But Sontag uses the word "avidity" with noticeable frequency, usually applying it with admiration to her heroes; and the renunciation of avidity, the ceasing to admire it in others whom one desires to emulate, is, given the cultural role she has assumed, all too difficult.

The strength of Sontag's own personality—her own avidity for ideas and detail—is demonstrated in the virtuoso essay on Syberberg's *Hitler, a Film*. This movie . . . is enormously long, but her avidity is equal to the absorption of what must be its multitudinous detail. Moreover, she gives a convincing account of its precursors in film, photography, and music, especially Wagner. Syberberg appeals to Sontag's Romantic view of art: "a truly great work must seem to break with an old order" and "extend the reach of art," she claims; and she finds in the film a strong apocalyptic strain. . . . Being a work of genius, Sontag would argue, *Hitler, a Film* demands from us *fealty*.

An interesting expression, which suggests the chivalric quality of the author's dedication to the idea of greatness. A little halting, a little hectic in its exposition, this essay is nevertheless of more importance than the one that deftly puts down Leni Riefenstahl and does a good Barthesian job on the Nazi iconography of sado-masochism. It is under the stress of excitement, the solemnities of affirmed fealty, that occasional clumsinesses occur, almost as signs of homage, indices of an avid deference. But the cooler reader must make what he can of the heat and rush of Sontag's prose; it beckons him on with its offer of an intelligible heroism. Perhaps she will, in due time, follow Canetti's advice: learn to breathe, seek something beyond the gathering of power. (p. 43)

Frank Kermode, *"Alien Sages," in* The New York Review of Books, *Vol. XXVII, No. 17, November 6, 1980, pp. 42-3.*

LEO BRAUDY

In *Under the Sign of Saturn* Sontag is at work again reshaping the canon of modern European literature. Her particular polemic—a strong element in the general thrust of postwar New York literary criticism—is to celebrate the leopards in the temple of literature, not those cool and calm consciousnesses (like the Sophocles and Shakespeare of Matthew Arnold) who abided all questions and saw life whole, but those whose own derangement allowed them to explode the lies of order so that better forms might be discovered. In her criticism she labors to turn even the most self-isolating, uncompromising, and personally outrageous of such figures (I think here especially of Artaud) into humane teachers, whose flame, all the brighter for being trimmed, she will pass on to future generations.

In the 1960s such a critical project was both exuberant and expansive. But as Sontag wrote further and became part of the critical establishment herself, her tone became more sober and somber, until in *Saturn* she finds a moral and emotional benchmark in the melancholic temperament (specifically Benjamin's), with its "self-conscious and unforgivable relation to the self, which can never be taken for granted," born under "the star of the slowest revolution, the planet of detours and delays." Sontag's heroes are, therefore, those writers whose acute sense of the difficulties of using language properly allows them, paradoxically, to pierce its veil and see into the heart of things. Without being system-builders, they search for the core of a newly whole reality that gives due respect to the fragmentations of 20th-century knowledge and perception. (pp. 43-4)

Reality is a crucial term for Sontag, not least because, for all her appreciation of movies, she is specifically hostile to what she calls nominalism, the view that there are no absolute concepts or ideas, only words that are socially accepted ways of communicating. Of course, the philosophical realist need not live entirely in a world of Platonic ideas and the nominalist is hardly happy only when he contemplates fragments and ruins. But Sontag's sympathies are clear. Her goal is an understanding of what is essential and what is real, and those she most admires retain a Platonic sensitivity to the disorder of the world and a Platonic faith in the ability of mind to penetrate that disorder and find truth. (p. 44)

To pursue the life of the mind and maintain its vitality in the face of both the dehumanizing horrors of 20th-century war and the more subtle dehumanizations of technological advance and aesthetic democratization, implies Sontag, requires the self-questioning detachment of the melancholic critic/artist, whose essentially passive objectivity her own style seems to imitate. Ever since the Renaissance, melancholy has been the mark of the artist whose work or aspiration made claims on the philosophic and eternal. Sometimes the melancholic artist, separated from ordinary men by his link to what is permanent,

could be a satirist as easily as a high-stalking dreamer of the divine. . . . Sontag's essays are in fact filled with traditional satiric themes—the incoherence of public sources of information, the corrupt emptiness of theatrical versions of reality, the pressure that time and bodily decay put on human aspirations—even though she never writes satire as such. . . . Instead, she is fascinated with the effort, through writing and sometimes film, of creative individuals to be Romantic eccentrics in a time of mass societies. The strategies of such an assertion obviously have changed since the days of Wordsworth, Byron, and Napoleon. But Sontag adds her own emphasis on the importance of the melancholic's corrosive self-awareness. In the view that she derives primarily from Benjamin, 20th-century history has forced the critic/artist to take up a custodial relation to the world—collecting, deciphering, rearranging what is discovered into patterns that in their turn must be criticized. Enter, then, the interpreter of such writers, who deciphers *their* references and fragments not by the piecemeal process of ascertaining the meaning of each but by enlightening us about the cultural significance of such fragmented referentiality.

Such a role suited Sontag well in her earlier incarnation as a questioner of critical and cultural clichés, when her special status as an émigré by adoption allowed her to champion many artists and thinkers whose moral purpose was often less clear than her own. But in our climate of confusion over what political, aesthetic, or spiritual leadership might be, *Under the Sign of Saturn* raises more questions than its ideals can satisfy. Where Sontag once strode the marches in search of outlandish but crucial sensibilities to bring back struggling and vital to the general reader, her trophies now have the slightly greenish tinge of the coterie or the salon. The fault lies more in her net than in her quarry.

In essence, I think it is difficult for Sontag to maintain an argument that attacks one side of Romantic individualism (that leads to political megalomania) in order to accept another (that leads to artistic self-aggrandizement). I hardly want to equate the two myself: strutting artists do much less harm than strutting dictators. But the paradox of the grandly assertive work of art that attacks the grandly assertive gesture in the public world of politics is a delicate one indeed, and Sontag is unconvincing about the terms of the competition, perhaps because she is so caught up in it herself. Syberberg's *Our Hitler* is Sontag's set piece here—"probably the most ambitious Symbolist work of this century"—and *Saturn*'s structure very carefully poises it against Riefenstahl's *Triumph of the Will*. In this implicit contrast Syberberg is the modernist virtuoso of fragments, playing in the spray of 20th-century images, constantly aware of the lie and deceit of all visual insignia, while Riefenstahl is the monolithic God's-eye director, soaring over the world like her subject, reducing all to pattern, sentimentally invoking the coercive abstractions of leader, nation, and body, and leaving her film unetched by any nuance of individual life and doubt.

In this contest the palm is clearly to Syberberg (or to Sontag's account of him). But from the competition seeps a corruption of means and terminology. Sontag devotes some telling comments to Syberberg's ambivalent relation to Wagner (who plays second fiddle to Hitler in the film), but scants the extent to which Syberberg, with his seven-hour film, administers an aesthetic dictatorship to his audience in order to purge the political dictatorship whose paraphernalia he portrays. Movies especially raise the question of how to draw the line between aesthetic and political control. . . . Must the artist counter the sins of political absolutism by an absolute gesture of his own?

Sontag no doubt thinks that melancholic self-questioning can keep the true artist and critic from such indulgences. But the coolness of her own style belies her prescriptions for self-awareness. . . . Sontag remarks on the fact that many of the exemplary thinkers she treats—from the modernist monk Artaud to the goliard intellectual Goodman—were riven by the worry that they hadn't been appreciated, hadn't become famous enough. (pp. 44-5)

For the secular writer and artist, musing on the face of death and the failure of the body and mind, the question of fame is crucial. . . . *Under the Sign of Saturn* is [Sontag's] effort to reassess the public aspect of her pursuit of a career that has been defined historically by its distaste for public life and display. Searching for the shape of other careers, she implicitly meditates on her own: what am I to make of this pile of books that in some way is me? The question is all too modern. At the end of the Middle Ages Chaucer's *House of Fame* described statues of the great writers of antiquity, each holding up his greatest work. By the 18th century, in Pope's rewriting of Chaucer, *The Temple of Fame*, they are standing on top of their books. Sontag similarly first dons the costumes of her various heroes and villains and then packs each neatly away in the cultural closet. As always, her intelligence makes her essays refreshing, even though we may often learn less about her subjects than about what she thinks of them and how their ideas affected her. In pursuit of new connections she has fashioned a rhetoric of subordination that puts her forward as the humble lightning rod of culture. This is my tradition, she seems to say, these are my boys, and thus the Romantic project of finding the heart of a culture in its eccentrics winds up recommending instead the eccentricity of its own quest. (pp. 45-6)

Leo Braudy, "A Genealogy of Mind," in The New Republic, Vol. 183, No. 22, November 29, 1980, pp. 43-6.

ELIZABETH HARDWICK

Susan Sontag: the name is a resonance of qualities, of quality itself. The drama of the idea, the composition, a recognition from the past that tells us what the present may bestow when we see her name. The term "essay" itself is somewhat flat as a definition of the liberality of her floating, restless expositions. *A Susan Sontag Reader*, a choice from her criticism and fiction, is in no way scant, but it interested me to note that one could regret the omission of almost any piece of her writing, any square of the mosaic that is in the end an extraordinarily beautiful, expansive, and unique talent.

Her writings are *hers*, intimately and obsessively one might say. They bear, each one, the mark of a large and coherent sensibility, the mark of her *interests*, her sense of the aesthetic and moral world around us. Almost none of her work comes out of the mere occasion, the book published, the film released, or the fad acknowledged. I suppose her theme is the wide, elusive, variegated sensibility of modernism—a reach of attitude and feeling that will include great works of art, the modern disturbance of the sense of self seen in "camp" and in pornography, and account for the social, historical disturbance represented by the contemporary glut of photographic images. Modernism is style and the large figures of culture she likes to reflect upon leave in their styles the signature of wishes, attractions, morals, and, always, ideas.

Susan Sontag is not drawn to her themes as a specialty, as one might choose the eighteenth century, but rather as expressions of her own taste, her own being, her own style perhaps. Her imagination is obstinate, stubborn in its insistence upon the heroic efforts of certain moving, complex modern princes of temperament such as Walter Benjamin, Artaud, Roland Barthes, Lévi-Strauss, Canetti, and the tragic moral philosopher Simone Weil. The modern sensibility in her view is democratic; it embraces the aristocratic spirit of the films made by Godard, Bresson, Bergman, and Syberberg. The listing of her "interests" shows an almost spendthrift openness to example and precept and vivacious practice. But her thoughts surprise. Films, writers, philosophers are, as it were, excavated, brought up to the topsoil to be viewed in the round. This is a particular vision, the defining glance of cultural history in which each thing is itself, unique and to some degree "against interpretation"— and yet reflecting a disjunctive modern consciousness that is historical. On this theme and its fascinations each of her essays has a profound authority, a rather anxious and tender authority—the reward of passion. (pp. ix-x)

The writers she has chosen to reflect upon are somewhat daunting and I do not think she would place herself among the undaunted. The tone of her writing is speculative, studious and yet undogmatic; even in the end it is still inquiring. There remains what Henry James called the "soreness of confusion," the reminder of the unaccountable and inexhaustible in great talents. This remnant of wonder is her way of honoring the exceptional, the finally inimitable. (p. xi)

She, like Barthes and Benjamin, chose philosophy as a student. . . . Her metaphysical vocabulary retains this habit of mind and she has Nietzsche and Plato as readily at hand as bits of memorized poetry. . . . Conceptualization from instances gathered from afar is her method. There is seldom anything whimsical or indulgent in this far-flung patterning. The structure is genuine, convincing, and the gathering-in is an illumination.

She practices delicately and lightheartedly the aphoristic summation, rather than the aphoristic interruption. . . . Her style, her prose language, is clear, fresh, not meant to tease or to confound. However, the extremity of her subjects will often demand that the expositor be a gymnast. Waywardness attracts her and in waywardness there is humor, outrageousness, the unpredictable, along with extremity. In that sense her work is sensual and many of her essays are about heroic insatiability, as in the instance of the brilliant "Syberberg's Hitler."

"Notes on Camp" is an early, exhilarating work about "style" at an ineffable outpost of sensibility. "Camp" is parochial in that it can only be fulfilled in the city with its infinite byways. "Camp is the answer to the problem: how to be a dandy in the age of mass culture." If the word is beyond definition, it is not beyond reflection, example, listing. The essay is amused, a sophisticated precondition for a pose that elevates the amusing to a criterion. The camp sensibility is not a text to be held in the hand. The only text is finally this essay, with its incorporation of the exemplar of the camp mode—the epigrams of Oscar Wilde. The essay is intuition, observation, tolerance for the inverted, the willful. (pp. xii-xiii)

In 1966 a number of essays by Miss Sontag which had appeared in magazines were collected into a published book, *Against Interpretation*. "Appeared" is to the point in this case since it leads to the personal, the noticeable, the theatrical element in taste and in "point of view" when the observer is a foraging pluralist. This first book of essays was provoking, meaning to unsettle by an insistent avant-gardism, by aesthetic irregularities such as "camp," science fiction, and the film *Flaming Creatures*, "the poetry of transvestism," closed on the ground of obscenity by the police. These diversions are bright, poisonous poppies, flaming about Simone Weil, Lévi-Strauss, Camus, and others. There is an anarchic, intrepid stretch to the book. In it we are invited to a "new sensibility," in which the "beauty of a machine or of the solution to a mathematical problem, of a painting by Jasper Johns, or a film by Jean-Luc Godard, and of the personalities and music of the Beatles is equally accessible." Youthful, brilliant, and so ardently interesting and unmistakably hers. And a mood that would at last disappoint, or if not disappoint, fall into familiarity and thereby ask of her intelligence some steadier and more difficult refinement.

Her essays gradually became longer, and perhaps more serene, and certainly less imploring. The labyrinthine perfectionism, the pathos of a "dissatisfied" spirit like Walter Benjamin came to her, I think, as a model, and certainly as an object of *love*, the word in no way out of bounds. It is love that makes her start her essay on Benjamin by looking at a few scattered photographs. Benjamin is not an image to us; his is one of those faces that dissolve. It would seem that his body and soul are not friends. And so we can never be surrounded, illuminated as we are by the face of Kafka, a face of absolute rightness. The wish to find Benjamin as a face is touching, subjective, venerating. And this is the mood of much of her recent work, particularly the majestic honoring of Barthes and the homage to Canetti, himself a great and complicated "admirer" of his own chosen instances of genius.

Thinking about Susan Sontag in the middle of her career is to feel the happiness of more, more, nothing ended. An exquisite responsiveness of this kind is unpredictable, although one of the intentions of her work is to find the central, to tell us what we are thinking, what is happening to our minds and to culture. There are politics, fashions, art itself, and of course the storehouse of learning to be looked at again and again in her own way. I notice that in her late work she stresses the notion of pleasure in the arts, pleasure in thinking. Only the serious can offer us that rare, warm, bright-hearted felicity. (pp. xiv-xv)

> *Elizabeth Hardwick, in an introduction to* A Susan Sontag Reader *by Susan Sontag, Farrar/Straus/Giroux, 1982, pp. ix-xv.*

WALTER KENDRICK

A fully established American figure, Sontag is ready for the archive; and so, appropriately, we have *A Susan Sontag Reader*. It's not *the* Reader—maybe there will be a sequel—but it offers a heavy sampling of her work, from her first novel, *The Benefactor* (1963), through her obituary essay on Roland Barthes (1981), all selected by Sontag herself. Ordinarily, writers are dead or incapacitated before Readers are bestowed on them. Sontag is neither—though you'd never know it from Elizabeth Hardwick's elegiac introduction [see excerpt above], which croons of "unique talent" and "profound authority" till you can fairly smell the formaldehyde.

There's too much of Sontag's fiction here—a harmless gesture of vanity on its author's part, but an unwelcome reminder to the reader of how dull and derivative that fiction is. . . .

Her nonfiction, however, is always vivacious, even when its polemic is blurry and its impact has grown blunt with time. Her most famous essays are here—"Against Interpretation," "Notes on 'Camp,'" "The Pornographic Imagination," "Fascinating Fascism"—along with others that are less well known but equally provocative, such as "On Style" and "The Aesthetics of Silence." . . . Everything here has been published before, some of it more than once; but now the arrangement is strictly chronological, so that you can follow (or at least look for) signs of development in Sontag's thought.

I couldn't find any, except perhaps the loss of ardency, and gain of serenity, that Hardwick notes in her introduction. But, because the *Reader* is apparently a self-portrait, the absence of a piece can be as revealing as its presence. Many of the short, early pieces from *Against Interpretation* were probably omitted because they are too slight or too closely tied to works and events that appear minor in hindsight. "Trip to Hanoi" might have been passed over for reasons of space, or because it reeks too much of 1968; but I'd rather have had it than *The Benefactor*. Without that troubled, ambivalent attempt to come to terms with herself as a "citizen of the American empire," the *Reader* makes Sontag look much more placidly detached, much more of a nabob, than she in fact has been. But this effect may very well be deliberate.

The total omission of *Illness as Metaphor* is undoubtedly so: even more clearly than *On Photography,* this little book demonstrates Sontag's inability to sustain an extended argument. Her considerable talents as a writer are confined to the fashioning of memorable phrases and elegant sentences; sometimes she can even make a paragraph hang together. But when it comes to a sequence of paragraphs, she slips and slides; and when that sequence must form itself into the larger structures that constitute a coherent book, she collapses. Her best essays are either formless by design, like "Notes on 'Camp,'" or else propped up on the ready-made structure of someone else's film, novel or *oeuvre*.

Her essay on Walter Benjamin ("Under the Sign of Saturn"), for example, is a graceful blending of biography, appreciation and criticism. For Sontag, Benjamin's life and his writing were both shaped by his "Saturnine temperament," and under that rubric she is able to move smoothly back and forth between the man and his work, producing a stylish literary portrait. . . .

When Sontag's subjects are less clearcut, however, she habitually starts, stops, starts again and finally loses her way. "Camp" may be such a scatterbrained phenomenon that a shoal of fifty-eight "notes" is an appropriate form for discussing it, but even such an apparently unified essay as "The Pornographic Imagination" moves at the same jerky, uncertain pace. (p. 404)

Sontag's best writing is impressionistic, and the limits of her thought are those of esthetic impressionism. *On Photography* and *Illness as Metaphor* reveal her limitations most plainly, but they hem in all her work and are more than merely formal. Her "exquisite responsiveness" (Hardwick's phrase) is genuine and often beguiling, but her responses are dictated by a time-worn understanding of the world that is no longer adequate to what the world contains. Sontag's eminence in American letters is disproportionate to the quality of her thought; she perpetuates a tradition of philosophical naïveté that has always kept America subservient to Europe and that surely should have run its course by now. (p. 405)

In the early 1960s, when her most controversial essays were written, Sontag might have looked avant-garde; but since then, her constant devotion to the Anglo-American tradition of genteel literary discourse has sorely outmoded her. She seems to know nothing of semiotics, deconstruction, the reinterpretation of Freud, Nietzsche, Hegel and Marx—the true leading edge of the European intelligentsia. . . .

Sontag's only concession to the actual avant-garde has been her appropriation of Roland Barthes. "Writing Itself," her eulogy of him, concludes the *Reader* and is a fine example of Sontag at her most Sontagian. Barthes is an ideal subject for Sontag, because in his late work he seemed to turn away from the scary semiotic radicalism of his middle career, producing a series of gentle, impressionistic books that even Matthew Arnold would have found congenial. In Sontag's hands, Barthes becomes just another sensibility on tour; the essay is heartfelt and touching, but it represses the danger in Barthes and distorts the multifaceted intellectual movement of which he was an important part.

If the *Reader* is in fact Sontag's self-portrait, what she shows us is an unexpectedly conservative, philosophically retrograde writer whose primary function has always been domestication. She introduced American culture to several artists who would have remained obscure much longer without her aid. But in the process she also made them safe, accommodating them to a familiar vocabulary of appreciation and evaluation. That vocabulary has hardly changed since the eighteenth century. When Samuel Johnson spoke of "sensibility," the term meant something definite to him and to his limited, homogeneous audience; when Matthew Arnold used the term, he was already defending the citadel against the noisy rabble; when Sontag uses it, it means nothing except that her unanalyzed preconceptions must at all costs be soothed.

None of this would make any difference if Sontag didn't have such important influence on somebody, somewhere. I must confess, I don't know anyone who looks to Sontag for esthetic guidance. But she takes herself so seriously, and her publisher treats her with such awe, that I can only presume the existence of a vast, anonymous readership, hungry for Sontag's pearls. If these readers exist, their reverence is Sontag's only real achievement—a notable achievement, to be sure, but a far more trenchant criticism of the world of American letters than any essay she ever wrote. (p. 406)

> Walter Kendrick, "In a Gulf of Her Own," in The Nation, Vol. 235, No. 13, October 23, 1982, pp. 404-06.

JAY PARINI

Sontag has done an able job of editing [*A Barthes Reader*], and her introduction is thoughtful, an elegiac retrospective, what in the eighteenth century would have been called an *éloge*— a commemoration of the illustrious dead. This introduction to Barthes forms the concluding essay in her own selection, *A Susan Sontag Reader*. . . . It is quite instructive to read the Barthes and Sontag *Readers* in tandem; the real thing looks even more real beside the imitation.

Sontag's ability to stay one step ahead of Continental Thinking has earned her high marks in the world of intellectual journalism. She is always a half-step ahead of the fashion, with a knack for saying the outrageous thing—*à la* Barthes—but without the impishness and controlled ambivalence of her master. Where Sontag is correct, she is often sophomoric; where she is wrong, she is irritating and, frequently, pretentious. Her

style reflects this pompousness, as when she writes: "Spirituality = plans, terminologies, ideas of deportment aimed at resolving the painful structural contradictions inherent in the human situation, at the completion of human consciousness, at transcendence." Were her essays (and fiction) not bestrewn with such stuff, one would have to assume she was kidding.

Sontag is always dead serious, even when she is "being funny." Her first book was *The Benefactor* (1963), a novel about a young man called Hippolyte (move over, Racine!) who has strange dreams and then, for some reason, attempts to duplicate them in his life. Says her hero: "I am surprised dreams are not outlawed. What a promise the dream is! How delightful! How private! And one needs no partner, one need not enlist the cooperation of anyone, female or male. Dreams are the onanism of the spirit." Perhaps this is meant to be funny. Sontag's *Reader* begins with eighty-five pages of this stiff, almost unreadable novel.

Five essays from *Against Interpretation* (1966) follow. They are written in a style reminiscent of Oscar Wilde and Barthes but with the suppleness of neither. "Against Interpretation," the title essay, argues that "all Western consciousness of and reflection upon art have remained within the confines staked out by the Greek theory of art as mimesis or representation." This is backed up by a sophomoric excursion into what Plato meant by mimesis. What is wrong here is that Sontag assumes a naive dichotomy of form and content, thus allowing herself (in the tradition of aestheticism) to champion form-as-style over content-as-message. She casts aspersions on all "reactionary" critics who stifle us with their boring "interpretations," pleading for "an erotics of art" in place of sterile academic hermeneutics. Her rhetoric is all fizz, without intellectual rigor or moral force. (pp. 415-16)

One has to wonder if Sontag is serious much of the time. Attempting on the one hand to abolish the distinctions between "high" and "low" art, she focuses [in "Notes on 'Camp'"] repeatedly on works that might be called Camp Highbrow: Pierre Louÿs's *Trois Filles de leur Mère*, George Bataille's *Histoire de l'Oeil* and *Madame Edwards*, the *Mystica Theologia* of Dionysius the Areopagite, and so forth. She uses the old trick of name-dropping to a ludicrous degree; unlike, say, George Steiner, whose excessive name-dropping at least suggests the resonating chamber of a deeply learned mind, Sontag does not call up the sense of connected worlds. The reader is asked to admire her range, which is all breadth and no depth, not enter into a process of thought with her. (p. 417)

There is also another novel-excerpt, from *Death Kit* (1967), which concerns the feeble attempts of one "Diddy" to figure out whether or not he really did (*did he?* = Diddy) murder a workman in a train tunnel. Though very brief, the excerpt is unspeakably tedious—a thing no novelist can afford to be. The setting is entirely abstract, impalpable, idealized. Critical aphorisms (which sound like parodies of Barthes) jump out of the narrative to assert Sontag's presence: "Dying is overwork" or "The splendor of children is never, really, more than pathos." One marvels at Sontag's willingness to type out such a novel.

Her best work is certainly in the criticism, and one does find patches of brilliance, as in "The Image-World," taken from *On Photography* (1977). . . .

Perhaps the main problem in Sontag is that she wants everything all ways: a "radical" stance (with the implicit choices involved) and the cool amoral impartiality of Wildean aestheticism. She wants to be a democrat, but she clings to Camp exclusiveness. She disdains critics who still separate content from style, then she does just that when it suits her argument. (p. 418)

Both Sontag and Barthes argue from a position that cannot, finally, withstand excessive scrutiny. The aesthete can never resist putting key words in quotation marks, thus undermining the seriousness of any statement. Art is a form of play, but it is serious play—as is the play of children—what Auden called ''a game of knowledge.'' Art depends upon what Wallace Stevens called ''the necessary angel / of reality.'' If art is not a criticism of life, per se, as Matthew Arnold would have it, it is nonetheless an interpretation of it. Barthes, at his best, interprets the world-as-text, tacitly rendering judgments that can only be called moral. Sontag is just too dead-set against interpretation to read the world at all. (p. 419)

Jay Parini, ''Reading the Readers: Barthes and Sontag,'' in The Hudson Review, *Vol. XXXVI, No. 2, Summer, 1983, pp. 411-19.**

Frank (Arthur) Swinnerton

1884-1982

English novelist, critic, and biographer.

Swinnerton's reputation as a writer rests on his chronicles of the activities and concerns of the Georgian movement in English literature, which began with the onset of the First World War and lasted into the 1940s. His penchant for amusing detail, which often lends a gossipy quality to his work, contributes to the comprehensive literary portraits he created.

In his novels Swinnerton stressed realism and clear, detailed characterizations, projecting his pragmatic view of life. Of his more than forty novels, *Nocturne* (1917) is generally considered the best. Critics have praised its nearly flawless structure, convincing characterizations, and Swinnerton's compassion in depicting a harsh and disappointing world. His last novel, *Some Achieve Greatness* (1976), reveals that even past the age of ninety Swinnerton upheld the same artistic and moral positions evident in his earliest works.

Swinnerton's *The Georgian Literary Scene* (1934) is often cited as an important critical history of this era in English literature. In this large volume, Swinnerton offers insightful descriptions of the Georgian circle of writers, tempering his insider's viewpoint with objectivity. *The Georgian Literary Scene* provides intimate sketches of such writers as G. K. Chesterton, A. A. Milne, Arnold Bennett, and Hilaire Belloc. Swinnerton's subsequent literary memoirs, *Swinnerton: An Autobiography* (1936) and *Figures in the Foreground* (1963), which include information and personalities of the post-Georgian period, exhibit the same confident ease of presentation which makes *The Georgian Literary Scene* enjoyable reading.

(See also *Contemporary Authors*, Vol. 108 [obituary].)

H. G. WELLS

[Mr. Swinnerton] sees life and renders it with a steadiness and detachment and patience quite foreign to my disposition. He has no underlying motive. He sees and tells. His aim is the attainment of that beauty which comes with exquisite presentation. Seen through his art, life is seen as one sees things through a crystal lens, more intensely, more completed, and with less turbidity. There the business begins and ends for him. He does not want you or any one to do anything. (p. x)

Mr. Swinnerton, like Mr. James Joyce, does not repudiate the depths for the sake of the surface. His people are not splashes of appearance, but living minds. Jenny and Emmy in [*Nocturne*] are realities inside and out; they are imaginative creatures so complete that one can think with ease of Jenny ten years hence or of Emmy as a baby. The fickle Alf is one of the most perfect Cockneys—a type so easy to caricature and so hard to get true—in fiction. If there exists a better writing of vulgar lovemaking, so base, so honest, so touchingly mean and so touchingly full of the carving for happiness than this that we have here in the chapter called *After the Theatre*, I do not know it. Only a novelist who has had his troubles can understand fully what a dance among china cups, what a skating over thin ice, what a tight-rope performance is achieved in this astound-

ing chapter. A false note, one fatal line, would have ruined it all. On the one hand lay brutality; a hundred imitative louts could have written a similar chapter brutally, with the soul left out, we've loads of such "strong stuff" and it is nothing; on the other side was the still more dreadful fall into sentimentality, the tear of conscious tenderness, the redeeming glimpse of "better things" in Alf or Emmy that would at one stroke have converted their reality into a genteel masquerade. (pp. xi-xii)

Mr. Swinnerton has written four or five other novels before this one, but none of them compare with it in quality. His earlier books were strongly influenced by the work of George Gissing; they have something of the same fatigued greyness of texture and little of the artistic completeness and intense vision of *Nocturne*. . . . I add an intimate and personal satisfaction to my pleasant task of saluting this fine work that ends a brilliant apprenticeship and ranks Swinnerton as Master. This is a book that will not die. It is perfect, authentic, and alive. Whether a large and immediate popularity will fall to it I cannot say, but certainly the discriminating will find it and keep it and keep it alive. If Mr. Swinnerton were never to write another word I think he might count on this much of his work living, as much of the work of Mary Austen, W. H. Hudson, and Stephen Crane will live, when many of the more portentous reputations of to-day may have served their purpose in the world and become no more than fading names. (pp. xiii-xiv)

H. G. Wells, in an introduction to Nocturne *by Frank Swinnerton, George H. Doran Company, 1917, pp. vii-xiv.*

H. W. BOYNTON

[*Nocturne*] is neither grey nor gay, neither realism in its docket nor romance in its pigeon-hole. It is a book of fact but also of arrangement, of insight as well as observation; of dramatic action as well as sympathy. In short, it is a work of imaginative art, holding its magic mirror (and not a mere reflector) up to nature. To this roundness and fulness within its slender bounds [H. G.] Wells is paying tribute when he writes to Mr. Bennett, "You know, Arnold, he achieves a perfection in *Nocturne* that you and I never get within streets of." Mr. Wells enlarges upon his enthusiasm in his Introduction. "This is a book that will not die," he concludes. "It is perfect, authentic, and alive." Authentic or artistic—we may use either word in the effort to express our sense of this story as "the real thing." But I think the main point, which does not seem to be altogether clear to Mr. Wells, is that this is the real thing *as a story*. The Cockney family: Jenny, the milliner's girl; Emmy, the domestic slave; Pa Blanchard, the paralytic remnant of a reckless fellow . . . Alf, the vague satellite. . . . These people with their dingy surroundings fairly offer themselves to the grey method of a Gissing or the jaunty method of a Bennett or the inquisitive method of a Wells. The Swinnerton method is none of these. It is the method of the interpreter who frankly makes truth salient by his skilful manipulation of facts. Here, for example, it is his purpose to compass or focus the meaning of four lives in the events of a single night. To that end he employs without hesitation the familiar instruments of the romancer. He is after, not a slice of life, but a distilled and golden drop of life. That immortal tool of the narrative or dramatic artist which we call "the long arm of coincidence," and mock at when it is perfunctorily wielded, is here employed with bland consummate skill. . . . [All events in the plot] are compassed at the will of the storyteller; but so compassed that we accept them with rich gratitude as setting us free from the stupid casual incompletion of "fact." It is the tense and compacted method of drama in contrast with the elaborate haphazard of fiction as it is so often written to-day. As for the meaning or moral of the story, it is inherent, not appended. One feels its quality to be tragic, not sentimental or occasional.

For all its lesser realism of detail, its economy of materials, and its restraint of manner, the book is charged with high emotion. . . . (pp. 567-68)

H. W. Boynton, "Peace-Time Novels," in The Bookman, *New York, Vol. XLVII, No. 5, July, 1918, pp. 564-70.**

LOLA RIDGE

The structure of [*Nocturne*] is almost classic. The events take place in the course of a single night. And each chapter folds upon the other without visible apertures or creaking joints, so that in retrospect the mind encompasses the whole with a single gesture.

In theme and treatment is seems to usher in a coming democratization of art. Here is no preoccupation with the commonplace from the contemptuous elevation of the intellectual aristocrat—Mr. Swinnerton approaches the vulgarest of his creatures with a genial tolerance. At the same time his book emphasizes the revival of that indiscriminate realism already apparent in the work of two very different writers, Wyndham Lewis and James Joyce. But though he etches accessory details with the minuteness of the author of *Dubliners,* he does not achieve the latter's biting phrases. In the work of Joyce one is always conscious of looking through a piquant and intensely individual personal atmosphere. But in *Nocturne,* as Mr. Wells says succinctly: "Life is seen as through a crystal lens." And in spite of the warmth and color of the book and the physical glamor of the soft London darkness, the characters challenge one's vision like objects seen in a too strong light. (p. 323)

Lola Ridge, "A Study of the Commonplace," in The New Republic, *Vol. XVI, No. 206, October 12, 1918, pp. 320, 323.*

H. W. BOYNTON

One secret of the charm of Frank Swinnerton's **"Nocturne"** is what may be called the warm disinterest, or sympathetic detachment, of the chronicler. He doesn't mean his little episode to "teach" anything: it is simply there before us, yet by no means as a "slice of life", for what makes it alive is the radiant energy of creative art. The artist's self as well as his skill informs it. Irony would be too cold a word for its mood, for there is something glowing here. As we enter that mood, we feel ourselves lifted to something like the wisdom and tenderness of the gods, glimpsing elements of beauty in the children of dust, and in the dust itself. **"Shops and Houses"** is a less sublimated kind of fiction. Its emotion is less intense and less from within. And it labors somewhat from the outset under the burden of an "idea". At once we are, so to speak, confronted with Beckwith, an English provincial town which is confessedly and unhappily typical. Beckwith is an ancient village but fifteen miles from London, half spoiled by the advent of railway and factories, yet still self-centered. It is a place of rigid class distinctions, raw social nerves, and ruthless tongues of censure or surmise. . . . It is a village of snobs, such as from Miss Mitford to E. F. Benson has made itself familiar to American readers as a kind of stronghold of Briticism. What gives Mr. Swinnerton's handling freshness is his explicit conviction that this narrow, ingrowing, pharisaical life of the Beckwiths of old England is a damnable thing, and not merely a quaint and amusing thing.

The opening situation is intensely British. The unchallenged social supremacy in Beckwith belongs to the Vechantors. . . . The Vechantors are a family of a good deal of charm, dwelling serene and contented on their high eminence, not haughty in bearing and of really gentle breeding, but half-consciously basking in their sense of superiority and precedence. Vechantor senior is a quiet paterfamilias, fond of his own company and a few old books. Louis, the oldest son, does what a gentleman may in a local bank. All is serene enough when falls a bolt from the blue in the person of a forgotten Vechantor cousin blundering into town in the place of a retiring grocer. Horrible! The village feels the outrage, and the incoming Vechantor and his luckless family feel it, and not least of all the reigning Vechantors on their eminence. The very presence of the interlopers, Vechantors behind a counter, is a vague menace to that eminence. The queen-mother herself, gentle and generous woman that she is by nature, shares the universal distress. And this Louis presently makes intolerable by actually showing a slight civility toward his cousins. The elder Vechantors ignore them; and there is presently a parental decree forbidding the grown-up Louis further intercourse with these people who have the insolence to be relatives without permission.

Louis is a bold Briton. He defies the decree; and in the end, with the approval of his converted elders, makes choice of his charming cousin, the grocer's daughter, as against the conventional Beckwithian female who has almost hooked him. But Beckwith is not to be lived in and remodeled by them or the new forces their union represents. . . . And Louis and his Dorothy, though they love the country and Beckwith itself, as the place nature made it, dare not try to live out their lives there. Nor is it Beckwith as an isolated spot they shrink from. (pp. 51-3)

So they choose London, where shops and houses are at least more indifferent, if not more kindly, to one another. Apart from this idea, and the two interesting lovers who struggle with it—and more vividly than either, perhaps—I expect to remember this book for its portrait of the "nice girl" Veronica, so "common" and unmoral beneath her surface conformity—an indubitable portrait of female Victorianism at its nadir. (p. 53)

> *H. W. Boynton, "Novels of Character and Atmosphere," in* The Bookman, *New York, Vol. XLIX, No. 1, March, 1919, pp. 50-6.**

REBECCA WEST

It is not clear why Mr. Frank Swinnerton has called his new novel *Coquette*. A coquette, one had always understood, was a lady who loved the work for its own sake, who found the evocation and frustration of desire a satisfying sport in itself; but his Sally Minto was moved in her first encounter with a man by real passion and in her second by ambition. A novel about a coquette would be primarily . . . a discussion of the mystery of athleticism, that passion which leads human beings to spend their lives attaining proficiency in occupations which are obviously not of a kind that will print through this world into the next and be placed to their credit in eternity. But Sally Minto's story is something far other than this. It is first of all a virtuosic study of character. Throughout the book there are signs that Mr. Swinnerton is capable of talking conventional nonsense about women in general. He subscribes, for instance, to the legend that a set of girls will inevitably be jealous of the most attractive of their number, and makes all the hands in the dressmaking establishment where Sally works look on her with disfavour. This is Victorian. Experience is all against it; every pretty schoolgirl collects a train of plainer girl adorers, and while there may be rivalry among such leaders there is no jealousy felt by the plain against the pretty. This is not to say that there is no jealousy between women. There is, just as there is between men, but it is the jealousy the unhappy feel against the happy. . . . But the jealousy Mr. Swinnerton ascribes to the girls at Madame Gala's is a dusty convention with which a writer of his realist ambition ought to have nothing to do. It does in fact deprive him of one chance of exhibiting Sally's character. She would have shown her quality nicely in exploiting her adorers just to keep her hand in.

But Sally herself is a magnificent piece of work. . . . Her slenderness is half the desirable slenderness of youth and half the thinness of a dustheap cat. She is a child of Murderous London. . . . She is a most characteristic member of the class of murderers, who invariably have something genteel and select about them . . . , who have something really respectable and pathetic about them so diligently do they set about their work,

and with such an air of being compelled to act in despite of their own hearts' kindliness by some darker sister of Necessity. Admirably does Mr. Swinnerton depict the season of aspiration to loot taking the place of normal adolescence in this nipped creature's heart, which sends her out to henna her hair and find a place in a West End workroom. There is not a false note in the subtle and intricate adventure in which he has enmeshed her. She would inevitably have liked the young brute Toby just as she would inevitably have liked a pickle and a cup of hot strong tea. For her it would have been possible to have had a genuine and transcending passion for Toby, and yet have felt it absolutely necessary to marry Madame Gala's weakly son Gaga because that meant wealth and power. It is in the description of Sally's relations with Gaga that Mr. Swinnerton shows, for the first time since *Nocturne,* to what intensity his imagination can attain.

One's only complaint against Mr. Swinnerton is that his brushwork is often not beautiful. He has some theory of writing that forbids the conspicuously brilliant phrase, the dazzlingly appropriate image. It is his intention to give his prose a matt surface. But there are times when it is more than matt; it is almost dingy. That is perhaps due to the fact that Mr. Swinnerton was in his literary beginnings greatly influenced by Gissing, whose drab prose is one of the most painful examples of the disastrous effect that too close application to the classics has upon the style. . . .

It is a pity that Mr. Swinnerton evidently swallowed the art of Gissing whole, and felt it necessary to retain the habit of writing tedious prose along with the habit of conceiving inquisitive and lively imaginations.

> *Rebecca West, in a review of "Coquette," in* New Statesman, *Vol. XVII, No. 438, September 3, 1921, p. 597.*

RAYMOND MORTIMER

Every page of [*Young Felix*] shows the author to be a perceptive and thoughtful person. But ever since I finished reading it, I have been wondering what it is that he has been attempting. *Young Felix* is the story of the first thirty years of a man's life. Is it only a prologue to an enormous work five times its length, in which case its shapelessness is only apparent? If so, Mr. Swinnerton is unfair to himself in not giving us warning. If not, what are we to make of it? There must have been a moment when Mr. Swinnerton first saw his story in the lovely light that plays upon an idea when first it rises to the surface of our minds. What has happened since? In some respect the conception lacked vitality, and the author's talent is wasted—at least as far as other people are concerned. He may have learnt a lot in the writing of his book, but we have learnt nothing that we did not know before—that Mr. Swinnerton is a serious and conscientious writer, with a good sense of comedy of which he hardly makes sufficient use. The first few pages seem to adumbrate the shape that Mr. Swinnerton intended his book should take, but the book hardly begins to take it. Why? If this review is a series of unanswered questions, it is really Mr. Swinnerton's fault. He should make more allowance for the stupidity of critics.

> *Raymond Mortimer, in a review of "Young Felix," in* New Statesman, *Vol. XXII, No. 548, October 13, 1923, p. 18.*

P. C. KENNEDY

[Here] is a literary problem for you. Read the following passage, and guess who wrote it:

> Mr. Sims was in a better position than either Mr. Leicester or Mr. Twist. At a word from Mr. Sims, both Mr. Twist and Mr. Leicester would have been forced to leave the firm. They, although they had worked there for fifteen years and a quarter of a century respectively, and although they knew the business through and through, and could produce the papers unaided, had no status. They could be dismissed at a month's notice. Mr. Sims could not be dismissed. Although the junior, he was, by his purchase of a larger share, the principal partner in the firm. Mr. Twist and Mr. Leicester could run the business, and Mr. Sims could not do so; but Mr. Sims had had the good fortune to possess a rather wealthy uncle, and he was for this reason favourably situated. It might have been supposed that Mr. Sims thought highly of Mr. Twist and Mr. Leicester, and valued them for their long service and experience. He did not so value them. To him they were both merely employees, to be kept or dismissed at his own will.

Whom have you guessed? Of course, Mr. Arnold Bennett. The manner, the mannerisms, and the moral: the repetitions, and the avoidance of repetition: the blend of staccato and rhythmical effects—all, all are Bennett, pure and perfect Bennett. But they happen, in this instance, to be Mr. Swinnerton. And I dwell on this point because I think it supremely important in the estimation of Mr. Swinnerton's genius and achievement. He has a powerful and original mind: that is obvious. It is also obvious that, consciously or unconsciously, he has been very much influenced by Mr. Bennett. One might do worse, no doubt, than be influenced by Mr. Bennett, whose mind is indubitably among the *most* powerful and original of his generation. But the point is that Mr. Swinnerton is too good to be influenced, to that extent, by anybody. It is only when he is writing of a subject with which he is not at home that he puts on the Bennett armour. For his own subject, the depth of rare and intimate emotion, he has a style exquisitely appropriate and individual. The plot of his new novel [*The Elder Sister*] is simple. Anne and Vera are sisters. They are both utterly in love with Mortimer, who is a handsome, weak, selfish, snivelling cad. (There is nothing improbable in the baseness of Mortimer: Goneril and Regan *were* naughty girls: and cads are often loved, for the world must be peopled). Mortimer breaks Vera's heart by marrying Anne, and Anne's heart by running away with Vera. That is all. There are a few subordinate characters, lightly but surely touched in—the sisters' "Dad" and "Mum," and their stuffy little home in Kilburn, make a little masterpiece in themselves; and then there is Mr. Sims at Anne's office, and Mr. Harrow at Vera's. But the story is the story of Vera's weak, terrible, seeking, destroying passion, and Anne's difficult but indomitable greatness of heart. It is a beautiful story, beautifully told—told with reticence, with lyrical ardour, with the very exactness of fine sense.

> *P. C. Kennedy, in a review of "The Elder Sister,"* in New Statesman, *Vol. XXVI, No. 652, October 24, 1925, p. 50.*

RUTH CAPERS McKAY

[The following essay is part of a thesis presented at The University of Pennsylvania in 1927.]

To speak of Swinnerton's novels in general we may say that he writes principally of the lower middle class life in London and in the cheaper suburbs. The exceptions to this are the three successful studies of the upper middle classes found in *The Casement, Shops and Houses* and *September.* His greatest weakness is in plot work; few of his endings have a finished effect, the reader is left dangling, dissatisfied. This is notable particularly in *The Happy Family, On the Staircase,* and *Young Felix.* His best motivation is achieved through character analysis as in the case of *September.* When he is unable to proceed by that method, he is at a loss and finds it necessary to use the various devices which are only too familiar to the reader.

For settings Swinnerton is at his best in the business streets of London and in the commonplace suburbs with their rows of little houses all alike. His London seems to be seen largely from the top of a swaying omnibus. The West End and all the abodes of fashion and affluence are hidden in an unrevealed grandeur. *The Three Lovers* presents a part of the semi-fashionable town life which is not typical of Swinnerton's field. He does not belong in the bright cabaret but with Gladys Verren in the small parlor-sitting room of one of the ninety-six identical flats which comprise "Culverin Mansions", or walking quietly in Hyde Park with Mortimer, Anne and Vera who have come out to listen to the public band concert. His men are largely occupied in printing offices, the only business we may judge with which Swinnerton is familiar; his girls, if of the working class, are stenographers—a limitation which even the most idealistic analysis cannot completely overcome.

It is in his portrayals of young women that Swinnerton does his most convincing and original work; in fact, one is led to say that his novels are all written from the feminine point of view. His analysis of their restless half-formed thought bears a naturalness delightful to the reader. The men, that is the young men, are all modern editions of the Gissing type with, of course, such variations as would be expected. Young girls in the early teens such as Rachel Lane in *Summer Storm* or Edith Dennett in *The Happy Family* are well drawn, and this is an age that few novelists are able to present successfully; the majority feel that they must have either the child, or the woman, or the definite child-woman, never attaining that intermediate something which is none of these but has a quality essentially its own.

Swinnerton writes on one theme, love; no matter of what he is speaking his constant preoccupation is with sex. That is the reason, I think, why one sees signs of exhaustion in [*Summer Storm*]. After reading it many would say that he was "written out". The difficulty is in knowing just how long a writer can last who has only one theme. Is, say, fourteen novels his limit? In *Shops and Houses* Swinnerton broke away and allowed other motives and other thoughts as well as those of love to sway his characters. In *Young Felix,* by means of a new style, a broader vision was glimpsed. But as many must have seen, when Swinnerton published his following novel, *The Elder Sister,* he had not continued any of his new developments but reverted to the unrestricted pursuit of his original theme, love. His future novels must invade new fields: *Nocturne, Coquette, September,* and *The Elder Sister* cannot be repeated; their possibilities have been exhausted. (pp. 88-9)

Ruth Capers McKay, in her George Gissing and His Critic: Frank Swinnerton, *University of Pennsylvania, 1933, 88 p.*

BASIL DAVENPORT

In ["**The Georgian House**"] the author has assembled a number of well-tried and generally reliable ingredients: an old-fashioned house with a secret panel; a hero who is at the beginning of the book living under an assumed name and is evidently under some sort of romantic cloud, from which he is called home to take his inheritance; a wise old lady who understands the young things; a missing will; a thorough-paced villainess; a black-mailing lawyer's clerk; and other stand-bys too numerous to mention. The sort of book that results from such a combination is in most cases excellent entertainment, and of that we cannot have too much. If "**The Georgian House**" kept its promise of good traditional melodrama it would be a pleasure to read and recommend it. But unfortunately the good old melodrama never quite comes off.

There appear to be several reasons for its failure. The various parts are not sufficiently connected. And there are many minor characters, treated at considerable length, who have no effect upon the plot at all. In another sort of book, this would matter less; but in a book in which the plot is so insisted on as it is here, where every few pages there is an intimation that we shall see more of this or that there is more in that than meets the eye; it is difficult to realize that there are whole scenes that are meant to stand only by their own interest.

Mr. Swinnerton appears to have tried to write a melodramatic novel in which the chief interest should not be in the story, nor in the principal figures, but in the setting, the lesser actors, and other elements. This of course can be done; Dickens did it, though not by design, in almost every book he wrote; and it is no doubt tempting to a writer of Mr. Swinnerton's technical skill. But though it can be done, it cannot be done by hurrying over the crises of the melodrama at the rate that "**The Georgian House**" does. . . . [Each of the three turning points of the action] is given a treatment which is so sketchy as to be positively shamefaced. . . . it would seem that Mr. Swinnerton had attempted a melodramatic novel which should avoid the melodrama's vices, and had unfortunately succeeded in avoiding the melodrama's virtues as well.

Basil Davenport, "A Novel of Setting," in The Saturday Review of Literature, *Vol. IX, No. 18, November 19, 1932, p. 252.*

GEORGE DANGERFIELD

Readers with a general curiosity about the last twenty-five years of English literature need look no further than ["**The Georgian Scene**"]. There are, no doubt, more brilliant writers and better critics in England than Mr. Swinnerton, but I doubt if any writer is better informed. It is precisely its information which gives this book its melancholy value—this, and its author's extraordinarily pleasant manners.

"Melancholy" because so few of the writers it mentions can one remember any more; and more melancholy still because one realizes how precious few of them were worth remembering. "**The Georgian Scene**" is not merely a record of English writers from 1910 until today, it is also the record of thousands of tons of forgotten printed paper; and it says much for Mr. Swinnerton that he can make this literary mausoleum

a pleasant place to linger in, instead of simply a place which gives you the creeps.

I have only one real criticism of Mr. Swinnerton's comprehensive and dutiful book. Its title is misleading. Surely the real Georgian scene was the scene which was never played out, which young prewar England never had time to finish, which ended abruptly with the death of Rupert Brooke in 1915; a scene which was mostly written in terms of a sentimentalism too mild to be poisonous, and prompted only by the magnificent, unfulfilled voices of Shaw and Wells. For if the Georgian scene actually continued beyond the war and into our year 1934, then it isn't finished yet—not so long as King George the Fifth lives to preside over the uncertain destinies of such as Spender and Auden. And it is something more than unfinished—it is practically meaningless unless you discuss politics and economics along with your literature.

Mr. Swinnerton, however, is purely a shrewd literary gossip. As such, it is difficult to praise him too highly. He knows his facts; and there never was such an array of facts, dates, and information as you will find here. Nor can you disagree with any of the judgments which he passes upon the hundreds of writers who throng this book; you can't disagree with them because they don't go deep enough. Indeed, Mr. Swinnerton invariably says the right thing: and, while the right thing about writers we haven't read and no longer remember is refreshing and useful, the right thing about writers we know pretty well is merely tedious.

While Mr. Swinnerton accurately describes his twenty-five years' scene, somehow or other he never gives it a shape. He is far too avuncular. From his kindly pages one can merely deduce a shape; the hollow and feverish five pre-war years; the so-called "purgation" of the war, and the curiously dispirited levels of today. This is the sad drama of English literature, and Mr. Swinnerton is too much in the drama to see it as a whole; nor can one see it simply in terms of literature. The reason is not a literary one. (pp. 305, 311)

In English life, the most violent changes have been made by men who did not believe in change; in English literature, the most startling innovations have been the work of innate conservatives. And so when—in post-war England—everything began to dissolve and melt together into some disordered jelly; when the old, comfortable world was given over to such scared and shifty figures as Baldwin and MacDonald; when the institutions that had once been fought against, in the happy belief that they were invincible, began to reel—then the English man of letters lost his grip. In an apparently broken society, he could neither build nor break. He became an Aldous Huxley, or a Noel Coward, or a pacifist; he turned his back on reality. . . .

Mr. Swinnerton is obviously troubled by this situation, but does his best to ignore it. He cannot see the dilemma of a non-revolutionary literature in a revolutionary age. But he does contend very shrewdly that the new writers are too educated, and that the common man is scarcely heard any more. Perhaps the answer to the problem which haunts "**The Georgian Scene**" lies there; perhaps from the less educated classes which make up the larger part of that various, resourceful, and (if the word be allowed me) passionate race will come the new great writers. Meanwhile—and this is implicit in the text of "**The Georgian Scene**"—English literature has competently, and charmingly, and sometimes even brilliantly gone bankrupt. (p. 311)

George Dangerfield, "Brilliant Bankruptcy," in The Saturday Review of Literature, *Vol. XI, No. 19, November 24, 1934, pp. 305, 311.*

JOSEPH WOOD KRUTCH

[*The Georgian Scene*] contains essays on approximately seventy-five writers who range in time from Henry James to T. S. Eliot and in importance from Shaw and Bennett to Edgar Wallace and Noel Coward. A few of the discussions are quite perfunctory, and the space devoted to each often seems to bear little relation to either the popularity or the significance of the subject, but the best are genuinely illuminating and nearly all both informative and readable. Mr. Swinnerton quite frankly discusses his authors from the point of view of an enthusiastic reader of catholic taste rather than from that of a critic with dogmatic ideas. He walks around each subject, noting significant biographical details and, in a very large number of cases, supplying personal reminiscences. He proposes no standards other than very general ones and he makes no final judgments. But he does achieve a panorama, and few men are better qualified than he to do just that. . . .

In so far as **"The Georgian Scene"** has a theory, it seems to be that a fairly distinct mode of writing emerged about the time that the Henry James method went into bankruptcy, and that it held the field more or less unchallenged until the rise of what Mr. Swinnerton calls the New Academicism of T. S. Eliot and his disciples. Probably the best of all the essays is the first, on James himself, and according to that the central defect of James was his ambition to be, as he himself stated it, "just literary." The tenuousness of his writing was not due simply to his detachment but to the fact that he was not merely detached from but actually ignorant of both the material background and the driving motives of his characters, who were compelled to live in a spiritual as well as a material vacuum. He did not know precisely what forced Roderick Hudson's wayward young woman to marry a man she did not want to marry any more than he knew the precise nature of that humble household article from the manufacture of which the chief personages in "The Ambassadors" derived their income. . . .

Wells and Bennett sacrificed much of the artfulness of James for the sake of communicating the concrete things they knew, and it is with the writers of their period that Mr. Swinnerton obviously has the greatest sympathy. They managed to keep a common touch which most of our strictly contemporary writers—especially those most praised by the cliques—have lost, and they reaped the reward of a larger, more substantial influence. Mr. Swinnerton has many kind things to say about the younger men; he does not deny the force of Lawrence or of Joyce, but he quite frankly does not like them very much, and unless I am oversystematizing his opinion it seems to be that they have failed to maintain an equilibrium formerly maintained between the writer's tendency to exploit either his art as such or his gift for self-expression and the duty to report and interpret an actual, familiar world. Neurotic self-absorption gets the best of Lawrence, virtuosity gets the best of Joyce, and pedantry gets the best of Eliot.

Mr. Swinnerton's attitude is not fashionable at the moment and is, of course, arguable. He himself does not insist upon it at any length as deducible from an abstract principle, and it serves chiefly as a method of holding loosely together what is primarily a "panorama." Those who seek in his book a well-knit history will be disappointed, as will also those who want to be told dogmatically what to think, or what limited number of books are "significant" from the point of view of this or that critical school. On the other hand, **"The Georgian Scene"** is an admirable introduction and guide for anyone who wishes to read comprehensively in the literature of the recent past. It is also good reading for those who are already familiar with the literature but who would like to discuss favorite books with a man who has read widely and enthusiastically.

Joseph Wood Krutch, "Panorama of Recent Writing," in The Nation, *Vol. CXXXIX, No. 3623, December 12, 1934, p. 681.*

GEORGE DANGERFIELD

"Swinnerton" leaps, as it were, from ring to ring. Its sub-title should be changed from "An Autobiography" to "A Circus," and I make this suggestion without rancor, for there are many things less pleasant than a circus, and few more calculated to take our minds away from fact. In a circus all the performers have a glamor which is not false, but fictitious: and only if we are very small children do we think that they are what they so beautifully pretend to be. . . .

"Swinnerton" is the kind of autobiography which has leaped into that category over the back fence, about one foot ahead of the critics. The more considerable part of it is about other people, and a charming troupe they are—all talented, all good talkers, and all of them liking Mr. Swinnerton. About Mr. Swinnerton himself one learns less. At first you cannot convince yourself that you know much more about him than that he has a "thousand dollar smile," a description which occurs as late as p. 331, was handed to him by an American lady, and not restored to her. You accept this, of course, but you find yourself wishing that there was rather less of that smile in his book. That is why, when the smile grows faintly acid, as it occasionally does, you draw a long breath of gratitude.

These remarks are intended to convey the thought that to be kind in print (and Mr. Swinnerton has met and is kind to almost everybody English and literary) is something of a modern vice. The public is being trained not to accept abuse and venom, which are both useful things if not overemployed, and were highly thought of among the Greeks and the Elizabethans and the eighteen century wits and other good people.

Yet Mr. Swinnerton is not always just a Smile in Wonderland. A careful consideration of this book reveals another man, a novelist whose **"Nocturne,"** had I read it, I am sure I should have admired; a skilful writer, and a man of warm and singular feelings. This man is discovered, infrequently, in those portions of **"Swinnerton"** which are legitimately autobiographical and which are also infrequent: in the first chapters, and especially those chapters in which he speaks of early days in the publishing business. There was a person at J. M. Dent's who always wore a frock coat, not because he was formal, but because he had once sat down on a pair of scissors and was indisposed to take that chance again: and there is only one character more lovable in the whole book, and that is the character of Arnold Bennett. Arnold Bennett has escaped the circus. The pages that deal with him are not written to satisfy our curiosity, but to appease an emotion in Mr. Swinnerton. "Have I the power to make you see my friend as I saw him?" That sentence has another intonation, the intonation of literature. . . .

The last chapter, about Mr. Swinnerton and his wife and their cat, is also literature. When you read this, and the early chapters, and the story of Arnold Bennett, and one or two other passages, it does seem as if the top of the Big Tent had blown off: and above us, through the fog, we can almost see the stars, which in their courses fight for men and against them, and which are real.

> George Dangerfield, "Kindness in Print," in The Saturday Review of Literature, *Vol. XV, No. 4, November 21, 1936, p. 11.*

THE TIMES LITERARY SUPPLEMENT

To use the word "old-fashioned" in describing [*Harvest Comedy*] is to praise it highly, for it is old-fashioned in the sense that it tells a gripping story and that it gives to each character a scrupulous care that is reminiscent of the method of Dickens. . . . The story traces the careers of [the three main characters] in London, with their various ups and downs, their marriages and their love affairs, but it does much more than this: it shows us the inside of every life. . . . In another sense, too, the book is old-fashioned in that the good boy comes out on top while the two bad boys, who seemed to flourish like the green bay tree at first, got their deserts. But even for them, with their very human weaknesses, Mr. Swinnerton arouses sympathy; and, although the ending of the book could, in other hands, read like a Sunday School prize of our youth, in his it has the convincingness of life.

> A review of "Harvest Comedy," in The Times Literary Supplement, *No. 1857, September 4, 1937, p. 640.*

COMMONWEAL

Possibly the lowest sort of reviewing is the type which borrows overgenerously from the blurb on the highly colored book jacket—that eye-catcher which proudly quotes the welcome bouquets of a favored few who have seen the masterpiece in galleys or in manuscript. . . . In the case of **"A Woman in Sunshine"** the yellow jacket is misleading. . . . It purports to describe a novel concerned chiefly with "a good woman who is also an exciting one." . . .

The woman in question, Letitia Boldero, is 53 and gravely concerned about the marital status of her two sons, as well as that of the daughter-in-law in question. It is only in the final pages that she herself makes any impression in the field of feminine attractiveness—only because an old friend who is stricken with a painful and apparently fatal illness turns to her for sympathy. It may have something to do with her age, but how many readers will in fact find Letitia anywhere near as "exciting" as they are supposed to? **"A Woman in Sunshine"** deals primarily with other matters. The impression it leaves is one compounded of the dreariness of London, the ennui of bourgeois married life and the depths to which some scoundrels will descend. Not to mention the author's irony and pity.

Mr. Swinnerton is indeed a trained hand in the art of depicting ugliness in many forms. He is a true master of the repulsive. Most fascinating of all is the way he spins out the workings of a rascal's mind. Letitia and her household despite the intensity of their emotional problems pale before the machinations of her renegade brother, R. F. The ravages of time noted in Letitia's circle are practically non-existent when compared with the revulsion which Mr. Swinnerton's portrayal of her sister-in-law Thelma, her sister Muriel, and her tyrannical invalid mother inspire. Their looks, their mannerisms and their

outlook are so repellent as to become at last rather attractive in a morbid sort of way. Mr. Swinnerton's irony is often marked. For that quality his title rivals Edith Wharton's "The Age of Innocence." (p. 567)

Rivaling this fascination with ugliness, and closely interwoven with it, is a skilfully developed story of crime. R. F.'s plans to make away with a very nice nest egg are artfully developed. And he makes use not only of all the powers of attraction he can command from long experience in cadging, but he even mistakenly resorts to terrorization of his sister, Muriel, who at 57 is as pitiful a character as one would ever want to see. The author works it all out so neatly—with increasing suspense and all the rest—that for long stretches **"A Woman in Sunshine"** qualifies as a real thriller. From these rambling remarks it should be clear at least that Mr. Swinnerton boasts of great gifts in the narrative art. His book is difficult to pigeonhole because of its many angles. Perhaps its most engaging aspect is the study it provides of a cheerfully calculating, rascally mind. (p. 568)

> "Irony and Pity," in Commonweal, *Vol. XLI, No. 23, March 23, 1945, pp. 567-68.*

THE TIMES LITERARY SUPPLEMENT

The title of Mr. Swinnerton's new book [*The Doctor's Wife Comes to Stay*] is Trollopean, and so in a sense is the story. An energetic and successful young artist, egotistical but attractive, finds that his wife is not content merely with household duties, nor even with the small celebrity of occasional parts in "little theatre" productions. The immense success of the play in which she is acting obtains for her an offer of the leading part in its American production; and she goes to America, leaving her husband at home in the care of her apple-cheeked Victorian mother who comes on a prolonged visit. This lady is the doctor's wife of the title; the doctor himself is an impressively puritanical, sharp-tongued and untidy Scot.

The most unpromising themes may be turned to good fictional use; and Mr. Swinnerton's story, which sounds perhaps even more like Hollywood than like Trollope, is in fact written most carefully and intelligently in the manner of Henry James. At the end of it we are left with a kind of Jamesian problem, and Mr. Swinnerton evokes with remarkable skill that sense of horror, mystery and fascination in the past which comes through so clearly in the master's work. *The Doctor's Wife Comes to Stay* is not an altogether easy book to read, although it is written with much humour; its subject, obliquely revealed, is really the artist's investigation of the secret lying in the Victorian mother's past. Mr. Swinnerton prepares us for the final dramatic scenes—which cannot be disclosed without affecting the reader's pleasure—with admirable artistry.

> "Past and Future," in The Times Literary Supplement, *No. 2500, December 30, 1949, p. 853.**

WALTER ALLEN

Those who have read Frank Swinnerton's earlier volume of literary reminiscences, **"Background With Chorus,"** know what to expect of **"Figures in the Foreground."** It is, as the author says himself, "a book of personal gossip," but it is the gossip of a man who writes from experience at first hand. Mr. Swinnerton has spent his life among books and among those who make them. . . .

In his new book he draws on his memories of British literary life between 1917 and 1940. He is—and no one knows it better than he—a survivor from a past age. He is, as he says in a characteristic phrase, "worm-eaten with Liberalism"; and of himself before World War I he writes:

"It never occurred to me that one day men would consider it disgraceful for a writer to earn money by the popularity of his writings. The authors I admired, whether dead or living, from Shakespeare to Shaw, had all done this; we who followed hoped to share our interest and pleasure in life with innumerable fellow-creatures, and not only the esoteric few. We aimed at being professionals."

That is precisely what he became, and for the most part his reminiscences are of fellow-professionals. His book is discursive, but a backbone is provided for it by extracts from his more than 20 years' correspondence with Hugh Walpole.

They make a nice contrast: Swinnerton cool, skeptical, the embodiment of common sense; Walpole enthusiastic, impulsive, avid of popularity and success almost to the point of morbidity. No question, Walpole emerges as more than slightly absurb, as when, for instance, he proposed to entertain his 50 'best" friends on his 50th birthday. But, as Swinnerton presents him through his letters, he is touching in his absurdity. . . .

There are, too, American interludes, recollections of lecture tours, a study of the personality of the publisher George Doran, the report of a single, awkward interview with Fitzgerald, and some perceptive pages on Sinclair Lewis. . . .

Many of the figures in Swinnerton's foreground are now almost forgotten and much of what he relates of the literary gang-wars of the twenties seems remote indeed. This does not matter. He brings a literary epoch to life with a sharp clarity; and, as with all epochs, we understand the bigger figures the better for being made aware of the smaller. He gives us the background to history, which is gossip preserved and reported.

> *Walter Allen, "Some Literary Gang-Wars of Yesterday," in* The New York Times Book Review, *June 14, 1964, p. 6.*

ERNEST BUCKLER

Near 80, Verdi composed "Falstaff"; at 80, England's Frank Swinnerton writes **"Quadrille." "Quadrille"** is no "Falstaff," to be sure, but it is a like example of perdurable creative power. Mr. Swinnerton has composed upward of 50 books in his lifetime. Of this number, at least 35 are novels. . . . This novel is certainly among his best. The final installment of a quartet (the others were **"The Woman From Sicily," "A Tigress in Prothero"** and **"The Grace Divorce"**) it continues the author's observation—again, over more than half a century—of the changing tactics in another, timeless war, this time between men and women. The wit, marksmanship, spanking pace and impeccable technique are still there, brighter than new.

It is a rather old-fashioned novel, in that it has a forthright plot, assertive characters and no more allegorical lint than a scalpel; but its grasp of the moneyed and artistic life in St. John's Wood is as up-to-date as Kansas City. The title may be taken in either meaning: the book covers the "game" of life and the "dance" of life equally well. Reminiscent of Maugham's lucidity and shrewdness, it meshes like clockwork, without a waste word. Sniffers at Maugham (or at literary clock

work of any kind) may sniff at **"Quadrille,"** but it is whacking good and substantial entertainment nevertheless.

The time is 1960, and the story pivots on young concert pianist Laura Grace, through the hurdles of career, involvement with some way-out esthetes (deliciously skewered) and a fateful infatuation, to true love at last with a solid fellow artist. The Grace clan . . . are all "good" people. It is the author's prime feat that he makes each of them also distinctive and interesting.

They are not quite so interesting, though, as the seamier types whose lives involve theirs. . . .

There is plenty of good melodrama, including a cliff-hanger inquest . . . but the book's chief force lies in its unerring blend of detail and occasion. The epigraph is: "In tragic life, God wot / No villain need be! Passions spin the plot / We are betrayed by what is false within." It is taken from Meredith's "Modern Love," which charts the dark undertows that menace fervency. The subject here is less restricted and the over-all tone nothing like as grim as Meredith's, but in this case (see the chapters labeled "Panic," "Bitterness," "What Is Jealousy?"), the novelist renders such carcinogens of the spirit more tellingly than the poet.

Mr. Swinnerton dips into no psychological arcana. Though he avoids such immersions, his eagle eye and darting net miss little that is galvanic in human relations. **"Quadrille"** really swings.

> *Ernest Buckler, "Skulduggery in St. John's Wood," in* The New York Times Book Review, *June 27, 1965, p. 30.*

THE TIMES LITERARY SUPPLEMENT

For the past forty years, two-thirds of his long career as a writer, Mr. Frank Swinnerton has lived in a restored seventeenth-century cottage in the Surrey village of Cranleigh. . . . At least, he calls it a village, for, in spite of all the urbanization of the Home Counties, he has managed to remain confidently under the impression that he lives deep in the English countryside. Indeed, one of the attractions of *Reflections from a Village* comes from the otherwise by no means unsophisticated author's naive discovery of the garden, the village green and the commonest of wild birds and flowers. . . . There is nothing affected about this, however, for Mr. Swinnerton has preserved into old age much of the excitement with which he first began "to notice such things".

Old people do not merely remember the past, they carry part of it with them, and Mr. Swinnerton appears to wear, like a jacket, something of the warmth of a period earlier than that of the 1920s when he first came to his cottage. For he did not really fit into the age of Lawrence, Fitzgerald and Aldous Huxley; he belonged more to what he himself called "the Georgian Literary Scene". His writer friends were men like H. G. Wells and Walter de la Mare. . . .

Perhaps, in his admiration for the Georgians, Mr. Swinnerton repeats some of their bad habits, including a tendency towards "belle-lettrism" on subjects about which he does not know very much, such as spiders. But he has their merits too: a genuine enjoyment of life, a sharp eye for the homely and familiar, and a capacity for friendship. Even his occasional blindnesses help to recapture the opinions and prejudices of a past age—he believes, for instance, that "superfine critics" still despise the work of Charles Dickens. *Reflections from a*

Village is a rambling, companionable, agreeably old-fashioned book and though W. H. Hudson and Hilaire Belloc and the rest of Mr. Swinnerton's more country-minded friends would not have regarded his Surrey garden as being in the heart of rural England, they would certainly have agreed that he has made the most of it.

"Late Georgian," in The Times Literary Supplement, *No. 3499, March 20, 1969, p. 292.**

THE TIMES LITERARY SUPPLEMENT

It would be hard to maintain that *Nor All Thy Tears* comes up to the standard of [Swinnerton's] best fiction, since despite its lively construction and wide range of characters, there is a certain lack of verisimilitude about much of their behaviour which, alas, depends largely on the way they talk and the attitudes they express—inescapably those of an earlier age. The tough twenty-five-year-old heiress to a Fleet Street empire, who is the focus of attention, is somewhat inclined to shriek and glare and collapse, particularly after a glass or two of champagne with her oily legal adviser, in the manner of a Victorian heroine rather than the dogged and indeed pig-headed new broom who decides to liven up the old firm with more sex and sophistication. . . .

Frank Swinnerton is never at a loss for incident; there are both office and domestic tensions interwoven here, and he has managed his two big scenes—the office dinner and a jolly discussion, on politics and such . . .—with considerable aplomb and expertise. He is a good deal less convincing on the interior monologues in which most of the women characters spend some time indulging. . . . Those who actually know Fleet Street office life may raise an eyebrow or two, but they will nevertheless find much to entertain in the remarkably agile and fluent narrative that Mr. Swinnerton invents. . . .

"Paper Tigers," in The Times Literary Supplement, *No. 3669, June 23, 1972, p. 705.*

PETER ACKROYD

What a familiar ring it has, 'the novel.' A comfort to the spinster and the secretary, and a temporary refuge for 'the reader' in an imagined world. A world in which effect follows cause, emotions are excited only to be soothed, adventure and surprise are muted in the pianissimo of a final chapter. The novel is now the armchair of our culture. I would hate to be considered a rabid experimentalist, but I often wish that contemporary English writing were something other than the fag-end of the nineteenth century.

Gloomy reflections like these occurred to me after reading Swinnerton's *Rosalind Passes.* It is Mr Swinnerton's fortieth novel and his writing career must, as they say of another profession, have given pleasure to millions. I may be a juvenile carper, but I found nothing commendable in this novel. It has that unctuous and enveloping quality which I associate with afternoon music on Radio Two. And perhaps this is its context, for the writing is of the romance-and-intrigue variety which commonly appeals to the silent majority. *Rosalind Passes* transpires in the world of the middle-classes. At the centre of the narrative are Clarissa, an amateur artist, and her husband Henry, a senior civil servant with an interest in Druids. Clarissa meets Rosalind through Daphne, a bright old friend, and the death of Rosalind (was it murder or was it suicide?) involves them all in a nexus of tea and suffering.

Mr Swinnerton's prose is constructed in what can only be called a mannered style. Here is a description which I have picked at random: "Clarissa's lips, too full for perfect beauty, although she would have been described as a handsome woman, closed tightly . . ." which adequately fits the generally fussy tenor of the narrative. There is something remarkably prosaic about even the most lyrical passages: "'Do you know what suspicion is? Black terrible suspicion.' Tears filled the lovely eyes." The lovely eyes are those of Rosalind at this juncture, but they might have been those of any of the females. Sentiment of this kind has its place, but in a novel of emotional intrigue it makes the action a little stereotyped.

Human reactions are reduced (raised, some might say) to the status of middle-class caricature. Conversations are permanently conducted in that bright and brittle fashion which novelists generally assume when they aspire to 'real' conversation. More surprisingly, at moments of stress the characters commune with themselves in exactly the same style. Their interior lives are like a very long cocktail party, thus holding the attention for less than a moment. And as a counterpoint to the yearnings of these women who were born to better things, Swinnerton has created for us a charming working-class couple who have worked their way up in the world (remember, this is the 'twenties). They are appropriately named George and Doris. No working-class Mum would dare call her daughter Clarissa, of course, and the aforesaid child would never dream of 'taking up' painting. But the roles of Doris and George are peripheral, and the emotional heat is generated in rather more discreet surroundings. Chapters are entitled 'Henry Turns To Philosophy' and 'Clarissa Is a Comfort.' Which of course she is, to any frustrated and semi-intelligent woman who wants to feel—vicariously—both sorry for herself and appeased with her lot. (pp. 282-83)

Peter Ackroyd, *"Insubstantial Pageant,"* in The Spectator, *Vol. 231, No. 7575, September 1, 1973, pp. 282-83.**

JAMES BROCKWAY

A new novel by Frank Swinnerton published in his 92nd year. I make no apology for referring to the author's age. It is utterly relevant. And what do we see opposite the title-page? No less than forty fiction titles listed, followed by fifteen other titles. What an achievement. It makes another man blush for shame.

Only yesterday I received a card from a celebrated woman author, intellectual and sometime contributor to *b&b* . . . saying: 'What, I ask myself, *is* a bookman? Have I ever met one?'. Now, I can answer her: Frank Swinnerton.

Before discussing [*Some Achieve Greatness*], I should declare an interest, then claim disinterest—in the correct sense of that word, on which Mr Swinnerton, particularly, would insist: the need to take an objective view, which is every author's right to expect. The interest is twofold. In the first place, Frank Swinnerton is a respected contributor to *b&b*. In the second place, quite unknown to him, I owe him a great debt of gratitude. I also owe one to the late Adolf Hitler—to whom he is related as the North Pole is to the South: each at opposite ends of our world. . . . Hitler's starting of the war rescued me from an unwanted civil service career and Swinnerton's *The Georgian Literary Scene,* read at an RAF station in 1940, while waiting for Hitler to invade, confirmed me in my ideas about what really interested me in life.

I am not one for 'books on books on books'? . . . Yet there is one book of this kind I still take down from the shelf . . . and that is Frank Swinnerton's classic. So I have novelist and bookman Frank Swinnerton in large measure to thank for (a) my doing more or less, or something like, what I wanted to do in life; (b) remaining relatively impecunious; and, third blessing, (c) achieving what in the very last words of his new novel he describes as the first of the many blessings enjoyed by his leading character, Florence Marvell: 'contentment with her own lot'. (pp. 56-7)

So, in view of all this, how can I approach this novel objectively, as I should and as the author deserves that I should? I must try. . . .

[The story] amounts to a moral tale, too realistic in detail, too worldly-wise, to be called a fairytale and too lively and witty to be called a homily. Though sweetness and light prevail, all through the novel there is a very present sense of the author's knowing quite well that in real life they mostly do not. In addition to his picture of British Justice at work, there is also a chapter entitled 'Politics', with sufficient insights into that world to put anyone (except Sir Roderick?) off wanting to be part and parcel of it.

With the exception of the young people . . . all the characters and minor figures are excellently drawn. The narrative . . . sags towards the middle, when both Florrie and Roderick become too full of self-questioning and speculation: 'Should I? Would he? Will it?'. The situation, however, is saved and the final impression is of a story well and most entertainingly told.

A middlebrow novel? Yes—and I don't think the author would pretend it was anything else. He has none of the pretension of those who scorn Gilbert and Sullivan and he quotes Gilbert when it suits him . . . as his characters would do, too.

The novel of an elderly man, whose values and opinions were shaped in a safer, more confined world than ours today? Most certainly—and again the author makes no bones about that. Indeed, he goes out of his way in his very first sentence to stress it, and in several other places too. No make-believe here, either.

The world he describes—a small, parochial affair, like British politics today? Yes, again. And a world, too, of decent values made possible only because it was a privileged and protected world. (p. 57)

James Brockway, "A Real Bookman," in Books and Bookmen, *Vol. 21, No. 10, July, 1976, pp. 56-7.*

D(onald) M(ichael) Thomas

1935-

English novelist, poet, translator, editor, and critic.

Thomas became a literary celebrity with the publication of *The White Hotel* (1980). Thomas's earlier work is also respected but was less widely reviewed. It includes several volumes of poems noted for their science fiction slant and two novels, *The Flute Player* (1979) and *Birthstone* (1980). Thomas has also translated some works of the Russian poets Anna Akhmatova and Alexander Pushkin.

The poems in Thomas's collections *Dreaming in Bronze* (1981) and *Selected Poems* (1983) range from graphic accounts of atrocities committed at Nazi concentration camps to interpretations of Freudian concepts of human sexuality. Many critics view Thomas's thematic concerns as "obsessions" with sex and death. These are also prominent themes in *The White Hotel*. The novel begins with a twelve-page erotic poem attributed to Lisa Erdman, a young Jewish woman whose hysterical sexual fantasies lead her to seek treatment with Sigmund Freud. Later, during World War II, Lisa's fears of physical mutilation are realized when she is killed during a pogrom in the Russian town of Babi Yar. Critics were impressed with Thomas's creative use of various narrative viewpoints—historical, psychological, and ethical—to convey the intensity of Lisa's fantasies and her fate.

In *Ararat* (1983) Thomas again examines the themes of sexual imagery and violent death. Constructed as several separate yet thematically linked stories, the novel exhibits Thomas's technical skill in translation, his surrealistic verse, and his knowledge of European culture. The major theme in *Ararat*, fantasy versus reality, is developed through a famous Soviet poet who entertains his lover by composing erotic tales about past and present Russian artists. Within these stories, each character travels to Mount Ararat, where Noah's Ark is said to have ended its journey; it was also the site of an Armenian massacre by the Turks in 1915. Although critics have pointed out similarities between this work and *The White Hotel*, *Ararat* received less favorable attention. While the theme and originality of the book have been commended, a number of critics maintain that Thomas's multilayered narrative lacks unity and focus. Others have contended that the violence in *Ararat* is less relevant to the story than in *The White Hotel*. Thomas's recent novel *Swallow* (1984) is the first of a projected series of sequels to *Ararat*.

(See also *CLC*, Vols. 13, 22 and *Contemporary Authors*, Vols. 61-64.)

DICK DAVIS

There is nothing underwritten about D. M. Thomas's new book of poems [*Dreaming in Bronze*]; many of them are vigorous monologues by the neurotic and obsessed. Mr Thomas is clearly a writer who takes it as axiomatic that obsession is artistically fruitful, and that extreme states of mind are in some way more real than sanity. (See his novel, *The White Hotel*.) Those who share these notions will enjoy most of the book; those who look to poetry as a means of providing a sane perspective on

© Nancy Crampton

life will find less to attract them, though at least three of the poems, 'The Clearing', 'The Handkerchief or Ghost Tree' and 'Still Life', are worth their close attention. (p. 22)

Dick Davis, "Missed Worlds," in The Listener, *Vol. 107, No. 2742, January 7, 1982, pp. 22-3.**

ALASDAIR D. F. MACRAE

For some years [Thomas's] poetry was best known for a science fiction element but his collection *The Honeymoon Voyage* (1978 . . .) displayed a wide range of subject matter and was very well received. [*Dreaming in Bronze*] shows a continued progress in material and technique. The collection is divided into two sections. In the first, the poems are in the form of letters, journals or accounts by characters set in literary or historical context; Freud appears both as a character and as an influence on how the other characters are seen in situations of violence, repression and frustration. The importance of Freud continues in the second section where many of the poems are more personal, more immediately attached to the author, in his musings about growing up and his links with his family. The combination of a strongly erotic element with the familiar is sometimes brutal and discomfiting. Thomas's poems are never dull and they excite by pulling together different areas of life and different times. . . . Fantasy remains central to his poetry but what appeared as invention in earlier poems now operates as an extension of reverie and self-examination. His poems have scant involvement with places of work or the press of practical problems but, in their wit, speculation, intelligence and an underlying humaneness, they do comment, often profoundly, on our shared problems.

> *Alasdair D. F. Macrae, in a review of "Dreaming in Bronze," in* British Book News, *February, 1982, p. 114.*

BOOKLIST

[Thomas] considers himself primarily a poet, even in his fiction, which shares with his verse a preoccupation, or rather, an obsession, with sex and death. [In *Selected Poems,* the] graveyards and scenes of departure, particularly of Mother, are sufficiently depressing. But the "love" poems are more unpleasant. Though filled with sexual details, language, and symbols, the impression these often coarse and quirky lines convey is not so much erotic or sensual as gross and fetid. The voyeuristic camera sweeps over scenes of sweaty passion but is often obscured by a filter smudged with murky imagery scraped from that catch basin conveniently called the collective unconscious. Yet there is a curious mix of sparseness, even Oriental subtlety, amid these gross contrivances, unfortunately not extended to the tortured language, which is singularly without music or charm.

> *A review of "Selected Poems," in* Booklist, *Vol. 79, No. 4, October 15, 1982, p. 290.*

PUBLISHERS WEEKLY

Thomas's poems are condensed narratives in much the same way that his prose is a logical extension of years of immersion in the poetic form. He is an unusual hybrid who has cultivated his own consciousness to create a personal myth composed of equal parts of morbid eroticism, his memory of a Cornwall childhood, a romanticization of Freud and Jung and a profound fascination for the Slavic variety of *Weltschmerz.* As poetry, [Thomas's *Selected Poems*] are most valuable for their obdurate shock value. More generally, they are admirable for their quirky, perseverant genius—an independence of mind and a courage of personal vision that are increasingly rare in the literary marketplace.

> *A review of "Selected Poems," in* Publishers Weekly, *Vol. 222, No. 24, December 17, 1982, p. 72.*

ANTHONY BURGESS

Admirers of *The White Hotel* will find that the technique of that pseudo-novel (the term implies no disparagement) has been put to a similar use [in *Ararat*]—meaning that long stretches of verse, documentary facts about atrocities, journeys that get nowhere, insertions that look like pastiche but are straight translation, are in the service less of a structure than of an artfully deceptive object. The object—measurable and weighable—is a book, and the book looks like a novel. Indeed, it sometimes reads like a novel, but it is no more a novel than was *The White Hotel.* . . .

Let me put it this way: if *Madame Bovary* and *The Great Gatsby* and *The Rainbow* are novels, then *Ararat* is a sort of poem. What matters in fiction is character and the action that character begets: things happen, people change, tentative conclusions are reached. What matters in *Ararat* is the title (this is true also of *The White Hotel*) and the cluster of symbols that Mr Thomas has thrown at it, trusting that most of them will stick. What matters also is Mr Thomas's devotion to Russian literature. His portrait on the back cover shows him brooding . . . against bookspines, Pushkin pushing his name out above all.

A poet's book, naturally, and like, say, Auden's *Orators,* less of a structural unit than the poet hopes to persuade us to consider it. You can make such a book by taking various disparate items and pretending to glue them together. The glue will hold for a couple of readings but it turns out to be spittle. [*Ararat*] itself, being unclassifiable, will have to be called a novel, but it is only one in a very Pickwickian sense. Mr Thomas is to be watched, but with great suspicion. (p. 77)

> *Anthony Burgess, "Let's Parler Yidglish!" in* Punch, *Vol. 284, No. 7423, March 2, 1983, pp. 76-7.**

DIANE JOHNSON

Readers of "*Ararat*," D. M. Thomas's new novel, will recognize its similarities to his earlier "*The White Hotel.*" . . . To many critics "*The White Hotel*" seemed an unusual and major work, attempting to treat the largest subjects of our time—World War II, its relation to modern consciousness as described by Freud, and the implications of Freud for the writer of fiction—through the story of a young woman patient of Freud. "*Ararat*" shares these preoccupations—in particular the Freudian conjunction of sexuality and death; this time they are approached through the story of Cleopatra and her lovers and in the reminiscences of a mysterious figure, encountered on a dreamlike sea voyage, who obsessively recounts his part in all of the terrible massacres of modern history. Like the earlier work, "*Ararat*" provides an abundant display of the author's astonishing virtuosity in poetry, in prose, in translating—a writer combining an impassioned European soul with the formal instincts of a spider weaving an immensely complex, elegant and sophisticated web.

A close description of "*Ararat*" reveals a congruity of subject and form, that of a story within a story within a story. In the first framing story, a Russian poet, Rozanov, travels to Gorki on an erotic whim, to sleep with a blind woman who has written a fan letter to him, but whom, in the event, he finds boring. To beguile the night that he must in all politeness spend with her, he improvises a narrative to amuse her on a subject of her choosing: "Improvisation." His narrative begins with a second framing story in which three writers, drinking together in an Armenian hotel, challenge each other to a competition of improvisations; Rozanov then improvises these improvisations. The first teller begins a tale of Surkov, a Russian poet on his way to America by sea. On shipboard Surkov completes an unfinished fragment of Pushkin's "Egyptian Nights."

In Pushkin's fragment, a Russian poet, Charsky, befriends an Italian *improvvisatore,* who gives a dazzling public performance in verse on a subject proposed by someone in the fashionable St. Petersburg audience Charsky has assembled for him. The improviser's subject is Cleopatra and her lovers, three men who have by lot drawn the chance to spend a night with her and who will face execution in the morning. The third lover is a youth, very beautiful, at the beginning of life. Pushkin's fragment breaks off here. D. M. Thomas's Rozanov's Surkov's *improvvisatore* continues the tale to a satisfactory and amusing conclusion. Surkov must then go on to finish the tale of Charsky and the improviser; Rozanov must finish the tale of Surkov and two other tales, ostensibly by the two other writers.

The second writer continues the story of Surkov, now arriving in America by plane, the sea voyage having been only an anxiety dream in the mind of the apprehensive traveler, who, now in New York, plans to set down on paper the amazing improvisation on Pushkin which he has dreamed. Surkov's tale ceases, but he figures in the tale of the last speaker, an American writer of Armenian descent, who brings the two earlier speakers and herself to Ararat, the sacred Armenian mountain where in tradition Noah's ark came to rest. Then in an epilogue we return to Rozanov, and a reminder that these stories are only his contrivances which, in the course of our reading, have absorbed us in their reality.

The power of an artist, in his work, is absolute. When Surkov is finishing Pushkin's tale, he brings Charsky and the Italian improviser to a conclusion he does not like: The improviser has been made to face a duel, and when he and Charsky arrive at the appointed place, they hear that Pushkin has just been fatally wounded in an earlier duel with his brother-in-law D'Anthes (a historical fact). Surkov decides that if his improvisation had not included certain things, Pushkin would not have fought, and he rewrites the ending, in the second version sacrificing the improviser and attempting thereby to alter history. . . .

In this tale the artist is God creating order, and he can be as arbitrary. In elaborately framed narratives such as these, the reader may resent being torn from one interesting situation and made to face another. But Mr. Thomas's powers are such, and the faintly repellent qualities of his protagonists are such, and the formal elements are so clearly going to prevail over the purely narrative elements, that we do not mind; in fact part of the pleasure we take in the work is in seeing the pieces fit together, and in Mr. Thomas's omniscient foresight: Art—or fiction—is the true subject of "Ararat."

Mr. Thomas's elaborate constructions have provoked reproaches for not being all "made up." "The White Hotel" draws upon the recorded testimony of a woman who had been at Babi Yar, material from Freud, lines from Yeats—all properly attributed, of course, by Mr. Thomas, who had done no more than the author of any "true-life novel" to document the congruence of truth and fiction. Yet the uneasiness provoked by "The White Hotel" seemed to testify more to a general discomfort with his protean powers of projection and assimilation—his witchery: "I can't help being others. I can't help becoming others. Everyone, everything," exclaims the writer Surkov in "Ararat."

We usually admire extremes of artifice—things made in miniature, purses made of stitches too tiny to see, projects which reveal that the artist has gone to an immense lot of trouble to make a thing that seems like nature but is not. Yet some critics have faulted "The White Hotel" for the conjunction of its ambitious themes—eros and thanatos, the Holocaust—and its formal virtuosity, as if fiction, with its elements of artifice and imitation, somehow does a disservice to the reality of events; implicit in this criticism is the notion that some aspects of history are so solemn they can never be a suitable subject for art (which is one theory of why there are no great Holocaust novels, unless you consider "The White Hotel" one). But if some subjects can be too large for art, there must be other subjects of perfect proportion; "Ararat," a work of artifice

about artifice, a formal work about form, risks less, perhaps, but seems a work of perfect proportion. (p. 7)

> Diane Johnson, "Story within Story within Story," in The New York Times Book Review, March 27, 1983, pp. 7, 39.

ANNE TYLER

It's not really necessary, of course, for a reviewer to make the plot entirely clear to prospective readers. But in *Ararat,* the whole point is the plot—its devilish cleverness, or its maddening obscurity, however you choose to view it. In any case, it's not an honest plot. If a contract exists between writer and reader that the writer will do his best to draw the reader in and the reader will do his best to follow, D. M. Thomas reneged on his part of the deal. To be fair, he didn't even agree to make the deal. He blurs events—the whole point is their blurring—and he swerves and doubles back in hope of losing us. And if we hang on, against all odds, and stick with his tale to the end, we're not rewarded with the final "Ah, now I see!" that would have made the hanging on worthwhile.

The central male figures of these stories—even Pushkin . . .— tend to melt together; no distinction is made between their various personalities. In fact, there's a deliberate attempt to merge them, to imply that these are really inner chambers of one and the same man. All of them are self-centered, self-indulgent, and unlikable. Rozanov is sleeping with the blind woman because "he had never slept with a blind woman," but he's disgusted by her thin legs and her "wandering, unattached pupils." The dream Surkov deflowers a childish little Polish gymnast and then feels oppressed by her ("I burn up women as a marathon runner burns up his flesh," he says), and the real-life Surkov, who shares Rozanov's distaste for thin legs, has the same attitude of conquest toward all the women he meets. Even the Armenian . . . , while a gentler man than the others, cannot function sexually until his partner has bitten his hand to draw blood and he has called her a "foul name." In general, sex on these pages is violent, unloving, and unpleasant.

The book's effect, a publisher's blurb tells us, is that of opening one of those little Russian dolls and finding other dolls inside. But it's not, exactly. The dolls inside those Russian dolls are different from each other, each with its own unique little face and costume. The dolls inside this novel are indistinguishable. Evidently the point is that there is no true invention in storytelling. Willy-nilly, the narrator passes his own traits and prejudices on to his characters; his characters are inextricable from him.

Ararat takes its title from its preoccupation with the Armenian diaspora of 1915. The shipboard Surkov, the one of the dream, is followed about by an old man who compulsively relates all the atrocities he has committed in his lifetime—or in several lifetimes, perhaps, for what he's describing is every instance of mass brutality that occurred during the twentieth century. . . . Special emphasis, however, is placed upon the Armenian events, and it's a mark of this book's strangeness that these horrors—chillingly, meticulously described—fill the only scenes in this book where there's the slightest bit of humor. If humor is what you want to call it.

The old man's appalling coolness as he catalogs his crimes is in itself funny, in a dreadful way. ". . . altogether there has, been great exaggeration of the numbers killed," he says. "It is certain that no more than a million were killed.'' (pp. 30-1)

In *The White Hotel,* the account of the Nazi atrocities appeared to have some point; everything led up to it, and there was a moment where the reader heard that satisfying click of things coming together. *The White Hotel* was disturbing to read, but one felt it was necessarily disturbing. *Ararat* disturbs without purpose. The Armenian tragedy is merely one more quirky scene in a book that's full of quirky scenes.

Finally, *Ararat* lacks power. It seems almost to be consciously undermining its power—breaking off each narrative sweep the moment we're caught up in it, beaching us once again, leaving us looking around in bewilderment. Books are meant to carry us to other lives, I figure. When a book drives its readers to diagraming the plot, you know it's not going to carry you very far. (p. 32)

Anne Tyler, "Stories within Stories," in The New Republic, Vol. 188, No. 13, April 4, 1983, pp. 30-2.

CHRISTOPHER DRIVER

Ararat is a shorter book than [*The White Hotel*], but it picks its way through similar no man's lands between fact and fiction, life and literature, erotic fantasy and historic massacre. The poetic or cinematic structure challenges the reader to absorption, as into a hall of mirrors, without any tiresome demand to follow the sequence of thought and event: it is *fides quaerens intellectum.* The listener to Rozanov's story is blind, and the listener-by-extension to the story-within-the-story sometimes feels like a blindfold hostage, permitted glimpses of half-recognised street furniture that leave him well short of secure orientation. Unless, perhaps, he is as familiar as Thomas is with the life and work of Pushkin, whose 'Egyptian Nights' is translated and reinterpreted as the structural core of the book. The lambent presence of Pushkin, the author's guru or second skin, saves *Ararat* from being written off as a relatively lightweight re-creation of a popular success, and it also rescues Thomas's writing from sprawling psychoanalytical self-indulgence. Perhaps it is with justice that Pushkin's elegant strength is sometimes compared with Mozart's.

Certainly the effect of moving as a reader from *The White Hotel* to *Ararat* recalls a process familiar in the history of musical composition. Ideas, themes, patterns and juxtapositions of tonality that have been employed for a large-scale work often suggest to a composer in their working-out a further series of possibilities which demand subsequent exploration in a more intimate medium, a quartet or a sonata. In chamber music, tone can be lightened or darkened and an atmosphere changed in the space of a bar or two, without portentous build-up. This happens here with the mixture of emotion and embarrassment in the love-making of two Armenians, Khandjian and Mariam, at the close of Rozanov's long improvisation. When the couple begin to share 'the sorrows and miracles of their origins' in the holocaust and diaspora of their people, they are able to pass from affection to violence, and from a 'soapy erection' under the shower to a snowy vision of Ararat from an upstairs window, in the space of a paragraph or two, without apprehension of the mixture curdling under pressure of haste. . . .

The central role allotted to Pushkin in this book allows Thomas the poet to deploy his virtuosity with translation from the Russian. But it is also important at a deeper level to Thomas the novelist. In *The White Hotel* —the hotel which was 'just my life, you see' in the dream the young Lisa Erdman related to Freud—Pushkin was parenthetical, but he was significantly present at the climax, after Lisa and her stepson had arrived at Kiev in September 1941. At Babi Yar:

> During the night, the bodies settled. A hand would adjust, by a fraction, causing another's head to turn slightly. Features imperceptibly altered. 'The trembling of the sleeping night', Pushkin called it; only he was referring to the settling of a house.

This apparently casual quotation precedes the unifying paragraph of the whole novel, where fantasy meets reality and unites the dreamer-victim not only with the Jewish dead but with their German and Russian exterminators, who had encouraged each other—as a perceptive concentration camp graduate once remarked—to act out in public the most secret fantasies of the European mind. 'The soul of man is a far country, which cannot be approached or explored.'

For the coda to that fearsome climax Thomas then side-slipped into a curiously Bunyan-like vision of a workaday heaven where a routine of human service freely given is punctuated by specifically Biblical references evocative of transcendence and inexhaustible resource: the wine at Cana, maternal milk, the image of an infinitely expandable refugee camp 'where Israel's tents do shine by night'. Pushkin, too, admired Bunyan, and wrote a poem called 'The Pilgrim'. He also lived an adventurous sexual life and died in his duel with d'Anthès as a jealous cuckold, which probably helps rather than hinders a modern writer's appreciation of his far-reaching humanism, his instinct for the universal. Pushkin, according to one critic, 'could think and speak as a pagan, a Christian, a medieval knight, a Renaissance man, a votary of Voltaire and a disciple of Rousseau'. It is surely as his disciple that Thomas in these two books seeks to embrace in the same unifying vision both the characteristic horrors and the fresh starts of the 20th century: in *The White Hotel,* the holocaust and Freud; in *Ararat,* the Armenian genocide and the Cold War.

Christopher Driver, "Pushkin's Pupil," in London Review of Books, April 1 to April 20, 1983, p. 11.

JASCHA KESSLER

When a novel called *The White Hotel* became a bestseller in 1981-1982, its author, D. M. Thomas, was not generally known as a poet. . . . Thomas is a Cornishman, not an American, and indeed his strange and fascinating novel had not become famous in Great Britain at all. Those who have read *The White Hotel* know that its title is the name of the long narrative poem that opens its pages, an erotic, even rather pornographic poem, and that The White Hotel of the poem is itself a fantastic place, a symbol of the female body itself, the mother's body, as projected from the deepest layer of Oedipal fantasy. . . . For some theorists, that place remains potentially retrievable, not in the imagination, but in reality; but how such a thing should be possible remains a mystery. Perhaps the problem of remembering the preconscious paradise of the womb's universe of oceanic bliss, and its continuation for some at the breasts of the mother is the chief problem of the human animal and the source of all our strivings for the (re)creation of Utopian worlds, for individual maturation, and the source of the religious impulse that seeks heaven beyond death in an afterworld of eternal beatitude. Certainly such a dream-fantasy poses what is perhaps the most formidable obstacle towards the understanding and acceptance of reality itself for the human animal, and for its reconciliation with existence itself. At any rate Thomas' exceptionally interesting and provocative novel is the work of an unusual imaginative intelligence, and is clearly the work of a *thinking* poet. . . . The long poem that prefaces and introduces [*The White Hotel*] was written by the patient at a point in her psychoanalysis by Freud when all progress towards the resolution of her illness had been blocked: she goes for a vacation, and the poem erupts from her unknown, unconscious self.

I mention all of this because a portion of that poem appears in print now in a volume by D. M. Thomas entitled *Selected Poems* where it's called *"from* **Don Giovanni."** It is as though Thomas sees this poem as part of his work through his several books, for he is primarily a poet, and now he has decided to select those of his pieces that still live for him and still represent "different phases and stages of [his] work," as he puts it in his Preface. This volume of selected poems is really quite an interesting one, and I would hope that all those readers who prefer fiction to poetry and who liked *The White Hotel* . . . will consider buying and reading his poetry too, for it will surely shed some interesting light upon this writer and his work.

Thomas has divided [*Selected Poems*] into three parts. The first contains love poems or erotic poems, which are not necessarily the same sort of thing; the second part contains a lot of poems that fill in our sense of his Cornish background, as well as his early years in Australia and the United States. The third part offers poems that handle broader themes, from history, culture, myth. What we have therefore is a compendium that provides us with much that this writer cannot show us in the novels, and is a kind of exposure and exhibition of the artist's personality as a whole. . . . One point strikes one with great force at a first reading: Thomas is not only various and wide-ranging in his imagination, but also humorous, witty, and really quite fantastical, even rather daring, willing to risk grotesqueries and brutalities. He is also satirical. A poet who indulges in erotomania, in passional love, in intellectual fantasies, as well as offering wide-ranging themes taken from history, psychology and anthropology, is a poet who will stimulate our own imaginations strongly. . . .

[In **"Peter Kürten to the Witnesses (Düsseldorf, 1931)"** Thomas depicts the trial of a mass-murderer.] His note to the poem says, "When Kürten, the notorious mass-murderer was arrested and tried, the liberal German government agonised over whether he should be executed. The guillotine, in fact, had become rusted from disuse." What Thomas tells us in this one poem is more interesting and significant, I think, than whole libraries of works about the mentality of Nazi criminals during the years of Hitler's power. Thomas' imagination works itself into the quality of this man's mind and being, makes the inarticulate speak to us, and speak oh so clearly indeed about the years of Hitler that were to come; so that we must think again about our judgments of the values of life and death. . . .

[If *Selected Poems*] brings to our attention [Thomas'] decades of writing poetry, that is his good luck and ours. I trust I have suggested that his work is fascinating in both modes, and well worth considering as a whole. There are other good poets who have written novels, but their work doesn't seem quite as much all of a piece as does Thomas'.

Jascha Kessler, "D. M. Thomas: 'Selected Poems'," in a radio broadcast on KUSC-FM—Los Angeles, CA, May 18, 1983.

GEORGE KEARNS

[In *Ararat*, D. M. Thomas attempts a balancing act somewhat like Umberto Eco's in *The Name of the Rose*]: on the one hand the book is loaded with Significance; on the other it's all Fiction Games receding in an infinite series. This creates an annoyingly schizophrenic effect in which the serious is undercut by the clever, and the clever made heavy by the portentous. It's a puzzling book, partly because it's made out of puzzles, partly because after two readings I'm still not sure exactly who's who or what's going on. On the game side of Thomas' brain the book is an improvisation on the word *improvisation,* or an M. C. Escher drawing of a hand that's drawing a hand that draws the hand that is drawing it, and so on. Many find this endlessly fascinating. Others find that once you've got the Concept there's no place much to go. (p. 556)

Then there's the Portentous side, a litany of the atrocities, genocide, massacres that have written themselves on the pages of our century: much about the Turkish slaughter of the Armenians in 1915, the Gulag, Babi Yar, Indo-China, Dachau, Treblinka, Charles Manson, Beria, and others. And there's a lot of sex, extremely coarsely presented, most of it of the numbed or bored variety. Sex, of course, is linked with violence. What are we to make of all this? That we live in a world that is horror in public, waste land in private, and that all that is left to do is improvise stories? I don't know. Surely Thomas is a clever and learned writer, at his best when he's performing acts of mimicry, and he can be a very funny mimic, one with perfect pitch. . . . The publisher finds *Ararat* a "brutally funny" book. Brutal, yes; funny, not often enough. Imagine Nabokov, coming toward you with Messages, wringing his hands over atrocities, sweating ever so slightly from the exertion required to perform his admittedly clever stunts. (pp. 558-59)

George Kearns, "World Well Lost," in The Hudson Review, *Vol. XXXVI, No. 3, Autumn, 1983, pp. 549-62.**

JOHN BEMROSE

Swallow picks up where *Ararat* left off. Once again [Thomas] confronts his readers with the indefatigable Russian poet Rozanov, a womanizer with an extraordinary talent for literary improvisation. And once again Thomas's ability to weave a number of disparate stories into an uncannily unified whole has yielded a highly entertaining piece of fiction.

In *Swallow* Rozanov has not quite extracted himself from the dilemma into which he blundered in *Ararat,* a commitment to spending a night with Olga, a blind, unattractive scholar. Instead of sleeping with her, he held her spellbound with stories filled with enthralling characters who told even more stories. That technique, repeated in *Swallow,* has produced a literary hall of mirrors in which fact and fantasy become indistinguishable.

One of the most pervasive themes of the various tales is the mystery of literary creation. Rozanov tells Olga the story of an imaginary international Olympiad in which the competitors are literary improvisers. The Italian entry bitterly divides her listeners with a dark, passionate harangue. Surprisingly, some of the most intriguing passages in *Swallow* consist of the judges' private debates on that entry. It is a treat to hear an intelligent discussion of literature without cant or pointless complexity. But those passages also illustrate that literary taste is dominated by far deeper powers than rational discourse. Most of the judges initially dislike her offering, but they eventually approve of it—for no apparent reason. . . .

Swallow is often affecting, especially in the sections in which Thomas recreates the unhappy period he spent as an adolescent in Australia. He presents that story as the original prose version of the poem improvised by Southerland, the English contestant. Southerland commits suicide when he realizes that the judges have discovered he has stolen his material. Thomas seems to be offering up Southerland as a somewhat ironic sacrifice to critics who charged him with plagiarizing the descriptions of the Babi Yar massacre in *The White Hotel*.

The author seems to have remained essentially convinced of his right to borrow and change the work of other writers. He makes his defiance clear by including sections of H. Rider Haggard's 1886 novel, *King Solomon's Mines*. As Thomas writes in his preface, he has "scandalously amended" those excerpts by peppering them with hilariously obscene epithets. Most readers will not mind the transformation of the rather prim Haggard. Indeed, readers can forgive Thomas almost anything in return for his unflaggingly witty and charming book.

John Bemrose, "Tales of Brilliant Wit," in Maclean's Magazine, *Vol. 97, No. 26, June 25, 1984, p. 51.*

HARRIETT GILBERT

Whatever else may be said of D. M. Thomas, he certainly knows how to stir up the literary shit. My dentist, who is Jewish, nearly rammed the drill through my windpipe when describing his reaction to *The White Hotel*: its detailed, almost loving account of the massacre at Babi Yar was perceived by him as a pornographic insult to those whom the Nazis butchered there.

Others were more outraged by what they saw as that passage's plagiarism (from the writer Anatoli Kuznetsov), while others, me included, have been generally upset by Thomas's female characters. From his first novel, *The Flute-Player*, to last year's outpouring, *Ararat*, their primary function seems to have been as receptacles for brutality.

Swallow is *Ararat*'s sequel: number two in a threatened sequence 'of improvisational novels . . . [concerning] the mysterious way in which a word, an image, a dream, a story, calls up another, connected yet independent'. But if *Ararat*'s improvisations felt like a pointlessly nasty game, those in the new book begin to acquire a not uninteresting purpose. From his 'Author's Note' on, Thomas is challenging his critics. What, he is asking, does plagiarism mean when *all* stories are triggered off by something the author has heard or read? And why, come to that, do we place so much value on words that are fixed to a page?

It now transpires that the stories-within-stories of *Ararat* were being told by Corinna Riznich, an italian *improvisatrice*, as her contribution to the final heat of a story-telling Olympiad. The judges of the contest represent the 'detached' voice of literary criticism but, in his many-layered narrative . . . , Thomas shows how the critics, too, are enmeshed in the common fantasies, symbols and myths of the story-tellers. The world of the imagination (unlike that of nationalistic or cold-war, East-West politics) is not disfigured by boundaries. Its language is universal.

At the same time, we all of us speak it differently. And, despite an integrity more obvious than in his earlier books, Thomas's accent still jars. Making his principal character a woman is a facile response to feminist quarrels with his work—his female characters still live only as breasts and cunts to be conquered. An anti-nuclear-war theme is invoked with embarrassing gaucheness; a narrative poem (17 pages) reads like a car engine failing to start. Thomas is certainly more original than some of his detractors maintain, but his shocks to the system are still too like those of a consciously outrageous adolescent.

Harriett Gilbert, "Echo Chamber," in New Statesman, *Vol. 107, No. 2780, June 29, 1984, p. 26.**

Luisa Valenzuela

1938-

Argentine novelist, short story writer, journalist, and script-writer.

Valenzuela is recognized as one of the significant authors to have emerged in Argentina since the "boom" in Latin American literature during the 1960s. Like many of her literary contemporaries, Valenzuela introduces fantastic events into socially realistic settings—a technique known as magic realism which allows fiction to reflect the extraordinary qualities of life in Latin America.

Valenzuela's use of magic realism emphasizes the surreal and bizarre more so than does the fiction of such pioneers of the technique as Gabriel García Márquez and Julio Cortázar. Accordingly, some critics find her stories less reflective of social or psychological reality than those of her contemporaries and claim that she is more interested in experimenting with literary form than in telling stories. Valenzuela experiments with narrative structure through a constantly shifting point of view and through self-conscious language that examines the creative process of art while relating stories. She has been praised for her inventive use of image, metaphor, and symbol in examining themes of violence, political oppression, and cultural repression, especially as the latter relates to women. These aspects of Valenzuela's writings reflect her statement that "magic realism was a beautiful resting place, but the thing to do is go forward."

Valenzuela first gained attention with *Hay que sonreír* (1966), a novel that depicts the submissive state of women in Argentina. This novel, which appeared in English in *Clara: Thirteen Short Stories and a Novel* (1976), interrelates themes dealing with violence, women, and politics through the encounters of Clara, a beautiful young woman whose innocent dreams conflict with the values of her culture. Critics admired Valenzuela's infusion of magic realism into the novel's conventional structure. However, her short stories have met with a mixed critical response. Critics generally concluded that her stories appeal to ambitious readers who are willing to search through surreal presentations for meaning. Valenzuela's recent novel *The Lizard's Tail* (1983) is a fictional biography of a despotic government official who is also a sorcerer. This novel has been especially praised for Valenzuela's use of sorcery as a metaphor for the means by which political power is used to control people and is considered by some critics to be her most important work. Valenzuela presently lives in New York City.

(See also *Contemporary Authors*, Vol. 101.)

Photograph by Layle Silbert

to politics to philosophical quest, in each one the threat of violence lurks close to the surface. Valenzuela's Argentina is a place where any ordinary parcel may contain a bomb, where any car may belong to the secret police, where even the conversation of children turns to talk of guns. . . .

On the whole, . . . the collection gives a vivid, eerie, and affecting sense of life in a society where a cruel tension is the governing condition.

> [*Amanda Y. Heller*], *in a review of "Strange Things Happen Here,"* in The Atlantic Monthly, *Vol. 244, No. 1, July, 1979, p. 80.*

[AMANDA Y. HELLER]

Although the collection [*Strange Things Happen Here*] is prosaically subtitled "Twenty-six Short Stories and a Novel," it comprises a variety of forms, from single-page sketches to a novella-length fiction [*He Who Searches*] that shifts scene and point of view with unnerving abandon.

Throughout, these pieces offer a surrealistic picture of life in a fascist state. Though the themes of the stories vary from sex

ROGER SALE

Maybe Luisa Valenzuela is not, as her American publishers allege, "one of Argentina's foremost writers and journalists," but if she is even close to that, Buenos Aires is no place for anyone to point his cultural telescope at in hopes of seeing anything new. **"Strange Things Happen Here,"** which attempts nothing if not being up-to-date, is a collection of very short stories and an interminable short novel: "One more person dead in the city. It's getting to be a vice." "If we want to blame somebody, let's blame ourselves for being alive in this part of the world in these times." "I suppose I could ask them to stop munching celery at three in the morning, but that doesn't seem right. What with the price of celery these days.'' Even the height of banality for ''these days'' talk: ''So many things are confused now that the abnormal is imitating the natural and vice versa.''

And those who don't have the celery munchies do predictably abnormal things: burn their feet, find pubic hairs in their soup, make horizontal ladders, dial FR (Frontal Rapists), ''the well-known Argentine branch of the U.R.U. (United Rapes Unlimited) with headquarters in Des Moines, Iowa, and important branches all over the United States.'' There's a story called **''Meaningless Story,''** another is **''Silly Talk About Suicide,''** and a third is **''Neither the Most Terrifying Nor the Least Memorable.''** The titles are strictly accurate, though to find the least memorable among these 26 would be very difficult.

You can get away with this kind of stuff only by pretending that this writing, this snipping off of bits of irrelevance, is somehow more with it than a poor decent cluck of a reader is. To believe that ordinary things can happen, too, that life indeed has consequential moments, that it is important to try to make other people matter—all that is idly and inconsequentially repudiated. And of course such writing is anything but brand new; avant-garde writers have been exhausting themselves for a century trying to outdo one another in saying that nothing matters, only the impossible happens, and only the boring is worth writing about.

Still, there are moments of perkiness and whimsy in the stories, and if you don't like one, it is very soon over, and you can sample another piece of stale Turkish Delight. The novel, on the other hand, **''He Who Searches,''** is unrelievedly awful, and precisely as up-to-date as a Surrealist movie I saw 30 years ago called ''Dreams That Money Can Buy.'' (p. 10)

From 8,000 miles away, it is impossible to know much about what really goes on in Buenos Aires. But from any distance, it is clear that Miss Valenzuela is just playing around in a sandbox filled with trite words and events that she, and, one hopes, not very many others, find fascinating, the latest thing in fictions, words and lives. (p. 19)

> *Roger Sale, ''Argentine Modernism,'' in* The New York Times Book Review, *July 1, 1979, pp. 10, 19.*

JULIO CORTÁZAR

After a long period during which Argentine literature (and Latin American literature in general) was almost always cast in molds imposed by foreign examples or by internal limitations, we have been witnessing over the past thirty years the appearance of creativity that is at last free, at last our own. But, as always happens in times of liberation, many of the new writers have fallen too easily into the trap of exaggeration and verbal libertinism. . . . Little by little, however, we are beginning to map perplexing territories, and the best Argentine writers labor in search for—and often the discovery of—that difficult balance from which great literature has always sprung. Luisa Valenzuela seems to me to be a perfect example of what I am asserting.

Courageous—with neither self-censorship or prejudice—careful of her language—which is excessive when necessary but magnificently refined and modest as well, whenever reality is—Luisa Valenzuela travels through her various books, lucidly charting the seldom-chosen course of a woman deeply anchored in her condition, conscious of discriminations that are still

horrible all over our continent, but, at the same time, filled with a joy in life that permits her to surmount both the elementary stages of protest and an overestimation of women in order to put herself on a perfectly equal footing with any literature—masculine or not. To read her is to enter *our* reality fully, where plurality surpasses the limitations of the past; to read her is to participate in a search for Latin American identity, which offers its rewards beforehand. Luisa Valenzuela's books are our present but they also contain much of our future; there is true resplendence, true love, true freedom on each of her pages.

> *Julio Cortázar, ''Luisa Valenzuela,'' in* Review, No. 24, 1979, p. 44.

CLARA CLAIBORNE PARK

Some of the stories [in *Strange Things Happen Here*] aren't half a page long; two pages is average. Mostly they're finished before we know what they're up to. There's one about a woman in a bus who picks the pocket of a man who feels her ass. It's well done, but it's over in a paragraph. What did we miss? The point, obviously. There's one about a pampas thistle that ''thrives in a city that has eradicated green by decree,'' ''a prickly, ugly little thistle, which even so looks radiantly beautiful to many.'' A dissident group, initially in pursuit of noble ends, turns it into a false idol and is co-opted by the tyrannical government. There is no hope in greenery or anything else. Maybe it's safer to stick to parable and mysterious vignette if you want to go on living and publishing in Argentina, where Valenzuela is a prominent journalist. Or to write anti-novels. *He Who Searches*, the anti-novella included in *Strange Things*, was not banned in Argentina, though it begins with interrogation and torture and ends with the detonation of a bomb. It seems a world which Puig has prepared us to understand. Not so, though; between beginning and end obtain the weary puzzlements of that orphaned form, the *nouveau roman*. . . . To read Valenzuela after Puig is to experience the difference between narrative subtlety in the service of worthy subject and compelling story, and the artfulness that ''gives priority to the means over the end.'' If this is the price of writing in Argentina it is a heavy one.

> *Clara Claiborne Park, in a review of ''Strange Things Happen Here,'' in* The Hudson Review, *Vol. XXXII, No. 4, Winter, 1979-80, p. 577.*

FIMIE RICHIE

Considering the political content of several of the twenty-six short stories and of the last segment of the novel included in [*Strange Things Happen Here*], the present regime of Argentina would appear to be less repressive than Luisa Valenzuela . . . herself represents it. . . .

The obscurity of the novel [*He Who Searches*] cannot be attributed to the translation but rather to a style reminiscent of Carlos Fuentes' *Where the Air is Clear* or García Marquez' *One Hundred Years of Solitude*. Her writing also bears comparison to that of Kurt Vonnegut and Günther Grass. Vonnegut does not have the thick social protest that pervades the work of Valenzuela, but they are alike in the shifting points of view and the blunt, scatological language.

Three themes are found in the majority of the stories. Fifteen concern political repression and, closely linked to this, the poverty of the Latin-American populace. Each contains a streak of pornography, especially "**The Verb to Kill,**" "**Porno Flick,**" and "**United Rapes Unlimited, Argentina.**"

Two stories, "**Vision out of the Corner of the Eye**" and "**A Meaningless Story,**" are unusual for her in that they simply narrate a slice of life, with no special overtones. . . .

Seemingly, [in *He Who Searches*] an Argentine psychiatrist-professor in Barcelona re-encounters a prostitute (a Che Guevara Tania-type) whom he had met fifteen years earlier in Buenos Aires; and after long pages of his probing into her psyche and soma, she vanishes inexplicably. He returns to Buenos Aires via a peyote ceremony in Mexico (shades of D. H. Lawrence) and joins in the fight against "hunger and ignominy." There, he finds her apotheosized and enshrined a la Eva Perón. There, we leave him on the brink of a horrifying extinction, as we already knew from "page zero."

None of this is edifying nor pleasurable reading. Naturally there is some evocation of Borges. Her literary lineage traces back to Jorge Icaza's *Huasipungo* and mainstreams into the protest stories of the late sixties and early seventies in the United States.

> *Fimie Richie, in a review of "Strange Things Happen Here," in* Studies in Short Fiction, *Vol. XVII, No. 2, Spring, 1980, p. 190.*

PUBLISHERS WEEKLY

The historical events gaudily disguised and deeply interred in ["**The Lizard's Tail**"], while recognizable enough, must be gleaned from the swirling, spiraling masses of language, image, metaphor, folklore, imaginative conceit, hallucination. One by one the events are exhumed: Eva (the "Venerated Dead Woman"); Isabel (the "Intruder" or "Madame President"); the Generalissimo; the succession of brutal, absurd, strutting, bloody-minded colonels and generals, pretenders and juntists who have made a nightmare of that enchanted dreamscape. Fantasy, myth, magical transformations, bizarre ritual, caustic satire prevail over any semblance of conventional narrative, much less plot. By turns exuberant, ribald, excessively self-indulgent, the novel is also modish in mocking some of the buzzwords and ideas of advanced literary theory and avant-garde writing: deconstruction, semiotics, textuality, direct entry by the author into the work. Readers may regard the novel as a stylish feat of imagination or as an exercise in literary chic, depending on their penchant. (pp. 59-60)

> *A review of "The Lizard's Tail," in* Publishers Weekly, *Vol. 223, No. 21, May 27, 1983, pp. 59-60.*

W. A. LUCHTING

The Argentine writer Luisa Valenzuela . . . is what, after due apologies, still may be called a women's novelist: talkative, impulsive and full of unexpected turns in the flow of her stories. Her earlier work was regarded highly: the novels *Hay que sonreír* (1966) and *Como en la guerra* (1977); the short-story collections *Los heréticos* (1967), *Aquí pasan cosas raras* (1975) and *Libro que no muerde* (1980). . . . (p. 438)

[*Cambio de armas*] contains five stories of varying length. All have as theme the relationship between men and women, mostly in the form of love affairs that are either successful or not (in the title story the woman, in the final line of the book, points a revolver at the man—and presumably shoots). The feminist point of view is unmistakable but not obtrusive. Nevertheless, the overall impression created by the stories (except the final selection) is that the women suffer injustice. As behooves recent Argentine narrative, politics invade the stories with cruel consequences; and as behooves modern narrative in general, the stories, to varying degrees, engage in narrative self-reflection. At times this turns into self-indulgence (especially in "Cuarta versión," the first and longest of the stories). All in all, while they are not Valenzuela's best tales and are, moreover, of uneven quality, the texts of *Cambio de armas* are interesting to read. (pp. 438-39)

> *W. A. Luchting, in a review of "Cambio de armas," in* World Literature Today, *Vol. 57, No. 3, Summer, 1983, pp. 438-39.*

ALLEN JOSEPHS

"**The Lizard's Tail**" by Luisa Valenzuela is an exotic *roman à clef* based loosely on the life of José López Rega, one of Isabel Perón's despotic ministers. Yet much more than fictionalized biography, the novel is a baroque and parodistic fantasy centered on and in the mind of a nameless mad Sorcerer. In this plotless, rambling and episodic novel, Miss Valenzuela attempts to plumb the depths of unmitigated evil by examining the Sorcerer's frenzied and bizarre machinations. From his stream-of-consciousness monologues, sometimes called his novel or diary, and from Miss Valenzuela's first- and third-person narration, the reader gradually pieces together the life story of this unusual personage—his childhood, his usurpation of power, his expulsion by the military, his plot to return to power and his demise, prophesied on the book's first page, in a river of blood.

Any summary is, however, misleading, as is the use of the pronoun "his," since the Sorcerer is not exactly a man but a strange androgynous being with three testicles, one of which he refers to as his "sister," Estrella. Then, too, there are the witch 730-Wrinkles, the eunuch Egret, the Sorcerer's mother (whom he boils into bouillon and drinks), the Generalissimo, the revered and enshrined Dead Woman Eva, the Intruder Isabel and perhaps the most interesting character in the book, Miss Valenzuela herself.

"**The Lizard's Tail**," which understandably was not published in Argentina, is an ingenious, original and often intriguing satire that will no doubt delight many of Miss Valenzuela's readers (this is her third book to be translated into English). The witchcraft, the drugs, the violence, the sadism, the perversity and the utterly evil character of the Sorcerer cast a deadly charm. At the same time, Miss Valenzuela, who now lives in New York, possesses a magician's bag of literary tricks that keep the reader constantly on guard.

Yet her attempt at virtuosity tends to undermine the novel. In order to convince the reader of the Sorcerer's madness and narcissistic depravity, she resorts to surrealism, hyperbole and self-indulgent prose. The parody becomes increasingly self-conscious as the novel proceeds, especially when Miss Valenzuela becomes disgusted with herself "for believing that literature can save us, for doubting that literature can save us." As a result, she trivializes her subject matter. Although she writes artfully out of the tradition of Latin American magical realism, Miss Valenzuela sometimes seems to forget García Márquez's dictum that you can get away with anything as long as you make it believable. (p. 15)

Allen Josephs, "Sorcerers and Despots," in The New York Times Book Review, *October 2, 1983, pp. 15, 26.*

ANNE MARIE SCHULTHEIS

The Lizard's Tail opens with a narrative stylistically similar to the Benjy section of Faulkner's *The Sound and the Fury*. Details and shreds of insight seem never to fuse. Each sentence starts a string of thoughts which remain dangling, unknotted by the paragraph's end. And understandably, this makes for frustrating reading.

Faulkner's narrator is an idiot; Valenzuela's is a messianic maniac, a Sorcerer and witchdoc. (p. 287)

The power source for this witchdoc is his third testicle, an appendage which he believes to be his sister, Estrella. By means of this third testicle he plans to conceive a son who will regain the power the Sorcerer himself once wielded.

The difficulty with this magical/realistic plot lies in the narrative technique and writing style Valenzuela employs. The Sorcerer tells his story through fits of rage, perversity, deviousness, and self-indulgence. One emotional outburst ignites another and thus a chain of associations forms. The line between fantasy and reality becomes difficult to distinguish. Ideas and facts mix completely, creating a waking-dreamlike effect.

This novel is so full of intricate images, poetic juxtapositions of words and symbols, and half-expressed ideas (which Valenzuela challenges the reader to complete), that the reading is slow going and often confusing. In spite of the density of the novel, Valenzuela does communicate well her ideas on power, politics, and magic through the form of magical realism. Her achievement lies in this blend of fact and fantasy. (pp. 287-88)

Anne Marie Schultheis, in a review of "The Lizard's Tail," in Best Sellers, *Vol. 43, No. 8, November, 1983, pp. 287-88.*

SHARON MAGNARELLI

Unquestionably, one of the most characteristic qualities of Valenzuela's prose is the plurality to which Cortázar has referred [see excerpt above], for her work inevitably offers or even demands a multiplicity of readings and interpretations. At times deceptively simple, always subtly political and/or feminist but never sententious, her prose rarely offers solutions to the problems it posits, for that is not her intent. Instead, her work examines life, reality and sociopolitical structures from different vantage points and in a variety of contexts in order to suggest new definitions or even a plurality of interpretations for situations not necessarily recognized as problematic. Much of the wealth and beauty of her writing resides in the fact that she often touches upon areas and topics which are ostensibly irrefragable, already settled or even taboo.

In this respect her work continually undermines social and political myths, but unlike so many writers with a political bent, Valenzuela steadfastly refuses to replace the old mythic structures with new but equally arbitrary and potentially equally authoritative ones. . . . [Valenzuela] attempts to present situations in ways that subject them to different interpretations and possibly unique, more productive solutions. But again the final diagnosis or cure for these social ills, if any exists, rests

with the reader, who must be actively involved in the text and also in life outside the text. (p. 10)

In this sense her work is characterized by *una búsqueda eterna,* always pursuing those uncharted truths which will necessarily challenge and redefine that absolute, orthodox Truth (which, as Valenzuela insinuates, may be a misnomer) that is so facilely accepted as it surreptitiously dominates and engulfs us all. And of course this search is necessarily predicated on and conducted through the medium of language, and Valenzuela is a virtuosa of language. Her unique style is unfailingly vibrant, crisp and clever—paradoxically, at times almost classical, at others patently baroque. For example, *Como en la guerra* is neatly structured on the ever-inescapable, classic, heroic myth with its preordained discovery, subsequent loss, journey and final encounter. *El gato eficaz,* at the other extreme, is filled with typically baroque conceptism and linguistic play. Continually self-conscious, with narrators frequently critical of their stance as well as their task, her prose has been correctly labeled "una aventura verbal," as we are caught up in and by the language and the linguistic twists and turns.

Nevertheless, to speak of language as if it were a separate entity does not mean to suggest that language in Valenzuela's work is somehow alien to her thematic concerns. Quite the contrary. Her discourse is not only the means of expression but also the subject of that expression, for Valenzuela's work centers on three intricately related preoccupations: language, women and politics. Her work is clearly an attempt to free language and women from the shackles of society and in so doing to liberate us all from language and the sociopolitical structures and prisons which are the products of that discourse. Although such thematic concerns might easily produce a prosaic, pedantic, pretentious literature, such is certainly not the case with Valenzuela, for her work is circumscribed by its playfulness and its humor as she toys with, manipulates and pushes language to its ultimate possibilities. Thus, in spite of her serious thematic interests, her work is amusing and entertaining. There can be little doubt, however, that the playfulness and wit, as much as we relish them, are anything but innocent or harmless. On the contrary, both the humor and the games are bitter, perhaps even biting decoys or distractions for her deadly, if indeed subtle, attacks.

But again, herein lies the richness of Valenzuela's prose, for her novels and stories can, indeed must, be read on several levels, both individually and collectively. We can read and be amused by the language and the puns, as in *El gato eficaz,* where the narrator plays with the linguistic permutations and idiomatic expressions based on or formed by the words *gato* and *perro;* or, on another level, we can read for plot or story, as perhaps in *Hay que sonreír* or *Como en la guerra.* If we insist on literature with a serious, moral, social, philosophical, political message, however (and we do), these also shape each of the Valenzuela texts as indicated; yet the reader can probably ignore these messages, should he so choose, and many have done so.

Still, let us be more specific and examine the abovementioned characteristics in two Valenzuela works which chronologically mark opposite extremes of her career to date: *Hay que sonreír* (1966) and *Cambio de armas* (1982). . . . *Hay que sonreír* is the tale of a young woman who comes to Buenos Aires from the provinces without enough money for a pretty blouse she sees in a shop window. Prostitution supplies the money for the blouse and a means of survival for Clara, whose only desires are to see the ocean and to be somebody by using her head—

not unreasonable longings, but ones which ultimately prove fatal. As the novel continues, we follow the protagonist, an unpretentious, childlike young woman, in her pseudoprogression from the domination of one male to that of another. . . . (pp. 10-11)

The novel is very tightly structured on the classic triad of Western religion and civilization, as it is divided into three clearly delineated sections: "El cuerpo," "Transición," "La cabeza." Such division not only reflects but also ultimately undermines the Western propensity to envision sociopolitical development as a progression away from the baser elements (the physical, the body) upward toward the rational and the spiritual (the head). In the first section Clara's body is the center of attention as the rest of the characters essentially ignore any aspect of her being other than the physical. In "Transición" she finds that her body can lure the man of her dreams, but since he proves so inferior to her idealization of him, she recognizes that perhaps the body is not the answer and that the head may cloud the issue. . . . When she meets the fortune-teller, her destiny leads her to follow him and use her head. . . . What she soon discovers, however, is that using her head also has its limitations. . . . Clara becomes a mere circus act, a head with no body. Finally, in the eloquent act of violence, hatred and aggression which concludes the novel, Alejandro [the fortune-teller] severs that head from that body, and she becomes on a very literal level a body without a head, or vice versa.

Significantly, in spite of all this, Clara never becomes a tragic figure, nor does she elicit great pathos. Valenzuela is far more subtle. One of the main themes of the text is unquestionably contemporary woman's plight with the social expectations that she will be passive, silent, industrious (but only in areas of minor import), possessed by a male (be he her father, husband or pimp) and that she will continue to smile (*hay que sonreír*) in spite of the exploitation or violence perpetrated against her. Poignantly, Clara never challenges these principles. . . . Clara, a woman whom society has never allowed to mature fully and assume complete responsibility for herself, asks the questions a child might ask—why? Why can't she go to the sea? Why must she always wait? Why must she always belong to someone? Why must the wife obey her husband and follow him everywhere? Why can't she speak? Why is the drawing of a car either moral or immoral? Simple questions, to be sure, and ones we tend to dismiss as childish; yet they are questions which, if taken seriously and answered honestly, are not only totally subversive but threaten to undermine the foundations of Western society and thought. (p. 11)

The novel ends, however, as it began, with Clara waiting for a man, this time for Alejandro, . . . as he licks his lips and prepares to slit her throat and make her the head without a body. Thus, in perfect circularity, like the face of a clock, the text ends with the body now physically rather than philosophically or psychologically severed from the head. The central concern of *Hay que sonreír*, then, rests in the sociolinguistically produced dichotomy between the body (physical, tractable reality) and the head (soul, dreams, rationality) as it is envisioned by Western society. Carefully analyzed, Clara has been using her head all along, for she is a dreamer. The incongruity results from the fact that her dreams, as created by the discourse of popular culture, are not reconcilable with the reality which surrounds her physical being in the world. As Valenzuela shows, it is not that there is any inherent disjunction between body and mind but rather that we are surrounded by contradictory discourse designed to oppress.

Although distanced by sixteen years and ostensibly completely dissimilar, "Cuarta versión," the first story in *Cambio de armas,* reflects many of the same preoccupations as *Hay que sonreír*. It is structured with the same circularity, ending as Pedro begins to narrate the story of Bella which we have just read. Like *Hay que sonreír* too, it sets for itself the task of reexamining our social, political and rhetorical mythic structures. "Cuarta versión," however, is a narrative marked by an even greater multiplicity of levels than any other Valenzuela work to date. The story, in fact, proffers at least five distinct possible readings, focal points or levels of interpretation, and it is precisely these readings which lead us to the principal concerns of the story.

First, the text offers a political story, but it is a political story hidden beneath and disguised by a love story; as the narrator notes, a love story signals that which can be articulated openly, a political story that which cannot. . . . In this sense, what is not said becomes even more important than what is said, and the story centers on an absence, a silence. . . . Thus the narrator's concern, and in turn the reader's, is precisely this silence, this blank space. . . . (p. 12)

At the same time, the work is a detective story on at least two levels. Not only must the reader continually attempt to fill this void, this blank space, the unmentionable which pervades the text, but the very act of writing, the narration, becomes a search for clues, a quest for that one paradigmatic moment or event which will summarize all, make all else significant and become a viable synecdoche for the ineffable experience. The narrator is presumably writing the fourth version of the story, working from other written documents, as she creates her narration using details selected from the "mar de papeles." . . . The narrator acknowledges that she is omitting what is most important as she searches for the crucial clue; again the focal point is the void. . . . Thus both the reader and the writer become detectives trying to decipher the clues and discover the cause of the final murder. Unlike the traditional detective story, however, "Cuarta versión" is just that—the fourth, not the definitive version—and the mystery remains unsolved again, perhaps because the solution too marks that which cannot be expressed.

Yet, on still another level, we are presented with a modern-day fairy tale—Sleeping Beauty, "la bella durmiente," who will awaken with the proper (male?) stimulus. . . . But it is a fairy tale reexamined under the light of twentieth-century politics and feminism. Unlike the fairy-tale Sleeping Beauty, whose tale is a love story and who awakens to live happily ever after at the side of her Prince Charming (that is, whose sleeping inactivity is converted into waking inactivity), Bella's trajectory is the reverse. Inactive, apparently politically ignorant at the beginning, Bella metaphorically awakens to the political atrocities occurring in her unnamed country and takes an active role in opposing the tyrannical regime. Bella's awakening, however, paradoxically leads to her death. (pp. 12-13)

Finally, "Cuarta versión," as the title suggests, is also the story of writing. It is writing about the act of writing, discourse which watches and analyzes itself as it writes. In this story we again encounter the linguistic virtuosity which characterized *El gato eficaz,* but here the narrative stance is even more self-conscious. The story examines the literary gesture while at the same time it dramatizes the inevitable internalization of the subject of reading and writing as the narrator identifies with and eventually becomes the protagonist herself (whom she is both reading and writing)—or is it the other way around? . . . The writing itself becomes a distraction, a diversion of attention which disguises the void, for the text is composed of alternating sections, some of which tell the story of Bella, and others, in italics, which tell the story of writing. The latter patently divert our attention away from the main story each time that story appears to be getting dangerously close to the unspeakable. Significantly, as the text progresses, the division between the two forms of discourse becomes less and less discernible, until in the final chapter the italicized discourse, like the act of narrating, becomes indistinguishable from the narrative itself. Discourse and being have become one.

Perhaps the principal difference between Clara and Bella is that the latter is an actress in both the literal and the etymological sense of the word. Her life, like her story, is a performance as she dons a series of roles, a succession of masks. . . . Whereas Clara merely allows herself to be swept along with the flow of life and those who surround her, Bella actively assumes the leading role. . . . Unfortunately, however, the script has been written by others, and her leading role is that of pawn. The story ends as Pedro begins to retell her story, but significantly his narration exhibits a change of center. . . . Thus her place on center stage is usurped by the male. In fact, the play which is rehearsed during the course of the action might well be considered a mirror reflection of the narrative itself. . . . Again, the show is an invitation to act much as the narrative itself is. But, as pointed out at the beginning of this essay, it is the reader who must now act, for literature is not life. It merely posits some possibilities for action in life. (p. 13)

Sharon Magnarelli, "Luisa Valenzuela: From 'Hay que sonreír' to 'Cambio de armas'," in World Literature Today, *Vol. 58, No. 1, Winter, 1984, pp. 9-13.*

(Jorge) Mario (Pedro) Vargas Llosa

1936-

Peruvian novelist, short story writer, critic, essayist, and journalist.

Vargas Llosa is one of the younger writers associated with "El Boom," the flowering of Latin American literature that occurred in the 1960s. During this time, such authors as Gabriel García Márquez and Julio Cortázar reached international prominence, and several other Latin American authors enjoyed immediate acclaim with their initial works of fiction, Vargas Llosa and Carlos Fuentes in particular. This almost simultaneous production of major works by a number of authors led to sudden critical and popular recognition of the important contributions to modern literature being made by contemporary Latin American authors.

Like most of the writers linked with El Boom, Vargas Llosa freely experiments with the form and structure of the novel and short story in order to attain a distinctive method that can reflect the more colorful qualities of life in Latin America. He has been particularly praised for his successful experiments with narrative structure. Specifically, Vargas Llosa employs disordered chronological development, rapidly shifting narrative perspectives, and complex structures to mirror the political, social, and personal chaos of his settings and characters.

Vargas Llosa first gained critical attention with *La ciudad y los perros* (1963; *The Time of the Hero*), which satirizes the way of life in a Peruvian military academy. This partly autobiographical novel explores the cultural concept of *machismo* and its effects on individuals and society. Some readers viewed the military academy as a microcosm for Latin America, and many were impressed with Vargas Llosa's observations on how *machismo* contributes to the violent political and social realities of Peru and Latin America. *La casa verde* (1966; *The Green House*), his next novel, won wide critical acclaim and established Vargas Llosa as an important literary figure. In this novel, seemingly disparate stories are interwoven in a narrative structure that mixes objective and subjective perspectives and gradually becomes a unified whole. *The Green House* is set, in part, in the jungles of Peru, and draws upon myths and legends of both past and modern Peruvian culture. While some critics attacked the multitude of characters in this novel as undeveloped, most praised Vargas Llosa's technical procedures which convey an ambiguous view of reality through the fragile and mysterious identities of the characters.

Conversación en la catedral (1969; *Conversation in the Cathedral*) was also favorably received. In this novel, as in earlier works, Vargas Llosa subordinates cohesive plot development in favor of a structurally complex narrative. In his presentation of a world torn by corruption and social friction, Vargas Llosa uses a montage-like structure with rapidly shifting points of view and quick changes of setting. Critics were impressed with his ability to employ such techniques which are more often associated with cinema than with literature. However, some readers and reviewers found the novel's labyrinthine structure difficult to penetrate.

With *Pantaleón y las visitadoras* (1973; *Captain Pantoja and the Special Service*) Vargas Llosa's satirical fiction became

more humorous. While some critics claimed that this novel lacked the intensity and social significance of his earlier works, many praised his deft use of irony to achieve comedic effects. *La tía Julia y el escribador* (1977; *Aunt Julia and the Scriptwriter*) furthers Vargas Llosa's use of humor. While this novel is structurally less complicated than his earlier works, Vargas Llosa's manipulation of point of view is of primary importance. Half of the chapters are overtly autobiographical, relating events in Vargas Llosa's life as a young man. The alternate chapters are works by a soap opera scriptwriter whose elaborately complex plots and dedication to his art are fantastic, yet they mirror the real life situation of Vargas Llosa's persona. As with *Captain Pantoja and the Special Service*, Vargas Llosa uses comedy to satirize those people and institutions whom he had previously disparaged. Critics noted that *Aunt Julia and the Scriptwriter* contained a thematic richness and density not found in *Captain Pantoja and the Special Service*.

(See also *CLC*, Vols. 3, 6, 9, 10, 15 and *Contemporary Authors*, Vols. 73-76.)

GENE BELL-VILLADA

With frustrated soldiers going sexually amok in Amazon outposts, and civilian fathers and husbands up in arms about this lewd misconduct, the Peruvian top brass appoint loyal career administrator Capt. Pantaleón Pantoja to solve the problem. And solve it he does [in *Captain Pantoja and the Special Service*]—too well and none too wisely. In the heat of the tropical rainforest, covert in mufti, with his mother, wife and new-born daughter housed away in civilian secrecy, a diligent Pantoja quietly launches the "Special Service for Garrisons, Frontier and Related Installations (SSGFRI)." This mouthful of officialese denotes what will become a vast network of mobile brothels, staffed by experienced dames who gladly trade in the rigors of night life for regimentation, steady pay, Sundays off and other such perks, while the Special Service, armed with surveys, accountants, a river boat, a hydroplane, a colorful flag and even a bouncy hymn (sung to the "Mexican Hat Dance"), soars to dizzying success, becomes the Peruvian military's most efficient single organism. . . .

Seem raunchy? And yet, with his masterful technique and his fascinating protagonist, Vargas Llosa pulls it off with high artistry. Capt. Pantoja is your classic organization man—loyal to the team and to authority, obsessed with order and work, zealous to a fault. Acclaimed by all as an administrative genius, he falls as a result of his own bland innocence, his incapacity to distinguish between what might or might not be deemed legitimate administrative material. Strangely naive, even saintly (his pre-Special Service record was absolutely perfect), the Captain duly stands up for his subordinates—hookers included. (p. 346)

Though easy and amusing from page to page, *Captain Pantoja* is no pop-realist puff job—no "straight" third- or first-person narratives here. The entire story is told through an artful combination of dry military dispatches, juicy personal letters, verbose radio rhetoric, and lurid sensationalist news reports (with campy headlines about "BLOOD, PASSION AND BASE INSTINCTS"). For those doomsayers who proclaim the death of the Novel, Vargas Llosa further develops his own third-person device—the intermixing of dialogue from totally different situations, times and places, with action and description placed not around the talking but rather fitted into those old cracks, the "he said-she said" portions. . . . Some of those in-between descriptions eventually become full-length paragraphs that summarize entire scenes—Vargas Llosa thereby turning novelistic procedure literally inside-out. . . .

As in the author's earlier books, *Captain Pantoja* sniffs out corruption in high places, but it also presents something of a break, Vargas Llosa here shedding his high seriousness and adopting a humorous, ribald tone. The plot is funny enough, but the real laughs come from Vargas Llosa's variegated linguistic registers—ranging from the earthily colloquial to the deadpan-bureaucratic. (p. 347)

Gene Bell-Villada, "From the Ribald to the Bureaucratic," in Commonweal, *Vol. 106, No. 11, June 8, 1979, pp. 346-47.*

JEROME CHARYN

A pox on translations! We long for a writer's natural line, and we usually get a voice that sounds broken and silly. It may not even be the translator's fault. How do you render the "music" of one language into another and still manage to hold on to the meaning of a word? And what if the prose has an unconventional "music," a rhythm that depends heavily on the exact placement of words? Such is the predicament of **"The Cubs"** (**"Los Cachorros"**), the title piece of Mario Vargas

Llosa's first collection of stories in English ["**The Cubs and Other Stories**"]. . . .

Vargas Llosa himself has said that **"The Cubs"** is "a story more sung than told and, therefore, each syllable was chosen as much for musical as for narrative reasons. I don't know why, but I felt in this case that the verisimilitude depended on the reader's having the impression of listening, not reading, that the story should get to him through his ears."

This is the sadness of it: the story's special song is lost in translation. There are only a few moments in which the "liturgy" of the prose survives. The story has a collective narrator, a "choral voice" that is composed of the Cubs themselves, teen-agers from Miraflores, a suburb of Lima. Here are the Cubs, telling about their friend, P. P. Cuéllar, who has been emasculated by a dog and is afraid to ask the girl he loves to go steady with him: ". . . and anyway you can't go on like this, growing bitter, getting thinner, wasting away: he should ask her right away. And Lalo [said] how could he doubt it? He'd ask her, he'd have a girlfriend and [P. P. said] what would I do? and Choto [said] he'd make out and Manny [said] he'd hold her hand and Chingolo [said] he'd kiss her and Lalo [said] he'd fool around with her a little." This sort of choral music isn't sustained throughout the text as the narrative seems to sputter along and spill out its words.

The story is remarkable nonetheless. Even through the translation, it gives us the skin and bones of a particular time and place: Miraflores in the 1950's and its *barrio* of friendship and puppy love. . . . Into this tribe comes Cuéllar, the bookworm, with his terrible wound, which leaves him without "a scratch on his face or hands," but unable to cope with Miraflores. He can't pursue any of the rituals of courtship, and the Cubs fear that "he'll end up a drunk, outlaw, madman." He dies in a car crash, and his friends mourn him with the recognition of their own deteriorating lives. . . .

The other six stories, written while Vargas Llosa was a student in Lima, are more conventional and easier to read, but they lack the nervous power of **"The Cubs."** The best of these stories, **"The Challenge,"** describes a knife fight between two local toughs, and here again some of Vargas Llosa's music snakes through the text. The fight itself becomes a sexual dance, with one of the combatants "offering his body and whisking it away, slippery, agile, tempting and rejecting his opponent like a woman in heat."

"The Cubs and Other Stories" provides a good counterpoint to Vargas Llosa's novels, which create his own private *barrio* of friendship, betrayal and loss in a universe that has gotten ugly and gone a little mad.

Jerome Charyn, "In Vargas Llosa's Peru," in The New York Times Book Review, *September 23, 1979, p. 12.*

MICHAEL WOOD

People go to the movies in Vargas Llosa's *The Cubs and Other Stories,* but the book itself evokes other books rather than films. Not because it makes allusions or seems derivative, but because it aspires so transparently to literature, conjures up so clearly the decorous company of sensitive, intelligent, well-written texts it wishes to join. Vargas Llosa himself, in an engaging and modest preface written for this translation, says the book *is* derivative, attributes one story to the influence of Paul Bowles, and calls another "an out-of-tune echo of Malraux's novel *Man's Hope.*" (p. 45)

The Cubs and Other Stories is an early work, a young man's book. The title piece, a novella, was written when Vargas Llosa was twenty-nine, but the other six stories were written when he was between seventeen and twenty-one. It is a young man's book in another sense. It is *about* youth; about the fights and hesitations and prejudices that go with growing up in the closed world of a school or a neighborhood or a farm or a familiar city. Only the young have such moments, as Conrad said. There is a story, called **"The Leaders,"** about a failed school strike which is really a personal battle between the strike's competing organizers. Another story depicts a rivalry for a girl which sends two boys out to ride the Pacific surf in a wintry mist, where they almost drown in cold and terror; another shows a boy coming home to a harsh and bigoted country life, and learning how to assert himself against his older brother. These scenes and quarrels are rendered sharply and economically, with impressive professional skill. . . .

The novella in the collection, **"The Cubs,"** is more ambitious. A boy is savaged and emasculated by an angry dog, and Vargas Llosa became interested, he says, in that "strange wound that, in contrast to others, time would open rather than close." The boy grows up, passes through adolescence into adult life, getting more and more unhappy, desperate when his pals have girlfriends, miserable when he himself falls briefly in love. He leaves Lima, loses touch with his old chums, who hardly speak to him when he returns to visit. . . . His friends meanwhile have settled down, have wives and children, are getting fat, wearing glasses, worrying about age spots and wrinkles.

There is a certain shallowness in the work, a failure to find the depths the subject seemed to promise. The boy's difficulty never acquires a psychological face, seems to remain a problem of engineering. We don't see who he is or how he feels, we see what he has lost: a manhood that is, oddly, both too particular and too abstract. But then this is perhaps a reason for the success of the novella's remarkable collective narrative. . . , alternating between tenses and idioms, and between first and third person ("They were wearing long pants by then, we slicked our hair with tonic, and they had grown. . ."). The gang can't really imagine a man without a member, so the story can't either. The boy parades the unthinkable through their lives, a ruined monster, and their lives thus become the true subject of the fiction: normality, the proper sequence of aging, doing what others do.

The technical bravura of the piece—"I wanted 'The Cubs' to be a story more sung than told," Vargas Llosa says, "and, therefore, each syllable was chosen as much for musical as for narrative reasons"—serves to create a community, a universe of shared hopes and assumptions and styles, the happiest time of a life. It is not the happiest time of the wounded boy's life, but his exclusion is what convinces us of the happiness of the others: that is why we feel so sorry for him, and for them when they turn into dreary men. What the boy has missed is not adult sexuality, but the long magical moment of passage toward it, youth itself. Only the young have such moments; and some of them have no moments at all.

Captain Pantoja and the Special Service is a lighter, later work first published in Spanish in 1973. Both the Spanish and the English blurbs describe it as a farce. . . .

The central joke is rather laborious, and returns us, in a disturbing way, to the title story of **"The Cubs."** Instead of a

monstrous absence of virility we have here an exuberant masculine rampage, but the subject is still sexual power. ***Captain Pantoja*** recalls Gabriel Chevallier's *Clochemerle,* or any one of a dozen other French fantasies about rural paradises of the libido; and I wonder, hesitating about being a damp old spoilsport, whether grievous sexual worries do not regularly hide behind such emphatic jollity on the subject of sex.

Nevertheless, the technical high jinks of ***Captain Pantoja*** are very appealing. Vargas Llosa uses a quickfire, unlikely dialogue which seems to come from Queneau, amasses piles of mock reports and requests supposedly passed between various branches of the army; he imitates newspapers, letters, and generally conjures up a universe of documents which resembles that of Manuel Puig. But for Puig the space between death and a coroner's report, say, is usually a space of pain and pathos, while for Vargas Llosa, at least in this book, the gaps between reality and language are comic—indeed they provide the fun that the plot of the novel can't quite deliver. (p. 46)

> *Michael Wood, "The Claims of Mischief," in* The New York Review of Books, *Vol. XXVI, Nos. 21 & 22, January 24, 1980, pp. 43-7.**

WILLIAM KENNEDY

And now for something entirely different from Latin America: a comic novel that is genuinely funny. This screwball fantasy [**"Aunt Julia and the Scriptwriter"**]—interwoven with a realistic tale of an improbable romance—is the Peruvian novelist Mario Vargas Llosa's homage to two people who gave shape to his artistic and personal life during his adolescence: an ascetic Bolivian who all day, every day, wrote scripts for radio soap operas, and the author's Aunt Julia.

The two become marvelous fictional creations in a novel that was originally conceived as half-autobiographical, and elements of autobiography still cling to it. The narrator is a young man named Mario, sometimes called Varguitas, which is a diminutive of the author's surname. The narrator precociously courts and marries his delectable Aunt Julia, as did Vargas Llosa, whose first wife was an aunt (but not a blood relative) named Julia. This book is dedicated to her. Also, Vargas Llosa, as a young radio newsman in Lima in 1953, worked with a singular Bolivian named Raúl Salmón, and he has said that he based his fictional scriptwriter, Pedro Camacho, on Salmón.

The fictional characters do not need this authentication, but the matter deserves at least a mention since the *roman à clef* element has generated talk of Vargas Llosa's indiscretion. Also, it is nifty gossip for Vargas Llosa fans, whose numbers are increasing. For he is one of the most widely known Latin American writers of this age, a scholar, a critic, a playwright, a novelist (**"The Green House" "Conversation in the Cathedral"**) whose work has made him a progenitor of the so-called Boom in modern Latin American literature. (p. 1)

He creates his Aunt Julia as a lovely, intelligent coquette, a 32-year-old divorcée with a splendid lack of common sense about love. When Mario, 18, steals a kiss from her on the dance floor, she is stunned and resists: "Me, seducing a kid? Never!" He persists, opening his heart, telling her his dream of going off to France and living in a garret, dedicating his heart and soul to literature. Julia's taste in literature runs to Frank Yerby, but she listens, and a romance blooms. (pp. 1, 14)

All this is narrated in the first person by Mario, in an amiable and sometimes suspenseful style; but lovely as Julia is when she's on the page, Mario's telling of her tale is overlong in its reconstruction of the ordinary. The story of Mario's working life at the radio station is also a bit tedious but is saved by Pedro Camacho, the heroic writer of soap-opera scripts. . . .

Camacho is little more than a cartoon at first, but as the story progresses Mario views him with increasing awe. And as we are exposed to his soaps—which are related at length—the man becomes a cartoon of substance, a brain worth scanning. The problems that beset Camacho—his fear of aging, his niggling comic hatred of Argentines (he has his reasons), his constipation, his championing of masturbation for actors and priests—turn into the stuff of his scripts, their mundane reality carried to dramatic extremes. And so the soaps become the blueprints of Camacho's imagination, and what we are given is a privileged view of the arcane and volcanic reaches of a writer's psyche.

The book's principal achievement is the rendering of this vast comic landscape, with its heroes, victims and villains—all populating a world that grows increasingly complex as the novel progresses but that never ceases to entertain. Camacho's imagination is that of a surreal clown; in person he is as solemn as a totem pole. . . .

Camacho lives monastically, loathes money, snubs the fame his serials give him. When he writes, he assumes roles physically, wearing false mustaches, a fireman's hat, the mask of a fat woman. Mario finds him at his enormous typewriter, writing about the birth of triplets. He is in a white smock, surgeon's skullcap and long, rabbinical black beard. "I'll do a Caesarean on the girl," he tells his visitor, "and then I'll go have . . . tea with you."

Camacho's soaps are written as narratives in the novel, not as scripts, and they alternate with the realistic story of Mario and Aunt Julia. . . .

A Peruvian critic some years ago asked Vargas Llosa the meaning of this novel, and he said one of his intentions was to prove that his own early world and the world of soap opera were not so very different from each other. His tale of Aunt Julia is low-key, timid soap, but then suddenly violence impends: Mario's father hears of the unholy romance and comes to Lima with murder on his mind. . . .

Vargas Llosa also intends his book as satire of myriad social types and classes, and as in much comic writing, he creates extreme creatures. But Julia and Camacho have also endured in his memory as beings worthy of affection, and he dogs them with small and humanizing detail—Julia's common sense and selfless ways, the squalor of Camacho's lonely life. And by the book's end they both have become unexpectedly real and rise to moments of poignant revelation.

Vargas Llosa once said he didn't like novels with a moral, and he hasn't imposed one here, though any book which is so well wrought, which defines a world with such unarguable accuracy, is moral; and what's more, it made me laugh out loud.

Perhaps it carries an antimoral—that soap opera is good for you. It is a work that celebrates story: story that gives pleasure to a large number of people, story also as a pleasure principle for the writer. Whether it is Vargas Llosa creating a wacko scriptwriter creating a compulsive ear licker, the process is the same: giving shape to beings who never before existed outside dream or daydream. They prove here to be very unlikely citizens, but then again who doesn't? (p. 14)

> William Kennedy, "Peruvian Soap Opera," in The New York Times Book Review, *August 1, 1982, pp. 1, 14.*

RONALD de FEO

With his last novel, *Captain Pantoja and the Special Service,* the Peruvian writer Mario Vargas Llosa surprised many of his admirers by joining the literary carnival. Prior to this dizzyingly playful account of an army officer assigned to supply a party of prostitutes to deprived jungle soldiers, the author had produced a stark short-story collection, translated as *The Cubs,* and three long, increasingly complex novels, *The Time of the Hero, The Green House,* and *Conversation in the Cathedral,* all exploring with a near-savage seriousness and single-mindedness themes of social and political corruption. In the novels, Vargas Llosa employed with great skill a variety of narrative techniques (fractured chronology, interlocking stories, shifts in point of view, cinematiclike cuts, parallel and contrapuntal dialogues) that turned the old social-realist novel upside down and inside out. Though narrative experimentation was still very much in evidence in *Captain Pantoja,* a new, unexpected element entered Vargas Llosa's work: an unrestrained sense of humor. It was as if the author had decided to join the great big party going on around him.

The fun continues in *Aunt Julia and the Scriptwriter,* but with some very significant differences. Not only is the new book longer and much broader in scope, but it has a thematic richness and density the other book lacked. The technical fireworks are, surprisingly, kept to a minimum. In fact, this is a relatively restrained performance for the author. Yet he has managed to create a work that is both challenging and absolutely captivating, a multilayered, high-spirited, and in the end terribly affecting text about the interplay of fiction and reality, the transformation of life into art, and life seen and sometimes even lived as fiction. Using as a foundation an actual period in his life during the early 1950s when he was employed as a newswriter for Lima's Radio Panamericana, Vargas Llosa proceeds to work on two distinct narrative planes. On the "real" level he writes in first-person what is, from all reports, a fairly solid autobiographical account of his experiences at the radio station and of his romance with and ultimate marriage to his Aunt Julia, his first wife (to whom the book is dedicated)—an event that created a family scandal as well as a host of problems for the eighteen-year-old Mario and his thirty-two-year-old aunt. On the purely fictive level, he presents what might be described as straight narrative renderings or adaptations of the various soap operas written by Pedro Comacho, an amazingly prolific scriptwriter recently hired by Panamericana's neighboring radio station because of his unique ability and the popular success he enjoyed in Bolivar. The autobiographical chapters alternate with the soap opera chapters, each of which tells a different and ultimately incomplete story (for soap situations are never quite resolved). Most of them are, to say the least, bizarre, even crazy by soap opera standards—from the story of a haunted rodent exterminator whose obsessive mission is to kill every rat in Peru, to the tale of a traveling medical supplies salesman who is persuaded by an unorthodox psychiatrist that he did not run over a child by accident. . . . (pp. 38-9)

Surprisingly enough, the alternating narrative lines are not as jarring as one might expect. Though the "real" story of Mario and Julia never quite approaches the sheer madness and intensity of Comacho's stories, it too contains the stuff of melodrama: furtive meetings, partings, reconciliations, scandal, family threats, and final flight. . . .

It is worth mentioning that Comacho's stories, though admittedly superficial and fantastic and hardly the stuff of your typical soaps, are quite gripping. So taken are we by these fictions that when Comacho begins to go mad and starts populating one soap opera with characters from another, arbitrarily changing their professions, histories, and relationships, killing them off and resurrecting them at will, we are disturbed by the shattering of the illusion, by, as Comacho's boss so wonderfully puts it, "these modernist gimmicks." After all, the reader takes pleasure in the unreal as well.

At times the reader wishes that aunt Julia were a more substantial creation, and at times he can't quite believe that an unsophisticated hack like Comacho could produce such ingeniously cockeyed scripts or that their physical qualities could have been realized on radio. These, however, are minor qualms. The novel may sometimes recall Nathanael West's *The Day of the Locust*, Stanley Elkin's radio novel *The Dick Gibson Show*, and Puig's campy treatments of characters living B-movie lives. But it is such a clever, complex, and enjoyable work that it very much makes its own special mark. If with his last novel Vargas Llosa joined the Latin American literary party, with *Aunt Julia and the Scriptwriter* he becomes, along with his friend García Márquez, the life of that party. (p. 39)

> Ronald De Feo, "Life As Fiction, Fiction As Life," in The New Republic, Vol. 187, Nos. 7 & 8, August 16 & 23, 1982, pp. 38-9.

CAROLYN CLAY

Here, fresh off the boat from Peru, is the exception to prove the rule that all autobiographical novels about growing up to be a writer are alike, noisy with the clacking of John-Boy's typewriter and the howl of the Wolfe. As far as the Andes are from Walton's Mountain is Mario Vargas Llosa's *Aunt Julia and the Scriptwriter* from most efforts to shake literary pay dirt from the author's roots. The story, set in Lima in the fifties, traces the eighteen-year-old narrator's pristine secret courtship of his Aunt Julia, a sensuous but pragmatic Bolivian divorcée, and his simultaneous fascination with the squirrelly Pedro Camacho, a consummate artist-cum-one-man industry dedicated to the cranking out of radio serials. This is a curious yet seductive book that layers truth, in the guise of the author's own story, with fiction, in the form of Camacho's modern gothic soapers. . . .

Underneath it all, *Aunt Julia and the Scriptwriter* is a treatise on the art of writing, on the relationship of stimulus to imagination. Varguitas—as young Mario is known to his intimates—is in love for the first time with something other than his fantasies of authorship. . . .

As the young newshound—increasingly smitten with Aunt Julia and determined to marry her if he has to travel to Las Vegas by llama to pull it off—watches his own heretofore art-oriented existence lather up, he becomes captivated by the grotesque Pedro Camacho, who is both a successful hack *and* a martyr to his art. . . .

There can be no question that Camacho is committed; in fact, when his characters start juggling professions and perversions and leaping serials, he is packed off to an institution (proving once again, ho hum, that the line between creativity and madness is a thin one). . . .

What makes the book bizarre—and as maddening as a channel flipper—is that every other chapter is an episode of one of Camacho's serials: In re-creating them, Vargas Llosa engages in a kind of narrative teasing in that we never find out how any of the weird tales turn out. But then neither do Camacho's listeners, since in an effort to save his sanity he resorts to killing everyone off in apocalyptic fashion. . . .

The notion of characters controlling their creator is a tradition in Spanish literature going back to Cervantes. Vargas Llosa plays with it, but he himself is no puppet. Sure, there are times when he seems to have turned his typewriter over to Pedro Camacho (how will this May-December matrimonial melodrama of Miraflores end?), but there is irony in surrender. *Aunt Julia and the Scriptwriter* develops into both a parodic tour de force and a tender tale of youth brandishing its way to maturity. Putting it all together to form a meditation on art is a game for the reader amused enough to be patient.

And Varguitas's story, unlike those of Camacho, has an ending—less grisly than what the scriptwriter might have devised but sad in the way that real life, its passions muted, so often is. The narrator—older, expatriated, and published—returns to Lima with his second wife and runs into just about everybody he used to know, including the artistically emasculated "Balzac of Peru." Though little is said, it is achingly clear that Varguitas, the writer now, is as grown up as Camacho is burned out—and that the two states are much the same.

> Carolyn Clay, "South American Soap," in New York Magazine, Vol. 15, No. 33, August 23, 1982, p. 90.

EDWARD TICK

A writer's coming of age is at once ridiculous and sublime. Mario Vargas Llosa, Peru's best-known modern author, provides a good dose of both emotions in his newly translated semi-autobiographical novel [*Aunt Julia and the Scriptwriter*]. With this work we have the story of a writer's transformation and emergence in contemporary South America. . . .

The tone, pace and coloring of his language are at times reminiscent of adult fairy tales, of stories told to symbolically prepare children for the harsh realities of grownup life. Mario, a passionate 18-year-old Peruvian law student and would-be writer, certainly needs to be initiated into adulthood. . . .

Mario might have passed his life trifling with short stories and eventually scratching out a law degree and a living. But he comes upon two individuals who change him from a mere product of his surroundings into its keen observer and wry commentator.

The first is Aunt Julia, whom Mario bumps into at one of many lunches with his extended family. . . . Julia is a 32-year-old divorcée, a forerunner of the liberated woman who flouts decorum by reckless dating. She represents the perfect conquest for young Mario. From their first meeting the competition is set.

Much of the novel is devoted to their sometimes funny, sometimes ironic, always clandestine courting. . . . In time they elope. . . . [The] couple embarks on a trek to the primitive villages and jungles of Peru to find a justice of the peace who will illegally marry a minor and a divorcée from Bolivia.

This hilarious adventure is one of the high points of the novel. We get a comprehensive portrait-in-passing of mid-20th century Peru, from its urban grandeur and squalor through its villages tenuously linked by the remnants of a transit system, to its outposts and jungles where natives fish, drink, spawn, and seriocomically attempt to conform to a bureaucracy that makes no sense to them yet is respected and feared. Unwittingly, we come to know the intricate and contradictory South American landscape.

Julia meanwhile enables Mario to sexually and romantically mature. This is not really a matter of love and we are more fascinated with their doings than with their personalities. But what is missing in them is more than compensated for in the scriptwriter, Pedro Camacho.

With this character the novel becomes special. Pedro Camacho is one of those creations who is fascinating and incisive because of his sufferings and deformity. . . .

Part Ahab, part Joycean expatriate, part buffoon, Pedro Camacho is also the obsessed writer, the megalomaniac pitting his ego against the cosmos. . . .

Camacho enables Llosa to give his novel a fascinating structure. Alternating chapters are Camacho's short stories, where we glimpse the inner workings of a person wholly dedicated to expressing his version of truth, no matter what the personal consequences. (p. 16)

Each of Camacho's increasingly decadent stories destroys the surface respectability of some social institution—religion, family, legal system, business—to expose the horrors underneath. As Nietzsche observed, though, one who experiences the annihilation of nature experiences inner annihilation: In the course of revealing the decay of his culture, Camacho's personality fragments. Like so many artists in the modern age, he becomes a victim of the processes he scrutinizes. . . .

Aunt Julia and the Scriptwriter is successful on many levels, but it has the weaknesses of the soap operas it emulates. We are, at times, too close to the banalities, to the details of family dinners and petty intrigues. We long for the relief of deterioration, much as many people long for the six o'clock news to excite them with another important crisis.

The weaknesses are purposeful, however. By the end of the book, we know the people in it intimately. We know how young Marito grew up to be Mario Vargas Llosa. We have observed both the tedium and the fantasies of the mind in obsessed love and creative turmoil. We have seen how love and creativity grow and how they die. Most important, we have, along with Mario, answered some of the questions he struggles with. (p. 17)

> *Edward Tick, "A Portrait of the Artist As a Young Peruvian," in* The New Leader, *Vol. LXV, No. 21, November 15, 1982, pp. 16-17.*

SELDEN RODMAN

From the beginning Vargas Llosa was accused by the friendliest of his critics of "the bad habit of withholding vital information." In his impressive first novel, *La Ciudad y los Perros,* what the dog-eat-dog violence of a military school is intended to symbolize depends on a series of interior monologues in the mind of a character whose identity is not revealed until the end of the book. The young novelist idolized Faulkner and may have copied from him this lack of respect for the reader, but he had rejected Faulkner's subjectivity from the outset. In his next novel, *La Casa Verde,* Vargas Llosa commits even graver sins of obfuscation, telling simultaneously five stories about essentially anonymous characters and providing no clues to place or time.

In comparison with those predecessors, *Aunt Julia and the Scriptwriter* is a model of straightforwardness. The plots of Pedro Camacho's radio soap operas . . . are simply and dramatically unfolded—at least until the scriptwriter goes completely wacky and confuses new characters with old ones. But the unfolding love affair of the young novelist with his middle-aged Bolivian aunt-by-marriage, which develops in alternating chapters until their clandestine marriage is consummated at the end, is told with high spirits, gusto, humor, and tenderness—and with no attempt to conceal what apparently happened in real life. The chapter in which the lovers drive all over central Peru trying to circumvent the author's horrified parents, and the couple's lack of funds to bribe officialdom, is a comic masterpiece.

It is only toward the end of the novel that things get unnecessarily mixed up. When he first appears Pedro Camacho is a brilliant evocation of the obsessive artist. . . .

Perhaps this is where the novel should have ended. Or with the marriage to lovely, laughing, uncomplicated Aunt Julia that follows. But the final disintegration of the soap operas—how different these bizarre tales are from our soaps with their suave middle-class motivations of money and adultery!—into hopeless confusions foreclosing continuations, serves only to bring the author back into sync with his existentialist colleagues; and make of Peru, hitherto described with so much affection and understanding, another neo-Marxist parable of Third World hopelessness. To see Pedro Camacho lugged off to the insane asylum and then return to the radio station as a fawning lackey doing odd jobs, is sad. Maybe that's the way it was in "real life," but it brings a great comic novel, and a promising new beginning for a very talented writer, to a tame conclusion. (p. 1560)

> *Selden Rodman, "Writing on Air," in* National Review, *Vol. XXXIV, No. 24, December 10, 1982, pp. 1559-60.*

MARGHANITA LASKI

The belief that the craft of narrative fiction is alive, well, and putting on flesh in South America seemed for many pages verified by Mario Vargas Llosa's novel, *Aunt Julia and the Scriptwriter,* originally published in Peru in 1977. Not only is Llosa immediately acceptable as a proper storyteller: his stories are set in, to us, exotic Lima, and they are clearly going to be fashionably fickle and freckled, peppering the promising narration by 18-year-old Mario of the mutual love that unfolds between him and his 32-year-old aunt-by-marriage Julia, a divorcée from Bolivia. . . .

Well presented, then, a good scene, and not only Mario's: interspersed are what seem to be poised to develop into nourishing subplots—the episode of the incestuously pregnant bride, of the Kaspar-Hauser of a naked nigger, doomed literally for the trash-heap, of the dubiously unchaste Jehovah's Witness—and so right is the pitch of the telling, so exotically unknown the settings, that it is only about half-way through, at what would, in one of today's more usual single-stranded novels, be the climactical point, that quaintness rather than originality seems to be the mode and encroaching boredom the response, with some impatience forcing the question of where we are being taken.

It is only then (tardily, if you so decide, but pardonably because always ready to be a sucker for a story) that one realises that the interposed stories are never going to thicken the novel up, are no more to do with the novel proper than by being the soap operas churned out by the compulsively creative, self-styled artist, the scriptwriter, whom the station has brought in from Bolivia. 'I learned that everything, without exception, could be turned into the subject of a short story,' says young Mario, who is forever trying to write one, but not everything can be turned into a good short story, and not every short story, we come sadly to decide, can fit into a would-be novel or, indeed, pass as the stuff of soap. Certainly these stories, even before they deliberately disintegrate, could never have been such enrapturing soaps to the women of Lima that the station could even afford to disregard their deliberate insults to the Argentines.

It is by intention that the internal stories degenerate into confusion as the soap operas degenerate with the disintegration of the scriptwriter's brain. But the presentation of mental degeneration needs genius, which this has not, if we are not to be as bemused, and then as restless, as the story-starved women of Lima. But if . . . we place our expectations on the principal narrative thread, we are baulked again, for nothing much ever happens, apart from a set-piece, over-drawn-out search for a mayor who will marry underage Mario to divorced Julia; while the attendant characters play their stock roles. . . . They are rather in a zoetrope than in life, and it is delightful to watch them twitching for the first few twirls, but soon too far distanced to be lifesize as they are, it finally seems, distanced by time from the apparently autobiographical author, now living in Paris with a new young wife and an annual trip home to replenish the roots.

Llosa has, the blurb tells us, written plays, and these we should be greatly interested to see, for the undoubted talents of this long prose narrative (or, rather, this narrative device for threading short stories) augurs well for drama. . . .

> *Marghanita Laski, "Stories Galore," in* The Spectator, *Vol. 250, No. 8079, May 14, 1983, p. 22.*

RICHARD LOCKE

The work of the Peruvian novelist Mario Vargas Llosa . . . has established him as a major figure in contemporary Latin American letters. His new book [*The War of the End of the World*] should confirm this: even in translation it overshadows the majority of novels published here in the past few years. Indeed, it makes most recent American fiction seem very small, very private, very gray, and very timid.

The War of the End of the World is based on a true incident that occurred in Brazil in the final years of the 19th century. Slavery had been abolished in 1888, and a republic succeeded the monarchy in 1889. Four years later, in a desolate part of the northern state of Bahia, a charismatic religious leader established a peasant community that shared his belief in the imminent end of the world and his radical rejection of the secular state. This community was seen as a violent, atavistic

threat to the progressive ideals and political stability of the new republic. The story of this community and its destruction is the plot of the novel. It explores a series of interactive delusions: apocalyptic religion, revolutionary idealism, military absolutism, and peasant machismo. Its historical and political vision is closer to that of Conrad or Orwell than either Che Guevara or Ronald Reagan.

The story is not told chronologically; there are flashbacks and crosscuts, frequent shifts between the past and present tenses, and, as we follow the lives of more than 50 characters, more than a dozen different points of view. But this is never obscure, or surrealistic, or arty; each of the chapters and sub-sections is dense with clear, realistic narrative and concrete detail. The difficulty of the book arises from the sheer mass of unfamiliar historical incidents and personalities that are gradually animated before our eyes. (pp. 1, 11)

Vargas Llosa is so saturated with his subject, so grasping in his imagination of it, that he brings it to urgent life. We not only see the development of the Counselor's band of true believers, and the complex growth and organization of his holy village of Canudos, but we follow the intricate political maneuvering back in the state capital and the progress of the four military campaigns. We are close to the lives of some two dozen major characters. . . . We observe many varieties of religious experience and witness the social, political, and moral transformations such belief can effect. But Vargas Llosa rarely sentimentalizes; he is both sympathetic and unsparing of these religious and political fanatics, of the peasants, soldiers, and landowners alike.

A great deal of time is spent on the picaresque adventures of various bandits who join the company of the elect and on the fortunes of a demented Scottish anarchist (and phrenologist), a devotee of Proudhon and Bakunin, a veteran of the Paris Commune, who desperately tries to get to Canudos [the peasant community] to cast his lot with its primitive socialist revolution. There is much to do with a terrified, nearsighted journalist who is caught between the lines and gets closer to the war story than he ever imagined he could. And there is an enormous amount of military detail—transportation, skirmishes, battles, hand-to-hand combat—and a large number of rapes, mutilations, and atrocities: cinematic Goya.

The novel concludes with a return to the brutal *status quo ante* and a curious burst of sexual narrative: in the depths of this degradation the journalist discovers true love in the arms of a stoic peasant girl, and the Baron is inspired by this to rape his mad wife's maid. This is portrayed as a triumph of life over death, but it's most unconvincing. In general, Vargas Llosa does poorly with the women in this book.

Although he is more ambitious than precise in the construction of this large novel—he hasn't the architectonic skill that Garcia Márquez commands, nor his humor—Vargas Llosa has abundant energy, stamina, and intellectual curiosity. His violent realistic narrative enlarges our understanding of political and religious fanaticism and reaffirms the rich variety and strength of contemporary Latin American literature. (p. 11)

> *Richard Locke, "A Voice Crying in the Wilderness," in* Book World—The Washington Post, *August 26, 1984, pp. 1, 11.*

SALMAN RUSHDIE

In his loudly acclaimed novel *The War of the End of the World* . . . Vargas Llosa sets down with appalling and ferocious clarity his vision of the tragic consequences for ordinary people of millenarianism of whatever kind. He has written before, in his novel *Captain Pantoja and the Special Service,* about the emergence in remote rural parts of an ascetic figure who becomes a focus of resistance to a militaristic state. That was primarily a comic novel, however, whereas the new book is as dark as spilled blood. And while it is most impressively got up as a historical novel—based, we are told, on a "real" episode in Brazilian history—its value as a text is entirely contemporary. In an age such as ours, plagued by bloodthirsty armies and equally violent gods, an account of a fight to the finish between God and Mammon could be nothing else, even though Vargas has placed his war in one of the most remote corners—the "ends"—of the world, that is, in the northeastern part of Brazil in the nineteenth century. . . .

The Counselor . . . [a messiah figure] is a thin, awe-inspiring holy man who wanders the backlands of the province of Bahia in the last decade or so of the nineteenth century, advising the peons of their spiritual obligations in clear and comprehensible language, encouraging them to help him repair the region's many dilapidated and priestless churches, slowly gathering about himself an inner circle or band of apostles, and warning eloquently of the fearsome apocalypse that is to arrive with the millennium. . . .

Bahia, in which slavery has not been abolished for very long and which remains in the two-fisted grip of autocratic feudal landowners and in extreme ignorance of the outside world, begins to hear about ominous developments. A Republic has been proclaimed; it intends to make a census, and worse, to levy taxes. These are the last straws for the people of the backlands. Why would the Republic want everyone counted and described, except to re-impose slavery? And, again, "animal instinct, common sense and centuries of experience made the townspeople realize immediately . . . that the tax collectors would be greedier than the vultures and the bandits." The Counselor gives expression to their worst fears. He announces that "the Antichrist was abroad in the world; his name was Republic." Then he withdraws, with all who wish to follow him, to the fastness of Canudos, part of the lands of the Baron de Canabrava, the largest of the feudal landlords and chief of the Bahian Autonomist Party—which, ironically, is just as hostile to the new Republic, though for wholly profane reasons of self-interest.

In Canudos the Counselor sets about the construction and fortification of "Belo Monte," a city and a church, a new Jerusalem against which the Antichrist must hurl his armies. There will be four fires, the Counselor tells his flock (which numbers, at its peak, more than thirty thousand souls). He will quench three and permit the fourth to consume them. So the four battles of the war of Canudos are prophesied in advance. What follows has the slow, somber inevitability of a Greek tragedy—though one played out in a jungle. Our knowledge of the end serves only to increase our pain.

Vargas Llosa's writing has been working up to this book throughout his remarkable career; the prose has been getting simpler, the forms clearer. It is a long way from the structural complexities and the sometimes willful-seeming obscurity of

his very striking early novels, *The Time of the Hero* and *The Green House,* via the comic accessibility, even zaniness, of *Captain Pantoja* and *Aunt Julia and the Scriptwriter,* to the much more solid, crafted, traditional virtues of the present novel. It must not be supposed, though, that this represents some kind of descent into populism. Rather, Vargas Llosa would appear to have been moving, gradually, from one form of complexity toward another. Or, to be precise, from complexity of form to complexity of ideas. *The War of the End of the World* does certainly offer many of the conventional satisfactions of the long, meticulous, historical novel—the recreation of a lost world; leisurely, well-paced exposition; a sense of elbowroom, and of being in safe hands. But it also gives us a fictional universe bursting with intellectual argument, one whose inhabitants are perfectly willing and able to dispute matters both political and spiritual at great length and with considerable verve.

But the greatest qualities of this excellent novel are, I believe, neither its inexorable Greek progress toward the slaughter of the innocents with which it climaxes, nor its intellectual rigor. They are, rather, its refusal ever to abandon the human dimension in a story that could so easily have become grandiose; also a sense of ambiguity, which enables Vargas Llosa to keep his characters three-dimensional, and not merely the representatives of Good, or Evil, or some such abstraction; and finally, a profound awareness of the tragic irony that makes tens of thousands of ordinary women and men die fighting against the Republic that was created, in theory, precisely to serve them, and to protect them against the rapacity of their former feudal overlords. (p. 26)

The political vision of *The War of the End of the World* is bleak, and it would be possible to take issue with such absolute bleakness. But it is hard for a writer in the late years of this savage century not to have a tragic view of life, and Mario Vargas Llosa has written a modern tragedy on the grand scale, though not, mercifully, in the grand manner. At the end of its 550 pages, two images dominate its seething portrait of death, corruption, and faith. One is of the tracker Rufino, and anarchist Galileo Gall, each the somewhat absurd servant of an idea, hacking one another slowly to death; this image would seem to crystallize Vargas Llosa's political vision.

The second image, however, is redemptive. Thirty thousand people die in Canudos, and it would be easy to think that a God who demanded such sacrifices was a God to avoid like the plague. But Vargas Llosa, with the generosity of spirit that informs the entire novel, is willing to allow the last word to someone who accepts that the catastrophe was also a kind of triumph. The victorious soldiers, mopping up after the leveling of Canudos, are anxious to account for the one leader whose body has not been found. An old woman asks Colonel Macedo if he wants to know what happened to Abbot Joao and the Colonel nods eagerly. "Archangels took him up to heaven," she says, clacking her tongue. "I saw them." (p. 27)

Salman Rushdie, "Peruvian Master," in The New Republic, *Vol. 191, No. 15, October 8, 1984, pp. 25-7.*

Rebecca West

1892-1983

(Pseudonym of Cicily Isabel Fairfield) English journalist, novelist, and critic.

West wrote of equality for women in the workplace, the voting booth, and in the pursuit of pleasure. Hers were radical ideas in 1911, the year she began her career writing for *The Freewoman*, a feminist publication. Although she expanded her talents into literary criticism and, eventually, into fiction, her best-known and most respected work was in journalism. West once said that were she to begin again, she would write only novels, but ironically, her novels are thought to be the least effective of her works. Critics attribute this to her journalistic style which allows for little warmth, spontaneity, or imagination.

Prominent among West's early books are the biographies *Henry James* (1916) and *St. Augustine* (1933). The latter, one of the first psychohistories, is written with a heavily Freudian emphasis. Although the books were praised for their historical accuracy, many critics felt that the psychoanalytical language presented an unnecessary distraction.

West's early fiction, including her novels *Harriet Hume* (1929) and *The Thinking Reed* (1936) and her collection of four short novels, *The Harsh Voice* (1935), were not well received. Critics generally find her fiction undistinguished because of its heavy emphasis on didacticism and the unbelievability of her plots and characters. Perhaps as a result of the demands placed upon her by her journalistic work, West published only two novels after *The Thinking Reed*. However, one of these, *The Fountain Overflows* (1956), was praised for its depiction of a young girl growing up in a failing London family and is seen as West's most sensitive piece of fiction.

West's journalism and criticism are considered by critics to be her most important and enduring work. In these fields she forcefully conveys her strong opinions and liberal political views. *The Strange Necessity* (1928) is a collection of critical essays which focuses on the historical and contemporary role of art and the artist; this is a major theme in much of West's criticism. Her interest in the nature of patriotism and the motivations underlying the decision to betray are discussed in *The Meaning of Treason* (1947). A related idea explored in *The Court and the Castle* (1957) is how corruption affects the individual who is ruled by the pursuit and acquisition of power. The book which has been called her masterpiece, *Black Lamb and Grey Falcon* (1941), recounts West's travels through Yugoslavia; essentially, however, it is a commentary on the politics, history, social attitudes, and living conditions among the people of that country. Although her writing is consistently praised for being technically accomplished, this book has been criticized for historical misinterpretations.

Among the most frequent complaints about West's work are its digressive wordiness and the author's reliance upon personal observation rather than research. However, critics consistently appreciate her "felicity of phrase," and many enjoy her passionate, often eccentric, opinions. In her work and in her life, West was true to those issues she wrote about. Even in the early *Freewoman* pieces, she decries injustice, berates

© Jerry Bauer

stupidity, scorns laziness, and despises cowardice. Her wry wit and sardonic humor were applied unsparingly to whatever aroused her dissatisfaction.

(See also *CLC*, Vols. 7, 9; *Contemporary Authors*, Vols. 5-8, rev. ed., Vol. 109 [obituary]; and *Dictionary of Literary Biography Yearbook: 1983*.)

PHILIP LITTELL

What kind of book about Henry James would you expect from a vivid and eager young radical, whose own interest in politics and history is prodigious, who has a keen appetite for almost every kind of life except the life lived in English country houses, and who detests, with all her many gifts of detestation, the predominance of sex in the relations of men and women? You would do well not to expect a delineative book, which defines Henry James with a portrait-painter's hand, or a luminously expository book, which makes him plainer to readers who could not understand for themselves.

[In **"Henry James"**] Miss West has given us neither of these things. One would have been astonished if she had, and yet not more astonished, I think, than one is by the book she has actually written, which with all its brilliant arrogance and cockiness, with all its impatience at the difference between yesterday's mode and to-day's, with all its failures in sympathy and in understanding—there is an amazingly unperceiving passage about "The Awkward Age"—does glow with such a beauty of admiration for Henry James that one gets the strongest incentive to read him all over again. . . .

Miss West's book has wit and beauty and intelligence and stupidity. It has hardly more than a scrap of anything you could call insight. You would never learn from it that Henry James's life was among other things a long discarding of naïveté. You would never learn from it that his books were a series of attempts to put his newer ideas of distinction and its opposite into the place once occupied by his earliest ideas of right and wrong. Some day Miss West will find her real subject. But, being only twenty-four, she need not hurry. (p. 3)

> Philip Littell, "Rebecca West on Henry James," in The New Republic, Vol. IX, No. 107, November 18, 1916, pp. 2-3.

HENRY B. FULLER

What first interests me in [*The Return of the Soldier*] is its length, or rather its brevity: all is done within one hundred and eighty-five pages. . . . Miss West's "novella" is an episode, a situation involving but a few days—or would be, were it not for a chronological backthrow which provides perspective, complications, and the road to a highly effective climax.

We think, at the start, that we have to deal with Rebecca West as still the brisk and brusque young radical of "The Free-woman" and "The New Republic," walking through life in a trim tailor-made, with her feet setting themselves down firmly and her elbows in vigorous action. Well, she is all of that—in certain phases of her social criticism; but she is much more.

Later on we incline to image Miss West as a spirited young filly, speeding it over her race track. For two-thirds of her course she trots, true to form, on the old well-known course, though she covers it with a quickened stride; then comes a moment of tangled hoofs and a threat to bolt the regular track and to finish up before the judges' stand anyhow. It is this that makes the fifth of her six chapters, which is crowded with unskilled transitions, both the worst and the best; surely it is the most novel and moving.

"The Return of the Soldier" is of course a war-story—a story of shell-shock, amnesia, and the suppressed wish. The author is of the new day, and the new nomenclature shall not fail. But she throws out a decisive arm and tames science to art—all with a tense economy of means that helps open a fresh era for the novel. (p. 299)

One's sense at the beginning is that the book may be a contraption ad hoc: it indeed derives from the war, and it rests on a combination of circumstances impossible before our own day; but one presently perceives that it is animated by a higher and better spirit, and one willingly meets the applied psychology which, exercised near the end of the basis of homely domestic detail, brings the clouded mind safely through the labyrinth and throws a last grateful light on a memorable and essentially lovable heroine.

It is in the social setting of her scene that Miss West seems most her radical self. Though she loves the changing aspects of nature and is lavish with vignettes portraying them, she is severe upon the landscape-gardening of the country-house and upon all its implications. . . .

Miss West's diction (I may even call it style) is of a richness—a tempestuous, tangled richness that keeps one interested and excited. She lavishes it alike on her landscape and on the psychology of her people. Truth to tell, as regards this last, she is her own brusque, peremptory self, and sometimes does rather cursorily what, with due regard to the mysterious temple of the human mind, might justly enlist a little more leisure and finesse. But she has set her own limits and done her best—a pretty good best—within them. (p. 300)

> Henry B. Fuller, "Rebecca West—Novelist," in The Dial, Vol. LXIV, No. 763, March 28, 1918, pp. 299-300.

THE NEW YORK TIMES BOOK REVIEW

Rebecca West's new novel ["**The Judge**"] is a brilliant piece of work, forceful, impressive, haunting with a sense of instance. . . . Her one previous novel, her critical work, and her essays have shown her to possess a keenly probing intellect, a rich mental background and a notable gift for the art of writing. All this, in fuller, richer development and in finer quality, is evident in "**The Judge**," but through its pages there shines, too, the clear, unmistakable light of genius. In its insight into the deeps of human nature, and especially of feminine human nature, in its treatment of the drama of human life, in the richness of its fabric and in the force and power and skill with which it uses, for the purposes of the story, the element of personality in its characters, the novel is comparable with the work of George Eliot at her best, although falling short, in some respects, of the measure of her artistic excellence. But it is as different from her fiction as this age is different from George Eliot's period. For it is franker, truer, comes to closer grips with the forces of life, seeks more ruthlessly to find the roots of motive, the sources of character, the causes of action.

It is a long novel containing close upon two hundred thousand words, and its story could be boiled down into the compass of half a dozen sentences. Nevertheless, with such skill has Miss West painted her characters, marshaled her temperaments, used her emotional elements, that the attention is at once enlisted and the interest grows constantly deeper and more absorbing until the end. Stripped down to its last essentials, it is a story of the love of a man for the girl he intends to marry cutting across his love for his mother. But it would be as inadequate to describe it thus as to say of a tempestuous, thrilling, dramatic conflagration merely that "a fire burned down such and such a block yesterday." for this situation of a man greatly loving his promised wife and yet being deeply absorbed in his lifelong love of his mother not only flowers out into drama in the present, but opens the doors into the past and shows the fateful story being enacted, step by step, that lives on from one generation to the next. It is out of this sense of continuing destiny that the novel takes its title, for "the Judge" is the mother of children, the woman who by her choice of their father determines their fate, visits upon them their destiny. . . .

Through the first half of the book the outstanding figure is Ellen Melville, 17 years old, child of an Irish father and a Scotch mother, a vivid, dreaming, practical, ambitious, red-haired typist in a lawyer's office in Edinburgh. It was an audacious thing for an author to conceive in the first place and then to attempt to work out and put down in cold type such a conglomerate of opposed qualities as Miss West has fused together in Ellen, with her Scotch mentality and her Scotch-Irish temperament. But the attempt is successful, for Ellen, with all her moods and her surprises and her contrarieties, her ardent generosities and her thrift and her forethoughtedness, her tempers and her glowing joys, is a logical, convincing character. One knows her, believes in her, loves her and rejoices always in her presence. In a novel notable for the variety and unusual quality of its character portrayal she stands easily first as the most clearly and vividly painted personality in the book. . . .

[The second] half of the book, doubtless in part because its elements are those of which human agonies and human ecstacies are chiefly made, holds the interest at a higher tension than does the first half. But in part this is due also to the closer, more rapid treatment of the theme. The author does not so often stand off and speculate, nor does she so frequently stop to hold the spotlight a little longer on a result or a situation already sufficiently elucidated—a fault too often evident in the first half of the story. In this second part she herself seemed to have become so absorbed that the emotional intensity of the narrative forced her pen rapidly on and on and forbade her to stop for necessary words.

Although it is a drama of many tragedies that drives its way inexorably on to its final tragic scenes, there is in it much of sunshine and laughter, crisp humor and happy hours. . . . The author has an epigrammatic wit that sparkles frequently, especially when she is mentioning some characteristic of the Scotch, whom she calls "an unsensuous race inordinately and mistakenly vain of its knees." And she has a happy faculty of phrasing neatly, sometimes poetically, an interesting or a significant thought. . . .

The book is, pre-eminently, a woman's book, because woman is the vessel of creation, and herein she is shown busy, body, soul, and mind. In the business for which nature demands her services. The men in the novel are brilliantly portrayed, but they are not quite as convincing as the women, do not carry in their lineaments the assurance of quite such fullness of knowledge in the mind of their creator. And one somehow gets the impression from them that Rebecca West hasn't a very high opinion of men. (p. 19)

A review of "The Judge," in The New York Times
Book Review, August 20, 1922, pp. 19, 27.

NEW STATESMAN

The Strange Necessity is almost as tedious as *Das Kapital,* and with much less justification. It is so intrinsically unreadable that the printer's reader will surely be the last and only man who will ever be able to claim that he has read all through the sixty or seventy thousand words of it. In the first place, in so far as it contains any fresh or useful idea on the problem of aesthetics—and we are not sure that it does—the adequate expression of that idea need certainly not have occupied more than a quarter of the space it does. A very great deal of the essay seems to be just incoherent rambling, and the amount of sheer self-repetition in it is, to say the least, irritating. Page after page upon which Miss West seeks to trace the connection and sequence of her own thoughts and feelings, reads more like an exercise in elementary Pelmanism than anything else we know of, and since the whole is clothed in the jargon of psychoanalysis imperfectly comprehended, the result is inevitably most depressing. . . .

The title of the essay refers to the "strange necessity" of art in life. Art, in Miss West's view, is the force which enables

the "will to live" to triumph over the "will to die"; but it is difficult to disentangle from her torrent of long words what her ideas of art really are, and therefore it is difficult to discuss them. If they seem to us a little naive, that may be because we have not grasped her intended meaning. When she asserts, for example, that "it is no use saying that what we call beauty in life is that which is most useful to man in life" or "that what we call beauty in art is that which is most useful to man in art," there seems to be no comment to make save the question, "Who ever has said any such things?" On another page, discussing the difficulty of defining what we mean by the difference between good art and bad art Miss West writes:

> If one says that one likes meat if it is good and dislikes it if it is bad, one knows as one speaks that one means by good meat that which has been well fed when it walked this earth, has been killed in the right way, kept the right time after killing, and has been properly cooked so that it is tender and juicy and full of flavour, and by bad meat that which, not having been as justly dealt with, is stringy and dry and tasteless. But good art . . .

Surely if Miss West had pursued this line of thought a little more closely she would have realised that there is no greater difficulty in defining good art than in defining good meat. A good picture is one which has been composed of the right materials, has been painted in the right tradition by the right man—who has rightly apprehended the essential possibilities of his subject—has been properly framed and hung, and, in the result, produces a poignant and enlightening effect upon our aesthetic sensibilities. This definition begs no more questions than Miss West's definition of good meat. In both cases we are able in fact to judge only by the result. Does the steak please our palate? Does the picture produce the aesthetic emotion we are looking for? One sensibility may be more delicate, more sublime than the other, but the only possible criterion in either case is the same. . . . It is just as easy and just as impossible for the gourmet as for the art critic to define his sensations. Apart from the difference of plane the parallel is in all respects exact. A realisation of this fact must surely be the starting point of any valuable contribution to the science of aesthetics.

A great part of Miss West's essay is devoted to a discussion of the artistic value of Mr. James Joyce's *Ulysses*. But even here, when she is on her own ground, it is very difficult to make out what is her real opinion of that at any rate remarkable book. She refers to Mr. Joyce as a writer of "majestic genius" and speaks of his "titanic imagination," but elsewhere she suggests that in composing his masterpiece he "simply did not understand what he was doing." . . . This is characteristic of Miss West's fundamentally sentimental view of the nature of art. Art is something which marvellously happens, and the intellect must not be allowed to have anything to do with it. The artist must "achieve identity" with what he makes. In one place Miss West tells us that "to communicate his experience to an audience is no trouble to an artist"; in another, apropos of Ingres, she writes "astoundingly his medium seemed a friend and not the enemy—which it is to nearly all artists." What is one to make of such contradictions?

These strictures, however, are by no means intended to imply an opinion that Miss West's essay is all rubbish. Certainly a good deal of it is rubbish, or, more exactly, a medley of imperfectly digested external impressions and subjective ideas.

But she has some excellent things to say, particularly for example about the tremendous handicap under which an artist inevitably works if he is divorced, by choice or circumstances, from his own land, that is to say from a body of tradition which he has imbibed from his earliest youth, and does not have to think about because it is part of himself. In general, however, Miss West gives the impression of having thought too little about her subject, of being too glib, of having treated one of the greatest and most difficult problems in the world with much the same quality of care and attention as she might reasonably devote to a newspaper review of the latest novel of Mr. Swinnerton or Mr. Galsworthy. She is insufficiently critical of her own work, too apt to be influenced by the glamour of her own sentences. She appears to think in words rather than in ideas. If a good phrase has bubbled up in her mind it must be a just phrase; if a sentence that pleases her has somehow found its way on to her writing block she cannot bring herself to believe that it does not embody some essential and profound truth. That, we suppose, is why so much of her work is superficial and contradictory. Thinking in words is for the journalist an excellent and most useful habit, but for anyone who aspires to be more than that it is a very bad habit indeed—suicidal. Miss West's final conclusion about art is that it is nothing less than "a way of making joys perpetual." It is the word "less" that may shock artists. Nothing *less* indeed! (pp. 566-67)

> "Miss Rebecca West on Art," in New Statesman,
> Vol. XXXI, No. 798, August 11, 1928, pp. 566-67.

ERNEST SUTHERLAND BATES

["St. Augustine"] stands out above its predecessors both in beauty of style and significance of thought. A popular biography only in being easy and delightful to read, Miss West's flexible and trenchant style here wholly at her command, mingling wit and eloquence without disharmony, her book is also a keen analysis of the character and meaning of one of the world's greatest men. Here with a subject worthy of her steel, Miss West has risen above her lesser self, somewhat too generous of casual impressions, and has given us a volume rich in reflection as well as daringly alive in treatment. Augustine stands before us almost a contemporary, a tortured spirit, fellow with Tolstoy, Lawrence, Proust, and Joyce, yet at the same time a citizen of the dying Roman Empire when under the strokes of Goth and Vandal and the weight of its own decrepitude an age-old civilization was breaking up much as Western civilization seems to many to be breaking up today.

Miss West's volume begins appropriately with a letter from Bishop Cyprian of Carthage to a Roman official in which the Christian attributes the manifest decline of civilization to the weakening of the forces of nature. . . . It is against this background of a failing world that the portrait of Augustine is limned, its exponent and interpreter. . . . The sack of Rome by the Goths which broke the aged heart of Saint Jerome aroused in Augustine a fiery exultation and inspired "The City of God," a work which Miss West, while applauding its genius, fearlessly recognizes as "a shocking and barbarous book." Shocking and barbarous Augustine himself often appears in her work, in his arrogance and tactlessness and in his cruel persecution of heretics, but the arrogance and tactlessness arise out of timidity, and his heresy hunting out of an anguished need for an infallible other-worldly religion. Miss West, it is true, speaks of him in several places as "a lion," but the picture which she draws is not at all leonine. It is that of a poet-philosopher, sick at heart over the intrinsic vileness of mankind and seeking a great cleansing. . . .

With [the] more impersonal part of his work Miss West was prevented from dealing by limitations of space, which is a pity, as the pungent and provocative comments scattered throughout her book suggest that her handling of this phase of Augustine would also have been new and vital.

> *Ernest Sutherland Bates, "A Tortured Spirit," in*
> The Saturday Review of Literature, *Vol. IX, No. 40,*
> *April 29, 1933, p. 559.*

WILLIAM PLOMER

[The] four "short novels" which Miss Rebecca West has collected under the title of *The Harsh Voice* are a significant expression of current truths, though she may not be the first to make their significance real. Some of the current truths upon which she has most firmly seized are these: that in love and marriage today the intermingling of love and hate has taken on a new complexity, partly on account of changes in manners and the variable economic conditions, particularly in America; [and] that America in particular has evolved a new kind of woman, extremely capable, "hard-boiled," influential, but certainly not devoid of feminine feelings. . . . All four stories are about rich people; three are about Americans; three are principally about problems of the married; and in all may be heard that "harsh voice we hear when money talks, or hate." It is noticeable that with one exception Miss West accords her women justice, mercy and admiration, and that she seems to find them definitely more important and worthy of respect and affection than the men, who leave an impression that they are little more than foils to the women, than commercial and domestic functionaries—with one exception, who is dominated by vanity. This exception appears in the most brilliant and characteristic of the four stories, the one called "There is no Conversation." It shows to the best advantage Miss West's sophistication, her respect for wealth and power, and her ingenuity and resourcefulness as a story-teller. . . . Two individuals belonging to entirely different worlds are brought by chance into a close association. . . . The Marquis de Sevenac, at luncheon with some Americans in Paris, was "thrown back on" a Mrs. Sarle, who did not seem to him what in fact she was, an extremely shrewd woman of big business. Being at the time in a state of loneliness and frustrated tenderness, he conceived a sentimental affection for her, to which, in her own more cautious and much more serious way, she responded. He failed her, and she was left in a position where she felt bound to avenge herself. So much for the situation. How does Miss West manage it? She contrives that the narrator shall be so placed as to get from each of the leading actors their own version of the affair, and the result is a highly sardonic revelation of the obtuseness of the *mondain* male, and of the Napoleonic nature of the female whom he had actually presumed to pity. Another of the stories is an exposure of the dreadfulness of being good: "Alice," a man tells his wife, "you're the salt of the earth. . . . The point is that nobody likes having salt rubbed into their wounds. . . ." Another provides a pleasing portrait of a chorus-girl turned faithful mistress. These stories are likely to be read by those who care for excellent writing, acuteness and wit, applied to the "seizure of certain current truths." I cannot help feeling that Henry James would have been interested to find an English writer so extraordinarily knowledgeable about certain of his compatriots, and so sympathetic towards them.

William Plomer, in a review of "The Harsh Voice,"
in The Spectator, No. 5560, January 18, 1935, p.
96.

EDITH H. WALTON

Turning her agile talent to a rather difficult medium Rebecca West has produced four miniature novels, or long short stories, which are chiefly remarkable for their technical brilliance. They have a smooth high glaze, a competence of construction, reminiscent of Somerset Maugham at his slickest and most suave. Only a very good craftsman could have written **"The Harsh Voice,"** but its brittleness and its occasional meretriciousness seem to prove that something besides craftsmanship is required.

Miss West's attitude . . . is curiously literary. One is perpetually aware that these tales are contrived, and contrived for a maximum dramatic effect. They do not proceed simply and naturally with the rhythm of life, but respond to expert guidance from the author, who is always stationed watchfully in the wings. Nothing is left to chance. The reader is led firmly and with precision to the desired point, is forced to react in just the fashion Miss West has so carefully planned.

Such cleverness can overreach itself, as in **"There Is No Conversation."** . . .

Miss West tacks on a twist ending which is utterly unforeseen. Surprising and effective as it is, it quite destroys the integrity of the story—leaving one saying "how clever" instead of "how tragic."

There is the same sense of artificiality in **"The Abiding Vision,"** a far better piece of work. . . . The story has a certain amount of warmth and vigor, but the ironic theme is dragged in once more at the end with a patness and abruptness which are destructive of illusion.

Both these stories pretend to be straightforward and turn out to be tricky. **"The Salt of the Earth"** is more successful than either because its trickiness and ingenuity are apparent from the start. . . .

The fourth and most inferior of the stories also has an American background. From the fact that all of the tales except **"The Salt of the Earth"** deal at least in part with America, and from the fact that there are acknowledgments to popular American magazines, one can gather that Miss West has been doing a little deliberate pot-boiling outside her own country. Most authors do so at times, and Rebecca West in her off moments is still, in a sense, Rebecca West. She is incapable of slovenly writing, of being anything but witty and entertaining. Nevertheless it seems a pity that she should squander her fine gifts on a book so inconsiderable as **"The Harsh Voice."**

Edith H. Walton, "Four Stories by Rebecca West,"
in The New York Times Book Review, February 3,
1935, p. 7.

MARY ROSS

"Man is but a reed, the most feeble thing in nature; but he is a thinking reed," wrote Pascal in the passage from which the title of Rebecca West's new novel [**"The Thinking Reed"**] is taken. The phrase is curiously suggestive of Miss West's own work. "Thinking," none could deny who watched the flashing wit in her essays of feminism many years ago; nor in the subsequent volumes of her literary essays, at all too widely spaced intervals. But a reed also is something through which music may be made, and even in Miss West's critical writing (sometimes, I have suspected, in spite of herself) there often has been a lyrical note with both depth and distinction. Her lyricism had a chance for fuller expression in the novels—in **"The Return of the Soldier"** in 1925 and **"Harriet Hume"** four years later. And in the four short novels published together in 1935 as **"The Harsh Voice,"** there seemed to be a surer unity of wit and feeling than I had been aware of previously in her work.

Both strains reappear in this far more ambitious book. . . . [The] essence of the story is not in the mood of one outside, looking on. It has the directness of the novelist, not the detachment of the critic. Its substance is the conflict within a woman between her idea of herself and her pride in herself and her need and capacity to love. . . .

[The two principal characters, Isabelle and Marc,] are real, especially Marc. Real, because one not only sees but feels their hopes and desires and shortcomings and frustrations. But behind them, like an elaborate backdrop in a play, stands a throng of their contemporaries.

What is extraordinary about these people is that they seem to exist not as human beings with whom Isabelle and Marc have some human contact, but as embodiments of impersonal forces—one might almost say of social conditions—with which those two struggle because they are among the rich and highly placed. Wealth and power, one gathers, are corrupting and depersonalizing both to those who rest on it and those who grasp for it. Marc would seem to have escaped because he has work and strength in himself and a heritage of work as well as money; Isabelle, perhaps because of the detachment of her orphanhood.

Now this view may be true. I suspect that to a considerable extent it is true. It would be more convincing, however, if one felt that in these cosmopolitans of Continental resorts there were something more than acid or flaccid sawdust. It is highly amusing to see the sawdust squirt when Miss West pricks neatly; a bit disconcerting, when occasionally she flays with fury. These furious lashings do not stir one, however, because these people are not real enough to matter. They exist on a plane wholly different from that of Marc and Isabelle.

The only explanation I can offer of that duality is that at points Miss West, the critic, has stepped into the place of Miss West, the novelist. To use other persons for one's own purposes is likely to be as dehumanizing in fiction as it is in real life. To make a generalization in terms of individuals is equally dangerous on the intellectual side.

These assertions do not mean to imply that Miss West's fictionalized social criticisms are to be deprecated. They are often brilliantly amusing and provocative. They show the reaction of a sentient mind to questions that are not at all amusing, though much of that reaction, as is the case in most of our contemporaries, seems to be frustration and confusion. For the purposes of this book, however, I wish the generalised criticism and the specific story had been divorced. We would have had the first more clearly and more cogently. And the other—which is the best fiction by Miss West with which I am acquainted; which to my mind means very good and very moving fiction indeed—would have had a better chance to have been read for its distinguished self.

Mary Ross, "A Woman's Need and Capacity to Love,"
in New York Herald Tribune Books, March 8, 1936,
p. 5.

CLIFTON FADIMAN

When someone as responsible as Rebecca West sets herself to write, and succeeds in writing, over half a million words about Yugoslavia, one can be pretty sure that she has more than Yugoslavia on her mind. Penetrate the fastnesses of her two cyclopean volumes called **"Black Lamb and Grey Falcon"** and you encounter far more than an impassioned survey of the history, topography, and peoples of Yugoslavia. Here's what you will meet: glittering bits and pieces of a philosophy of history; an assemblage of characters shaped in the round by the hand of a skilled novelist; a profound meditation on the central core of Fascism; a witty running commentary on the fixed differences between men and women; soliloquies, ranging from the tragic to the humorous, on the wayward nature of the human animal; literary conversations as searching and brilliant as anything of their kind since the famous Shakespeare colloquy in James Joyce's "Ulysses;" prophecies dire and thrilling utterances of exaltation; in brief, the mind of a rich, various, and fallible being revealed in a prose of fascinating complexity and beauty. . . .

We must understand, first of all, that this book, like others in its class, such as T. E. Lawrence's "Seven Pillars of Wisdom" and C. M. Doughty's "Arabia Deserta," is not a mere record, however fine, of travel or adventure. It is superbly disguised personal confession. **"Black Lamb and Grey Falcon"** is as much autobiography as anything else. It arises not so much out of an interest in Yugoslavia's towns, peasants, castles, monasteries, embroideries, scandals, murders, kings, superstitions, and songs as out of an emotion inside Miss West so rich one must call it religious, an emotion that happened to find release and clarification, when she visited Yugoslavia. The country possesses for her a symbolic, almost a talismanic value. It is the Calais imprinted on her heart. . . .

"In Yugoslavia," she writes, "there was an intensity of feeling that was not only of immense and exhilarating force, but had an honourable origin, proceeding from realist passion, from whole belief." In this sentence lies the deep source of these 1,150 beautiful, often profound, often (some will think) capricious pages. Yugoslavia satisfied in her a passion for a kind of life that seemed to be dying out in Europe, a life of nobility, richness, ardor, even ferocity. Mass propaganda, the rise of dictatorship, and the mechanization of man had conspired to throttle in western European life the one quality that, I should venture, moves Miss West more than any other—the quality of intensity. (p. 76)

"Black Lamb and Grey Falcon" is one of the great books of spiritual revolt against the twentieth century, just as the work of D. H. Lawrence, considered as a whole, is. To the Chamberlain world, the Laval world, the Hitler world, Miss West opposes her proud, violent, beautiful, generous Yugoslavia. . . . She admires whole-souledly the Slav temperament, with its "infinite capacity for enquiry and speculation." This admiration for the heroic, like Lawrence's admiration for the primitive, sometimes runs to extravagance, but in both cases it is more meaningful to note the fertility of the emotion than to carp at its excesses. (p. 77)

Perhaps I am giving the impression that this is a heavy, a dense book. It is not. On the contrary, it glints with wit—I suppose Miss West must be one of the wittiest of living Englishwomen—and its theoretical passages are constantly relieved by others that are merely graceful or amusing or lively. A certain narrative thread is provided by the astonishing and presumably non-fictional figure of Constantine, a Serb poet who accompanies Miss West and her husband . . . on most of their travels. . . . The disintegration of Constantine may be said to be the "plot" of the book. It is the subtle symbol of Miss West's theory of what is wrong with Western civilization.

There is no doubt that Yugoslavia is Miss West's King Charles's head. Those less Balkanomane than herself will not always be able to see her Slavs as she sees them. . . . [Just] as there is a little too much of Constantine, so there is a little too much of everything in this book. . . . But on the whole the book is not overwritten; it is merely too long, which is not quite the same thing. That it is Miss West's magnum opus goes without saying, but I am almost sure that, of its sort, it is also one of the great books of our time. (pp. 77-8)

> *Clifton Fadiman, "Magnum Opus," in* The New Yorker, *Vol. XVII, No. 37, October 25, 1941, pp. 76-8.*

DONALD A. STAUFFER

Style is the man. The adage need not be changed in gender to include Miss West, for she writes with such force as to make most male writers appear effeminate. A rich style therefore demands a well-furnished mind, and this Rebecca West possesses. It would be easy to turn this review [of **"The Meaning of Treason"**] into grouped quotations to display the vigor of her thought, the shape of her sentences, her knowledge of psychology, her sense of terror and of exile, her humor, the profundity of her ethical judgments, her vignettes of people and her panoramas of places.

Surprisingly, considering the subject, this book contains intimate descriptions of buildings in London, interiors and exteriors, that make it, in my judgment, the best writing on architecture and the looks of cities since Ruskin. This sense of solid reality is a part of the maturity of Miss West's style, which tacitly assumes literary culture, and builds on the creative inventions of Shakespeare and Dickens and Dostoevsky and Henry James and D. H. Lawrence. . . .

Only in structure is the book open to cavil. . . . [The first two-thirds, the story of William Joyce, are] full and well proportioned. But the last two sections, which tell of John Amery and some less-known figures, fall off in interest as the pattern of horror repeats itself less dramatically; and the epilogue, generalized and in a different key, does not equal in power the moral meditations casually interspersed in earlier pages. Perhaps Miss West wishes to show the littleness, the dull mechanical pattern of evil. Perhaps she does not wish to rest her case for the meaning of treason upon one or two traitors. But the structure over-all is not successful, for the first two-thirds is greater than the whole. . . .

Even if presented in a fumbling fashion, however, the theme of this book would be impressive. . . .

Though [Miss West] reveals heart-sickening sordidness and treachery in her sad subjects, she witnesses that even in these caged half-men "time revealed to them, which they had not expected, that man can score a victory over fate other than its reversal." She is not a preacher, but a tragic moralist. Like Auden, she realizes that "the guilt is everywhere." . . .

For all its sharp detail, the book has limitless horizons. By implication it contains fundamental criticism of those fantastic nightmare empires of Hitler and Mussolini. The story of William Joyce as an outcast in London helps us to understand the bitter creations of Karl Marx. Miss West can take a trial at the Old Bailey, or in Nuremberg, or in a Carolina town, and make it ring with the overtones of Kafka's "The Trial," see it with the sharp compassion of Dickens' "Bleak House." . . .

Courage is in this book, as well as treason. The theme is not desperate, for conscience and the need for truth move some of the trapped traitors as well as the judges and the juries. Certainly this is one of the best books to come out of the war: a great subject seriously treated, in spite of its horrifying materials.

It has a passionate, almost a religious, integrity. Yet as Rebecca West handles it, it is a good story also, more exciting than any detective shocker, and filled with people in the London air.

> *Donald A. Stauffer, "Miss West Considers Some English Traitors of World War II," in* The New York Times Book Review, *December 14, 1947, p. 3.*

ELIZABETH JANEWAY

[Fifteen] years after **"Black Lamb and Grey Falcon,"** Miss West publishes a new novel [**"The Fountain Overflows"**], a real Dickensian Christmas pudding of a book. In fact, it is very like Dickens. It is as full of characters—odd and even, but mostly odd—as a pudding of plums; full of incident, full of family delights, full of parties and partings, strange bits of London, the lobby of the House of Commons, a classic murder with portraits of the murderer, the murderee and a couple of innocent bystanders, bill collectors, kitchen fires, good food, and a considerable quota of ghosts. . . . In short, this is a very novelish sort of novel—old-fashioned, busy and extremely readable. (p. 1)

[The] most remarkable thing about **"The Fountain Overflows"** is how good, how enjoyable a book Miss West's talent makes it. It is extravagant and melodramatic and full of coincidences in quite the nineteenth-century way. So, of course, are many avant-garde novels—but in these, symbolism is offered as an explanation of the artifices: indeed, most avant-garde authors are so intent upon their symbols that the fact that they have produced melodrama quite escapes their attention. Miss West, however, is not working with symbols. Her people are people, their desperate situations are desperate situations, not allegories. Can she, then, be forgiven for extravagance and melodrama?

I think she can. If she is not working with symbols, she is working toward signification. Life has meaning, she wishes to say; and in order to show that meaning clearly, she must use extreme situations. Also, she must invoke unfashionable abstractions: honor, generosity, devotion, dedication, love. These are words that are easy to use as words, and that have been contaminated by over-use by all the positive thinkers. To this degree, Miss West's message is weakened: it arouses unfortunate echoes.

But Miss West does not use these words as words at all, she creates, brilliantly and decisively, situations which illustrate them in action. If she fails to convince fully—and I do not think she brings off this difficult task with complete success—it is a failure of technique, not of intention. Unlike poor Cordelia, she knows what she is doing, she knows the demands of art. She *does* walk the edge of sentimentality and put a foot wrong here or there. She still wields the broom of generalized *obiter dicta* with a sweep that occasionally knocks down character and reader alike. She is, I have a sneaking suspicion, a

bit too fond of some of her creations: just a little, she dotes. All this tends to reduce by a degree the size of the world that she is creating, and to lessen its importance; but, to flourish a generalization of my own, it is still a world that she is creating, and creating in the right way. Also, it is still a world that is a delight to enter and to live in, warm and vital, inventive and constantly entertaining. (pp. 1, 18)

> *Elizabeth Janeway, "It All Happens within the Family," in* The New York Times Book Review, *December 9, 1956, pp. 1, 18.*

WILLIAM ESTY

As a novelist, Rebecca West resembles Cordelia, one of the characters in her own book, **The Fountain Overflows,** a hopelessly unmusical girl in a musical family, whose unflagging industry at violin practice produces not one note that satisfies her talented sisters and mother. Miss West inflicts on the reader the same painful sensation that the Aubrey family felt when poor Cordelia sawed away so indefatigably: why can't she realize she has no gift for this sort of thing?

The intention is clear enough. Miss West wished to write a big, heartwarming novel of Edwardian family life, to invite the reader into the Aubrey's chaotic but wonderful household, where he would be caught up in their love for each other, the display of their talents, the frequent near-disasters.

But the novel of nostalgic sentimentality depends upon the keeping of the reader's sympathy. He must never cease to accept the characters at the author's valuation. If the thread of sympathy snaps, the failure is total.

Why does one not love the Aubreys? . . . [Why] are they such insufferable bores? . . .

We don't love them because their lovableness is crammed down our throats. It is not only the narrator who tells us unceasingly about the goodness of the "good" characters; their goodness, as in Elizabethan drama, is always recognized and acclaimed by all the other characters. Not one sour note is heard in the chorus of praise. Even the "baddies" are struck by the virtue of the "goodies," though they may treat them meanly.

The Good and the Bad alike bear their distinguishing signs. For instance, the "good" Aubreys all possess extrasensory perception and some of them can exorcise poltergeists by their mere presence. The "baddies," by mechanical contrast, lack ESP but have a reprehensible interest in spiritualism and mind-reading.

The unsparing emphasis on the Aubreys' goodness affects us as Jane Austen's novels affected Mark Twain: we are in Heaven and we don't like it, we positively look for reasons to disbelieve in it.

> *William Esty, "Sugar and Spice . . . Everything Nice," in* The New Republic, *Vol. 135, No. 27, December 31, 1956, p. 18.*

THE TIMES LITERARY SUPPLEMENT

The Fountain Overflows is Miss Rebecca West's first novel for twenty-one years and is indeed only her sixth work of fiction. That this should be so is no doubt the price she has had to pay for her versatility as a writer. Are we to think of her primarily as a brilliant reporter, a great journalist? That she certainly is. But during her career as a writer she has played many parts:

she has been, among other things, an admirable literary critic and a wonderfully astringent reviewer. Yet the publication of *The Fountain Overflows* proves that what she is above all, and what she ought to be, is a novelist; and in the light of this new novel, it is impossible not to regret her long years of absence from fiction.

It is not news that Miss West possesses a most formidable intelligence. Intellectually, she is, one feels, armed at all points; and though a formidable intelligence is not the first requisite of a novelist, other things being equal he will be a better novelist for having it. In point of fact, Miss West's early novels were not quite satisfactory as novels. She was one of the first English authors to grasp the value of psycho-analysis as part of the novelist's necessary equipment towards the understanding of human nature. In her earlier fiction, however, the formal element of psycho-analysis is altogether too obtrusive, so much so that *The Return of the Soldier,* her first novel, now reads like a dramatization of a case-history. In a too overt illustration of the working of the Oedipus Complex, it finally ruins her second novel, *The Judge.* Yet *The Judge* remains a work of real interest and distinction; it announces in character and theme some of its author's abiding preoccupations. First, there is the character of the heroine. However the novel may fail at the end, Ellen Melville is surely one of the most striking representations in all English fiction of a young woman. She is as passionate and as sure of herself as a Brontë heroine. . . .

In her conscious feminism, of course, she goes far beyond the heroines of the Brontës and James. She is not the "New Woman"; she is of a later generation and can therefore take her rights for granted; but however different she may be from the male of the species she knows that she is his equal. She does so in part from the evidence of her intelligence, which is as formidable as her creator's; Ellen is very young, and Miss West's attitude towards her is one of affectionate irony, but reading the novel we do not for a moment question the brilliance of her mind. At the same time, she is firmly set in the context of her place and period, Edinburgh in the first decade of the century, during the suffragette campaign.

Then there is the quality of Miss West's imagination, which is very close to that of Ellen. Miss West is a romantic in much the way James and Conrad were. She chooses her characters from the exceptional, not the ordinary; she demands minds that are at once large and clear-thinking, ambitions that are lofty. And she uses her prose, which is richer in texture, more coloured and more sustained in imagery than contemporary prose normally is, to heighten her characters.

Finally, there is Miss West's view of the nature of life. It is by no means fully expressed in *The Judge,* but it may be felt there all the same and realized the more surely by the reader when he goes back to the novel after *The Thinking Reed* and *The Fountain Overflows.* There is, on the one hand, a passionate apprehension of the necessity and beauty of order, the lovely fruit of self-discipline and self-knowledge, and, on the other, an equally vivid apprehension that order is in constant danger from the forces of violence and destruction. In her later fiction Miss West seems to equate order with the female principle and the forces of destruction with the male. . . .

In *Harriet Hume,* Miss West's third novel, this relationship between the male and the female is presented almost in Jungian terms, as the relationship between an ambitious, power-seeking politician and his anima. *Harriet Hume* is perhaps an ironical, fantastic parable rather than a novel and it can hardly be thought

a success. Its irony is a little too easy, and its calculated artificiality of manner begins to embarrass. Yet *Harriet Hume* takes on a new interest in the light of *The Fountain Overflows,* for through the anima-figure, Harriet, a concert-pianist, we find first suggested the notion, so strong in *The Fountain Overflows,* that the value of music and no doubt of art generally lies in its creation of an order that is at once ideal and real and that in some sense provides a standard by which the disorderliness of life may be judged.

The notion is not heard in Miss West's next fictions, the long short stories of *The Harsh Voice* and the novel *The Thinking Reed.* In these we are in the international world of the very rich, in which money itself is the agent of destruction. *The Thinking Reed* remains an admirable novel. Again we have the young woman of formidable intelligence who can scarcely help thinking justly of reaching just conclusions, the American girl Isabelle, whose natural impulse to create a still centre of happiness and harmony is frustrated by the destructive impulses of the restless and arbitrary male will, first of her lover and then of her husband, and who is compelled, to save herself and her husband, to resort herself to at least the simulation of violence. It is in *The Thinking Reed* that Miss West most thoroughly explores the relationship between men and women. They are seen as existing in a state of polarity. . . . Miss West, in fact, is describing the state of unregenerate human nature. Still, it is enough for her purposes that Isabelle realizes that she is defenceless against others and herself except for the possession of "an insatiable craving for goodness."

In a sense, *The Fountain Overflows* takes up where *The Thinking Reed* leaves off; in her new novel, all the themes implicit in Miss West's earlier fiction come together. *The Fountain Overflows* is the first of what is planned to be a series of novels which will record the chronicles of the Aubrey family until the end of the Second World War, but it is complete in itself and can be judged as a single work. It has a richness and a solidity beyond any novel Miss West has written before, and it is technically a triumph. The fortunes of the Aubreys are related, from the vantage-point of almost half a century later, by the youngest of the three daughters, Rose; and Miss West conveys beautifully the brilliance of the child that Rose was and the formidable quality of her intelligence now. . . .

Piers Aubrey, who stands for the forces of destruction in the novel, is a masterly creation. He is a brilliant journalist and pamphleteer, the dedicated crusader in the service of every cause that wins his allegiance. In the ordinary traffic of life, however, he is an impossible person. . . .

As much as Marc in *The Thinking Reed,* Piers Aubrey does "not belong to the same race as women," and it is with the race of women that Miss West is almost exclusively concerned in *The Fountain Overflows;* of the only two other significant male characters in the novel, the one, Cousin Jock, is also a representative of the principle of destruction, and the other, Richard Quin, the Aubrey girls' beloved younger brother, is curiously unconvincing. . . .

[Rarely has] the solidity and the glow of family life been more beautifully described than in [*The Fountain Overflows*]. There is, however, a rebel in the family midst, the eldest daughter, Cordelia. Mary and Rose are intransigent in their apartness from the South London suburb in which they live: Cordelia pines for the normality it represents. No musician at all, according to her mother's standards, Cordelia still sees her violin as the weapon with which she will win acceptance from the world. To her sisters' horror, as a schoolgirl she becomes a leading executant of Raff's Cavatina at parish-hall concerts; in the end she is forced to face the truth about herself and her talent. . . .

Whether, as it might seem, Miss West is merely offering us a new variation of the doctrine of election, or whether music itself is a powerful enough symbol of the serenity of order that she wishes to oppose to the destructive impulse, we must wait for the later novels to find out. Meanwhile, in *The Fountain Overflows* she has written a novel of much more than ordinary distinction and seriousness.

"Rebecca West Returns to the Novel," in The Times Literary Supplement, *No. 2867, February 8, 1957, p. 80.*

JACOB KORG

The Court and the Castle is a series of critical observations about various literary works held loosely together by a concern with how great writers from Shakespeare to Kafka have treated the problem of salvation. Miss West begins with the interesting theory that the king in Shakespeare's plays is fated to misuse the power he possesses, yet the usurper who stands ready to unseat him is invariably evil. Noting that this paradox of power does not seem relevant to actual political life, Miss West confesses that she would not be at all surprised if Shakespeare thought of his kings as symbols of the will, of their courts as symbols of personality, and of the usurpers as symbols of the will's futile attempts to reform itself. She seems unaware that the pattern she has observed is a form of the institution of the dying god described in *The Golden Bough*. Instead she considers that Shakespeare's plays about royalty are protests against the Renaissance heresy that man is capable of achieving his own salvation. This interpretation may make Shakespeare a sound theologian, but it also makes him a very poor allegorist, because it involves the use of one symbol for the will itself and another for the will in a struggle to reform. The usurper is thus required to be an activity of the king and the symbolism obviously breaks down.

Miss West does not succeed, in her later chapters, in showing that such novelists as Jane Austen, Fielding, Thackeray and Trollope had much to say either about the relations of kings and courtiers or about the spiritual situation they are supposed to represent. As she herself seems to realize when she complains that the novel cannot reveal "deepest truth," English fiction was usually occupied, not with ultimate spiritual matters, but with problems of character and social life. A similar difficulty besets her attempt to impose a theological message upon Proust. She is bound to find Proust's handling of moral values unsatisfactory, because for Proust morality was merely subject-matter, not theme. It is on the whole a pity that Miss West should have devoted the charm and ingenuity displayed in *The Court and the Castle* to an ill-conceived attempt to harmonize some of the world's most unorthodox literature with the *Summa Theological*. (p. 15)

Jacob Korg, "Strained Conclusions," in The Nation, *Vol. 186, No. 1, January 4, 1958, pp. 15-16.**

NICHOLAS KING

Miss West, or Dame Rebecca as she is now styled, may still have an Ibsen conscience, but her world has flowered well beyond introspection, and [*Rebecca West: A Celebration*] has

collected much of it. Some will say too much, for it is made up of many subjects and cannot easily be read through. It celebrates the milestones of her long career, journalistic, novelistic, and biographical, and includes large chunks of her most famous work, *Black Lamb and Grey Falcon*. . . .

The publishers, looking back now from a different age, tend to present her work as centered on two themes, feminism and the modern fatality of war. Certainly, the fact of Dame Rebecca's womanhood informs her point of view constantly, but her feminism is of the old-fashioned, more practical kind—that of a woman who has succeeded in clearing the requisite space around her in society and has proved that she is as good as a man at her job; indeed, is every bit as energetic and well-educated, and has, in addition, that sensibility and tenderness which temper the steel to its finest edge and point.

Unlike the feminists of our day, she is a writer first, not a careerist. She does not want to play the role of a self-satisfied sacrificial victim. She wants to do right, not to be right, a distinction she applies with much effect to the inner drives of various balkan peoples who have dealt with history in the belief that the gate of heaven is open only to the defeated. Her politics tend, therefore, to draw on the common-sensical and the humane—the hallmarks of the British liberal spirit between the world Wars and before them, the period which was her seedbed. (p. 35)

Dame Rebecca writes within a framework of Christian manners—it would hardly be possible to write about the Balkans, much less St. Augustine, without such a framework—which gives bone and sinew to her observations. For although Christianity came late to the Balkans, it was there most lately defended. *Black Lamb and Grey Falcon* is a reading of a country by an ambitious talent, and remains unquestionably her best work.

Otherwise, Dame Rebecca is known for her own brand of journalism, specifically her reporting of criminal traits. . . . Her best-remembered accounts are those of the postwar Nuremberg trials and—in *The Meaning of Treason*—the case of William Joyce, the Lord Haw-Haw of the German radio broadcasts. The question—at this remove, when people have forgotten or never been taught who these traitors and war criminals were—is: How well does she convey their importance? More bluntly, are these pieces of journalism worth reading again? The answer, inevitably, is: Insofar as these subjects interest you. They are drawn from sources of history, but they are not history themselves.

For Dame Rebecca's way of presenting things is not reporting at all. It is more like meditation, often searching, often purring, cross-hatched by loosely presented facts—at the time of writing, be it remembered, familiar to everyone—and plumped out with great patches of needlepoint. (pp. 35-6)

To be fair, Dame Rebecca makes no claim for her own literary profile. "I had never used my writing to make a continuous disclosure of my own personality to others," she says at the end of *Black Lamb*, "but to discover for my own edification what I knew about various subjects which I found to be important to me." This remark is used to show how difficult it is to define her as a writer, but it fits well if you think of an artist in needlepoint facing the challenge of a difficult design. It is a challenge which shows up most directly in her portrait of St. Augustine, an inspired sketch for a dossal to dominate the furnishings in her temple of ideas.

There is much in being a good craftsman; in using words well and knowing their meaning; in exhibiting discrimination in regard to landscape and architecture; in being sympathetic to unsympathetic yet deserving historical personages. Dame Rebecca is successful in these fields. She is successful, too, in that terrible contest of making what one writes stand up well, for nothing ages like journalism. And, like a good and conscientious craftsman, she has enjoyed her work. But although she may be honestly and creditably satisfied—and although this book is a creditable attempt at conveying that satisfaction—many people won't be. (pp. 36-7)

> Nicholas King, "A Literary Profile," in National Review, *Vol. XXX, No. 1, January 6, 1978, pp. 35-7.*

ROSEMARY DINNAGE

The current interest in Rebecca West's work, even if it is partly due to the pursuit of every and any feminist writer and partly homage to her age, is well deserved. But she is a critic's nightmare. How can anyone have written so well and so badly? Have worked in so many different genres? Be so resistant to fitting any particular pigeonhole? If [*The Return of the Soldier, Harriet Hume, The Young Rebecca,* and *1900*] were representative of her life's work, she need not be taken too seriously; but in fact they are oddments from the very beginning and very end of her long writing career. One could say that they are interesting mainly because of their relation to the other books—except that it is so hard to relate the different parts of her work to each other.

She writes, she once said in a radio talk, to explore character: an unexceptionable explanation from a writer half of whose *oeuvre* has been fiction, except that it is only outside her novels that she really does so. When she has to invent, she generally flusters and fails; but once she has a theme, whether a journey or a political trial or a critical exposition, her gift for observing character and then fitting it into great sweeping generalizations and moral patterns comes into its own. She needs her characters to be somewhat at a distance: a fourth-century saint (Augustine), the peasants and monks and chambermaids and children of her Balkan journey, the human dregs in the dock at Nuremberg. Watching these like a hawk, interpreting them *sub specie aeternitas,* she is stunningly magisterial. "Who does she think she is?" we are inclined to ask as she explicates history, sorts out morality, defines our condition and destiny. Someone exceptionally well up to the job or doing so, is the answer.

But then there are tremendous failures. Here we have reissues of two early novels, from 1918 and 1929. In her early book reviews reprinted in *The Young Rebecca* she is hilariously cruel about what has displeased her, so let me borrow some of her cheek (if not her wit) and say that they are awful. It is their very awfulness that is endearing: we see that his powerful writer is not in fact the Archbishop of Canterbury and Regius Professor of History and Lord Chief Justice rolled into one, but an uneven writer who spans extremes of brilliance and disaster. . . .

[*The Return of the Soldier*] is a curious amalgam of some of West's themes: the necessity for truth at all costs; the ineffectuality of men as compared to women; the awfulness, however, of a certain kind of woman. But there is another element in her view of the sexes—and this is going to make modern readers squirm, for I assume the following to be serious:

> . . . it was my dear Chris and my dear Margaret who sat thus englobed in peace as in a crystal sphere, [and] I knew it was the most significant as it was the loveliest attitude in the world. It means that the woman has gathered the soul of the man into her soul and is keeping it warm in love and peace so that his body can rest quiet for a little time. That is a great thing for a woman to do.

True. But it has been better put (Shakespeare, John Donne, Ella Wheeler Wilcox . . .).

Harriet Hume is even more of an oddity, given that it was written eleven years later, when West was in her mid-thirties and had meantime published a successful volume of essays and reviews, *The Strange Necessity*. Victoria Glendinning in her introduction to the novel charitably calls it "an exercise in the higher whimsy." If the higher whimsy is what you want, it is your book; if not, it is simply embarrassing. West is nothing if not solid and vigorous and prosy, and this arch fantasy about two manikins (or manikin and womanikin) dances like an elephant. Dialogue such as, "You are riding softly down the moments as a snowflake rides down the airs, white, oh, so white, and weightless as anything in this ponderous universe, and you are trembling, trembling, trembling," is neither serious nor a skit; simply skittish. (p. 12)

Harriet, who mews and twitters and scampers about on teeny birdlike feet, embodies things it would seem well worth rejecting; Condorex as masculinity, however, is simply a shit. They pursue each other through baroque landscapes and through the years, and the moral seems to be that the two principles must complement each other.

In fact, though, the female once again has the whip hand, for not only has Harriet the psychic gift of reading Condorex's thoughts instantly—reasonable enough grounds for his eventual murder of her, one would imagine—but she is the one who enlightens him about what the two of them represent. . . . In spite of [a] kindly pat on the head the Masculine Principle remains understandably gloomy, and the closing wish for the two ghosts—"A Very Happy Eternity"—seems unlikely to come true.

And this is the author who dismissed *The Waves* as pre-Raphaelite flummery! It is the crudeness of the revenge fantasy—superior women putting down inferior men—that stifles imaginative vitality in these novels. In *The Thinking Reed* of 1936, a much better book, this has been overcome. . . . But perhaps it is a handicap, in writing about the relationship between men and women, to be conclusive. To be aghast and muddled and fascinated is at least a good start.

Rebecca West's long and unsatisfactory liaison with H. G. Wells has been well known at least since it was made the subject of a book in 1974. Writers' personal lives, perhaps, shouldn't be raked over while they are still alive; but since West the feminist has much to say about men and women, one cannot pretend that her life story is irrelevant. The experience clearly hampered and damaged her, but perhaps also enriched her writing by making her so well aware of the irrationality of passion and the inadequacy of brisk solutions. (pp. 12-13)

Perhaps this early love affair was an influence on the guiding theme that runs through all West's mature work: that man is crucially divided between affirmative and self-destructive passions. When she pursued the married and rather notorious Wells via two suicide attempts she was a brilliant twenty-year-old at the start of a successful career; what could have been more self-obstructing? But the strength of her best work is this very recognition of our partition between Eros and Thanatos; in this, without benefit of jargon, she is one of the few true Freudians. (p. 13)

[*Black Lamb and Grey Falcon*] is a marvelous work that outshines everything else she has written: poetic, declamatory, shrewd, funny, immensely ambitious. . . . In the Balkans, with their extremes of cruelty and heroism, poverty and beauty, she finds a metaphor for this struggle between light and darkness; though the book returns continually to the tragic and abominable, it is suffused with a kind of glow of sensuous appreciation for everything beautiful—especially human beings. . . . Rebecca West celebrates woman as the first sex, the strong sex, and this is a constant throughout her work. But where the early novels are clogged with daydream and anger, *Black Lamb and Grey Falcon* radiates good humor. Her husband (she made a happy late marriage) is made an important character in the book, teased, admired, and given sagacious speeches (while a German woman who accompanied them is an embodiment of the anti-life principle). Simply, everyone is in a fix: men are insecure creatures with the double burden of physical strength and dependence on women; women are committed to maternity, but vulnerable to men's revengefulness and unreliability.

In *The Young Rebecca* we have the first of the three versions of her feminism, a version genuinely innocent of pain and complexity, the early writings of a prodigiously talented and high-spirited girl just out of her teens. These pieces have the humor and glow of her later work without its dark side. . . . Her easiest targets are the antifeminists of the time; they go down like ninepins. . . . And (since this was before the time of trying to grapple with the strong-tender-fingers problem herself) she has a remorseless way with the sentimental novelist: "I was held from the very first page, whereon I read: 'There were reservoirs of love in her—of wife-love and of mother-love—accumulating reservoirs, which had never been tapped'. . . . The conception of fate as a Metropolitan Water Board regulating the flow of spiritual liquids is immense."

But she is as sharp as a knife, too, over women and the things they get away with. . . . For the middle-class lady "loafing about the house with only a flabby mind for company" she has no mercy. Nor has she for the creed of "virtue" and self-sacrifice. (pp. 13-14)

For the working woman she fights like a tiger; feminism never distracted her from economic injustice. [A vintage essay] from *The Clarion*, 1913, [shows] her at the top of her form. In **"The Sheltered Sex: 'Lotus-Eating' on Seven-and-Six a Week"** she casts an eye on a politician's pronouncement that something must be done about women drawing too much welfare benefit. In a blazing rage she compares statements about the sanctity of motherhood with the wages that women in "the graceful feminine occupation of chain-making" are getting for an eighty-hour week.

A writing career of seventy-one years is a rare phenomenon; 1911 seems immeasurably distant even to those of us who are middle-aged. What consistency is there between the young journalist and the eighty-nine-year-old author of the text of *1900* (a better-than-average picture book based on that year) and the author of the books and articles in between? Certainly the twenty-year-old who wrote loftily that "the only way to medicine the ravages of this fever of life is to treat sex lightly, . . . to think no more hardly of two lovers who part soon than we do of spring for leaving the earth at the coming of June" differs from the writer who struggled ambivalently but more realistically with the relation between men and women. The red-hot socialist of 1913 is not the same as the grave indicter of communism and its spies. . . .

But in *1900* . . . the young writer is still clearly visible. The wit is as sharp as ever . . . , and the hauteur . . . , and the wry view of the sex war . . . , and the empathy for the working woman. . . . And what could be more remarkable than that? (p. 14)

Rosemary Dinnage, "Staying the Course," in The New York Review of Books, *Vol. XXIX, No. 13, August 12, 1982, pp. 12-14.*

Joy Williams
1944-

American novelist and short story writer.

In Williams's fiction, the ordinary events of daily life are susceptible to bizarre turns of horror and individuals are lost in their private selves, unable to comprehend the forces which shape their lives. Although Williams occasionally alleviates her bleak vision with humor, a sense of hopelessness and despair remains central to her work. Her first novel, *State of Grace* (1973), was hailed by critics as the work of a promising talent. While faulted for its lack of structural cohesiveness, the novel impressed critics with its powerful evocation of a fictional world.

***The Changeling* (1978), Williams's second novel, disappointed most critics. Some reviewers again commended Williams's surrealistic intensity, but they generally considered her treatment of the fine line between psychosis and reality unconvincing and her character development inadequate. Williams's first collection of short stories, *Taking Care* (1982), received mixed reviews. Although two of the stories are affirmations of love, most of them depict unsuccessful marriages, ineffective communication, and aimless, encumbered characters who fail to gain insight into their lives or their selves. While critics generally view this as an uneven collection, they praise Williams's crisp writing and her skillful representation of the characters' subjective realities.**

(See also *Contemporary Authors*, Vols. 41-44, rev. ed.)

© Nancy Crampton

GAIL GODWIN

The fated heroine of this bleak but beautifully-crafted first novel ["**State of Grace**"] may well be the final, perfected archetype of all the "sad ladies," that formidably fashionable sorority which has impinged on the past decade or so of American fiction. But I'll remember Kate Jackson; I'll reread her stubbornly depressing story, picking out those cleverly-hidden but ever-present clues of grace. Kate is no simple "slice-of-despair" character; her sad story becomes, through the author's skill and intention, transsubstantiated into significant myth. This book is neither a self-indulgent journal of despair, nor journalism of despair. It is premeditated, articulate, artistic—a novel. (p. 2)

> Gail Godwin, "Her Heart Belongs to Daddy," in
> The New York Times Book Review, *April 22, 1973,*
> *pp. 2-3.*

RUST HILLS

State of Grace is a "difficult" novel, hard to get into and even then not easy to stay with. Williams is not [Jacqueline] Susann, after all. Time shifts are sometimes confusing, and the plotting is in parts outlandish. I once attempted a plot summary, and it sounded like Tolstoy's vicious précis of *King Lear*. The novel was written some years ago, and some of Williams' best stories have been written since. It may be that she is at her best as a short-story writer, or it may be that she's learned how to write a novel by writing this; time will tell. Clearly parts of it don't

seem to fit, have little or no apparent relation to the whole or other parts.

But open the novel to virtually any page and you'll instantly see it—a kind of strange phosphorescent style describing disquieting, dark and funny goings-on. Sentences are brilliant, gorgeous, surprising, which is strange because Williams uses the simple declarative sentence almost exclusively; I doubt if there's more than one subordinate clause per page in the whole book. This syntax somehow enhances the probing, prowling restlessness of intention and method. Not easy to read, perhaps; but also not easy to forget. (p. 26)

For despite the lack of cohesiveness of the novel, and especially if it is read in conjunction with her short stories, Williams does create a unique "world" through the interaction of her unique fictional elements—unpredictable character, bizarre event, savage description, raunchy dialogue, and so on—in the way any fine writer creates a world. We easily recognize "Hemingway's world," "Fitzgerald's world," and so on, but there are as many such worlds as there are successful authors. In terms of form, such worlds are mostly created by language, but in terms of content they are essentially a vision. Geoff Ward, editor of *Audience,* once said to me of Williams' work, "She sees things no one else ever sees, thank God." . . . Over and over, in brilliant set-pieces of thoroughly convincing but truly crazy dialogue, her characters show themselves to be obsessed by all the wrong things. One laughs, as is intended—but nervously, conscious of some menace implicit in all this derangement.

No writer springs full-blown in a first novel, and there are recalls here—of John Hawkes and of John Cheever and of others—but it is distinctively Williams' world we enter in this intriguing first novel, an absolute guarantee of extraordinary work to come. (p. 28)

> *Rust Hills, in a review of "State of Grace," in* Esquire, *Vol. LXXX, No. 1, July, 1973, pp. 26, 28.*

DAVID BROMWICH

[In *State of Grace*] Joy Williams is pouring forth a tepid Creative Writing ooze which has become stock in trade at the universities, and which is strictly a habit of the permanently would-be novelist. Here are a few of her more wonderfully worked-over set pieces: "Almost all arms and noons and lips and anger are the same and love." "I don't look at all pregnant and never would have thought it of myself, but I've been told firmly that it's so. I peed into a paper cup and now I know." . . . And in a metaphor that deliberately mixes the organs of speech and sex, Miss Williams has gone well beyond John Updike at his coyest:

> I want to have him love me. The fact that he does already troubles both of us. I prop the pillow behind my back and begin a conversation. The room is close. I've spilled some scent and it's in the carpet. I open my lips and the words enter my furred mouth.

Miss Williams has not understood that whatever tries to be prose-poetry ends up with the worst of both worlds, and is at once ersatz prose and ersatz poetry.

The heroine of this novel is Kate—I almost said Kate Williams. But, though there are touches that look autobiographical, one cannot be sure. The novel brings Kate from her pregnancy to the birth of her child, with generous flashbacks to her religious childhood and her early free-living and free-loving adulthood. I will only say that as far as one can separate style from content, the first-person protagonist from the author who watches over her, Kate appears to share certain characteristics with her creator. She is self-indulgent and not obviously intelligent, and she stands in a passive relation to her experience. Just so does Miss Williams answer to the muse of an impersonal and artificially heightened style. When the author gets down to earthly affairs and listens to a secondary character, she simply does not hear the way he would sound. But then, as a backwoods type in her novel most ungracefully avers, "That's something which ain't easy at all!" Since there is no movement from Kate the child to the Kate who can have a child, the desert spaces of plot demand no summary. Though the religious episodes may have been deeply felt by the author, again one cannot be sure. "The Reverend is talking about the grave, how deep and insatiable it is, just like the barren womb. It's never satisfied, he is saying." Yes, thank you, we caught "insatiable" the first time around but are glad nevertheless to learn that Miss Williams knows what it means. Leaving aside the stylistic density, however, even the conceit which it supports is silly. In what sense is a grave or a barren womb insatiable? Like many of Miss Williams's metaphors, this one gives the impression of being old and sick with use and, at the same time, bad in a new way. Actually, the off-realism of this book—the air of disbelief—is less than calculated. The author just has not taught herself to write continuous prose. Of course, the worst feature of such a performance is that it holds the world of experience not too close up but too far away. Most sins are pardonable in a first novel, but perhaps not all. We cease to be concerned whether or not Miss Williams is true to herself, her manner in reaching the goal is so patently false. (pp. 85-6)

> *David Bromwich, in a review of "State of Grace," in* Commentary, *Vol. 56, No. 3, September, 1973, pp. 85-6.*

JOHN AGAR

Kate is the anesthetic woman [in *State of Grace*] whose life is too painful for her to face, who sees with a child's eye focused dissociatively on the foreground, who wants to be released from the burden of her selfhood. (p. 106)

"Everything I touch hurts," Kate says. But she touches only small things, for she can approach her suffering and humiliation only indirectly: through splinters in her hand or fables or half transmogrified memories. Williams' accomplishment is that of having dramatized the inertia of a mind too weary even to feel, much less resist suffering. Like a mosaic, *State of Grace* is full of color and intimations of movement, but without movement, and . . . Williams uses a miniaturist's art to achieve effects which are not small. (pp. 106-07)

As in [her previously published short story] **"Tripping,"** Williams relies on her control of rhythm and on the judicious use of detail to characterize the mind which is affected by narrated events. And because Williams' art is that of nuance, traumatic events are often elided—because they are too painful for a character to face—or undergo a sea-change in the character's sensibility. (p. 107)

But this kind of narrative also has soft spots. Williams' talent, at this point in her career, evidently is for introspective first person narrative, or narrative at least through the eyes of a character. In *State of Grace* she is aware of her strength and exploits it. But there are less satisfactory sections of the novel, particularly those . . . in which Kate must speak to "Daddy" and "Daddy" must reply. Indeed, Williams would be at a disadvantage here anyhow. The figure of the hellfire preacher who is sexually possessive—not to mention those of vacuous sorority girls and thick-waisted and thick-headed southern cops—come to her hand ready made. There is not a whole lot anyone can do with them. Hence "Daddy" is not really an impressive character until the middle of *State of Grace,* where Williams beautifully describes him through the eyes of the child-Kate.

Nor does Grady [Kate's husband] often talk like a believable person. This is somewhat surprising in that **"Tripping"** shows that Williams has an excellent ear for dialogue. Yet even that story reaches its resolution not through any confrontation between characters, but by a simple, perhaps awkward, shift of focus. . . . This problem conceded, however, *State of Grace*'s successes still easily overshadow its faults. . . . [*State of Grace*] is a powerful and lovely first novel. (pp. 107-08)

> *John Agar, in a review of "State of Grace," in* Carolina Quarterly, *Vol. XXV, No. 3, Fall, 1973, pp. 106-08.*

ANATOLE BROYARD

["**State of Grace**"] was a startlingly good novel, and it pains me to have to say that "**The Changeling**" is a startlingly bad one. Miss Williams likes to take large risks, to try to go where no one has gone before. She is more drastic in her approach to character than any other novelist I can think of who is writing today. In "**State of Grace**," she survives the risks by the skin of her teeth and her narrow escapes have the effect of intensifying the book even further. But harsh as it may sound, I find that almost nothing works in "**The Changeling**." I admire the first book so much that I am tempted to take the position that only a very talented person could write as badly as Miss Williams does in her second novel.

The eccentricity of the characters in "**State of Grace**" seems to arise out of a surplus of truth. They are so real, so close to the bone of feeling, that it is hard to get used to them. They are natural to an unnatural degree. Miss Williams's heroine, Kate, has answers to questions no one would ever think to ask. Pearl, in "**The Changeling**," has no answers, and to questions no one would want to ask. While Kate transcends the natural, Pearl falls below it. . . .

"**The Changeling**" suggests to me that two things ought to be done about avant-garde writing today. Readers ought to actively question its assumption that a character's mental disturbance is a symbol for a disturbed world. It is not invariably true; sometimes a character's aberration is a circumscribed function that concerns no more than two or three people. To try to stretch it to embrace our entire culture is either pretentious, lazy or simply mistaken.

And then I believe it would be a salutary exercise for both reader and writer if we begin to take the rhetoric of the avant-garde literally, to assume that the words on the page mean what the dictionary says they do. When Miss Williams writes, "Oh to bring back the days when stars spoke at the mouths of caves," I feel entitled, perhaps even obliged, to ask, "Which days were those?" When she writes, speaking of Pearl, that "she was young but some day she would be covered with ants," I want to know how the author can tell that she will be covered with ants and how I am expected to employ this information. . . .

When I read of the children's "condor eyes" or of "the tremendous human darkness," I am not going to give the author the benefit of the doubt. There have been too many doubts and too many benefits, and perhaps Miss Williams has fallen victim to them.

> Anatole Broyard, "New Joy Williams Novel," in The New York Times, *June 3, 1978, p. 17.*

ALICE ADAMS

[Joy Williams] is a talented, skillful writer. She evokes the feel and smell of certain moments with an eerie precision. . . . Certain characters, too, in her fiction, are entirely original and absolutely credible. . . . The evidence suggests that Miss Williams could and probably will write an excellent novel, which "**The Changeling**," unfortunately, is not.

Its action, more or less (Miss Williams does not exactly spell out her narrative), is this: A young woman, Pearl, is picked up while shoplifting by a man named Walker and taken to his family's 20,000-acre offshore (what shore is not specified) island, which they have owned for 100 years. Five semi-related and some unrelated children populate the island. Pearl bears a child named Sam to Walker, and then, disturbed by odd goings-on between the adults and children on the island . . . , she runs away—to be re-kidnapped, as it were, by Walker. On the plane back to the island, Pearl glimpses an unnatural-looking baby in the arms of a very old woman. The plane crashes; its survivors are hospitalized, and Pearl is handed a baby whose first gesture is a savage bite, tearing her breast. Walker is dead. With her new-old baby, Pearl again takes up life on the island. From then on, roughly the remaining three-fourths of the novel, events are murkier.

Pearl sits around the pool with the children, and she drinks a lot. . . . (p. 6)

Various sexual acts, mostly "unnatural," including a murderous copulation between two praying mantises, are observed and commented upon by Pearl and the children. (Miss Williams has a lurid sexual imagination, potentially comic, which is largely wasted here.) There are hints of animal worship, of children becoming animals, lots of dreams of animals. . . . Then, one terrible night, all the children seem to be lost, in a landscape of beetles and lizards. There is a bloody attack by some unidentified animals, and the book ends in a cataclysm of run-on sentences, about animals and children, sleep and death and change.

Trying to puzzle all this out, one has the unsettling sense of an unfamiliar mythology (Hindu? Norse?), perhaps of someone else's dream. What do all those animals mean? "Once, in the very earliest time, a human being could become an animal if he wanted to and an animal could become a human being." Does this sentence, occurring mid-novel, describe what has happened at the end, or has Pearl gone crazy? Or is she just drunk?

This borderland between psychosis and reality, the land of private mythology of the "grotesque," is dangerously tempting to writers: so easy to do badly, almost impossible to do well. . . . (pp. 6, 17)

If we don't know quite enough about a central character to be moved by his or her possible madness, or quite enough about the external events of the story to be sure what is actually going on, the result is an unconvincing and ultimately unsatisfactory novel, instead of the very good one that I believe Joy Williams could write. (p. 17)

> Alice Adams, "Someone Else's Dream," in The New York Times Book Review, *July 2, 1978, pp. 6, 17.*

THE VIRGINIA QUARTERLY REVIEW

Joy Williams, in [**The Changeling**], descends from the best of recent innovators in fiction. Like Cortázar and Márquez, she has a surrealistic intensity matched by an admirable control of word and metaphor. Like Pynchon, she keeps us guessing: does Pearl suffer a nervous breakdown or is she the straight woman in a psychotic universe? Williams lapses into experimental form only in the last two, unpunctuated, chapters, certainly the weakest. . . . But the ferocity of Williams's imagination makes the choppiness of her sentences beside the point. . . . [The] witty and horrifying **Changeling** establishes Williams as a major contemporary novelist.

> A review of "The Changeling," in The Virginia Quarterly Review, *Vol. 54, No. 4 (Autumn, 1978), p. 134.*

PATRICIA MEYER SPACKS

[The impossibility of accurate memory is dealt with] in the increasingly surrealistic account of *The Changeling,* which retreats altogether from the public realm into a self-indulgent phantasmagoria of privacy. The ambiguities of its plot reflect its explicit insistence on the hopelessness of attempts to know. Pearl, the protagonist, twenty years old at the outset, has trouble discerning meaning in her experience. "Nothing in her life had prepared Pearl for significance. Each moment that occurred lay mute within her, a buried stone, contained from and irrelevant to herself, an event with neither premonition nor consequence." Moreover, she cannot remember properly. . . . Pearl's interest in story creates the protean shapes of [her past]. Around her, others invent, remember, enact disturbing stories. Her own life follows a plot whose outlines she cannot grasp. . . . She lives with her husband's brother and an ever-changing collection of children on a strange island. She does not understand the people among whom she lives, nor does the reader— for whom, however, it hardly matters, so contrived are characters and happenings alike. The stories the children tell, which gradually come to control reality, concern human beings and animals and the relation between them, a matter which also preoccupies Pearl, given to wondering about how men evolve from lower forms or vice versa. It's all a problem of appearance and reality—a problem college sophomores typically discover with wonder as a fertile device for filling up their essays about philosophy, history, literature, just about anything. Joy Williams has the genuine sophomoric vision. (pp. 668-69)

Pearl may have problems about significance, but . . . the novel's narrator feels no shyness about offering frequent overblown announcements of meaning. Lavish statements about story, memory, appearance, the changeability of the past, prepare for the ambiguous ending, in which either all the children turn to animals and kill the grown-ups or Pearl goes crazy and believes this to have happened. The novel has proceeded from the flat, tough, Joan Didion-ish prose of its early sequences . . . to a dreary unpunctuated stream of consciousness. . . . The stylistic shift corresponds to the change in focus from outer to inner events, but . . . it also reflects unsure novelistic purpose. Neither memory nor imagination, *The Changeling* insists, tells the truth; the arbitrariness of fictional technique reflects the arbitrariness of meaning. Memory here makes nothing permanent; the absence of belief in the possibility of even personal preservation of the past—what person? what past?—expresses itself in a novel which, despite its cloudy grandiosity, constantly reminds us that novels don't, can't, matter. (p. 669)

> Patricia Meyer Spacks, *"Necessities of Memory,"* in The Hudson Review, *Vol. XXXI, No. 4, Winter, 1978-79, pp. 663-76.**

DAVID QUAMMEN

[Joy Williams's **"Taking Care"** contains some] wonderfully crisp writing and patches of bleak humor that made me guffaw. Social disjunction and the discontinuity of relationships are . . . chief concerns, with most of the stories in **"Taking Care"** focused on the imperfect efforts of husbands and wives trying marriage for the second or third time, and on the children surviving (in various degrees of disability) from the earlier attempts. Also dogs: There are many waifish canines from these broken homes, all of them portrayed with high sympathy and most cast as important secondary characters. Joy Williams has dogs the way John Irving has bears. And in fact Miss Williams

seems to judge her people largely on these two bases: whether or not they can make a better second marriage and whether they get along well with dogs. The criteria are probably sounder than most.

But again the state of affairs, and of marriages, as seen by Miss Williams, is not cheerful. "By the time they were in Manhattan," she says in one story, "they were arguing. They had been married for eleven years. Both had had brief marriages before. They could argue about anything." With variations on the number eleven, this could apply to almost every couple in the book. Miss Williams depicts failing communication and death of love and willful emotional brutality and betrayal, all at epidemic levels. . . .

In even her dreariest pieces, Miss Williams is consistently percipient and witty. But she ends the collection triumphantly with a pair of stories, very different from each other, that are both masterly creations and also—pleasant surprise—moving affirmations.

"Taking Care" portrays an aging preacher named Jones, a steadfastly loving man who assumes the roles of mother and father to his infant granddaughter while the child's mother (his daughter) sows her oats in Mexico and his own cherished wife is dying of leukemia. **"Breakfast"** describes a watershed morning in the lives of four beings finding each other: a young woman named Liberty, her half-blind German shepherd called Clem, a neglected 7-year-old neighbor boy named Teddy, and Charlie, a hulking Cajun alcoholic. . . .

These final two stories, one a delicate treasure, the other overflowing with mad comic energy, are alone worth the price of the book. (p. 34)

> David Quammen, *"Women in Crisis," in* The New York Times Book Review, *February 14, 1982, pp. 11, 34.**

JOYCE KORNBLATT

With prose of indiscriminate radiance, Williams creates a landscape for [the tales in *Taking Care*] at once geographic and spiritual. . . .

These stories seem closest in spirit to the fictions of Flannery O'Connor and Joyce Carol Oates. Madness, murder, the surrender of hope become commonplace rather than extreme behaviors, and even those characters who sustain the ability to love seem perplexed, even encumbered, by their triumph. . . .

Williams' characters lack grounding, and the stories purposefully withhold any larger frames of reference which might accommodate, explain, help contain the formlessness of subjective life. In *Taking Care,* the world seems to exist only as each character imagines it to be. No person's reality is like another's, each man and woman and child dreams his or her own life. In **"The Shepherd,"** a dog breeder observes: "We are all asleep and dreaming, you know. If we could actually comprehend our true position, we would not be able to bear it, we would have to find a way out." Whereas the characters in O'Connor and Oates tales move precisely *to* that comprehension of their true position, the people in Williams' stories seldom get that far. They remain inchoate. Death itself fails to jolt them into awareness and if it does, they sink again even more deeply into their private worlds. In these stories people do not change; they simply exist in the ongoing mysteries, tawdry or pure, that are their lives.

This vision is both comforting and disturbing, and one cannot leave Joy Williams' work without deep ambivalence. As in all myths—and these stories are modern myths—we are connected again to what is elemental. However horrific, the primal dramas speak to our yearning for what is authentic, for what exists beneath the name-brand patina, the media polish, the intellectual armor that defines and distorts our age. Transcending religious and political systems of belief, Williams speaks to us from a plane of pure feeling. Like fine music, these stories circumvent the intellect; Williams seems to make the works themselves transparent and we gaze directly into the souls of her characters. This opportunity for communion—with the writer as a kind of spiritual medium—is one of the gifts of good fiction. . . .

Yet the refusal of most of these stories to take us beyond states of feeling into conscious awareness, even change, leaves a reader disquieted. What can one believe in if people lose the will to believe, if they forget how to do it, if they can no longer manage it? Instead of being a communal solace, faith turns into a solitary ordeal, the dreamer alone forever in his or her own dream. Jones, the preacher [in "Taking Care"], "is gaunt with belief." Yet the title story suggests that he must persist in spite of his doubt and exhaustion. His wife dying, his daughter lost to him, Jones leaps yet again in his life over despair into the delusion of hope. "For insurance purposes, Jones' wife is brought out to the car in a wheelchair. She is thin and beautiful. Jones is grateful and confused. He has a mad wish to tip the orderly. Have so many years really passed? Is this not his wife, his love, fresh from giving birth?"

Of course, we know that it is not. He is hallucinating, dreaming with his eyes opened. But his delusion empowers him and we support him in his fabrication. It is redemptive. It imposes meaning on a world infinitely indifferent to his needs. In one of the few rebellions in this volume against the world's fierce neutrality, "Jones helps his wife up the steps to the door. Together they enter the shining rooms." In these fragile gestures of *Taking Care*—a sick woman leaning on her husband's arm, a wife catching sight of "her little family," during a tense vacation, a girl mourning the loss of her dog—we glimpse, merely glimpse, an order of being that eschews randomness, that ascribes value, that insists on love in the face of destructiveness.

        Joyce Kornblatt, "Madness, Murder and the Surrender of Hope," in Book World—The Washington Post, March 21, 1982, p. 4.

BRINA CAPLAN

Taking Care, story by story and incident by incident, withdraws meaning from the lives it represents. In each case, what remains is a gem of despair, worked into the shape of finality by skillful sleights of hand.

Williams's characters usually live in the suburbs or the small coastal towns of Florida and New England. They are divorced or remarried, in their mid 20s or 30s, the parents of small children. There are exceptions. . . . On the whole, though, Williams focuses on ordinary moments in familiar lives. Ordinary moments, as she conceives them, are the most vulnerable to horror. . . .

In prose as coldly intense as fluorescent lighting, Williams displays the wares of everyday life, a collection of objects that in the aggregate exert pressure on her characters, urging them toward madness. . . . Williams's men and women find themselves suddenly stranded in the surreal, like shoppers in a no-exit supermarket. And the goods banked up in aisles around them have their own frightening, inhuman order—an order that trivializes human experience. . . .

At times it seems that madness will culminate in a superb sanity; that is, by negation, the lives of Williams's characters will define some essential good missing from a world encumbered with goods. Regrettably, Williams uses her narrative skill to another end, to make all sources of suffering appear equally mysterious and all sources of reparation equally futile. For example, in *Taking Care*, ties of familiarity or family are as easily slipped as knots tied in butter. . . . In Williams's world, the cruelties of contemporary folkways ultimately have no more pattern than mechanical or natural disasters—death by automobile, heart failure or anaphylactic shock. All losses are equally disrupting and equally random.

One of Williams's characters, Jenny, a small child haunted by visions, announces to her nursery school teacher that "the crayons are dead, the swings are dead." For her, a private debate with pain leads to compelling equations that nonetheless falsify reality. Jenny says

> that she has no toys, that she lives with machinery she cannot run, that she lives in a house with no windows, no view of the street, that she lives with strangers.

Jenny shares her conclusion of victimization with other central characters in *Taking Care* and her method of deriving it with Williams herself—for not only character but author deny the consoling possibilities of home and work, solitude and company, family and friends. Perhaps, also like Jenny, Joy Williams conducts a private debate in which the satisfaction of balancing arguments at zero exceeds the pleasure of arriving at certain sums. In any event, the result of her imagining is a world brilliantly rendered and simultaneously nullified—without doubt "its own place." (p. 502)

        Brina Caplan, "Mind Games," in The Nation, Vol. 234, No. 16, April 24, 1982, pp. 500-02.*

A(braham) B. Yehoshua

1936-

Israeli novelist, short story writer, essayist, scriptwriter, and dramatist.

Yehoshua is one of Israel's foremost contemporary fiction writers. He is a member of "the generation of the state," the first generation to come of age after Israel was proclaimed an independent state in 1948. Yehoshua's fiction treats concerns which have arisen in this generation: such political problems as the Arab-Israeli conflict; such moral dilemmas as the danger of clinging to the Zionist dream without facing the reality of Palestinian demands; and such social issues as the emigration from Israel of the younger generation and its loss of faith in the Zionist ideology which created Israel. Although much of Yehoshua's work is centered on Israeli concerns, certain characteristics give his fiction universal significance: his underlying theme of the alienation and isolation of humankind and the careful development of the psychological state of his characters.

Critics of Yehoshua's early story collections, *Mot ha-zaken* (1962) and *Mul ha-ye'arot* (1968; the latter volume published in the United States under the title *Three Days and a Child*), compared him to Franz Kafka because of the abstract and surrealistic nature of his stories. Many of these stories, which one critic called "modern fables," are not grounded in a particular time and place; instead Yehoshua uses allegory to comment on contemporary Israel and humanity in general. He makes extensive use of symbolism in these stories, a characteristic which some critics have found overwhelming. Yehoshua explained in an interview, "I am still not able, in dealing with reality, to be content with a spontaneous selection from the passing stream. I am compelled always to seek out the intellectual, symbolic aspects and to see reality as representing the general idea." More recently, Yehoshua has moved towards realistic modes of expression which deal more explicitly with Israel and in which the symbolism is less obtrusive.

"Facing the Forests," which appeared in *Three Days and a Child,* has evoked much critical discussion for its controversial subject matter. In this story, a frustrated and disaffected Israeli graduate student takes a job as a forest ranger. He ultimately acts as a silent accomplice when an Arab burns down the forest that had displaced his village. Critics have offered a variety of interpretations of this story. In the context of the Arab-Israeli conflict, "Facing the Forests" has been seen as an illustration of the younger generation's ambivalence and lack of faith in Israel. On a more universal level, the story has been interpreted as a commentary on humanity's tendency towards unmotivated evil and isolation. In another story, "The Lengthening Silence of a Poet," Yehoshua again offers a dim prognosis for Israel's future. In his depiction of a formerly great poet, who no longer writes, and an imbecile son, who tries and fails to continue the father's work, Yehoshua portrays the impotence of the older generation and the lack of inner resources of the younger one. The other stories in this collection are similarly negative. The world Yehoshua portrays is sterile and oppressive; the characters are imprisoned and alienated. According to critic Jerome Greenfield, "In the existential despair, the pessimism, the sense of dislocation and

Photograph by Alex Goffryd

alienation that pervade his work, Yehoshua establishes a bridge between modern Israeli writing and a dominant stream of some of the best Western literature of our age . . . without abandoning . . . the everyday reality of Israeli life."

As Yehoshua's work moved away from surrealism and towards realism, he turned from short stories to novels. His first novel, *The Lover* (1977), was followed by *A Late Divorce* (1983), which critics have compared to William Faulkner's *The Sound and the Fury* as a family saga which employs a series of different narrators to explore psychological and moral questions. *A Late Divorce* concerns an Israeli who has immigrated to the United States and later returns home to obtain a divorce. The man finds his family in a state of decay, which some critics considered a symbol for the decline of Israel. Yehoshua explained, "I don't claim the family is a symbol of Israel, but there is a layer of allegory—the imbalance between the father and mother, which does not create proper relations for the health of the family. Like the father, who gives up his responsibilities and goes to America, Jews who leave Israel for America are escaping their responsibility."

Critical reaction to Yehoshua's work has often focused more on its ideological than its literary aspects, but both have been almost uniformly praised. Yehoshua is commended for his storytelling abilities, the psychological depth of his characters, his precise and evocative use of language, and his structural innovations. He is acknowledged as one of Israel's most important social critics. His political and social commentary appears both in his fiction and as essays in Israeli newspapers and magazines. He has published a collection of essays, *Between Right and Right* (1981), which Harold Bloom described as "a polemic against the Diaspora. . . . [These essays are] efforts to reformulate the terms of identity, Jew, Zionist, Israeli." Yehoshua's works have been translated into numerous languages and two of his books, *Three Days and a Child* and *Early in the Summer of 1970*, have been adapted as films.

(See also *CLC*, Vol. 13 and *Contemporary Authors*, Vols. 33-36, rev. ed.)

ROBERT ALTER

[*The following excerpt was taken from an essay which originally appeared in* Commentary, *June, 1969, entitled "New Israeli Fiction."*]

For Amos Oz, and in a more restricted way for A. B. Yehoshua, there is something uncannily semantic about Israeli reality. Topographical, architectural, even institutional actualities allude to things beyond themselves, and though both writers have been guilty on occasion of symbolic contrivance (Oz much more glaringly), one gets some sense that their cultural predicament has made symbolists out of them. One of Yehoshua's narrators in fact comments on the temptations of symbolism which the setting offers: "For everyone here is addicted to symbols. With all their passion for symbolism the Jerusalemites imagine that they themselves are symbols. . . ." There is, patently, an acerbic ironic perspective here on the excesses of symbol-hunting and symbol-making; the ironic intelligence points to the admirable artistic restraint with which Yehoshua, in his second volume of fiction, *Opposite the Forests* [also translated as *Facing the Forests*] (1968), develops a distinctive mode of symbolism that is quietly suggestive and for the most part not obtrusive. (pp. 216-17)

The work of both Oz and Yehoshua raises an interesting question about Israel's peculiar cultural situation. Their concerns, as I have already intimated, are if not quite apolitical then metapolitical, seeking to come to grips with the ultimate facts about human nature and social existence which issue in political events, institutions, and conflicts. But given the explosively charged nature of Israel's political situation, it is not surprising that a good many readers should see directly political, even "subversive," implications in this new kind of Hebrew fiction. (pp. 218-19)

Yehoshua writes a much cooler, more understated kind of fiction than Oz, sometimes arranging his narrative materials in generalizing designs that place them almost at the distance of parable from the reader; but there are certain affinities in theme between the two writers. Several of Yehoshua's protagonists, like those of Oz, bear within them a deep sexual wound that humiliates them, drives them to acts of hostility. Without a trace of Oz's mythopoeic imagination or his interest in an erotic underworld, Yehoshua also often sees lurking animal instincts beneath the façade of the civilized self; his educated, ostensibly pacific, ineffectual personages frequently harbor a murderous impulse to destroy whatever stands in their way or whatever is associated with those who have given them pain. (p. 225)

Also like Oz is Yehoshua's fascination with destruction for its own sake, the desires civilization breeds in people to escape its imposed order and rational framework. Yehoshua treated one variant of this condition in an early story, "**The Tropville Evening Express**" [also translated as "**The Evening Journey of Yatir**"], about a quiet little town that is pitifully *de trop* in a world of vast wars and so its citizens conspire to cause a trainwreck simply to make something happen in the dead air of their empty existence. More memorably, this time using materials from Israel's political situation, Yehoshua deals with the same problem in the title story of *Opposite the Forests*. (p. 226)

The political applicátion of the story is transparent, and for anyone accustomed to thinking of Israel in official Zionist terms, it may seem more comprehensively "subversive" than anything in Oz. Yehoshua, let me emphasize, is unswervingly committed to Israel's survival and to the constructive development of Israeli society—he is, of all things, Dean of Students at Haifa University—and the story must properly be seen as an unflinching exploration of the shadowy underside of ambivalence in Israeli consciousness within the state of siege. A more general human ambivalence is also implied in the story's use of the local situation; as we move in a typical Yehoshua pattern from frustrations of impotence—here, the unwritten paper—to the thirst for destruction, we get a sense of the balked consciousness of civilized man secretly longing for the cataclysm that will raze all the artificial hedging structures of human culture. (p. 227)

The unnamed graduate student at once becomes an exemplar of contemporary futility, purposelessness, deracination, but with none of the self-conscious reaching for the effects of a Kafka parable that one finds in some of Yehoshua's earlier stories. The language is unpretentious, the diction largely colloquial, the references to the details of student life factually precise yet formulated to make their paradigmatic implications evident. The first sentences of the story introduce us immediately to the characteristic Yehoshua world, which is, in a word, a world of incompletions. Characters undertake all kinds of projects which they are incapable of seeing to an end—a thesis, a poem, a love affair, the building of a dam in Africa. As this protagonist's fatigue with language suggests, the individual is confirmed in his radical loneliness because the instruments of communication seem so pathetically inadequate, or futile. "Is it still possible to say anything?" asks another Yehoshua protagonist at the end of his disillusioning experiences. Most of Yehoshua's stories are models of the difficulties of communication; . . . he delights in juxtaposing mutually incomprehensible figures. . . . I alluded earlier to Yehoshua's ironic intelligence; one is especially aware of its presence in the wryly comic effects of poignant farce through which he frequently conveys the breakdown of communication, the failure of human relation. (pp. 227-28)

Such a bleak view of humanity as this would be utterly depressing were it not articulated with a quality of imaginative wit, as a critique of mankind's inadequacies, a sort of ultimate satire, that is finally moral in purpose. If, as I have suggested, there is some relationship to Kafka in the earlier Yehoshua, he stands at about the same distance from the German writer as Isaac Rosenfeld. Like Rosenfeld, he offers us in place of Kafka's neurotic visionary intensity a critical shrewdness in the manipulation of narrative, a certain muted intellectual verve, an ironic perspective in which sympathy for the characters and their predicaments is continuous with rigorous judgment of them. Because of this effect of broad critical overview in his fiction, Yehoshua is able at times to project with the greatest naturalness a general image of human existence out of the particular tensions, strains, fears, and ambiguities of life in an Israel surrounded by enemies. The suggestive connection between particular and universal is especially clear in a story called **"The Last Commander,"** which is included in *The Death of the Old Man* [1962]. (pp. 228-29)

[We] are presented with a world that is based on Israeli reality but not a direct representation of it. Reflections and refractions of particular facts of Israeli existence glimmer through the story. . . . However, only one place name, presumably Arab, is given in the entire story, the few names of characters offered have no clear national identity, and the war that has been fought is not specifically the war of 1948-49 but an archetypal "seven year's war" with an anonymous enemy who remains completely faceless.

The story finally is not "about" Israel's security situation but about human effort, will, and the strain of maintaining the disciplines of civilization in an utterly indifferent cosmos. (pp. 229-30)

If one tried to restrict the story to a purely political frame of reference, it would emerge as a parable of encounter with a fascist ethos. The writer, however, offers a number of important indications that the meaning of the events demands a broader and more complex perspective. We are made significantly aware of the presence of the elemental desert over against the sky, described at the very end as "the stretches of whitish glare called the heavens"; we note equally the descent of the commander out of the fierce blue like an implacable god, and the six days of creation through which the soldiers labor on their exhausting and futile tasks. . . . The story maintains a fine balance of perspective to the end; the narrator makes us feel the voluptuous attraction of sleep, and more sleep, for the exhausted men, but we are also led to see that this orgy of indolence signifies moral and physical paralysis, is finally a sour parody of death.

Both Yehoshua and Oz, then, achieve the widest reverberations of meaning not when they attempt self-consciously to be universal but precisely when they use their fiction as an instrument to probe the most troubling implications of their own cultural and political reality. One is tempted to see them as a kind of Faulkner-Hemingway polarity of talents, Oz having the greater range—in resources of style, in realization of character, in sheer mimetic ability—and Yehoshua a greater degree of poise, efficiency, artistic cunning. Either of them, I believe, would be an exciting writer in any national literature. Their appearance on the Hebrew literary scene bears witness to the ability of Israeli society to maintain under the shadow of the sword a complex culture that is both a medium of self-knowledge and an authentic voice in the larger culture of men. (pp. 230-31)

> Robert Alter, "Fiction in a State of Siege," in his Defenses of the Imagination: Jewish Writers and Modern Historical Crisis, *The Jewish Publication Society of America*, 1977, pp. 213-32.*

HUGH NISSENSON

[In **"Three Days and a Child,"** Yehoshua's] talent is immediately apparent. He has been influenced by Kafka and, like

him, has managed to convey, by the specifics of objective reality, a unique inner world. He is a fabulist; his characters inhabit a familiar but mysterious universe in which meaning and emotion are expressed by many esthetic elements: leitmotif, counterpoint, and, when he is in full control, over-all structure.

"Flood Tide" is the one story in the collection that doesn't make it at all. It is too abstract, too remote from the natural world (the landscape of Israel) to be convincing. The title story, however, is fascinating; too diffuse, like some of the others, but an extraordinary study of what the Bible, the great Talmudists and Hassidic masters called "the evil impulse."

Anguished by jealousy, the narrator wants to kill the child of a woman he once loved. It takes place in Jerusalem, where, "after nine in the evening, you'll be walking through a city of the dead." The empty streets, a thorn, a viper accidentally loosed in an apartment fill the story with the same menace that seems to emanate from the protagonist. He is an alienated intellectual, a type who appears in almost all of Yehoshua's stories: the rational man, sundered from his roots, who is confounded by his impulse to do evil. . . .

Yehoshua is immensely popular in Israel, particularly with the young. It speaks well for them to recognize and respond to such a writer. I hope that Americans will also respond. . . .

> Hugh Nissenson, "Evil, Muted but Omnipresent," in The New York Times Book Review, *October 25, 1970, p. 56.*

JEROME GREENFIELD

It is a depressing vision of the human condition that Yehoshua projects in [*Three Days and a Child*]. In each of its five stories attention is focused on a protagonist trapped within the prison of some inner despair and alienation that constantly threatens to break out—and sometimes does—into some kind of disaster. Everywhere there hovers the smell of danger, the nuance of menace. . . .

Yehoshua's many talents come through powerfully. . . . His observation of the details of Israeli life—its cities, its implacable summers, its landscape—are done with deftness and vivid simplicity. (p. 27)

In the existential despair, the pessimism, the sense of dislocation and alienation that pervade his work, Yehoshua establishes a bridge between modern Israeli writing and a dominant stream of some of the best Western literature of our age—and he does this without abandoning, except for the single exception of **"Flood Tide,"** the everyday reality of Israeli life. No mean achievement this, in the case of a national life so completely conceived in ideology and dream as Israel has been. It is, no doubt, because of this achievement that in Israel he has earned the reputation of being one of the most authentic voices of the younger generation of writers. But it is this, too, that poses a problem, creates a paradox. (pp. 27-8)

[The] problem that Yehoshua poses is how we are to relate his unrelenting morbidity, the invariable isolation of his protagonists, their destructive self-negation, their total unadjustment to their forests, their deserts, their climate and cities to [the other, more positive] image we have of Israeli life and, indeed, that Israelis generally have themselves.

We cannot rationalize away his despairing vision as sickly atypical since, as has been noted, he commands the respect of a large portion of the younger intelligentzia in the country. The kind of world he projects, in other words, represents in some dimension, on some level, as much of a reality in modern Israel as does the more common image of Israel as a land of fulfillment, hope and redemption. In fact, **"Facing the Forests"** can be read as a head-on clash between these two realities. The tormented, frustrated, alienated protagonist at first does not believe that real forests even exist in Israel. . . . But when reaching his fire-post he sees a real forest, with full grown trees stretching to the horizon, he is fascinated, almost hypnotized by the view—which in some way is the very thing that leads him eventually to maneuver the old Arab into setting it ablaze.

In other words, the protagonist's impulse to burn down the forest—pride of the Afforestation Department's director, planted with the help of funds donated by American Zionists, symbol of the whole idea of Zionist redemption and hope—has no rationale, is done with no bitterness or feeling of revenge, but is, on the contrary, completely unmotivated, almost evil for its own sake, suggestive of Gide's concept of *l'acte gratuite*. It is as though the author himself were posing the problem in very explicit, very ultimate terms; asserting the persistence of human irrationality and destructiveness and the need of such feelings for outlet at the expense of civilized, constructive rationality.

Yehoshua deals with a universal theme in a milieu that intensifies its ramifications. There seems to be a hint of danger that in its pursuit he will—as in **"Flood Tide"**—be tempted to remove his theme from this milieu, attempt to explore it in completely abstract and metaphysical terms. For a writer with his ability to deal with concrete details this would be a loss. It would be a loss, too, for readers interested in understanding how people living in such a determinedly extroverted country like Israel deal with their inner lives.

At the moment he is by any literary standards a writer to be watched. (p. 28)

> *Jerome Greenfield, in a review of "Three Days and a Child," in* Jewish Frontier, *Vol. XXXVII, No. 10, December, 1970, pp. 27-8.*

HAROLD FISCH

One of the most serious Israeli writers of the present generation . . . is A. B. Yehoshua, who is fortunately also a most competent storyteller. Yehoshua lacks as yet the epic range, but the remarkable gift displayed so far in his short fiction holds within it a brilliant promise. The title story in the present collection, **"Three Days and a Child,"** reads at one level as though it had been written as a model for the delectation of structural analysts. It opens on a note of dilemma. The narrator, Dov, a research student in mathematics at the Hebrew University who has long loved a kibbutz girl but has failed to win her, cannot solve a quadrilateral equation on which his university thesis depends; and the story, constructed with a kind of mathematical precision, is in some way an attempt to solve the equation. It sets up a series of dialectical and parallel relationships among the characters, each of whom has a different professional and avocational interest. . . . There is, in fact, a perfect balance of unresolved tensions. Into the center of this tangle is injected Yahli, the three-year-old child of Haya, whom

the narrator is asked to look after for three days. He is overcome with love for the child in whom he sees the image of the mother, but he also dreams fantastically of the boy's death as a means of revenge on Haya.

In pursuit of this object Dov drags the child through the fierce meridian heat of Jerusalem in sickness and mortal danger. The Jerusalem of dryness, rockiness, menace, and death (the time is pre-1967, when the guns of the Arab Legion stand poised over the Jewish city) is contrasted with the fertile countryside from which Haya derives. But Jerusalem will reveal its "secret fertility" when, on the final day of the story, summer wonderfully gives way to autumn and at that precise moment the narrator breaks out of the love/hate syndrome. (pp. 75-6)

Yehoshua's story **"Facing the Forests,"** also included in the present collection, has been much criticized in Israel as a gratuitous offense to the whole Zionist state enterprise. Its hero-narrator is a frustrated intellectual, a failed scholar (a kind of brother to Dov) who, when placed in charge of a forest planted by the Jewish National Fund on the ruins of an abandoned Arab village, stands idly by and even rejoices as a crazed Arab laborer "takes a firebrand and rushes through the trees like an evil spirit." From one point of view, the tale can indeed be regarded as a nihilistic work. . . . It speaks of obsessive responsibility (fire-watching), of fatal and debilitating inadequacy (the failed scholar), of menace and hate (the fire in the eyes of the Arab, the fire in the forest). Nor is the link between the narrator and the Arab any simple matter: through it runs a madness and pain going back to the period of the Crusades when both Arabs and Jews suffered at the hands of the Christian invader. Of course, it need hardly be said that Yehoshua no more approves of putting JNF forests to the torch than he does of letting little children get bitten by poisonous snakes; but he does have nightmares about both, and he seeks to resolve those nightmares by the means available to the imagination.

Yet the controversy over the real "meaning" of Yehoshua's stories—especially insofar as they seem to have disturbing social implications—is itself indicative of the deeply "relevant" quality of contemporary Israeli fiction even at its most abstract or symbolic level. Israeli writers, no matter how they may strive for the Kafkaesque effect, cannot successfully achieve the kind of symbolic autonomy that is the mark of Kafka's genius. . . . In the world of a Kafka story the specific subject matter is transformed by the imagination into a kind of literary Esperanto, a universal language of symbolic signs and patterns. But in the best Israeli fiction these signs and patterns, however abstractly they may be interpreted (as for instance in another Yehoshua story, **"Flood Tide"**), are nevertheless inescapably weighted with Jewish history and with Jewish historical consciousness. Throughout the work of writers like Amos Oz, A. B. Yehoshua, Aharon Megged, and others, there runs a sense of tragic responsibility, of a task to be discharged, and of dangers threatening the accomplishment of the task from within and from without. It is this existential condition which writers like Yehoshua make real. To expect something more universal is to expect too much—or perhaps too little. (p. 77)

> *Harold Fisch, "Unique and Universal," in* Commentary, *Vol. 54, No. 2, August, 1972, pp. 74-7.**

ANAT FEINBERG

For someone familiar with Yehoshua's short stories there is hardly any surprise in the fascination the theatrical medium has for this writer. For in each of his stories,—for instance in such a multi-symbolic story as **"Mul Hayaarot"** (**"Opposite the Forests"**) as well as in the more intimate expression of a complex relationship between a man and the family of a long-loved woman (**"Three Days and a Child"**)—there is always a strong dramatic kernel, a striking and unmistakable focus of tension and struggle which dictates the development of plot and simultaneously serves as the climax of narration. Moreover, the dramatic culmination—this artistically contrived turning point—very often takes the form of a catastrophe, an absolutely subverting disaster which inevitably leads to a new perspective of life, its meaning and values. This is the case, for instance, in the story **"The Evening Journey of Yatir"**: the inhabitants of a god-forsaken village dream, yearn and finally scheme and realize a terrible disaster for the train which regularly passes the small village on its way to Jerusalem. This is an unconscious attempt to solve their personal problems through a demonic apocalypse and to endow their lives with a new meaning; what Yeats called a "terrible beauty", which is born in a moment of death and utter destruction.

The first of the two plays—*A Night in May* (written after the Six Day War . . .) moves towards a dramatic and political climax. The action on stage is condensed to less than twelve hours—the night between May 22nd and 23rd, 1967. On the morning of the new day the announcer of the Israeli radio informs both the characters on the stage and the audience of Nasser's decision to close the straits of Tiran to Israeli shipping. War is the inevitable consequence; that war which has been hovering throughout the entire play and inducing at least part of the dramatic tension and atmosphere of the drama.

The dénouement is thus only a seeming resolution. The gunpowder barrel is still to explode. The external catastrophe may or may not (possibly will not) solve the personal problems of each and every one of the characters involved. In the play itself—during that long journey into the night—the special circumstances and the everpresent threat of war function as a catalyst for the shaping and clarification of psychic attitudes of every member in the 'septet', and serve as an indirect opportunity—or cause—for inter-personal confrontations.

Hence, the drama moves on three levels: it is the drama of a nation—a historical turning point yet to be 'born'. It is the drama of seven human beings, each burdened with his own complex idiosyncratic load of living. It is the drama of the 'clock'—the constant reminder of permanent motion of time, of the ceaseless division drawn between past, present and future. One is tempted to speak of the dimension of time as an additional actor in the play, perhaps even the major character who takes upon himself the burden of the drama. The radio-set, the news bulletins, the watch and various other references to time turn time from a mere abstract notion to what might be considered a three dimensional feature in the play. (pp. 43-4)

As far as pure dramatic skill is concerned—the argument that the second play, *Last Treatments,* is theatrically superior to the first—cannot be refuted. The play is shorter, more compact and obtains greater unity. The dialogues and monologues are far shorter, bordering sometimes on asthmatic expression which produces great dramatic impact. One has the feeling that A. B. Yehoshua has freed himself from the bondage of narrative in favour of theatrical requirements. I, for one, liked the first play better in spite of its incompleteness. For in *Last Treatments* I found myself puzzled by ideas and metaphysical evocations

rather than being fascinated—the way I was in the first play—by the characters. The major protagonists in *Last Treatments* stand for a certain concept. Mr. Herman, an old bookdealer, personifies the latent human desire to cut oneself off from one's past by external manifestation such as getting rid of an enormous collection of books, reorganizing his lodging as well as by his conscious efforts to forget. Mr. Shatz—his opponent—'symbolizes' the other extreme: his present existence is justified through the recapitulation of the past. Thus he constantly re-lives his memories and tries to share past experiences with people whom he once knew and who played a part in his life. (p. 46)

Nothing like what Buber called "the I-Thou relationship" is established. Mr. Herman is rude and inconsiderate to Shatz as well as to the young couple who seek the help of his wife. He who once had a human attitude to books shows no compassion and understanding when it comes to human beings. No wonder then that reading (or watching) the play one senses its deep debt to the Theatre of the Absurd: the somewhat Ionescian function of objects, the fragmentary and often twisted building of human relations and the paradoxical starting point in the pursuit of identity. Israel is not as yet blessed with too many gifted and skillful playwrights. One ought, I believe, to welcome Yehoshua's venture into the theatre and hope that by exploring and 'living' this particular medium more intensely, and becoming acquainted with its secrets—A. B. Yehoshua will enrich our theatrical literature while still adhering to his own idiosyncratic artistic vision of life. (p. 47)

Anat Feinberg, "A. B. Yehoshua As Playwright," in Modern Hebrew Literature, *Vol. 1, No. 1, Spring, 1975, pp. 43-7.*

CURTIS ARNSON

Regardless of the specific plot, there is a great deal of consistency between the early stories and Yehoshua's later work. In each of the stories [included in the retrospective collection *Ad Horef 1974*] there is the theme of withdrawal from the surrounding society and the isolation of an individual, usually self-imposed. This underlying idea is skillfully handled by the author and in some cases adds a considerable amount of tension to the narrative of an ostensibly banal story. While in many cases there is a stressed allegorical-political element to a story, the underlying theme of isolation turns it into more than merely sophisticated polemics. This element is added subtly to each work but in each case is there for the reader to discern.

My only criticism of this collection is that the ten stories together become a bit too much to take at one sitting. Yehoshua's short stories, as is the case with the short stories of many writers in all languages, can be fully enjoyed only when read separately.

Curtis Arnson, in a review of "Ad Horef 1974," in Books Abroad, *Vol. 49, No. 4, Autumn, 1975, p. 848.*

WILLIAM NOVAK

To live in Israel is to live with unremitting tension unremittingly; private life is intruded upon 24 hours a day by the real world in the form of hourly news broadcasts, which come into the home, the office, even the public buses.

Such is the psychological climate facing the Israeli writer, and no one has dealt with it so directly as Avraham B. Yehoshua. . . .

The schoolteacher in the title story [of *Early in the Summer of 1970*] was to have retired in 1967. But three years later he is still working. At the time of his scheduled retirement, most of the younger teachers were called up to fight in the war. Now, in 1970, there is a different kind of war—a war of attrition. It brings fewer casualties, yet each day brings news of another death. . . .

One day the [man] . . . goes off to teach and is informed that his son has been killed in the Jordan Valley. In a daze, he drags himself to the boy's army unit. There, to his shock and confusion, the corpse is unfamiliar; he examines it, and realizes it is not his son. Driving on, he eventually finds his son alive and well—and slightly annoyed at the arrival of this unexpected visitor. The father feels foolish—and joyful and sad. In truth, he doesn't know *how* to feel on a day like this, in a swell of contradictory emotions, when he has been the victim of the ultimate breakdown in the public-private balance. A soldier has died, after all, and in Israel one feels every loss. On the other hand, his son is alive. As he is assimilating all of this, the American wife to whom the father has never been able to relate, arrives on the scene. She is relieved, of course, but through the father we sense that she never believed in the possibility of tragedy in the first place.

This is a tricky and delicate theme to handle, and Yehoshua moves slowly and cautiously, peering intensely over the emotional landscape of his characters, sensitive to the slightest nuance, the faintest doubt, the subtlest gesture, and even then understating everything. His characters emerge fully drawn and emotionally complex and, although they must live in something smaller than a novel, they are not easily forgotten.

Yehoshua is always mindful of what is called in Israel "the situation," and even when the stories seem to be about universal expressions, there are always reminders that they could take place only in Israel. Some stories, though, are more forceful reminders of the public backdrop against which Israelis play out their lives. . . .

[Intensity] is the mark of all of Yehoshua's stories. They deal with complex and whole and often troubled human beings who reach out, mostly in vain, to connect with their relatives and their friends, only to connect most profoundly with themselves—and then, perhaps, with the big events they must live through. Yehoshua's stories find their way right to the unconscious; of his eight stories in English, at least five are as good as anything that has appeared since 1945. Nobel prizes have been given for less.

> William Novak, "*Terrible Events Are Imminent,*" in The Village Voice, *Vol. XXII, No. 17, April 25, 1977, p. 72.*

ALAN MINTZ

Nostalgia for an idealized past, the frenzied search for a transcendent future—it is one of the marks of A. B. Yehoshua's achievement as a writer that he refuses to give way to either of these temptations. In his new collection, *Early in the Summer of 1970,* as in a previous collection, *Three Days and a Child,* Yehoshua sticks resolutely to the harrowing confines of the present, even though, within those confines, he often works with the touch not of a realist but of a fabulist. The stories in the new collection take place in the period between 1967 and 1973, a time of wearying stalemate between Israel and its Arab neighbors, punctuated by random, sporadic death. In Yehoshua's imaginative reconstruction of this period, the larger collective purposes of the national existence have lost their clarity; his characters struggle on, but the struggle discloses no meaning to them. If there is any heroism in Yehoshua's world, it consists in the courage to face facts as they are and still proceed with the business of life.

The nameless hero of "**Missile Base 612**" cannot muster such courage. Rather, he persists in demanding some revelation that will explain the disorientation of his existence. Like the aimless fighting between Israel and Egypt along the Suez Canal, his life has become a permanent battle fought from fixed positions. . . . Thus, when he is asked to spend a day lecturing in the Sinai to army troops, he is grateful for the chance to break out of his isolation. Yet he who has come to lecture is actually the one in need of enlightenment. The army is full of people who have adapted to the conditions of uncertainty and attrition, and his fumbling and grandiloquent overtures to the men are met by stupefaction or bemused skepticism.

Finally, he steals a close look at the missiles on the base and is electrified by the spectacle they present of impersonal, erotic power. But he characteristically fails to grasp the nature of this power. Searching for an epiphany that will explain, and release him from, the deadlock of his own life, he cannot understand that the purpose of the missiles is *not* to be fired, that they are there to prevent an apocalypse by remaining in check.

Loss of meaning, and the baffled search for a way to overcome that loss, is similarly at the center of the title story, "**Early in the Summer of 1970,**" Yehoshua's brilliant recasting of the motif of the sacrifice of Isaac. (p. 66)

The story is told with an obsessive, almost painful, allegiance to the point of view of the father, who returns constantly in his mind to the moment when he was given the news of his son's "death." With each repetition, it becomes clearer that instead of reliving a moment of pain, the father is actually reliving a moment in which his son's life, and his own, seem finally to have taken on meaning. He sees himself, guilty and bereft, but somehow heroic, offering up his son on the altar of national existence, and he sees his son as a willing martyr in the same cause. As in the biblical tale, however, the son is allowed to live. But whereas in Abraham's case it was trust in God that was being tested and revealed, in the case of Yehoshua's story what is being tested is only the father's desperate and misplaced faith in a deliverance wrought by others. And whereas in the biblical story, ordeal is followed by covenant, by the striking of a new redemptive relation between God and His chosen ones, "**Early in the Summer of 1970**" ends back in unillusioned reality: the ordeal will simply continue.

Yehoshua's stories sound grim and severe when stripped to their moral burden, but as works of art they are marvelously accomplished, rich and precise in language and startlingly inventive in their use of non-realistic modes of narration. As a moralist, Yehoshua is relentless, and he shows his characters no quarter. Conspicuously absent from his work is just that element of sympathy toward the yearning for deliverance which runs like a scarlet thread through so much serious Jewish writing in this century—and not only in this century.

Still, what Yehoshua does share with almost all Hebrew writers of the modern period, and with many contemporary Israeli writers in particular, is a highly charged sense of obligation toward his material, an obligation not only to depict faithfully but also to evaluate and comment upon the twists and turns of the national consciousness as they reveal themselves in character and incident. (pp. 66-7)

Alan Mintz, "New Israeli Writing," in Commentary, Vol. 65, No. 1, January, 1978, pp. 64-7.*

NILI WACHTEL

Of the vast amount of critical commentary that followed publication of A. B. Yehoshua's latest work, *The Lover,* the majority dealt not so much with the literary merit of the work, or with any great truths it might have revealed, as with its political and social implications.

Increasingly Yehoshua's writing focuses on situations in Israeli life; it might appear that he is becoming increasingly parochial. But as with others, so with him: the situations he chooses revolve around certain recurring themes—universal human themes—and it is they that constitute the essential Yehoshua.

These themes were evident even in his first published work, *The Death of the Old Man,* a collection of short parable-like stories showing the influence both of Agnon and Kafka. The stories are symbolic in style, and, contrary to his later work, rooted in no particular place and no particular time.

In the first of these, the title story, a very old man, "maybe a thousand years old, maybe more," refuses to die. Demanding that he remove himself from the affairs of this world, complaining that "he is so burdened with memories that he cannot see the world around him," and that they are simply tired, "too tired to carry him," his neighbors declare him dead and forcibly bury him. But burying the old man brings them neither comfort nor exhilaration. There is only a sense of emptiness: eyeing an abandoned spade, the narrator wistfully wonders whether to dig the old man up, or to dig a grave for himself.

The story suggests, of course, the attempt of present day Israelis to unburden themselves of the founder-generation and of its 2000 year old memory. But at the same time, the situation described is a thoroughly familiar and a universal situation: it is the modern world, divested of the beliefs and values of the past, become in the process an empty and a meaningless place. Indeed, the futility of man's efforts to understand or control his existence animates the remaining stories in this volume. (p. 48)

The same themes appear in Yehoshua's second book, *Facing the Forests,* except that here they are set within a recognizable Israeli landscape and clothed in recognizable Israeli situations. They acquire, as a result, a greater vitality, are far more persuasive, and certain nuances not apparent in the more abstract treatment reveal themselves here.

"The Death of the Old Man" has its counterpart in **"The Lengthening Silence of a Poet."** An aging poet is raising, and thoroughly dominating, his son—a slow, feeble-minded, "border-line" boy. . . . [In both works], a portrait is drawn of a weak, afflicted generation, a generation which has nothing of its own—the added implication here being that the sons are what they are because the fathers were what they were.

The title story, **"Facing the Forests,"** provides insight into this afflicted generation. . . .

On the face of it, the story is about conflicts in the Middle East, but **"Facing the Forests"** also has a great deal to say about the problematics of human existence. A generation of poets, of visionaries, was succeeded by what Yehoshua called in his play, *One Night in May,* a generation of "perplexed people." The clarity and certainty of the parents' dream disintegrated for the sons into a nightmare of contradictions. "We have in our lives some extremely serious repressions regarding the Israeli-Arab problem, the entire problem of our existence here," Yehoshua was to say following publication of **"Facing the Forests."** (p. 49)

It is unfortunate, perhaps, that Yehoshua tells his story through the Zionist dream, a dream sacred to Jews everywhere as the means for Jewish survival. And yet, the Zionist dream as metaphor can serve to show the gap that exists between man's vision and his reality. And it is this gap, and the pain of living in it, which is the essence of Yehoshua's fiction.

The predicaments of Yehoshua's characters stem from his conviction that reality is complex, composed of conflict and contradiction. It does not present itself to man in a series of neatly-separated clearly-defined alternatives, but as a blend in which opposites exist together. Man, for example, possesses the highest spiritual aspirations *and* primitive animal instincts. To achieve some sort of balance between them is the burden of his life, but he would rather dwell in the comfort and security of one sphere or the other. Thus, for example, in **"The Conclusion,"** . . . Yehoshua shows the results of life lived exclusively in the realm of reason and ideas, while in **"The Rising Tide"** he shows the existence of subterranean non-rational emotions and drives which cannot be escaped. (pp. 49-50)

The problem for Yehoshua's heroes is that one force without the other is not reality; and yet to bring them together is impossible. And so, whether they face the paradoxes inherent in the Zionist enterprise or in life itself, they are portrayed as hesitant, ambivalent, weak, and ineffectual men, poised between two warring camps, stuck between two radio stations (**"Missile Base 612"**), between two worlds and unable to get to the essence (**"Facing the Forests"**), often described as straddling a dividing line of some kind—a fence, a border, a river— unable to move. The typical Yehoshua hero, in other words, inhabits a hopelessly polarized world, a world whose conflicting claims he feels helpless to reconcile. He either lives his life in a state much like sleep, or else he longs for some catastrophe that will solve his problem by destroying it.

A good example is the last story in the volume—a novella really—**"Three Days and a Child."** The story takes place against the background of a series of opposites. The Jerusalem of the story is truly a divided city: a bustling modern western metropolis on the one hand, and, on the other, an ageless mound of parched rocks, ancient olive trees, and Muslim cemeteries. . . .

People in the story are also grouped into opposing types. There are those who live as if every action and event is symbolic of something higher. . . . And then there are the members of the Nature Lovers Society; they "go along at a snail's pace, all but creeping over the ground . . ."; they "examine every detail of their surroundings . . . out of a sacred principle." . . . And at the center of all this is Dov, suspended between all the extremes. Described as living "without soil or sky," he is stuck in a "logical contradiction," an equation he cannot solve, at work on a thesis he cannot finish.

The story begins when a child, Yali—like the forest, a veiled reference to Israel—is entrusted to Dov. Like the forest, he both accepts and rejects this charge, and spends the better part of the story trying to destroy it. At one point he brings the child to the home of an elderly couple, representing the parent generation, and there to a swing—more an altar than a swing. He places the child on the swing—the swing prepared by the elderly couple—and in a scene highly reminiscent of the biblical sacrifice of Isaac, he sends the child high into the sky. All this to suggest, once again, that it is the parent generation which prepared the bind in which the present generation finds itself.

This theme of the sacrifice of Isaac, the sacrifice of sons for the beliefs and visions of the fathers, has been prominent among Israeli writers since 1948. . . . What is special about Yehoshua, as was stated before, is that he goes beyond the situation at hand, and points to the nature of man's dreams and the nature of reality. (p. 50)

This pattern is often seen in Yehoshua: something small, and couched in reality, begins to swell and grow until it overtakes reality. It is exceedingly easy, Yehoshua shows, for the fragile and intricate relationships that make up real life to be disrupted, easy for legitimate drives to become all-consuming passions, for one-half of the whole to become the whole. . . .

Early in the Summer of 1970, in barest outline, is the story of a father informed of his son's death during the War of Attrition. He is invited to identify the body, but the body produced for him is not his son's. The son later turns up elsewhere, alive.

There are those who see Christological elements in *Early in the Summer of 1970*—particularly in the recollection of the main event in three slightly differing versions—and conclude that *Early in the Summer of 1970* is one more reworking of the father-sacrificing-son motif, perhaps the ultimate reworking, right down to the son's eventual resurrection. But to say this is to miss all the fine nuances and rich details that combine to make the very point of the story. . . .

The irony of the situation is that the younger generation, a perplexed and troubled generation, would like nothing better than genuine inspiration, real purpose—the slow-witted son of **"The Lengthening Silence of a Poet"** desperately prods his father to write—but the parent generation has nothing to give. The visions dragged up by the parents do not speak to the sons' reality. . . . Confronting his father in the uproar of battle, the son of *Early in the Summer of 1970* confesses that he sees no meaning in it. The father, this time, is silent. . . .

The fathers, in other words, pay homage to grand, but distant and abstract, ideals, while the sons are mired in ugly reality. The fathers' dreams are too far removed from conditions of the battlefield, in many ways the real condition of life. (p. 51)

The problem with visions, Yehoshua seems to be saying, is that sooner or later they clash with real life. The old father of *Early in the Summer of 1970* also, when plunged into the realities of battle, realizes with a shock that he, a lifelong teacher of Bible, has forgotten every bit of Bible he knew. . . . And it is this—that in the clash between the dream and the reality it is the dream that must give way—which is, finally, the main point of *Early in the Summer of 1970*.

Throughout the story it is entirely unclear who it is who is actually losing his life: the son or the father. Repeatedly it is the father who appears bound up. . . . Also, as the three ver-

sions of the story succeed each other, the figure of the father seems to lose something, his "condition" weakening with every re-telling. . . . At the same time, he progressively loses his hold over his students until, again at the end, he realizes that neither he nor his values are alive for his students. . . . (pp. 51-2)

One of Israel's most noted literary critics, Gershon Shaked, sees in *Early in the Summer of 1970* a turning point in Yehoshua's work, because, he says, the younger generation is portrayed as having found something new for themselves, some new "message." In connection with the theme of the resurrection, Shaked suggests that they come to life because of having linked on to some new reality.

And indeed, the promise of something new does seem to be in the air. The son of the story returns home to his father from overseas, where he was studying, "by way of the Orient." He brings with him . . . all the paraphernalia of the disaffected youth of the 1950s and 60s. . . . The new message, then, would seem to be that this generation finally caught up with the outlook prevailing in the Western world: the pacifism, the uncertainty about values, the disenchantment with ideologies, with rationalist optimism, with the pretense that it is possible to make sense of human experience.

But that this is a turning point in Yehoshua is not strictly true. These thoughts have been articulated by Yehoshua's characters almost from the beginning. The difference is that before they were expressed by individuals, by outsiders, men at odds with their society, whereas now they are presented as the prevailing mood of mainstream Israeli society. This became even more pronounced after the Yom Kippur War when, as Yehoshua notes, Israeli society lost much of its self-confidence. "There is . . . no point," writes Shimon Sandbank about the post-1973 Yehoshua—and this is the real turning point—"in [his] repeating what he did in *Facing the Forests*. . . . Instead, his alienated protagonist can now return to the fold which has itself become alienated from its former certainties. His characters, in other words, can now move to the center of Israeli life."

These forces all come together in Yehoshua's latest work, and his first novel, *The Lover*. Written in the aftermath of the Yom Kippur War, *The Lover* depicts a society in turmoil. All sorts of hidden doubts and fears about Jewish existence in Israel, about human existence in general, broke out into the open. . . . Combing the roads at night, Adam, one of the central characters, comes across the night life, the inner life, of Israelis: they are stuck on the roads. The truth is, under all the tumult and the frantic activity, Israeli inner life is stuck. The country was swept into a mad, senseless rush, whose purpose has vanished. (p. 52)

On another level, Yehoshua tells a parallel story, the story of Zionism. Old lady Veducha is Grandmother Zionism. . . . She lies in a hospital for degenerative diseases, reliving all the stages of her development: how she began small and simple, how she began to spread out, becoming swollen and monstrous, progressively showing fewer signs of life and response to reality.

This is Yehoshua's graphic representation of Zionism gone messianic. Zionism began, he says, by seeking a little Jewish freedom. . . . But progressively it expanded its aims, thereby changing its character. (pp. 52-3)

The Lover was, predictably, greeted with storms: "Yehoshua's vision of the end of Zionism," proclaimed one reviewer. But it is not a question of Yehoshua's prognosis for Zionism. The book is a description of what he sees around him. . . . The nation has been caught napping. It was living in dreams, not reality. This is why Yehoshua populates *The Lover* with people who live in their dreams. . . . [Adam's wife] Asya's exceptionally well-ordered room is not of this place, her severe and old-fashioned clothes are not of this place or time, her interest in equality and social revolution is all theory, her cures for humanity's ills are all rational and painless. She lives terrified that reality will intrude on her dreams: her dreams are well-ordered and manageable, while reality holds the unexpected. Even Adam himself is in love more with the idea that he formed of his wife than with his wife herself. . . . He is perfectly content to love her from afar. . . . The very title of the book in Hebrew, in fact, suggests one who loves from a distance, one who does not really love: *ha-Me'ahev*, and not *ha-Ohev*.

This, then, is the fundamental sin operating in Yehoshua's world: loving from afar. It permits one to love without "effort," without an "obligation." And guilty of it are all who live in the passion of their ideal without having to face the palpable consequences. . . .

It is not the Arab-Israeli conflict *per se* which causes Yehoshua to question the Zionist dream. The protracted conflict and the recurring wars, however, serve as constant reminders that something basic remains unresolved. (p. 53)

To Yehoshua, the various disputed territories, the State, the government, were all means to an end, not the end itself. This is why he considers their "sanctification" a "betrayal of Zionism." The end was freedom, freedom for the nation to rule itself, to grow and develop normally, to shed some unwholesome tendencies acquired in Diaspora. In Zionism, he says, there was a "delicate balance": the creation of a Jewish state attentive to the needs and survival of Jews everywhere, but at the same time, the creation of a "new hybrid," a Jew rooted in and attuned to this land, drawing life from its own inner life and vitality. This is Gingit, the girl-soldier of **"Missile Base 612,"** with hair the color of the desert, at home in the desert. (pp. 53-4)

Yehoshua's greatest disappointment with the dream's implementation, by the same token, is again not the Arab-Israeli conflict alone, but the fact that this "new hybrid" was not really created, that Israelis living on their own land react to events with notions and excesses developed for life in Diaspora. And it is here, finally, that he sees the roots of the nation's uneasy existence in Zion—that it lives in Zion like a lover from afar.

What will be the next installment? Yehoshua does not say. Beyond suggesting, that is, that a time of national self-searching is an opportunity for returning to basics, for facing reality. . . .

One suspects that living with reality, for Yehoshua, remains in the final analysis what it was in **"The Wedding of Galia":** a stubborn journey, with no answers, no certainties, with nothing but the making and re-making of one's way. (p. 54)

> *Nili Wachtel, "A. B. Yehoshua: Between the Dream and the Reality," in* Midstream, *Vol. XXV, No. 7, August-September, 1979, pp. 48-54.*

HAROLD BLOOM

"The question of the *Golah* (Exile) is the most important and profound question a Jew must pose to himself when trying to probe the essence of the Jewish people." Whether that is true or not, it is central to the art and thought of the Israeli writer A. B. Yehoshua. The quotation is not from the admirable novel under review ["**A Late Divorce**"] but from Mr. Yehoshua's polemic against the Diaspora, **"Between Right and Right"** (1981), which deserves more attention than it has received. In his fiction, Mr. Yehoshua is subtle, indirect and sometimes visionary, even phantasmagoric. His polemical essays are fierce, hyperbolic efforts to reformulate the terms of identity, Jew, Zionist, Israeli.

Reading "**A Late Divorce**" . . . persuades me that Mr. Yehoshua, though still only 47, has now integrated his art and his argument and joins himself, with this book, to what is strongest in contemporary Israeli literature—the poetry of Dan Pagis and Yehuda Amichai and the fiction of Amos Oz. "**A Late Divorce**" ought to attract a wide readership here, since it is authentic storytelling, acutely representative of current social realities in Israel and marked by extraordinary psychological insight throughout.

Though it is set entirely in Israel's three major cities, Jerusalem, Tel Aviv and Haifa, its hidden subject is Mr. Yehoshua's obsessive theme of "the great debate between Israel and the *Golah*." The words are his own, and so indeed mostly is the overt debate, at least until now. But many readers of "**A Late Divorce**" are unlikely to realize the ultimate designs of this absorbing family saga, a well-told tale of marital calamity, madness, estrangement between generations, sexual malaise and thwarted intellectual and spiritual ambitions, in a society always at war or between wars and almost always in economic and social crisis.

Though there is a deft symbolic dimension to Mr. Yehoshua's novel, it is secondary to the naturalistic pathos that dominates plot, character, point of view and stylistic presentation. Like his Israeli precursor, S. Yizhar, author of "The Days of Ziklag," Mr. Yehoshua writes in the shadow of Faulkner, with an admixture of Joyce, and it is the achievement of "**A Late Divorce**" that it successfully synthesizes the antithetical modes of naturalism and symbolism. Though it perhaps harbors such an ambition, it cannot be called an Israeli "The Sound and the Fury," but perhaps Mr. Yehoshua, on its evidence, may yet surpass S. Yizhar as a kind of Israeli Faulkner.

The novel's exile is Yehuda Kaminka, a marginal intellectual and teacher, who in his 60's has gone off to Minnesota in quest of a new life. He returns to Israel for the nine days up through the first day of Passover in order to obtain his estranged wife's consent to a divorce so as to marry his pregnant American mistress. . . . His nine days are told in sequence by Kaminka's stolid 10-year-old grandson; his hyperactive lawyer son-in-law; his beautiful daughter-in-law, an aspirant writer; his insecure son, a lecturer in history; a homosexual son and the son's lover, a banker, in a Joycean dialogue, followed by a Svevo-like analytical session between the homosexual son and his astonishingly brilliant therapist; a monologue by Kaminka's selfless daughter, who is married to the lawyer; then by the psychotic Mrs. Kaminka; and at last by the bemused Kaminka himself. This catalogue of narrators may sound wearisome or artificial, but Mr. Yehoshua is marvelously resourceful in varying the personal stance of each figure.

A reader could react unkindly by reflecting that Mr. Yehoshua has rendered a caricature of an Israeli family, since the Kaminkas sometimes seem to be on the verge of becoming Jewish Snopeses. So grand are the talents of this novelist that there is a certain danger of the local color becoming too vivid or the powerful humor turning rancid. But for the better part of the novel, Mr. Yehoshua maintains firm control so that some scenes attain an uncanny magnificence. (pp. 1, 31)

Beyond his undoubted gifts for naturalistic pathos and hallucinatory comedy, Mr. Yehoshua is an idealist with a fixed idea, the necessity for gathering the spiritual remnants of Jewry, lest Jewry and Israel both perish. On an undoubted symbolic level, there is an identity between the disturbed Mrs. Kaminka and the land of Israel. More problematical is the relation between Yehuda Kaminka and the Jew as wayward father, exiling himself from the mother-homeland, going off to the new Egypt that is America.

It is both touching and sly of Mr. Yehoshua that he allows into his novel, before it ends, the American son of Yehuda, brought to Israel at the age of 3. The boy is named Moses and is a stutterer, like his fabled namesake. This is Mr. Yehoshua's hint and wish that a new Moses might rise among American Jewry and lead it back to Israel. I doubt that Mr. Yehoshua will be numbered among the prophets of his people, but I prophesy a high place for him among its storytellers. (p. 31)

Harold Bloom, "Domestic Derangements," in The New York Times Book Review, *February 19, 1984, pp. 1, 31.*

JOSEPH COHEN

Faulkner's presence is everywhere felt in this remarkable novel ["**A Late Divorce**"]. It is a presence that both exhilarates and depresses, so sustained is the emotional intensity of the story, not just recalling but indeed being structured upon what many regard as the Southern writer's single most important work, "The Sound and the Fury." Not simply derivative, "**A Late Divorce**" is a Faulknerian tour de force, with enormous power in its own originality, enabling it to function organically and soundly in its own right. . . .

[The] sheer lyrical quality of Yehoshua's prose [is] a poetic accomplishment which was also a noteworthy feature of Faulkner's writing. Though both books are fiction of an exceptionally high order, each functions somewhat as poetry does, communicating on an emotional level, making it easy for the reader to relate to the characters and to respond to their actions. . . .

What do all these nice Israelis have to do with Southern gothicism? In the first place, with one exception, they are not so nice. Beyond that, they are no different from anyone else under extreme stress.

Secondly, Yehoshua, whose stories, like Faulkner's, concentrate attention on psychological and moral problems, involves Faulkner at the beginning of his book, hinting broadly (but imprecisely, on purpose) at its outcome in his use of an epigraph to the first chapter, taken from "The Sound and the Fury." This chapter, related by Gaddi, Kaminka's seven-year-old grandson, is introduced with the quotation "Benjy knew it when DaMuddy died." . . .

Narrative technique, style and characterization apart, Yehoshua imitates Faulkner further by naming his chapters for days of the week just as Faulkner used dates for his chapter headings, and the books of both authors end on holidays of corresponding seasonal significance, Yehoshua's on the first day of Passover, Faulkner's on Easter Sunday.

Everything in both books leads up to these holidays, which serve as moral backdrops against which the weaknesses and follies of the characters in both works are accentuated.

Just as Faulkner did, Yehoshua makes it clear by implication that redemptive religious values are everywhere present but are ignored or, at best, merely paid lip-service, by people hurling themselves toward their own destruction.

Finally, the basic theme of both books is identical. Each demonstrates for us the impact of the loss of love within the family unit, and the devastating effect this loss has, first on the children, and in time on society as a whole. It is a lesson every generation must learn anew whether it is located in the turn-of-the-century American South or in contemporary Israel.

That Yehoshua has dealt so masterfully with this message both independently of and in conjunction with Faulkner's "The Sound and the Fury" is no small achievement.

Joseph Cohen, "Faulknerian Tale from Israel's A. B. Yehoshua," in The Detroit Jewish News, *March 2, 1984, p. 12.*

LEON WIESELTIER

The most important decision that a writer must make is probably not the decision about subject. It is the decision about scale. . . . Scale, in this sense, is the measure of a writer's seriousness. Also, of his ambition, which in the best instances consists in a shocking belief in the possibility of greatness. (p. 38)

[A Late Divorce] is, in its subject and its scale, a large novel. [Yehoshua's] subject is the fate of a family, or more precisely, the family as the instrument of fate. Rarely have the crippling consequences of the extraordinary closeness in which all lives begin, the banal derailments of fathers and mothers and sons and daughters and sisters and brothers and husbands and wives by one another, been captured with this much wisdom. (pp. 38-9)

The story of the mortification of the Kaminkas is told by Yehoshua in a brilliant series of monologues. . . . [His characters] all tell the story slowly, one after the other, until it reaches its crazy and catastrophic end.

The compassion with which Yehoshua creates all these smashed-up people is remarkable. His model, quite obviously, is Faulkner, *The Sound and The Fury* in particular; and while he does not achieve the raw sublimity of his model, the range of his human sympathies and his utterly unsentimental understanding of everybody's reasons are sufficient to show that a part of Faulkner's mantle has landed in, of all places, Israel.

When Yehoshua's novel was published in Israel . . . it occasioned great debates in the papers about its meaning. . . . Some critics took it to be an allegory. It is at least plausible that the flight of Kaminka from Israel, from the wife who almost destroyed him, originates in Yehoshua's obsessive concern with the failure of the Jewish state to sustain all the Jews, too many are leaving and not too many are coming. And Kaminka does not survive the return to the homeland—a land that devours its inhabitants, as the spies from Canaan warned. Yehoshua is hardly dead to these dimensions of his saga. He is not only a talented novelist, he is a talented intellectual, too. . . .

Still, this is no *roman à thèse*. Its symbols are swamped by its reality. To be sure, it is a portrait of the inner life of Israelis who are worn down. To treat it mainly as a document, however, would be to condescend to its literary achievement. Yehoshua has frequently written on behalf of "the normalization of the Jewish people," that great Zionist slogan for the great Zionist dream; but his novel, insofar as it is not dominated by the public subjects that have dominated so much Israeli writing in the past, is itself a measure of how much normality has been snatched from the decades of adversity. More and more Israeli writing is becoming less and less "Israeli." (p. 39)

There is only one thing missing from *A Late Divorce*. That is transcendence. The novel is a little too psychological, a little too schematic in its classification of the forms of familial suffering. It has its visionary moments, its passages of phantasmagoric humor, its spots of lyrical delirium, but these all lead back only to a kind of analytic sophistication. All this misery would seem to deserve a mystery. Or perhaps that is the final secret of family life. It may be that it includes no mystery. The pain may be completely understood. The tragedy may be without transcendence. Love may turn unwittingly into power, and every divorce is late. (pp. 39-40)

Leon Wieseltier, "The Fall of a Family," in The New Republic, *Vol. 190, No. 10, March 12, 1984, pp. 38-40.*

Appendix

The following is a listing of all sources used in Volume 31 of *Contemporary Literary Criticism*. Included in this list are all copyright and reprint rights and acknowledgements for those essays for which permission was obtained. Every effort has been made to trace copyright, but if omissions have been made, please let us know.

THE EXCERPTS IN CLC, VOLUME 31, WERE REPRINTED FROM THE FOLLOWING PERIODICALS:

America, v. 146, April 17, 1982 for a review of "A Mother and Two Daughters" by John B. Breslin; v. 147, December 18, 1982 for a review of "Visions from San Francisco Bay" by Tom Alessandri; v. 150, January 14, 1984 for a review of "One Day of Life" by Edward J. Curtin, Jr. © 1982, 1984. All rights reserved. All reprinted with permission of the respective authors./ v. 111, July 4, 1964; v. 112, January 16, 1965; v. 132, January 11, 1975. © 1964, 1965, 1975. All rights reserved. All reprinted with permission of America Press, Inc.

The American Book Review, v. 4, January-February, 1982. © 1982 by *The American Book Review*. Reprinted by permission.

American Indian Quarterly, v. 5, May, 1979. Copyright © Society for American Indian Studies & Research 1979. Reprinted by permission.

American Literature, v. 53, May, 1981. Copyright © 1981 by Duke University Press, Durham, North Carolina. Reprinted by permission of the publisher.

The American Poetry Review, v. 5, May-June, 1976 for "Marvin Bell: 'Time's Determinant. / Once I Knew You'" by Arthur Oberg. Copyright © 1976 by World Poetry, Inc. Reprinted by permission of the publisher and the Literary Estate of Arthur Oberg.

Américas, v. 24, February, 1972. Reprinted by permission from *Américas*, a bimonthly magazine published by the General Secretariat of the Organization of American States in English and Spanish.

Analog Science Fiction/Science Fact, v. CIX, February, 1984 for a review of "The Neverending Story" by Tom Easton. © 1984 by Davis Publications, Inc. Reprinted by permission of the author.

The Antioch Review, v. XL, Spring, 1982. Copyright © 1982 by the Antioch Review Inc. Reprinted by permission of the Editors.

Arizona Quarterly, v. 35, Autumn, 1979 for a review of "American Indian Fiction" by Larry Evers; v. 36, Summer, 1980 for "From Semblance to Selfhood: The Evolution of Woman in H. D.'s Neo-Epic 'Helen in Egypt'" by L. M. Friebert; v. 38, Spring, 1982 for a review of "HERmione" by Lucy M. Friebert; v. 39, Spring, 1983 for a review of "The Gift" by Lucy M. Friebert. Copyright © 1979, 1980, 1982, 1983 by Arizona Board of Regents. All reprinted by permission of the publisher and the respective authors.

The Atlantic Monthly, v. 244, July, 1979 for a review of "Strange Things Happen Here" by Amanda Y. Heller. Reprinted by permission of the author.

Atlas, v. 11, June, 1966. © 1966 copyright by Aspen Publishing Company, Inc. Now published as *World Press Review*. Reprinted by permission.

Appendix

1918, 1956, 1967, 1969, 1977, 1978, 1980, 1981, 1982, 1983, 1984 The New Republic, Inc. All reprinted by permission of *The New Republic*.

New Statesman, v. XVII, September 3, 1921; v. XXII, October 13, 1923; v. XXVI, October 24, 1925; v. XXXI, August 11, 1928; v. LXIX, March 19, 1965; v. LXIX, April 2, 1965; v. LXIX, April 16, 1965; v. LXIX, June 18, 1965; v. LXX, September 24, 1965; v. 71, April 1, 1966; v. 71, April 29, 1966; v. 73, October 7, 1966; v. 73, June 16, 1967; v. 76, September 20, 1968; v. 76, October 4, 1968; v. 78, August 8, 1969; v. 78, September 5, 1969; v. 84, March 24, 1972; v. 84, April 14, 1972; v. 83, June 16, 1972; v. 87, January 18, 1974; v. 90, November 28, 1975; v. 94, September 30, 1977; v. 99, May 9, 1980; v. 99, June 6, 1980; v. 100, July 4, 1980; v. 100, October 24, 1980; v. 101, June 5, 1981; v. 102, July 10, 1981; v. 102, September 4, 1981; v. 102, October 9, 1981; v. 103, March 12, 1982; v. 103, April 30, 1982; v. 103, May 21, 1982; v. 103, June 25, 1982; v. 104, September 10, 1982; v. 104, December 17 & 24, 1982; v. 105, February 25, 1983; v. 106, August 5, 1983; v. 106, September 2, 1983; v. 106, September 16, 1983; v. 107, January 27, 1984; v. 107, March 23, 1984; v. 107, June 29, 1984. © 1921, 1923, 1925, 1928, 1965, 1966, 1967, 1968, 1969, 1972, 1974, 1975, 1977, 1980, 1981, 1982, 1983, 1984 The Statesman & Nation Publishing Co. Ltd. All reprinted by permission.

The New Statesman & Nation, v. 75, February 9, 1968; v. 86, July 20, 1973; v. 104, December 17-24, 1982. © 1968, 1973, 1982 The Statesman & Nation Publishing Co. Ltd. All reprinted by permission.

New York Herald Tribune Book Review, October 17, 1954; January 15, 1956; July 20, 1958; April 12, 1959; September 20, 1959; March 27, 1960. © 1954, 1956, 1958, 1959, 1960 I.H.T. Corporation. All reprinted by permission.

New York Herald Tribune Books, October 15, 1939; July 21, 1940; October 27, 1940; April 6, 1941./ March 10, 1929; March 8, 1936. © 1929, 1936 I.H.T. Corporation. Both reprinted by permission./ November 18, 1934; June 9, 1935; March 14, 1937; April 24, 1938. © 1934, renewed 1962; © 1935, renewed 1963; © 1937, renewed 1965; © 1938, renewed 1966 I.H.T. Corporation. All reprinted by permission.

New York Herald Tribune Weekly Book Review, August 5, 1945; September 11, 1949. © 1945, 1949 I.H.T. Corporation. Both reprinted by permission.

New York Magazine, v. 15, August 23, 1982 for "South American Soap" by Carolyn Clay; v. 17, January 16, 1984 for "Castle Rackrent" by Quentin Crisp. Copyright © 1982, 1984 by News Group Publications, Inc. All reprinted by permission of the respective authors./ v. 16, April 11, 1983; v. 16, May 9, 1983; v. 16, November 28, 1983; v. 17, June 13, 1984. Copyright © 1983, 1984 by News Group Publications, Inc. All reprinted with the permission of *New York* Magazine.

New York Post, December 22, 1966; November 12, 1971; April 7, 1981; May 19, 1981; March 28, 1983; May 31, 1983. © 1966, 1971, 1981, 1983, New York Post Corporation. All reprinted from the *New York Post* by permission.

The New York Review of Books, v. III, January 14, 1965 for "Novels from Abroad" by Stanley Kauffmann. Copyright © 1965 Nyrev, Inc. Reprinted by permission of Brandt & Brandt Literary Agents, Inc./ v. VII, December 1, 1966; v. XXII, January 22, 1976; v. XXIII, May 27, 1976; v. XXIII, June 10, 1976; v. XXVI, July 19, 1979; v. XXVI, January 24, 1980; v. XXVII, November 6, 1980; v. XXVIII, June 25, 1981; v. XXIX, May 13, 1982; v. XXIX, August 12, 1982; v. XXX, December 8, 1983; v. XXXI, March 15, 1984; v. XXXI, April 12, 1984. Copyright © 1966, 1976, 1979, 1980, 1981, 1982, 1983, 1984 Nyrev, Inc. All reprinted with permission from *The New York Review of Books*.

The New York Times, March 4, 1968; December 2, 1968; April 3, 1969; June 3, 1978; February 12, 1980; February 4, 1981; April 7, 1981; May 20, 1981; January 10, 1982; February 23, 1982; December 29, 1982; March 28, 1983; April 3, 1983; April 8, 1983; May 31, 1983; August 20, 1983; September 6, 1983; October 19, 1983; October 28, 1983; November 2, 1983; November 17, 1983; December 12, 1983. Copyright © 1968, 1969, 1978, 1980, 1981, 1982, 1983 by The New York Times Company. All reprinted by permission.

The New York Times Book Review, August 20, 1922; September 28, 1924; March 6, 1927; October 21, 1928; February 16, 1930; April 10, 1932; June 19, 1932; April 9, 1933; March 18, 1934; June 10, 1934; February 3, 1935; March 31, 1935; June 16, 1935; October 27, 1935; March 7, 1937; August 14, 1938; January 1, 1939; August 20, 1939; October 8, 1939; July 21, 1940; October 27, 1940; March 30, 1941; September 14, 1941; May 31, 1942; October 31, 1943; November 18, 1945; December 2, 1945; December 14, 1947; August 26, 1951; August 3, 1952; February 8, 1953; January 8, 1956; December 9, 1956; June 22, 1958; June 7, 1959; October 4, 1959; December 6, 1959; May 1, 1960; July 31, 1960; December 11, 1960; March 12, 1961; October 22, 1961; June 14, 1964; June 27, 1965; July 31, 1966; February 5, 1967; January 28, 1968; September 15, 1968; May 18, 1969; September 28, 1969; January 11, 1970; March 29, 1970; October 25, 1970; February 28, 1971; January 30, 1972; October 22, 1972; December 10, 1972; April 22, 1973; July 15, 1973; November 23, 1975; September 19, 1976; July 10, 1977; August 7, 1977; July 2, 1978; January 14, 1979; February 11, 1979; May 6, 1979; July 1, 1979; September 23, 1979; March 9, 1980; June 15, 1980; August 31, 1980; November 2, 1980; May 10, 1981; September 13, 1981; February 14, 1982; February 28, 1982; June 20, 1982; August 1, 1982; September 26, 1982; October 3, 1982; October 17, 1982; November 7, 1982; November 21, 1982; January 16, 1983; January 23, 1983; March 27, 1983; May 1, 1983; June 26, 1983; July 17, 1983; August 21, 1983; September 18, 1983; October 2, 1983; October 16, 1983; October 30, 1983; November 3, 1983; November 6, 1983; November 20, 1983; January 22, 1984; February 19, 1984; March 25, 1984; April 1, 1984; June 17, 1984; September 2, 1984. Copyright © 1922, 1924, 1927, 1928, 1930, 1932, 1933, 1934, 1935, 1937, 1938, 1939, 1940, 1941, 1942, 1943, 1945, 1947, 1951, 1952, 1953, 1956, 1958, 1959, 1960, 1961, 1964, 1965, 1966, 1967, 1968, 1969, 1970, 1971, 1972, 1973, 1975, 1976, 1977, 1978, 1979, 1980, 1981, 1982, 1983, 1984 by The New York Times Company. All reprinted by permission.

The New Yorker, v. LIX, November 14, 1983 for "Baggy Monsters" by John Updike; v. LX, March 19, 1984 for "From Fragments a World Perfect at Last" by Helen Vendler. © 1983, 1984 by the respective authors. Both reprinted by permission./ v. XVII, October 25, 1941 for "Magnum Opus" by Clifton Fadiman. Copyright © 1941, 1969 by The New Yorker Magazine, Inc. Reprinted by permission of

THE EXCERPTS IN CLC, VOLUME 31, WERE REPRINTED FROM THE FOLLOWING BOOKS:

Ansorge, Peter. From *Disrupting the Spectacle: Five Years of Experimental and Fringe Theatre in Britain*. Pitman Publishing, 1975. © Peter Ansorge 1975. All rights reserved. Reproduced by kind permission of A. & C. Black (Publishers) Ltd.

Ascher, Carol. From *Simone De Beauvoir: A Life of Freedom*. Beacon Press, 1981. Copyright © 1981 by Carol Ascher. All rights reserved. Reprinted by permission of Beacon Press.

Barthes, Roland. From *Critical Essays*. Translated by Richard Howard. Northwestern University Press, 1972. Copyright © 1971 by Northwestern University Press, Evanston, Ill. All rights reserved. Reprinted by permission.

Besser, Gretchen Rous. From *Nathalie Sarraute*. Twayne, 1979. Copyright © 1979 by Twayne Publishers. All rights reserved. Reprinted with the permission of Twayne Publishers, a Division of G. K. Hall & Co., Boston.

Bjornson, Richard. From "Reviews of Professional Works: 'The Novel in the Third World'," in *Yearbook of Comparative General Literature, No. 28*. Edited by Horst Frenze. Indiana University, 1979. Copyright 1980 Comparative Literature Committee, Indiana University, Bloomington, Indiana. Reprinted by permission.

Brotherston, Gordon. From *Latin American Poetry: Origins and Presence*. Cambridge University Press, 1975. © Cambridge University Press 1975. Reprinted by permission.

Cohan, Steven. From "From Subtext to Dream Text: The Brutal Egoism of Iris Murdoch's Male Narrators," in *Men by Women*. Edited by Janet Todd. Holmes & Meier, 1981. Copyright © 1981 by Holmes & Meier Publishers, Inc. All rights reserved. Reprinted by permission of Holmes & Meier Publishers, Inc., IUB Building, 30 Irving Place, New York, NY 10003.

Copland, R. A. From *Frank Sargeson*. Oxford University Press, Wellington, 1976. © Oxford University Press 1976. Reprinted by permission.

Durham, Frank. From an introduction to *Collected Short Stories of Julia Peterkin*. By Julia Peterkin, edited by Frank Durham. University of South Carolina Press, 1970. Copyright © 1970 University of South Carolina Press. Reprinted by permission.

Friar, Kimon. From "Introduction: The Social Poets," in *Modern Greek Poetry*. Edited and translated by Kimon Friar. Simon & Schuster, 1973. Copyright © 1973 by Kimon Friar. Reprinted by permission of Simon & Schuster, Inc.

Friedman, Susan Stanford. From *Psyche Reborn: The Emergence of H. D*. Indiana University Press, 1981. Copyright © 1981 by Susan Stanford Friedman. Reprinted by permission.

Grant, Steve. From "Voicing the Protest: The New Writers," in *Dreams and Deconstructions: Alternative Theatre in Britain*. Edited by Sandy Craig. Amber Lane Press, 1980. Copyright © Amber Lane Press Limited, 1980. All rights reserved. Reprinted by permission.

Hardwick, Elizabeth. From an introduction to *A Susan Sontag Reader*. By Susan Sontag. Farrar, Straus and Giroux, 1982. Introduction copyright © 1982 by Farrar, Straus and Giroux, Inc. All rights reserved. Reprinted by permission of Farrar, Straus and Giroux, Inc.

Hatcher, Harlan. From *Creating the Modern American Novel*. Farrar & Rinehart, 1935. Copyright, 1935, renewed 1962, by Harlan Hatcher. All rights reserved. Reprinted by permission of the author.

Johnson, Robert K. From *Neil Simon*. Twayne, 1983. Copyright 1983 by Twayne Publishers. All rights reserved. Reprinted with the permission of Twayne Publishers, a division of G. K. Hall & Co., Boston.

Keeley, Edmund. From an introduction to *Ritsos in Parentheses*. By Yannis Ritsos, edited and translated by Edmund Keeley. Princeton University Press, 1979. Copyright © 1979 by Edmund Keeley. Excerpts reprinted by permission of Princeton University Press.

Kerensky, Oleg. From *The New British Drama: Fourteen Playwrights Since Osborne and Pinter*. Hamilton, 1977. Taplinger, 1979. Copyright © 1977 by Oleg Kerensky. All rights reserved. Published and reprinted by permission of Taplinger Publishing Co., Inc., NY. In Canada by Hamish Hamilton Ltd.

Kessler, Jascha. For radio broadcasts on April 15, 1981; May 18, 1983; December 7, 1983; February 29, 1984 on KUSC-FM—Los Angeles, CA. All reprinted by permission.

King, Bruce. From *The New English Literatures: Cultural Nationalism in a Changing World*. St. Martin's Press, 1980. © Bruce King 1980. Reprinted by permission of St. Martin's Press, Inc. In Canada by Macmillan, London and Basingstoke.

Landess, Thomas H. From *Julia Peterkin*. Twayne, 1976. Copyright 1976 by Twayne Publishers. All rights reserved. Reprinted with the permission of Twayne Publishers, a division of G. K. Hall & Co., Boston.

Appendix

Cumulative Index to Authors

This index lists all author entries in the Gale Literary Criticism Series and includes cross-references to other Gale sources. References in the index are identified as follows:

Author Index

Author Index

Author Index

Author Index

Author Index

Author Index

Author Index

Cumulative Index to Critics

Critic Index

Critic Index

Critic Index

Critic Index

Critic Index

Critic Index

Critic Index

Critic Index

Critic Index

Critic Index

Critic Index

Critic Index

Critic Index

Critic Index

Critic Index

Critic Index

Critic Index

Critic Index

Critic Index

Critic Index

Critic Index

Critic Index

Critic Index

Critic Index

637

Critic Index

Critic Index

Critic Index

Critic Index

Critic Index

Critic Index

Critic Index

Critic Index

Critic Index